THE EVERTON ENCYCLOPEDIA

THE EVERTON ENCYCLOPEDIA

JAMES CORBETT

ALSO BY

JAMES CORBETT

EVERTON:
THE SCHOOL OF SCIENCE

ENGLAND EXPECTS:
A HISTORY OF
THE ENGLAND FOOTBALL TEAM

THE WORLD CUP:
THE COMPLETE HISTORY
(WITH TERRY CROUCH)

NEVILLE SOUTHALL:
THE BINMAN CHRONICLES
(WITH NEVILLE SOUTHALL)

DEDICATION

For my children

SO THEY KNOW WHY
(AND HOW AND WHEN AND WHERE
AND BY HOW MANY)

And my wife

WHO SOMEHOW UNDERSTANDS

Published by
deCoubertin Books Ltd in 2012

deCoubertin Books,
145 - 157 St John Street,
London,
EC1V 4PW

www.decoubertin.co.uk

First Hardback Edition
Nil Satis Nisi Optimum Edition
ISBN: 978-0-9564313-4-9

Legends Edition
978-1-909245-04-4

A CIP catalogue record for
this book is available from the
British Library

Cover design and layout
by Leslie Priestley

Photographs courtesy of
Everton Football Club,
Getty Images, and the pivate
collections of the author and
other Evertonians.

Printed and bound by Korotan

Every effort has been made to
contact copyright holders for
photographs used in this book.
If we have overlooked you in any
way, please get in touch so that we
can rectify this in future editions.

Introduction

This book was a half a lifetime in the making. It was born in the dying days of Joe Royle's term as Everton manager, when I was still living in my home city of Liverpool; a fiercely ambitious sixth former, juggling A Levels with editorship of a fanzine and trying to contemplate which was the best path for me to fulfil my ambitions of being an author and journalist. The writing was concluded amidst a similar winter of discontent for one of Royle's successors, David Moyes. I was in exile in London in my early-thirties, juggling a career in journalism and publishing with bringing up two lively young children. The hinterland of my life had changed inexorably and many of my ambitions realised, but one thing was constant – my devotion to Everton Football Club.

BEFORE reaching its present form – entries on each of the 800 plus men to play for Everton, including more than 400 full entries, some 330,000 words, 652 pages and 400 or so photographs – this work took on a number of guises and went through several phases. It started as a book of profiles of the 100 greatest Everton players, but the lack of primary material available in the mid-1990s showed through and I eventually shelved plans to publish in collaboration with the club. Some of that research did, however, come in useful when my narrative history of the club, Everton: The School of Science, was published in 2003 (and reissued by deCoubertin Books in 2010). The decision to work on an Encyclopedia came in 2008, and although there was a hiatus of a couple of years to concentrate on my responsibilities as an international sports correspondent (at the time of the greatest corruption crisis to ever hit world football), I worked in earnest on finishing this book through the second half of 2011. Its publication is probably two years late but I hope the wait is worth it.

Contained in this book are biographical details of every man to play for Everton Football Club. Around half of these players have full in depth profiles. My methodology for selecting those with full profiles was as follows: every player to make more than 15 starts since 1960; every player to make more than 30 appearances between 1945-59; every player to make more than 50 appearances in the interwar years; every player to make more than 100 appearances in the club's first years; all of Everton's managers and other significant individuals in the club's history. In addition there are articles on aspects of Everton's history, their rivals and landmark events in the club's rich and illustrious history. This book is based on new and original research, particularly centred on the first 80 years of its history. At times I have utilised interviews and anecdotes from my career as a journalist, but it is based primarily on original documentary research and is the first major book to take advantage of the magnificent Everton Collection, since it opened at Liverpool Central Library in 2009.

Completing a work of this size would not have been possible without the help of many, many people, the development of key new research facilities and the encouragement of a small army of others.

FIRST and foremost on my list of acknowledgements is the book's designer, Leslie Priestley. He first approached me about the project out of the blue when it was lying semi-dormant and has since accompanied me every subsequent inch of the way. His excellence as a designer and enthusiasm for the work shines through on every page and for that I am very grateful.

David France, the father of Evertonia and inspiration for a slew of Everton-related initiatives, also played a fundamental role in making this happen. His incredible work as a collector bore the aforementioned Everton Collection, without which it would be inconceivable that I could have conducted a book of such in-depth research.

David is also founder of the EFC Heritage society, whose fellow members have always been so helpful. Its members include the largely unheralded but incredible Billy Smith, who has spent years in newspaper archives collating every single Everton report from the club's lengthy history, then publishing it in his books and on his website. Without Billy's research this book may well have been delayed by another couple of years. Another member is George Orr, a friend of almost two decades, former editor of the Blue Blood fanzine and author of distinguished Everton books of his own. George has always been there: a fount of encouragement, timely responder to even the most obscure requests for help, and someone to keep my enthusiasm for David Moyes in check. Philip Ross of the Everton Former Players Charity assisted me in several matters. Les Read of EFC Memorabilia has been a brilliant link with the icons of Everton's past. I would also like to thank Steve Johnson, Lyndon Lloyd, Eric Howell, Ed Bottomley,

Simon Paul, Mark O'Brien, Brendan Connolly and Paul Wharton. Peter 'Ped' McPartland was responsible for one of Goodison's less-auspicious occasions, namely my appearance as a footballer upon its hallowed turf in May 2011. I will always be grateful for that opportunity and for many other things.

Publication has been assisted by many people. I would like to thank Ian Allen, Anna Corbett, Daniel Lewis and Gary Stone, who all had important roles in producing and promoting this work too.

Living and working with someone involved in such Stakhanovite endeavours has, I would imagine, at times been testing, but people have always been kind and patient. When, at a conference in the Middle East, about three weeks from when I completed the first draft a delegate said to me 'Aren't you constantly in the last stages of finishing this Everton book?' I realised it was time to pull my finger out and get it finished.

Many of my endeavours in the final, exhausting straight of copy editing and fact checking would not have been possible without the kindness of my mother and father in law, James and Noreen Miller, and my sister in law, Mary, who for a short but crucial few months uncomplainingly shouldered many of my domestic duties and gave me the time and space to think and work.

From the strange but compelling worlds of football politics and sports journalism, I would like to thank: Jens Andersen, David Barrett, Mark Bisson, Jonathan Calvert, Jerome Champagne, Mike Collett, John Dureden, Jesse Fink, Oliver Fowler, Andrew Jennings, Louis Massarella, Bonita Mersiades, James Montague, Osasu Obayiuwana, Richard Padula, Dave Prentice, Andrew Warshaw, Jonathan Wilson, Martyn Ziegler. In London: Aline Conus, Claudia Kim, Julien Moulin, Hannes Niemitz, Claire and Patrick Cogan, Mukul Devichand. Former players: the late Alan Ball, Ian Callaghan, Howard Kendall, Bob Latchford, Ken Rea, Graeme Sharp, Neville Southall, Derek Temple. At Everton FC: Carena Duffy, Darren Griffiths, John Howard, Mark Rowan and – of course – David Moyes, who gave me an hour of his time a couple of years ago that I will never forget.

From my match-going gang: my father, John Corbett; my brothers, David, Andrew and Michael Corbett; my cousins, Ben and Tom Mills, Lucy O'Connor and her husband, Mark; my uncles, Charles and Peter Mills; our post-match leader of ceremonies, Joe Wright; my European tourmaster, Peter 'Frank' Francis; and, of course, my grandfather, Charles Mills. He recalls chats with his own grandfather, who watched Everton in the Victorian era – thus exists an unbroken family link to the club's virgin days. My mother, Mary Corbett, has been subjected to many of this motley cast for a lifetime, and it is worth recording her (usually) unending patience in the teeth of Everton mania.

THIS BOOK is dedicated to my young children, Joshua and Eleanor, who, while aware of Everton, haven't fully grasped its significance. Hopefully, in years to come, this book will help them appreciate the club's hold over their family. I hope also, even in these relatively dark days, that they experience some of the unbridled if not intermittent joy the club has given me. The book is also dedicated to my wife, Catherine, who somehow understands the compulsion that drives me to devote so long to such a study.

A book of this size is always prone to have errors, no matter how many years of work go to perfecting it. I can be contacted via www.jamescorbett.co.uk to rectify any mistakes in future editions.

James Corbett
Greenwich and Ireland
DECEMBER 2011 - AUGUST 2012

EVERTON
·ENCYCLOPEDIA·

Abandoned Fixtures, Walter **Abbott,** Gary **Ablett,** Jimmy **Adams,** Neil **Adams,** Hugh **Adamson, Africa** and Everton, Alan **Ainscow,** Hope **Akpan,** Niclas **Alexandersson,** Frank **Alford,** Graham **Allen,** Daniel **Amokachi, Anderson** Da Silva, Brett **Angell,** Jack **Angus,** John Alexander **Angus,** Victor **Anichebe,** Bill **Archer,** Jim **Arnold,** Smart **Arridge, Arsenal** and Everton, Mikel **Arteta,** Alec **Ashworth,** Sam **Ashworth, Aston Villa** and Everton, Ian **Atkins,** Record **Attendances,** Ray **Atteveld,** Arthur **Attwood**

Abandoned Fixtures

Only seven matches have been abandoned in Everton's long history, most recently against Bolton Wanderers in 1979

V SMALL HEATH [H]

28 DECEMBER 1895

Played on a quagmire of a Goodison pitch, on 37 minutes and with Everton leading due to John Bell's goal, the referee gathered the players and it was decided to abandon the match. Everton won the replayed game 3-0 six weeks later.

V WOOLWICH ARSENAL [A]

26 NOVEMBER 1904

The game that cost Everton the League Championship: Everton were leading Arsenal 3-1 when thick fog led to the game's abandonment. When the game was replayed the following April Arsenal won 2-1 and Everton eventually lost the title by a single point.

V STOCKPORT COUNTY [H]

11 JANUARY 1913

Arctic conditions led to the FA Cup tie's abandonment after 50 minutes with the scores level at 1-1; Everton won the replay 5-1.

IN THE REPLAYED GAME
IN MID-APRIL 1915
EVERTON WON 2-1
AND TWELVE DAYS LATER
LIFTED THE TITLE
BY A SINGLE POINT

V BRADFORD PARK AVENUE [A]

15 FEBRUARY 1915

Just as Everton effectively lost the title in 1905 after their notorious abandoned game v Woolwich Arsenal, so the weather favoured them a decade later. They were 3-0 down when a snowstorm whipped in over the Pennines, forcing the referee finally to call a halt to proceedings. In the replayed game in mid-April Everton won 2-1 and twelve days later lifted the title by a single point.

V MIDDLESBROUGH [H]

4 FEBRUARY 1922

With Everton leading 1-0 with 12 minutes of the second half played, proceedings were ended because of stormy conditions. Everton won the rematch 4-1.

V TOTTENHAM HOTSPUR [A]

17 DECEMBER 1969

The breakdown of a nearby electricity substation caused the floodlights to fail after 30 minutes with the match goalless. The referee waited nearly 50 minutes before abandoning the game; Everton won the replayed match 1-0 the following March.

V BOLTON WANDERERS [A]

1 JANUARY 1979

A game notorious for a horrific broken leg suffered by Peter Reid, following a collision with Everton goalkeeper George Wood, was played on a virtual ice rink and called off at half-time with the scores level at 1-1. Bolton won the rematch 3-1 in April.

Abbott, Walter

Illustrious left half who was a stalwart during the early twentieth century

Everton FA Cup Winners 1906

ELLIOTT (TRAINER) MAKEPEACE BALMER W. TAYLOR (C) SCOTT CRELLEY ABBOTT
SHARP BOLTON YOUNG SETTLE HARDMAN

Expectations were high in the summer of 1899 when Everton shelled out £250 to bring Walter Abbott, Small Heath's prolific inside forward, to Goodison Park.

THE PREVIOUS SEASON the 21-year-old had scored 34 Second Division goals for Small Heath, forerunners of modern-day Birmingham City.

Yet hopes that Abbott would revitalise Everton's shot-shy attack were soon confounded. Three games into his Everton career he was dropped, with his new club propping up the First Division having suffered three straight defeats. He returned midway through the 1899/1900 season as a converted half back, a position in which he remained for nearly a decade, adding skill, solidity and dependability to one of Everton's finest ever teams. Abbott quickly earned national prominence for his role in the Everton defence.

He was, wrote William Gibson and Alfred Pickford, 'one of a great line, and one who has made hard shooting from long range quite a speciality, some of his shots being like cannon shots, and often scoring when his own forwards are completely inoperative.' Indeed his long-range shooting, honed while playing as a young inside forward, were a notable part of his repertoire. His 'cannon shots', wrote the Everton historian Thomas Keates, 'so frequently successful, were a fascinating feature of his game, and installed him as a great favourite'.

His form earned him an England call-up against Wales in 1902, but

he played at a time when the national team's line-up was in a constant state of flux and riven between 'gentlemen' amateurs and mere professionals such as himself.

> **'ONE WHO HAS MADE HARD SHOOTING FROM LONG RANGE QUITE A SPECIALITY, SOME OF HIS SHOTS BEING LIKE CANNON SHOTS'**
>
> **WILLIAM GIBSON AND ALFRED PICKFORD**

Frequently the gentlemen found their social standing to be a better asset than their footballing ability in the selector's eyes, and so found themselves picked ahead of professionals – such as Abbott – who were looked down upon by the class-obsessed snobs who ran football.

Abbott won just one cap, but perhaps a truer indication of his standing came by virtue of his selection for the Football League XI on four occasions.

EVERTON IN THIS ERA were perennial nearly men, finishing First Division runners-up in 1901/02 and 1904/05 and FA Cup runners-up in 1907. They also finished third on another two occasions. Abbott, however, did experience glory in 1906, when he was part of the team that lifted the FA Cup.

Indeed, the left half played a key part in Everton's victorious run. Facing Liverpool in the semi-final in his home city of Birmingham, Everton's rivals dominated the early stages of the game. However, in the second half Abbott transformed proceedings with a long-range shot, which took a wicked deflection off the Liverpool left back Billy Dunlop and crept into the back of the goal. Liverpool were thrown into disarray and a minute later Jack Sharp set up Harold Hardman, who gave Everton an unassailable 2-0 lead.

[FACTFILE]

BORN
Birmingham,
7 December 1877
DIED
Birmingham,
1 February 1941
POSITION
Inside left/left half
OTHER CLUBS
Small Heath (1895-99);
Burnley (1908-10);
Birmingham City (1910-11)
HONOURS
FA Cup 1906
1 England cap (1902)

Yet less than two years after lifting the FA Cup, in spring 1908, Abbott lost his place to Hugh Adamson. Now aged 31, Everton sold him to Burnley, where he spent two years. In the veteran stage of his career he returned to the Midlands, playing out his career with Birmingham City. After leaving professional football he worked in his home city's nascent automobile industry.

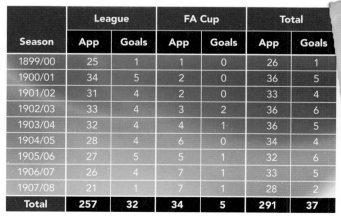

Season	League		FA Cup		Total	
	App	Goals	App	Goals	App	Goals
1899/00	25	1	1	0	26	1
1900/01	34	5	2	0	36	5
1901/02	31	4	2	0	33	4
1902/03	33	4	3	2	36	6
1903/04	32	4	4	1	36	5
1904/05	28	4	6	0	34	4
1905/06	27	5	5	1	32	6
1906/07	26	4	7	1	33	5
1907/08	21	1	7	1	28	2
Total	**257**	**32**	**34**	**5**	**291**	**37**

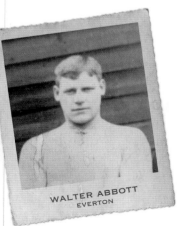

WALTER ABBOTT
EVERTON

Ablett, Gary

Local defender who became the only player to lift the FA Cup with both Merseyside teams

Signed for £750,000 in January 1992, Gary Ablett arrived at Goodison after a long and successful career on the other side of Stanley Park with Liverpool. A title winner in 1988 and 1990 and part of the team that defeated Everton in the 1989 FA Cup Final, Ablett was an accomplished centre half and left back, though perhaps lacked the additional ruthlessness that may have brought full England honours to add to his England B and Under-21 caps.

> POWERFUL IN THE AIR HE POSSESSED A RARE COMPOSURE IN POSSESSION

Tall and gaunt, perhaps lacking a little pace, Ablett was nevertheless powerful in the air and possessed a rare composure in possession. Occasionally concentration eluded him, never more traumatically so than when he conceded a comical own goal when Everton faced Wimbledon on the last day of the 1994/95 season, needing to win to avoid relegation.

As left back under Joe Royle he was part of the team that won the 1995 FA Cup, but the following season, after the arrival of Craig Short and Andy Hinchcliffe's reversion to full back, he found opportunities more difficult to come by. After a loan spell at Howard Kendall's Sheffield United, and past his thirtieth

birthday, he was allowed to join Birmingham City in summer 1996, where he formed a central defensive pairing with former Manchester United captain Steve Bruce.

Following spells in the lower leagues and in the United States, Ablett turned to coaching. In 2002 he became Everton's under-17 coach and over the subsequent four years held down roles within the Everton academy. In summer 2006 he returned to Anfield to become Liverpool's reserve manager. Later there was a spell in charge of Stockport County and as Roy Keane's assistant manager at Ipswich Town.

IN 2010 Ablett was diagnosed with a rare form of non-Hodgkin's lymphoma. The disease spread with devastating ferocity, but Ablett fought it bravely and in the public eye, raising awareness of all forms of cancer. He succumbed to the illness on the first day of 2012, uniting Merseyside in mourning. At his funeral at the Anglican cathedral a week later it was fitting that the service began with a rendition of 'You'll Never Walk Alone' and concluded with the theme from Z-Cars.

[FACTFILE]

BORN
Liverpool, 19 November 1965
DIED
Liverpool, 1 January 2012
POSITION
Left Back/Centre Back
OTHER CLUBS
Liverpool (1983-92);
Derby County (Loan, 1985);
Hull City (Loan, 1986);
Sheffied United (Loan, 1996);
Birmingham City (1996-99);
Wycombe Wanderers (1999);
Blackpool (2000);
Long Island Rough Riders (US, 2000-01)
AS MANAGER
Stockport County (2009-10)
HONOURS
1995 FA Cup

Season	League		FA Cup		League Cup		Other		Total	
	App	Gls	App	Gls	App	Gls	App	Gls	App	Gls
1991/92	17	1	1	0	0	0	-	-	18	1
1992/93	40	0	2	0	6	0	-	-	48	0
1993/94	32	1	2	0	5	0	-	-	39	1
1994/95	26	3	4	0	0	0	-	-	30	3
1995/96	13	0	3	1	1	0	4	0	21	1
Total	**128**	**5**	**12**	**1**	**12**	**0**	**4**	**0**	**156**	**5**

Adams, Jimmy

Scotland international full back of Everton's early years

Season	League		FA Cup		Total	
	App	Goals	App	Goals	App	Goals
1894/95	12	0	0	0	12	0
1895/96'	28	1	3	0	31	1
Total	**40**	**1**	**3**	**0**	**43**	**1**

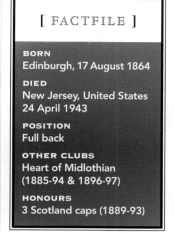

[FACTFILE]

BORN
Edinburgh, 17 August 1864
DIED
New Jersey, United States
24 April 1943
POSITION
Full back
OTHER CLUBS
Heart of Midlothian
(1885-94 & 1896-97)
HONOURS
3 Scotland caps (1889-93)

Adams, Neil

Young right winger who lifted the 1987 League Championship

The Victoria Ground provided a fertile source of Goodison talent in the 1980s, and in swapping Stoke City for Everton, Neil Adams followed a tradition set by Adrian Heath and Paul Bracewell (via Sunderland).

AFTER A hugely impressive debut season in the Potteries, Howard Kendall had deemed the 19-year-old a sound investment for the future, paying £150,000 in the summer of 1986.

An attacking midfielder with pace and skill, Adams was best suited to the right wing, but played through the middle as well. During his debut season he made enough appearances to earn a League Championship medal, and selection for the England under-21 team was just reward for a player who impressed in flashes. Alas for Adams, after Kendall's departure in June 1987, he failed to find favour with Colin Harvey and his chances were subsequently limited. In January

ADAMS DESCRIBED
EVERTON AS
THE BEST CLUB
HE EVER
PLAYED FOR:

'EVERTON WAS
FANTASTIC'

1989 he joined Oldham Athletic on loan, a deal that was in June made permanent for a fee of £100,000. Ironically Trevor Steven had just left the club: who knows how Adams might have prospered given an extended chance in his place?

Certainly, Adams always did well when pitted against his former club. He won promotion with Oldham in 1991, and when facing Everton in February 1993 scored two late goals to earn a 2-2 draw. In summer 1994 he joined Norwich City and, as he did at Boundary Park, put in a solid five-year stint. He later returned to Oldham, and on his retirement joined Norwich as a youth coach.

IN 2008, Adams described Everton as the best club he ever played for: 'Everton was fantastic, I was a young kid when I went to Everton, I was 19 years old. Everton at the time were the equivalent of Manchester United now, probably one of the best clubs in Europe. The dressing room banter at the time was phenomenal. Players will always tell you that the dressing room will get you half of the way there, obviously you have to have the talent or you won't do it... Any team that has a bond in the side as we had at Everton... has a good chance.'

[FACTFILE]

BORN
Stoke, 23 November 1965
POSITION
Midfield
OTHER CLUBS
Stoke City (1985-86)
Oldham Athletic (1989-94)
Norwich City (1994-99)
Oldham Athletic
(1999-2001)
HONOURS
1986/87 League
Championship

Season	League		FA Cup		League Cup		Other		Total	
	App	Goals	App	Goals	App	Goals	App	Goals	App	Goals
1986/87	10 (2)	0	0	0	3	0	4 (1)	0	17 (3)	0
1987/88	7 (1)	0	0	0	1	1	1 (1)	0	9 (2)	1
1988/89	0	0	0	0	0 (1)	0	0	0	0 (1)	0
Total	**17 (3)**	**0**	**0**	**0**	**4 (1)**	**1**	**5 (2)**	**0**	**26 (6)**	**1**

Adamson, Hugh

Scottish wing half who deputised for Walter Abbott and Harry Makepeace

	League		FA Cup		Total	
Season	App	Goals	App	Goals	App	Goals
1907/08	16	0	0	0	16	0
1908/09	7	0	0	0	7	0
1909/10	2	0	0	0	2	0
Total	25	0	0	0	25	0

[FACTFILE]

BORN
Scotland, 21 April 1885
POSITION
Wing half
OTHER CLUBS
Dunfermline Athletic
Lochgelly United
Bolton Wanderers (1909-11)
South Liverpool

Africa, and Everton

Eight African players have followed in Daniel Amokachi's footsteps in playing for Everton

ABEL XAVIER *Born in Mozambique, but represented Portugal;*
IBRAHIMA BAKAYOKO *Ivory Coast;*
ALEX NYARKO *Ghana;*
MATTEO FERRARI *born Algeria, but represented Italy;*
STEVEN PIENAAR *South Africa;*
DANIEL AMOKACHI *Nigeria;*

VICTOR ANICHEBE *Nigeria;*
JOSEPH YOBO *Nigeria;*
YAKUBU AIYEGBENI *Nigeria*

Everton also had Egyptian international defender Ibrahim Said on loan for six months in 2003, although he never played a game.

Ainscow, Alan

Experienced midfielder who was among Howard Kendall's first signings

One of Howard Kendall's so-called 'Magnificent Seven', Alan Ainscow was the most experienced of the manager's glut of signings in the summer of 1981.

ARRIVING at goodison with 300 appearances to his name, garnered from spells at Blackpool and Birmingham, the £250,000 midfielder was seen by the new manager as the sort of dependable and dedicated professional who might aid the progress of some of Everton's promising younger players. Doughty, reliable, but never the sort of flamboyant player who might earn the unending affection of fans, Ainscow scored on his debut against Birmingham, but thereafter struggled to make his mark in a transitional Everton team.

In November 1981, Ainscow suffered a broken leg against Notts County and, although he returned the following spring, thereafter he found himself part of Kendall's tactical experimentations and unable to hold down a regular spot. Released at the end of the 1982/83 season, he had a spell with Hong Kong's Eastern Athletic before returning to England to play out his veteran years in the lower leagues.

[FACTFILE]

BORN
Bolton, 15 July 1983
POSITION
Midfield
OTHER CLUBS
Blackpool (1971-78)
Birmingham City (1978-81)
Barnsley (loan) (1982-83)
Eastern Athletic (1983-84)
Wolverhampton Wanderers (1984-86)
Blackburn Rovers (1986-89)
Rochdale (1989-90)

	League		FA Cup		League Cup		Total	
Season	App	Goals	App	Goals	App	Goals	App	Goals
1981/82	15 (2)	2	0	0	1 (1)	0	16 (3)	2
1982/83	9 (2)	1	0	0	0	0	9 (2)	1
Total	24 (4)	3	0	0	1 (1)	0	25 (5)	3

Akpan, Hope

Home-grown midfielder who made just a solitary first-team outing

	League		FA Cup		League Cup		Europe		Total	
Season	App	Goals	App	Goals	App	Goals	App	Goals	App	Goals
2009/10	0	0	0	0	0	0	1	0	1	0
Total	0	0	0	0	0	0	1	0	1	0

Alexandersson, Niclas

Disappointing right midfielder who made little impact in an Everton shirt

Signed for a hefty £2.2million from freshly relegated Sheffield Wednesday in the summer of 2000, Niclas Alexandersson arrived at Goodison with a reputation as a sensible if unspectacular midfielder with an eye for goal. A Swedish international, who had played in the Champions League with IFK Gothenburg before joining Wednesday for £750,000 in 1997, he was a favourite at Hillsborough in a struggling side.

A somewhat pedestrian right-sided midfielder – he lacked the pace and skill to ever really be considered an out-and-out winger – his patent mediocrity was in keeping with Walter Smith's dismal teams of the early 2000s. Although he struggled with injuries, he continued to play a more telling role for his national team than he did his club, scoring against England at the 2002 World Cup Finals. Following David Moyes's arrival, despite scoring in two of his first three games as manager, the Swede lost his place and his last game came in the 1-2 FA Cup defeat to Shrewsbury Town in January 2003. For Everton he played no part in the 2003/04 season and thereafter he played on loan at West Ham, and on his release in 2004 rejoined Gothenburg.

	League		FA Cup		League Cup		Total	
Season	App	Goals	App	Goals	App	Goals	App	Goals
2000/01	17 (3)	2	1	0	2	0	20 (3)	2
2001/02	28 (3)	2	3 (1)	0	0	0	31 (4)	2
2002/03	4 (3)	0	0 (1)	1	0	0	4 (4)	1
2003/04	0	0	0	0	0	0	0	0
Total	49 (9)	4	4 (2)	1	2	0	55 (11)	5

Alford, Frank

Early-1920s winger who made just a couple of first team appearances

Season	League		FA Cup		Total	
	App	Goals	App	Goals	App	Goals
1921/22	2	0	0	0	2	0
Total	2	0	0	0	2	0

[FACTFILE]

BORN
Swindon, 14 May 1901
DIED
1982
POSITION
Outside left
OTHER CLUBS
Swindon Town; Darwen;
Barrow (1923–24);
Lincoln City (1925);
Scunthorpe United

Allen, Graham

Home-grown defender who later enjoyed a solid career at Tranmere

Season	League		FA Cup		League Cup		Total	
	App	Goals	App	Goals	App	Goals	App	Goals
1996/97	0 (1)	0	0	0	0	0	0 (1)	0
1997/98	2 (3)	0	0	0	0	0	2 (3)	0
Total	2 (4)	0	0	0	0	0	2 (4)	0

[FACTFILE]

BORN
Bolton, 6 April 1977
POSITION
Centre back
OTHER CLUBS
Tranmere Rovers
(1998–2004);
Rushden & Diamonds
(2004–06);
Chester City (2006–07)

Amokachi, Daniel

Everton's first African player, whose FA Cup goals secured a place at Wembley

When Daniel Amokachi became the first African to play for Everton in August 1994, the euphoria that surrounded his £3million arrival hinted that he might be the biggest thing to pull on a blue shirt since Dixie Dean.

Previously without a significant black player in their ranks, Everton had been tarred with unsubstantiated accusations of racism within the club's hierarchy and among its support. Yet the sheer scale of the Nigerian's welcome put paid to any such suggestions for good, and although Amokachi failed to live up to the substantial expectations placed on his broad shoulders, most Evertonians will remember his two-year Goodison sojourn with fondness.

Born in the northern Nigerian city of Kaduna in December 1972, after a spell with Ranchers Bees of his native Kaduna, Amokachi followed the traditional route of many young African footballers and moved to Belgium. Here, with labour restrictions on non-EU immigrants less strict, he was able to join the youth side of Club Bruges. By 18 he had moved up to the seniors after his trademark rampaging, attacking style impressed coaches.

Outstanding performances in the Belgian league and European competitions catapulted Amokachi, known as 'The Bull', to fame and several awards, including the Ebony Boot for Best African Player in Belgium. At the 1994 World Cup Finals in the US, his renown became global after a 25-yard goal against Greece was one of the tournament's best: taking the ball just past the halfway line, he slalomed past four Greek defenders before letting fly with an unstoppable shot from the penalty area's D.

HIS MOVE TO EVERTON just weeks later was meant to herald the onset of Peter Johnson's Everton revolution after a hitherto frustrating summer in the transfer market. Big-money moves to bring in players such as Jurgen Klinsmann, Martin Dahlin and the Brazilian, Muller, had all collapsed, so Amokachi's signing

was not just greeted with elation, but relief, too.

Unable to play immediately due to work-permit restrictions, he had to wait a fortnight to make his debut, in a 3-0 defeat at Blackburn, but a goal on his home debut against QPR had Evertonians in raptures about a player who claimed he could run 100 metres in 10.1 seconds. Amokachi certainly had pace, but it became apparent that he lacked the spontaneity in front of goal to turn around the club's worst ever start to a season. When Mike Walker was sacked in November, Amokachi figured in only the first of Joe Royle's games as manager before a prolonged spell in the reserves.

Indeed, Royle, it seemed, did not rate Amokachi at first, even picking the hapless Brett Angell ahead of him. Part of the Nigerian's

problem was that he was not an out-and-out striker, nor was he a traditional target man. Instead his best position – the one he played for Nigeria – was as a deep-lying forward, operating in the so-called 'hole' behind a front man or forward pairing. But Royle had rebuilt Everton around a tight defence and compact midfield; put simply, there was no room for a luxury player like Amokachi.

Only when faced with an injury crisis in spring 1995 did Royle see fit to recall Amokachi and he was on the substitute's bench when Everton faced Tottenham Hotspur in the FA Cup semi-final at Elland Road. On this day the forward entered Everton lore.

EVERTON WERE LEADING a closely fought contest 2-1 when, on 67 minutes, Paul Rideout picked up a knock and Amokachi was told to warm up. As he was about to be brought on, Les Helm, Everton's physiotherapist, indicated to the bench that Rideout would be fine to continue. Amokachi either did not notice this – or pretended not to – and entered play before the Everton bench could stop him.

The game's pivotal moment came fourteen minutes later when Neville Southall saved magnificently with his legs. What could have been 2-2 promptly became 3-1 as Southall's clearance was manoeuvred upfield by Anders Limpar. Barry Horne's lay-off was crossed to the far post where Amokachi met it with a

downward header. Nine minutes later, Amokachi made Everton's FA Cup Final place a certainty when he scored a second – and Everton's fourth – following link-up play between Limpar and Gary Ablett.

Rehabilitated by his semi-final exploits, Amokachi was a second-half substitute in the FA Cup Final victory over Manchester United. Through the 1995/96 season the African showed glimpses of his potential, but was again noted more for his inconsistency in front of goal. Having signed only a three-year contract

when he first joined the club, the onset of the 'Bosman ruling' meant that Everton were faced with the very real risk of losing him for nothing. When, in August 1996, Turkish side Besiktas made a £1.9million bid, Royle decided to cut Everton's losses and sell the African. Amokachi left just days after scoring in the Olympic final against Argentina, adding an Olympic gold to his FA Cup winner's medal.

In Turkey, Amokachi prospered at first, but after the 1998 World Cup Finals struggled with a persistent knee injury that brought his career to an end by his mid-twenties. Besiktas released him in 1999 and a multinational search for a club – that took in France, Germany, the US, Qatar and even Tranmere Rovers – yielded him nothing. In his early thirties he became involved in the coaching set-up of the Nigerian national team, but left in 2005 to become manager of Nigerian Premier League side, Nassarawa FC. Later that decade he served as assistant manager of the Nigerian national team over two spells.

[FACTFILE]

BORN
Kaduna, Nigeria, 30 December 1972
POSITION
Forward
OTHER CLUBS
Rancher Bees (1989–90);
Club Brugge (1990–94);
Besiktas (1996–99)
HONOURS
FA Cup 1995;
Olympic gold medal (Nigeria) 1996;
42 Nigeria caps (14 goals)

Season	League		FA Cup		League Cup		Europe		Total	
	App	Goals	App	Goals	App	Goals	App	Goals	App	Goals
1994/95	17 (1)	4	0 (2)	2	2	0	-	-	19 (3)	6
1995/96	17 (8)	6	2 (1)	1	1	0	3	1	23 (9)	8
Total	**34 (9)**	**10**	**2 (3)**	**3**	**3**	**0**	**3**	**1**	**42 (12)**	**14**

Anderson Da Silva

Brazilian midfielder who experienced just three minutes of first team action

[FACTFILE]

BORN
Sao Paolo, Brazil, 28 August 1982
POSITION
Midfield
OTHER CLUBS
Nacional (Uruguay, 2002–05);
Montevideo Wanderers
(Uruguay, loan, 2003);
Racing Santander (Spain, 2003–05);
Malaga (loan, 2005–06);
Barnsley (2007 3 x loan spells & 2008–10);
Nacional (2011–)

Season	League		FA Cup		League Cup		Europe		Total	
	App	Goals	App	Goals	App	Goals	App	Goals	App	Goals
2006/07	0 (1)	0	0	0	0	0	0	0	0 (1)	0
Total	**0 (1)**	**0**	**0**	**0**	**0**	**0**	**0**	**0**	**0 (1)**	**0**

Angell, Brett

Prolific lower-league centre forward caught out of his depth at Goodison

When Mike Walker paid Southend United £500,000 to make Brett Angell his first signing as Everton manager in January 1994, it was hoped that the club's lengthy search for a target man was at an end. Not since Graeme Sharp left the club 30 months earlier had they possessed a centre forward who could add muscle to the club's usually diminutive forward line. Unfortunately, Angell – a prolific lower-league scorer – was no fitting successor to a tradition set by Dixie Dean et al.

A lumbering giant of a man, Angell seemed bewildered by the tempo and standard of Premier League football. When Walker signed him, he had already been sent back to Southend after a loan period under Howard Kendall proved fruitless. He was, opined one fanzine, 'A dead ringer for Frankenstein's monster.

Arguably the X-movie creature was more mobile and a tad more skilful.'

Perhaps such a view does a disservice to a man who scored freely in the lower leagues and never gave anything but his all in an Everton shirt. Unfortunately it was never quite enough and in March 1995 Joe Royle sold him to Sunderland for a £100,000 profit.

[FACTFILE]

BORN
Marlborough, 20 August 1968
POSITION
Centre forward
OTHER CLUBS
Portsmouth (1986–87);
Cheltenham Town (1987–88);
Derby County (1988);
Stockport County (1988–90);
Southend United (1990–94);
Sunderland (1995–96);
Sheffield United (loan, 1996);
West Bromwich Albion (loan, 1996);
Stockport County (1996–2000);
Notts County (loan, 2000);
Preston North End (loan, 2000);
Walsall (2000–02);
Rushden & Diamonds (2002);
Port Vale (2002);
Queens Park Rangers (2002–03)

Season	League		FA Cup		League Cup		Total	
	App	Goals	App	Goals	App	Goals	App	Goals
1993/94	13 (3)	1	0	0	0	0	13 (3)	1
1994/95	3 (1)	0	0	0	0 (1)	0	3 (2)	0
Total	16 (4)	1	0	0	0 (1)	0	16 (5)	1

Angus, Jack

Goalkeeper during Everton's first League Championship winning season

Season	League		FA Cup		Total	
	App	Goals	App	Goals	App	Goals
1890/91	11	0	1	0	12	0
Total	11	0	1	0	12	0

[FACTFILE]

BORN
Unknown
POSITION
Goalkeeper
OTHER CLUBS
Kings Park; Sunderland Albion
HONOURS
1890/91 League Championship

Angus, John Alexander 'Jack'

Outside left during Everton's Football League debut

Season	League		FA Cup		Total	
	App	Goals	App	Goals	App	Goals
1888/89	5	0	-	-	5	0
Total	5	0	-	-	5	0

[FACTFILE]

BORN
Unknown
POSITION
Outside left
OTHER CLUBS
Newcastle West End;
Gainsborough Trinity

Anichebe,
Victor

Home-grown Nigerian international forward who earned Olympic silver

Born in Lagos, brought up in Crosby, before representing the country of his birth in an Olympic football final – the career of Victor Anichebe represents one of the more unconventional paths to football stardom. What makes this all the more extraordinary is that it was achieved before his 21st birthday.

Born in the Nigerian capital in 1988, Anichebe and his family immigrated to England while he was still a baby, living in Toxteth before settling in the north Liverpool suburb of Crosby. Part of a family of great sporting pedigree, his cousin Iffy Onuora was a lower-league centre forward in the 1990s and another cousin, Anyika Onuora, was a Commonwealth silver medallist sprinter.

Spotted by Everton's youth academy, Anichebe worked his way through the ranks, making his reserve team debut at 15. Two years later, in January 2006, he made his senior debut in an FA Cup fourth round tie against Chelsea. His first goal came in the dramatic 2-2 draw on the last day of the 2005/06 season. In an emotionally charged match, coming days after the death of Brian Labone and on Duncan Ferguson's last Everton appearance, Anichebe led a late fightback after Everton had fallen 2-0 behind to already-relegated West Bromwich Albion. The substitute's turn and shot six minutes from full time brought Everton back into the match, before Ferguson's last-ditch goal brought equilibrium.

Tall, powerful and muscular, Anichebe was typically used as a late-impact substitute and filled an important squad role following the retirement of Ferguson. His physicality often saw his fine all-round play overlooked and although never prolific he has shown a fine goal-poacher's instinct, as witness the Christmas brace he scored at home to Newcastle United on the penultimate day of 2006.

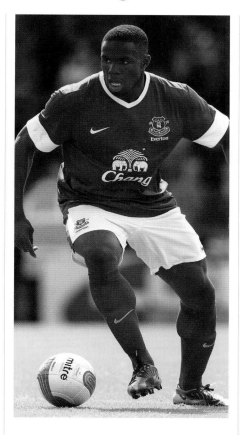

Anichebe's best form typically came in Europe, with continental teams ill at ease with his physicality and pace. Few goals he scored were better than his effort two minutes from full time against FC Nuremburg in the UEFA Cup in 2007. Breaking down the right wing, he ran 40 yards, shaking off the attention of his marker before slipping Everton's second goal of the night past the goalkeeper from an oblique angle. Pointing to the penalty he had won just minutes earlier, David Moyes said: 'Victor made some impact, what a way to finish that was. He has been struggling with a broken hand and I wasn't sure whether to put him on. Just shows what I know.'

Anichebe's form earned him international recognition with Nigeria and a call-up as part of his country's 2008 Olympic squad for Beijing. He scored the deciding goal in Nigeria's group match against Japan and came on as a second-half substitute in the 4-1 semi-final win over Belgium. That result guaranteed him a medal, but coming up against the Argentina of Lionel Messi, Juan Angel Riquelme and Sergio Aguerro proved one step too far for the Super Eagles as they fell to a 1-0 defeat in the Bird's Nest Stadium.

Anichebe returned to Merseyside with an Olympic silver medal, but a starting berth for Everton was usually elusive, except in a right-midfield role that he often seemed ill at ease in. His 2008/09 season was brought to an abrupt end after a horrific high challenge from Kevin Nolan when Everton faced Newcastle in February 2009. The injury it caused kept him out of action for 11 months – causing him to miss the FA Cup Final – and Anichebe later won an out-of-court settlement for loss of earnings against Nolan.

He nevertheless made a full recovery and signed a new contract in 2011 and although his is never the first name on the teamsheet he seems to be part of Everton's long-term plans.

> **[FACTFILE]**
>
> **BORN**
> Lagos, Nigeria, 23 April 1988
> **POSITION**
> Centre forward / right midfielder
> **HONOURS**
> 2008 Olympic silver medal;
> 11 Nigeria caps (1 goal) (2008-)

	League		FA Cup		League Cup		Europe		Total	
Season	App	Goals	App	Goals	App	Goals	App	Goals	App	Goals
2005/06	0 (2)	1	0 (1)	0	0	0	0	0	0 (3)	1
2006/07	5 (14)	3	1	0	1 (2)	1	-	-	7 (16)	4
2007/08	10 (17)	1	0 (1)	0	1 (3)	0	1 (8)	4	12 (29)	5
2008/09	5 (12)	1	3	0	0	0	1 (1)	0	9 (13)	1
2009/10	6 (5)	1	0	0	0	0	0	0	6 (5)	1
2010/11	8 (8)	0	0 (3)	0	0	0	-	-	8 (11)	0
2011/12	5 (7)	5	1 (2)	0	1	1	-	-	7 (9)	6
Total	**39 (65)**	**12**	**5 (7)**	**0**	**3 (5)**	**2**	**2 (9)**	**4**	**49 (86)**	**18**

Archer, Bill

Understudy to Jock Thomson, a regular starting berth proved elusive

Season	League		FA Cup		Total	
	App	Goals	App	Goals	App	Goals
1932/33	3	0	0	0	3	0
1933/34	6	0	0	0	6	0
1934/35	0	0	0	0	0	0
1935/36	6	2	0	0	6	2
Total	**15**	**2**	**0**	**0**	**15**	**2**

[FACTFILE]

BORN
Wednesbury, 24 July 1908
DIED
1985
POSITION
Left half / left winger
OTHER CLUBS
Walsall (1929–30);
Coventry City (1936–38);
Plymouth Argyle (1936–38)

Arnold, Jim

Sturdy goalkeeper whose presence eased the emergence of Neville Southall

Shortly after the arrival of Howard Kendall as manager in the summer of 1981 from Blackburn Rovers, Jim Arnold followed his former boss from East Lancashire in a move that surprised many Blues fans.

Having already signed Neville Southall from Bury and with Irish international Jim McDonough in his squad, the addition of a third goalkeeper may have raised some eyebrows. McDonough was sold to Bolton Wanderers shortly after Arnold's arrival, and the former Blackburn keeper, it became clear, had been brought in to add some experience while Southall honed his rare, raw talent.

A former England amateur international, Arnold was a late arrival in professional football, not making his league debut until his late twenties. A capable goalkeeper and decent shot-stopper, he opened the 1981/82 campaign, losing his place to Southall in the second half of the season, before reclaiming it again the following year. Ultimately the prodigious Welshman's talent shone through and Arnold was relegated to his understudy. He continued to provide goalkeeping cover until August 1985 when he moved to Port Vale to conclude his league career.

[FACTFILE]

BORN
Stafford, 6 August 1950
POSITION
Goalkeeper
OTHER CLUBS
Blackburn Rovers
(1979–81);
Preston North End
(loan, 1982–83);
Port Vale (1985–87)

Season	League		FA Cup		League Cup		Total	
	App	Goals	App	Goals	App	Goals	App	Goals
1981/82	16	0	0	0	4	0	20	0
1982/83	25	0	5	0	2	0	32	0
1983/84	7	0	0	0	0	0	7	0
Total	**48**	**0**	**5**	**0**	**6**	**0**	**59**	**0**

Arridge, Smart

Welsh international left back in Everton's early years

| Season | League | | FA Cup | | Total | |
---	App	Goals	App	Goals	App	Goals
1893/94	2	0	0	0	2	0
1894/95	3	0	0	0	3	0
1895/96	23	0	2	0	25	0
1896/97	23	0	3	0	26	0
Total	**51**	**0**	**5**	**0**	**56**	**0**

[FACTFILE]

BORN
Southwick, 21 June 1872
DIED
1947
POSITION
Left back
OTHER CLUBS
Bangor City; Bootle (1892);
New Brighton Tower (1898–1900);
Stockport County (1901–02);
Bangor City
HONOURS
8 Wales caps (1893–96)

Arsenal, and Everton

One of the true thoroughbreds of English football, Arsenal are a team steeped in similar history, traditions and ethos to Everton

With 13 league titles and ten FA Cups, tallies significantly boosted under the managerial reign of Arsène Wenger, they now outstrip Everton in terms of success. But the club's inherent belief in good football and being run in the right manner by the right people is comparable to their northern cousins, and is increasingly rare in an era in which football is increasingly dominated by foreign businessmen.

Yet contrary to their reputation as sporting aristocrats, Arsenal were football's first wide boys. Founded as Dial Arsenal in 1886, by workers at the Royal Arsenal in London's docklands in southeast London, they subsequently renamed themselves Royal Arsenal and then, in 1891 on turning professional, Woolwich Arsenal. They joined the Football League two years later and won promotion to the First Division in 1904. But these years were dominated by mediocrity on the pitch and financial uncertainty off it.

In 1910 they were rescued by a colourful businessman named Henry Norris. Norris had already served as a Fulham director, had an indirect role in the creation of Chelsea, and would later be banned from football for life for using Arsenal's bank account for his personal use. Norris plucked Woolwich Arsenal from the comparatively remote and impoverished

southeast London and transplanted them to the more prosperous and populous north of the city. After the First World War he also used his influence to secure Arsenal's promotion back to the First Division, despite their having finished nowhere near the promotion places when football was suspended four years previously. Such shenanigans seem entirely out of keeping with Arsenal's modern image, but it was the making of the club and they have remained in the top flight ever since.

UNDER THE management of Herbert Chapman and George Allison during the 1930s and Tom Whittaker the following decade, Arsenal became English football's strongest force. They won the First Division title five times during the 1930s and twice more in the decade following the Second World War. Famous names that played for them at that time include Cliff Bastin, Alex James, Wilf Copping and Ted Drake.

AFTER WINNING the First Division title in 1952/53 a period of mediocrity set in. It was broken by the management of Bertie Mee, the club's former physiotherapist, under whom they won the 1970 Inter Cities Fairs Cup and the League and FA Cup double the following year. But by now the club were known as 'Boring, Boring Arsenal' – even by their own fans – and not even successes, such as the 1979

FA Cup win or the 1988/89 and 1990/91 league titles could alter this perception.

This changed dramatically with the appointment of Arsène Wenger as manager in 1996. An outstanding, forward-thinking Frenchman, Wenger completely transformed the north London club. With his nose for a bargain and an innate ability to draw the best from his existing players, he made Arsenal into one of the most attractive forces in the history of the game, wowing fans of all persuasions with their thrilling brand of football. Arsenal won their second and third doubles in 1997/98 and 2001/02. In winning the Premier League in 2003/04 they did so without losing a game, the first club to manage such an achievement since Preston's 'Invincibles' in the first year of league football.

Everton's ties with Arsenal are less entwined by geography, shared history and fate than they are with other key rivals. They did not meet until 1904 – this first match was to be one of their most fateful meetings (see below) – and not until the late 1920s did Arsenal emerge as significant challengers to Everton's might. Through the following decade Everton were the principal contenders to Arsenal's hold on English football, but thereafter they seemed to peak at different points in their history. Besides the 1988 League Cup semi-final – won by Arsenal over two legs – they have avoided each other in the latter stages of cup competitions.

In the early 1990s, Everton's chairman Philip Carter and Arsenal's powerful director David Dein were key architects of the Premier League, an institution that Arsenal have done rather better out of than Everton.

There has been a steady exchange of players between Everton and Arsenal over the years, with the London club doing particularly well out of such transactions. Joe Mercer, Tommy Lawton (via Chelsea, Notts County and Brentford), Alan Ball, Martin Keown and Mikel Arteta have all gone south, while Everton have got the likes of Anders Limpar and Kevin Campbell (via Nottingham Forest and Trabsonspor) from Arsenal.

Key figures

Alan Ball

Evertonians of a certain age are still traumatised and perplexed by Alan Ball's British record transfer to Arsenal, shortly before Christmas 1971. Earlier that year Harry Catterick had claimed Ball to be worth £1million – an inconceivable sum in the early 1970s – but by Christmas Ball was an Arsenal player and Everton were just £220,000 richer. Even until his death in 2007 Ball remained baffled by the move and said he never wanted to go. Although he played with distinction for the Gunners, he never reached the same heights as he did at Everton again.

Kevin Richardson

An unsung hero of Everton's great mid-1980s sides, Richardson often found himself overshadowed by Kevin Sheedy on the Everton left. A fine, solid player, the blond north-easterner had worked his way up through the Everton ranks, winning the FA Cup in 1984 and the league title a year later. But a first-team place was never assured, so in 1986 he left to join Watford, where he played

a single season before moving to Highbury. Richardson was a dependable part of George Graham's team that pipped Liverpool to the 1988/89 league title in the last minute of the last match of the season.

Francis Jeffers

Arguably the most promising of Everton's late-1990s 'golden generation', Francis Jeffers seemed destined for big things. A lithe, skilful forward, whose outstanding movement, predatory instincts and speed of thought were reminiscent of a young Ian Rush, it was his misfortune to make a Goodison breakthrough at a time when the club's finances were in disarray. Arsène Wenger singled him out as a key addition to his squad, spending £9million to bring a player he dubbed 'the fox in the box' to Highbury in 2001. But Jeffers played just a handful of games for the Gunners, before returning to Goodison for an ill-fated year-long loan in 2003. A year later he joined Charlton and his career fizzled into a long decline.

Key meetings

26 NOVEMBER 1904
First Division
Woolwich Arsenal v Everton
Everton's first fixture with Arsenal – although never completed – was arguably its most significant. Played in the Gunners' former south London home, Everton had gone into a seemingly unassailable 3-1 lead when the referee, influenced by the Arsenal captain Jimmy Jackson, decided that the thick swirling fog was too much and abandoned the game with 20

minutes remaining. Although irritating at the time, few could have guessed the full consequences of his actions. When the game was replayed the following April, a fixture build-up caused by Everton's FA Cup run left them needing to play three away games in four days. It proved a challenge too much: Woolwich Arsenal won the replayed game 2-1 and Everton missed out on the title by a single point.

5 MAY 1928
First Division
Everton 3 Arsenal 3
One of the most dramatic conclusions to a season in Everton history, with the First Division title already in the bag this game was all about Dixie Dean and his quest for an unprecedented haul of 60 league goals. A week earlier he had scored four against Burnley to draw him within two goals of George Camsell's record of 57. Now he needed a hat-trick to complete his task. Arsenal set out to spoil the party and took an early lead, but Dean soon set about doing what he did best. He bundled a Critchley corner home to equalise, and three minutes later scored a penalty. Everton played at a frantic pace, but as the game neared its conclusion time seemed to be running out. Then, with seven minutes remaining, Alec Troup hit an out-swinging corner, Dean rose above the Arsenal defence and the record was his.

Everton
Davies, Cresswell, O'Donnell, Kelly, Hart, Virr, Critchley, Martin, Dean, Weldon, Troup
Scorer: Dean 3

Arsenal
Patters, Parker, John, Baker, Butler, Blythe, Hulme, Buchan, Shaw, Brain, Peel
Scorers:
Shaw 2, O'Donnell (own goal)

19 OCTOBER 2002
FA Premiership
Everton 2 Arsenal 1
This was the day a legend was born, the kind of match Evertonians who were there will tell their grandchildren about in 50 years time. In the build-up to it, Arsène Wenger had spoken about his team – unbeaten in 29 matches – going through an entire season without losing; it was a mark of how good they were that no one mocked his temerity. But Everton matched Arsenal on this autumn afternoon, and despite conceding an early goal to Freddie Ljungberg, pulled level through Tomasz Radzinski. With ten minutes remaining, David Moyes brought Wayne Rooney on as substitute. The game had entered stoppage time when Thomas Gravesen's hopeful punt was brought down by the teenager, who turned and then unleashed an unstoppable, swirling shot into the top-left corner of the Arsenal net. 'Remember the name! WAYNE ROONEY!' screamed ITV's Clive Tydlesley as Goodison erupted.

Everton
Wright, Hibbert, Weir, Yobo, Unsworth, Carsley (Stubbs), Gravesen, Li Tie (Linderoth), Pembridge, Radzinski (Rooney), Campbell
Scorers: Radzinski, Rooney

Arsenal
Seaman, Lauren, Campbell, Cygan, Cole, Ljungberg (Edu), Gilberto Silva, Viera, Toure (Wiltord), Kanu (Jeffers), Henry
Scorer: Ljungberg
Attendance: 39,038

Arteta, Mikel

The finest Spaniard Goodison ever knew

By the time of his 22nd birthday, Mikel Arteta had played for four clubs in three different countries. He had graduated from Barcelona's legendary Mestalla academy and lined up alongside some of the greatest players – Xavi Hernandez, Ronaldinho, Carlos Puyol – of his era. But he had still not found a place he could call home.

While he languished in an unhappy spell with Real Sociedad in his native Basque region, little could the former Barcelona, Glasgow Rangers and Paris Saint-Germain player have imagined that that place would be Goodison Park. But when David Moyes made an unexpected deadline-day loan move for the midfielder in January 2005, the Spaniard unexpectedly found a place where he belonged.

Arteta's arrival was initially a short-term attempt to bolster Everton's 2004/05 push for Champions League qualification and followed Thomas Gravesen's surprise move to Real Madrid. Skilful, creative, technically outstanding and double-footed, Arteta started out on the flank and added impetus to the closing stages of Everton's most successful league campaign in a generation. With his dashing dark good looks and the manner in which he beckoned opponents before whirling past them in the blink of an eye, it was as if watching a great matador mocking a bull before plunging in for the kill. He made just ten league starts in the remainder of the campaign, but his influence was keenly felt – never more so than when he delivered a pitch-perfect free kick onto the head of Duncan Ferguson, whose goal brought a famous win against Manchester United and effectively secured Champions League qualification.

When first bringing him to Goodison, Moyes had wisely agreed a £2.8million fixed fee with

Real Sociedad to make the loan permanent. It was one of the wisest bits of business conducted in Everton's modern history and an option he took up that summer after protracted negotiations over personal terms. The welcome he had received at Goodison helped make up the Spaniard's mind. 'I was very surprised by the club, the people and the fans when I came here,' Arteta said after signing a five-year contract. 'What we did last season was so very important for everybody. I was so happy and felt so close to the club. I was very surprised that the fans were trying to make me feel an Everton player and an important player very quickly. I much appreciated that from the first minute.'

EVERTON held high hopes for the 2005/06 season, but these were quickly dashed as the club lost ten of their first twelve games and were dumped out in the Champions League qualifying round. It became evident that the rebuilding plans put in place by Moyes needed to go further. In the two years after Arteta's permanent arrival the manager made several key signings, including Joleon Lescott, Steven Pienaar and Yakubu Aiyegbeni, which added pace and guile and provided the Spaniard with team-mates that performed at a similar level.

The Everton midfield purred with energy and at times looked as if it might well propel the team on to great things. In the 2007/08 season many tipped Everton for UEFA Cup glory after they strolled through the group stage. In the last sixteen of the competition, Everton came up against Fiorentina boasting the best group record in the competition. But despite coming into the first leg in Florence on the back of five straight wins, they put in an anaemic performance and lost 0-2.

'I WAS SO HAPPY AND FELT SO CLOSE TO THE CLUB'

AT GOODISON – which was a veritable cauldren of noise – one week later Everton were as good as they had been bad in Italy, inspired by the talismanic Arteta. Andy Johnson put Everton in front early on and Arteta's long-range drive brought the house down on 67 minutes. Everton laid siege to the Italian goal but could not find a way through and somehow the game went to penalties, which

Fiorentina won 4-2. The result stunted Everton's momentum and a second Champions League spot slipped from their grasp, although they still finished fifth.

Arteta had by now dropped into the heart of the team and had taken the number 10 shirt – the playmaker's number in the continental football culture in which he was so versed. When he hummed Everton ticked; he oozed class and composure and was an important contributor of goals in a team that usually won by tight margins. He was Everton's designated penalty taker and scored from free kicks in a manner that was occasionally reminiscent of his great predecessor, Kevin Sheedy.

Disaster struck Arteta in the final part of the 2008/09 season when he snapped a cruciate ligament in a sterile away match at Newcastle. The injury kept him out for ten months and with it he lost the chance to play in the 2009 FA Cup semi-final and his best chance of silverware. High hopes rested on his return but with the insidious petro-billions of Manchester City's owners being wafted around many feared he would follow Joleon Lescott down the M62. But in August 2010 Arteta signed a new five-year contract that, with reputed wages of £75,000 per week, made him the highest-paid player in the club's history. 'Mikel Arteta is one of the finest players ever to wear an Everton shirt and over the past few weeks his pride in wearing that shirt has helped our conversations hugely,' said Bill Kenwright on concluding the deal. 'Alongside several others in the squad, we are both passionate Evertonians.'

Arteta continued to be one of Everton's most influential players throughout the 2010/11 season, although some of his magic had faded with the injury. In particular, he was less potent from set-pieces, which seemed to bounce off their opponents with alarming regularity. But perhaps expectations were just higher than ever following his new contract.

Everton under Kenwright had, alas, become a club where to sell was to survive and losing the best players carried a sense of looming inevitability. In the summer of 2011 there was no money for new signings and the banks were barking at the Goodison boardroom door. An unseemly leaked conversation between the chairman and a fans' group laid bare many of Everton's problems. Vultures loomed again, and on deadline day Arsenal made a £10million offer for the midfielder, which was accepted. Resignation rather than anger – as had accompanied the sales of Lescott and Rooney on previous deadline days – greeted the mood. Arteta was somehow different and his exit was conducted in a manner that befitted the way he played football: with dignity and a touch of class.

'Leaving Everton means the world to me. This is my family and I can see from the reaction people have had with me that it is a proper family. Everyone was devastated,' he said in an emotional farewell.

'I have Everton in my heart and I'm not going to earn more money, I just think it's the right time to move and hopefully they will understand. I appreciate what they have done for me and it has been an absolute pleasure to play in front of them … I just want to thank the fans. Some will get upset. What I can say is that I have given all I have for Everton… everything. I could play better or worse but I always try my best. I made my decision for the best of the club. Thanks a million times for the love, the support and how good they have been with me and my family. I am always going to be an Everton supporter… there's no doubt about it.'

Season	League		FA Cup		League Cup		Europe		Total	
	App	Goals	App	Goals	App	Goals	App	Goals	App	Goals
2004/05	10 (2)	1	1	0	0	0	-	-	11 (2)	1
2005/06	27 (2)	1	4	1	1	0	3	1	35 (2)	3
2006/07	35	9	1	0	2 (1)	0	-	-	38 (1)	9
2007/08	27 (1)	1	0	0	2	0	6 (1)	3	35 (2)	4
2008/09	26	6	3	1	0	0	2	0	31	7
2009/10	11 (2)	6	0 (1)	0	0	0	2	0	13 (3)	6
2010/11	29	3	3	0	0 (1)	0	-	-	32 (1)	3
2011/12	1 (1)	1	0	0	1	1	-	-	2 (1)	2
Total	**166(8)**	**28**	**12 (1)**	**2**	**6 (2)**	**1**	**13 (1)**	**4**	**196(12)**	**35**

[FACTFILE]

BORN
San Sebastian, Spain, 26 March 1982
POSITION
Midfield
OTHER CLUBS
Barcelona (1999–2002);
Paris Saint-Germain (loan, 2000–02);
Glasgow Rangers (2002–04);
Arsenal (2011–)

Ashworth, Alec

Home-grown inside forward who later appeared in the 1964 FA Cup Final for Preston

Season	League		FA Cup		Total	
	App	Goals	App	Goals	App	Goals
1957/58	4	3	0	0	4	3
1958/59	6	0	0	0	6	0
1959/60	2	0	0	0	2	0
Total	**12**	**3**	**0**	**0**	**12**	**3**

[FACTFILE]

BORN
Southport, 1 October 1939
POSITION
Inside forward
OTHER CLUBS
Luton Town (1960–62);
Northampton Town (1962–63);
Preston North End (1963–66)

Ashworth, Sam

Well travelled amateur footballer who lifted the 1904 FA Cup with Manchester City

[FACTFILE]

BORN
Fenton, Staffordshire, March 1877
DIED
30 December 1925
POSITION
Outside defender
OTHER CLUBS
Stoke City (1901–03);
Oxford City (1903);
Manchester City (1903–04);
Reading (1904); Burslem
Port Vale (1905–06)

Season	League		FA Cup		Total	
	App	Goals	App	Goals	App	Goals
1904/05	11	0	0	0	11	0
Total	**11**	**0**	**0**	**0**	**11**	**0**

Aston Villa, and Everton

Midland rivals that played a key part in Everton's ascent to league football

Aston Villa were among the first aristocrats of English football, one of the great powers of Victorian football and a driving force behind the creation of the Football League in 1888. Although many of their trophies were won before the outbreak of the First World War, and despite falling on lean times in several periods during the twentieth century, they re-emerged to win the First Division title and European Cup in the early 1980s. They remain one of the best-supported clubs in England and the club's home, Villa Park, is one of the country's great venues.

Like Everton, Villa's origins lie as a church team and they were founded in 1874 by members of the Villa Cross Wesleyan Chapel in the Handsworth suburb of Birmingham. Villa quickly emerged as one of the leading Midland clubs and in 1887 won the FA Cup. In an era of local football, the FA Cup was the sole competition with genuine national scope. Although there were also a plethora of local cup competitions, most games were still friendlies which often had limited appeal to spectators and were hastily arranged and frequently cancelled.

Everton's first historian, Thomas Keates, was all too aware of the problem: 'The contrast in the attendances at cup ties and ordinary matches, the trifling interest taken in the latter by the public and the insignificance had long vexed the souls of club managers. How can we vitalise the torpid? That was the question.'

RECOGNISING THE LIMITATIONS in football's organisational structure was one of Villa's committeemen, William McGregor, a local draper. He proposed a regular, competitive system of fixtures involving only the top clubs, along the lines of the County Cricket Championship. The season would still allow for local cup competitions and the FA Cup, but interest would be maintained after a team had been knocked out in the early stages.

McGregor quickly garnered support among leading football clubs and in a meeting at Manchester's Royal Hotel in April 1888, the Football League was formally created. Everton were among its twelve founder members, to no little consternation. Local rivals, Bootle, felt they had better credentials, while the FA Cup semi-finalists Crewe Alexandra and Derby Junction were also absent.

BUT IT SEEMS THAT MCGREGOR influenced Everton's inclusion. He had been impressed by the reception Villa received after playing an exhibition game against them. In terms of the league he was interested only in professional clubs and favoured representatives from the major towns and cities (although that did not preclude Accrington's inclusion), both of which worked in Everton's favour. He was also a staunch Methodist, which, given Everton's origins as a church team, may also have influenced his thinking.

In his new invention, Everton initially led the way over Villa, winning the First Division title in 1890/91, but thereafter it was all Villa, who won the league five times over seven years during that decade. In 1897 Villa beat Everton 3-2 in the FA Cup Final at Crystal Palace to claim an historic double. Villa won a sixth league title in 1909/10, but over the following century won just one more championship.

MILK CUP SEMI-FINAL 2ND LEG, VILLA PARK, 1984 *Bailey, Heath and Sharp celebrate Everton's 2-1 aggregate victory over Aston Villa to reach the 1984 Milk Cup Final*

> EVERTON INITIALLY LED THE WAY OVER VILLA, WINNING THE FIRST DIVISION TITLE IN 1890/91

Indeed Villa spent many years in mediocrity and during the 1970s even slipped down into the Third Division. They remained well supported, nevertheless, and a good cup team. Under the management of Joe Mercer in the early 1960s they won the inaugural League Cup, a competition in which they became specialists, winning it five times – including a 1977 victory over Everton.

The transfer of leading players between the two clubs has been comparatively limited and often involved promising young players going from one to the other and embarking on distinguished careers. Notable examples include Jack Sharp and Martin Keown, who both left Villa as youngsters and had excellent Everton careers, and Ken McNaught, a young defender with Everton in the 1970s who won the First Division title and European Cup with Villa in the early 1980s. Joe Mercer and Ron Saunders, a young fringe player at Everton in the 1950s, both managed Villa with considerable success, while Gordon Lee followed a lengthy playing career at Villa Park with a stint as Everton boss in the 1970s.

Key figures

William McGregor

A Scottish-born Methodist who earned his fortune as a Birmingham draper with a profitable sideline in sporting goods, McGregor was one of the leading Victorian sports administrators. He sat on the Aston Villa committee that steered the club from a church team to the top English club of the 1890s. But it was his role in forming the Football League which remains his most enduring contribution to football and Everton – for it seems it was his support which brought Everton into the fold as founder members in 1888.

Jack Sharp

One of sport's great all-rounders, Jack Sharp starred for England at both football and cricket, in so doing becoming one of just a dozen dual internationals. For Everton he won the FA Cup in 1906 and was three times a league runner-up. Later he served on the board of directors. But it was at Villa Park where his footballing career took off. Although he made just 23 appearances for the Midlanders, he did so in one of

their most distinguished sides, winning the league title in before moving to Goodison that summer.

Joe Mercer

Mercer was one of the great footballers of the 1930s and 1940s, a key member of Everton's 1938/39 League Championship winning team, who was infatuated with his boyhood club. He left to join Arsenal in 1946 after falling out with manager Theo Kelly, captaining them to further success. One of the most loved and respected figures in the game, he seemed destined for a successful managerial career. After starting out with Sheffield United in the mid-1950s, he became Villa manager in 1958. Although he was unable to prevent their relegation later that season, he won the Second Division championship in 1959/60 and the inaugural League Cup a year later. He developed a talented young team known as 'Mercer's Minors', but after suffering a stroke in 1964 was – disgracefully – sacked by the Villa board. Later he managed Manchester City with considerable success.

Key matches

Aston Villa 3 Everton 2

10 APRIL 1897 **FA Cup Final, Crystal Palace**

One of the first great FA Cup Finals, this was an epic battle between two of Victorian football's finest powers. It was, recalled William Gibson and Alfred Pickford, 'a remarkable match – many good judges think it was the best game the final ever furnished'. Villa took the lead on 18 minutes, but five minutes later John Bell – the game's outstanding presence – equalised. On 28 minutes Boyle put Everton in front, but it was short-lived and by half-time Villa had not just equalised, but gone 3-2 up. The Midlanders were a formidable force – they had just won the First Division title by a margin of 11 points – and held out in the second half to claim the double.

Everton
Menham, Meecham, Storrier, Boyle, Holt, Stewart, Taylor, Bell, Hartley, Chadwick, Milward
Scorers: Bell, Boyle

Attendance: 65,891

Aston Villa
Whitehouse, Spencer, Evans, Reynolds, James Cowan, Crabtree, Athersmith, Devey, Campbell, Wheldon, John Cowan
Scorers:
Campbell, Wheldon, Crabtree

Aston Villa 3 Everton 2 [AET]
13 APRIL 1977
League Cup Final
second replay, Old Trafford

A game, or rather series of games, that seemed to typify Everton's 1970s, ending in agonising late defeat at Old Trafford. It followed three attempts played over 330 minutes, spanning a calendar month. Everton were desperate to creep out of Liverpool's shadows with some silverware, but after a 0-0 bore draw at Wembley on 12 March they were forced into a replay at Hillsborough four days later. There, Roger Kenyon's late own goal seemed certain to give Villa victory, until Bob Latchford slammed home an equaliser from close range.

Nearly a month passed before the second replay. On 38 minutes Ken McNaught flicked on a Goodlass free kick and Latchford put Everton in front. Villa attacked incessantly, but just as it seemed as if Everton would hold out they struck two goals in two minutes. Mick Lyons scored a quick-fire equaliser and the game entered extra time. It seemed to be heading for penalties – a first in domestic football – when, two minutes from the end, a deflection off Goodlass wrongfooted the Everton defence and nobody could prevent Brian Little from grabbing a winner. And so, Everton's search for a trophy continued.

Everton
Lawson, Robinson, Darracott, Lyons, McNaught, King, Hamilton, Dobson, Latchford, Pearson (Seargeant), Goodlass
Scorers: Latchford, Lyons

Aston Villa
Burridge, Gidman (Smith), Robson, Phillips, Nichol, Mortimer, Graydon, Little, Deehan, Cropley, Cowans
Scorers: Nicholl, Little 2

Attendance: 54,749

Everton 2 Aston Villa 0
15 FEBRUARY 1984
Milk Cup semi final 1st leg,
Goodison Park

For years Evertonians had suffered false dawn after false dawn in their long wait for success. But Everton's Milk Cup semi-final win was the latest sign that times were changing. The previous month there had been famous cup wins over Stoke City and Oxford United and Everton's league campaign was gathering momentum. The tie with Villa was a poor, scrappy encounter decided by Kevin Sheedy's bobbling cross shot and Kevin Richardson's fierce drive. Villa won the second leg 1-0 a week later, but Everton had done enough to go through on aggregate. It was a clear sign that Everton were on the up, but not even the most optimistic fan could have foreseen the adventures that were to follow.

Everton
Southall, Stevens, Bailey, Ratcliffe, Mountfield, Reid, Irvine, Heath, Sharp, Richardson, Sheedy
Scorers: Sheedy, Richardson

Aston Villa
Spink, Williams, Gibson, Evans, Bremner, Mortimer, Curbishley, Shaw, Withe, McMahon, Walters

Attendance: 40,006

Atkins, Ian

Well-travelled midfielder who played a cameo during the Club's greatest season

[FACTFILE]

BORN
Sheldon, 16 January 1957
POSITION
Midfield
OTHER CLUBS
Shrewsbury Town (1975–82);
Sunderland (1982–84);
Ipswich Town (1985–88);
Birmingham City (1988–90);
Colchester United
(as player-manager, 1990–91);
Birmingham City (1991–92);
Cambridge United
(as player-manager, 1992–93);
Sunderland (1993);
Doncaster United
(as player-manager, 1993–94)

Season	League		FA Cup		League Cup		Europe		Total	
	App	Goals	App	Goals	App	Goals	App	Goals	App	Goals
1984/85	6	1	0 (1)	0	0	0	0 (1)	0	6 (2)	1
1985/86	0 (1)	0	0	0	0	0	0	0	0 (1)	0
Total	**6 (1)**	**1**	**0 (1)**	**0**	**0**	**0**	**0 (1)**	**0**	**6 (3)**	**1**

Attendances, Record

GOODISON PARK has boasted crowds of more than 70,000 on 16 occasions; all were in the 16 seasons that immediately followed the Second World War. The last, against Liverpool in 1962, greeted the first Merseyside derby in seven years.

All fixtures were in the First Division unless otherwise stated.

Attendance	Date	Opponents
78,299	18 September 1948	Liverpool, 1-1
77,920	14 February 1953	Manchester United, 2-1 (FA Cup fifth round)
76,839	28 August 1954	Preston North End, 1-0
75,818	29 January 1958	Blackburn Rovers, 1-2 (FA Cup fourth round)
75,322	27 December 1954	Wolves, 3-2
74,867	27 December 1960	Burnley, 0-3
74,782	28 January 1959	Charlton Athletic, 4-1 (FA Cup fourth round replay)
72,921	11 February 1950	Tottenham Hotspur, 1-0 (FA Cup fifth round)
72,569	31 January 1948	Wolves, 3-2 (FA Cup fourth round replay)
72,488	22 September 1962	Liverpool, 2-2
72,000	29 January 1955	Liverpool, 0-4 (FA Cup fourth round)
71, 868	4 September 1957	Manchester United, 3-3
71,587	14 February 1948	Fulham, 0-1 (FA Cup fifth round replay)
71,150	16 September 1950	Liverpool, 1-3
71,088	7 April 1950	Blackpool, 3-0
70,812	27 August 1949	Liverpool, 0-0

Atteveld, Ray

Trail-blazing foreign signing who provided competent if unexceptional service

Hailed as the most promising player to emerge from Eredivisie side, Haarlam, since the great Ruud Gullit, Ray Atteveld was part of the first batch of Everton's foreign signings.

Signed by Colin Harvey in the summer of 1989 – shortly after Stefan Rehn arrived at Goodison – Atteveld was a right back cum right midfielder. His belated debut in December 1989 came after Rehn's last action for the club and

his attributes made him better suited for First Division football than the Swede. And yet, while clearly a competent squad member, there was nothing that particularly distinguished Atteveld's play. Rather than for his football, at Goodison he is best remembered for stripping down to his underpants on the last day of the 1989/90 season and throwing his entire kit into the crowd.

> AT GOODISON HE IS BEST REMEMBERED FOR STRIPPING DOWN TO HIS UNDERPANTS AND THROWING HIS ENTIRE KIT INTO THE CROWD

Although he played in the famous 4-4 draw with Liverpool in February 1991, Howard Kendall's return three months before that game marked the beginning of the end of his Goodison career. There followed a brief loan spell at West Ham before a £250,000 move to Bristol City. Within a year he had returned to the Netherlands, where he would play out a journeyman's career.

Season	League		FA Cup		League Cup		Other		Total	
	App	Goals	App	Goals	App	Goals	App	Goals	App	Goals
1989/90	16 (2)	1	3 (1)	0	0	0	-	-	19 (3)	1
1990/91	17 (3)	0	3	0	3	0	0 (1)	0	23 (4)	0
1991/92	8 (5)	0	0	0	3 (1)	1	0 (2)	0	11(8)	0
Total	41 (10)	1	6 (1)	0	3 (1)	1	0 (3)	0	53 (15)	2

Arthur Attwood

Attwood, Arthur

Late-1920s understudy to Dixie Dean

Season	League		FA Cup		Total	
	App	Goals	App	Goals	App	Goals
1928/29	1	0	0	0	1	0
1929/30	2	0	0	0	2	0
Total	3	0	0	0	3	0

THE

EVERTON
·ENCYCLOPEDIA·

John **Bailey,** David **Bain,** Leighton **Baines,** Ibrahima **Bakayoko, Alan Ball,** Michael **Ball,** William and Robert **Balmer,** Bert **Banks,** Arthur **Barber,** John **Bardsley,** George **Barker,** Ross **Barkley,** George **Barlow,** John **Barlow,** Stuart **Barlow,** Nick **Barmby,** Geoff **Barnett,** Earl **Barrett,** John **Barton,** The **Battle of Goodison,** Dr James Clement **Baxter,** Jose **Baxter,** Peter **Beagrie,** Peter **Beardsley,** George **Beare,** James **Beattie,** Jermaine **Beckford,** Rod **Belfitt,** John **Bell,** Robert 'Bunny' **Bell,** Laurie **Bell, Bellefield,** Harry **Bennett,** Marcus **Bent,** Stanley **Bentham,** Jack **Bentley,** Mike **Bernard,** Arthur **Berry,** C.H.**Berry,** William **Berwick,** Robert **Beveridge,** Jake **Bidwell,** Alan **Biley,** Slaven **Bilić,** Peter **Billing,** Diniyar **Bilyaletdinov,** Billy **Bingham,** Ken **Birch,** Alex **Birnie,** Ian **Bishop,** William **Black,** John **Blair,** Jesper **Blomqvist,** Joe **Blythe,** Bill **Bocking,** Hugh **Bolton,** Johnnie **Bone,** Tom **Booth,** Brian **Borrows,** John **Borthwick, Bosman Ruling,** Adam **Bowman,** Wally **Boyes,** Dan **Boyle,** Richard **Boyle,** Paul **Bracewell,** Frank **Bradshaw,** George **Bradshaw,** Alec **Brady,** John **Bramwell,** Michael **Branch,** Drew **Brand,** James **Brannick,** John **Brearley,** George **Brewster,** Harry **Briggs,** Billy **Brindle,** William **Briscoe, British Championship,** Jimmy **Broad,** William **Bromilow,** Andy **Browell,** Tommy **Browell,** Sandy **Brown,** William **Brown** (b. 1865), William **Brown** (b. 1897), Ian **Buchan,** Harry **Buck,** Ted **Buckle,** Mick **Buckley,** George **Burnett,** David **Burrows,** Andy **Burton**

Bailey, John

Left back and court jester of the Kendall glory days

Perhaps the most enduring image of Everton's 1984 FA Cup Final victory over Watford was that of left back John Bailey celebrating victory. Squat and beaming, he danced in the sun, bedecked in an Everton-decorated top hat and comical blue sunglasses. The picture seemed to encapsulate Bailey, for he was always more than just a valued team-member.

Fittingly for a man born on April Fool's Day he was the dressing room prankster, the man who defused tension in a crisis and led the obligatory post-victory party. Read any account of Everton in this era, and tales of Bailey's merry-making will invariably feature.

> 'PELE TRIED IT ONCE,' HE LIKES TO SAY OF HIS STUPENDOUS GOAL AGAINST LUTON ALL THOSE YEARS AGO, 'BUT HE MISSED!'

[FACTFILE]

BORN
Liverpool, 1 April 1957
POSITION
Left back
OTHER CLUBS
Blackburn Rovers (1975–79);
Newcastle United (1985–88);
Bristol City (1988–91)
HONOURS
1984 FA Cup;
1984/85
League Championship

Yet Bailey was more than just a clown: he was a good player – good enough to win FA Cup and League winner's medals, as well as a solitary England B cap. Were it not for the ruthlessness of Howard Kendall, who in 1985 believed the Everton defence needed hardening up, he may well also have added to the 219 appearances he made over seven years in an Everton shirt. And who could possibly forget the goal he scored from his own half against Luton Town, one week before Christmas 1982?

ALTHOUGH BORN in Liverpool the left back started out at Blackburn Rovers, clocking 120 appearances before Gordon Lee paid £300,000 for the highly rated 22-year-old in the summer of 1979. Diminutive and quick, Bailey was fine on the overlap, bursting into the opposition half to send in testing crosses. A solid defender, he sometimes lacked the physical presence necessary to challenge more daunting opponents.

Perhaps it was this that led Howard Kendall to sign the more abrasive Pat Van den Hauwe – a hard man in every sense of the word – in September

1984. Bailey nevertheless made enough appearances to claim a title medal that season before his departure to Newcastle in an £80,000 deal in October 1985. He later played out his career with Bristol City.

Bailey briefly returned to Everton in the 1990s as a coach before drifting out of the game, although he still attends Goodison every week. Now in his fifties, he is able to reflect on an accomplished career and at least one unprecedented achievement. 'Pele tried it once,' he likes to say of his stupendous goal against Luton all those years ago, 'but he missed!'

Season	League		FA Cup		League Cup		Other		Total	
	App	Goals	App	Goals	App	Goals	App	Goals	App	Goals
1979/80	42	2	6	0	5	0	2	0	55	2
1980/81	31	0	4	0	1 (1)	0	-	-	36 (1)	0
1981/82	12	0	0	0	3	0	-	-	15	0
1982/83	37	1	5	0	2	0	-	-	44	1
1983/84	33	0	7	0	7	0	-	-	47	0
1984/85	15	0	0	0	1	0	5	0	21	0
1985/86	1	0	0	0	1	0	0 (1)	-	2 (1)	0
Total	**171**	**3**	**22**	**0**	**20 (1)**	**0**	**7 (1)**	**0**	**220 (2)**	**3**

Bain, David

Forward turned defender who provided cover in the early Dixie Dean era

Season	League		FA Cup		Total	
	App	Goals	App	Goals	App	Goals
1924/25	3	0	1	0	4	0
1924/25	23	0	2	0	25	0
1926/27	10	3	2	0	12	3
1927/28	2	0	0	0	2	0
Total	38	3	5	0	43	3

[FACTFILE]

BORN
Rutherglen, Scotland,
5 August 1900
POSITION
Forward
OTHER CLUBS
Manchester United
(1922–24);
Bristol City (1928–29);
Halifax Town (1930–31);
Rochdale (1932–33)

Baines, Leighton

Outstanding England international who has become the finest exponent of the left back art since Ray Wilson

In completing a £6million move from Wigan Athletic to Everton in July 2007, Leighton Baines fulfilled a lifelong ambition to join his boyhood club. It was also the conclusion of a journey that had seen him rejected as a schoolboy by Liverpool and rise from the Second Division to the Premier League. At Goodison his progression continued, bringing him an FA Cup Final appearance, England recognition and a reputation as one of the finest full backs in the Premier League. At Goodison many now consider him the best left back the club has possessed since Ray Wilson.

Born and brought up in Kirkby, Baines first attracted notice as a left winger with Liverpool Schoolboys, following a tradition set by Brian Labone. He was attached to the Liverpool Centre of Excellence but released as a teenager. After interest from Wolverhampton Wanderers he joined Wigan Athletic, making his debut in the Second Division in 2002. His progress was swift and he helped earn promotion to Division One in the 2002/03 season. Two years later Wigan were promoted to the Premier League.

THE SON of a Liverpool supporter, Baines changed allegiance to the blue side of Merseyside as a young boy and followed Everton to the 1995 FA Cup Final when he was aged 10. 'I started watching Everton properly when I was about 14,' he told wthe Guardian in 2007. 'My mum wouldn't let me go on my own but my cousin was three years older than me so we'd get the bus, 50p from Kirkby, and then hang around outside until we could sneak in. We'd wait until they opened the gates after 75 minutes for the early-leavers to go. There were stewards on the gates and if they were in a good mood they would wink and let us in. One guy, in particular, used to look out for us. But sometimes, if we were unlucky, there would be a jobsworth on the door and we wouldn't get to see anything.'

His move to Goodison came after two impressive seasons in the Premier League with Wigan, a period in which he brought his tally of England under-21 appearances up to a total of 16. But although he had impressed at the highest level of English football, his early displays for Everton were marked by unusual hesitancy and lapses of concentration. It took 18 months for him to make the left back berth his own, with Joleon Lescott and Nuno Valente often preferred ahead of him. Sometimes he was selected in left midfield.

Midway through the 2008/09 season injuries to Valente and Joseph Yobo forced David Moyes

to give Baines an extended run in his preferred position and he excelled, remaining there ever since. Quick, skilful, a fine, intelligent overlapping attacker, Baines combines attacking prowess down the flank with defensive solidity at the back. In particular he forged an exceptional left-sided partnership with Steven Pienaar, and their understanding proved – at times – subliminal. 'He is probably the best player I have ever played with because he is so selfless as well,' said Baines after Pienaar's return to Goodison on loan in January 2012. 'The

shift he has put in after not playing very often and training once is unbelievable. He gives everything. He does all the work you would want him to do and more. Sometimes he was over on the right and trying to make things happen. When it breaks down he is not the type to take his rest there, he will get back and help out as well.'

Baines's set-piece technique is formidable too, and he has a fine record as a taker of both penalties and free kicks. By the end of the 2011/12 season he had scored

nine out of ten of the penalties he had taken for Everton. Few of his free kicks have been struck with such magnificent velocity – or provided a more dramatic conclusion to a game – as that which almost burst the Chelsea net in the last minute of extra time in a 2011 FA Cup fourth round replay at Stamford Bridge.

His form first saw him called up to the England squad in March 2009 and he made his international debut against Egypt in March the following year. His subsequent omission that summer

from England's World Cup squad – with the unheralded Stephen Warnock taking his place – caused consternation and befuddlement. He made a successful return to the international fold and was included in England's squad for the 2012 European Championships. Only the continued excellence of Ashley Cole in the England left back position has limited him to fewer than ten caps.

Season	League		FA Cup		League Cup		Europe		Total	
	App	Goals	App	Goals	App	Goals	App	Goals	App	Goals
2007/08	13 (9)	0	1	0	0 (1)	0	3 (2)	0	17 (12)	0
2008/09	26 (5)	1	7	0	0	0	1	0	34 (5)	1
2009/10	37	1	2	1	1	0	8	0	48	2
2010/11	38	5	4	2	2	0	-	-	44	7
2011/12	33	4	5 (1)	1	3	0	-	-	41 (1)	5
Total	147(14)	11	19 (1)	4	6 (1)	0	12 (2)	0	184(18)	15

[FACTFILE]

BORN
Kirkby, 11 December 1984
POSITION
Left back
OTHER CLUB
Wigan Athletic
HONOURS
8 England caps (2010–)

Bakayoko, Ibrahima

Misfiring striker of mysterious origins

Signed from Montpellier by Walter Smith for £4.5million in October 1998, Ibrahima Bakayoko was heralded as one of the Premiership's most exciting foreign arrivals. Considered a player of pace and promise, the 21-year-old striker was thrust into a Merseyside derby on his debut and almost realised Evertonians' hopes in the opening stages when he nearly bundled the ball home. Alas, this set the pattern for a disappointing eight months at Everton in which he remained very much a nearly man.

Glimpses of his potential were fitful: though quick and lively and

possessing a formidable shot, he struggled with the aggression and intensity of English football. There were, however, magnificent braces at Bristol City (the first from a late free kick of majestic velocity) and Blackburn Rovers, as well as a deftly taken winner at home to Southampton. But increasingly he found himself a marginalised figure, more so after the arrival of Kevin Campbell in March 1999, and by May Smith was prepared to cut his losses and sell him to Marseille for £4million.

The first Muslim to play for Everton – his daily prayers at Bellefield were the source of respectful curiosity among his colleagues – questions were nevertheless asked about Bakayoko's origins. One French coach claimed in the late 1990s

that Bakayoko was at least eight years older than he said he was, having seen him play for the Ivory Coast's under-21 team at the start of the decade. Other rumours hinted that a move to Arsenal had collapsed because a bone scan revealed him to be older than he claimed.

SUCH innuendo remains questionable, however. In October 2007 Bakayoko, now aged 30 (or a sprightly 38, depending on your view), made a surprise return to Goodison with Greek side Larissa in the UEFA Cup group stage. Although his goal had helped knock out Blackburn Rovers in the previous round, as with many of his other showings at Goodison he had a quiet night as his former team ran out easy 3-1 winners.

[FACTFILE]

BORN
Seguela, Ivory Coast
31 December 1976
POSITION
Striker
OTHER CLUBS
Stade d'Abdijan (1994–95);
Montpellier (1995–98);
Marseille (1999–2003);
Osasuna (Spain, 2003–04);
FC Istres (France, 2004–05);
Livorno (Italy, 2005–07);
Messina (Italy, 2007);
FC Larissa (2007–08);
PAOK Salonika (2008–09);
PAS Giannina (2009–)
HONOURS
11 Ivory Coast caps
(14 goals) (1996–2002)

Season	League		FA Cup		League Cup		Total	
	App	Goals	App	Goals	App	Goals	App	Goals
1998/99	17(6)	4	1 (2)	2	2	1	20(8)	7
Total	17(6)	4	1 (2)	2	2	1	20(8)	7

Ball, Alan

World Cup winning midfielder who belongs to the highest pantheon of Everton greats

When Bill Shankly described Alan Ball as 'one of the greatest players since the war', he spoke for virtually all followers of English football through the 1960s and 1970s. The midfielder, who cut a distinctive figure because of a shock of flame-red hair – matched by a fiery temperament – was a World Cup winner in July 1966, aged just 21, and an Everton player a month later.

The ultimate self-made footballer, fiercely driven and ambitious after suffering rejection by Bolton Wanderers as a teenager, he excelled at Goodison for five years, winning a league title in 1970 and forming part of the so-called 'Holy Trinity' with Colin Harvey and Howard Kendall.

Born in Farnworth, the Bolton suburb that also bred Tommy Lawton, Ball inherited something of a footballing pedigree, for his father – Alan Ball senior – was a lower-league journeyman with Southport, Birmingham City and Oldham, and later a coach and manager. Rejected by his home-town club – the trauma of rejection would be a formative experience – he signed for Blackpool at 15 and promised his father that he would play for England by the time he was 20.

Self-belief was never a problem for the young footballer. As a 16-year-old he found himself playing in practice games alongside Sir Stanley Matthews and during one session played a pass inside the full back, inviting the great man to run on to it. Matthews demanded that the ball be passed to his feet, only to be told: 'It's your job to bloody run and

get it.' Matthews may have been unimpressed, but Ball was soon to play his first league game for Blackpool in a 2-1 win at Liverpool.

He also maintained his promise to his father, making his international debut against Yugoslavia in May 1965, three days before his 20th birthday. Little over a year later he was lining up in the World Cup Final against West Germany; in extra time, Ball was the game's best player, seen with his socks around his ankles, willing his team-mates on and inspiring them with his running. He provided the cross for the second of Geoff Hurst's goals – the one that hit the underside of the crossbar – and could be seen in space, screaming for the ball, when Hurst hit his late third.

IN HIS CLASSIC coaching study, Soccer For Thinkers, Malcolm Allison recalled what Ball said about the closing minutes of the 1966 final when he saw the ball run loose. 'I thought, oh no! I can't get that one – I'm finished. I had already died twice and been looking for a chance to have a breather for 10 minutes. But that [Karl-Heinz] Schnellinger was already shooting after it. Well, I'd been beating him all afternoon so there was no reason why I couldn't do it again. Here we go again, I thought. This time I am really finished.'

'How fast he raced to the ball I could not judge,' Allison remembered. 'Certainly it was faster than anyone else at that particular distance.'

Such energy and commitment made the inside forward a coveted player indeed, and it was inevitable that he would leave Blackpool for a bigger club. Leeds United seemed the most likely destination – in fact it later emerged that so desperate was their manager, Don Revie, to sign Ball that he arranged a series of surreptitious meetings with the player on Saddleworth Moor in which cash-filled envelopes were handed over to the player in an attempt to tap him up – but the Elland Road board were split over whether to meet Blackpool's asking price: £110,000 – a British record.

Instead, Harry Catterick, always a wily manoeuvrer in the transfer market, slipped in and on 15 August 1966 met Blackpool's price.

HE EXCELLED AT GOODISON FOR FIVE YEARS, WINNING A LEAGUE TITLE IN 1970

Despite winning the FA Cup in May 1966, Everton's league form the previous season had been hugely disappointing and after a lethargic display in the Charity Shield against Liverpool, Catterick deemed it necessary to bolster his midfield. Ball marked his Everton debut against Fulham on 20 August with the only goal of the game, although the best was still to come from the pocket dynamo. On 27 August, the second Saturday of the season, Everton met Liverpool for the first league derby of the season. According to

Catterick, Ball's arrival had already lifted the standard of the other player's contributions 'by 10 per cent' but what happened that afternoon was more indicative of Ball's influence than his manager's rhetoric. On ten minutes Ball put Everton ahead after finishing off a Johnny Morrissey shot which had deflected into his path. Seven minutes later he took advantage of a mix-up between Ron Yeats and Gordon Milne to crash the ball into the roof of the net and put Everton 2-0 up. Despite a Tommy Smith goal, Liverpool were unable to force a comeback and Sandy Brown sealed a 3-1 victory seven minutes from time. 'When the second one went in,' Ball said later, 'I'd never heard so many people singing my name or encouraging me like that in my life – even by comparison with the World Cup – and I've never experienced it again.'

SEVEN MONTHS later Ball re-affirmed his reputation as Liverpool's bête noire when he hit the winner in an FA Cup fifth round tie. Such was the anticipation preceding the game, 105,000 tickets to watch the game, both live at Goodison and relayed on television screens at Anfield, had been sold within just three hours. Ball's angled volley was the only goal of the match and brought an unprecedented roar from Evertonians watching from both the club's current and former homes. 'I smacked the volley from an acute angle right in the other corner,' Ball recalled. 'I've never hit a volley as sweetly in all my life. I finished up right in the corner by the flag, and I don't think I got away from there for about three minutes. These days, I'd have been charged with bringing the game into disrepute!'

Unquestionably a vital and regular source of goals from the middle of the park – Ball scored 56 times in his first three seasons – his goalscoring should not overshadow his other attributes. His blend of ferocious aggression and delicate skill was unusual, but Ball carried it off to his own magnificent standards. Quick and energetic, a harrier and a chaser, though elegant too, Ball would not have looked out of place in the modern game.

Along with the World Cup, it was his midfield partnership with Colin Harvey and Howard Kendall for which he is most remembered. Goodison's 'Holy Trinity' was considered to be a work of 'perpetual motion' and won many of the team's plaudits. 'As three players we hardly ever needed any coaching,' Ball would recall. 'We could find each other in the dark.'

Colin Harvey would say: 'Howard, Alan and myself were all different but when we came together as a midfield three we just clicked and gelled. He was the one who did everything at 100 miles an hour and he had such a great big heart as well as fantastic ability. It was a privilege to have played with him.'

Although only 5ft 6in tall, Ball was the proverbial giant among men, omnipresent – and it wasn't just his red hair and famous white boots which made him easy to pick out. The possessor of a fierce temper, team-mates and opposing players alike were often on the receiving end of a tongue-lashing from the midfielder if things went awry. Sent off twice in his early years at the club and given a five-week ban for poor discipline at a crucial stage in the 1969/70 season, Catterick took the unusual step of appointing Ball captain in an attempt to positively channel his aggression. Explaining the appointment, Everton's manager said: 'It was a psychological move to give Alan more responsibility and make him more aware of referees' and players' problems.'

BALL LED Everton for the first time against Tottenham in March 1970 and played one of his best games in a blue shirt, getting on the scoresheet in a 2-1 victory. A six-match winning streak followed and Ball's leadership was integral to Everton's successful title challenge. Invariably, he enjoyed the added responsibility, which occurred as a result of an injury to Brian Labone. 'I don't think anything will change my temperament, but being captain helped me keep out of trouble,' he said. 'I could ask questions of referees instead of screaming at them as I used to do.'

Perhaps surprisingly, the 1970 League Championship was the only domestic medal Ball ever won, but for a period he was considered priceless. When Harry Catterick was asked for a valuation of Ball in spring 1971 he said, 'I would not dream of selling him, but of course every player has his price. Alan's is one million pounds.' When asked if such a sum were offered, would he sell, Catterick replied, 'No, but I would consider it first.'

'I'D NEVER HEARD SO MANY PEOPLE SINGING MY NAME OR ENCOURAGING ME LIKE THAT IN MY LIFE'

Season	League		FA Cup		League Cup		Europe		Total	
	App	Goals	App	Goals	App	Goals	App	Goals	App	Goals
1966/67	41	15	6	2	-	-	4	1	51	18
1967/68	34	20	4	0	2	0	-	-	40	20
1968/69	40	16	5	0	4	2	-	-	49	18
1969/70	37	10	1	1	3	1	-	-	41	12
1970/71	39	2	6	3	1	0	6	3	52	8
1971/72	17	3	0	0	0	0	-	-	17	3
Total	**208**	**66**	**21**	**5**	**10**	**3**	**10**	**4**	**250**	**79**

Also played: 1970 Charity Shield

But Catterick was unpredictable and ruthless. Nine months later, in December 1971, he sold the midfielder to double-winners Arsenal for £220,000 – another British record fee. Ball was 'flabbergasted' by his own account and did not want to go. Catterick, according to Ball, responded: 'It's business, son. I am doubling my money. I've had you for six years. I am making a profit on you and I have had an awful lot out of you. Football's business, son.' With those words, Ball was no longer an Everton player.

Most Evertonians were up in arms over the deal and many still recall the news with shock. The Everton historian George Orr believes there was more to the transfer than was immediately apparent, however, and later wrote of the deal in his book Everton in the Seventies: Singing the Blues:

There were rumours about gambling debts and unrest in the dressing room. I was at his last match at Derby and remember Howard Kendall playing a blinder and only making one bad pass, Ball turned round and screamed at him. Kendall walked toward Ball and gave him a look that could kill. This to me was the fault, Ball was a great player but his mouth was never shut, arguing with referees or linesmen cost him many bookings and forced Everton into team changes for avoidable suspensions. If you look back, players from that team, Lyons, Darracott, Kendall, Harvey and Royle have all gone on to serve the club in some form of management but there has never been a place for Ball, isn't there a pointer there?

Ball served Arsenal for five years, also captaining England for a short time while at Highbury. He joined Southampton midway through the 1976/77 season and

remained there until 1978. He then headed to the United States, spending two years playing in the NASL, first with Philadelphia Fury, then in Canada with Vancouver Whitecaps. In 1980 he left America for a short unsuccessful spell as Blackpool player-manager before returning to The Dell for a second spell as a Southampton player.

In 1982 one of the periodic attempts to stimulate football in Hong Kong brought Alan Ball to the former colony. His friend and fellow World Cup winner, Bobby Moore, had recently been appointed coach of Eastern Athletic by the club's wealthy owners, and sought out Ball for some of the passion and guile that were trademarks over a 20-year-long career. 'It was a great move,' said Ball. 'I would be linking up with Bobby again and there was plenty of money.' So much, in fact, that he was able to turn his back on Southampton. A year later he returned to England, playing out his career with Bristol Rovers.

A MANAGERIAL CAREER of varying success followed. With Portsmouth, who he managed between 1984 and 1989, he won promotion to the First Division in 1987 and was considered the club's best manager since the 1950s. At Stoke City (1989–91) he struggled, but at Exeter City (1991–94) he was a relative success, bringing some order and good times to a club whose history was replete with uncertainty and struggles. This led to 18 months in charge at Southampton (1994–95) where again Ball was a modest success, attaining mid-table respectability and bringing the best from the Saints' mercurial star Matthew Le Tissier. In the summer of 1995 he was allowed to join Manchester City, but the move was disastrous; City were relegated from the Premiership and Ball resigned three games into the 1996/97 season. A brief spell back at Portsmouth in the late 1990s was fruitless.

> 'FOR ME HE WAS THE GREATEST EVERTONIAN OF ALL TIME'
> **COLIN HARVEY**

By the first years of the 21st century, Ball's football career was all but over. An occasional pundit and prized after-dinner speaker, he was always a popular guest at Goodison and at reunion dinners was treated with the same reverence with which he had been greeted in his heyday. The death of his wife, Lesley, in 2004 hit him hard and was detailed with candour in his autobiography Playing Extra Time, published later that year. Ball, always sprightly, courteous and with a word for everyone, put on a brave face and remained positive. It shocked the world of football and Evertonians in particular when he died suddenly at his home in April 2007.

'I supported Everton as a boy, played there, coached there and managed there,' said Colin Harvey after his friend's death. 'For me he was the greatest Evertonian of all time. Obviously I never saw Dixie Dean play, but in my time Alan was the greatest I have seen at Everton. The fact that he was the man of the match in a World Cup Final at 21 years of age says it all.' Phil Neville, Ball's modern successor as Everton captain, said: 'I will always recall he was nothing other than an absolute gentleman. He is a legend through being part of the '66 team, and an Everton legend through his faultless performances on the pitch. He was, and still is, an inspiration for all current Everton players.'

GOODISON PARK saw the best of Alan Ball's firebrand football and it was here where his heart lay. Shortly before his death Ball said: 'When you have been touched by football clubs – when you've played for them, when you've represented them and when you've managed them – they are always there with you, they never change. But I have got to say that I am an Evertonian. The worse things get, the better the fans get, and that is why Everton is such a fantastic football club. And that is why players that play for Everton know exactly what is needed.

'I would love to play at Goodison again. It held so many memories for me. It was just such a wonderful place to play ... in front of people who appreciated players giving 100 per cent. That is what Goodison is all about and that is what the club is all about.'

For many players, winning the World Cup at 21 could mean complacency or a downwards spiral, but Ball prevented his career from fizzling into anticlimax through a continual and tireless dedication to improve his game. When he was feted as an England hero in 1966 he said, 'People say I am a success but I have won

nothing. No cup medal, no League medal, no European honour.' Even when he won the League in 1970 his relentless search for perfection continued – although no more medals were ever to come Alan Ball's way.

Books:

ALAN BALL, *Ball of Fire*, Pelham, 1969
ALAN BALL, *It's All About A Ball*, WH Allen, 1978
ALAN BALL, *Playing Extra Time*, Sidgwick and Jackson, London, 2004
DAVID FRANCE AND BECKY TALLENTIRE, *Goodison's Holy Trinity*, Skript, 2001

[FACTFILE]

BORN
Farnworth, 12 May 1945

DIED
Warsash, 25 April 2007

POSITION
Inside forward / midfield

OTHER CLUBS
Blackpool (1962–66);
Arsenal (1971–76);
Southampton (1976–78);
Philadelphia Fury (US, 1978–79);
Vancouver Whitecaps (US, 1979–80);
Blackpool (player-manager, 1980–81);
Southampton (1981–82);
Eastern Athletic (Hong Kong, 1982–83);
Bristol Rovers (1983–84)

AS MANAGER
Blackpool (1980–81);
Portsmouth (1984–89);
Stoke City (1989–91);
Exeter City (1991–94);
Southampton (1994–95);
Manchester City (1995–96);
Portsmouth (1998–99)

HONOURS
1969/70 League Championship;
1966 World Cup;
72 England caps (8 goals) (1965–75);
MBE

Ball, Michael

Outstanding young prospect who fell foul of Walter Smith

Michael Ball was one of the first of an outstanding crop of young players to emerge from the Everton youth system in the late 1990s.

The left-sided defender and graduate of the FA National School was handed his Everton debut during Dave Watson's caretaker spell in charge at the end of the 1996/97 season and despite Everton's perilous position at the time, never looked anything but a model of composure. Even at the age of just 17, the tall blond defender seemed the very antithesis of the typical English defensive player. Composed on the ball and the possessor of an exceptional first touch and with assured and confident distribution, it was clear that Ball was a cut above many of his contemporaries. And yet he possessed the strength and aerial presence that suited the hurly-burly of the Premier League. During Howard Kendall's disastrous third reign as manager, Ball was one of the few players to flourish. Given an extended run as a left wing back, Ball's confident displays were enough for Kendall to deem Andy Hinchcliffe – England's sometime left back, no less – surplus to requirements mid-season. An England under-21 call-up was just reward for a player whose sterling displays helped keep Everton from sliding into the abyss.

Through the 1998/99 season Ball kept his place in the Everton team, although under Walter Smith's management – which at times seemed preoccupied with filling the team with as many defenders as possible – Ball was often asked to fill in as a left midfielder, which was unsuited for the young defender. His performances waned and he fell foul of Smith, whose disciplinarian style had little patience with the perceived excesses of the younger players. With Richard Dunne, Ball was publicly admonished for missing training after the millennium celebrations, and later disciplined for having the temerity to laugh on the team coach after a League Cup defeat.

DURING THE 2000/01 season a long-term injury to Richard Gough saw Ball revert to centre half, where he excelled. Twice he was called up to the England squad, making his debut against Spain in February 2001 in Sven-Goran Eriksson's first game as manager. Ball was awarded the club's player of the year award but should have recognised that this was a curse: the two previous recipients – Nick Barmby and Don Hutchison – had been sold without playing another game after receiving the accolade.

On the basis of his excellent form, Ball requested a revised contract, but these negotiations soon fell down. Smith used the opportunity to rid the club of a player who he seemed to disdain – this despite Ball's perennial excellence and youth. Still aged only 21 he was sold to Glasgow Rangers for £6.5million in August 2001.

Ball made no secret of the fact that he did not wish to leave. 'I went to the training ground to say my goodbyes but I had to leave because I was getting too emotional,' he said. 'It was a sad moment for me as I'd been at the club since I was 14 and never expected to leave. The tears were on their way and I didn't want my friends to see me like that so I cut my goodbyes short and got in my car.'

His time at Rangers was undermined by persistent injuries – the result of playing on with painkilling injections while at Everton. Ball later said: 'I was disappointed with Everton because they went with the cheapest option at the time to get me fit. The injections rather than the operation, and I was naive perhaps. When you think back, they were fighting relegation and then they sell me in the six weeks that my knee is good from the injection.' In all it cost him 18 months on the sidelines and diminished some of his earlier promise. When he recovered Rangers refused to play him, lest he play more than 60 games and so trigger an extra payment to Everton. The impasse was eventually resolved after much public posturing and Ball lifted wwwwthe Scottish title in 2005.

Shortly after he was sold to PSV Eindhoven for £500,000, where he spent an unsuccessful 18-month spell. He returned to the Premier League in January 2007 with Manchester City, initially on a short-term deal. That summer rumours linked Ball with a return to Everton, but a move was not forthcoming and he took up the option of a new contract at Eastlands. When that expired in 2009 he spent two years out of the game, but returned to Leicester, then managed by Eriksson, in the summer of 2011. The experience ended unhappily; just three games into his Leicester career he was dismissed after receiving an FA fine for making homophobic comments on a social media site.

Season	League App	League Goals	FA Cup App	FA Cup Goals	League Cup App	League Cup Goals	Total App	Total Goals
1996/97	2 (3)	0	0	0	0	0	2 (3)	0
1997/98	21 (4)	1	1	0	1 (1)	0	23(5)	1
1998/99	36 (1)	3	3	0	3 (1)	0	42 (2)	3
1999/2000	14 (11)	1	1 (1)	0	2	0	17 (12)	1
2000/01	29	3	2	0	1 (1)	0	32 (1)	3
Total	**102 (19)**	**8**	**7 (1)**	**0**	**7 (3)**	**0**	**116 (23)**	**8**

Balmer, William and Robert

Full back brothers who kept opposing wingers in check during careers marked by fraternal excellence

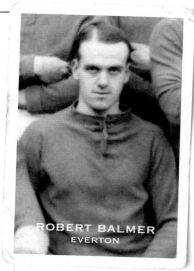

ROBERT BALMER
EVERTON

Like their lives, the careers of the brothers William and Robert Balmer are so inextricably linked that is appropriate to consider both men in the same entry. Both rugged full backs, between them they made more than 500 Everton appearances, with William earning international recognition and winning the 1906 FA Cup – a triumph that came at the expense of his younger brother, who was dropped for the match.

William first broke into the Everton team in the 1897/98 season, ousting Peter Meecham from the right back position and making it his own to such an extent that the novice was selected for all of Everton's games in an FA Cup run that took them to the semi-finals. He impressed immediately for his tenacity and ruggedness. He was a player, wrote one correspondent at time, who 'simply revelled in downright hard and effective work'. This may be seen as the motto that dictated his whole career.

WILLIAM BALMER
EVERTON

Everton's back line at the time had a reputation for its footballing principles, but the addition of William Balmer added some steely resolve that was probably much needed. Sometimes this would get him into trouble. Of the September 1898 derby match, the Liverpool Courier's correspondent noted: 'Balmer early in the game showed indiscreet tactics, and he never recovered; for all through he failed to do himself justice and a kindly admonition from the skipper Owen proved abortive.

THE CLIMAX was reached when he whipped Robertson's leg from under him when only a few yards from the posts, and the game was then decided. Otherwise the contest was remarkably free from foul play especially considering the high tension, which the combatants were working, and probably the lesson will prove salutary to the capable right back, as it was decisive.'
On another occasion, the same journalist wrote admonishingly: 'Balmer would do well to control himself, even when under trying conditions and ablutions of temper are not conducive to the best interests of one's side, particularly when occurring within the penalty limit.' William's play saw him pick up a solitary England cap in February 1905, when he was picked against Ireland in a 1-1 draw at Ayresome Park.

He was joined in the Everton squad for the 1902/03 season by his brother Robert, who was four years his junior. The younger Balmer was two inches shorter and stockier, but just as uncompromising and hard-working in his play. From being a bit-part player and occasional reserve for his elder brother, by the 1905/06 season he was starting to establish a regular berth.

This would lead to one of the most difficult dilemmas to ever face an Everton official. Robert had been ably deputising for his brother and also Jack Crelley through large parts of the campaign and had played in the FA Cup semi-final win over Liverpool alongside Crelley. His brother, by contrast, had missed that match and been in and out of the team ahead of the final against Newcastle at Crystal Palace. Crelley would definitely play in the final, but who would be the other full back: William or Robert?

EVERTON'S preparations in a country hotel in Chingford were based on the total relaxation of its squad, but the question over which Balmer would play hung heavily. On the morning of the match the Liverpool Courier reported: 'The men will take the field fresh as paint, eager for the fray, and confident of victory. The exact constitution of the team will not be decided until the morning, there being just a doubt, so Mr Cuff informs me, as to which of the Brothers Balmer will partner Crelley at back. The younger brother, Robert, has so greatly improved that he may possibly fill the position.'

Not until half an hour from the start of the game did it transpire which Balmer would appear in the right back position. 'A short consultation on the part of the Everton directors resulted in the elder Balmer being selected to partner Crelly,' recorded the Courier. William did not let Evertonians down as the club lifted its first FA Cup. 'W. Balmer probably never played a better game than on Saturday,' the same newspaper reported. 'He tackled

coolly, and kept a good length with his punts. He was a trifle shaky at the close, but on the whole his performance was of a sterling character.'

The following campaign Robert ousted Crelley from the Everton starting XI. When Everton made the FA Cup Final for a second year running there was no dilemma for the directors and both brothers were picked to play against Sheffield Wednesday. But it was not a happy day. Everton were outplayed and beaten 2-1. The Balmer brothers, moreover, were picked out for criticism. 'The backs on both sides were curiously weak, the mistakes being quite extraordinarily frequent and the two Balmers made fully their share,' noted one correspondent. 'The defence they presented was not steady, and with the Wednesday forwards playing right up to them they were often in extreme difficulty.'

Both brothers played together through the deeply disappointing 1907/08 campaign. At the season's end many of the squad's more established names were transfer-listed, but both Balmers were retained. And yet William never played for the first team again and disappeared from view. Quite what happened is not clear, but it may be linked to an incident prior to the start of the 1908/09 season, when he was disciplined for missing training. The club transfer-listed him for £100 and

he played several games for the reserves during the 1908/09 season. Some sources say that he played for Croydon Common in the Southern League but Everton certainly retained his playing registration until 1911. In October 1909 the Everton board agreed to a loan move to Southport Central, although the club's minute books don't record whether the transfer went through. By 1911 William Balmer was listed in the census as a West Derby newsagent.

Robert continued playing for the Everton first team for a further three years. In December 1908, while his brother sat in the footballing wilderness, he was awarded a benefit match, which he shared with Harry Makepeace. It earned both players £500 and the club hosted a dinner in honour of the beneficiaries.

He was ultimately edged out of the team by William Stevenson, who added new resolve to the Everton defence as the club pushed hard for League Championship honours. These would prove elusive, as would

further games for Robert, whose registration was nevertheless retained by Everton until at least the summer of 1915 – four years after his last appearance in a blue shirt.

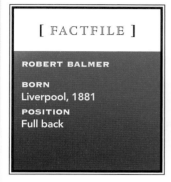

[FACTFILE]

ROBERT BALMER

BORN
Liverpool, 1881

POSITION
Full back

[FACTFILE]

WILLIAM BALMER

BORN
Liverpool, 12 July 1877

DIED
1937

POSITION
Right back

HONOURS
1906 FA Cup;
1 England cap (1905)

Balmer, Robert

Season	League		FA Cup		Total	
	App	Goals	App	Goals	App	Goals
1902/03	1	0	0	0	1	0
1903/04	3	0	0	0	3	0
1904/05	11	0	3	0	14	0
1905/06	20	0	2	0	22	0
1906/07	25	0	8	0	33	0
1907/08	26	0	7	0	33	0
1908/09	35	0	2	0	33	0
1909/10	20	0	0	0	37	0
1910/11	23	0	1	0	20	0
1911/12	1	0	0	0	1	0
Total	**165**	**0**	**23**	**0**	**188**	**0**

Balmer, William

Season	League		FA Cup		Total	
	App	Goals	App	Goals	App	Goals
1897/98	12	0	5	0	17	0
1898/99	23	0	2	0	25	0
1899/1900	32	1	1	0	33	1
1900/01	31	0	2	0	33	0
1901/02	28	0	2	0	30	0
1902/03	28	0	3	0	31	0
1903/04	32	0	1	0	33	0
1904/05	30	0	3	0	33	0
1905/06	18	0	5	0	23	0
1906/07	33	0	8	0	41	0
1907/08	26	0	6	0	32	0
Total	**293**	**1**	**38**	**0**	**331**	**1**

Banks,
Herbert Ernest 'Bert'

Seaforth Highlander turned professional footballer

[FACTFILE]

BORN
Coventry, 1874

DIED
1947

POSITION
Inside left/ centre forward

OTHER CLUBS
St Mirren; Third Lanark; Millwall Athletic; Aston Villa (1901); Bristol City (1901–02); Watford; Coventry City; Stafford Rangers; Verity's Athletic

Season	League		FA Cup		Total	
	App	Goals	App	Goals	App	Goals
1896/97	2	0	0	0	2	0
Total	**2**	**0**	**0**	**0**	**2**	**0**

Barber, Arthur

Home-grown winger who made a League Championship-season cameo

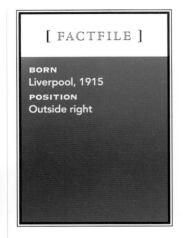
Season	League		FA Cup		Total	
	App	Goals	App	Goals	App	Goals
1938/39	2	0	0	0	2	0
Total	**2**	**0**	**0**	**0**	**2**	**0**

Bardsley, John

Left back who made a solitary first-team appearance

Season	League		FA Cup		Total	
	App	Goals	App	Goals	App	Goals
1909/10	1	0	0	0	1	0
Total	**1**	**0**	**0**	**0**	**1**	**0**

Barker, George

Deputy full back in the late 1890s

Season	League		FA Cup		Total	
	App	Goals	App	Goals	App	Goals
1896/97	4	0	0	0	4	0
1897/98	6	0	0	0	6	0
Total	**10**	**0**	**0**	**0**	**10**	**0**

Barkley, Ross

'England youth international for whom hopes are high'

Season	League		FA Cup		League Cup		Total	
	App	Goals	App	Goals	App	Goals	App	Goals
2011/12	2 (4)	0	0 (1)	0	2	0	4 (5)	0
Total	**2 (4)**	**0**	**0 (1)**	**0**	**2**	**0**	**4 (5)**	**0**

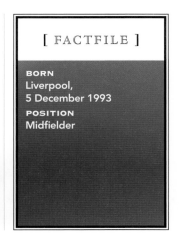

[FACTFILE]

BORN
Liverpool,
5 December 1993
POSITION
Midfielder

Barlow, George

Amateur winger who was part of Great Britain's 1908 Olympic gold medal-winning squad

Season	League		FA Cup		Total	
	App	Goals	App	Goals	App	Goals
1908/09	23	4	1	0	24	4
1909/10	6	0	7	1	13	1
1910/11	5	1	0	0	5	1
Total	**34**	**5**	**8**	**1**	**42**	**6**

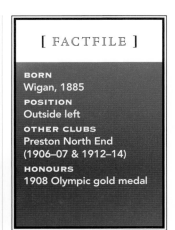

[FACTFILE]

BORN
Wigan, 1885
POSITION
Outside left
OTHER CLUBS
Preston North End
(1906–07 & 1912–14)
HONOURS
1908 Olympic gold medal

Barlow, John

Reserve winger who had a fleeting late-Victorian era career

Season	League		FA Cup		Total	
	App	Goals	App	Goals	App	Goals
1897/98	2	0	0	0	2	0
1898/99	2	0	0	0	2	0
Total	**4**	**0**	**0**	**0**	**4**	**0**

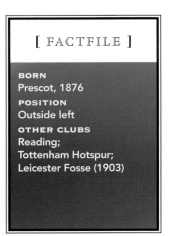

[FACTFILE]

BORN
Prescot, 1876
POSITION
Outside left
OTHER CLUBS
Reading;
Tottenham Hotspur;
Leicester Fosse (1903)

Barlow, Stuart

Fleet-footed striker noted for his profligacy in front of goal

Cruelly dubbed 'Jigsaw' (on one occasion on by the ITV prime-time police thriller Cracker) on account of his tendency to 'fall apart in the box', Stuart Barlow was a selfless and hard-working squad player during the lean early 1990s.

A PROLIFIC goalscorer for the reserves, Barlow, who possessed an extraordinary turn of pace and knack of getting himself in one-on-one situations, struggled to apply the finishing touches in the first team. Indeed, on occasion, it seemed inevitable that a chance would go begging, touching the woodwork or somehow scraping agonisingly past the wrong side of the goalpost.

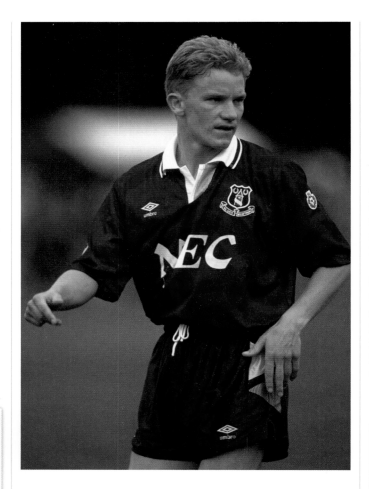

> AS OTHER PLAYERS DASHED FOR THE TUNNEL, BARLOW COULD BE SEEN HALF-BURIED UNDER MASSES OF ECSTATIC FANS, CELEBRATING EVERTON'S SURVIVAL

Afterwards, as other players dashed for the tunnel, Barlow could be seen half-buried under masses of ecstatic fans, celebrating Everton's survival.

Sold to Oldham Athletic for £350,000 in November 1995, he seemed to find his level in the lower leagues, and was still turning out as a semi-professional for Southport just short of his 40th birthday.

The former butcher carved a niche in the Everton squad in the early 1990s after starting out in the old A team as an amateur. It was, perhaps, his misfortune that he was an Everton player during a period when, because of the utterly threadbare nature of the squad, an unfair burden of expectation rested on his slender shoulders.

Frustrated though Evertonians often were with the striker, that never turned to ire and he remained popular for his work rate in trying circumstances. Barlow played a crucial part in the build-up to Graham Stuart's second goal against Wimbledon on the last day of the 1994/95 season that saved Everton from relegation.

[FACTFILE]

BORN
Liverpool, 16 July 1968
POSITION
Striker
OTHER CLUBS
Rotherham United (loan, 1992)
Oldham Athletic (1995–98)
Wigan Athletic (1998–2000)
Tranmere Rovers (2000–03)
Stockport County (2003–05)
Bury (2005–06)
Morecambe (2006)
Southport (2006–07)

Season	League		FA Cup		League Cup		Europe		Total	
	App	Goals	App	Goals	App	Goals	App	Goals	App	Goals
1990/91	0 (2)	0	0	0	0	0	-	-	0 (2)	0
1991/92	3 (4)	0	0	0	0	0	-	-	3 (4)	0
1992/93	8 (18)	5	1 (1)	0	2 (2)	1	-	-	11 (21)	6
1993/94	6 (16)	3	1 (1)	2	1 (2)	0	-	-	8 (19)	5
1994/95	7 (4)	2	2 (1)	0	0	0	-	-	9 (5)	2
1995/96	0 (3)	0	0	0	0 (1)	0	0 (2)	0	0 (6)	0
Total	**24 (47)**	**10**	**4 (3)**	**2**	**3 (5)**	**1**	**0 (2)**	**0**	**31 (57)**	**13**

Barmby, Nick

Underachieving prodigy of questionable loyalty

When Joe Royle made Middlesbrough's clever young inside forward Nick Barmby Everton's record signing in October 1996 he was buying a player not just of unquestioned potential, but a man of experience too.

A member of the England squad, Barmby had, at the age of 22, already partnered the likes of Gary Lineker, Jurgen Klinsmann, Fabrizio Ravanelli, Alan Shearer and Teddy Sheringham in a career of tremendous promise. Royle's £5.75million signing had often been likened to Kenny Dalglish and Peter Beardsley, whom he replaced in the England team. Even Pele suggested that Barmby was destined for greatness while watching him at the previous summer's European Championship Finals. Indeed, few watching Barmby's performance against Southampton, less than a fortnight after his Goodison arrival, could have disagreed with the Brazilian. Everton's new signing scored one goal, made four others, and after the 7-1 demolition was complete walked away with the man-of-the-match champagne. Alas, Barmby's Everton career was to be more fizz than of any real vintage.

Born in Hull, Barmby was an early

graduate of the FA's School of Excellence at Lilleshall, joining Tottenham Hotspur on his graduation and forcing his way into the first team by the time he was 18. He would make more

than 100 appearances for Spurs, but after losing his place in the 1994/95 season, joined Middlesbrough in a £5.25million deal. He stayed on Teesside for a year, earning an international call-up, but once more lost his place, to Juninho, the diminutive and brilliant Brazilian, and when he asked for a transfer Royle came in.

SHORT AND ADROIT, though never particularly quick, Barmby was a technically gifted player with a powerful, accurate finish and an eye for a defence-splitting pass. He preferred to play in the so-called 'hole' behind a front man or forward pairing, but as Royle's time as Everton manager unravelled, so he found himself marginalised, a luxury player without the wherewithal to impose himself on games. The comparisons with Beardsley soon proved to be premature as he was patently never of the same calibre. He also lost his place in the England team.

Walter Smith reinvented Barmby as a left-sided midfielder in the 1999/2000 season, a campaign in which he was arguably the club's best player. The highlight for Barmby was a hat trick in a 4-0 mauling of West Ham at Upton Park. Everton's new owner, Bill Kenwright, led calls for Barmby's England recall, which he earned, and at the season's end he deservedly took his place in the squad for the European Championship Finals in Belgium and the Netherlands. Kenwright also promised a new contract, making Barmby the club's best-paid player on his return.

Barmby's response to Kenwright's loyalty and Smith's perseverance represented the avarice and twisted loyalties of modern football at its very worst. He demanded a transfer away from Goodison, so that he could complete a 'dream move' to Liverpool who, it suddenly

emerged, were the player's boyhood club. Smith gave short shrift to such antics, quickly selling him for £6million and making Barmby the first player to leave Goodison for Anfield in some forty years. With retrospect, the anguish of Evertonians was premature for it represented a good price for a player with only a year left on his contract.

At Liverpool Barmby was a moderate success in his first year, winning a treble of cups, but thereafter he faded, once more the proverbial round peg in a square hole. He joined Leeds United in 2002 as the club stood on the precipice of financial ruin, but by the 2003/04 season was being loaned out to Nottingham Forest, now in the Championship. At the end of that season, still aged only 30, and to whoops of schadenfreude from Evertonians, he dropped down yet another division and joined his home-town club, Hull City.

> HE DEMANDED A TRANSFER FROM GOODISON SO HE COULD COMPLETE A DREAM MOVE TO LIVERPOOL

[FACTFILE]

BORN
Hull, 27 February 1974

POSITION
Attacking left midfielder / forward

OTHER CLUBS
Tottenham Hotspur (1991–95);
Middlesbrough (1995–96);
Liverpool (2000–02);
Leeds United (2002–04);
Nottingham Forest (loan, 2003-04);
Hull City (2004–12)

AS MANAGER
Hull City (2011–)

HONOURS
23 England caps (4 goals) (1995–2001)

Season	League		FA Cup		League Cup		Total	
	App	Goals	App	Goals	App	Goals	App	Goals
1996/97	22 (3)	4	2	1	0	0	24 (3)	5
1997/98	26 (4)	2	1	0	1 (1)	3	28 (5)	5
1998/99	20(4)	3	4	1	1 (1)	0	25 (5)	4
1999/2000	37	9	5	1	0 (1)	0	42 (1)	10
Total	**105 (11)**	**18**	**12**	**3**	**2 (3)**	**3**	**119 (14)**	**24**

Barnett, Geoff

England under-23 goalkeeper who found it hard to dislodge Gordon West

Season	League		FA Cup		League Cup		Total	
	App	Goals	App	Goals	App	Goals	App	Goals
1965/66	9	0	0	0	0	0	9	0
1966/67	0	0	0	0	0	0	0	0
1967/68	1	0	0	0	-	-	1	0
Total	10	0	0	0	0	0	10	0

[FACTFILE]

BORN
Northwich, 16 October 1946

POSITION
Goalkeeper

OTHER CLUBS
Arsenal (1969–76);
Minnesota Kicks (1976–80)

Barrett, Earl

Athletic right back who struggled to win over the Goodison faithful

Right back Earl Barrett was one of Joe Royle's first signings, arriving from Aston Villa for £1.7million in January 1995. Under Royle's management at Oldham Athletic, Barrett, who had previously languished in Manchester City's reserves, had briefly risen to the England team, before a £2.5million move to Villa Park in February 1992 made him England's most expensive defender.

Quick, athletic and a cloying defender, Barrett nevertheless struggled to win over the Goodison crowd. His distribution frequently let him down, while his tendency to stand off a player rather than jump into a tackle was unendearing – no matter how effective it might have been. Moreover, he replaced the popular Matt Jackson, who had done little discernibly wrong. Indeed, right back seemed to be a position with which Royle perpetually struggled, also signing Marc Hottiger, a comical Swiss defender, in December 1996.

Cup-tied at the time of his arrival, Barrett missed Everton's successful FA Cup run, which was perhaps a blessing given the way that Jackson set up the winner in the final against Manchester United. In the 1995/96 season his presence in the Everton team was brought to an abrupt end when he was injured in October and missed the remainder of the campaign.

[FACTFILE]

BORN
Rochdale, 28 April 1967

POSITION
Right back

OTHER CLUBS
Manchester City (1985–87);
Chester City (loan, 1986);
Oldham Athletic (1987–92);
Aston Villa (1992–95);
Sheffield United (loan, 1998);
Sheffield Wednesday (1998–2000)

HONOURS
3 England caps (1991–93)

He returned the following August and as Everton laboured under Royle, Barrett put in the best performances of his Everton career, also deputising as centre back.

Howard Kendall's arrival as manager in June 1997 stymied Barrett's Everton career and after a spell on loan at Sheffield United he was free to join Sheffield Wednesday in 1998, where injuries forced his retirement in 2000, aged just 32.

Season	League		FA Cup		League Cup		Other		Total	
	App	Goals	App	Goals	App	Goals	App	Goals	App	Goals
1994/95	17	0	0	0	0	0	-	-	17	0
1995/96	8	0	0	0	2	0	3	0	13	0
1996/97	36	0	2	0	2	0	-	-	40	0
1998/99	12 (1)	0	0	0	0	0	-	-	12 (1)	0
Total	73 (1)	0	2	0	4	0	3	0	81 (1)	0

Barton, John

Right back who made the transition from non-league to the big time

In November 1978 John Barton was part of the Worcester City team that knocked Malcolm Allison's Plymouth Argyle out of the FA Cup, causing the shock of the first round. A week later Gordon Lee paid £25,000 – a record for a non-league player – to bring the 25-year-old right back to Goodison. If the move caused ripples of surprise among Evertonians, when the rookie was introduced the following spring he provided competent cover for Colin Todd – who quickly tipped him for an international future.

LEAN, ATHLETIC and a willing overlapper, Barton started the 1979/80 season as Everton's first-choice right back. However, his progress was abruptly halted that autumn when he suffered a broken leg. The road to recovery was long, and when he regained his fitness John Gidman had taken his place. In March 1982, having failed to make an appearance under Howard Kendall, Barton was released and joined Derby County. He later made a return to non-league, and turned his hand to management with Burton Albion and Worcester City.

Season	League		FA Cup		League Cup		Europe		Total	
	App	Goals	App	Goals	App	Goals	App	Goals	App	Goals
1978/79	9 (1)	0	0	0	0	0	0	0	9 (1)	0
1979/80	6 (1)	0	0	0	3	0	2	0	11 (1)	0
1980/81	3	0	0	0	0	0	-	-	3	0
Total	**18 (2)**	**0**	**0**	**0**	**3**	**0**	**2**	**0**	**23 (2)**	**0**

Battle of Goodison, The

Goodison Park has seen many epic tussles in its 120-year-long history. But few have been as vicious or notorious as the meeting between Everton and Leeds United on 7 November 1964.

Everton in the 1960s had a reputation for free-flowing attacking football, their School of Science reputation enhanced by such delightfully skilled players as Alex Young, Colin Harvey and Alex Scott. But they were no shrinking violets either, and as skilled and sublime as certain individuals were, Harry Catterick's teams were underpinned by basic concepts of pace and power. Men such as Dennis Stevens, Tony Kay, Johnny Morrissey and Jimmy Gabriel were all eminently capable of looking after themselves – and their team-mates too. When Everton played Manchester United in September 1964, the referee, J. E. Carr, needed to call both teams into the centre circle and warn them to calm down.

Don Revie's newly promoted Leeds United were a different proposition. They were steel without silk; a side characterised by niggling, nasty fouls, intimidation of officials, time-wasting and gamesmanship. They could play a bit too, but to most people they were simply 'Dirty Leeds'.

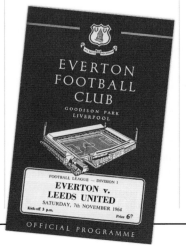

A simmering feud with Everton had built up over the previous couple of years. Some attributed it to Bobby Collins' sale to Elland Road in March 1962, others to a bone-crunching FA Cup fourth round tie in January 1964, which Everton won after a replay. Either way it took just seconds for the clubs' first league meeting in four-and-a-half years to explode.

On four minutes Sandy Brown and Johnny Giles were contesting the ball outside the Everton penalty area. Giles kicked Brown in the chest ('Our legs accidentally became entangled as we fell to the ground,' Giles later claimed), Brown complained, while also exacting retribution with his left fist. The referee, Ken Stokes, sent Brown to the dressing room.

It was the fastest sending off in Everton history. But if it represented an attempt by Stokes to exert a deterrent to further excess it backfired. The crowd were whipped up into a paroxysm of fury at this perceived injustice. Foul followed foul. Leeds took the lead through Willie Bell on 14 minutes, which only heightened the sense of outrage. 'It was not the attitude of the players which was causing so much concern, but the attitude of the crowd,' recalled Jack Charlton. 'I'll make no bones about it – the Goodison Park crowd was the worst before which I have ever played.'

On 39 minutes came the moment for which the game has achieved notoriety. Derek Temple was hurtling down the wing when Bell

let fly with a waist-high challenge that left the winger prone on the side of the pitch. Years later Brian Labone told me that he thought Bell had 'killed' his team-mate. Goodison went wild. 'You could feel the hate in the air and fans started throwing things on the pitch,' recalled George Orr in his diary of the era. Both trainers came on and Bell was urged to stay on the ground as the fury of the crowd failed to relent. Bottles and other missiles rained down upon the pitch.

'That was the most frightening moment I have ever experienced on a soccer pitch,' recalled Giles. 'I had the feeling that, at any moment, the fans – all 55,000 of them – would invade the field, just as they try to do in parts of South America, where players have to be protected by moats, barbed wire and riot police.'

EVERTON'S players surrounded Stokes, demanding Bell be sent off. Instead the referee signalled that both teams leave the field for what was termed in the following day's press a 'cooling-down' period. It was an unprecedented situation in English football. A Tannoy announcement by the Everton secretary warned that if further missiles were launched onto the pitch the referee would abandon the match. Stokes visited both dressing rooms to warn both teams about their conduct.

They returned to the pitch ten minutes later, Everton with just nine men, although Temple returned shortly before half-time carrying an injury. 'The crowd had calmed down, and there was no further trouble in that direction … even though there was still a lot of ill feeling among the players,' recalled Giles. The Liverpool Echo even reported 'a remarkable spell … of five minutes without a foul'.

The scenes caused national opprobrium and prompted a debate over the conduct of players on the field and fans off it. 'Goodison Park has already gained an unsavoury tribal reputation for vandalism,' reported The Times. 'Leeds United have earned black marks for ill temper on the field. The marriage of these two dangerous elements sparked an explosion.' Yet Leeds escaped sanction

while Everton were fined £250 for failure to control the crowd. Brown was suspended for two weeks.

IN THE MINDS of the opposing players, Goodison's reputation as the most intimidating stadium in England had been secured. 'With the Everton fans there always seems to be a threatening attitude, a vicious undertone to their remarks,' complained Charlton. 'You never feel this is a football atmosphere – it creates more a sense of fear.'

'THE MOST FRIGHTENING MOMENT I HAVE EVER EXPERIENCED ON A SOCCER PITCH'

JOHNNY GILES
LEEDS UNITED

Baxter, Dr James Clement

Liverpool physician whose generosity ensured the switch to Goodison

The elevation of James Baxter (1857–1928) onto the Everton board of directors in 1889 was to have seismic implications not just for the club he and his family would serve for 65 unbroken years, but for English football too. His ascent with George Mahon, a Liverpool accountant, was to bolster the faction within the Everton committee unhappy with the state of affairs at Anfield and the club's exploitative chairman, John Houlding.

Baxter was a well-known physician and prominent member of Liverpool's Liberal and Catholic communities. Among many of the local Irish community, who were beginning to form Anfield's core constituency, he was a familiar face. Like Houlding, he was to make a name for himself as a local politician, representing the Liberal Party on the city council from 1906 to 1920.

He loved football and Everton and sought from the outset to ensure the club's future via ownership of its own home. The club's home at Anfield was sublet by Houlding at a rental rate that was increasing beyond the comfort zone of some of Everton's members. Soon after Baxter and Mahon's arrival onto the management committee they made attempts to form the club into a limited liability company for the express purpose of acquiring the purchase of Anfield. Their demand was put in the form of an official resolution at a special committee meeting. The opening shot in what would emerge as a civil war with Houlding had been fired.

Everton would experience their first League Championship success at Anfield, but it soon became clear that further glories lay elsewhere. An extraordinary general meeting on 15 September 1891 carried a motion by Mahon that Everton should negotiate to seek pastures new. The problem was that Everton had no new venue. Moreover, the forfeiture of Anfield's stands was costly enough to be almost unthinkable, yet retention of them was clearly an obstacle.

A special general meeting was convened on 25 January 1892 at which Mahon revealed that a new site had been found at Mere Green Field, an area of land on the other side of Stanley Park on which he had gained an option (today it is known by a more familiar name: Goodison Park). To fund the relocation Everton formed a limited liability company with 2500 ordinary shares of £1 apiece and 100 mortgage debenture bonds of £10 each.

Mahon still lived uneasily with the barren bank account that stood at the end of the many outlays on Everton's new home. With little in the way of assets and before transfer fees had seriously become an issue, a bad season may have put Everton's future in doubt. Knowing of these concerns, in stepped Dr Baxter. He

advanced the club a £1000 loan, free of interest or security (the equivalent of approximately £500,000 today, based on the average earnings index, or £80,000 based on RPI).

Baxter's generosity helped secure Everton's future, but in their empty Anfield home a new team were formed. Liverpool FC would cast a shadow over Everton and make a huge impression on the shape of English and European football history.

Everton flourished in their new home and the last instalment of Dr Baxter's debenture was paid off as early as October 1894. The following summer Baxter was elected Everton chairman, a position he held until June 1904. 'When he occupied the chair, if heat generated in a discussion he soon cooled it down by his tranquillity, which provocation by the offensive could not disturb,' wrote his fellow director and Everton historian Thomas Keates. After stepping down as chairman he continued to serve the club as medical advisor and director. He also served the Football League's management committee for 15 years and the FA council for a further four.

BAXTER died in January 1928 at the age of 71. 'The immensity of the concourse of mourners at his graveside, astonished even those who were most intimate with the gentle geniality and perennial facial sunshine,' wrote Keates. At the subsequent board meeting: 'The Chairman reported the death of Dr. J. C. Baxter & in doing so deeply deplored the loss of one of their colleagues who had been associated with the club since its inception & who had been a valiant worker in the club's interest during the whole of the period. He was sure they would all agree with them that his loss would be severely felt.' At the next meeting it was unanimously decided to co-opt his son, Dr Cecil Baxter, to replace him on the board. Like his father he would serve Everton as chairman. His own death in 1954 broke a family chain that extended back some 65 years.

'Everton made tremendous strides under the stewardship of Baxter and Mahon,' wrote David France – a subsequent 'Dr Everton'. 'They constructed one of the first purpose-built stadiums in Europe, attracted quality professional footballers from around the country and earned a world-wide reputation for cultured play. In addition, the club captured the League Championship and English Cup and was unfortunate not to win both trophies on several other occasions around the turn of the century.'

Baxter, Jose

Promising midfielder who as a 16 year-old became Everton's youngest ever debutant

[FACTFILE]

BORN
Liverpool, 7 February 1992
POSITION
Forward
OTHER CLUBS
Tranmere Rovers (2011–12);
Crystal Palace (2012–)

Season	League		FA Cup		League Cup		Europe		Total	
	App	Goals	App	Goals	App	Goals	App	Goals	App	Goals
2008-09	1 (2)	0	0	0	0 (1)	0	0	0	1 (3)	0
2009-10	0 (2)	0	0	0	0	0	1 (4)	0	1 (6)	0
2010-11	0 (1)	0	0 (1)	0	0	0	-	-	0 (2)	0
2011-12	0 (1)	0	0	0	0 (1)	0	-	-	0 (2)	0
Total	1 (6)	0	0 (1)	0	0 (2)	0	1 (4)	0	2 (13)	0

Beagrie, Peter

Back-flipping winger who brought colour to pallid years

In November 1989, the Liverpool manager Kenny Dalglish called his friend and former Scotland colleague Graeme Sharp to say that he'd booked him into a private clinic for a cartilage operation. A confused Sharp told him there was nothing wrong with his cartilage. 'There will be, Sharpy, there will be,' came the droll reply. 'You've just signed Peter Beagrie, so you'll be in the box, out the box, in the box, out the box.'

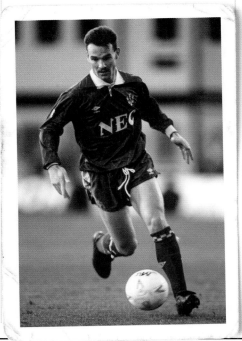

Bought for £750,000 from Stoke City, Beagrie was a winger of undoubted but maddeningly mercurial talents prone to gross over-elaboration. Dalglish's joke referred to his habit, frequently witnessed in an Everton shirt, of beating his man, checking and trying to beat him again. By his own account the new signing 'infuriated' Sharp.

YET BEAGRIE could also be a thrilling player, a throwback to the great wideman of the sepia-toned days of Stanley Matthews, Tom Finney and Alec Troup. Possessing dash, control and a sharp turn of pace, he would lull defenders in before suddenly changing direction and darting past them. His knack of nicking the ball away just as a defender thought he was about to win it delighted the alarmingly diminished crowds that attended Goodison in the early 1990s. And when goals came they were celebrated in exuberant fashion: Beagrie was an early exponent of the extravagant back-flipping celebration more commonly seen in recent years.

> BEAGRIE WAS A WINGER
> OF UNDOUBTED
> BUT MADDENINGLY
> MERCURIAL TALENTS

HIS EARLY days at Everton were replete with disappointment and Beagrie cut an erratic, isolated figure, often left to cameo run-outs from the substitute's bench. Indeed it took 30 games for Evertonians to witness his famous somersault goal celebration. By the summer of 1991, when he infamously crashed a moped through the glass doors of a Spanish hotel lobby while on a pre-season tour, it seemed inevitable that Beagrie's Everton career would end. A loan spell at Sunderland followed, but he was recalled to help lift the torpor that increasingly consumed the club.

Finally assured of a first-team place, Beagrie became one of the few bright lights in a succession of dull Everton teams. With the departure of Peter Beardsley to Newcastle in 1993, he was the club's most creative player and responded magnificently in the early months of the 1993/94 season when, despite the team's struggles, he always displayed class and guile. Given this form it seemed surprising that Mike Walker accepted a £1.1million bid from Manchester City on transfer-deadline day in March 1994, although with Anders Limpar set to arrive his absence was less keenly felt.

Beagrie returned for a loan spell at the tail-end of the 1997/98 season – an indicator of the paucity of resources left to Howard Kendall in his third spell as manager. He performed reasonably, inspiring a home win against high-flying Leeds United that may ultimately have kept Everton up. He subsequently made a Premiership return with Bradford City before playing out his career in the lower leagues, turning out for Grimsby and Scunthorpe past his 40th birthday. Now retired from playing, he is a popular television pundit.

[FACTFILE]

BORN
Middlesbrough, 28 November 1965
POSITION
Winger
OTHER CLUBS
Middlesbrough (1984–86);
Sheffield United (1986–88);
Stoke City (1988–89);
Sunderland (loan, 1991);
Manchester City (1994–97);
Bradford City (1997–2001);
Wigan Athletic (loan, 2001);
Scunthorpe United (2001–06);
Grimsby Town (2006)

Season	League App	League Goals	FA Cup App	FA Cup Goals	League Cup App	League Cup Goals	Other App	Other Goals	Total App	Total Goals
1989/90	14 (5)	0	2 (1)	0	0	0	-	-	16 (6)	0
1990/91	14 (3)	2	1 (1)	0	0	0	5	1	20 (4)	0
1991/92	20 (7)	3	2	0	1 (1)	2	0 (1)	0	23 (9)	0
1992/93	11 (11)	3	0	0	3 (1)	0	-	-	14 (12)	0
1993/94	29	3	2	0	3	1	-	-	34	0
1997/98	4 (2)	0	0	0	0	0			4 (2)	0
Total	**92 (28)**	**11**	**7 (2)**	**0**	**7 (2)**	**3**	**5 (1)**	**1**	**111 (33)**	**0**

Beardsley, Peter

Outstandingly gifted forward, whose modest genius harked back to a gentler era

As English football entered its cash-laden Premier League era of excess, Peter Beardsley was a refreshing antidote to such gauche times. A quiet man, a teetotaller in an era when to be so was considered exceptional, who preferred life away from the limelight which so many professional footballers enforce upon themselves, Beardsley was also one of the select few who have played for – and captured the imagination of – both of Merseyside's 'big two'.

During a two-year spell at Goodison Park he scored more than thirty goals – an impressive tally for a man who was in his thirties when Howard Kendall paid £1million to bring him across Stanley Park. As well as the goals that assured Everton's top-flight survival in lean times, Beardsley captured blue hearts and minds with his array of neat skills and incisive play. Born in Newcastle in 1961, Beardsley was a graduate of the famous Wallsend Boys Club, whose alumni included the likes of Alan Shearer and Steve Bruce. Like Bruce and Shearer he slipped under the radar of his home-town club, eventually getting his break with Carlisle United where he emerged as one of the lower leagues' most exciting young talents. Former England and Leeds player Johnny Giles was an early admirer of Beardsley and signed him in 1981 while coaching the Canadian side, Vancouver Whitecaps, for £275,000.

In 1982, after impressing in a pre-season friendly against Manchester United, Ron Atkinson gave him a six-month extended loan-trial at Old Trafford but never took up the option to sign him, and Beardsley returned to Canada where he played for a further year. When the NASL neared collapse in 1983, Beardsley was brought back across the Atlantic by Newcastle, where, alongside the likes of Kevin Keegan and Chris Waddle, he won the Second Division title in 1984. In 1987 Liverpool made him a British record signing, paying £1.9million to bring him to Anfield, where he spent four years, picking up two Championship medals and also played a leading role in the 1990 World Cup, where England reached the semi-finals.

On falling out with new Liverpool manager Graeme Souness, Beardsley was allowed to

> A DEEP-LYING FORWARD
> OF GRACE AND SKILL,
> BEARDSLEY TOOK LITTLE TIME
> TO SETTLE IN AT GOODISON

join Everton in the summer of 1991. A deep-lying forward of grace and skill, Beardsley took little time to settle in at Goodison. Early highlights included a hat-trick against Coventry City in September and his form earned him many plaudits, some saying he was worthy of an England recall. Surprisingly the England manager, Graham Taylor, made clear that he did not feature in his plans.

Although Everton's football at this time was occasionally slick and entertaining, the team struggled for form and crowds were poor. Two goals by Beardsley in March 1992 against Oldham Athletic gave Everton their first home win for exactly three months, which was telling of the way in which the team struggled. Beardsley nevertheless ended the season with 20 league and cup goals and 12 assists.

Everton were again disappointing in his second season, finishing 13th and exiting the League and FA Cups at an early stage. Beardsley still managed 12 goals, including a late winner in the Goodison derby, which he described as one of the 'most satisfying' goals he had ever scored.

That summer, with transfer funds at a premium and Kendall in the market for a target man, he accepted £1.2million bids from Derby County and Newcastle for Beardsley, with the forward opting for the latter club, where he was

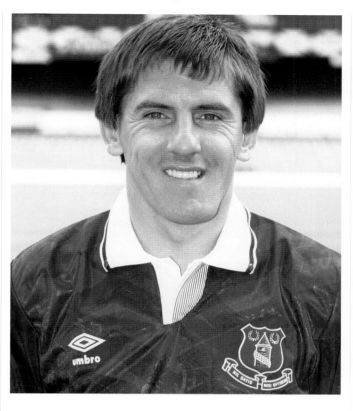

reunited with Kevin Keegan, now manager. Ironically Kendall never got his target man and the Goodison career of one of Everton's most gifted individuals was over.

AT NEWCASTLE Beardsley enjoyed something of a renaissance, earning an England recall and spearheading

Newcastle's resurgence under Keegan. On leaving St James's Park in 1997 his career resembled a road atlas, appearing for six different clubs in barely two years. On calling time on his playing career he assisted Keegan when he was England manager, later taking up a variety of coaching roles at St James's Park.

Beardsley's time at Goodison was probably best encapsulated in one sublime moment in a 3-0 win over Nottingham Forest in March 1993. After intercepting the ball just past the halfway line and spotting the goalkeeper off his line, he made an audacious lob. The end result, however, was indicative of Everton's fortunes at the time. It hit the bar.

[FACTFILE]

BORN
Newcastle-upon-Tyne,
18 January 1961
POSITION
Forward
OTHER CLUBS
Carlisle United (1979–82)
Vancouver Whitecaps
(1981–83)
Manchester United
(loan, 1982–83)
Newcastle United (1983–87)
Liverpool (1987–91)
Newcastle United (1993–97)
Bolton Wanderers (1997–98)
Manchester City (loan, 1998)
Fulham (1998)
Hartlepool United (1998–99)
Melbourne Knights (1999)
Doncaster Rovers (1999)
HONOURS
59 England caps (9 goals)
(1986–96); MBE

Season	League		FA Cup		League Cup		Other		Total	
	App	Goals	App	Goals	App	Goals	App	Goals	App	Goals
1991/92	42	15	2	1	4	3	2	1	50	20
1992/93	39	10	2	0	4	2	-	-	45	12
Total	81	25	4	1	8	5	2	1	95	32

Beare, George

Cricket-playing outside forward who illuminated the Goodison wing

In signing for Everton from Blackpool in November 1910, wideman George Beare joined a flourishing early-twentieth century Goodison tradition. Not just a fine footballer,

Beare combined his footballing pursuits with those on the cricket field during the summer months in his native Southampton. In serving as a cricket professional he followed

an Everton tradition set by Jack Sharp, Harry Makepeace (who played for Lancashire as an amateur), Bob Turner, all countymen, as well as James Meunier and the Balmers. 'Soon,' quipped one local reporter on his arrival, 'We shall be able to run the Everton County Cricket Club in summer months.'

BEARE started out as a footballer with Southampton, where he played in the Southern League. The Saints held his registration

'HE WAS STREETS AHEAD OF THE OTHER ATTACKERS'
LIVERPOOL ECHO

after he moved north to play for Blackpool in 1908. After he impressed in a Lancashire Senior Cup tie against Everton ('He was streets ahead of the other attackers, and his shooting

was strong and the ball invariably kept low,' reported the Liverpool Echo) he was signed immediately.

Optimism greeted the winger's arrival at Goodison. 'He loves his work and wants plenty of it,' reported the Echo. 'In truth he is known to sulk if he does not get sufficient chances of showing his powers. Fast and sure of centre he is able to play on the extreme left or right, but the right wing is his favourite and most useful position.' Beare went straight into the team, initially at outside left where he replaced his follow cricketer, Turner. He also deputised at inside forward

It was at outside right, however, where Beare played most of his football for Everton. He was ever present for the first three-quarters of the 1911/12 season as Everton challenged at the top of the table. Goals, however, were not easy to come by – just 46 all campaign – and the lack of them probably cost Everton the League Championship – they finished

runners up, three points behind champions Blackburn Rovers.

The next season Everton fell to the uncharted depths of eleventh. Although Beare missed just a solitary league game, thereafter he found his position under threat from Johnny Houston. Everton were now a team in transition and after making just a dozen

appearances through the 1913/14 campaign he was sold to Cardiff City.

Season	League		FA Cup		Total	
	App	Goals	App	Goals	App	Goals
1910/11	26	8	3	0	29	8
1911/12	30	3	5	1	35	4
1912/13	37	7	5	0	42	7
1913/14	11	0	1	0	12	0
Total	104	18	14	1	118	19

[FACTFILE]

BORN
Southampton,
2 October 1885
DIED
1970
POSITION
Outside forward
OTHER CLUBS
Southampton;
Blackpool (1908–10);
Cardiff City
(1914-20 & 1922);
Bristol City (1921);
Oswestry Town

Beattie, James

One-time record signing whose sluggish demeanour seldom set pulses racing

In January 2005 when the twice-yearly transfer window opened, David Moyes made Southampton centre forward James Beattie Everton's record signing in a £6million deal. Beattie had 18 months earlier finished top English scorer in the Premier League, scoring 23 league goals as Southampton also reached the FA Cup Final. His form earned him the first of five England caps.

AND YET as Everton successfully battled to reach fourth spot and claim a coveted Champions League place, the new record signing added little to the cause. Beattie looked slovenly and off the

pace, while a red card in one of his first outings for a bizarre head-butt on Chelsea's William Gallas scarcely endeared him to the Everton faithful.

Beattie, a schoolboy champion swimmer, had started his career with Blackburn Rovers in the mid-1990s as an understudy to Alan Shearer. He made a handful of non-scoring appearances before being sold to Southampton in July 1998 as a £1million makeweight

in a deal that brought Kevin Davies to Ewood Park. His five-and-a-half years on the south coast were troubled by injury and inconsistency – Beattie could be brilliant one month and hopeless the next – but by the time he reached his mid-twenties he looked as though he might be realising his potential.

Alas it was not to be. Even when fully fit for Everton during the 2005/06 season, Beattie looked

'THE GOALSCORING TOUCH THAT ONCE BROUGHT INTERNATIONAL RECOGNITION REMAINED ELUSIVE'

slow and leaden, his first touch ungainly, while the goal-scoring touch that once brought international recognition usually remained elusive. He hit a purple patch in spring 2006, and there were glimpses of previous form: a sublime chip against Fulham hinted at past potential. Beattie talked up his England chances ahead of that summer's World Cup in Germany, but the forward himself seemed to be the only person who considered this a possibility.

In summer 2006, Andrew Johnson replaced Beattie as Everton's record signing, and although Moyes tried to perm them as a striking partnership it was clear to all that this was no winning formula. More poor form and injuries had, by the end of the

season, relegated Beattie to fourth choice among Everton's strikers.

Beattie's parting contribution came on the final day of the 2006/07 season against Chelsea when, straying into an offside position, he led to James McFadden's late strike being disallowed. McFadden's goal would have resulted in Chelsea manager Jose Mourinho's first home defeat in five years as a manager and elevated Everton to fifth position. The moment seemed to perfectly encapsulate Beattie's wretched time at Everton.

Beattie was sold to newly relegated Sheffield United in August 2007 for £4million. In 85 appearances he had scored just 15 times, a poor total inflated by four fiercely struck penalties – the only emphatic thing about Beattie's time at Goodison. In the second tier he seemed to find his level, although his repeated complaints that Moyes never gave him a proper chance continued to ring hollow.

	League		FA Cup		Europe		Other		Total	
Season	App	Goals	App	Goals	App	Goals	App	Goals	App	Goals
2004/05	7 (4)	1	2	1	0	0	-	-	9 (4)	2
2005/06	29 (3)	10	2 (1)	0	1	0	1 (1)	1 (1)	33 (5)	11
2006/07	15 (18)	2	0	0	1 (1)	0	-	-	16 (19)	2
Total	**51 (25)**	**13**	**4 (1)**	**1**	**2 (1)**	**0**	**1 (1)**	**1 (1)**	**58 (28)**	**15**

Beckford,
Jermaine

Pacey striker who failed to convince he was worthy of a longer Goodison stint

When Everton played Chelsea on the final day of the 2010/11 season, Jermaine Beckford plundered one of the finest goals Goodison has witnessed. Collecting the ball 15 yards inside the Everton half, Beckford ran at the Chelsea defence – and kept on running. A ricochet near the halfway line saw the ball balloon up kindly for the forward; as it fell he controlled it deftly and, losing three opposing defenders, suddenly found himself clear. He ran in on the Chelsea goal, and coolly chipped Petr Cech, continuing his 70-yard run to celebrate his wonder strike with an ecstatic Gwladys Street.

For the 27-year-old, the goal had special pertinence. A decade

earlier Beckford had been released as a trainee by Chelsea and, unwanted by other league clubs, rebuilt his career in non-league. He joined Leeds United in 2006 where, after loan moves at Carlisle and Scunthorpe United, he found his feet in the Championship. The move to Everton on a Bosman free in June 2010 represented a belated and circuitous return to the top level.

Lithe and pacey, Beckford typically played off the last man hunting for chances. At the outset his first season might have been seen as a top-flight apprenticeship and he generally came through it passably. Often asked to play as a lone forward or without a run of starts to his name, expectations were high for one lacking experience at such a level. Beckford never shirked from the

challenge, but there were times when his finishing was erratic. Before his wonder goal against Chelsea one shot flew so far wide that it went out for a throw in.

There was, nevertheless, also a sense that he never enjoyed the full confidence of David Moyes. Beckford started the opening game of the 2011/12, but was dropped days later for a League Cup tie. A week after that, with the banks biting at Everton's door, a deadline day bid of £2.5million was accepted from Leicester City.

	League		FA Cup		League Cup		Total	
Season	App	Goals	App	Goals	App	Goals	App	Goals
2010/11	14 (18)	8	2 (2)	1	1 (1)	1	17 (21)	10
2011/12	1 (1)	0	0	0	0	0	1 (1)	0
Total	**15 (19)**	**8**	**2 (2)**	**1**	**1 (1)**	**1**	**18 (22)**	**10**

Belfitt, Rod

Centre forward whose Goodison arrival represented a bad deal

A fringe member of Don Revie's 'Leeds Machine', Rod Belfitt had garnered a reputation through the 1960s as a hard-working, dependable centre forward – the sort of resolute Yorkshireman for which Revie's teams had become famed and feared.

He started out as an amateur with Arsenal, but joined Leeds without having made an appearance. Admired by the Leeds faithful for his work ethic, which allowed more

> BELFITT HAD GARNERED A REPUTATION THROUGH THE 1960S AS A HARD-WORKING, DEPENDABLE CENTRE FORWARD

glamorous players to prosper, he never made the breakthrough as a first-team regular. In November 1971 he joined Bobby Robson's Ipswich and became a popular and important part of a rapidly improving team. When Harry Catterick exchanged David Johnson plus £50,000 a year later, Ipswich fans were left scratching their heads as to why Robson had allowed him to leave.

They were not as mystified as Everton fans, however. Belfitt was an honest trier, but lacked the finesse to meet the lofty expectations of the Goodison faithful. Johnson, on the other hand, was viewed as an outstanding prospect, and his subsequent successes with Liverpool and England hammered home how badly Catterick had misjudged this piece of transfer business.

Following Billy Bingham's appointment as Catterick's successor in summer 1973,

Belfitt disappeared from first-team view. In October 1973 he moved on to Sunderland, later playing out his career with Huddersfield.

[FACTFILE]

BORN
Doncaster, 30 October 1945
POSITION
Centre forward
OTHER CLUBS
Arsenal (1961–63);
Leeds United (1963–71);
Ipswich Town (1971–72);
Sunderland (1973–75);
Fulham (loan, 1974);
Huddersfield Town (1974–76)

Season	League		FA Cup		League Cup		Other		Total	
	App	Goals	App	Goals	App	Goals	App	Goals	App	Goals
1972/73	14 (2)	2	2	1	0	0	-	-	16 (2)	3
1973/74	0	0	0	0	0	0	1	0	1	0
Total	14 (2)	2	2	1	0	0	1	0	17 (2)	3

Bell, John

Scottish wing wizard whose greatest days lay at Goodison

In the last years of the nineteenth century, Dumbarton proved a fertile poaching ground for Everton Football Club. With the Scottish town's various football clubs stubbornly refusing to give up their amateur status, their best players were attracted to Merseyside by the promise of a professional contract and the riches it could bring.

Richard Boyle, Johnny Holt and Abraham Hartley were all lured south by Everton, but perhaps the most distinguished part of this crop was John Bell, a star of Dumbarton's

back-to-back Scottish Championship wins at the start of the 1890s. A winger of great skill, he was to make one short of 200 Everton appearances, which spanned two spells and 10 years, also weighing in with 70 goals – an impressive haul for a man better known as a master dribbler than goalscorer. 'One swallow does not make a summer,' noted the early Everton historian Thomas Keates, 'but one player of outstanding ability in a football team

> 'ONE SWALLOW DOES NOT MAKE A SUMMER BUT ONE PLAYER OF OUTSTANDING ABILITY IN A FOOTBALL TEAM MAKES A GREAT DIFFERENCE IN ITS AGGREGATE RESULTS'
> **THOMAS KEATES**

makes a great difference in its aggregate results.' After making his Everton debut at the end of the 1892/93 season – Goodison's inaugural campaign – Bell made his place on the Everton wing his own the following campaign.

Like all of the great mavericks, Bell has become a near-mythical figure. Sam Crosbie, an early Everton fan, wrote of an incredible incident involving Bell in Keates' 1928 history of the club. 'At one game we noticed a player circling around as if very dizzy. Jack Bell ran to him, took hold of his head, put his shoulders between his knees, pulled his head with all his might, and in a few minutes the player joined in the game. It turned out he had dislocated his neck, and would have been a dead man in a few minutes had not Jack Bell adjusted the dislocation.' On another occasion Bell was run over by a cab on the Strand on the eve of an England v. Scotland meeting at the Crystal Palace. He brushed himself down, making little fuss of his injuries, and turned out the next day. Scotland won 2-1.

In all he would make 10 appearances for his country in an international career that spanned a decade. It is worth noting, however, that this tally might have been much higher were it not for the fact that Scotland's selectors usually overlooked the 'Anglos' – as Bell and others who played south of the border were referred – and that the bulk of his caps came while at Dumbarton at the start of his career, and Celtic near its end.

Perhaps Bell's finest game for Everton came in the 1897 FA Cup Final, when he harangued Aston Villa all afternoon. 'This was a remarkable match – many good judges think it was the best game the final ever furnished,' wrote Gibson and Pickford in their seminal Association Football and the Men Who Made It.

Villa took an early lead and, seizing the early initiative, could have gone further in front. But then Abraham Hartley played in Bell, who sidestepped past a defender and waited for James Whitehouse, the Villa goalkeeper, to advance, before rolling the ball past him and into the empty net. Everton then took the lead through Boyle – but it was all to no avail and Villa fought back to win 3-2 and lift a league and FA Cup double.

'Everton played moderately in the first half, but in the second they were different, and better men, and were only beaten by a goal,' Gibson and Pickford noted. 'The game was made memorable by John Bell's extraordinary efforts to win the match for his side, and no one admired his wonderful ability more than the supporters of Aston Villa ...'

Bell was an erudite figure and an articulate spokesman for players'

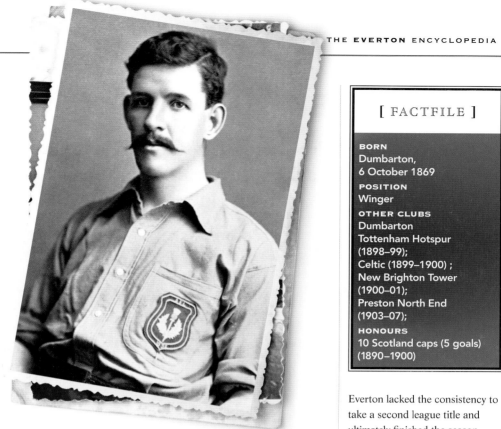

[FACTFILE]

BORN
Dumbarton,
6 October 1869
POSITION
Winger
OTHER CLUBS
Dumbarton
Tottenham Hotspur
(1898–99);
Celtic (1899–1900) ;
New Brighton Tower
(1900–01);
Preston North End
(1903–07);
HONOURS
10 Scotland caps (5 goals)
(1890–1900)

rights. In February 1898, in a response to moves by Football League clubs to limit footballers' wages, Bell was one of the leading agitators against this, helping form the first ever player's union, the Association Footballer's Union (AFU), of which he became chairman.

His work with the nascent Player's Union brought him into conflict with Everton's management, and for a while – as the 1897/98 season drew to its close – it seemed as if Bell might walk away from football altogether. Instead he joined Tottenham, then of the Southern League, and subsequently returned to Scotland, where he signed for Celtic. By now players in Scotland faced no impediment to their earning power. His departure back north of the border – combined with several notable player defections to the Southern League, which was also free from proposed wage constraints –marked the death knell of the AFU, seriously diminishing its credibility. Bell had previously campaigned against transfer fees, but had no objection to the £300 he cost Celtic, as he received a cut of it.

He returned to Merseyside after a two-year hiatus, joining New Brighton Tower in 1900, and returning to Goodison a year later. Through the 1901/02 season he galvanised a team in flux, scoring twice on his second debut against Manchester City, as Everton led the league through much of the first half of the season. Yet despite the veteran's best efforts,

Everton lacked the consistency to take a second league title and ultimately finished the season runners-up, three points behind Sunderland. 'One match dazzling, next puzzling,' recorded Keates. 'Puzzling to the players as well as to the spectators. Good teams often get in a tangle and fail to win the very matches they feel confident they could, and would, win.'

This baffling inconsistency carried over to the next campaign, as Everton finished 12th – their worst position yet. At the end of the 1902/03 season, Everton's directors sought fresh blood and Bell, who was now nearing his 34th birthday, was deemed expendable. Harold Hardman replaced him on the Everton flank and the Scot moved to Preston.

Here he would enjoy an Indian summer, helping revive football's first great team. He inspired their Second Division championship victory in 1903/04 and brought them to within a few points of a league title in 1905/06. A year later, he brought an end to his lengthy career and Preston would never come so close to a championship again. Bell continued to work as a coach at Deepdale, later emigrating to Canada.

	League		FA Cup		Total	
Season	App	Goals	App	Goals	App	Goals
1892/93	3	0	0	0	3	0
1893/94	24	9	1	0	25	9
1894/95	27	15	3	3	30	18
1895/96	27	9	3	1	3	10
1896/97	27	15	5	2	32	17
1897/98	22	4	5	0	27	4
1901/02	24	5	2	0	26	5
1902/03	23	5	3	2	26	7
Total	**177**	**62**	**22**	**8**	**199**	**70**

Bell, Robert 'Bunny'

Prolific understudy to Dean and Lawton, for Tranmere he once scored nine in a single match

Season	League		FA Cup		Total	
	App	Goals	App	Goals	App	Goals
1935/36	2	3	0	0	2	3
1936/37	3	1	0	0	3	1
1937/38	5	2	0	0	5	2
1938/39	4	3	0	0	4	3
Total	**14**	**9**	**0**	**0**	**14**	**9**

[FACTFILE]

BORN
Birkenhead, 10 April 1911
DIED
25 December 1988
POSITION
Centre forward
OTHER CLUB
Tranmere Rovers

Bell, Stanley Lawrence 'Laurie'

Scottish centre forward of a late-Victorian vintage

Season	League		FA Cup		Total	
	App	Goals	App	Goals	App	Goals
1897/98	23	12	5	3	28	15
1898/99	18	5	2	0	20	5
Total	**41**	**17**	**7**	**3**	**48**	**20**

[FACTFILE]

BORN
Langbank, 6 October 1869
POSITION
Centre forward /
outside right
OTHER CLUBS
Langbank; Dumbarton; Third Lanark; Sheffield Wednesday (1895–97);
Bolton Wanderers (1899–1902);
Brentford; West Bromwich Albion (1904);
Hibernian

Bellefield

For more than 60 years Everton's training ground was Bellefield, a complex located approximately three miles from the club's main home of Goodison Park. At one time one of the most advanced training facilities in the country, Everton eventually outgrew its amenities and in 2007 moved to the new Finch Farm complex in Halewood.

Originally the training ground for employees of the White Star Shipping Line, by the interwar years it incorporated a cricket pitch, bowling greens and tennis courts, which were used for company sports days. In 1935 the Liverpool building merchant William Tyson bought the land and leased it to the Co-op, which used it for staff events too.

EVERTON at this time used Goodison Park to train its players but German bomb damage during the Second World War meant some £5000 of repairs were needed to be carried out at Goodison. The club switched some of its training sessions over to Bellefield while this work was carried out and the players spent Tuesdays and Thursdays there.

In 1964 the club decided to make Bellefield their permanent training base and paid more than £25,000 for the land. Its cricket pavilion was pulled down and a two-storey building, incorporating changing rooms, a gym, physio rooms and later even a sauna, were built. There was a sports hall with an artificial pitch and other training pitches on the campus. It was a training base that was the envy of English football and many players say it swung their decision to join Everton.

The complex was officially opened by Football League President Joe Richards in July 1966. But by the time pre-season training for the

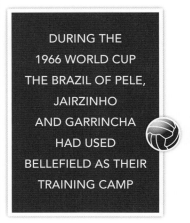

DURING THE 1966 WORLD CUP THE BRAZIL OF PELE, JAIRZINHO AND GARRINCHA HAD USED BELLEFIELD AS THEIR TRAINING CAMP

1966/67 season started Bellefield had already had some illustrious occupants. During that summer's World Cup the Brazil of Pele, Jairzinho and Garrincha had used it as their training camp.

'BELLEFIELD stood apart from other modern training grounds because of its intimacy,' the Liverpool Echo's long-standing Everton correspondent, Dave Prentice, would write. 'Recognised as one of the most modern and well-equipped complexes of its type, it was still small … its compact nature meant that each visit entailed interaction with everyone there.'

For the next 40 years it was, in effect, the Everton team's day-to-day home. Training was carried out there, contracts negotiated and signed, new players transferred in and old ones sold. Writing in the Observer Sport Monthly in 2003, Martin Baker described the Bellefield building as:

> **a neat and clean bit of 1950s architecture surrounded by a car park, three full-size pitches and other bits of parkland. Downstairs are the changing rooms, the kit rooms and a corridor leading to a vast gym hall with its full-size Astroturf pitch. Upstairs are the offices and the canteen. [David] Moyes has his own office, as do Irene, his personal assistant, the guy who runs Prozone (a hi-tech match analysis facility) and (inevitably, these days) the website manager. There is also a communal office for Moyes's managerial team. Bigger than the rest, it looks like something from the Fifties with its cheery, bright, functional desks and chairs — but with Sky Sports News playing in the corner. This is where Moyes meets the management team every morning.**

It was in many ways a nondescript place, where few Evertonians ever ventured. But for the players and the staff it formed many memories.

For Everton's most successful captain, Kevin Ratcliffe, it was the staff that made the place. 'You go upstairs after training and you all eat together but it was that little bit of banter after training,' he told EvertonTV in 2007. 'There were not too many clubs that had their own training grounds in those days and now everybody has got it.'

Yet by the early 21st century Everton were outgrowing Bellefield. It was a time when sports science facilities were being expanded, and increased youth development schemes made greater demands on facilities. The Everton youth academy for several years was left to train at the Littlewoods training grounds in Netherton, with staff based in Portakabins. It was an unsatisfactory state of affairs that was resolved with the move to Finch Farm. Bellefield was eventually sold to property developer Bestway for a sum reputed to be £8million.

'Unfortunately this place does not have the structure to go state-of-the-art because it is not big enough but you have got to move with the times,' said Ratcliffe when it finally shut its doors. 'It will be sad but if you want to progress you have got to move.'

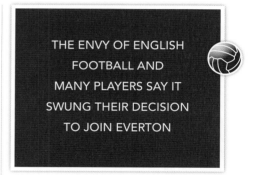

THE ENVY OF ENGLISH FOOTBALL AND MANY PLAYERS SAY IT SWUNG THEIR DECISION TO JOIN EVERTON

Bennett, Harry

Season	League		FA Cup		League Cup		Total	
	App	Goals	App	Goals	App	Goals	App	Goals
1967-68	2 (1)	0	0	0	0	0	2 (1)	0
1968-69	0	0	0	0	0	0	0	0
1969-70	0	0	0	0	1	0	1	0
Total	2 (1)	0	0	0	1	0	3 (1)	0

[FACTFILE]

BORN
Liverpool, 16 May 1949
POSITION
Wing half
OTHER CLUBS
Aldershot (1970–73)
Crewe Alexandra (1973–74)

Bent, Marcus

Wandering striker who lacked finishing touches necessary to realise his potential

[FACTFILE]

BORN
Hammersmith, 19 May 1978
POSITION
Striker
OTHER CLUBS
Brentford (1995–98)
Crystal Palace (1998–99)
Port Vale (1999)
Sheffield United (1999–2000) Blackburn
Rovers (2000–01)
Ipswich Town (2001–04)
Leicester City (loan, 2003–04) Charlton
Athletic (2006–08)
Wigan Athletic (loan, 2007-08)
Birmingham City (2008–11)
Middlesbrough (loan, 2009–10)
Queens Park Rangers (loan, 2010)
Wolverhampton Wanderers (loan, 2010–11)
Sheffield United (loan, 2011)
Mitra Kukar (Indonesia, 2011–12)

2004 represented a turbulent summer in Everton's recent history. Fans were bewildered by an array of rumours concerning the club's financial plight and the destiny not just of star player Wayne Rooney, but the very future ownership of Everton too. Amid this rancour, the arrival of Marcus Bent for a nominal fee from Ipswich Town went almost unheralded. As Rooney agitated for his move to Manchester United, the realisation that the £450,000 journeyman was, in essence, the brilliant teenager's replacement was scarcely edifying to Evertonians.

And yet, as the 2004/05 season got under way and David Moyes settled on a five-man midfield, with Bent a lone striker, he struck a winning formula. Everton upset the Premier League form book and challenged at the top of the table, with Bent a key component of their success.

INDEED Bent's problem was seemingly that he did not realise just how good he was. Although his finishing was at times erratic, his overall contribution to the team was excellent and he possessed all the attributes that befit a top modern striker: pace, aerial ability, technical skill. Playing alongside James Beattie, signed for a record fee the following January, Bent always looked a better bet than the man that had cost more than twelve times as much as him.

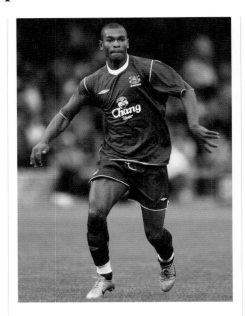

So just what held Marcus Bent back? Possibly it was his nomadic career. After starting out as a Brentford trainee in the mid-1990s he embarked on a footballing journey that took in Crystal Palace, Port Vale, Sheffield United, Blackburn Rovers, Ipswich Town and a lengthy loan period at Leicester City in the six years that preceded his move to Goodison. A lack of self-belief, perhaps, also stopped him from making the step up from decent squad player to first-choice striker. Nor did he get the goals his all-round play often merited.

Everton's fourth-placed position at the end of the 2004/05 season owed much to Bent's substantial but often unheralded contribution. Never was he better than when he almost lifted the net from the goalposts with a rasping last-minute equaliser against Southampton in February which kept Everton's campaign on track.

THE following season, however, he became frustrated at a lack of opportunities, often playing second fiddle to the hapless Beattie, who did little to merit his inclusion ahead of him. When David Moyes received a £2.2million bid for Bent from Charlton the following January he happily quadrupled his money on a player from whom he had got much. Although relegated with Charlton a year later, Marcus Bent returned to the Premier League with Wigan Athletic in August 2007. A subsequent move to Birmingham proved unsuccessful and after a plethora of loan moves in 2011 he wound up in Indonesia in 2011 with Mitra Kukar, club number 15.

Season	League		FA Cup		League Cup		Europe		Total	
	App	Goals	App	Goals	App	Goals	App	Goals	App	Goals
2004/05	31 (6)	6	2 (1)	0	1 (1)	1	-	-	34 (8)	7
2005/06	7 (11)	1	1	0	0 (1)	0	2 (2)	0	10 (14)	1
Total	38 (17)	7	3 (1)	0	1 (2)	1	2 (2)	0	44 (22)	8

Bentham, Stanley

Unsung stalwart of the 1939 title-winning side who served as a coach through the 1950s

Over three decades, Stan Bentham was a valued member of the Goodison set-up, first serving with distinction as a player, winning the League Championship in 1939, then as a member of the coaching staff.

BENTHAM MISSED JUST ONE GAME IN THE 1938/39 SEASON WHEN EVERTON WON THE CHAMPIONSHIP

An inside right by number, Bentham was a pioneer of the roving midfield role, becoming the 'extra man' in the middle of the team, at hand whenever Everton were on the attack, but always ready to drop back when the defence needed assistance.

He learned his early football with his church team, Lowton St Mary's, in the Leigh and District Sunday League, and had a series of trials with Bolton before signing professional forms with Wigan Athletic in December 1933. Within weeks he found himself scouted by top clubs, but chose Everton, making the Goodison switch with Springfield Park team-mate Terry Kavanagh in February 1934.

KAVANAGH never made the Goodison grade but, after working his way up through the youth and reserve sides, Bentham made his debut in November 1935, scoring twice in a 4-0 away victory against Grimsby Town. Despite the dream debut it took him a further three years to establish himself in the Everton starting line-up, but when he did his influence was considerable.

Bentham missed just one game in the 1938/39 season when Everton won the Championship, and he was able to round off a glorious campaign with a hat-trick in the 6-2 victory over Sunderland on 10 April, which virtually sealed the League title for Everton. The following day the Liverpool Echo ran a cartoon singing his praises, and its caption read: 'Bentham had a plaster on his head, a cut over his eye and was kicked in the ribs, yet he scored 3 goals… As Bentham seems to thrive on injuries there is no knowing how many he would have scored if he had received a few more bumps!'

AS WITH many of the highly promising players of his generation, Bentham had his career wrecked by the war. When he came back from the fighting, despite missing just five games in the 1946/47 season, he struggled to hold on to his first-team place. He was appointed to the coaching staff on his retirement from playing in 1949, a position which he kept until he left Goodison in 1962 to take up a similar role at Luton Town.

A fine amateur cricketer who scored several centuries for Newton Le Willows, Bentham lived quietly on Merseyside until his death in May 2002 in a Southport nursing home.

Season	League		FA Cup		Total	
	App	Goals	App	Goals	App	Goals
1935/36	7	4	1	0	8	4
1936/37	2	0	0	0	2	0
1937/38	0	0	0	0	0	0
1938/39	41	9	5	0	46	9
1945/46	-	-	2	0	2	0
1946/47	37	3	2	0	39	3
1947/48	10	0	5	0	15	0
1948/49	13	1	0	0	13	1
Total	**110**	**17**	**15**	**0**	**125**	**17**

[FACTFILE]

BORN
Leigh, 17 March 1915
DIED
Southport, 29 May 2002
OTHER CLUB
Wigan Athletic (1933–34)
HONOURS
1938/39 League Championship

Bentley, Jack

Centre forward who subsequently enjoyed incredible non-league success

Season	League		FA Cup		Total	
	App	Goals	App	Goals	App	Goals
1960/61	1	0	0	0	1	0
Total	**1**	**0**	**0**	**0**	**1**	**0**

[FACTFILE]

BORN
Liverpool, 17 February 1941
DIED
26 May 2007
POSITION
Centre forward
OTHER CLUBS
Stockport County (1961–63)
Wellington Town
(subsequently Telford United)
(1963–77)

Bernard, Mike

Brave and reliable midfielder cum right back

In May 1972, Harry Catterick paid £140,000 to bring former England under-23 international Mike Bernard to Goodison. Earmarked as an important part of the Everton manager's rebuilding programme, it was hoped the arrival of Bernard – who had just helped Stoke City to win the League Cup – would bring some of the competitive spirit lacking since Alan Ball's controversial departure to Arsenal the previous December.

WITH HIS solid, somewhat chunky physique, Bernard was an archetypal ball winner in an era of midfield hard men. Tough, competitive and a tireless worker, he was the sort of player that allowed more attack-minded colleagues to express themselves. Arguably, he lacked some of the cut-and-thrust and dirty tricks that saw other midfield harriers elevated to international level, but Bernard could sometimes take his

competitiveness too far – as witness his sending off in Everton's bad-tempered UEFA Cup tie with AC Milan in 1975.

By then he had been converted by Billy Bingham to right back, a position that was hitherto alien to him. He proved a competent rather than outstanding defender, but his competitive spirit and enthusiasm never wavered and he always gave his best in a position that was problematic for Everton throughout the 1970s.

Following Gordon Lee's arrival as manager in January 1977, Bernard fell behind Terry Darracott and Steve Sergeant in the pecking order. He nevertheless made a rare appearance in the first replay of the League Cup Final with Aston Villa, playing on through extra time despite being injured – a performance that one veteran Evertonian described to this author as the most outstandingly brave he had witnessed. It was this sort of resilience that seemed to typify the player.

THIS virtually represented his last action as an Everton player, and in July 1977 he joined Oldham Athletic, whom he served briefly before injury forced his premature retirement from the game.

> HIS COMPETITIVE SPIRIT AND ENTHUSIASM NEVER WAVERED AND HE ALWAYS GAVE HIS BEST

[FACTFILE]

BORN
Shrewsbury, 10 January 1948
POSITION
Midfield / right back
OTHER CLUBS
Stoke City (1965–72)
Oldham Athletic (1977–79)

Season	League		FA Cup		League Cup		Other		Total	
	App	Goals	App	Goals	App	Goals	App	Goals	App	Goals
1972/73	30 (2)	1	2	0	1	0	-	-	33 (2)	1
1973/74	35 (2)	4	3	0	2	0	0 (1)	0	40 (3)	4
1974/75	31 (2)	0	2 (1)	0	2	0	-	-	35 (3)	0
1975/76	29 (1)	2	1	0	2 (1)	0	1	0	33 (2)	2
1976/77	14 (1)	1	1	0	4	0	-	-	19 (1)	1
Total	139 (8)	8	9 (1)	0	11 (1)	0	1 (1)	0	160 (11)	8

Berry, Arthur

Amateur winger and double Olympic champion

Season	League		FA Cup		Total	
	App	Goals	App	Goals	App	Goals
1909/10	6	2	0	0	6	2
1910/11	21	5	2	0	23	5
Total	27	7	2	0	29	7

[FACTFILE]

BORN
3 January 1888
POSITION
Outside right
OTHER CLUB
Liverpool (1907–09 & 1912)
HONOURS
England cap (1909),
2 Olympic gold medals (1908 & 1912)

Berry, C.H.

Reserve goalkeeper during the early Edwardian era

Season	League App	League Goals	FA Cup App	FA Cup Goals	Total App	Total Goals
1908/09	2	0	0	0	0	2
1909/10	0	0	0	0	0	0
1910/11	0	0	0	0	0	0
1911/12	1	0	0	0	0	1
Total	**3**	**0**	**0**	**0**	**0**	**3**

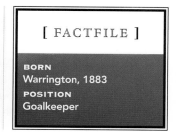

[FACTFILE]

BORN
Warrington, 1883
POSITION
Goalkeeper

Berwick, William

Full back who made just a solitary appearance

Season	League App	League Goals	FA Cup App	FA Cup Goals	Total App	Total Goals
1919/20	1	0	0	0	1	0
Total	**1**	**0**	**0**	**0**	**1**	**0**

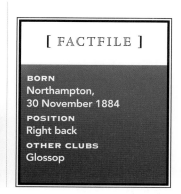

[FACTFILE]

BORN
Northampton,
30 November 1884
POSITION
Right back
OTHER CLUBS
Glossop

Beveridge, Robert

Misfiring centre forward given the briefest of chances

Season	League App	League Goals	FA Cup App	FA Cup Goals	Total App	Total Goals
1900/01	4	0	0	0	4	0
Total	**4**	**0**	**0**	**0**	**4**	**0**

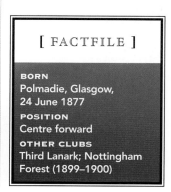

[FACTFILE]

BORN
Polmadie, Glasgow,
24 June 1877
POSITION
Centre forward
OTHER CLUBS
Third Lanark; Nottingham
Forest (1899–1900)

Bidwell, Jake

Home grown left back who is Everton's youngest ever player to make a European appearance

Season	League App	League Goals	FA Cup App	FA Cup Goals	League Cup App	League Cup Goals	Europe App	Europe Goals	Total App	Total Goals
2009/10	0	0	0	0	0	0	1	0	1	0
Total	**0**	**0**	**0**	**0**	**0**	**0**	**1**	**0**	**1**	**0**

[FACTFILE]

BORN
Southport, 21 March 1993
POSITION
Left back
OTHER CLUB
Brentford (loan) (2011-12)

Biley, Alan

Charismatic forward who struggled to make the top-flight grade

When Howard Kendall made him one of his first signings as Everton manager, it meant Alan Biley had finally worked his way up through all the English divisions to make it to the top flight.

A £300,000 acquisition in July 1981, Biley had been a prolific marksman with Cambridge

> A SMART CHIP ON HIS DEBUT AGAINST BIRMINGHAM HELPED SECURE A 3-1 WIN, AND HE STRUCK AN EARLY GOAL IN EVERTON'S NEXT FIXTURE, AGAINST LEEDS UNITED

United and Derby County. At these clubs his explosive turn of pace and intuitive sense of timing had garnered him a reputation as a penalty area predator. With his spiky Rod Stewart haircut and penchant for a lively quip, he seemed to have the personality for the big time too. Indeed, all the early signs were good. A smart chip on his debut against Birmingham helped secure a 3-1 win, and he struck an early goal in Everton's next fixture, against Leeds United.

BUT THEN the goals dried up and Biley lost his place to Graeme Sharp. He was loaned to Stoke City after Everton signed Adrian Heath from them, but this proved fruitless. Just over a year after his arrival he was sold for £125,000 to Portsmouth, where the goals flowed once more. However, Alan Biley would never return to the top flight.

'I've got extremely fond memories of everywhere I've been but my time at Everton was probably the most frustrating,' he later told evertonfc.com. 'You'll never be able to put your finger on why it didn't have longevity. Everybody will have their own thoughts on it. For me it was about not being played in the right position but at the time Howard Kendall was new to the post and he was trying everybody.'

[FACTFILE]

BORN
Leighton Buzzard, 26 February 1957
POSITION
Striker
OTHER CLUBS
Cambridge United (1975–80);
Derby County (1980–81);
Portsmouth (1982–85);
Brighton & Hove Albion (1985–86);
Cambridge United (1987)

Season	League		FA Cup		League Cup		Total	
	App	Goals	App	Goals	App	Goals	App	Goals
1981/82	16 (3)	3	0	0	2	0	18 (3)	3
Total	16 (3)	3	0	0	2	0	18 (3)	3

Bilić, Slaven

Underperforming defender of vast pedigree

Vast, imposing centre back Slaven Bilić first appeared in English football with West Ham following a £1.3million transfer from Karlsruher SC in January 1996. With a good first touch and astute reading of the game, he immediately impressed for the Hammers, turning out for Croatia at that summer's European Championships in England. His performances attracted the notice of Joe Royle, who was in the market for a long-term replacement for Dave Watson, and in March 1997 he agreed a £4.5million deal for the defender.

BILIĆ, who was always idiosyncratic and sought his own path, refused to leave West Ham immediately, saying he owed them a 'debt of loyalty', which he chose to express as helping them out of a relegation battle. (It was later alleged that he stayed to collect a £200,000 loyalty bonus.) However, by the time he completed his move that summer, Royle had left Everton and Bilić was left to forge his career amid the chaos that defined Howard Kendall's third spell as Everton manager.

Not that Bilić did much to alleviate Everton's plight. Sent off three times, he missed one quarter of the 1997/98 season to suspension and when he did play did little to allay Everton's descent to the

relegation zone. Tellingly he was left out of the season's crucial game, at home to Coventry City, where a wretched Everton team barely staved off relegation.

PERHAPS unbelievably, Bilić appeared just five more times in an Everton shirt after that tumultuous day. Although these last days were purportedly confounded by persistent injuries, he would somehow recover in order to play for his national team and seemed to spend as much time recovering in his homeland as he did at Bellefield.

Without a first-team appearance in more than a year, in February 2000 Everton gave Bilić a £1 million payoff, which represented half the balance of his contract, also writing off the transfer fee. Within days he joined Hadjuk Split, where he played out his career.

An erudite, intelligent man and qualified lawyer, Bilić later managed Croatia, masterminding England's demise in the 2008 European Championship qualifiers.

SENT OFF THREE TIMES, HE MISSED ONE QUARTER OF THE 1997/98 SEASON TO SUSPENSION

When fees, wages and his payoff had been taken into account, Bilić cost Everton around £250,000 per match. Yet during this time his only notable contribution to football was an outrageous dive in the World Cup semi-final, which saw the France captain, Laurent Blanc, banned for the final. Blanc, like Everton Football Club, had every right to feel cheated.

[FACTFILE]

BORN
Split, Yugoslavia (now Croatia)
11 September 1968
POSITION
Centre back
OTHER CLUBS
Hadjuk Split (1987–1993);
Karlsruher SC (1993–96);
West Ham United (1996–97);
Hadjuk Split (2000–01)
AS MANAGER
Hadjuk Split (2001-02)
Croatia under-21 (2004-06),
Croatia (2006-12),
Lokomotiv Moscow (2012-)
HONOURS
44 Croatia caps (3 goals)
(1990–99)

Season	League		FA Cup		League Cup		Total	
	App	Goals	App	Goals	App	Goals	App	Goals
1997/98	22 (2)	0	0	0	3	0	25 (2)	0
1998/99	4	0	1	0	0	0	5	0
1999/2000	0	0	0	0	0	0	0	0
Total	**26 (2)**	**0**	**1**	**0**	**3**	**0**	**30 (2)**	**0**

Billing, Peter

Defender plucked from local non-league ranks who forged a solid top-flight career with Coventry

[FACTFILE]

BORN
Liverpool, 24 October 1964
POSITION
Centre back
OTHER CLUBS
South Liverpool
Crewe Alexandra (1986–89)
Coventry City (1989–93)
Port Vale (1993–95)
Hartlepool United (1995–96)
Crewe Alexandra (1996–97)
Northwich Victoria (1997)

Season	League		FA Cup		Europe		Other		Total	
	App	Goals	App	Goals	App	Goals	App	Goals	App	Goals
1985/86	1	0	0	0	0	0	2	0	3	0
1986/87	0	0	0	0	0	0	2	0	2	0
Total	**1**	**0**	**0**	**0**	**0**	**0**	**4**	**0**	**5**	**0**

Bilyaletdinov, Diniyar

Enigmatic Russian international who returned to his home nation after 28 frustrating months

At £8.9million Russian international Diniyar Bilyaletdinov became the third most expensive player in Everton's history when he joined the club at the end of the August 2009 transfer window. The son of a former professional player and influential coach at Lokomotiv Mosow, Rinat Bilyaletdinov, there were high hopes of a player who carried great potential. In concluding the deal David Moyes ended a nine-month-long pursuit of him.

Indeed, on unveiling his new signing, Moyes likened the young Tartar to Kevin Sheedy. 'He's a left-sided player and he's actually got a bit of Kevin Sheedy about him,' said the Everton manager. 'He can also play on the right and can fill several roles in the team. [Russia manager] Guus Hiddink has even used him as an emergency left back in the past.'

Bilyaletdinov was given a role in one of the most talented midfields in Everton history, lining up alongside the likes of Marouane Fellaini, Mikel Arteta and Steven Pienaar. But while showing intelligence in his passing and movement, the physicality and intensity of the Premier League seemed too much for the Russian and he had a tendency to go missing from the action. On just seven occasions during the 2009/10 season did he complete 90 minutes in a league match.

And yet his talent was obvious. There was a shot that struck the back of the Manchester United net with such mighty velocity that it left the usually imperious Edwin Van Der Sar standing still and set Everton on the way to a fine victory in February 2010. There was a similarly net-bursting long-distance goal against Portsmouth with virtually the last kick of his debut season that whetted the Evertonian appetite further.

But despite these glimpses of his pedigree, Bilyaletdinov and English football did not appear to be made for each other. A regular starting berth proved elusive and so did the form that saw Moyes pay such a hefty fee. He started just ten league games in the 2010/11 season and similarly struggled the following campaign. Seeking to revitalise his team, in January 2012 Moyes cut his losses, selling the midfielder to Spartak Moscow for a fee believed to be around £5million. With the funds he signed Darron Gibson and Nikica Jelavic and Everton once more prospered.

[FACTFILE]

BORN
Moscow, 27 February 1985
POSITION
Left winger / midfielder
OTHER CLUBS
Lokomotiv Moscow
(2004–09);
Spartak Moscow (2012–)
HONOURS
46 Russia caps (2005–)

Season	League		FA Cup		League Cup		Europe		Total	
	App	Goals	App	Goals	App	Goals	App	Goals	App	Goals
2009/10	16 (7)	6	2	0	1	0	6 (1)	1	25 (8)	7
2010/11	10 (16)	2	3 (1)	0	1 (1)	0	-	-	14(18)	2
2011/12	7 (3)	0	1	0	1	0	-	-	9 (3)	0
Total	**33(26)**	**8**	**6 (1)**	**0**	**3 (1)**	**0**	**6 (1)**	**1**	**48 (29)**	**9**

Bingham, Billy

Member of the 1963 League Championship winning team who went on to manage Everton

For many men an unsuccessful spell as Everton manager has signalled the end of their top-class managerial career and sometimes seen a slide towards obscurity. Gordon Lee, Colin Harvey and Mike Walker all failed to maintain the managerial heights after leaving the Everton top job. Yet Billy Bingham, who failed to achieve the success demanded by the club in a three-and-a-half year term as manager in the mid-1970s, left Goodison to guide Northern Ireland to the pinnacle of the country's football history. Previous to his managerial career, Bingham had served Everton with distinction as a player, culminating in the 1962/63 League Championship.

Born in the midst of the great depression and brought up through years of poverty and war, Bingham was raised in the shadow of Belfast's great shipyards. A schoolboy prodigy, he was nevertheless versed in the realities of working life, working as an apprentice in one of the yard's manufacturing shops. Aged 17 he turned professional with Glentoran and, although some deemed him too lightweight to make it, by the 1949/50 season the winger was a first-team regular and called up to represent the Irish League against the Scottish League.

Such progress drew the attention of English scouts and in October

1950 Bingham joined Sunderland for £8000. He spent seven years at Roker Park, for a period combining his shipyard apprenticeship with football for the Wearsiders and the Northern Ireland team. Sunderland in this period were perennial nearly-men and Bingham played in some thrilling teams. His time in the Northeast was to end in acrimony, however, as Sunderland were engulfed in financial scandal midway through the 1957/58 season. The club was found to have paid players more than the permitted maximum wage and the club received a hefty fine. In disarray, Sunderland were relegated and Bingham joined Luton Town.

That summer the winger was elevated to the global stage and appeared for Northern Ireland at the World Cup finals in Sweden. In qualifying for the tournament the Irish had already dismissed Italy and Portugal and in the finals they knocked out Argentina and Czechoslovakia before falling to Just Fontaine's France.

Bingham did well at Luton, who briefly topped the First Division and made the FA Cup Final during the 1958/59 campaign. A year later, however, they were relegated and the Irishman sought a fresh start. Negotiations with Arsenal broke down, but in October 1960 Luton accepted a part-exchange deal that saw John Bramwell and Alec Ashworth move to Kenilworth Road along with £10,000 and Bingham move north to Everton.

BINGHAM was a classic, jinking winger, who liked inviting in opponents before cutting inside and letting fly with a shot or cross. His goal ratio was healthy and he would more than play his part in Everton's early-1960s ascent. To facilitate his arrival, manager Johnny Carey switched Mickey Lill, Everton's joint top scorer in the previous campaign, to the

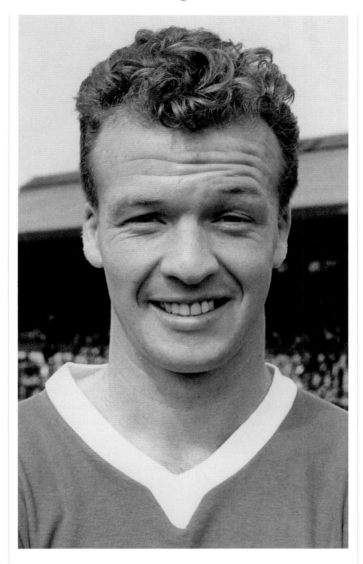

other wing. Bingham soon built up a keen understanding with the Scottish international full back Alex Parker. Horace Yates wrote in the Daily Post: 'Everton now possess the most goalworthy pair of wingers they have had for many a year.' Parker was equally enthusiastic about his new team-mate: 'He's probably the best winger I've played with. He can read me and I can read him and that's why we play so well together.'

Bingham soon emerged as a favourite in an expansive, attractive team that was undermined by its inconsistency. Carey had brought in players like Alex Young and Roy Vernon but Everton lacked killer instinct. A run of nine league defeats in 12 games in early 1961 killed off Everton's title hopes and Carey's chances of holding on to his job. Everton finished 1960/61 fifth, their best league placing since the war, but Carey was replaced by Harry Catterick. 'In army terms,' Bingham would recall, 'Harry was sergeant major and Johnny an officer.'

CATTERICK would bring discipline to the Everton team. The club finished one better in 1961/62, with Bingham appearing in all but five of Everton's league outings. But the new manager was also ruthless and always seeking to improve his starting XI. Midway through the 1962/63 season, as football ground to a halt under the conditions of the most bitter winter in a generation, Catterick signed Scottish winger Alex Scott from Glasgow Rangers.

Bingham was bullish about the signing, saying: 'I am looking at [Scott's signing] merely as a challenge and I am prepared to battle for my place.' The reality was that in an era without substitutions it was a losing battle he faced. He played just twice more for Everton, but had made enough appearances to merit a League Championship winner's medal at the season's end. 'There was a nice mixture of the Scottish, Welsh, Irish and English,' he later remembered. 'It was a great team to play in and I really enjoyed my playing days at Everton.'

Bingham joined Port Vale several months after Everton's title win, playing for two further years before a broken leg ended his career. From the Potteries, Bingham returned to Merseyside, where he enjoyed a three-year tenure as manager of Southport, which ended with a move to Plymouth Argyle, a role he combined with taking charge of Northern Ireland. But his record in Devon was mixed: relegated from the Second Division, fifth in the Third Division, then sacked for breach of contract after travelling to Wrexham for a training session with the Northern Ireland Under-23 team.

A brief spell as boss of Linfield followed but this ended (after they'd been crowned Northern Irish champions) when the Greek FA made him an offer to become manager of their national team. Following his failure to take Greece to the 1974 World Cup Finals in West Germany his contract was not renewed.

Somehow this mixed CV led Bingham back to Merseyside in May 1973. Harry Catterick had been shifted to an undefined executive role following a period of ill health and a decline in Everton's fortunes, and the chairman, John Moores, was frustrated in his attempts to hire names such as Don Revie and

Brian Clough in his place. Instead he appointed Bingham, who – given his eclectic CV – possessed a reputation as a coach of progressive methods and discipline. A wave of optimism spread through the club. Moores described the new manager as a 'true Evertonian' and Bingham said he was 'dying to have a go at the job'.

EVERTON still ranked among English football's big spenders in this era and Bingham was given a hefty £300,000 transfer budget for the purchase of new players. However, he started the 1973/74 season without having made any major forays into the transfer market. He also brought his disciplinarian creed into the dressing room. Players were fined for breaking curfews and new scientific training methods, which combined running and gym-based routines even on match days, were introduced. Bingham was also

> MOORES DESCRIBED THE NEW MANAGER AS A 'TRUE EVERTONIAN' AND BINGHAM SAID HE WAS 'DYING TO HAVE A GO AT THE JOB'

quick to change the coaching staff, replacing Tommy Eggleston with Ray Henderson and using Catterick in a scouting role. His methods were not universally liked and would eventually bring him into conflict with his squad.

Despite a slow start to the season, he started to gel his desired side together, picking up the October Manager of the Month award after a 100 per cent record. In February 1974, Bingham made his first major transfer deal, acquiring Bob Latchford from Birmingham City in a British record deal. The move, however, wasn't without controversy and it sent Howard Kendall – Everton's best player – and Archie Styles in the opposite direction. With Joe Royle's powers declining, however, Everton needed goals. Latchford's contribution was virtually immediate and he scored seven times in the remaining 13 games of the season as Everton finished Bingham's first season seventh.

Over the summer and first months of the 1974/75 season, Bingham continued to make his impression. He sold Royle and Colin Harvey, the last stalwarts of the League Championship winning season, and brought in Jim Pearson, Dave Clements and Martin Dobson. At Anfield an epoch had ended with Bill Shankly's retirement and

many felt dominance shifting back to the blue half of Merseyside. Catterick tipped Everton to win the League and FA Cup double. Of Bingham's new team, he added: 'He's also winning games attractively.' Not everybody agreed with the former manager's view. The Derby County assistant manager, Des Anderson, branded Bingham's side 'robots' and the London press nicknamed Everton (with reference to their orange away strip) the 'Clockwork Orange'.

Bingham had certainly made Everton difficult to beat. Fifteen games into the 1974/75 season they had lost just once in the league. Yet they also won just four matches and this inordinate number of stalemates would cost them dearly at the season's end. Still, in a tightly matched division, it stood them in good stead: after beating Derby County shortly before Christmas they went top for the first time in 26 months.

Everton would spend most of the first three months of 1975 at the top of the First Division. Bingham's team were effective, but lacked a certain ruthlessness. They were beaten 3-2 at home by Carlisle United, despite leading 2-0 at half-time, and knocked out of the FA Cup fifth round at home to Second Division Fulham. Yet seven games from the end of the season Everton remained top and Bingham promised: 'The chase is almost over and the prize is almost won. We are not cracking at the crunch.'

THESE words would soon come back to haunt him. On 29 March Everton travelled to Carlisle, who would end their only top-flight season bottom. The league leaders were turned over 3-0. A win at Coventry restored Everton to the top, but then they travelled to Luton, who would also be relegated. Everton took the lead through a first-half Latchford goal, could not add to it, and Luton secured an improbable win after scoring twice in four second-half minutes. Everton dropped to fourth. Three points from their remaining three games were not enough to improve this position and Derby County took the title. In essence, it would have been Everton's had they managed to beat Carlisle or to win more than two of their final ten matches. Everton, reported the Observer, 'had made an unscheduled stop at the top on the way to becoming a good team'. It was probably a fair assessment.

As a Player

Season	League		FA Cup		League Cup		Europe		Total	
	App	Goals	App	Goals	App	Goals	App	Goals	App	Goals
1960/61	26	9	1	0	3	1	-	-	30	10
1961/62	37	9	3	1	-	-	-	-	40	10
1962/63	23	5	3	1	-	-	2	0	28	6
Total	**86**	**23**	**7**	**2**	**3**	**1**	**2**	**0**	**98**	**26**

As a Manager

Season	P	W	L	D	F	A	Pts	Position	FA Cup	League Cup	Europe
1973/74	42	16	12	14	50	48	44	7th	4th Round	3rd Round	-
1974/75	42	16	18	8	56	52	50	4th	5th Round	2nd Round	-
1975/76	42	15	12	15	60	66	42	12th	3rd Round	2nd Round	1st Round
1976/77*	42	14	14	14	62	64	42	9th	Semi	Runners-up	-

*Bingham sacked 8 January 1977 with Everton in 13th place, in the fourth round of the FA Cup and in the League Cup semi-final

Everton started the 1975/76 season with no major additions to their squad. The bad form of the latter stages of the previous campaign carried on. A 4-1 opening day home defeat to Coventry City set the tone. Everton fell at the first stage of the FA Cup and UEFA Cups and finished eleventh. The club's average attendance dropped by 13,000 and Bingham's disciplinary style brought him into conflict with his players. Gary Jones and Mick Buckley were sold after a half-time dressing-room row during a defeat at Manchester City in February.

Fresh hope greeted the start of the 1975/76 season. Everton beat the previous season's runners-up Queens Park Rangers 4-0 on the opening day and rose to second by October. Andy King, a bargain buy from Luton Town at the end of the previous season, looked an inspired acquisition. Although Everton reached the semi-finals of

the League Cup, the team lacked consistency in the league and supporters' patience with the dour football was wearing thin. In a final attempt to turn the situation around Bingham signed Scottish international midfielder Bruce Rioch and Duncan McKenzie, a showman forward. League results did not improve and after a poor Christmas he was sacked. 'I've had pressures from every quarter and I have tried to do the job as well as I could,' he reflected. 'Some people may debate whether that was the right way, but it was the best I could do.'

BINGHAM returned to Greece, where he spent a short spell later that year managing PAOK Salonika. In March 1978 he returned to English club management with Mansfield Town, but his record was poor and he left in July 1979 after falling out with his chairman. Six months later he again took over as manager of the Northern Ireland

national team. He held this job for 14 years and his managerial career is defined by this reign. During that time he took the team to the 1982 World Cup Finals in Spain, beating the host nation along the way, and to qualification for the 1986 tournament in Mexico. In 1990 Bingham was awarded the MBE for his services to football.

As a player, Bingham's unstinting contribution to Everton's renaissance under Johnny Carey and Harry Catterick will never be forgotten, nor the important part he played in Everton's 1963 League Championship win. As a manager, despite bringing stars such as Bob Latchford, Martin Dobson and Duncan McKenzie to Goodison, there remain some regrets that his team of 'robots' could not bring the title back to Goodison and transform the era of the clockwork orange into one tinged with more golden memories.

Birch, Ken

Wing half who combined to make history with T. G. Jones

Ken Birch's football career was defined by one of the great episodes of Welsh football history.

In 1962, Bangor City of the Cheshire League (managed by Everton legend T. G. Jones) were drawn against Italian giants Napoli in the preliminary round of the European Cup Winner's Cup. Captained by Birch, they recorded an improbable 2-0 win at their tiny Farrar Road Stadium, Birch scoring the second goal from the penalty spot. In Naples they fell three goals behind when, with five minutes remaining, Birch launched a long throw-in into the Napoli penalty area. It caused havoc and in the melee Bangor

scored to bring the scores to 3-1 on the night, 3-3 on aggregate. Alas, this was an era before away goals counted double. The match went to a replay at Highbury and Napoli edged through 2-1 winners. But Birch had made his way into football lore.

THIS WAS a great epilogue to a career spent on the fringes of professional football. The wing half was signed by Everton as a teenager in September 1950 and was engaged on the Goodison ground staff on wages of £6 per week. His career was interrupted by national service and he had to wait until April 1956 before making his first-team debut, in a

1-1 draw at Sheffield United. He was a regular through the 1956/57 season, but lost his place to Ken Rea the following campaign and in March 1958 a £6000 bid was accepted from Southampton.

Birch spent just 15 months at The Dell before dropping into non-league football with Chelmsford City and, in August 1960, Bangor City. He subsequently played out his career as player-manager of Benoni in South Africa.

	League		FA Cup		Total	
Season	**App**	**Goals**	**App**	**Goals**	**App**	**Goals**
1955/56	4	0	0	0	4	0
1956/57	29	1	1	0	30	1
1957/58	10	0	1	0	11	0
Total	**43**	**1**	**2**	**0**	**45**	**1**

Birnie, Alex

Scottish winger who made cameos during the 1905/06 season

[FACTFILE]

BORN
Aberdeen, 11 January 1884
POSITION
Outside right
OTHER CLUBS
Chatham Dockyard;
West Ham United;
Sittingbourne;
Norwich City;
Southend United;
Bury (1908–11)

Season	League		FA Cup		Total	
	App	Goals	App	Goals	App	Goals
1905/06	3	0	0	0	3	0
Total	3	0	0	0	3	0

Black, William

[FACTFILE]

BORN
Isle of Mull,
30 November 1883
POSITION
Right half
OTHER CLUBS
Enfield Star;
Dalziel Rovers;
Queens Park;
Celtic

Season	League		FA Cup		Total	
	App	Goals	App	Goals	App	Goals
1905/06	13	0	0	0	13	0
1906/07	7	0	0	0	7	0
Total	20	0	0	0	20	0

Bishop, Ian

Gifted midfielder who forged a stellar top-flight career beyond Goodison

[FACTFILE]

BORN
Liverpool, 29 May 1965
POSITION
Midfield
OTHER CLUBS
Crewe Alexandra
(loan, 1984);
Carlisle United (1984–88);
Bournemouth (1988–89);
Manchester City
(1989 & 1998–2001);
West Ham (1989–98);
Miami Fusion (2001–02);
Barry Town (2002);
Rochdale (2002–03);
Radcliffe Borough (2003–04);
New Orleans Shell Shockers
(2004)

Season	League		FA Cup		League Cup		Total	
	App	Goals	App	Goals	App	Goals	App	Goals
1983/84	1	0	0	0	0	0	1	0
Total	1	0	0	0	0	0	1	0

Blair, John

University graduate and England amateur international centre forward

[FACTFILE]

BORN
Liverpool, 21 October 1898
DIED
1974
POSITION
Centre forward
OTHER CLUBS
Liverpool University;
Northern Nomads;
Congleton Town;
Oldham Athletic (192-24);
Mold,
Arsenal (1926);
Ilford;
Derbyshire Amateurs

Season	League		FA Cup		Total	
	App	Goals	App	Goals	App	Goals
1919/20	3	2	0	0	3	2
1920/21	0	0	1	0	1	0
1921/22	2	1	0	0	2	1
Total	5	3	1	0	6	3

Blomqvist, Jesper

Former prodigy who failed to recapture past glories at Goodison

Swedish winger Jesper Blomqvist joined Everton towards the end of a high profile but injury interrupted career. Alas, like so many such players signed under Walter Smith's tenure, he failed to replicate the sparkling form that had once seen him hailed as one of Europe's brightest talents.

BLOMQVIST first came to prominence with Umea FC in 1992, and was signed by IFK Gothenburg as a 19-year-old. His thrilling performances helped IFK to the quarter finals of the Champions League and saw him elevated to the Sweden national squad that finished third at the 1994 World Cup. Fast and direct with an eye for a spectacular goal a glittering future seemed assured.

In 1996 he joined AC Milan, who had dominated Italian and European football for most of the previous decade, but the move ended in failure. Milan finished a disastrous eleventh and Blomqvist joined Parma at the season's end. He spent 12 months there and in the summer of 1998 moved to Manchester United for £4.4million as Ryan Giggs's understudy.

He was a qualified success at United. In his first year he was part of the team that lifted an unprecedented treble, starting just enough matches to earn a Premier League medal, named as an unused FA Cup Final substitute and starting the Champions League Final. But serious knee injury wrecked his Old Trafford career and he was released at the end of his contract in 2001 having scarcely played over the previous two years.

Into this void stepped Everton. Still aged only 27 when he joined on a free transfer a revival may have been hoped for. Blomqvist proved capable in a poor Everton team, scoring against Sunderland in the dying days of the Smith regime. But the old magic was gone and after a public altercation with Smith's successor, David Moyes, his Goodison career seemed doomed. He was released in the summer of 2002.

Attempts to revive his career with Charlton ended in failure and Blomqvist returned to his homeland. After retiring he began coaching in 2005 and made a surprise playing return in his mid-thirties.

[FACTFILE]

BORN
Tavelsjo, Sweden, 5 February 1974

POSITION
Winger

OTHER CLUBS
Umea (1992–93);
IFK Gothenburg (1993–96);
AC Milan (1996–97);
Parma (1997–98);
Manchester United (1998–2001);
Charlton Athletic (2002–03);
Djugarden (2003–05);
Enkoping (2008);
Hammarby (2010)

HONOURS
30 Sweden caps (1994)

Season	League		FA Cup		League Cup		Total	
	App	Goals	App	Goals	App	Goals	App	Goals
2001/02	10 (5)	1	2 (1)	0	0	0	12 (6)	1
Total	**10 (5)**	**1**	**2 (1)**	**0**	**0**	**0**	**12 (6)**	**1**

Blythe, John 'Joe'
Left half who later enjoyed an assured career in the Southern League

[FACTFILE]

BORN
Berwick-on-Tweed, 1881
POSITION
Left half
OTHER CLUBS
Delaval Villa;
Blyth;
Jarrow;
West Ham United;
Millwall Athletic;
Watford;
Blyth Spartans

Season	League App	League Gls	FA Cup App	FA Cup Gls	Total App	Total Gls
1898/99	8	0	0	0	8	0
1899/1900	19	1	1	0	20	1
1900/01	1	0	0	0	1	0
1901/02	6	0	0	0	6	0
Total	**34**	**1**	**1**	**0**	**35**	**1**

W. BOCKING

Bocking, Bill
Steady right back who won the 1932 League Championship

[FACTFILE]

BORN
Stockport, 11 June 1905
POSITION
Right back
OTHER CLUBS
Hyde United; Stockport
County (1924–30 & 1934–37)
HONOURS
1931/32 League Championship

Season	League App	League Gls	FA Cup App	FA Cup Gls	Other App	Other Gls	Total App	Total Gls
1930/31	1	0	0	0	-	-	1	0
1931/32	10	0	1	0	-	-	11	0
1932/33	3	0	0	0	-	-	3	0
1933/34	1	0	0	0	1	0	2	0
Total	**15**	**0**	**1**	**0**	**1**	**0**	**17**	**0**

Bolton, Hugh
Prolific inside forward who appeared in the 1907 FA Cup Final

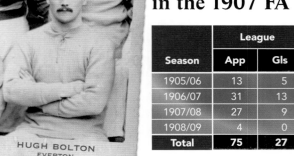

HUGH BOLTON
EVERTON

[FACTFILE]

BORN
Port Glasgow, 1880
POSITION
Inside forward
OTHER CLUBS
Clydeville;
Port Glasgow Athletic;
Newcastle United (1905);
Bradford Park Avenue
(1908–09);
Greenock Morton;
Glentoran

Season	League App	League Gls	FA Cup App	FA Cup Gls	Total App	Total Gls
1905/06	13	5	4	1	17	6
1906/07	31	13	2	0	33	13
1907/08	27	9	6	6	33	15
1908/09	4	0	0	0	4	0
Total	**75**	**27**	**12**	**7**	**87**	**34**

Bone, Johnnie

Inside forward who hailed from Bill Shankly's home village

[FACTFILE]

BORN
Glenbuck, 1880
POSITION
Inside left

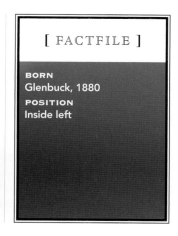

	League		FA Cup		Total	
Season	App	Goals	App	Goals	App	Goals
1901/02	2	0	0	0	2	0
Total	2	0	0	0	2	0

Booth, Tom

Centre back and captain who was Everton's first line of attack in the early 20th century

Centre half Tom Booth was an Everton stalwart through the first years of the twentieth-century, an unfailingly reliable defender who was desperately unlucky not to get his hands on silverware during his time at the club. Twice he was part of teams that finished runners-up; and twice Everton made the final of the FA Cup, although on each occasion he was absent from the starting XI.

Booth was captain of Blackburn Rovers in the last years of the 19th century and impressed while on a visit to Goodison in April 1900. Blackburn's defenders, reported the Liverpool Mercury of the goalless draw, 'were more persistent than the home backs, Booth rendering splendid service by his untiring and zealous efforts'. The Everton board immediately sought his signature, a £325 fee enough to bring him to Merseyside.

Installed in the Everton back line for the start of the 1900/01 season, the Mancunian immediately impressed. 'At half back most interest was centred in Booth, and it may at once be stated that he proved himself as resourceful as ever,' reported the Mercury. 'When danger threatened he anticipated its quarter… and avoiding aimless kicking always placed the ball to the best advantage. The value of his work cannot be overestimated, and his inclusion will undoubtedly tend to cement the attractive style of play between forwards and halves that football spectators of to-day delight in.'

EVERTON finished his debut season seventh, but the following year they registered a huge improvement. With Booth both captain and ever-present, the club finished runners-up – narrowly missing out on the title to Sunderland. Booth retained his captaincy through 1902/03 and 1903/04, seasons in which he remained virtually ever-present. He was always more than just a rugged centre half though, and the Everton defence in this period was always the first line of their attack. 'The Everton speedy outside men were almost continually on the move, for Booth and his halves fed them as if they had been starved for six months,' said one contemporaneous account.

Playing against Preston North End in September 1904 disaster struck the defender. 'Booth was so badly kicked above the ankle shortly after the interval that he had to retire permanently,' recorded the Mercury's correspondent. Booth struggled thereafter to get his place back from Harry Makepeace, who stepped into the breach left by his colleague.

From thereon the Mancunian was a peripheral player at Goodison; an adept reserve, but never able to force his way back into the first team as a regular. He travelled with the team to the FA Cup Finals of 1906 and 1907, but was overlooked both times. After making just eight appearances through the 1907/08 season he was released by the club. James Baxter led a boardroom effort to re-sign him later in 1908, but his motion was defeated.

BOOTH was capped twice by England, in 1898 against Wales while still at Blackburn, and five years later against Scotland.

	League		FA Cup		Total	
Season	App	Gls	App	Gls	App	Gls
1900/01	31	0	2	0	33	0
1901/02	34	1	2	0	36	1
1902/03	29	2	3	1	32	3
1903/04	34	4	1	0	35	4
1904/05	8	0	0	0	8	0
1905/06	17	0	2	1	19	1
1906/07	14	1	0	0	14	1
1907/08	8	1	0	0	8	1
Total	175	9	10	2	185	11

[FACTFILE]

BORN
Ardwick, Manchester,
25 April 1874
DIED
Blackpool, 7 September 1939
POSITION
Half back
OTHER CLUBS
Blackburn Rovers
(1896–1900);
Preston North End (1908);
Carlisle United (1908–10)
HONOURS
2 England caps (1898 & 1903)

Borrows, Brian

Proficient right back edged from contention by Gary Stevens

Having struggled to adequately replace Tommy Wright through much of the 1970s, in the early 1980s Everton were suddenly blessed with a surfeit of gifted right backs. John Gidman, Gary Stevens and Brian Borrows were all fine custodians of the number two shirt, providing the appropriate mix of defensive solidity and attacking verve.

Following Howard Kendall's arrival as manager in May 1981, the experienced Gidman was an early departure, raising much-needed transfer funds. Kendall started the season with Billy Wright in the right back berth, but after the early stages of the new campaign alternated between Stevens and Borrows, both of whom had graduated through Everton's youth ranks. Neither let the new manager down. Borrows was, perhaps, the more complete footballer, confident and polished in possession and a fine outlet on the overlap. What Stevens lacked in élan he made up for with his athleticism and pace. Although Borrows was no slouch, it was this that ultimately saw Stevens win through.

FOLLOWING Everton's November 1982 derby day massacre, Borrows was dropped and never regained his place. The following March Kendall accepted a bid for his services from Bolton Wanderers. Borrows returned to the top flight with Coventry City in 1985, and put in a lengthy and distinguished stint in the Midlands.

> PROVIDING THE APPROPRIATE MIX OF DEFENSIVE SOLIDITY AND ATTACKING VERVE

[FACTFILE]

BORN
Liverpool, 20 December 1960
POSITION
Right back
OTHER CLUBS
Bolton Wanderers (1983–85);
Coventry City (1985–97);
Bristol City (loan, 1993);
Swindon Town (1997–99)

Season	League		FA Cup		League Cup		Total	
	App	Goals	App	Goals	App	Goals	App	Goals
1981/82	15	0	0	0	0	0	15	0
1982/83	12	0	0	0	2	0	14	0
Total	27	0	0	0	2	0	29	0

Borthwick, John

Centre half understudy to the great Jack Taylor

[FACTFILE]

BORN
1882
POSITION
Centre half
OTHER CLUBS
Wemyss Violet; Lochgelly United;
Hibernian; Millwall Athletic

Season	League		FA Cup		Total	
	App	Goals	App	Goals	App	Goals
1907/08	1	0	0	0	1	0
1908/09	1	0	0	0	1	0
1909/10	19	0	0	0	19	0
1910/11	4	0	0	0	4	0
Total	25	0	0	0	25	0

Bosman Ruling

European court case that revolutionised football transfers

The so-called Bosman Ruling was a 1995 European Court of Justice decision concerning freedom of movement of workers within the European Union. It had a profound effect on the transfer of footballers within the EU and beyond.

ITS NAME refers to Jean-Marc Bosman, a former Belgian youth international, who first brought the case to court. Bosman was a journeyman player for RFC Liege in the Belgian First Division. In 1990 his contract expired and he sought a transfer to the French club Dunkerque. Liege, however, refused to let him go and put an

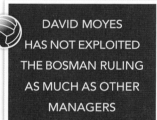

DAVID MOYES HAS NOT EXPLOITED THE BOSMAN RULING AS MUCH AS OTHER MANAGERS

Everton's Bosman Free Signings		
Date	**Player**	**Signed from**
Jul 1998	Alex Cleland	Glasgow Rangers
May 1999	Richard Gough	San Jose Clash
Nov 1999	Joe-Max Moore	New England Revolution
Jul 2001	Alan Stubbs	Celtic
Aug 2004	Eddy Bosnar	Sturm Graz
Aug 2008	Lars Jacobsen	1 FC Nuremberg
Sep 2009	Lucas Neill	Unattached
Jul 2010	Jermaine Beckford	Leeds United
Jul 2010	Jan Mucha	Legia Warsaw
Sep 2011	Marcus Hahnemann	Unattached
Oct 2011	James McFadden	Unattached

inflated price tag on his head, while simultaneously dropping him to the reserves, causing a drop in wages. Bosman sued for restraint of trade and, after a gruelling legal battle, in December 1995 the European Court of Justice ruled in his favour. As a result Bosman and all other EU footballers were granted a free transfer at the end of their contracts. This was later expanded to include footballers worldwide. By the time of the ruling Bosman was aged 31 and his career had been ruined.

Besides the freedom of movement it allowed, the main consequence of the Bosman case was a massive upward spiral in the level of players' remuneration. Initially some players let their contract run down and moved for free, often pocketing for themselves the equivalent of the transfer fee their new clubs would have paid under the old system. Celtic's John Collins and Liverpool's Steve McManaman were two early examples of players to follow this route.

To avert this damaging scenario clubs began to raise footballers' salaries, offering their best players long-term contracts on dramatically improved wages. Even in the late 1990s it was preferable to pay a player worth £5million an annual wage of £1million rather than risk losing him for nothing. If a club protected itself that way, it could still always sell a player on. To put the upward trajectory of players' wages into context: in 1988 Tony Cottee became a British transfer record signing, with wages of £1500 per week; 20 years later, in 2008, Robinho, the new record transfer signing, was reputedly pocketing £150,000 per week from Manchester City. Player values also dropped considerably in the last year of their contracts, as clubs sought to get some sort of return from want-away stars.

Not until 1998 did Everton benefit from a Bosman free transfer, when Alec Cleland joined after the expiry of his contract from Rangers. Walter Smith proved an early master of the new ruling, signing players who neared the end of their contracts for fees substantially lower than their market value. Smith also acquired several good freebies, notably Richard Gough and Alan Stubbs. He was also certain to move players on who neared the end of their Everton contracts and had been slow to re-sign. Unlike many of their rivals, Everton are still to lose a significant player for nothing.

AS THE system has evolved and matured it has become an important part of many clubs' transfer strategies, particularly with the signing of squad players. Perhaps surprisingly, given the financial circumstances with which he has often been faced, David Moyes has not exploited the Bosman ruling as much as other managers.

Bowman, Adam

Reserve centre forward who forged a fine career at Blackburn and elsewhere

Season	League		FA Cup		Total	
	App	**Goals**	**App**	**Goals**	**App**	**Goals**
1901/02	4	1	2	0	6	1
1902/03	5	2	0	0	5	2
Total	**9**	**3**	**2**	**0**	**11**	**3**

[FACTFILE]

BORN
Forfar, 12 August 1868
POSITION
Centre forward
OTHER CLUBS
St Johnstone;
East Stirlingshire;
Blackburn Rovers (1902–06);
Brentford; Leeds City (1908);
Brentford; Portsmouth;
Leith Athletic;
Accrington Stanley

Boyes, Wally

Diminutive winger who enjoyed championship success in 1939

Winger Wally Boyes was a dashing flanker in an era defined by thrilling wide men. He joined a club that had in its recent past possessed such players as Jackie Coulter, Albert Geldard, Torry Gillick and Jimmy Stein, and still found a way into the hearts of supporters spoiled for choice by its wingers.

WINGER WALLY BOYES WAS A DASHING FLANKER IN AN ERA DEFINED BY THRILLING WIDE MEN

STANDING just 5ft 3in tall, Derbyshire-born Boyes had been a schoolboy prodigy in nearby Sheffield, but ultimately made his way as a professional with West Bromwich Albion. In 1935 he came up against his boyhood team, Sheffield Wednesday, in the FA Cup Final, but despite scoring, Wednesday proved too strong and ran out 4-2 winners.

Success that proved elusive at the Hawthorns came quickly at Goodison. Signed for £6000 in March 1938 he immediately replaced Torry Gillick in the Everton team, and played 36 times as the Blues lifted the 1938/39 league title. Already an England international, he added a further two caps to the one he had picked up while in the Midlands and with Joe Mercer and Tommy Lawton playing alongside him, Everton looked set to have a decisive say in the fortunes of the national team for years to come.

Such hopes proved cruelly elusive. War struck, and by its conclusion Boyes, like so many of his team-mates, was past his best. He was ever-present during the Football League North season of 1945/46, but when the First Division resumed the following year Everton struggled and he lost his place to Tommy Eglington.

NOW in the veteran stage of his career, he would remain at Goodison past his 35th birthday, but seldom getting a run-out for the first XI. Norwich City offered him the chance to become

player-coach, but the board would only release the winger if he gave up his share of the benefit – a significant sum in a time of austerity. Boyes remained, eventually joining Notts County, where he was reunited with Lawton, whom he had partnered with such distinction a decade previously.

Season	League		FA Cup		Total	
	App	Gls	App	Gls	App	Gls
1937/38	13	3	0	0	13	3
1938/39	36	4	5	4	41	8
1945/46	-	-	2	0	2	0
1946/47	9	3	0	0	9	3
1947/48	4	1	0	0	4	1
1948/49	4	0	0	0	4	0
Total	**66**	**11**	**7**	**4**	**73**	**15**

Boyle, Dan

Right half who deputised for Sam Wolstenholme during the 1901/02 season

Season	League		FA Cup		Total	
	App	Goals	App	Goals	App	Goals
1901/02	7	0	0	0	7	0
Total	7	0	0	0	7	0

Boyle, Richard

Distinguished half back whose lengthy Goodison career ended barren

Nowhere in the last years of the 19th century was a more fertile poaching ground for Everton than the royal Scottish burgh of Dumbarton. In the first days of the Football League no fewer than four of the town's players made the journey south to Liverpool. For more than twenty years these men – Alex Latta, John Bell, Abe Hartley and Richard Boyle – were to dominate the ranks of Everton Football Club and play telling parts in Goodison Park's early glories.

FEW WERE more distinguished than Boyle, who, with his waxed moustache and raffish good looks, was the archetype of the Victorian sporting hero. The half back joined Everton in August 1892 as the club lay on the cusp of an exciting new era at their new stadium, Goodison Park. He made an immediate impact for Everton and was renowned for his dashes up the field and fearsome long-range shots, which were – for all their frequency – not often matched with goals. Rarely did a defender pick up plaudits like Boyle. 'Boyle's brilliancy was indeed a treat, and was lavishly noticed throughout the game,' recorded one admirer after a friendly against Gorton Villa in 1893.

With Bob Kelso and Johnny Holt he formed a solid back line, whose footballing ethos – always to play the ball rather than hoof aimlessly – made them the first line of the Everton attack. 'The halfback passing game has another great advantage as it draws away the first line of defence in the opposing halfbacks and thus leaves the forwards free when they do get the ball,' wrote the Liverpool Mercury of the ploy in 1895. It was, the same paper recorded on another occasion, through the defenders' 'untiring cleverness' that Everton were able to assume such a 'tremendous lead'.

WELL LIKED and respected, Boyle was made Everton captain for the 1895/96 season, a position he gave up to Billy Stewart for a year, before taking it up again for the 1897/98 campaign. Few had any doubts about his suitability for the role. Boyle, recorded an 1896 tribute, 'has not only proved worthy of support by his skill on the field, where his individual

RICHARD BOYLE
EVERTON

excellence has commanded admiration from supporters and opponents alike, but his gentlemanly and courteous demeanour has combined to make him a universal favourite.'

Boyle's 243 Everton games would never yield him the medals his service surely deserved. But there were brushes with glory. In 1894/95 he finished a league runner-up and two years later he reached the FA Cup Final, where Everton met Aston Villa. His first-half free kick would give Everton a 2-1 lead, but within 15 minutes of scoring Villa had not only equalised but taken a 3-2 lead, which they would not relinquish.

Not until the 1901/02 season, when they finished runners-up again, would Everton come so close to winning a trophy again. Boyle by then had slipped from first-team view and at the end of the season was released by the club.

Season	League		FA Cup		Total	
	App	Goals	App	Goals	App	Goals
1892/93	24	0	7	0	31	0
1893/94	21	1	0	0	21	1
1894/95	30	2	4	0	34	2
1895/96	30	3	3	0	33	3
1896/97	29	0	5	1	34	1
1897/98	22	0	0	0	22	0
1898/99	34	1	2	0	36	1
1899/1900	29	0	0	0	29	0
1900/01	2	0	0	0	2	0
Total	221	7	21	1	242	8

Bracewell, Paul

Elegant midfielder whose Goodison years were shattered by injury

At the start of 1986, Paul Bracewell was a footballer with the world at his feet. Often likened in style to Howard Kendall, alongside whom he briefly played when at Stoke City in the late 1970s, the 23-year-old midfielder was already an England international, a league champion and European winner and had narrowly missed out on the PFA Young Footballer of the Year award in 1984.

On New Year's Day 1986 Bracewell limped off during a 2-2 draw with Newcastle United. Although medical examinations initially proved inconclusive and he continued to play for the rest of the season, it was to mark the start of an injury nightmare from which he never fully recovered.

Exploratory surgery at the end of the campaign found a loose piece of bone in his ankle and he played no further part in Everton's plans for two years. When he did eventually return a series of niggling injuries further hampered his chances. Finally, in 1989, he was sold to Sunderland and Everton lost one of their most promising talents.

Perhaps only the injustice of injury prevented Paul Bracewell from turning a career of great potential into greatness itself. After starting

out in the Potteries, Howard Kendall paid Sunderland £250,000 for the Wirral-born midfielder in May 1984 and he made his debut at Wembley in the Charity Shield against Liverpool the following August. Everton won 1-0, and afterwards pundits pointed to the poise and control of Bracewell and his midfield partner, Peter Reid. As Everton swept all-comers over the 1984/85 season, theirs was a crucial component of the team's success.

REID had initially been sceptical about the partnership: 'I remember thinking when we bought him that we might be too similar to be effective. We were both tacklers, getting the ball and giving it, engine room players. But it worked. We stayed solid in the middle and left Trevor Steven and Kevin Sheedy to get on with it wide.' Bracewell was always more than just a 'tackler' though, and while lacking some pace and goal-scoring prowess, he compensated with accurate passing and great vision, often leading to strikes further up the field. Reid also spoke of a 'telepathic' understanding between them. 'If he went forward I was always in behind him, we had it worked out to a T,' he said. 'As a midfield partnership we played against all the top teams and I don't remember us coming off second best to anyone.'

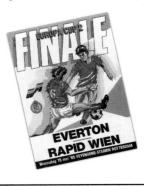

Season	League		FA Cup		League Cup		Other		Total	
	App	Goals	App	Goals	App	Goals	App	Goals	App	Goals
1984/85	37	2	7	0	4	1	9	1	57	4
1985/86	38	3	6	0	5	1	5	0	54	4
1986/87	0	0	0	0	0	0	-	-	0	0
1987/88	0	0	0 (2)	0	1	0	1	0	2 (2)	0
1988/89	20	2	6	0	1	0	2 (2)	0	29 (2)	2
Total	95	7	19 (2)	0	11	2	17 (2)	1	142 (4)	10

A member of the England under-21 team that won the European Championships in 1984, Bracewell gained full international recognition at the end of the 1984/85 season, winning the first of three England caps against West Germany. Before his New Year's Day injury it looked as though he would join the England squad travelling to Mexico for the World Cup Finals.

Not only did he miss out on Mexico, where Everton players dominated Bobby Robson's team, Bracewell also missed the chance to win a second championship medal when injury ruled him out of the entire 1986/87 campaign. When he did try to relaunch his Everton career in the League Cup semi-final against Arsenal the following season his comeback was cruelly halted by an ankle tendon injury, completely unconnected with the previous ailment. After a spell of rehabilitation at Lilleshall he returned to playing duties at the start of the 1988/89 season, initially with the reserves, and eventually re-established himself in the first team, playing in the FA Cup Final defeat to Liverpool in May.

This, however, proved to be the final sortie in Bracewell's five-year-long Everton career: just as it had started with a Wembley derby, so it ended, and he was allowed to rejoin Sunderland that summer.

AT ROKER PARK he helped lead Sunderland's charge for promotion and within a year of his signing they had restored their top-flight status, although their spell in the First Division lasted

just a year. In 1992 he captained Sunderland to the FA Cup Final, where they faced Liverpool, but for the third time in a cup final against them Bracewell came out a loser.

That summer he joined Kevin Keegan's Newcastle United, helping them to the First Division Championship and promotion to the Premier League. He enjoyed two more productive seasons at St James's Park before returning to Sunderland for a third spell, where he was reunited with Peter Reid, now the Black Cats manager, before playing out his career with Fulham.

In 1999 he was made Fulham manager, after Kevin Keegan was appointed England boss, but was sacked within a year after failing to bring the Cottagers promotion to the Premier League. He later had a brief, unproductive spell in charge of Halifax Town in 2000/01, and subsequently spent a couple of years as an FA coach. Bracewell is currently involved in sports marketing.

[FACTFILE]

BORN
Heswall, 19 July 1962
POSITION
Midfield
OTHER CLUBS
Stoke City (1979–83);
Sunderland (1983–84);
Sunderland (1989–92);
Newcastle United (1992–95);
Sunderland (1995–97);
Fulham (1997–99)
AS MANAGER
Fulham (1999–2000); Halifax Town (2000–01)
HONOURS
League Championship 1984/85
European Cup Winners' Cup, 1985;
3 England caps (1985)

Bradshaw, Frank

Distinguished amateur inside forward who scored a hat-trick on his only international appearance

[FACTFILE]

BORN
Sheffield, 31 May 1884
POSITION
Inside forward
OTHER CLUBS
Sheffield Wednesday (1905–10);
Northampton Town (1910–11);
Arsenal (1914–22)
HONOURS
1 England cap
(3 goals) (1908)

Season	League		FA Cup		Total	
	App	Gls	App	Gls	App	Gls
1911/12	21	8	4	0	25	8
1912/13	34	10	3	1	37	11
1913/14	11	1	1	1	12	2
Total	66	19	8	2	74	21

Bradshaw, George

Reserve goalkeeper who enjoyed a lengthy career beyond Goodison Park

[FACTFILE]

BORN
Southport, 10 March 1913
DIED
1989
POSITION
Goalkeeper
OTHER CLUBS
Southport (1931);
New Brighton (1932–34);
Arsenal (1935);
Doncaster Rovers (1936–37);
Bury (1938–49);
Oldham Athletic (1950)

Season	League		FA Cup		Total	
	App	Goals	App	Goals	App	Goals
1934/35	2	0	0	0	2	0
Total	2	0	0	0	2	0

Brady, Alec

Inside forward whose goals helped bring Everton their first League Championship

[FACTFILE]

BORN
Cathcart, 2 April 1865
POSITION
Inside / outside forward
OTHER CLUBS
Cowie Wanderers; Renton Thistle;
Burnley (1888–89);
Celtic (1891–92);
Sheffield Wednesday (1892–98)
HONOURS
1890/91 League Championship

Season	League		FA Cup		Total	
	App	Goals	App	Goals	App	Goals
1889/90	13	8	2	3	15	11
1890/91	21	9	0	0	21	9
Total	**34**	**17**	**2**	**3**	**36**	**20**

Bramwell, John

Defender who rose from non-League to have professional career

Defender John Bramwell was a £3,500 signing from non-league Wigan Athletic in April 1958. His arrival came between an era when the club relied on such cheap prospects as himself and a time when the Moores millions were starting to make an impression on the complexion of the Everton team.

The young rookie was soon given a chance to impress and after Jimmy Tansey and Bryan Griffiths had been used unsuccessfully at left back in the opening stages of the 1958/59 season, Bramwell was drafted in and remained ever-present through the rest of the season.

This was a period that saw the arrival of Johnny Carey as manager, the introduction of players such as Bobby Collins and Alex Parker, and, of course, Everton's record 4-10 defeat to Tottenham Hotspur. They were, recalled one observer of the era, 'a team that could win 4-0 one week and lose by the same scoreline the next'. Quite often they did just that.

Initially favoured in this wildly inconsistent team, Bramwell fell victim to Carey's attempts to find the winning formula the next campaign. During the 1959/60 season, a young Brian Labone was favoured at centre half and in order to accommodate him the club captain T. E. Jones was shifted to left back. Bramwell made just 15 appearances in his second full season.

In October 1960 Everton bid for Luton Town's Northern Ireland international winger Billy Bingham. In exchange the Hatters asked for £10,000, the inside forward Alec Ashworth and Bramwell, who was without a game in the 1960/61 campaign. All parties agreed to the deal and Bramwell went on to serve Luton over almost 200 appearances.

EVERTON 1959
*Back - **Sharples, Parker, Labone, Dunlop, Gabriel, Meagan, Bramwell***
*Front - **Lill, Collins, Harris, Vernon, Ring***

[FACTFILE]

BORN
Ashton-in-Makerfield, 1 March 1937
POSITION
Full back
OTHER CLUBS
Wigan Athletic (1952–58);
Luton Town (1960–65)

Season	League		FA Cup		Total	
	App	Goals	App	Goals	App	Goals
1958/59	37	0	4	0	41	0
1959/60	15	0	0	0	15	0
Total	**52**	**0**	**4**	**0**	**56**	**0**

Branch, Michael

Teenage prodigy overburdened by the weight of expectation

After years in which Everton's best young players were thoroughly overshadowed by those emerging from Liverpool's youth development programme, Michael Branch was hailed as the player that Evertonians had been waiting for. The England youth international and graduate of the FA National School of Excellence was a quicksilver striker blessed with control, pace and a knack of intelligent movement.

Handed his debut as a 17-year-old during the 1995/96 season, Branch showed many encouraging signs: willingness, electrifying speed and inherent natural ability. What he lacked, perhaps, was ruthlessness in front of goal. Joe Royle, himself once a teenage centre forward, included him more often in the opening stages of the 1996/97 season. In only his second start, against Sheffield Wednesday in September 1996, Branch ravaged his experienced opponents – Des Walker and Steve Nicol – setting up both of Everton's goals in a performance that had pundits purring. 'In only his second full appearance, and at just 17, he showed heartwarming potential,' reported The Times. 'He is impudent, linear, and his style of play uncannily similar to a certain Robbie Fowler from across the other side of Stanley Park.'

BUT AS Royle's managerial reign unravelled, Branch suffered. Too often he was called upon as a substitute, expected to turn around the fortunes of an out-of-form team. In short, it was too much of a burden for his young shoulders to carry. His progress plateaued during the 1997/98 season, when he was hampered by injuries and overshadowed by Danny Cadamarteri. The following campaign Walter Smith seemed equally reluctant to use Branch or sell him – both Manchester City and Portsmouth sought the forward.

A surprise inclusion when Everton met Liverpool in April 1999, Smith's wild-card selection failed to pay off. It was the first and last time the Everton manager started Branch. At the end of the 1998/99 season he was transfer-listed. In January 2000, Branch joined Wolves in a £500,000 deal, but failed to make an impact. His subsequent career in the lower leagues was a sorry tale of unrealised potential.

[FACTFILE]

BORN
Liverpool, 18 October 1978
POSITION
Forward
OTHER CLUBS
Manchester City (loan, 1998);
Birmingham City (loan, 1999);
Wolverhampton Wanderers
(loan, then permanent
transfer, 1999–2003);
Reading (loan, 2002);
Hull City (loan, 2002–03);
Bradford City (2003–04);
Chester City (2004–06);
Halifax Town (2007)

Season	League		FA Cup		League Cup		Europe		Total	
	App	Goals	App	Goals	App	Goals	App	Goals	App	Goals
1995/96	1 (2)	0	0	0	0	0	0	0	1 (2)	0
1996/97	13 (12)	3	1	0	0 (1)	0	-	-	14(13)	3
1997/98	1 (5)	0	0	0	0	0	-	-	1 (5)	0
1998/99	1 (6)	0	0 (2)	0	0	0	-	-	1 (8)	0
1999/2000	0	0	0	0	0	0	-	-	0	0
Total	**16(25)**	**3**	**1 (2)**	**0**	**0 (1)**	**0**	**0**	**0**	**17(28)**	**3**

Brand, Drew

Scotland under-21 goalkeeper who failed to gain a regular first-team berth

[FACTFILE]

BORN
8 November, 1957
POSITION
Goalkeeper
OTHER CLUBS
Crewe Alexandra
(loan, 1976–77 & 1978–79);
Hereford United (1980–83);
Wrexham (loan, 1982–83);
Witton Albion (1983–84);
Blackpool (1984)

Season	League		FA Cup		League Cup		Total	
	App	Gls	App	Gls	App	Gls	App	Gls
1975/76	1	0	0	0	0	0	1	0
1976/77	1	0	0	0	0	0	1	0
Total	**2**	**0**	**0**	**0**	**0**	**0**	**2**	**0**

Brannick, James

Inside forward who enjoyed a fleeting Everton first-team career

[FACTFILE]

BORN
1888
POSITION
Inside right
OTHER CLUBS
St Mirren

Season	League		FA Cup		Total	
	App	Goals	App	Goals	App	Goals
1912/13	3	2	0	0	3	2
Total	3	2	0	0	3	2

Brearley, John

Inside forward who was top scorer in his only season at Goodison

[FACTFILE]

BORN
West Derby, 1875
DIED
1944
POSITION
Inside right / right half
OTHER CLUBS
Kettering; Notts County (1897); Chatham (1898–99); Millwall Athletic (1899–1900); Notts County (1900); Middlesbrough (1900–01); Tottenham Hotspur (1903–07); Crystal Palace (1907–09); Millwall Athletic (1909–11)

Season	League		FA Cup		Total	
	App	Goals	App	Goals	App	Goals
1902/03	22	7	2	1	24	8
Total	22	7	2	1	24	8

Brewster, George

Powerhouse Scottish defender who struggled to find top form on Merseyside

G. BREWSTER
602 EVERTON

Unable to defend their 1914/15 league title for four years owing to the interruption of war, Everton struggled to regain top form when peace came and the 1919/20 season ensued. By the start of 1920, the champions found themselves as low as 13th and the Everton board rang the changes. Scottish defender George Brewster was at the heart of their rebuilding plans and a boardroom delegation were dispatched to Aberdeen to sign him. Vested with the authority to spend '£200–300 either side of £2000' they got their man for a club record fee of £2400.

On Merseyside relief greeted his arrival. 'He is a veritable giant as footballers go, standing 6ft high and weighing 13 stone,' reported

the Liverpool Courier. 'Twenty-five years of age Brewster is probably one of the finest if not the best middle man playing in Scotland. He has been playing centre half with Aberdeen, but he is a most versatile exponent of the code, and can fill most positions on the field. He is not only a fine defender, but also looks after the wants of the front line, beside which he can shoot when the opportunity arise, and in this respect has scored several goals for Aberdeen. Everton have made a really great capture.'

BREWSTER had initially been reluctant to join Everton and at first he struggled to adapt to the English game, making just five appearances during the remainder of the 1919/20 season. His form

improved considerably at the start of the 1920/21 campaign, despite facing a month-long suspension for a sending off against Huddersfield Town in October. When Everton beat Newcastle in an FA Cup third round tie, the 'formidable' half back line he formed with Tom Fleetwood and Louis Weller was praised. 'They

had a capital understanding with the forwards, and assisted them with excellent constructive play.' Brewster, believed the Liverpool Courier, 'was the mainstay of the halves, his breaking up being good while he also shot at times with force and precision'.

AT THE START of the 1922/23 season, Brewster was awarded the captaincy, but this precipitated a dramatic decline in fortunes. Everton's form was poor and the captain was singled out for criticism. 'Brewster failed to touch his best form save in heading,' reported the Daily Post after a 2-0 defeat at Tottenham. 'Perhaps the cares of captaincy bother him. Whatever it was he started ill at

Season	League		FA Cup		Total	
	App	Goals	App	Goals	App	Goals
1919/20	5	0	0	0	5	0
1920/21	29	0	4	1	33	1
1921/22	25	3	0	0	25	3
1922/23	5	1	0	0	5	1
Total	64	4	4	1	68	5

ease, and never really became a constructive half back.' Twelve days later Everton fell to a 5-1 defeat at Blackburn. Brewster was dropped and never played for the first team again.

Scarcely a month later the Everton directors were hawking their captain around, attempting to swap him for Airdrieonians' centre back, Jock McDougall. Brewster played on for the reserves, even keeping goal in the Central League derby after Ernie Salt was injured. His heroics helped earn Everton a 3-2 win.

In November 1922 Everton accepted a £3250 bid from Wolverhampton Wanderers for Brewster and Stan Fazackerley. He later dropped down to non-league football, then spent time in the US coaching, before a spell as manager of Inverness Caledonian.

Briggs, Harry

Enjoyed a brief spell in the Everton goal during Goodison's first days

Season	League App	League Goals	FA Cup App	FA Cup Goals	Total App	Total Goals
1895/96	1	0	0	0	1	0
1896/97	10	0	0	0	10	0
Total	**11**	**0**	**0**	**0**	**11**	**0**

[FACTFILE]

BORN
1895
POSITION
Goalkeeper
OTHER CLUBS
Darwen (1893–95)

Brindle, Billy

Young prospect who dropped down to non-league ranks after failing to make the grade

Season	League App	League Goals	FA Cup App	FA Cup Goals	League Cup App	League Cup Goals	Total App	Total Goals
1967/68	1	0	0	0	0	0	1	0
1968/69	0	0	0	0	0	0	0	0
1969/70	0	0	0	0	1	0	1	0
Total	1	0	0	0	1	0	2	0

[FACTFILE]

BORN
Liverpool, 29 January 1950
POSITION
Midfield
OTHER CLUBS
Barnsley (1970–71); Runcorn

Briscoe, William

Occasional inside forward during Everton's first league season

Season	League App	League Gls	FA Cup App	FA Cup Gls	Total App	Total Gls
1887/88	-	-	1	0	1	0
1888/89	3	0	0	0	3	0
Total	**3**	**0**	**1**	**0**	**4**	**0**

[FACTFILE]

BORN
Culsalmond, Aberdeenshire, 7 May 1893
DIED
1963
POSITION
Centre half
OTHER CLUBS
Aberdeen (1913–20); Wolverhampton Wanderers (1922–23)
HONOURS
1 Scotland cap (1921)

[FACTFILE]

BORN
1865
POSITION
Inside left

British Championship

Anglo-Scottish competition which has taken on various forms

The notion of a British Championship, centred on the best clubs of England and Scotland, is one that has been periodically floated through the history of football in the two countries. Given the appalling state of Scottish football in the 21st century it seems easy to forget the historical strength of the game north of the border and how desirable it once was for English clubs to test themselves against their neighbours.

Besides Scottish clubs appearing in the early years of the FA Cup, only in the early 1970s was there an officially sanctioned Anglo-Scottish tournament – the Texaco Cup – which Everton competed in during the 1973/74 season. This competition was a failure, abandoned a year later amid lack of interest from clubs and supporters.

> A WONDERFUL BLEND DEVELOPED BETWEEN THE PLAYERS, WHICH RESULTED IN A FAR CLOSER TEAM SPIRIT
>
> **TOMMY LAWTON**

EVERTON have competed in several unofficial British Championships, a tradition that extends back to the start of the last century. In 1902 they competed in the British League Cup, a four-team competition staged between the winners and runners-up of the English and Scottish Leagues to raise funds for the victims of the Ibrox Stadium disaster, which claimed the lives of 25 Rangers fans. Everton drew their semi final 1-1 to Rangers before losing a replay 3-2 two days later.

In 1938 they played in the Empire Exhibition Trophy, an Anglo-Scottish tournament held as part of Glasgow's British Empire Exhibition. Everton were late inclusions to the tournament and were expected to exit early having been drawn against Rangers. But they prevailed 2-0, giving 'a brilliant exhibition of high class football, to which even a Rangers team had no reply' according to 'Stork' in the Liverpool Echo. 'Against Aberdeen they were not so sprightly,' he added of their semi-final. 'They did not reproduce the snap of cleverness which qualified for the semi-final, but they had a defence which was capital of holding the Dons out after they (Everton) had taken the lead.' In the final against Celtic at Ibrox, 82,761 turned out to watch the match. Everton lost Jimmy Cunliffe to injury and had an Alex Stevenson goal disallowed. Despite fierce local support their ten men held their opponents until John Crum hit Celtic's winner in the 95th minute.

Their appearance in Scotland had a profound effect on the Everton dressing room. It had involved a month-long stay in the west-coast holiday town of Largs and served as the turning point between a young struggling side with lots of potential and a great one. 'The reason was that we began to know each other as people, not just players,' reflected Tommy Lawton.

'People with different personalities, faults, varying moods, likes and dislikes... a wonderful blend developed between the players, which resulted in a far closer team spirit.' The following season Everton lifted the First Division in breathtaking style.

Twenty-five years later, Everton, as League Champions, faced Scottish champions Rangers in a two-legged British Championship match. Everton arrived at Ibrox on 27 November 1963 to chants of 'Easy, easy, easy' from the Rangers fans. Defending tightly, they punished the Glaswegians on the break, with efforts by Alex Scott and Alex Young silencing their compatriots. With Derek Temple also scoring, Everton left Ibrox 3-1 victors. The return at Goodison was marred by crowd violence. Scottish fans in the Upper Bullens stand rained a hail of glass bottles and other ammunition onto those unfortunate enough to be in the Paddock, and onto the pitch. Everton drew 1-1 through a Young goal to take the contest 4-1 on aggregate. 'The whole length of the running track from the Street End to the halfway line was full of bottles and glasses that had been taken from the Rangers fans, there were fights everywhere,' recorded George Orr in his diary of the era. 'We were the champions of Britain. I suppose it didn't mean a lot to most of our fans but I suppose the club saw it as an honour won.'

ANOTHER quarter-century passed and Everton faced Rangers in a further unofficial British Championship match. On this occasion they played in Dubai's Al Maktoum Stadium and led 2-0 until the 80th minute through Kevin Sheedy and Dave Watson goals. But two late strikes from Rangers resulted in a penalty shootout, which the Glasgow team won 8-7 on sudden death after Ian Snodin failed to convert his effort.

British League Cup

1 MAY 1902
SEMI-FINAL V GLASGOW RANGERS (AT IBROX), 1-1 (YOUNG)
Kitchen, Eccles, Watson, Wolstenholme, Blyth, Abbott, Taylor, Brearley, Young, Bell, Dilly

3 MAY 1902
SEMI-FINAL REPLAY V GLASGOW RANGERS (AT CELTIC PARK), 2-3 (BREARLEY, DILLY)
Kitchen, Henderson, R. Balmer, Rankin, Clark, Abbott, Taylor, Brearley, Young, Bell, Dilly

Empire Exhibition Trophy

30 MAY 1938
FIRST ROUND V GLASGOW RANGERS (AT IBROX), 2-0 (LAWTON, CUNLIFFE)
Sagar, Cook, Greenhalgh, Mercer, Jones, Thomson, Gillick, Cunliffe, Lawton, Stevenson, Boyes

6 JUNE 1938
SEMI-FINAL V ABERDEEN (AT IBROX), 3-2 (GILLICK, BOYES, LAWTON)
Sagar, Cook, Greenhalgh, Mercer, Jones, Thomson, Gillick, Cunliffe, Lawton, Stevenson, Boyes

10 JUNE 1938
FINAL V GLASGOW CELTIC (AT IBROX) 0-1
Sagar, Cook, Greenhalgh, Mercer, Jones, Thomson, Gillick, Cunliffe, Lawton, Stevenson, Boyes

British Championship

27 NOVEMBER 1963
V GLASGOW RANGERS [A] 3-1 (SCOTT, TEMPLE, YOUNG)
Rankin, Brown, Meagan, Harris, Heslop, Kay, Scott, Stevens, Young, Vernon, Temple

2 DECEMBER 1963
V GLASGOW RANGERS [H] 1-1 (YOUNG)
Rankin, Brown, Meagan, Gabriel (Harvey), Heslop, Harris, Scott, Stevens, Young, Vernon, Temple

Dubai Champions Cup

8 DECEMBER 1987
V GLASGOW RANGERS (AT THE AL MAKTOUM STADIUM, DUBAI), 2-2 (SHEEDY, WATSON)
(Rangers win 8-7 on penalties)
Southall, Stevens, Pointon, Ratcliffe, Watson, Reid, Steven, Heath, Sharp, Snodin, Sheedy

Broad, Jimmy

Well-travelled journeyman forward who lost his place to Dixie Dean

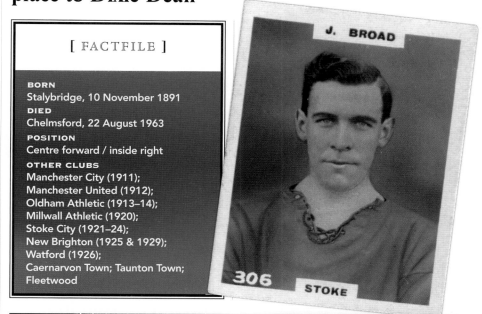

[FACTFILE]

BORN
Stalybridge, 10 November 1891
DIED
Chelmsford, 22 August 1963
POSITION
Centre forward / inside right
OTHER CLUBS
Manchester City (1911);
Manchester United (1912);
Oldham Athletic (1913–14);
Millwall Athletic (1920);
Stoke City (1921–24);
New Brighton (1925 & 1929);
Watford (1926);
Caernarvon Town; Taunton Town;
Fleetwood

Season	League		FA Cup		Total	
	App	Goals	App	Goals	App	Goals
1924/25	14	8	3	0	17	8
1925/26	4	0	0	0	4	0
Total	**18**	**8**	**3**	**0**	**21**	**8**

Bromilow, William

Local goalkeeper whose first-team career lasted just 90 minutes

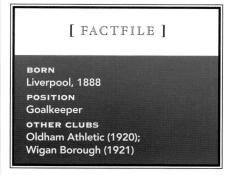

[FACTFILE]

BORN
Liverpool, 1888
POSITION
Goalkeeper
OTHER CLUBS
Oldham Athletic (1920);
Wigan Borough (1921)

Season	League		FA Cup		Total	
	App	Goals	App	Goals	App	Goals
1912/13	1	0	0	0	1	0
Total	**1**	**0**	**0**	**0**	**1**	**0**

Browell,
Anthony 'Andy'

One-game wonder who previously served Hull City well

Season	League		FA Cup		Total	
	App	Goals	App	Goals	App	Goals
1912/13	1	0	0	0	1	0
Total	1	0	0	0	1	0

Browell,
Tommy

Prolific inside forward who later wrote himself into Manchester City folklore

Season	League		FA Cup		Total	
	App	Goals	App	Goals	App	Goals
1911/12	17	12	5	7	22	19
1912/13	26	12	5	4	31	16
1913/14	7	2	0	0	7	2
Total	50	26	10	11	60	37

Brown, Alexander 'Sandy'

Invaluable utility player, best remembered for his spectacular derby day own goal

Without question, the defining moment in Sandy Brown's Everton career came in the Goodison derby of December 1969 and tainted an otherwise exemplary spell with the club. Trailing 1-0 and chasing the game, the Liverpool forward Peter Thompson burst forward and struck a cross into the Everton penalty area, which had it been left would have drifted harmlessly wide. And yet, under little pressure and inexplicably misjudging the flight of the ball, there was Sandy Brown, diving in to head the ball into his own net. It was, and remains, a classic own goal, becoming part of the local football lexicon. Even 40 years later, when Liverpool's John Arne Riise headed a similarly catastrophic effort into his own goal in a Champions League semi-final, it was referred to by gleeful Evertonians and distraught Liverpudlians as 'a Sandy Brown'.

Real Zaragoza in the 1966/67 European Cup Winners' Cup and his headed goal in the Goodison derby earlier that season. In his favoured role of overlapping full back, Brown would probably have made the grade in most other First Division sides.

His game was sometimes overly reliant on his physical presence, which tended to compensate for an occasionally inconsistent reading of the game, and also found him trouble with referees. It was Brown's sending off for punching Johnny Giles in the early stages of a November 1964 league game against Leeds that precipitated the so-called 'Battle of Goodison'.

DESPITE playing four times in Everton's march on Wembley in 1966, he was left out of the team that won the FA Cup against Sheffield Wednesday. Yet when Everton won the League Championship four years later,

IT WAS, AND REMAINS, A CLASSIC OWN GOAL, BECOMING PART OF THE LOCAL FOOTBALL LEXICON

he played a part in all but six games, starting 31 times.

A popular character, both on the terraces and in the dressing room, as Catterick broke up his second Championship-winning team Brown was sold to Shrewsbury Town in 1971. He returned to Merseyside a year later and helped Southport to the 1972/73 Fourth Division title before moving into non-league football with Fleetwood. In later years he ran a Blackpool guest house and worked in a biscuit factory.

The own goal was uncharacteristic of Brown, who provided Everton with eight years of unstintingly reliable if unspectacular service. However, as every successful manager will attest, behind every great team is a staunch utility player, a man who can be counted upon to fill an unfamiliar role, give his all, and carry off the trick with composure and skill. In Everton's so-called 'golden era', Sandy Brown was that man.

SIGNED from Partick Thistle in September 1963 for £38,000, he filled every position in his Everton career – including goalkeeper on one occasion, after Gordon West was sent off – without ever really making any position his own, something more attributable to the excellence of his team-mates than any fundamental flaw in his play. Ostensibly a defender, he also slotted in as an auxiliary centre forward – as witness his goal-scoring appearances against

Season	League		FA Cup		League Cup		Europe		Total	
	App	Goals	App	Goals	App	Goals	App	Goals	App	Goals
1963/64	30	0	5	0	-	-	0	0	35	0
1964/65	28	5	1	0	-	-	4	0	33	5
1965/66	14 (2)	0	4	0	-	-	1	0	19 (2)	0
1966/67	15 (5)	1	1 (3)	0	-	-	1	1	17 (8)	2
1967/68	12 (13)	1	0 (2)	0	2	1	-	-	14 (15)	2
1968/69	40	1	5	0	4	0	-	-	49	1
1969/70	31 (5)	0	0 (1)	0	4	0	-	-	35 (6)	0
1970/71	6 (8)	1	0 (2)	0	-	-	0 (2)	0	6 (12)	1
Total	**176 (33)**	**9**	**16 (8)**	**0**	**10**	**1**	**6 (2)**	**1**	**208(43)**	**11**

[FACTFILE]

BORN
Grangemouth, Scotland,
24 March 1939
POSITION
Utility player / full back
OTHER CLUBS
Partick Thistle (1957–63);
Shrewsbury Town (1971–72);
Southport (1972–73)
HONOURS
1970 League Championship

Brown, William (b. 1865)

Versatile squad member during Everton's first league season

Season	League		FA Cup		Total	
	App	Goals	App	Goals	App	Goals
1888/89	6	2	-	-	6	2
Total	**6**	**2**	**-**	**-**	**6**	**2**

[FACTFILE]

BORN
1865
POSITION
Outside left / centre forward

·EFC·

Brown, William (b.1897)

Reliable half back whose lengthy service was not enough to secure an elusive medal

William Brown's Everton career began and ended with League Championship winning seasons, but the Scottish half back left Goodison after a 14-year career without a medal to his name.

BROWN joined Everton in May 1914 as a 17-year-old from the Scottish junior club Cambuslang Rangers, having impressed a watching director. Everton donated £10 to the Lanarkshire club for his services and it proved to be a fine investment indeed.

He made his Everton debut in the 1914/15 season but with only four appearances to his name did not collect a League Championship medal at the season's end. Indeed, with the intervention of war, it would take him the best part of a decade to make an Everton shirt his own.

With Neil McBain and Hunter Hart in the mid-1920s he formed a distinguished half-back line,

whose modus operandi was to keep the ball on the ground during a time when other half backs had a propensity to loft it aimlessly into the air. He was, wrote Ernest 'Bee' Edwards, a half back of 'customary excellence' with an ability to hold a 'vice-like grip' on his opponents. On occasion he deputised at right back and was a reliable if unspectacular defensive shield. 'Brown who played a capital defensive game proved a thorn in the Burnley attack,' reported the Liverpool Courier of his performance against Burnley in November 1925. 'Time after time he held up the visitor's front line when it seemed well on the way towards the Blues' citadel.'

Pace, however, was never one of his great virtues and in a side threatened by relegation in the 1926/27 season this failing was cruelly exploited. After a 6-2 hammering at Leicester City in February 1927, Brown was

Season	League		FA Cup		Total	
	App	Goals	App	Goals	App	Goals
1914/15	4	0	0	0	4	0
1919/20	20	0	1	0	21	0
1920/21	10	0	0	0	10	0
1921/22	16	0	1	0	17	0
1922/23	8	0	2	0	10	0
1923/24	37	0	2	0	39	0
1924/25	20	0	3	0	23	0
1925/26	28	0	0	0	28	0
1926/27	25	0	0	0	25	0
1927/28	2	0	0	0	2	0
Total	**170**	**0**	**9**	**0**	**179**	**0**

heavily criticised for his performance. 'The chief cause of the debacle was the inability of the wing half backs Reid and Brown to hold up the speedy wing play of the City,' reported the Liverpool Post and Mercury. 'They were distinctly poor. They were neither good in defence nor construction, and as a consequence their forwards had to work out their own salvation, and were not successful in their task, while the defence had double duty to perform.'

Brown lost his place in the side to Jerry Kelly and although he deputised twice in the 1927/28 season. once more it was not enough to claim an elusive League Championship medal. At the season's end he joined Nottingham Forest for £500, the Everton board meanly refusing to award the player his share of the 'benefit'.

[FACTFILE]

BORN
Cambuslang, 10 May 1897
POSITION
Half back
OTHER CLUB
Nottingham Forest (1928–30)

Buchan, Ian

Everton 'team coach' whose authority over the club's affairs remains open to question

The appointment of Loughborough University PT lecturer Ian Buchan as Everton team coach in May 1956 was at once a highly progressive and strange move by the Everton board. In seeking a man at the forefront of sports science, the board recognised the changing face of football and the growing emphasis on physical conditioning. And yet at the same time he came with no experience of professional football.

Previously a Scotland amateur international forward who had played for the famous Glasgow amateur club Queens Park, in becoming Everton manager Buchan had seen off the candidacies of former players Maurice Lindley and T.G. Jones, plus the former England captain George Hardwick. Unlike his predecessor Cliff Britton, Buchan was not afforded the title of manager, instead holding the position of 'team coach'.

Indeed it seems unclear the influence and say over team affairs that the Scot possessed. Certainly by comparison to Britton, Johnny Carey and Harry Catterick, his name in the Everton ledgers of this era is largely conspicuous by its absence and he seemed to be at the beck and call of the directors. It is not clear how much leeway he was ever given in the transfer market, although the return of Dave Hickson for the start of the 1957/58 season was a popular one – whether it was Buchan's choice or the board's.

Because of his background in sports science, Everton had a reputation as the fittest team in the First Division through this era.

As Everton Manager									
Season	P	W	L	D	F	A	Pts	Position	FA Cup
1956/57	42	14	10	18	61	79	38	15	5th Round
1957/58	42	13	11	18	65	75	37	16	4th Round
1958/59*	42	17	4	21	71	87	38	16	5th Round

*Buchan was relieved of his duties on 8 September 1957 with Everton bottom after losing their first five games

How true this was is a moot point. Certainly results didn't match up to this billing. Indeed Buchan's start to life at Goodison was an unmitigated disaster, with Everton losing six of their first seven matches, including a 5-1 defeat on the opening day of the season to Leeds United. Results did pick up, however, and from being relegation candidates, Everton finished the campaign 15th.

Despite the £6500 re-signing of Hickson over the summer of 1957, the emphasis remained on youth. Derek Temple and Brian Labone were given their debuts on Buchan's watch, the former becoming a first-team regular over the 1957/58 season; while Brian Harris also enjoyed a regular berth for the first time.

With a settled team, Everton rose as high as second in the early stages of the 1957/58 season, but this was a temporary diversion on the road to mediocrity. In the final four months of the season Everton won just five times in the league, back-to-back wins in the last two matches averting a closer brush with the relegation zone. Buchan was unable to halt this malaise in the first stages of the following season as Everton lost their first six matches.

At a board meeting on 8 September 1958 proposals were put forward to alter the complexion of the Everton training staff. A boardroom minute records: 'Mr. Buchan stated that in his opinion the proposed changes would not solve any of the present problems.' The board did not like this, and placed Gordon Watson in charge of first-team affairs, with 'the question of the relative positions of Messrs. I.C. Buchan and A.W. Fielding … deferred for discussion next week'.

At this subsequent meeting it was resolved that the club hire a full team manager and Buchan was offered the role of 'tactical advisor'. But these two decisions were incompatible. The board moved swiftly to appoint Johnny Carey, and the Scot was ushered out of the club and left professional football. Buchan died seven years later, aged just 45, in a car crash in Glasgow.

[FACTFILE]

BORN
1920
DIED
Glasgow, 1965
CLUB AS A PLAYER
Queens Park

Buck, Harry

Former Tranmere winger who made a 90-minute cameo in royal blue

[FACTFILE]

BORN
1883
POSITION
Outside right
OTHER CLUBS
Tranmere Rovers

Season	League		FA Cup		Total	
	App	Goals	App	Goals	App	Goals
1908/09	1	0	0	0	1	0
Total	1	0	0	0	1	0

Buckle, Ted

Tall winger who struggled to make an impression through Everton's bleakest year

High hopes rested on the slender shoulders of winger Ted Buckle when he joined Everton from Manchester United for a fee of £6500 in November 1949. The club was struggling to find its way in the post-war years and the arrival of the tall Londoner from one of the best sides of the era was considered something of a coup. Within 24 hours of signing he was lining up against his former team-mates and played his part in a 0-0 draw, which lifted Everton from the relegation zone.

ALAS, most of Buckle's Goodison career was to be consigned to the depths of one of the deepest depressions in Everton history. Although he played in every match in Everton's run to the semi-finals of the 1950 FA Cup – also playing at the same stage of the competition three years later – it was his misfortune to be part of the team that was relegated in April 1951 and subsequently the side that plunged to 16th in Division Two in 1952/53, the nadir of Everton history. For some, Buckle provided a glimmer of light during hard times.

'This long and lanky winger proved in a very short time that his direct methods and goal-scoring penchant were just what our forward line needed,' a generous profile in the club programme recorded. 'Ted is a real character, who frequently has the dressing room in an uproar with his antics. His style of play is most distinctive, his most noticeable trait being an eel-like twist of the body when passing opponents with the ball.'

Buckle was a regular through the first half of the 1953/54 season, which saw Everton win promotion back to the top flight. However, the re-emergence of Eddie Wainwright following a lengthy injury battle saw his place under threat. On Everton's return to Division One he made just a single appearance and in June 1955 a deal worth £2000 was concluded for his transfer to Exeter City.

[FACTFILE]

BORN
Southwark, 28 October 1924
DIED
Manchester, 24 October 1990
POSITION
Winger
OTHER CLUBS
Manchester United (1945–49);
Exeter City (1955–57)

Season	League		FA Cup		Total	
	App	Goals	App	Goals	App	Goals
1949/50	26	6	5	2	31	8
1950/51	22	5	0	0	22	5
1951/52	15	12	1	0	16	12
1952/53	14	5	4	0	18	5
1953/54	19	3	0	0	19	3
1954/55	1	0	0	0	1	0
Total	97	31	10	2	107	33

Buckley, Mick

Midfield prodigy who was a stalwart during the tumultuous seventies

An England Youth international midfielder, who in May 1972 scored his country's winner in the final of the 'Little World Cup' in Brazil, Mick Buckley seemed destined for a glittering career. Two months earlier, aged 18, he had been given his Everton debut by Harry Catterick and shown much promise in the closing stages of the 1971/72 season. A goal against Southampton in April 1972 brought Everton their first league victory in three months.

Born in Manchester in 1953, Buckley spurned the advances of his home city's clubs to join the formidable youth set-up at Goodison. With the

> BUCKLEY WAS AN ENGLAND YOUTH INTERNATIONAL MIDFIELDER, WHO IN MAY 1972 SCORED HIS COUNTRY'S WINNER IN THE FINAL OF THE 'LITTLE WORLD CUP' IN BRAZIL

likes of David Johnson, Gary Jones and Ronnie Goodlass he was part of a talented generation to emerge during this period, but like so many of his contemporaries he would ultimately fail to live up to his lofty potential.

After the arrival of Billy Bingham in the summer of 1973 he cemented a regular starting position, in place of the oft-injured Colin Harvey. A slight figure who strutted around the middle of the field, Buckley was a fine ball player, technically accomplished, always willing and alert to attacking opportunities. Nevertheless, a lack of genuine pace and aggression along with a poor strike rate prevented him from matching some of his illustrious predecessors.

INDEED the football writer Ivan Ponting described Buckley as a 'less inspired' version of Harvey – but the comparison is somewhat unfair. When Harvey was a 20-year-old staking his first-team claim a decade earlier, he played alongside Goodison immortals such as Alex Young and Brian Labone. Buckley, on the other hand, had to make his name with players like the unlamented Mike Bernard and Terry Darracott.

Despite being a regular through Bingham's first years at the club, it was Buckley who initiated the beginning of the end of his manager's reign. Having been genuine title contenders during the 1974/75 season, Everton slipped considerably the following year. Things came to

a head after a 0-3 away defeat at Manchester City on 21 February 1976, which left Everton 15th. After the game a number of fans protested outside the players' entrance. Inside the dressing room a furious argument broke out which ended with Gary Jones and Mike Buckley demanding transfers. It was, according to the Liverpool Echo's Michael Charters, 'as poor a performance as I can recall from an Everton team', the dressing room revolt 'unprecedented in my knowledge of Goodison affairs'.

Buckley declined to comment, but speculation linked him with a move to Leeds. After dropping Buckley for a game, Bingham held clear-the-air talks a few days later, but the dispute was the first clear sign of the growing dressing room disenchantment, from which the Everton manager never recovered.

Injuries and discord made Buckley a peripheral figure for the remainder of Bingham's reign and he slipped down the pecking order under Gordon Lee. In August 1978 Everton accepted an £80,000 bid from Sunderland, and the midfielder continued to provide spirited service for a succession of northern clubs before his retirement in 1985.

More recently he has returned to the spotlight as an eloquent and moving spokesman for the Everton Former Player's Foundation, which helped him after he fell on hard times.

[FACTFILE]

BORN
Manchester, 4 November 1953
POSITION
Midfield
OTHER CLUBS
Sunderland (1978–83);
Hartlepool (1983);
Carlisle United (1983–84);
Middlesbrough (1984–85)

Season	League		FA Cup		League Cup		Other		Total	
	App	Goals	App	Goals	App	Goals	App	Goals	App	Goals
1971/72	6	1	0	0	0	0	-	-	6	1
1972/73	9	1	2	0	2	0	-	-	13	1
1973/74	33	3	3	0	1	1	2	0	39	4
1974/75	31 (2)	2	4	0	2	0	-	-	37 (2)	2
1975/76	30 (1)	1	0	0	5	0	2	0	37 (1)	1
1976/77	7 (4)	0	2	0	0	0	-	-	9 (4)	0
1977/78	12	2	0	0	3	0	-	-	15	2
Total	**128(7)**	**10**	**11**	**0**	**13**	**1**	**2**	**0**	**156**	**11**

Burnett, George

Long-standing understudy to Ted Sagar

Despite spending his 14-year Goodison career largely in the long shadow cast by Ted Sagar, goalkeeper George Burnett's time at the club is littered with all manner of odd happenings and coincidences.

There was, for instance, his transfer to South Liverpool in 1951, which must surely represent one of the quickest transfers in football history. Desperate for first-team football, Burnett had been transfer-listed earlier that year at £7500 – but unsurprisingly no league club were prepared to pay so vast a fee for a reserve goalkeeper. So instead Burnett joined South Liverpool as an amateur. But within 24 hours of joining, Everton were beset by an injury crisis and so Cliff Britton re-signed him. The hapless Burnett was placed immediately in the team for a relegation showdown with Sheffield Wednesday and promptly conceded six goals without reply as Everton were relegated in one of the most infamous capitulations in the club's history.

Then there was the time Everton were looking for promotion back to the First Division three years later. They needed to beat Oldham Athletic to secure a top-flight return; by six goals they would have gone up as Second Division champions. Facing them in the Oldham goal was none other than Burnett. By half-time he had let in four and although he did enough to stave off further concessions, for years dark rumours that he had been too generous to his former team-mates followed him.

> **BURNETT'S TIME AT THE CLUB IS LITTERED WITH ALL MANNER OF ODD HAPPENINGS AND COINCIDENCES**

The Sheffield Wednesday fiasco was the last action in a long Everton career that saw first-team opportunities limited by the war and the ubiquitous Sagar. The local lad had first signed as a junior in the 1930s, but aged 19 – a time when he should have perhaps been looking to the first team – war broke out and changed everything. From 1941 he was Everton's regular goalkeeper and from April 1943 made more than 130 consecutive wartime appearances – no mean feat when troop movements and guest appearances radically altered the complexion of a team week in week out.

WHEN PEACE came and the Football League re-commenced in August 1946, Burnett retained his place, but it wasn't for long. Twelve games in to the 1946/47 season Sagar returned and for most of the rest of his Everton career Burnett played second fiddle to the veteran until his £2000 transfer to Oldham at the end of the disastrous 1950/51 season.

He remained phlegmatic about his fate as Sagar's understudy. 'Playing staffs were much bigger in those days,' he said in 1969. 'You couldn't afford to be temperamental if you wanted a game. You had to fight for a place in the team and it was a real honour to pull on an Everton or Liverpool jersey.'

Season	League		FA Cup		Total	
	App	Goals	App	Goals	App	Goals
1946/47	13	0	0	0	13	0
1947/48	0	0	0	0	0	0
1948/49	2	0	0	0	2	0
1949/50	24	0	5	0	29	0
1950/51	8	0	0	0	8	0
Total	47	0	5	0	52	0

Burrows, David

Unpopular left back never given a chance by the Goodison faithful

In the history of Everton Football Club, has there been a less popular player to pull on the famous royal blue shirt than David Burrows?

Signed by Mike Walker in a part-exchange deal that saw Tony Cottee return to West Ham, Burrows was greeted by a chorus of boos when he made his Everton debut away to Blackburn in September 1994. This was scarcely fair to a player whose form had previously seen him rise to the fringes of the England squad. But it

BURROWS WAS GREETED BY A CHORUS OF BOOS WHEN HE MADE HIS EVERTON DEBUT

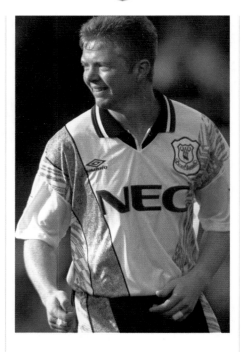

was unsurprising for a man who had made his reputation at Liverpool – where he won a league title and FA Cup – as a hard man, hated by opposing fans.

A SOLID, abrasive left back, what Burrows lacked in pace and elegance he made up for with competitive spirit. Still, this was not enough to help turn around Everton's worst

ever start to a season. Within two months of his arrival Walker was sacked and under his successor, Joe Royle, Burrows scarcely featured. In March 1995 he joined Coventry City for £1.1million, his departure unlamented by Everton's unforgiving fans.

THREE years later, Burrows nearly exacted his revenge upon Evertonians: his cross, in Everton's so-called 'Great Escape' against Coventry on the last day of the 1997/98 season, set up the goal that should have dealt relegation to his former club. But Everton held on, and Burrows played out his career in the second tier.

[FACTFILE]

BORN
Dudley, 25 October 1968
POSITION
Left back
OTHER CLUBS
West Bromwich Albion (1985–88);
Liverpool (1988–93);
West Ham (1993–94);
Coventry City (1995–2000);
Birmingham City (2000–01);
Sheffield Wednesday (2001–03)

Season	League		FA Cup		League Cup		Total	
	App	Goals	App	Goals	App	Goals	App	Goals
1994/95	19	0	2	0	2	0	23	0
Total	19	0	2	0	2	0	23	0

Burton, Andy

Inside forward who appeared briefly during the 1911/12 season

[FACTFILE]

BORN
Lochgelly, 1884
POSITION
Inside left
OTHER CLUBS
Thomson Rovers; Lochgelly Rovers;
Lochgelly United; Motherwell; Bristol
City (1905–11); Reading; East Fife

Season	League		FA Cup		Total	
	App	Goals	App	Goals	App	Goals
1911/12	12	4	0	0	12	4
Total	12	4	0	0	12	4

THE
EVERTON
· ENCYCLOPEDIA ·

Danny **Cadamarteri**, Tim **Cahill**, Bob **Cain**, Tom **Cain**, James **Caldwell**, Daniel **Cameron**, John **Cameron**, Kevin **Campbell**, William **Campbell**, Johnny **Carey**, Lee **Carsley**, Sir Philip **Carter**, Jimmy **Caskie**, James **Cassidy**, Segundo **Castillo**, Harry **Catterick**, Eddie **Cavanagh**, Arthur **Chadwick**, Edgar **Chadwick**, J. **Chadwick**, Nick **Chadwick**, Thomas **Chadwick**, Wilf **Chadwick**, Reverend Ben Swift **Chambers**, Sam **Chedgzoy**, Archie **Clark**, Charles **Clark**, Harold **Clarke**, Peter **Clarke**, Wayne **Clarke**, Alec **Cleland**, Dave **Clements**, Joe **Clennell**, Bob **Clifford**, Tommy **Clinton**, **Club Atlético Everton**, **Club Everton La Plata**, Jack **Cock**, Billy **Coggins**, Tim **Coleman**, Séamus **Coleman**, Bobby **Collins**, Harry **Collins**, John **Collins** (b. 1870), John **Collins** (b. 1968), Ted **Common**, John **Connolly**, Billy **Cook**, George **Cook**, Harry **Cooke**, Peter **Corr**, Thomas **Corrin**, James **Costley**, Tony **Cottee**, Jackie **Coulter**, George **Couper**, Walter **Cox**, Bernard **Coyle**, Darrin **Coyle**, **Coyne**, Nathan **Craig**, Jack **Crelley**, Warney **Cresswell**, Ted **Critchley**, Thomas **Crompton**, Charlie **Crossley**, Will **Cuff**, George **Cummins**, Jimmy **Cunliffe**, Terry **Curran**

Cadamarteri, Danny

Dreadlocked striker whose immense promise washed away in a fug of excess

In spring 1997 two teenage strikers appeared for the first time on either side of the Merseyside football divide.

AT ANFIELD, the fleet-footed Michael Owen was regarded as the club's best prospect since Robbie Fowler some years earlier; at Goodison, Danny Cadamarteri, Bradford-born but of exotic parentage, had impressed for the youth team and with his guile and abundant pace when appearing on the last day of the 1996/97 season against Chelsea. And while his arrival was unheralded by comparison to Owen's, when the two youngsters came face-to-face in the Goodison derby it was Cadamarteri who thoroughly overshadowed his Liverpudlian rival. After terrorising the Liverpool defence all afternoon with his dribbling, 15 minutes from the end he ran clear of Bjørn Tore Kvame, checked and struck a fierce low drive past David James to seal a 2-0 win.

Invariably dubbed 'Cadamagic', the young tyro was rewarded with a lucrative contract and seemed to have a glittering career ahead of him. Incredibly quick and agile, the sight of the dreadlocked teenager running at an opponent's defence was something to behold.

And yet something went badly wrong in Danny Cadamarteri's

career. For sure, it didn't help that he was initially expected to make his mark in the worst Everton team in modern history; nor that Walter Smith – who seemed to struggle in his man-management of Everton's youngsters – became manager in the summer of 1998. Injuries also stunted Cadamarteri's progress and he put on weight. The nadir came

when he went on trial in 2001 and was found guilty of assaulting a woman outside a Liverpool nightclub and fined.

Still aged only 22 when he was released from Everton in 2002 he traversed the lower leagues, but struggled to make his mark. In 2006 he failed a drugs test and despite pleading his innocence, claiming it was attributable to a flu remedy, received a six-month ban from football. He made a return with Leicester City after a spell in non-league, but as time draws to an end on what should have been a glittering career, Danny Cadamarteri will surely rue his wasted opportunities.

> DUBBED 'CADAMAGIC', THE YOUNG TYRO WAS REWARDED WITH A LUCRATIVE CONTRACT AND SEEMED TO HAVE A GLITTERING CAREER AHEAD OF HIM

[FACTFILE]

BORN
Cleckheaton, West Yorkshire, 12 October 1979
POSITION
Striker
OTHER CLUBS
Fulham (loan, 1999); Bradford City (2002–04); Leeds United (2004); Sheffield United (2004–05); Bradford City (2005–06); Grays Athletic (2006–07); Leicester City (2006–07); Doncaster Rovers (loan, 2007); Huddersfield Town (2007–09); Dundee United (2009–11); Huddersfield Town (2011–)

Season	League		FA Cup		League Cup		Total	
	App	Goals	App	Goals	App	Goals	App	Goals
1996/97	0 (1)	0	0	0	0	0	0 (1)	0
1997/98	15 (11)	4	1	0	1 (2)	1	17 (13)	5
1998/99	11 (19)	4	3 (1)	0	3 (1)	0	17 (21)	4
1999/2000	3 (14)	1	0 (2)	0	2	1	5 (16)	2
2000/01	7 (9)	4	2	0	0	0	9 (9)	4
2001/02	2 (1)	0	0	0	0	0	2 (1)	0
Total	**38 (55)**	**13**	**6 (3)**	**0**	**6 (3)**	**2**	**50 (61)**	**15**

Cahill,
Tim

Australian midfielder turned forward who stands among the Everton greats

As the summer of 2004 drew to its disappointing conclusion, with Wayne Rooney Manchester United-bound in a £27million transfer deal, the £1.5million signing of Australian midfielder Tim Cahill from Millwall passed largely unnoticed. Scarcely could Evertonians have imagined then the impact that Cahill, a 24-year-old without a top-flight game to his name, would have on the club's fortunes or that he would establish himself as the first Everton great of the 21st century.

Born in Sydney to an English father and Samoan mother, Cahill had paid his own airfare to England as a teenager in the mid-1990s in the hope that he would find a club. Ferociously ambitious and dedicated to his craft, these were the first steps on his path to being a top-class professional, and indicative of the hard work and desire that became hallmarks throughout his career. Signed by Millwall, he swiftly became an integral part of the south London team, helping them earn promotion in 2001 and an unlikely place in the 2004 FA Cup Final.

Cahill's headed goal in Millwall's FA Cup semi-final win over Sunderland elevated him to national prominence and alerted Premier League clubs to his availability. Throughout the summer of 2004 it seemed as if he might make the short journey

across south London to newly promoted Crystal Palace. But when that transfer broke down due to a row over payments to Cahill's agents, Everton stepped in. The £1.5million fee proved to be a fine bargain indeed.

A TENACIOUS, energetic midfield warrior, supremely fit and committed to his cause, Cahill brought real energy and verve to the Everton team. But it was his aerial ability and goalscoring prowess that elevated him to excellence. Standing just 5ft 10in tall, Cahill was one of the finest headers of the ball Goodison had seen in years. Despite his comparatively slight frame he had

perfected the art of 'floating' in the air and his timing was imperious. In front of goal he was deadly, possessing a striker's ruthlessness and utilising his aerial prowess to lethal perfection.

Cahill's force was soon felt on the Premier League. In only his second game in an Everton shirt he headed the winner against Manchester City in one of their first matches at Eastlands – only to be sent off for an over-exuberant celebration. He repeated the trick on his Premier League return against Portsmouth a fortnight later, scoring the only goal of the game and this time remaining on the field.

Pushed to an auxiliary forward position, usually playing off Marcus Bent, Cahill was crucial to Everton through the 2004/05 season, finishing top scorer with 12 goals as they finished fourth and qualified for the Champions League. It was fitting that his strike against Newcastle in the last home match of the season effectively secured the coveted fourth spot and his place in Everton hearts.

CAHILL'S excellent debut season brought a new and improved contract, and over the following year he earned global renown. His debut for Australia was delayed until he was aged almost 25, owing to appearances he made for Western Samoa's under-20 team when he was aged just 14. FIFA's initial unwillingness to scrub this from their records almost brought legal action when Cahill initially sought to play for the Republic of Ireland in the 2002 World Cup. A resolution came in 2004, by which stage he was firmly committed to the country of his birth. The following year Cahill was named Oceania Player of the Year as Australia qualified for the World Cup Finals for the first time since 1974, and Cahill was included in the country's squad for Germany. His introduction as a substitute in the first group match against Japan changed the flow of the game and his two late goals helped bring a 3-1 victory. Australia eventually qualified for the second round and were unlucky to fall to eventual World Champions Italy. Cahill was one

Season	League		FA Cup		League Cup		Other		Total	
	App	Goals	App	Goals	App	Goals	App	Goals	App	Goals
2004/05	33	11	1 (1)	1	2 (1)	0	-	-	36 (2)	12
2005/06	32	6	3	1	0	0	4	1	39	8
2006/07	17 (1)	5	0	0	2 (1)	2	-	-	19 (2)	7
2007/08	18	7	0	0	3 (1)	1	6	2	27 (1)	10
2008/09	28 (2)	8	7	1	0 (1)	0	2	0	37 (3)	9
2009/10	33	8	2	1	1	0	7	1	43	10
2010/11	22 (5)	9	1	0	0	0	-	-	23 (5)	9
2011/12	27 (8)	2	4	1	1 (1)	0	-	-	32 (9)	3
Total	**210(16)**	**56**	**18 (1)**	**5**	**9 (5)**	**3**	**19**	**4**	**256(22)**	**68**

of 50 players nominated for the Ballon d'Or the following October, the first time an Everton player had been nominated in 18 years. He also appeared at the 2010 World Cup in South Africa and the 2011 Asian Cup in Qatar.

Domestically he continued to shine, and was often asked to lead the Everton front line. Off the pitch what immediately set Cahill apart from other players was an inherent understanding of what the club meant to the fans and what it was to be an Evertonian. He took his responsibilities as a royal blue icon seriously. In interviews he spoke with humility about the honour of playing for a club that had given him worldwide renown.

Asked in 2009 if he regretted not playing for a club that regularly appeared in the Champions League, he replied: 'Is the grass always greener? Is it the right situation for you and your family and you as a player? I feel that I am achieving a lot at Everton. It's unfortunate that I haven't won them big awards. But who knows? Maybe one day. But beating Liverpool is like winning an FA Cup. Once you've played for Everton and know what it is to be a Blue, then you know what it means to beat Liverpool.'

Derby matches were games Cahill seemed to particularly relish and they always seemed to inspire the best in him. Besides Dixie Dean no other Everton player has scored more times at Anfield than Cahill and the intensity of his performance always seemed to rise a notch when he came up against Everton's great rivals. His display in the October 2010 Goodison derby was among the finest seen by an Everton player in years and he coupled an excellent goal with an effervescent, unrelenting display that battered his opponents into submission.

Afterwards, the blogger Ed Bottomley paid the following tribute on his Dixie's 60 website:

> **Tim Cahill is 30 years old. Many players peak sooner, some, usually defenders and keepers, peak later, but the Australian has reached the apex of his playing career and is currently a fearsome combination of physical strength and footballing craft. Gorge your eyes on him, tell yourself to remember, remember, remember. Those of us lucky enough to have seen Alan Ball in his pomp always regret we did not see more of him, make not the same mistake with Tim Cahill. In years to come children and grandchildren, nephews and nieces and vague passing acquaintances will ask 'what was he like?' On Sunday this player passed two landmarks, one mathematical the other mythical: His 34th minute strike was his fifth league derby goal, a post war record for a Blue, but it was his overall match performance, along with thirty or forty of equal intensity in recent years, that finally took him through the shimmering veil which separates the merely good, from the truly great. Though nominally operating in his accustomed role, playing just off the lone striker, Cahill was everywhere; at one moment auxiliary defender, the next supporting Arteta in midfield and then popping up to harass and to penetrate the Liverpool rearguard. It was all that we have come to expect from the Aussie, a performance of passion, intelligence and leadership.**

Cahill had by then committed to a new long-term contract that will take him to his mid-thirties and ten-year anniversary with the club. 'The chairman knows my thoughts,' he said after putting pen to paper. 'I will sign here for life. He knows my thoughts on what I love about this club. I respect everyone so much and hopefully I will be here for a long time.'

At times since then there have been questions asked about Cahill's continued effectiveness in an Everton shirt. Certainly the relentless effort, the long-haul travel to represent his country, the battering by Premier League defenders has sometimes appeared to take its toll. The 2011 calendar year passed without a Cahill goal. But he has adapted his game, taken on more midfield responsibilities and continues to be one of Everton's most important players.

Few goals in his Everton career were better or more important than his instinctive twisting header against Sunderland in 2012 FA Cup quarter-final and it showed that he is far from finished. After scoring he ran to the corner flag and unleashed his famous kangaroo boxing celebration that has become his trademark. Few sights at Goodison were more beautiful or pleasing than this in the early-twenty-first century, but all good things have to come to an end. The following summer Cahill joined the New York Red Bulls in MLS for an enticing swansong.

[FACTFILE]

BORN
Sydney, Australia,
6 December 1979
POSITION
Midfielder / forward
OTHER CLUBS
Millwall (1998–2004);
New York Red Bulls (2012–)
HONOURS
55 Australia caps (24 goals) (2004–);
Oceania Player of the Year (2005)

Cain, Bob

Defence-minded player during Everton's second league campaign

Season	League		FA Cup		Total	
	App	Goals	App	Goals	App	Goals
1889/90	10	0	0	0	10	0
Total	**10**	**0**	**0**	**0**	**10**	**0**

[FACTFILE]

BORN
Slamannan, Scotland, 13 February 1866
POSITION
Left back / right half
OTHER CLUBS
Airdrieonians; Bootle;
Sheffield United (1892–97);
Tottenham Hotspur;
Albion Rovers; Small Heath

Cain, Tom

Stand-in goalkeeper who failed to make long-term impression

Season	League		FA Cup		Total	
	App	Goals	App	Goals	App	Goals
1894/95	11	0	1	0	12	0
Total	**11**	**0**	**1**	**0**	**12**	**0**

[FACTFILE]

BORN
Sunderland, 1872
DIED
1952
POSITION
Goalkeeper
OTHER CLUBS
Hebburn Argyle; Stoke City (1893);
Southampton; Grimsby Town (1896);
Hebburn Argyle; West Stanley

Caldwell, James

Widely travelled goalkeeper rejected after just a season of first-team action

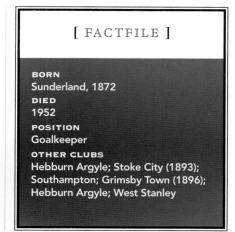

Season	League		FA Cup		Total	
	App	Goals	App	Goals	App	Goals
1912/13	31	0	5	0	36	0
Total	**31**	**0**	**5**	**0**	**36**	**0**

[FACTFILE]

BORN
Carronshore, Scotland, 1886
POSITION
Goalkeeper
OTHER CLUBS
Carron Thistle;
Dunipace;
East Stirlingshire;
Tottenham Hotspur (1908);
Reading;
Woolwich Arsenal (1913); Reading

Cameron, Daniel

Irish centre half who was limited to a solitary first-team appearance

Season	League		FA Cup		Total	
	App	Goals	App	Goals	App	Goals
1948/49	1	0	0	0	1	0
Total	**1**	**0**	**0**	**0**	**1**	**0**

[FACTFILE]

BORN
Dublin, 16 June 1922
POSITION
Centre half
OTHER CLUBS
Shamrock Rovers;
Sligo Rovers

Cameron, John

Rebellious Scottish forward who later put in a fine stint as Tottenham boss

Season	League		FA Cup		Total	
	App	Goals	App	Goals	App	Goals
1895/96	13	4	3	1	16	5
1896/97	15	5	0	0	15	5
1897/98	14	3	3	1	17	4
Total	**42**	**12**	**6**	**2**	**48**	**14**

[FACTFILE]

BORN
Ayr, 13 April 1872
DIED
1935
POSITION
Centre forward / inside left
OTHER CLUBS
Ayr Parkhouse; Queens Park;
Tottenham Hotspur
AS MANAGER
Tottenham Hotspur (1899–1907);
Dresdner SC; Ayr United (1918–19)
HONOURS
1 Scotland cap (1896)

Campbell,
Kevin

Everton's first black captain, his goals saved the club from the abyss

It was a curious irony of Walter Smith's prolific transfer activity, that his signings which seemed to hold least promise for Everton supporters turned out to be his most successful. The arrivals of Richard Gough, David Weir and Lee Carsley each barely mustered a shrug from Evertonians, but all went on to have excellent Goodison careers. Even more unheralded, and arguably more crucial to the club's history, was the arrival of Kevin Campbell on a loan deal in March 1999.

Considered something of a journeyman when Smith signed him, Campbell had been the last

of a crop of outstanding black London players to break into the Arsenal team during the 1980s. Following a tradition set by Paul Davis, David Rocastle and Michael Thomas, the centre forward established himself in the first team during the 1990/91 season, scoring eight times in ten games as Arsenal lifted the First Division title. Although he was overshadowed in subsequent years by Ian Wright, Campbell played an important role in Arsenal's FA Cup and League Cup successes in 1993, and their European Cup Winners' Cup victory a year later.

The forward joined Nottingham Forest for £2.8million in July 1995, and was part of the side that was relegated in 1997. He helped Forest to promotion the following year, but chose to make a personally lucrative move to Turkish team Trabzonspor over a return to the Premier League. That transfer soon unravelled after Campbell suffered a torrent of racist abuse from his chairman, who publicly derided him as 'discoloured' and a 'cannibal'.

Alerted to Campbell's obvious distress, Walter Smith moved to sign the 29-year-old on loan for the rest of the season. It was hoped that Campbell might fill the void controversially left

earlier that season by Duncan Ferguson, and the misfiring Ibrahima Bakayoko.

CAMPBELL'S home debut, against Sheffield Wednesday, was a disaster for Everton, who conspired to commit defensive suicide and lose 1-2, dropping into the relegation places. 'The signs are that no one at Goodison Park believes they can drag themselves back from the brink this time,' reported the Independent after the match. 'After 45 consecutive seasons of top flight football,' added The Times, 'this could be the year that Everton go down in flames.'

Nobody, however, had banked on Campbell, who showed some deft touches amid the debacle.

Indeed the impression of a clumsy and wayward striker, garnered in his last days at Arsenal, was actually unfair, and took no account of the fact that he was often asked to play out of position, wide on the right. Campbell was very much a hustling, bustling centre forward, very much in the tradition of the Everton number nine. Indeed his movement was good and link-up play excellent, and he possessed a poacher's eye for goal – an instinct not always apparent in the departed Ferguson. If there were any lingering doubts about Campbell, the centre forward was to dispel them over the final weeks of the season.

Six days after the Sheffield Wednesday game came another 'six-pointer', this time against Coventry City. Campbell scored twice as Everton recorded a 2-0 win. One week later, against Newcastle United, Everton won 3-1, their first win at St James's Park since they had last won the title. It suddenly meant that Everton were five points clear of the third

Season	League		FA Cup		League Cup		Total	
	App	Goals	App	Goals	App	Goals	App	Goals
1998/99	8	9	0	0	0	0	8	9
1999/2000	26	12	5	0	0 (2)	0	31(2)	12
2000/01	27 (2)	9	1	0	1 (1)	1	29 (3)	10
2001/02	21 (2)	4	3	3	1	0	25 (2)	7
2002/03	31 (5)	10	0	0	3	2	34 (5)	12
2003/04	8 (9)	1	0 (1)	0	0	0	8 (10)	1
2004/05	4 (2)	0	0	0	0 (1)	0	4 (3)	0
Total	**125(20)**	**45**	**9 (1)**	**3**	**5 (4)**	**3**	**139(25)**	**51**

relegation spot going into the meeting with its occupants, Charlton Athletic, at Goodison. Knowing that a win would effectively secure survival, Everton took to the task with gusto, with Francis Jeffers and Campbell running amok in a 4-1 win. Again Campbell scored a brace. A fortnight later he hit a hat-trick in the 6-0 demolition of West Ham, which took his end-of-season tally to nine goals in eight games, and gave Everton the security of 14th place. Almost single-handedly, Campbell had saved his new club.

SMITH MADE the deal to sign Campbell permanent that summer, amid crippling financial problems. He scored 12 league goals in 26 appearances in 1999/2000, including a derby winner at Anfield, and his experience and ability aided the development of the promising Jeffers. Perhaps surprisingly,

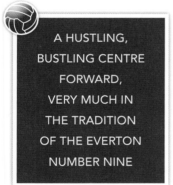

A HUSTLING, BUSTLING CENTRE FORWARD, VERY MUCH IN THE TRADITION OF THE EVERTON NUMBER NINE

Smith rewarded Campbell, now aged 30, with an improved five-year contract at the end of that season. Worth a reputed £30,000 per week, it made Campbell the most highly paid player in the club's history and was to place constraints upon Everton's transfer-market muscle in subsequent seasons. If that raised a few eyebrows, the award of the captaincy to Campbell – Everton's first black captain – was seen as a deserved reward for a popular and consummate professional.

THE inevitable toll of age and injuries lessened Campbell's effectiveness as the Walter Smith era petered out under a fug of disappointment. Yet following the arrival of David Moyes in March 2002, Campbell was revitalised and his fitness and movement improved. Although he conceded the captaincy, he was to end the 2002/03 season top scorer, having played in almost all of Everton's games. Moreover his experience and composure aided the development of Wayne Rooney, as it once had Jeffers.

From thereon, however, injuries made Campbell a peripheral figure at Goodison. When he was fit, which was not often, his pace and power had obviously diminished markedly. In his final two seasons

at Goodison he was to start just a dozen league games, scoring only once. Although he is due respect for his earlier achievements, his plight emphasised the folly – committed all too often under Smith's watch – of awarding large and long contracts to aging players.

In January 2005, Campbell was given a free transfer and joined West Bromwich Albion, helping them avoid relegation from the Premier League that season. He subsequently had a short but fruitless spell with Cardiff City, before retiring in 2007 to pursue business interests.

A former England under-21 and England B international, Campbell holds the distinction of being the Premier League's leading English scorer never to have won a full cap.

[FACTFILE]

BORN
Lewisham, 4 February 1970
POSITION
Centre forward
OTHER CLUBS
Arsenal (1988–95);
Leyton Orient (loan, 1989);
Leicester City (loan, 1989);
Nottingham Forest (1995–98);
Trabzonspor (1998–99);
West Bromwich Albion (2005–06);
Cardiff City (2006–07)

Campbell, William

League Championship winning defender

Season	League		FA Cup		Total	
	App	Goals	App	Goals	App	Goals
1890/91	13	1	0	0	13	1
1891/92	4	0	0	0	4	0
1896/97	3	1	0	0	3	1
Total	20	2	0	0	20	2

[FACTFILE]

BORN
Unknown
POSITION
Left half / centre half / inside left
OTHER CLUBS
Bootle;
Clyde
HONOURS
1890/91 League Championship

Carey, Johnny

Widely respected Irish manager who lacked the ruthless streak demanded by John Moores

The three managers who have won major trophies with Everton – Messrs Catterick, Kendall and Royle – all displayed a ruthless streak in their respective quests for glory. One of the Everton managers who never won anything – except for many friends – was Johnny Carey, a softly spoken Dubliner whose sides played nice football but were never quite able to stamp down the authority necessary for major honours.

CAREY, an accomplished Gaelic footballer in his youth, had been captain of Manchester United's post-war side in the pre-Busby Babes era, helping them to League runners-up position for three consecutive seasons and to the FA Cup Final, which they won in 1948. He played with distinction, picking up 29 caps for the Republic of Ireland (and 7 for Northern Ireland) and also captained the Rest of the World against Great Britain in 1947 in a match to raise money for FIFA. He was the Footballer Writers' Association Player of the Year in 1949, only the second player to win the award, and made nearly 350 appearances for United before his retirement as a player in 1953. He declined an Old Trafford coaching position to take up the Blackburn Rovers manager's job in August that year.

> IN SIGNING A FIVE-YEAR CONTRACT TO BECOME EVERTON MANAGER, CAREY BECAME ONE OF THE BEST-PAID FIGURES IN ENGLISH FOOTBALL

Carey was a footballing purist, a man whose motto was purportedly, 'Only the keeper stops the ball.' He was not without success at Ewood Park and in 1957/58 led Blackburn to the top flight as Second Division runners-up. Everton, who were in a dire state, may have been set to replace them. They lost the first six games of the 1958/59 season and head coach Ian Buchan was sacked. In searching for a replacement Everton went to Ewood Park and Carey accepted the challenge of restoring glory to Goodison.

In signing a five-year contract to become Everton manager, Carey became one of the best-paid figures in English football. He earned £3000 per year at a time when most of his players earned one-sixth of that amount, and was given a house for a peppercorn rent. The task facing him was onerous. A fortnight before first formally managing Everton the club fell to its record defeat, a 4-10 hammering at Tottenham. Everton were deep in relegation trouble. Carey nevertheless eased these concerns, elevating Everton to 16th place by the season's end.

At this time John Moores' millions were starting to make an impression on the club and big signings were beginning to arrive at Goodison. Bobby Collins joined from Celtic a month before Carey's arrival and Alex Parker from Falkirk a month after. Carey took a year to start to make a big impression at Goodison and when he did it was not for a signing but a departure. On Friday 6 November 1959 a £10,000 offer from Liverpool for the club idol, Dave Hickson, was accepted.

FOR EVERTONIANS the news was deeply traumatic. 'I protest at the abominable treatment afforded Dave Hickson. Everton supporters know that Hickson is not the best centre forward in football, but of the centre forwards on Everton's books he is by far the

best,' wrote J.D. Pierce of L11 to the Football Echo. 'It seems ridiculous that other players in the team can play badly and still retain their places while Hickson, who has played his heart out (and incidentally, is leading goalscorer) should be dropped.' 'Is Mr Carey using Hickson to cover mistakes by rash buying?' pondered C. Purvis of L24.

The club were, at the time, in 19th position, and the day Hickson's sale was revealed they lost 8-2 at Newcastle. Carey was in the market for a centre forward but had been foiled in attempts to sign Joe Baker and Denis Law. Instead, the doughty trier, Alan Shackleton, was persisted with until the end of the season. But other new signings over coming months helped ease the burden of Hickson's loss. Wingers Tommy Ring and Micky Lill, wing half Jimmy Gabriel and, from Blackburn, the rapier-like forward Roy Vernon all arrived before the end of the season.

Yet despite the changes, Everton again finished 16th and although their football could be thrilling, they could also frustrate. They won 13 of their 19 home matches, but won none away. An autumn series of results saw a 6-1 win over Leicester, the 2-8 defeat at Newcastle and then a 4-0 win over Birmingham. A similar sequence in spring witnessed a 4-0 win, a 2-2 draw, a 6-1 victory and a 2-6 defeat. Evertonians did not know if they were going to witness a humiliation being handed out or received.

In the dressing room Carey got a mixed response. 'I thought his ideas on football were good, but I didn't like him as a man,' Derek Temple said in 2011. 'He was a very sarcastic man. I've spoken to other players and they felt the same. Some liked him as well. But you always get that: some players that like managers, and others that detest them.' Ken Rea was similarly unimpressed. 'Carey was useless,' he said. 'He would come in at half-time and say, "I want you all to listen to this." But he never told us anything! We were at Arsenal and losing 2-0 and he said, "I want you to go out there and meet the ball and play football." But I thought that was part of the

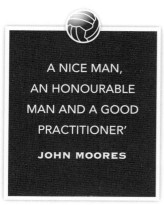

'A NICE MAN, AN HONOURABLE MAN AND A GOOD PRACTITIONER'

JOHN MOORES

game, meeting the ball and playing football! He was a terrible manager! People might say he's okay, but he was a terrible manager. Terrible!'

Off-the-field developments over the summer of 1960 would have a dramatic impact on the club. At the Annual General Meeting on 23 June, the chairman, Fred Micklesfield, revealed that Moores had offered £56,000 to the club free of interest 'to enable star players to be secured'. Micklesfield offered words of confidence about the club's future before retiring from the chair, to which Moores was elected. Over the course of the 1960/61 season Billy Bingham and Alex Young would be added to Carey's expensive new squad.

While the away form remained indifferent, Everton were unstoppable at Goodison and by Christmas lay in third place. A 3-1 win at league champions Burnley on Boxing Day underlined Everton's title credentials. But then it all started to go horribly wrong. Burnley visited Goodison the following day and won 3-1. It sparked a run of nine matches without a win, encompassing eight defeats and FA Cup and League Cup exits to Sheffield United and Shrewsbury Town. Carey was suddenly a man under pressure and scrutiny, and from March whisperings in the press suggested his days were numbered.

On Friday 14 April 1961, Carey and Moores travelled to London for an FA meeting.

Although Everton had beaten Newcastle United 4-0 at St James's Park the previous Saturday, speculation was more intense than ever about Carey's future. Wanting clarification, he demanded a meeting with his chairman. Moores suggested that they reconvene and the two men took a taxi to the Grosvenor Hotel. During that journey, Carey repeated his request for clarification on his future. Moores, always a man of principle, was straight and to the point. He told Carey that he was being replaced.

The following day Everton faced Cardiff City at Goodison. Moores' appearance in the director's box shortly before kick-off was greeted with boos, slow handclapping and 'We want Carey' chants. Just before the team left the dressing

room to come onto the pitch, the captain Bobby Collins made a speech thanking Carey on behalf of him and all the rest of the players and expressed their regret at his departure. Cardiff were beaten 5-1 thanks to a hat-trick by Bobby Collins and a brace by Alex Young. After the game around 30 to 40 fans waited around Carey's car to thank him for everything he had done for the club. 'That touched me very much,' he said, 'And so did the players' little speech before a match which was for me, one of the greatest and yet one of the saddest of my career.'

BUT THERE was no stay of execution. 'Mr Moores deserved better,' recalled Young. 'As did Johnny. He was a wonderful Irish gentleman of immense dignity who knew football and had played

the game at the highest level. His approach had been uncomplicated. He required us to emphasise neat passing and ball skills at all times in training and in matches.'

Carey returned to football with Orient a few months later and took them to the unprecedented heights of the First Division within a year of assuming command. In 1963 he became Nottingham Forest manager and would lead them to runners-up spot in the First Division in 1966/67 as well as the FA Cup semi-final. His final job in football came back at Ewood Park, but he failed to bring success back to East Lancashire and left in 1971 after Blackburn suffered relegation to the Third Division. He subsequently worked for a textile company and in the treasurer's office of Trafford Borough Council. He died in 1995 and at Goodison will always be remembered best in the words of John Moores: 'A nice man, an honourable man and a good practitioner.'

[FACTFILE]

BORN
Dublin, 23 February 1919
DIED
Macclesfield, 22 August 1995
POSITION
Centre forward
OTHER CLUBS
(as a player) Manchester United (1936–53);
(as a manager) Blackburn Rovers (1953–58 and 1969–71); Orient (1961–63); Nottingham Forest (1963–68)
HONOURS
29 Republic of Ireland caps (1937–53),
7 Northern Ireland caps (1946–49);
1949 Football Writers' Player of the Year

Season	P	W	L	D	F	A	Pts	Position	FA Cup	League Cup
1958/59	42	17	4	21	71	87	38	16th	5th Round	N/A*
1959/60	42	13	11	18	73	78	37	16th	3rd Round	N/A
1960/61	42	22	6	14	87	69	50	5th	3rd Round	5th Round**

*Appointed 25 October 1958   ** Dismissed 15 April 1961

Carsley, Lee

Hugely dependable stalwart of the Moyes era

Signed from Coventry City in a £1.9million deal in the final days of Walter Smith's managerial reign, Lee Carsley arrived at Goodison with the unenviable reputation of being relegated at each of his two previous clubs. With his new club facing another relegation battle, scarcely could many Evertonians – who feared the jinx might continue – have imagined that the 27-year-old would be one of the lynchpins around whom successive pushes for European football were based.

Born in Birmingham, but of Irish parentage, Carsley started his career with Derby County, cultivating a reputation as a tough but composed midfield anchor. He joined Blackburn Rovers in a £3.5million deal in March 1999, although his presence was unable to help the Lancashire club stave off relegation that season. Promoted to club captain, he finished the 1999/2000 season as Rovers' top scorer after being designated penalty-taker.

But after failing to win promotion that year, Carsley was allowed to join Coventry City in December 2000 for £2.5million. Six months later the relegation curse struck again, and as Coventry were subsequently beset by financial crisis Carsley was sold to Everton in February 2002. Initially derided, Carsley's signing would prove to be one of Smith's shrewdest pieces of transfer business.

At first Carsley struggled to make a discernible impact at his new club, holding a variety of roles across the middle of the park without the effect that would mark his latter career. At the start of the 2004/05 season, David Moyes was forced to radically reshape his team in the wake of Wayne Rooney's departure to Manchester United, adopting a 4-1-4-1 formation. Carsley dropped back into a holding position just in front of the back four and he, and Everton, flourished.

PHYSICAL AND ADROIT, powerful yet composed, Carsley mastered this difficult position immediately. His experience allowed him to read the game to perfection, but even though he was entering the veteran stage of his career, he remained a fine athlete, working tirelessly to do the defensive work that allowed more attacking players, such as Leon Osman, Tim Cahill and – notably – Thomas Gravesen to flourish. Gravesen, whose Everton career had previously been beset by inconsistency, suddenly freed from his defensive responsibilities became one of the Premier League's most effective attacking midfielders, earning a surprise January move to Real Madrid. It was joked that Madrid had mistaken Gravesen, who resembled his bald colleague, for Carsley and signed the wrong man.

Without question, Carsley's finest moment in a blue shirt came in the December 2004 Goodison derby. A typically close-fought game was deadlocked when, in the 68th minute, Carsley met Leon Osman's cutback on the edge of the Liverpool area and curled a low shot past Chris Kirkland, Liverpool's unsighted goalkeeper, for the game's only goal. A photograph that captured the team piled on top of Carsley in celebration became so iconic at Goodison Park that David Moyes ordered a framed copy for every member of his squad, but Carsley joked three years later: 'I find it ironic, because I'm still asked to sign that picture of my goal celebrations and I'm the only Everton player not on it.'

HIS IMPORTANCE to a team that finished fourth was underlined when Carsley was forced to miss most of the 2005/06 season through a serious knee injury sustained in a pre-season friendly. In the early stages of the season, Everton were scarcely able to cope without him, as they crashed out of Europe, losing 11 of their first 14 fixtures. When he returned for the 2006/07 season, he was ever-present as Everton finished sixth, again qualifying for Europe, and he missed just four league games as Everton went one place better the next season.

> CARSLEY'S SIGNING WOULD PROVE TO BE ONE OF SMITH'S SHREWDEST PIECES OF TRANSFER BUSINESS

Aged 34 at the end of the 2007/08 season, Carsley was offered a new contract, but instead chose to take up an offer with Birmingham City, citing a need to be near his Midlands home and his disabled son. While the club and supporters respected his decision, his departure was nevertheless mourned, and on the pitch Everton initially struggled to cope without his composure in the early stages of the 2008/09 season.

An inherently decent man and popular member of the first-team squad, Carsley also made 39 appearances for the Republic of Ireland, appearing at the 2002 World Cup Finals.

[FACTFILE]

BORN
Birmingham,
28 February 1974

POSITION
Midfielder

OTHER CLUBS
Derby County (1992–99); Blackburn Rovers (1999–2000); Coventry (2000–02); Birmingham City (2008–10); Coventry City (2010–11)

HONOURS
39 Ireland caps (1997–2006)

Season	League		FA Cup		League Cup		Europe		Total	
	App	Goals	App	Goals	App	Goals	App	Goals	App	Goals
2001/02	8	1	0	0	0	0	-	-	8	1
2002/03	21 (3)	3	1	0	2	0	-	-	24 (3)	3
2003/04	15 (6)	2	2	0	2	0	-	-	19 (6)	2
2004/05	35 (1)	4	3	0	2	1	-	-	40 (1)	5
2005/06	3 (2)	0	0 (1)	0	0	0	0	0	3 (3)	0
2006/07	38	1	1	0	3	0			42	1
2007/08	33 (1)	1	1	0	5	0	9	0	48 (1)	1
Total	**153(13)**	**12**	**8 (1)**	**0**	**14**	**1**	**9**	**0**	**184(14)**	**13**

Carter, Sir Philip

Longstanding chairman who oversaw Everton's glory years and the Premier League's birth

Born in Glasgow and educated at Waterloo Grammar School, Philip Carter (b.1927), came to Liverpool with his family as a two-year-old and never left. He first visited Goodison when he was four and was immediately cast by its spell. During the war he served with the Fleet Air Arm as a pilot, and in 1948 joined the retailing division of Littlewoods, John Moores' pools and shopping conglomerate. Carter was a successful careerist within the corporation, rising to store manager, chief buyer and eventually, in 1976, managing director.

In 1973 Carter was made an Everton director and in 1978 became chairman, succeeding T.H.W. Scott. It followed a tradition set by his mentor John Moores, who led both Littlewoods and Everton at the same time. It was a position he held for the next 13 years, before stepping down in the summer of 1991, to be succeeded by Dr David Marsh.

Carter has become synonymous with Everton's mid-1980s glory years and, in particular, the decision not to sack Howard Kendall in 1983 when there was fierce pressure for him to do so.

EVERTON HAD MANAGED just seven goals in the opening ten fixtures of the 1983/84 season, and at the end of their tenth game, a 1-0 win over Watford, Carter delivered a vote of confidence in Kendall. 'We are not complacent about our present problems – we are most concerned – but let us state unequivocally that our manager Howard Kendall has the absolute support of the board,' he said. 'This is not just a club chairman trotting out a hackneyed phrase; I am stating that categorically.' Even when leaflets were distributed by fans calling for his and the manager's removal, he held firm. Six months later, Everton lifted the FA Cup and the rest is history.

Carter took early retirement from Littlewoods in 1983, allowing him to focus on Everton and an extraordinary range of other interests. He became President of the Football League in 1986, a Vice President of the Football Association, a member of the Merseyside Development Corporation and an influential figure for a score of charities. As chairman of the Merseyside Tourism Board he oversaw Liverpool's rise as a popular tourist destination.

In his role at the Football League, Carter was a controversial figure. Unlike his eleven predecessors as president he had never served on the league's management committee, immediately casting him a maverick outsider among some of his contemporaries. This was heightened when he led the so-called 'big five' clubs – Everton, Liverpool, Manchester United, Arsenal and Tottenham – to negotiate more money and power within the league's structure. Rather than protecting the league, this breakaway movement eventually, in the early-1990s, led to the break-up of the 104-year-old league and the creation of the Premier League. Carter is credited as being one of the Premier League's key architects.

As a Tory grandee – he was chairman of the Liverpool Conservative Association at the height of Thatcherism – at the time of Merseyside's economic nadir, Carter was not always going to be a popular figure among Evertonians. Some supporters have since accused him of not sufficiently building upon the club's mid-1980s successes. Other criticisms have focused on his role in creating the Premier League, in which Everton have fared badly.

AS CHAIRMAN, Carter always backed his managers to the best of his ability. Twice Gordon Lee broke the Everton transfer record, Howard Kendall did so three times and Colin Harvey broke the British transfer record with the £2.2million signing of Tony Cottee. Even when Everton were in terrible financial health in the early 1980s, Carter changed Everton's bankers to one that would sanction the £60,000 overdraft needed to purchase Peter Reid.

As chairman his managerial appointments – Howard Kendall, Colin Harvey and David Moyes – have either been inspired or, as in Harvey's case, satisfied supporter's demands.

Carter made a dramatic return to the Everton boardroom as chairman in December 1998, following the resignation of Peter Johnson. Everton were in disarray at the time and Carter was seen as the sort of safe pair of hands needed to guide the club out of the mess. Yet his deputy chairman Bill Kenwright was seen as the prime mover in the boardroom, particularly after he became the club's majority shareholder a year later.

Although the direct role Carter played in the day-to-day running of the club in his second spell as chairman was never quite clear, what followed over the next six years on and off the pitch was one of the most tumultuous in the club's history.

During this time Everton lurched from crisis to crisis off the pitch. In 2000 a massive media deal with the cable company NTL fell through at the last minute, after the board had sanctioned a summer spending spree. The club's crippling financial situation forced Everton to mortgage their future season-ticket sales against a £25million loan from Bear Stearns. A proposed move to an iconic stadium at Kings Dock fell through because Everton could not come up with the necessary cash. A succession of Everton's best players – Olivier Dacourt, Marco Materazzi, Nick Barmby, Michael Ball and Francis Jeffers – were sold, while the wheels were already in motion on the transfer that saw Wayne Rooney leave for Manchester United when Carter stepped down from the board. On the pitch – notwithstanding the exhilarating 2002/03 season – the football was dire, with relegation flirtations a regular feature.

In June 2004 Kenwright succeeded Carter as chairman, and the 78-year-old was made Life President of the club. He returned to the Everton boardroom again in August 2008, more than three decades after his first appointment as a director. As of April 2012 he remains Everton's fifth largest private shareholder with a 2 per cent stake in the club.

Caskie, Jimmy

Flying winger whose Goodison career was wrecked by war

Season	League		FA Cup		Total	
	App	Goals	App	Goals	App	Goals
1938/39	5	1	0	0	5	1
Total	5	1	0	0	5	1

Cassidy, James

Forward whose brief flirtation with Everton was the prelude to a successful career in Bolton

Season	League		FA Cup		Total	
	App	Goals	App	Goals	App	Goals
1887/88	-	-	2	0	2	0
Total	-	-	2	0	2	0

Castillo, Segundo

Ecuadorian loan star

Season	League		FA Cup		League Cup		Europe		Total	
	App	Goals	App	Goals	App	Goals	App	Goals	App	Goals
2008/09	5 (4)	0	1 (1)	0	1	0	1	1	8 (5)	1
Total	5 (4)	0	1 (1)	0	1	0	1	1	8 (5)	1

Catterick, Harry

Diligent centre forward who managed the club through its defining golden era

Following Johnny Carey's much-publicised departure in April 1961, the Everton board were left with the unenviable task of bringing in a manager who could clinch Everton's first trophy in more than a generation. Carey's successor, Harry Catterick, completed the task within two years of his appointment and went on to be Everton's longest serving boss in a career which lasted 12 years. His name, and iron rule, dominated what became known as Everton's golden era.

CATTERICK had already experienced 15 years as a centre forward with the club when he returned to Goodison Park in the summer of 1961. He had first signed in April 1937 as a part-time professional while continuing an apprenticeship as a marine engineer. As a youngster making his way in the A team and reserves, he shared a dressing room with Dixie Dean, then in the final days of his Goodison career. But with the likes of Tommy Lawton and Robert 'Bunny' Bell ahead of him, Catterick had to wait until after the Second World War to make his league debut in an Everton shirt, although he did make 73 wartime appearances, scoring 56 times.

After the war, although no less accomplished than many of his contemporaries, he struggled to claim the number nine shirt on a regular basis. Among Evertonians of a certain era, like many of his team-mates he has tended to fade by comparison to his illustrious forbears. And yet his scoring record in a struggling side was by no means a disgrace and he attracted plaudits on the way. 'Catterick has for years shown a virility, sense of direction, shooting, urge and general football stamp that earned him a regular place in a senior side,' wrote Leslie Edwards in October 1948. 'He did not get his deserts through misfortune, injury and the luck of the game… He is wrong in his outlook when he essays to help the defence but at least he shows forthright thoroughness and willingness to work.'

Catterick did, however, have his occasional moments of glory, such as a hat-trick scored in a 5-1 away thrashing of Fulham in October 1950. At the end of that season Everton were relegated and after playing a part in just three more first-team games, in December 1951 he left to become player-manager of Crewe Alexandra. His work at Gresty Road and, from 1953, at Rochdale was quietly efficient, stabilising Third Division strugglers into steady forces. In August 1958 he was appointed Sheffield Wednesday manager, a move that proved to be the making of Catterick. In his first full season he led them to the Second Division Championship, in his second to fifth in the First Division – eleven places above Everton. In 1960/61 Wednesday might have won the League Championship had it not been for the formidable Tottenham double winners of Mackay, Blanchflower and Jones.

BY THIS TIME 'The Catt' had established a reputation as one of the finest managers in the country. He had the verve, winning mentality and discipline that many believed the popular Johnny Carey did not have. Amid heavy speculation about his future, on 14 April 1961, the day before Everton played a home match with Cardiff City, Everton's chairman John Moores sacked Carey while on their way to a Football League meeting in London. The Irishman was in the process of leading Everton to their highest post-war position of fifth. Catterick replaced him days later.

Moores later said of his decision to appoint Catterick: 'I believed Harry had the drive we needed and I didn't give him two years to bring us trophies, or even say anything like that.

I told him to aim for a place in the top six by playing good football, and by doing that I was sure that success would come.'

Carey had already laid the foundations of a very good side and his dismissal divided opinion, with some arguing that he was unlucky to be sacked. Among his expensively assembled squad were players like Billy Bingham, Jimmy Gabriel, Brian Harris, Brian Labone, Mick Meagan, Derek Temple, Roy Vernon and Alex Young. All would be important players for Catterick.

'THE CATT' HAD ESTABLISHED A REPUTATION AS ONE OF THE FINEST MANAGERS IN THE COUNTRY

The new manager laid down an immediate marker for his style as Everton boss. On the club's end-of-season tour to the US he sent home his captain and star player, Roy Vernon, for 'disciplinary reasons'. In doing so Catterick had shown that he would give short shrift to anyone who crossed him, even a player as crucial to his cause as the Welshman. He would have not just the deference of the Everton players, but their fear too.

MANY YEARS LATER, this author came into conversation with a player who was managed by both Catterick and his England counterpart, Alf Ramsey. The two shared many qualities: tactical mastery; dour, almost emotionless

personas; winning mentalities. I asked the player what the differences were between the Everton and England managers. 'We respected Alf,' he said. 'And we respected Catterick too. But we feared him more than anything.'

BUT FEAR also played a part in Catterick's own mindset. In John Moores he had one of the most demanding and exacting bosses in British business. As he had shown with Carey, he had little patience with those who failed in his pursuit of success. 'I am only paid for one thing – to get results,' Catterick told the News of the World's Bob Pennington. 'If I don't get results for any reason then I'm no good to my employer and I should be OUT.'

During his first full season, the 1961/62 campaign, the new manager only made a few additions to the side he inherited, bringing in 19-year-old Gordon West from Blackpool and adding some steel to the heart of his team with the acquisition of Dennis Stevens. In signing West, Everton had paid a record fee for a goalkeeper and Catterick had no issues in breaching transfer records. Twice under his rule the British transfer record would be shattered by one of his purchases. 'I haven't got a copyright in this transfer business,' he would say. 'Other managers also buy big and sell big. But the important thing is to think big.'

EVERTON finished the 1961/62 season in fourth place, an improvement of one position from Carey's last season, but Catterick's management had seen Everton shore up their previously leaky defence and add discipline and consistency. They conceded 15 fewer goals than in the previous campaign. Gone were the days of the late 1950s when the Blues could lose by five or six goals. And yet they were still capable of emphatically demolishing their

opponents as they had done on occasion when Carey was boss. Cardiff City discovered this in the penultimate game of Catterick's first season when Everton knocked eight past them.

During the summer of 1962 Catterick added only Liverpool's winger Johnny Morrissey to his side – a move that initially inspired mystification on both sides of Stanley Park. The £10,000 fee was to prove one of the finest bargains in Everton history. But the confidence Catterick had in his existing squad – the basis of which was inherited from Carey – was justified. Goodison had become a veritable fortress under Catterick and this was underlined by the fact that they lost just four home games in his first three seasons as manager and remained undefeated there through 1962/63. The Goodison crowd had a huge effect upon the team's performance – something which the Observer noted in September 1962: 'Visiting teams must survive matches at this ground in the certain knowledge that if Everton don't get them the crowd will. This has become an inferno... frightening, ferocious, and often with some of the malevolence of a latter day Rome in it.'

BY LATE November 1962 Catterick's team were second and well placed for an assault on the League Championship. But England was about to be struck by its coldest winter of the century. The big freeze halted English football. From 22 December Everton went seven weeks without a league game and more than two months without a home match. They came out of the blizzard strongly, the squad augmented by the signings of midfielder Tony Kay – Catterick's captain at Sheffield Wednesday – and winger Alex Scott.

Bill Nicholson took his great Spurs team to Fortress Goodison on 20 April 1963 with the winner

expected to eventually take the Championship. Everton were in third position with 50 points, with Leicester and Spurs ahead of them on 51. An Alex Young header divided the teams and virtually ensured that the League Championship was Goodison-bound. The title was secured on the last day of the season when a Roy Vernon hat-trick saw off Fulham. Catterick, recalled Young, 'had taken Johnny Carey's men, added a few of his own and transformed us from entertainers into winners. He then fine-tuned us into champions.'

Everton would start the 1963/64 season badly, falling as low as 16th position by October and being knocked out of the European Cup in the opening round by Inter Milan. However, the side was boosted in March 1964 by the £85,000 arrival of Blackburn Rovers centre forward Fred Pickering, a British domestic transfer record. By the end of the month Everton were sat at the top of the table with just five games remaining. But Everton were unhinged by the match-fixing scandal that led to Tony Kay's ban and lost three of their remaining games, drawing a fourth. Everton finished third.

Catterick's new signings – and those, such as Colin Harvey, who were plucked from the youth team – were forming the basis of his next great team. But in the dressing room there was unease among the crop of highly talented players he had inherited from Carey. Years later, Young wrote: 'I remain convinced that the only men he wanted to succeed were those he'd brought through the ranks and the ones he'd spent money on.' Vernon became increasingly peripheral through the 1964/65 season and was sold to Stoke City and Tommy Wright replaced Alex Parker at right back. England full back Ray Wilson replaced Mick Meagan and even Young found himself out of favour.

This was to the consternation of some fans, who produced placards bearing such wisdom as 'Sack Catterick, Bring Back Young'.

CATTERICK was a remote figure, rarely seen on the training pitch unless press cameras or the chairman were present. Players sensed his presence by seeing gaps open in the blinds of his office at their new Bellefield training ground. Much of the day-to-day business was conducted by his trainer, Tommy Egglestone. He was never revered like his contemporaries, Don Revie, Bill Shankly and Matt Busby.

Catterick justified his aloofness to the sportswriter Alan Hoby in a revealing interview in March 1967, saying that it was a consequence of the city's goldfish bowl mentality. 'There is a different atmosphere in Liverpool to anywhere else in the country,' he said. 'The intensity of feeling, the personal involvement is unique. I know, because I manage one of the country's leading teams in a city where football is a religion. Of course, working as I do amid all this emotion, it would be fatal for me to become part of it. You've got to keep a cool head in this business. Otherwise, you'd never be able to make any decisions.'

Everton had finished the 1964/65 season fourth, but expectations were mounting. So too was discontent with the manager. This was to bubble over spectacularly midway through the following campaign. In January 1966, with Everton labouring in 11th place, the team travelled to Blackpool. Catterick caused shock and consternation by dropping Young in place of a 16-year-old debutant, named Joe Royle. Everton lost 2-0 and afterwards a crowd of supporters gathered around the team bus, and Catterick was jostled and jeered at and fell. Afterwards it was claimed in the national press that he was attacked. Catterick labelled the fans 'cowards' and the Everton director E. Holland-Hughes described it a 'dastardly attack'. Others suggested that it was exaggerated. Brian Labone said years later that Catterick slipped and stumbled, that the only real damage was to his pride. As Young wrote 40 years later: 'Blue folklore contains no shortage of misinformation about "The Blackpool Rumble".' But what is certain is that it showed an extreme example of the extraordinary ambivalence sections of the support felt for their manager.

A week later Young was restored to the line-up for an FA Cup third round tie against Sunderland. He scored in a 3-0 win. Some Evertonians felt that his omission was a piece of kidology, designed to kick-start his season.

If that was the case it certainly reaped rich dividends. For the first time in 33 years Everton returned to Wembley, overcoming a disappointing league campaign and a 2-0 deficit in the final against Sheffield Wednesday to lift the FA Cup for just the third time. Catterick described the win over his former club as 'the thrill of my footballing life'. Years later, in semi-retirement, he reflected: 'That was my greatest moment. The Cup hadn't been to

Everton for many years and it was wonderful to bring it back to Merseyside and receive the acclaim of the crowds as we returned to the city.'

BUT CATTERICK didn't rest easily. In the 18 months following the FA Cup Final win he reconstituted his team again, edging out Scott, Young and Gabriel and bringing fresh blood in the shape of Royle, Alan Ball and Howard Kendall. Ball was a £110,000 British record signing from Blackpool, Kendall cost £80,000 from Preston North End. Tommy Wright later told me that Catterick's biggest attribute was signing the right players at the right time. 'Gelling the players, that's what Harry Catterick was good at,' he said when we met in the mid-1990s. 'Buying the right players to fit into the team, not having the team fit around a player, which a lot of teams tend to do.' They fitted the new complexion of football, which was becoming harder, more defensive, more tactically astute.

Speaking in 1967 Catterick acknowledged the changing landscape of the English game. 'Football today,' he said, 'is much more punishing physically than when I was playing. More and more emphasis is laid on the physical side of the game … upon destroying … wrecking. In fact, if the trend goes on, there is a danger that the skills which make football the great entertainment it is will gradually melt away.' Players like Kendall, Ball and Colin Harvey – who formed the exquisite heartbeat of his new team – merged the skill and physicality to excel in this new world.

Everton returned to Wembley in 1968 and were unlucky not to recapture the FA Cup, falling to a single extra-time goal against West Bromwich Albion. Catterick remained loyal to his squad and no new faces were brought in over the summer of 1968. Of the side that started the first game of the 1968/69 season eight played 40 or more League games, something which bears testament to Catterick's loyalty and confidence in his players.

Many believe that the Everton of the 1968/69 season played better and more stylish football than the one that was to win the title a year later. But for an indifferent start and a poor finish, Catterick's side may well have clinched the title in 1969 too. In the end they claimed third spot, but many sides had been given a lesson in football from the School Of Science ruled over by the iron fist of its headmaster Catterick. The most emphatic win came against Leicester City in November when the Blues stuck seven past a young Peter Shilton. The 'strolling maestroes of Goodison fulfilled

the promise they have been parading in recent weeks', recorded the Daily Post.

His team's potential was realised in the 1969/70 season, when Everton strolled to the League Championship. 'They have won it by playing football, by applying their individual skills to the team as a whole,' said Catterick. 'And I would like to believe they have also managed to entertain spectators all over the country in the process … Our success has been a team effort and the effort must be shared all round.' Jibes about the 'Merseyside Millionaires' no longer held true. The team had cost just £275,000 to build, with £112,000 of that spent on Ball. Harvey, Hurst, Husband, Labone, Royle, Whittle and Wright had all been home-grown players and the average age was just 24. Ball confidently predicted, 'I can see five great seasons ahead. This team is certain to go better. We have lots of skill and every player works hard for each other. With that behind us, how can we fail?'

WHAT HAPPENED over the following three years counts as one of the great mysteries in Everton history. Everton started the 1970/71 season slowly but built up momentum in cup competitions, reaching the quarter-finals of the European Cup against Panathinaikos and the semi-finals of the FA Cup against Liverpool. Within the space of

'THE THRILL OF MY FOOTBALLING LIFE'

HARRY CATTERICK ON WINNING THE 1966 FA CUP

three days they were dumped out of both competitions – on away goals by the Greek side and 2-1 against Liverpool having first taken the lead – and Catterick's team seemed to die. They finished the season 14th, having won just one of their last 13 league and FA Cup games.

Things did not improve in the 1971/72 season. Within its first month Catterick effectively lost Labone and Wright to serious injury. Then in December he sold Alan Ball for a British record fee to Arsenal. The move shocked English football. Catterick announced that Ball's departure marked the start of the construction of a new team. 'I have been extremely patient, giving them every chance to regain their form and attitude to the game. Now my patience has ended.'

But, normally so astute in his transfers, Catterick's judgement began to fail him. Large sums were frittered on players like Henry Newton, Bernie Wright and Joe Harper. The highly promising David Johnson was part-exchanged for the less-than-satisfactory Geoff Nulty.

Things worsened for the Everton manager. In January 1972 Catterick suffered a heart attack while driving back from Sheffield where he'd been watching a game. Although he was back at the centre of things within ten weeks, he later estimated that it took him 'eighteen months' to fully recuperate. When that period had elapsed time had run out for him. Finishes of 15th and 17th saw him ushered upstairs to a largely undefined 'executive' role and Billy Bingham took over.

CATTERICK had anticipated that such a day would come, when he spoke to Alan Hoby six years earlier. 'It's a strain at times and it can be lonely,' he said. 'Every Saturday you are on trial. Of course there are bound to be pressures. If things go wrong naturally you get the bird. You are the target. But that's what I'm paid for. I certainly wouldn't like to be in some backwater where there is no excitement, no atmosphere. What really keeps you on your toes is the fact that you've got this big duty to the public … That you're completely involved with the team and its future. Football is a business. You've got to sell it like any other commodity. And, like any other business, there is no room for complacency.'

Two years later he was appointed manager of Preston North End but failed to bring back success to the once mighty Lancastrian club.

After leaving that job in 1977 his football career ended. Fittingly it was at Goodison Park where Catterick died on 9 March 1985 after watching a 2-2 draw with Ipswich Town in the FA Cup. Everton's manager that day was Howard Kendall, the second of four Catterick players to have learned sufficient managerial lessons from the 'master' to go on and manage the club.

After winning the Championship in 1970 Catterick shared his football philosophy with the world. 'When I go to a match,' he said, 'wherever it may be and whoever might be playing, I go to watch a contest. I go to be entertained … Quality of performance is so important.' For many years, by vigorously adhering to Everton's famous Nil Satis Nisi Optimum motto, Catterick did just that.

[FACTFILE]

BORN
Darlington, 26 November 1919
DIED
Goodison Park, Liverpool, 9 March 1985
POSITION
Centre forward
OTHER CLUB
Crewe Alexandra (1951-53);
AS MANAGER
Rochdale (1953-58),
Sheffield Wednesday (1958-61)
Preston North End (1975-77)

As a Player

Season	League		FA Cup		Total	
	App	Goals	App	Goals	App	Goals
1946/47	3	0	0	0	3	0
1947/48	9	2	4	1	13	3
1948/49	10	3	1	0	11	3
1949/50	20	9	5	3	25	12
1950/51	13	5	0	0	13	5
1951/52	4	0	0	0	4	0
Total	**49**	**19**	**10**	**4**	**59**	**23**

As a Manager

Season	P	W	L	D	F	A	Pts	Position	FA Cup	League Cup
1961/62	42	20	11	11	88	54	51	4th	5th Round	-
1962/63	42	25	11	6	84	42	61	1st	5th Round	-
1963/64	42	21	10	11	84	64	52	3rd	5th Round	-
1964/65	42	17	15	10	69	60	49	4th	4th Round	-
1965/66	42	15	11	16	56	62	41	11th	Winners	-
1966/67	42	19	10	13	65	46	48	6th	6th Round	-
1967/68	42	23	6	13	67	40	52	5th	Runners Up	3rd Round
1968/69	42	21	15	6	77	36	57	3rd	Semi-final	4th Round
1969/70	42	29	8	5	72	34	66	1st	3rd Round	4th Round
1970/71	42	12	13	17	54	60	37	14th	Semi-final	-
1971/72	42	9	18	15	37	48	36	15th	5th Round	2nd Round
1972/73	42	13	11	18	41	49	37	17th	4th Round	2nd Round

Catterick's European record

1962/63	Inter Cities Fairs Cup	1st Round
1963/64	European Cup	1st Round
1964/65	Inter Cities Fairs Cup	3rd Round
1965/66	Inter Cities Fairs Cup	2nd Round
1966/67	European Cup Winners' Cup	2nd Round
1970/71	European Cup	Quarter-finals

…TIS NISI OPTIMUM

EVERTON
TRIBUTE TO HARRY CATTERICK

Cavanagh, Eddie

Staunch Evertonian whose 'Wembley cup run' brought global fame

It was the 1966 FA Cup Final and Everton were on their way to the impossible. Two goals down after 57 minutes, on 64 minutes they were level after Mike Trebilcock's quick-fire brace.

For one fan, Eddie Cavanagh, the excitement became too much. 'I think the crowd got to you more than anything,' he would recall to the authors of Three Sides of the Mersey. 'They were all screaming. You'd have to see it to believe it. I couldn't explain that.' Seizing the moment, he climbed the Wembley perimeter fence and, evading the attention of police, made his way onto the pitch. He remembered:

I'd seen Trebilcock and I went for him first. Well, he didn't know me but I grabbed him, pulled him on the ground. He shit himself because he didn't know me. We all played in blue and white, didn't we. Sheffield were in blue and white, and we're in blue and white, so he didn't know who I was.

When I got him down, I was coming across then to Westy. I was going to say, 'Gordon, for God's sake don't let no more in, we'll get that now.' But I'd seen this busy [policeman] came after me and he caught up with me and got me by the coat. But I just took it off ...

RUNNING FULL PELT across the Wembley turf, this hysterically jubilant fan was chased by a procession of police officers. One grabbed Cavanagh's coat tails, but he wriggled out of his jacket and the policeman fell to the turf, holding Cavanagh's empty coat. A second officer gave up the chase, throwing his hat to the ground in frustration.

A third officer, coming from a different direction, caught Cavanagh unawares – 'I didn't see him coming because he wouldn't have caught me,' he recalled – and floored him with a rugby tackle before he could reach West's goal. A bevy of policemen piled onto Cavanagh, then threw him out of the ground. But Cavanagh was indomitable: he climbed back in and was able to see Derek Temple's sublime winner and Brian Labone lift the Cup. A well-known figure among Evertonians even before his famous cameo, Cavanagh remained a regular at Goodison until his death in December 1999.

'I DIDN'T SEE HIM COMING BECAUSE HE WOULDN'T HAVE CAUGHT ME'

Chadwick, Arthur

Full back who had a fleeting role in Everton's first years

Season	League		FA Cup		Total	
	App	Goals	App	Goals	App	Goals
1888/89	2	0	-	-	2	0
1890/91	0	0	0	0	0	0
1891/92	0	0	0	0	0	0
1892/93	3	0	0	0	3	0
Total	**5**	**0**	**0**	**0**	**5**	**0**

[FACTFILE]

BORN
Church, 1868
POSITION
Left back
OTHER CLUB
Accrington

Chadwick, Edgar

Inside forward who illuminated Everton's first decade of league football

Edgar Chadwick was one of Everton's first giants. An inside forward of pace, skill and fine finishing, he illuminated Anfield and Goodison during the club's first decade of league football. During that time he made 300 appearances for the Blues, winning the League Championship, seven England caps and appearing in two FA Cup Finals. The impression he left was lasting. 'Edgar Chadwick is still recalled with pride and affection by the older generation of soccer followers in this city,' said a 1930s article. 'Never ruffled, never in a hurry, Chadwick almost invariably managed to "get there" thanks to his powers of body swerve, plus an ability to send opponents the wrong way looking for the ball.'

Born in Blackburn in 1869, as a teenager he played for his home-town clubs Blackburn Olympic and Rovers while working as a baker. But with the onset of league football in 1888 he was lured away from Everton's fellow founder league members and to Anfield, where he was paid wages of 35 shillings per week. In a side that struggled to find its way in the Football League's first season he was one constant, an ever-present whose six goals made him Everton's top goalscorer.

A SLIGHT PLAYER, standing just 5ft 5in tall, some accounts say that it was suggested he was too frail for the rigours of league football. Chadwick was to prove any doubters wrong and was ever-present through Everton's first three league campaigns, missing just one game in their fourth. He was, recorded David Prentice and David France in Virgin Blues, an account of Everton's first season of league football, 'an exciting forward famed for his blistering pace and keen eye for an opening'. He was, added a contemporary account, 'the foremost with the tricky bite of play'.

Chadwick would form a formidable left-wing partnership with Alf Milward. As Everton found their way in the brave new world of league football they were the cornerstones of a formidable attack and in 1890/91 – the season Everton first lifted the League Championship – they combined to score 22 goals between them, with the centre forward, Fred Geary, adding another 20.

Everton's outstanding forward line was one of the distinguishing features of early league football. An account in the Liverpool Mercury of a 7-1 hammering of champions Sunderland in September 1893 is instructive of how potent they were. Playing in front of Ebenezer Cobb Morely – the Football Association's founding father – and several members of Liverpool City Council, with their play 'of the most spirited kind' Everton 'looked likely to again lower the visitors' colours every minute'. Chadwick set up Jack Southworth for a goal, finished an Alex Latta centre himself, struck a second goal from long range and forced Gibson into scoring an own goal (which appears to have been credited to him – thus giving him a hat-trick). He was, mused the Mercury later that season, a player with a 'profundity' of skill.

CHADWICK earned the first of seven England caps against Wales in 1891. It was an international career that saw him score three times for his national team, most memorably after just 30 seconds against Scotland in England's 4-1 victory in Glasgow in 1892.

> AN EXCITING FORWARD FAMED FOR HIS BLISTERING PACE AND KEEN EYE FOR AN OPENING

Season	League		FA Cup		Total	
	App	Goals	App	Goals	App	Goals
1888/89	22	6	0	0	22	6
1889/90	22	9	2	0	24	9
1890/91	22	10	1	0	23	10
1891/92	25	10	1	1	26	11
1892/93	27	10	7	3	34	13
1893/94	24	13	0	0	24	13
1894/95	28	11	4	3	32	14
1895/96	28	11	3	1	31	12
1896/97	28	7	5	2	33	9
1897/98	22	8	5	2	27	10
1898/99	22	2	2	1	24	3
Total	**270**	**97**	**30**	**13**	**300**	**110**

For Everton, further honours after the 1890/91 League Championship were elusive. He appeared on the losing sides in the 1893 and 1897 FA Cup Finals, and would do so again as a Southampton player in 1902.

The move to Southampton came after a spell with Burnley in 1899/1900 after he had been transfer-listed at the end of the 1898/99 season. The decision was a surprising one, but his replacement – Jimmy Settle – was worthy. He then made the move that several of his League Championship winning team-mates had made by joining John Houding's Liverpool. He played out his career with Blackpool, Glossop North End and Darwen.

In retirement his career took a remarkable twist when he went to coach in the Netherlands. As well as spells in charge of HVV Den Haag and Koninklijke HFC, Chadwick was appointed the first manager of the Dutch national team and led them to the 1908 and 1912 Olympics, where they won bronze medals in both football tournaments. In March 1913 he led the Dutch team to a 2-1 victory over the England amateur team, a stupendous result that hinted at the shifting sands in European football. Chadwick went on to manage Vitesse Arnhem and Sparta Rotterdam, leading the latter to the Dutch League Championship in 1915.

Chadwick's career came to an abrupt halt after the First World War. He had been involved in football for more than 30 years but after returning to his home town of Blackburn he resumed his original vocation – as a baker. It was a mundane end to a career less ordinary.

Chadwick, J.

Mystery man who made a solitary appearance on the left wing

[FACTFILE]

BORN
Unknown
POSITION
Outside left

Season	League		FA Cup		Total	
	App	Goals	App	Goals	App	Goals
1901/02	1	0	0	0	1	0
Total	1	0	0	0	1	0

Chadwick, Nick

Young home grown centre forward who went on to enjoy a solid lower league career

[FACTFILE]

BORN
Stoke-on-Trent, 26 October 1982
POSITION
Centre forward
OTHER CLUBS
Derby County (loan, 2003);
Millwall (loan, 2003–04);
Plymouth Argyle (2005–08);
Hereford United (2008–09);
Shrewsbury Town (2009);
Chester City (2009–10);
Barrow (2010–11);
Stockport County (2011–12);
Plymouth Argyle (2011–)*

[FACTFILE]

BORN
Blackburn, 14 June 1869
DIED
Blackburn, 14 February 1942
POSITION
Inside left
OTHER CLUBS
Blackburn Olympic (1886–87);
Blackburn Rovers (1887–88);
Burnley (1899–1900);
Southampton (1900–02); Liverpool (1902–04); Blackpool (1904–05);
Blackpool (1904–05); Glossop North End (1905–06); Darwen (1906–08)
AS MANAGER
Netherlands (1908–13);
Sparta Rotterdam; HVV Den Haag;
Koninklijke HFC; Vitesse Arnhem

Season	League		FA Cup		League Cup		Total	
	App	Goals	App	Goals	App	Goals	App	Goals
2001/02	2 (7)	3	0 (1)	0	0 (1)	0	2 (9)	3
2002/03	0 (1)	0	0	0	0	0	0 (1)	0
2003/04	1 (2)	0	0	0	1	1	2 (2)	1
2004/05	0 (1)	0	0 (2)	1	0 (2)	1	0 (5)	2
Total	3 (11)	3	0 (3)	1	1 (3)	2	4 (17)	6

* permanent after initial loan spell

Chadwick, Thomas

Versatile reserve defender of the early twentieth century

Season	League		FA Cup		Total	
	App	Goals	App	Goals	App	Goals
1904/05	3	0	0	0	3	0
1905/06	4	0	0	0	4	0
1906/07	10	0	1	0	10	0
1907/08	3	0	0	0	3	0
Total	**20**	**0**	**1**	**0**	**20**	**0**

[FACTFILE]

BORN
Blackburn, 2 March 1882
DIED
1960
POSITION
Centre half / wing half
OTHER CLUBS
Blackburn Rovers (1900–01);
Preston North End (1908)

Chadwick, Wilf

Inside forward with roller-coaster fortunes

Inside forward Wilf Chadwick enjoyed one of the most meteoric rises in English football history and within a 26-month period went from playing amateur football to leading the First Division scoring chart.

Signed from non-league Rossendale for £350 in February 1922, he joined a club that was haunted by the spectre of relegation to the Second Division for the first time in its history. Two reserve-team outings yielded three goals and within weeks of leaving non-league ranks he unexpectedly found himself leading the Everton first-team forward line. Up against Bradford City, the 21-year-old debutant did not disappoint, scoring a brace on his debut. 'Everton have found another good centre forward in Chadwick, who can justly be called an opportunist,' recorded the Liverpool Echo. 'But he does not finish at that, for his passes to the wings were always accurate and well conceived, while he placed himself well when there was a likelihood of a centre coming his way.'

Tall, direct, and an accurate, effective finisher, the youngster suffered by comparison to his more polished forward team-mates – Bobby Irvine, Sam Chedgzoy, Jack Cock and Alec Troup. His lack of pace also saw him singled out for criticism in the local press through his Everton career. 'Chadwick keeps on scoring, and such a fine opportunist deserves every encouragement,' reported the Liverpool Courier after his second appearance also yielded a goal. 'He is on the slow side yet,

but knows where the net lies, and with more experience will be a decided acquisition.'

CHADWICK'S annus mirabilis came in the 1923/24 season when he outshone his more celebrated team-mates to top the First Division scoring charts. Playing in Everton's most settled side in years suited him, as did the presence of the brilliant left winger Alec Troup for all but one game. 'Chadwick is a better footballer and a better shot than has been given credit for, and he has shown more genuine football this season than has been generally recognised,' opined the Daily Post early in the campaign. 'His shots are always so forceful that he should be left severely alone in the matter of tactics and speed. He is gaining experience every day and he is reaping a rich harvest through playing alongside Troup.' It was an accurate prediction and Chadwick's haul of 28 goals included four goals against Manchester City and a hat-trick in the final home game of the season against Tottenham Hotspur. Yet within less than a year of topping the First Division scoring charts, Chadwick found himself out of favour at Goodison. The promise shown in the previous campaign subsided and when relegation became a possibility, the board of directors dismantled the team, selling Jack Cock and bringing in Manchester United's Fred Kennedy, who replaced Chadwick. The board resisted offers from Bradford City,

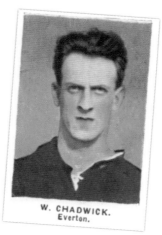

W. CHADWICK.
Everton.

Leicester City and Swansea Town for Chadwick but in November 1925 sold him to Leeds United for £2,500. He later enjoyed good spells with Wolves and Stoke City, but the heights once reached at Goodison remained elusive.

[FACTFILE]

BORN
Bury, 7 October 1900
DIED
14 February 1973
POSITION
Inside forward
OTHER CLUBS
Bury (1917–20); Nelson (1920–21);
Rossendale (1921–22);
Leeds United (1925–26);
Wolverhampton Wanderers (1926–29);
Stoke City (1929–30);
Halifax Town (1930–32)

Season	League		FA Cup		Total	
	App	Goals	App	Goals	App	Goals
1921/22	4	3	0	0	4	3
1922/23	27	13	1	0	28	13
1923/24	42	28	2	2	44	30
1924/25	27	6	4	3	31	9
1925/26	2	0	0	0	2	0
Total	**102**	**50**	**7**	**5**	**109**	**55**

Chambers,
Reverend Ben Swift

Hitherto unheralded founding father of Merseyside football

Although one of the crucial influences in the creation of Everton Football Club, until recently the role of Reverend Ben Swift Chambers, a Methodist minister at St Domingo's Church, has been overlooked. It was his intervention and form of 'muscular Christianity' that first bore the football club in 1878, as an offshoot of the popular parish cricket team he had founded a year earlier. After his death in 1901 he became largely forgotten until new research a century later cast fresh light on his life, times and influence.

Born in Stocksmoor, a hamlet six miles outside Huddersfield, on 30 August 1845, and brought up in nearby Shepley, as a youth Chambers taught at Sunday school. He trained as an apprentice engraver, but aged 22 entered the Methodist ministry. The Methodist circuit saw a journey around the north of England like that of an itinerant footballer: stints in Ashton-under-Lyme, Stockport, Halifax, Barrow, Gateshead and finally, in July 1877, Liverpool, where Chambers, now aged 32, was appointed circuit superintendent and minister of St Domingo Chapel, Everton.

CHAMBERS was an energetic, dedicated minister, concerned with the social welfare of his parishioners. According to one account he possessed 'a powerful and winning personality' and was 'a manly, affectionate, kindly, pleasant, happy, noble being,

eager to serve, anxious to do good, a never-failing friend'. He was keenly involved with the Band of Hope Union, a national anti-temperance society that preached the dangers of drink. This was a popular Victorian concern, with alcohol intrinsically linked in many eyes to violent crime, child neglect and poverty.

Another popular Victorian idea was 'muscular Christianity'. The notion dated back to the 1830s and placed great emphasis on the redemption by physical activity. The origins of football as an organised sport are tied to this concept: public schoolmasters seeking to tire out their unruly pupils introduced medieval versions of football to their curricula. Each school had their own distinct version of the game, but when these pupils left and entered university they wanted to continue playing football. A unified set of rules was needed and thus, in 1863, they were agreed, with a new body – the Football Association – created to govern them.

Chambers, it seems certain, was committed to these ideals. Almost immediately after joining St Domingo's he formed a parish cricket club, which began playing in Oakfield Road over the summer of 1877. The following year the cricket club really took off, and

its enthusiastic members decided it would be worthwhile adopting a winter sport so as to keep fit. Thus, in the autumn of 1878, St Domingo's Football Club began playing in a corner of Stanley Park. Scarcely could Ben Chambers have imagined the force he had just created.

HIS ROLE WITHIN this rapidly evolving sporting club is not recorded, nor what he thought about St Domingo's FC being renamed Everton in 1880. In 1882, after five years in Everton, he left the parish to become superintendent minister of the Southport circuit. Eight years later he returned to Everton for a further four years at St Domingo's church. By then Everton FC were a professional team, competing in the Football League. Chambers would have known many of Everton's leading members, notably George Mahon, who combined duties as St Domingo's organist with leading Everton from Anfield to Goodison Park, and St Domingo's choirmaster, Will Cuff – later Everton's illustrious secretary and chairman.

Chambers left St Domingo's in 1894, and soon after was struck by terminal illness. He fought it for four years, but on 24 November 1901 finally succumbed. He was buried in Shepley, the Yorkshire village where he had grown up.

For more than a century he was consigned to obscurity, meriting barely a footnote in histories of the Merseyside clubs, until the author Peter Lupson tracked him down. Lupson, author of Thank God For Football, a 2006 book

ONE OF THE CRUCIAL INFLUENCES IN THE CREATION OF EVERTON FOOTBALL CLUB

which detailed English clubs' origins as church teams, uncovered Chambers' story and discovered his unkempt grave at Shepley. Lupson campaigned for the Merseyside clubs to restore Chambers' grave and in July 2008, the two clubs' chaplains conducted a joint service of commemoration at Shepley Methodist Church.

'There are few things more important on Merseyside than football,' Sir Philip Carter told the congregation. 'Both Liverpool and Everton have a proud heritage, and the history of our clubs is a source of immense pride to our supporters. To honour a gentleman who was so pivotal to the creation of football in our city is entirely appropriate. Ben Chambers was a visionary and everyone with an interest in football in Merseyside owes him a debt of gratitude.'

See also:
LUPSON, PETER, *Thank God for Football*, Azure, 2006.
LUPSON, PETER, *Everton FC & Liverpool FC: Across The Park*, Common Ground, Trinity Sport Media, 2009.

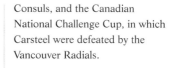

S. CHEDGZOY

Chedgzoy, Sam

Long-serving winger who precipitated a change to the football rule book

It was an incident involving Sam Chedgzoy on 12 April 1924 which led to a quite remarkable and almost immediate change in the laws of football. Chedgzoy had been asked by Ernest 'Bee' Edwards, a local sports reporter, to carry out an experiment during an away game against Tottenham Hotspur. When Everton were awarded a first-half corner Chedgzoy placed the ball by the corner flag and waited for the attacking players to line up in anticipation for his cross. The cross never came as Chedgzoy, to the amazement of his fellow players and fans, proceeded to dribble the ball inside before shooting into the net.

The referee's first inclination was to penalise Chedgzoy's audacity, but at half-time he was persuaded to consult his rule book which showed that he had been incorrect to disallow the goal: it was legal to score from a corner with no mention being made of the taker being restricted to one touch of the ball. The referee's error led to the rule being swiftly amended by the Football Association.

That one incident by no means defined Chedgzoy's name. He was an Everton player for some 15 years and won a League Championship medal in 1915. Although his career was restricted by the war Chedgzoy continued with some brilliance after most of the Championship side had either left or retired.

Born in Ellesmere Port in 1889, for a time he played as an amateur alongside Joe Mercer's father for Burnell Ironworks, where he was spotted by Fred Geary, now working on the Goodison ground staff. He made his Everton debut in the 1910/11 season, although it took this quick, industrious outside right until the latter stages of the 1913/14 season to hold down a regular first-team place.

Many of Everton's 1914/15 Championship winning side faded after the war, but Chedgzoy only seemed to improve with age. During the famous rule-changing encounter with Spurs, his friend 'Bee' reported: 'Chedgzoy has never played better than on this occasion … [scoring] a delightful oblique shot which struck the underside of the cross-bar and into the net … He was here, there and everywhere, showing a command of the ball and accuracy of touch which was at times amazing.'

IN HIS later years at Goodison, Chedgzoy, now aged in his mid-thirties, nurtured a young Dixie Dean – the striker described his fellow Wirraler as 'a great old china' – also supplying many of the crosses for his early Everton goals.

FINALLY, in 1926, Chedgzoy left Everton, immigrating to North America, where he had spent the summer of 1924 coaching the Grenadier Guards team. He joined the New Bedford Whalers of the American Soccer League, making 164 appearances over four seasons. Chedgzoy then returned to Canada, where he had previously coached, joining Montreal Carsteel as player-coach. Here, he became something of a Canadian sports hero: Carsteel were one of the country's best teams, and Chedgzoy continued playing for them well into his forties. Aged 50 he appeared in the 1939 National Soccer League Final, which Carsteel lost to Toronto British Consuls, and the Canadian National Challenge Cup, in which Carsteel were defeated by the Vancouver Radials.

Chedgzoy made eight appearances for England between 1920 and 1924, his last cap against Northern Ireland fittingly won at Goodison Park. His son Sid also joined Everton but never made the first team. Although Chedgzoy visited England regularly in his retirement, Canada became his adopted home and he remained there until his death in 1967. In 1999 Chedgzoy was named one of Everton's 'Millennium Giants' and more recently has been inducted into the Canadian Soccer Hall of Fame.

AN EVERTON STAR FOR SOME 15 YEARS

Season	League		FA Cup		Total	
	App	Goals	App	Goals	App	Goals
1910/11	3	0	0	0	3	0
1911/12	0	0	0	0	0	0
1912/13	1	0	0	0	1	0
1913/14	7	1	0	0	7	1
1914/15	30	2	5	1	35	3
1919/20	18	3	1	0	19	3
1920/21	35	5	5	0	40	5
1921/22	35	5	1	0	36	5
1922/23	36	3	2	1	38	4
1923/24	38	5	2	1	40	6
1924/25	38	2	3	0	41	2
1925/26	38	7	2	0	40	7
Total	279	33	21	3	300	36

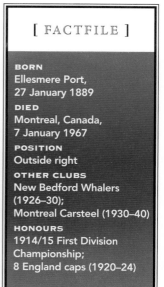

[FACTFILE]

BORN
Ellesmere Port,
27 January 1889
DIED
Montreal, Canada,
7 January 1967
POSITION
Outside right
OTHER CLUBS
New Bedford Whalers
(1926–30);
Montreal Carsteel (1930–40)
HONOURS
1914/15 First Division
Championship;
8 England caps (1920–24)

Clark, Archie

League Championship winning defender whose career spiralled into mysterious decline

[FACTFILE]

BORN
Shoreham, 4 April 1904
DIED
January 1967
POSITION
Centre half
OTHER CLUBS
Brentford (1926);
Arsenal (1927);
Luton Town (1928–30);
Tranmere Rovers (1935–38)
AS MANAGER
Gillingham (1939–58)
HONOURS
1931/32 League
Championship

Season	League		FA Cup		Total	
	App	Goals	App	Goals	App	Goals
1931/32	39	1	1	0	40	1
1932/33	0	0	0	0	0	0
1933/34	0	0	0	0	0	0
1934/35	2	0	0	0	2	0
Total	**41**	**1**	**1**	**0**	**42**	**1**

Clark, Charles

Reserve centre half who went on to enjoy a long career with Plymouth

[FACTFILE]

BORN
1881
POSITION
Right half / centre half
OTHER CLUBS
Plymouth Argyle;
Crystal Palace

Season	League		FA Cup		Total	
	App	Goals	App	Goals	App	Goals
1901/02	3	0	0	0	3	0
1902/03	3	1	1	0	4	1
Total	**6**	**1**	**1**	**0**	**7**	**1**

Clarke, Harold

Winger who enjoyed a solitary season in the Goodison sun

[FACTFILE]

BORN
Walsall, 1875
POSITION
Outside right
OTHER CLUBS
Portsmouth

Season	League		FA Cup		Total	
	App	Goals	App	Goals	App	Goals
1898/99	12	2	0	0	12	2
Total	**12**	**2**	**0**	**0**	**12**	**2**

Clarke, Peter

Commanding England under-21 centre back who enjoyed a distinguished lower-league career

[FACTFILE]

BORN
Southport, 3 January 1982
POSITION
Centre half
OTHER CLUBS
Blackpool (loan, 2002); Port Vale (loan, 2003); Coventry City (loan, 2004); Blackpool (2004–06); Southend United (2006–09); Huddersfield Town (2009–)

Season	League		FA Cup		League Cup		Total	
	App	Goals	App	Goals	App	Goals	App	Goals
2000/01	0 (1)	0	0	0	0	0	0 (1)	1
2001/02	5 (2)	0	3	0	0	0	8 (2)	0
2002/03	0	0	1	0	0	0	1	0
2003/04	1	0	0	0	0 (1)	0	1 (1)	0
Total	**6 (3)**	**0**	**4**	**0**	**0 (1)**	**0**	**10 (4)**	**1**

Clarke,
Wayne

Youngest member of a footballing dynasty, his goals pushed Everton over the line for their ninth League Championship

Signed from Birmingham City for £300,000 in March 1987 as Everton edged towards their ninth League Championship, Clarke was instrumental in the season's run-in, scoring several vital goals that pushed the club towards glory. The youngest of five footballing brothers – the most

> 'I'D GONE FROM BIRMINGHAM TO WINNING THE CHAMPIONSHIP IN THE SPACE OF A FEW MONTHS'

famous of whom was Allan, Leeds and England's goal-poaching talisman in the early 1970s – Clarke was brought in to relieve the striking burden, enforced after injury to Graeme Sharp. Clarke immediately repaid his modest price tag. An outstanding 25-yard lob over Arsenal goalkeeper John Lukic was the only goal of Everton's visit to Highbury and he coolly dispatched a hat-trick against Newcastle United on Easter Monday that put Everton into a virtually unassailable lead at the top of the First Division. A few weeks later Everton were crowned champions, and Clarke, who had spent his early career ambling around the lower reaches of the division with Wolves and Birmingham, was a winner for the first time. 'It probably took a while to sink in,' he told the Evertonian in 2008. 'I'd gone from Birmingham to winning the Championship in the space of a few months.'

FURTHER brushes with glory were not far away. Clarke scored the only goal of the Charity Shield match, against Coventry City at Wembley the following August. Although Everton's 1987/88 season was largely disappointing, his strike against Liverpool in the Goodison derby in March – a cool tap home after Bruce Grobbelaar flapped at a corner – was memorable. Unbeaten since the start of the season, had Everton failed to beat Liverpool it would have seen their rivals surpass Leeds United's record 29-game unbeaten start to a season; a record set in 1974, in part because of the efforts of Clarke's older brother Allan.

With the British record signing of Tony Cottee the following August, opportunities for Clarke were rarer in the 1988/89 season, although he did score a penalty in the 1-1 league draw with Liverpool in December. Disappointed to be left out of the 1989 FA Cup Final squad, he joined Leicester City that summer, a makeweight in the deal that brought Mike Newell to Goodison. Clarke was later reunited with Howard Kendall at Manchester City, before embarking on a lower-league tour in the early 1990s, including a brief spell as Telford United manager. Now living back in his native Midlands, Clarke works as a travelling rep for Coca-Cola.

[FACTFILE]

BORN
Wolverhampton,
28 February 1961
POSITION
Centre forward
OTHER CLUBS
Wolverhampton Wanderers
(1977–84);
Birmingham City (1984–87);
Leicester City (1989–90);
Manchester City (1990–92);
Shrewsbury Town
(loan, 1990);
Stoke City (loan, 1991);
Wolverhampton Wanderers
(loan, 1991);
Walsall (1992–93);
Shrewsbury Town (1993–95)
HONOURS
1987 First Division
Championship

Season	League		FA Cup		League Cup		Other		Total	
	App	Goals	App	Goals	App	Goals	App	Goals	App	Goals
1986/87	10	5	0	0	0	0	0	0	10	5
1987/88	24 (3)	10	1 (6)	0	3 (2)	1	1	1	29(11)	12
1988/89	12 (8)	3	1 (2)	0	0 (1)	0	2	2	15(11)	5
Total	**46(11)**	**18**	**2 (8)**	**0**	**3 (3)**	**1**	**3**	**3**	**54(22)**	**22**

Cleland,
Alec

Everton's first Bosman signing, his Goodison career was hampered by injury

Acquired by Howard Kendall on a Bosman free transfer, scarcely could Alec Cleland have imagined when he agreed to join Everton in spring 1998 that on completing his transfer the following summer he would immediately be reunited with Walter Smith. The right

back's career had long been entwined with Kendall's successor: Smith had coached him as a Dundee United youngster and in 1995 signed him when Rangers manager. And so it came to pass that when he turned up for pre-season training with Everton

in July 1998, Smith had been installed as Goodison boss.

CLELAND started the 1998/99 season as Everton's first-choice right back. A solid if somewhat unremarkable player, Cleland was comfortable in possession and

Season	League		FA Cup		League Cup		Total	
	App	Goals	App	Goals	App	Goals	App	Goals
1998/99	16 (2)	0	1	0	2 (1)	0	19 (3)	0
1999/2000	3 (6)	0	1	0	2	0	6 (6)	0
2000/01	2 (3)	0	0	0	1 (1)	0	3 (4)	0
2001/02	0 (3)	0	0	0	0	0	0 (3)	0
Total	**21(14)**	**0**	**2**	**0**	**5 (2)**	**0**	**28(16)**	**0**

going forward as well as a competent defender, always preferring to jockey an opponent out of possession than dive in with a crunching tackle.

But despite their shared past, Smith never seemed entirely convinced by him, eventually preferring to play an assortment of midfielders and centre halves out of position at right back instead of him. Within months of his arrival he was no more than a squad player and a succession of calf injuries limited his impact in the first years of the new century. Shortly after his contract expired in 2002, Cleland called time on his playing career.

[FACTFILE]

BORN
Glasgow, 10 December 1970
POSITION
Right back
OTHER CLUBS
Dundee United (1987–95);
Rangers (1995–98)

Clements, Dave

Northern Ireland midfielder who simultaneously served his country as manager and Everton as a player

A widely respected player, Dave Clements was a footballer of calm and composure who, in 1975, captained Everton to within a few points of the league title.

After breaking through as a teenage left winger with Portadown in the early 1960s, Clements was scouted by Wolves and signed for them as an 18-year-old in 1963. After failing to make an appearance at Molineux, in 1964 he signed for Coventry City, making the first of 48 Northern Ireland appearances during the 1964/65 season. In 1967 he was an important part of the team that lifted the Second Division title, and he continued to make an impression in the First Division. In 1971 he joined Sheffield Wednesday in a part-exchange deal valued at £100,000. A versatile player who was capable of fitting in at left back, defensive midfield or the left side of midfield, his versatility clearly made him attractive to Billy Bingham, who paid Wednesday £60,000 for him in September 1973.

TALL, MUSCULAR and cultured in possession, Clements played most of his Everton career in defensive roles. For the 1974/75 season he was made club captain as Everton went close to lifting the league title, and was also appointed penalty-taker. An influential and distinguished player, his lack of pace meant he could never quite live up to the illustrious example set by Howard Kendall, who he came to replace. Through the 1975/76 season he was replaced in midfield, usually reverting to left back as Everton lost their way under Bingham.

An erudite and intelligent man, who also captained his country, in March 1975 he replaced Terry Neill as Northern Ireland manager, simultaneously serving as a player.

In February 1976, Clements received a lucrative offer to join up with Pele at New York Cosmos in the NASL. In 1977 he was reputedly interviewed as a successor to Bingham as Everton manager, but the job went to Gordon Lee. His break as a coach came in 1978 when he became player-manager of Colorado Caribous for the only year of its existence. Through the 1980s he coached at Denver Avalanche, St Louis Steamers and Kansas City Comets in the Major Indoor Soccer League.

[FACTFILE]

BORN
Larne, 15 September 1945
POSITION
Midfield / left back
OTHER CLUBS
Portadown (1962–63);
Wolverhampton Wanderers
(1963–64); Coventry City
(1964–71); Sheffield
Wednesday (1971–73); New
York Cosmos (1976);
Colorado Caribous (as
player-manager, 1978)
HONOURS
48 Northern Ireland caps
(1965–76)
(player-manager, 1975–76)

FOR THE 1974/75 SEASON HE WAS MADE CLUB CAPTAIN AS EVERTON WENT CLOSE TO LIFTING THE LEAGUE TITLE, AND WAS ALSO APPOINTED PENALTY-TAKER

Season	League		FA Cup		League Cup		Europe		Total	
	App	Goals	App	Goals	App	Goals	App	Goals	App	Goals
1973/74	31	3	2	1	2	0	-	-	35	4
1974/75	39 (1)	1	4	1	2	0	-	-	45 (1)	2
1975/76	11 (1)	2	0	0	4	0	0 (1)	0	15 (2)	2
Total	81 (2)	6	6	2	8	0	0 (1)	0	95 (3)	8

Clennell, Joe

Inside forward with a knack for scoring opportune goals

Everton's pursuit of inside left Joe Clennell extended for more than three years at the start of the 1910s, but when they finally got their man his impact upon his new club was immediate.

Twice, in November 1910 and March 1911, Everton had been thwarted in their attempts to wrest the talented youngster from Blackpool, who were holding out for around double the £500 Everton put on the table. Clennell joined Blackburn Rovers instead, but after a good start he lost his place to Eddie Latheron. Everton's third attempt to buy Clennell was successful but the price of £1500 was high. He soon started to pay it back. Two minutes into his Everton debut, at home to Aston Villa, Clennell scored; it was his first kick in a blue shirt and evidence that he was a lucky player.

Standing just 5ft 5in tall, the diminutive Clennell was, wrote the Liverpool Echo, 'a popular player, [with] a magnificent fine shot, and an opportunist'. He was the Central League's leading goalscorer at the time of his arrival and hopes were high. He did not let anyone down and earned a reputation for scoring crucial goals at crucial times.

Four goals in 12 games through to the end of the 1913/14 season gave a taste of his talent, but it was the following campaign Clennell made the most telling contribution. Everton lifted the League Championship and his goals were crucial to their success. A hat-trick on the opening day at Tottenham laid a marker and he scored a brace in the 5-0 hammering of Liverpool a month later. But a more crucial strike was to follow: the one that practically sealed Everton's second title.

IN A CLOSE-FOUGHT away game at Manchester City – the penultimate match of the season: 'Parker got in a strong drive, which Smith, with outstretched left arm, was unable to clear, with the result that Clennell, rushing up, met the ball, and it rolled into the net,' reported 'Rover' in the Evening Express. It was the only goal of the game and sent Everton top. Nine days later their title victory was confirmed. Clennell was a regular in the regional leagues during the First World War and scored a phenomenal amount of goals: 128 in 124 games. But when the Football League restarted in 1919 his regular place came under threat and after losing it to Charlie Crossley he moved on, enjoying a lengthy Indian summer in the lower leagues.

[FACTFILE]

BORN
New Silksworth, Sunderland, 19 February 1889
DIED
1965
POSITION
Inside forward
OTHER CLUBS
Blackpool (1901–11);
Blackburn Rovers (1911–13);
Cardiff City (1921–24);
Stoke City (1924–26);
Bristol Rovers (1926–27);
Rochdale (1927)
HONOURS
1914/15 League Championship

Season	League		FA Cup		Total	
	App	Goals	App	Goals	App	Goals
1913/14	12	4	0	0	12	4
1914/15	36	14	5	3	41	17
1919/20	18	12	1	0	19	12
1920/21	1	0	0	0	1	0
1921/22	1	0	0	0	1	0
Total	**68**	**30**	**6**	**3**	**74**	**33**

Clifford, Bob

Versatile defender never quite able to make a first-team place his own

[FACTFILE]

BORN
Rankinston, 12 November 1883
POSITION
Defender
OTHER CLUBS
Bolton Wanderers (1903–08);
South Liverpool; Fulham (1911)

Season	League		FA Cup		Total	
	App	Goals	App	Goals	App	Goals
1908/09	9	0	1	0	10	0
1909/10	23	0	7	0	30	0
1910/11	5	0	0	0	5	0
Total	**37**	**0**	**8**	**0**	**45**	**0**

Clinton, Tommy

Rugged Irish full back infamous for his crucial penalty miss

In March 1948 Tommy Clinton signed for Everton under some of the most unusual circumstances in the club's history. Manager Theo Kelly had been tipped off about the young Irish defender and arranged to meet him to discuss a transfer at Dundalk station. During the meeting, Clinton's train arrived and he signed the papers agreeing to a £2000 move to Goodison from Dundalk through the window of the train as it pulled away.

The right back had been spotted a year earlier by the director, Dick Searle, and after serving an apprenticeship in the Central League was given his debut against Burnley in February 1949. Over seven years with the club he made just 80 appearances, often finding himself overlooked in favour of more polished colleagues.

Alas, the moment for which Clinton is most synonymous marked the nadir of his career. Playing in the 1953 FA Cup semi-final against Bolton Wanderers, Everton were 4-0 down when, minutes before half-time, they were given a glimmer of hope when a penalty was awarded in their favour. Clinton boldly stepped up to take it, but could only send it wide of the Bolton goal. The enormity of his mistake was only realised later, after Everton brought the score back to 4-3 – but could not manage an equaliser. Clinton never seemed to recover from his error and scarcely featured for Everton again.

ALWAYS A PLAYER who relied on his physical strength rather than any great natural ability, Clinton justifiably earned a reputation as a hard man. 'I liked to make contact,' he once said. 'I suppose I was one of those full backs who would have kicked their grandfather over the stand if they had been asked to.'

He played the majority of his Everton career outside the First Division – or during the 1950/51 campaign when the club were careering out of it – but was nevertheless good enough to be picked for his country on three occasions.

Having made just six appearances in the promotion-winning 1953/54 season, when Blackburn Rovers made a £3000 bid for the defender in April 1955, the Everton board accepted it.

The deal was structured so that Blackburn would make £1000 payments for each ten games Clinton played for them up to the £3000 threshold. Clinton, however, played just six games for Rovers before joining Tranmere a year later. Here his career fizzled out and he retired in 1957.

POST-FOOTBALL, Clinton made Liverpool his home, continuing to live in his old club house on Goodison Road and working as a superintendent with the Pioneer Life Assurance company. 'It's a great city,' he said in an interview in 1969, 'and they serve draught Guinness here, so why move?'

	League		FA Cup		Total	
Season	App	Goals	App	Goals	App	Goals
1948/49	4	0	0	0	4	0
1949/50	0	0	0	0	0	0
1950/51	15	0	0	0	15	0
1951/52	26	4	2	0	28	4
1952/53	22	0	5	1	27	1
1953/54	6	0	0	0	6	0
1954/55	0	0	0	0	0	0
Total	73	4	7	1	80	5

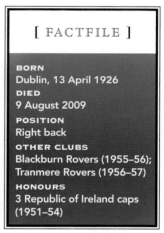

[FACTFILE]

BORN
Dublin, 13 April 1926
DIED
9 August 2009
POSITION
Right back
OTHER CLUBS
Blackburn Rovers (1955–56);
Tranmere Rovers (1956–57)
HONOURS
3 Republic of Ireland caps
(1951–54)

Club Atlético Everton

Uruguayan team that bears Everton's name in tribute to the club's 1909 South American tour

Situated in the small south-eastern city of Rosario, Club Atlético Everton were founded in 1920 by railway workers who were completing the line from the Uruguayan capital, Montevideo. Eleven years earlier Everton FC, while on their groundbreaking tour of South America, had defeated a Uruguayan League XI in the capital, and the name still carried resonance within the country.

A tiny club by comparison to its English and Chilean namesakes, the club serves as a focal point for its local community. It possesses its own bar, indoor sports hall, restaurant area and 'bocha' court (a form of bowls). It has won the local Rosarina League Championship on nine occasions.

IN 2009 the club were visited by members of Ruleteros Society, the organisation formed to promote closer links between Everton FC and its South American cousins. The delegation were guests of honour at Club Atlético Everton's 89th birthday celebrations and exchanged commemorative gifts with club officials.

'It is amazing that, across the three countries that make up the southern cone (Cono Sur) of South America, there should be three clubs named after Everton FC,' recorded Paul Wharton, who travelled with the Ruleteros. 'Especially in the absence of any other British club name in the region (with the exception of Rangers in the Chilean town of Talca); Liverpool in Uruguay was actually named after our fair city.

'All three clubs had shown incredible hospitality to the visiting party – from the terraces to the Board Room... The one thing that united them all was the name "Everton" – all Evertonians following their own particular colour and flavour of the great name.'

Club Everton La Plata

Argentine club which changed its name to honour Everton's 1909 South America tour

Situated in the capital of Buenos Aires Province, La Plata, Club Everton are the oldest club in the city of 570,000 and have lifted the La Plata Championship on nine occasions. Founded in 1905 as '25 de Mayo', four years later the club's members voted to change its name to Club Everton in tribute to the English club. That year Everton and Tottenham had just completed a successful tour of South America, playing the first ever professional games on the continent.

CLUB EVERTON were not the first Buenos Aires team to adopt Everton's name, nor were they the last. There had already been an Everton FC in Buenos Aires, founded in 1906 (the year of Everton's FA Cup Final victory over Newcastle). In 1910, in Escobar, Buenos Aires Province, clubs were named after both Everton and Spurs (the only known example of the latter). These merged to form Escobar FC who again merged in 1912 to form CA Independiente.

In 1910, the town of Alberdi, 200 miles west of Buenos Aires, also founded its own Club Everton. Two years later, Everton from San Jorge, Santa Fé, merged with For Ever to form CA San Jorge, still thriving in the 21st century. In 1914, in Cañada de Gómez, Santa Fe Province, yet another Everton was founded, which today plays under the name of Asociación Deportiva Everton Olimpia.

But it is Club Everton La Plata that has proved most enduring. Since its formation a century ago the club has gone from strength to strength and is at the heart of the local community. Part football club, part community organisation, it provides its 1000 members with access to a range of activities from skating and gymnastics to taekwondo and, of course, football. It possesses three fully floodlit pitches, changing and restaurant facilities as well as a library.

Cock, Jack

Actor and war hero who played up for the Toffees

Few players in Everton history can boast a life less ordinary in the fashion of 1920s centre forward Jack Cock. By the time of his arrival at Goodison, he could already lay claim to being a war hero, big-screen actor, as well as the first Cornishman to play for England.

[FACTFILE]

BORN
Hayle, Cornwall, 14 November 1893
DIED
Kensington, 16 April 1966
POSITION
Centre forward
OTHER CLUBS
Brentford (1914);
Huddersfield Town (1914–19);
Chelsea (1919–23);
Plymouth Argyle (1925–27);
Millwall (1927–30)
AS MANAGER
Millwall (1944–48)
HONOURS
2 England caps (2 goals)
(1919–20)

Born in Hayle in 1893, he made his way through a succession of London amateur clubs before turning out for Second Division Brentford as a 20-year-old amateur, then signing in 1914 for Huddersfield Town. But Cock was one of the generation of players who saw his early career wrecked by the outbreak of the First World War and he wouldn't play league football again until his mid-twenties.

IN THE TRENCHES he served with distinction, rising to the rank of sergeant major and earning the Distinguished Conduct Medal and Military Medal for gallantry. During breaks from war duty he played for Croydon Common and Brentford and when peace resumed his form for Huddersfield in the early part of the 1919/20 season saw him selected for England in a victory international against Wales in October 1919. That same month he joined Chelsea for a club record £2500 and was prolific, scoring 22 goals in 30 games during his first season. His popularity saw him picked for England twice more and he played himself in the 1920 film, The Winning Game.

In January 1923 he joined an Everton team that had struggled for goals since the end of the war. The £2000 fee – with Cock getting a meagre £10 signing-on fee – was deemed good business for such a player. At 5ft 11in tall, Cock was nimble-footed and pacey rather than the centre forward archetype. 'Cock, without doing anything brilliant, was quite satisfactory,' the Daily Post and Mercury reported of his debut against Stoke City. 'He frequently used his head effectively, and his experience in knowing where to place himself for a pass was of considerable help to the inside forwards. He made one splendid solo run in the second half, and instead of doing the obvious, shooting for goal, he placed the ball perfectly in the right wing.'

A WAR HERO, BIG-SCREEN ACTOR, AS WELL AS THE FIRST CORNISHMAN TO PLAY FOR ENGLAND

Everton won that game 4-0, with Cock scoring on his debut. Facing the same opponents a week later they lost 4-1, which exemplified some of the club's problems at the time. Nevertheless the Cornishman scored nine goals in 15 matches in his first months at Goodison, helping them rise from 13th to fifth at the season's end. He missed the early stages of the 1923/24 season because of flu, but after his return was ever-present as Everton once more finished fifth. One observer praised how he 'controlled the younger forwards in nice style. He tells them what to do, when he will pass and how he will pass, and then encourages them to go on with the good work. His generalship counts for something.' Indeed it did. Cock's 23-year-old forward partner, Wilf Chadwick,

Season	League		FA Cup		Total	
	App	Goals	App	Goals	App	Goals
1922/23	15	9	0	0	15	9
1923/24	35	15	2	2	37	17
1924/25	19	5	1	0	20	5
Total	**69**	**29**	**3**	**2**	**72**	**31**

ended the season as the First Division's top goalscorer with 28 league goals.

However, a partnership that had yielded 43 goals in 1923/24 stuttered the next season. Everton scored just six times in the opening ten games and with relegation a threat Cock found himself dropped at Christmas.

He played just twice more for the Blues, his last match the February 1925 derby in which he missed two open goals as Everton fell to a 3-1 defeat. A month later the Everton board accepted a £2100 bid by Third Division Plymouth Argyle for Cock and Fred Forbes. Only three months earlier the club had resisted an offer from Arsenal for the forward, but at

that stage hadn't a replacement lined up. The man they ultimately brought in a week before Cock left turned out to be rather good. His name? Dixie Dean.

AT PLYMOUTH Cock broke scoring records and was sold on to Millwall at a profit in 1927; within a year he helped win the club's first promotion to Division Two. In 1930 he appeared alongside a young Rex Harrison in the film The Great Game and although he had by now dropped out of league football he continued to turn out as a semi-professional until in his late thirties. Later he served as Millwall manager and also ran a pub near its south London home.

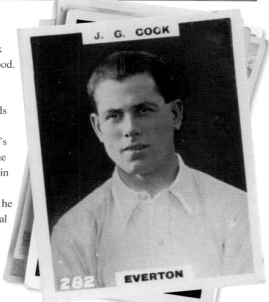

J. G. COCK

282 EVERTON

Coggins,
Billy

Popular custodian who found himself overshadowed by the great Ted Sagar

Signed from Bristol City in March 1930 for £1500, Billy Coggins was brought in to Goodison to help avert a goalkeeping crisis. Arthur Davies had suffered a drop in form and rookie Ted Sagar was not yet deemed ready for the relegation battle in which Everton found themselves embroiled.

COGGINS, whose thick West Country accent saw him marked out by other players as a figure of fun, particularly Dixie Dean, was soon a popular member of the dressing room. His inclusion in the Everton team at the end of the 1929/30 season led to a dramatic upturn in form. Everton won four of their last five games, but it was not enough to lift them from bottom spot and the nightmare of relegation.

Coggins, nevertheless, had done enough to impress the Everton management and was ever-present as Everton lifted the Second Division Championship in record-breaking fashion. There were some lingering doubts, though, about a player who still managed to concede 66 league goals, 17 more than the second-placed team let in. When Everton faced West Bromwich Albion in the FA Cup

semi-final at Old Trafford, Coggins was caught off guard when a cross shot was carried over his head for the game's only goal.

Still, the 1930/31 season was a triumphant one and the high point of Coggins' career. But just days after the season ended, the Everton goalkeeper was rushed to hospital with severe appendicitis. Complications emerged and two months later, with Coggins only just well enough to leave a convalescence home, the Everton board started seeking a replacement for the new season.

Ultimately the board kept faith with Ted Sagar, and so perpetually excellent was he that Coggins played just three further games for Everton.

HIS FATE in the reserve team epitomised the lack of player power in this era. Not until January 1934 was he transfer-listed, and then the Everton directors demanded £1000 or £750 from the likes of Brentford and Chester City. Such sums were beyond the likes of these clubs, and by September 1934, the board resolved to ask Luton Town for £400 – or whatever they would be willing to pay!

Coggins eventually joined Queens Park Rangers and played out his career with Bath City.

[FACTFILE]

BORN
Bristol, 16 September 1901
POSITION
Goalkeeper
OTHER CLUBS
Bristol City (1925–30);
Queens Park Rangers (1935–36)
HONOURS
1930/31 Second Division
Championship

PLAYER'S CIGARETTES.

W. COGGINS.
BRISTOL CITY.

Season	League		FA Cup		Total	
	App	Goals	App	Goals	App	Goals
1929/30	6	0	0	0	6	0
1930/31	42	0	5	0	47	0
1931/32	1	0	0	0	1	0
1932/33	0	0	0	0	0	0
1933/34	2	0	0	0	2	0
Total	51	0	5	0	56	0

Coleman, John 'Tim'

Distinguished forward and defender of players' rights whose goals almost brought Everton the title

Season	League		FA Cup		Total	
	App	Goals	App	Goals	App	Goals
1907/08	13	5	0	0	13	5
1908/09	33	19	2	1	35	20
1909/10	23	5	0	0	23	5
Total	**69**	**29**	**2**	**1**	**71**	**30**

[FACTFILE]

BORN
Kettering, 26 October 1881
DIED
20 November, 1940
POSITION
Forward
OTHER CLUBS
Kettering Town;
Northampton Town
(1901–02);
Woolwich Arsenal (1902–08);
Sunderland (1910–11);
Fulham (1911–14);
Nottingham Forest (1914–15)
HONOURS
1 England cap (1907)

Coleman, Séamus

Gaelic footballer turned emergent international midfield star

In making the transition from top-class Gaelic player to top-class professional association footballer, Séamus Coleman continued a tradition first set by his countryman Val Harris a century earlier. If his entry in an Everton shirt was traumatic – played out of position in a 5-0 mauling in Benfica – his subsequent ascent has been impressive indeed.

Originally a Gaelic footballer, playing to county level in his native Donegal, he was spotted as a 17-year-old and offered the chance to play professional soccer with Sligo Rovers in Ireland's Premier League, earning a salary of €150 per week. Admitting it was a tough choice to turn his back on the sport he had played all his life, his initial plan was to try out soccer and turn back to the Gaelic game if things didn't work out.

But his performances as Sligo Rovers' right back confirmed his all-round pedigree and he was soon attracting the notice of

English scouts. Everton saw off reputed interest from Celtic to sign him for just £60,000 in January 2009.

Initially blooded as a full back, Coleman came into his own on the right side of the Everton midfield where his pace, verve and fearlessness saw him soar past more heralded opponents.

The nightmare of Benfica was swiftly obliterated. In December 2009, making only his second Premier League appearance, he was introduced as a substitute at home to Tottenham Hotspur. With Everton lucky to be trailing just 2-0 nobody had counted on the young novice. Played in down the right on 78 minutes, Coleman cut past Gareth Bale with ease before playing the ball in to Louis

Saha who finished at the near post. On 86 minutes Coleman again found himself in space on the right side of the penalty area. His low cross caused havoc and when Leighton Baines drilled it back in from the right Tim Cahill stooped to equalise. It was quite an introduction to the top flight.

Coleman was subsequently loaned out to Blackpool and played an important part in their successful promotion push, appearing in the 2010 playoff final. His return to Goodison the following season was a success, and his form kept out £8.9million signing Diniyar Bilyatedinov and earned him a nomination for the PFA Young Player of the Year, the first time an Everton player had been short-listed for the award since Wayne Rooney.

He captained Ireland's under-21 team and was called up to the full national squad in October 2010, making his international debut against Wales in February 2011.

His strength and honesty have endeared him to Evertonians and Coleman ascribes them to his roots in the Gaelic game. 'I think some of my Gaelic experience has been useful here,' he told the Guardian in October 2011. 'It's a harder game for a start. If you get pushed you get straight back up. You don't roll around looking at the referee for a free kick and you wouldn't get one if you did in Gaelic. It's a fight – nothing too serious, but it is pure determination and I think I brought that with me here. I just had to play soccer the way I played Gaelic and thankfully it has worked out.'

[FACTFILE]

BORN
Killybegs, Ireland,
11 October 1988
POSITION
Right back / right midfield
OTHER CLUBS
Sligo Rovers (2006–09);
Blackpool (loan, 2010)

Season	League		FA Cup		League Cup		Europe		Total	
	App	Goals	App	Goals	App	Goals	App	Goals	App	Goals
2009/10	0 (3)	0	0 (1)	0	0	0	3	0	3 (4)	0
2010/11	25 (9)	4	4	1	2	1	-	-	31 (9)	6
2011/12	14 (4)	0	2 (2)	0	1 (1)	0	-	-	17 (7)	0
Total	**39 (16)**	**4**	**6 (3)**	**1**	**3 (1)**	**1**	**3**	**0**	**51 (20)**	**6**

Collins, Bobby

Everton's pocket general and saviour

Baby-faced and standing no taller than 5ft 4in, Bobby Collins was a giant in an Everton shirt; an improbable mix of tenacious skill, biting aggression and impish brilliance. Such was his contribution during his first two seasons at Goodison that he can lay claim to saving their First Division lives, and thereafter being the basis of their 1960s revival.

Signed for £24,000 from Celtic in September 1958, Collins' arrival made front-page news on Merseyside. Everton were without a manager following the sacking of Ian Buchan and on a run of six straight defeats. The new boy's impact was immediate: within a day of his arrival he had inspired Everton to their first win of the season, a 3-1 victory over Manchester City. 'First appearances suggest that Collins will be well worth every penny of his transfer fee and although one man may not be the complete answer to Everton's troubles, he can go a great part of the way to restoring Everton's glamour,' was the prescient view of his debut by the Liverpool Football Echo. Two minutes before full time the debutant produced a 'story book finale' with a shot so powerful that it slipped through the goalkeeper's grasp to make it 3-1.

COLLINS, ironically, could have been an Everton player more than a decade earlier. In 1947 he came to Goodison from Scottish junior side Pollock as a raw 16-year-old but left just weeks later, complaining of home-sickness. Upset at losing such a promising young star, Everton complained to the Scottish FA and Collins had to serve a six-week ban as punishment for his indecision. Back in Scotland he joined Celtic and won a glut of honours for his boyhood club. Gradually disenchanted by life in Glasgow, he requested a transfer and Everton came in almost immediately.

Short, stocky, ferocious in the tackle, Collins never stopped running or shouting at and encouraging his team-mates. He was dubbed the 'Little General' and 'Pocket Napoleon' and when Johnny Carey was made manager a month after his return to Goodison, he was quick to recognise that Collins' mere presence on the pitch inspired his fellow players and made him captain. Amid a team short on confidence, Collins continually demanded the ball, driving Everton forward and bringing his colleagues into play. He was a prolific goalscorer too, and finished the 1959/60 season top scorer with 14, a total he bettered by three goals the following year. For a couple of years Collins seemed to be the fulcrum of everything positive at Goodison.

If Collins was Everton's saviour in these first days at Goodison, the inside forward fully blossomed with the arrivals of Alex Young and Roy Vernon in 1960. Under Carey's watch, Everton's attacking football was considered among the best in the club's history and Collins – with his unusual brand of tenacity and skill – flourished. Yet Everton's problems rested in defence and a title challenge in 1960/61 faltered mid-season amid lapses at the back. Nothing Collins could do could save Carey, not even a hat trick in a 5-1 drubbing of Cardiff City in April – Carey's final match as Everton manager.

His replacement, Harry Catterick, brought with him his own ideas and unpredictable ruthlessness. In March 1962 he sold Collins, now aged 31, to Leeds United for £30,000, bringing in Dennis Stevens from Bolton as his replacement. This would be the first of several significant transfers that Catterick would make in the teeth of supporter opinion, but Collins remained phlegmatic about his departure. 'I couldn't have been that good,' he quipped in later life, 'because they won the league the next season!'

THERE REMAINS an indisputable sense that Collins was allowed to leave Everton too early. At Don Revie's Leeds he enjoyed a prolonged Indian summer, helping transform a side perilously close to relegation to the Third Division into one that was unlucky to miss out on a League and FA Cup double in 1965 – the year he collected the Football Writers' Association Player of the Year award.

Collins was unsentimental on his returns to Goodison, meting out the same ferociousness that had once been his hallmark in an Everton shirt. In November 1964 he was part of the Leeds team that partook in the infamous 'Battle of Goodison', when the two teams were led off the pitch for a cooling-off period. 'We came back out and Everton were even harder,' Collins would recall. 'People talk about that game, but the following January we met them in the Cup and it was even worse than the original match.'

After five years' distinguished service at Elland Road, Collins was allowed to join Bury on a free transfer in 1967. There were subsequent spells in Australia and for Morton and Oldham Athletic before he finally hung up his boots aged 42. Managerial spells at Huddersfield Town, Hull City and Barnsley were all destined to end in failure.

Despite such all-round brilliance in a playing career which spanned a quarter of a century and more than 600 games, Collins' football philosophy remained simple: 'I went out and tried to be the best,' he would say – and more often than not he succeeded in achieving just that.

Further reading:
SAFFER, DAVID, *Bobby Collins: Scotland's Mighty Atom,* NPI Media, 2004

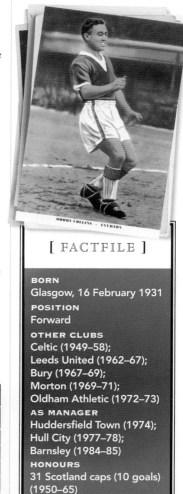

[**FACTFILE**]

BORN
Glasgow, 16 February 1931
POSITION
Forward
OTHER CLUBS
Celtic (1949–58);
Leeds United (1962–67);
Bury (1967–69);
Morton (1969–71);
Oldham Athletic (1972–73)
AS MANAGER
Huddersfield Town (1974);
Hull City (1977–78);
Barnsley (1984–85)
HONOURS
31 Scotland caps (10 goals)
(1950–65)

Season	League		FA Cup		League Cup		Total	
	App	Goals	App	Goals	App	Goals	App	Goals
1958/59	32	7	4	3	-	-	36	10
1959/60	42	14	1	0	-	-	43	14
1960/61	40	16	1	0	5	1	46	17
1961/62	19	5	3	2	-	-	22	7
Total	**133**	**42**	**9**	**5**	**5**	**1**	**147**	**48**

Collins, Harry

Irish goalkeeper with the briefest Goodison career

Season	League		FA Cup		Total	
	App	Goals	App	Goals	App	Goals
1905/06	3	0	0	0	3	0
Total	3	0	0	0	3	0

Collins, John (b.1870)

Left back whose Everton career traversed the infamous 'split' of 1892

Season	League		FA Cup		Total	
	App	Goals	App	Goals	App	Goals
1891/92	6	0	0	0	6	0
1892/93	9	0	0	0	9	0
Total	15	0	0	0	15	0

Collins, John (b.1968)

Scottish international midfielder of considerable repute, his time at Goodison was underwhelming

With the advent of the Bosman ruling during the 1995/96 season – allowing the freedom of movement for out of contract players – for a period it looked as though Celtic's elegant midfielder, John Collins, might become Everton's first Bosman 'free' at the end of that season. In the event he plumped for AS Monaco, but Goodison only had to wait a further two years to see Collins pull on an Everton shirt – signed, as he was, for £2.5million in July 1998.

He arrived on Merseyside having played at the World Cup in France that summer – he drilled home a penalty against holders Brazil in the tournament's opening match – and with his reputation enhanced after two years in the French league, the first of which saw him lift the Ligue 1 trophy. A small, tough midfielder, cultured and skilful, it was hoped that Collins would be the creative lynchpin of a team bolstered by several expensive summer signings.

ON HIS debut, at home to Aston Villa, he missed a penalty – a dark hint of the disappointments which were to follow. Put simply, Collins didn't look up to the pace of the Premiership and often seemed ponderous on the ball, with an infuriating propensity to get caught in possession. His play lacked incisiveness and he usually preferred a safe sideways ball than anything more penetrative. At Christmas 1998, he revealed he had been playing since the World Cup with a broken toe and when that was operated upon in the New Year he missed the remainder of the season.

Hopes that this had held him back dissipated when he returned at the start of the 1999/2000 season without a discernible upturn in form, and it was only the following spring, when he claimed the captain's armband from Don Hutchison, that Goodison saw him at his best. Suddenly he seemed galvanised and in the closing stages of the season hinted at the calibre of player Evertonians thought had arrived two years earlier.

Despite reaffirming his commitment to Everton, with the appointment of former Monaco manager Jean Tigana as Fulham boss, Collins suddenly got itchy feet, and after agitating for a move left for Craven Cottage for £2.5million that summer. He helped Fulham to promotion to the Premiership in the 2000/01 season, but seemed no more able to stamp his authority on the top flight with them than he had with Everton. When his contract expired in 2003 he retired from playing, aged 35, later turning to management with Hibernian.

Season	League		FA Cup		League Cup		Total	
	App	Goals	App	Goals	App	Goals	App	Goals
1998/99	19(1)	1	0	0	2(2)	1	21(3)	2
1999/2000	33(2)	2	4	0	1	0	38(2)	2
Total	52(3)	3	4	0	3(2)	1	59(5)	4

Common, Ted

Reserve full back whose brief Goodison career coincided with a royal blue slump

Season	League		FA Cup		Total	
	App	Goals	App	Goals	App	Goals
1928/29	10	0	0	0	10	0
1929/30	4	0	0	0	4	0
Total	14	0	0	0	14	0

[FACTFILE]

BORN
Seaton Delaval, 25 January 1901
DIED
1958
POSITION
Full back
OTHER CLUBS
Blyth Spartans;
Preston North End (1933);
Chester City (1935–38)

Connolly, John

Scottish winger who failed to fulfil early promise

So highly did Harry Catterick rate John Connolly, a dashing 21-year-old winger, that he left his sick bed, where he was recovering from a heart attack, to complete the Scot's £75,000 signing from St Johnstone.

It was March 1972 and the Everton manager was seeking to rebuild the League Championship winning side of two years earlier, which had since suffered a dramatic loss of form. Connolly was slated as a replacement for Johnny Morrissey, who was nearing the end of his lengthy Goodison career. Through the troubled 1972/73 season, in which he was almost ever-present, playing more games than any of his colleagues, Connolly was virtually the only bright spot as Catterick's reign fizzled out to its disappointing end. 'Connolly was really playing well and had scored some great goals,' recorded George Orr in his diary of the era, Singing the Blues.

WIRY, exceptionally quick and on his day an electrifying presence, Connolly harked back to the era of great Scottish wingers. Like Joe Harper, Connolly was one of the most highly rated young footballers in Scotland but similarly struggled to consistently replicate his north of the border form in England. At St Johnstone he possessed an extraordinary goalscoring record, scoring nearly a goal every other game. At Goodison such feats were harder to replicate, although his form was nevertheless good enough to win him a solitary Scotland cap in 1973.

Entering a team in transition, he struggled to consistently maintain his form, and his confidence diminished after Catterick's departure. Billy Bingham utilised him in the first half of the 1973/74 season, but then preferred George Telfer. After regaining his place at the start of the next season he suffered an appalling broken leg in an FA Cup tie against Altrincham in January 1975 and dropped out of a team challenging

for the title. After a year on the sidelines he made his return for the disappointing run-in to the 1975/76 season. But as Bingham sought to rejig his resources the following summer, Connolly was deemed expendable and sold to Birmingham City for £75,000. There followed spells with Newcastle United and Hibernian, but the bountiful potential once shown in his youth was never quite realised.

On his retirement there were brief spells in management. Most recently Connolly was working for a player scouting agency.

> 'CONNOLLY WAS REALLY PLAYING WELL AND HAD SCORED SOME GREAT GOALS'

[FACTFILE]

BORN
Glasgow, 13 June 1950
POSITION
Winger
OTHER CLUBS
St Johnstone (1967–72);
Birmingham City (1976–78);
Newcastle United (1978–80);
Hibernian (1980–82)
AS MANAGER
Queen of the South (2000–04);
St Johnstone (2004–05)
HONOURS
1 Scotland cap (1973)

Season	League		FA Cup		League Cup		Europe		Total	
	App	Goals	App	Goals	App	Goals	App	Goals	App	Goals
1971/72	2	0	0	0	0	0	-	-	2	0
1972/73	41	7	2	0	1	0	-	-	44	7
1973/74	26	5	0	0	1	0	-	-	27	5
1974/75	22 (2)	3	1	0	2	0	-	-	25 (2)	3
1975/76	14 (1)	1	0 (1)	0	0	0	0	0	14 (2)	1
Total	105 (3)	16	3 (1)	0	4	0	0	0	112 (4)	16

Cook, Billy

Right back who reigned supreme through the era of Dean and Lawton

Everton's signing of Irish international full back Billy Cook on the last day of 1932 simultaneously represented both a major transfer shock and coup. In leaving Glasgow Celtic it was the first time in its history the Scottish club had lost an established player mid-season. For Everton it meant they had acquired one of the best defenders in Britain.

Born in Coleraine, Cook had been plucked from the anonymity of junior football by Celtic in February 1930 and plunged straight into action for the Glaswegian giants, making his debut within a week of signing. It was soon clear that Celtic had a major talent on its hands. In his first full season he won the Scottish Cup and the following year, in September 1932, he made his international debut for Ireland against Scotland at Windsor Park. Scouts had started to come in their droves, and when Everton sent up their former player, Hunter Hart, to watch him he reported back to the Everton board 'that he was the best two-footed back he had seen for years'. Everton immediately dispatched their secretary to Scotland with powers to sign him for up to £4000. Everton got him for £3000.

Everton immediately pitched him into the New Year's Eve league match against West Bromwich Albion. Everton lost 2-1 and the local newspapers were critical. 'Stork', in the Liverpool Post and Mercury, claimed Cook was played out of position on the right. 'His kicking with his left foot was prodigious and sure,' he wrote. 'His tackling was keen, and as time goes on he will realise that speed is an essential in English football.' It was a theme 'Pilot' picked up on in the Evening Express. He believed Cook's arrival did not solve Everton's 'full back problem'. He wrote: 'His display against West Bromwich showed conclusively that he is a natural left back, and not a right back … His left foot kicking was magnificent, but rarely did he trust his right to punting. It was the same with tackling. When Cook cut across to the Albion right flank his interception was good, but when he had to make a right hand tackle he was inclined to turn his back to

his man and content himself with sliding the ball into touch.'

The unfortunate Cook had been an Everton player a matter of hours when such hasty judgements were wired to newsdesks. But by the time Everton played Leicester City in the FA Cup third round a few weeks later, 'Bee' in the Liverpool Post and Mercury reported how he improved in front of his eyes: 'Cook played better the longer the game progressed, and finally he did many clever things to make one forget the daring he displayed when in the first half he back-heeled a ball, although he was in his own penalty area.'

EVERTON beat Leicester 3-2 at Filbert Street and there was growing momentum behind the FA Cup run as the club sought to overcome a disappointing league campaign. Before FA Cup matches the team would be secreted in the spa town of Buxton as they made their preparations. Bury were seen off 3-1 in the fourth round and Leeds 2-0 in the fifth. In the quarter-finals Luton were cannon fodder, beaten 6-0, and West Ham were edged out 2-1 in the semi-finals.

It set up a final versus Manchester City, but Cook had a more pressing engagement and had to leave the training camp days before the final. He returned to Scotland to see his wife and newborn baby daughter for the first time before returning to Derbyshire and the Everton training base.

HE was by now a firm favourite and an ever-present since his arrival. Of one match in the run-up to the final, the previously dismissive 'Pilot' wrote: 'the big man of the game was Cook, the Everton right back. His sparkling, tenacious work roused the crowd and constituted the one bright spot in the display.' Before the FA Cup Final he added: 'They are thinking of entering him for the Grand National next year as he will go through anything. Besides negotiating a "Brook" will be his special Wembley task.'

The Brook in question was City's exquisite outside left, Eric. Cook entirely subdued him and Everton were 3-0 winners. He had outdone even the meteoric start to his Celtic career by becoming a cup winner in less than six months.

Standing just 5ft 7in tall, but weighing 11¼ stone, Cook was short and robust. Double-footed and endlessly enthusiastic, he was the sort of pocket hard man fans love and opposing supporters loathe. Contemporary accounts of his play suggest that he was like a prototype Stuart Pearce. 'Though he took some time to settle down in the English style he has now developed into one of the best backs in the League,' wrote one correspondent. 'Tackles and kicks with great gusto, and he thoroughly enjoys his game.'

Cook was a leader among a team of strong characters and would succeed Dixie Dean as captain in 1937. After his own training duties he drilled the youngsters with customary relish. 'He was a hard man. He would give you a kick at times,' the youth team goalkeeper Fred Roberts told the Denbighshire Free Press as an octogenarian in 2011. 'He said: "Right, Ginger. Show me what you can do!"'

Jock Thomson succeeded Cook as captain ahead of the 1938/39 season, but he was the senior

Season	League		FA Cup		Total	
	App	Goals	App	Goals	App	Goals
1932/33	20	0	6	0	26	0
1933/34	35	0	1	0	36	0
1934/35	29	0	5	0	34	0
1935/36	25	0	1	0	26	0
1936/37	41	0	4	0	45	0
1937/38	35	0	2	0	37	0
1938/39	40	5	5	1	45	6
Total	**225**	**5**	**24**	**1**	**249**	**6**

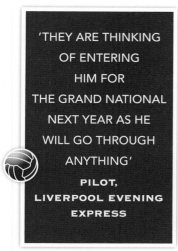

Cook, George

Itinerant defender who made a solitary Blues appearance

Season	League		FA Cup		Total	
	App	Goals	App	Goals	App	Goals
1930/31	1	0	0	0	1	0
Total	**1**	**0**	**0**	**0**	**1**	**0**

[FACTFILE]

BORN
Shankhouse,
20 November 1904
POSITION
Full back
OTHER CLUBS
Gillingham (1924);
Preston North End (1924–25)
Torquay United (1927);
Carlisle United (1928);
Sittingbourne;
Tranmere Rovers (1931);
Carlisle United (1932)

player when injury deprived his fellow full back of captaining Everton to their fifth title the following April. Then war intervened and changed everything. Cook was stationed in India and when league football returned he was nearing his 38th birthday. He played briefly for Wrexham before embarking on a managerial career that took in all points from Bergen to Baghdad, Lima and Wigan.

[FACTFILE]

BORN
Coleraine, 20 January 1909
DIED
Liverpool,
11 December 1992
POSITION
Right back
OTHER CLUBS
Celtic (1930–32);
Wrexham (1945–46)
AS MANAGER
SK Brann Bergen (1947 &
1949–51); Peru (1952–53);
Portadown (1954–55); Iraq
(1955–56); Wigan Athletic
(1956–57)
HONOURS
1933 FA Cup; 1938/39
League Championship;
15 Ireland Caps (1932–39)

Cooke, Henry Edward (Harry)

Inspirational player turned trainer whose career spanned more than 50 years

With his perpetually half-finished cigarette hanging out the corner of his mouth and his iodine-soaked rag, Harry Cooke was one of the most recognisable figures at Goodison through the first half of the 20th century. His association with the club spanned roles as player, trainer, mentor, coach and scout, and for generations of Everton teams he was, quite literally, 12th man. Smartly kitted out in a three-piece suit, he appeared on most team photographs from the 1920s onwards. On match days he was a constant presence, fag invariably in hand, bucket and sponge at his feet; a man who had, in the words of David France, 'developed his own therapeutic massage treatment involving a propriety blend of iodine and wayward cigarette ash'.

Cooke's association with Everton began in the first years of the 20th century as a reserve forward who was utilised occasionally in the first team during the 1905/06 season. Of his debut in the FA Cup second round against Chesterfield, the Liverpool Courier reported: 'Cooke made a creditable debut, as partner to Sharp, who, despite one particularly bad miss was by far the most conspicuous forward on the field.' He was, another report noted later in the season, a 'thorough trier' but with men such as Sharp, Sandy Young, Jimmy Settle and George Wilson ahead of him, establishing a regular first-team role was always going to be challenging and his first-team career began and ended in 1906.

COOKE continued playing for the reserves but in August 1908 a board minute records: 'The temporary engagement of H. Cooke as assistant trainer at 25/- per week was confirmed.' Thus began in earnest one of the most remarkable associations in the club's history.

In an era before a proper team manager and long before the concept of sports science, tactics, advanced physiotherapy or any other concepts we would consider essential parts of modern football, it is difficult to emphasise the importance of someone like Cooke. In his rudimentary way he encompassed all of these roles and many more.

The stories about him are legion, but his most famous association was with Dixie Dean, whom he nurtured back from multiple injuries. In his career he was to undergo 15 operations and Cooke would preserve bits of Dean's bone in jam-jars and thrust them under the noses of new

recruits, saying, 'That's what it takes to be a real player!' Ahead of Everton's famous match with Arsenal in May 1928, with Dean needing a hat-trick to beat George Camsell's scoring record, it was only through the assiduousness of Cooke that Dean was fit to play. Cooke was a constant presence at the forward's side in the week leading up to the match, staying with Dean at his Claughton home. 'Harry was bandaging and putting plasters on my right leg through the week,' remembered Dean.

'He stuck with me right to the morning of the match and we went across to Goodison together.' Dixie, of course, broke the record, but Cooke's part in helping him has usually been overlooked.

Cooke had a good reputation through football and during the 1930s was hired by the FA as trainer and team attendant to an England XI. 'Popular with all and sundry. He lives through every moment of every match and by his encouragement in his quiet way puts an atmosphere in the dressing room,' recorded one contemporary report. He was fixated with Everton and every New Year's Eve would turn up at Goodison to let the New Year in.

EVEN WHEN Everton dispensed with the secretary-manager system and appointed a manager in the modern sense of the word in Cliff Britton, Cooke was retained. He was, recalled the 1950s goalkeeper Jimmy O'Neill, 'the main trainer in those days' and 'a character in his own right'. He recalled in Three Sides of the Mersey: 'Anybody who ever had an operation, a cartilage out, or a bone out of his knee, or a bone out of his ankle, Harry used to keep all these bones in glass jam-jars. He used to preserve all these bones. I think he had a piece of Dixie's skull.'

Brian Labone recalled: 'When I joined in 1957, Harry must have been about 75 then, and he used to have this dirty old cloth, and he just used to rub your leg. Whatever was wrong with you, he just used to rub your leg with oil and stuff. He had this dirty old cloth which hadn't seen soap and water, I don't know, since Dixie Dean's day perhaps, and, after he'd rubbed your leg down, your

leg would break out in a rash or something a few days later. That's how basic it was in those days.'

While Cooke may sometimes seem like a caricature from football's past, his value to Everton was recognised. After Everton won the 1931/32 League Championship, 'Pilot' in the Liverpool Evening Express filed the headline 'WHAT GOODISON OWES TO HARRY COOKE'. He wrote: 'This is a tribute to Harry Cooke the Everton trainer, who has been one of the vital factors in Everton's championship success. It is Harry Cooke's fifth season as Everton trainer, and during that time the club has won the First Division twice; the Second Division once, and reached the semi-final of the FA Cup. He is conscientious in his work, and nothing is too much trouble for him, he has made a special study of each player, so that he knows just what each man requires to attain and maintain fitness. All the players appreciate what Harry Cooke, who first played for Everton in 1906, has done for them. In praising Everton, let us not forget that hard worker.'

COOKE continued to serve Everton through the managerial reigns of Britton, Ian Buchan and Johnny Carey. The arrival of Harry Catterick in April 1961, however, signalled the end of an association that spanned nearly 60 years. In June that year the board resolved that Cooke be retired on a pension of £5 per week.

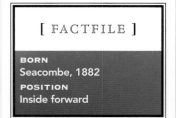

[FACTFILE]

BORN
Seacombe, 1882
POSITION
Inside forward

	League		FA Cup		Total	
Season	App	Goals	App	Goals	App	Goals
1905/06	7	3	2	0	9	3
Total	7	3	2	0	9	3

Corr, Peter

Irish international winger who struggled to hold down a regular place during dark days

[FACTFILE]

BORN
Dundalk, 23 June 1923
DIED
Goosnargh, 1 June 2001
POSITION
Outside right
OTHER CLUBS
Dundalk (1939–47);
Preston North End (1947–48)
Bangor City (1949–52);
Wigan Athletic (1952–53)
HONOURS
4 Ireland caps (1949)

	League		FA Cup		Total	
Season	App	Goals	App	Goals	App	Goals
1948/49	10	1	0	0	10	1
1949/50	14	1	0	0	14	1
Total	24	2	0	0	24	2

Corrin, Thomas

Reserve winger who struggled to hold down a regular place during the early 20th century

[FACTFILE]

BORN
1880
POSITION
Outside left
OTHER CLUBS
Portsmouth;
Reading;
Plymouth Argyle;
Millwall Athletic

	League		FA Cup		Total	
Season	App	Goals	App	Goals	App	Goals
1900/01	3	0	0	0	3	0
1901/02	0	0	0	0	0	0
1902/03	0	0	0	0	0	0
1903/04	8	1	1	0	9	1
Total	11	1	1	0	12	1

Costley, James

Outside left who played six games in Everton's debut league season

Season	League		FA Cup		Total	
	App	Goals	App	Goals	App	Goals
1888/89	6	3	-	-	6	3
Total	**6**	**3**	-	-	**6**	**3**

[FACTFILE]

BORN
1862
POSITION
Inside forward
OTHER CLUB
Blackburn Olympic

Cottee, Tony

British record signing who sampled mixed fortunes on Merseyside

Summer 1988 was a time of intense transfer speculation surrounding the hottest property in the First Division. Since making his professional debut in 1983, Tony Cottee had established himself as one of the deadliest young strikers in the league, amassing 92 goals in 212 games for West Ham United, earning an England debut at 21 and the PFA Young Player of the Year award in 1986. Now the young striker saw his future elsewhere and Everton and Arsenal became embroiled in a race for his signature, a battle which Everton ultimately won – though only after spending a British record transfer fee of £2.3million.

'Signing for Arsenal would have been easy for me,' he recalled. 'But coming up to Merseyside and sampling a new culture was an option for me too. Basically I felt that Everton wanted me more than Arsenal.' Though he never said so, it was a decision he would surely come to rue: for while Arsenal won the League Championship twice in the next three seasons, Everton set upon a precipitous decline with Cottee central to many fans' deep-lying frustrations.

With Cottee's price tag and the acquisitions of Pat Nevin, Stuart McCall and Neil McDonald, expectations for the 1988/89 season were higher than ever as Colin Harvey sought to make his mark as manager. The season's opener, against Newcastle United, saw what many, including Cottee, believe was his finest performance in an Everton shirt, in which he plundered a hat-trick. 'I would have thought it was my best performance,' he said in 1995.

'And it was probably the best thing and the worst thing that I ever did. Obviously, it was the best thing because of the performance which I put in, but from an expectation point of view, everyone thought that I could get a hat-trick every game and I felt that I put a lot of pressure on myself.'

SHORT, quick and with an uncanny knack of being in the right place at the right time, Cottee was the archetypal six-yard box predator. Despite his size, he possessed good upper body strength and held his own so long as the ball was played to his feet. His first touch was good, his all-round team play less so.

'BASICALLY I FELT THAT EVERTON WANTED ME MORE THAN ARSENAL'

The following week Cottee scored again, against Coventry City, earning an England recall. In all he made seven appearances for the national team, the first coming in September 1986 against Sweden, the last against Scotland three years later.

YET IT TOOK Cottee a further month to score again for Everton and such inconsistency came to typify his Everton career. Although the pressure of being Britain's most expensive footballer was onerous, his form was – without question – disappointing. Nevertheless, he still finished the season as top scorer in all competitions with 15 goals, despite failing to contribute any to the team's FA Cup run.

In summer 1989 Harvey paid £1.1million for Leicester City's Mike Newell and Cottee spent the early part of the season on the substitutes bench. Within little over a year Britain's first £2million player had become a mere reserve – this in an era when squad rotation was an unknown concept. When Cottee lost his place a second time in January 1990 he demanded a transfer, but after returning to the side hit top form, finishing top scorer with 13 league goals.

Yet despite wanting to leave Everton, no one came in for the striker. A stomach virus kept him out of action in the early part of the 1990/91 season, and when he did regain fitness he lost his place again after the sacking of Colin Harvey, and flitted in and out of the side for the remainder of the season.

He did, however, hit a personal high point in the famous 4-4 draw with Liverpool in February 1991 when he came on as a late substitute and equalised twice. That game restored some confidence and he asked for his name to be removed from the transfer list. He also managed to hold down a regular place for the last eleven league games, scoring seven times. Despite being in and out of the team, by

the season's end he had scored an impressive 22 goals in 29 starts in all competitions – an achievement that should be caveated by the recollection that three of these goals were against Wrexham in the League Cup and a further seven against lesser opposition in the Zenith Data Systems Trophy. Cottee possessed an infuriating tendency to boost his scoring ratio against lower league opposition in cup competitions while going for long periods without a goal in the league. Graeme Sharp later stated that he would get 'very angry' after games in which Everton lost but Cottee scored, for his colleague would consider it 'job done … whereas I was more concerned with the final result'.

AGAIN Cottee found himself out of favour in the 1991/92 campaign; after failing to click with new strike partner Peter Beardsley he found himself dropped and, after a poor showing for the reserves, in the A team at Morecambe for whom his window cleaner was playing! Following the signing of Maurice Johnston and a loss of form (he didn't score at all after the start of December 1991) his time at Everton looked as though it would draw to a disappointing close.

Injury problems curtailed his contribution in the first half of the 1992/93 campaign but the chance to play with Paul Rideout in the latter half of the season saw him finally play alongside the target man he had for so long coveted. With Peter Beardsley's departure at the end of the season the two were given an extended run in the 1993/94 season. As much

as anything Cottee's 16 goals, including hat-tricks against Sheffield United and Swindon Town, saved Everton from relegation.

YET WITH the influx of fresh investment, Mike Walker considered Cottee expendable and in September 1994 used him as bait to sign David Burrows from West Ham, Cottee's former club.

Here he prospered briefly but many Hammers fans saw that he was a shadow of the young tyro they had once adored and expensive foreign signings soon meant that his chances were limited. Aged 31, he moved to Malaysia for a year, but in 1997 returned to England with Martin O'Neill's Leicester City, where as a veteran he enjoyed three productive years, winning the League Cup in 2000: his first honour at the age of 34.

Released by Leicester the following September to join Norwich City for what would be a short spell as player-coach, in 2000/01 Cottee became the first player to play in all four professional divisions in a single season, after a short period as player-manager of Barnet and a couple of appearances for Millwall. On his retirement at the end of that season he turned to media work, and is now a commentator for Sky Sports.

[FACTFILE]

BORN
Plaistow, 11 July 1965
POSITION
Striker
OTHER CLUBS
West Ham (1982–88, 1994–96);
Selangor (Malaysia, 1996–97);
Leicester City (1997–2000);
Birmingham City (loan, 1997);
Norwich City (2000);
Barnet (player-manager, 2000–01);
Millwall (2001)
HONOURS
7 England caps (1986–89),
1986 PFA Young Footballer of the Year

Season	League		FA Cup		League Cup		Europe		Total	
	App	Goals	App	Goals	App	Goals	App	Goals	App	Goals
1988/89	35 (1)	13	8	0	5	2	5	3	53 (1)	18
1989/90	25 (2)	13	3 (2)	2	1 (2)	0	-	-	29 (6)	15
1990/91	20 (9)	10	2 (3)	2	3	4	4 (2)	8	29(14)	24
1991/92	17 (7)	8	1 (1)	0	3 (1)	1	2	1	23 (9)	10
1992/93	25 (1)	12	0	0	2 (1)	1	-	-	27 (2)	13
1993/94	36 (3)	16	2	0	5	3	-	-	43 (3)	19
1994/95	3	0	-	-	-	-	-	-	3	0
Total	**161 (23)**	**72**	**15 (6)**	**4**	**19 (4)**	**11**	**11 (2)**	**12**	**206(35)**	**99**

Coulter, Jackie

Wide man destined for greatness who was cut down by the cruellest of blows

Jackie Coulter was a dazzling Irish winger who played a telling role in one of Goodison's finest games, seeming destined for greatness until his career was savaged by an horrendous injury.

An outstanding flanker of intricate footwork, back-heels and dummies, he was first spotted by an Everton director, Mr J. Fare, in September 1933 playing for Ireland versus Scotland. That he wasn't immediately snapped up was because

of doubts over his size, but the Everton board remained keenly interested, watching him on several occasions before bringing him to Goodison from Belfast Celtic for a fee of £2750 in February the following year.

EVERTON at the time were between two great sides – that which had won back-to-back Second and First Division titles at the start of the decade, and the team which would win the league title again in 1939 – and the board were seeking fresh blood to reinvigorate their charges. Coulter was eased into this transitional team, but soon excited whispers were emanating from his virtuoso appearances for the reserves.

Having made three appearances at the end of 1933/34, he made the outside left position his own from autumn 1934, replacing Jimmy Stein. An extraordinary goal in the home defeat to Manchester City in November had the watching

Ernest 'Bee' Edwards salivating. 'Coulter was out on his own,' he wrote. 'The goalkeeper came out to anticipation of the ball being centred, but Coulter cutely lobbed the ball behind him and into the empty net. It was a brilliantly conceived goal and if Coulter intended to do what he did then he must be given top mark, for only a thinking footballer would have thought of such a plan.'
His greatest moments came during one of Goodison's finest hours, in January 1935. An FA Cup fourth round replay brought Sunderland to Merseyside. Despite playing on a Wednesday afternoon, just short of 60,000 packed Goodison, with many more locked out and casualties reported in the scrum to see the game. People even stood on the roofs of nearby tramcars trying to catch a glimpse of the action. Coulter opened the scoring on 13 minutes: from the left wing he span 180 degrees, losing two markers in an instant. His rasping shot

was parried into the path of Dixie Dean, who couldn't finish, but Coulter did. Eighteen minutes later he doubled the lead from close range before going at Sunderland again, beating five men with one dribble before being dispossessed by a sixth. Sunderland pulled a goal back, but Stevenson made it 3-1 on 74 minutes.

The game, however, was still to burst into greatness. Sunderland pulled a goal back and in the final minute did the unthinkable and equalised. Everton were shattered but Coulter was indomitable, driving home Dean's knockdown two minutes into extra time to complete his hat-trick. His fellow flanker Albert Geldard was in similarly inspired form, adding two more goals as the match finished 6-4 to Everton. 'It was a wonderful

day and one we will never forget as long as we live,' was the view of the watching Will Cuff.

Many tipped Everton to repeat their 1933 FA Cup success. When Coulter scored a brace in the 3-1 fifth round victory those hopes intensified. A new record crowd of 67,696 crammed into Goodison for the quarter-final against Bolton Wanderers. Coulter made the scoresheet, but it was an 83rd-minute consolation in a grim 2-1 defeat. 'Everton were slow moving; uncertain in front of goal, and not at all clean in their methods, while the referee gave Everton the benefit of the doubt about a penalty kick that probably entered none of the minds of the 60,000 spectators,' lamented 'Bee'. Four weeks later, Coulter was struck by personal disaster.

Playing for Ireland against Wales at Wrexham's Racecourse Ground he challenged his Everton team-mate Ben Williams, who was clearing the ball. The men fell in a heap and next thing Williams was seen cradling Coulter in his arms 'like a baby'. The Irishman had fractured his right fibia – an appalling fate for a footballer in a time of primitive healthcare.

Coulter missed all of the 1935/36 season and although he returned to the Everton team for the start of the 1936/37 campaign, much of the old magic proved elusive. He fought for his place in the team, but the selectors eventually favoured Torry Gillick switching from the right flank. Middlesbrough and Bolton both made moves for the showman, but it was from Grimsby Town that

Everton accepted a £1500 offer in October 1937. He joined Chester City the following summer and in 1939 Swansea Town, after a brief spell with Chelmsford. The outbreak of war just weeks later brought that move and his playing career to an unsatisfactory and premature end.

When peace came he worked as a Manchester City scout under his old team-mate Jock Thomson, who was Maine Road manager. Later he returned to his native Belfast, where he found work in a shipyard.

[FACTFILE]

BORN
Whiteabbey, 1912
DIED
Belfast, January 1981
POSITION
Winger
OTHER CLUBS
Belfast Celtic (1929–34);
Grimsby Town (1937–38);
Chester City (1938–39);
Chelmsford City (1939);
Swansea Town (1939–40)
HONOURS
11 Ireland caps (1 goal)
(1933–38)

Season	League		FA Cup		Total	
	App	Goals	App	Goals	App	Goals
1933/34	3	0	0	0	3	0
1934/35	24	11	5	6	29	17
1935/36	0	0	0	0	0	0
1936/37	21	5	3	2	24	7
1937/38	2	0	0	0	2	0
Total	**50**	**16**	**8**	**8**	**58**	**24**

Couper, George

Scottish winger who was unable to hold down a regular first team berth

[FACTFILE]

BORN
1880
POSITION
Outside right
OTHER CLUB
Heart of Midlothian

Season	League		FA Cup		Total	
	App	Goals	App	Goals	App	Goals
1906/07	3	1	0	0	3	1
1907/08	1	0	0	0	1	0
Total	**4**	**1**	**0**	**0**	**4**	**1**

Cox, Walter

Scottish goalkeeper who failed to find favour with the Anfield selectors

[FACTFILE]

BORN
Scotland, 1863
POSITION
Goalkeeper
OTHER CLUBS
Hibernian (1879–86);
Burnley (1888–89);
Nottingham Forest

Season	League		FA Cup		Total	
	App	Goals	App	Goals	App	Goals
1889/90	4	0	0	0	4	0
Total	**4**	**0**	**0**	**0**	**4**	**0**

Coyle, Bernard

Reserve player who made a solitary appearance days before the 1893 FA Cup semi-final

[FACTFILE]

BORN
Unknown
POSITION
Defender

	League		FA Cup		Total	
Season	App	Goals	App	Goals	App	Goals
1892/93	1	0	0	0	1	0
Total	1	0	0	0	1	0

Coyle, Darrin

Ulster defender who gave up football to join the police

[FACTFILE]

BORN
Belfast, 27 March 1965
POSITION
Defender
OTHER CLUBS
Linfield (1982–85 & 1988–91)

	League		FA Cup		League Cup		Other		Total	
Season	App	Goals	App	Goals	App	Goals	App	Goals	App	Goals
1985/86	0	0	0	0	0	0	2	0	2	0
Total	0	0	0	0	0	0	2	0	2	0

Coyne

Mystery man who scored on his Everton debut

[FACTFILE]

BORN
1864
POSITION
Inside forward

	League		FA Cup		Total	
Season	App	Goals	App	Goals	App	Goals
1888/89	2	1	-	-	2	1
Total	2	1	-	-	2	1

Craig, Nathan

Welsh under-21 international midfielder who made a solitary Europa League appearance

[FACTFILE]

BORN
Caernarfon,
25 October 1991
POSITION
Midfielder
OTHER CLUBS
Caernarfon Town (2011–12)
Torquay United (2012–)

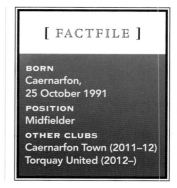

Season	League		FA Cup		League Cup		Other		Total	
	App	Goals	App	Goals	App	Goals	App	Goals	App	Goals
2009/10	0	0	0	0	0	0	1	0	1	0
Total	0	0	0	0	0	0	1	0	1	0

Crelley, Jack

Full back who was part of Everton's first FA Cup winning team

Defender Jack Crelley was one of a handful of local-born players who appeared in the team that won Everton their first FA Cup, in 1906. It marked the highlight of a two-spell Goodison career that initially saw him blooded in the first team as a raw teenager.

That first appearance came in April 1900, but Crelley would have to wait two and a half further years before making an impression in an Everton shirt. The hiatus included a year-long spell with Southern League club Millwall Athletic, but he returned in time for the 1902/03 season and finally got a run in the first XI.

The Liverpool Mercury gave a cautious welcome after his second debut, saying he was 'worthy of a continued trial'. But when Everton played Derby County in November he came up against England's record goalscorer, Steve Bloomer, and was considered to have 'shaped well' against his 'tricky' opponent. Crelley kept his place in the Everton team.

He was a player, according to one correspondent, 'whose tackling was well timed and kicking both clean and well directed'. After a 3-0 home defeat to Sunderland in March 1903, the Mercury wrote: 'Amidst a host of failure, there was one redeeming feature in the display of the Everton team, and that [was] Crelley did give the splendid exhibition at left back. He had the strongest portion of the Sunderland attack to face, and he came out of the ordeal with distinct credit; in fact, on this form there can be no doubt about his claims to a permanent place in the team. His tackling was grand, and this was accomplished not by a mad lunge at the ball or the man, nor by recklessly flinging himself wholesale on to an opponent, but was the result of purely superior skill in dispossessing the forward and coolly placing to one of his own side. His style reminded one forcibly of [George] Molyneux at his best.'

IN 1903/04 Crelley made 30 league and FA Cup appearances, a figure he bettered by two the following campaign. But there was a sense that a first-team shirt was never quite his own and he faced competition for it from the Balmer brothers. He did, nevertheless, see off the younger brother, Robert, to appear in the 1906 FA Cup Final win against Newcastle. A year later Everton returned to Crystal Palace but Robert Balmer had by now largely assumed the left back shirt.

It was the sign of things to come, and after making just three appearances in the 1907/08 season he was transferred to Exeter City.

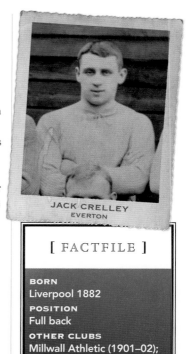

JACK CRELLEY
EVERTON

[FACTFILE]

BORN
Liverpool 1882
POSITION
Full back
OTHER CLUBS
Millwall Athletic (1901–02);
Exeter City
HONOURS
1906 FA Cup

APPEARED IN THE TEAM THAT WON EVERTON THEIR FIRST FA CUP
1906

Season	League		FA Cup		Total	
	App	Goals	App	Goals	App	Goals
1899/1900	1	0	0	0	1	0
1900/01	1	0	0	0	1	0
1902/03	18	0	1	0	19	0
1903/04	29	0	1	0	30	0
1904/05	26	0	6	0	32	0
1905/06	23	0	3	0	26	0
1906/07	15	0	0	0	15	0
1907/08	3	0	0	0	3	0
Total	116	0	11	0	127	0

Cresswell, Warney

Goodison's iceman who was subject of a world record transfer fee

For a period in the 1920s Warneford (Warney) Cresswell held the distinction of being the most expensive footballer in the world. The elegant defender, dubbed the 'Prince of full backs', signed for Everton as he was about to advance into the veteran stage of his career but nevertheless shone for nine years, encompassing more than 300 appearances, and winning every honour available to an inter-war footballer.

W. CRESSWELL

THE ELEGANT DEFENDER WAS DUBBED THE 'PRINCE OF FULL BACKS'

Born and raised in South Tyneside, Cresswell represented South Shields and England Schoolboys as a youngster, but the outbreak of the First World War, when he was aged 17, prevented the onset of his professional football career. He guested for Scottish clubs Morton, Heart of Midlothian and Hibernian, as well as Tottenham Hotspur, during the war and when peace came he signed for South Shields, then of the Second Division. He played just under 100 games for the club before the record transfer to Sunderland in 1922 – the £5500 fee they paid their neighbours beating a record set earlier that year, when the forward Syd Puddefoot left West Ham for Falkirk for £5000.

CRESSWELL was by then an England international and would collect seven caps over the period 1921–29. He came close to winning the league title with an accomplished Sunderland team, which finished third three times as well as runners-up during his time at Roker Park. In February 1927 Everton bid £4900 for the full back in an attempt to plug a defence that would leak 90 goals by the end of the season.

Surprisingly Sunderland accepted and Cresswell – who remained the most expensive player in the world until Bolton's David Jack joined Arsenal for £10,890 the following year – became an Everton player and was appointed captain. His experience and composure helped lift Everton from a relegation battle.

The impact he made on a talented but erratic team has often been overlooked because of Dixie Dean's staggering goalscoring feats during the 1927/28 season. In scoring 60 goals Dean won Everton the League Championship and bought himself footballing immortality. But Everton's defence shipped 24 fewer goals with Cresswell in the side compared to a year earlier. His nickname in Sunderland had been 'the iceberg', because of his cool demeanour when faced by attackers. He was entirely unflappable, repelling opposition attacks and mopping up what others left behind. Always one to favour a timely interception to a desperate lunge, he was soon attracting plaudits.

'Cresswell was the more polished, and at times he seemed to carry his nonchalance to excess,' wrote the Liverpool Post and Mercury of his performance in the first game of the 1927/28 season, against Sheffield Wednesday. 'But he was always quick to recover, and often to the surprise of his opponents.'

In 15 months as an Everton player Cresswell achieved what he had frequently threatened – but never managed – in five years at Roker Park – the League Championship. On awarding the trophy to him in May 1928, League President John McKenna – once an Everton committeeman before the notorious split of 1892 – paid tribute to a team that had been dominated by Dean's goals. 'I need not tell you what a pleasure it is for me to be here to present this cup, this is the third time

Everton have achieved championship honours,' he said from the steps of the Goodison Main Stand. 'The first time was thirty-seven years ago, in 1891. The team that won then were a similar body of experts at their business as the present team and they were the same again because they were gentlemen on and off the field. I congratulate the directors on having such a fine team and also for showing such fine judgement in selecting the players. It is a policy that Everton have always followed to get the best and place them on the field. The team are a credit to the club, a credit to themselves and to the game they play.' Cresswell responded: 'As captain I am proud to receive the cup, it has been a great season, and if all goes well I hope we achieve the self-same honour next season.'

YET EVERTON suffered an alarming decline after their title win. They finished the 1928/29 season 18th and came bottom in the 1929/30 campaign. The slide baffled as much as it hurt but it precipitated one of the most successful periods in the club's history – three trophies in three years: the 1930/31 Division Two title, the League Championship a year later and the 1933 FA Cup.

Cresswell, by now in his mid-thirties, was integral to Everton's renaissance. His 'coolness and methodical football was one of the features', noted one observer of his performances, who added that he helped present 'an almost insurmountable barrier' to his opponents.

THE FA CUP WIN was the crowning glory of a distinguished career, but Cresswell suffered surprising pre-match nerves. As kick-off approached, the mood in the Everton dressing room was one of high excitement and nerves and Cresswell asked to leave the room. According to Will Cuff he asked a police constable if there

EVERTON F.C. - F.A. CUP WINNERS 1933

LEFT TO RIGHT - BACK ROW :- H.F.COOKE (Trainer), BRITTON, CRESSWELL, SAGAR, COOK, WHITE, THOMSON.
FRONT ROW :- GELDARD, DUNN, DEAN, JOHNSON, STEIN, CRITCHLEY.

was a private room where he could smoke before going onto the pitch, 'To settle me nerves, d'ye know, man!' The policeman obliged, Cresswell smoked his pipe and went off to join his team-mates, and was the day's most consummate performer.

'[City inside forward Alec] Herd, tried at centre-forward, ploughing a lonely field and doing best with his head, but being utterly unable to get through the avenue that was "surrounded" by [Tommy] White, Cresswell, and [Billy] Cook,' wrote one Merseyside correspondent. 'City piled on pressure and pace without finality; the more they tried the more they broke their own curbed belief; they ran into the clinches; they were easy prey for two men of direct opposite tastes in defence; Cook the lover of the lusty kick and Cresswell the fine-art dealer who with head and the took all raids as his special pleasure. He shattered them all.'

'Cresswell was the team's steadying influence,' recalled Joe Mercer years later. 'Apparently wise and imperturbable as an owl.'

Everton's board, however, could be entirely ruthless. The next season Everton faded to mediocrity again. A poor performance in an FA Cup third round defeat at Tottenham, in which Cresswell was responsible for a goal, had alarm bells sounding. The Liverpool Post and Mercury correspondent wrote: 'Cresswell battling bravely and at times very cleverly was not always secure.' 'Pilot' writing in the Evening Express went further: 'Everton's dismissal from the F.A. Cup by 3-0 at Tottenham may in time, prove a blessing in disguise. Although it was by no means an inglorious failure, the match showed up weaknesses in the Everton side — weaknesses which have been duly noted by the ruling officials — and I anticipate that immediate action will be taken to

remedy them. I know that the directors have made up their minds to infuse more youth into the League meet tomorrow night some sensational changes may be made. It must not be imagined that the directors are disgusted at the Cup failure. They are not. They think, however, that now is the time to set the Goodison house in order, and even if they fail in their bid to secure new men, especially forwards, I have reason to believe that some youngsters will be given a chance to make a name for themselves.'

These proved prescient words indeed and for the next game, at Sheffield Wednesday, Cresswell lost his place to Ben Williams. Although he regained his place for a period the next season, it marked the beginning of the end for Cresswell at Goodison. Through the 1935/36 season he made just four appearances for the first team and was starting to eye managerial positions. His last games for Everton came in the Liverpool Senior Cup Final against Liverpool, with the clubs sharing the trophy after tying a replay 1-1. 'Williams and Cresswell proved sound and cool and got through a lot of work, rarely putting a foot wrong,' recorded the Post and Mercury.

A month later Cresswell became Port Vale manager. He had already shown his aptitude for spotting fresh talent while at Goodison. In one of his Central League appearances, against Stoke City, he spent the first half being given the run-around by an unknown youngster who had been hugging the Stoke City flank. At half-time, a club director happened to be in the dressing room and Cresswell urged him to snap his opponent up: 'You see this boy. Go and buy him. Sell the Royal Liver Building to get him if you have to – but get him.' The young pretender was Stanley Matthews.

AT PORT VALE, he introduced strict fitness-based training methods and after a year moved to Northampton Town, where he was in charge

until the outbreak of the Second World War. Post-war he drifted into non-league football and when work dried up he returned to his native Northeast, running a Sunderland pub. His son, Corbet Cresswell, was in the Bishop Auckland team that won the FA Vase three years in a row in the 1950s and his great granddaughter, Kate Haywood, is an Olympic swimmer, named BBC Young Sports Personality of the Year in 2003. In 2006 she was a Commonwealth Games silver medallist.

EVERTON 1933
*Back row - **Cooke (Trainer), Britton, Cresswell, Sagar, Cook, White, Thomson***
*Front - **Geldard, Dunn, Dean, Johnson, Stein, Critchley***

[FACTFILE]

BORN
Liverpool 1882
DIED
20 October 1973
POSITION
Right back
OTHER CLUBS
South Shields (1919–22);
Sunderland (1922–26)
AS MANAGER
Port Vale (1936–37);
Northampton Town (1937–39)
HONOURS
League Championship
1927/28, 1931/32;
Second Division
Championship 1930/31;
FA Cup 1933;
7 England caps (1921–29)

Season	League		FA Cup		Total	
	App	Goals	App	Goals	App	Goals
1926/27	15	0	0	0	15	0
1927/28	36	0	2	0	38	0
1928/29	32	1	1	0	33	1
1929/30	30	0	0	0	30	0
1930/31	42	0	5	0	47	0
1931/32	40	0	0	0	40	0
1932/33	41	0	6	0	47	0
1933/34	25	0	1	0	26	0
1934/35	25	0	1	0	26	0
1935/36	4	0	0	0	4	0
Total	**290**	**1**	**16**	**0**	**306**	**1**

Critchley, Ted

Dazzling outside right who became one of the most decorated players in Everton history

The December 1926 signing of Ted Critchley marked the conclusion of a hunt for the outside right that had lasted almost the entire year. Everton's directors hummed and hawed over his acquisition from Stockport County, but Arthur Riley Wade and Jack Sharp – who he had impressed – had the deciding say and £1500 was enough to secure his signature on the same day that Welsh centre half Tom Griffiths joined the club. It was to be a good investment and one that Critchley repaid many times.

The Everton he joined was a club which, despite the presence of William 'Dixie' Dean, was flirting perilously close to the relegation spots. He made his debut on Christmas Day 1926 and impressed immediately in a 5-4 win. 'Forward Critchley was on view for the first time, and the Stockport boy did very well indeed,' reported the Liverpool Echo. 'His one run the full length of the field was something to memorise, but allowing for his over-anxiety, which made him run the ball out. I thought his old mannerisms and passes and centres augur well for the future days.'

> 'THERE WASN'T A BETTER CLUB IN THE COUNTRY TO PLAY FOR THAN EVERTON,' HE REMEMBERED IN HIS LAST INTERVIEW. 'EVERYTHING WAS THE BEST. IT WAS FIRST CLASS ALL THE WAY'

Critchley was a dazzling winger of pace and verve, a man whose breakneck pace could in an instant switch the flow of a game. Interviewed as an old man, he was asked how quick he was. Critchley replied: 'Let's put it this way. I could do half an hour in twenty-five minutes!' He was not without critics among the Goodison faithful, however, who lamented his poor record in front of goal and, occasionally, the quality of his delivery. But he would be vital to Everton, playing his part in numerous successes that would see him number among the most decorated players in club history.

Nobody among his team-mates was better than Dean, the club's talisman and goalscorer extraordinaire. 'Bill was just an ordinary bloke as a person, but his positional play as a footballer was outstanding,' Critchley said in a late-1990s interview with the Stockport County website. 'When I went down the wing to the by-line, you had no need to look for him. He was always in the perfect position for a good centre... I told Bill not to be frightened of heading the lace because I'd always make sure it was on the other side of the ball when I crossed it.'

The team that had struggled through the mid-1920s suddenly gelled in the 1927/28 season. Dean's incredible 60 goals were the foundation point for the title

win, but his fellow forwards – Critchley, Alec Troup, Dick Forshaw and Tony Weldon – would make crucial contributions to his haul and the 102 the team scored between them. 'His record will never be beaten,' said Critchley of the 60 goals, while the League Championship win was, he said, 'the best moment' of his career.

YET EVERTON were baffling inconsistent. Unable to build on their title win they slipped to eighteenth in 1928/29 and were bottom and relegated a year later. Critchley featured heavily in both disappointing seasons but escaped the clear-out that came with the humiliation of relegation.

Indeed the Mancunian was to be one of the key men behind Everton's subsequent renaissance. He played 37 times as Everton lifted the Second Division title, scoring 13 times. He played as many times the following year as he became one of just a handful of players to lift two League Championships with Everton. And yet, recorded the Liverpool Echo, Critchley was a player 'with many critics who never appear to forgive'.

John Peel in the Liverpool Post and Mercury wrote that he believed Critchley was a key component in Everton's title success – a success that saw them

find the net on no fewer than 116 occasions. 'At the present time Everton seem to have adopted the right plan of forward movement, and the part Critchley is playing is a great factor in the scheme,' he wrote. 'For it is a recognised fact that if Dean gets the ball from the wings in a proper way, there is no more dangerous centre-forward in the land. I have always held the view that when Critchley mastered the art of centring the ball in the right way and at the right time he would prove a distinct asset to any club. He seems to have developed in the direction desired, and he has only to maintain such form to reach the pinnacle of his profession.' The Liverpool Courier correspondent added: 'I might add that the [Tommy] White–Critchley wing is one of the best in the land at the moment.'

The Everton board remained hungry for success, however, and were not afraid to bring change. In November 1932 they abruptly halted Critchley's Everton career, bringing in Bradford Park Avenue's boy wonder, Albert Geldard. After six years service Critchley was dropped immediately.

After four months on the sidelines his return, in February 1933, was dramatic. Injury saw Geldard miss the FA Cup quarter-final with Luton Town and Critchley was selected again. Everton won 6-0. Greater dramas came three weeks later in the semi-final against West Ham at Molineux. With the scores balanced at 1-1, Critchley was the man that, in the words of the Liverpool Evening Express's Football Edition 'did the trick'.

'For once [West Ham centre half Jim] Barrett failed,' it reported. 'He delayed his tackle, and Critchley slipped through well inside the penalty area. Critchley feinted to pass to Dean, but cut in between two players and scored with a shot that hit Watson, bounced up over the goalkeeper and a yard over the line.'

'Collins ran into the net and booted the ball out, but it had already counted for Everton, whose players leapt down the field like Indians doing a war dance at their success. There were tremendous scenes of enthusiasm at the finish. Johnson raced for the ball and picked it up, while crowds of Everton supporters rushed on the field to congratulate the players. Dean and Watson shook hands, and had to have a cordon of police, to escort them to the dressing room.'

Dean, interviewed after the match, said: 'This is our dream coming true. I do not think we played quite up to our standard, but West Ham proved themselves a fine enthusiastic side. It is a glorious thing for Everton, and we hope to beat the City in the final.'

THE DEFINING moment of Ted Critchley's Everton career was soon followed by its most disappointing. A twisted knee in a

Central League match against Leeds United left him bed-bound. Although there was speculation he would return for the final, such hopes were over-optimistic. Everton beat Manchester City 3-0 but Critchley was a frustrated figure. 'I had everything that all the other players had, apart from the medal. That was the only thing missing,' he recalled. 'There was nothing I could do about it. I was injured and that was that.'

Geldard increasingly held the favour of the selectors and although Critchley returned for a spell during the 1933/34 campaign, his Everton career was drawing to a close. In 1934 Everton accepted a £2000 bid from Preston North End and he later played for Port Vale. But it was Everton that remained foremost in his affections. 'There wasn't a better club in the country to play for than Everton,' he remembered in his last interview. 'Everything was the best. It was first class all the way.'

[FACTFILE]

BORN
Ashton-under-Lyme,
31 December 1903
POSITION
Right winger
OTHER CLUBS
Stockport County (1922–26);
Preston North End (1934);
Port Vale (1934–35)
HONOURS
League Championship
1927/28 & 1931/32;
Second Division
Championship 1930/31

Season	League		FA Cup		Total	
	App	Goals	App	Goals	App	Goals
1926/27	15	0	0	0	15	0
1927/28	40	6	2	0	42	6
1928/29	25	1	0	0	25	1
1929/30	30	4	2	2	32	6
1930/31	37	13	4	2	41	15
1931/32	37	8	1	0	38	8
1932/33	17	2	2	1	19	3
1933/34	16	3	1	0	17	3
Total	217	37	12	5	229	42

Crompton, Thomas

Centre forward who had the briefest of Goodison careers before slipping into obscurity

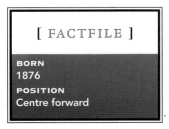

[FACTFILE]

BORN
1876
POSITION
Centre forward

Season	League		FA Cup		Total	
	App	Goals	App	Goals	App	Goals
1898/99	3	1	1	0	4	1
Total	3	1	1	0	4	1

Crossley, Charlie

Forward who rose from amateur ranks to finish top goalscorer during the 1920/21 campaign

Inside forward Charlie Crossley was one of a generation whose career was ravaged by the First World War, but who nevertheless managed to overcome this and enjoy a solid career in both amateur and professional ranks either side of the conflict.

BORN IN a suburb of Birmingham, Crossley initially escaped the notice of Football League clubs, instead forging an amateur career with Hednesford Town in the Birmingham Combination League. In 1913 he joined Walsall, then of the Southern League, and in February 1914, Sunderland. He was a success, despite the war-interrupted years at Roker Park (he was called up for the Royal Navy and worked as a stoker onboard a submarine destroyer), and in February 1920 was called up for an England trial, in which he represented the North versus England. Full honours were nevertheless elusive.

In March 1920, Sunderland offered Crossley to Everton for £2500. A delegation visited the Northeast to watch him, with permission to spend £2000 on his transfer. They came back empty-handed but returned a month later and a £2750 fee was accepted for the forward.

A short, stocky, powerful player, he was described in the local press as a 'deadly shooter' and 'opportunist'. But contemporaneous reports, which tended to favour more natural showmen, were always reticent in their praise.

A REGULAR THROUGH THE 1920/21 SEASON HE FINISHED EVERTON'S TOP SCORER

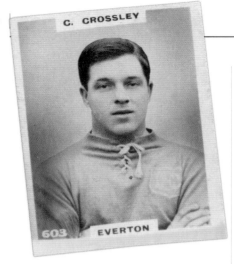

C. CROSSLEY

603 EVERTON

CROSSLEY was a regular through the 1920/21 season, finishing Everton's top scorer. His finest moments came in an FA Cup third round tie at home to Newcastle United in which he scored a brace. Crossley, reported the Daily Post and Mercury, 'was in great form, and his deadly shooting, forceful attack, and wise passes to Harrison made him the outstanding forward'.

Everton showed some promise that season, but lacked the consistency to sustain a title challenge. The following season Everton's weaknesses were more apparent and Crossley found himself overlooked in favour of David Reid and Alec Wall. The signing of Billy Williams from Darwen effectively spelled the end, and in June 1922 he joined West Ham for £1000. He helped the Hammers to promotion in 1922/23, but failed to make the team that appeared against Bolton in Wembley's first FA Cup Final in April 1923. Crossley then joined Swindon Town and in 1925 signed for Ebbw Vale as player-manager. A year later they won the Welsh Cup for the only time in their history.

[FACTFILE]

BORN
Short Heath, 17 December 1891
DIED
Wolverhampton, 29 April 1965
POSITION
Inside forward
OTHER CLUBS
Walsall (1913–14);
Sunderland (1914–21);
West Ham United (1922–23);
Swindon Town (1923–25)

Season	League		FA Cup		Total	
	App	Goals	App	Goals	App	Goals
1920/21	35	15	5	3	40	18
1921/22	15	3	0	0	15	3
Total	**50**	**18**	**5**	**3**	**55**	**21**

Cuff, Will

Everton's last link to St Domingo's, Cuff was a key administrator for Everton and English football

Will Cuff's career at Everton – incorporating numerous roles, including member, director, secretary, reserve-team manager, board member and chairman – spanned the virgin days of St Domingo's, the era of Dixie Dean, and the post-war world, in which attendance records were broken by the week and a creeping – and, to Cuff, unpalatable – commercialism was infiltrating the game.

If George Mahon and Dr James Clement Baxter can be credited with laying the foundations of Goodison Park, it was Cuff who sustained this momentum and forged the modern institution today's Evertonians know. Unlike his fellow founding fathers, Cuff eschewed local politics, but forged a career in football's committee rooms, embarking on a career that would take him to the summit of English football power politics.

CUFF WAS BORN IN LIVERPOOL on 19 August 1868, the son of a prosperous butcher and a Welsh-speaking mother. His father, Henry, was a devoted churchman and later became a trustee of St Domingo Chapel, serving the chapel until his death in

1911. After first living in Byrom Street, Liverpool, they moved to 34 Spellow Lane where Will grew up.

It has been speculated that Cuff played for St Domingo's or Everton in his youth. Nothing confirms this – he would have been too young to play for St Domingo's anyway – but it is known that he was a useful player for Walton Breck FC and Mount FC, where injury forced him to retire.

In 1890 Cuff became a member of Everton FC. He was a friend of George Mahon, St Domingo's organist, while Cuff was its choirmaster. He supported Mahon's stand against John Houlding, which led to Everton's move from Anfield in 1892. Cuff also became a shareholder. In 1894, still aged only 26, he became a director of Everton FC – although this was a position less steeped in prestige than its contemporary equivalent. Directors were expected to serve as match-day stewards, as well as run the club from the boardroom.

In 1901 Cuff was appointed Everton's secretary, (the only paid position in the club's

Will Cuff

management structure). As secretary, as well as the general running of the club, he had a say in team selection and signings, although training was not among his responsibilities. Under his charge Everton lifted the FA Cup in 1906 and won the First Division title in 1914/15, but at other times seemed to be perennial nearly-men. In 1901/02, 1904/05, 1908/09 and 1911/12 they finished league runners-up and lost the 1907 FA Cup Final to Sheffield Wednesday too.

CUFF was a visionary too, and sought to promote Everton beyond Britain. In 1909 he was behind the decision to send Everton on a

South American tour. The most lasting result of this exotic sojourn was the creation of Everton de Chile in Valparaiso.

In 1919 he took a three-year hiatus to concentrate on his successful legal practice, Cuff-Roberts, a Liverpool firm that lived long after his death (it was taken over and incorporated into Halliwells in 2004). In 1922 he returned as Everton chairman, and the Midas touch returned. Dixie Dean was signed in 1925, and Everton won the First Division Championship in 1928 and 1932, and the 1933 FA Cup. Off the pitch, Goodison was redeveloped by the architect Archibald Leitch.

Cuff was highly moralistic and ran Everton according to his personal principles. He would profess that he did not mind defeat so long as the team had played the 'Everton way'. There was an unspoken understanding that Goodison would be the crucible of attractive football. He supported the creation of the Everton Shareholders Association in 1938, seeing it as a vehicle through which the democratic principles envisaged by George Mahon could be protected. 'It existed to further the welfare of Everton and not primarily to fill seats on the board with its own nominees,' he said. 'So long as [it] was satisfied with this, the Association would continue to have his support.' A year later he opposed 'one vote per share', fearing bloc-voting would rest too much power in the hands of wealthy members.

Such inherent decency saw him well liked and seemingly admired by all who encountered him. Dixie Dean referred to him as 'the master', a tribute that seemed to be echoed by all who shared a view about him. In the 1910s the Liverpool magazine Porcupine profiled Cuff, offering a revealing insight into his personality:

EVERTON FOOTBALL CLUB 1904/05

Although a solicitor of the Supreme Court of Judicature, there is nothing in his personality that smacks of the hard and crude fossildom of the typical man of the law ... his breezy temperament carries with it an infectious atmosphere of geniality ... he is one of the men who gets things done, done thoroughly, and yet in such a fashion that the disciplinary machinery seems to run on oiled wheels ...

And yet Will ever 'bobs up' with an unruffled exterior, and in his own electric individuality inspires everyone from Chairman of Directors to message boy with that espirit-de-corps which has, in so large a measure, contributed to the success of the world famed Association football club of which he may justly claim to be the bright particular star.

Cuff served as Everton chairman until the 1938/39 season, when they won their fifth First Division title, and continued to serve on the board of directors for another decade.

In tandem with his career at Everton, Cuff also developed a reputation as one of football's great power brokers. He was an FA vice president and served on the Football League Management Committee from 1925. In 1939 he was made President of the Football League. He used this position to bring gradual change, such as the compulsory numbering of shirts, but was resolutely against other innovations, such as the football pools. One wonders what he would have made of John Moores' later involvement with Everton. Throughout the 1930s Cuff, in his role with the Football League, and Moores, head of Littlewoods Pools, were constantly at odds. Cuff also wanted to retain the competitive ethos that made the Football League so vibrant and was working towards a transfer ceiling of £20,000 at the time of his death.

PERHAPS his most important work for the league came during the Second World War. A generation earlier football emerged from the First World War with its reputation muddied. Football was labelled unpatriotic because it continued until May 1915 while men died in the trenches. Rugby union and cricket, by contrast, had ceased playing virtually immediately. Thanks to the work of Cuff and the FA Secretary, Stanley Rous, football was well prepared this time and plans were hatched long before 1939 to cover the eventuality of war. The Football League season was abandoned as soon as fighting broke out in September 1939, and reorganised into regional leagues. Player contracts were abandoned and players allowed to 'guest' for other clubs. Football provided an important diversion during the privations of war, and was an important fundraising

activity too, with many thousands diverted into war charities.

Cuff was, however, an arch-conservative and many of his ideas were steeped in the days when football was still an amateur sport. At Goodison there was little of the innovativeness that set Arsenal apart on and off the field in the 1920s and 1930s. His unwillingness to countenance the game's developments, such as the football pools, is a reflection of his personality, and in some respects it held Everton and football in general back. By 1935, £800,000 was bet on football pools every week – some 16 times as much as was spent on attending games. In his role at the Football League, Cuff refused to formalise a link between football and gambling, even when a proportion of these vast revenues was offered back to the game by the pools companies. How might English football, and its infrastructure, have been improved by some of these riches? We will never know.

EVERTON were also one of the last clubs to ditch the old-style secretary-manager and by the 1940s the attitude of Theo Kelly, who treated players as mere minions, was utterly outmoded. Indeed it had a disastrous effect, seeing the departures of Tommy Lawton and Joe Mercer, and contributing substantially to Everton's post-war decline. Tactically the unrelenting pursuit of attractive, attacking football, while pleasingly idealistic, was increasingly naive and outmoded as other teams' approaches became more sophisticated.

A CAREER THAT WOULD TAKE HIM TO THE SUMMIT OF ENGLISH FOOTBALL POWER POLITICS

On the other hand the panache and verve that earned Everton the reputation as the 'School of Science' has never died, even during troubled times. Perhaps that, in its way, represents Will Cuff's greatest legacy.

Towards the end of his life, in the mid-1940s, he fell out with his colleagues on the Everton board as a power struggle was played out. While remaining on the board, he joined the shareholders' association and was elected its president. 'They have convinced me that their whole object is the welfare of the Everton club, which in my view has lost a lot of its prestige,' he said. 'I am very sorry to have to say that. It is up to you to regain that prestige and you can count on me to work heart and soul with this object in view. If we are going to fight this conflict, and it is a conflict, we must do it as gentlemen. I want us to have clean hands.'

THINGS QUICKLY turned nasty, with Cuff accused by his enemies of vote rigging as part of a plot to return as chairman. Cuff furiously refuted the insinuations levelled against him. 'It forges the latest link in a chain of insults levelled at me by so-called colleagues during the past seven years.' [i.e. since he had retired as chairman.]

As Everton struggled to come to terms with their place in the post-war football order, finishing their first seasons back 10th and 14th, Cuff spoke of his fears for the club's prospects. 'I am very apprehensive about the future of the Everton club,' he said. 'I consider its prestige has deteriorated considerably in the last few years. It is now up to the shareholders to mend matters. All along my sole interest has been the well-being and welfare of Everton.'

Finally Cuff resigned his directorship at the end of the 1947/48 season, so bitterly opposed was he to the way the club was being run. He was not the only great figure to leave Goodison under a shadow in this time.

His wife of 54 years had died in February 1948 and Cuff spent the last year of his life living in the Holywell Hotel, Parkgate, still taking an interest in FA and Football League affairs and his law firm in Castle Street. But in the winter of 1949, after returning from London where he had helped make the FA Cup draw, he fell ill.

Cuff died on 6 February 1949. His funeral took place in Liverpool four days later and was presided over by the Reverend James Jackson, a former Liverpool player. A mile-long procession followed his cortege to Anfield Cemetery.

'In that later era of aeroplanes and floodlights, Will Cuff would have been an anachronism,' recorded Simon Inglis in his 1988 history of the Football League. 'His death in 1949 coincided with both the peak of an era, and the start of a downward slide that would not be arrested fully until the 1960s. Cuff led the League into the post-war world, but he could not have taken it any further, not in his stiff collar.'

PERHAPS the best reflection of Cuff the man came from one of his enemies. Jimmy Guthrie was captain of Portsmouth's 1939 Cup winning team and leader of the PFA; he was a belligerent character, who devoted much of his life to battling football's bosses. But despite coming up against Cuff time and again – he was, said Guthrie 'a doughty opponent in negotiations' – he conceded that Cuff was 'a great man' for the League. 'We admired him for his fighting qualities,' Guthrie admitted. 'He stood up for what he believed right.'

> THE 'SCHOOL OF SCIENCE' HAS NEVER DIED, EVEN DURING TROUBLED TIMES. PERHAPS THAT, IN ITS WAY, REPRESENTS WILL CUFF'S GREATEST LEGACY

Cummins, George

Irish international forward for whom the scoring touch proved strangely elusive

Season	League		FA Cup		Total	
	App	Goals	App	Goals	App	Goals
1951/52	5	0	0	0	5	0
1952/53	19	0	5	0	24	0
Total	**24**	**0**	**5**	**0**	**29**	**0**

[FACTFILE]

BORN
Dublin, 12 March 1931
DIED
Southport,
29 November 2009
POSITION
Inside forward
OTHER CLUBS
Luton Town (1953–61);
Cambridge City (1961–62);
Hull City (1962–63)
HONOURS
19 Republic of Ireland caps
(5 goals) (1953–61)

Cunliffe, Jimmy 'Nat'

Talented inside forward who earned England honours

But for his more illustrious team-mates, the impact that James 'Nat' Cunliffe made upon the royal blue consciousness might have been considerably greater than the last impression he made during a 16-year Goodison career. Although naturally a centre forward, he spent most of his career partnering William Ralph 'Dixie' Dean and then Tommy Lawton in the inside right position. For an egoist it was a nightmare situation; for a footballer happy to ply his trade wherever he was asked it was perfection.

Cunliffe came to Goodison in 1930 from Aldington FC after quitting his job as an apprentice plater. Following three years in the A and Central League teams, the young Lancastrian finally got his break in spring 1933 when he played two league games against Aston Villa (marking his debut with a goal) and Middlesbrough. The Liverpool Post and Mercury was scathing about his contribution: 'Cunliffe, and [Gordon] Watson, the young men who were "on trial" were lost from the first minute onwards, except when they caused one to look at the programme to find out who had missed an acceptable chance.'

The newspaper's attitude would soon change. In the first months of the 1933/34 season, Everton – with an injury-stricken Dean – were faltering and there were growing calls for Cunliffe to be given a chance. A reserve-team appearance against Preston in early November was characterised by Cunliffe's 'bright display' in which he showed 'confidence and progressive ideas'. A week later he replaced Tommy White as centre forward in the first-team fixture versus Sheffield United and immediately struck a chord.

'The introduction of Cunliffe for Dean and [Ted] Critchley for [Albert] Geldard lent life and pace and a youthful strain to the attack of the Everton side,' reported Ernest 'Bee' Edwards in the Liverpool Post and Mercury. 'Cunliffe did not get a goal because he got under his drives and gave them loft. Yet he played well, and his run through the middle is a thing of danger.' 'Pilot' added in the Evening Express that he 'came through the game with the utmost credit. He was fast and elusive, and revealed good ball control. He was always leading Holmes a merry dance. I admired his willingness to take a shot from all angles and if he can contrive to get over the ball instead of under it when shooting, he will keep goalkeepers busy. That is his fault, judging from this game. Several lightning drives flashed over the top, whereas had he kept over the ball they would have found a resting-place in the net. Still, everyone admires a trier, and Cunliffe did try.'

THE ROOKIE was virtually ever-present, mostly as inside right, through the remainder of the 1933/34 season, scoring nine league goals. But he really thrived when playing alongside Dean, who was largely fit through the duration of the 1934/35 campaign. Cunliffe played in all but three of Everton's league games, scoring 15 times, and adding another two goals in the FA Cup, including the one which set up a famous FA Cup fourth round replay with Sunderland.

HIS FINEST season was the 1935/36 campaign, when he outshone even Dean's scoring exploits and finished Everton's top league goalscorer with 23. Twice he scored four goals in a single match. 'The game between Everton and Stoke City at Goodison Road was a complete triumph for Cunliffe, the Everton inside left, who scored four of the five goals against the one obtained by the Potters,' recorded the Daily Post in November 1935. 'He was in brilliant form, apart from his goals, for he tripped along with the ball at toe to make clever passes, so that the line moved along smoothly and well.

'It was, of course, as a goal scorer that he made his big hit, for each of his goals was a magnificent effort, particularly his third, for it was practically a self-made point from start to finish. He beat a number of Stoke defenders before finally coaxing Lewis out of goal and then turning the ball right away and out of reach of the Stoke custodian. I have never seen Cunliffe so sure with his shooting.' Cunliffe's form that season elevated him to the England team and he won his solitary cap against Belgium in Brussels. But the Everton team to which he contributed so much were in transition, stuck in a limbo between the eras of Dean and Lawton – the latter even briefly supplanting him as inside right. Everton finished the 1936/37 season (the last full campaign with Dean) 15th and the next (the first one with Lawton) just one place better.

CUNLIFFE had been a regular throughout these years, but when the 1938/39 season dawned he suddenly found himself out of favour, with Stan Bentham preferred in his place. He made just seven appearances that year, which was deemed too few to warrant a League Championship winners' medal.

An accomplished crown bowler and a dressing room joker who was described by Joe Mercer as 'the quickest thing on two feet', Cunliffe was a popular figure at Goodison. After the interruption of the war, he was allowed to leave Everton and he played out his career with Rochdale.

	League		FA Cup		Total	
Season	**App**	**Goals**	**App**	**Goals**	**App**	**Goals**
1932/33	2	1	0	0	2	1
1933/34	27	9	1	0	28	9
1934/35	39	15	5	2	44	17
1935/36	37	23	1	0	38	23
1936/37	28	9	4	1	32	10
1937/38	34	13	2	0	36	13
1938/39	7	3	0	0	7	3
Total	**174**	**73**	**13**	**3**	**187**	**76**

[FACTFILE]

BORN
Blackrod, 5 July, 1912
DIED
1986
POSITION
Inside forward
OTHER CLUB
Rochdale (1946–47)
HONOURS
1 England cap (1936)

Curran, Terry

Flamboyant and elusive winger ultimately overshadowed by younger blood

When Howard Kendall sought to revive Everton's flagging form midway through the 1982/83 season he brought in Sheffield United's Terry Curran on loan. Curran, a flamboyant, highly skilful Yorkshireman, was a throwback to the mavericks of a previous generation.

As a rookie in the mid-1970s, he had been among Brian Clough's first acquisitions as Nottingham Forest manager, but since then his career had been that of a journeyman, with five different clubs in the half-decade since he had left the City Ground.

With a dip of his shoulders and a twirl of his feet, he was the sort of player who could meander through opposing defences at will, illuminating even the darkest days of the early 1980s. But acknowledgement of Curran's glorious talent was tempered by the realisation that he could be a frustrating player, prone to over-elaboration, tactical indiscipline and sulking.

WHEN KENDALL brought him into the fold, the loanee immediately impressed, inspiring several wins as Everton's form set on an upward trajectory. Cries of 'sign him up' from the Goodison terraces were heeded as the Everton manager tried to make the deal permanent, but Sheffield United upped their price and Kendall had neither the means nor inclination to meet it.

Curran returned to Yorkshire, but at the season's end a £90,000 deal was struck. On his return to Goodison, however, the winger was constantly beset by injuries, and when fit found himself third

choice on the Everton flank, behind Alan Irvine and Trevor Steven. Through the 1983/84 season he made just eight league starts, and none in either of Everton's cup runs. Everton's glorious title-winning season a year later was watched mostly from the substitutes bench or, more often, the sidelines. At the end of the 1984/85 season, Curran was released and set off on the nomad's trail once more.

> HE WAS THE SORT OF PLAYER WHO COULD MEANDER THROUGH OPPOSING DEFENCES AT WILL

[FACTFILE]

BORN
Kinsley, 20 March 1955
POSITION
Winger
OTHER CLUBS
Doncaster Rovers (1973–75);
Nottingham Forest (1975–76);
Bury (loan, 1977);
Derby County (1977–78);
Southampton (1978–79);
Sheffield Wednesday (1979–82);
Sheffield United (1982–83);
Huddersfield Town (1985–86)
Panionios (1986);
Hull City (1986);
Sunderland (1986);
Grantham Town (1986–87);
Grimsby Town (1987);
Chesterfield (1987–88)

Season	League		FA Cup		League Cup		Europe		Total	
	App	Goals	App	Goals	App	Goals	App	Goals	App	Goals
1982/83	7	1	0	0	0	0	-	-	7	1
1983/84	8	0	0	0	0	0	-	-	8	0
1984/85	4 (4)	0	1	0	0	0	3 (1)	0	8 (5)	0
Total	**19 (4)**	**1**	**1**	**0**	**0**	**0**	**3 (1)**	**0**	**23 (5)**	**1**

THE
EVERTON
·ENCYCLOPEDIA·

Olivier **Dacourt**, Jason **Danskin**, Frank **D'Arcy**, Terry **Darracott**, Willie **Davidson**, George **Davie**, Arthur **Davies**, Dai **Davies**, Jack **Davies**, Joe **Davies**, Simon **Davies**, Stan **Davies**, Harold **Dawson**, William Ralph 'Dixie' **Dean**, Peter **Degn**, Robert **Depledge**, James **Dewar**, Alec **Dick**, Alfred **Dickinson**, Tommy **Dilly**, Sylvain **Distin**, John **Divers**, George **Dobson**, Martin **Dobson**, Jock **Dodds**, **Dogs of War**, Art **Dominy**, John **Donaldson**, Don **Donovan**, Landon **Donovan**, Peter **Dougal**, Dickie **Downs**, Dan **Doyle**, Shane **Duffy**, Royston **Drenthe**, Gordon **Dugdale**, Albert **Dunlop**, Jimmy **Dunn**, Richard **Dunne**, Iain **Durrant**

Dacourt,
Olivier

Supremely talented French international, his best days lay elsewhere

For more than two decades successive Everton managers have grappled with the same issue: finding a midfield dynamo who might prove a worthy successor to Peter Reid. Of all the pretenders to have filled that role, Olivier Dacourt may have come closest to filling the boots of his illustrious predecessor. Certainly he had all the technical attributes – steely determination, an unflinching tackle, a keen eye for a pass (not to mention pace and a good shot – qualities never shared by Reid) – to write his name into Everton lore, and in happier times he may well have done.

After impressing Walter Smith while playing for Strasbourg against Rangers in the UEFA Cup, Everton's new manager made the midfield general one of his first signings in the summer of 1998, paying £3.8million. Displaying a sense of urgency and will to win that was not immediately evident in his team-mates, Dacourt impressed straight away, winning a string of man-of-the-match awards and showing rare pedigree in an otherwise struggling team.

Quickly loved by Evertonians he was, alas, a target for referees and yellow cards came at a rate of one every other game. 'It has got to the stage where the fear of picking up a yellow card has started to affect my game,' he admitted later on in the season. 'In the game at Manchester United, I had to let one of their players go past me as I had already been booked.'

ALTHOUGH EVERTON fought off relegation, Dacourt was one of a few bright lights. Yet as financial troubles beset the club in the summer of 1999, Dacourt, one of the most saleable assets, was among the first to be sold – to RC Lens for £6.5million – in an effort to balance the books.

He returned to the Premiership a year later with Leeds United and spent three injury-hampered years at Elland Road, a period in which he made the step up to the French national team,

before he was again sold, this time to AS Roma, to avert financial problems. In Rome he was a key component in one of Serie A's most formidable powers, before switching to Internazionale in 2006, where he was reunited with Marco Materazzi, winning back-to-back Scudetto in 2007 and 2008.

[FACTFILE]

BORN
Montreuil, France, 25 September 1974
POSITION
Midfielder
OTHER CLUBS
Strasbourg (1992–98);
RC Lens (1999–2000);
Leeds United (2000–03);
AS Roma (2003–06);
Internazionale (2006–09);
Fulham (loan, 2009);
Standard Liege (2009–10)
HONOURS
21 France caps (1 goal) (2001–04)

Season	League		FA Cup		League Cup		Total	
	App	Goals	App	Goals	App	Goals	App	Goals
1998/99	28 (2)	2	2	0	4	1	34 (2)	3
Total	28 (2)	2	2	0	4	1	34 (2)	3

Danskin,
Jason
Young trainee midfielder who failed to make the Goodison grade

[FACTFILE]

BORN
Winsford, 28 December 1967
POSITION
Midfielder
OTHER CLUBS
Mansfield Town (1986–87);
Hartlepool United (loan, 1987–88)

Season	League		FA Cup		League Cup		Europe		Total	
	App	Goals	App	Goals	App	Goals	App	Goals	App	Goals
1984/85	1	0	0	0	0	0	0	0	1	0
Total	1	0	0	0	0	0	0	0	1	0

D'Arcy, Frank

Home-grown full back who never made a first-team shirt his own

EVERTON 1970 CHAMPIONS
Back row - Kendall, Harvey, Whittle, Wright, Brown, Husband, Royle, Morrissey, Newton
Front - Jackson, Kenyon, Catterick (Manager), Dickinson (Director), Labone, Ball, West, Dixon, Hurst, D'Arcy

Season	League		FA Cup		League Cup		Europe		Total	
	App	Goals	App	Goals	App	Goals	App	Goals	App	Goals
1965/66	1	0	0	0	-	-	0	0	1	0
1966/67	0	0	0	0	-	-	0	0	0	0
1967/68	4	0	0	0	0	0	-	-	4	0
1968/69	1 (2)	0	0 (1)	0	0	0	-	-	1 (3)	0
1969/70	0 (5)	0	0	0	0	0	-	-	0 (5)	0
1970/71	2 (1)	0	0	0	0	0	0	0	2 (1)	0
Total	**8 (8)**	**0**	**0 (1)**	**0**	**0**	**0**	**0**	**0**	**8 (9)**	**0**

[FACTFILE]

BORN
Liverpool, 8 December 1946
POSITION
Full back
OTHER CLUBS
Tranmere Rovers (1972–73)

Darracott, Terry

Doughty and long-serving defender and coach

Terry Darracott was one of a select band whose Goodison career dovetailed Everton's two golden eras. As a rookie full back in the late 1960s he was a bit-part player in Harry Catterick's second great Everton team, eventually becoming a stalwart of the following decade. He returned to the club, via a spell in the US and a year at Wrexham, as part of the youth coaching staff in the mid-1980s, later serving as Colin Harvey's assistant.

It was an Everton career that lasted some 18 years – 13 as a player and five as a coach – and yet Darracott never seemed to find a way into Evertonian affections. A boyhood fan, whose commitment and enthusiasm could never be called into question, the response from the terraces was often muted. Later, as Everton's mid-1980s team broke up, Darracott – now assistant manager – was made a scapegoat by some fans for the club's decline. It was a harsh outcome for a dedicated servant, but maybe symptomatic of the fact that he had again come to prominence just as Everton waned.

DARRACOTT made his debut as a 17-year-old apprentice in April 1968, deputising for Ray Wilson as left back. Over the next three years Evertonians caught mere glimpses of the youngster, but when his chance came early in the 1971/72 season he was deputising for the injured Colin Harvey in midfield. For the rest of the decade, he would be like a latter-day Sandy Brown, filling in every position across the back line and also in midfield. In only one season – 1973/74 – was he a guaranteed starter in his favoured right back position.

Wherever he was called upon to play, Darracott did so with passion and bravery. But for fans of a club stuck in Liverpool's shadows it was never quite enough. A rough and ready defender who made up what he lacked in finesse with unstinting dedication to the Everton cause, he was an effective man-marker and occasionally indomitable presence. George Best was one big name he subdued in an early encounter. On another occasion, Darracott's bravery was plain for all to see: after colliding with an opponent he bit through his lip, but played on despite gore foaming from his mouth.

Alas, many Evertonians' memories of the 1970s are defined by the team's shortcomings. Darracott is perhaps best remembered for his part in the calamity of the errors that led to Aston Villa's winner in the 1977 League Cup Final: a Villa cross clipped off Ronnie Goodlass, wrong-footing Darracott – who would ordinarily have cleared easily – and letting in Brian Little to score. It was the cruellest of blows.

> WHEREVER HE WAS CALLED UPON TO PLAY, DARRACOTT DID SO WITH PASSION AND BRAVERY

[FACTFILE]

BORN
6 December 1950
POSITION
Defender
OTHER CLUBS
Tulsa Roughnecks (1979); Wrexham (1979–80)

In 1979 Darracott joined Tulsa Roughnecks in the NASL. He returned to English football with Wrexham, later turning to coaching. After serving Everton in a variety of coaching roles through the 1980s, he became youth coach at Manchester City in 1991, later holding down similar roles at Blackburn Rovers and Bolton. In October 2008 he was appointed assistant manager of Wrexham, a position he held for a year, before he joined Bolton as part of its scouting team led by Colin Harvey.

Season	League		FA Cup		League Cup		Europe		Total	
	App	Goals	App	Goals	App	Goals	App	Goals	App	Goals
1967/68	1	0	0	0	0	0	-	-	1	0
1968/69	1	0	0	0	0	0	-	-	1	0
1969/70	0	0	0	0	0	0	-	-	0	0
1970/71	2	0	0	0	0	0	0	0	2	0
1971/72	16 (1)	0	2	0	1	0	-	-	19 (1)	0
1972/73	11 (5)	0	0	0	0	0	-	-	11 (5)	0
1973/74	36	0	3	0	2	0	-	-	41	0
1974/75	5	0	0	0	0	0	-	-	5	0
1975/76	20	0	1	0	1	0	0 (1)	0	22 (1)	0
1976/77	20 (3)	0	4	0	5	0	-	-	29 (3)	0
1977/78	19 (1)	0	1	0	2	0	-	-	22 (1)	0
1978/79	7	0	1	0	1	0	4	0	13	0
Total	**138(10)**	**0**	**12**	**0**	**12**	**0**	**4 (1)**	**0**	**166(11)**	**0**

Davidson, Willie

Scottish flanker whose wing play almost helped bring the title to Goodison

[FACTFILE]

BORN
Glasgow, 1888
POSITION
Outside left
OTHER CLUBS
Queen's Park; Falkirk; Middlesbrough (1910-11); St Mirren

Season	League		FA Cup		Total	
	App	Goals	App	Goals	App	Goals
1911/12	25	3	4	1	29	0
1912/13	13	0	3	0	16	0
Total	**38**	**3**	**7**	**1**	**45**	**4**

Davie, George

Scottish centre forward who made two outings in Everton's first league season

[FACTFILE]

BORN
Cardross, 19 April 1864
POSITION
Centre forward
OTHER CLUBS
Sunderland; Renton; Woolwich Arsenal

Season	League		FA Cup		Total	
	App	Goals	App	Goals	App	Goals
1888/89	2	0	0	0	2	0
Total	**2**	**0**	**0**	**0**	**2**	**0**

Davies, Arthur

Goalkeeper who played his part in Everton's 1928 League Championship run-in

EVERTON 1928
Back - *T.H.McKintosh, Kelly, Hart (Captain), Davies, O'Donnell, Virr, H.E.Cooke*
Front - *Critchley, Martin, Dean, Cresswell, Weldon, Troup*

Goalkeeper Arthur Davies had dropped out of league football, having previously appeared on the books of New Brighton, when he was picked up by Everton after impressing in a trial match in the summer of 1926. Within months he was making his Everton debut, lining up alongside his fellow Wirralian, Dixie Dean, and within two years he had collected a League Championship winner's medal.

It marked a dramatic turnaround for a player whose career had seemed to be petering out, but Davies impressed from the off in an Everton shirt. His Everton debut came in a goalless draw versus Huddersfield Town in October 1926 and he attracted the notice of the watching Liverpool Post and Mercury correspondent. Under the headline 'DAVIES MAKES GOOD' he reported: 'Davies, who appeared in the Everton goal in place of [Ben Howard-] Baker, inspired confidence by his safe handling of several difficult shots, and early on he made a capital clearance that showed he had a safe pair of hands.'

The new signing supplanted Howard-Baker between the Everton posts and was, according to a contemporary report, 'cool and safe in the Everton goal'. But Everton struggled through the 1926/27 season, eventually finishing 20th, just four points and a place off relegation. The Everton selectors also tried Harry Hardy and Ted Taylor in the Everton goal but without great success.

For the start of the famous 1927/28 campaign the Everton board preferred Taylor, who appeared in most of Everton's first 30 games of the season. But when injury struck him down, Hardy and Davies were picked for the season run-in. A Dean-inspired Everton had propelled the club to the top of the league and with Davies appearing in eight of the last nine games – including the occasion of Dean's 60th league goal – they moved over the finish line as League Champions.

THROUGH the deeply disappointing 1928/29 season, Davies was ever-present but Everton finished 18th. He retained his place for the

EVERTON DIVISION 1 CHAMPIONS 1928

subsequent campaign, but Everton's form failed to pick up and by Christmas they were in the relegation places. At a fateful away match to Arsenal on 8 February, Everton started well but a Davies mistake let in the home side for a goal and it shattered Everton's fragile confidence. 'The air of misfortune spread around the team,' wrote Ernest 'Bee' Edwards in the Liverpool Post and Mercury. 'The players went from good to bad from bad to worse, till finally the visiting side packed up and realised that this was not their day out.' Arsenal won 4-0 and Davies never played for Everton again.

IN AUGUST 1930 Exeter City inquired about taking the goalkeeper on loan. Everton responded that they could have him for £250 and Davies moved south. He played league football for a further decade, also appearing for Southport and Plymouth Argyle, before the Second World War intervened, ending his career.

> WITHIN TWO YEARS OF JOINING EVERTON HE HAD COLLECTED A LEAGUE CHAMPIONSHIP WINNER'S MEDAL

[FACTFILE]

BORN
Wallasey, 3 January 1905
DIED
Plymouth, December 1939
POSITION
Goalkeeper
OTHER CLUBS
New Brighton (1924–25);
Exeter City (1930–35);
Plymouth Argyle (1935–37);
Southport (1937–38);
Plymouth Argyle (1938–39)
HONOURS
1927/28 League Championship

Season	League		FA Cup		Other		Total	
	App	Goals	App	Goals	App	Goals	App	Goals
1926/27	10	0	1	0	-	-	11	0
1927/28	10	0	0	0	-	-	10	0
1928/29	42	0	1	0	1	0	44	0
1929/30	28	0	1	0	-	-	29	0
Total	**90**	**0**	**3**	**0**	**1**	**0**	**94**	**0**

Davies, David (Dai)

Welsh international goalkeeper who never won over the Goodison faithful

In December 1970, Harry Catterick paid Swansea City £20,000 for their promising young goalkeeper, Dai Davies. When he sold Andy Rankin to Watford the following year, it seemed as if Davies was the preferred long-term successor to Gordon West. However, the record-breaking acquisition of David Lawson in summer 1972 seemingly put paid to such hopes and, save for a couple of appearances in spring 1971, Evertonians did not get a glimpse of Davies until September 1974.

A former PE teacher who had forgone the profession to make his way as a footballer with Swansea, Davies was a big, brave goalkeeper and fine shot-stopper. His inclusion in the Everton team near the start of the 1974/75 season coincided with an ultimately unsuccessful league title challenge and the start of a distinguished international career for Davies.

And yet the Welshman never really convinced between the Everton posts. He was prone to frustrating inconsistency – a world-beater one week, erratic the next – that fomented uncertainty among the defence and earned him the unwelcome nickname 'Dai the Drop'. Having been between the posts for most of the 1974/75 season, he lost his place to Lawson at the start of the following campaign and spent most of the next two years alternating with his rival. The signing of George Wood in summer 1977 spelled the end for Davies, who joined Wrexham for £8000 in September that year.

ALWAYS ONE of football's more colourful characters – his autobiography *Hanner Cystal a' Nhad ('Half the Man my Father Was')* was a rare Welsh-language football book, and he was reputedly inducted into a community of druids while still a player – Davies continued to represent Wales until 1982, when he lost his place to Neville Southall. After retiring in 1984 he opened a craft shop in Mold but was called out of retirement in 1985 by Bangor, who utilised his experience against Frederikstad FK and Atletico Madrid in the European Cup Winners' Cup. The following season he rejoined Wrexham, playing in their successful challenge for the Welsh FA Cup as their regular goalkeeper was cup-tied. Davies combines work as a Welsh-language football pundit for S4C with the running of a natural healing centre.

[FACTFILE]

BORN
Ammanford, 1 April 1948
POSITION
Goalkeeper
OTHER CLUBS
Swansea City (1969–70 & 1974, on loan); Wrexham (1977–81); Swansea City (1981–83); Tranmere Rovers (1983–84); Bangor City (1985); Wrexham (1986)
HONOURS
52 Wales caps (1975–82)

Season	League App	League Goals	FA Cup App	FA Cup Goals	League Cup App	League Cup Goals	Europe App	Europe Goals	Total App	Total Goals
1970/71	2	0	0	0	0	0	0	0	2	0
1971/72	0	0	0	0	0	0	-	-	0	0
1972/73	0	0	0	0	0	0	-	-	0	0
1973/74	0	0	0	0	0	0	-	-	0	0
1974/75	35	0	4	0	0	0	-	-	39	0
1975/76	19	0	1	0	2	0	1	0	23	0
1976/77	26	0	0	0	4	0	-	-	30	0
Total	**82**	**0**	**5**	**0**	**6**	**0**	**1**	**0**	**94**	**0**

Davies, Jack

Welsh wing half confined to a solitary appearance in a war-interrupted decade at Goodison

[FACTFILE]

BORN
Holt, 14 November 1916
POSITION
Wing half
OTHER CLUBS
Chester City (1934–37); Plymouth Argyle (1947–48); Bristol City (1948)

Season	League App	League Goals	FA Cup App	FA Cup Goals	Total App	Total Goals
1946/47	1	0	0	0	1	0
Total	**1**	**0**	**0**	**0**	**1**	**0**

Davies, Joe

Welsh international forward who partook in Everton's very first league season

[FACTFILE]

BORN
Chirk, 1870
POSITION
Inside forward / outside right
OTHER CLUBS
Ardwick (1892–93); Sheffield United (1894–95); Ardwick (1895); Millwall Athletic; Reading; Manchester City (1900); Stockport County (1901)
HONOURS
11 Wales caps (1889–1900)

Season	League App	League Goals	FA Cup App	FA Cup Goals	Total App	Total Goals
1888/89	8	2	-	-	8	2
Total	**8**	**2**	**-**	**-**	**8**	**2**

Davies, Simon

Disappointing midfielder whose Goodison career was brought to an early end

Previously linked to a £10million move to Manchester United, where he was once touted as a long-term successor to David Beckham, in May 2005 David Moyes paid £3.5million to bring Simon Davies to Goodison from Tottenham Hotspur. The versatile midfielder, who could play at right wing, wing back or through the centre, had started out at Peterborough United in the late 1990s, before George Graham brought him to White Hart Lane in a double deal with fellow teenage wide man, Matthew Etherington. Hopes that the Welsh international would bring additional pace and creativity to the Everton midfield were soon confounded, however.

Davies had spent his latter years at Spurs in the thrall of injury and this seemed to have diminished the acceleration and dynamism that had previously seen him so highly rated. Only one goal in an Everton shirt points at his lack of potency and it is difficult to recall what he actually brought to a blue shirt. Although David Moyes initially maintained his patience with Davies, his inclusion ahead of the underrated Leon Osman seemed difficult to justify and he was eventually dropped. Chances in the 2006/07 season were limited as Moyes seemed to settle on a successful formation without the need for Davies, and in the following January's transfer window when a £2.5million bid came in from Fulham it seemed like good business for the Everton manager to cut his losses.

[FACTFILE]

BORN
Haverfordwest,
23 October 1979
POSITION
Midfield
OTHER CLUBS
Peterborough United
(1997–2000);
Tottenham Hotspur (2000–05)
Fulham (2007–)
HONOURS
58 Wales caps (6 goals)
(2001–10)

Season	League		FA Cup		League Cup		Europe		Total	
	App	Goals	App	Goals	App	Goals	App	Goals	App	Goals
2005/06	22 (8)	1	1 (1)	0	1	0	3	0	27 (9)	1
2006/07	13 (2)	0	0	0	2	0	-	-	15 (2)	0
Total	35 (10)	1	1 (1)	0	3	0	3	0	42 (11)	1

Davies, Stan

Welsh international forward who failed to make his mark at Goodison

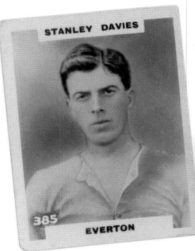

Season	League		FA Cup		Total	
	App	Goals	App	Goals	App	Goals
1920/21	10	4	2	1	12	5
1921/22	10	5	0	0	10	5
Total	20	9	2	1	22	10

[FACTFILE]

BORN
Chirk, 24 March 1898
POSITION
Inside forward/centre forward
OTHER CLUBS
Preston North End (1919–21);
West Bromwich Albion
(1921–27); Birmingham City
(1927–28); Cardiff City
(1928–29); Rotherham United
(1929–30); Barnsley (1930)
HONOURS
18 Wales caps (5 goals)
(1920–30)

Dawson, Harold

Left winger who made cameo appearances during the 1908/09 campaign

Season	League		FA Cup		Total	
	App	Goals	App	Goals	App	Goals
1908/09	4	0	1	0	5	0
Total	4	0	1	0	5	0

[FACTFILE]

BORN
Rossendale, 1884
POSITION
Outside left
OTHER CLUBS
Blackpool (1908–10);
Croydon Common;
West Ham United;
Gillingham

Dean, William Ralph 'Dixie'

The greatest goalscorer in British football history

In football history, few men have ever been so synonymous with the club they played for as William Ralph 'Dixie' Dean and Everton. Just as mention of Pele instantly conjures the name Santos, or Alfredo Di Stefano Real Madrid, so Dean and Everton seem intrinsically linked.

For 13 years, Goodison became 'Dixieland', ruled on and off the pitch by his effusive personality. On it, Dean's goals defined Everton's fate and helped bring them an array of trophies. Off it, Dean the man was – as one colleague remembered – 'bigger and better than life', his extrovert character a colossal presence in the dressing room yet also somehow transcending the traditional barriers that existed between players and fans. Perhaps this was because Dean was both an Everton player and supporter himself.

Schoolboys idolised him. Grown men idolised him. His own team-mates idolised him. Even decades after his death, Evertonians still idolise him – the magnificent statue bearing his likeness is each Saturday transformed into a shrine to the greatest goalscorer football's founding nation has ever seen.

A SCOUSE LEGEND, Dean's roots nevertheless lie on the other side of the River Mersey, in Birkenhead. Born in January 1907, the young Dean quickly emerged as a local footballing

prodigy. The nickname 'Dixie' – which he disliked, preferring to be called Bill – may have originated from his boyhood, when friends dubbed him 'Digsy'. Never the most naturally athletic or tallest of players, he honed incredible shooting power and aerial prowess, and was said to 'hang' in the air awaiting crosses.

From an early age football took all of his spare time, much of which was spent practising his heading. 'When I was 12 or 13 I used to practice by tossing the ball onto a low chapel roof and heading it as it dropped,' he later recounted. 'Once the ball was on the roof it was out of sight and I only had a split second when it came back into vision. I then tried to head the ball into the opposite direction to that which I was running. I got so good that I could hit virtually any square of the net later on!' Dean also possessed a fearsome shot: in one game one of his 'bullets' was said to have broken the goalkeeper's arm.

As a schoolboy he played for an array of teams – Laird Street School, Birkenhead Boys, Parkside, Birkenhead Melville and occasionally Upton Hamlet and Wirral Railways – sometimes playing two or three games on a single day.

Tranmere Rovers signed him in 1923, pitching him in the first team before his 17th birthday. He established himself during the 1924/25 season and was a phenomenon, scoring 27 league goals in 27 appearances. Newcastle and Arsenal were said to be interested in the young star, but for Dixie there was only ever one team: Everton.

The young player's love affair with Everton began as a seven-year-old, when his father, a railwayman, took him to Goodison in its 1914/15 Championship-winning season. From that day he knew his destiny lay at Goodison.

Everton's secretary-manager Tom McIntosh had already seen the teenager perform well on a number of occasions across the Mersey. He recognised that his outstanding ability both in the air and on the ground fitted in with the club's credo (later professed by Will Cuff) that, 'It has always been an unwritten but rigid policy of the board, handed down from one generation of directors to another, that only the classical and stylish type of player should be signed. The kick-and-rush type has never appealed to them.'

EVERTON F.C. - F.A.CUP WINNERS 1933

DIXIE DEAN

In March 1925, Everton paid £3000 for the 18-year-old. As the Daily Post put it: 'He is a natural footballer with a stout heart, a willing pair of feet and a constitution that will stand him in good stead.' At the time of his transfer Dean had scored 27 of Tranmere's 44 goals and they were second bottom of Division Three North.

Everton were faring scarcely better in the top flight, sitting in 20th place, a single position over the two relegation spots. At the campaign's conclusion they had scored only 40 times, conceding 60 and finishing 17th. Dean added two goals to that measly tally in his seven appearances. His debut, a 3-1 defeat at Arsenal on 21 March 1925, passed without him finding the net, although that was soon rectified when he made his Goodison debut against Aston Villa and hammered home the first of his 377 Everton goals, a feat marked by a standing ovation from the Goodison crowd.

Dean began the 1925/26 season in the reserves, missing the first four first-team matches of the campaign. Recalled in mid-September, Dean took a few weeks to settle and then the goals started to flow at a rate that would barely subside through the rest of his Goodison career. His first hat-trick came against Burnley on 17 October 1925 and another a week later at Goodison against Leeds. By the end of the season he

had scored 32 goals in just 38 games and the roar 'Give it to Dixie' came to reverberate around Goodison whenever an Everton attack started. A new star had been born.

Dean was always more than just a goal machine though, and part of his enduring appeal are the stories about him, which on Merseyside are legion. One that persists even decades after his death concerns his mythical heading power. On a motorcycling outing during the 1926 close season Dean was involved in head-on collision with another bike. For 36 hours he lay in a coma, having suffered an appalling array of injuries, including a fractured skull and jaw. Although he made a full recovery, a legend emerged that Dean had had a metal plate inserted into his forehead, enabling him to use his head like a battering ram. The story was nonsense, but since Dean could head the ball as powerfully as some players kicked it, it was unsurprising some fans thought it true.

THIRTY THOUSAND PEOPLE turned out to see Dean's return for the reserves in October. On a sodden pitch, with a heavy ball, any fears of the long-term effects – psychological or physical – were soon forgotten when he powered home a header from a Ted Critchley corner. Thomas Keates marvelled: 'The romance of Dean's recovery and the amazing increase in his skill are psychological, physiological and supernatural occurrences.' During the 1926/27 season Dean scored a further 23 goals

in 30 league and cup appearances, but once more Everton's woeful defence let them down (conceding 94 goals) and they slumped to 20th position, a single place off relegation

'I GOT SO GOOD THAT I COULD HIT VIRTUALLY ANY SQUARE OF THE NET'

At the end of the 1924/25 season, the Football Association had changed the offside law in order to promote attacking play. The number of opponents required between the attacker and goal line was now reduced to two from three.

IT SEEMED a minor alteration, but the impact on the 'goals for' columns was dramatic. In the Football League the number of goals scored rose from 4,700 in 1924/25 to 6,373 the following campaign. As defences struggled to get to grips with the new rule, it was a boom time for strikers. George Camsell was the first major beneficiary, scoring an astonishing 59 goals for Middlesbrough in the Second Division during the 1926/27 season.

Spurred on by Camsell's feats, Dean began the 1927/28 season in mesmerising fashion. By the end of November he had played 15 matches and scored 27 times. His haul included hat-tricks against Portsmouth and Leicester, plus all five when Everton beat Manchester United at the start of October.

By Christmas Everton were top of the Football League and Dean started the New Year with 35 goals. 1928 brought more goals: two against Blackburn on 2 January; another brace against Camsell's Middlesbrough on the seventh.

On 22 January Dean celebrated his 21st birthday and a week later he scored another two goals in the fourth round of the FA Cup against Arsenal, which ended in a 3-4 defeat.

When Everton met Liverpool at Anfield on 25 February his tally stood at 40 goals. Up against his great friend and rival Elisha Scott in the Liverpool goal, he hit a hat-trick, which pulled him level with Ted Harper's First Division record set two years earlier.

> **NO INDIVIDUAL HAS COME WITHIN A SNIFF OF DEAN'S 60-GOAL RECORD**

It took Dean a further month to beat Harper's tally, with a brace against Derby County on 25 March, which sealed a 2-2 draw. Camsell's record, which had been spoken about among Evertonians with confidence just a month earlier, now seemed to be slipping away from Dean.

In the last nine games of the 1927/28 season, Dean needed to score 17 times to attain the magical 60 – and one of those

matches would be missed through international duty. Odds of 10,000–1 against Dean breaking the record were supposedly offered locally but, undeterred, he went back to doing what he did best: scoring. Fourteen goals in seven starts followed. Everton had already lifted the First Division title: to beat Camsell's record all Dixie needed was a hat-trick at Goodison on the last day of the season, 5 May 1928, against the mighty Arsenal. Such feats belonged to the pages of Rover and The Wizard, comic book fantasy. No mortal could possibly manage such feats, could they?

The day got off to a bad start and Goodison was silenced when Arsenal took a 1-0 lead on three minutes. Two minutes later the hush turned to elation as Dean equalised with a typically stupendous header – from outside the Arsenal area. One down, two to go, and on seven minutes Dean made it 2-1 from the penalty spot.

Camsell's record had been equalled, but with almost the entire match remaining Dean struggled to beat it. Chances passed and Arsenal equalised, but still the magical 60th goal would not come. Then on 82 minutes Everton got a corner. Alec Troup, provider of so many of Dixie's goals, swung it in and Dean stooped to head his 60th goal into an empty net.

'You talk about explosions and loud applause,' an ageing Thomas Keates recalled. 'We have heard many explosions and much applause in our loud pilgrimage but believe us, we have never heard before such a prolonged roar of thundering congratulatory applause as that which ascended to heaven when Dixie broke his record.' Dean marked his 60th goal with a simple bow, but Goodison went wild. 'Somebody ran on the pitch and stuck his whiskers in my face and tried to kiss me,' he recalled. 'Well! I'd never seen a supporter run onto the pitch until that day.' He was congratulated by the Arsenal players and the first man to shake his hand was Bill Paterson, the Arsenal goalkeeper. 'I looked at Dean and he seemed shocked,' he remembered. 'I smiled and, God forgive me, I went over and shook hands with him.'

The final minutes of the season were played out amid wild cheering. 'It was the signal for the pantomime dames and gentry to take up their stance,' remembered the watching Will Cuff. 'The crowd raced onto the field, the game appeared as if it would never be restarted. Players leapt into the air; nobody cared a brass farthing for the remaining minutes of the match.'

IN ALL DEAN HAD SCORED in 29 of his 39 First Division appearances – eight singles, 14 doubles, five hat-tricks, a four and a five; 29 at home, 31 away; 40 from shots, 20 from headers. Only West Ham and Sunderland escaped his goals and they each featured in two of the three games Dean didn't play. But just how great was Dean's achievement? There is an idea that defending was far more lax in the 1920s, but actually the notion that defences were uniquely generous pre-war is false. In winning the First Division in 1928 Everton scored 102 goals; but even in the early 1960s such a tally was regularly trumped. As Premier League champions in 2010, Chelsea scored 103 times in just 38 games. Yet no individual has come within a sniff of Dean's 60-goal record.

Modern defending may be more sophisticated, but Dean had to contend with unrestrained violence. As a youngster he lost a testicle after one horror tackle, while the Everton trainer, Harry Cooke, collected pieces of Dean's cartilage from the numerous operations he underwent. Conditions and equipment were rudimentary too. Games were often played on quagmires and the boots Dixie wore are more akin to today's health and safety footwear on building sites.

Aston Villa's 'Pongo' Waring (another Birkenhead boy) came nearest to Dean's 60 with 49 top-flight goals in 1930/31, but nobody else has ever come close. Only Arthur Rowley scored more league goals than Dixie's career total of 379, but while Dean played most of his career in the top flight, only two years of Rowley's career were spent outside the lower leagues.

DEAN went on scoring. He had already made the first of 16 England appearances a year earlier, and would score 18 goals for his country. Staggeringly he only played four more times for his country after the age of 21, the last of these appearances coming in 1932 against Northern Ireland.

For two years after his 60-goal haul, Dean would be troubled by persistent injuries that would ultimately have disastrous consequences for Everton. With his appearances restricted by rheumatism and an ankle operation, Everton finished the 1928/29 season 18th, a position considerably worsened after an alarming run of eight defeats in their last nine games. Despite a stop-start campaign, Dean still managed a highly credible 26 goals from 29 league appearances.

However, the 1929/30 season would be an unmitigated disaster for Everton. An injury-ravaged Dean bagged 25 goals from 27 league and cup appearances, but goals weren't the problem: Everton scored 80, but conceded a disastrous total of 92. They finished the season bottom, albeit just four points off 14th-placed Arsenal, and were relegated for the first time.

When the players reported for pre-season training on 1 August 1930, first there for duty was Dean – an annual custom he maintained throughout his Everton career. It was a sign of intent, and with Everton's maestro

putting his injury problems behind him, few anticipated the stay in football's second tier to be a long one. Unburdened by his injury woes, Dean went on the rampage, scoring 39 goals in 37 matches as Everton lifted the Second Division title, and a further nine in the FA Cup, where they reached the semi-final.

MORE RECORDS came Dean's way. He completed his double-century of goals on 8 November 1930 in only his 207th appearance. He was 23 years, 290 days old – exactly the same age as Jimmy Greaves when he completed the same feat more than 30 years later. He was presented with a commemorative medal and the Daily Post noted: 'It is a fine record considering his comparatively short career. No footballer in history had a record of such consistency in league soccer, or ever will, perhaps.' On the day Dean scored his 200th Everton goal with a brace against Bradford City, Everton were guaranteed promotion back to the top flight.

By then, many people were paying the admission just to see him play and it was reckoned Dean was adding 5,000 onto the average gate. It was known that some fans asked at the turnstile, 'Is he playing?' If the answer were negative then they would go home. One biographer has pondered that if that were the case throughout his Everton career it would have yielded the club an additional total of two million on their gates.

Off the field his pleasures included a pint of beer and a cigarette, which merely added to his appeal. Tales of him drinking ten pints in the Wilnslow pub opposite Goodison the night before scoring a hat-trick are mostly apocryphal, but he remained a man of the

people and was frequently seen socialising with fans. Although easy-going, certain things nevertheless riled Dean. He hated what the German Nazi Party represented, and when Everton visited Dresden on a pre-season tour in 1932, he refused to let his team conduct a Heil Hitler salute in front of a crowd that included Hermann Goering.

Dean became Everton captain for the 1931/32 season and went at First Division defences mercilessly. He scored 45 league goals – the third-highest tally in top-flight history (behind his own record and Pongo Waring's 49) – as Everton romped home to their fourth league title. Dean scored five in the 9-3 win over Sheffield Wednesday on 17 October and again when Everton beat Chelsea 7-2 on 14 November. Comparisons were soon made with the 1927/28 season and whether Dean could break his own amazing record – but this time, despite his staggering tally, the goals were shared.

Amid an inconsistent defence of the league title in 1932/33, solace was found in the FA Cup, the only honour Dean was still to win. He scored in the third round (a 3-2 win over Leicester), the fourth round (Bury, 3-1), fifth round (Leeds, 2-0) and the sixth round (Luton 6-0), but not when Everton met West Ham in the semi-final at Molineux, Ted Critchley and Jimmy Dunn grabbing the goals in a 2-1 victory.

The final – Everton's first appearance at Wembley – was notable for being the first match where players' shirts were officially numbered – Everton wore 1–11; Manchester City 12–22 – so that Dean, doyen of centre forwards, became the original number nine. All afternoon Dean tormented his opponents. As Matt Busby in the City half back line put it: 'To play against Dixie Dean was at once a delight and a nightmare. He was a perfect specimen of an athlete, beautifully proportioned, with immense strength, adept on the ground but with extraordinary skill in the air.' Jimmy Stein opened the scoring shortly before half-time after Dean pressured the City goalkeeper into dropping the ball. Dean scored a second, powering home the ball and goalkeeper from Cliff Britton's centre, and Jimmy Dunn completed the rout ten minutes from the end.

At the age of 25 Dean had now accomplished everything in football. 'I'll never forget going up to the royal box at Wembley to collect the FA Cup,' he recalled. 'I received it off the Duchess of York [the late Queen Mother]. She congratulated me and said it was a very good

game. She really smiled and said she had enjoyed it. That made me feel so proud. I was walking ten feet tall because it meant I had won every honour in the game. That cup medal completed my collection.'

Although he continued to be a formidable force, by his own impossible standards Dean was a declining force after 1933. Injuries persistently blighted him. He made just 12 appearances in 1933/34, as Everton slipped to 14th, but still scored nine goals – including his 300th league goal.

A REVIVED Dean returned for the 1934/35 season and scored 26 goals in 38 appearances as Everton finished 16th. But this was an Everton side in transition, prone to unexpected lapses (as witness the double-header with Sunderland – Everton beating them 6-2 on Christmas Day and losing 0-7 the following day), and never in serious contention for the league.

Dean was again blighted by injury through the 1935/36 season, but still found the net 17 times in 29 appearances. Of lasting consequence to the forward's own prospects was the death of secretary-manager Tom McIntosh in December and his replacement with the machiavellian Theo Kelly. A self-publicising and egotistical man, Kelly's relationship with Dean was destined to failure.

In the short term, a resurgent Dean did not let this impair his goalscoring. He was to grab 24 goals in 36 appearances in 1936/37, passing Steve Bloomer's league scoring record at the start of the season.

DIXIE DEAN

By now Dean had entered the veteran stage of his career. Still aged only 29, although he had retained his instinct in front of goal, he was stockier and slower and injuries had impaired his movement. A long-term replacement in Tommy Lawton had been bought mid-season from Burnley, and although Dean took the young forward under his wing he sensed that Kelly was trying to oust him.

'This chap Kelly had no time for the older lads,' Dean would say. 'I just couldn't get on with him. He was secretary but I didn't care what he was. I knew what was happening. He wanted to get rid of me and also one or two other people who looked like being in with a chance of becoming manager one day.'

Three games into the 1937/38 season, Dean was dropped and Lawton handed the number nine shirt. He was to play just twice more for the first team, his 399th and final game coming at home to Birmingham City on 11 December, 1937. He continued to play for the reserves, eventually winning a Central League Championship medal, but Kelly had cut off any prospect of his returning back to the first team. Dean recalled: 'Kelly started telling lies about me and things got worse. He wanted to have that manager's job and definitely wanted to get rid of me. I could see that. So I had it out with him and decided to move on.'

On 11 March 1938, the unthinkable happened. Dean was sold to Notts County for £3000. Astute as ever, Kelly made certain that Everton recouped the money paid to Tranmere thirteen years earlier. 'I didn't want to leave Everton,' Dean said years later. 'But Kelly was the reason I did leave. It wasn't on account of Tommy Lawton arriving – it was nothing to do with that. That fella Kelly just didn't want me there long.' Disgracefully, though, Everton's greatest ever player was allowed to leave without a farewell or thanks. Perhaps understandably, he did not return to Goodison for many years.

DEAN'S SPELL in Nottingham was brief and not entirely auspicious. He played out his career in Ireland with Sligo Rovers where he won the Irish FA Cup, returning to Britain on the outbreak of the war.

Although one of the most revered players in football history, like most of his contemporaries Dean's extraordinary exploits never made him rich. He earned the statutory maximum basic wage of around £8 a week – worth about £375 in today's money. By contrast, in the same era the baseball player Babe Ruth earned $80,000 each year ($1,000,000 today) – 25 times as much as Dean. On his retirement he ran a Chester pub, the Dublin Packet, but gave it up in 1961. Aged 54, Dean was given a job by the Everton chairman and Littlewoods pools magnate John Moores – but there was no glamour: he was a security guard, then porter in Littlewoods headquarters. Moores, nevertheless, granted Dean Everton's first ever testimonial game in 1964, which raised £10,000.

On 1 March 1980, Dean, along with Bill Shankly, was a guest of the journalist John Keith at a lunch in Liverpool. Keith recalled: 'Shanks stood up and eulogised Dixie, coming out with a wonderful quote, "Dean remains in the company of the supremely great, like Beethoven, Rembrandt and Shakespeare." Dixie actually started to cry.' Afterwards the men reconvened to Goodison, where Keith was covering the Merseyside derby for the Daily Express. It was a bad-tempered match, won 2-1 by Liverpool, but the result was soon forgotten. News had broken that Dean had collapsed with a heart attack during the game and died in Goodison's gymnasium. 'It was an amazing, incredibly poignant day,'

said Keith. 'With Shanks' speech, Dixie had heard his own obituary.'

It was somehow fitting that Dean spent his final moments at Goodison, for being an Evertonian was elemental to his existence. Despite all his goals, it was his pride at being taken to Evertonians' hearts that brought most pleasure. 'I'll never forget the Everton fans for the way they treated me, not only when I was playing but long after I left the club,' he said late in his life. 'I felt that these fans belonged to me and I belonged to them. I was born and bred an Evertonian and I knew I would never change.'

'WITH SHANKS' SPEECH, DIXIE HAD HEARD HIS OWN OBITUARY'

As to the 60 goals, even at the end of his life Dean was adamant that the record was beatable. 'People ask me if that 60-goal record will ever be beaten,' he reflected. 'I think it will. But there's only one man who'll do it. That's the fella who walks on water. I think he's about the only one.'

Season	League		FA Cup		Other		Total	
	App	Goals	App	Goals	App	Goals	App	Goals
1924/25	7	2	0	0	-	-	7	2
1925/26	38	32	2	1	-	-	40	33
1926/27	27	21	4	3	-	-	31	24
1927/28	39	60	2	3	-	-	41	63
1928/29	29	26	1	0	1	2	31	28
1929/30	25	23	2	2	-	-	27	25
1930/31	37	39	5	9	-	-	42	48
1931/32	38	45	1	1	-	-	39	46
1932/33	39	24	6	5	1	4	46	43
1933/34	12	9	0	0	0	0	12	9
1934/35	38	26	5	1	-	-	43	27
1935/36	29	17	0	0	-	-	29	17
1936/37	36	24	4	3	-	-	40	27
1937/38	5	1	0	0	-	-	5	1
Total	**399**	**349**	**32**	**28**	**2**	**6**	**433**	**388**

[FACTFILE]

BORN
Birkenhead, 22 January 1907
DIED
Goodison, 1 March 1980
POSITION
Centre forward
OTHER CLUBS
Tranmere Rovers (1923–25);
Notts County (1938–39);
Sligo Rovers (1939)
HONOURS
League Championship
1927/28, 1931/32;
Second Division Championship
1930/31;
FA Cup 1933;
16 England caps (18 goals)
(1927–32)

Further reading:

KEITH, JOHN, *Dixie Dean: The Inside Story of a Football Icon,* Robson Books, 2001
ROBERTS, JOHN, *Dixie Dean: The Forgotten Tapes,* Trinity Mirror, 2008
ROGERS, KEN (ed.), *Dixie Dean Uncut: The Lost Interview,* Trinity Mirror 2005
UPTON, GILBERT, *Dixie Dean of Tranmere Rovers,* 1992
WALSH, NICK, *Dixie Dean: The Life of a Goalscoring Legend,* MacDonald and James, 1977

Degn, Peter

Denmark under-21 international found out of his depth at Goodison

Season	League		FA Cup		League Cup		Total	
	App	Goals	App	Goals	App	Goals	App	Goals
1998/99	0 (4)	0	0	0	0	0	0 (4)	0
1999/2000	0	0	0	0	1	0	1	0
Total	0 (4)	0	0	0	1	0	1 (4)	0

Depledge, Robert

Local goalkeeper whose career was limited to a solitary outing

Season	League		FA Cup		Total	
	App	Goals	App	Goals	App	Goals
1906/07	1	0	0	0	1	0
Total	1	0	0	0	1	0

Dewar, James

Left back who was a one-game wonder

Season	League		FA Cup		Total	
	App	Goals	App	Goals	App	Goals
1892/93	1	0	0	0	1	0
Total	1	0	0	0	1	0

Dick, Alec

Fiery defender who was Everton's first professional

A FINE PLAYER WITH SEEMINGLY PSYCHOPATHIC TENDENCIES

Along with Bolton Wanderers' George Dobson, in the summer of 1885 Alec Dick became Everton's first professional footballer. The policy of paying the best players had gone on under the table for several years, and so that summer the Football Association sought to control what they had previously banned and sanctioned professionalism. Dick, who joined from Kilmarnock, and Dobson were a fine line of defence, although the latter would play much of his football for Everton further up the field.

Dick, wrote Thomas Keates in his history of the club, was 'a daring, reckless full back'; according to him, 'the two "D's", Dobson and Dick, proved to be a most formidable barrier to advancing forwards; their sensational kicking was an entertaining feature of matches.' By the onset of the Football League in September 1888, Dick was still a mainstay of the Everton defence, partnering the cultured Nick Ross in Everton's first league game against Accrington. Dick was a fine player with seemingly psychopathic tendencies. This saw him marked out by opponents and drew the animalistic tendencies of purportedly mild crowds.

WHEN EVERTON travelled to face Notts County in October 1888 things came to a dramatic head. The denizens of an unusually hostile crowd demanded, 'Which is Dick?' and marked him out for such epithets as 'dog' and 'pig'. This clearly irked the Everton defender, who let out his frustration with a punch in the

back of an opponent. In turn this increased the ire of the crowd and at the end of the game they invaded the pitch to attack the Everton man with sticks.

Dick was left with a 'severe wound' to the side of his head, according to a Nottingham newspaper. Police and Notts County players protected him in the club's pavilion while his injuries were tended.

By all accounts Dick was the victim of what was termed 'a cowardly outrage'. But instead of receiving sympathy, when he recovered from injuries which kept him out of Everton's next two games, he was hauled before an FA disciplinary commission in Birmingham. There the FA's honorary secretary Charles Alcock and the Bolton Wanderers secretary Fitzroy Norris banned the Everton player for eleven weeks.

THEIR RATIONALE for doing so has been lost to the sands of time, but was Alec Dick the victim of a stitch-up? Certainly Alcock was

no fan of professional players, believing that playing for money debased the sport and produced such aggressive players as Alec Dick. And Norris had his own score to settle with Everton, after shenanigans in the previous year's FA Cup saw a Bolton win over Everton overturned on a technicality and his club knocked out in the replayed match.

Dick played twice more for Everton after returning from his ban, but lost his place to Andrew Hannah for the 1889/90 season. Quite possibly he suffered serious injury, for while he was still on the

Everton books he did not appear for the senior side, or seemingly the reserves either. He was awarded a benefit match against Darwen in March 1891, with the proceeds shared with George Farmer and the goalkeeper Charles Jolliffe. Thereafter he drifted into obscurity.

[FACTFILE]

BORN
1865
POSITION
Full back
OTHER CLUBS
Kilmarnock

	League		FA Cup		Total	
Season	App	Goals	App	Goals	App	Goals
1887/88	-	-	4	0	4	0
1888/89	9	0	-	-	9	0
Total	9	0	4	0	13	0

Dickinson, Alfred

Inside forward from the Welsh border lands who made just a single appearance

[FACTFILE]

BORN
Saltney Ferry,
10 February 1914
DIED
1998
POSITION
Inside left
OTHER CLUBS
Port Vale (1936);
Northampton Town (1937–38)

	League		FA Cup		Total	
Season	App	Goals	App	Goals	App	Goals
1934/35	1	0	0	0	1	0
Total	1	0	0	0	1	0

Dilly, Tommy

Well-travelled forward who struggled for first-team openings at Everton

[FACTFILE]

BORN
Arbroath, November 1882
POSITION
Outside left/ inside left
OTHER CLUBS
Forfar County; Arbroath;
Heart of Midlothian;
West Bromwich Albion
(1905–07);
Derby County (1907);
Bradford Park Avenue
(1908);
Walsall; Shrewsbury Town;
Worcester City;
Kidderminster Harriers

	League		FA Cup		Total	
Season	App	Goals	App	Goals	App	Goals
1902/03	6	0	0	0	6	0
1903/04	0	0	0	0	0	0
1904/05	1	0	0	0	1	0
1905/06	2	2	0	0	2	2
Total	9	2	0	0	9	2

Distin, Sylvain

Former Manchester City and Portsmouth captain who proved an effective addition to the Everton defence

Signed from financially stricken Portsmouth at the end of the summer 2009 transfer window, Sylvain Distin was a straight replacement for Joleon Lescott who had joined one of Distin's former clubs – Manchester City – in acrimonious circumstances days earlier. A tall, physically imposing player with impressive pace given that he was already in his thirties, Distin had captained both City and Portsmouth and impressed in a loan spell with Newcastle United earlier in the decade.

Distin was a late developer, having been released by the Paris Saint-Germain academy as a teenager. For a player later renowned for his professionalism it seems surprising that he was let go for his own personal excesses. 'For me football was always a game, I never thought it would be a job,' he admitted to the Evertonian in 2009. 'I never worked at my game, I just used my natural ability and that worked fine for me. But one day they asked me to slow down on the nights out and I didn't, so I got sacked.'

He worked his way back into the game with US Joué-lès-Tours in France's sixth tier and at the age of 21 signed his first professional contract with Gueugnon. A surprising run that saw the small-town club win the French

League Cup brought him national attention and PSG signed him back. He played alongside Ronaldinho and Mikel Arteta before moving to England in 2001, initially on loan at Newcastle. Eight years later he was an Everton player.

With Phil Jagielka recovering from long-term injury and Phil Neville deputising at centre back, the £5million acquisition provided some desperately needed respite for Everton's stretched defence. He proved to be a fine, committed defender, albeit prone to some excruciating lapses of concentration. A rash challenge late in Everton's Round of 32 Europa League game against Sporting Lisbon saw his dismissal, gifted a penalty to the Portuguese and completely altered the complexion of a tie in which Everton had been cruising.

It was certainly true that his partnership with Joseph Yobo and Phil Jagielka had some weaknesses when compared to how those players paired with Lescott. But alongside Johnny Heitinga he seemed a different player and their partnership through the 2011/12 season proved the cornerstone on which Everton's progress was built.

Articulate and well rounded, Distin has emerged as one of the most popular members of the Everton dressing room. 'Sylvain is not normal,' his former team-mate Louis Saha told the Liverpool Echo in May 2012. 'He is a superhuman like a cyborg. Believe me, he works very hard in every training session – that's the norm at Everton anyway and he goes beyond that.'

Distin connects with supporters via the social media site Twitter, and there is a healthy respect between the player and fans. This was heightened following the 2012 FA Cup semi-final defeat to Liverpool, which proved a personal catastrophe for the Frenchman.

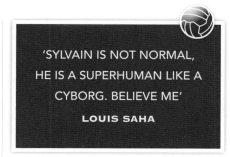

> 'SYLVAIN IS NOT NORMAL, HE IS A SUPERHUMAN LIKE A CYBORG. BELIEVE ME'
>
> **LOUIS SAHA**

A stray back-pass on the hour mark let in Luis Suarez who equalised for Liverpool and altered the flow of the match. But afterwards a distraught Distin came to the Everton fans to apologise and memories of his aberration were quickly replaced by admiration for his honesty and respect.

In May 2012 Distin signed a one-year contract extension that will take him past his 35th birthday. 'I don't need any boost to go into next season. I love my job and I know how lucky I am to do this kind of job,' he said. 'I want to carry on as long as I can. No matter what happens, you can be sure I'll be there the next day. It's a good squad here with a great atmosphere. I feel so comfortable with the lads, so it's a pleasure.'

[FACTFILE]

BORN
Bagnolet, France, 16 December 1977
POSITION
Centre back / left back
OTHER CLUBS
US Joué-lès-Tours (1997–98);
Tours (1998–99);
Gueugnon (1999–2000);
Paris Saint-Germain (2000–02);
Newcastle United (loan, 2001–02);
Manchester City (2002–07);
Portsmouth (2007–09)

Season	League		FA Cup		League Cup		Other		Total	
	App	Goals	App	Goals	App	Goals	App	Goals	App	Goals
2009/10	29	0	1	0	2	0	6	2	38	2
2010/11	38	2	4	0	2	0	-	-	44	2
2011/12	24 (3)	0	5	0	1	0	-	-	30 (3)	0
Total	**91 (3)**	**2**	**10**	**0**	**5**	**0**	**6**	**2**	**112 (3)**	**4**

Divers, John

Scottish international winger who briefly dazzled on Merseyside

[FACTFILE]

BORN
19 September 1873
POSITION
Outside left/ inside forward
OTHER CLUBS
Celtic; Hibernian
HONOURS
1 Scotland cap (1 goal) (1895)

Season	League		FA Cup		Total	
	App	Goals	App	Goals	App	Goals
1897/98	26	11	2	0	28	11
1898/99	4	0	0	0	4	0
Total	30	11	2	0	32	11

Dobson, George

One of Everton's first professionals, he partook in the advent of league football

[FACTFILE]

BORN
1862
POSITION
Full back
OTHER CLUB
Bolton Wanderers

Season	League		FA Cup		Total	
	App	Goals	App	Goals	App	Goals
1887/88	-	-	4	0	4	0
1888/89	18	0	-	-	18	0
Total	18	0	4	0	22	0

Dobson, Martin

Stylish midfielder whose grace and poise were not enough to bring glory days back to Goodison

Billy Bingham set a new British cash record in August 1974, when he paid Burnley £300,000 to sign their elegant England international midfielder, Martin Dobson. The value of the deal matched that which brought Bob Latchford to Goodison Park the previous February and it was hoped that the two big-money buys would bring success back to Goodison after the break-up of Harry Catterick's 1970 Championship winning team.

Dobson started out as a centre forward, but as a youth player with Bolton Wanderers was not offered professional terms at 18. Several years earlier, Alan Ball had suffered a similar fate at Burnden Park, before making his name elsewhere in Lancashire, with Blackpool, ahead of a record move to Everton, and so history would repeat itself for Dobson.

Taken on by Burnley, under the management of Jimmy Adamson the six-foot-tall player was moved into central midfield. This was to be such an inspired switch that he became, at the age of just 21, club captain. Dobson made his England debut in 1974 against Portugal, in Sir Alf Ramsey's last match in charge. Seen as almost a continental- type player, with calm, fluent distribution, but who almost strolled around the pitch, his doubters wondered whether

such a player could be accommodated within the hustle of the modern game.

Attention heightened after Billy Bingham paid Burnley a record fee in August 1974 and the midfielder initially struggled. Dobson admitted years later: 'I found it difficult to adapt from a small town club to one in a big city and didn't do myself justice at first.'

Indeed the high-tempo style of play under Bingham was very different to that played at Burnley. Although Everton challenged for the league title in Dobson's debut season, it was only after an absence over the Christmas period that Evertonians saw the best of him. Bryan Hamilton later attributed a tendency to fall out of games to Dobson 'probably playing better with the ball than without it', and it was acknowledged that Dobson played his best when the Blues were dominating proceedings.

GOODISON saw the very best from Dobson after the signing of Bruce Rioch in December 1976, who complemented his style of play superbly. Duncan McKenzie

said: '[Dobson] oozed ability and almost had the look of a continental-type player when he was on the pitch. Martin was very elegant on the pitch and would be the perfect complement to Rioch. A playmaker to his hard man.'

Despite making the League Cup Final in 1977 before finishing third in 1978 and fourth in 1979, playing in the shadow cast by Liverpool Everton were perpetually seen as second best, no matter how well they played. Dobson was sold back to Burnley at the end of the 1978/79 season for £100,000. At the age of 31, Everton were only prepared to offer him a two-year contract when the midfielder wanted three years. In all he played 230 League and Cup games for Everton, scoring an impressive 40 goals including a hat-trick in the League Cup tie against Wimbledon – an achievement somewhat overshadowed by Bob Latchford's five goals in the same game.

'It was brilliant coming to Everton,' he said in 2007. 'That was another level for me, playing for a big-city club in front of 40,000 fans. I'll always be grateful

for the support that the Evertonians gave me, they are so passionate and want you to succeed.'

ALTHOUGH it was felt that he was coming to the end of his career Dobson continued to played for another five years at Turf Moor, helping Burnley to the Third Division title in 1982 and appearing alongside a young Trevor Steven. In March 1984 he moved to Bury as player-manager where he spent five years, gaining promotion in 1985, but after failing to re-negotiate a contract he was subsequently out of the game for two years. He returned to management with Bristol Rovers in 1991 but left after just three months saying, 'I went there with a lot of enthusiasm and plenty of ideas but the bottom line is results and the team just didn't get them.'

Subsequently Dobson held positions on the peripheries of the game – a spell as Bolton youth coach in the mid-1990s, most recently scouting work for Ipswich. In 2007 Dobson published a football novel for teenagers. Now in his sixties, he still attends Goodison regularly from his home in Lancashire.

Season	League		FA Cup		League Cup		Europe		Total	
	App	Goals	App	Goals	App	Goals	App	Goals	App	Goals
1974/75	30	5	3	0	2	0	-	-	35	5
1975/76	42	5	1	0	5	1	2	0	50	6
1976/77	40	8	6	1	8	2	-	-	54	11
1977/78	38	7	2	0	4	1	-	-	44	8
1978/79	40	4	1	1	3	4	3	1	47	10
Total	**190**	**29**	**13**	**2**	**22**	**8**	**5**	**1**	**230**	**40**

[FACTFILE]

BORN
Rishton, 14 February 1948
POSITION
Midfield
OTHER CLUBS
Burnley (1967–74, 1978–83); Bury (player-manager, 1984–89)
HONOURS
5 England caps (1974)

Dodds, Ephraim (Jock)

Veteran striker who replaced Tommy Lawton in the post-war years

A giant, no-nonsense centre forward, Jock Dodds' imposing frame propped Everton up in the immediate post-war years, as the pre-war champions struggled to make an impression in football's new era.

BORN in Grangemouth in 1915, but raised in Durham, Dodds had started his career at Huddersfield Town, but was unable to make a breakthrough at a club considered among the best in the country. In May 1934 he joined Second Division Sheffield United and here the goals – 114 in 178 league outings – flowed. He helped United to the 1936 FA Cup Final, which they lost to Arsenal, and to promotion in 1938/39. By then Dodds was a Blackpool player, having moved for family reasons two months from the end of the season. War intervened, but Dodds remained in Blackpool as a PT instructor, turning out in the wartime leagues and for Scotland. Goals came in Dixie-like proportions: 65 in the 1941/42 season, and 47 the next campaign.

WHEN peace came and league football resumed, Dodds was aged 31, and after finding himself in dispute with Blackpool, became a target for Everton, whose attack was blunted by the departure of Tommy Lawton, and signed for £8500. 'With his bulk, power and fearless drive', he was, believed Brian Glanville, 'the epitome of the marauding centre forward, more prevalent between the wars than later'. Even playing in some lamentable Everton teams, he found the net with astounding regularity, including 17 goals in 21 games during the 1946/47 season. Dodds also finished the 1947/48 season top scorer for a second time.

But nothing at Goodison made much sense during these years. Everton started the 1948/49 season in abysmal fashion, shipping 28 goals in the opening ten fixtures and propping up the First Division. Despite this disarray, Dodds managed six goals in seven games, including a hat-trick against Preston. His reward? A £6000 transfer to Second Division Lincoln City. It would take several years and relegation before Everton could claim an adequate replacement in the form of Dave Hickson.

Now a veteran, Dodds was a prolific lower league striker, but his career was to end in controversy two years later. Colombian teams, operating outside the auspices of FIFA, had started poaching some of the best players from across the planet, such as Alfredo di Stefano, with lucrative wages on offer. Dodds became a recruiting agent for the Colombians, arranging the transfers of Neil Franklin, George Mountford and Charlie Mitten. For his troubles he was banned by the Football League, bringing an end, at the age of 35, to his playing days.

Post-football, Dodds retired to Blackpool, where his enterprises included a hotel and a rock-making factory. He remained there until his death in February 2009.

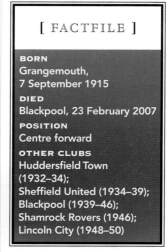

[FACTFILE]

BORN
Grangemouth, 7 September 1915
DIED
Blackpool, 23 February 2007
POSITION
Centre forward
OTHER CLUBS
Huddersfield Town (1932–34); Sheffield United (1934–39); Blackpool (1939–46); Shamrock Rovers (1946); Lincoln City (1948–50)

Season	League		FA Cup		Total	
	App	Goals	App	Goals	App	Goals
1946/47	21	17	2	0	23	17
1947/48	27	13	1	1	28	14
1948/49	7	6	0	0	7	6
Total	**55**	**36**	**3**	**1**	**58**	**37**

Dogs of War

The key to Everton's salvation during the dramatic 1994/95 season

The 'Dogs of War' – the midfield triumvirate of John Ebbrell, Barry Horne and Joe Parkinson – have become synonymous with Joe Royle's tenure as Everton manager. Certainly they were crucial to Everton's revival during the 1994/95 season, ensuring the club's Premiership survival and serving as the foundation stone for its FA Cup success. However, Royle came to regret the term, which was born as a quip early in his time as Everton manager. Asked why he overlooked Vinny Samways, the gifted but erratic midfielder, Royle replied, 'What we need is a "Dogs of War" mentality rather than a "School of Science" one.' The tag stuck, but Royle came to see its continued use in the media as a slight on his emerging team.

WHEN ROYLE was appointed Everton manager in November 1994, he inherited a side in dire straits. Bottom of the league, their troubled start to the season was characterised by the insipidness and lack of fight from the team. Royle radically reconstituted the team, packing the midfield with a defensive-minded core, containing Parkinson, Ebbrell and Horne. Their task was to scrap, harry and chase every ball as if their very lives depended upon it. After his revitalised team beat Liverpool in Royle's opening match, they embarked on a remarkable run that culminated in survival and the FA Cup Final victory over Manchester United.

There were a number of factors behind this remarkable turnaround – the enhanced sense of responsibility of the senior players; the form of hitherto under-performing stars like Duncan Ferguson and Anders Limpar; the set pieces of Andy Hinchcliffe and the renewed team spirit engendered by Royle – but the Dogs of War were at the centre of Everton's revival.

'High-profile players have since told me that they didn't look forward to playing against us,' Barry Horne told Becky Tallentire in Still Talking Blue. 'There was something of a reputation about the whole team, not just individuals. While it's always nice to know that people don't look forward to playing you, I felt people focused too much on that aspect of my game and overlooked others.'

AFTER WINNING the FA Cup, Royle insisted that Everton were now more 'Crufts' than 'Dogs of War'. But while he sought a more expansive style, introducing more gifted ball players like Tony Grant and Gary Speed to his midfield, Everton largely remained a rough-and-ready team.

Royle was notoriously sensitive about press coverage and disliked allusions to the 'Dogs of War'. 'I did live to regret making the remark because it was held over our heads like a sword through my time at the club,' he recalled in his autobiography.

Indeed Royle's relations with the press deteriorated rapidly over the winter of 1996–97, culminating in his banning journalists from Bellefield. At the root of this rupture was Royle's sensitivity to criticisms of Everton's style and tactics, particularly from the Liverpool Echo. The Dogs of War, it seemed, always came back to bite him. Certainly none of this messy dispute enhanced his reputation, and arguably it played a crucial role in his departure from the Everton manager's seat in March 1997.

By then the Dogs of War had been broken up. Barry Horne had joined Birmingham City the previous summer, and John Ebbrell was sold to Sheffield United in February 1997. Only Joe Parkinson remained, but he was playing with an injury that ended his career by the age of 28. It was an inauspicious end for a group of players who had been so vital to Everton.

Dominy, Arthur 'Art'

Dixie Dean's forward partner as he made his first steps to greatness

[FACTFILE]

BORN
South Stoneham, 11 February 1893
DIED
1974
POSITION
Inside forward
OTHER CLUBS
Southampton (1920–25); Gillingham (1927–28); Clapton Orient (1929)

Season	League		FA Cup		Total	
	App	Goals	App	Goals	App	Goals
1926/27	28	12	4	1	32	12
1927/28	1	0	0	0	1	0
Total	29	12	4	1	33	13

Donaldson, John

Scottish left half whose Everton career was limited to two appearances

[FACTFILE]

BORN
Cardross, 19 April 1864
POSITION
Centre forward
OTHER CLUBS
Sunderland; Renton; Woolwich Arsenal

Season	League		FA Cup		Total	
	App	Goals	App	Goals	App	Goals
1905/06	2	0	0	0	2	0
Total	2	0	0	0	2	0

Donovan, Don

Reliable full back and utility man through Everton's darkest era

Don Donovan was one of a succession of committed Irish players who served the club with loyalty and diligence through the dark days of the 1950s. Signed as an inside forward in May 1949, the Cork man made a transition down the left of the Everton team, evolving into an international-class full back, having also served as wing half and even centre half.

Donovan's arrival as a 20-year-old at Goodison saw him placed among familiar company. Fellow Irishmen – including Jimmy O'Neil, Peter Farrell, Tommy Eglington and Tommy Clinton – formed the spine of the Everton team and the basis for huge popularity in the Emerald Isle. Alas, this team laboured through historic lows: relegation in 1951 and 16th place in Division Two in 1952/53.

Donovan did not make his full debut until August 1951 and made just seven appearances the following season – the year of Everton's nadir. He admitted later: 'It took me nearly a year to reach the playing fitness need for English soccer. During this long period I struggled for promotion and wondered whether I had made the right decision [in leaving Ireland].'

The breakthrough came in a reserve match at Huddersfield in late 1950 when he was deployed as an emergency wing half. Ted Sagar gave rave notices of his performance to Cliff Britton and the transformation from attacker to destroyer was born. Early in the 1951/52 season he was given a run at wing half, although he later lost his place to Cyril Lello, who had returned from long-term injury.

A hiatus from first-team affairs followed and Donovan scarcely appeared through the dire 1952/53 season. His return the following campaign was triumphant: the Irishman was ever-present as Everton won promotion back to the top flight. By now the majority of his appearances came as full back and he appeared on either flank of defence. He was also, on more than one occasion, selected as centre half. Marking the great John Charles in a match against Leeds at Goodison in November 1953, he put in a fine performance as Everton ran out 2-1 winners. Donovan was in no doubt which position he preferred. 'After a few minutes at full back I settled down delightedly,' he told Charles Buchan's Football Monthly in 1956. 'There seemed to be much more space in which to use the ball and I thoroughly enjoyed our positional movements.'

International honours arrived in November 1954 when he faced Norway at Dalymount Park. But in total he would win just five caps. Donovan was a regular in the team that sought to re-establish Everton as a top-flight force. Perhaps surprisingly he found himself transferred away from Goodison following a dressing room reshuffle in 1958. He joined Grimsby and put in a fine stint that extended his career until his mid-thirties and took his career total beyond 400 first-class appearances.

But it is Everton with whom his name remains synonymous. 'Everton expect hard work from anyone they sign,' he said in 1956. 'But if one puts one's back into the job, then they supply everything which can lead to a wonderful career.'

[FACTFILE]

BORN
Cork, 23 December 1929
POSITION
Full back
OTHER CLUBS
Grimsby Town (1958–65);
Boston United (player-manager, 1965–67)
HONOURS
5 Republic of Ireland caps (1954–57)

Season	League		FA Cup		Total	
	App	Goals	App	Goals	App	Goals
1951/52	22	0	2	0	24	0
1952/53	7	0	0	0	7	0
1953/54	42	0	2	0	44	0
1954/55	35	0	0	0	35	0
1955/56	8	1	0	0	8	1
1956/57	36	1	3	0	39	1
1957/58	29	0	1	0	30	0
Total	**179**	**2**	**8**	**0**	**187**	**2**

Donovan, Landon

American loan star who captured royal blue hearts and rejuvenated his adopted team

American international Landon Donovan's Everton career lasted just two 10-week spells, but during those brief periods he won the universal admiration of Evertonians and found a permanent place for the club in his own heart.

Arguably the greatest American footballer of all time, Donovan joined Everton on three months' loan from LA Galaxy in January 2010. Major League Soccer plays to a summer calendar, affording its players the opportunity to turn out in Europe. A year earlier Donovan had appeared on loan at Bayern Munich. Lithe, pacey and a fine finisher, Donovan added élan and guile to the right side of an impressive Everton midfield. He joined a team that had struggled to find form in the first half of the 2009/10 season and his presence, wearing the famous number nine shirt, helped rejuvenate the team. After his arrival Everton lost just twice more in the league that campaign and fine goals against Sunderland and Hull City cemented his reputation as a crowd favourite. Indeed, Donovan established a close rapport with Evertonians and said that he would 'jump' at the chance to sign for Everton. But when his spell came to an end in March 2010 LA Galaxy

wanted to hold on to their man and the money to buy him was not there in any case.

'I'm 28 years old now and I've played over 100 times for my country, I've also played a lot of league games in different parts of the world,' he told EvertonTV in an emotional farewell interview. 'But I've never met a fan base like this, either playing for them or as an away player. Forget about football for a moment, this is a experience I'll never forget.'

TWO years later, with Everton struggling after a slow start to the 2011/12 season, Donovan returned on a similar deal. His

'THIS IS AN EXPERIENCE I'LL NEVER FORGET'

pace and urgency lifted his team-mates and added fresh impetus to a flagging season. He returned to California in February 2012 without any further goals to his name, but with his special relationship reinforced.

[FACTFILE]

BORN
Ontario, California, 4 March 1982
POSITION
Winger / forward
OTHER CLUBS
Bayer Leverkusen (1999–2005);
San Jose Earthquakes (loan, 2001–04);
LA Galaxy (2005–);
Bayern Munich (loan, 2000)
HONOURS
138 USA caps (46 goals) (2000–)

Season	League		FA Cup		League Cup		Europe		Total	
	App	Goals	App	Goals	App	Goals	App	Goals	App	Goals
2009/10	7 (3)	2	1	0	0	0	2	0	10 (3)	2
2011/12	7	0	2	0	0	0	-	-	9	0
Total	**14(3)**	**2**	**3**	**0**	**0**	**0**	**2**	**0**	**19(3)**	**2**

Dougal, Peter

Widely travelled inside left who was one of the first British football exports to France

[FACTFILE]

BORN
Falkirk, 21 March 1909
DIED
12 June 1974
POSITION
Inside left
OTHER CLUBS
Burnley (1926–29);
Clyde (1929);
Southampton (1929–32);
Séte (France) (1932–33);
Arsenal (1933–37);
Bury (1938–40)

Season	League		FA Cup		Total	
	App	Goals	App	Goals	App	Goals
1937/38	11	0	0	0	11	0
Total	**11**	**0**	**0**	**0**	**11**	**0**

Downs, Richard 'Dickie'

Attack-minded full back whose career enjoyed an Indian summer in the blue of Everton

In electing to join Everton at the age of 33, Richard 'Dickie' Downs fulfilled an ambition that had eluded him through a long and distinguished career with Barnsley. Twice – in 1910 and 1912 – he had appeared in FA Cup Finals for the Yorkshire club, winning it at the second time of asking, but First Division recognition always proved elusive. So committed was he to his goal of seeing Barnsley in the top flight that he repeatedly ignored the covetous attentions of bigger clubs.

The First World War cut out the prime of his career and he may,

on returning to league football as a 33-year-old, have feared that the chance of playing at the highest level had passed him by. But following Barnsley's FA Cup exit in 1920 he requested a transfer and Everton gladly paid £2400 to bring him to Goodison Park.

The Liverpool Post and Mercury reported that he was 'one of the soundest backs in the League', adding, 'he is a sturdy player, with ideals of his own, and in recent games with Barnsley, when his side were doing badly, went from full back to centre forward – once in the cup-tie at Plymouth – and scored goals. Several clubs were

after his signature.' Downs came straight into what was a highly transitional Everton team and immediately impressed. On his home debut, a 0-0 draw with Manchester United, he struck the post and was described as the best player on the pitch. 'The ex-Barnsley player made a wonderful difference to the Everton defence, which was certainly the best part of the side,' recorded the Liverpool Courier.

Downs was elected captain for the 1920/21 season and missed just two matches. His fine form saw him selected, at the age of 34, for England in October 1920 for a Home Championship game against Ireland at Roker Park. Everton finished the league campaign in seventh position, but were unable to build on this progress. The 1921/22 season was the worst in the club's history at that stage and they finished just a place off relegation. Changes were sought and the following campaign Downs lost his place to David Raitt. At the end of the 1923/24 season, in which Downs made just 3 appearances, he was placed on the transfer list. In August 1924 Brighton and Hove Albion bid £96 for his services a week after the player's 38th birthday, and the board accepted, giving Downs the fee as his accrued share of the benefit.

Season	League		FA Cup		Total	
	App	Goals	App	Goals	App	Goals
1919/20	12	0	0	0	12	0
1920/21	40	0	5	0	45	0
1921/22	28	0	0	0	28	0
1922/23	9	0	0	0	9	0
1923/24	3	0	0	0	3	0
Total	92	0	5	0	97	0

[FACTFILE]

BORN
Middridge, Newton Aycliffe, Country Durham, 13 August 1886
DIED
24 March 1949
POSITION
Full back
OTHER CLUBS
Barnsley (1909–20); Brighton and Hove Albion (1923)
HONOURS
1 England cap (1920)

Doyle, Dan

Wild man of the Everton back line during the Victorian era

One of the most formidable footballers of his generation, Dan Doyle was an outstanding left back for Everton and Scotland and a figure who earned renown for his wild antics on and off the football field. Highly talented, aggressive and always controversial, he can be seen as Everton's first 'psycho' – a forerunner of Pat Van Den Hauwe, who succeeded him in the number three shirt a century later.

Born in Paisley in 1864, Doyle started working life down the Strathclyde coalmines that would later breed a succession of football immortals. The horror of the pit instilled in him a relentless will that if he could ever escape he would make sure he would never have to return. It bred behaviour that might be regarded as mercenary, but which Doyle surely considered necessary.

He started out as an amateur left back in the mid-1880s, simultaneously playing for East Stirlingshire and Hibernian. Scottish football, unlike its English counterpart, was still resolutely amateur – although under-the-table payments were the norm – and when Doyle was offered

the chance to sign professional terms with Grimsby Town in 1888 he seized it.

While playing at Clee Park, in November 1888 Doyle was involved in an incident that forever marred his reputation. He collided with an opponent, who was left writhing around on the ground in agony before being stretchered off – within hours he had died. Although there was no malicious intent, Doyle was called before a court where he was exonerated. Being a defender who had killed an opposing player on the field was, however, something fans and other players would never forget.

Yet his footballing reputation preceded him and in the summer of 1889 two of the Football League's founder members – Everton and Bolton – were involved in a lengthy tussle for his services. Doyle signed for both clubs, simultaneously taking a salary from both boardrooms before finally plumping for Everton. Such boldness was not uncharacteristic.

Although he had a reputation as a hard player, Doyle was also cultured on the ball – a man who could not only kick the ball further, but also with more accuracy than many of his contemporaries. With Andrew Hannah he built up the league's best full back partnership. They were, according to one contemporary account, 'great barriers, tacklers and sensational kickers'. His football philosophy was always simple, however. In a rare interview with Scottish Sport in 1894, he professed: 'There is only one way. Let the man go bang into the game with the determination to win.'

He was an important member of the team that lifted the Football League title in 1891, but Doyle had become disillusioned with life at Anfield. He believed he was being paid £3 per week less than some of his team-mates and so began a flirtation with Celtic. They were still bound by Scottish football's amateurism, but had offered him tenancy of a pub, which was worth £5 a week, plus payment per game.

The dispute was played out in the Victorian media. In the August 1891 edition of Field Sports it reported that the Everton committeemen said they would 'see Doyle ******* hang first' before they would let him go.

Eventually Doyle came back with an ultimatum to Everton's pleas to honour his contract. He would stay if they gave him £100 for the previous two years and increased his pay from £3 to £4 per week. 'He enjoyed wielding power over directors and committeemen,' wrote his biographer Marie Rowan. 'Already a hardened coal miner by the age of 16, Doyle had learned a lot during these dark days down the pit and he knew exactly how to get his pound of flesh.'

On 1 August 1891 he met the Everton committee and told them of his intent to play on for the forthcoming season after they agreed to a rise. He even telegraphed the Athletic News: 'Kindly insert I intend playing for Everton, certain.'

But a week later, on 8 August, he wired Everton to say he had agreed to sign for Celtic after all. Everton were furious, and tried to get the FA to take up a case against Celtic via the Scottish FA for breaching its rules on amateurism. The whole messy dispute rumbled on for months and was only resolved when Doyle agreed to pay back some of the £100 wages Everton advanced him at the end of the 1890/91 season.

Doyle went on to be one of Celtic and Scotland's great stars of the 1890s, and was one of the most famous footballers of his generation. Despite his controversial departure, Evertonians retained a great affection for him and he was the subject of continued speculation that he might return to Merseyside.

When he did come back to Liverpool, in April 1894, to appear for the Scottish League against the English League, he got a rousing reception: Scottish Sport reported that he received 'the warmest of welcomes from the Liverpudlians both at the start and at half time'.

Later that year Dick Molyneux met with Doyle in an attempt to bring about his return. Everton offered him a 19-year lease of his favourite Liverpool pub, worth £5 per week, in return for signing for two more years, but he preferred to play on for Celtic.

Doyle retired at the end of the decade and ran the Horse Shoe Bar in Belshill. Always a heavy drinker and gambler, however, he ran into financial difficulties and lost ownership of the pub in 1910. He died eight years later, still a well-recognised figure in Glasgow, but reduced to penury after years of excess.

Further reading:

ROWAN, MARIE, *Dan Doyle: The Life and Death of a Wild Rover*, Black and White Publishing, 2007

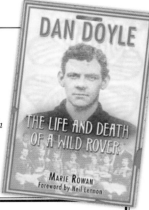

[FACTFILE]

BORN
Paisley, 16 September 1864
DIED
8 April 1918
POSITION
Left back
OTHER CLUBS
East Stirlingshire (1886–88);
Hibernian (1886–88)*;
Grimsby Town (1888–89);
Bolton Wanderers (1889);
Celtic (1891–99)
HONOURS
1890/91 League Championship;
8 Scotland caps (1892–98)

*Doyle played simultaneously for these two clubs before turning professional.

Season	League App	League Goals	FA Cup App	FA Cup Goals	Total App	Total Goals
1889/90	22	0	2	1	24	1
1890/91	20	3	1	0	21	3
Total	**42**	**3**	**3**	**1**	**45**	**4**

Duffy, Shane

Promising Irish centre half for whom great hopes are held

Season	League App	League Goals	FA Cup App	FA Cup Goals	League Cup App	League Cup Goals	Europe App	Europe Goals	Total App	Total Goals
2009/10	0	0	0	0	0	0	1 (1)	0	1 (1)	0
2010/11	0	0	0	0	0	0	-	-	0	0
2011/12	2 (2)	0	1	0	0	0	-	-	3 (2)	0
Total	**2 (2)**	**0**	**1**	**0**	**0**	**0**	**1 (1)**	**0**	**4 (3)**	**0**

[FACTFILE]

BORN
Derry, 1 January 1992
POSITION
Centre half
OTHER CLUBS
Burnley (loan) (2011),
Scunthorpe united (loan) (2011)

Drenthe,
Royston Ricky

Live-wire winger who fell foul of David Moyes after impressive loan spell

Signed amid the frustrating summer of 2011, the loan signing of Royston Drenthe offered Evertonians real hope for the forthcoming season. The diminutive, explosive winger had once been considered among the most promising young players in Europe, signing for Real Madrid in a €14million deal after starring in the Netherlands' successful UEFA Under-21 Championship challenge in 2007.

Drenthe was named player of the tournament then and hopes were still high four years later. Small, adroit, pacey, and with a thunderous shot, he had the talent and potential to shine at the highest level of European football. But chances were hard to come by in the Spanish capital and he laboured under several managerial changes. 'Given few opportunities, unable to choose the right studs, a-skidding and a-sliding his way across pitches all over the country, he scored just two league goals in three seasons and, although he memorably described one of them as "fuckin' good" before being asked if he'd mind describing it again in language that could actually get broadcast, few remembered them,' recorded the distinguished Spanish football journalist, Sid Lowe.

There were also questions posed about his temperament and a promising loan spell with Hercules ended with Drenthe on strike, simultaneously playing villain and victim.

The move to Everton offered him some form of redemption and Moyes's reputation for turning around the careers of gifted but wayward stars augured well. Certainly the early signs were good and there were some fine goals and no questions about his outstanding technical ability. But his temperament seemed at times to be suspect and his temper sometimes bubbled over. In an FA Cup quarter-final with Sunderland he repeatedly had to be calmed by his own team-mates before being substituted, seemingly for his own good.

That was virtually his last act in an Everton shirt. After turning up late for training one time too many he was told to stay away from the club by Moyes. This was a shame, for it coincided with Everton's FA Cup semi-final with Liverpool, which ultimately ended in defeat. With Steven Pienaar cup-tied, how Everton could have used the inspiration of such a gifted player.

[FACTFILE]

BORN
Rotterdam, Netherlands, 8 April 1987
POSITION
Winger
OTHER CLUBS
Feyenoord (2005–07);
Real Madrid (2007–12);
Hercules (loan, 2010–11)
HONOURS
1 Netherlands cap (2010)

Season	League		FA Cup		League Cup		Total	
	App	Goals	App	Goals	App	Goals	App	Goals
2011/12	10 (11)	3	2 (2)	1	2	0	14 (13)	4
Total	10 (11)	3	2 (2)	1	2	0	14 (13)	4

Dugdale,
Gordon

Promising left back whose career was wrecked by illness

By his mid-twenties, Gordon Dugdale seemed to have the world at his feet. After establishing himself as Everton's first-choice left back – in the process displacing the club captain, Norman Greenhalgh – he was tipped as a possible member of Walter Winterbottom's England squad for the 1950 World Cup Finals in Brazil.

But then disaster struck. A heart complaint linked to the rheumatic fever he suffered as a Fleet Air Arm pilot in the US during the war resurfaced. Aged just 25 he was forced to call time on a career that had seemed full of potential. Dugdale, who had long defied doctors orders having been told as a 19-year-old that he would never play football again, remained phlegmatic about his fate. 'In view of what happened, I consider myself lucky to have got in three years with them,' he said in 1969. After wartime service, Dugdale had signed professional terms with Everton in 1946. His debut came in October 1947 against Wolves and after vying with Greenhalgh and Jack Hedley for the number three shirt over the next 18 months, by spring 1949 he looked to have finally made it his own. Yet Dugdale had less than a year as a first choice, his career ending in December 1949 after just 63 appearances.

AFTER RETIRING, Dugdale became a successful local businessman, with interests in accountancy and property. He also served as a city councillor for the Conservative Party, as a coach with Marine and director of South Liverpool FC.

Season	League		FA Cup		Total	
	App	Goals	App	Goals	App	Goals
1947/48	19	0	4	0	23	0
1948/49	19	0	1	0	20	0
1949/50	20	0	0	0	20	0
Total	58	0	5	0	63	0

[FACTFILE]

BORN
Liverpool, 21 February
POSITION
Left back

Dunlop, Albert

Controversial custodian who became embroiled in doping allegations

Long-serving goalkeeper Albert Dunlop was one of a handful of figures in Everton history whose background may euphemistically be described as 'colourful'.

Signed by the club as a local teenager he had to wait some eight years to make his debut, serving as Everton's number one for six seasons before losing his place to Gordon West. Off the pitch flirtations with dodgy business interests and drug taking were followed by a series of tawdry tabloid allegations made after his Goodison departure.

He was, recalled a colleague, a 'menacing character' and 'troublemaker'; memories that tend to overshadow his capabilities as a goalkeeper.

Indeed, Dunlop was a fine custodian of the Everton net. He made his debut in October 1956 against the mighty Busby Babes at Old Trafford.

ALBERT DUNLOP · EVERTON F.C. (1957)

Up against the reigning league champions, Dunlop – with his team-mates – put in an astonishing performance as Everton won 5-2.

Never the tallest of goalkeepers, he overcame a lack of physical presence in his area with bravery and athleticism. 'The vociferous Albert was also renowned for pointing out team-mates' mistakes – real or imaginary – almost every time he was beaten,' added the distinguished football historian, Ivan Ponting. Certainly in this era there was plenty of time for shouting. In October 1958 Dunlop would pick the ball out of his own net ten times as Everton fell to a record 10-4 defeat.

DUNLOP WAS A FINE CUSTODIAN OF THE EVERTON NET

As the 1960s dawned, a new era infused with the Moores millions, Dunlop remained a constant. But under the arch-disciplinarian Harry Catterick it was only a matter of time before he fell foul of the new manager.

THE GOALKEEPER, a former team-mate of Catterick, had already had numerous brushes with the club before Harry's return as manager in April 1961. 'Albert had few friends at the club and was known as something of a menacing character,' recalled Alex Young. 'He had always been a troublemaker … Like most of my team-mates, I thought of him as someone to be avoided.' In 1960

he opened a licensed club near to Goodison but was ordered by the board to sever all his connections. After Catterick's return he sought to borrow money from the board to tide over his business interests. The board acceded to his request, but when Catterick found out he 'reported that in his opinion Albert Dunlop's business interests were not in the best interests of the Club, and it was agreed not to proceed with the arrangements to make him a loan'.

By then Dunlop had been edged out of the first team by West. He returned for the 1962/63 season conclusion, appearing in Everton's last four games. When they lifted the League Championship on the last day of the season with a 4-1 win over Fulham, it would be his final appearance in an Everton shirt.

WEST was progressing well at Goodison, but Dunlop and Catterick never saw eye to eye. According to Young he 'threatened' the manager 'numerous times'. When West was dropped the following season, Andy Rankin – and not Dunlop – took his place. At the end of the campaign he was sold to Wrexham, fuelling the shunned custodian's anger.

HE WAS not long wreaking his revenge. In September 1964 Dunlop turned on his former team-mates, selling his story to the Sunday tabloid, the People. In it he included salacious allegations about drug taking among the Everton squad. He claimed that his former team-mates took Drinamyl, popularly known as 'purple hearts'.

'Many of the players started taking Benzedrine regularly early in 1961,' he alleged. 'I cannot remember how they came first to be offered to us. But they were distributed in the dressing room … we didn't have to take them, but most of the players did … They were used throughout the 1961/62 season and the championship season which followed it. 'Drug-taking had previously been virtually unknown at the club. But once it started we could take as many tablets as we liked. On match days they were handed out to most players as a matter of course. Soon, some players could not do without drugs. It became a sort of ritual for them to be handed out on Saturdays and other match days by our head trainer, Tommy Egglestone.'

According to Young, Dunlop was embittered at being sold to Wrexham 'and swore to get even'. Years later he described the story as 'a mindless act of vengeance by a troubled soul who had been discarded by his employer'.

MOREOVER, Young claimed that Dunlop 'was no stranger to drugs' and had himself become addicted. While in rehab, Young claimed, he had decided to sell his story to the People. The FA and Football League cleared Everton

during investigations into the allegations, although as Ivan Waddington and Andy Smith muse in An Introduction to Drugs in Sport, 'it is difficult to see what action the Football League … could have taken, for though the use of stimulants was increasingly coming to be regarded as morally questionable, there were at that time no specific rules banning their use.'

Dunlop was subsequently player-manager of Rhyl. In 1979 he was found guilty of three charges of deception. He died in March 1990.

Season	League		FA Cup		League Cup		Europe		Total	
	App	Goals	App	Goals	App	Goals	App	Goals	App	Goals
1956/57	29	0	3	0	-	-	-	-	32	0
1957/58	36	0	3	0	-	-	-	-	39	0
1958/59	33	0	4	0	-	-	-	-	37	0
1959/60	37	0	1	0	-	-	-	-	38	0
1960/61	42	0	1	0	5	0	-	-	48	0
1961/62	30	0	3	0	-	-	-	-	33	0
1962/63	4	0	0	0	0	0	0	0	4	0
Total	**211**	**0**	**15**	**0**	**5**	**0**	**0**	**0**	**231**	**0**

Dunn, Jimmy

Wembley Wizard who won every honour possible for an inter-war player

Within days of signing for Everton in April 1928, Scottish international inside forward Jimmy Dunn witnessed what was arguably Goodison's greatest occasion. On the day that Everton sealed the 1927/28 League Championship, Dunn was named as twelfth man, the player who was on stand by lest any of the First XI unexpectedly withdrew before kick off. Not only was he a close witness to his new team-mates lifting the title after a 3-3 draw with Arsenal, he watched his new forward partner William Ralph 'Dixie' Dean score his 58th, 59th and 60th goals of the season and enter football immortality.

IT WAS A reminder to the Scot of the lofty expectations he would have to live up to, but Dunn had already experienced highs of his own. Five weeks earlier he was one of the 'Wembley Wizards' – the incomparable Scottish team that beat England 5-1 on the

site of 1920s football's greatest temple. Dunn's £5000 transfer to Goodison from Hibernian in April 1928 concluded a 15-month pursuit of the player. Everton's directors made several visits north of the border in an attempt to sign Dunn and his team-mate, the winger Harry Ritchie, but the Edinburgh club would not relent. Finally they accepted a £5000 offer for Dunn just weeks after the Wembley massacre, resisting an £8000 joint bid for the pair. On the same day Jimmy Stein arrived from Dunfirmline. Everton would have to wait until the end of the summer before Ritchie was also an Everton player. Expectation was soon higher than ever.

Gallaher's Cigarettes.

JAS. DUNN
EVERTON

After appearing in the annual Blues v. Whites trial match Dunn received rave notices. 'Naturally, chief interest centred on the appearance of Dunn, one of the men who helped Scotland to nip the English rose "in the bud" at Wembley last season, and they went home convinced that in this diminutive auburn-haired Scot the champions had found a man with football written all over him,' wrote the Liverpool Courier. 'This was only a trial game, it is true, but [good] football in the main, just the same as truth in all walks of life, will out. Possessed of a most deceptive body swerve, he manipulates the ball with rare skill, and passes with extreme delicacy. Quick to size up a situation, he passed last evening to the right man nine times out of ten, and with this link in the chain (that was missing for a greater part of last campaign) fully forged, it was no wonder that Dean and company had a merry time, much to the discomfiture of the White's defence. Dunn will fit in splendidly with the Goodison scheme of things.'

Days later Everton captured Ritchie and expectation rose even higher. After beating Bolton on the opening day of 1928/29 the Courier pondered: 'A Championship again and an FA Cup?' Of Dunn it wrote that he 'showed that he is a player who believes in making the ball do the work, and many of

the most deadly of the champions' thrusts could be traced back to his astute initiation.'

ALAS SUCH hopes appeared misplaced. Everton lost the last six games of the season and finished 18th. It set a worrying precedent. In the 1929/30 season they finished bottom, Dunn making just 12 league appearances.

What followed over the following three years was as remarkable as Everton's sudden fall. In 1930/31 they stormed to the Division Two title, Dunn scoring 14 goals in 28 games – only Dean managing more. A year later Everton were First Division Champions, Dunn this time managing to earn a medal for the triumph he had witnessed just days into his Everton career. A year after that, in April 1933, Dunn was back at Wembley – the scene of his greatest day – adding another unforgettable occasion to his memory bank. Everton beat Manchester City 3-0, Dunn heading home Everton's third from a corner.

The importance of Dunn's contribution was not limited to a sucker-punch goal. Everton had utilised their forwards in withdrawn positions to nullify City's own potent forward line and their diligence reaped dividends. 'One could not describe this as a thrilling game. Yet it was a match which thoroughly satisfied the football student and that is why I term it a joyous final,' recorded 'Pilot' in the Liverpool Evening Express.

'Everton served up delightful football. It was not quite according to their usual plan, for [fellow inside forward Tommy] Johnson and Dunn lay back more than is their usual wont. Yet this was according to a preconceived move to counteract the match-winning methods of the City, which had been studied for six weeks. Everton knew the Manchester's goal-scoring moves were developed by Busby, the right half-back sweeping a square pass cross to McMullan, the inside left, in that way the complete outlook of the game was changed.

The blues knew all about it, and so Johnson came back to force Busby to part, and Jimmy Dunn lay on McMullan, so keeping him out of action. What was the result? The City floundered for want of a good move. Most of the Everton raiding was left to Dean, and the wingers and they played their parts well. Johnson and Dunn were parted defenders but they could make those lovely sweeping passes up the middle or out to the wings after drawing the opposition.'

The Cup winning triumph was the end for the great team of the early 1930s and Everton entered a period of transition. Dunn lost his place to Jimmy 'Nat' Cunliffe midway through the 1933/34 season and played only intermittently thereafter. He appears to have been a victim of the maximum wage system inflicted on players at the time. While still an Everton player his financial difficulties were discussed in the Everton

DUNN WAS BACK AT WEMBLEY – THE SCENE OF HIS GREATEST DAY –

boardroom but 'no action taken'. In December 1936 he offered his FA Cup medals for sale for 5 guineas, but the Everton board said 'no'.

IN 1935 Dunn joined Exeter for £350 and subsequently played for Runcorn before turning to coaching. In January 1945 a minute of the Everton board records: 'Good reports on the play of this young son of James Dunn, former player of ours, were received & it was agreed that the Secretary pursue efforts to obtain the boy's services.' But Jimmy junior – perhaps put off by his father's inhospitable treatment – never joined Everton, instead pursuing a distinguished career with Wolves and Derby County, lifting the 1949 FA Cup with the former after a 3-1 victory over Leicester.

Season	League		FA Cup		Other		Total	
	App	Goals	App	Goals	App	Goals	App	Goals
1928/29	24	4	1	0	0	0	25	4
1929/30	12	0	1	0	-	-	13	0
1930/31	28	14	5	3	-	-	33	17
1931/32	22	10	0	0	-	-	22	10
1932/33	25	10	6	4	0	0	31	14
1933/34	23	4	1	0	1	0	25	4
1934/35	6	0	0	0	-	-	6	0
Total	**140**	**42**	**14**	**7**	**1**	**0**	**155**	**49**

[FACTFILE]

BORN
25 November 1900
DIED
20 August 1963
POSITION
Inside forward
OTHER CLUBS
Hibernian (1920–28);
Exeter City (1935–36)
HONOURS
6 Scotland Caps (2 goals)
(1925–29);
1931/32 First Division
Championship;
1930/31 Second Division
Championship;
1933 FA Cup

Dunne, Richard

Promising Irish defender who fell foul of Walter Smith

Initially signed as a raw teenager from Home Farm in 1995 – a period in which the Dublin club served as a feeder team to Everton – centre back Dunne was the archetypal 'Man-Boy', towering above even Dave Watson when he made his first-team debut alongside him in an FA Cup tie against Swindon Town, in January 1997. Invariably commanding for such a physically imposing player, Dunne seemed a ready-made replacement for the Everton captain, who was now in the veteran part of his career.

INDEED, when Watson became caretaker manager three months later, perhaps seeing something of himself in the young Irishman, he thrust Dunne into the limelight, making him the youngest player to turn out in a Merseyside derby, a distinction he held for just 25 minutes when Michael Ball – eleven days his junior – joined him as an early substitute. He responded superbly, putting in a performance of composure and maturity in a game that ended in a 1-1 draw, simultaneously ending Liverpool's title challenge and easing Everton's

relegation worries. An international call-up for the 17-year-old followed just weeks later.

ALTHOUGH HIS progress was limited under Howard Kendall in the 1997/98 season, along with Leon Osman, Danny Cadamarteri, Francis Jeffers and Tony Hibbert, Dunne was part of the team that lifted the FA Youth Cup that year, following a two-legged final victory over Blackburn Rovers.

He made his breakthrough into the Everton squad the following year, with new manager Walter Smith deploying him at wing back, a position totally unsuited to Dunne's attributes. The young Irishman nevertheless impressed in patches, and continued to receive call-ups to his national squad. Yet only on the rare occasions he was given a chance at centre half did he show his true potential. Calm and unruffled, firm in the tackle and with a good first touch, it was clear even from a young age that he had all the facets necessary to cut it at the top level.

And yet indiscipline on and off the field tempered that realisation – and would ultimately cost him his career at Everton. Dunne suffered periodic lapses in concentration, which would sometimes result in a howling error or an unnecessary red or yellow card. Never the most naturally athletic player, he sometimes struggled with his weight, which invariably

affected his match fitness. A series of escapades, tame by comparison to some of modern football's excesses, were allowed to escalate under Smith's man-management to a point where they reached the national press: on one occasion he ill-advisedly took Everton to an FA tribunal after claiming a two-week fine for missing training contravened his contract; on another, he was dropped after being caught laughing on the team coach following a League Cup defeat to Bristol Rovers, rather than spending the journey home in silent introspection.

Indeed the latter incident led directly to Dunne's £3million departure to Manchester City days later. Dunne plodded on, eventually putting his disciplinary problems behind him, becoming club captain at Eastlands and one of the Premier League's most formidable defenders.

Season	League		FA Cup		League Cup		Total	
	App	Goals	App	Goals	App	Goals	App	Goals
1996/97	6 (1)	0	1	0	0	0	7 (1)	0
1997/98	2 (1)	0	1	0	0	0	3 (1)	0
1998/99	15 (1)	0	2	0	2	0	19 (1)	0
1999/2000	27 (4)	0	4	0	1	0	32 (4)	0
2000/01	3	0	0	0	1	0	4	0
Total	53 (7)	0	8	0	4	0	65 (7)	0

[FACTFILE]

BORN
Dublin, 21 September 1979
POSITION
Central defender
OTHER CLUBS
Manchester City (2000–9),
Aston Villa (2009–)
HONOURS
71 Ireland caps (8 goals) (2000–)

Durrant, Iain

Loan star who arrived in the same deal that brought Duncan Ferguson to Goodison

Season	League		FA Cup		League Cup		Total	
	App	Goals	App	Goals	App	Goals	App	Goals
1994/95	4 (1)	0	0	0	0	0	4 (1)	0
Total	4 (1)	0	0	0	0	0	4 (1)	0

[FACTFILE]

BORN
Glasgow, 29 October 1966
POSITION
Midfielder
OTHER CLUBS
Glasgow Rangers (1984–98);
Kilmarnock (1998–2002)
HONOURS
20 Scotland caps (1986–2000)

THE
EVERTON
·ENCYCLOPEDIA·

Jack **Earp,** Joe **Easthorpe,** Peter **Eastoe,** Bill **Easton,** John **Ebbrell,** George **Eccles,** Tommy **Eglington,** Jack **Elliott,** Thomas **Elliott,** Everton and **England, European Cup, European Cup Winners Cup,** UEFA **Europa League,** Billy **Evans,** The **Everton Collection, Everton de Viña del Mar**

Earp,
Jack

Deputy full back from Everton's final Anfield campaign

[FACTFILE]

BORN
Nottingham,
6 September 1872
POSITION
Full back
OTHER CLUBS
Nottingham Forest;
Sheffield Wednesday
(1893–99);
Stockport County (1900)

Season	League		FA Cup		Total	
	App	Goals	App	Goals	App	Goals
1891/92	9	0	1	0	10	0
Total	9	0	1	0	10	0

Easthope,
Joe

Left winger whose two appearances came in Everton's darkest season

[FACTFILE]

BORN
26 September 1929
POSITION
Outside left
OTHER CLUB
Stockport County

Season	League		FA Cup		Total	
	App	Goals	App	Goals	App	Goals
1952/53	2	0	0	0	2	0
Total	2	0	0	0	2	0

Eastoe, Peter

Selfless forward who lifted Everton during lean years

Peter Eastoe arrived at Goodison in March 1979 as Bob Latchford's latest forward partner. Despite his finest, most selfless efforts, he was unable to revive his team-mate's once formidable goalscoring form, but would later assist the development of another great Everton number nine – Graeme Sharp.

STARTING OUT at Wolves, Eastoe, a former England Youth international, had seemed destined for great things, but struggled to

IN 1980/81
HE WAS EVERTON'S
TOP SCORER
WITH 19 LEAGUE AND
CUP GOALS

make an impression in a squad that included such names as Derek Dougan and John Richards. In 1973 he joined Swindon Town for £80,000 and after averaging a goal every other game, made the step up to the First Division in March 1976 with Queens Park Rangers. Exactly three years later he came to Everton in an exchange deal that saw Mick Walsh join a Rangers team doomed to relegation.

He came into an Everton team that was showing the first signs of decline under Gordon Lee. A strong, diligent front man, he was the sort of hard-working foil for Bob Latchford that Lee had long sought – certainly more the breed of player he preferred to the gifted but wayward showman, Duncan McKenzie. With his intelligent running off the ball and neat shimmies and touches, his play drew comparisons to Kenny Dalglish – although playing in a

faltering Everton team, he was invariably considered the 'poor man's' answer to the great Liverpool forward.

Injury limited Eastoe's impact during the 1979/80 season, but the following year he was Everton's top scorer with 19 league and cup goals – including the opener in Everton's FA Cup fourth round victory over Liverpool. Everton, however, could muster only 15th

position and Gordon Lee was out of a job. As Howard Kendall moved on many of Lee's signings that summer, Eastoe was a player he retained. During the 1981/82 season, he aided the emergence of a young Graeme Sharp. 'He was,' Sharp recalled, 'a far better player than a lot of people gave him credit for... He could shield the ball superbly well, hold it up when he got it and he had a terrific first touch. We had a very good partnership.'

FOLLOWING THE arrival of Adrian Heath in January 1982, Eastoe's opportunities became more limited. In August that year, seeking to make his own impression on the club, Kendall swapped the forward for West Bromwich Albion's Andy King. After a trail of loan moves there followed a period in Portugal, where he played out his career in the sun.

[FACTFILE]

BORN
Tamworth, 2 August 1953
POSITION
Forward
OTHER CLUBS
Wolverhampton Wanderers (1971–73);
Swindon Town (1973–76);
Queens Park Rangers (1976–79);
West Bromwich Albion (1982–85);
Leicester City (loan, 1983 & 1984);
Huddersfield Town (loan, 1983);
Walsall (1984);
Wolverhampton Wanderers (1985);
SG Farense (Portugal, 1985–87)

Season	League		FA Cup		League Cup		Europe		Total	
	App	Goals	App	Goals	App	Goals	App	Goals	App	Goals
1978/79	7 (1)	0	0	0	0	0	0	0	7 (1)	0
1979/80	23 (3)	6	5	2	3	0	2	0	33 (3)	8
1980/81	41 (1)	15	6	3	3	1	-	-	50 (1)	19
1981/82	17 (2)	5	1	1	0	0	-	-	18 (2)	6
Total	88 (7)	26	12	6	6	1	2	0	108(7)	33

Easton, Bill

Inside forward who played a supporting cameo during Dixie's greatest season

[FACTFILE]

BORN
Newcastle, 10 March 1906
POSITION
Inside forward
OTHER CLUBS
Rotherham County;
Montreal Maroons;
Blyth Spartans;
Swansea Town (1929–30);
Port Vale (1931–32);
Aldershot (1933);
Workington

Season	League		FA Cup		Total	
	App	Goals	App	Goals	App	Goals
1927/28	3	1	0	0	3	1
1928/29	12	2	0	0	12	2
Total	15	3	0	0	15	3

Eccles, George

Reliable defender who was never quite able to make a full back berth his own

[FACTFILE]

BORN
Newcastle-under-Lyme, 1874
DIED
18 December, 1945
POSITION
Full back
OTHER CLUBS
Burslem Port Vale (1893–95);
Wolverhampton Wanderers (1896–97);
Preston North End (1901);
West Ham United;
Bolton Wanderers (1904)

Season	League		FA Cup		Total	
	App	Goals	App	Goals	App	Goals
1898/99	10	0	0	0	10	0
1899/1900	20	0	1	0	21	0
1900/01	12	0	2	0	14	0
1901/02	14	0	1	0	15	0
Total	56	0	4	0	60	0

Ebbrell, John

Promising midfielder who struggled to fulfil his lofty potential

Although recently renowned for producing plenty of vastly talented young players, when John Ebbrell broke into the Everton team in the 1989/90 season his rise came in the midst of a long barren patch for the club's youth academies.

Not since Kevin Richardson and Gary Stevens came through to the first team in 1981 had a home-grown player made the cut, and it would be several more years before David Unsworth made a similar breakthrough. When Evertonians first caught a proper sight of the 20-year-old midfielder, it was obvious that he was worth the wait.

FRESH-FACED and composed, the energetic midfielder seemed to exert a confidence and maturity that belied his young years. A graduate of the FA School of Excellence at Lilleshall who would go on to captain the England under-21 team, Ebbrell was soon spoken of as a future Everton captain. A clean and accurate passer of the ball with a formidable work rate, he established himself as a regular in the transitional teams of the early 1990s.

Allied to this work ethic, Ebbrell was a brave and strong tackler. Never was this better exemplified when a crunching challenge by Liverpool's Steve McMahon in the 1991 FA Cup tie was met unflinchingly by the Everton player. McMahon, a vilified figure at Goodison, came off worst and was substituted. Two decades on, it is, perhaps, what Evertonians best remember Ebbrell for.

As Everton's transitional period became one of more marked decline, Ebbrell's promise seemed to eviscerate. Shortcomings – notably in front of goal – that were once excused on account of his inexperience became picked up

ONE OF
THE ORIGINAL
'DOGS OF WAR'

on by the club's notoriously demanding fans. For several years, fans spoke of it being 'make or break' for Ebbrell, but the progression from promising youngster to a mainstay of the Everton team never seemed to come. Maybe he would have fared better in a stronger team.

When Joe Royle became Everton manager in November 1994, Ebbrell was one of the original 'Dogs of War' – a harrier and a scrapper whose primary objective was to break up the opposition's play. But as Royle sought a more expansive style, he preferred Barry Horne and Joe Parkinson as his central midfield pairing. When Everton reached the FA Cup Final the following May, Ebbrell did not even make the substitute's bench: leaving him out, said Royle, was

the 'hardest decision' of his managerial career. Ebbrell at first seemed crushed by this omission, but made his way back into the team during the 1995/96 season. Alas, some wayward performances even made him the target of abuse from sections of his own support. With Royle eventually preferring Tony Grant and even the hapless Claus Thomsen to Ebbrell over the 1996/97 season, it was clear that his time at Everton was drawing to a close.

With his contract running out in summer 1997 and the new Bosman ruling allowing him a lucrative free transfer to the continent, Royle reluctantly sold Ebbrell to First Division Sheffield United for £1million in February that year. Here he was reunited with Howard Kendall, who was managing the Blades, but Ebbrell was to make just a single appearance at Bramall Lane.

A succession of ankle injuries picked up at the tail-end of his Everton career had been aggravated when Ebbrell played on to ease an injury crisis. His ankle was operated on but became infected and he was forced to retire while still short of his 30th birthday. Ebbrell returned to Everton in 2000 as Walter Smith's chief scout, but left after the arrival of David Moyes. He briefly worked as an agent and in 2010 became Tranmere Rovers' centre of excellence manager.

[FACTFILE]

BORN
Bromborough,
1 October 1969
POSITION
Central midfield
OTHER CLUB
Sheffield United (1997–99)

Season	League		FA Cup		League Cup		Europe		Total	
	App	Goals	App	Goals	App	Goals	App	Goals	App	Goals
1986/87	0	0	0	0	0	0	0 (1)	0	0 (1)	0
1987/88	0	0	0	0	0	0	0	0	0	0
1988/89	1 (3)	0	0	0	0	0	0 (1)	0	1 (4)	0
1989/90	13 (4)	0	2	0	2	0	-	-	17 (4)	0
1990/91	34 (2)	3	6	2	3	1	5	1	48(1)	7
1991/92	39	1	2	0	4	0	1	0	46	1
1992/93	24	1	2	0	2	0	-	-	28	1
1993/94	39	4	1	0	5	0	-	-	45	4
1994/95	26	0	3	0	0	0	-	-	29	0
1995/96	24 (1)	4	4	1	0	0	3	1	31 (1)	6
1996/97	7	0	0	0	1	0	-	-	8	0
Total	207(10)	13	20	3	17	1	9 (2)	2	253(12)	19

Eglington, Tommy

Long-serving outside left, capped by both Ireland and Northern Ireland

Widely considered one of the finest left wingers of his era, Tommy Eglington was a name that sent shivers down the spines of right backs across the country during the 1940s and 1950s. Renowned for his blistering pace, he earned 24 Ireland caps and 6 Northern Ireland caps at a time when Irish players could appear on both sides of their nation's divide.

TOMMY EGLINGTON · EVERTON F.C. (1955)

Already an accomplished and successful player in Ireland, who had played in three FAI Cup Finals during the war years, Eglington signed for Everton with Peter Farrell from Shamrock Rovers for a combined fee of £10,000 in 1946. Although he came into an Everton team struggling at the wrong end of the First Division, his devastating pace, close control and fierce shot helped illuminate an often dour Goodison Park.

Speaking in 2004, Dave Hickson said: 'Tommy was one of the best wingers I ever played with. When Tommy went down that wing, I always knew that he was going to find me. As well as supplying goals, he used to score a few himself. But I won't remember him for scoring goals, I'll remember him for making them!'

BEFORE IRELAND'S modern obsession with Manchester United and Liverpool, Everton were perhaps the most widely admired English club there, and many supporters made the journey across the Irish Sea to Goodison. Later in his life, Eglington recalled the popularity of his club at the time: 'Back in the fifties, Everton was the team in Ireland. We had a number of Irish players then and the boats would be full of fans coming over every Friday night to watch us.'

Everton were relegated in 1951 but Eglington played an important part in their revival, scoring eleven times when they regained

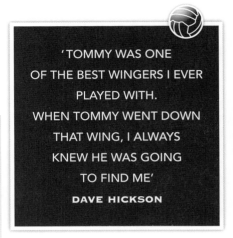

top-flight status in 1954. This was after he had single-handedly demolished Doncaster Rovers in September 1952 with five goals in a 7-1 win. He scored twice in the first half and in the second added a further three goals to his tally. The Daily Post's Leslie Edwards reported: 'Eglington's three in the second half, two with his trusty left foot and one glorious header from yet another Harris centre completed the business for the day and no Evertonian can be cross with anyone this week.'

PROMOTION IN 1954 was the highlight of Eglington's career and he later recalled: 'It was a wonderful feeling to be back in the First Division, particularly as we had done it with virtually the same team that had taken the team down.'

Speaking to the Everton match-day programme in 1991, he said: 'I suppose the greatest satisfaction was getting promotion from the Second Division in 1954. We went to Oldham on a Wednesday night needing to win 6-0 to pip Leicester for the title.

'When we went four up at half-time we felt we might do it, but we didn't score any more. Yet it was a great feeling that after having been in the team that went down three years earlier we had got the club back into the First Division.

'Apart from the result, my outstanding memory is of the support we had that night. We travelled along the East Lancashire Road and it was packed with Everton supporters waving blue and white favours and cheering us on. It was an amazing sight.'

Season	League		FA Cup		Total	
	App	Goals	App	Goals	App	Goals
1946/47	34	5	2	0	36	5
1947/48	29	3	5	1	34	4
1948/49	34	7	2	0	36	7
1949/50	34	1	5	0	39	1
1950/51	39	8	1	0	40	8
1951/52	38	8	2	0	40	8
1952/53	39	14	5	2	44	16
1953/54	41	11	3	1	44	12
1954/55	41	9	2	0	43	9
1955/56	38	8	4	2	42	10
1956/57	27	2	3	0	30	2
Total	**394**	**76**	**34**	**6**	**428**	**82**

THE IRISHMAN was also something of an entrepreneur, running a grocery store on Stanley Road. Writing in the Liverpool Echo in January 2008, Evertonian Mike Kelly, recalled:

> Tommy appeared to live over the shop and on the counter was a glass cabinet full of Tommy Eglington's Irish international caps. Many a time you would have to shout to get service, because whoever was on duty would be in the back of the shop. Tommy's international caps would still be on the counter so there was fear of them being taken by a sneak thief.

Eglington remained at Everton until 1957 when he was sold to Tranmere Rovers, now managed by Peter Farrell, where he enjoyed four productive years. In 1961 he returned to Ireland, where he spent two seasons with Cork Hibernians, making, between the ages of 38 and 40, four appearances for the League of Ireland Representative side and a fourth FAI Final appearance in 1963, before calling time on his career.

EGLINGTON then returned to his native County Dublin, where he ran a butcher's shop. A keen and skilled amateur golfer, he was a popular and regular visitor to Goodison right up until his death in 2004.

[FACTFILE]

BORN
Donneycarney, County Dublin,
15 January 1923
DIED
Raheny, County Dublin,
18 February 2004
POSITION
Winger
OTHER CLUBS
Shamrock Rovers (1942–46);
Tranmere Rovers (1957–61);
Cork Hibernians (1961–63)
HONOURS
24 Republic of Ireland caps (2 goals)
(1946–55);
6 Northern Ireland caps (1946–48)

Elliott, Jack

Attack-minded utility man during Goodison's first years

[FACTFILE]

BORN
Unknown
POSITION
Utility player

Season	League		FA Cup		Total	
	App	Goals	App	Goals	App	Goals
1890/91	1	0	0	0	1	0
1891/92	1	0	0	0	1	0
1892/93	4	1	0	0	4	1
1893/94	3	0	0	0	3	0
1894/95	4	0	1	0	5	0
1895/96	1	0	0	0	1	0
Total	**14**	**1**	**1**	**0**	**15**	**1**

Elliott, Thomas

Inside forward who partook in Everton's first post-war competitive matches

[FACTFILE]

BORN
Liverpool, 30 November 1922
POSITION
Inside forward

Season	League		FA Cup		Total	
	App	Goals	App	Goals	App	Goals
1945/46	-	-	2	0	2	0
Total	**-**	**-**	**2**	**0**	**2**	**0**

England, Everton and

Everton – and Evertonians – possess a traditionally difficult relationship with their national team. Although two of its players, Ray Wilson and soon-to-be-signed Alan Ball, were part of the 1966 World Cup winning team, there is a sense that throughout the national team's history Everton players have been under-represented and overlooked. William Ralph 'Dixie' Dean made just 16 national team appearances and none at all after his 25th birthday. Colin Harvey was picked just once for England and Howard Kendall never. Brian Labone's England debut against France in 1962 was the first time in nearly a quarter-century that an Everton player was selected for the national side.

More recently that ambivalence has been returned by Everton fans and there is an inevitable sense that a national team call-up is bad news for the club's players. Such apprehension is not misplaced and there is a long list of players who have sought moves elsewhere after allegedly having their heads turned in the England dressing room. Gary Lineker, Martin Keown, Nick Barmby, Wayne Rooney and Joleon Lescott have all departed elsewhere soon after impressing for their country.

ENGLAND PLAYED their first international in 1871, but Everton had to wait until March 1890 for Johnny Holt to became its first international when he was selected against Wales. Fred Geary followed him into the national team later that year against Ireland. Over the next quarter-century most of Everton's great players were recognised by their country, including Harold Makepeace, Jimmy Settle, Bertie Freeman and Edgar Chadwick.

This was an era when international football was defined by Home International matches and gaining a regular stint or hatful of caps was difficult. Although Chadwick and Makepeace were regularly picked for the most important match on the calendar – that versus Scotland – it would be difficult to describe any Everton player as a long-term international regular until Wilson and Ball in the 1960s.

EVERTON'S relationship with the national team was given explosive momentum by the ascent of Dean. In February 1927, aged 19, Dean marked his debut against Wales in Wrexham with a brace of goals in a 3-2 win. Seven weeks later, England travelled to Hampden to face Scotland where England were without a win since April 1904. It was a miserable run that everybody south of Hadrian's Wall was desperate to bring to an end. England, nevertheless, got off to a nervous start and fell behind. Dean, however, was never a man to pass up the opportunity of a goal. When Sidney Bishop sent him free in the 65th minute, he had no hesitation in hitting an equaliser past Harkness. As the minutes passed, a draw seemed the most likely conclusion, until Dean once more intervened. 'One defender came for him,' wrote the Daily Express's 'Broadcaster', 'and then another, and then another. They all seemed around him, but although he did not seem to be travelling much faster than they were, he stuck to the ball like a leech, kept them off somehow, and, as the goalkeeper came out, slipped the ball neatly past him for the winner.'

The Scottish crowd were dumbstruck. 'You've heard all about the Hampden roar,' recalled Dean. 'Well, when our first one went in you could have heard a pin drop. And when I got the second in the old onion bag I thought I was playing in a cemetery.'

On England's summer tour, Dean hit hat-tricks against Belgium and Luxembourg and a brace against France. Not even 21, he had struck 12 goals in his first five games. He played five more times in 1928, but in the last 11 years of his professional career just four more times for England. His fate was characteristic of an era when selection of the England team was privy to the whims of remote selectors, often biased towards players at London clubs.

The next generation of great Everton players – Cliff Britton, Joe Mercer and Tommy Lawton – all seized chances to shine for the England team. But after that there was the hiatus before Labone's arrival on the international scene. Even that represented a strange kind of glory for the defender, who turned down the chance to play at the 1966 World Cup finals – and possible football immortality – in order to get married. Instead it was left to Ray Wilson to become the first Everton player to appear in the World Cup finals (Roy Vernon, Alex Parker and Billy Bingham all played in 1958 before joining the Blues) and the only serving player to win the greatest prize of all: the World Cup.

Many tipped England to retain the trophy in 1970 when players – Labone, Ball, Keith Newton and Tommy Wright – from Everton's League Championship winning side dominated the ranks. It was a similar story when England returned to Mexico 16 years later. Four Everton players – Gary Stevens, Trevor Steven, Peter Reid and Gary Lineker – starred for England, with Lineker winning the Golden Boot after scoring six goals. But the outcome was the same and England fell, as they had done

DEAN HIT HAT-TRICKS AGAINST BELGIUM AND LUXEMBOURG AND A BRACE AGAINST FRANCE

in 1970, at the quarter-final stage. Strangely, no Everton player has appeared in an England World Cup squad since.

Not every Evertonian would mourn this fact. Among some there is a suspicion, perhaps paranoia, that their players' heads are inevitably turned when put in a dressing room with better paid colleagues from more 'glamorous' clubs. Certainly this has been borne out by experience and a string of high-profile defections that have followed England call-ups. Even 140 years after the first England international only Wilson and Ball have enjoyed careers as bona fide regulars over the course of more than three years.

ONE PLAYER who has enjoyed a lengthy England career is Wayne Rooney. As an Everton player his England debut came as a substitute in a friendly against Australia in February 2003, making him the youngest ever England player, at 17 years and 111 days. This broke a record that had stood since 1879, although it was subsequently broken again by Theo Walcott. Still only mid-career, Rooney threatens to break all manner of international records and the finest England player of his generation may go on to be his country's greatest ever servant. The tragedy is that his contribution to this record as a Manchester United player will inevitably overshadow that as a young Everton star.

European Cup
(now known as, UEFA Champions League)

Club football's ultimate prize, Everton's history in the competition is tainted with controversy

Europe's premier club competition was conceived in 1955 by Gabriel Hanot, editor of the influential French sports newspaper, L'Équipe. Hanot had been irritated by British newspapers' proclamation of Wolverhampton Wanderers as 'European Champions' on account of their victories over the mighty Spartak Moscow and Honvéd at Molineux in exhibition games in late 1954.

THE IDEA THAT English newspapers raised – that Wolves were best, simply on the back of two friendly wins – was seen as wearingly typical of a country oblivious to its true standing in European football. 'We had better wait until the Wolves travel to Moscow and Budapest to proclaim their invincibility,' he wrote in his editorial a few days after Wolves' win over Spartak. 'But if the English are so sure about their hegemony in football, this is the time to create a European tournament.'

Hanot was more than just a man of words, however. Within days he had drafted a plan for a 'European Champions Cup' based around 16 participants, who would contest a knockout competition. Games would be played in midweek and in the evenings (still a rarity in the 1950s) and be sponsored by a television station or newspaper of the participating country. When the proposals were put to UEFA the following March, European football's recently created governing body were hesitant in their support, but a month later, at a meeting convened by L'Équipe in Paris, consisting of the chairmen and presidents of Europe's leading clubs, the plan met enthusiastic backing. When L'Équipe held another meeting with UEFA in May 1955, this time their proposals met greater support, and UEFA agreed to organise the competition and respect all the decisions already approved.

On 4 September 1955, in Lisbon, the European Champions Cup kicked off with a match between Sporting Lisbon and Yugoslavia's FK Partizan. Real Madrid won the inaugural competition – as they did in each of its first five seasons – beating Stade Reims 4-3 in the first final in Paris.

The first round was expanded to include 32 teams from 1962/63 (a preliminary round restricted clubs from footballing backwaters) and remained virtually unchanged for the next 30 years.

FROM THE 1991/92 season, the European Cup incorporated a group stage. This took several formats. Initially it replaced the quarter-final stage, with two mini-leagues of four teams, from which the top team in each group progressed to the final. From 1993/94 the top two teams from the groups qualified for semi-finals; and from 1994/95 16 teams partook in the group stage with the top two teams from the four groups progressing to the quarter-finals. Several variations on this format have since taken place, but have remained largely true to the 1994/95 format.

The competition was renamed the Champions League from the 1992/93 season, although the historic trophy was retained. Backed by massive television and sponsorship rights it became football's ultimate cash cow. From 1997/98 runners-up from top European leagues were

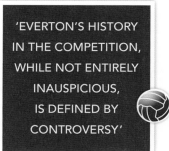

'EVERTON'S HISTORY IN THE COMPETITION, WHILE NOT ENTIRELY INAUSPICIOUS, IS DEFINED BY CONTROVERSY'

permitted to enter; from the 1999/2000 season this was extended to four clubs.

Although Newcastle United and Leeds United competed in the first years of the expanded competition, the revised Champions League ultimately led to the creation of a so-called 'Big Four' in English football, consisting of Manchester United, Chelsea, Arsenal and Liverpool. The extra revenue derived from the competition gave them vast spending power enabling them to bring their squads to such a standard that they were virtually untouchable in the league. Everton were one of the few teams to break this clique in 2004/05, and Tottenham Hotspur and the petro-dollar-subsidised Manchester City have done so since.

EVERTON'S HISTORY in the competition, while not entirely inauspicious, is nevertheless defined by controversy. In particular the fact that the post-Heysel ban on English clubs in Europe meant they were not allowed to compete in it during the mid-1980s – at a time when they were favourites – still rankles more than a quarter of a century later.

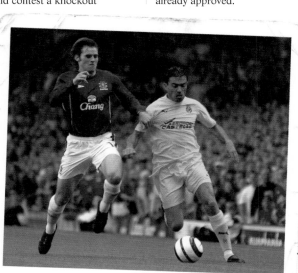

EVERTON'S European Cup debut came following their 1963 League Championship success. In an unseeded first round draw they could have drawn Real Madrid, who had already won it five times, or Benfica, European champions in 1961 and 1962, but escaped such a fate. Instead, they got Helenio Herrera's Inter Milan, who were at the start of one of the greatest periods in Inter's history and possessing such illustrious names as Sandro Mazzola, Giacinto Facchetti, Luis Suarez and the Brazilian winger, Jair.

The first leg was played at Goodison – 62,000 turned up, despite increased prices – and after being slightly overawed by their opponents in a goalless first half, Everton stepped up the pressure in the second. The game's crucial moment came in the 80th minute when Roy Vernon latched onto a Dennis Stevens pass and prodded home; the goal was disallowed for offside, a decision Brian Labone insisted was wrong until his dying day.

In the second leg at the San Siro a week later, Everton largely held their own in a game notable for Colin Harvey's debut. A minute after the interval Jair caught a glimmer of Gordon West's goal and fired a shot into the top corner from a tight angle. 'Everton were bound to play this game defensively as we did at Goodison Park and until the interval I wasn't sure whether they were going to succeed or not,' said Herrera afterwards. Inter went on to beat the Real Madrid of Puskas and Di Stefano in the final in Austria, and ended the year World Club Champions after beating Argentina's Independiente.

Seven years later, the European Cup's first round was expanded to include 32 teams, giving Everton a somewhat easier start to the 1970/71 campaign. This time they played the Icelandic part-timers Keflavik. A nervy opening to the Goodison leg saw Everton fall behind after a Gordon West own goal (West then reacted to crowd barracking by flicking a V-sign; Harry Catterick took a dim view and dropped him for Everton's next game), but recovered to win 6-2. The away leg was a 3-0 stroll.

Next were Bundesliga champions, Borussia Monchengladbach, who included the likes of Bertie Vogts and Gunter Netzer among their number. In the away leg, Everton fell behind to a first-half Vogts goal and struggled at times to control their opponents. They got back into the game through bizarre circumstances. Fans had lobbed toilet rolls onto the pitch, and the German goalkeeper, Wolfgang Kleff, was clearing his goalmouth when caught unawares by a Kendall shot.

The 1-1 draw gave Everton a crucial away goal, and in the second leg they were a side transformed. Johnny Morrissey opened the scoring and they were at times rampant, with only Kleff's heroics keeping the Germans in it. The balance of the game changed, however, when Herbert Laumen equalised and both teams became more cautious. Extra time followed, then penalties – a new concept in European competition. Joe Royle missed Everton's first spot kick, but Laumen missed for the Germans. The scores were level at 3-3 with one penalty remaining. Sandy Brown made it 4-3, and up stepped the veteran defender Ludwig Muller. He hit it sweetly, but Andy Rankin – in for the out-of-favour West – swooped acrobatically to his right, palming it away and igniting the Goodison crowd.

FOUR MONTHS later, in the quarter-finals, Everton met Panathinaikos of Greece at Goodison on 9 March 1971. The Greeks were considered the easiest of the eight quarter-finalists. Managed by Ferenc Puskas they mixed a well-organised defence with a touch of gamesmanship and were aided against Everton by great luck. Royle had a header cleared off the line, Tommy Wright's header hit the bar and Alan Ball missed an easy chance. The onslaught went on, and Rankin was not called upon until the 66th minute. A quarter of an hour later, with only their second shot of the night, and entirely against the run of play, the Greeks went in front through Antoniadis. Everton laid siege to the Greek goal and the breakthrough came in the final minute from Everton's 17th corner of the night, when David Johnson slammed the ball past the Panathinaikos goalkeeper. Catterick, who had earlier spoken of the necessity of taking a three-goal lead to Greece said, 'We played all the football. We created sufficient chances to have won easily – but we didn't stick them in the net.'

Two weeks later, Everton travelled to Greece. Like the England team in the previous summer's World Cup, they were plagued by bad fortune and intimidation: the plane was not able to land until the early hours of the morning; the hotel was circled by cars beeping their horns well into the following night; and the Everton secretary, Bill Dickinson, received a death threat before the game. Once play eventually began things got little better. On a rock-hard, bumpy pitch the Greeks closed Everton out by fair means and foul – 'They were spitting in our faces and gouging at our eyes by sticking their fingers into them,' complained Catterick – holding on for a 0-0 draw and progression to the next round via away goals. Everton's European dream was over.

There followed a 34-year-long hiatus from the European Cup, through no fault of anyone connected to Everton FC. Then in the 2004/05 season a miracle occurred: upsetting all predictions, including those of its own fans, Everton finished fourth in the Premier League. It put them through to the Champions League third qualifying round ahead of Liverpool.

But even this happy event was overshadowed by Liverpool's unexpected Champions League final victory over AC Milan. All summer the FA and UEFA procrastinated over which Merseyside team should be entered, even though the rules were clear that it should be Everton. Eventually both started in the Champions League qualifying round – Liverpool so they could defend the trophy they had just won – but the suspicion remained that UEFA were deeply unhappy at the arrangement and would like to see at least one English team eliminated at the earliest possibility.

The subsequent draw prompted immediate whisperings of conspiracy. While Everton were drawn against the previous season's La Liga runners-up, Villarreal – virtually the hardest opponents they could have faced – the other English entrants, Manchester United and Liverpool, faced Hungarians Debreceni and CSKA Sofia respectively.

Villarreal took the first leg at Goodison 2-1, where Everton looked nervy in their first European match in a decade. But it was in Spain where controversy dominated. Everton

Everton's Record

1963/64

18 SEPTEMBER 1963

RD 1, 1ST LEG V INTER MILAN [H] 0-0; 62,408

West, Parker, Harris, Gabriel, Labone, Kay, Scott, Stevens, Young, Vernon, Temple

25 SEPTEMBER 1963

RD 1, 2ND LEG V INTER MILAN [A] 0-1 (AGGREGATE 0-1); 70,000

West, Parker, Harris, Stevens, Labone, Kay, Scott, Harvey, Young, Vernon, Temple

1970/71

16 SEPTEMBER 1970

RD 1, 1ST LEG V KEFLAVIK [H] 6-2 BALL 3, ROYLE 2, KENDALL; 28,444

West, Wright, K. Newton, Kendall, Kenyon, Harvey, Husband (Whittle), Ball, Royle, Hurst, Morrissey

30 SEPTEMBER 1970

RD 1, 2ND LEG V KEFLAVIK [A] 3-0 (AGGREGATE 9-2) ROYLE 2, WHITTLE; 9,500

Rankin, Wright, K. Newton, Kendall, Labone, Harvey (Brown), Whittle, Ball (Jackson), Royle, Hurst, Morrissey

21 OCTOBER 1970

RD 2, 1ST LEG V BORUSSIA MONCHENGLADBACH [A] 1-1 KENDALL; 32,000

Rankin, Wright, K. Newton (Brown), Kendall, Kenyon, Harvey, Whittle (Husband), Ball, Royle, Hurst, Morrissey

4 NOVEMBER 1970

RD 2, 2ND LEG V BORUSSIA MONCHENGLADBACH [H] 1-1 (AET) (AGGREGATE 2-2; EVERTON WON 4-3 ON PENALTIES) MORRISSEY; 42,744

Rankin, Wright, K. Newton (Brown), Kendall, Kenyon, Harvey, Whittle (Husband), Ball, Royle, Hurst, Morrissey

9 MARCH 1971

QUARTER-FINAL 1ST LEG V PANATHINAIKOS [H] 1-1 JOHNSON; 46,407

Rankin, Wright, K. Newton, Kendall, Kenyon, Harvey, Husband (Johnson), Ball, Royle, Hurst, Morrissey

24 MARCH 1971

QUARTER-FINAL 2ND LEG V PANATHINAIKOS [A] 0-0 (AGGREGATE 1-1; PANATHINAIKOS WIN ON AWAY GOALS); 25,000

Rankin, Wright, K. Newton, Kendall, Labone, Harvey, Whittle, Ball, Royle, Hurst, Morrissey (Johnson)

2005/06

9 AUGUST 2005

3RD QUALIFYING ROUND, 1ST LEG V VILLARREAL (H) 1-2 BEATTIE; 37,685

Martyn, Hibbert, Yobo, Weir, Pistone (McFadden), Davies, Arteta, Neville, Cahill, Kilbane (Ferguson), Beattie (Bent)

24 AUGUST 2005

3RD QUALIFYING ROUND 2ND LEG V VILLARREAL [A] 1-2 (AGGREGATE 2-4) ARTETA; 22,000

Martyn, Hibbert, Yobo, Weir, Kilbane (Osman), Arteta, Cahill, Neville, Davies (McFadden), Bent, Ferguson

fell further behind after a first-half shot cruelly deflected off David Weir, but they needed two goals anyway.

For a long time this seemed a distant prospect, but on 69 minutes Mikel Arteta's brilliantly executed free kick made it 1-1 on the night and Everton were suddenly in the ascendancy. Soon after a corner was curled in and Duncan Ferguson rose to plant a textbook header into the back of the Villarreal net.

2-1 Everton on the night, 3-3 on aggregate and suddenly all to play for. But there was no goal. Pierluigi Collina, previously a World Cup final referee and reputedly the best in the world, had blown for a foul, even though it was clear that there had been no infringement. The Everton players were incandescent, but Collina merely ushered them away, allegedly telling them not to question 'the best referee in the world'.

The incident – which bore echoes of Bryan Hamilton's ghost goal against Liverpool a generation earlier – took the momentum from Everton and they were finished off by Diego Forlan's last-gasp goal.

Afterwards the only talk was of Collina's decision. 'I am so frustrated with him,' said Mikel Arteta. 'Duncan did nothing wrong. I asked him why he had disallowed the goal but he just said: "Walk away, walk away". Afterwards he said he spotted a foul before the corner, but then why didn't he blow before I took the corner? We feel we should be in the group stages but we need to get over the fact that we are not very quickly and start again.'

It was to prove not only Everton's last action in the Champions League, but Collina's final act as a referee. Four days later he announced his shock retirement as a referee, fanning another generation of conspiracy theories.

·EFC·

European Cup Winners Cup

Late lamented competition which saw Everton's only European success

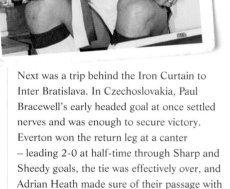

EVERTON 1985
*Back row - **Mountfield,
Gray, Steven, Sharp, Sheedy, Bracewell,**
Front - **Stevens, Southall, Ratcliffe
(Captain), Van Den Hauwe, Reid***

The European Cup Winners' Cup was a competition staged for the winners of Europe's domestic cup competitions. Founded in 1960, it ran until the end of the 1998/99 season, when it was merged with the UEFA Cup. It consisted of a straight knockout contest, with two-legged ties leading up to a final played at a neutral venue.

EVERTON APPEARED in the competition three times – in 1966/67, 1984/85 and 1995/96 – and were it not for the post-Heysel ban would probably have appeared a fourth time in 1986/87, after Liverpool claimed a First Division and FA Cup double the previous season.

Of course, the European Cup Winners' Cup saw Everton's only triumph in European competition, when they won it in 1985.

GIVEN THE GLORIES that were to follow that season, it is perhaps surprising that Everton nearly fell at the very first hurdle, against the most inauspicious opponents. University College Dublin (UCD) was, quite literally, a student team, which had risen through the Irish football pyramid to play in the top flight of the League of Ireland. Former players included the Manchester United defender Kevin Moran, and the previous season they had stunned Irish football by beating Shamrock Rovers to lift the FAI Cup. Everton were expected to beat them easily – the previous season Spurs had beaten Drogheda United 14-0 on aggregate in the

UEFA Cup, which was seen as indicative of Irish football's standard during this time.

Yet no avalanche of goals followed. UCD defended obstinately in Dublin and held out for a 0-0 draw. At Goodison a fortnight later, on ten minutes neat interplay by Trevor Steven and Adrian Heath played in Graeme Sharp to put Everton 1-0 in front. Although the thin Goodison crowd expected more goals, the Irish team continued to defend stoutly – UCD's goalkeeper, a civil servant called Alan O'Neill, was named man of the match in both legs – and was not breached again. Near the end, Ken O'Doherty skimmed the Everton bar with an effort that would have put the Blues out on away goals.

> THE EUROPEAN CUP WINNERS CUP SAW EVERTON'S ONLY TRIUMPH IN EUROPEAN COMPETITION WHEN THEY WON IT IN 1985

Next was a trip behind the Iron Curtain to Inter Bratislava. In Czechoslovakia, Paul Bracewell's early headed goal at once settled nerves and was enough to secure victory. Everton won the return leg at a canter – leading 2-0 at half-time through Sharp and Sheedy goals, the tie was effectively over, and Adrian Heath made sure of their passage with a third goal on 63 minutes.

For the quarter-finals Everton were touched with fortune, avoiding AS Roma and Bayern Munich, and instead being handed a tie with Fortuna Sittard, a Dutch team whose ranks were replete with semi-professionals. They were, however, wily opponents and in the first leg at Goodison, held Everton to a first-half stalemate. The 26,000 crowd showed signs of restiveness at the interval, but Andy Gray soon took charge of proceedings. Shortly after the break he opened the scoring with a low stab after the Fortuna goalkeeper failed to hold on to Peter Reid's shot. The game was still tightly balanced as the game entered its final quarter. But Gray put paid to Sittard's hopes, first when

he met Terry Curran's cross with a diving header, then when he completed his hat-trick by hitting home Sheedy's cross. In the return leg, Graeme Sharp killed the tie after just 15 minutes, scoring a crucial away goal. There was no collapse from the Dutch team, but Peter Reid's late goal secured an emphatic 5-0 aggregate win.

In the semi-finals, Everton were drawn against the competition's favourites, Bayern Munich. What followed became part of Everton folklore.

The away leg in Bavaria came first and promised Everton's sternest test. Marshalled by Lothar Matthaus, Bayern were an outstanding team and packed with internationals, including Belgian goalkeeper, Jean-Marie Pfaff; the defenders Klaus Augenthaler and Wolfgang Dremmler; Danish winger, Soren Lerby; and the deadly forward pairing of Dieter Hoeness and Ludwig Kogl, who possessed a ferocious combination of power and pace. Everton's task was made more difficult after Sheedy and Gray failed fitness tests on the morning of the match. Kevin Richardson and Alan Harper were brought in and neither let their team-mates down in a performance of iron resolve. With magnificent discipline and determination, the Everton team stuck to their task of withstanding the Bayern attack.

Only once did Bayern break through in a packed Olympic stadium: Michael Rummenigge, younger brother of the legendary Karl-Heinz, beating Southall with a shot only to see Richardson clear it off the line. It maintained a stalemate and gave Everton an excellent chance in the second leg.

The return leg, on 24 April 1985, perhaps saw Goodison's greatest night. On a balmy evening, Bayern Munich were outfought on the pitch by the players and sung off the park by nearly 50,000 Evertonians. Gray and Reid were fit again, meaning Everton were at full strength.

IT WAS BAYERN who took the lead on 38 minutes, when Southall conceded his first goal in the competition to Dieter Hoeness. Yet Everton were unfortunate to go in at half-time a goal down. In the early moments of the game, Trevor Steven had flashed a shot wide and Kevin Sheedy had twice gone close, first being denied only by the onrushing Pfaff and again with a trademark free kick that left the Bayern goalkeeper scrambling to his far post. In the middle of the park, Reid and Bracewell were dominating their more experienced opponents as Everton took the game to the Germans.

At half-time Kendall told his players to maintain their tempo and continue to attack Bayern. They entered the second half to a wall of such noise from the Goodison crowd as had rarely been heard before. As Gray put it, 'I don't think I've ever been overcome by so much noise and you could see that Bayern was suffering.' Both players and fans were abundantly aware of the size of the task: that Everton needed two goals to overcome the Germans, who now had a crucial away goal.

WITHIN THREE minutes they got one back. Gray back-headed Stevens' long throw in and Sharp glanced home his 29th goal of the season. The Goodison crowd roared the team on and on 73 minutes they got their reward in a reverse of the roles that had led to the first goal. Stevens' launched another long throw into the Bayern area, this time Sharp flicked it on and with Pfluger inadvertently impeding his own goalkeeper, Gray was allowed to steal in with a header and make the score 2-1. All night long the physical presence of Gray had unsettled the Bayern Munich defence and one of their centre backs had had his nose broken after an overzealous challenge by the Scot. Now his strength and bravery had cost them again.

Everton's third and final goal came late on. Paul Bracewell played a ball to the buccaneering Gray who found himself in space, just inside the Bayern half. He played the ball first time, without looking up, into the path of Trevor Steven. Steven raced clear of the straggling Bayern defence, held his nerve and calmly drew Pfaff out of his goal as he advanced unchallenged, then dispatched the ball past the exposed goalkeeper and into the bottom corner of the Gwladys Street net to secure Everton's place in the final. 'The noise from the fans behind the goal sent the roof of the Gwladys Street [stand] soaring into the air before miraculously falling back into place,' recalled Mike Owen in his history of Everton in Europe, Der Ball ist Rund. 'Around the ground there were so many men kissing each other that it looked like a Gay Pride festival. The Germans looked at each other, crestfallen, as from the heavens came the sound of Tchaikovsky's 1812 Overture, with cannons exploding.'

Given such excitement, the final in Rotterdam against Rapid Vienna might have seemed anticlimactic. As they would in later years in

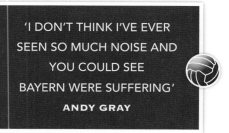

Villareal, Nuremburg and Liege, Evertonians invaded foreign soil, taking over Holland's second city. It was a carnival atmosphere, with epic games of football played in the city's main square against local policemen beforehand, and vast quantities of local beer consumed.

As to the game, Rapid Vienna seemed nervous and Everton were in control throughout. Perhaps surprisingly it took Everton 57 minutes to break the deadlock. Gray, who had already seen a goal disallowed, scored after Sharp intercepted Weinhofer's back-pass and pulled the ball back for his fellow Scot to volley home. Fifteen minutes later Everton doubled their lead through Steven's far post shot after Sheedy's corner. With six minutes remaining Hans Krankl scored an unexpected goal, but any concerns were short-lived. A minute later Sheedy shimmied through the Rapid Vienna defence to score Everton's third goal and seal the club's first and, to date, only European trophy.

The richly deserved win was generously acknowledged by the Rapid Vienna manager, Otto Baric. 'Everton were the better team and we could not cope with their speed and aggression,' he said. 'We were without three important midfield players, but even on our best form we could not have lived with Everton tonight.' Howard Kendall was genuinely thrilled by what he had seen. 'It was something special tonight, a truly tremendous performance,' he told reporters. 'We showed everybody what a good side we are. In terms of possession football you will see nothing better. Everyone in the side was magnificent. We deserved every bit of our win.'

Everton's Record

1966/67

28 SEPTEMBER 1966
RD 1, 1ST LEG V AALBORG [A] 0-0;
11,385
West, Wright, Wilson, Gabriel, Labone,
Harvey, Temple, Ball, Young, Trebilcock,
Morrissey

11 OCTOBER 1966
RD 1, 2ND LEG V AALBORG [H] 2-1
(AGGREGATE 2-1) MORRISSEY, BALL;
36,628
West, Wright, Wilson, Gabriel, Labone,
Harvey, Temple, Ball, Young, Husband,
Morrissey

9 NOVEMBER 1966
RD 2, 1ST LEG V REAL ZARAGOZA [A]
0-2; 14,364
West, Wright, Wilson, Gabriel, Labone,
Harvey, Scott, Ball, Young, Temple,
Morrissey

23 NOVEMBER 1966
RD 2, 2ND LEG V REAL ZARAGOZA [H]
1-0 (AGGREGATE 1-2) BROWN;
56,077
West, Wright, Wilson, Gabriel, Labone,
Harvey, Scott, Ball, Young, Brown, Temple

1984/85

19 SEPTEMBER 1984
RD 1, 1ST LEG V UNIVERSITY COLLEGE
DUBLIN [A] 0-0; 9,750
Southall, Stevens, Bailey, Ratcliffe,
Mountfield, Reid, Steven (Curran), Heath,
Sharp, Bracewell, Sheedy

2 OCTOBER 1984
RD 1, 2ND LEG V UNIVERSITY COLLEGE
DUBLIN [H] 1-0 (AGGREGATE 1-0)
SHARP; 16,277
Southall, Stevens, Bailey, Ratcliffe,
Mountfield, Reid, Steven, Heath
(Wakenshaw), Sharp, Bracewell, Curran

24 OCTOBER 1984
RD 2, 1ST LEG V INTER BRATISLAVA [A]
1-0 BRACEWELL; 15,000
Southall, Stevens, Bailey, Ratcliffe,
Mountfield, Reid, Steven, Heath, Sharp,
Bracewell, Harper

7 NOVEMBER 1984
RD 2, 2ND LEG V INTER BRATISLAVA
[H] 3-0 (AGGREGATE 4-0) HEATH,
SHARP, SHEEDY; 25,007
Southall, Stevens, Bailey, Ratcliffe,
Mountfield, Reid (Harper), Steven, Heath,
Sharp, Bracewell, Sheedy (Morrissey)

6 MARCH 1985
QUARTER-FINAL 1ST LEG V FORTUNA
SITTARD [H] 3-0 GRAY 3; 25,782
Southall, Stevens, Van den Hauwe, Ratcliffe,
Mountfield, Reid (Richardson), Steven,
Curran, Gray, Bracewell, Richardson

20 MARCH 1985
QUARTER-FINAL 2ND LEG V FORTUNA
SITTARD [A] 2-0 (AGGREGATE 5-0)
REID, SHARP; 16,425
Southall, Stevens, Van den Hauwe, Ratcliffe
(Atkins), Mountfield, Reid, Steven, Curran,
Sharp (Wakenshaw), Harper, Richardson

10 APRIL 1985
SEMI-FINAL 1ST LEG V BAYERN MUNICH
[A] 0-0; 67,000
Southall, Stevens, Van den Hauwe, Ratcliffe,
Mountfield, Reid, Steven, Harper, Sharp,
Bracewell, Richardson

24 APRIL 1985
SEMI-FINAL 2ND LEG
V BAYERN MUNICH [H] 3-1
(AGGREGATE 3-1)
GRAY, SHARP, STEVEN; 49,476
Southall, Stevens, Van den Hauwe,
Ratcliffe, Mountfield, Reid, Steven,
Sharp, Gray, Bracewell, Sheedy

15 MAY 1985
FINAL V RAPID VIENNA (ROTTERDAM)
3-1 GRAY, SHEEDY, STEVEN; 40,000
Southall, Stevens, Van den Hauwe, Ratcliffe,
Mountfield, Reid, Steven, Sharp,
Gray, Bracewell, Sheedy

1995/96

14 SEPTEMBER 1995
RD 1, 1ST LEG V KR REYKJAVIK [A] 3-2
EBBRELL, UNSWORTH (PEN),
AMOKACHI; 5,956
Southall, Jackson (Holmes), Watson,
Unsworth, Ablett, Limpar (Grant),
Parkinson, Ebbrell, Hinchcliffe, Amokachi,
Rideout

28 SEPTEMBER 1995
RD 1, 2ND LEG V KR REYKJAVIK [H]
3-1 (AGGREGATE 6-3) STUART,
GRANT, RIDEOUT; 18,422
Southall, Barrett, Short, Unsworth,
Hinchcliffe, Grant, Parkinson, Ebbrell,
Limpar, Amokachi (Stuart), Rideout

19 OCTOBER 1995
RD 2, 1ST LEG V FEYENOORD [H] 0-0;
27,526
Southall, Jackson (Holmes), Barrett, Short,
Ablett, Unsworth, Samways, Horne, Limpar
(Barlow), Stuart, Rideout

2 NOVEMBER 1995
RD 2, 2ND LEG V FEYENOORD [A] 0-1
(AGGREGATE 0-1); 40,289
Southall, Jackson, Short, Watson, Ablett
(Barlow), Hinchcliffe, Stuart, Ebbrell
(Grant), Horne, Amokachi, Rideout

Europa League, UEFA

Third incarnation of UEFA's second-tier cup competition

Created in 2009, UEFA's Europa League represented the third incarnation of its second-tier competition, following the Fairs Cup and UEFA Cup. The rebranding included a merger with the oft-maligned Intertoto Cup, an enlarged competition format and an expanded group stage. Greater prize money was provided by UEFA in an attempt to reduce the economic polarisation between regular Champions League qualifiers and the rest of the pack. UEFA also used the competition as a testing ground for various experiments, including the use of two additional match officials.

Everton entered the inaugural round of the competition in 2009, reaching the Round of 32 before falling to Sporting Lisbon.

Everton's Record

2009/10

20 AUGUST 2009
PLAYOFF ROUND 1ST LEG
V SIGMA OLOMOUC [H] 4-0
SAHA 2, RODWELL 2;
27,433
Howard, Hibbert, Yobo, Neville, Baines, Osman, Cahill, Rodwell (Gosling), Fellaini, Pienaar (Vaughan), Saha (Jô)

27 AUGUST 2009
PLAYOFF ROUND 2ND LEG
V SIGMA OLOMOUC [A] 1-1
(AGGREGATE 5-1) PIENAAR;
10,212
Howard, Hibbert, Yobo, Neville, Baines, Gosling, Osman (Baxter), Rodwell, Pienaar (Wallace), Fellaini, Jô (Yakubu)

17 SEPTEMBER 2009
GROUP I MATCH
V AEK ATHENS [H] 4-0
YOBO, DISTIN, PIENAAR, JÔ;
26,747
Howard, Gosling, Yobo, Distin, Baines, Pienaar (Saha), Cahill (Osman), Rodwell, Fallaini, Bilyaletdinov (Yakubu), Jô

1 OCTOBER 2009
GROUP I MATCH
V FC BATE BORISOV [A]* 2-1
FELLAINI, CAHILL; 23,000
Howard, Gosling, Hibbert, Distin, Baines, Cahill, Osman, Fellaini, Bilyaletdinov (Baxter), Jô, Yakubu (Agard)

22 OCTOBER 2009
GROUP I MATCH V BENFICA
[A] 0-5; 44,534
Howard, Gosling, Hibbert, Distin, Coleman, Cahill, Fellaini, Rodwell, Bilyaletdinov (Saha), Jô, Yakubu (Baxter)

5 NOVEMBER 2009
GROUP I MATCH
V BENFICA [H] 0-2;
30,790
Howard, Hibbert, Yobo, Distin, Baines, Gosling (Jô), Cahill, Rodwell, Fellaini, Bilyaletdinov, Yakubu (Agard)

2 DECEMBER 2009
GROUP I MATCH
V AEK ATHENS [A] 1-0
BILYALETDINOV; 15,000
Howard, Coleman, Hibbert, Distin (Duffy), Baines, Gosling (Baxter), Pienaar, Fellaini, Bilyaletdinov, Cahill, Jô (Yakubu)

17 DECEMBER 2009
GROUP I MATCH V FC BATE
BORISOV [H] 0-1; 18,242
Nash, Coleman, Duffy, Hibbert (Mustafi), Bidwell, Forshaw, Osman (Craig), Rodwell (Akpan), Baxter, Agard, Yakubu

Group I Table

Team	P	W	D	L	GF	GA	GD	Pts
Benfica	6	5	0	1	13	3	10	15
Everton	6	3	0	3	7	9	-2	9
FC BATE Borisov	6	2	1	3	7	9	-2	7
AEK Athens	6	1	1	4	5	11	-6	4

* Played at the Dinamo Stadium, Minsk

16 FEBRUARY 2010
ROUND OF 32
V SPORTING LISBON [H]
2-1 PIENAAR, DISTIN;
28,131
Howard, Neville, Yobo, Distin, Baines, Donovan, Osman, Arteta (Rodwell), Pienaar, Cahill (Yakubu), Saha (Bilyaletdinov)

25 FEBRUARY 2010
ROUND OF 32
V SPORTING LISBON [A]
0-3 (AGGREGATE 2-4);
17,609
Howard, Neville, Yobo, Senderos (Jagielka), Baines, Bilyaletdinov (Rodwell), Osman, Arteta, Pienaar, Donovan (Yakubu), Saha

Evans, Billy

Little-used full back who made his mark beyond Goodison

[FACTFILE]

BORN
Llanglos, 1899
POSITION
Full back
OTHER CLUBS
Swansea Town (1920);
Southend United (1921–23);
Queens Park Rangers (1924)

	League		FA Cup		Total	
Season	App	Goals	App	Goals	App	Goals
1919/20	2	0	0	0	2	0
Total	**2**	**0**	**0**	**0**	**0**	**0**

The **Everton Collection** (also known as the David France Collection)

AS A YOUNG BOY in the 1950s, a keen Evertonian named David France began assembling a collection of programmes at his Widnes home. Always infatuated with the Blues, his boyhood hobby later became an adult obsession as he put together a vast collection of artefacts, letters and other ephemera. A successful businessman, he moved to the United States, always with one eye on Everton, still accumulating, still collecting. By the turn of the century, France's collection had become, according to the auction house Christies, 'the finest and most comprehensive collection of its type relating to a single football club'. Together it was valued in the millions.

Yet France's collection was more than just a mountain of ephemera. It represented a timeline of Everton history stemming from the very roots of the club's existence to the present day. It included some of football's rarest artefacts and comprised 10,000 collated items, many of which pre-dated the formative years of the Football League. The collection included:

- An anthology of programmes dating back to 1886, containing 6065 programmes covering the club's participation in league, cup competitions, friendly games and reserve team fixtures between 1886 and 2001.

- Everton ledgers: Considered by France to be the 'DNA of Everton Football Club', the official club ledgers consist of a complete run of 29 volumes chronicling all of the scheduled weekly meetings and emergency meetings of the early management committee and later board of directors from 1886 to 1964.

- Everton medals: 40 medals covering all of the major competitions won by Everton between 1890 and 1985.

- Everton tickets, including of a run of 11 season tickets/ members cards from 1881–92, featuring seasons at Stanley Park, Priory Road and Anfield.

- Victorian-era photographs including the first known Everton team group from 1881 and the only known photograph of the first championship-winning side of 1891.

- Miscellaneous ephemera, including official hand-written tenders for the construction of Anfield, examples of players' contracts from 1890–1940, a complete set of Everton cigarette cards from 1897–1939, 20 Victorian-era post-cards featuring early team groups, several album pages of pre-war autographs and various examples of turn-of-the-century club correspondence. Other items include over 100 Everton books (every known volume), foreign tour itineraries, club function menus as well as club and international shirts and England caps.

Everton de Viña del Mar, or Club Deportes (CD) Everton

Leading Chilean club named in tribute to their English cousins

The formation of a Chilean football club bearing Everton's name is the most enduring result of Everton's groundbreaking 1909 tour of South America.

THREE WEEKS AFTER the end of the 1908/09 season, in which Everton had finished First Division runners-up, the squad made the three-week steamer journey from Southampton to Buenos Aires. They were joined by Tottenham Hotspur, that year's Second Division runners-up, on what was essentially a tour to spread the gospel of football through South America.

Within hours of their arrival, the two English clubs played the first game ever played between two professional clubs in South America – a 2-2 draw watched by the Argentine President, José Figueroa Alcorta. Although all but one of the exhibition games Everton and Spurs played was in Argentina, the excitement of their visit transcended the country's borders.

ON 24 JUNE 1909 – a day before Everton headed back to England – in the Chilean port of Valparaiso, a group of Anglo-Chileans formed a football club and decided to call it Everton. Valparaiso was a well-known stopover for British sailors and the eight included two expatriates, Cornishman Frank Boundy and Scot Malcolm Frazer, who would both return home on the outbreak of war five years later, and lose their lives on the Somme in July 1916. The leader of the group was David Newton Foxley Chapman (more commonly referred to as Eduardo de la Barra), a third-year humanities student whose parents had emigrated from Liverpool in 1859 and set up the port's first steam-driven flour mill.

In its early days the club played friendly games against mostly expatriate opponents in the winter and practised athletics in the summer. In 1919 the name was changed to Club Deportes Everton, to reflect its prominence as a sporting club at both national and international level. Two Everton athletes – Rodolfo Hammersley and

Harold Rosenqvist – had already been crowned South American champions by this stage.

In 1944 CD Everton were elected members of the Chilean national professional league on condition of their moving five miles up the coast to Viña del Mar. The transition was a success. In 1950 they became the first provincial club to lift the league title, a feat they repeated two years later. Further league titles came in 1976 and, following a dramatic play-off victory over giants Colo Colo, 2008. CD Everton have won one Copa Chile, in 1984.

The club's Estadio Sausalito hosted group, quarter-final and semi-final games during the 1962 World Cup finals, just as Goodison would do four years later.

Since 2002 ties between the English and Chilean teams have greatly increased with the formation of the Ruleteros society, a fan-based organisation aimed at promoting friendship between the clubs.

Although the founding fathers of the two clubs never encountered each other, there are remarkable similarities in terms of ethos and tradition. 'Our club certainly became a watchword for reliability and trustworthiness,' Alfredo Aravena recorded on CD Everton's 50th anniversary in 1959. 'There is one point that should not be forgotten, and that is out of Everton grew the Corinthian spirit of sport.

'It is for this reason that the current board and future directors should strive to ensure that this aspect of the game be safeguarded and encouraged in order to provide our youngsters with a healthy and enjoyable form of entertainment, which may, in turn, provide a sound basis for those who aspire to practise the sport at a professional level.'

On 4 August 2010 the close ties between the two clubs reached their apotheosis when Everton's Chilean cousins made the long journey from South America for a pre-season friendly. Everton FC ran out 2-0 winners on a memorable evening, with goals from Jermaine Beckford and Marouane Fellaini.

France's dream was always for the collection to eventually rest in the hands of Everton. To this end negotiations opened with the club in 2003 for the purchase of the collection. Although valued at between £1.2million and £2million, loathe to see his work divided among private collectors, France offered the entire body of material to Everton for £800,000, only to be told the club could not afford or justify the outlay. Instead it helped launch a charitable trust to raise the necessary funds.

EVERTON'S DECISION was criticised by some fans, although it pledged £250,000 towards the total needed and promised to donate its own holdings of memorabilia to complement France's incredible collection. There followed a lengthy and exhausting fundraising campaign, with the charitable trust also lobbying for lottery funding.

In November 2007 it was revealed that a £1million bid for lottery funding had been successful. Hailing this announcement, Lord Grantchester said: 'This means that the history of Everton Football Club and indeed the history of football on Merseyside has been safeguarded for future generations.' David Stoker, manager of the Liverpool Record Office where the collection was to be housed, added: 'We are very proud and extremely excited to be providing a home for this remarkable football archive, which has important information on Liverpool FC as well as Everton FC.'

Over the following two years, fans were treated to 'tasters' of the Everton Collection, before it was finally made available to the public – via the Liverpool Public Records Office and an extensive website – in September 2009.

THE

EVERTON
·ENCYCLOPEDIA·

FA Community Shield, FA Cup, Ted **Falder, Fanzines,** Adam **Farley,** Alec **Farrall,** Peter **Farrell,** Gareth **Farrelly,** Stan **Fazackerley,** Jimmy **Fell,** Marouane **Fellaini,** Duncan **Ferguson,** Mick **Ferguson,** Tom **Fern,** Manuel **Fernandes,** Matteo **Ferrari,** Wally **Fielding, Finch Farm,** Harold **Finnis,** Tom **Fleetwood,** George **Fleming,** Albert **Flewitt, Footballing innovations and landmarks, Football League,** Fred **Forbes, Foreign players,** Adam **Forshaw,** Dick **Forshaw,** David **France,** Bert **Freeman, Full Members Cup**

FA Community Shield
(also known as the Charity Shield)

Opening match of the English football season, which Everton have won nine times

The Community Shield is the traditional curtain-raiser to the English football season, played on the weekend preceding the opening top-flight fixtures.

IT WAS FIRST contested in 1908 and has since taken on a variety of guises. It initially succeeded the Sheriff of London Charity Shield, introduced in 1898 as a professionals versus amateurs cup ('gentlemen versus the players'). Following a falling-out between leading amateur clubs and the FA, football's governing body initiated its own trophy to be played between the First Division champions and the Southern League champions. There followed several variations of this: from 1913 it was staged between amateurs and professionals; in 1921 it was contested between the Football League and FA Cup winners for the first time, and over the next decade or so alternated between these two formats.

In 1930 the Football League winner versus FA Cup winner format returned and, with a couple of exceptions, has remained ever since. From 1959 it has been staged before the start of the league season – rather than midweek in autumn as had often previously been the case. The game was first staged at Wembley in 1974. In 2002 it was renamed the Community Shield, after a government report said that the FA had breached fund-raising regulations in the way it handled cash raised by the game. The renaming of the competition removed it from the jurisdiction of the Charity Commission.

EVERTON FIRST CONTESTED the Charity Shield in 1928 and have one of the best records in the competition, winning it eight times and sharing it on another occasion.

24 OCTOBER 1928
v Blackburn Rovers (Old Trafford) 2-1
Dean 2; **4000**
Davies, Cresswell, O'Donnell, Griffiths, Hart, Virr, Ritchie, Forshaw, Dean, Weldon, Troup

12 OCTOBER 1932
v Newcastle United (St James' Park) 5-3
Dean 4, **Johnson;** 10,000
Sagar, Williams, Cresswell, Britton, White, Thomson, Critchley, McGourty, Dean, Johnson, Stein

18 OCTOBER 1933
v Arsenal (Goodison) 0-3; 18,000
Sagar, Cook, Bocking, Britton, Gee, Thomson, Geldard, Dunn, White, Johnson, Stein

17 AUGUST 1963
v Manchester United (Goodison) 4-0
Gabriel, Stevens, Temple, Vernon; **54,844**
West, Parker, Meagan, Gabriel, Labone, Kay, Scott, Stevens, Young, Vernon, Temple

13 August 1966
v Liverpool (Goodison) 0-1; 63,329
West, Wright, Wilson, Gabriel, Labone, Glover, Scott, Young, Trebilcock, Harvey, Temple

8 August 1970
v Chelsea (Stamford Bridge) 2-1
Whittle, Kendall; 43,547
West, Wright, Newton, Kendall, Labone, Harvey, Husband, Ball, Royle, Hurst, Whittle

18 AUGUST 1984
v Liverpool (Wembley) 1-0
Grobbelaar (Own Goal); **100,000**
Southall, Stevens, Bailey, Ratcliffe, Mountfield, Reid, Steven, Heath, Sharp, Bracewell, Richardson

10 AUGUST 1985
v Manchester United (Wembley) 2-0
Steven, Heath; **82,000**
Southall, Stevens, Van Den Hauwe (Bailey), Ratcliffe, Mountfield, Reid, Steven, Lineker (Heath), Sharp, Bracewell, Sheedy

16 AUGUST 1986
v Liverpool (Wembley) 1-1 ***Heath;***
88,231 (Trophy Shared)
Mimms, Harper, Power, Ratcliffe, Marshall, Langley, Steven, Heath, Sharp, Richardson, Sheedy (Adams (Wilkinson))

1 AUGUST 1987
v Coventry City (Wembley) 1-0 ***Clarke;***
88,000
Mimms, Harper, Power, Ratcliffe, Watson, Reid, Steven, Clarke, Sharp, Heath, Sheedy (Pointon)

13 AUGUST 1995
v Blackburn Rovers (Wembley) 1-0
***Samways;* (40,169)**
Southall, Barrett, Ablett, Unsworth, Hinchcliffe, Grant (Watson), Horne, Parkinson, Samways, Limpar, Rideout

EVERTON 1987
Back row - **Reid, Mimms, Harper, Watson, Marshall, Power, Mountfield, Jones**
Front - **Ratcliffe (Captain), Steven, Clarke, Sharp, Sheedy, Heath, Adams, Pointon**

FA Cup,
Everton and the

The most famous domestic cup competition in world football

The FA Cup is the oldest and most distinguished national cup competition in the world, with a tradition that spans some 140 years and a fame that reaches every far corner of the globe. Everton have always been one of the FA Cup's great competitors, winning the competition five times and appearing in 13 finals and 25 semi-finals. Many of its most enduring moments – particularly the dramatic 1966 final – are the result of Everton's participation.

The competition was created in 1871, when association football was still in its infancy. It was the idea of the FA's Honorary Secretary, Charles Alcock, a key influence in elevating football from the pursuit of the few to the obsession of the masses. He was the principal force behind the first international matches between England and Scotland in the early 1870s, but his most enduring legacy is the creation of the FA Cup.

AT HARROW School, Alcock had played in inter-house 'sudden death' competitions and remembered vividly the thrill of these schoolboy encounters. Among his colleagues at the FA and the Sportsman newspaper (for which Alcock was a regular contributor) he floated the idea of initiating a knockout competition along similar lines and found it met with enthusiastic approval. The FA swiftly agreed to his proposal and on 20 July 1871 put out the announcement: 'That it is

EVERTON BOAST A PROUD RECORD IN THE COMPETITION

desirable that a Challenge Cup should be established in connection with the Association for which all clubs belonging to the Association should be invited to compete.' Thus, in a single short sentence, the FA Cup was born.

STANDING JUST 18 inches high in its original form, the FA Cup towers high in the history of football. (The original trophy was stolen in 1895 and never recovered. The second trophy was presented to Lord Kinnaird to commemorate his 21st year as FA President in 1911; the third trophy was replaced with an exact replica in 1992 – the cup that we know today.) In its first year just 15 of the Football Association's 50 members entered, almost all London-based, and Alcock himself captained Wanderers to a 1-0 victory over Royal Engineers in the final. Although the first seven finals would each see either Alcock's men or Royal Engineers emerge with their name inscribed across the trophy's base, with every passing year the competition – the only national football competition at that time – increased in strength: the number of entrants rose exponentially and the level of interest it attracted changed football from being the leisure pursuit of a few former public schoolboys to a sport which attracted national attention – and participation.

The key year in the competition's evolution was 1883, when Blackburn Olympic beat Old Etonians 2-1 in the final at Kennington Oval. From then on, the dominance of the old, southern-based public schoolboys and amateurs diminished and it became a genuine national competition.

In these first years Everton were content with the excitement of local cup competitions, but in the 1886/87 season entered the FA Cup for the first time. Their first match came against Glasgow Rangers – this being a time when Scottish teams still entered the FA Cup – in autumn 1886. Yet when Rangers arrived at Anfield, Everton, on discovering they had an ineligible player, forfeited the tie and a friendly was played instead, which they lost 0-1.

A year later Everton tried again in contentious circumstances. This time they were drawn away at Bolton Wanderers, but what followed was to epitomise the petty bickering that plagued local football rivalries in the period. After the first match – a 1-0 defeat – was declared null when a Bolton player was ruled ineligible, Everton played out two draws before finally seeing off the Lancastrians 2-1. They went on to be turned over

6-0 by Preston North End in the second round. But by then Bolton had launched a counter-appeal that Everton had also fielded ineligible players. The FA ruled against Everton, and, unable to kick them out of the FA Cup, ordered that Anfield be closed for a month. Everton did not appear in the competition again until January 1890, when they famously hit Derby County for 11 goals in what remains their record victory.

A FIRST FA Cup final appearance came in 1893, ending in defeat to Wolves. In 1897 Everton lost to Aston Villa in the final at Crystal Palace, but nine years later finally had their moment of glory, beating favourites Newcastle 1-0. In 1933 Everton became the first Merseyside team to appear at Wembley, beating Manchester City 3-0, to win the competition a second time. Seventy-six years later they would be the first team from Liverpool to appear at the new Wembley, when they defeated Manchester United on penalties to win the 2009 semi-final.

Between those two dates are interspersed all manner of dramas and stories. From the heroics of Dave Hickson in 1953 and the comeback kids of 1966, to the agonies of 1968 – when nothing seemed to go Everton's way in the final against West Bromwich Albion – and 1985, via the high drama of the 4-4 derby draw in 1991, and humiliations at the hands of clubs like Shrewsbury, Oldham and Tranmere Rovers. Although it has lost some of its lustre, the FA Cup remains the premier domestic cup competition in the world, and its finals are watched by global audiences of hundreds of millions in some 200 countries.

Sponsorship was introduced to the competition in 1994/95, when Littlewoods signed a three-year deal to endorse it. Perhaps fittingly, given the late John Moores' links to the club, Everton were the first winners of the Littlewoods-sponsored FA Cup. AXA insurance and E.ON energy company have since had sponsorship deals with the competition. Budweiser took over sponsorship for the 2012 competition with a three-year deal.

EVERTON boast a proud record in the competition. Although seven other teams have won it more times than their five wins, only Arsenal and Manchester United have made more semi-final and final appearances than Everton. In lean stretches of the club's history – such as the 1950s and 1990s – the competition provided one of the few distractions from the mediocrity that otherwise consumed the club.

Everton in the FA Cup Final

1893 Everton had every right to be confident going into their first FA Cup final. Only a week earlier they had faced Wolves at Molineux and, despite fielding a reserve team, ran out 4-2 winners.

At Manchester's Fallowfield stadium, Everton boasted six internationals and were overwhelming favourites for the match. But nothing seemed to go quite right for them and when Wolves centre back Harry Allen let fly with a spectacular shot, Everton's goalkeeper Dick Williams found himself blinded by the sun and conceded. Despite Everton's best efforts, Allen's was the only goal of the game.

25 MARCH
**v Wolverhampton Wanderers
(Fallowfield, Manchester) 0-1; 45,067**
Williams, Kelso, Howarth, Boyle, Holt, Stewart, Latta, Gordon, Maxwell, Chadwick, Milward

1897 Considered one of the classic Victorian FA Cup finals, 1897 saw the two footballing heavyweights of the decade come face to face.

A record crowd for a final saw Villa take an early lead, but thereafter Everton really took the game to the Midlanders. John Bell, in particular, was in mesmerising form. 'The game was made memorable by John Bell's extraordinary efforts to win the match for his side, and no one admired his wonderful ability more than the supporters of Aston Villa,' record William Gibson and Alfred Pickford in their seminal history of English football.

Everton took a 2-1 lead through Bell and Richard Boyle, but their defensive frailties let them down. Bob Menham, their hapless goalkeeper, was singled out for criticism as Everton fell 3-2 behind by the 35th minute. Extraordinarily, given the dramas that preceded it, the score remained the same until the final whistle.

10 APRIL
**v Aston Villa (Crystal Palace)
2-3** *Bell, Boyle;* **65,891**
Menham, Meecham, Storrier, Boyle, Holt, Stewart, Taylor, Bell, Hartley, Chadwick, Milward

1906 In contrast to some of the excitement that accompanied Everton's early FA Cup adventures, the 1906 final was a drab affair. But it was the result that mattered, and Sandy Young's 77th-minute goal brought the famous trophy to Goodison for the first time.

'The winners found their feet from the start, and with the exception of a few fitful excursions and alarms of their so-called opponents, they were top-dog all the way,' reported the Morning Leader. 'Everton ... took off the FA Cup after a hard struggle, in which, whatever their rivals Newcastle United did, they did themselves full justice, and gained a well merited victory,' recorded the Sporting Chronicle.

21 APRIL
**v Newcastle United (Crystal Palace)
1-0** *Young;* **75,609**
Scott, W. Balmer, Crelley, Makepeace, Taylor, Abbott, Sharp, Bolton, Young, Settle, Hardman

1907 Everton had the chance to retain the FA Cup when they faced Sheffield Wednesday – the previous year's vanquished quarter-finalists – at Crystal Palace. But the build-up to the final was disrupted by a dispute between George Wilson – Everton's brilliant inside forward – and the directors, who omitted him from the starting line-up, despite his scoring in the semi-final. The decision bewildered both fans and neutral onlookers, including the Football League's founding father, William McGregor.

Wednesday took an early lead, but Jack Sharp ensured the half-time score stood at 1-1. But Everton were unable to seize control of a scrappy game and six minutes from the end, Simpson's goal won the FA Cup for Wednesday.

20 APRIL
**v Sheffield Wednesday (Crystal Palace)
1-2** *Sharp;* **84,594**
Scott, W. Balmer, R. Balmer, Makepeace, Taylor, Abbott, Sharp, Bolton, Young, Settle, Hardman

1933 Everton's first Wembley appearance ended in a crushing victory for the Blues over Manchester City.

They took a 1-0 half-time lead, after City's goalkeeper Len Langford, under pressure from Dixie Dean, spilled a Cliff Britton cross at Jimmy Stein's feet. On 52 minutes Dean bundled both the hapless Langford and the ball into the net to make it 2-0, and Jimmy Dunn's header ten minutes from full time assured a comprehensive victory.

'One feels it is a grand achievement after forty-one years with the club. I was present at the final in 1897, 1906 and 1907 and today was a happy consummation as it were,' said Will Cuff. 'I would like to pay tribute to our doughty opponents, Manchester City. We are delighted at the sporting way in which they accepted the verdict although one expected nothing but that from such good sportsmen.'

29 APRIL
v Manchester City (Wembley) 3-0
Stein, Dean, Dunn; **92,950**
Sagar, Cook, Cresswell, Britton, White, Thomson, Geldard, Dunn, Dean, Johnson, Stein

1966 In one of the most dramatic finals in FA Cup history, Everton overcame a two-goal deficit with barely half an hour remaining to take the tie 3-2 at the final whistle.

After falling behind to an early Sheffield Wednesday goal, Everton had been unlucky to go in a goal down at half-time: Alex Young had what seemed a legitimate goal ruled out for offside, then saw a penalty appeal waved away. Wednesday doubled their lead on 57 minutes and commentator Kenneth Wolstenholme declared it 'Wednesday's Cup'.

But no one had banked on Mike Trebilcock, a rookie striker in for the injured Fred Pickering. His quickfire double on 59 and 64 minutes transformed the tie. With 17 minutes remaining Derek Temple broke clear and, one-on-one with the Wednesday keeper Ron Springett, struck a low winner.

'The match which no one save the two cities concerned wanted had become the match which thrilled millions,' Leslie Edwards recorded in the Liverpool Echo. 'I congratulate the club, the team and everyone concerned – and especially the scout who îfoundî Trebilcock – on a Wembley victory any club will find it hard to equal much less surpass.'

14 MAY
v Sheffield Wednesday (Wembley) 3-2 *Trebilcock 2, Temple;* **100,000**
West, Wright, Wilson, Gabriel, Labone, Harris, Scott, Trebilcock, Young, Harvey, Temple

1968 The 1968 FA Cup final represents one of the great disappointments in the club's so-called 'golden era'. Two months before Everton and West Brom met at Wembley, Everton had visited the Hawthorns and played Albion off the park in a 6-2 annihilation.

IN REACHING WEMBLEY, Everton had faced and beaten the mighty Leeds United in the semi-final, while the majestic Kendall-Harvey-Ball 'holy trinity' was showing its first stirrings of greatness. But in an underwhelming final, Everton struggled to make a breakthrough. The best chance came four minutes from the end of normal time, when Jimmy Husband missed from close range – but that was as close as Everton came. The game seemed to be drifting towards a replay when – four minutes from the end of extra time – Jeff Astle struck the game's only goal from the edge of the Everton area.

'It just didn't work for the team. We weren't firing,' Joe Royle recalled in his autobiography. 'West Brom were a physical side and they did set about us. I'm afraid we didn't respond to that challenge as well as we might have and we could have no complaints.'

18 MAY
v West Bromwich Albion (Wembley) 0-1; **100,000**
West, Wright, Wilson, Kendall, Labone, Harvey, Husband, Ball, Royle, Hurst, Morrissey

1984 The 1984 FA Cup final marked the dawn of a new golden era for Everton, after years spent in Liverpool's shadow.

Watford had the best of the early exchanges, but once Graeme Sharp's turn and shot put Everton ahead on 37 minutes, there was only one team in it. On 52 minutes, Andy Gray's controversial header – there were claims he fouled the Watford goalkeeper, Steve Sherwood – made it 2-0 and an unassailable lead.

'It shows that when people talk about a crisis at a football club, they should think in terms of the whole season,' said Howard Kendall after victory had been ensured. 'Fortunately the chairman and the board had faith. I am delighted for everyone that we have taken a major trophy back to Merseyside that belongs to Everton for a change.'

He continued, 'To win the FA Cup is fantastic, but in the long run it is the championship, achieved over 42 games, that has to be the main objective. The Cup was the icing, now we want the cake.'

19 MAY
v Watford (Wembley) 2-0
Sharp, Gray; **100,000**
Southall, Stevens, Bailey, Ratcliffe, Mountfield, Reid, Steven, Sharp, Gray, Richardson, Heath

1985 Everton went into the 1985 FA Cup final already crowned league champions and chasing an unprecedented treble. Days earlier they had lifted the European Cup Winners' Cup, after a 3-1 win over Rapid Vienna in Rotterdam.

Twice already that season, Everton had beaten their opponents Manchester United, including a 5-0 hammering at Goodison considered by many Evertonians the most complete team performance they had ever witnessed. But as Everton knew from 1968, past form counted for little in an FA Cup final.

In a largely humdrum affair – remembered mostly for Kevin Moran's sending off for a foul on Peter Reid and Norman Whiteside's outstanding curled winner – Everton could not summon enough strength to overcome United.

'We lost because we were shattered,' Graeme Sharp recalled in his autobiography. 'It was purely and simply one game too far in a long, long season. The whole campaign and the emotions that had come with it, had finally caught up with us.'

18 MAY
v Manchester United (Wembley) 0-1; **100,000**
Southall, Stevens, Van Den Hauwe, Ratcliffe, Mountfield, Reid, Steven, Sharp, Gray, Bracewell, Sheedy

1986 After almost a century of Merseyside derbies and four FA Cup semi-final derby encounters, Everton finally came face to face with their neighbours and great rivals in the final. A week earlier Liverpool had wrested the First Division title from Everton at the last, after a stunning run of wins in the latter part of the season overhauled Everton's lead at the top of the table. Now Everton were bent on revenge.

Everton took a 27th-minute lead when Gary Lineker latched on to Peter Reid's outstanding through ball and took it past Bruce Grobelaar. With Everton deserved leaders at half-time, Liverpool's unease was demonstrated by a flare-up between Grobelaar and Jim Beglin. Both Kevin Sheedy and Trevor Steven went close to doubling Everton's lead after the interval.

But then Jan Molby intercepted Gary Stevens' aimless crossfield ball and played in Ian Rush, who sidestepped Bobby Mimms and made it 1-1. Soon after a back-pedalling Grobelaar tipped over Graeme Sharp's header, and Everton's best chance of regaining the lead was gone. Craig Johnston put Liverpool ahead, and Rush made it 3-1 to Liverpool with six minutes remaining.

10 MAY
v Liverpool (Wembley) 1-3 *Lineker;* **98,000**
Mimms, Stevens (Heath), Van Den Hauwe, Ratcliffe, Mountfield, Reid, Steven, Lineker, Sharp, Bracewell, Sheedy

1989 The FA Cup final that many argue should never have been played came just six weeks after the Hillsborough disaster at which 96 Liverpool fans lost their lives prior to the semi-final against Nottingham Forest.

In Everton's eleventh Wembley appearance in five years, for a long part of the match it looked like John Aldridge's fourth-minute goal would be enough to separate the two teams. Liverpool dominated for long stretches, and it was not until injury time that substitute Stuart McCall scrambled an Everton equaliser. Ian Rush put Liverpool back in front early in extra time, only for McCall to unleash a stunning volley from the edge of the Liverpool area to make it 2-2. Rush, however, had the final say, scoring a winner in the 104th minute.

'The game was very competitive,' said Colin Harvey afterwards. 'What both teams wanted was a game played in the right spirit, and the crowd to watch it in the right spirit, which they did.'

20 MAY
v Liverpool (Wembley) 2-3 (aet)
McCall 2; **82,800**
Southall, McDonald, Van Den Hauwe, Ratcliffe, Watson, Bracewell (McCall), Nevin, Steven, Sharp, Cottee, Sheedy (Wilson)

1995 This was the final act of one of the most dramatic seasons in Everton's history. Having suffered their worst ever start to a season under Mike Walker, new manager Joe Royle dragged Everton from the spectre of relegation to an unlikely FA Cup final. Manchester United, thwarted on the last day of the season from a third consecutive Premiership title, were, however, hot favourites.

But despite heavy United pressure throughout, it was Everton who found the necessary cutting edge. On the half-hour mark, Anders Limpar led a lightning Everton breakaway. He switched the ball to Matt Jackson on the Everton right, who cut inside and played in Graham Stuart; his shot crashed off the underside of the United crossbar, but Paul Rideout reacted quickest to head home the rebound. A string of outstanding saves from Neville Southall assured the goal was enough for an Everton victory.

'I'm happy with the way the season has turned out but I'm not happy with the way things were,' said Southall afterwards. 'We were a disgrace for part of the season. We gave our fans a torrid time and staying in the Premiership was the main achievement. But we had to do something like this for all those people who went to places like Wimbledon and Crystal Palace on cold wet nights. They deserve this – it's for them.'

20 MAY
v Manchester United (Wembley) 1-0 *Rideout;*
79,592
Southall, Jackson, Ablett, Watson, Unsworth, Hinchcliffe, Parkinson, Horne, Stuart, Limpar (Amokachi), Rideout (Ferguson)

2009 Having faced one of the toughest FA Cup runs in history – Everton dispatched Premier League champions Manchester United and runners-up Liverpool as well as a fine Aston Villa team in reaching Wembley – the Blues came up against a formidable Chelsea team in the final.

Yet it took just 25 seconds for Louis Saha to put Everton in front with the quickest goal in FA Cup final history. Thereafter, however, Chelsea dominated, ultimately proving too much for an Everton team that was crippled by injuries to such key personnel as Mikel Arteta, Phil Jagielka and Yakubu.

'For us to finish fifth and reach the FA Cup final, then come here and not look out of place was a great achievement,' said David Moyes. 'We played Chelsea twice this season and drew and this was only 2-1. I'm really keen that the players are recognised for how well they have done this season because they have been outstanding.'

30 MAY
v Chelsea (Wembley) 1-2 *Saha;* **89,391**
Howard, Hibbert (Jacobsen), Yobo, Lescott, Baines, Osman (Gosling), Neville, Cahill, Pienaar, Fellaini, Saha (Vaughan)

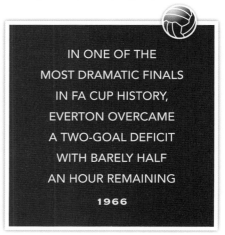

IN ONE OF THE MOST DRAMATIC FINALS IN FA CUP HISTORY, EVERTON OVERCAME A TWO-GOAL DEFICIT WITH BARELY HALF AN HOUR REMAINING

1966

Everton in the FA Cup Semi-final

4 MARCH 1893
**v Preston North End
(Bramall Lane) 2-2**
Chadwick, Gordon; **26,000**
*Williams, Kelso, Howarth, Boyle,
Holt, Stewart, Latta, Gordon,
Maxwell, Chadwick, Milward*

Replay: **16 MARCH 1893**
**v Preston North End
(Ewood Park) 0-0;** **15,000**
*Williams, Kelso, Howarth, Boyle,
Holt, Stewart, Latta, Gordon,
Maxwell, Chadwick, Milward*

2nd Replay: **20 MARCH 1893**
**v Preston North End
(Trent Bridge, Nottingham) 2-1**
Maxwell, Gordon; **18,000**
*Williams, Kelso, Howarth, Boyle,
Holt, Stewart, Latta, Gordon,
Maxwell, Chadwick, Milward*

20 MARCH 1897
**v Derby County (Victoria
Ground, Stoke) 3-2** *Chadwick,
Hartley, Milward;* **25,000**
*Menham, Meecham, Storrier,
Boyle, Holt, Stewart, Taylor, Bell,
Hartley, Chadwick, Milward*

19 MARCH 1898
v Derby County (Molineux) 1-3
Chadwick; **25,000**
*Muir, W. Balmer, Storrier,
Stewart, Holt, Robertson, Taylor,
Divers, L. Bell, Chadwick, J. Bell*

25 MARCH 1905
**v Aston Villa
(Victoria Ground, Stoke) 1-1**
Sharp; **35,000**
*Roose, W. Balmer, Crelley,
Makepeace, Taylor, Abbott,
Sharp, McDermott, Young,
Settle, Hardman*

Replay:
29 MARCH 1905
**v Aston Villa (Trent Bridge,
Nottingham) 1-2** *Sharp;* **25,000**
*Roose, W. Balmer, Crelley,
Makepeace, Taylor, Abbott,
Sharp, McDermott, Young,
Settle, Hardman*

31 MARCH 1906
v Liverpool (Villa Park) 2-0
Abbott, Hardman; **37,000**
*Scott, R. Balmer, Crelley,
Makepeace, Taylor, Abbott, Sharp,
Bolton, Young, Settle, Hardman*

23 MARCH 1907
**v West Bromwich Albion
(Burnden Park, Bolton) 2-1**
Sharp, Wilson; **32,381**
*Scott, W. Balmer, R. Balmer,
Makepeace, Taylor, Abbott, Sharp,
Settle, Young, Wilson, Hardman*

26 MARCH 1910
v Barnsley (Elland Road) 0-0;
36,000
*Scott, Clifford, Maconnachie,
Harris, Taylor, Makepeace, Sharp,
White, Freeman, Young, Barlow*

Replay:
31 MARCH 1910
v Barnsley (Old Trafford) 0-3;
55,000
*Scott, Clifford, Maconnachie,
Harris, Taylor (retired injured),
Makepeace, Sharp, White,
Freeman, Young, Barlow*

27 March 1915
v Chelsea (Villa Park) 0-2;
22,000
*Mitchell, Thompson, Simpson,
Fleetwood, Galt, Makepeace,
Chedgzoy, Kirsopp, Parker,
Clennell, Harrison*

18 MARCH 1933
**v West Ham United (Molineux)
2-1** *Dunn, Critchley;* **37,936**
*Sagar, Cook, Cresswell, Britton,
White, Thomson, Critchley,
Dunn, Dean, Johnson, Stein*

25 MARCH 1950
v Liverpool (Maine Road) 0-2;
72,000
*Burnett, Moore, Hedley,
Grant, Falder, Farrell,
Buckle, Wainwright, Catterick,
Fielding, Eglington*

21 MARCH 1953
**v Bolton Wanderers
(Maine Road) 3-4**
Parker 2, Farrell; **75,213**
*O'Neill, Clinton, Lindsay, Farrell,
Jones, Lello, Buckle, Cummins,
Hickson, Parker, Eglington*

23 APRIL 1966
**v Manchester United
(Burnden Park, Bolton) 1-0**
Harvey; **60,000**
*West, Brown, Wilson, Gabriel,
Labone, Harris, Scott, Trebilcock,
Young, Harvey, Temple*

27 APRIL 1968
**v Leeds United (Old Trafford)
1-0** *Morrissey (pen);* **63,000**
*West, Wright, Wilson,
Jackson, Labone, Harvey,
Husband (Young), Kenyon,
Royle, Kendall, Morrissey*

22 MARCH 1969
**v Manchester City (Villa Park)
0-1;** **63,025**
*West, Wright, Brown,
Kendall (Jackson), Labone,
Harvey, Husband, Ball,
Royle, Hurst, Morrissey*

27 MARCH 1971
v Liverpool (Old Trafford) 1-2
Ball; **62,144**
*Rankin, Wright, K. Newton,
Kendall, Labone (Brown),
Harvey, Whittle, Ball,
Royle, Hurst, Morrissey*

23 APRIL 1977
v Liverpool (Maine Road) 2-2
McKenzie, Rioch; **52,637**
*Lawson, Darracott, Pejic, Lyons,
McNaught, Rioch, Buckley,
Dobson (Hamilton), Pearson,
McKenzie, Goodlass*

Replay: **27 APRIL 1977**
v Liverpool (Maine Road) 0-3;
52,579
*Lawson, Darracott, Pejic, Lyons,
McNaught, Rioch, Buckley,
Dobson (King), Pearson,
McKenzie, Goodlass*

14 APRIL 1984
**v Southampton (Highbury)
1-0 (aet)** *Heath;* **46,587**
*Southall, Stevens, Bailey, Ratcliffe,
Mountfield, Reid, Curran, Heath,
Gray, Steven (Sharp), Richardson*

13 APRIL 1985
**v Luton Town (Villa Park) 2-1
(aet)** *Sheedy, Mountfield;* **45,289**
*Southall, Stevens, Van Den
Hauwe, Ratcliffe, Mountfield,
Reid, Steven, Sharp, Gray,
Bracewell, Sheedy*

5 APRIL 1986
**v Sheffield Wednesday (Villa
Park) 2-1 (aet)** *Harper, Sharp;*
47,711
*Mimms, Stevens, Van den Hauwe,
Ratcliffe, Mountfield, Reid
(Harper), Steven, Heath, Sharp,
Bracewell, Richardson*

15 APRIL 1989
**v Norwich City (Villa Park)
1-0** *Nevin;* **46,553**
*Southall, McDonald,
Van den Hauwe, Ratcliffe,
Watson, Bracewell, Nevin,
Steven, Sharp, Cottee, Sheedy*

9 APRIL 1995
**v Tottenham Hotspur (Elland
Road) 4-1** *Jackson, Stuart,
Amokachi 2;* **38,226**
*Southall, Jackson, Watson,
Unsworth, Ablett, Limpar,
Horne, Parkinson, Hinchcliffe,
Stuart, Rideout (Amokachi)*

19 APRIL 2009
**v Manchester United
(Wembley) 0-0 (aet; Everton
won 4-2 on penalties);** **88,141**
*Howard, Hibbert, Jagielka,
Lescott, Baines, Osman, Neville,
Cahill, Pienaar, Fellaini
(Vaughan), Saha (Rodwell)*

14 APRIL 2012
v Liverpool (Wembley) 1-2
Jelavić; **87,231**
*Howard, Neville, Heitinga,
Distin, Baines (Anichebe),
Gibson, Fellaini, Osman, Cahill,
Gueye (Coleman), Jelavić*

Falder,
David 'Ted'

Defender who came with the approval of the 'Prince of Centre Halves'

David 'Ted' Falder first arrived at Goodison following the recommendation of a member of the Goodison aristocracy, and although he never lived up to the reputation of his illustrious predecessor it spoke much of the abundant potential he held. Stationed with T.G. Jones in the RAF during the Second World War, the Prince of Centre Halves recommended the young novice for Goodison trials. He was a success and aged 23 he signed as a professional a week before Christmas 1945.

> THE PRINCE OF CENTRE HALVES RECOMMENDED THE YOUNG NOVICE FOR GOODISON TRIALS

Progress was nevertheless slow for the young hopeful and the Everton management toyed several times with the prospect of letting him leave without blooding him in the first team. During the 1949/50 season, however, circumstances demanded drastic action. Everton were leaking goals and slipping towards relegation. Cliff Britton moved desperately to resolve the situation and brought in Jack Hedley in place of George Saunders at left back and Falder, ironically, in place of Jones, whose frosty relations with the manager had become martial.

It proved enough to steady Everton's faltering season. The club had conceded an average of two goals a game before Christmas, but after Falder's introduction on 27 December the arrears were halved. He was ever-present for the remainder of the season, playing in the FA Cup run that took Everton to the semi-finals.

EVERTON IN this era were in a truly dismal state and a poor start to the 1950/51 season saw Falder dropped five games in. He played just once more for the club and his successor – T.E. Jones – was unable to halt the slide into the Second Division.

In September 1951 Falder was transfer-listed. Tranmere Rovers tried to buy him in a part-exchange deal for Harold Bell, with Saunders also heading to Prenton Park, but injury waylaid the deal. Further attempts to swap him for Crewe's Frank Blunstone, a future England winger, came to nothing. In July 1952 he joined Ellesmere Port and, nearing his thirties, never saw league football again.

Season	League		FA Cup		Total	
	App	Goals	App	Goals	App	Goals
1949/50	19	0	5	0	24	0
1950/51	6	0	0	0	6	0
Total	**25**	**0**	**5**	**0**	**36**	**0**

> [FACTFILE]
>
> **BORN**
> Liverpool, 21 October 1922
> **POSITION**
> Centre half

Fanzines

The unofficial voice of the masses

FANZINES ARE non-professional publications written by fans, for fans. In Britain, they possess a tradition dating back to the 1960s and 1970s when typewritten and photocopied band tributes were produced and sold at concerts and in record shops. Football started to attract such publications in the early 1980s.

Among the best known of this early batch was The End, notionally devoted to Liverpool FC, but whose remit extended to music, fashion and popular culture. In many ways it transcended footballing allegiance and its co-editor, Peter Hooton, later the front man of The Farm, could sometimes be seen at Goodison selling copies to Evertonians.

By the late 1980s Everton were one of the few big clubs still without a fanzine to their name. In December 1988 the seminal When Skies Are Grey was founded by Chris Collins.

Initially based out of Porthmadog, it was type-written, smeared with globules of Tipp-Ex and replete with spelling mistakes. Collins' first editorial boasted: 'At last you the fan's have you're own platform to air you're views on Everton FC ... I will not make any apologies for ruffling any feathers though. What's got to be said will be said, unlike the programme which would have us believe that all is rosy in the Goodison Garden. The football I've seen over the last eighteen months or so tells me otherwise.' (Sic)

The Daily Post's Len Capeling welcomed its arrival: 'Hardened Everton fans who've suffered the slings and the arrows (plus the occasional bouquets) of the last 20 years will instantly warm to the tone of torment in the Goodison fanzine WSAG. Of course the title gives the game away. Depressingly downbeat, it forcibly reminds us that every silver lining has a cloud.'

FANZINES STRUCK a chord with fans who were increasingly dispossessed, alienated and treated appallingly by their clubs and the football authorities. Amateurishly produced, often libellous and bitingly funny, they made for essential half-time reading and were always more pertinent than the match-day programme. To a certain extent they suffered with the ascent of the internet in the late 1990s. Their original success was because fans did not have a say; with the arrival of blogs, fan sites, messageboards and so on, everyone suddenly had a forum.

EVERTON HAVE POSSESSED a handful of fanzines, some of which are still in production.

When Skies Are Grey (1988–): The original and best Everton fanzine, still going strong after more than 170 issues and for many years supplemented by a lively and popular (now sadly defunct) website. Among its editors is Mark O'Brien, one of the most gifted and perceptive commentators on the club.

Blue Wail: (1988–89): Now a collectors' item. The fanzine was pulled after inadvertent comments about Liverpool fans that the editors feared might have been misconstrued following the Hillsborough disaster.

Speke From The Harbour (1989–): Originally published by Everton's Northern Ireland Supporters Club. A longstanding and irreverent addition to the fanzine annals.

Gwladys Sings The Blues (1994–97): Co-edited by four Crosby school friends, including this author, this ran for 16 issues and a 'Best Of', covering the eventful Joe Royle years.

Satis (1998–2002): Published with the mantra 'We Don't Hate Liverpool; We Don't Hate Man Utd; We Don't Hate Anyone', Satis was charged with the gloomy task of covering the Walter Smith years.

Blueblood (2002–12): Run by George Orr, prolific Everton writer and historian, it specialised in the rich lore of the club and ran for 100 editions.

Farley, Adam

FA Youth Cup winning centre back who forged a local non-league career

[FACTFILE]

BORN
Liverpool, 12 January 1980
POSITION
Centre half
OTHER CLUBS
Altrincham (2000–01);
Drolysden (2001–04);
Witton Albion (2004–05);
Marine (2005–09);
Leigh Genesis (2010);
Formby (2010–11);
Burscough (2011–12);
AFC Liverpool (2012–)

Season	League App	League Goals	FA Cup App	FA Cup Goals	League Cup App	League Cup Goals	Total App	Total Goals
1998/99	1	0	0	0	0	0	1	0
Total	1	0	0	0	0	0	1	0

Farrall, Alec

Local midfielder who forged a solid lower-league career

[FACTFILE]

BORN
West Kirby, 3 March 1936
POSITION
Midfield
OTHER CLUBS
Preston North End (1957–60);
Gillingham (1960–65);
Lincoln City (1965–66);
Watford (1966–68)

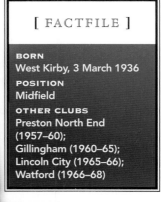

Season	League App	League Gls	FA Cup App	FA Cup Gls	Total App	Total Gls
1952/53	1	0	0	0	1	0
1953/54	1	0	0	0	1	0
1954/55	1	0	0	0	1	0
1955/56	1	0	0	0	1	0
1956/57	1	0	0	0	1	0
Total	5	0	0	0	5	0

Farrell, Peter

Long-standing Irish servant who ranks among the greats

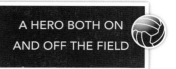
On 21 September 1949, a Peter Farrell lob made safe a famous Goodison Park victory.

However the goal which secured the 2-0 win wasn't scored in the royal blue of Everton, and although playing on his home turf Farrell was actually turning out for the away side. In fact he was playing in the green of Ireland, who, thanks to their strong Everton contingent, had recorded a rare victory over a seemingly indestructible England team. Indeed it was the first time football's founding nation had ever been defeated by a 'foreign' nation. That famous encounter was just one appearance in a 28-cap Ireland career enjoyed by Farrell, who also played seven times for Northern Ireland because of a ruling which meant they could use players from the Republic for the Home International Championship.

FARRELL first came to Goodison in 1946 from Shamrock Rovers along with Tommy Eglington in a £10,000 double deal. Between them they made over 850 appearances, representing some

of the shrewdest business the Blues have ever completed. Farrell quickly established himself as a sturdy wing half whose steely tackling served as an inspiration to his team-mates. It was in light of this that manager Cliff Britton appointed him captain at the end of the ill-fated 1950/51 season when Everton were relegated.

Farrell was one of the few Everton players to emerge with credit from this calamitous season. Writing after the 2-1 home defeat to Aston Villa that virtually sealed Everton's fate, 'Ranger' wrote in the Liverpool Echo of Everton's lack of 'tenacity or courage to send the spectators away with even the slight consolation that the Blues had gone down fighting'. The Irishman, he added, was one of only two players to emerge with credit. 'Farrell set a great example and Potts ran himself almost to a standstill,' he wrote. 'But the rest seemed as infirm of purpose and lacking in determination as though it made no difference whether they won or lost.'

A hero both on and off the field, Farrell socialised freely with the supporters in his typically down-to-earth manner. After Everton had lost to Bolton in the 1953 FA Cup semi-final, man of the people Farrell took the defeat worse than many of his team-mates. 'I didn't look at anyone,' he later revealed. 'I got onto the bus and sat down. I heard a banging on the window and when I looked up I saw the coach was surrounded by our supporters. There must have been six thousand of them. Those nearest gave the thumbs up sign and shouted, "Don't worry, Peter, we'll do it next time!"'

The disappointments of 1953 were forgotten the following year when he captained Everton to promotion back to Division One, after a 4-0 win against Oldham on the last day of the season guaranteed a runners-up spot. 'We have no star man. Our success has been due to all-round work as a team and with such a great bunch of colleagues, my job as captain has been made easy,' proclaimed the Everton captain at the time. Years later he was more emotional still. 'I was in tears in the dressing room,' he remembered. 'I knew how much promotion meant to the people.'

Sixty years later Dave Hickson claimed that the shock of relegation in 1951 and Farrell's love for the club saw him assume personal responsibility for getting Everton back to the top flight. 'I was in the army when Everton

were relegated and joined them as a Division Two team,' Hickson told the Liverpool Echo in 2011. 'Peter Farrell was the captain and there was never a bigger Evertonian than him. I think he felt partly responsible for the relegation and he was so happy when we were promoted again.'

Farrell remained at Goodison for a further three years, helping a shaky Everton team consolidate their top-flight status, before, at the age 33, he took up the chance to manage Tranmere Rovers. He was as popular in Birkenhead as he had been on the other side of the Mersey and average attendances rose to a record high. He stayed at Prenton Park until December 1960 before taking over as boss of Welsh League club Holyhead Town, but later returned to Ireland to continue in management with St Patrick's Athletic. On leaving football altogether, Farrell – the friend of the fans – took up a job with a Dublin insurance firm.

Season	League		FA Cup		Total	
	App	Gls	App	Gls	App	Gls
1946/47	27	0	2	0	29	0
1947/48	38	2	3	1	41	3
1948/49	38	0	2	0	40	0
1949/50	41	2	5	0	46	2
1950/51	42	3	1	0	43	3
1951/52	40	0	2	0	42	0
1952/53	38	1	5	1	43	2
1953/54	39	1	3	0	42	1
1954/55	41	0	2	0	43	0
1955/56	42	1	4	1	46	2
1956/57	36	3	2	1	38	4
Total	**422**	**13**	**31**	**4**	**453**	**17**

PETER FARRELL - EVERTON F.C. (1953)

[FACTFILE]

BORN
Dalkey, Co. Dublin, Ireland, 16 August 1922

DIED
Dalkey, Co. Dublin, Ireland, 16 March 1999

POSITION
Right half/ inside forward

OTHER CLUBS
Shamrock Rovers (1939–46); Tranmere Rovers (player-manager, 1957–60); Sligo Rovers (player-manager, 1961))

AS MANAGER
Holyhead Town (1961–62); St Patrick's Athletic

HONOURS
28 Republic of Ireland caps (3 goals) (1946–57); 7 Northern Ireland caps (1946–49)

Farrelly, Gareth

Underwhelming midfielder whose moment of glory saved Everton's skin

Signed for £700,000 from Aston Villa just days after Howard Kendall's return as Everton manager in June 1997, Farrelly was a highly regarded Irish playmaker who had struggled to make the breakthrough to the Villa first team. On concluding the deal Kendall declared the midfielder had the potential to be a household name, although few Evertonians could have envisaged the dramatic way that this prophesy would unfold.

Thrust into one of the poorest Everton teams in the club's history, Farrelly struggled to make an impression as his new club lagged towards the relegation places. Perhaps it was unfair to place such a burden on his young shoulders, but he continually looked off-pace, while the execution of his passing and finishing left much to be desired.

That was until the final day of the 1997/98 season. Everton faced Coventry City implanted in the relegation places and relying on Bolton, a single place above them, not to win at Chelsea. Six minutes in Farrelly lofted an aimless ball into the penalty area; Duncan Ferguson's leap saw it bouncing invitingly back into the path of the Irishman, who struck a right-footed half-volley past Marcus Hedman and in off the goalkeeper's left-hand post. It was his first league goal for Everton and a wonderful strike. Coventry scored a late equaliser, but Bolton lost to Chelsea. Farrelly's goal saved Everton from the abyss – just.

'It was my first goal of the season and it couldn't have been a better one,' he said afterwards. 'I have never scored a more important goal.'

Perhaps surprisingly, Everton's hero of the hour made just one more fleeting appearance for the club, as a substitute in a League Cup game. He was sold to Bolton – ironically, the club he had condemned a year earlier – in December 1999 for £300,000. After a loan tour of England's lower leagues, in August 2004 Farrelly became player/manager of FAI side, Bohemians, shortly before his 29th birthday. His time in charge lasted just two years, and he subsequently played for Blackpool and Cork City. Here his career was brought to a tragic conclusion when he was diagnosed with a pancreatic tumour in 2008. In 2010 he returned to football, signing for Unibond Premier League team, Warrington Town.

Season	League		FA Cup		League Cup		Total	
	App	Goals	App	Goals	App	Goals	App	Goals
1997/98	18 (8)	1	1	0	1	1	20 (8)	2
1998/99	0 (1)	0	0	0	0	0	0 (1)	0
1999/20	0	0	0	0	0	0	0	0
Total	**18 (9)**	**1**	**1**	**0**	**1**	**1**	**20 (9)**	**2**

Fazackerley, Stan

Prolific inside forward who fell foul of the Everton board

The £4000 record signing of Stan Fazackerley from Sheffield United in November 1920 marked the conclusion of an eight-month-long pursuit of the inside forward.

It had started in March that year when the Everton board were alerted to his unhappiness at Sheffield United. A board minute recorded: 'Secy. reported that this player had informed him of his desire to leave his club but that the latter, on being approached, had declined to part.' A stand-off emerged over the following summer, with Fazackerley refusing to sign new terms at Bramall Lane. Eventually he relented but Everton did not give up their hunt. In November, with hopes of a title challenge in the Goodison air, a delegation was dispatched to Yorkshire to sign the player. This time they got their man, beating Bolton Wanderers in a bidding war.

Nearing his 30th birthday at the time of his Goodison arrival, Fazackerley was an accomplished and experienced addition to the Blues' squad. He had spent eight war-interrupted years in Sheffield, the highlight of which was the club's 1915 FA Cup final win over Chelsea, in which he scored the second of three goals. Previously he had turned out for Hull City and Accrington Stanley.

HOPES WERE high that the new boy would form a good partnership with outside right Sam Chedgzoy, and he did not disappoint. 'The entrance of Fazackerley into the Everton team on Saturday led to some good

FAZACKERLEY WAS EVERTON'S LEADING GOALSCORER

results,' reported the Liverpool Daily Post and Mercury of his debut, a 2-2 draw with Bradford City. 'The ex-Sheffield United player has art to recommend him in a year when artistry is rarely seen. With his skilled edging of the ball, feinting and dribbling, so Fazackerley has come to the right team. Then he has added confidence to a side that lacked it. Moreover, he has the necessary

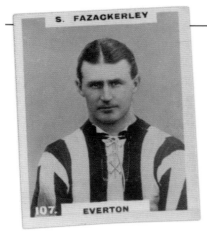

S. FAZACKERLEY

107. EVERTON

height where heading of the ball is necessary. All told, he comes at the right time to mend a disjointed side. There was more "forward" play by Everton on Saturday than had been seen throughout the season.'

Standing 6ft tall, Fazackerley added some presence to the Everton forward line, but an assault on the top of the table never came, Everton finishing the season in seventh. Fazackerly scored eight goals, including a hat-trick at home to Chelsea, when he was used as an auxiliary centre forward.

The following campaign was a disaster for Everton. After opening the season with a 5-0 thrashing of Manchester United the club then spent most of the season floundering around the bottom of the table. Fazackerley was Everton's leading goalscorer, but amid the gloom he fell out of favour spectacularly. Allowed by the club to live in Preston and train three days per week on Merseyside, the agreement broke down in early March 1922. Everton suspended him for 'disobedience' and he played just four times more for the club. In November 1922 Everton accepted a £1750 bid for the player from Wolverhampton Wanderers and the inside forward played out his career in the Midlands at Molineux and with Derby County.

[FACTFILE]

BORN
Doncaster, 30 October 1945
DIED
1946
POSITION
Inside right
OTHER CLUBS
Preston North End (1909);
Charlestown (USA);
Accrington Stanley; Hull City (1911–12);
Wolverhampton Wanderers (1922–24);
Derby County (1925)

Season	League		FA Cup		Total	
	App	Goals	App	Goals	App	Goals
1920/21	20	8	5	0	25	8
1921/22	29	12	1	0	30	12
1922/23	2	1	0	0	2	1
Total	**51**	**21**	**6**	**0**	**57**	**21**

Fell, Jimmy

Chemist turned professional footballer who played out wide in the early 1960s

Season	League		FA Cup		Total	
	App	Goals	App	Goals	App	Goals
1960/61	6	0	0	0	6	0
1961/62	21	4	1	1	22	5
Total	**27**	**4**	**1**	**1**	**28**	**5**

[FACTFILE]

BORN
Cleethorpes, 4 January 1936
DIED
Grimsby, 2 February 2011
POSITION
Outside left
OTHER CLUBS
Grimsby Town (1956–61);
Newcastle United (1962–63);
Walsall (1963–64);
Lincoln City (1964–65);
Boston United (1965–69)

Fellaini, Marouane

Belgian international midfielder of grace and skill who is the club's record signing

The dramatic signing of 20-year-old Belgium international midfielder Marouane Fellaini in the closing minutes of the 2008 summer transfer window concluded one of the most dramatic pieces of transfer business in the club's history. David Moyes had tracked the Standard Liege midfielder for more than six months, but it wasn't until the window drew to its close that it became clear if he would get his man. Last-ditch machinations – which at one stage included the dispatch of a private jet – saw the deal close moments before the midnight deadline. At £15million Fellaini became the most expensive player in Everton's history.

Born to Moroccan parents from Tangier and brought up in Brussels, Fellaini came from footballing stock. His father Abdellatif Fellaini had played in goal with Raja Casablanca and Hassania Agadir and earned a move to Racing Mechelen but was unable to play because his former Belgian club refused to release his paperwork. His son was picked up by the Anderlecht academy when he was aged just seven, eventually signing as a professional for Standard Liege as a 17-year-old. He represented Belgium at U-18, U-19 and U-21 level and, a year after breaking into the Liege team in 2006, the Belgian national team. He was awarded the Ebony Shoe in 2008, the prize given to the best player of African descent. Daniel Amokachi had been awarded the same prize twice while playing for Club Bruges in the early 1990s.

FELLAINI had by then attracted a reputation as the best box-to-box midfielder in the Belgian league. A tall, rangy player, he combined the guile of a long-distance runner with the grace of a ballerina. Despite his imposing frame he possessed the knack of being able to delicately pluck the ball from the air and spray it across the pitch. His technique was simple; his passing accuracy formidable. Standing 6ft 4½in he offered an imposing physical and aerial threat. In short he possessed all the facets one would expect from a modern midfield dynamo.

And yet with sky-high expectations from the Goodison crowd, his first days at the club were undermined by inconsistency. At times the new signing looked lost in the hurly-burly maelstrom of the Premier League. His acute football brain was never in doubt, but questions were posed of his aptitude amid the pace and intensity of English football.

His slightly awkward gait also saw him singled out by referees and he collected ten bookings in his first three months at the club. At times Moyes even deployed him as a makeshift centre forward.

Slowly but surely he got to grips with the Premier League and by the start of 2009 was flourishing. Among supporters he became something of a cult figure, with fans wearing Afro wigs in homage to their new hero. There were goals too, none more important than that which set Everton on their way to an FA Cup quarter-final victory against Middlesbrough. In the FA Cup Final against Chelsea it was Fellaini's knockdown that Louis Saha smashed home to put Everton in front after just 25 seconds. At the end of his debut season he was Everton's joint top goalscorer with nine goals and awarded the club's Young Player of the Season.

LONG-TERM injury to Mikel Arteta had by this stage made Fellaini more central to Everton's play. He took on more responsibilities and became the focal point of the midfield. Although never a spectacular player, there were some breathtaking flourishes, such as a 360-degree pirouette on the ball during Everton's 2-0 victory over Manchester City in January 2010. Following Arteta's departure in 2011 his importance to the Everton cause increased. Statistically he became Everton's most vital player. The Everton tactics blog, Executioner's Bong, made the following assessment in March 2012:

Fellaini's athleticism is there for all to see; he is in the top 1% of midfielders in terms of energy and distance covered during matches. He has the 4th highest average distance run per game in the top flight, clocking up a whopping 6.65 miles per match. His notable marathon matches this season include 7.5 miles in the derby defeat and 7mile+ outings in the away games at Man City and Fulham. He is also more than useful in the opposition box despite often playing quite deep ... he made it into double figures for goals in his first season on Merseyside and has scored in all 3 competitions this campaign. Perhaps the biggest impact he makes in the final third though is in terms of attracting the attention of several markers / blockers and causing general chaos particularly at set pieces.

Newspaper speculation has often linked Fellaini with a move beyond Goodison, with both Chelsea and Real Madrid said to be coveting his services. But in November 2011 and with just 18 months left on his existing contract, Fellaini signed a new deal with Everton committing him to the club until 2016. 'We are delighted to have secured the services of Marouane for the long term,' said Everton chief executive Robert Elstone. 'As everyone is aware these negotiations have been ongoing for some time but both parties remained positive that we would reach agreement. Marouane has been a hugely influential player for Everton since his arrival in 2008 and we hope that remains to be the case for the next five years.'

> [FACTFILE]
>
> **BORN**
> Etterbeek, Belgium,
> 22 November 1987
> **POSITION**
> Midfielder
> **OTHER CLUB**
> Standard Liege (2004-08)
> **HONOURS**
> 35 Belgium caps
> (5 goals) (2007–)

Season	League		FA Cup		League Cup		Other		Total	
	App	Goals	App	Goals	App	Goals	App	Goals	App	Goals
2008/09	28 (2)	8	4	1	1	0	0	0	33 (2)	9
2009/10	20 (3)	2	2	0	1 (1)	0	7	1	30 (4)	3
2010/11	19 (1)	1	3	1	2	1	-	-	24 (1)	3
2011/12	31 (3)	3	6	1	3	1	-	-	40 (3)	5
Total	**98 (9)**	**14**	**15**	**3**	**7 (1)**	**2**	**7**	**1**	**127(10)**	**20**

Ferguson, Duncan

Enigmatic centre forward adored by the Goodison faithful

ALWAYS A MAN with a gift for a quip, never was Joe Royle more prescient than when he observed, shortly after signing him in 1994, that Duncan Ferguson had become 'a legend before he was a player'. More than a decade later, as Ferguson drew time on his long, injury-interrupted footballing career, Evertonians were left to rue that same, strange paradox first voiced by Royle.

On the one hand, Ferguson was a man they had taken to their hearts, who had inspired and been inspired by the Goodison crowd, who, in his flourishes, had been one of the very few to lift the torpor that consumed Everton through lean years. And yet, there was an unmistakeable sense that he had wasted the prodigious gifts that once made him Britain's most expensive footballer, that because of this underachievement he had contributed to the mediocrity that defined the club during his time on Merseyside. As Ferguson made his way to Spain, where he lived with his family in quiet retirement for five years before a surprise

Goodison return, so the debate about his actual importance to Everton's history rumbles on among the club's support.

BORN IN the medieval town of Stirling in 1971, Ferguson was heralded as the most promising Scottish footballer of his generation. A centre forward, he played for his country's youth teams alongside Alex Young's son, Jason, and was signed by Dundee United, making his debut in November 1990, and establishing himself as a first-team regular by that season's end.

Two years later, in July 1993, he became a British record signing, when he joined Glasgow Rangers for £4million, in the process rejecting the opportunity of moving to England, where a number of clubs – including Everton – were linked to him. Ferguson was far from a success at Rangers, notching just one goal in his first season, although he was kept out for much of it with a broken leg.

WORSE STILL, his off-the-pitch antics earned him unwanted headlines. Ferguson had already been involved in three assault cases in two years when he was handed a 12-match ban by the Scottish Football Association for head-butting Raith Rovers defender John McStay during a league match at Ibrox in April 1994. The referee missed the incident, but it was captured on television and although Ferguson appealed against the ban, he was also charged with assault by Strathclyde Police and left facing the prospect of a custodial sentence.

It was with this cloud hanging over him that Ferguson arrived at Goodison in October 1994 in a loan deal with the midfielder, Iain Durrant. Many fans viewed the expensive deal with some scepticism, seeing it as a last-ditch attempt by Mike Walker to save his job as manager after Everton's worst ever start to a season.

Although Ferguson impressed in flashes under Walker, he failed to score and just weeks into his three-month loan spell Walker was sacked. Walker's replacement, Joe Royle, was well versed in the lore of Everton centre forwards, and under his management Ferguson seemed to be galvanised. In Royle's first game as manager, a derby match against Liverpool with Everton propping up the Premier League, Ferguson scored his first goal in an Everton shirt – a header from a ferocious Andy Hinchcliffe corner. Later in the game, pressure from Ferguson enabled Paul Rideout to score a second.

Suddenly the anti-hero, who had been charged with drink-driving the previous night, was Goodison's new darling. 'Duncan went to war in the second half,' said Royle after the game. A fortnight later, Royle made the loan deal permanent at a cost of £4.5million – then the second highest fee ever paid by an English club. 'I don't think he came here to play for Everton,' Royle would say. 'I think he came to get out of Scotland. But then he found the place was growing on him, and suddenly there was this adulation which has to be seen to be believed. You walk round Goodison today, and they've all got Ferguson shirts on. The big fella has got a charisma about him. He is a bit of a gunslinger, sometimes an anti-hero in people's eyes, but they absolutely adore him.'

Though noted for his physicality and aerial prowess – at 6ft 4in, Ferguson was a giant in a time before English football was dominated by such players – this belied a deft touch and quick feet. A succession of top defenders, such as Arsenal's Tony Adams and Manchester United's Gary Pallister, lined up to describe him as their toughest opponent. Never the most instinctive finisher, he nevertheless possessed a fierce shot and was capable of

> 'HE IS A BIT OF A GUNSLINGER, SOMETIMES AN ANTIHERO IN PEOPLES' EYES, BUT THEY ABSOLUTELY ADORE HIM'
> **JOE ROYLE**

spectacular strikes. A good team player, who brought colleagues into the game, at times Ferguson was perhaps not selfish enough in the penalty area. Before injuries ravaged his career he possessed a reasonable turn of pace too.

In short, he possessed all the attributes to be a top-class centre forward. On his day he was unplayable, and there were few sights more majestic than Ferguson rising to head home a cross. What seemed to hold him back, however, was a suspect temperament. The times when he was at his best could in most seasons be counted on one hand. Joe Royle later hinted that Ferguson was actually uninterested in football, and certainly there were occasions when he seemed to struggle to motivate himself and games passed him by. Nor did he score the number of goals one would expect from a top-class striker. Ferguson's best ever tally came in 1997/98 when he scored 12 goals.

The violence that dogged his life in Scotland – on and off the pitch – persisted, and although Ferguson found himself a marked man by referees and was unfairly targeted on occasion, there were times when he literally blew up, elbowing or punching opponents. Sometimes these were memorable and went unpunished – who could forget him pushing over Liverpool's Paul Ince or throttling Jason McAteer? But often they cost Everton dearly. In total he received eight red cards while an Everton player – an unenviable Premier League record he shares with Patrick Vieira.

> 'THE BIGGER THE REPUTATION OF THE OPPOSITION, THE MORE HE'S UP FOR IT'
> **JOE ROYLE**

Despite facing the wrath of many a referee, and the injuries that forced him to miss much of the latter stages of the 1994/95 season, Ferguson still managed to add to his burgeoning reputation. He scored the winner when Everton met Manchester United in February, and celebrated by whipping off his shirt and swinging it around his head. Three months later he collected an FA Cup winners' medal against the same opponents after coming on as a late substitute, although his contribution to the win was ultimately minimal, having missed most of Everton's FA Cup run through injury or suspension.

The 1995/96 season was a bad one for Ferguson. After missing the early stages of the season with a groin injury, in October he became the first professional footballer to serve a jail term for on-the-field violence when a Scottish sheriff's court sentenced him to three months' imprisonment for the McStay incident. Ferguson served six weeks but his return was once more curtailed by injury, and again he missed the latter stages of the season, and consequently Scotland's participation in the European Championship Finals.

WHEN HE returned at the start of the 1996/97 season he seemed rejuvenated, putting in immense displays against Newcastle and Manchester United. 'The bigger the reputation of the opposition, the more he's up for it,' said his Scotland team-mate, Gary McAllister. 'He acquires that strut as if he's saying: "You might be [Steve] Bruce or Pallister, but now Fergie's arrived." It turns him on.' However the old problems soon returned: another ludicrous sending off at Blackburn – this time for 'industrial language' – then further surgery, this time on his knee.

Suddenly Ferguson was under the microscope again, and it was noted that in his first two years at Goodison he had missed half of Everton's games through injury or suspension. Ferguson, who refused to speak to the press, challenged such scepticism on the pitch, usually in front of the TV cameras. A spectacular turn and shot, which levelled the scores in the April Goodison derby, was one such retort, and the point that this earned simultaneously ensured Everton's Premier League status and ended Liverpool's narrow hopes of the title. Such interludes heightened Goodison's adoration for the player.

During Howard Kendall's third spell as manager in 1997/98, Ferguson enjoyed his most prolific season. He announced his retirement from international football – it was said that he still hadn't forgiven the SFA for their part in the McStay affair – and after Gary Speed left Goodison in January 1998 took over the captaincy. The added responsibility seemed to galvanise him and it was his goals – including a hat-trick against Bolton and another derby goal – that again ensured Everton's survival.

In the summer of 1998 Ferguson was reunited with new boss Walter Smith, who had been his manager first at Dundee United, then Rangers. Fresh investment brought new hope to Goodison, but in November chairman Peter Johnson tried to balance the books and

Ferguson was sold to Newcastle United in an £8million deal. The transfer was conducted without Smith's knowledge and Johnson's already diminishing credibility was destroyed. With the manager threatening to resign, it led to a dramatic boardroom coup: Johnson stepped down, to be succeeded by Sir Philip Carter as chairman and Kenwright as vice-chairman, and he subsequently sold the club to a Kenwright-led consortium.

At Newcastle, where he partnered Alan Shearer, Ferguson was a qualified success, although injuries and disciplinary problems – those perpetual bugbears – limited him to just 30 league and cup starts. By July 2000, Newcastle were ready to cut their losses on him, and he returned to Goodison in a £4.5million deal.

His second coming was less than triumphant, however, and for a long time Ferguson, the club's top earner, was a costly burden. His paltry number of league starts say everything about how injuries damaged his career: just nine in 2000/01, 17 in 2001/02 and none at all in 2002/03. By the summer of 2004 there was talk of Ferguson being paid off for the final year of his contract – but he flatly rejected the offer. Then in December that year it looked as though Ferguson's Everton career would draw to an even more ignominious close when he was told to stay away from Bellefield after a furious row with David Moyes. The Everton manager and player resolved their differences and Ferguson returned to the Everton squad.

THERE WAS an element of Roy of the Rovers fantasy about what followed. As Everton chased an unprecedented Champions League place, Ferguson, now a grizzled veteran, became something of a talisman, usually brought on from the bench to wreak chaos in the opposition penalty area, and he played a decisive part in Everton's race for fourth place. His finest moment, indeed arguably his finest hour as an Everton player, came on 20 April 2005, when Everton met Manchester United under floodlights at Goodison. Ferguson went to war, playing with the skill and bombast of a man a decade younger. He captured the game's

THE 1995 F.A. CUP FINAL
SPONSORED BY LITTLEWOODS POOLS

Everton v Manchester United
SATURDAY 20 MAY KICK OFF 3.00PM

decisive moment when he dived through a maelstrom of United defenders to somehow head home Mikel Arteta's free kick into the Gwladys Street goal. The 1-0 win, Everton's first league victory against United since Ferguson had scored at the same end ten years earlier, virtually assured them of a Champions League place.

Rewarded with a new year-long contract, Ferguson almost played a decisive part in their Champions League qualifier against Villarreal the following August, scoring a late header that would have brought an away-goals victory. However, referee Pierluigi Collina inexplicably disallowed the goal. Collina had become the world's most famous referee by studying players' movements and behaviour prior to games. Once more, it seemed, Ferguson's reputation had preceded him.

Ferguson's role was less substantial in 2005/06, and by the final day, when Everton met already relegated West Bromwich Albion at Goodison, it became clear that his contract would not be renewed. Ferguson, accompanied by his children, who were mascots, led Everton out one last time as captain on an emotional day – Brian Labone had died just days earlier and the game was preceded by a heart-rending tribute. Albion took an unexpected two-goal lead, but Everton fought back, first through a Victor Anichebe goal, then, in the dying seconds they were awarded a penalty. Ferguson, without a goal all season, stepped

up to take it, but Albion's goalkeeper, Tomasz Kuszczak, who had been in inspired form all afternoon, saved it. Ferguson had the last word, however, and with the final kick of his Everton career converted the rebound.

AS THE TEAM went on a lap of honour, a tearful Ferguson waved at the fans, many of whom shared his emotional state, for the last time. It was a strange thing, the bonds that united the centre forward with his support, for although his career was marked by occasional moments of brilliance, it was ultimately one of immense underachievement. Plenty of men with less formidable talent outperformed him during his Goodison years yet without sharing the same affinity with the crowd.

Enigmatic he may have been, but Ferguson was the ultimate cult figure. As a younger man, wild stories about his nightclub antics – sometimes apocryphal or exaggerated in the telling – proliferated among Evertonians, adding to his legend. There was the pigeon fancying and the Everton tattoo, designed by a fan after a competition in the club magazine. Then there was the incident, in 2001, when Ferguson confronted burglars in his home and put one of them in hospital for three days.

Ferguson's life even inspired an orchestral piece, Barlinnie Nine,

composed by the Finnish composer, Osmo Tapio Räihälä. Of his work, Räihälä said, 'I got the idea for it when he was facing jail and had just become something of a cult figure for Everton. It takes into account the contradictions in him: he has an aggressive side but there is a lyrical undertone to him, as the fact that he keeps pigeons shows.' Barlinnie Nine premiered on 20 April 2005 by the Finnish Radio Symphony Orchestra – the same night Ferguson scored his famous goal against Manchester United. The significance of this was not lost on Räihälä, who said: 'There I was describing Duncan as a failure in Finland, and thousands of miles away at Everton he rises like a phoenix from the ashes to score against Manchester United. If there are gods of football up there, this proves they have got a most twisted sense of humour.'

In April 2007, Ferguson broke his long-standing public silence to speak out against Everton's proposed move to Kirkby. He said: 'During my time at Everton, Goodison Park came to feel like a second home, with the supporters of the club, and the people of the city becoming a second family to me. If you were to take Everton out of the city, I firmly believe the club could no longer call itself the "People's Club" and I give my whole-hearted support to the campaign to keep Everton in the city.'

THE LATE Tommy Lawton once said that Ferguson 'could be the greatest [number nine] the club has ever had', sentiments echoed by Joe Royle. Before the injuries, the talent was patently there, but the application never seemed to match it. Jim Baxter, a predecessor at Rangers, once quipped: 'I hear he likes a few pints, loves to stay out late and gives a bit of lip in training. In my book he has all the ingredients of a great footballer.' Maybe, just maybe, it was those same 'ingredients' that held Duncan Ferguson back from true greatness.

[FACTFILE]

BORN
Stirling, 27 December 1971
POSITION
Centre forward
OTHER CLUBS
Dundee United (1990–93);
Glasgow Rangers (1993–4);
Newcastle United (1998–2000)
HONOURS
7 Scotland caps (1992–97);
1995 FA Cup

FERGUSON 'COULD BE THE GREATEST [NUMBER NINE] THE CLUB HAS EVER HAD'
TOMMY LAWTON

Season	League		FA Cup		League Cup		Other		Total	
	App	Goals	App	Goals	App	Goals	App	Goals	App	Goals
1994/95	22 (1)	7	3 (1)	1	1	0	–	–	26 (2)	8
1995/96	16 (2)	5	2	2	0	0	0	0	18 (2)	7
1996/97	31 (2)	10	2	1	1	0	–	–	34 (2)	11
1997/98	28 (1)	11	1	0	2	0	–	–	31 (1)	11
1998/99	13	4	0	0	4	1	–	–	17	5
2000/01	9 (3)	0	1	0	0	0	–	–	10 (3)	0
2001/02	17 (5)	6	2	1	1	1	-	-	20 (5)	8
2002/03	0 (7)	0	0	0	0 (1)	0	-	-	0 (8)	0
2003/04	13 (7)	5	2	2	2	2	-	-	17 (7)	9
2004/05	6 (29)	5	0	0	2	1	-	-	8 (29)	6
2005/06	7 (20)	1	1 (1)	0	0	0	2 (2)	0	10 (23)	1
Total	162 (77)	60	14 (2)	7	13 (1)	5	2 (2)	0	191 (82)	72

Ferguson, Mick

A member of Howard Kendall's so-called 'magnificent seven' whose star failed to shine

Season	League		FA Cup		League Cup		Total	
	App	Goals	App	Goals	App	Goals	App	Goals
1981/82	7 (1)	4	0	0	3 (1)	2	10 (2)	6
Total	**7 (1)**	**4**	**0**	**0**	**3 (1)**	**2**	**10 (2)**	**6**

[FACTFILE]

BORN
Newcastle-upon-Tyne,
3 October 1957
POSITION
Centre forward
OTHER CLUBS
Coventry City (1971–81);
Birmingham City (1982–84);
Coventry City (loan, 1984);
Brighton and Hove Albion
(1984–86);
Colchester United (1986–87)

Fern, Tom

Reliable custodian whose safe hands helped lift the 1915 League title

The December 1913 signing of goalkeeper Tom Fern was a happy accident that served Everton excellently for more than a decade. A couple of weeks previously an Everton director had been dispatched to Leeds to watch the Lincoln City centre forward David MacFarlane. The front man missed out through injury, but the scout returned to Merseyside with a 'strong recommendation' to sign the goalkeeper. £1500 sealed the deal and the new player made his first appearance alongside fellow debutant, centre forward Bobby Parker, when Everton faced Sheffield Wednesday on 6 December 1913.

Both would be resounding successes at Goodison, but it was the goalkeeper who attracted the notice of the Liverpool Courier. 'Everton's angling at Lincoln has resulted in a big catch,' its correspondent wrote. 'Though he has figured for such a long time in Second Division football, Fern is reckoned a keeper of the highest class, and certainly

he has performed wonderful work for Lincoln City during the four and a half seasons he has been with them. On his only appearance in the city – against Everton Reserves in a Central League game – Fern, in addition to making several grand clearances, had the distinction of stopping a couple of penalty kicks.'

A bulky player, Fern had made over 160 consecutive appearances for the Citizens, and quickly captured the imagination of a home support that had lacked the presence of a reliable goalkeeper since Billy Scott's departure several years earlier. 'The Everton directors have undoubtedly been fortunate in securing the services of Fern, whose custodianship bore the hall-mark of class,' the Courier wrote of his second appearance, away at Bolton. 'His anticipation of shots turned out accurate in every instance, and the grit and persistency with which he on one occasion saved his charge, at a time a host of opponents were endeavouring to force the ball into

the net, merited the unstinted applause of the big gathering. He gave early evidence of his ability in dealing with high and low shots, and his safe-keeping no doubt inspired confidence among his backs, each of whom was seen to great advantage.'

Fern appeared in all but two of Everton's league matches as they lifted the League Championship for the second time in 1914/15. Indeed further glory may have come his way that year. Everton progressed to the FA Cup semi-final but a finger injury kept him out and Fred Mitchell took his place instead. The stand-in had a nightmare, having a clearance charged down, which led to Chelsea's first goal, and diving late to a long shot for the second. Fern returned for the crucial league run-in, but an historic double was elusive.

War led to football's suspension for four years and Fern played intermittently in the regional leagues. But when peace came,

although now in his mid-thirties, he returned to the first team and gave four more years' service, eventually making way for Alfie Harland.

In June 1924 he joined Port Vale, apparently so he could retain his Liverpool home and his position as secretary of Fazackerly Cricket Club. Fern put in a request to the Everton board to use the club's training facilities, but the board recorded, 'This player's application for permission to train on the ground was not entertained.'

And in one mean-spirited gesture, thus ended the career of one of Everton's finest custodians.

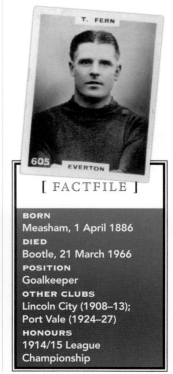

Season	League		FA Cup		Total	
	App	Gls	App	Gls	App	Gls
1913/14	21	0	1	0	22	0
1914/15	36	0	4	0	40	0
1919/20	34	0	1	0	35	0
1920/21	40	0	5	0	45	0
1921/22	38	0	1	0	39	0
1922/23	25	0	0	0	25	0
1923/24	25	0	0	0	25	0
Total	**219**	**0**	**12**	**0**	**231**	**0**

[FACTFILE]

BORN
Measham, 1 April 1886
DIED
Bootle, 21 March 1966
POSITION
Goalkeeper
OTHER CLUBS
Lincoln City (1908–13);
Port Vale (1924–27)
HONOURS
1914/15 League
Championship

Fernandes,
Manuel

Enigmatic midfielder who failed to take his second chance

FERNANDES QUICKLY IMPRESSED THE GOODISON FAITHFUL

First signed by David Moyes in a loan deal from Benfica in the January 2007 transfer window, Portuguese international midfielder Fernandes quickly impressed the Goodison faithful as his new team made a successful assault on UEFA Cup qualification.

A quick, physically imposing player, Fernandes had initially been billed by his compatriot, Jose Mourinho, as a defensive midfielder like Claude Makele, but it soon became apparent that his strengths lay in going forward. A box-to-box player, Fernandes showed a wide range of passing – his speciality was a quick slide-rule pass that sometimes caught out his less gifted team-mates – and a formidable shot. His bullet from the edge of the Manchester United penalty area in April 2007 almost ripped the Gwladys Street goal net from its stanchions.

At the end of the 2006/07 season, Moyes tried to sign Fernandes on a permanent deal. This was complicated by the fact that Fernandes was partly owned by the Global Sports Agency (GSA), a consortium that bought the rights to promising young players. Partial ownership is banned by the Premier League, so Everton were forced to enter complex negotiations with GSA and Benfica. Just as a £12million transfer seemed to be agreed in August 2007, Fernandes walked away and joined Valencia to shock and consternation.

HOWEVER, Valencia were in a state of financial and on-the-field turmoil and when Ronald Koeman became coach, shortly after Fernandes' arrival at the Mestalla, the midfielder was frozen out. A second loan move was agreed in January 2008, but despite being forgiven his earlier snub, Fernandes failed to impress in his second spell at Goodison.

Season	League		FA Cup		League Cup		Europe		Total	
	App	Goals	App	Goals	App	Goals	App	Goals	App	Goals
2006/07	8 (1)	2	0	0	0	0	-	-	8 (1)	2
2007/08	9 (3)	0	0	0	1	0	1 (1)	0	11 (4)	0
Total	17 (4)	2	0	0	1	0	1 (1)	0	19 (5)	2

[FACTFILE]

BORN
Lisbon, Portugal, 6 February 1986
POSITION
Midfield
OTHER CLUBS
Benfica (2005–07);
Portsmouth (loan, 2006);
Valencia (2007); Besiktas (2011–)
HONOURS
8 Portugal caps (2 goals) (2005–)

Ferrari,
Matteo

Elegant Italian international defender who impressed during Goodison loan spell

Season	League		FA Cup		League Cup		Europe		Total	
	App	Goals	App	Goals	App	Goals	App	Goals	App	Goals
2005/06	6 (2)	0	3	0	1	0	1	0	11 (2)	0
Total	6 (2)	0	3	0	1	0	1	0	11 (2)	0

[FACTFILE]

BORN
Aflou, Algeria, 5 December 1979
POSITION
Centre back
OTHER CLUBS
Internazionale (1997–2001);
Genoa (loan, 1997–98);
Lecce (loan, 1998–99);
Bari (loan, 1999–2000);
Parma (2001–04);
AS Roma (2004–08);
Genoa (2008–09);
Besiktas (2009–11); Montreal Impact (2012–)
HONOURS
11 Italy caps (2002–04)

WALLY FIELDING · EVERTON F.C. (1955)

Fielding, Alfred 'Wally'

Long-serving inside right who illuminated the post-war years

During the 1940s and throughout most of the 1950s, Everton possessed an inside right of incisiveness and skill, capable in a single devastating moment of alleviating the gloom in a moribund Goodison Park. Alfred Walter Fielding wore the Everton number ten shirt for a dozen seasons before departing to Southport in his late thirties. But while Fielding was one of Everton's most distinguished and capable servants, he left Goodison without any trophies or international recognition from a career which had once promised to bring much success to his name.

'NOBBY', as he was affectionately known by both fans and fellow players, might never have become an Everton player had Charlton Athletic had their way. Fielding had turned out for the south London club as a junior, but the war intervened before he was able to sign professionally. While stationed in Italy he was spotted by Jack Sharp junior (who went on to become an Everton director and then chairman), a major in the Royal Ordnance Corps at Bari, who recommended him to the Everton manager, Theo Kelly. Kelly signed him, but in doing so sparked a furious debate with Charlton, who claimed that Everton had snatched their player.

EVERTON prevailed in the dispute, and over the following thirteen years Fielding proved a brilliant strategist and ball player, invariably at

> 'I STILL REGARD THE GREATEST MOMENT OF MY CAREER AS THE DAY I SIGNED FOR EVERTON'

the centre of most creative moves in a succession of predominantly lacklustre Everton teams. Initially a master at floating past defenders with a deceptive swerve of the body, as age diminished his pace, his considerable skill still shone through. Even as he approached his 40th birthday he still possessed the cool authority and athleticism of a man a decade younger.

These were lean years for Everton, but rarely has Goodison been so well attended. 'I can remember the days when the players had a shilling sweep on the attendance, and if anybody predicted less than 60,000 we thought he was off his trolley,' said Fielding, later in life.

But despite his prodigious gifts, the nearest Fielding ever came to winning an England cap was when he turned out for the International XI in the Bolton Disaster Fund match at Manchester in 1946. 'I really enjoyed that,' he said. 'But not long afterwards I was sent off at Goodison Park playing against Preston and our manager Cliff Britton told me that I might

never get picked for England again. He was right and it was a major disappointment. I always felt that no matter how well I played I would not even be considered.' There were other high points though and he was an integral part of the 1953 FA Cup run and of the promotion-winning side the following year.

One of the few Jewish players to ever pull on an Everton shirt, he had a fearsome streak, often encountered by team-mates with the temerity to make a mistake. As Johnny King, later manager of Tranmere Rovers, put it: 'If you were playing, you were there to get him his bonus, which was four pounds.'

FIELDING was sold to Southport in 1959 after record-signing Bobby Collins, took his place in the team. By then he was nearly forty, and few doubted that Everton had seen his best years.

Although he had a spell working at the Vauxhall factory in Luton, Fielding spent most of his career in football, being appointed coach at Luton Town in 1960. He was also a coach at Watford before scouting for Spurs. He lived in Cornwall during his retirement, but Everton always remained close to his heart. 'I still regard the greatest moment of my career as the day I signed for Everton,' he said in 1991. 'When I walked into Goodison Park, I felt 20 feet tall. I had achieved my ambition of becoming a professional footballer.'

Season	League		FA Cup		Total	
	App	Goals	App	Goals	App	Goals
1945/46	0	0	2	0	2	0
1946/47	31	4	2	1	33	5
1947/48	33	8	5	2	38	10
1948/49	36	1	2	0	38	1
1949/50	14	0	3	0	17	0
1950/51	34	3	1	0	35	3
1951/52	37	4	2	0	39	4
1952/53	26	5	1	1	27	6
1953/54	39	5	3	0	42	5
1954/55	33	4	2	1	35	5
1955/56	29	3	4	0	33	3
1956/57	34	6	3	0	37	6
1957/58	24	4	0	0	24	4
1958/59	10	2	0	0	10	2
Total	**380**	**49**	**30**	**5**	**410**	**54**

[FACTFILE]

BORN
London, 26 November 1919
DIED
Cornwall, 18 January 2008
POSITION
Inside forward
OTHER CLUB
Southport (1959–60)

Finch Farm

State-of-the-art training complex, home to Everton since 2007

Opened in October 2007, Finch Farm, located in Halewood, south Liverpool, represented a great leap into the future by Everton. It marked the end of a 60-year association with the Bellefield training facility, which by the end of its existence was showing its age. It also incorporated the vastly expanded academy, which had previously occupied a shabby, temporary facility in Netherton.

THE £14 MILLION facility boasts some of the finest training facilities in the world, and features 10 full-size grass pitches on three plateaus, one of which is floodlit, along with an additional floodlit synthetic pitch and specialist training areas for fitness work and goalkeepers. There is also an exact replica of the Goodison pitch.

David Moyes heralded its opening, saying the new facility 'shows the signs Everton are making progress'. He added, 'We are determined to bring ourselves up to date with all the things the players require, and it is certainly good. Most clubs have got the facilities so we had to get it.'

Development of the site took 150 weeks including pitch construction and landscaping. It was according to Everton 'a massive undertaking' with '69,000 ceramic tiles, 68,000 concrete blocks, 4376 carpet tiles, 550 tins of paint, 265 tonnes of steel and 1400 cubic metres of concrete used on a building that boasts 6410 square metres of space for the academy and first team to utilise'. The complex was funded through a leaseback scheme, with Everton effectively paying annual rent until the middle of the century.

EVERTON'S chief executive Keith Wyness said at the opening: 'We're proud of the facility we now have at Finch Farm. Bellefield was ground-breaking when it was developed in the 1960s but times have changed and, in this

modern era, it was vitally important to ensure we had the very finest training complex for the first team.

'Everton has always been a club intent on innovation and moving forward. Being able to now boast one of the most advanced training facilities in world football maintains that tradition and further underlines our determination to continue the great progress made on and off the field in recent seasons.'

In 2012, the Everton supporter's trust, Trust Everton, announced long-term plans to try to buy back the lease on the complex.

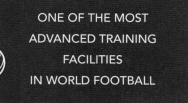

ONE OF THE MOST ADVANCED TRAINING FACILITIES IN WORLD FOOTBALL

Finnis, Harold

Left back who was a one-game wonder

[FACTFILE]

BORN
Liverpool, 21 November 1920
POSITION
Left back

Season	League		FA Cup		Total	
	App	Goals	App	Goals	App	Goals
1946/47	1	0	0	0	1	0
Total	1	0	0	0	1	0

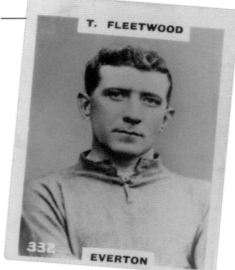

T. FLEETWOOD

332 EVERTON

Fleetwood, Tom

Forward turned defensive lynchpin who captained Everton in the interwar era

Tom Fleetwood was one of Goodison's first great stalwarts, a man who made some 400 appearances – including 121 during the First World War – and lifted the League Championship in 1915, while playing in an array of positions. This saw him start his Goodison career as an inside forward, play most of his career in defence and even make a brief appearance in the Everton goal.

A SON of the city in which he played most of his career, Fleetwood nevertheless started out at Rochdale. He was spotted by Everton's former captain, Jack Taylor, who recommended his signing to the board. £425 captured the forward's signature in March 1911 and it was to be an investment he repaid many times.

Despite a lack of top-flight pedigree, Fleetwood was drafted straight into the starting XI as Everton sought to bolster their flagging First Division title challenge. A goalless draw

at home to Bradford was a disappointing start and the following week Everton fell to fellow title challengers, Aston Villa. The Liverpool Echo nevertheless took some solace from the newcomer's input. 'One of the best features of a good clean game, in which much artistry was shown, was the footwork of Fleetwood, the new Walton forward,' its correspondent reported. 'Resolute yet fearless, Fleetwood was always a source of danger, and could have got a goal had he not lost the ball when [defender James] Logan charged him hard.'

Everton finished the 1910/11 season fourth, with Fleetwood playing the final game at half back in place of Robert Young. It was to be a portent of what was to follow and over the summer of 1911 Fleetwood continued the transition from hopeful First Division forward to top-class defender. In the annual whites v blues trial match, it was reported that the 'half-backs line was strong and Fleetwood's continued appearances at half-back instead of forward seems likely to bear good fruit'.

Young started the 1911/12 season in the half back position, while Fleetwood sat out in the reserves. But this was to be just a temporary situation. Everton started the season slowly and after Fleetwood had appeared three times as centre forward, he supplanted the Scot in the Everton defence.

Not everyone was pleased by these changes. 'Young and Fleetwood have defects in common, and the faster the pace the less effective

these deliberate players are,' reported the Liverpool Post and Mercury. 'The result of slow thinking and lumbersome action in a centre forward is extremely difficult to neutralise by other more desirable qualities. It was hoped Fleetwood would develop more craft, alertness, and keenness in his new position, but up to date he remains the slowest man of a pretty fast line ... His nomadic tendencies [do] not promote the necessary cohesion, and hence the attack was frequently finessing to regain advantage, which had been practically frittered away. A centre forward who is slow to see his chances must necessary always be late in endeavouring to profit by them. Everton certainly want more dash and initiative in the centre.'

But Fleetwood's switch marked an about-turn in Everton's fortunes. Sixteenth at the start of October, they rose to second by mid-January. 'Fleetwood pleased immensely at centre half, and has

steadied down wonderfully,' reported the same newspaper later in the season. 'He showed great self-control and never indulged in over-vigorous tactics... Nowadays Fleetwood's passes are kept low and are seldom overdone.'

EVERTON, the perennial nearly-men of the era, finished the 1911/12 season runners-up, three points behind Blackburn Rovers who beat them 3-1 in what was effectively the title decider four games from the end of the season. Fleetwood was now a first-team regular and although he faced a brief challenge from Billy Wareing he regained his place in time for the 1914/15 season when he made 35 league appearances as Everton won their second First Division title.

WAR BY THEN had taken hold and resulted in football's reorganisation into regional leagues. Unlike some of his team-mates, Fleetwood continued to turn out regularly for Everton.

> FLEETWOOD'S SWITCH TO DEFENCE MARKED AN ABOUT-TURN IN EVERTON'S FORTUNES

EVERTON FOOTBALL CLUB 1918/19

Season	League		FA Cup		Total	
	App	Gls	App	Gls	App	Gls
1910/11	8	1	0	0	8	1
1911/12	34	1	5	0	39	1
1912/13	28	1	2	1	30	2
1913/14	27	1	1	0	28	1
1914/15	35	2	5	0	40	2
1919/20	37	1	1	0	38	1
1920/21	39	1	4	0	43	1
1921/22	33	1	1	0	34	1
1922/23	23	0	2	0	25	0
Total	**264**	**9**	**21**	**1**	**285**	**10**

He also appeared for England in two victory internationals against Scotland in April and May 1919. When peace came he was the first name on the Everton teamsheet and was elected captain for the 1919/20 season. Once he even – in October 1921 – appeared as goalkeeper after Tom Fern was injured in a match against Oldham.

The club, nevertheless, was in a period of transition. In 1919/20, the first season back, Everton finished 16th, then a more promising sixth. But in 1921/22 they had slipped back to 20th and missed out on relegation by just four points. Fleetwood, now in the veteran stage of his career, was facing challenges from Hunter Hart and Joe Peacock – another forward-cum-defender– but it was the arrival of Neil McBain from Manchester United midway through the 1922/23 campaign that saw him off. When the 1923/24 season kicked off Everton had its most settled look in years but there was no sign of Fleetwood. A month into the campaign a board minute recorded: 'The Chairman reported an offer

made by Mr D. G. Ashworth on behalf of the Oldham Athletic F.C. of £750 for this player's transfer, the amount to be paid in two instalments viz half on 30th October and half on 30th November and interest on the money at the rate of 5% to be paid. It was stated that the player would be entitled to an accrued share of benefit of about £300. It was agreed to accept this offer and to give the Club permission to approach.' Fleetwood accepted Oldham's offer and the career of one of Everton's most reliable and versatile sons was over.

[FACTFILE]

BORN
Liverpool, 6 December 1888
POSITION
Defender / forward
OTHER CLUBS
Rochdale (1911);
Oldham Athletic (1923)
HONOURS
1914/15 League
Championship;
2 England caps
(Victory internationals, 1919)

Fleming,
George

Scorer of Everton's first ever league goals

[FACTFILE]

BORN
1863
POSITION
Outside right

Season	League		FA Cup		Total	
	App	Goals	App	Goals	App	Goals
1887/88	-	-	1	0	1	0
1888/89	4	2	0	0	4	2
Total	**4**	**2**	**1**	**0**	**5**	**2**

Flewitt,
Albert

Inside forward who gained representative honours for the Football League

[FACTFILE]

BORN
Beeston, 2 February 1872
POSITION
Inside forward
OTHER CLUBS
Lincoln City (1893–94);
West Bromwich Albion
(1895–98)

Season	League		FA Cup		Total	
	App	Goals	App	Goals	App	Goals
1895/96	3	1	0	0	3	1
Total	**3**	**1**	**0**	**0**	**3**	**1**

Footballing innovations and landmarks

Since the club's creation, Everton have always been at the forefront of innovation

As well as being founder members of the Football League in 1888, the Premier League in 1992, and the first club to play 100 top-flight league seasons, Everton have been at the fore of all manner of innovations and firsts.

Goal nets

EVERTON WERE not the first club to use goal nets in their matches – they were first used at a match between Nottingham Forest v Bolton Wanderers in 1890 – but it was an Evertonian who dreamed up the idea. As Liverpool city engineer, John Brodie (1858– 1934) would find fame as the designer of the Mersey Tunnel and the Queens Drive ring road, but it was his most simple invention that was his most enduring gift to the world. Watching an Everton match in 1889, he saw the game erupt into controversy after the referee could not decide whether the ball had passed between the goalposts or not. The result was a 'net pocket', patented by Brodie, for 'improvements in or applicable to goals used in football, lacrosse, or other like games'.

Goodison Park

Today it might appear less salubrious than many of its more modernised neighbours, but Goodison is positively steeped in history. In 1892, when they left Anfield, Everton became the first English club to move into a purpose-built stadium. In 1894 Goodison was the first Football League ground to host an FA Cup Final.

In 1913 Goodison became the first ground visited by a reigning monarch. The first covered dugouts in England were installed in 1931. Seven years later, after Archibald Leitch designed renovations to the Gwladys Street end, Goodison became the country's first continuously two-tiered ground.

In 1949 Goodison was the scene of England's first defeat on home soil by a nation from beyond the home nations, namely the Republic of Ireland. In May 1958 Goodison became the first British ground to have undersoil heating installed. The current Main Stand, built in 1970, was the first triple-decker stand in Britain. In 2006/07 Goodison became the first stadium to host 100 seasons of top-flight football.

First overseas tour

IN 1905 EVERTON set out on a groundbreaking tour of the Austro-Hungarian empire, in so doing becoming the first professional club to leave these shores. The three-week-long excursion took in seven games, including two exhibition matches against Tottenham Hotspur, then of the Southern League. In football's early days, such games had a huge effect in arousing interest in the game beyond Britain. Four years later, in 1909, Everton and Spurs played the first ever professional game in South America, in so doing inspiring three different clubs – in Argentina, Uruguay and, most notably, Chile – to take Everton's name.

Five match officials

IN SEPTEMBER 2009, the first Europa League match day was notable for the introduction of five match officials: a referee, two linesmen and two further officials positioned in the penalty area to watch for infractions and to check if the ball had crossed the line when a team had scored. Everton's 4-0 win over AEK Athens at Goodison passed without the additional officials being tested by significant incidents.

Everton Free School

In November 2011 Britain's coalition government announced that Everton would be the first football club in the country to have a school attached to it. Aimed at 14–19-year-olds its stated aim was to 'use the power of sport to engage pupils and their wider families with an alternative learning experience'. Funded by the government and administered by Everton's charitable arm, Everton in the Community, the school's unveiling was hailed as a landmark for both the club and the local community. 'This will represent a fantastic opportunity for Everton Football Club and its charitable arm, Everton in the Community, to further extend its reach into a wide variety of communities across the Merseyside region,' said David Moyes. 'It will, unquestionably, provide a real chance for some less-privileged, less-fortunate children to embrace – and benefit from – a high-quality education.'

Football League

Football's first league, of which Everton were founder members and ruled over nine times

Founded in 1888 by the Birmingham draper William McGregor, the Football League was the first such national competition in the world and the premier one in English and Welsh football for more than a century.

Everton were among its founder members and one of its dominant forces, lifting its First Division title nine times – a feat bettered only by Arsenal and Liverpool – and appearing in the top flight for all but four seasons. In 1992 the First Division clubs broke away from the Football League to form the FA Premier League. This ended the mutuality that was for years the Football League's pervading ethos and afforded fresh power to English football's elite to negotiate lucrative new TV and commercial deals, which came to revolutionise English football.

During the 1880s, McGregor, a 41-year-old Scot and Aston Villa

committeeman, witnessed at first hand football's ascent from the fancy of the few to the obsession of the masses. He was aware of the limitations of football's organisational structure and that the system was ad hoc and open to petty rivalries. Games were prone to cancellation when opponents were lured into a fixture that promised higher gate receipts, while 'scratch' teams sent in their place were not uncommon. The lack of organisation meant that in the days before professionalism was legalised players often switched allegiance to whoever could offer them a game or financial inducements. The Everton director Thomas Keates was keenly aware of the problem too: 'The contrast in the attendances at cup ties and ordinary matches, the trifling interest taken in the latter by the public and the insignificance had long vexed the souls of club managers. How can we vitalise the torpid? That was the question.'

MCGREGOR'S answer was a regular, competitive system of fixtures involving only the top clubs, along the lines of the County Cricket Championship. The season would still allow for local cup competitions and the FA Cup, but interest would be maintained after a team had been knocked out in the early stages. The Scot toured the country, seeking the support of his colleagues at other clubs during the 1886/87 season. The response he got was not always favourable and concerns were voiced about upsetting the FA and the cost of regularised fixtures.

McGregor made his first formal move on 2 March 1888, writing to five clubs – Blackburn Rovers, Bolton Wanderers, Preston North End, West Bromwich Albion and Aston Villa (but not Everton) – laying out his ideas: a division of ten or twelve clubs who would play each other in home and away matches played under FA rules, and a formal association to be managed by representatives from each member. He also asked for suggestions for additional members. Of the two replies he received, neither appeared to advocate Everton's inclusion. When several representatives from prospective league members met in London at the end of March, prior to the FA Cup Final between West Bromwich Albion and Preston North End, again Everton were not present.

A FURTHER MEETING WAS scheduled in Manchester's Royal Hotel on 17 April 1888. Here the Football League was formally created. Alexander Nisbet was present to sign Everton up as founder members along with Accrington, Aston Villa, Blackburn Rovers, Bolton Wanderers, Burnley, Derby County, Notts County, Preston North End, Stoke City, West Bromwich Albion and Wolverhampton Wanderers. According to McGregor: 'The League should never aspire to be a legislating body ... by the very nature of things the League must be a selfish body. Its interests are wholly bound up in the welfare of its affiliated clubs, and what happens outside is, in a sense, of secondary importance ... The League has work to do; the Association has its work to do and there need be no clashing.'

Everton's inclusion was something of a surprise, and to this day the rationale remains a mystery. Local rivals Bootle felt that they had a better case for membership and two of that season's FA Cup semi-finalists, Crewe Alexandra and Derby Junction, were also conspicuous by their absence. The Athletic News noted: 'Some of the "twelve most prominent" Association clubs, who are to form the new league, have been knocked into smithereens by teams who, so far, have been left out in the cold.'

The Football League's expansion was rapid. In 1892 the First Division was enlarged to 16 clubs and a new 12-club Second Division was established, taking many members from the rival Football Alliance. By 1898 the League consisted of two 18-club divisions, with its overall

membership expanded to 40 in 1905. Its constituency was still largely based on the North-west and Midlands, but the incorporation of the Southern League to make the Third Division in 1920 and the creation of a northern section of the bottom tier (Third Division (North)) a year later brought its total membership up to 88. The Football League, 33 years after its creation, was now a genuinely national venture.

> **EVERTON ESTABLISHED THEMSELVES AMONG THE NOBILITY OF THIS MAGNIFICENT VENTURE, WINNING THE FIRST DIVISION TWICE BEFORE ITS ENFORCED WARTIME HIATUS**

Everton established themselves among the nobility of this magnificent venture, winning the First Division twice before its enforced wartime hiatus and a further three times in the interwar years. They also won the Second Division Championship in 1930/31. As befitted its stature as one of the game's leading clubs it was well represented in the Football League's management structure. Robert Molyneux (1893–98), Dr James Baxter (1904–19) and Will Cuff (1925–36) were all members of the League's management committee, the ruling council that was elected by the clubs to govern its affairs. From 1936–39 Cuff served as the Football League's vice president and from 1939–49 its President.

THE FOOTBALL LEAGUE presented itself as the counterpoint of the FA, which remained dominated by the public school and university-educated amateurs that first founded

the organisation. In reality it was equally conservative, requiring a three-quarters majority to make alterations to its constitution or rules, which frustrated even modest reforms.

In 1958 the regional elements of the Third Division were removed and the leagues merged to create nationally based Third and Fourth Divisions. In 1960 it started its own cup competition, the League Cup.

UNDER THE League Secretary (later Director General) Alan Hardaker (1957–80), the league took on an insular petty-xenophobic complexion, obstructing Chelsea from competing in the first European Cup and opening up the club versus country debate. It became increasingly belligerent on certain issues, such as the relationship with the pools companies and players' remuneration, taking both parties on in the courts. From the pools its won a settlement for the use of its fixtures, but in 1961 it lost a bitterly fought battle to limit players' wages.

THE FOOTBALL LEAGUE was slow to adapt to the television revolution that swept through the sport from the 1960s. Even in the early 1980s games were seldom shown live on television and the medium was viewed suspiciously. The league remained caught in the past, although the mutuality that existed in the English game was a distinguishing factor. Gate receipts were shared until 1983 and an equality of competition existed. At the same time hooliganism, crumbling stadia and rapidly declining crowds plunged the game to breaking point in the 1980s. England's best players started to move elsewhere.

Under the presidency of Everton chairman Sir Philip Carter, from 1986, the larger clubs started to rebel against this status quo. Seeing the potential from more lucrative television deals – without the need to divvy up money between football's 'have nots' – there was an agitation from the elite clubs to create a 'Super League'. Football League plans for power sharing were rejected by the FA, which in 1991 produced its own 'Blueprint for the Future of Football'. This laid the basis for a breakaway with FA support and in 1992 the entire First Division resigned from the Football League and formed the FA Premier League.

In the teeth of this seismic change, the 72-member Football League not only survived, but flourished. Today the Championship (the former Second Division) is the fourth best-supported league in Europe. While the financial divisions between the Premier League and the Football League are widening, the older body has found renewed purpose adopting eminently sensible governance measures, such as a salary cap and controls on ownership, that have brought increased stability to the English game.

But for Everton, besides its annual participation in the League Cup, the league with which they were once so synonymous has now become a spectre, a nightmare to be endured only if they ever suffer the indignity of relegation.

> UNDER THE PRESIDENCY OF EVERTON CHAIRMAN SIR PHILIP CARTER, FROM 1986, THE LARGER CLUBS STARTED TO REBEL AGAINST THIS STATUS QUO

Forbes, Fred

Scottish inside forward from the transitional early 1920s

EVERTON F. C.

EVERTON 1923
Back row - **Hart, Brewster, Peacock, Fern, McDonald, Chedgzoy**
Front - **Harrison, Downs, Irvine, Forbes, Williams**

Season	League		FA Cup		Total	
	App	Goals	App	Goals	App	Goals
1922/23	10	4	0	0	10	4
1923/24	3	0	0	0	3	0
1924/25	1	0	0	0	1	0
Total	**14**	**4**	**0**	**0**	**14**	**4**

[FACTFILE]

BORN
Leith, 5 August 1894
POSITION
Inside forward
OTHER CLUBS
Heart of Midlothian;
Plymouth Argyle (1924–28);
Bristol Rovers (1929–30);
Northampton Town (1932);
Airdrieonians

Foreign players, and Everton

The overseas revolution that all began with a Swede in 1989

Since Swede Stefan Rehn became Everton's first foreign player in 1989, some 67 overseas players from 31 different countries have played for Everton.

Many of their careers have been fleeting, others have been more successful. Joseph Yobo has the most appearances of an overseas player with 240 appearances during his nine-year Goodison career; Anderson Da Silva has the least, with a single two-minute substitute cameo to his name.

The countries represented are as follows:

*Netherlands
(six players);
France, Sweden and Denmark
(five);
Nigeria, the USA
(four);
Brazil, Italy, Portugal, Australia
(three);
Norway, China, Russia,
Switzerland, Croatia, Germany
(two);
Argentina, Greece, Slovakia,
South Africa, Iceland, Ecuador,
Belgium, Poland, Yugoslavia,
Switzerland, Ivory Coast,
Ghana, Israel, Canada, Spain
(one each).*

The players *(in chronological order of appearance):*

Stefan Rehn
Sweden — 1989-90
Raymond Atteveld
Netherlands — 1989-92
Robert Warzycha
Poland — 1991-94
Predrag Radosavljevic (Preki)
Yugoslavia — 1992-94
Jason Kearton
Australia — 1993-94
Anders Limpar
Sweden — 1994-97
Daniel Amokachi
Nigeria — 1994-96
Andrei Kanchelskis
Russia — 1995-97
Marc Hottiger
Switzerland — 1996-97
Claus Thomsen
Denmark — 1997-98
Slaven Bilić
Croatia — 1997-2000
Mickael Madar
France — 1997-1999
Thomas Myhre
Norway — 1997-2001
Marco Materazzi
Italy — 1998-99
Olivier Dacourt
France — 1998-99
Peter Degn
Denmark — 1999-2001
Ibrahima Bakayoko
Ivory Coast — 1998-99
Abel Xavier
Portugal — 1999-2002
Joe Max Moore
USA — 1999-2002
Alessandro Pistone
Italy — 2000-07
Alex Nyarko
Ghana — 2000-04
Niclas Alexandersson
Sweden — 2000-04
Thomas Gravesen
Denmark — 2000-05 & 2007-08

Idan Tal
Israel — 2000-03
Tomasz Radzinski
Canada — 2001-04
Jesper Blomqvist
Sweden — 2001-02
Tobias Linderoth
Sweden — 2002-04
David Ginola
France — 2002
Joseph Yobo
Nigeria — 2002-
Li Wei Feng
China — 2002
Li Tie
China — 2002-06
Juliano Rodrigo
Brazil — 2002-03
Brian McBride
USA — 2003
Espen Barrdsen
Norway — 2003
Tim Cahill
Australia — 2004-
Mikel Arteta
Spain — 2005-11
Per Kroldrup
Denmark — 2005-06
Matteo Ferrari
Italy — 2005-06
Nuno Valente
Portugal — 2005-09
Andy Van Der Meyde
Netherlands — 2005-09
Sander Westerveld
Netherlands — 2006
Victor Anichebe
Nigeria — 2006-
Tim Howard
USA — 2006-
Anderson Da Silva
Brazil — 2007-08
Manuel Ferdandes
Portugal — 2007 & 2008
Steven Pienaar
South Africa — 2007-11 & 2012-

Yakubu Aiyegbeni
Nigeria — 2007-11
Stefan Wessels
Germany — 2007-08
Bjarni Vidarsson
Iceland — 2004-08
Lars Jacobsen
Denmark — 2008-09
Segundo Castillo
Ecuador — 2008-09
Louis Saha
France — 2008-12
Marouane Fellaini
Belgium — 2008-
Jo
Brazil — 2009
Johnny Heitinga
Netherlands — 2009-
Dinyar Bilyaletdinov
Russia — 2009-12
Lucas Neill
Australia — 2009-10
Sylvain Distin
France — 2009-
Shkodran Mustafi
Germany — 2009-12
Landon Donovan
USA — 2010 & 2012
Phillipe Senderos
Switzerland — 2010
Apostolos Velios
Greece — 2010-
Magaya Gueye
France — 2010-
Jan Mucha
Slovakia — 2010-
Denis Stracqualursi
Argentina — 2011-
Royston Drenthe
Netherlands — 2011-
Nikica Jelavić
Croatia — 2012-

Forshaw, Adam

Young midfielder who made first-team bow in Europa League tie

[FACTFILE]

BORN
Liverpool, 8 October 1991
POSITION
Midfield
OTHER CLUB
Brentford (loan, 2012)

Season	League		FA Cup		League Cup		Europe		Total	
	App	Goals	App	Goals	App	Goals	App	Goals	App	Goals
2009/10	0	0	0	0	0	0	1	0	1	0
Total	0	0	0	0	0	0	1	0	1	0

Forshaw, Dick

Inside forward who crossed the Merseyside football divide

[FACTFILE]

BORN
20 August, 1895
DIED
1963
POSITION
Inside forward
OTHER CLUBS
Liverpool (1919–27);
Wolverhampton Wanderers
(1929–30)
HONOURS
1927/28 League
Championship

Season	League		FA Cup		Other		Total	
	App	Goals	App	Goals	App	Goals	App	Goals
1926/27	10	2	0	0	-	-	10	2
1927/28	23	5	0	0	-	-	23	5
1928/29	8	1	0	0	1	0	9	1
Total	41	8	0	0	1	0	42	8

France, David

Philanthropist, historian and fan who made outstanding contributions to 'Evertonia'

AS AUTHOR, philanthropist, historian, collector and Evertonian, the contribution of David France (b.1948) to the dissemination of the club's history and culture stands tall. His legacies include a library of fine Everton-related books, the Gwladys Street Hall of Fame, the Everton Former Players' Foundation and the Everton Collection.

Born in modest surroundings in Widnes, France was dismissed as a 'slow learner' as a schoolboy and was unable to read until the age of 14. He began working life as an apprentice gas-fitter, but later resumed his education with great success, gaining several university degrees, including a PhD in chemical engineering. He subsequently immigrated to the United States, where he worked in the oil industry and served as a consultant to NASA. In 1990, aged 42, he ended his working life to concentrate on what he termed 'good deeds'.

An intensely driven man who has run 100 marathons over the years,

his love of Everton Football Club manifested itself in many ways. Its first expression came in book form and over the years France would prove a prolific and outstanding author on his great passion. His debut came in 1997 with Toffeecards, an A5-size softback book offering an illustrated and concise pre-World War Two history of Everton through the medium of cigarette cards. He followed this up the same year with Toffeepages, which described the post-war years at Goodison Park through the medium of football programmes.

Other significant works included Gwladys Street's Holy Trinity

BERT FREEMAN
EVERTON F.C.

(2001; with Becky Tallentire) about the great Harvey-Kendall-Ball triumvirate; Virgin Blues (2002, with David Prentice), an outstanding account of Everton's early years; Everton Treasures (2005; later republished as Dr France's Magnificent Obsession) about the accumulation of his famous memorabilia collection; and Alex Young: The Golden Vision (2008), a fabulous biography of the icon who is France's hero.

> THIS WAS THE
> FIRST SUCH BENEVOLENT FUND
> OF ITS KIND
> IN WORLD FOOTBALL,
> AND UEFA HAVE ADOPTED IT
> AS ITS MODEL

In 1998 Dr France conceived the Gwladys Street Hall of Fame 'as a tribute to the individuals who have aided the development of the first club of Merseyside'. He established a panel of Evertonians to elect Goodison greats into the inaugural Hall of Fame, and subsequent elections were held among the wider fan base. Players and officials were inducted at raucous dinners at Liverpool's Adelphi Hotel. Several illustrated books were produced by France to mark the Hall of Fame, with the proceeds donated to Alder Hey children's hospital.

PARTLY AS A RESULT of his work in putting the Hall of Fame together, France then set about establishing the Everton Former Players Foundation to help old pros fallen on hard times. Any player to have made one or more first-team appearances for Everton was eligible for assistance, and the foundation has helped dozens of former players adjust to life after football. This was the first such benevolent fund of its kind in world football, and UEFA have adopted it as its model.

But his most amazing legacy is surely the most comprehensive single-club collection of historical footballing artefacts and memorabilia the world has ever seen. For decades he collected just about anything and everything of significance related to the club's history. His archives, as recounted by his friend and frequent collaborator David Prentice, included 'ledgers, cash-books, gate-books, handbooks, (a complete run of) programmes, season-tickets, photographs, postcards, cigarette-cards, bubble gum cards, postal covers, players' contracts, financial accounts, articles of association, travel itineraries, celebration menus and other ephemera.'

France's self-styled 'magnificent obsession' started as a boy, when a neighbour would give him his old Everton programmes, which he scrupulously filed away. He then spent years trawling antique markets and auction houses, and tracking down former players, adding to his remarkable collection.

AFTER SUFFERING ill health, at the start of the 21st century France sought to sell his great labour of love. But rather than separate the collection to maximise his own financial gain, he wished to keep it together to maintain its integrity and have it as a record for future generations of Evertonians. Despite initial disinterest, then obfuscation by Everton, a charitable trust was eventually set up to purchase the collection and, backed by heritage-lottery funds, the purchase was finally completed. The collection – with additional artefacts provided by Everton itself – finally went on public display at Liverpool's Picton Library in 2009.

It represented the culmination of an outstanding contribution to Everton history and culture by a remarkable man. Applauded for his work, France always displays characteristic humility. 'Don't thank me,' he once told a pair of admirers. 'Being a blue is my reward.'

Freeman, Bert

Aston Villa reject turned goal-poacher extraordinaire

Bertie Freeman was one of the most extraordinary goalscorers in Everton history, an explosive poacher par excellence who became the first player to hit more than 30 league goals in a single campaign, also topping the First Division scoring charts.

HE HAD STARTED out with Aston Villa in his native Birmingham, but left without making an impression to join Woolwich Arsenal. In south London he was prolific but without ever making the centre forward shirt his own.

Woolwich Arsenal were perpetually cash-strapped and to sell was to survive. In 1907/08 Everton eyed some of their players with avarice as they sought to rejuvenate a disappointing league campaign. In February 1908 the Everton board made a double bid for Arsenal's England international inside forward Tim Coleman and Freeman. Coleman was allowed to leave for Goodison, but for Freeman Everton had to wait another two months. Then, £350 was enough to buy the player. For the London club it was, reflected Tony Matthews in the Arsenal Who's Who, 'one of the great transfer blunders of those early years'. Freeman and Coleman were an incredible success together.

They appeared briefly at the end of the 1907/08 season, but it was only with the onset of the following campaign that Goodison witnessed their full potential. A brace apiece on the opening day at, ironically, Woolwich Arsenal set the tone. Once they started scoring they couldn't stop – 57 league goals combined, with 38 from 36 appearances for Freeman. This included four hat-tricks and seven braces, including one in a 5-0 hammering of Liverpool as well as a run of ten straight scoring appearances.

THERE SEEMED to be no great elegance to Freeman's technique. He got the ball and put it into the goal; he was a finisher, a rabid poacher – there were no thrills other than the ball hitting the back of the net. After scoring both goals versus Bristol City in the second game of the campaign the Liverpool Courier recorded: 'Freeman has the requisite heights and weights, and though he may not be endowed with the gifts in the direction of knitting the wings together, which distinguish really great pivots, he possesses the happy faculty of seizing an opportunity for forcing his way through by sheer weight and determination, and shooting with deadly effect.' Later that season, the same publication wrote: 'Freeman still adopts the same brisk methods that characterised his play when a member of the Arsenal team, but he has improved immensely with his juggling with the ball, and I should say he is now one of the cleverest forwards in the League.'

Freeman was called up to the England team and Everton shot to the top of the league, winning 13 of their first 18 matches and losing just twice. But their form collapsed dramatically in the second half of the campaign and they won just five of their last 20 matches. It was enough for runners-up spot, but they were well behind League Champions Newcastle United.

Freeman started the 1909/10 campaign where he had left off the previous one. He scored ten goals in Everton's first eight league matches. 'The great feature was Freeman's return to form,' reported the Liverpool Courier after he struck a hat-trick against Sheffield United. 'Not only was he responsible for the hat-trick, but his play throughout was a marked advance upon anything he has given this season. He distributed the play better, and his trapping of the ball combined with his marvellous dexterity in seizing openings was reminiscent of his best days.'

Although Everton shared the goals out this campaign, they remained heavily reliant on

Freeman's prowess. When he plundered Everton shone; when he struggled for goals and form, the team laboured. Everton finished tenth and reached the FA Cup semi-final, but the Everton board had started to refashion the team. Coleman had started to be edged out and Jack Sharp retired; Freeman would struggle in this new team.

He opened the 1910/11 season with a brace, but while the form of the team was good, his was poor. When Everton faced Woolwich Arsenal in early November he had gone two months without scoring. 'Freeman's play was erratic,' reported the Liverpool Courier. 'Early on he gave us a taste of his old time dash and good intention and worked for openings, but the spectators are still waiting for that goal. Frequently they concluded that this was forthcoming, only to be disappointed, however, by the centre's wild kicking over the bar.' Freeman, it added, 'made a miserable attempt with a splendid opening'.

A WEEK LATER, against Bradford City, he was dropped and Sandy Young returned as centre forward. Freeman played just once more for Everton. Less than 18 months had passed between him topping the First Division scoring charts and his axing from the Everton first team.

In April 1911 Freeman was transfer-listed for £800. Burnley moved quickly and with Harry Mountford he moved across Lancashire later that same month for a joint fee of £850. There was, however, still plenty of life – and goals – in the forward. His staggering prowess returned at Turf Moor and he scored 64 league goals in his first two seasons for Burnley. In 1914 and before King George V – the first reigning monarch to attend an FA Cup Final – he scored the only goal of the match when Burnley beat Liverpool to lift the cup for the only time.

War interrupted his career, like so many others of his era, but he returned to football afterwards, putting in another season with Burnley before dropping down to non-league with Wigan Borough. Shortly before he left Turf Moor, he received the following newspaper

tribute, which is worth recalling in full, because it says much of the player, the man and his achievements:

Freeman may justly be described as one of the most remarkable players of the past 20 years, a centre-forward who was a leader in deed as well as name. The modern tendency is for the leaders of attack to wait for opportunities to be provided for them. They have to be spoon fed to succeed, merely relying upon pace, weight and ability to shoot. Freeman could burst through with the best; moreover he could also engineer openings for his colleagues and was an artist with the ball at his toes.

That queer, short step of his misled many defenders and it was one of the surprises of football when in 1909 Everton decided that his playing days were over. So far from the fact did the Everton judgment prove that Freeman led Burnley to promotion and to victory in the English Cup. He has been with the Turf Moor club for 11 years and has taken part in 300 games for them in which he has scored 174 goals – a wonderful record for a player supposed to be at the end of his career. He will be greatly missed at Turf Moor, where he made himself one of the most popular players the club has ever possessed.

[FACTFILE]

BORN
Handsworth, Birmingham,
1 October 1885
DIED
11 August 1955
POSITION
Centre forward
OTHER CLUBS
Aston Villa (1904–05);
Woolwich Arsenal (1905–08);
Burnley (1911–21);
Wigan Borough (1922–24)
HONOURS
5 England caps (3 goals) (1909–12)

Season	League		FA Cup		Total	
	App	Goals	App	Goals	App	Goals
1907/08	4	1	0	0	4	1
1908/09	37	38	1	0	38	38
1909/10	34	22	7	4	41	26
1910/11	11	2	0	0	11	2
Total	**86**	**63**	**8**	**4**	**94**	**67**

Full Members' Cup

(also known as the Simod Cup and Zenith Data Systems Cup)

Unlamented cup competition that offered a poor alternative to European football

Introduced in 1985 after English clubs were banned from Europe, the Full Members' Cup was a knockout trophy designed to drum up additional attendances in the midst of football's financial crisis. A Full Member – although this was never quite clear to the public – was one of the 44 clubs in the First or Second Division. It was a straight knockout competition, but singularly failed to capture the imagination of the public. In 1986/87 gates of 821 and 817 were recorded at First Division Charlton, and only four attendances in the entire competition reached five figures that year.

The competition was rescued by the sports manufacturers Simod, who sponsored it in 1988 and 1989. The prize money on offer – £60,000 for the winners, £30,000 for the runners-up and £15,000 for the semi-finalists – was comparatively generous by the standards of the time. The American computer manufacturer Zenith Data Systems sponsored the competition between 1990 and 1992. When this deal ran out, the ambivalence of clubs and the public plus the onset of the Premier League meant the competition was disbanded.

HAVING boycotted the inaugural competition, Everton entered for the first time in 1986/87, but were knocked out in the quarter-final on penalties by Charlton. The game came in the midst of the League Championship run-in, but Howard Kendall nevertheless put out a strong side, that included a debut for John Ebbrell. Everton did not enter in 1987/88, but the following year reached the final, in which they were beaten in a half-empty Wembley by Nottingham Forest. Again, Everton did not enter in 1989/90.

By 1990/91 the competition was split into north–south regional sections, which drummed up slightly more public interest. Everton beat Leeds United in the northern final, but in the national final at Wembley were torn apart in extra time by Crystal Palace, losing 4–1. Everton entered the competition's finale in 1991/92, but were knocked out by Leicester City early in the competition.

EVERTONIANS' ambivalence to this maligned competition is best surmised by the numbers who actually attended these games. Goodison hosted just seven Full Members' Cup ties, and yet the old stadium's five lowest record attendances for a senior match are all in this short-lived competition.

1986/87

3 DECEMBER 1986
Rd 3 v Newcastle United [H] 5-2 *Sheedy, Heath, Sharp 3;* 7530
Southall, Harper, Pointon, Ratcliffe, Watson, Power (Mountfield), Steven, Heath, Sharp, Adams, Sheedy

3 MARCH 1987
Quarter-final v Charlton Athletic [H] 2-2 (Charlton win 6-5 on penalties) *Wilkinson, Steven;* 7914
Southall, Van Den Hauwe, Pointon, Mountfield, Watson, Harper (Ebbrell), Steven (Langley), Heath, Wilkinson, Snodin, Adams

1988/89

20 DECEMBER 1988
Rd 3 v Millwall [H] 2-0 *Hurlock og, Cottee;* 3703
Stowell, McDonald, Pointon, Ratcliffe (Ebbrell), Watson, Bravewell, Steven, Reid, Nevin, Cottee, Sheedy

18 JANUARY 1989
Quarter-final v Wimbledon [A] 2-1 *Clarke 2;* 2477
Southall, McDonald, Pointon, Ratcliffe, Watson, Steven (Wilson), Nevin, McCall, Clarke, Cottee, Sheedy

28 FEBRUARY 1989
Semi-final v Queens Park Rangers [H] 1-0 *Nevin;* 7072
Southall, McDonald (Bracewell), Pointon, Ratcliffe, Watson, Snodin, Nevin, McCall, Clarke, Cottee, Sheedy

30 APRIL 1989
Final v Nottingham Forest (Wembley) 3-4 [AET] *Cottee 2, Sharp;* 46,606
Southall, McDonald, Van den Hauwe, Ratcliffe, Watson, Bracewell (McCall), Nevin, Steven, Sharp, Cottee, Sheedy

1990/91

18 DECEMBER 1990
Rd 2 v Blackburn Rovers [A] 4-1 *Newell, Cottee, Watson 2;* 5410
Southall, McDonald, Hinchcliffe, Ratcliffe, Watson, Ebbrell, Nevin, McCall, Newell, Cottee, Beagrie

22 JANUARY 1991
Rd 3 v Sunderland [H] 4-0 *Cottee 4;* 4609
Southall, McDonald, Ebbrell, Ratcliffe, Keown, McCall, Nevin, Cottee, Sharp (Atteveld), Sheedy (Milligan), Beagrie

13 MARCH 1991
Northern semi-final v Barnsley [A] 1-0 *Cottee;* 10,287
Southall, Keown, Ebbrell, Ratcliffe, Watson, Milligan, Nevin, McCall, Newell, Cottee, Beagrie (McDonald)

19 MARCH 1991
Northern final (1st leg) v Leeds United [A] 3-3 *Beagrie, Warzycha, Milligan;* 13,387
Southall, McDonald, Ebbrell, Ratcliffe, Watson, Keown, Warzycha (Nevin), McCall, Newell (Cottee), Milligan, Beagrie

21 MARCH 1991
Northern final (2nd leg) v Leeds United [H] 3-1 [AET] *Cottee 2, Ebbrell;* 12,603
Southall, McDonald (Cottee), Ebbrell, Ratcliffe, Watson, Keown, Warzycha, McCall, Newell, Milligan, Beagrie (Nevin)

7 APRIL 1991
Final v Crystal Palace (Wembley) 1-4 [AET] *Warzycha;* 52,460
Southall, McDonald, Hinchcliffe, Keown (Ratcliffe), Watson, Milligan, Warzycha, McCall, Newell (Nevin), Cottee, Sheedy

1991/92

1 OCTOBER 1991
Rd 2 v Oldham Athletic [H] 3-2 *Newell, Watson, Cottee;* 4588
Southall, Harper, Hinchcliffe, Ebbrell, Watson, Youds, Nevin, Beardsley, Newell (Atteveld), Cottee, Sheedy

27 NOVEMBER 1991
Rd 3 v Leicester City [A] 1-2 *Beardsley;* 13,242
Southall, Jackson (Atteveld), Hinchcliffe, Harper, Watson, Keown, Warzycha, Beardsley, Johnston, Cottee, Ward

EVERTON
·ENCYCLOPEDIA·

Jimmy **Gabriel**, Jimmy **Galt**, Mick **Gannon**, Thomas **Gardner**, Paul **Gascoigne**, Jimmy **Gauld**, Ernie **Gault**, Fred **Geary**, Charlie **Gee**, Albert **Geldard**, Scot **Gemmill**, Paul **Gerrard**, Billy **Gibson**, Darron **Gibson**, David **Gibson**, John **Gidman**, Torry **Gillick**, David **Ginola**, Jimmy **Glazzard**, Gerry **Glover**, Brian **Godfrey**, Hugh **Goldie**, Ronnie **Goodlass**, Patrick **Gordon**, Dan **Gosling**, H. **Goudie**, Richard **Gough**, James **Gourlay**, Tom **Gracie**, Bobby **Graham**, Jackie **Grant**, Tony **Grant**, Thomas **Gravesen**, Andy **Gray**, **Great Escapes**, Colin **Green**, Norman **Greenhalgh**

Gabriel, Jimmy

Popular 1960s wing half, who returned as a Goodison coach in the 1990s

When Jimmy Gabriel became temporary manager following Howard Kendall's resignation in December 1993 he boasted a 100 per cent record from a previous spell as caretaker boss, after Colin Harvey's sacking in 1990.

Granted, it was only one game – a 3-0 victory over Queens Park Rangers – but he still held the brief and unusual distinction of having Everton's best ever managerial record. 'If things go okay,' he said at the time of taking over again, 'I might be interested in the job.' Five defeats and two draws later he decided that the Goodison hot seat was not for him.

As a 1960s wing half, however, Jimmy Gabriel excelled, winning the admiration of fans and players for his complete commitment. Alex Young once remarked, 'Jimmy would run through a brick wall and just blink' – sentiments shared by virtually anyone who saw him play. Yet there was far more to Gabriel's game than pure aggression, and as well as his physical qualities, he possessed the skill and aerial ability to control the right side of the Everton midfield for some years. Gabriel was mentally tough too: when, just three games into his Everton career, he was given a torrid time by West Bromwich Albion's Derek Kevan, who scored five times in a thrashing at the Hawthorns, he possessed the

resilience at just 19 years of age to react positively to the humiliation by working to improve his game.

SIGNED FOR £30,000 from Dundee in March 1960, his exploits had already won the teenager comparisons with fellow-countryman Dave Mackay, who had joined Spurs a year earlier. Gabriel quickly forged a strong partnership with Brian Harris, then Tony Kay, occasionally deputising as centre forward too.

A charismatic and popular member of the dressing room, he earned a reputation as a minder and mentor to the younger players – despite his own tender years. The likes of Tommy Wright and Colin Harvey benefited from this as they pushed their way into the first team. Harvey later said: 'Whoever came in, if you were a bit young, Jimmy took you under his arm and looked after you.' Such was the youngster's regard for his team-mate that when he was Everton manager he made Gabriel his reserve team manager.

GABRIEL WON a Championship medal in 1963 and three years later was another stalwart as Everton lifted the FA Cup. Gabriel's cup final display

still evokes fond memories among older supporters after he provided one of the most memorable moments in an unforgettable match: with just minutes remaining he played the ball against the corner flag, egging on the Sheffield Wednesday players to try and dispossess him. On eventually winning a throw-in he lifted his arms in the air as if he had just scored the winning goal.

The ruthless Harry Catterick moved quickly to break up the cup winning team, however, and Gabriel was one of the first to go: sold to Southampton at the end of the 1966/67 season to make way for Howard Kendall.

[FACTFILE]

BORN
Dundee, 10 October 1940
POSITION
Wing half
OTHER CLUBS
Dundee (1957–60);
Southampton (1967–72);
Bournemouth (1972–74);
Swindon Town (loan, 1973);
Brentford (1974); Seattle
Sounders (1974–79)
HONOURS
1962/63 League
Championship,
FA Cup 1966,
2 Scotland caps (1961–64)

Season	League		FA Cup		League Cup		Europe		Total	
	App	Goals	App	Goals	App	Goals	App	Goals	App	Goals
1959/60	8	0	0	0	-	-	-	-	8	0
1960/61	40	1	1	0	5	0	-	-	46	1
1961/62	42	6	3	0	-	-	-	-	45	6
1962/63	40	5	3	1	-	-	2	0	45	6
1963/64	33	5	5	1	-	-	1	0	39	6
1964/65	37	4	4	0	-	-	5	0	46	4
1965/66	24	6	6	0	-	-	3	1	33	7
1966/67	31 (1)	6	3	0	-	-	4	0	38 (1)	6
Total	**255 (1)**	**33**	**25**	**2**	**5**	**0**	**15**	**1**	**300(1)**	**36**

A GOODISON RETURN with Southampton four years later was less than happy for the Scot, as Everton won 8-0 – their biggest win in 41 years. 'Southampton were a side who could do that sort of thing,' Gabriel said years later. 'One day we'd take on the top team in the country and beat them, the next we'd get battered.' He spent the day as a makeshift right back with the unenviable task of marking Alan Whittle. 'He was twice as fast as me,' he recalled. 'He kept knocking the ball past me and running on to it … and big Joe Royle was in the middle smashing them in from the crosses.' Royle ended the day with four goals and David Johnson also netted a hat-trick.

For Scotland, only Mackay's excellence at right half restricted Gabriel to two international caps, the first coming in 1961 against Wales, the latter as substitute against Norway three years later.

Gabriel moved to Bournemouth in 1972, and later played for Swindon Town and Brentford. In 1974 he moved to the NASL where he spent five productive years with Seattle Sounders, the latter two as manager. In 1977 he won the National Conference and took Sounders to the Soccer Bowl – football's answer to the Super Bowl – but they lost to a New York Cosmos team that included Pele and Franz Beckenbauer. Between 1980 and 1982 Gabriel managed San Jose Earthquakes, whose players included George Best and Colin Bell.

He returned to England in 1986 as coach at Bournemouth, then to Goodison as part of Colin Harvey's backroom staff in 1990. As reserve team manager he oversaw the development of players such as Michael Ball and David Unsworth, as well as twice stepping in as caretaker manager.

Gabriel returned to Seattle in 1997, ostensibly to be reunited with family who lived there, although he continued coaching, first at the Washington Huskies, then as assistant manager at Sounders. On winning the US Second Division title in October 2005, Gabriel, now aged 65, called time on a football career that had spanned almost half a century.

> AS RESERVE TEAM MANAGER HE OVERSAW THE DEVELOPMENT OF PLAYERS SUCH AS MICHAEL BALL AND DAVID UNSWORTH

Galt, Jimmy

Captain of Everton's 1914/15 League Championship winning side

Few players in Everton's history have made so great an impression in so short a period as Scottish defender Jimmy Galt. His Everton first-team career effectively lasted just eight months and 36 appearances, but in that short time he captained the club to its second League Championship.

A FORMER Scotland international, Galt came to Goodison with almost a decade's worth of trophy-studded experience at Glasgow Rangers. A former left half who had converted to centre back, he came 'into English football with a splendid reputation, which he earned whilst with the Rangers across the border', recorded the Football Echo of his £1250 transfer. 'He has been chosen to captain the "Blues" and much will be expected of him. May hopes be fully realised.' Galt quickly met those expectations, making, reported the Liverpool Post and Mercury 'a pleasing debut' against Tottenham Hotspur. 'He exhibited much good judgment and fed his forwards capitally.' Another correspondent wrote of his leadership skills, saying that he was a player that 'generalled his forces with much skill'.

The 1914/15 season would be one of the closest on record, with just eighteen points separating the top and bottom clubs at the season's end and three points dividing the top eight teams. Everton's strengths lay in the amazing goals tally of striker Bobby Parker and its miserly defence. Galt played his part in this.

The First World War hung over Everton's triumphant season and after the league was abandoned Galt scarcely appeared in wartime matches. Times were evidently hard during these years. In February 1919 Galt wrote to the Everton board concerning his 'present status'. The minuted response suggests that he was after more money: 'Resolved that he cannot be paid

> FEW PLAYERS IN EVERTON'S HISTORY HAVE MADE SO GREAT AN IMPRESSION

more than the amount stipulated by the League for players taking part in matches, & that we cannot undertake to find him employment.'

Now in his mid-thirties and with his top-class playing career presumed to be over, Galt had returned to Glasgow. The Everton board, however, retained his playing registration and sought £500 for it. It probably scuppered a move to Kilmarnock in his native Ayrshire. Galt tried to have his playing registration freed by the club, but for 18 months they refused to relent. Finally on 28 September 1920 they gave Galt the free transfer he sought and he joined Third Lanark.

ON LEAVING football he went into business with his former Rangers team-mate Jimmy Gordon and ran a series of billiards halls. He was offered the position of Everton's Scotland scout in early 1935 but declined. Later that year he passed away.

[FACTFILE]

BORN
Saltcoats, 11 August 1885

DIED
17 November 1935

POSITION
Centre back

OTHER CLUBS
Glasgow Rangers (1906–14); Third Lanark

HONOURS
1914/15 League Championship, 2 Scotland caps (1 goal) (1908)

Season	League		FA Cup		Total	
	App	Goals	App	Goals	App	Goals
1914/15	32	2	4	2	36	4
Total	32	2	4	2	36	4

Gannon,
Mick

Young understudy to Brian Labone who forged a solid lower league career

[FACTFILE]

BORN
Liverpool, 2 February 1943
POSITION
Defender
OTHER CLUBS
Scunthorpe United (1962–64);
Crewe Alexandra (1964–70)

Season	League		FA Cup		Total	
	App	Goals	App	Goals	App	Goals
1961/62	3	0	0	0	3	0
Total	3	0	0	0	3	0

Gardner,
Thomas

One-game wonder on the Everton wing

[FACTFILE]

BORN
Liverpool, 17 March 1923
POSITION
Right wing

Season	League		FA Cup		Total	
	App	Goals	App	Goals	App	Goals
1947/48	1	0	0	0	1	0
Total	1	0	0	0	1	0

Gascoigne,
Paul

Finest English footballer of his generation, whose Goodison spell was symptomatic of a sad decline

When Everton signed Paul Gascoigne in the summer of 2000 most Evertonians were unsure whether to laugh or cry.

On the one hand, Gascoigne was the finest and best-known English footballer of his generation, and yet the litany of personal demons – boozing, burping, wife-beating – were well known. As a footballer, fans were perpetually left to wonder if Gascoigne could put those behind him, whether they would see him at his best again – the brilliant player who propelled England to within a whisker of the 1990 World Cup. In Scotland, Walter Smith had at times got the best from Gascoigne, and Evertonians wondered if he could repeat the trick at Goodison.

Put simply, Smith was unable to do this. On the rare occasions Gascoigne was unleashed, it was to witness a footballing tragedy unfold. For here was a man whose footballing brain was as sharp as ever, but whose body – through injuries and the effects of years of boozing and excess – was unable to keep pace with it.

WHAT WAS particularly infuriating about Smith was that he sheltered Gazza, whose personal excesses were wildly rumoured on Merseyside but not revealed until his unusually candid autobiography was published in 2004, while not giving quality young players, like Michael Ball, an inch.

Gauld,
Jimmy

Controversial figure who was subsequently embroiled in the Tony Kay bribery scandal

[FACTFILE]

BORN
Aberdeen, 9 May 1931
POSITION
Inside forward
OTHER CLUBS
Charlton Athletic (1955–57);
Plymouth Argyle (1957–59);
Swindon Town (1959–60);
St Johnstone (1960–61);
Mansfield Town (1961)

Season	League		FA Cup		Total	
	App	Goals	App	Goals	App	Goals
1956/57	23	7	3	1	26	8
Total	23	7	3	1	26	8

WITHIN DAYS of David Moyes' arrival in March 2002, Gascoigne joined Burnley. From there a desperately sad odyssey for a role within the game – any role – took in the Chinese Second Division and various lower league outposts in English football.

An oblivion of drink and drug abuse followed and his sectioning under the Mental Health Act in February 2008 had an aura of sad inevitability.

Further reading:
GASCOIGNE, PAUL, AND HUNTER DAVIES,
Gazza: My Story, Headline, 2004

[FACTFILE]

BORN
Dunston, 27 May 1967
POSITION
Midfield
OTHER CLUBS
Newcastle United (1984–88);
Tottenham Hotspur (1988–92);
Lazio (1992–95);
Glasgow Rangers (1995–98);
Middlesbrough (1998–2000);
Burnley (2002);
Gansu Tianma (China, 2003);
Boston United (2004)
HONOURS
57 England caps
(10 goals) (1988–98)

Gault,
William Ernest 'Ernie'

Northumberland born forward whose Everton career extended across two spells

[FACTFILE]

BORN
Wallsend, 20 September 1889
DIED
1980
POSITION
Inside forward
OTHER CLUBS
Stockport County
(1913–14 & 1920–21);
Cardiff City (1920);
New Brighton

Season	League		FA Cup		League Cup		Total	
	App	Goals	App	Goals	App	Goals	App	Goals
2000/01	10 (4)	0	0	0	0 (1)	0	10(5)	0
2001/02	8 (10)	1	3 (1)	0	1	0	12(11)	1
Total	18(14)	1	3 (1)	0	1 (1)	0	22(16)	1

Season	League		FA Cup		Total	
	App	Goals	App	Goals	App	Goals
1912/13	8	1	0	0	8	1
1919/20	21	12	1	0	22	12
Total	29	13	1	0	30	13

Geary, Fred

Prolific front man who gave birth to the Everton centre forward tradition

Fred Geary started a tradition that has become synonymous with Everton's history: the illustrious centre forward. A staggering scoring record in his six seasons at Anfield and Goodison put him almost on a par with Dixie Dean on a goals-per-game ratio. And yet diminutive, slight and fleet-footed as Geary was, he could not have been further from the Everton centre forward archetype.

> 20 GOALS
> IN 22 APPEARANCES
> HELPED PROPEL
> THE CLUB TO THEIR
> FIRST LEAGUE TITLE

Born in Nottingham, Geary made his name in local football with Bothwell Rangers, Basford Rovers and latterly Notts Rangers, who competed in the Midland League. 'Inducements of a pleasant kind', according to one local newspaper, saw him join Everton in the summer of 1889 and he was an immediate hit at Anfield, scoring a brace on his debut. 'Geary was the hero of the match, his sprinting capabilities were a revelation to all, and the way he ran round his opponents visibly astonished them,' recorded the Liverpool Mercury.

SPEED WAS Geary's great asset and opposing defences found him impossible to deal with. Crucially, he could run with the ball faster than many players could without, in so doing

wreaking terror among his opponents. Describing one incident (that didn't yield a goal) in his debut season, the Mercury reported: 'Geary, when not far from his own goal, became possessed of the sphere and rushed away at a slashing rate, passing all in front of him, and finishing by kicking into the home custodian's hands.'

He ended his debut season with 25 goals from 20 games as Everton finished runners-up to Preston North End by just two points. His goals had undoubtedly made a huge and crucial difference compared to Everton's fitful debut season of league football. 'Geary's great speed, his lightness of foot, and his agility are eminently useful qualities, and it is a sight to [see] him scouring down the field with the ball at his toe, [followed] by hopeful but leaden-footed opponents,' wrote the Liverpool Echo in an early profile. 'The estimation in which the speedy forward is held may be gauged to some extent by the result of a competition recently organised by an athletic paper, Geary being voted the best forward in England. Although that is a matter for discussion, there can be no doubt he is one of the best centre forwards in the country.'

GEARY'S SUCCESS in an Everton shirt saw him elevated to the England team in March 1890, against Ireland. Geary scored a hat-trick in a 9-1 win but only appeared once more for England. For Everton his scoring dropped to below a goal a game in 1890/91, but only just, 20 goals in 22 appearances helping propel the club to their first league title.

Geary unquestionably seized many of the plaudits in Everton's first great team, but his contribution was played down by his captain, Andrew Hannah. 'Geary is apt to be too fast sometimes,' he said in an interview with the Liverpool Echo. 'If he gets clean right past the backs he can beat them, but it does not always come off; and the centre forward should feed his wing. Geary goes in sometimes for single-handed play, and it looks brilliant.

It might come off twice in half-a-dozen times, but it can't always come off. This is a little defect that can always be remedied.'

Injury limited him to just 11 league and FA Cup appearances in the 1891/92 season, but Geary made a triumphant return the following year, scoring 23 in 27 matches during Goodison's debut season. Injuries curtailed his last two seasons at the club and he and his wife suffered tragedy when their only child passed away. Jack Southworth then Abraham Hartley took up residence in the centre forward's berth and when Everton finished runners-up in 1894/95 Geary played just eight times.

AT THE END of that campaign he returned to Anfield, where Liverpool had set up home. He scored 11 times as the club won the Second Division Championship in his debut season, but he was a bit-part player on their return to the top flight. Age and injuries had increasingly robbed him of his greatest asset: his pace.

[FACTFILE]

BORN
Nottingham, 23 January 1868

DIED
8 January 1955

POSITION
Striker

OTHER CLUBS
Notts Rangers (1886–87);
Grimsby Town (1887–88);
Notts Rangers (1888–89);
Liverpool (1895–99)

HONOURS
1890/91 League Championship;
2 England caps (3 goals) (1890–91)

Season	League		FA Cup		Total	
	App	Goals	App	Goals	App	Goals
1889/90	18	21	2	4	20	25
1890/91	22	20	1	0	23	20
1891/92	10	6	0	0	10	6
1892/93	24	19	3	4	27	23
1893/94	9	8	0	0	9	8
1894/95	8	4	1	0	9	4
Total	**91**	**78**	**7**	**8**	**98**	**86**

Gee, Charlie

Reliable and committed centre back for club and country

From signing for Everton as an unknown centre back from Stockport County in July 1930 to making his England debut against Wales in November the following year, Charlie Gee completed an astonishing ascent to the top of English football.

Over the following decade he would make more than 200 appearances for Everton, becoming a stalwart of one of the club's finest teams.

When Gee arrived at Goodison winning a first-team place was no easy feat. Ahead of him in the pecking order were Tom Griffiths and Tommy White, Welsh and English internationals respectively. But Gee buckled down in the Central League and made a big impression playing for the reserves. Within months of his arrival he had replaced the injured Griffiths as Everton's first-choice centre back and claimed a Second Division championship medal. A year later he had added a First Division title to his collection.

An old-school defender who relished physical battle, Gee's unstinting commitment instantly made him a crowd favourite. His progress into the Everton team was eased by Dixie Dean, who gave him the lowdown on centre forwards' tricks and flourishes. 'Dixie was a very astute judge,' he would recall, 'and his advice made me an experienced centre half. He used to tip me off about the strengths and weaknesses of centre forwards I was playing against.'

WITHIN A YEAR of his debut he was called up to the England squad, making his debut against Wales at Anfield in November 1931. His opposite number that day was the unlucky Griffiths, who would move on to Bolton Wanderers soon after.

Gee was, a profile later concluded, 'A strong, determined pivot. Particularly effective in the use of his head. At one period inclined to be rather impetuous. A powerful tackler and uses the ball much better than formerly.'

A second cap came against Spain at Highbury in December 1931 in what was Dixie Dean's last international appearance. Dean bet Gee his £6 match fee that England would put more than five goals past Ricardo Zamora, Spain's flamboyant goalkeeper, to which the defender agreed. Dean scored just once, but England won 7-1 and Dean collected his winnings.

It would take Gee a further five years to earn back his match fee. He was struck down by injuries that necessitated a cartilage operation – a career-threatening procedure in those days of unrefined surgical procedures – and he missed most of the 1932/33 season. A third and final international cap did not come until 1936.

ALTHOUGH STILL only in his late twenties, Gee began to fall out of favour with the Everton management. In November 1937, the pendulum swung back in favour of a Welsh centre half and Gee lost his place to T.G. Jones. A month later the Everton board consented to his moving house to Manchester, a rare allowance at a time when clubs liked their players to live within sight of the stadium. The following April Gee rejected the terms offered him, a development that would not endear him to the boardroom. He seems to have belatedly accepted a new contract, but thereafter was a peripheral figure.

Gee's impact on Everton's history transcended his own playing days. When, in 1930, he had the chance to choose between several First Division clubs, his trainer at Stockport – Harry Catterick senior – advised him to go to Goodison. Later that decade Gee was able to return the favour: his old coach told him that his son – Harry Catterick – who was playing as an amateur for Stockport was ready for bigger

GEE'S IMPACT ON EVERTON'S HISTORY TRANSCENDED HIS OWN PLAYING DAYS

things and Gee promptly passed on word to the Everton management.

'I was there with Theo Kelly in the Tory Club at Stockport when young Harry signed the forms,' Gee said in 1969. And so began one of the most enduring relationships in the club's history.

Gee played more than 200 games for Everton, but bad luck ultimately prevented him from winning more medals. His cartilage problems kept him out of the FA Cup winning team in 1933, and by the time of Everton's title win in 1939 he had lost his place to the more polished T.G. Jones.

POST-FOOTBALL, Gee became a woodwork teacher in Manchester, later retiring to St Asaph in North Wales.

Season	League		FA Cup		Total	
	App	Goals	App	Goals	App	Goals
1930/31	20	2	5	0	25	2
1931/32	38	0	1	0	39	0
1932/33	7	0	0	0	7	0
1933/34	29	0	0	0	29	0
1934/35	37	0	5	0	42	0
1935/36	9	0	0	0	9	0
1936/37	40	0	4	0	44	0
1937/38	14	0	0	0	14	0
1938/39	2	0	0	0	2	0
Total	**196**	**2**	**15**	**0**	**211**	**2**

[FACTFILE]

BORN
Stockport, 6 April 1909
DIED
1981
POSITION
Centre half
OTHER CLUBS
Stockport County (1928–30)
HONOURS
1930/31 Second Division Championship;
1931/32 First Division Championship

Geldard, Albert

Pacy winger who frustrated and delighted in equal measure

For nearly eighty years Albert Geldard was the youngest player to turn out in a Football League match. In September 1929, aged 15 years, 158 days, Geldard appeared for Bradford Park Avenue against Millwall, setting a record which he shared with Wrexham's Ken Roberts until Barnsley's Reuben Noble-Lazarus trumped it – aged 15 years 45 days – in autumn 2008. It was the first distinction of a lengthy and illustrious career that would take in England recognition and an FA Cup win.

A fine all-rounder, Geldard could have taken up cricket professionally and later cited not playing county cricket for his beloved Yorkshire as one of his biggest disappointments. For Bradford he was no flash-in-the-pan and soon developed a reputation as the Yorkshire club's most exciting player. A right winger who possessed fine close control and an electric turn of pace, he soon attracted the notice of bigger clubs.

Bradford Park Avenue had already turned down a £5000 bid from Huddersfield when financial necessity forced them to sell Geldard to Everton for £4000 in November 1932. Geldard was introduced straight into the Everton team in place of the unfortunate Ted Critchley.

After scoring on his debut at Middlesbrough, Geldard gave Evertonians a glimpse of his sumptuous talents on his home debut, versus Bolton. Dean took possession on the right wing and, seeing Geldard sprint into the centre forward position, played him through. Geldard still had much work to do, however. But his pace carried him past two onrushing defenders; he then drew the goalkeeper and glided past him, before strolling the ball over the goal line.

Although Everton were inconsistent in the league during the 1932/33 season, they made great strides in the FA Cup. Geldard was struggling with an ankle injury, however, and missed the quarter-final annihilation of Luton Town and also the semi-final against West Ham. Critchley returned to take his place and scored Everton's late winner in the semi.

A month later, in the run-up to the final, there were still doubts about Geldard's fitness. But at Everton's pre-final retreat at Buxton, he received extensive massages from Harry Cooke, Everton's famous trainer, and recovered in time to play. The unlucky Critchley missed out and Geldard provided the cross for Jimmy Dunn's third goal.

At the end of the 1932/33 season Geldard's form for Everton saw him included, along with Tommy White, for England's end of season tour of Italy. The visit included a now notorious meeting with Mussolini. Geldard received the first of four international caps in a 1-1 draw in Rome against Italy just a fortnight after lifting the FA Cup with Everton.

Through the 1933/34 season he shared responsibilities on Everton's right with Critchley. But after his team-mate's sale to Preston in June 1934 he was first choice on the Everton wing. In particular he developed a fine understanding with Cliff Britton, the Everton right half. Geldard's biographer, John Rowlands, recalled:

> Cliff Britton was Albert's best friend on and off the field and whenever Albert was crowded into a corner Cliff always appeared to receive the pass. On one occasion, against Leeds at Goodison Park, he dribbled through the whole team from his own half, but hit the side netting as he had no strength left to score. The crowd applauded for ten minutes. Albert regards him as Everton's finest player and a joy to play with. Cliff would take the ball within six inches of an opponent, lean back and suddenly be past him.

On Boxing Day 1935 Geldard 'fulfilled a long ambition' when he deputised for Ted Sagar for 20 minutes while the goalkeeper was off the field receiving treatment. At one point he leapt at full stretch and felt something flick his wrists. 'He landed facing Tommy White,' recalled Rowlands. '"Where is it, Tommy?" he asked. "Tha's aw reight, it ower bloody top," he replied. Albert could have hugged him.'

In 1937/38 Geldard was in exceptional form and was recalled to the England team for the 5-1 win over Ireland. Ireland shifted Billy Cook to left back to mark his Everton team-mate and his aggressive defensive play overwhelmed Geldard. Next time England played he was replaced by Stanley Matthews. Geldard was inconsistent, however, and sometimes earned catcalls from his own supporters. He said at the time: 'Players delight to play away from home rather than hear the catcalls of home spectators who, being sportsmen, should try to help a player rather than hinder him.' Twice, in 1936 and 1937, he requested a transfer, but only at the third time of asking, in June 1938, did the board accede to his request, and Geldard joined Bolton Wanderers.

A year later war intervened, but when peace came Geldard was still only in his early thirties and he played on for another year with Bolton. Geldard vigorously campaigned to improve the working conditions of professional footballers and was the Player's Association representative when he was at Burnden Park. A colourful figure, Geldard was a part-time magician and member of the Liverpool Mahatma Circle of Magicians. Later he turned to journalism and wrote for the Sunday Post.

Further reading:
GELDARD, ALBERT AND JOHN ROWLANDS, *Life and Times of a Professional Footballer*, Countryside, 1990

Season	League		FA Cup		Total	
	App	Goals	App	Goals	App	Goals
1932/33	26	5	4	0	30	5
1933/34	24	5	0	0	24	5
1934/35	31	5	5	5	36	10
1935/36	39	7	1	1	40	8
1936/37	13	3	1	0	14	3
1937/38	34	6	1	0	35	6
Total	167	31	12	6	179	37

[FACTFILE]

BORN
Bradford, 11 April 1914
DIED
8 October 1989
POSITION
Right winger
OTHER CLUBS
Bradford Park Avenue (1928–32);
Bolton Wanderers (1938–47)
HONOURS
1933 FA Cup;
4 England caps (1933–37)

· EFC ·

G

Gemmill,
Scotland 'Scot'

Scottish international who played during Everton's hard times

The son of the former Scottish international midfielder Archie Gemmill, Scot Gemmill followed the tradition set by his father, appearing as he had done for Nottingham Forest and Scotland through the 1990s. A box-to-box midfielder with a good first touch, Gemmill was signed by Walter Smith on transfer deadline day in March 1999 for a cut-price fee of £200,000. If Evertonians feared they had bought a player whose star was on the wane, some of these concerns were allayed when, in one of his early games, at Newcastle, his sizzling 20-yard volley sealed an important victory that helped lift Everton from the relegation mire.

A useful squad player but with a tendency to drift out of games, Gemmill was to be a regular in Walter Smith's faltering Everton sides at the start of the millennium. After the arrival of David Moyes in 2002 he became increasingly marginalised, not even making a single appearance in the final year of his contract. Gemmill subsequently played for Preston, Leicester City and Oxford United, concluding his career in the Australian A League with the New Zealand Knights.

Season	League		FA Cup		League Cup		Total	
	App	Goals	App	Goals	App	Goals	App	Goals
1998/99	7	1	0	0	0	0	7	1
1999/2000	6 (8)	1	0 (1)	0	2	0	8 (9)	1
2000/01	25 (3)	2	1 (1)	0	0	0	26 (4)	2
2001/02	31 (1)	1	5	0	0	0	36 (1)	1
2002/03	10 (6)	0	1	0	1 (1)	0	12 (7)	0
2003/04	0	0	0	0	0	0	0	0
Total	79(18)	5	7 (2)	0	3 (1)	0	89(21)	5

[FACTFILE]

BORN
Paisley, 2 January 1971
POSITION
Midfielder
OTHER CLUBS
Nottingham Forest (1990–99);
Preston (2004);
Leicester City (2004–06);
Oxford United (2006);
New Zealand Knights (2006–07)
HONOURS
26 Scotland caps (1 goal) (1995–2003)

Gerrard, Paul

Highly rated goalkeeper who failed to fulfil his early promise

When Joe Royle went back to his former club Oldham in July 1996 to buy goalkeeper Paul Gerrard, it was hoped that the highly rated 23-year-old would go on to be a long-term successor to the ageing Neville Southall. An established England under-21 international, with a good record – 12 clean sheets in 18 appearances – had made him the most highly rated young goalkeeper in the country, placing a price of £1 million on his head.

INITIALLY SERVING as Southall's understudy, Gerrard's chance came in February 1997, when the Welshman was made scapegoat during Joe Royle's winter of discontent, and dropped for the first time in 15 years following five successive defeats. Alas, Gerrard was unable to change Everton's luck, conceding four goals against Newcastle in his first start. Given further opportunities over the following

year, Gerrard failed to grasp them, looking edgy and short of confidence. The Norwegian international, Thomas Myhre, was acquired in November 1997, and the England under-21 international Steve Simonsen the following summer, severely limiting Gerrard's chances.

Myhre's early promise in an Everton shirt was brought to an abrupt halt with a broken ankle in the summer of 1999, and Gerrard was brought back to the fore. For the next two years, he was largely Everton's first-choice goalkeeper and, given an extended run, seemed to grow in confidence.

A good shot-stopper who commanded his area reasonably well, he was nevertheless prone

to some excruciating lapses. These included the concession of an improbable 44-yard free kick by Liverpool's Gary McAllister in the last minute of the 2001 Goodison derby and an ugly collision with Abel Xavier in a home defeat to Newcastle the following October. Gerrard had come charging off his line, missed the ball entirely, sent his defender to hospital and left Newcastle striker Craig Bellamy with an empty net. This proved to be one error too many for Walter Smith, who dropped him. Although he was to remain an Everton player

[FACTFILE]

BORN
Heywood, 22 January 1973
POSITION
Goalkeeper
OTHER CLUBS
Oldham Athletic (1991–96);
Oxford United (loan, 1998–99);
Ipswich Town (loan, 2002);
Sheffield United (loan, 2003);
Nottingham Forest (loan, 2004);
Nottingham Forest (2004–06);
Sheffield United (2006–08);
Blackpool (loan, 2008);
Stockport County (2009–10);
Oldham Athletic (2010–)

for another four years, Gerrard barely featured again, as he fell behind Simonsen, Richard Wright and latterly Nigel Martyn and Iain Turner in the pecking order. Despite a series of loan moves, the club was unable to offload him until the expiry of his contract in the summer of 2005.

Season	League App	League Goals	FA Cup App	FA Cup Goals	League Cup App	League Cup Goals	Total App	Total Goals
1996/97	4 (1)	0	0	0	0	0	4 (1)	0
1997/98	4	0	0	0	2	0	6	0
1998/99	0	0	0	0	1	0	1	0
1999/2000	34	0	3	0	0	0	37	0
2000/01	32	0	0	0	2	0	34	0
2001/02	13	0	0	0	1	0	14	0
2002/03	2	0	0	0	0	0	2	0
2003/04	0	0	0	0	0	0	0	0
2004/05	0	0	0	0	0	0	0	0
Total	**89 (1)**	**0**	**3**	**0**	**6**	**0**	**98(1)**	**0**

Gibson, Billy

One of the 'virgin blues', he played in Everton's first FA Cup run

[FACTFILE]

BORN
1866
POSITION
Centre half

Season	FA Cup App	FA Cup Goals	Total App	Total Goals
1887/88	4	0	4	0
Total	**4**	**0**	**4**	**0**

Gibson, Darron

Republic of Ireland international who quickly became Everton's lucky mascot

The £500,000 acquisition of the hitherto unheralded Manchester United midfielder Darron Gibson in January 2012 represented Everton's first cash purchase in a staggering 28 months. If it set few Evertonian pulses racing at first, the Irishman quickly set about proving his doubters wrong.

A product of Manchester United's famed youth academy, Gibson found opportunities difficult to come by at Old Trafford. In seven years he made just 14 Premier League starts, but showed promise in loan spells at United's feeder club, Royal Antwerp, and Wolves. During his loan spell at Molineux in the 2007/08 season he earned his first Republic of Ireland caps.

Nevertheless, with his club career stagnating he was urged by Ireland manager Giovanni Trapattoni to leave United to further his career. A transfer to Sunderland was agreed in summer 2011 but fell down over personal terms. Six months later he joined Everton for an undisclosed fee, thought to be worth just £500,000. 'I can see a hunger,' said David Moyes. 'He is young and wants to prove himself.'

A steady rather than spectacular player, Gibson sits in front of the Everton back four, keeping play moving and allowing other more expressive players, such as Marouane Fellaini, to flourish. His passing is crisp and accurate – he gets and gives and moves into space and continues the shift up the pitch – and his presence immediately provided a solidity previously lacking in the Everton midfield. He possesses a fierce shot, and his deflected effort from the edge of the penalty area brought a memorable victory against Manchester City a month after his arrival. At the time of joining Everton Gibson had gone 20 months without appearing on the losing side in a league match (for Manchester United). Remarkably, he extended this

record until beyond the end of his debut season at Everton.

'I have always liked Darron and thought there was something there,' Moyes told journalists in an early assessment of the player. 'It is going to take time and there is more to come. He probably needs a wee bit of the treatment as well. He will need to get whipped a couple of times. I am sure he has had that with his previous manager as well. We will try to get him to be a bit braver in a lot of the things he does.'

[FACTFILE]

BORN
Derry, 25 October 1987
POSITION
Midfielder
OTHER CLUBS
Manchester United
(2005–12);
Royal Antwerp
(loan, 2006–07);
Wolverhampton Wanderers
(loan, 2007–08)
HONOURS
19 Republic of Ireland caps
(1 goal) (2007–)

Season	League App	League Goals	FA Cup App	FA Cup Goals	League Cup App	League Cup Goals	Total App	Total Goals
2011/12	11	1	4	0	0	0	15	1
Total	**11**	**1**	**4**	**0**	**0**	**0**	**15**	**1**

Gibson, David

Young winger who made three appearances during Everton's hard times

Season	League		FA Cup		Total	
	App	Goals	App	Goals	App	Goals
1950/51	1	0	0	0	1	0
1951/52	2	0	0	0	2	0
Total	3	0	0	0	3	0

[FACTFILE]

BORN
Runcorn, 18 March 1931
POSITION
Outside right
OTHER CLUB
Swindon Town

Gidman, John

Swashbuckling right back whose best days lay beyond Goodison

A one-time Liverpool apprentice who was rejected as a teenager by Bill Shankly, John Gidman triumphed over this early setback to forge a successful career with Aston Villa. Moving to the Midlands as a teenager, the right back was an instrumental part of the Villa teams that rose from the Third to the First Division. During this time he also overcame a horrific fireworks accident that left him blind in one eye and played in the 1977 League Cup Final defeat of Everton.

Signed in a club record £650,000 deal in October 1979 that sent Pat Heard in the opposite direction, Gidman filled a right back berth that had proved troublesome to Everton since Tommy Wright's enforced retirement at the start of the decade.

A DEFENDER with pace and élan, he was an overlapping full back

whose attacking instincts were an important part of his team's forward play. Possessing the natural skills ordinarily found in midfield players, his storming runs on the Everton right were the prompt for a memorable Gwladys Street chant: 'Ashes to ashes/ dust to dust/ if Gidman doesn't get him/ then [John] Bailey must'. And yet, while Gidman became a staunch crowd favourite amid lean times, his presence was not enough to arrest the club's alarming decline under Gordon Lee. After finishing the 1977/78 season third and the following campaign fourth, Everton

dropped to 19th, then 15th during his two seasons at the club.

Following Howard Kendall's arrival in May 1981, Gidman was an early casualty. The right back was exchanged with Manchester United for winger Mickey Thomas as Kendall sought to bolster his attacking options. The full back's departure was widely mourned, but eventually led to opportunities going the way of Gary Stevens.

GIDMAN GAVE United five years' service and was part of the team that defeated Everton in the 1985 FA Cup Final. A year later he joined Manchester City, later playing out his career with Stoke City and Darlington.

[FACTFILE]

BORN
Liverpool, 10 January 1954
OTHER CLUBS
Aston Villa (1972–79);
Manchester United
(1981–86);
Manchester City (1986–88);
Stoke City (1988–89);
Darlington (1989)
HONOURS
1 England cap (1977)

Season	League		FA Cup		League Cup		Europe		Total	
	App	Goals	App	Goals	App	Goals	App	Goals	App	Goals
1979/80	29	1	6	0	0	0	0	0	35	1
1980/81	35	1	5	0	3	1	-	-	43	2
Total	64	2	11	0	3	1	0	0	78	3

Gillick, Torrance 'Torry'

The top Scottish winger of his day – and any other day

Torrance Gillick signed for Everton from Glasgow Rangers having played in every forward position for the Scottish club. He spent most of his time at Goodison on the right wing, occasionally switching to the left in order to accommodate Albert Geldard, but no matter where he played he rarely failed to do what he did best: entertain. A natural showman, Gillick could, at will, effortlessly waltz past defenders with some of the most flamboyant trickery Evertonians have ever seen.

Born in Airdrie during the First World War, Gillick first came to prominence with Petershill, a famous Glasgow junior club. After being spotted by Rangers long-serving manager Bill Struth, he was signed shortly after his 18th birthday and won successive league and Scottish Cup doubles with the Glasgow giants.

PERHAPS SURPRISINGLY, when Everton came in with a club record offer of £8000 for the 20-year-old in the summer of 1935, Rangers accepted it. Gillick quickly became a Goodison favourite.

While his pace made him an exhilarating sight when in full flight, his major shortcoming seemed to be his outlook on the game. Gillick, sometimes to the annoyance of his team-mates, played for laughs. At times he could prove to be entirely ineffective, as if his mind was elsewhere, and then in a moment of genius could turn a game with a piece of skill.

ON OCCASIONS, however, this carefree attitude brought him into conflict with the club authorities. In Glasgow, he clashed with manager Bill Struth, a dour Calvinistic type who obsessed about issues such as proper diet and the correct way of dressing. Rangers players were expected to wear bowler hats as a way of distinguishing them from the common crowd; but as Archie McPherson, the famous Scottish commentator, noted: 'Gillick, an inside forward right out of the old school, would rather have fed the bowler hat to his greyhounds than wear one, and only brought it out of a bag a few yards before entering the stadium.'

Gillick's form was greatly helped by the introduction of the dogged inside right Stan Bentham to the first team at the start of the 1938/39 season. Bentham provided Gillick with an even more regular supply of the ball and the two men proved to be stars of a Championship winning side. 'As far as I'm concerned,' Bentham later said, 'Torry just stayed on the wing, not interested. But suddenly he'd tune in and go past three or four blokes as easy as anything, and either score, or put over a great cross.'

The late Gordon Watson told David France and Dave Prentice in the Gwladys Street Blue Book: 'Torry Gillick was an outrageous crowd pleaser. The outside-right was tremendously gifted and

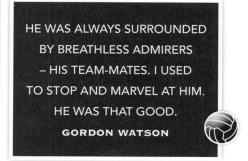

> HE WAS ALWAYS SURROUNDED BY BREATHLESS ADMIRERS – HIS TEAM-MATES. I USED TO STOP AND MARVEL AT HIM. HE WAS THAT GOOD.
> **GORDON WATSON**

his sublime footwork set up a bonanza of goals during our 1939 championship triumph. He was always surrounded by breathless admirers – his team-mates. I used to stop and marvel at him. He was that good. Torry had the world at his feet but was denied further success by the outbreak of World War II. Torry was the top Scottish winger of his day and possibly any other day.'

Gillick returned to Scotland at the start of the war and played for Rangers during wartime friendlies, officially rejoining them in 1945. He formed an effective partnership with Rangers left winger Willie Waddell, lifting the Scottish League Championship in 1946/47 and the Scottish Cup a year later, as well as two Scottish League Cups (1947 and 1949). He left Rangers for Partick Thistle in 1951, where he played for a single season. On retiring he later ran the greyhound track next to Ibrox.

[FACTFILE]

BORN
Airdrie, 19 May 1915

DIED
12 December 1971

POSITION
Inside forward and winger

OTHER CLUBS
Glasgow Rangers (1933–35 & 1945–51);
Partick Thistle (1951–52)

HONOURS
1938/39 League Championship;
5 Scotland caps (3 goals) (1937–38)

Season	League		FA Cup		Total	
	App	Goals	App	Goals	App	Goals
1935/36	23	9	1	0	24	9
1936/37	42	14	4	2	46	16
1937/38	16	3	2	0	18	3
1938/39	40	14	5	2	45	16
Total	**121**	**40**	**12**	**4**	**133**	**44**

Ginola, David

The last of Walter Smith's white elephants

David Ginola arrived at Goodison Park in the dying days of Walter Smith's managerial reign and as his own distinguished career was drawing to its close. In his heyday a tall, powerful, yet flamboyant and formidably gifted winger, Ginola had been one of the first high-profile foreigners to play in the Premier League.

A former French Footballer of the Year and France international, Ginola joined Newcastle in 1995, where he spent two successful seasons before joining Tottenham in a £2.5million deal. Ginola won the Football Writers' and PFA

Player of the Year awards in 1999, but was sold to Aston Villa the following year in a £3million deal. Now aged 33, he struggled at Villa Park, and after falling foul of Villa's manager, John Gregory, was allowed to join Everton on a free transfer in February 2002.

The sight of an aged Ginola in a blue shirt seemed to represent a final and desperate throw of the dice for Smith's ailing regime. To many Evertonians it was another low and symbolised all their manager's shortcomings, for he was always a man more comfortable giving opportunities to ageing professionals than investing his faith in youth.

GINOLA MADE just four starts in a blue shirt, and was unable to save Smith, who was fired less than five weeks after his arrival. After a final substitute appearance on the last day of the 2001/02 season, Ginola announced his retirement. He has subsequently carved out a post-football career as a pundit, actor and vintner.

> AFTER A FINAL SUBSTITUTE APPEARANCE ON THE LAST DAY OF THE 2001/02 SEASON, GINOLA ANNOUNCED HIS RETIREMENT

[FACTFILE]

BORN
Gassin, France, 25 January 1967

POSITION
Winger

OTHER CLUBS
Toulon (1985–88);
Racing Club Paris (1988–90);
Brest (1990–92);
Paris Saint-Germain (1992–95);
Newcastle United (1995–97);
Tottenham Hotspur (1997–2000);
Aston Villa (2000–02)

HONOURS
17 France caps (3 goals) (1990–95);
French Footballer of the Year (1994);
PFA Footballer of the Year (1999);
Football Writers' Player of the Year (1999)

Season	League		FA Cup		League Cup		Total	
	App	Goals	App	Goals	App	Goals	App	Goals
2001/02	2 (3)	0	2	0	0	0	4 (3)	0
Total	**2 (3)**	**0**	**2**	**0**	**0**	**0**	**4 (3)**	**0**

Glazzard, Jimmy

Prolific lower league striker for whom the goalscoring touch proved elusive in the big time

EVERTON F.C. 1956–57

EVERTON 1956/57
Back row - **Sutherland, Tansey, O'Neill, Jones, Kirby**
Front - **McNamara, Eglington, Farrell, Llewellyn, Glazzard, Rea**

[FACTFILE]

BORN
Normanton, West Yorkshire, 23 April 1923

DIED
1995

POSITION
Centre forward

OTHER CLUBS
Huddersfield Town (1946–56);
Mansfield Town (1956–57)

Season	League		FA Cup		Total	
	App	Goals	App	Goals	App	Goals
1956/57	3	0	0	0	3	0
Total	**3**	**0**	**0**	**0**	**3**	**0**

Glover, Gerry

Young prodigy whose handful of appearances included the 1966 Charity Shield

Season	League		FA Cup		Other		Total	
	App	Goals	App	Goals	App	Goals	App	Goals
1964/65	1	0	0	0	0	0	1	0
1965/66	1 (1)	0	0	0	0	0	1 (1)	0
1966/67	0	0	0	0	1	0	1	0
Total	**2 (1)**	**0**	**0**	**0**	**1**	**0**	**3 (1)**	**0**

[FACTFILE]

BORN
Liverpool, 27 September 1946
POSITION
Midfield
OTHER CLUBS
Mansfield Town (1967–68);
Northwich Victoria;
Marine

Godfrey, Brian

One-game wonder who had a fruitful career beyond Goodison

[FACTFILE]

BORN
Flint, 1 May 1940
DIED
Cyprus, 11 February 2010
POSITION
Striker
OTHER CLUBS
Scunthorpe United (1960–63);
Preston North End (1963–67);
Aston Villa (1967–71);
Bristol Rovers (1971–73);
Newport County (1973–75);
Portland Timbers (1975);
Bath City (1976–78)
HONOURS
3 Wales caps (2 goals) (1964–65)

Season	League		FA Cup		Total	
	App	Goals	App	Goals	App	Goals
1959/60	1	0	0	0	1	0
Total	**1**	**0**	**0**	**0**	**1**	**0**

Goldie, Hugh

Right half whose career north of the border brought him Scottish League honours

Season	League		FA Cup		Total	
	App	Goals	App	Goals	App	Goals
1895/96	15	1	1	0	16	1
1896/97	3	0	0	0	3	0
Total	**18**	**1**	**1**	**0**	**19**	**1**

[FACTFILE]

BORN
Dairy, 10 February 1874
POSITION
Right half
OTHER CLUBS
St Mirren; Celtic; Dundee;
Barry Town; Millwall Athletic; Dundee;
New Brompton

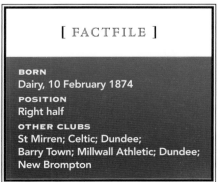

·EFC·

Goodlass,
Ronnie

Cult winger who has since become a distinguished radio voice

A piece of impudent brilliance from Goodlass still lingers long in the memory of many Evertonians.

UPTON PARK, April 1977, and Everton are edging away from a relegation battle. The ball is laid back to Goodlass on the halfway line and, spotting Mervyn Day off his line, the left-winger chips the ball over the hapless goalkeeper's head and into the empty net. It remains one of the most memorable goals in Everton's history. 'It is always nice when people bring up the goal

from the halfway line,' Goodlass told the Liverpool Echo in 2009. 'People always remind me I did it before David Beckham. I reply, "David who?"'

IT CAPPED a memorable season for Goodlass, who had made the breakthrough from young hopeful to first-team regular. A local lad, he had graduated through the Everton youth system, making a belated debut, aged 22, in December 1975. He was an old-school winger, stocky and adroit, who relished skipping past tackles. An accurate and potent source of crosses for Bob Latchford, with his hands invariably hidden under long sleeves he cut a distinctive figure on the Everton wing.

But just as quickly as he had established himself in the Everton team, so he faded from view. During summer 1977 Gordon Lee signed Dave Thomas and, after watching most of the start of the 1977/78 season

[FACTFILE]

BORN
Liverpool,
6 September 1953
POSITION
Winger
OTHER CLUBS
NAC Breda (1978–80);
Fulham (1980–81);
South China AA (1982–83);
Tranmere Rovers (1983–85)

from the sidelines, Goodlass sought a fresh challenge with the Dutch club NAC Breda, who he joined for £100,000 in October. He returned to England two years later, but never again played in the top flight.

During the mid-1990s, Goodlass briefly returned to Everton, serving as a youth coach under Joe Royle. Still involved in local youth football in his native Merseyside, he has since also established a reputation as an erudite and perceptive match analyst for Radio Merseyside.

IT REMAINS ONE OF THE MOST MEMORABLE GOALS IN EVERTON'S HISTORY

Season	League		FA Cup		League Cup		Europe		Total	
	App	Goals	App	Goals	App	Goals	App	Goals	App	Goals
1975/76	2 (1)	0	0	0	0	0	0	0	2 (1)	0
1976/77	29 (2)	2	7	0	9	0	-	-	45 (2)	2
1977/78	0 (1)	0	0	0	0	0	-	-	0 (1)	0
Total	**31 (4)**	**2**	**7**	**0**	**9**	**0**	**0**	**0**	**47 (4)**	**2**

Gordon, Patrick

Scottish winger who remained at Anfield following the great 'split' of 1892

Season	League		FA Cup		Total	
	App	Goals	App	Goals	App	Goals
1890/91	3	0	0	0	3	0
1891/92	4	1	0	0	4	1
1892/93	11	2	4	2	15	4
Total	**18**	**3**	**4**	**2**	**22**	**5**

[FACTFILE]

BORN
Renton, 18 August 1864
POSITION
Outside right
OTHER CLUBS
Liverpool (1893–94);
Blackburn Rovers (1894);
Liverpool South End

Gosling, Dan

Scorer of dramatic FA Cup winner whose Goodison career ended acrimoniously

Dan Gosling's brief Everton career will forever be remembered for his dramatic last-gasp FA Cup fourth round replay goal against Liverpool during the club's run to the 2009 final. Goalless, deep into extra time and with the match headed towards a penalty shootout, Andy Van Der Meyde's searching right-wing cross found Gosling in space on the left-hand edge of the Liverpool six-yard box. Gosling's first touch was poor, but he controlled it past a challenge from Dirk Kuyt, then adroitly turned Alvaro Arbeloa before curling a delicious right-footed shot in off Pepe Reina's goalpost. Goodison exploded, the February air turning blue with joy.

Gosling's stunning intervention came in just his fifth appearance in an Everton shirt and only six weeks after his debut. Yet he ended the season at Wembley, coming on as a second-half substitute for Leon Osman as Everton chased the FA Cup Final against Chelsea.

David Moyes had signed Gosling as a 17-year-old tyro from Plymouth Argyle in January 2008 for an undisclosed fee. Nominally a right back, he made most of his Everton appearances on the right side of midfield, where his roving runs and eye for goal were most effectively deployed. A slight lack of pace and defensive naivety suggested that this was where his future may ultimately lie.

In the 2009/10 season he was a regular in European competition but in the league deployed most often from the bench. His performances for Everton would see him gain England under-21 recognition, following appearances for his country at U17, U18 and U19 level. However, after such a promising start his Goodison career was to end in acrimony.

WHILE RECOVERING from a cruciate ligament injury in spring 2010, contract talks between Gosling's agent and the club broke down irrevocably. Everton claimed that a verbal contract offer had been agreed with the player, although his contract stipulated that this needed to be put in writing before a May 2010 deadline. The player then rejected the offer and walked away for nothing under a free transfer – the loophole Gosling had exploited costing Everton an estimated £4million in compensation and Plymouth, which would face financial administration a year later – any sell-on fee as part of the agreement.

Everton appealed to the Premier League but to no avail. Gosling joined Newcastle, memories of that goal but a glorious memory of a career that didn't see its Goodison potential reached.

[FACTFILE]

BORN
Brixham, 1 February 1990
POSITION
Right midfield
OTHER CLUBS
Plymouth Argyle (2006–8);
Newcastle United (2010–)

Season	League		FA Cup		League Cup		Europe		Total	
	App	Goals	App	Goals	App	Goals	App	Goals	App	Goals
2008/09	6 (5)	2	1 (5)	1	0	0	0	0	7 (10)	3
2009/10	3 (8)	2	0	0	2	1	6 (1)	0	11 (9)	3
Total	**9 (13)**	**4**	**1 (5)**	**1**	**2**	**1**	**6 (1)**	**0**	**18 (19)**	**6**

Goudie, H.

Centre forward from Everton's first FA Cup run, he did not last to see league football

Season	FA Cup		Total	
	App	Goals	App	Goals
1887/88	4	1	4	1
Total	**4**	**1**	**4**	**1**

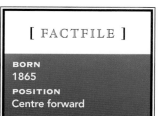

[FACTFILE]

BORN
1865
POSITION
Centre forward

Gough, Richard

Veteran defender, who overcame scepticism to wow Goodison

When, in the summer of 1999, Walter Smith signed Richard Gough, a distinguished former Scotland international defender, the move was greeted with shrugs of bemusement and cynicism. Past his 37th birthday and at the end of his career, Gough had been consigned to the graveyard of America's MLS since mid-decade, yet was slated as a replacement for the departed Marco Materazzi – 11 years his junior.

Gough had been Smith's captain at Rangers, where he won nine consecutive league titles, and the suspicion was that he was just another old boy out for a final pay day. Gough, however, soon confounded such scepticism. Hard, immensely fit and with impeccable reading of the game, Gough brought a veteran's calm to an Everton defence notable in previous seasons only for its erraticism and ill discipline. He was a distinguished leader too, and as Dave Watson faded from first-team view he took many of his responsibilities, serving as

Smith's on-the-field lieutenant. Sometimes this desire was too much for some of his colleagues. In one game, against Coventry City in October 1999, Don Hutchison, serving as team captain, took exception to Gough's involvement and took a well-publicised swing at him.

BORN IN SWEDEN to a Scottish father and Swedish mother, and subsequently brought up in South Africa, Gough had started out with Dundee United in the early 1980s, first coming into contact with Smith, who was winding down his playing career and setting out as a coach. He was a key member of Jim McLean's remarkably successful teams, lifting the Scottish League title in 1983. He spent a year at Tottenham in 1986/87, returning to Scotland with Rangers at the end of the season. In the veteran stage of his career he moved to the nascent MLS, returning to Britain for brief spells with Rangers and Nottingham Forest. After impressing at the latter, Smith made his move.

Gough's form through 1999/2000 was rewarded with a generous two-year contract and the club captaincy. Three games into the 2000/01 season, however, he was struck down with knee ligament damage, and although he returned intermittently was never the same again. Nor indeed, was Everton's defence, and without his leadership a promising start to the season slipped away. At the end of the season, Gough, now aged 39, retired. Arguably, Walter Smith's reign never recovered from the loss of his talisman.

Season	League		FA Cup		League Cup		Total	
	App	Goals	App	Goals	App	Goals	App	Goals
1999/2000	29	1	3	0	0	0	32	1
2000/01	9	0	0 (1)	0	0	0	9 (1)	0
Total	**38**	**1**	**3 (1)**	**0**	**0**	**0**	**41(1)**	**1**

[FACTFILE]

BORN
Stockholm, 5 April 1962
POSITION
Centre half
OTHER CLUBS
Dundee United (1980–86);
Tottenham Hotspur (1986–87);
Rangers (1987–97);
Kansas City Wizards (1997);
Rangers (1997–98);
San Jose Clash (1998–99);
Nottingham Forest (1999)
AS MANAGER
Livingston (2004–05)
HONOURS
61 Scotland caps (6 goals) (1983–93)

Gourlay, James

Scottish inside forward who won league representative honours in his home country

Season	League		FA Cup		Total	
	App	Goals	App	Goals	App	Goals
1909/10	4	2	0	0	4	2
1910/11	28	4	2	1	30	5
1911/12	16	2	1	0	17	2
1912/13	6	0	1	0	7	0
Total	**54**	**8**	**4**	**1**	**58**	**9**

[FACTFILE]

BORN
Annbank, 1884
POSITION
Inside forward
OTHER CLUBS
Port Glasgow; Morton

Gracie,
Tom

Scottish centre forward who crossed the Mersey divide then died of leukaemia while serving during the First World War

[FACTFILE]

BORN
Glasgow, 12 June 1889
DIED
Glasgow, 23 October 1915
POSITION
Centre forward
OTHER CLUBS
Airdrieonians (1907–08);
Hamilton Academical (1908–09);
Arthurlie (1909);
Morton (1909–11);
Liverpool (1912–14);
Heart of Midlothian

Season	League		FA Cup		Total	
	App	Goals	App	Goals	App	Goals
1910/11	7	1	0	0	7	1
1911/12	6	0	0	0	6	0
Total	13	1	0	0	13	1

Graham,
Bobby

Inside right whose Goodison career failed to take off

[FACTFILE]

BORN
Glasgow, 1879
POSITION
Inside right
OTHER CLUBS
Cartha;
Queen's Park Strollers;
Fulham;
Third Lanark;
Bolton Wanderers;
Third Lanark

Season	League		FA Cup		Total	
	App	Goals	App	Goals	App	Goals
1906/07	2	0	0	0	2	0
1907/08	0	0	1	0	1	0
Total	2	0	1	0	3	0

Grant,
Jackie

Popular post-war right half and utility man

Jackie Grant was one of a number of highly committed players charged with reviving Everton's post-war fortunes, but who ultimately proved short of the standard required.

AN EVERTON CAREER
THAT SPANNED
MORE THAN 17 YEARS

In an Everton career that spanned more than 17 years, Grant was a dedicated servant who never gave anything other than unstinting dedication, despite never really being able to call a first-team shirt his own.

The exception was the 1950/51 season, when he was ever-present in the number four shirt, deputising for the injured Cyril Lello. But despite his best efforts, the season was an unmitigated disaster and Everton were relegated after finishing bottom of the First Division.

Born in County Durham, Grant first came to Everton as a 14-year-old amateur in 1939. Yet the outbreak of war later that year forced his return to the Northeast and for the next three years he played for High Spen juniors. He returned to Merseyside in 1942, and from the following year was a regular in Everton's wartime teams, taking the place of Joe Mercer, who had been stationed away from Merseyside.

When peace came and the Football League resumed in August 1946, Grant found himself in and out of the team. He was a skilful right half, but was often called to play in unfamiliar positions throughout his Everton career. Popular in the dressing room, he captained Everton's reserve team when absent from the first XI.

HIS FINEST MOMENT in an Everton shirt came in Everton's epic FA Cup fourth round replay against Wolves in January 1948. Played in front of 72,569 spectators, it was the ninth highest attendance in Goodison's history. Yet the day seemed destined to end in disappointment, with Wolves entering the last minute

2-1 in front. Everton were then awarded a corner kick.

'Nobby Fielding took the corner with about 30 seconds left,' Grant recalled in 1970. 'Bill Shorthouse went up for it, but the ball landed at my feet. All I did was thump it. I was told later that the people outside heard the roar, realised it was the equaliser and then tried to get back into the ground for the 30 minutes of extra time. It was bedlam inside the ground, too. We went on to beat them 3-2.

It's nice to think back and remember how they carried me on their shoulders at the end.'

After slipping out of first-team consideration by the mid-1950s, in June 1956 his former team-mate Harry Catterick – now manager of Rochdale – paid £2500 to bring Grant to Spotland. He made more than 100 appearances for Rochdale before ending his career with Southport.

Season	League		FA Cup		Total	
	App	Goals	App	Goals	App	Goals
1946/47	5	1	0	0	5	1
1947/48	18	4	5	1	23	5
1948/49	7	0	1	0	8	0
1949/50	23	3	5	0	28	3
1950/51	42	2	1	0	43	2
1951/52	5	0	0	0	5	0
1952/53	17	0	0	0	17	0
1953/54	3	0	0	0	3	0
1954/55	1	0	0	0	1	0
Total	**121**	**10**	**12**	**1**	**133**	**11**

[FACTFILE]

BORN
Gateshead,
8 September 1924
POSITION
Right half
OTHER CLUBS
Rochdale (1956–59);
Southport (1959–60)

Gravesen, Thomas

Eccentric midfielder who delighted and frustrated in equal measure

With a pump of his fists and a wave in the air, Danish international midfielder Thomas Gravesen could whip up the Goodison crowd like few of his contemporaries. On his day the Dane was one of the most exciting players in the Premier League, with his close control and willingness to make runs from midfield a potent attacking weapon. At other times, however, Gravesen looked tactically ill disciplined, his endless enthusiasm making him look like a schoolboy on a playground kickaround, chasing every ball. While his two-spell Goodison career can – perhaps – ultimately be regarded a success, it was, for large parts, undermined by such inconsistency.

Gravesen started his career with his home-town club, Vejle Boldklub (VB), in the mid-1990s, playing as both a sweeper and defensive midfielder. Here he first came to the attention of Walter Smith, then Rangers manager, who considered a move for him, but in 1997 Gravesen joined SV Hamburg. Here he developed a reputation as one of the best foreigners in the Bundesliga and in 1999/2000 helped his club qualify for the Champions League.

Alerted to the fact that Gravesen only had a year remaining on his Hamburg contract, Smith finally made his move for the Dane, paying a cut-price £2.5million to bring him to Goodison in summer 2000.

ALTHOUGH HE would continue to be classed a defensive midfielder throughout his Everton career, it was clear that Gravesen's abilities were best suited to the final third of the field. From here he would lung-busting marches, showing attributes that were increasingly rare in the

modern midfield player: the willingness and ability to run with the ball. All too rarely, however, did Gravesen show this on a consistent basis. His tackling was often reckless, earning him an unenviable disciplinary record, and his passing could be wayward, sometimes marked by an entire lack of concentration. Likewise his positional play was frequently erratic. Nor did he score enough goals. However, it was clear to seasoned Evertonians that despite such lapses, within the 24-year-old was the genesis of a very good player.

Thrown into an almost entirely reconstructed midfield, with the likes of Paul Gascoigne and Alex Nyarko, Gravesen impressed in flashes, but like many of his contemporaries struggled to

ON HIS DAY THE DANE WAS ONE OF THE MOST EXCITING PLAYERS IN THE PREMIER LEAGUE

consistently live up to his potential amid the grimness of Smith's managerial reign. Within barely a year of his arrival reports began to surface in the Danish and German press that Gravesen was unimpressed by Everton's lack of ambition and unhappy on Merseyside. By the end of 2001, Smith had seemingly started to freeze Gravesen out of the Everton team.

HE RETURNED to the team for David Moyes' debut as manager against Fulham in March 2002, but was sent off after just 28 minutes for two bookings – the sort of petulant display that had driven fans to distraction since his arrival. Moyes, however, persisted with him and for the next two years Gravesen frustrated and delighted in equal measure. Off the field and on it, he maintained a good rapport with fans, frequently showing the humour that earned him the sobriquet 'Mad Dog'. Memorable japes included punching the air while being stretchered off, and joining in the fans' booing of Tomasz Radzinski on his 2004 return to Goodison with Fulham.

At the start of the 2004/05 season, limited financial resources and dressing room disarray forced Moyes to entirely rejig his line-up. By necessity he adopted a 4-1-4-1 formation that removed many of Gravesen's defensive responsibilities, enabling him to float around Everton's lone striker, make charges into the penalty area and serve as Everton's playmaker. He was anointed Everton's principal set-piece taker, showing his composure and technical skills to serve up a string of assists. As Everton soared up the Premier League table, Gravesen flourished, playing the best football of his Everton career.

And yet, with his existing deal running out, a new contract lay unsigned. Speculation that agreement was imminent lingered through the last months of 2004. Then in the January transfer window, something entirely unexpected happened: Real Madrid came in for Gravesen. Faced with the option of losing him for nothing the following summer, or selling him for £2.5million, Moyes let Gravesen join up with Zidane, Beckham, Figo and the rest of the Galacticos.

His spell in Spain lasted 18 months before he returned to Britain with Celtic in August 2006. His time at Parkhead was less than happy, amid discord between Gravesen and manager

Gordon Strachan. Persistent rumours linked him with a move to England, but not until the August 2007 transfer deadline did this happen, when, to widespread delight, he rejoined Everton on a season-long loan.

WITHIN days of his return, a Gravesen corner had set up a last-minute winner against Bolton, but hopes of an Indian summer were never realised. Gravesen, now aged 31, looked shorn of the athleticism that had propelled him to such heights three years previous, and his appearances in a blue shirt were limited to cameos. At the end of the 2007/08 season, Moyes announced that he would not be taking up an option to buy the midfielder, who returned to Parkhead. Here his contract was promptly paid up, and Gravesen released. After being unable to find another club, in January 2009 he announced his retirement from the game, aged 32.

A Danish international, Gravesen made 66 appearances for his country, appearing at the 2002 World Cup Finals and the 2000 and 2004 European Championships.

[FACTFILE]

BORN
Vejle, Denmark, 11 March 1976
POSITION
Midfielder
OTHER CLUBS
Vejle Boldklub (Denmark, 1995–97);
SV Hamburg (1997–2000);
Real Madrid (2005–06);
Celtic (2006–08)
HONOURS
66 Denmark caps (5 goals) (1998-2006)

Season	League		FA Cup		League Cup		Europe		Total	
	App	Goals	App	Goals	App	Goals	App	Goals	App	Goals
2000/01	30 (2)	2	2	0	1	0	-	-	33 (2)	2
2001/02	22 (3)	2	0 (1)	0	0	0	-	-	22 (4)	2
2002/03	30 (3)	1	1	0	1	0	-	-	32 (3)	1
2003/04	29 (1)	2	3	0	3	0	-	-	35 (1)	2
2004/05	20 (1)	4	0 (1)	0	1	1	-	-	21 (2)	5
2007/08	1 (7)	0	1	0	0 (1)	0	1 (2)	0	3 (10)	0
Total	**132(17)**	**11**	**7 (2)**	**0**	**6 (1)**	**1**	**1 (2)**	**0**	**146(22)**	**12**

Gray, Andy

Effusive Scot whose arrival inspired Everton to greatness

IN THE HISTORY of Everton Football Club, no single figure has made so vast an impression in so short a time as Andy Gray did in the mid-1980s. His arrival at Goodison in late 1983 coincided with what seemed at the time an unlikely revival of Everton's fortunes, his presence galvanising a hitherto struggling team that would – within a year – emerge as one of the best in the world. What makes Gray's impact all the more remarkable is that his time at the club spanned just 19 months. Yet when he left Goodison he possessed one of the most impressive medal hauls of any Everton player, while simultaneously capturing a place in every Evertonian's heart.

Born in Glasgow, Gray started out at Dundee United, where as a teenager he garnered a reputation as a cavalier and free-scoring centre forward who would win at all costs. Still aged only 19, he joined Aston Villa in October 1975, a move that was hugely successful. In 1976/77 Gray won both the PFA Player of the Year and Young Player of the Year award (a feat not repeated until 2007, when Cristiano Ronaldo scooped both prizes), as well as the First

WHEN HE LEFT GOODISON
HE POSSESSED
ONE OF THE MOST IMPRESSIVE
MEDAL HAULS
OF ANY EVERTON PLAYER

Division Golden Boot, after scoring 25 league goals. In 1979 he joined Wolves in a British record deal worth £1.5million, but after a promising start his form suffered as a result of injuries and backroom rancour.

As such, when Howard Kendall made a £250,000 move for him in November 1983, Gray was very much seen as yesterday's man – a player who had failed to continue the outstanding form of his youth. 'I was grateful to have the money available to buy such a quality forward,' Kendall said at the time. 'In this price bracket Gray is top of the list and I see an exciting partnership ahead with Graeme Sharp.'

Asked by journalists why he had come to Everton, Gray answered: 'To win things.' When this was derided and Gray told that such hyperbole had been heard many times before, he replied: 'You've never heard it from me.' This was the first demonstration to Evertonians of Gray's incredible confidence, which would have a huge impact on a beleaguered dressing room.

INITIALLY SIGNED on a month's loan in order to beat a transfer deadline, Gray made his debut against Nottingham Forest in a 1-0 home victory. His first goal came a month later, against former club Aston Villa in a 1-1 home draw, and although Everton's form was slow to pick up, Gray had already made a great impression upon the Everton dressing room. 'He was just the sort of character we needed,' Graeme Sharp recalled. 'He was terrific: a breath of fresh air. And you could hear him long before you saw him. He had an unbelievable will and a desire to win football matches and, although our fortunes didn't turn around immediately, he made sure we were never down for too long after a poor result, which is important to a group of young players.'

There were several turning points in the 1983/84 season, one of which was an FA Cup third round tie at Stoke. Gray opened the scoring on 67 minutes with a stupendous diving header, and Everton never looked back. His new team seemed suddenly galvanised by his desire, courage and bravery. Nothing epitomised Gray better than his FA Cup quarter-final winner against Notts County. With the game balanced

at 1-1, after 47 minutes Everton gained a free kick. Kevin Sheedy lifted the ball over the heads of Graeme Sharp and his marker David Hunt to the back post where Gray appeared horizontally and, virtually touching the ground, headed the deciding goal. Cup-tied for Everton's Milk (League) Cup run, Gray returned for the FA Cup Final against Watford, scoring Everton's second in a 2-0 win with a 51st-minute back-post header.

With the onset of the 1984-85 season, Gray's chances were initially limited by the continued excellence of Adrian Heath. But a cruel injury to Heath in early December saw the Scot restored to the team and he seized his opportunity: Everton embarked on a league run that saw them drop just nine points in six months, with Gray averaging a goal every other game, and lift the league title.

AT NO POINT, however, was Gray more impressive than in Everton's European Cup Winners' Cup run. He effectively wrapped up the quarter-final against Fortuna Sittard with a first-leg hat-trick. Absent through injury from the first leg of the semi-final against Bayern Munich, he made a triumphant return for the return tie at Goodison. Trailing 1-0 at half-time, Gray battered Bayern into submission, scoring Everton's second, decisive goal as they claimed a famous 3-1 win. Asked about the difference between his side's performance in the first and second legs Kendall replied, 'They hadn't seen Andy Gray in the first leg.' 'Gray,' claimed the Bayern coach, Uli Hoeness, 'should be playing rugby, not football.' Invariably he played a lead role in the final, volleying Everton's first in a 3-1 victory over Rapid Vienna.

Mocked eighteen months earlier for claiming he had come to Goodison to win things, with an FA Cup, European Cup Winners' Cup and League Championship medal, it was Gray now having the last laugh. But having written his way into Everton lore, Gray's Goodison career was, in July 1985, brought to an abrupt halt. After signing Gary Lineker for a club record fee, Kendall – already with Graeme Sharp, Adrian Heath and England under-21 striker Paul Wilkinson at his disposal – accepted a £150,000 bid from Aston Villa. Later, he claimed that he couldn't face the prospect of having to leave Gray out of his starting line-up in the forthcoming season.

Not since Dave Hickson was sold to Liverpool in 1959 had Evertonians been so outraged by a transfer. Petitions were drawn up and hundreds wrote to the club begging for Gray to stay. But it was all to no avail.

[FACTFILE]

BORN
Glasgow,
30 November 1955
POSITION
Centre forward
OTHER CLUBS
Dundee United (1973–75);
Aston Villa (1975–79);
Wolverhampton Wanderers (1979–83);
Aston Villa (1985–87);
Notts County (loan, 1987);
West Bromwich Albion (1987–88);
Rangers (1988–89)
HONOURS
FA Cup 1984, 1984/85
League Championship,
European Cup Winners' Cup 1985;
20 Scotland caps (7 goals) (1975–85)

Season	League		FA Cup		League Cup		Other		Total	
	App	Goals	App	Goals	App	Goals	App	Goals	App	Goals
1983/84	23	5	7 (1)	3	0	0	-	-	30 (1)	8
1984/85	21 (5)	9	7	0	0 (1)	0	3	5	31 (6)	14
Total	**44 (5)**	**14**	**14 (1)**	**3**	**0 (1)**	**0**	**3**	**5**	**61 (7)**	**22**

MAYBE KENDALL was right to sell the Scot when he did. Now in his thirties, a succession of knee injures meant that Gray never again reached such heights, either during his second period at Villa Park or in subsequent spells with Notts County, West Bromwich Albion and Glasgow Rangers. Following his retirement in the summer of 1989, after winning a Scottish Championship medal with Rangers, he embarked on a career in the media, also briefly holding down a role as Ron Atkinson's assistant at Aston Villa. When Sky TV won the right to screen Premier League football, Gray took up his media role full-time and has become one of television's leading pundits.

In summer 1997 it seemed for a period as if Gray would make an unexpected return to Goodison – as Everton manager. Linked to the position, Gray said: 'This is a job I am interested in discussing because Everton is in my heart and soul. I loved my time at the club and I think the supporters know I've got blue blood running through my veins.' Yet a week later he announced, to the 'shock and bewilderment' of Everton, that he was to remain at Sky.

THERE WAS MUCH claim and counterclaim about why Gray never became Everton manager, souring some of the outstanding memories had of him. Despite all this, for the majority of those to witness this swashbuckling talisman, Gray's place among the pantheon of Everton legends is beyond doubt.

GRAY'S PLACE AMONG THE PANTHEON OF EVERTON LEGENDS IS BEYOND DOUBT

Gray, Robert

Scottish forward who failed to make a first-team shirt his own

[FACTFILE]

BORN
Scotland, 1876
POSITION
Outside / inside left
OTHER CLUBS
Partick Thistle;
Southampton

Season	League		FA Cup		Total	
	App	Goals	App	Goals	App	Goals
1899/1900	15	1	1	0	16	1
1900/01	5	0	0	0	5	0
Total	20	1	1	0	21	1

Great Escapes

Last-gasp bids to beat the drop that typified Everton's dismal 1990s

Everton's 1990s can be defined by three epic matches. At one end of the spectrum was the 1995 FA Cup Final victory over Manchester United, the ultimate expression of triumph over adversity.

Everton had overcome their worst ever start to the season to avoid relegation and then beat United, who were overwhelming favourites, at Wembley. In doing so, there was a solitary ray of light in a miserable decade.

The other two memorable matches also came at the conclusion of long seasons that were momentous for the wrong reasons. Rather than looking for trophies, Everton were staring relegation down the nose, needing final-day wins and for results to go their way in order to avoid the abyss of second-tier football.

In 1993/94, years of under-investment and a season replete with managerial uncertainty combined with near devastating consequences at its end. Howard Kendall's second managerial reign had ended in December 1993, and under caretaker manager Jimmy Gabriel form slid dramatically. Mike Walker succeeded Kendall in mid-January, but after a bright start results dried up. When Everton visited Norwich on 20 March his former club routed Everton 3-0. Relegation started to become a distinct threat: Sheffield Wednesday thrashed Everton 5-1 at Hillsborough and 3-0 reversals at Blackburn and Leeds pushed Everton closer towards the trapdoor. Only a win at West Ham stemmed a seemingly irreversible tide.

It meant Everton approached the final match of the season against Wimbledon occupying the third

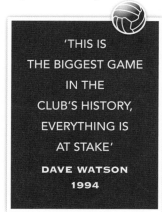

'THIS IS THE BIGGEST GAME IN THE CLUB'S HISTORY, EVERYTHING IS AT STAKE'
**DAVE WATSON
1994**

relegation spot, lying behind Sheffield United, whose result against Chelsea Everton would need to better in order to survive.

'This is the biggest game in the club's history,' declared captain Dave Watson beforehand. 'Everything is at stake. We simply must win and hope other results go our way. Everything is on the line against Wimbledon.'

THAT DAY, 7 May 1994 has justly gone down in Goodison folklore. A crowd of 31,000, some queuing from before midday, packed the three-sided ground – the old Park Stand was now entirely demolished ahead of construction of its replacement – with hundreds more watching from the trees of Stanley Park.

Wimbledon were coming to the end of their best ever season and hunting a fifth-place finish. Their charismatic chairman, Sam Hamman, promised them a trip to Las Vegas if they managed to upset Everton.

THE NIGHT before the match, the game was given an added edge when the Wimbledon team coach was burned out by arsonists. The former football hooligan and author, Andy Nicholls, claims in his book Scally that it was an opportunistic attack by a group of Everton supporters, who spotted the coach at a Warrington hotel while on their way back from a nearby rave.

Wimbledon appeared singed, but unperturbed. Indeed from the earliest stages of the game Everton looked doomed. In the fourth minute Limpar mysteriously handled inside his own area. Dean Holdsworth gratefully stepped up to take the resulting penalty and score his 24th goal of the season, the ball trickling agonisingly into the net after Southall had got both hands to it. Worse was to follow. Sixteen minutes later Dave Watson and David Unsworth jumped for the same high ball. It dropped to Andy Clarke, whose mis-hit shot found the net via Gary Ablett's shin. Goodison, which had earlier been a cauldron of noise, was hushed.

FOUR MINUTES later the crowd was stirred back into life. Limpar, desperate to atone for the bizarre penalty he had given away, ghosted into the left of the Wimbledon penalty area. As he sought to shuffle past Peter Fear, he appeared to have been caught and crashed to the ground. The referee awarded a dubious penalty. No one but Graham Stuart, still a rookie who had never previously taken a spot kick, volunteered to take it. He held his nerve, scoring to give Everton a lifeline.

Despite Stuart's goal, in the second half Wimbledon still looked the most likely to score. Holdsworth twice went close, and missed from four yards on a third occasion. At the other end Stuart nearly scored with a low, near-post drive after a mazy run, but one was still left to ponder where an Everton goal might come from.

Then, on 67 minutes, came a miracle. Barry Horne, hitherto an under-performer for Everton, seized the ball on the edge of the centre circle. Surging forward, the ball sat up invitingly and he crashed a volley from 30 yards into the top corner of Hans Segers' net. In 102 years of Goodison history it was one of the finest goals the old stadium had ever witnessed.

Everton surged forward in search for a winner. Walker brought Stuart Barlow on for John Ebbrell with ten minutes remaining. With his first piece of action he ran down the right flank and played the ball to Cottee. His flick found Stuart who, from the edge of the area, hit a tame shot which squeezed in under the body of Segers to make it 3-2. It was a scoreline Everton managed to hold until the referee's final whistle nine minutes later signalled that they were safe.

The game has nevertheless since been dogged by allegations of skulduggery. The following March, Wimbledon's goalkeeper, Segers, was arrested on suspicion of match fixing and subsequently charged. At the subsequent trial, he was asked about a payment of £19,000 into a Swiss bank account six days after Everton's great escape. It was one of a number of mysterious payments totalling £160,000 that had been made over a period of two years. Segers denied any wrongdoing, claiming the payments were from legitimate business interests. When the jury made its deliberations in March 1997 it was deadlocked. At the retrial that summer Segers was acquitted. But in some minds the whiff of scandal surrounding Everton's great escape has never quite evaporated.

The prevailing message after the Wimbledon game was 'never again'. But in two of the subsequent three seasons, Everton had further brushes with the dreaded drop. In the fourth, the 1997/98 season, Everton were such a shambles on and off the field that they should indeed have gone down.

After losing the penultimate game of the season 4-0 at champions-elect Arsenal, Everton plummeted back into the relegation mire. They went into the final game of the season against Coventry City needing to get a result better than Bolton, who were away at Chelsea. If Bolton won, Everton were relegated.

By the time 10 May 1998, the season's final day, rolled around there was an air of resignation over Goodison Park. Unlike the Wimbledon game four years earlier, only the most optimistic Evertonians expected to survive. That they eventually did was not down to the efforts of the team, nor a moment of inspiration, like Horne's thunderous equaliser. So excruciatingly awful were they that Everton could not even beat a Coventry City side notable only for their own mediocrity.

EVERTON, nevertheless, started the Coventry game well and in the sixth minute they took the lead. Gareth Farrelly, who had been out of sorts all season, let fly with a shot from 25 yards that nestled into the roof of the Coventry net. Goodison erupted, but the goal failed to settle the team. Coventry took control of the game, and the longer it went on, the more edgy Evertonians and their team became.

Tempers were becoming frayed on the pitch, when, with 15 minutes left, a sudden roar, unconnected with events on the pitch, erupted. Chelsea had scored through their player-manager Gianluca Vialli. Goodison began to reverberate with the echo of his name.

With five minutes remaining, Danny Cadamarteri was played through by Nick Barmby's flick header. He was cleanly tackled by Paul Williams, Coventry's centre half, but the referee Paul Alcock inexplicably gave a penalty. With the chance to put Everton into a 2-0 lead, and probably ensure Premiership survival, Barmby was charged with the task of taking the penalty. However, he shot poorly and Marcus Hedman saved.

The game then took a darker turn. Four minutes later David Burrows surged down the left, and from his cross Dion Dublin's header slipped out of Thomas Myhre's grasp and into the Everton goal.

THE CROWD bayed for the final whistle to bring an end to this most wretched of seasons. In among the whistles and jeers from the crowd came a second roar, as news came through that Jody Morris had added a second for Chelsea. Moments later came the final whistle at Goodison and the players ran for the dressing room as the crowd stormed onto the pitch, singing and dancing in relief.

'Everton had survived because of another club's inadequacies, rather than their own efforts, a grimly fitting way to end a season that had stumbled from one catastrophe to another,' wrote the Liverpool Echo's David Prentice – an eloquent, but ordinarily restrained voice. 'The last time that happen club officials declared, "Never again". The message this time must be: Never say never again. Whatever it takes, just get it right. Mid-table mediocrity would be nice for a start.'

7 MAY 1994
v Wimbledon 3-2 [H]
Stuart 2, Horne; **31,297**
Southall, Snodin, Ablett, Watson, Unsworth, Stuart, Ebbrell (Barlow), Horne, Limpar, Cottee, Rideout

10 MAY 1998
v Coventry City [H] 1-1 *Farrelly;* **40,109**
Myhre, O'Kane, Short, Watson, Tiler, Ball, Hutchison, Barmby, Farrelly (McCann), Ferguson, Madar (Cadamarteri)

> **'HORNE'S WAS ONE OF THE FINEST GOALS THE OLD STADIUM HAD EVER WITNESSED'**

Green, Colin

Young Welsh full back who gained international recognition beyond Goodison

Season	League App	League Goals	FA Cup App	FA Cup Goals	League Cup App	League Cup Goals	Total App	Total Goals
1960/61	7	0	0	0	1	0	8	0
1961/62	8	1	2	0	-	-	10	1
Total	**15**	**1**	**2**	**0**	**1**	**0**	**18**	**1**

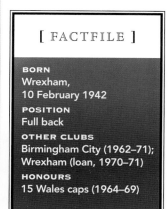

[FACTFILE]

BORN
Wrexham,
10 February 1942
POSITION
Full back
OTHER CLUBS
Birmingham City (1962–71);
Wrexham (loan, 1970–71)
HONOURS
15 Wales caps (1964–69)

Greenhalgh, Norman

Unsung hero and captain of the 1938/39 Championship-winning team

Starting out at Bolton Wanderers in the early 1930s, Norman Greenhalgh honed his trade in the rough and ready world of Division Three North, a league in which hardness had to be combined with footballing ability in order to survive. As a young half back he possessed both, as well as the guile and mental toughness necessary to succeed. His relentless will to win marked him out as a natural leader, yet there was no rapid ascent. In 1935 he joined New Brighton and converted to full back, where he emerged as a formidable young talent.

> **HIS RELENTLESS WILL TO WIN MARKED HIM OUT AS A NATURAL LEADER**

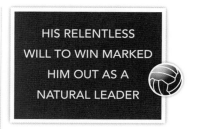

IN FEBRUARY 1938, Everton paid their neighbours £3000 for Greenhalgh, who was given a contract worth £6 per week, rising to £7 after he played eight league games. His progress was impressive. After deputising for Billy Cook at right back, he came in for Jack Jones on the left side of Everton's defence. By the end of the 1937/38 season he had made the number three shirt his own, and by the start of the following campaign he was captaining Everton.

Greenhalgh, recalled Stan Bentham in Three Sides of the Mersey, 'was a very wholehearted player, and he didn't take much from any of the outside-rights. He made a good captain; not always too popular, I don't think, because he opened his mouth a bit to try to get the best out of the players.'

For an opposing winger he was a formidable sight, and Stanley Matthews was one such player known to hate coming up against him. 'Norman was the only one who could get much out of Matthews,' said Bentham. 'He was known for his sliding tackle, and I've seen Matthews jump out of the way: "Mind me legs, Mind me legs."'

Season	League App	League Goals	FA Cup App	FA Cup Goals	Total App	Total Goals
1937/38	12	0	0	0	12	0
1938/39	42	1	5	0	47	1
1945/46	-	-	2	0	2	0
1946/47	38	0	2	0	40	0
1947/48	12	0	0	0	12	0
1948/49	2	0	0	0	2	0
Total	**106**	**1**	**9**	**0**	**115**	**1**

THE IMPRESSION he made upon a team renowned for their attacking play – and yet not necessarily a winning mentality – was considerable. Everton had finished 16th, 17th and 14th the previous three seasons; yet they won the 1938/39 First Division title in breathtaking fashion. In a side possessing players like T.G. Jones, Tommy Lawton, Torry Gillick and Joe Mercer, the input of the likes of Greenhalgh – the proverbial 'water carrier' – tends to be overlooked. But his contribution unquestionably allowed others to flourish.

Greatness seemed to beckon for Everton, but three games into the 1939/40 season war came and changed everything. Greenhalgh made nearly 300 wartime appearances for Everton, but it was never the same. 'We won the League and Portsmouth won the Cup, and we were supposed to play them in the Charity Shield,' he told the authors of Three Sides of the Mersey. 'What happened? Bloody Adolf Hitler stepped in, didn't he, and the bloody war was on, and I lost a medal. That was always a bone of contention for me.'

[FACTFILE]

BORN
Bolton, 10 August 1914
POSITION
Full back
OTHER CLUBS
Bolton Wanderers (1933–35);
New Brighton (1935–38)
HONOURS
1938/39 First Division Championship

By the time football recommenced in September 1946, Greenhalgh had been shorn of his pace by the passing years. Although he played most of Everton's games in the 1946/47 season, thereafter he found Gordon Dugdale and Jack Hedley picked ahead of him. After appearing on the wrong side of a 6-0 mauling against Chelsea in September 1948, he never played for Everton again. He joined Bangor City on a free transfer and later worked in the pub trade.

'WITH GREENHALGH CAPTAIN EVERTON WON THE 1938/39 FIRST DIVISION TITLE IN BREATHTAKING FASHION'

Grenyer, Alan

Half back who made a decisive contribution in Everton's second league title win

Left half Alan Grenyer's Everton career was hugely interrupted by the onset of the First World War, limiting him to less than 150 senior appearances in a Goodison career that spanned more than 14 years. But he was to make a decisive contribution to Everton history, scoring the goal in April 1915 that propelled Everton towards their second League Championship win.

Born in North Shields in August 1892, Grenyer caught the eye of Everton scouts while playing as an 18-year-old amateur for North Shields. They had been scouting for a centre forward named Dawson, but upon seeing Grenyer convened an emergency board meeting at which a £125 transfer fee and 50 shillings weekly wages were authorised. A condition of the players engagement was that he be permitted to complete his apprenticeship as a riveter with a local firm.

GRENYER had to wait a couple of years before getting a run in the first team, when injury to the brilliant cricketer-footballer Harry Makepeace gave him his chance. Little in contemporaneous reports suggest that he particularly shone and Makepeace, fitness permitting, remained first choice.

But when injury robbed Makepeace of his first-team place near the end of the 1914/15 season, Grenyer got his chance again. A disastrous run of three defeats had knocked Everton out of the FA Cup at the semi-final stage and in many minds also ended the club's league challenge. But a comprehensive victory at Sunderland bred some hope. 'Grenyer played a capital game yesterday,' reported 'Critic' in the Liverpool Evening Courier after the 3-0 win. 'Now that he has had two or three games on the run the ability he undoubtedly possesses is beginning to show itself.'

Optimism intensified after a 2-1 victory at West Bromwich Albion. Next was a visit to Bradford Park Avenue. 'When Everton visited Bradford before in the snowstorm the Yorkshiremen were

winning easily when the match was abandoned, so that the replay proved quite a lucky stroke for the Blues,' reported the Courier. 'The conditions were quite summerlike on this occasion. Everton were the better side throughout. It is pleasing to record that the "new" forward, Grenyer, shaped exceedingly well, and he had the satisfaction of scoring the winning goal.' That came after he combined with Sam Chedgzoy and his strike was described as 'beautiful'. The following Saturday Everton went top with a 1-0 win over Manchester City. Their rivals, Oldham, then lost their two games in hand, effectively ensuring Everton's title on goal average. They then went a point clear after drawing their final game with Chelsea.

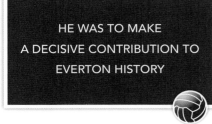

HE WAS TO MAKE A DECISIVE CONTRIBUTION TO EVERTON HISTORY

Celebrations, coming some ten months into the First World War, were understandably muted. 'Our gratification was chilled by the catastrophe of the Great War,' recorded the club historian and former director, Thomas Keates. The Football League was abandoned and teams played in regional leagues. Grenyer was a regular throughout this period, playing more than 120 games. He was also recognised by England, playing a Victory international against Wales in October 1919.

BY THEN league football had resumed and observers took comfort in the solidity of the reigning champions' defence. 'The half back line – [Tom] Fleetwood, [Billy] Wareing and Grenyer, who were the mainstay of the team during the past season or two, will again do duty, and here again there is no cause for anxiety,' recorded one correspondent on the eve of the 1919/20 season.

HOWEVER, more than four years away from league football had seen Everton go into decline. Grenyer, now approaching his thirties, found Joe Peacock then Hunter Hart preferred at left half. In October 1924, having failed to make the first team in 20 months, his transfer back to the Northeast, to South Shields, was agreed. He later crossed town, to where he had started, when he was appointed North Shields coach in 1931.

Season	League		FA Cup		Total	
	App	Goals	App	Goals	App	Goals
1910/11	1	0	0	0	1	0
1911/12	3	0	0	0	3	0
1912/13	26	0	4	0	30	0
1913/14	22	0	0	0	22	0
1914/15	14	1	0	0	14	1
1919/20	33	5	1	0	34	5
1920/21	23	1	1	0	24	1
1921/22	13	1	0	0	13	1
1922/23	7	1	0	0	7	1
Total	**142**	**9**	**6**	**0**	**148**	**9**

[FACTFILE]

BORN
North Shields,
31 August, 1892
POSITION
Half back
OTHER CLUB
South Shields (1924–28)
HONOURS
1914/15 League
Championship;
1 England (victory) cap (1919)

Griffiths, Bryan

Home-grown full back who later became a well-known figure in Merseyside non-league football

[FACTFILE]

BORN
Liverpool, 27 November 1938
POSITION
Full back
OTHER CLUB
Southport (1960–63)

Season	League		FA Cup		Total	
	App	Goals	App	Goals	App	Goals
1958/59	2	0	0	0	2	0
Total	**2**	**0**	**0**	**0**	**2**	**0**

Griffiths, Philip

Reserve winger who briefly lined up alongside the illustrious Dixie Dean

[FACTFILE]

BORN
Tylorstown, Glamorgan,
25 October 1905
DIED
14 May 1978
POSITION
Outside right
OTHER CLUBS
Port Vale (1926–30);
West Bromwich Albion (1933);
Cardiff City (1934)

Season	League		FA Cup		Total	
	App	Goals	App	Goals	App	Goals
1931/32	7	3	0	0	7	3
1932/33	1	0	0	0	1	0
Total	**8**	**3**	**0**	**0**	**8**	**3**

Grant, Tony

Mercurial midfielder, out muscled by the modern game

In many ways, Tony Grant was a hark to a bygone, more cultured and less physical age; his style of football infused with traditions established at Goodison by the likes of Wally Fielding, Martin Dobson and Colin Harvey.

The local midfielder made his breakthrough into the Everton team of the mid-1990s. A slight, technically gifted player, whose passing sometimes seemed to be on a different plane to some of his colleagues, Evertonians soon realized that he was a special prospect indeed, dubbing him 'Grantona' for some of the similarities he shared with the Manchester United talisman.

Before he could truly make his mark and call a starting place his own, however, the midfielder's progress was halted by a series of debilitating injuries, which disrupted his most promising spells. At the same time, Grant, who was a footballing aristocrat,

was forced to make his mark in a team of yeoman. In short, the odds were always stacked against him.

Transfer listed by Walter Smith at the end of the 1998/99 season, he joined up with Joe Royle at Manchester City the following

December, later playing for Burnley, before embarking on a tour of the lower leagues, his potential never quite realised.

Season	League		FA Cup		League Cup		Other		Total	
	App	Goals	App	Goals	App	Goals	App	Goals	App	Goals
1994/95	1 (4)	0	0	0	0	0	-	-	1 (4)	0
1995/96	11 (2)	1	0 (1)	0	2	0	2 (2)	1	15 (5)	2
1996/97	11 (7)	0	0 (2)	0	1	0	-	-	12 (8)	0
1997/98	7	1	1	0	1	0	-	-	9	1
1998/99	13 (3)	0	3 (1)	0	1 (1)	0	-	-	17 (5)	0
1999/2000	0 (2)	0	0	0	0	0	-	-	0 (2)	0
Total	43(18)	2	4 (4)	0	5 (1)	0	2 (2)	1	54 (25)	3

[FACTFILE]

BORN
Liverpool, 14 November, 1974
POSITION
Midfield
OTHER CLUBS
Swindon Town (loan) (1996);
Tranmere Rovers (loan) (1999);
Manchester City (1999-2001);
West Bromwich Albion (loan)
(2000-01); Burnley (2001-05);
Bristol City (2005-06);
Crewe Alexander (2006-07);
Chester City (2007-08)

Griffiths, Tom

Wales defender who overcame nightmare debut

Welsh international centre back Tom Griffiths joined Everton midway through the 1926/27 season and was plunged straight into the first team.

The mauling he received on his debut – a 6-2 defeat to Leicester – was so traumatic as to almost finish his Goodison career before it had even begun. But the defender recovered sufficiently to have a solid spell with the Blues and continued appearing in the top flight through the 1930s.

BORN NEAR Wrexham, he played 36 times for his home-town club after starting out as an amateur.

Scouted by Everton, in December 1926 he moved to Merseyside on the same day as Stockport County's Ted Critchley for a fee of £1500. His debut two months later was a fiasco. 'It was small wonder that Leicester won by 6 goals to 2,' reported the Liverpool Post and Mercury. 'The secret of Leicester's success was that the forwards and half-backs linked up with each other. The forwards were fast and were accurate in the passing. They were also quick to take up position, and although Chandler only scored one goal he was for ever a dangerous raider, and Griffiths had a trying time against him and his colleagues Hine and Lochhead. The former Wrexham player had a poor first half, but improved considerably after half-time.'

Griffiths was dropped and Goodison did not see him for another 20 months. Happily his 'second' debut was a more successful occasion – a 4-2 win at West Ham. 'One of the most gratifying features was the auspicious debut [sic] of Griffiths

at right-half,' reported the Post and Mercury. 'After some minutes in which to settle down he proceeded to give an excellent exhibition of honest football, coupled with some tenacious tackling and a serious of delightful accurate low passes down the middle. He gave Dunn and Ritchie admirable support and fitted in well with Cresswell.'

The Welshman appeared in the Charity Shield victory four days later and settled well into an Everton team that struggled to match the heights of Dean's 60-goal season. 'His tackle is hard and definite, with little recovery if he is beaten,' recorded one newspaperman. 'But his method of swinging the ball about to his wingmen is his forte, and it is a happy inspiration to Everton for the future.'

EVERTON finished the 1928/29 season 18th, having lost their last six league games. It was a worrying portent for the following campaign, which ended with them bottom and relegated for the first

time. Griffiths had appeared 26 times in the calamitous league campaign, once more than the much-missed Dixie.

The stay in the second tier was short and Griffiths was ever-present through the first half of the 1930/31 campaign. But when an unexpected and huge offer of £6500 came in from Bolton Wanderers in December 1930, the board decided it was too good to turn down and sold Griffiths. He was replaced by Charlie Gee, who went on to earn England honours.

Griffiths later turned out for Middlesbrough and Aston Villa, finishing his career at Wrexham, where he also had spells as coach and a club director.

[FACTFILE]

BORN
Moss, Wrexham,
21 February 1906
DIED
Moss, Wrexham,
25 December 1981
POSITION
Centre half
OTHER CLUBS
Wrexham (1922–26);
Bolton Wanderers (1931–33);
Middlesbrough (1933–35);
Aston Villa (1935–38);
Wrexham (1938–39)
HONOURS
1930/31 Second Division
Championship;
21 Wales caps (3 goals)
(1927–37)

Season	League		FA Cup		Oher		Total	
	App	Goals	App	Goals	App	Goals	App	Goals
1926/27	1	0	0	0	-	-	1	0
1927/28	0	0	0	0	-	-	0	0
1928/29	26	2	1	0	1	0	28	2
1929/30	26	4	1	0	-	-	27	4
1930/31	23	3	0	0	-	-	23	3
Total	76	9	2	0	1	0	79	9

NISI OPTIMUM

Grundy, Harry

Season	League		FA Cup		Total	
	App	Goals	App	Goals	App	Goals
1905/06	2	0	0	0	2	0
Total	2	0	0	0	2	0

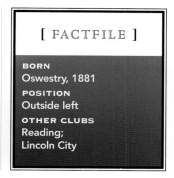

[FACTFILE]

BORN
Oswestry, 1881
POSITION
Outside left
OTHER CLUBS
Reading;
Lincoln City

Gueye, Magaye

French under-21 international who has a bright future

Signed in summer 2010 from Strasbourg for a fee understood to be worth up to £1million, Evertonians hold high hopes for the future of French forward Magaye Gueye. Having represented France at every youth level and at under-21 level too, his potential is beyond question.

Limited to cameos in his debut season at Goodison, he played through Everton's run to the FA Cup semi-final and was outstanding in the quarter-final replay against Sunderland. His first goal for Everton came in a league match against the same opponents ten days later.

'His energy, his effort and his link-up play were first class,' said the Everton assistant manager Steve Round after that game

'I'm really pleased for the lad. He's a nice lad, he's a good character, he trains well and he's certainly got ability.'

FIVE DAYS later Gueye started at Wembley against Liverpool. Alas, that occasion proved too much for him, and he was disappointing as Everton fell to defeat, but the experience will surely be useful as he seeks to make the Goodison grade.

GUEYE WAS OUTSTANDING IN EVERTON'S 2012 FA CUP QUARTER FINAL REPLAY WIN

[FACTFILE]

BORN
Nogent-sur-Marne, France,
6 July 1990
POSITION
Winger
OTHER CLUB
Strasbourg (2008–10)

Season	League		FA Cup		League Cup		Total	
	App	Goals	App	Goals	App	Goals	App	Goals
2010/11	2 (3)	0	0 (1)	0	2	0	4 (4)	0
2011/12	3 (14)	1	5 (1)	0	0 (1)	0	8 (16)	1
Total	5 (17)	1	5 (2)	0	2 (1)	0	12 (20)	1

Bryan **Hamilton**, Herbert **Hamilton**, Harry **Hammond**, Alan **Hampson**, Andrew **Hannah**, John **Hannah**, Peter **Harburn**, Harold **Hardman**, Harry **Hardy**, Frank **Hargreaves**, Alfie **Harland**, Alan **Harper**, Joe **Harper**, Bert **Harris**, Brian **Harris**, Jimmy **Harris**, Joe **Harris**, Val **Harris**, George **Harrison**, Hunter **Hart**, Asa **Hartford**, Billy **Hartill**, Abraham **Hartley**, Colin **Harvey**, William **Haughey**, Pat **Heard**, Adrian **Heath**, Jack **Hedley**, Johnny **Heitinga**, Bill **Henderson**, George **Heslop**, Tony **Hibbert**, Dave **Hickson**, Billy **Higgins**, Mark **Higgins**, Mike **Higgins**, **High-scoring games**, Norman **Higham**, Jimmy **Hill**, Percy **Hill**, Jack **Hillman**, John **Hills**, Andy **Hinchcliffe**, Martin **Hodge**, William **Hodge**, Walter **Holbem**, Oscar **Hold**, Paul **Holmes**, Johnny **Holt**, Barry **Horne**, Harold **Houghton**, Johnny **Houston**, Tim **Howard**, Benjamin **Howard-Baker**, Bob **Howarth**, Harold **Howarth**, Darren **Hughes**, Mark **Hughes** (b.1963), Mark **Hughes** (b.1986), Ted **Hughes**, Gerry **Humphreys**, Jack **Humphreys**, Ernie **Hunt**, Eli **Hurel**, John **Hurst**, Don **Hutchison**, Jimmy **Husband**

Hamilton, Bryan

Northern Ireland midfielder whose Everton career is still defined by FA Cup injustice

More than 30 years after leaving Everton Bryan Hamilton's name still conjures memories of one of the most bitter moments in the club's history. On 23 April 1977 Everton met Liverpool in the FA Cup semi-final at Maine Road.

Late in the game and with the scores balanced at 2-2 Ronnie Goodlass cut in from the byline and played a centre for Hamilton, who deflected the ball into the Liverpool net. While the Evertonians celebrated wildly and Liverpool players contemplated the inevitability of defeat, the referee, Clive Thomas, inexplicably disallowed the goal. The game ended a draw and Liverpool, with a certain inevitability, won the replay 3-0. Everton's seven-year-long search for a trophy would extend for a further seven years.

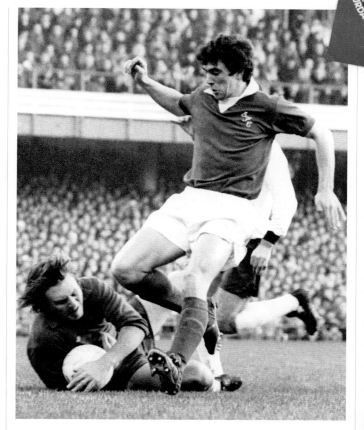

> BRYAN HAMILTON'S NAME STILL CONJURES MEMORIES OF ONE OF THE MOST BITTER MOMENTS IN THE CLUB'S HISTORY

Why did Thomas disallow the goal? Even today, no one really knows. During the match he told Ken McNaught that Hamilton had 'obviously handled the ball'. But afterwards all he would say was that there had been 'an infringement of the rules of the Football Association'. The following Monday Thomas said that Hamilton was offside, despite the linesman failing to flag. Video replays show that Thomas was 25 yards behind play – although he still refuses to admit he made a mistake. He later told the authors of A Celebration of the Merseyside

Derby: 'From the angle of the cross there was no way Bryan Hamilton could have controlled the ball without the use of his arm. In no way could I say that from behind I could have seen the ball make contact with his hand or his arm. But I was 100 per cent certain that he couldn't have controlled it any other way. So I disallowed it. For handball.'

Hamilton had been a £40,000 signing from Ipswich Town in November 1975, where he carried a reputation as a goalscoring midfielder. At Goodison, however,

the Northern Ireland midfielder failed to live up to this reputation, although no one faulted his effort. Although he worked tirelessly down the right side of midfield, Hamilton never became a regular and, already into his thirties, he was sold to Millwall for £25,000 in the summer of 1977. After a spell with Swindon Town he turned to management, embarking on a lengthy and varied career, which he combined with extensive media work, providing one of the game's most articulate and distinguished voices.

[FACTFILE]

BORN
Belfast, 21 December 1946

POSITION
Midfielder

OTHER CLUBS
Distillery (1964–66);
Linfield (1966–71);
Ipswich Town (1971–75);
Millwall (1977–78);
Swindon Town (1978–80);
Tranmere Rovers
(player-manager, 1980–85)

AS MANAGER
Wigan Athletic (1985–86);
Leicester City (1986–87);
Wigan Athletic (1989–93);
Northern Ireland (1994–98);
Norwich City (2000)

HONOURS
50 Northern Ireland caps
(1969–80)

Season	League		FA Cup		League Cup		Total	
	App	Goals	App	Goals	App	Goals	App	Goals
1975/76	22 (1)	5	1	0	0	0	23 (1)	5
1976/77	16 (2)	0	1 (2)	0	7 (2)	0	24 (6)	0
Total	**38 (3)**	**5**	**2 (2)**	**0**	**7 (2)**	**0**	**47 (7)**	**5**

Hamilton, Herbert

One-game wonder who forged a successful lower league career

[FACTFILE]

BORN
Wallasey, 27 March 1906
DIED
1951
POSITION
Right back
OTHER CLUBS
New Brighton (1923); Preston North End (1927–30); Chesterfield (1931–36); Tranmere Rovers (1937–38); Accrington Stanley (1938); Bangor City; Marine

Season	League		FA Cup		Total	
	App	Goals	App	Goals	App	Goals
1926/27	1	0	0	0	1	0
Total	1	0	0	0	1	0

Hammond, Harry

Early left back who made just a solitary Anfield appearance

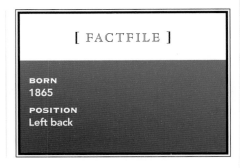

[FACTFILE]

BORN
1865
POSITION
Left back

Season	League		FA Cup		Total	
	App	Goals	App	Goals	App	Goals
1889/90	1	0	0	0	1	0
Total	1	0	0	0	1	0

Hampson, Alan

Inside forward whose solitary outing came during Everton's last relegation season

[FACTFILE]

BORN
Prescot, 27 December 1927
POSITION
Inside forward
OTHER CLUBS
Halifax Town (1952–56); Bradford City (1956–57); Prescot Cables

Season	League		FA Cup		Total	
	App	Goals	App	Goals	App	Goals
1950/51	1	0	0	0	1	0
Total	1	0	0	0	1	0

Hannah, Andrew

Everton's first League Championship winning captain

A right back of pace and tenacity, Andrew Hannah was Everton's first great captain, leading the club to their first League Championship in 1891.

Signed from his home-town club of Renton, Hannah had established a reputation as a leading light in one of Victorian football's most formidable teams. Renton had won the 1889 Scottish Cup and then proved their superiority over the English by conquering 'the Invincibles' of Preston North End, who had won the League Championship without losing a single game. The Evening Telegraph described Hannah as a 'man to be respected by opponents, for he could break up an attack either by skilful tackling or robust charging'.

A renowned athlete in his native Dunbartonshire, he was a championship 'jumper' and sprinter and had competed at the Highland Games. He later claimed in an interview with the Liverpool Echo that he earned more £300 in prize money from these exploits – this at a time when a professional footballer took home around £3 per week.

He was installed as captain on arriving at Anfield ahead of the 1889 season and made a great impact, revitalising the previous season's strugglers and elevating them into genuine title challengers.

'Mr. Hannah,' wrote the Echo in an interview in November 1889, 'is a quiet unassuming gentlemanly young Scotchman without very much appearance of the professional athlete about him.' The Everton captain explained how he had started playing football 'as soon as I was able to walk' and 'seriously aged fourteen' and went on to detail his athletic career – jumping exploits and all. He said that Everton should aspire for the level of 'scientific football' shown by Renton and Preston, who 'are the two best for scientific play'.

'The great art of football is the short passing game,' he said. 'It is better to tackle a man

when they are all closed up than it is in long passing. The short passing is the best playing game right up to the goal, when you have the best chance of shooting through. The best rule is to work well up to the goal, and then "Don't hesitate to shoot".'

Everton were top at the time, and – Hannah said – would be favourites for the title if they beat Preston North End on the Saturday. A record crowd at Anfield – 18,000 – turned out in hope and expectation, but were left disappointed. Everton lost 5-1 and the Championship remained at Deepdale. Everton finished runners-up by just two points.

A year later, however, Hannah captained Everton to their first title, as they finished two points ahead of Preston. However, he rejected the chance to build on this success, returning to Renton – who were to be admitted to the Scottish League as professionals for the first time – at the end of the season.

He returned to Anfield a year later as part of John Houlding's renegades and played in Liverpool's first league match in 1893. His experience and natural authority helped Everton's rivals through these early years of struggle and established them as a football force.

Season	League		FA Cup		Total	
	App	Goals	App	Goals	App	Goals
1889/90	22	0	2	0	24	0
1890/91	20	0	0	0	20	0
Total	42	0	2	0	44	0

Hannah, John

Full back whose solitary outing came on Boxing Day 1905

Season	League		FA Cup		Total	
	App	Goals	App	Goals	App	Goals
1905/06	1	0	0	0	1	0
Total	1	0	0	0	1	0

Harburn, Peter

Lower league forward for whom the toils of the top flight proved too much

Season	League		FA Cup		Total	
	App	Goals	App	Goals	App	Goals
1958/59	4	1	0	0	4	1
Total	4	1	0	0	4	1

Hardman, Harold

Outstanding outside left and famous administrator, Hardman was the last of the 'gentleman footballers'

Harold Hardman was among the last of the generation of gentleman footballers, the group of keen, middle-class amateurs who played for love of the game and were crucial to the development of football during the 19th century.

Contrary to its reputation as a working-class game, football was established as an organised sport by middle-class enthusiasts in the 1860s. With a missionary zeal they spread word of football throughout the world, retained control of the Football Association and dominated the ranks of the England team until the early 1900s. Many of these gentlemen players frowned upon the creation of the Football League in 1888 and would have nothing to do with professionals, who they thought undermined the sense of fair play they deemed inherent to their sport.

Hardman was a diminutive winger who graced the Everton flank on a Saturday and bestrode the chambers of his

> **HIS FINEST MOMENTS FOR EVERTON CAME DURING ITS VICTORIOUS FA CUP RUN IN 1906**

Manchester law firm during the week, where he practised as a solicitor. Unlike many of his 'gentleman' contemporaries, he seemingly had no problem reconciling his affluent background with his role for Everton.

Born in suburban Manchester in 1882, Hardman started his career at Blackpool, joining Everton in 1903 for £100. A left winger of skill and panache, he immediately formed a formidable left-sided partnership with Jimmy Settle. They were an outstanding supply line for Sandy Young, who blossomed when playing alongside them.

'The season 1903/04 marked a revival, the club securing third place on the chart,' wrote Thomas Keates. 'Taking it all through, the team, varied at times, combined well and gave some entrancing displays.' In particular, Everton's first historian singled Hardman and Settle out 'for excellence on the left wing'.

EVERTON came within a whisker of winning the league title the next season, losing out to Newcastle by only a point after losing a rearranged match to Woolwich Arsenal, having led the abandoned game 3-1 the previous autumn. Hardman's superb displays for Everton were nevertheless rewarded with a full England cap, when his country faced Wales at the Racecourse Ground in March. In total he would win four caps, but his most telling contribution would come for England's amateur team.

Perhaps his finest moments for Everton came during its victorious FA Cup run in 1906. On 31 March 1906 Birmingham was taken over by the blue, red and white ribbons of Everton and Liverpool fans who had converged on the city to see their respective teams at Villa Park vying for a place in the FA Cup Final. The Liverpool team had stayed overnight in Tamworth, and Everton had taken a morning train

journey, arriving in time for lunch at the Grand Hotel.

Once hostilities commenced on the pitch it was Liverpool who took the early initiative, holding much of the possession and having the best chances. Everton defended doughtily and made occasional counterattacks, particularly down the right. As the game progressed into the second half, Everton began to come to terms with their opponents and became more confident in their attacks. In one of their forays into the Liverpool half, Walter Abbott let fly with one of his characteristic long shots and, via the forlorn Liverpool defender Dunlop, it crept into the back of the goal. With Liverpool disorientated, Hardman seized the moment. A minute later he took possession, ran towards goal and shot. Hardy saved his effort, but the ball fell only as far as Jack Sharp. He played it back to Hardman, who tapped home the goal that sent Everton to their third FA Cup final, in which they defeated Newcastle United 1-0.

As evidenced by his playing record from the 1906/07 season, Hardman was finding it harder to combine work as a solicitor with football for Everton. He played a game, missed a game, played a brace of games and missed a couple, and so it went on. He was a close friend of Everton's secretary, Will Cuff, a fellow solicitor who would rise through football's committee rooms to have a huge influence on the wider game. The two shared a lengthy correspondence, in which Cuff empathised with Hardman's struggles at combining training with Everton in Liverpool with work as a solicitor in Manchester. Perhaps it was this empathy that led to Hardman's release at the end of the 1907/08 season so that he could concentrate on his profession.

HARDMAN JOINED Northern Nomads, one of the leading amateur clubs of the era. They

HAROLD HARDMAN
EVERTON

had reached the first round of the FA Cup that year and would later win the FA Amateur Cup. While playing for them Hardman was part of the England team that won the 1908 Olympic football tournament in London. In winning gold he was Everton's only successful Olympian until Daniel Amokachi matched his achievement at Atlanta in 1996.

NORTHERN Nomads, who didn't even have their own home, were no fit stage for Hardman, however, and he had joined Manchester United by the end of 1908. After just a handful of appearances he joined Bradford City in 1909, playing in their first two seasons in the First Division. In April 1909 he made an emotional return to Goodison, playing in Bradford's 1-0 win over Everton – a victory that ultimately secured Bradford's survival as a First Division team. In 1910 he joined Stoke City where he played out the remainder of his top-class career.

In 1912 Hardman returned to Old Trafford as a director and thus began his third career, as a football administrator. Like his friend Will Cuff he blazed a trail through football's committee rooms and would serve on the FA Council.

In 1951 he became Manchester United chairman and his leadership of the club – in partnership with Matt Busby – is credited with the making of United as the modern institution known today. Certainly he took the lead in supporting United's groundbreaking entry into European football in 1956, a move that ended in tragedy two years

later when Busby's great team was decimated by the Munich air disaster. 'United will rise again,' proclaimed Hardman, and they did – although the club's hierarchy was accused of ignoring the plight of many of the survivors and the victims' families.

Hardman lived long enough to see the advent of George Best and United's renaissance under Busby. He also saw Everton lift the league title once more in 1963, a feat that had eluded him as a player. Quite what he made of Johnny Morrissey and Derek Temple dodging a path down the Goodison flank we do not know, but one thing is certain – Hardman was every bit as illustrious as these revered figures who succeeded him on the Everton flank.

[FACTFILE]

BORN
Manchester, 4 April 1882
DIED
9 June 1965
POSITION
Outside left
OTHER CLUBS
Blackpool (1899–1903);
Manchester United (1908–09);
Bradford City (1909–10);
Stoke City (1910–13)
HONOURS
1906 FA Cup;
1908 Olympic gold medal;
4 England caps (1 goal) (1905–08)

Season	League		FA Cup		Total	
	App	Goals	App	Goals	App	Goals
1903/04	26	5	0	0	26	5
1904/05	32	8	6	1	38	9
1905/06	31	6	6	2	37	8
1906/07	19	3	7	1	26	4
1907/08	22	3	7	0	29	3
Total	**130**	**25**	**26**	**4**	**156**	**29**

Hardy, Harry

England international goalkeeper who provided safe hands in the era of Dixie Dean

[FACTFILE]

BORN
Stockport, 14 January 1895
DIED
17 February 1969
POSITION
Goalkeeper
OTHER CLUBS
Stockport County (1918–25);
Bury (1929)
HONOURS
1 England cap (1924)

Season	League		FA Cup		Total	
	App	Goals	App	Goals	App	Goals
1925/26	27	0	2	0	29	0
1926/27	7	0	3	0	10	0
1927/28	6	0	0	0	6	0
Total	**40**	**0**	**5**	**0**	**45**	**0**

Hargreaves, Frank

Inside forward who failed to make his mark in a time of transition

[FACTFILE]

BORN
Ashton under Lyme, 1902
POSITION
Inside forward
OTHER CLUBS
Oldham Athletic (1923 & 1925–29);
Rochdale (1930);
Bournemouth (1931);
Watford (1931);
Oldham Athletic (1932)

Season	League		FA Cup		Total	
	App	Goals	App	Goals	App	Goals
1924/25	9	2	0	0	9	2
Total	**9**	**2**	**0**	**0**	**9**	**2**

Harland, Alfie

Irish international unable to win Everton's green jersey on a long-term basis

Alfie Harland was one of a succession of talented goalkeepers whose Everton careers were sandwiched between those of two giants of the club, Billy Scott and Ted Sagar. Like many such players his career suffered by comparison to his great royal blue compatriots in the Everton goal.

HE CAME to Goodison in 1922 having won the Irish League Championship with Linfield, represented the Irish League and won his first Ireland caps. Everton's directors were suitably impressed by his performances for the Irish League to spend £1500 on his signature and he replaced the injured Tom Fern in goal to make his debut on 4 November 1922 in a 1-0 victory over Arsenal.

'Interest centred in the debut of Harland, the Irish international goalkeeper recently signed by Everton,' reported the Liverpool Daily Post and Mercury. 'The test was by no means a severe one but Harland gave sufficient evidence of his ability to justify the excellent opinion formed of his skill on previous occasions. The stiffest task came when Dr [James] Patterson sent in a high shot that almost went under the bar, and Harland showed resource in the way he got the ball over the bar after appearing to misjudge

the flight of the ball. From a spectators' point of view, the contest was well nigh featureless, because the forward work of both sides was extremely poor … The goalkeeper certainly had little to do in the first half, but afterwards there was more liveliness, and with Arsenal always threatening to rob Everton of their small lead, interest was maintained.'

Harland gained the respect of his fellow players and fans, who quickly considered him a safe pair of hands. 'Harland was at his best in goal, the Irishman saving several fine shots when Chelsea were at their best in the first half, and his safe catching and prompt clearances inspired confidence,' recorded 'FMN' in the Liverpool Courier of one match against the London club.

BUT THIS was an era in which goalkeepers were battered around by opposing forwards and thus exceedingly vulnerable to injury. Having made a string of appearances in place of the injured Fern, in February 1923 Harland was himself injured and Fern regained his place, holding it for a year. Harland regained the green jersey for the second half of the 1923/24 campaign but then lost it to another goalkeeper – Jack Kendall – for the first half of 1924/25 before regaining it once more. Kendall was seen off but when Everton signed Harry Hardy in 1925 it spelled the end for Harland.

He suffered from a series of injuries through his final year at Goodison and a dispute over his medical bills was discussed at boardroom level. In August 1926 it was decided to grant the player a free transfer and he joined Runcorn.

[FACTFILE]

BORN
26 November 1897
POSITION
Goalkeeper
OTHER CLUBS
Linfield (1919–22);
Runcorn
HONOURS
2 Ireland caps (1922)

Harper, Alan

Utility player whose versatility was an important part of the 1980s glory days

Unglamorous and unrevered he might well have been, but few Evertonians will dispute the notion that Alan Harper was one of the most important players in Everton's mid-1980s glory years.

BORN INTO a Liverpool-supporting family in 1960, it seemed the natural progression for Harper to join the side he had idolised as a boy. Although a stalwart of the Liverpool reserve team, never did he receive the opportunity to play for the first team at Anfield and was released in the summer of 1983. Perhaps surprisingly, Howard Kendall moved for the 22-year-old – although over the years the Everton manager did well in acquiring Anfield cast-offs – Kevin Sheedy, Dave Watson and Peter Beardsley among them – and on the opening day of the 1983/84 season Harper replaced the highly rated Gary Stevens as right back.

Right back was always Harper's favoured position but the continued excellence of Stevens, who regained his place and was to become an England international, severely restricted his chances of regularly filling the berth. Instead Kendall used him to fill a variety

Season	League		FA Cup		Total	
	App	Goals	App	Goals	App	Goals
1922/23	17	0	2	0	19	0
1923/24	16	0	2	0	18	0
1924/25	27	0	2	0	29	0
1925/26	4	0	0	0	4	0
Total	**64**	**0**	**6**	**0**	**70**	**0**

of roles ranging from defence to attack, which he always did with enthusiasm and proficiency. When not deputising for injured players, in the days of just a solitary substitute Harper was left to sit on the bench and wait for his chance – an unenviable position, though one he carried out without complaint.

HE DID however enjoy his moments of glory, most notably when his first goal for

> EVERTONIANS HELD HARPER IN GENUINE AFFECTION, AFFORDING THE UTILITY MAN CULT STATUS

the club earned a point in the Goodison derby in March 1984. He also scored a spectacular long-range chip over Martin Hodge in the 1986 FA Cup semi-final against Sheffield Wednesday and a 25-yard thunderbolt shot against Chelsea in April 1987 which put Everton top. Such goalscoring was a rarity – he scored only five times in over 200 Everton appearances – but often seemed to come spectacularly and at crucial times, earning him the nickname 'Zico'. It might have been ironic, but Evertonians held Harper in genuine affection, affording the utility man cult status.

ALTHOUGH HE MADE just 13 appearances in the 1984/85 Championship side, an injury crisis in 1986/87 meant that 'Zico' played in almost all of the games that season. His was a

crucial role in a team that overcame the odds to lift their ninth league title.

What Harper yearned for – and what Everton seemed to be unable to give him – was a regular first-team place. Once more, with players fit again, Harper found chances limited in the 1987/88 campaign. When his contract expired in summer 1988 he opted for a move to Sheffield Wednesday. He was reunited with Howard Kendall at Manchester City 18 months later and when Kendall returned to Merseyside he took Harper with him at the cost of £300,000. It was the third time Kendall had signed Harper, testament to how highly he rated him.

After nearly two seasons at right back he lost his place to Matt Jackson, and went to Luton Town

on a free transfer. After playing an important part in Luton's 1994 FA Cup run, when they reached the semi-final, he became part of Adrian Heath's coaching staff at Burnley. Later, in the early 2000s, he returned to Goodison for a third time as a youth coach, in which time he oversaw Wayne Rooney's meteoric rise. He left in November 2005, later taking up a scouting position at Bolton Wanderers, where he worked under the club's chief scout, Colin Harvey. In 2010 he returned to Anfield as the club's chief scout.

[FACTFILE]

BORN
Liverpool,
1 November 1960
POSITION
Utility player / right back
OTHER CLUBS
Liverpool (1978–83);
Sheffield Wednesday
(1988–89);
Manchester City (1989–91);
Luton Town (1993–94);
Burnley (1994–96);
Cardiff City (loan, 1995)
HONOURS
1984/85
League Championship,
1986/87
League Championship

Season	League App	League Goals	FA Cup App	FA Cup Goals	League Cup App	League Cup Goals	Europe App	Europe Goals	Total App	Total Goals
1983/84	26 (3)	1	1 (1)	0	6 (1)	0	-	-	33 (5)	1
1984/85	10 (3)	0	1 (1)	0	1	0	3 (1)	0	15 (5)	0
1985/86	17 (4)	0	4 (2)	1	4	0	5	0	30 (6)	1
1986/87	29 (7)	3	1 (1)	0	4	0	3	0	37 (8)	3
1987/88	21 (7)	0	3 (3)	0	2 (1)	0	3	0	29 (11)	0
1991/92	29 (4)	0	1	0	1 (1)	0	2	0	33 (5)	0
1992/93	16 (2)	0	1 (1)	0	4	0	-	-	21 (3)	0
Total	**148 (30)**	**4**	**12 (9)**	**1**	**22 (3)**	**0**	**16 (1)**	**0**	**198(43)**	**5**

Harper, Joe

Bulky Scottish striker who failed to live up to expectations in England

FOR JOE HARPER, scoring goals in his native Scotland came as naturally as breathing. In England, as with so many Scottish players who try their luck down south, it was a different story. A spell with Huddersfield Town during the late 1960s ended with a swift return to his homeland. There, with Morton

and Aberdeen, he rehabilitated his reputation, finishing third top league scorer in all of Europe in the 1971/72 season, also earning a Scotland call-up.

Scouts flooded to Pittodrie, but it was Harry Catterick who got his man, concluding a club record

£180,000 deal in December 1972. For the Everton manager it was a last throw of the managerial dice, but in hindsight was to demonstrate once more how his once astute judgement of players had lapsed.

Harper was the archetypal goal-poacher, a great opportunist who was at his best in the six-yard box. The Scottish football journalist Paul Forsyth recorded that he was 'An instinctive player, he believed that the brain was quicker than the feet, that his meaty thighs need only be used to feed on scraps in and around the box. A bit of a chancer, he used to grab defenders by the testicles to gain half a yard, but it worked …'

On his debut against Tottenham, Harper set the tone of his Everton career with a missed penalty. Although he scored in Everton's two subsequent games, it was a tough time for a new player to settle as Catterick's reign flickered to its disappointing conclusion. As Everton languished, too often he would go missing. Harper nevertheless finished the 1972/73 season Everton's top scorer with eight goals.

Harper continued to partner Joe Royle or Mick Lyons in attack following Billy Bingham's arrival as manager in the summer of 1973. But the goals did not come, and the Everton manager concluded he needed a more reliable alternative. In February 1974 he cut Everton's losses, selling Harper to Hibernian for £120,000. Soon after Bingham made Bob Latchford a British transfer record signing.

In Scotland the goals flowed once more, and after returning to Pittodrie in 1976 the striker wrote himself into club lore with his scoring exploits.

> [FACTFILE]
>
> **BORN**
> Greenock, 11 January 1948
> **POSITION**
> Striker
> **OTHER CLUBS**
> Morton (1965–67);
> Huddersfield Town
> (1967–68);
> Morton (1968–69);
> Aberdeen (1969–72);
> Hibernian (1974–76);
> Aberdeen (1976–81)
> **HONOURS**
> 4 Scotland caps (2 goals)
> (1972–78)

Season	League		FA Cup		League Cup		Total	
	App	Goals	App	Goals	App	Goals	App	Goals
1972/73	20	7	2	1	0	0	22	8
1973/74	20 (3)	5	2	1	2	0	24 (3)	6
Total	40 (3)	12	4	2	2	0	46 (3)	14

Harris, Bert

Local goalkeeper who went on to be Tranmere and Southport's long-standing custodian

> [FACTFILE]
>
> **BORN**
> Bootle, 21 November 1931
> **POSITION**
> Goalkeeper
> **OTHER CLUBS**
> Tranmere Rovers (1957–60);
> Southport (1960–65)

Season	League		FA Cup		Total	
	App	Goals	App	Goals	App	Goals
1955/56	5	0	0	0	5	0
Total	5	0	0	0	5	0

Harris, Brian

Fun-loving wing half whose long career traversed the dismal 1950s and Everton's 'golden era'

Perhaps the defining image of Brian Harris came late in the 1966 FA Cup Final. Everton had just scored an improbable equaliser, having earlier trailed Sheffield Wednesday by two goals, and for one exuberant supporter, Eddie Kavanagh, the emotion famously became too much.

EMBARKING on a mazy run across the Wembley turf, he evaded one policeman, who groped forlornly at his empty jacket, before being rugby-tackled by a second, who lost his helmet in the process. As the still ecstatic supporter tried to free himself to embrace Brian Labone, a beaming Harris could be seen in the background, trying on the policemen's helmet for size.

The interlude was a very public exposition of Harris's wicked sense of humour, which even in moments of high drama was never far from the surface. Everton went on to beat Wednesday 3-2, and for Harris the day became the crowning glory of a 20-year career.

Born in Bebington on the Wirral, Harris was an outstanding schoolboy sportsman: an ace cricketer and, as a footballer, an England youth international. Perhaps surprisingly, he evaded the scouting networks of Merseyside's three league clubs until the age of 18 when Everton recruited him from non-league Port Sunlight in January 1954 for £10. The fee was to prove one of the finest bargains in the club's history. Initially a winger, Harris possessed great positional versatility and occupied every outfield position in an Everton career which spanned more than a decade.

While he spent much of his career as a left-sided wing half, the era's tactical shifts saw that position evolve so that he became a forerunner of the modern midfield destroyer. Even in a defensive role, however, the vision honed as schoolboy winger was still occasionally in evidence and a searching through ball would often pick out the run of Alex Young or Roy Vernon.

HARRIS MADE his Everton debut in August 1955, in the midst of a difficult period for the club. The great Dixie Dean and Tommy Lawton-inspired teams of the 1930s were a fading memory and the investment of John Moores, which would transform the club's fortunes in the 1960s, was still to come.

In a team of journeymen, Harris at first struggled to make an impression, but following the appointment of Johnny Carey as manager in October 1958 he flourished. As a player with Matt Busby's Manchester United, Carey had changed position from inside forward to wing half and, perhaps seeing something of himself in the young Harris,

moved him from the Everton flank to a more withdrawn role at wing half. In his new position, occasionally deputising at full back, Harris excelled, and even when the Moores money began to buy up some of British football's best players, the £10 signing kept his place among the 'Mersey Millionaires' – as Everton became known. Indeed, the underrated Harris was central to Everton's transformation from 1950s strugglers to one of the most accomplished English teams of the following decade.

In December 1962, midway through a League Championship winning season, Harry Catterick, who had replaced Carey a year earlier, signed Sheffield Wednesday's wing half Tony Kay in a record transfer deal. Harris, who had performed impressively in the opening half of the season, was harshly dropped.

Rather than demand a transfer, he bided his time in the reserves and his perseverance paid off in April 1964, when Kay was found to have been part of a match-fixing scam, subsequently being jailed and banned for life. Harris returned in Kay's place and went on to provide the best form of his career, culminating in the FA Cup win, where his was a calm head in an afternoon of high drama.

Catterick was a ruthless manager, however, and moved quickly to break up the Cup winning team. Harris was sold to Cardiff City the following October for £15,000, and over five years at Ninian Park his experience contributed hugely to one of Cardiff's most successful periods. In the 1967/68 season, Harris appeared in all of Cardiff's European Cup Winners'

Cup games as they reached the semi-final, losing narrowly over two legs to SV Hamburg.

IN 1971 he dropped down a couple of divisions, playing out his career with Newport County, whom he briefly managed. He returned to Cardiff as assistant manager in the late 1970s, then coached briefly at Bobby Robson's Ipswich Town.

On dropping out of professional football he returned to Wales, settling in Chepstow, where he managed the town's non-League club and ran a canvassing business with his sons. A gregarious, fun-loving character, always popular with team-mates and fans, in his later years Harris was a popular guest at Everton reunion dinners. It was with his first club that his heart lay, and it seemed appropriate that his funeral service in February 2008 was held at St Luke's Church, located at the corner of Goodison Park.

Further reading:
WESTCOTT, CHRIS, *Brian Harris: The Authorised Biography*, Tempus, Stroud, 2003

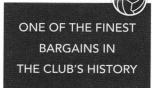

ONE OF THE FINEST BARGAINS IN THE CLUB'S HISTORY

[FACTFILE]

BORN
Bebington, Merseyside,
16 May 1935
DIED
Chepstow, Monmouthshire,
17 February 2008
POSITION
Wing half / midfielder
OTHER CLUBS
Cardiff City (1966–71);
Newport County (1971–74)
HONOURS
1962/63
League Championship,
FA Cup 1966

Season	League		FA Cup		League Cup		Europe		Total	
	App	Goals	App	Goals	App	Goals	App	Goals	App	Goals
1955/56	20	2	4	1	-	-	-	-	24	3
1956/57	3	0	0	0	-	-	-	-	3	0
1957/58	30	6	3	0	-	-	-	-	33	6
1958/59	35	1	4	0	-	-	-	-	39	1
1959/60	32	1	1	0	-	-	-	-	33	1
1960/61	30	3	1	0	5	0	-	-	36	3
1961/62	33	1	3	0	-	-	-	-	36	1
1962/63	24	1	1	1	-	-	2	0	27	2
1963/64	28	3	5	2	-	-	2	0	35	5
1964/65	31	3	1	0	-	-	4	0	36	3
1965/66	40	2	8	0	-	-	4	2	52	4
1966/67	4	0	0	0	-	-	0	0	4	0
Total	**310**	**23**	**31**	**4**	**5**	**0**	**12**	**2**	**358**	**29**

Harris,
Jimmy

Versatile attacker who brought verve to Goodison during lean times

Even more than half a century after Everton's record defeat to Tottenham Hotspur (which is also a record top-flight aggegate scoreline), few can be more perplexed by that strange day in autumn 1958 than Jimmy Harris. The Wirral-born player was a regular across the Everton forward lines of the late 1950s, in one year finishing top scorer, but never would he hit a hat-trick except for the day that Everton also happened to concede ten.

EVEN IF that minor detail overshadowed what should have been his finest hour in a blue shirt, Harris's Everton career was one of distinction, despite the hard times in which he often found himself playing.

Born in the shadow of Tranmere's Prenton Park, Harris signed for Everton after one of his aunts had recommended him for a trial. Not until August 1955 – just past his 22nd birthday – did he make his Everton debut, but his ascent to the first team brought great optimism, to the extent that Dave Hickson – Goodison's talisman – was sold to

Aston Villa partly in order to accommodate the forward.

HARRIS repaid this confidence, scoring 21 League and FA Cup goals in his debut season. Although Everton finished a disappointing 15th, they reached the quarter-finals of the FA Cup. 'We felt we had a good chance of reaching Wembley in 1956,' Harris later recalled. 'We went to Manchester City in the quarter-finals and put on a terrific display in the first half only to be frustrated by Bert Trautmann, their German goalkeeper. I managed to beat him once and it could have been 2-0 only for a terrific save from Eddie Wainwright just before the interval. But our defence fell away after that and we lost 2-1. That was a great disappointment after we'd played so well.'

Harris's outstanding debut season saw him rewarded with England under-23 recognition. With his whippet-like pace, close control and accurate finishing he looked set for more honours, but injuries and loss of form during the 1956/57 season saw him derided as a one-season wonder. However, the return of Hickson, the man he had been slated to replace, in summer 1957 witnessed a return to form.

Moved out to the right wing in order to accommodate the 'Cannonball Kid', Harris established himself as one of the country's deadliest wide men. The goals returned and he finished the 1957/58 season second top scorer with 14 goals – five more than Hickson.

After Hickson's shock departure to Liverpool in 1959, Harris was often asked to deputise as centre forward. Although selected for the Football League representative side in 1960, he found himself increasingly marginalised by the expensive signings brought in with John Moores' millions. With the

arrival of Alex Young in November 1960 and the emergence of Frank Wignall, Harris was deemed surplus by Johnny Carey and a £20,000 bid from Birmingham City in December 1960 was considered too good to turn down.

At St Andrews, Harris helped Birmingham reach the 1961 Inter City Fairs Final and win the 1963 League Cup. He later played for Oldham Athletic and the Dublin side St Patricks before briefly taking up a coaching job with Tranmere Rovers. On leaving football he found a job at the Vauxhall car plant on his native Wirral and remains a regular visitor to Goodison Park.

BORN
Birkenhead, 18 August 1933
POSITION
Centre forward/winger
OTHER CLUBS
Birmingham City (1960–64);
Oldham Athletic (1964–66)

Season	League		FA Cup		League Cup		Total	
	App	Goals	App	Goals	App	Goals	App	Goals
1955/56	40	19	4	2	-	-	44	21
1956/57	13	4	2	1	-	-	15	5
1957/58	41	14	3	1	-	-	44	15
1958/59	42	14	4	1	-	-	46	15
1959/60	36	9	1	0	-	-	37	9
1960/61	19	5	-	-	2	2	21	7
Total	**191**	**65**	**14**	**5**	**2**	**2**	**207**	**72**

HARRIS'S OUTSTANDING DEBUT SEASON SAW HIM REWARDED WITH ENGLAND UNDER-23 RECOGNITION

Harris,
Joe

Rookie winger who struggled to make a first-team shirt his own during Everton's dark days

[FACTFILE]

BORN
Liverpool,
20 December 1926
POSITION
Outside right
OTHER CLUBS
Bangor City

Season	League		FA Cup		Total	
	App	Goals	App	Goals	App	Goals
1950/51	1	0	0	0	1	0
1951/52	0	0	0	0	0	0
1952/53	13	4	0	0	13	4
Total	**14**	**4**	**0**	**0**	**14**	**4**

Harris, Val

Gaelic footballer who served Everton with distinction

Val Harris (Vailintín Ó hEarchaí) represented the first of a strong tradition of top-class Gaelic footballers – which would encompass the likes of Kevin Moran, Niall Quinn and Ronnie Whelan – crossing codes to serve at the highest level of association football. His remarkable playing career would extend into his forties and he later found success as a club and international manager.

Harris was an outstanding teenage Gaelic footballer, winning the All Ireland Championship – the sport's highest accolade – in 1901 with Dublin. As a club player he had also won the Dublin Championship twice with Isles of the Sea before even reaching adulthood. He made the crossover to football with Shelbourne in 1903, still aged only 19, and made his international debut three years later. During this period he also signed for West Bromwich Albion but never actually played a game.

Harris was nominally a right half but fitted in across a range of positions. He was a player, wrote one correspondent, 'neat and clever in every move'. It was this versatility and soundness of technique that made him attractive to the Everton board, who in spring 1908 moved to sign him.

His transfer was, however, complicated by this earlier deal with West Bromwich Albion. The exact details of this are confused, but it seems as though he had signed some form of contract with the Baggies around five years earlier but left without playing a game. Under football's draconian 'retain and transfer' system Albion retained his Football League playing registration and upon hearing of Everton's interest in Harris tried to obtain £150. Everton refused and sought adjudication from the Football League, which found in their favour. Harris's arrival to the Everton half-back line effectively marked the end of Walter Abbott's Everton career. Harris was virtually ever-present as his new club finished his debut season in 1908/09 runners-up, a near-miss which they would repeat three years later.

Everton's back line was the foundation upon which their side was built and made them viable challengers for high honours, and Harris played his part in this. He was a tough player and could handle himself when challenged. He was physically brave too. Reporting on a game versus Manchester City, the Liverpool Mercury correspondent recorded how Harris clashed heads with an opponent 'with considerable violence' and both players withdrew with cut heads. Harris, however, 'was quickly back in the field, but the City went on to play with ten men'.

Besides trophies – to which he came tantalisingly close – Harris's Everton career had everything. Everything, it seemed, but a goal. He broke his duck in spectacular fashion four and a half years into his Everton career in a game against Spurs, a 4-0 thumping on the opening day of the 1912/13 season.

'Val Harris during his five years' useful service with Everton, has never had the satisfaction of scoring a goal,' reported 'Cosmo' in the Liverpool Evening Express. 'He has tried hard, but somehow up to this afternoon ill luck has attended all his efforts. Twenty minutes after the start he scored as brilliant [a] goal as one could wish to see. He had wriggled his way right across to the left wing and then finding himself clear of the opposition he screwed in an oblique shot which entered the goal just under the bar, Iremonger being taken completely unawares. It was a great goal and at length the spell of ill-luck, it is to be hoped, has been broken. The spectators' delight knew no bounds and the cheering and waving of hats continued for several minutes.'

HARRIS was at the height of his powers but quite abruptly his Everton career came to an end. Following the end of the 1913/14 season he became embroiled in a pay dispute with the Everton board, who eventually acceded to his demands. But when they relaid their offer there was a shock in store. 'The Secretary read a letter from Harris in which he intimated that he had signed for Shelbourne,' recorded a board meeting minute. 'The Secretary also reported that he had written to the President of the League on the matter and that owing to some misunderstanding between the English League and the Irish League the arrangement

alleged between the two Leagues had not been ratified.'

Harris's timing was poor and within a year of his departure Everton were champions again. But back in his native Ireland he served Shelbourne with distinction. In 1920 he won the Irish Cup a second time, and a year later was part of the team that were founder members of the League of Ireland. In 1926, aged 41 – the same year he represented the League of Ireland XI – he lifted the League of Ireland Championship.

The following year he turned to coaching with Shelbourne and the Ireland national team. He managed Ireland versus the Netherlands in 1932 and found success with Shelbourne again, winning the FAI Cup in 1939, in which they overcame a Sligo Rovers team that included Dixie Dean.

Almost exactly a century after Harris's arrival at Goodison, the club's link with Gaelic football continued with the signing of Seamus Coleman, who gave up GAA to pursue a career in the association game.

Season	League		FA Cup		Total	
	App	Goals	App	Goals	App	Goals
1907/08	3	0	0	0	3	0*
1908/09	36	0	2	0	38	0
1909/10	31	0	7	0	38	0
1910/11	32	0	3	0	35	0
1911/12	34	0	5	0	39	0
1912/13	28	1	5	1	33	2
1913/14	26	0	1	0	27	0
Total	**190**	**1**	**23**	**1**	**213**	**2**

* Some accounts erroneously attribute an FA Cup appearance to Harris this season from when before he joined Everton

---

[FACTFILE]

BORN
Dublin, 23 June 1884
POSITION
Right half/utility player
OTHER CLUBS
Shelbourne
(1903–08 & 1914–27)
AS MANAGER
Shelbourne, Irish Free State
HONOURS
20 Ireland caps (1906–14)

Harrison, George

Pacey wide man who provided a thrilling partnership with Sam Chedgzoy

George Harrison was a flying winger and set-piece master, who, with Sam Chedgzoy, provided the First Division with its finest wing pairing of their generation. His career straddled both sides of the First World War, but there was no let up in standards during this four-year football hiatus and he earned honours on either side of the conflict.

HIS PACE AND INCISIVENESS ON THE EVERTON FLANK BROUGHT A NEW DIMENSION TO THEIR PLAY

The Derbyshire-born youngster started out with Gresley Rovers and got his break in professional football with Leicester Fosse while still a teenager. He served the Leicester first team for three years but financial difficulties at Filbert Street necessitated his departure in April 1913, when £750 was enough to secure his signature and that of full back Bob Thompson. 'He is exceedingly fast, centres well, and is also a good shot. In the past season he scored six goals (three from penalty kicks),' reported the Liverpool Post and Mercury of his arrival.

INDEED, Everton conducted brisk business over the summer and the Liverpool Courier remarked: 'Without paying any of the fancy prices now demanded for first class footballers, Everton have secured several new men who should prove of good service to the club. This, at least, was the opinion of many of the club supporters who witnessed the first practice game at Goodison Park.' Harrison, they added, was a player who could cross with 'unerring accuracy'.

Of Everton's plethora of new signings Harrison was the one who made the most lasting impact. His pace and incisiveness on the Everton flank brought a new dimension to their play and stretched Everton's opponents to their limit. He was potent from set pieces too, and his fierce shot was a testing weapon in the club's attacking armoury. He was, wrote the

Liverpool Courier, a player who can 'deliver a powerful left-footed drive that can score without the help of the inside forwards'. When Chedgzoy returned to the team for the 1914/15 season they helped propel Everton to the League Championship.

Harrison appeared in the first two years of the wartime leagues before being called up for service. But his partnership with Chedgzoy was one that was resumed for club and country after the four-year break for war. In October 1921 they appeared alongside each other for England in a 1-1 against Ireland in Belfast. 'Chedgzoy was the most brilliant player in the team, and Harrison his club mate was little inferior,' reported the Liverpool Courier. 'Harrison dropped the ball into the goal mouth for [Billy] Kirton to head into the net for the equaliser.'

Speculation around this time linked Harrison with a move to Manchester United. But a 1920s footballer's career was a precarious business. Virtually ever-present through the 1921/22 season, he suddenly found himself out of favour at the start of the following campaign. The signing of Alec Troup effectively spelled the end for him and while there was, wrote one correspondent, 'a certain amount of popular clamour – for the player was always a favourite with the spectators', his departure carried a degree of inevitability.

IN DECEMBER 1923 a £2000 bid from Preston North End was accepted and Harrison left for Deepdale, having collected a £650 benefit. He provided eight years excellent service for the Lilywhites, making nearly 300 league and cup appearances. A brief spell with Blackpool took his playing career almost up to his 40th birthday.

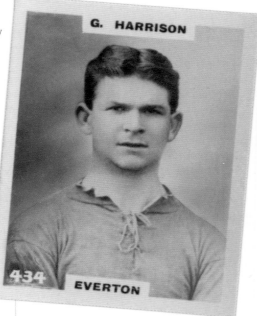

G. HARRISON

434 EVERTON

[FACTFILE]

BORN
Church Gresley, 18 July 1892
POSITION
Outside left
OTHER CLUBS
Leicester Fosse (1911–13);
Preston North End (1923–31);
Blackpool (1931)
HONOURS
1914/15 League Championship,
2 England caps (1921)

Season	League		FA Cup		Total	
	App	Goals	App	Goals	App	Goals
1913/14	35	1	1	0	36	1
1914/15	26	4	4	0	30	4
1919/20	25	0	1	0	26	0
1920/21	38	8	5	0	43	8
1921/22	40	2	1	0	41	2
1922/23	12	2	1	0	13	2
1923/24	1	0	0	0	1	0
Total	**177**	**17**	**13**	**0**	**190**	**17**

Hart, Hunter

Wing half, captain and dedicated servant through eighteen years at Goodison

Wing half Hunter Hart was a colossus for Everton through the 1920s, captaining the team for several years in a career that saw him make more than 300 Everton appearances, lift the League Championship in 1928 and serve the club in a variety of off-the-field roles.

The Glaswegian was a prodigious talent and despite only being born in the last years of the nineteenth century his career traversed both sides of the First World War. Spotted playing junior football by Airdreonians' famous manager John Chapman, he was signed up and thrust into senior football still aged only 15. War intervened, but in his early years he was one of the most highly rated young players in Scotland and many expected him to follow Chapman to England when he left to manage Manchester United in 1921.

It was Everton, however, that were the beneficiaries of his signature in January 1922, the fee £3100. 'English football should agree with Hart, and if he displays the same form at Everton as he did in Scotland, the Scottish selectors will not overlook him when the Internationals come round,' recorded the Liverpool Courier when he signed. Of his debut against Bolton Wanderers a few days later they reported: 'Even under such trying conditions he proved that he is a great footballer, both by his tackling and calculating way in which he pushed the leather up to his forwards. With further understanding of the men in front he should make the base of a scoring triangle.'

Hart was a powerful and tenacious half back, who would – as his career progressed – add some bite to a weak rearguard. He was capable of looking after himself too and sometimes the aggression of his play caused problems. In a match against Bradford six weeks after his arrival he was sent off for attempting to kick an opponent who had irked him. 'The decision seemed to be rather a severe one, as Hart had not hurt Hargreaves in any way, and many were of the opinion that a caution would have met the case. In any case, if one man deserved marching orders, one would imagine that they should have been given to both players,' recorded the Courier. Everton only narrowly avoided relegation in Hart's first season at the club, but his first full campaign – 1922/23 – was rather more promising as Everton finished fifth, with Hart captaining the team. He was to retain the captaincy for five seasons but some suggested it was a burden, not least when Everton again narrowly avoided relegation in 1926/27. When Warney Cresswell succeeded him the following campaign, Ernest 'Bee' Edwards wrote: 'Hart if anything played a better game than usual, thanks to being relieved of the cares of a side that was last season struggling from the first moment to the last kick.'

Having started as a left half, Hart had by then migrated to the centre of the Everton team. He was, wrote one admiring journalist, 'masterly in the centre – a skillful tactician'. The Daily Courier described him as 'the genius of the halves. His ideal place is pivot, although he has played at left-half.' However, the Scottish FA's preference for native-based players meant he was never picked to represent his country.

With Cresswell ascendant as captain and Hart thriving in the heart of the team, Everton – inspired by Dixie's 60 – romped to the League Championship in 1927/28. But their form was mystifyingly inconsistent. A year later they finished 18th and in 1929/30 succumbed

to the humiliation of relegation for the first time. Hart's season was ended in January after a 4-1 hammering at Blackburn and he never regained his place. He was to remain at Goodison for a further decade as a Central League player at a time when reserve attendances regularly reached five figures, and subsequently as reserve team manager, scout and member of the club administration.

His two decades at Goodison seem to have come to an ignominious end in November 1939. Everton's arch-machiavellian secretary Theo Kelly reported to the board bookkeeping discrepancies totalling £34. Hart and another employee were called in for questioning. 'The Sec'y. had interviewed Mr. Hart regarding these shortages & that Mr. Hart had declared himself responsible for two shortages, namely, the Petty Cash (£10.6.7) & Programme Petty Cash (£12.8.6),' reported a board minute. 'In reply, Mr. Hart agreed that he was responsible for those two accounts, but while he could not explain the full shortage, he stated that he had taken £7 (Seven pounds) from the Programme Petty Cash account, which he had not replaced.'

Hart had regularly reported to the Everton board on player matters, but his name disappears from board minutes thereafter. The incident appears to have marked the end of Hart's long and multifaceted association with the club; a sad end to a great and dedicated servant and an exit which – given Kelly's role in ousting the likes of Dean, Joe Mercer and T.G. Jones – may have even been devoid of wrongdoing.

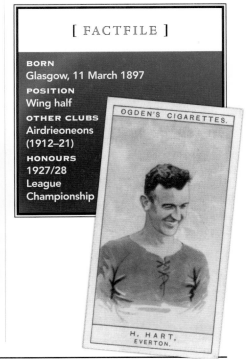

Season	League		FA Cup		League Cup		Total	
	App	Goals	App	Goals	App	Goals	App	Goals
1921/22	17	0	0	0	-	-	17	0
1922/23	40	1	2	0	-	-	42	1
1923/24	42	2	1	0	-	-	43	2
1924/25	24	0	0	0	-	-	24	0
1925/26	26	0	0	0	-	-	26	0
1926/27	39	1	3	0	-	-	42	1
1927/28	41	1	2	0	-	-	43	1
1928/29	40	0	1	0	1	0	41	0
1929/30	20	0	2	0	-	-	22	0
Total	**289**	**5**	**11**	**0**	**1**	**0**	**301**	**5**

Hartford, Richard 'Asa'

Gifted Scotland international midfielder unable to elevate Everton beyond mediocrity

Asa Hartford was meant to form the creative centrepiece of Gordon Lee's Everton team in the 1979/80 season, a side seeking to build on fourth and third-placed finishes. The sort of stylish midfield dynamo who would not have looked out of place in any of Everton's great post-war teams, the shortcomings and inexperience of his team-mates meant he was ultimately unable to lift the club beyond mediocrity.

Hartford had started out as a young midfielder with West Bromwich Albion in the late 1960s, garnering a reputation as one of English football's most exciting young talents. A transfer to Don Revie's Leeds United in 1971 fell through after a cardiac scan revealed a 'hole in his heart', and although it never otherwise undermined his career the whisperings about his health never quite went away. He made his Scotland debut in 1972 and was an international regular for much of the next decade, playing at the World Cups in Argentina in 1978 and Spain four years later. In 1974 he joined Manchester City, where his reputation grew.

In the summer of 1979, City made Hartford available for transfer, and Lee saw him as a direct replacement for Martin Dobson, whom he had recently sold to Burnley. He was involved in a transfer tussle with Brian Clough's Nottingham Forest, and Hartford eventually plumped for the European Champions over Everton. However, within weeks of signing for Forest he fell out with Clough, who transfer-listed him, and Lee finally got his man for a club record fee of £500,000.

A SKILFUL, industrious midfielder, who shared many of the characteristics of an old-style inside forward, Hartford was the sort of stylish midfielder that Evertonians instinctively took to their hearts. He formed a new-look midfield with Garry Stanley, but it was the Scot who impressed, despite Everton's poor form. Everton flirted with relegation,

finishing the 1979/80 season 19th, but Hartford was voted the club's player of the year.

HARTFORD remained modest about his contribution that year. 'I did not play as well as I had done in my last season with Manchester City, but I was quite happy with my form from Christmas onwards,' he told the Everton matchday programme at the start of the 1980/81 season. 'It's never easy for players to adjust to a new team. Some seem to be lucky in that they can move and settle straight away but for some it never works at all. I was somewhere in the middle of two extremes and now I'm looking forward to a more consistent season, both for myself and my club.'

Certainly he started the 1980/81 season well and was one of the main driving forces behind Everton's good start. By October Everton were third, with the top of the table in sight.

But his more inexperienced and less talented team-mates could not sustain the momentum and in the final seven months of the season Everton recorded just six league wins.

GORDON LEE exonerated the midfielder of any blame in another disappointing campaign. He used his programme notes for the last home game of the season to write: 'I don't think Asa has played better than at any time of his career.' It wasn't enough to save Lee's job, however, and that was the final time Goodison saw him as Everton manager. After finishing 1980/81 15th he was sacked and replaced by Howard Kendall.

Hartford initially survived the swingeing cuts of the new regime, but in October 1981 Manchester City bid £350,000 for their former star and Kendall decided to accept and invest the much-needed funds in creating his own vision for Everton. Hartford continued to play at Maine Road until 1984, before embarking on a tour of the lower leagues. He finished up as Shrewsbury Town player-manager in 1989, where he briefly lined up alongside David Moyes.

[FACTFILE]

BORN
Clydebank, 24 October, 1950

POSITION
Midfield

OTHER CLUBS
West Bromwich Albion (1967–74);
Manchester City (1974–79);
Nottingham Forest (1979);
Manchester City (1981–84);
Fort Lauderdale Sun (1984);
Norwich City (1984–85);
Bolton Wanderers (1985–87);
Stockport County
(as player-manager, 1987–89);
Oldham Athletic (1989);
Shrewsbury Town
(as player-manager, 1989–91)

HONOURS
50 Scotland caps (5 goals) (1972–82)

Season	League		FA Cup		League Cup		Europe		Total	
	App	Goals	App	Goals	App	Goals	App	Goals	App	Goals
1979/80	35	1	5	1	3	0	0	0	43	2
1980/81	39	5	6	0	3	0	-	-	48	5
1981/82	7	0	0	0	0	0	-	-	7	0
Total	81	6	11	1	6	0	0	0	98	7

Hartill, Billy

Wolves goal machine who failed to make the grade on either side of the Mersey divide

BILLY HARTILL
EVERTON

[FACTFILE]

BORN
Wolverhampton, 18 July 1905
DIED
1980
POSITION
Centre forward
OTHER CLUBS
Wolverhampton Wanderers
(1928–35); Liverpool (1935);
Bristol Rovers (1935–37)

Season	League		FA Cup		Total	
	App	Goals	App	Goals	App	Goals
1935/36	5	1	0	0	5	1
Total	**5**	**1**	**0**	**0**	**5**	**1**

Hartley, Abraham

Prolific Scottish forward who crossed Stanley Park

Season	League		FA Cup		Total	
	App	Goals	App	Goals	App	Goals
1892/93	1	1	0	0	1	1
1893/94	6	2	1	0	7	2
1894/95	11	5	4	1	15	6
1895/96	15	7	1	0	16	7
1896/97	14	6	5	3	19	9
1897/98	3	3	0	0	3	3
Total	**50**	**24**	**11**	**4**	**61**	**28**

[FACTFILE]

BORN
Dumbarton, 8 February 1872
DIED
Southampton, 9 October 1909
POSITION
Centre forward
OTHER CLUBS
Dumbarton (1890–93);
Liverpool (1897–98);
Southampton (1898–99);
Woolwich Arsenal (1899);
Burnley (1899–1900)

Harvey, Colin

Member of the Holy Trinity whose Everton career spanned five decades

It is something of an Everton tradition for talented youngsters to be given a baptism of fire. In 1984 Howard Kendall gave Paul Bracewell his Everton debut in front of 100,000 at Wembley in the Charity Shield against Liverpool. A decade later, Francis Jeffers, Michael Branch and Jonathan O'Connor were blooded in front of 55,000-strong Old Trafford crowds. And yet this is nothing compared to Colin Harvey's first senior game for Everton.

IN SEPTEMBER 1963, Harvey, an untried 18-year-old reserve ('who fans of the club have scarcely heard of', noted the Liverpool Echo), travelled with the Everton team for a European Cup tie with Internazionale. The youngster thought he was there merely to carry his colleagues' bags, but no one was more surprised than Harvey himself when he was included in place of the injured Jimmy Gabriel. Having played before no more than a few thousand in the Central League, Harvey was pitched in front of 80,000 passionate Italians in the San Siro, one of European football's great arenas. Harvey seemed unperturbed by the tumultuous atmosphere and the Liverpool Echo reported that he could 'look back on his first senior game with some pride since he fought hard, played at times with a veteran coolness and could have been a scorer'.

It took those Evertonians unable to travel to the San Siro another six months before they saw Harvey pull on a first-team shirt, when he made his league debut in a 2-1 win at Blackburn. But within little over a year of that memorable night in Italy, the inside forward had established himself in the first team.

An Evertonian since childhood, Harvey had stood in the Boys' Pen through the dark days of the 1950s. A supremely fit and dedicated trainer, Harvey had all the attributes that came to define the modern midfielder: speed, close control, an impeccable first touch, stamina. He would be renowned for his lung-busting surges from box to box, but it was his imaginative and supremely accurate distribution that brought him renown as 'the white Pele'. 'Colin was a very dedicated, hard-working individual who got to the top because he was prepared to do that little bit extra,' Terry Darracott recalled. 'He would always put in that extra half-hour after training, no matter what he had done in the morning.'

ALEX YOUNG later said that it was this dedication that was the difference between Harvey cutting it at the highest level and ending up in a backwater, like Southport, as many of Everton's young players did. He bulked up, said Young, and gained an extra yard of pace. 'He matured into a buzz-bomb of a footballer – an expert at precise and imaginative passing,' he recalled. 'Play and run, play and run – that was Colin. He was unselfish, recklessly brave and incredibly skilful.'

Although he was never a prolific goalscorer, Harvey had a knack of scoring important goals. His first in an Everton shirt came in the 4-0 win over Liverpool in September 1964. 'The ball came to me on the edge of the box,' Harvey later recalled. 'I chested it and as it bounced I just lobbed it into the top corner.'

> IT WAS HIS IMAGINATIVE AND SUPREMELY ACCURATE DISTRIBUTION THAT BROUGHT HIM RENOWN AS 'THE WHITE PELE'

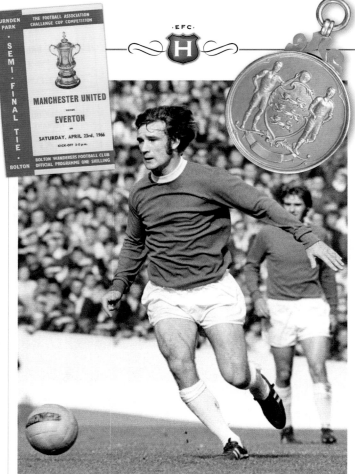

And yet, perhaps surprisingly, some Evertonians did not immediately take to him. Despite the obvious poise and elegance he brought to the team, in the early stages of his career – derby goal notwithstanding – he was rash in front of goal and fluffed chances. Catterick persevered with the youngster, lessening his attacking responsibilities. Eventually he would wear the number six shirt, but his experience reflected the positional transition of football at this time: from inside forward to wing half to something resembling a modern midfielder by the late 1960s.

By the age of 21, Harvey was one of the most important members of the team, and was virtually ever-present through the 1965/66 season. His crucial intervention that year came in the FA Cup semi-final against Manchester United at Burnden Park. In a tight, nervous encounter, his bobbling shot 12 minutes from the end was enough to separate the two teams. 'It was every supporter's dream to score the

goal that puts you through to the final,' he would recall. Three weeks later, he was part of the team that beat Sheffield Wednesday 3-2 at Wembley.

Harvey's ascent to greatness would be completed over the following season with the additions of Alan Ball and Howard Kendall to the Everton midfield. 'They were both different types of players but were outstanding in their own right,' said Harvey. 'Alan would chip in with some tremendous goals, while Howard was a great tackler. He had a special talent at passing the ball.' Through the latter part of the 1960s they emerged as one of the finest midfield triumvirates football has ever seen.

Harvey was already an England under-23 international when he was called up to England's 1969 tour of South America. Full international recognition would not come for a further two years, when he won a solitary cap against Malta.

During the 1969/70 season Harvey's career was put in real jeopardy when he lost the sight of his right eye following an infection. Specialist treatment and a complete break from football for two months followed and by mid-January, to the relief of the fans, he returned to the first team. His comeback was completed with the goal against West Bromwich Albion that secured Everton's seventh League Championship on 1 April. Few titles have ever been secured with such spectacular efforts and the strike has gone down in the annals of club history as one of the greatest goals Goodison has witnessed. 'First he moved towards goal, changed his mind and veered out, as though to bring Morrissey into play,' Horace Yates recorded in the Daily Post. 'Seeing Morrissey was covered he doubled back to the edge of the penalty area and while on the run sent a crashing drive soaring into the net with Osborne leaping spectacularly, but vainly across goal.'

With Harvey, Kendall and Ball still all only in their mid-twenties, many expected the revered trio to inspire Everton to further successes through the 1970s. They played more games together through the 1970/71 season than they had the previous year, but success was elusive. From 1971 injury started to haunt Harvey. Through the 1971/72 season he started just 17 league games, 24 the next campaign and just 15 in 1973/74. By now Billy Bingham was manager and, seeking to build on his own vision for the club, in September made Martin Dobson the most expensive midfielder in British football. Harvey was sold to Sheffield Wednesday for £70,000 in order to fund the deal.

In 2003, he told Bluekipper.com: 'I cried when I went out of the gate, I'll be honest with you – I thought it was the end. I thought the next time I come back it would be to watch a game. Billy Bingham was manager at the time, and I just

didn't seem to fit in with his plans. I was having trouble with my hip and the two seasons before I left I was missing training sessions and a few games... Because I wasn't training as hard my form had dipped and Billy Bingham had just bought Martin Dobson who was a good player and I wasn't getting a game. I don't care what you say, if you're a footballer, all you want to do is play football on a Saturday afternoon. That was the combination of things, and I just made a quick decision to move. The hip caused great difficulty over the next two years at Sheffield Wednesday, I used to train on a Friday, play on a Saturday then rest until the following Friday and Saturday. It became obvious at that time to call it a day from playing.'

But in 1976, after retiring, Harvey returned to Goodison as part of Bingham's coaching staff. He trained Everton's youngsters and oversaw the development of the likes of Gary Stevens, Kevin Ratcliffe and Kevin Richardson. In 1981 he was reunited with Kendall, who first made him reserve team manager, then in 1983 his assistant.

The switch coincided with a remarkable upturn in form. Goodison had been plagued with depression through the first stages of the 1983/84 season, with supporter-led campaigns calling for Kendall's sacking, but by the season's end the team had risen up the league and won the FA Cup. A glut of further honours awaited.

'Howard's strength was that he was very shrewd in judging a player I brought to him,' Harvey told Bluekipper. 'I was very passionate when it came to the training side of things, and was very passionate about video work as well. It was Howard who pulled it all together. It was certainly a great time to be at the club and for everyone connected with the club.'

Two league titles followed and when, in June 1987, Kendall left for Athletic Bilbao, Harvey was the natural successor. 'Everyone at the club, and I really mean everyone, had the utmost respect for Colin,' recalled Graeme Sharp. 'Although he had no top level management experience, he did seem to be the logical choice because he'd had such an influence on the success we'd enjoyed under Howard.'

In keeping with this sense of continuity, there was little change to the Everton team through the 1987/88 season. But when Everton finished a distant fourth to record-breaking champions Liverpool, there was a feeling at the season's end that the squad needed reconstruction.

In the summer of 1988 Harvey invested heavily on reinforcements, spending nearly £5million on Pat Nevin, Neil McDonald, Stuart McCall and Tony Cottee – the latter a British transfer record signing. After a positive start to

As a Player										
	League		FA Cup		League Cup		Europe		Total	
Season	App	Goals	App	Goals	App	Goals	App	Goals	App	Goals
1963/64	2	0	0	0	-	-	1	0	3	0
1964/65	32	2	4	1	-	-	4	2	40	5
1965/66	40	1	8	1	-	-	4	0	52	2
1966/67	42	1	6	0	-	-	4	0	52	1
1967/68	34	0	4	0	2	0	-	-	40	0
1968/69	36	4	4	0	4	0	-	-	44	4
1969/70	35	3	0	0	3	0	-	-	38	3
1970/71	36	2	5	1	0	0	6	0	47	3
1971/72	17	3	3	1	0	0	-	-	20	4
1972/73	24 (2)	0	0	0	1	0	-	-	25 (2)	0
1973/74	15 (1)	1	0	0	0 (1)	0	-	-	15 (2)	1
1974/75	4	1	0	0	0	0	-	-	4	1
Total	317 (3)	18	34	4	10 (1)	0	19	2	380 (4)	24

As a Manager										
Season	P	W	L	D	F	A	Pts	Position	FA Cup	League Cup
1987/88	40	19	8	13	53	27	70	4th	5th Round	Semi-Final
1988/89	38	14	12	12	50	45	54	8th	Runner-Up	4th R
1989/90	38	17	13	8	57	46	59	6th	5th Round	4th R
1990/91*	38	13	13	12	50	46	51	9th	QF	3rd R

* Harvey sacked 1 November 1990 with Everton in 18th place

the 1988/89 season, Everton's form fell apart. The new signings struggled with form and injuries, and there was talk of dressing room rifts between the new boys and the older generation of title-winning stars that seemed to permeate on the pitch. Everton finished eighth, a position that was flattered by their late-season form, also reaching the FA Cup Final, which was lost to Liverpool.

By the start of the 1989/90 season, such mid-80s stalwarts as Gary Stevens, Pat Van Den Hauwe, Trevor Steven, Peter Reid, Adrian Heath and Paul Bracewell had moved on. Harvey invested heavily again, signing Mike Newell, Norman Whiteside, Martin Keown and Stefan Rehn during the summer of 1989. Each, in their way, was an astute signing, but with the exception of the formidable Whiteside Harvey derived little benefit from them: Newell had his best years at Blackburn, Keown at Arsenal, and Rehn, whose time at Goodison was farcical, in Sweden. Everton started the new season well, and neared the top by November. But a 6-2 hammering at Aston Villa saw confidence ebb away and the dressing room splits became public. A team-building night out in a Chinese restaurant ended up in a well-publicised brawl between Keown and Kevin Sheedy. Everton showed signs of progress, but only finished the season sixth after winning just one of their last five games. But discontent was the prevailing mood within the club and on the terraces.

In the summer of 1990 Harvey signed just two players – Manchester City's left back Andy Hinchcliffe, and Oldham's promising midfielder Mike Milligan. But it would take more than four years for Goodison to see the best of the former, while Milligan was an acquisition doomed to failure. Harvey managed to hold on to Neville Southall who, in his unhappiness at the new order, had requested a transfer, but on the opening day of the 1990/91 season staged a one-man sit-down protest.

By the start of November, a disjointed Everton team had won just a single league game and sat in 18th place A 2-1 League Cup defeat to Sheffield United proved the final straw, and Harvey was sacked. One newspaper likened his departure to the death of a terminally ill friend: 'The sense of loss at the demise of a manager they idolised as a player and respected as a person was tempered by acceptance that the departure was the only way to end the suffering.'

Years later, Harvey was candid about the responsibility for his failings. 'I'm a believer that your fate is in your own hands,' he said. 'If players don't play as well as they should do, or they don't turn out as you thought they were going to, that's your fault, isn't it? I'm a great believer in that you are responsible for everything that you did yourself so if we didn't win anything, I was the only one to blame.' There was acknowledgement, too, that being Everton manager was 'probably the most frustrating time of my career'. He added: 'Every other period during my Everton career we had always won things, I've always been involved with winning teams. I wasn't then – even though we finished fourth, eighth, sixth and we got to the final of the FA Cup, the final of the Simod Cup, the semi-final of the Worthington [sic.] Cup. I really didn't enjoy being manager... I have got to consider that time as a failure due to the simple fact that we didn't win anything.'

After more than 25 years with the club, it looked like a sad ending for Harvey. But just days later he was reunited with Kendall, returning as his assistant manager. It was a move welcomed by many Evertonians, but the magic did not return. Following Kendall's resignation in December 1993, and Mike Walker's arrival a month later, Harvey left the club.

In November 1994 Harvey joined Oldham as assistant manager to Graeme Sharp. But the duo's time at Boundary Park ended in disappointment and Harvey left with Sharp in March 1997.

Four months later, Harvey returned to Everton, where he was reunited with Kendall yet again, this time as director of youth coaching. It was a similar position to that which he held in the late 1970s and was similarly productive. Within a year of his return to Goodison he again sampled success when he managed the youth team to victory in the FA Youth Cup Final with what he described as 'the best footballing side I have ever worked with'. Included in that crop of outstanding youngsters were Francis Jeffers, Richard Dunne, Danny Cadamarteri, Leon Osman and Tony Hibbert.

A few years later Harvey would be credited with the emergence of Wayne Rooney through Everton's youth set-up: it was Harvey who had first played Rooney in an Everton shirt, picking him for the under-19s, when he was aged just 14.

Rooney's emergence during the 2002/03 season would be Harvey's final achievement at Everton. At the end of that campaign he announced his retirement from football on account of a long-standing hip ailment dating back to his playing days. At the end of the season he was awarded a testimonial against Bologna, only the 11th former player to be given such an accolade. But in November 2007, Harvey came out of retirement when he was appointed Bolton Wanderers chief scout by Gary Megson, an early 1980s Goodison protégé of his.

It was heartening that someone who lived and breathed football still had something to offer the game in these veteran years.

> 'I CRIED WHEN I WENT OUT OF THE GATE, I'LL BE HONEST WITH YOU – I THOUGHT IT WAS THE END'
>
> **ON LEAVING FOR SHEFFIELD WEDNESDAY IN 1974**

But despite this new start, there was sense that Harvey's heart would always be at Goodison; for in his various guises he had spent almost his entire adult life at Everton, and was a man for whom, in the words of Tony Cottee, the club was his 'whole life'. Asked on the eve of his testimonial how he would best like to be remembered, Harvey answered simply: 'To have played for Everton and been an Evertonian myself.'

[FACTFILE]

BORN
Liverpool,
16 November 1944

POSITION
Midfield

OTHER CLUB
Sheffield Wednesday
(1974–76)

HONOURS
1966 FA Cup;
1969/70
League Championship;
1 England cap (1970)

Haughey, William

Inside forward signed from Lakhall Thistle who failed to make the step up from Scottish junior football

Season	League		FA Cup		Total	
	App	Goals	App	Goals	App	Goals
1956/57	3	1	0	0	3	1
1957/58	1	0	0	0	1	0
Total	**4**	**1**	**0**	**0**	**4**	**1**

[FACTFILE]

BORN
Falkirk, 20 December 1932
POSITION
Inside forward
OTHER CLUBS
Falkirk (1958–59);
St Johnstone (1959–60);
Stirling Albion (1960–61);
Albion Rovers (1961–62)

Heard, Pat

Versatile home-grown defender-cum-midfielder who forged a solid career beyond Goodison

Season	League		FA Cup		League Cup		Europe		Total	
	App	Goals	App	Goals	App	Goals	App	Goals	App	Goals
1978/79	9 (1)	0	0	0	0	0	0	0	9 (1)	0
1979/80	1	0	0	0	0	0	0	0	1	0
Total	**10 (1)**	**0**	**0**	**0**	**0**	**0**	**0**	**0**	**10 (1)**	**0**

[FACTFILE]

BORN
Hull, 17 March 1960
POSITION
Midfield / left back
OTHER CLUBS
Aston Villa (1979–83);
Sheffield Wednesday (1983–84);
Newcastle United (1984–85);
Middlesbrough (1985–86);
Hull City (1986–88);
Rotherham United (1988–90);
Cardiff City (1990–92);
Hull City (1992–93)

Heath, Adrian

Diminutive forward whose goals were central to Everton's 1980s revival

When, in January 1982, Everton signed a striker just shy of his 21st birthday for a club record fee of £700,000, many supporters expected Adrian Heath to immediately turn around the ailing club's fortunes. Such weighty expectations were almost impossible for the diminutive youngster, invariably dubbed 'Inchy', to realise. But almost exactly two years after his arrival Heath was to score the goal that would lift Everton, after years of mediocrity, to greatness.

Signed as a teenager by his local club, Stoke City, Heath first appeared as an 18-year-old alongside Howard Kendall, then in the veteran stage of his playing career. For the next two decades, the two men's careers would be closely linked. Indeed Kendall paid close attention to Heath even at such an early stage in his career. When, after becoming Everton manager in 1981, a club record attempt to buy West Bromwich Albion's Bryan Robson failed in autumn 1981, Kendall instead spent his transfer pot on the youngster.

HEATH MADE HIS DEBUT against Southampton and spent much of the remainder of the season flitting between a midfield and attacking role, scoring six times in 22 appearances, but failing to significantly impress sections of the expectant Goodison faithful. Eventually he found a niche for himself alongside Graeme Sharp, scoring ten times during the 1982/83 season.

But it was during the 1983/84 season that Heath really came into his own, finishing top scorer. Two of those goals, in particular, still stand out – even years later.

On 18 January 1984 Everton met Oxford United at the Manor Ground in a League Cup tie. The game came on the back of a disastrous run that had seen Everton win just one game in the previous seven and score only fourteen times in the first five months of the season. Kendall was under increasing pressure from the supporters, dissatisfied with a series of bad buys and form. The pitch that day was covered in frost, ideal for minnows looking for a scalp. When Bobby McDonald gave Oxford an early

lead it looked as though Everton's cup aspirations – and perhaps Kendall's managerial career – were coming to an end.

The pivotal moment came nine minutes from full time. Andy Gray, who was cup-tied, remembered it vividly: 'We were sitting on the bench and there's nothing we can do and nothing that Howard could do. Then Kevin Brock, God bless him, made a fatal error in judgement in trying a back pass which little Inchy read brilliantly.' Heath took the ball around the goalkeeper and, from a narrow angle, slotted home the equaliser. Everton and Kendall were saved.

HEATH'S SECOND vital goal came at Highbury in April, against Southampton in the FA Cup semi-final. Deep into extra time, the game was deadlocked at 0-0 when Graeme Sharp flicked on Peter Reid's free kick and Heath stole in to score the only goal of the game and send Everton to Wembley. A month later Heath pocketed his first ever medal after a 2-0 FA Cup Final victory over Watford.

These crucial goals inspired the best form of Heath's career and he started the 1984/85 season in mesmerising fashion: 11 goals in the first 15 league games and further strikes in the League Cup and European Cup Winners' Cup leading to talk of an England call-up. Before this could happen fate cruelly conspired against Heath: a late tackle by Sheffield

Wednesday's Brian Marwood in a league match at the start of December caused a serious knee injury. Heath missed the remainder of the season, including the FA Cup and European Cup Winners' Cup finals. Yet his early season contribution ultimately proved vital towards Everton's eventual league title triumph.

Heath returned for the 1985/86 season, but found his chances limited by the arrival of Gary Lineker. But the England forward's departure to Barcelona in July 1986 gave Heath a path back into the Everton team. Through the 1986/87 season he missed just one league game and his 11 goals again proved a valuable contribution to Everton's second Championship in three years.

IN OCTOBER 1988, following the British record signing of Tony Cottee, Heath was sold to Barcelona's second club, Espanyol.

After 12 months he returned to England with Aston Villa, but played just nine games before being reunited with Howard Kendall, now manager of Manchester City.

The joke at the time at Maine Road was that City were to change their kit from sky blue to royal blue, for Heath joined not just Kendall, but an entire contingent of former Everton players: Neil Pointon, Gary Megson, Alan Harper, Peter Reid, Mark Ward and Wayne Clarke. It was perhaps fitting that when Everton and City met in September 1990 it was Heath who scored the winner against his old club.

In 1991 Heath returned for a brief spell at Stoke City, before joining Burnley. In 1995 he was reunited with Kendall yet again, this time as a player-coach at Sheffield United, where Kendall was in charge. He left the following spring

IT WAS DURING THE 1983/84 SEASON THAT HEATH REALLY CAME INTO HIS OWN, FINISHING TOP SCORER

to take over as player-manager at Burnley, a position he held for 15 months, before the call came from Kendall once more. This time he was appointed Everton assistant manager for Kendall's ill-fated third spell in charge.

After Kendall's dismissal, Heath returned to Sheffield United for a brief spell as manager in 1999. He later hooked up with his old team-mate, Peter Reid, working in his backroom staff at Sunderland, Leeds United and Coventry City, where he was twice caretaker manager. In February 2008, Heath was appointed manager of the newly inaugurated American club, Austin Aztex, subsequently moving with the franchise when it relocated to Orlando and was rebranded Orlando City S.C.

[FACTFILE]

BORN
Newcastle-under-Lyme,
11 January 1961
POSITION
Midfield / forward
OTHER CLUBS
Stoke City (1979–82);
Espanyol (1988–89);
Aston Villa (1989–90);
Manchester City (1990–92);
Stoke City (1992);
Burnley (1992–95);
Sheffield United (1995–96);
Burnley
(player-manager, 1996–97)
HONOURS
1984 FA Cup,
1984/85 League
Championship,
1986/87 League
Championship

Season	League		FA Cup		League Cup		Other		Total	
	App	Goals	App	Goals	App	Goals	App	Goals	App	Goals
1981/82	22	6	0	0	0	0	-	-	22	6
1982/83	37 (1)	10	5	1	4	0	-	-	46 (1)	11
1983/84	36	12	7	2	11	4	-	-	54	18
1984/85	17	11	0	0	4	1	5	1	26	13
1985/86	24 (12)	10	2 (4)	2	3	1	3 (2)	2	32(18)	15
1986/87	41	11	3	0	4	3	4	2	52	16
1987/88	23 (6)	9	7 (1)	1	5 (2)	2	3	1	38 (9)	13
1988/89	6 (1)	2	0	0	2	0	0 (1)	-	8 (2)	2
Total	**206 (20)**	**71**	**24 (5)**	**6**	**33 (2)**	**11**	**15 (3)**	**6**	**278(30)**	**89**

EVERTON FOOTBALL CLUB 1948-49

LEFT TO RIGHT - BACK ROW :- STEVENSON, LINDLEY, SAUNDERS, SAGAR, HEDLEY, FARRELL, T.COOK (Trainer).
FRONT ROW :- CORR, BENTHAM, CATTERICK, FIELDING, EGLINGTON, JONES.

Hedley, Jack

Full back who tried to make his fortune in South America

IN THE SUMMER of 1950 a contingent of prominent First Division footballers fed up playing in front of crowds of 60,000 or more, but getting a maximum weekly wage of just £10, turned their backs on English football to try their luck in cash-rich Colombia. Lured by promises of vast signing-on fees and £130 weekly pay packets the group, led by the Stoke and England centre back Neil Franklin and Manchester United winger Charlie Mitten, rocked English football. Among their number were the Everton centre forward Billy Higgins and his team-mate, full back Jack Hedley.

While some, notably Mitten, stayed in South America and made relative fortunes, Hedley's stay was brief. He returned to Goodison in time for the 1950/51 season, but such was the stink caused in football's conservative corridors of power that Everton wanted nothing more to do with the player. Almost immediately they accepted a £10,375 bid from Sunderland and the 26-year-old returned to his native Northeast.

HEDLEY WAS a £500 signing from North Shields in January 1945. When the war ended he was slow to make an impression in the first team, making intermittent appearances in place of the regular full backs but never making a first-team shirt his own. His best run came in the second half of the 1949/50 season, when he replaced Gordon Dugdale as left back and played through Everton's FA Cup run that led them to a semi-final defeat to Liverpool.

EVERTON 1948/49
*Back - **Stevenson, Lindley, Saunders, Sagar, Hedley, Farrell, Cook** (Trainer)*
*Front - **Corr, Bentham, Catterick, Fielding, Eglington, Jones***

Then came his involvement with the 'Bogota Bandits' and the move to Sunderland, where he had the most successful period of his career, making nearly 300 appearances. A move to Gateshead in 1959 was less happy, as the club dropped out of the Football League a year after his arrival.

Season	League		FA Cup		Total	
	App	Goals	App	Goals	App	Goals
1947/48	13	0	0	0	13	0
1948/49	23	0	2	0	25	0
1949/50	18	0	5	0	23	0
Total	**54**	**0**	**7**	**0**	**61**	**0**

[FACTFILE]

BORN
Willington Quay,
11 December 1923
DIED
1985
POSITION
Full back
OTHER CLUBS
Sunderland (1950–59);
Gateshead (1959–60)

Heitinga, Johnny

Outstanding Dutch international defender

In July 2010 the Dutch international defender Johnny Heitinga followed Ray Wilson into the record books as only the second serving Everton player to appear in a World Cup Final. But while Wilson's day was one of the defining moments of his life, Heitinga's proved something of a nightmare. In a feisty, unpleasant encounter with Spain, 14 yellow cards were handed out; nine of these went to the Netherlands, two of which went to Heitinga. Seven minutes after his extra-time dismissal Andrés Iniesta scored the only goal of the match and the Dutch were doomed.

Heitinga was a £6.2million signing for Everton from Atlético Madrid the previous August. A former Dutch Footballer of the Year and product of the famed Ajax youth academy, the 25-year-old arrived at Goodison with considerable experience for both club and country and had already appeared in three major tournaments. Shortly after signing for Everton Heitinga made his 50th international appearance. He possessed the versatility to play in central midfield, at right back and centre half, although Moyes initially said that he saw his long-term prospects in central midfield.

A powerful defensive player, with excellent distribution over short and long distances, Heitinga overcame a shaky start to his Everton career to forge an

excellent central defensive partnership with Sylvain Distin. Indeed, after playing at both right back and in central midfield it was in the centre of the Everton defence that he looked most accomplished.

'This team makes you so welcome, and works so hard to help you,' Heitinga told the Daily Mirror four months after his arrival. 'I've been one of the team from the start, and if you have the feeling people are happy you're here, that helps and makes you play better.'

Doubts about his pedigree were soon overcome and he emerged as one of the most popular members of the Everton squad. With a snarl of his

teeth and pump of his fists, Heitinga knew how to lift the Goodison crowd. His form through the 2011/12 was imperious and he deservedly collected the club's Player of the Year Award. Many talk of him as a future Everton captain.

'It's always good if the fans like you, but you know how football is. One day you're a hero, the next you're not. So every game I play I give 100 per cent,' he said after collecting his Player of the Year award.

'When I came over from Atlético Madrid, the manager told me a lot of stories about Everton. After my first training session, the feeling was really good and now after three seasons here, I'm still really happy at Everton. I love playing for Everton and it feels like family.'

'I'M STILL REALLY HAPPY AT EVERTON. I LOVE PLAYING FOR EVERTON AND IT FEELS LIKE FAMILY'

[FACTFILE]

BORN
Alphen aan den Rijn, Netherlands,
15 November 1983
POSITION
Centre back / right back / defensive midfielder
OTHER CLUBS
Ajax Amsterdam (2001–08); Atlético Madrid (2008–09)
HONOURS
80 Netherland caps (7 goals) (2004–);
Dutch Footballer of the Year (Voetballer van het Jaar) (2008)

Season	League		FA Cup		League Cup		Europe		Total	
	App	Goals	App	Goals	App	Goals	App	Goals	App	Goals
2009/10	29 (2)	0	2	0	2	0	0	0	33 (2)	0
2010/11	23 (4)	1	2 (1)	0	1	0	-	-	26 (5)	1
2011/12	29 (1)	1	6	1	3	0	-	-	38 (1)	2
Total	81 (7)	2	10 (1)	1	6	0	0	0	97 (8)	3

Henderson,
Bill

Defender who enjoyed a successful career in the Southern League

[FACTFILE]

BORN
Broxburn, 30 November 1878
POSITION
Full back
OTHER CLUBS
Reading;
Southampton;
Clapton Orient

Season	League		FA Cup		Total	
	App	**Goals**	**App**	**Goals**	**App**	**Goals**
1902/03	13	0	2	0	15	0
1903/04	2	0	0	0	2	0
Total	**15**	**0**	**2**	**0**	**17**	**0**

Heslop,
George

Understudy to Brian Labone who went on to be part of Manchester City's greatest team

[FACTFILE]

BORN
Wallsend, 1 July 1940
DIED
17 September 2006
POSITION
Centre back
OTHER CLUBS
Newcastle United (1960–62);
Manchester City (1965–72);
Cape Town City (1972);
Bury (1972–73)

Season	League		FA Cup		League Cup		Total	
	App	**Goals**	**App**	**Goals**	**App**	**Goals**	**App**	**Goals**
1962/63	1	0	0	0	0	0	1	0
1963/64	8	0	1	0	0	0	9	0
1964/65	1	0	0	0	0	0	1	0
Total	**10**	**0**	**1**	**0**	**0**	**0**	**11**	**0**

Hibbert,
Tony

Longstanding defensive stalwart who has emerged as an unlikely cult figure

There have been few occasions in the history of Everton where an opposition goal has been applauded so raucously. With Everton cruising 3-0, 18 minutes from the end of the encounter with Newcastle United on the final day of the 2011/12 season a mix-up between Tim Howard and Tony Hibbert saw the veteran right back guide the ball past his own keeper with a goal-poacher's precision. More than ten years and 300 appearances into his Everton career Hibbert had finally scored, albeit into his own net. This didn't matter for the near capacity crowd, who delighted in his faux pas as if he had finished at the correct end. 'He scores when he wants, he scores when he wants, Oh, Tony Hibbert, he scores when he wants,' the crowd sang to the ashen-faced defender.

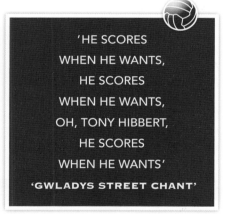

'HE SCORES WHEN HE WANTS, HE SCORES WHEN HE WANTS, OH, TONY HIBBERT, HE SCORES WHEN HE WANTS'
'GWLADYS STREET CHANT'

No outfield player in the club's history has gone longer without scoring a goal than Hibbert and his quest to find the back of the net has afforded the modest home-grown player unlikely cult status. The irony was that just a month earlier Hibbert had nearly broken his duck when a cross from the right flank struck the Norwich City crossbar.

A boyhood Evertonian, Hibbert emerged through the club's youth ranks and with Leon Osman and Francis Jeffers was part of the FA Youth Cup winning side of 1998. He made his

debit in a 2-0 victory over West Ham in March 2001, but it was the arrival of David Moyes a year later that saw him become a regular.

Quick, solid, dependable, hard, reliable; these were the key ingredients that made him a regular on the right side of the Everton defence. Naturally modest, he eschewed the limelight foisted upon modern footballers, kept his head down and did a fine job. Although his distribution was sometimes a cause for complaint, he worked on this and it improved considerably with time.

Sometimes he was guilty of rash challenges and the proverbial rush of blood to the head, but Hibbert never gave anything but his all and never let anyone down. Called into action as an auxiliary centre half at times of injury crisis he adapted with complaint and did his best. Never was he better than in Everton's memorable 1-0 victory over eventual champions Manchester City at Goodison in January 2012. Called into the unfamiliar centre back role he was a magnificent, stubborn, cloying presence all night, giving David Moyes his 150th league victory for Everton.

'Arguably it might have been the best,' said Moyes afterwards. 'The team we had, the players missing, we had to defend for long times

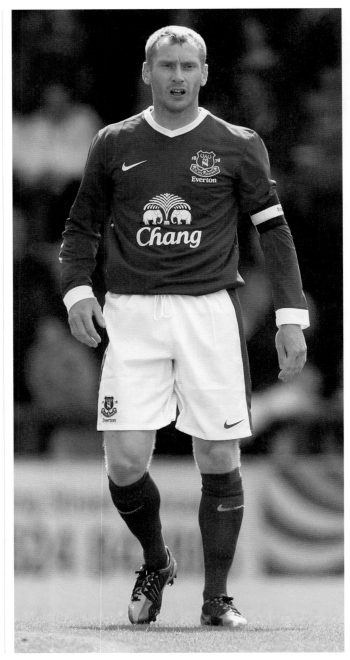

'HIBBERT SCORES WE RIOT'
PROMISED A MEMORABLE BANNER

but it was a great effort. That's as good as it has been at Everton for a long time.' Pointing to the input of the makeshift centre half, the Guardian's chief football writer, Daniel Taylor, added, 'Their performance was epitomised by the way Tony Hibbert, a right back by trade, handled his move to centre half.'

Cult status has come with time and a memorable banner at the 2009 FA Cup Final promised 'Hibbert scores, we riot'. The jovial nature of this relationship belies the deep respect that the club and its supporters have for the player. In 2012 Hibbert was awarded a testimonial match against AEK Athens.

Moyes has described Hibbert as 'part of the Everton brickwork' and said that he has a job for life at the club. 'Overall he's been great; consistent [and] reliable. I've always said he's part of the furniture here. He's tenacious, tough, committed and, probably the most important thing, I can rely on him,' he said. 'That's why he's been here so long and as long as I'm here, he'll be here.'

[FACTFILE]

BORN
Liverpool, 20 February 1981
POSITION
Right back

Season	League		FA Cup		League Cup		Other		Total	
	App	Goals	App	Goals	App	Goals	App	Goals	App	Goals
2000/01	1 (2)	0	0	0	0	0	-	-	1 (2)	0
2001/02	7 (3)	0	1	0	0 (1)	0	-	-	8 (4)	0
2002/03	23 (1)	0	0	0	1	0	-	-	24 (1)	0
2003/04	24 (1)	0	3	0	3	0	-	-	30 (1)	0
2004/05	35 (1)	0	1	0	3	0	-	-	39 (1)	0
2005/06	29	0	4	0	1	0	4	0	38	0
2006/07	12 (1)	0	0	0	0	0	-	-	12 (1)	0
2007/08	22 (2)	0	1	0	2	0	4 (4)	0	29 (6)	0
2008/09	16 (1)	0	6	0	0	0	1	0	23 (1)	0
2009/10	17 (3)	0	1	0	2	0	7	0	27 (3)	0
2010/11	17 (3)	0	1	0	0 (1)	0	-	-	18 (4)	0
2011/12	31 (1)	0	1 (1)	0	1 (1)	0	-	-	33 (3)	0
Total	**234(19)**	**0**	**19 (1)**	**0**	**13 (3)**	**0**	**16 (4)**	**0**	**282(27)**	**0**

Hickson, Dave

1950s idol who played on all three sides of the Mersey

Ask any Evertonian who grew up during the 1950s – that darkest of decades in the club's history – to name their favourite player and the answer is likely to be familiar and enthusiastically uttered. 'Dave Hickson was my all-time hero,' Billy Butler once told this author with all the wide-eyed enthusiasm of a young boy, 'and, like a lot of Evertonians, I went to see him when he was playing for Liverpool as well.'

Hickson, the only man to ever turn out for all three Merseyside teams, captivated the city during the 1950s with his outrageously brave centre forward play. A swashbuckling cavalier, he played like a human battering ram, running through opposing defences with the verve of a Boy's Own hero. With his trademark blond quiff, he looked the part too. But despite being idolised from all three sides of the Mersey, scoring a total of 169 goals to the delight of the masses at Anfield, Prenton and Goodison, he neither won a major trophy nor international honours.

WITHOUT QUESTION, it was at Everton where Hickson became the firmest favourite, his endeavours winning him a place among the pantheon of Everton greats. Like his illustrious forbears, Sam Chedgzoy and Joe Mercer, he was a son of Ellesmere Port and had come under the charge of Dixie Dean as a teenager while playing for the Cheshire Army cadets. Spotted playing non-league football by Cliff Britton, he was signed in 1948, but his early Everton career was put on hold so that he could complete national service.

On his return he was a prolific Central League player – once

scoring five in a reserve game against Sheffield Wednesday – and travelled with the first team as twelfth man on a number of occasions. But despite Everton playing some of the worst football in their history, suffering relegation at the end of the 1950/51 season, the madness that pervaded Goodison at this time meant that Hickson never got his chance until the start of the 1951/52 season, when he was aged nearly 22. He made his debut against Leeds United in a 2-0 victory, taking the place of Harry Catterick, and a week later scored his first goal in a 3-3 Goodison draw with Rotherham.

It was soon clear to watching Evertonians that Hickson was a player very much in the mould of the traditional English centre forward, a player, who, like his revered contemporaries Nat Lofthouse and Stan Mortenson, was a man they could vest all their hopes and aspirations in. Tall, lean, strong and supremely brave, Hickson possessed a ferocious shot and was formidable in the air. He relished battle, seeming to revel in scrapes with opposing defenders and referees too – he was always a player to attract the opprobrium of officialdom. And scarcely have there been braver players to pull on an Everton shirt: like Andy Gray three decades later, he was a player who would put his head where lesser men shirked putting their feet. 'I would have died for Everton,'

HICKSON, THE ONLY MAN TO EVER TURN OUT FOR ALL THREE MERSEYSIDE TEAMS

he once famously said, and few to witness him play would have disagreed. Often considered a mere bruiser, his attributes as a footballer are often overlooked: he was a talented target man, well able to hold up the ball or bring a colleague into play with a flick or a shimmy.

IN THIS DEBUT season the potential was there for all to see. He finished the season with 14 league goals from 31 outings, but his partnership with the inside forward John Willie Parker held the key to an Everton revival as they averaged more than a goal a game when permed together. Yet it wasn't enough to secure the anticipated recovery in the subsequent 1952/53 season: Everton finished 16th in the Second Division – the lowest position in the club's history.

That season would have been far harder to bear, were it not for an extraordinary FA Cup run that brought Everton within touching distance of the final. It also secured Hickson's place in Everton lore. The FA Cup run started with Hickson scoring twice in a 3-2 third round Goodison win over Ipswich Town, and Everton eased past Nottingham Forest in the fourth round.

The game that captured everybody's imagination, however, came on Valentine's Day 1953, when Everton were drawn with Manchester United for a fifth round tie at Goodison; 77,920 crammed in for the famous old ground's second highest ever attendance. United, possessing the first of Matt Busby's great teams, were reigning First Division champions and were strong favourites for the tie. Invariably, it seemed, they took a lead through a Jack Rowley goal midway through the first half.

But then Hickson seized the game by its throat. Seven minutes later, he played in Tommy Eglington, who rounded the United left back, Jack Aston, and let fly with a scorching right-footed shot which flew into the back of the United net. It was the Irishman's fifth goal in as many matches.

'I WOULD HAVE DIED FOR EVERTON'

Five minutes from the interval, Hickson dived in like a battering ram to try and connect with Jack Lindsay's cross, but in doing so caught a defender's boot and had to leave the field with blood streaming from his eye. Half-time came and went without the forward re-emerging. A minute into the second half he returned to cheers with a handkerchief, with which he dabbed his wound.

SHORTLY AFTER his return, he headed against the upright from a corner, which opened up the wound again. At this point the referee suggested to Peter Farrell, Everton's captain, that Hickson should leave the field. Although bloodied like a prize fighter, Hickson would hear none of it and stayed.

On 63 minutes came the game's crucial moment. Chasing Eglington's ball, Hickson beat one man, sidestepped another and thundered a right-footed shot beyond the reach of Ray Wood and into the United net. It was a worthy winner from the man who was the hero of a famous victory. 'Not only did he get the winning goal by sheer persistence,' recorded the Liverpool Echo. 'But with blood streaming down his face throughout the second half from a cut above his eye, gave a wonderful show of courage and fighting spirit.' Its correspondent recorded: 'Never in my whole life have I seen a player perform with such guts as Davie showed.'

In the quarter-final, at Aston Villa, Hickson's late thunderbolt was the only goal of the game. Afterwards he was lifted off in a throne of hands and arms by fans who had invaded the pitch. But in the semi-final against Bolton at Maine Road, Hickson found himself upstaged by Nat Lofthouse, England's 'Lion of Vienna'. Again, he had to leave the field through injury, and when he returned Everton were 3-0 down. Tommy Clinton missed a penalty and Bolton scored a fourth before half-time. Although Everton staged a second-half comeback, scoring three times, Bolton's lead was insurmountable. It was, Hickson would recall, 'the biggest disappointment of my career'. Never again would he come so close to winning a medal.

Hickson returned with a vengeance during the 1953/54 season, hitting 25 league goals as Everton won promotion back to the top flight. 'On the night we gained promotion,' he would recall, 'I said that the club would never go down again. That's been proved right and I'm proud of everything they've achieved ever since.'

HE AND PARKER resumed their prolific partnership in the 1954/55 season, scoring 31 league goals between them, and for a period Everton were considered League Championship dark horses, but faded to tenth after losing seven of their last ten matches. However, the failure of the Everton board to invest in the team meant Everton were never likely to make a sustained challenge for honours. Some of Cliff Britton's managerial decisions left much to be desired too. After Everton lost the opening two games of the 1955/56 season he dropped Hickson and Parker. Hickson demanded a transfer and two weeks later he was an Aston Villa player, sold for £19,500.

'He should do his new club the power of good and if he can finally conquer his rather pugnacious temperament – which he genuinely tried to do all last season – he has it in him to finally become one of the best centre forwards in the country …' recorded the Liverpool Echo. 'Hickson always gave to his last ounce of endeavour to the Everton cause. Many a time his great fighting spirit and sheer determination helped to achieve victory in a game which had seemed to be irretrievably lost.' Yet it was an unhappy experience and after netting just once in 12 Villa Park appearances, he was sold to Bill Shankly's Huddersfield Town two months later.

Without him Everton floundered, finishing the 1955/56 season 15th, the same position that they ended the subsequent campaign. Supporter unrest was now palpable. Britton left the club, but the parsimony of the board outraged fans. They needed someone to assuage this opprobrium, and in Dave Hickson they got him. His £6500 return from Huddersfield in the summer of 1957 delighted supporters, and probably the directors too, who could count on a handsome profit.

Hickson reclaimed the famous number nine shirt 'kept warm' for him by Jimmy Harris, George Kirby and Derek Temple and once again led the Everton forward line like a hero. Yet after a good start to the 1957/58 season, Everton faded and finished 16th, as they did the 1958/59 season. By now Hickson was nearing the veteran stage of his career and John Moores' millions were starting to make an impression on the Everton squad. After a stuttering start to the 1959/60 season, Hickson again found himself dropped.

If his 1955 transfer to Aston Villa attracted outrage it was nothing compared to what followed. In November 1959 Hickson was sold to Liverpool for £12,500, where he would be reunited with incoming manager Bill Shankly. Fans on both sides of the Mersey divide were incensed. 'I protest at the abominable treatment afforded Dave Hickson. Everton supporters know that Hickson is not the best centre forward in football, but of the centre forwards on Everton's books he is by far the best,' wrote J.D. Pierce of L11 to the Football Echo.

[FACTFILE]

BORN
Ellesmere Port, 30 October 1929

POSITION
Centre forward

OTHER CLUBS
Aston Villa (1955);
Huddersfield Town (1955–57);
Liverpool (1959–61);
Cambridge City (1961);
Bury (1961–62);
Tranmere Rovers (1962–64)

Season	League		FA Cup		Total	
	App	Goals	App	Goals	App	Goals
1951/52	31	14	2	0	33	14
1952/53	27	12	5	4	32	16
1953/54	40	25	3	3	43	28
1954/55	39	12	2	1	41	13
1955/56	2	0	0	0	2	0
1957/58	35	9	2	3	37	12
1958/59	39	17	4	5	43	22
1959/60	12	6	0	0	12	6
Total	**225**	**95**	**18**	**16**	**243**	**111**

'It seems ridiculous that other players in the team can play badly and still retain their places while Hickson, who has played his heart out (and incidentally, is leading goalscorer) should be dropped.' 'Whether Hickson joins Liverpool or not, I want to express the disgust of some Liverpool supporters of 30 years standing that the club should even consider a player who has been discarded by Everton Football Club (twice), Aston Villa and Huddersfield,' complained W. Parker of L8. 'After talking grandly of Clough, Baker and Holton, Liverpool have come down to this,' moaned A. Alan of L18, while A.A. Drury of L4 wrote, 'Everton will never be the same without Davy, and if he goes to Liverpool I, and I am sure many more, will willingly pay 2s to Liverpool just to watch him.'

This indeed was the case and many Evertonians went to watch him from the Kop. In 1961 he dropped out of league football, joining Cambridge City. Within a year he had returned to the Football League, with Bury. In 1962 he returned to Merseyside with Tranmere Rovers, later playing out his career with Ballymena and in non-league with Winsford United and Northwich Victoria.

Now in his eighties, he is still part of the hospitality team at Goodison, hosting visitors with the boyish relish he once attracted from its terraces. His quiff, now greyed, is still a popular sight around the ground on match-days, and Hickson remains as irrepressible as ever. After suffering a heart attack prior to Everton's game with Sunderland in November 2007, he was rushed to hospital and asked by nursing staff whether he expected to be playing in that fixture. Without missing a beat, he replied, 'Only in the last ten minutes.'

Higgins, Billy

Young forward whose career was wrecked by Bogotá controversy

Signed as an amateur from Tranmere Rovers for the recommencement of league football in September 1946, Billy Higgins' Everton career is defined by a single moment of glory at its midpoint and a tide of controversy and opprobrium at its end.

Born in Birkenhead, Higgins signed professional terms with Everton in May 1946, earning wages of £5 a week. Nominally a centre forward, he played across the Everton forward line without ever really making a first-team place his own. He appeared just seven times during the 1946/47 season and 14 times during the next campaign.

His crowning moment in an Everton shirt came in January 1949, when a crowd of 63,499 crammed into Goodison to see Everton take on Manchester City in an FA Cup third round tie. Twice Everton had faced City in the league over the Christmas holidays and both games had ended goalless. This time Higgins wore the famed number nine shirt and all afternoon tore into City with a tireless and effusive display – but still, as 90 minutes approached it remained goalless.

The game's deciding moment was its last. Alex Stevenson drove down the wing and accelerated past the City full back, before centring from the goal line. 'Higgins,' recorded the Liverpool Echo, 'hurled himself past Fagan to head the ball into the net – a mighty effort.'

'He would have required the wings of a dove to fly far away from his colleague's rapturous attention,' wrote Ernest 'Bee' Edwards in the Echo. 'They kissed him, they hugged him, they were aided in their congratulations by spectators entering the field to break all rules of a well-governed ground.' It was, concurred 'Stork' in the same pages, 'one of the greatest climaxes I have seen for an age.'

BUT IF HIGGINS expected this to be a breakthrough goal, he was sorely disappointed. When Everton faced Chelsea in the fourth round tie, he was dropped in favour of Harry Catterick and first-team outings thereafter remained as rare as ever.

In the summer of 1950, Higgins was approached by his former team-mate Jock Dodds with an incredible proposition. Dodds had recently retired and was working

as an agent for Colombian football clubs, who were awash with money at the time. Colombian teams had recently started acquiring some of the best foreign footballers in an attempt to boost the domestic league, luring them with vast wages. Because the country's football association had left FIFA, they were free from the jurisdiction of football's world governing body and could dispense with trifling matters like player registrations and transfer fees.

The wages on offer were extraordinary. Stoke's England defender, Neil Franklin, was offered £5000 per year plus a £5000 signing on fee, with half paid up front in sterling, to join Santa Fe. Given that a maximum wage was still imposed, a First Division player like Higgins was lucky to earn one tenth of that in a good year. Higgins followed the cash and secretly signed for Millionarios, where – and this seems the most extraordinary detail of all – he partnered a young Alfredo di Stefano in attack.

THE MOVE WAS ill fated and, like most of the so-called 'Bogotá Bandits', he suffered homesickness, returning to England after five months in an inevitable blaze of publicity. When he returned to the dockside, he and his two small children were met by a Pathé news crew, while his wife faced the cameras. 'As the wife of a professional footballer we never know where we are going to be next,' she said. 'All I want is a home to settle down with the children.'

	League		FA Cup		Total	
Season	**App**	**Goals**	**App**	**Goals**	**App**	**Goals**
1946/47	7	1	0	0	7	1
1947/48	13	3	0	0	13	3
1948/49	14	0	1	1	15	1
1949/50	14	4	0	0	14	4
Total	**48**	**8**	**1**	**1**	**49**	**9**

'ONE OF THE GREATEST CLIMAXES I HAVE SEEN FOR AN AGE'

The FA invariably took a dim view – despite the players only seeking a fair wage for themselves and their families – and handed the bandits hefty bans. Everton interceded on Higgins' behalf and got the ban reduced to six weeks – not that they intended on playing him again. Higgins was ostracised by the club and no other club would come in for such a notorious figure. There was talk of a move to Racing Club de Paris, before Higgins walked out of English football for a second time in December 1950 and joined Bangor City as a semi-professional.

[FACTFILE]

BORN
Birkenhead,
26 February 1924
POSITION
Forward
OTHER CLUBS
Tranmere Rovers (wartime);
Millionarios (1950);
Bangor City

Higgins, Mark

Captain and centre back whose Goodison career ended with Everton on the cusp of greatness

Mark Higgins' story ranks among the saddest in Everton's history and serves as a poignant reminder that football can deal the cruellest and most unexpected hands.

Born in Buxton, the tall centre back came from footballing stock. His father, John Higgins, served a distinguished career for Bolton Wanderers in the 1950s, twice reaching the FA Cup Final, and was part of the team that defeated the post-Munich Manchester United team in the 1958 final.

Higgins junior worked his way through the Everton youth teams, making his debut just past his 18th birthday in October 1976. His breakthrough came at the start of the 1977/78 campaign, when he was called to deputise for the injured Roger Kenyon through the first half of the season. Fast, composed and formidable in the air, seldom did he look out of

place in a team chasing for the title. Although Kenyon reclaimed his place mid-season, the teenager's progress had not gone unnoticed.

Yet there would be no meteoric rise. Over the next three years he played just 41 games, slipping behind his fellow young defender, Billy Wright, in the ranking, but when called upon to deputise showing all the composure and maturity that had first marked him out as a player to watch out for. His chance finally came during the 1981/82 season. Now managed by Howard Kendall, the new boss dropped his summer signing Mick Walsh, and Higgins took the number four shirt and made it his own. When Kendall subsequently lost faith in Mick Lyons, he made Higgins, still aged only 23, captain.

For the first time in his Everton career, Higgins was one of the

first names on the team sheet each week. Through the 1982/83 season and the first half of the following term he enjoyed the best football of his career until disaster struck. What was originally suspected to be a mere groin strain was diagnosed as a serious pelvic injury that specialists claimed would bring an end to his career. As his team-mates were lifting a glut of trophies, their former captain was forced to contemplate retirement while still only in his mid-twenties. Yet there was no giving up, and Higgins made a brief return with Ron Atkinson's Manchester United. He then played a further 120 games in the lower leagues with Bury, where he was reunited with Martin Dobson, now manager, and Stoke City, then managed by Alan Ball – making Higgins perhaps the only player to be coached or managed by each of the Harvey, Kendall, Ball 'Holy Trinity'.

After finally retiring in 1990, he returned to Derbyshire to take up a role with the bakery his family have run for generations.

[FACTFILE]

BORN
Buxton, 29 September 1958
POSITION
Centre back
OTHER CLUBS
Manchester United
(1985–87);
Bury (1987–88);
Stoke City (1988–90)

Season	League		FA Cup		League Cup		Europe		Total	
	App	Goals	App	Goals	App	Goals	App	Goals	App	Goals
1976/77	2	0	0	0	0	0	-	-	2	0
1977/78	25 (1)	1	1	0	5	0	-	-	31 (1)	1
1978/79	20 (1)	1	0	0	0	0	0 (2)	0	20 (3)	1
1979/80	19	0	0	0	5	0	2	0	26	0
1980/81	2	0	0	0	0	0	-	-	2	0
1981/82	29	3	1	0	2	0	-	-	32	3
1982/83	39	1	5	0	3	0	-	-	47	1
1983/84	14	0	0	0	5	0	-	-	19	0
Total	**150 (2)**	**6**	**7**	**0**	**20**	**0**	**2 (2)**	**0**	**179 (4)**	**6**

Higgins, Mike

Left half in Everton's first FA Cup run, he was unable to command a starting place with the onset of the Football League

Season	League		FA Cup		Total	
	App	Goals	App	Goals	App	Goals
1887/88	-	-	4	0	4	0
1888/89	1	0	-	-	1	0
Total	**1**	**0**	**4**	**0**	**5**	**0**

[FACTFILE]

BORN
1862
POSITION
Left half

High-scoring Games

Everton's record victory came early in their history, an 11-2 FA Cup demolition of Derby County in January 1890. Derby were no pushovers and were to finish the First Division season in a credible seventh position, but Everton were simply irrepressible.

Playing on a sodden pitch Derby took an early lead through Fred Goodall. After Fred Geary equalised for Everton, Derby regained the lead when Higgins' shot slipped through the grasp of Smalley. The Derby defence clearly had its deficiencies, and before half-time Milward put Everton 3-2 in front with a brace.

Defensive shortcomings or not, none of the Anfield crowd could have predicted what happened after the interval. Derby County simply collapsed. Alf Milward scored his third goal, and Geary also added a brace to complete his hat-trick. The excellence of Alex Brady perpetually confounded the beleaguered Derby defenders and he added three goals of his own to make a hat-trick of hat-tricks, while Doyle and Kirkwood each added a goal apiece to make it 11-2.

Evertonians had to wait 68 years before they saw a comparable goal rush – but this time they were on the receiving end. Facing Tottenham Hotspur at White Hart Lane in October 1958, they conceded ten goals – but still managed four in reply, with Jimmy Harris unlucky enough to grab a hat-trick on the one day that all eyes were on his opponents. The 14 goals witnessed in north London that afternoon remains a record aggregate top-flight score.

On 27 December 1930, in a Division Two match against Plymouth Argyle, Everton won 9-1 and embarked on one of the most prolific calendar years in its history. Through 1931 they beat Southport 9-1 in an FA Cup quarter-final; Newcastle United 8-1, Leicester City 9-2 and Sheffield Wednesday 9-3 in Division One, and also struck seven goals past both of Charlton Athletic and Chelsea.

Not since 1978 have Everton scored eight or more goals in a match, but they have scored seven goals on a couple of occasions – also conceding seven to Arsenal in May 2005.

Record Victories

11 goals scored
18 JANUARY 1890
FA Cup Rd 1 v. Derby County [H] 11-2 *Geary 3, Milward 3, Brady 3, Doyle, Kirkwood;* 10,000
Smalley, Hannah, Doyle, Kirkwood, Holt, Parry, Latta, Brady, Geary, Chadwick, Milward

9 Goals Scored
3 SEPTEMBER 1906
Division 1 v. Manchester City [H] 9-1 *Young 4, Settle 2, Abbott, Bolton, Taylor;* 16,000
Scott, Balmer, Crelley, Booth, Taylor, Abbott, Sharp, Bolton, Young, Settle, Wilson

27 DECEMBER 1930
Division 2 v. Plymouth Argyle [H] 9-1 *Stein 4, Dean 4, Johnson;* 37,018
Coggins, Williams, Cresswell, McPherson, Griffiths, Thomson, Critchley, Dunn, Dean, Johnson, Stein.

28 FEBRUARY 1931
FA Cup QF v. Southport [H] 9-1 *Dean 4, Dunn 2, Critchley 2, Johnson;* 45,647
Coggins, Williams, Cresswell, McClure, Gee, Thomson, Critchley, Dunn, Dean, Johnson, Stein

28 NOVEMBER 1931
Division 1 v. Leicester City [H] 9-2 *Dean 4, Johnson 2, White 2, Clark;* 33,513
Sagar, Williams, Cresswell, Clark, Gee, Thomson, Critchley, White, Dean, Johnson, Stein

17 OCTOBER 1931
Division 1 v. Sheffield Wednesday [H] 9-3 *Dean 5, Critchley, Thomson, White, Stein;* 38,186
Sagar, Williams, Cresswell, Clark, Gee, Thomson, Critchley, White, Dean, Johnson, Stein

8 goals scored

2 NOVEMBER 1889
Division 1 v. Stoke City [H] 8-0
Geary 3, Brady 2, Latta 2,
Milward; **7500**
Smalley, Hannah, Doyle, Parry,
Holt, Cain, Latta, Brady, Geary,
Chadwick, Milward

21 JANUARY 1939
**FA Cup Rd 4 v. Doncaster
Rovers [H] 8-0** Lawton 4, Boyes
2, Gillick, Stevenson; **41,115**
Sagar, Cook, Greenhalgh, Mercer,
Jones, Thomson, Gillick,
Bentham, Lawton, Stevenson,
Boyes

20 NOVEMBER 1971
Division 1 v. Southampton [H]
8-0 Royle 4, Johnson 3, Ball;
28,718
West, Wright, McLaughlin,
Kendall, Kenyon, Scott, Johnson,
Ball, Royle, Hurst, Whittle

29 AUGUST 1978
**League Cup Rd 2 v. Wimbledon
[H] 8-0** Latchford 5, Dobson 3;
23,137
Wood, Robinson, Pejic, Lyons,
Wright, Nulty, King, Dobson,
Latchford, Walsh (Ross), Thomas

21 OCTOBER 1893
Divison 1 v. Darwen [H] 8-1
Latta 2, Maxwell 2, Southworth 2
(1 pen), Bell, Chadwick; **9000**
Williams, Kelso, Howarth, Doyle,
Holt, Stewart, Latta, Maxwell,
Southworth, Chadwick, Bell

23 DECEMBER 1893
**Division 1 v. Sheffield
Wednesday [H] 8-1** Southworth
4, Bell 2, Chadwick, Latta; **9000**
Williams, Parry, Lindsay, Kelso,
Holt, Stewart, Latta, Bell,
Southworth, Chadwick, Milward

31 OCTOBER 1931
**Division 1 v. Newcastle United
[H] 8-1** Johnson 2, Dean 2,
White 2, Stein, Critchley; **30,765**
Sagar, Williams, Cresswell, Clark,
Gee, Thomson, Critchley, White,
Dean, Johnson, Stein

28 APRIL 1962
Division 1 v. Cardiff City [H]
8-3 Vernon 3, Bingham, Gabriel,
Stevens, Temple, Young; **31,186**
West, Meagan, Thomson, Gabriel,
Labone, Harris, Bingham,
Stevens, Young, Vernon, Temple

27 FEBRUARY 1954
**Division 2 v. Plymouth Argyle
[H] 8-4** Parker 4, Hickson 2,
Lello, Lindsay (pen); **44,496**
O'Neill, Donovan, Lindsay,
Farrell, Jones, Lello,
Wainwright, Fielding,
Hickson, Parker, Eglington

Record Defeats

11 OCTOBER 1958
**Division 1 v. Tottenham Hotspur
[A] 4-10** Harris 3, Collins; **37,794**
Dunlop, Sanders, Bramwell, King,
Jones, B. Harris, Fielding, J.
Harris, Hickson, Collins, O'Hara

7 OCTOBER 1959
**Division 1 v. Newcastle United
[A] 2-8** Thomas 2; **23,727**
Dunlop, Parker, Bramwell, King,
Jones, B. Harris, J. Harris, Thomas,
Shackleton, Collins, Laverick

Everton have also lost 7-0 on four occasions, all away from home and in
the top flight; versus Arsenal (2005), Portsmouth (1949), Wolves (1939)
and Sunderland (1934).

Higham, Norman

**Inside forward
who failed to
capture the
affection of
Everton
selectors despite
his fine scoring
record**

[FACTFILE]

BORN
Chorley, 14 February 1912
POSITION
Inside forward
OTHER CLUBS
Middlesbrough (1935–38);
Southampton (1939)

Season	League		FA Cup		Total	
	App	Goals	App	Goals	App	Goals
1933/34	13	6	0	0	13	6
1934/35	1	0	0	0	1	0
Total	14	6	0	0	14	6

Hill, Jimmy

**Northern
Ireland
international
winger who
struggled with
injuries and for
form during
Goodison spell**

[FACTFILE]

BORN
Carrickfergus,
31 October 1935
POSITION
Winger
OTHER CLUBS
Linfield;
Newcastle United (1957–59);
Norwich City (1959–63);
Port Vale (1965–67);
Derry City (1967–71);
AS MANAGER
Derry City (1968–71);
Linfield (1971–72);
Carrick Rangers (1988–91)
HONOURS
7 Northern Ireland caps
(1959–63)

Season	League		FA Cup		League Cup		Total	
	App	Goals	App	Goals	App	Goals	App	Goals
1963/64	7	1	0	0	0	0	7	1
Total	7	1	0	0	0	0	7	1

Hill, Percy

Reserve full back who played a role in Everton's first successful FA Cup run

Season	League		FA Cup		Total	
	App	Goals	App	Goals	App	Goals
1905/06	13	0	2	0	15	0
1906/07	1	0	0	0	1	0
Total	**14**	**0**	**2**	**0**	**16**	**0**

[FACTFILE]

BORN
1884
POSITION
Full back
OTHER CLUBS
Southampton;
Manchester City (1906–07);
Airdrieonians; Swindon Town

Hillman, Jack

Goalkeeper whose form after leaving Goodison earned him England honours

Season	League		FA Cup		Total	
	App	Goals	App	Goals	App	Goals
1894/95	6	0	0	0	6	0
1895/96	29	0	3	0	32	0
Total	**35**	**0**	**3**	**0**	**38**	**0**

[FACTFILE]

BORN
Tavistock, 30 October 1870
DIED
1955
POSITION
Goalkeeper
OTHER CLUBS
Burnley (1891–95);
Dundee (1896–98);
Burnley (1898–1901);
Manchester City (1901–05);
Millwall Athletic
HONOURS
1 England cap (1899)

Hills, John

Teenage full back with a searing cross signed as a young hopeful by Joe Royle

[FACTFILE]

BORN
Blackpool, 21 April 1978
POSITION
Full back
OTHER CLUBS
Blackpool
(1994–95 & 1998–2003);
Swansea City (2 loan spells, 1997);
Gillingham (2003–05);
Sheffield Wednesday (2005–07);
Blackpool (2007–08);
Fleetwood Town (2008–10)

Season	League		FA Cup		League Cup		Total	
	App	Goals	App	Goals	App	Goals	App	Goals
1996/97	1 (2)	0	0	0	0	0	1 (2)	0
Total	**1 (2)**	**0**	**0**	**0**	**0**	**0**	**1 (2)**	**0**

Hinchcliffe, Andy

Unassuming Mancunian who recovered from a slow start to become the finest Everton left back in a generation

When talking about his first match in charge of Everton, against Liverpool in November 1994, Joe Royle spoke of how Duncan Ferguson 'went to war' to help win the game for Everton. Such was his galvanising effect, said Royle after the game, that 'it was as if a bolt of lightning had struck him'. Yet Royle might have been talking about Andy Hinchcliffe, such was the transformation from that day in the defender's Goodison form and fortunes.

SIGNED BY Colin Harvey for £900,000 from Manchester City in the summer of 1990, Hinchcliffe was an outstanding all-rounder, and as a schoolboy he had represented Lancashire at cricket and lacrosse while also turning out for Manchester City's youth team on Sundays. As a young professional footballer, he had shown promise with other young Maine Road pretenders such as Paul Lake, David White and Ian Brightwell, so it was with some surprise that City manager Howard Kendall sold him to his former club.

At Goodison the England under-21 international at first looked to be an ideal long-term investment. Three months into his spell on Merseyside, however, Harvey was sacked and Kendall – with whom Hinchcliffe never seemed to click – returned from Maine Road. Injury and inconsistency combined to dog these first years at Everton, and by the time that Mike Walker was appointed manager in January 1994, Hinchcliffe's youthful potential looked as if it would remain untapped. Indeed Walker rarely picked Hinchcliffe, even signing the hugely unpopular David Burrows to replace him in September 1994.

TWO MONTHS later, Royle became Everton manager and Hinchcliffe was thrust back into the Everton first team. Playing as a left-sided midfielder, he was one of Royle's so-called 'dogs of war', ostensibly a defensive player whose magnificent – but hitherto unused – left-footed potency became one of Everton's main attacking outlets. On Royle's first, memorable, night as manager,

> **HE WAS ONE OF ROYLE'S SO-CALLED 'DOGS OF WAR'**

Season	League		FA Cup		League Cup		Other		Total	
	App	Goals	App	Goals	App	Goals	App	Goals	App	Goals
1990/91	21	1	5	0	2	0	2	0	30	1
1991/92	15 (3)	0	0	0	3	0	2	0	20 (3)	0
1992/93	25	1	0	0	3 (2)	0	-	-	28 (2)	1
1993/94	25 (1)	0	1	0	4	0	-	-	30 (1)	0
1994/95	28 (1)	2	5	1	2	0	-	-	35 (1)	3
1995/96	23 (5)	2	1 (2)	0	2	1	4	0	30 (7)	3
1996/97	18	1	0	0	2	0	-	-	20	1
1997/98	15 (2)	0	0	0	3	0	-	-	18 (2)	0
Total	**170 (12)**	**7**	**12 (2)**	**1**	**21 (2)**	**1**	**8**	**0**	**211(16)**	**9**

twice Hinchcliffe's pinpoint crosses met the head of Duncan Ferguson – one leading directly to a goal, the other to a knockdown, which Paul Rideout converted. A fortnight later, Everton met Leeds United at Goodison and Hinchcliffe swept the Yorkshiremen aside, with all three of Everton's goals coming as a result of his corners.

As Everton clawed their way to safety and an FA Cup win the following May, this became the pattern of their play, with Hinchcliffe's set pieces central to their renaissance. But when Royle began to tame his 'dogs of war' after safety was assured, moving Hinchcliffe back to his favoured left back position, so Evertonians saw the first signs of his completeness as a defender. Crisp in the tackle, pacy and with excellent short and long-range

distribution, Hinchcliffe fully deserved his call-up to Glenn Hoddle's first England squad for the World Cup qualifier against Moldova in September 1996.

FURTHER call-ups followed as Hinchcliffe thrived for club and country. But shortly before Christmas 1996, disaster struck. Playing in a dull match against a poor Leeds side, Hinchcliffe made an innocuous slip. After struggling on, he was clearly in pain and had to be substituted. 'No one realised the scale of the problem until the surgeon had operated,' he said afterwards. 'Then suddenly I wake up on Christmas Eve with my cruciate and a cartilage in a bottle beside my bed.'

Nine disastrous months on the sidelines followed, during which time Everton's form plummeted as the club was plagued by boardroom disarray. Royle was sacked as manager, and for a third time Hinchcliffe was reunited with Kendall. Invariably rumours about Hinchcliffe's future began to fly around. With less than a year remaining on his contract, some expected him to allow it to expire before making a personally lucrative free transfer under the terms of the Bosman ruling.

To the surprise and delight of Evertonians he affirmed his commitment to the club by signing a new long-term contract. Barely had the ink dried on his new deal, however, than he was sold to Sheffield Wednesday in a £2.7 million deal in January 1998. With the emergence of Michael Ball and chairman Peter Johnson refusing to allocate more transfer funds unless players were sold, Hinchcliffe had seemingly become an affordable sacrifice.

In Yorkshire Hinchcliffe briefly regained his place in the England squad, but injuries limited him to less than 90 appearances before he was forced to call time on his career in 2002. A quiet, thoughtful man, well liked by his team-mates, he later became involved in media punditry for local radio in Manchester.

[FACTFILE]

BORN
Manchester, 5 February 1969
POSITION
Left back / left midfield
OTHER CLUBS
Manchester City
(1986–1990);
Sheffield Wednesday
(1998–2002)
HONOURS
7 England caps (1996–98);
1995 FA Cup

Hodge,
Martin

Young goalkeeper who made his name beyond Goodison

Signed as a raw 20-year-old from Plymouth Argyle for £135,000 in July 1979, Martin Hodge was the latest in a long list of contenders to fill the gloves vacated by Gordon West at the start of the decade. Tall, brave and slightly ungainly, Hodge possessed outstanding reflexes and within months of his arrival had replaced George Wood as Everton's first-choice goalkeeper.

YET HODGE arrived amid trying times for Everton, and it was difficult for a young player – not

least one burdened with the challenge of keeping goal – to make an impression. Several of his latterly illustrious contemporaries, including the likes of Kevin Ratcliffe and Graeme Sharp, would take several years to do so. Towards the end of a promising first season, Wood reclaimed the number one shirt. Thereafter, with

the arrivals of Jim McDonagh, Jim Arnold and Neville Southall, as well as a serious knee injury, Hodge barely got a sniff of first-team action.

After several loan moves, Howard Wilkinson paid £50,000 to bring him to Sheffield Wednesday, where he blossomed and was an

essential part of the club's mid-1980s renaissance. In 1986 he was placed on standby for England's World Cup squad.

[FACTFILE]

BORN
Southport, 4 February 1959
OTHER CLUBS
Plymouth Argyle (1977–79);
Preston North End
(loan, 1981–82 & 1983);
Oldham Athletic
(loan, 1982);
Gillingham (loan, 1983);
Sheffield Wednesday
(1983–88);
Leicester City (1988–91);
Hartlepool (1991–93);
Rochdale (1993–94);
Plymouth Argyle (1994–96)

	League		FA Cup		League Cup		Europe		Total	
Season	App	Goals	App	Goals	App	Goals	App	Goals	App	Goals
1979/80	23	0	5	0	0	0	0	0	28	0
1980/81	2	0	1	0	0	0	-	-	3	0
1981/82	0	0	0	0	0	0	-	-	0	0
1982/83	0	0	0	0	0	0	-	-	0	0
Total	**25**	**0**	**6**	**0**	**0**	**0**	**0**	**0**	**31**	**0**

Hodge, William

Scottish goalkeeper who was unable to make the Everton green jersey his own

Season	League		FA Cup		Total	
	App	Goals	App	Goals	App	Goals
1912/13	6	0	0	0	6	0
1913/14	4	0	0	0	4	0
Total	10	0	0	0	10	0

[FACTFILE]

BORN
Kilwinning, 1885
POSITION
Goalkeeper

Holbem, Walter

Yorkshire defender who deputised at left back during the early 1910s

Season	League		FA Cup		Total	
	App	Goals	App	Goals	App	Goals
1911/12	11	0	0	0	11	0
1912/13	7	0	0	0	7	0
Total	18	0	0	0	18	0

[FACTFILE]

BORN
Sheffield, 1885
DIED
1930
POSITION
Left back
OTHER CLUBS
Sheffield Wednesday (1906–10);
St Mirren;
Preston North End (1913–14)

Hold, Oscar

Yorkshire-born forward unable to lift Everton's dark times, but who enjoyed a colourful managerial career

Season	League		FA Cup		Total	
	App	Goals	App	Goals	App	Goals
1949/50	1	0	0	0	1	0
1950/51	21	5	1	0	21	5
Total	22	5	1	0	22	5

[FACTFILE]

BORN
Barnsley, 19 October 1918
DIED
11 October 2005
POSITION
Inside forward
OTHER CLUBS
Barnsley (1937–39);
Aldershot (1946–47);
Norwich City (1946–49);
Chelmsford City (1949–50);
Queens Park Rangers (1951–53)
AS MANAGER
Doncaster Rovers (1962–64);
Fenerbahce (1964–65);
Ankara Demirspor (1965–67);
Goztepe (1975–76);
Apollon Limassol (1983–84)

Holmes, Paul

Lower league right back who struggled to make top-flight transition

> ATHLETIC AND STRONG ON THE OVERLAP, HE LACKED THE TALENT TO CUT IT AT THE HIGHEST LEVEL

The £100,000 signing of Paul Holmes in March 1993 epitomised the financial malaise at Goodison in the early 1990s. The previous month, Martin Keown – an England international – had been sold to Arsenal for £2million to balance the books. Holmes, along with a veteran Kenny Sansom acquired on a free, were the only defensive reinforcements the club could afford.

Aged 25, Holmes was something of a lower league journeyman when he joined Everton. Spells with Doncaster Rovers and Torquay United had resulted in a 1992 move to Birmingham City, and he was on the fringes of the Birmingham first team when Howard Kendall made him a surprise £100,000 signing. If his arrival was greeted with puzzlement, optimistic Evertonians looked back to Kendall's managerial heyday, when plucking unknown gems – such as Kevin Sheedy and Alan Harper – from other reserve teams was something of a habit.

ALAS, HOLMES had no such polish. Athletic and strong on the overlap, he lacked the talent to cut it at the highest level. The bulk of his appearances came at the start of the near-disastrous 1993/94 season and after losing his place to Matt Jackson he barely figured for the first team again. However, his Goodison experience served to reinvigorate his career, and there followed a productive spell with West Bromwich Albion before his return to Torquay at the end of the decade.

[FACTFILE]

BORN
Wortley, 18 February 1968
POSITION
Right back
OTHER CLUBS
Doncaster Rovers (1986–88);
Torquay United (1988–92);
Birmingham City (1992–93);
West Bromwich Albion
(1996–99);
Torquay United (1999–2002

Season	League		FA Cup		League Cup		Europe		Total	
	App	Goals	App	Goals	App	Goals	App	Goals	App	Goals
1992/93	4	0	0	0	0	0	-	-	4	0
1993/94	15	0	1	0	4	0	-	-	20	0
1994/95	1	0	0	0	0	0	-	-	1	0
1995/96	1	0	0	0	0	0	0 (2)	0	1 (2)	0
Total	**21**	**0**	**1**	**0**	**4**	**0**	**0 (2)**	**0**	**26 (2)**	**0**

Holt, Johnny

The 'Little Devil' who became Everton's first ever international

On 15 March 1890, Johnny Holt lined up for England against Wales in a 3-1 victory at Wrexham. In so doing he became Everton's first player of international standing and started a tradition that would include such luminaries as Dixie Dean, Ray Wilson, Neville Southall and Tim Cahill.

HOLT WAS one of Everton's 'virgin blues', the coterie of players who kick-started league football on Merseyside, and, with Edgar Chadwick, he would outlast all the original pioneers, partaking in all of Everton's early glories and near misses. He had started out playing junior football with Kings Own FC and Church FC before being spotted by Bootle, Everton's arch-rivals at the time. Everton were slightly fortuitous to assume a place in league football ahead of their near neighbours and Bootle's consternation was heightened by the acquisition of Holt.

He was an unlikely centre back, standing around 5ft 4in tall and weighing only 10 stone. But despite the slight physique he had real presence, even in the air where his team-mates stood over him. A newspaper report of a performance against Blackburn Rovers attested to this unlikely prowess: 'Holt's cranium had a rare grueling, and as the little man was in his best form it is little to be wondered at that the Rovers were not often successful in their attempts at combinations.'

League football represented quite a transition for Everton and over the course of their debut season they used a solid and eager defence as the cornerstone of their progress. Some, however, said that Everton's defenders were too zealous, notably Alec Dick, but also Holt – known as the 'Little Devil' – as well. Thomas Keates, Everton's first historian, told of how Holt was 'an artist in the perpetuation of clever minor fouls. When they were appealed for, his shocked look of indifference was side-splitting.' He had a reputation for winding up opponents too. 'Holt especially enjoyed great success in outing short aggressive tendencies by the Wanderers,' recorded a journalist of one performance.

> 'WITHOUT DOUBT ONE OF THE BEST HALF-BACKS IN ENGLAND'

But such uproar was caused by Everton's conduct that William Barclay felt obliged to write a defence of the club in the local press. 'A deliberate attempt is being made in certain quarters to disgrace and bring into disrepute the club and its players by distorted accounts of matches and untrue and biased statements about rough play on our part,' he wrote. 'The result is when we play away from home we play before a hostile

crowd, which is prepared to hoot at and ridicule any actions of ours it imagines to be of a shady character. I strongly protest against a continuance of this state of affairs.'

HOLT DID NOT let himself be distracted by such uproar. He was, said one newspaper tribute, 'without doubt one of the best half-backs in England, his tackling capabilities being what the old Dominie, termed "Prodigious!"' Another journalist said he was 'a veritable thorn', always 'the hardest working on the field [who] scored triumph upon triumph'.

Holt succeeded Andrew Hannah as Everton captain in the 1891/92 season and a year later led them out as captain at their new home at Goodison. He had been part of the League Championship winning team, but his Everton career might be characterised by its near misses: twice league runners-up, twice third, twice FA Cup runners-up. In September 1897, 3000 turned out to see a joint benefit for Holt and Edgar Chadwick. They were, wrote the Liverpool Mercury, 'two of the most popular players in the Everton team'. Although his talent was prodigious, he was not a man who got on easily with the Everton directors. The club minute books

from this era are full of references to meetings between the board and the player. Although he was a regular through the 1897/98 season, his failure to attend a friendly match against Gainsborough in April 1898 saw him suspended.

There was talk of emigration to Canada and giving up football altogether but Holt resurfaced the following season at Reading in the Southern League. It seems as if Everton retained his playing registration and the move was the cause for some dispute. But Holt's career in Berkshire enjoyed a revival and he was recalled to the England team, adding six international appearances to the four he had made while an Everton player.

[**FACTFILE**]

BORN
Church, Blackburn,
10 April 1865
POSITION
Centre half
OTHER CLUBS
Bootle (1887–88); Reading
HONOURS
1890/91 League
Championship, 10 England
caps (1890–1900)

Season	League		FA Cup		Total	
	App	Goals	App	Goals	App	Goals
1888/89	17	0	-	-	17	0
1889/90	21	1	2	0	23	1
1890/91	21	1	1	0	22	1
1891/92	21	0	1	0	22	0
1892/93	26	0	7	0	33	0
1893/94	26	0	1	0	27	0
1894/95	27	0	3	0	30	0
1895/96	14	0	2	0	16	0
1896/97	25	1	5	0	30	2
1897/98	27	0	5	0	32	0
Total	**225**	**3**	**27**	**1**	**252**	**4**

Horne, Barry

Battling midfielder whose Everton career was rejuvenated after vital wonder-goal

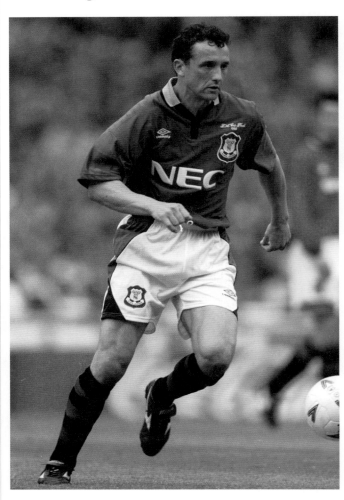

The Everton career of Welsh international midfielder Barry Horne can be divided into two roughly equal sections. The first two years of his four-year spell at Everton were a non-event, and with the team struggling, Horne's form was indifferent. Then came a flash of genius, delivered at a crucial juncture, and Horne was transformed, gaining immediate cult hero status among fans.

A late starter by professional standards, Horne's footballing career began in the mid-1980s with Wrexham, who he joined on completing a chemistry degree at Liverpool University. He signed for Portsmouth in 1987 and after 70 games moved along the south coast to join Southampton in 1989. A Welsh international, Horne became national captain following the international retirement of Kevin Ratcliffe.

AT THE START of the 1992/93 season he moved back north to join Everton, his boyhood team, in a £500,000 deal. Expectations of a player already past his 30th birthday were, perhaps, unfairly high after Howard Kendall's promise that Everton would be signing a midfielder 'in the Peter

Reid mould' – a tough billing for any player to live up to. Although he scored on his debut, Horne struggled in these early days and at one point found himself dropped in favour of the untried Billy Kenny.

Without question, the turning point in Barry Horne's Goodison career came on the final day of the 1993/94 season, when Everton faced Wimbledon needing a win to avoid relegation. At 2-1 down and with time running out, in the 67th minute the midfielder's moment arrived: a poor header by Vinnie Jones was picked up by Horne on the outside of the centre circle; beating his man, he checked and as the ball bobbled up let fly with a 30-yard half-volleyed shot which crashed into the top left-hand corner of the Wimbledon net. Goodison went crazy, having witnessed one of its great goals. Everton went on to win 3-2, saving themselves, and Horne's Everton career was transformed.

When Joe Royle was appointed manager the following November, with Everton once more propping up the Premier League, he handed Horne and the other senior professionals at the club – Dave Watson, Paul Rideout and Neville Southall – the responsibility of saving Everton from what seemed like the near-certainty of relegation. All four responded magnificently, providing the backbone to a team which lost just six more games that season and won the FA Cup – Horne's first trophy at the age of 33.

During the 1995/96 season, as a Welshman Horne found himself first a victim of UEFA's 'three foreigners' rule, then suspension. Although he occasionally deputised as captain in the absence of Dave Watson, Royle increasingly favoured Tony Grant and John Ebbrell as his central midfield pairing. At the season's end Horne, now aged 34, was allowed to join Birmingham City. It was a move Royle soon came to regret and in March 1997 the Everton manager tried to bring him back to Goodison as player-coach. When the Everton board refused to sanction the move, Royle resigned and Horne stayed at Birmingham. He left the Midlands for Huddersfield Town the following summer, later having spells at Sheffield Wednesday, Kidderminster Harriers and Walsall.

A THOUGHTFUL, intelligent man, on retiring from football he returned to the career path he had abandoned two decades earlier, becoming a chemistry teacher in a Chester school, a position he currently combines with extensive local media work.

[FACTFILE]

BORN
St Asaph, 18 May 1962
POSITION
Midfield
OTHER CLUBS
Wrexham (1984–87);
Portsmouth (1987–89);
Southampton (1989–92);
Birmingham City (1996–97);
Huddersfield Town
(1997–2000);
Sheffield Wednesday (2000);
Kidderminster Harriers
(2000–01);
Walsall (2001)
HONOURS
1995 FA Cup; 59 Wales caps
(2 goals) (1987–97)

Season	League		FA Cup		League Cup		Europe		Total	
	App	Goals	App	Goals	App	Goals	App	Goals	App	Goals
1992/93	34	1	0 (1)	0	5 (1)	0	-	-	39 (2)	1
1993/94	28 (4)	1	2	0	5	0	-	-	35 (4)	1
1994/95	31	0	5	0	0	0	-	-	36	0
1995/96	25 (1)	1	4	0	2	0	3	0	34 (1)	1
Total	**118 (5)**	**3**	**11 (1)**	**0**	**12 (1)**	**0**	**3**	**0**	**144(7)**	**3**

Houghton, Harold

Former England schoolboy international whose solitary appearance came in Dixie's most glorious season

[FACTFILE]

BORN
Liverpool, 26 August 1906
POSITION
Inside forward
OTHER CLUBS
Exeter City (1928–33);
Norwich City (1933–35);
Bristol Rovers (1935–36);
South Liverpool

Season	League		FA Cup		Total	
	App	Goals	App	Goals	App	Goals
1927/28	1	0	0	0	1	0
Total	**1**	**0**	**0**	**0**	**1**	**0**

Houston, Johnny

Irish international who won the Military Medal for gallantry during the First World War

[FACTFILE]

BORN
Belfast, 17 May 1889
POSITION
Outside right / centre forward
OTHER CLUBS
Linfield
(1911–13 & 1915–19);
Partick Thistle (1919–20)
HONOURS
6 Ireland caps (1912–14)

Season	League		FA Cup		Total	
	App	Goals	App	Goals	App	Goals
1912/13	7	0	2	0	9	0
1913/14	18	2	0	0	18	2
1914/15	1	0	0	0	1	0
Total	**26**	**2**	**2**	**0**	**28**	**2**

Howard, Tim

Goalscoring goalkeeper who has become a model of stability and excellence

On Wednesday, 4 January 2012, when Everton faced Bolton Wanderers at Goodison, Tim Howard accomplished what no other goalkeeper had done in 134 years of Everton history: he scored a goal. On a night with a fierce, swirling wind, Howard hoofed a back-pass up the pitch. It bounced on the edge of the Bolton D and caught a gust before looping over the head of Bolton's hapless goalkeeper, Adam Bogdan. Adhering to the unspoken rule of goalkeepers, Howard refused to celebrate. 'I feel for him. I have been beaten by a goalkeeper before and it is quite awful,' he said afterwards.

A loan signing from Manchester United following the retirement of Nigel Martyn in 2006, Howard signed permanently for £3million a year later after impressing through the 2006/07 season. He had first made his reputation as an outstanding young goalkeeper with New Jersey Imperials in United Systems of Independent Soccer Leagues in the late 1990s.

Such was his potential that he was snapped up almost immediately by the New York Metrostars and earned his first United States cap in 2002. Manchester United paid $4million to bring him to Old Trafford in 2003, and he replaced the club's World Cup winning goalkeeper Fabien Barthez. Howard made the PFA Team of the Year in his first season at Old

Trafford, but later lost his United place to Roy Carroll then Edwin Van der Sar.

Athletic, agile and brave, Howard possessed all the necessary facets one would expect from a top-class goalkeeper, but also brought the consistency lacking in many of the players who had tried to fill the Everton goal since the departure

Season	League		FA Cup		League Cup		Europe		Total	
	App	Goals	App	Goals	App	Goals	App	Goals	App	Goals
2006/07	36	0	1	0	1	0	-	-	38	0
2007/08	36	0	0	0	3	0	8	0	47	0
2008/09	38	0	7	0	1	0	2	0	48	0
2009/10	38	0	2	0	2	0	9	0	51	0
2010/11	38	0	4	0	0	0	-	-	42	0
2011/12	38	1	6	0	0	0	-	-	44	1
Total	**224**	**1**	**20**	**0**	**7**	**0**	**19**	**0**	**270**	**1**

> HOWARD ACCOMPLISHED
> WHAT NO OTHER
> GOALKEEPER HAD DONE
> IN 134 YEARS
> OF EVERTON HISTORY

of Neville Southall. There was great solidity in the Everton defence during his early days at the club. Of the five seasons in which Everton have conceded fewest goals in their entire history, three came in Howard's first three years with the club.

Certainly he played his part in this, but there were sometimes doubts about aspects of his game. At times he seemed susceptible to long-range shots and his record at saving penalties was – initially – poor. He did, nevertheless, improve on these shortcomings.

Howard came of age as Everton goalkeeper in the 2009 FA Cup semi-final when Everton faced Manchester United. After a goalless draw the match went to penalties. Tim Cahill missed Everton's opening penalty, but Howard rose to the occasion against his former club. First he swooped low to save Dimitar Berbatov's poorly

hit effort with his legs, then dived brilliantly to keep out Rio Ferdinand's shot. Everton went on to win 4-2, and after the win had been secured Everton's victorious players piled on top of their hero.

'I have to say because of the way things all worked out and on a personal level for me the semi-final at Wembley was my best match-day moment for a lot of reasons; playing against your old club particularly when it's Manchester United,' Howard told Bluekipper.com in 2010. 'Great atmosphere, great stadium, the moment was huge and also the icing on the cake was that I was in a cup final with Everton, which meant a huge amount to me, so that was definitely a day that I relish.'

Howard succeeded Kasey Keller as the United States' first-choice goalkeeper in 2007 and represented his country at the 2009 Confederations Cup (where he won the Golden Glove Award for the best goalkeeper), the 2010 World Cup and the 2011 Gold Cup.

In March 2012 he signed a four-year contract extension at Goodison, which – if he sees it out – will ensure that he has a decade's service at the club. 'I couldn't be happier. I've had a smile on my face ever since we finalised the deal,' Howard told evertontv. 'When you have a really good relationship in life and both sides are

eager to continue and keep that going, it's a no-brainer. This hasn't been a knockdown, drawn-out type of negotiation with meetings or anything like that. They were very happy to keep me here and I was very happy to stay. It's a place that is home for me.'

[FACTFILE]

BORN
North Brunswick, New Jersey,
6 March 1979
POSITION
Goalkeeper
OTHER CLUBS
North Jersey Imperials (1997–98);
New York Metrostars (1998–2003);
Manchester United (2003–07)
HONOURS
78 United States caps (2002–)

Howard-Baker,
Benjamin

England international goalkeeper who also twice competed as an Olympic high jumper

[FACTFILE]

BORN
Aigburth, 13 February 1892
DIED
Warminster, 10 September 1987
POSITION
Goalkeeper
OTHER CLUBS
Blackburn Rovers (1913–14);
Preston North End (1914–15);
Liverpool (1919–20);
Chelsea (1921–26);
Oldham Athletic (1928–29)
HONOURS
2 England caps (1921–25)

Season	League		FA Cup		Total	
	App	Goals	App	Goals	App	Goals
1920/21	2	0	0	0	2	0
1926/27	11	0	0	0	11	0
Total	**13**	**0**	**0**	**0**	**13**	**0**

Howarth, Bob

Preston invincible who served as Everton captain during their first Goodison years

[FACTFILE]

BORN
Preston, 20 June 1865
DIED
20 August 1938
POSITION
Defender
OTHER CLUB
Preston North End
(1888–91 & 1894–98)
HONOURS
4 England caps (1886–94)

Season	League App	League Goals	FA Cup App	FA Cup Goals	Total App	Total Goals
1892/93	26	0	7	0	33	0
1893/94	22	0	1	0	23	0
Total	**48**	**0**	**8**	**0**	**56**	**0**

Howarth, Harold

Local-born inside forward whose first-team chances were stymied by the outbreak of war

[FACTFILE]

BORN
Liverpool, 1889
POSITION
Inside forward

Season	League App	League Goals	FA Cup App	FA Cup Goals	Total App	Total Goals
1914/15	1	0	0	0	1	0
1919/20	7	2	0	0	7	2
Total	**8**	**2**	**0**	**0**	**8**	**2**

Hughes, Darren

1984 FA Youth Cup winner who became a lower league stalwart

[FACTFILE]

BORN
Prescot, 6 October 1965
POSITION
Left back
OTHER CLUBS
Shrewsbury Town (1985–86);
Brighton & Hove Albion (1986–87);
Port Vale (1987–94);
Northampton Town (1994–96);
Exeter City (1996–97); Morecambe

Season	League App	League Goals	FA Cup App	FA Cup Goals	League Cup App	League Cup Goals	Europe App	Europe Goals	Total App	Total Goals
1983/84	1	0	0	0	0	0	-	-	1	0
1984/85	2	0	0	0	0	0	0	0	2	0
Total	**3**	**0**	**0**	**0**	**0**	**0**	**0**	**0**	**3**	**0**

Hughes, Mark (b.1963)

Centre forward with an illustrious past, long past his best on reaching Goodison

Mark Hughes played for some of Europe's biggest clubs and had long written his name into Manchester United lore on joining Everton in March 2000. His arrival coincided with a contractual dispute between Don Hutchison and Walter Smith that saw the Everton manager exclude the auxiliary forward. To the hair-tearing frustration of Evertonians, Hughes was apparently on a bumper pay deal while Smith refused to give the younger man the rise to which he felt he was entitled, selling whim at the season's end.

Aged 36, Hughes arrived from Southampton where he had scored just twice in 50 starts. He still possessed all the aggression and fight that had once been his trademarks, but his movement and pace were virtually non-existent. While Hughes could battle, scrap and hold the ball up all day long, he was a negligible threat in front of goal. He scored just once in an Everton shirt, and while there was a man-of-the-match performance in a derby stalemate, little else of consequence occurred in a dismal seven-month Goodison sojourn.

> **HE STILL POSSESSED ALL THE AGGRESSION AND FIGHT**

HUGHES, who combined playing for Everton with management of Wales, joined Blackburn Rovers in October 2000, playing on for a further 18 months before switching to full-time management.

[FACTFILE]

BORN
Wrexham, 1 November 1963
POSITION
Centre forward
OTHER CLUBS
Manchester United (1980–86);
Barcelona (1986–88);
Bayern Munich
(loan, 1987–88);
Manchester United
(1988–95);
Chelsea (1995–98);
Southampton (1998–2000);
Blackburn Rovers (2000–02)
AS MANAGER
Wales (1999–2004);
Blackburn Rovers (2004–08);
Manchester City (2008–09);
Fulham (2010–11);
Queens Park Rangers
(2012–)
HONOURS
72 Wales caps (16 goals)
(1984–99);
PFA Player of the Year
(1989 & 1991);
PFA Young Player of the Year
(1985)

Season	League		FA Cup		League Cup		Total	
	App	Goals	App	Goals	App	Goals	App	Goals
1999/2000	9	1	0	0	0	0	9	1
2000/01	7 (3)	0	0	0	1	0	7 (3)	0
Total	**16 (3)**	**1**	**0**	**0**	**1**	**0**	**16 (3)**	**1**

Hughes, Mark (b.1986)

Reserve team captain whose best days lay beyond Goodison

[FACTFILE]

BORN
Liverpool, 9 December 1986
POSITION
Centre back
OTHER CLUBS
Stockport County
(loan, 2006);
Northampton Town
(2007–09);
Walsall (2009–10);
North Queensland Fury
(2010–11);
Bury (2011–)

Season	League		FA Cup		League Cup		Europe		Total	
	App	Goals	App	Goals	App	Goals	App	Goals	App	Goals
2006/07	0 (1)	0	0	0	1 (1)	0	0	0	1 (2)	0
Total	**0 (1)**	**0**	**0**	**0**	**1 (1)**	**0**	**0**	**0**	**1 (2)**	**0**

Hughes, Stephen

Promising midfielder who failed to deliver on the Goodison stage

Stephen Hughes was a rare thing: a young English footballer who broke through into Arsène Wenger's Arsenal team. The left-sided England under-21 midfielder played a part in the Gunners 1997/98 Premiership triumph, but subsequently struggled to make an impression at Highbury. Hughes possessed many of the hallmarks of a Wenger player: technique, movement, a good first touch and accurate passing – but perhaps lacked the pace and guile that would have earned him a regular berth.

Still spoken of as a potential England international when Walter Smith signed him in March 2000, Hughes was placed straight into the starting line-up. He settled quickly, but without standing out or seeming to justify the £3million price tag put on his head – a fee that subsequently turned out to be based on appearances and other clauses, of which Everton paid just £500,000. While showing some of the flourishes of an intelligent and inventive midfielder, as Smith's reign started to wane during the 2000/01 season Hughes degenerated into a pale, enigmatic presence, contributing little to a struggling team. Off the pitch there were questions asked of his attitude, which may have stemmed from an alleged half-time brawl involving Smith's assistant, Archie Knox, when Everton faced Bradford City in November 2000.

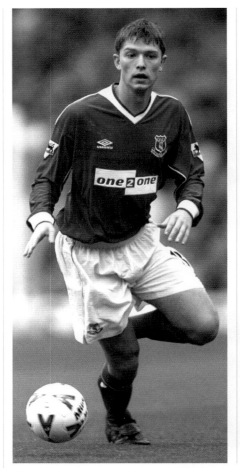

AMID TALK of homesickness, Hughes was edged out of the first team. There were rumours of a transfer to West Ham that failed to materialise, and at the end of the 2000/01 season he was released from his contract. Hughes joined Watford and played out a career of underachievement outside the top flight.

> A POTENTIAL ENGLAND INTERNATIONAL WHEN WALTER SMITH SIGNED HIM IN MARCH 2000

[FACTFILE]

BORN
Wokingham, 18 September 1976
POSITION
Midfield
OTHER CLUBS
Arsenal (1995–2000);
Fulham (loan, 1999);
Watford (2001–03);
Charlton Athletic (2003–04);
Coventry City (2004–08);
Walsall (2008–09)

Season	League		FA Cup		League Cup		Total	
	App	Goals	App	Goals	App	Goals	App	Goals
1999/2000	11	1	0	0	0	0	11	1
2000/01	16 (2)	0	2	1	1 (1)	0	19 (3)	1
Total	**27 (2)**	**1**	**2**	**1**	**1 (1)**	**0**	**30 (3)**	**2**

Hughes, Ted

Welsh international left half who made a name for himself with Tottenham Hotspur

Season	League		FA Cup		Total	
	App	Goals	App	Goals	App	Goals
1898/99	8	0	0	0	8	0
Total	**8**	**0**	**0**	**0**	**8**	**0**

[FACTFILE]

BORN
Ruabon, 1876
POSITION
Left half
OTHER CLUBS
Tottenham Hotspur (1899–1908);
Clyde
HONOURS
14 Wales caps
(1899–1907)

Humphreys, Gerry

Son of the 1940s defender who became a fringe member of Harry Catterick's great teams

EVERTON
Football Club
GOODISON PARK · LIVERPOOL

FOOTBALL LEAGUE — DIVISION 1
EVERTON V.
LEICESTER CITY
SATURDAY, 30th NOVEMBER, 1968
Kick-off 3 p.m.   Price 9d

OFFICIAL PROGRAMME

[FACTFILE]

BORN
Llandudno, 14 January 1946
POSITION
Winger
OTHER CLUBS
Crystal Palace (1970–71);
Crewe Alexandra (1971–77);
Rhyl

Season	League		FA Cup		League Cup		Europe		Total	
	App	Goals	App	Goals	App	Goals	App	Goals	App	Goals
1965/66	2	0	0	0	-	-	0	0	2	0
1966/67	0	0	0	0	-	-	0	0	0	0
1967/68	4	0	0	0	0	0	-	-	4	0
1968/69	5	2	0	0	1	0	-	-	6	2
1969/70	1	0	0	0	1	0	-	-	2	0
Total	**12**	**2**	**0**	**0**	**2**	**0**	**0**	**0**	**14**	**2**

Humphreys, Jack

Welsh international centre back whose prime was cut short by war

Jack Humphreys' nine-year-long Goodison career was limited to just 61 full appearances, a tally that would surely have been far greater had it not been for the intervention of the Second World War.

The war was a conflict in which Humphreys fought as a bombardier in the RAF, combining it with occasional appearances for Everton. The son of a schoolmaster and student at the renowned Loughborough College, he was spotted as an amateur in the summer of 1942 and signed professional terms with Everton the following April.

THE CENTRE BACK established a place for himself in the Everton team in the Football League North during the second part of the 1945/46 season. When the Football League restarted in August 1946 T.G. Jones took his place, but his fellow-countryman's disputes with the Everton management over subsequent years gave Humphreys playing time. A powerful defender, he, like many of his colleagues, suffered by comparison to the great pre-war League Championship winning team as Everton struggled to make an impression in the post-war years.

Appearances by the end of the 1940s had become harder to come by for Humphreys, so it was with some surprise that the club rejected a £12,000 bid for his services from Plymouth Argyle in October 1949. As T.G. Jones' dispute with Everton became martial over the following year, it was Humphreys' misfortune that he was suffering from injury, and Ted Falder instead stepped up to the mantle. Having made just a solitary appearance in the fateful relegation season of 1950/51 the club released Humphreys and he joined Llandudno Town.

HUMPHREYS died suddenly in September 1954, a month short of his 34th birthday. On being informed of his tragic demise the club paid a £50 grant to his widow and recommended that the Football League did likewise from its Jubilee Fund. His son Gerry played for Everton during the 1960s.

> HIS SON GERRY PLAYED FOR EVERTON DURING THE 1960S

[FACTFILE]

BORN
Llandudno, 28 October 1920
DIED
Llandudno,
14 September 1954
POSITION
Centre half
HONOURS
1 Wales cap (1947)

Season	League		FA Cup		Total	
	App	Goals	App	Goals	App	Goals
1945/46	-	-	2	0	2	0
1946/47	21	0	1	0	22	0
1947/48	18	0	5	0	23	0
1948/49	4	0	0	0	4	0
1949/50	9	0	0	0	9	0
1950/51	1	0	0	0	1	0
Total	**53**	**0**	**8**	**0**	**61**	**0**

Hunt,
Roger Patrick 'Ernie'

Famous as winner of Match of the Day's Goal of the Season, despite his heavy price tag he failed to make the Goodison grade

[FACTFILE]

BORN
Swindon, 17 March 1943
POSITION
Inside forward
OTHER CLUBS
Swindon Town (1959–65);
Wolverhampton Wanderers (1965–67);
Los Angeles Wolves (1967);
Coventry City (1968–73);
Doncaster Rovers (loan, 1973);
Bristol Rovers (1973–74)

Season	League		FA Cup		League Cup		Total	
	App	Goals	App	Goals	App	Goals	App	Goals
1967/68	12 (2)	3	1	0	1	0	14 (2)	3
Total	12 (2)	3	1	0	1	0	14 (2)	3

Hurel, Eli

Channel Islander who briefly deputised for Nat Cunliffe

[FACTFILE]

BORN
Jersey, 10 April 1915
POSITION
Inside forward
OTHER CLUBS
Northampton Town (1938–39)

Season	League		FA Cup		Total	
	App	Goals	App	Goals	App	Goals
1936/37	5	1	0	0	5	1
Total	5	1	0	0	5	1

Hurst, John

Cool and versatile defender every bit as unassuming as he was underrated

Hailed as the 'new Tommy Lawton' on his arrival at Goodison as an England schoolboy centre forward in May 1962, John Hurst made his name for Everton not as a striker but wing half, then central defender. In a lengthy – only 13 men have made more first-team appearances for Everton – and distinguished career, 'Gentleman Jack', the quiet man of the Everton dressing room, proved one of the First Division's most impeccable and consistent defenders, winning a league title medal in 1970 and providing sterling service through the first half of the new decade.

After plying his trade in the Central League and winning an FA Youth Cup Winners medal in 1965, Hurst made the step up to the senior side in August 1965 when he was named twelfth man for the opening-day clash with Northampton Town. He had to wait another week before making his debut as a substitute – the first in Everton's history – for Fred Pickering in an away fixture to Stoke City.

In this debut season, the teenager made 21 league appearances in a variety of roles, including wing half, centre back and centre forward, scoring twice, but failing to make a single appearance in Everton's successful FA Cup run.

AS HARRY Catterick reshaped the cup winning team over the 1966/67 season, Hurst found himself a regular place as Brian Labone's central defensive partner. Comfortable in possession, Hurst was an adept reader of the game, always more likely to make a timely interception than a last-ditch tackle. The quietest member of the dressing room, his ascent seemed somehow less meteoric than some of his less unassuming colleagues. But in March 1967, Hurst showed the football world his true value when he won the man-of-the-match award in the FA Cup epic against Liverpool. Entering the game as a largely unknown 20-year-old against Roger Hunt, a World Cup winner just months earlier, before more than 60,000 spectators Hurst proved unflustered and marked Hunt out of the game.

Everton subsequently fell in the FA Cup quarter-finals, but Hurst's Wembley chance came a year

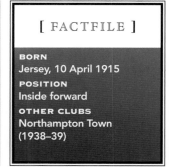

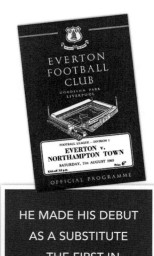

HE MADE HIS DEBUT AS A SUBSTITUTE – THE FIRST IN EVERTON'S HISTORY – FOR FRED PICKERING

Catterick was always, however, a taskmaster and said that Hurst's key weakness was a lack of self-belief. 'He has far more ability than he displays at times,' he added. 'He has greater attacking flair and when this situation is on for him to break from the back, he rarely does it. When he does, it usually means trouble for the opposition.'

later, when he recovered from jaundice to play on the losing side in the 1968 final. An ever-present over the following two seasons, he played a crucial role in the 1969/70 Championship triumph, also weighing in with some vital goals. His goal against Manchester United in only the second game of the season was described by the Daily Post's Horace Yates as 'a perfect cross shot'. Yates added: 'Here one of the greatest destroyers in modern football showed that he had not forgotten the schoolboy days when

he was England's centre forward. A scorer also at Arsenal on Saturday, he firmly underlined his claims to all-round status. His achievements made a mockery of the fact that Sir Alf Ramsey had named eight Everton players for his World Cup squad and still found it possible to omit Hurst.'

That Hurst's international hopes did not progress beyond the England under-23 team can be attributed to the continued excellence of Bobby Moore and then Colin Todd in his position. But for Harry Catterick, Hurst was a vital figure in his talented emerging team in the late 1960s.

Speaking in a full and frank television interview in December 1969, he said of the defender: 'John Hurst bolts up this defence along with Brian Labone. They play this twin centre half role so common in modern football. I think they complement one another very well. John has great defensive strengths because he's so powerful, he's very, very good in the air and he reads play exceptionally well.'

HURST continued to excel for Everton and by 1975 was, along with Roger Kenyon, the sole survivor of the 1970 title win. However, he was not part of Billy Bingham's long-term plans and was sold to Oldham Athletic in the summer of 1976, aged 29. He provided five years of effective service at Boundary Park, retiring in 1981. He returned to Everton in 1995 as youth team coach under Joe Royle, later rejoining his former team-mate when he took over as Manchester City manager.

Season	League App	League Goals	FA Cup App	FA Cup Goals	League Cup App	League Cup Goals	Other App	Other Goals	Total App	Total Goals
1965/66	19 (2)	2	0	0	-	-	0	0	19 (2)	2
1966/67	23 (2)	2	6	0	-	-	0	0	29 (2)	2
1967/68	40	5	5	0	2	0	-	-	47	5
1968/69	42	7	5	2	4	0	-	-	54	9
1969/70	42	5	1	0	3	0	-	-	46	5
1970/71	40	3	5	0	-	-	7	0	52	3
1971/72	28 (1)	0	1 (2)	1	1	0	-	-	30 (3)	1
1972/73	28 (1)	1	2	0	0	0	-	-	30 (1)	1
1973/74	39	3	3	1	2	0	2	0	44	4
1974/75	29 (2)	1	1	0	0	0	-	-	30 (2)	1
1975/76	6 (3)	0	1	0	1	0	0 (1)	0	8 (4)	0
Total	**336 (11)**	**29**	**30 (2)**	**4**	**13**	**1**	**9 (1)**	**0**	**388(14)**	**34**

[FACTFILE]

BORN
Blackpool, 6 February 1947
POSITION
Central defender
OTHER CLUB
Oldham Athletic (1976–81)
HONOURS
1969/70
League Championship

Husband, Jimmy

Tricky forward who faded after title triumph

'I shall never be able to forget it. I was standing almost under the West Brom bar and the cross was perfect. I could almost have swallowed it,' Jimmy Husband recalled years later of the moment that would have made him a Wembley hero. 'But just as I was about to stick it in, Alan Ball shouted. He did the right thing because he was probably in a good position but the call put me in two minds. It was my mistake. It was the biggest mistake I ever made. And I had to do it at Wembley.' It came four minutes from the end of the 1968 FA Cup final and with the score deadlocked at 0-0 would almost certainly have seen off West Bromwich Albion. But an extra-time winner from Jeff Astle – entirely against the run of play – won the cup for Albion and Husband's mistake has come to overshadow a largely impressive career.

Born in Newcastle, the young Geordie first attracted attention as a 15-year-old England schoolboy international, quickly attracting comparisons with Jackie Milburn. Everton beat off a plethora of clubs, including Newcastle, to sign the youngster, who started out as an inside right. With his quick feet, teasing skill and low centre of gravity – which contributed to a mesmerising body swerve – he impressed Harry Catterick, making his debut, aged just 17, against Fulham in April 1965. That same month he helped Everton win the FA Youth Cup for the first time since the competition's inauguration in 1953.

OVER THE following three seasons, Husband became established in the first team, picking up seven England under-23 caps, although full international honours eluded him. Catterick preferred him as an outside right, and it was here that he proved most potent, providing a supply line for the prolific Joe Royle. Husband nevertheless featured in most attacking positions, and was himself a regular name on the Everton scoresheet. His best season came in

1968/69 when he notched 20 goals in all competitions. The following term he played a part in the Blues' Championship win, although he was beset by injury, after which he seemed to lose confidence. Alan Whittle replaced him in the season's run-in, to immense effect.

Like so many of his team-mates, post-1970 Husband struggled to hit top form again. He joined Luton Town in November 1973, where he spent four years. Then, like many of his contemporaries, he moved to the US to try his luck in the NASL with the Memphis Rogues, where he came under the management of Malcolm Allison.

'HUSBAND CAME WITHIN MILLIMETRES OF BECOMING A WEMBLEY HERO'

[FACTFILE]

BORN
Newcastle, 15 October 1947
POSITION
Outside right / forward
OTHER CLUBS
Luton Town (1973–78);
Memphis Rogues (1978–80)
HONOURS
1969/70 League Championship

Season	League		FA Cup		League Cup		Other		Total	
	App	Goals	App	Goals	App	Goals	App	Goals	App	Goals
1964/65	1	0	0	0	-	-	0	0	1	0
1965/66	4	0	0	0	-	-	1	0	5	0
1966/67	19	6	6	4	-	-	1	0	26	10
1967/68	19 (1)	5	6	3	-	-	-	-	25 (1)	8
1968/69	36	19	5	0	2	1	-	-	43	19
1969/70	30	6	0	0	2	0	-	-	32	6
1970/71	15	6	4	3	-	-	3 (1)	0	22 (1)	9
1971/72	25 (2)	1	1	0	0	0	-	-	26 (2)	1
1972/73	8 (1)	0	0	0	0	0	-	-	8 (1)	0
1973/74	1 (3)	1	0	0	1	0	1	0	3 (3)	1
Total	**158 (7)**	**44**	**22**	**10**	**5**	**1**	**6 (1)**	**0**	**191(8)**	**55**

Hutchison,
Don

Effective midfielder who fell foul of Walter Smith's apparent parsimony

Signed from Sheffield United for £1.2million as Gary Speed's replacement amid the dark days of winter 1998, Don Hutchison's arrival at Everton raised some eyebrows among Evertonians and seemed to be another symbol of a club in decline. In the early 1990s Hutchison had been a promising midfielder at Liverpool, but had seen his Anfield career fade in the midst of drink-fuelled disciplinary problems. Subsequent spells at West Ham and Sheffield United hinted at a waning career.

YET HUTCHISON, who pleaded that his bad-boy days were behind him, confounded this initial scepticism, putting in some sound performances as Everton squeaked away from the relegation mire. A combative and physical midfielder with a good eye for a pass and a willingness to join attacks, he added some much needed robustness to Everton's midfield.

When fresh investment came over the following summer, Hutchison was expected to make way for such big-money signings as John Collins and Olivier Dacourt, but the adopted Scot easily overshadowed their contributions through the 1998/99 season. Indeed, Walter Smith was so impressed with Hutchison's contribution to the Everton midfield and as an auxiliary centre forward that he awarded him the captaincy in Dave Watson's absence. Never did he shirk these responsibilities, although sometimes it was reckoned he took them too far – as witness the punch he aimed at Richard Gough in an extraordinary on-the-pitch confrontation in October 1999.

BY NOW Hutchison was one of Everton's most consistent performers. With his contract due for renewal at the end of 2000/01, the club were keen to start negotiations lest he move on a lucrative free transfer under the Bosman ruling. Yet on Hutchison's basic salary of £9000 per week, Everton were only prepared to offer him an increase of £750.

In February 2000, Hutchison misguidedly described the offer as 'a disgrace'. Smith was furious, transfer-listing and dropping him. But this proved self-defeating and, without Hutchison, Everton embarked on a dismal run that extinguished vague hopes of European qualification. Although his comments were viewed with distaste, many supporters saw the manager's response as self-destructive. This sense was heightened when the injured Kevin Campbell was ruled out for the remainder of the season and rather than use Hutchison as an auxiliary centre forward, Smith signed the veteran Mark Hughes on wages said to be twice Hutchison's.

Before Smith could rid Everton of Hutchison, the player was embroiled in one final controversy. Recalled for the Good Friday derby meeting with Liverpool, the match was the usual tight tense affair, and seemed to be heading for its customary stalemate.

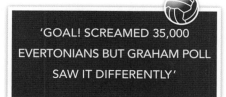

Then, 90 seconds into the two minutes of allocated stoppage time, Sander Westerveld took a free kick quickly, it hit Hutchison in the back as he was walking away, and flew over the Liverpool goalkeeper's head and into the back of his net. 'GOAL!' Screamed 35,000 Evertonians. But the referee, Graham Poll, saw it differently, claiming that he had already blown for full time. 'The players got excited and confused as they do in derby matches but it was clear in my mind,' Poll told reporters after the match. 'Strange, then,' noted The Times, 'that his hands should have been down by his sides as Westerveld took the kick.' Walter Smith was similarly bemused: 'The fourth official put up two minutes on the board, but the ball crossed the line 15 seconds short of that. We have a computer that measures it. I feel the referee has taken the easy way out.' The decision bore echoes of the Clive Thomas controversy 23 years earlier and Poll later admitted he'd got it wrong.

In summer 2000 came Hutchison's inevitable transfer, to Sunderland, who paid £2.5million. After a solitary season, he returned to West Ham in a £5million deal, but was beset by injuries. Given a free transfer in 2005, he played out his career in the lower leagues, with Millwall, Coventry City and Luton Town, calling time on his playing career in 2008.

[FACTFILE]

BORN
Gateshead, 9 May 1971

POSITION:
Midfield / forward

OTHER CLUBS
Hartlepool United (1990);
Liverpool (1990–94);
West Ham (1994–96);
Sheffield United (1996–98);
Sunderland (2000–01);
West Ham (2001–05);
Millwall (2005);
Coventry City (2005–07);
Luton Town (2007–08)

HONOURS
26 Scotland caps (6 goals) (1999–2003)

	League		FA Cup		League Cup		Total	
Season	App	Goals	App	Goals	App	Goals	App	Goals
1997/98	11	1	0	0	0	0	11	1
1998/99	29 (3)	3	4	0	3 (1)	1	36 (4)	4
1999/2000	28 (3)	6	5	0	1	0	34 (3)	6
Total	**68 (6)**	**10**	**9**	**0**	**4 (1)**	**1**	**81 (7)**	**11**

THE
EVERTON
·ENCYCLOPEDIA·

Individual Awards, Inter-Cities Fairs Cup, Record
Internationalists, Ireland and Everton, Alan **Irvine,**
Bobby **Irvine,** David **Irving,** Robert **Izzatt**

Individual Awards

From the Football Writers' Association Player of the Year to Oceania's, Everton personnel have largely been overlooked in the football awards

It is surprising, given Everton's excellence through the 1960s, and the achievements of players like Bob Latchford and Dave Hickson at other times, that no Everton player received an individual accolade until the mid-1980s.

FOOTBALL'S FIRST widely recognised individual award was the Football Writers' Association Player of the Year, created in 1947. It was the idea of Charlie Buchan, the former Arsenal and Sunderland player who had since embarked on a career as editor and publisher of his eponymous Football Monthly, for an award to be given 'to the professional player who by precept and example is considered by a ballot of members to be the footballer of the year'. It was voted by members of the Football Writers' Association. A quarter of a century later, in 1973, the Professional Footballers' Association launched its own Player of the Year award, also rewarding the best young player of the year. Both awards were voted for by its members.

In 1994 the League Managers' Association created its Manager of the Year award.

The Ballon D'or, or European Footballer of the Year, was created in 1956 by France Football magazine. The award is voted for by leading football journalists, but although Stanley Matthews won the inaugural prize it has traditionally been dominated by players from the Italian and Spanish leagues. Gary Lineker is the Everton player to come closest to winning the award, when he came second to Igor Belanov in 1986. From 1967/68 the European Golden Boot was awarded to the leading domestic goalscorer in European football.

Neither Bob Latchford in 1978 nor Lineker in 1986 – the two Everton players to top the English scoring charts since 1968 – came close to winning the award.

In 1991 FIFA launched its World Footballer of the Year award, voted for by captains and coaches of national teams.

No Everton player has won this award, although Tim Cahill has been long-listed for it. Cahill was in 2004 named Oceania Footballer of the Year. Joseph Yobo and

Steven Pienaar have been long-listed for the African Footballer of the Year award and in 1996 Daniel Amokachi came third in that year's voting.

GARY LINEKER IS THE EVERTON PLAYER TO COME CLOSEST TO WINNING THE AWARD

Football Writers' Player of the Year

1985 Neville Southall
1986 Gary Lineker

Professional Footballers' Association Footballer of the Year

1985 Peter Reid
1986 Gary Lineker

Oceania Footballer of the Year

2004 Tim Cahill

Bell's Manager of the Year

1985 Howard Kendall

League Managers' Association Manager of the Year

2003 David Moyes
2005 David Moyes
2009 David Moyes

Inter-Cities Fairs Cup

Precursor of the UEFA Cup, it witnessed Everton's first involvement in European competition

The Inter-Cities Fairs Cup was a European football competition played between 1955 and 1971.

It was formulated by the Swiss football pools magnate, Ernst Thonmen, the Italian league president, Ottorino Barassi, and Stanley Rous, the FA general secretary. Its creation was in keeping with the rising sense of cooperation and rapprochement in Europe at this time, and it was initially designed to be accompanied by international trade fairs. In its initial stages it was played between an amalgam of a city's teams (i.e. London, Vienna, Birmingham, and so on) and played over the duration of two and even three years.

From 1960/61 it followed a format – a two-legged knockout contest played between 'proper' clubs – that was virtually unchanged for the rest of its life, and most of the existence of its successor, the UEFA Cup, too.

Everton first entered in the 1962/63 season, but their debut was inauspicious and they fell at the first hurdle to Jock Stein's Dunfermline. They subsequently entered in 1964/65 and 1965/66, but were denied entry in the late 1960s because of a 'one club per city' rule. Because Liverpool finished ahead of them in the league, for the 1968/69 competition Chelsea qualified and for the 1969/70 competition Arsenal qualified – despite both finishing a league position behind Everton the previous year. Not for the last time would Everton be denied European qualification due to their neighbours.

In 1971 the competition came under UEFA's jurisdiction and was renamed the UEFA Cup. Four years later Everton fell victim of the 'one city' rule for a third time. This time, however, they appealed, arguing that it was anachronism, and won.

Everton's Record

1962/63

24 OCTOBER 1962
Rd 1 1st leg v. Dunfermline Athletic [H] 1-0
Stevens; 40,224
West, Parker, Thomson, Gabriel, Labone, Harris, Bingham, Stevens, Young, Vernon, Morrissey

31 OCTOBER 1962
Rd 1 2nd leg v. Dunfermline Athletic [A] 0-2 (aggregate 1-2); 21,813
West, Parker, Meagan, Gabriel, Labone, Harris, Bingham, Stevens, Young, Vernon, Morrissey

1964/65

23 SEPTEMBER 1964
Rd 1 1st leg v. Valerengen [A] 5-2 *Pickering 2, Harvey, Scott, Temple;* 17,952
Rankin, Harris, Brown, Gabriel, Labone, Stevens, Scott, Harvey, Pickering, Temple, Morrissey

14 OCTOBER 1964
Rd 1 2nd leg v. Valerengen [H] 4-2 (aggregate 9-4) *Young 2, Vernon, own goal;* 20,717
Rankin, Wright, Brown, Stevens, Labone, Harris, Scott, Young, Pickering, Vernon, Temple

11 NOVEMBER 1964
Rd 2 1st leg v. Kilmarnock [A] 2-0 *Temple, Morrissey;* 20,000
Rankin, Stevens, Brown, Gabriel, Labone, Stevens, Temple, Young, Pickering, Harvey, Morrissey

23 NOVEMBER 1964
Rd 2 2nd leg v. Kilmarnock [H] 4-1 (aggregate 6-1) *Pickering 2, Harvey, Young;* 30,727
Rankin, Harris, Brown, Gabriel, Labone, Stevens, Temple, Young, Pickering, Harvey, Morrissey

20 JANUARY 1965
Rd 3 1st leg v. Manchester United [A] 1-1
Pickering; 54,347
West, Wright, Wilson, Gabriel, Labone, Stevens, Scott, Harvey, Pickering, Vernon, Temple

4 FEBRUARY 1965
Rd 3 2nd leg v. Manchester United [H] 1-2 (aggregate 2-3) *Pickering;* 53,497
West, Wright, Wilson, Gabriel, Labone, Stevens, Scott, Harvey, Pickering, Vernon, Temple

1965/66

28 SEPTEMBER 1965
Rd 1 1st leg v. 1FC Nuremberg [A] 1-1
Harris; 10,000
West, Wright, Wilson, Gabriel, Brown, Harris, Temple, Stevens, Pickering, Harvey, Morrissey

12 OCTOBER 1965
Rd 1 2nd leg v. 1FC Nuremberg [H] 1-0 (aggregate 2-1) *Gabriel;* 39,033
West (Rankin), Wright, Wilson, Gabriel, Labone, Harris, Scott, Harvey, Pickering, Young, Temple

3 NOVEMBER 1965
Rd 2 1st leg v. Ujpest Dozsa [A] 0-3; 4000
Rankin, Wright, Wilson, Stevens, Labone, Harris, Scott, Harvey, Pickering, Temple, Morrissey

16 NOVEMBER 1965
Rd 2 2nd leg v. Ujpest Dozsa [H] 2-1 (aggregate 2-4) *Harris, own goal;* 24,201
Rankin, Wright, Wilson, Harvey, Labone, Harris, Temple, Gabriel, Young, Husband, Morrissey

Ireland, Everton and

Everton and the Emerald Isle have a lengthy shared past and present

Everton possessed so many Irish players in the mid-1950s that there was a contemporaneous joke that 20 minutes could pass without a Protestant touching the ball.

AT THE START of the 1956/57 season, for instance, Everton lined up with Jimmy O'Neill, Don Donavon, Peter Farrell and Tommy Eglington, while possessing several others in reserve, such as Mick Meagan and John Sutherland, who could also claim Irish passports. This led to a huge growth in the team's popularity in Ireland, and overnight ferries full of Irish fans would dock in Liverpool each match day. Since then the club's popularity in Ireland has been overtaken by Manchester United and Liverpool, but even in the 21st century it is not insignificant.

Jimmy 'Paddy' Sheridan was Everton's first Irish International. Sheridan made his debut in a 4-0 defeat to England at Molineux on 14 February, 1903. Since then Everton have possessed 17 further Ireland (pre-revolution) and Northern Ireland internationals. A further 21 have represented the Irish Free State or Republic of Ireland as of April 2012.

The clubs most noteworthy Ireland internationals were Peter Farrell and Tommy Eglington. They shared a footballing career that lasted more than 20 years, spanning four different decades and three clubs.

The two great friends started out as juniors with Shamrock Rovers in the late 1930s and spearheaded one of Rovers most successful teams, reaching the final of three successive FAI Finals, winning it in 1944 and 1945, and finishing runners-up in 1946. Soon after they signed for Everton and went on to play important roles in the Blues' first season back in competitive football following the war. Over the next 11 years they played a combined total of more than 800 League and FA Cup games, most in the same side as each other. Aged 34, in June 1957 Eglington joined Tranmere Rovers; Farrell followed him four months later. Farrell stayed at Prenton Park until 1960 when he finally left his team-mate for good, joining Holyhead Town. Eglington left Birkenhead a year later and played out his career with Cork Hibernians before working as a butcher in Dublin. Farrell returned to Ireland in 1962 and managed St Patricks Athletic, later running his own insurance business.

Everton have had two Irish managers, former Republic captain Johnny Carey (1958–61), and former (and future) Northern Ireland boss Billy Bingham (1973–77).

Although born and brought up in a Welsh border town, Kevin Sheedy, who claims Irish parentage, is Everton's greatest Irish player. In the 1980s, the unerring accuracy of his left foot elevated his adopted country into their first major finals: the 1988 European Championships in West Germany and 1990 World Cup in Italy. At the latter, Sheedy scored his country's first World Cup goal, rifling a late equaliser in Ireland's group match with England.

Jack Charlton's policy – continued by his successors – of selecting 'naturalised' Irish players (i.e. those born outside Ireland, but with an Irish parent or grandparent) has meant that of Everton's nine internationals wsince the mid-1980s, fewer than half – Darron Gibson, Seamus Coleman, Richard Dunne and Gareth Farrelly – were actually born in Ireland.

WHEN WAYNE ROONEY burst onto football's consciousness, Ireland manager Mick McCarthy tried to recruit him for the Republic's national team. Rooney dashed those slim hopes in 2003 when, shortly after his 17th birthday, he made his England debut against Australia.

Irvine, Alan

Traditional Scottish winger who returned to Goodison as David Moyes' assistant

Signed as a 23-year-old amateur from Queen's Park in May 1981, Alan Irvine had previously resisted the lure of professional football to complete his Chartered Insurance Institute exams. An old-school Scottish winger, he maintained a noble tradition set at Goodison by the likes of Alec Troup, Torry Gillick and Alex Scott. A good dribbler with pace and skill, he proved a natural crowd pleaser and at times defied the notion that his type of player was a dying breed.

Moyes and Irvine would enjoy one of the country's most prominent and longest serving managerial partnerships. From beyond Goodison the perception was that Irvine, a personable, friendly character, provided a contrast to Moyes's sharper edge.

'I don't think David was ever a bad cop but it is different as an assistant manager,' Irvine said of their partnership in 2009. 'The lads will turn to you a bit more because they know that you haven't picked the team. Even though it may well have been that David had gone with the team that I suggested. A massive thing for the assistant manager is that the players must never feel that you disagree with the manager. In private you might disagree, and we did on many occasions, but when he made the final decision we were all behind him.'

In November 2007, Irvine left Goodison to take on Moyes's former job as Preston North End manager, which he held for two years. A subsequent spell at Sheffield Wednesday was less happy.

Everton, however, still remained in his heart and in June 2011 he returned to Finch Farm to head Everton's academy. 'A big part of me will always belong to Everton,' he would reflect. 'I had a special time when I was there as a player and it was a special time when I was assistant manager. The club caught the imagination of my family and it is that kind of place.'

'I HAD A SPECIAL TIME WHEN I WAS THERE AS A PLAYER AND IT WAS A SPECIAL TIME WHEN I WAS ASSISTANT MANAGER'

And yet this was never quite enough for Irvine to make a regular place in the Everton team his own. Frustrated at biding his time in the Central League, he requested a transfer in September 1983. He stayed long enough to play a prominent role in Everton's two cup runs that season, appearing in both Milk Cup Final games against Liverpool, and in all of Everton's FA Cup games before the semi-final with Southampton. At the end of the season he joined Crystal Palace for £50,000 and subsequently had spells at Dundee United and Blackburn Rovers.

IN THE EARLY 1990s, Irvine embarked on a coaching career and in 1998 was made director of Newcastle's youth academy. Here his reputation quickly grew and in 2002 David Moyes offered him the assistant manager's job at Goodison. So highly was he rated at St James's Park that he was offered an unprecedented ten-year contract to stay, but Goodison was too alluring.

[FACTFILE]

BORN
Glasgow, 12 July 1958

POSITION
Winger

OTHER CLUBS
Queen's Park (1977–81);
Crystal Palace (1984–87);
Dundee United (1987–89);
Blackburn Rovers (1989–92)

AS MANAGER
Preston North End (2007–09),
Sheffield Wednesday (2010–11)

Season	League		FA Cup		League Cup		Total	
	App	Goals	App	Goals	App	Goals	App	Goals
1981/82	25	3	0	0	0	0	25	3
1982/83	7 (7)	1	2	0	0 (1)	0	9 (8)	1
1983/84	19 (2)	0	7	2	10	0	36 (2)	2
Total	**51 (9)**	**4**	**9**	**2**	**10 (1)**	**0**	**70 (10)**	**6**

EVERTON

1503 R. IRVINE

ROBERT IRVINE
EVERTON

Irvine, Bobby

Northern Irish inside forward who was 'better than Best'

Irish international Bobby Irvine was a thrilling inside right who illuminated Goodison through the 1920s. A brilliant showman, he was the finest Ulsterman to ever play football according to one of his colleagues. 'He was very good,' recalled his team-mate. 'He was better than Georgie Best at dribbling the ball. I've seen him bring it the length of the field beating man after man.' High praise indeed. And who would possibly argue with Dixie Dean?

SPOTTED PLAYING for Dunrummy, Irvine was invited over to Merseyside for a trial in the summer of 1921. The junior international impressed as a triallist in the annual Blues v. Whites match, but returned to Ireland while a four-way battle for his signature between Everton, Sunderland, Partick Thistle and Dundee was played out. Everton prevailed with £500 securing his arrival.

> HIS CHARGES INTO ENEMY TERRITORY WREAKED HAVOC AND YIELDED HIM A HEALTHY BOUNTY OF GOALS – 11 IN HIS 26 GAMES DURING THE 1921/22 SEASON

Irvine's forte was running with the ball at pace. His charges into enemy territory wreaked havoc and yielded him a healthy bounty of goals – 11 in his 26 games during the 1921/22 season. Not bad for a player immediately thrust into the hurly-burly of the First Division.

Initially he played as centre forward as Everton struggled desperately for form. Their lack of potency during Irvine's debut season almost led to relegation, but thereafter things improved.

The arrival of Jack Cock midway through the 1922/23 season saw Irvine switch to his preferred inside forward position and flourish. With Wilf Chadwick and Cock, Irvine formed part of the most potent forward line in the First Division during the 1923/24 season.

International recognition had by then arrived for the forward and he would make 15 appearances for Ireland. He attracted plenty of praise – Irvine 'worked like a horse both in attack and defence' was one verdict – but was not without critics either. Just as he could delight, so he could frustrate and he was often accused of overelaboration and not looking up. 'He dribbled to excess at times and one moment ran into a full back full tilt,' recalled one correspondent. 'He displeases many by his habit, which he cannot seen to throw off, of over-dribbling,' added the Liverpool Courier.

IRVINE'S brush with greatness came with the arrival of Dixie

Dean towards the end of the 1924/25 season. The centre forward became the fulcrum of the team, the dominant figure on and off the pitch. Along with his fellow inside forward Fred Kennedy, Irvine modified his game to allow Dean to flourish. 'It was noticeable that Everton's inside forwards, Kennedy and Irvine, were inclined to hang back a few yards, and the forward line gained by this, in addition to which the men named could give help to a harassed defence,' wrote Ernest 'Bee' Edwards of an early outing with Dean as the main man.

For two years Irvine helped Dean terrorise opposing defences and lined up alongside him as outside left on the opening day of the 1927/28 season. Everton won 4-0 but Irvine succumbed to injury. Ted Critchley took his place and Irvine struggled to find a way back into a team that was sweeping all comers. 'Irvine's appearance at inside left in view of Weldon's illness brought a new touch to the leaders' side, and though the Irishman showed all its old-time skill in dribbling, he hardly fitted the new Everton pattern of play,' recalled the Liverpool Courier of a rare appearance against Bury. Critchley, by contrast, 'played a smart game'.

Time was running out for Irvine and in March 1928 the Everton board sent a delegation to Scotland to coincide with the national team's game against England in an effort to sell him to one of the Glaswegian giants. That deal never came off, but Portsmouth

came in with a £3000 offer later that month. Irvine had played nine league games, one too few for a League Championship medal, at the end of that victorious season.

According to the Everton minute books the south coast club had difficulties meeting the second instalment of Irvine's fee, which may have led to his unexpected switch to the Cheshire League, with Connah's Quay, while still a full international. He returned to Ireland in 1930 and made a belated return to English League football, with Watford, while in the veteran stage of his career.

> [FACTFILE]
>
> **BORN**
> Lisburn, 29 April 1900
> **DIED**
> Ireland, 1979
> **POSITION**
> Inside forward
> **OTHER CLUBS**
> Dunrummy,
> Portsmouth (1928–29);
> Connah's Quay (1929–30);
> Derry City (1930–33);
> Watford (1933–35)
> **HONOURS**
> 15 Ireland caps (3 goals)
> (1922–31)

Season	League		FA Cup		Total	
	App	Goals	App	Goals	App	Goals
1921/22	25	11	1	0	26	11
1922/23	32	8	1	0	33	8
1923/24	40	9	2	0	42	9
1924/25	28	4	3	1	31	5
1925/26	31	8	2	0	33	8
1926/27	34	11	4	1	38	12
1927/28	9	3	2	1	11	4
Total	**199**	**54**	**15**	**3**	**214**	**57**

Internationalists, Record

Everton's international men of destiny

Total caps won at Everton (total caps won including other clubs given in brackets).

Player	Country	Caps won at Everton	(total caps won)
Alan Ball	England	39	(72)
David Weir	Scotland	45	(69)
Neville Southall	Wales	92	(92)
Alex Stevenson	Northern Ireland	14	(17)
Kevin Sheedy	Republic of Ireland	41	(45)

Irving, David

Rookie striker who found his feet in the United States

Season	League		FA Cup		League Cup		Other		Total	
	App	Goals	App	Goals	App	Goals	App	Goals	App	Goals
1973/74	0 (2)	0	0	0	0	0	0	0	0 (2)	0
1974/75	1	0	1	0	0	0	-	-	2	0
1975/76	3	0	0	0	1	1	0	0	4	1
Total	**4 (2)**	**0**	**1**	**0**	**1**	**1**	**0**	**0**	**6 (2)**	**1**

[FACTFILE]

BORN
Workington,
10 September 1951
POSITION
Forward
OTHER CLUBS
Workington (1970–73);
Sheffield United
(loan, 1975);
Oldham Athletic (1976–77);
Shamrock Rovers (1977–78);
Fort Lauderdale Strikers
(1978–80);
Tulsa Roughnecks (1980);
Atlanta Chiefs (1980);
San Jose Earthquakes
(1981);
Oulun Palloseura
(Finland, 1988)
AS MANAGER
Miami Freedom (1990–91);
Carolina Vipers (1994);
Wilmington Hammerheads
(1998–)

Izatt, Robert

Two-footed winger who was a veteran of Everton's first FA Cup run

Season	FA Cup		Total	
	App	Goals	App	Goals
1887/88	4	0	4	0
Total	**4**	**0**	**4**	**0**

[FACTFILE]

BORN
Scotland, 1864
POSITION
Outside right / left

THE EVERTON ENCYCLOPEDIA

George **Jackson,** Matthew **Jackson,** Tommy **Jackson,** Lars **Jacobsen,** Phil **Jagielka,** Jimmy **Jamieson,** R. **Jamieson,** David **Jardine,** Frank **Jefferis,** Francis **Jeffers,** Nikica **Jelavic,** Iain **Jenkins,** Phil **Jevons,** Jô, Albert **Johnson,** Andrew **Johnson,** David **Johnson,** Peter **Johnson,** Tommy **Johnson** (b. 1901), Tommy **Johnson** (b. 1971), Leslie **Johnston,** Maurice **Johnston,** Charles **Joliffe,** Dave **Jones,** Gary **Jones,** George **Jones,** Jack **Jones,** Robert **Jones,** Bob **Jones,** T.E.**Jones,** T.G.**Jones,** Willie **Jordan,** Albert **Juliussen,** Lucas **Jutkiewicz**

Jackson, George

Local full back who enjoyed a 20-year-long Goodison association

HE HAS FIGURED IN PRACTICALLY EVERY POSITION ON THE FIELD, FROM GOAL TO CENTRE FORWARD

Born in the shadow of Goodison Park, George Jackson was a full back who served Everton with redoubtable commitment and excellence in a career that spanned nearly two decades.
An alumnus of Arnot Street School, which bred many of Merseyside's finest players, he was spotted playing for Walton Parish by Everton in 1930 and signed on amateur terms. Loaned out to Marine, he played in their famous run to the FA Amateur Cup Final in 1932, which they lost to Dulwich Hamlet at Upton Park. He signed professionally for Everton soon after and made his first-team debut in February 1935, deputising for Warney Cresswell.

Thereafter he served Everton well, but was often unable to break the emergent full back partnership shared by Billy Cook and Norman Greenhalgh. Jackson made just two appearances in Everton's glorious 1938/39 campaign, but still managed to earn a place on the Football Association's 12-game summer tour of South Africa, where he lined up alongside Cliff Britton and Jack Jones.

War invariably interrupted the prime of his career, but Jackson was a stalwart of the Football League North and made 200 appearances in wartime football. Through the 1945/46 season he was ever-present in the Football League North.

Jackson, wrote the Liverpool Echo journalist 'Ranger' in March 1946, disproved 'the old adage of a "Jack of all trades and master of none". He has figured in practically every position on the field, from goal to centre forward, and has filled every one of them with at least satisfaction, some with distinction, and his real position of full back with brilliance. As a goalkeeper he was a revelation.'

'RANGER' went on to praise Jackson's kicking ability ('hear the resounding "whack" when he hits one of his full-blooded volleys') and sense of fair play ('I've never seen him guilty of a shady action'). 'He has confidence without showiness or swank, showing intelligent positioning and canny anticipation,' he wrote.

'In short he serves good, honest to goodness, skilful football, sturdy and robust, but with sufficient polish to make it attractive to watch.'

BUT AS with so many players, Jackson found wartime football a different proposition to the real thing. When the Football League recommenced in September 1946 he was nearing his 36th birthday. The pace and intensity of the First Division proved too much and he soon lost his place to George

Saunders. After making just two appearances in 1947/48 and none at all the following year, Jackson – now a veteran – was allowed to step into non-league with Caernarfon Town.

[FACTFILE]

BORN
Liverpool, 14 January 1911
POSITION
Full back

Season	League		FA Cup		Total	
	App	Goals	App	Goals	App	Goals
1934/35	8	0	1	0	9	0
1935/36	18	0	0	0	18	0
1936/37	26	0	0	0	26	0
1937/38	4	0	0	0	4	0
1938/39	2	0	0	0	2	0
1945/46	-	-	2	0	2	0
1946/47	15	0	1	0	16	0
1947/48	2	0	0	0	2	0
1948/49	0	0	0	0	0	0
Total	**75**	**0**	**4**	**0**	**79**	**0**

Jackson, Matthew

Right back whose attacking contribution to FA Cup run proved decisive

The cruellest irony of Matthew Jackson's Goodison career is that just as he was set to make his most important contribution in an Everton shirt, his first-team chances were to be severely restricted by the arrival of a new contender to his right back shirt.

THAT THE tall blond defender played on as if unperturbed by this challenge spoke volumes for his consummate maturity and professionalism – values that continue to shine through in his post-playing career as a BBC

pundit. Signed for £600,000 from Luton Town in October 1991, the Yorkshire-born defender made his debut on his 20th birthday, establishing himself as Everton's first-choice right back by the end of the 1991/92 season. Calm and composed, with a good turn of pace and displaying a willingness to join in attacks, Jackson also offered versatility, having started out as a centre back. His progress in a transitional Everton side was rewarded with an England under-21 call-up.

Perhaps if Jackson had played in a better Everton team or in a less traumatic point of their history, this early development may have advanced him towards full international recognition and a more prominent place in club lore. But as Everton laboured under Howard Kendall, then Mike Walker, Jackson's career trajectory seemed to freeze. Certainly playing in a defence as porous and disorganised as that which laboured under Walker's charge could do little for the confidence of a young defender.

Following Joe Royle's appointment as manager, one of his first acts, in January 1995, was to sign Earl Barrett, a former Oldham protégé. It seemed harsh on Jackson, who was no more culpable for the club's defensive shortcomings than any of his colleagues. Barrett came straight into the first team but was cup-tied, enabling the 23-year-old to reclaim his place for Everton's FA Cup run.

Jackson did this in emphatic fashion: as Barrett's signing was finalised his powerful drive from the edge of the area broke the deadlock late in a tricky fourth round tie at Bristol City. After partaking in the fifth and sixth round defensive shut-outs, Jackson's near-post header opened the scoring in Everton's thrilling semi-final victory over Tottenham. Left out of most of the remainder of Everton's league campaign, Jackson returned for the FA Cup Final. On 30 minutes, Jackson was played in down the right by Anders Limpar. He cut into the penalty area and coolly turned Gary Pallister to square the ball for Graham Stuart, whose shot onto the cross bar was converted by Paul Rideout for the game's only goal. Despite this outstanding riposte, there would be no comeback for Jackson. Many fans could not fathom Barrett's inclusion, for while he was a good defender, his poor distribution negated this impact. Indeed Royle even signed the hapless Swiss right back, Marc Hottiger, in March 1996, causing Jackson to slip further down the pecking order. When, in December that year, Mike Walker, now back at Norwich, came in with a £450,000 bid it was entirely logical for the defender to move on.

JACKSON provided five years of outstanding service at Carrow Road, mostly as captain. He joined Wigan Athletic in 2001 and captained them on an improbable rise from English football's third tier to the Premier League. In 2007 he joined Watford, and after a short loan spell at Blackpool called time on his playing career in August 2008. An articulate, erudite man, he has since set out on a career as a BBC radio pundit.

[FACTFILE]

BORN
Leeds, 19 October 1971
POSITION
Right back / centre back
OTHER CLUBS
Luton Town (1990–91); Preston North End (loan, 1991); Charlton Athletic (loan, 1996); Queens Park Rangers (loan, 1996); Birmingham City (loan, 1996); Norwich City (1996–2001); Wigan Athletic (2001–07); Watford (2007–08); Blackpool (loan, 2007)
HONOURS
1995 FA Cup

Season	League		FA Cup		League Cup		Europe		Total	
	App	Goals	App	Goals	App	Goals	App	Goals	App	Goals
1991/92	30	1	2	0	0	0	1	0	33	1
1992/93	25 (2)	3	2	0	3	0	-	-	30 (2)	3
1993/94	37 (1)	0	2	0	4	0	-	-	43 (1)	0
1994/95	26 (3)	0	6	2	1	0	-	-	33 (3)	2
1995/96	14	0	2	0	1	0	3	0	20	0
Total	**132 (6)**	**4**	**14**	**2**	**9**	**0**	**4**	**0**	**159 (6)**	**6**

Jackson, Tommy

Effective understudy to Gwladys Street's Holy Trinity

TOMMY JACKSON first came to prominence in unlikely circumstances. Aged just 20, Glentoran's defence-minded midfielder was called upon to man-mark Eusebio in the Northern Ireland club's October 1967 European Cup first round second leg tie with Benfica. In a performance of magnificent obduracy, Jackson repelled the Portuguese centre forward, leaving him to feed for scraps as his club earned an improbable goalless draw. Having drawn the first leg 1-1 in Belfast, however, Glentoran were the first club to fall victim to UEFA's away-goals rule. Jackson, however, had made his name and four months later joined Everton for £9000.

Solid and dependable, Jackson was drafted in as cover for Everton's famous midfield triumvirate. Among his first and most high-profile action was to serve as Alan Ball's replacement in the FA Cup semi-final with Leeds two months after joining.

ALL afternoon he scrapped and harried, subduing Billy Bremner and Johnny Giles as Everton sealed a 1-0 win. Called upon to deputise for Howard Kendall and Colin Harvey in 1969/70, he provided dependable cover and played on enough occasions to collect a Championship medal.

Alas, his performances were never quite good enough to make an Everton shirt his own and he left Everton in October 1970 as part of the £150,000 deal that brought Henry Newton to Goodison. He spent a spell at Manchester United mid-decade before returning to Northern Ireland as player-manager of Waterford. Through the 1980s and early 1990s, Jackson was a hugely successful manager in the province before his career petered out.

Season	League		FA Cup		League Cup		Europe		Total	
	App	Goals	App	Goals	App	Goals	App	Goals	App	Goals
1967/68	1(1)	0	1	0	0	0	-	-	2 (1)	0
1968/69	14	0	1 (1)	0	0	0	-	-	15 (1)	0
1969/70	14 (1)	0	2	0	0	0	-	-	16 (1)	0
1970/71	1	0	0	0	-	-	0 (1)	0	1 (1)	0
Total	**30 (2)**	**0**	**4 (1)**	**0**	**0**	**0**	**0 (1)**	**0**	**34 (4)**	**0**

Jacobsen, Lars

Not-so-great Dane who made a surprise appearance in the 2009 FA Cup Final

Season	League		FA Cup		League Cup		Europe		Total	
	App	Goals	App	Goals	App	Goals	App	Goals	App	Goals
2008/09	4 (1)	0	0 (1)	0	0	0	0	0	4 (2)	0
Total	**4 (1)**	**0**	**0 (1)**	**0**	**0**	**0**	**0**	**0**	**4 (2)**	**0**

Jagielka, Phil

England international centre half who has assumed the Goodison vice-captaincy

In joining Everton in July 2007, Phil Jagielka completed a football journey that had started out as a hopeful teenager at the Everton academy. His route had taken him to Stoke City and Manchester City, before he signed as a professional with Sheffield United in 1998, where he provided almost a decade of unstintingly reliable service. Back at Goodison he would progress even further, rising to the ranks of the England team and establishing himself as one of the Premier League's finest centre backs.

Jagielka's breakthrough to the Sheffield United team first came as a 17-year-old at the end of the 1999/2000 season, and he became a regular two years later. Talented, versatile and committed, he played in a variety of defensive positions – centre half, right back and central midfield – and was even considered good enough between the goalposts that United's manager, Neil Warnock, would eschew the use of a substitute goalkeeper. In a home match against Arsenal in December 2006, Jagielka was called into action after the Blades goalkeeper Paddy Kenny suffered an injury. With his side 1-0 up, Jagielka held his opponents at bay for the remaining 34 minutes and helped secure a famous victory. Such excellence and versatility have become his hallmarks.

Jagielka had played every minute when United were promoted to the Premier League in 2006, and would do so again when they were relegated a year later. However, he had proved that the Premier League was a fitting stage for his talents and in July 2007 David Moyes paid £4million to make him an Everton player.

He started his Everton career slowly, playing in central midfield and right back – positions to which he was less than well suited. Eventually he got a run at centre back and reduced Alan Stubbs – who had started the season as first choice in this position – to the role of a spectator. With his astute reading of the game, fine aerial ability and talent as an organiser of his defence he shared many of the facets of his predecessor. Although Jagielka suffered the heartbreak of missing the key penalty in a UEFA Cup Round of 16 shootout against Fiorentina, his debut season ended on a high with a call-up to the England squad and first cap against Trinidad and Tobago.

The 2008/09 season started with Jagielka as a first choice in the starting XI and when injury to Joseph Yobo saw Joleon Lescott shift from left back to centre back, the pair formed an imperious partnership. One run saw Everton go 643 minutes without conceding a goal. The 37 league goals conceded all season was one of the meanest defensive showings in the club's history.

Jagielka's finest moment was soon followed by his most harrowing. Having assisted in keeping another clean sheet in the FA Cup semi-final against Manchester

United, he bravely stood up and slotted home the deciding penalty in the shootout, exorcising the demons of Fiorentina. Six days later, however, disaster struck. Midway through the second half in a home match against Manchester City, Jagielka crumpled in a heap on the pitch. The centre back had torn his anterior cruciate ligament. It meant no FA Cup Final and a ten-month absence from the Everton team, thus effectively ruining his chances of travelling to the South Africa World Cup too.

'Football can be cruel at times,' an ashen-faced David Moyes said afterwards. 'When you're involved at the top end it can bring you great pleasure but also big downs.'

Jagielka returned to the Everton fold the following spring and has since made a full recovery. The brilliant partnership he formed with Lescott is still to be fully replicated with Sylvain Distin or Johnny Heitinga following Lescott's defection to Manchester City, but there are signs that

the defender is approaching his best form again. He was a worthy inclusion in Roy Hodgson's squad for the 2012 European Championships and has also assumed the Everton vice-captaincy.

Speaking to the Evertonian in 2010 he talked about his hopes to represent England at the 2014 World Cup in Brazil, but he also had a more pressing ambition, too. '[Brazil] is a long, long way away at the moment,' he said. 'I'd love to just do well with Everton and realise some other goals by getting to semi-finals and finals again and by trying to win something so I can walk up those Wembley steps and know what it's like to pick up a trophy.'

[FACTFILE]

BORN
Sale, 17 August 1982
POSITION
Centre back
OTHER CLUB
Sheffield United (2000-07)
HONOURS
12 England caps (2008–)

Season	League		FA Cup		League Cup		Europe		Total	
	App	Goals	App	Goals	App	Goals	App	Goals	App	Goals
2007/08	27 (7)	1	1	0	5	0	7 (2)	1	40 (9)	2
2008/09	33 (1)	0	6	0	1	0	2	1	42 (1)	1
2009/10	11 (1)	0	0	0	0	0	0 (1)	0	11 (2)	0
2010/11	31 (2)	1	2	0	1	0	-	-	34 (2)	1
2011/12	29 (1)	2	0 (1)	0	2	0	-	-	31 (2)	2
Total	**131(12)**	**4**	**9 (1)**	**0**	**9**	**0**	**9 (3)**	**2**	**158(16)**	**6**

Jamieson, Jimmy

Deputy left half who saw in Goodison's first season

[FACTFILE]

BORN
3 November 1867
POSITION
Left half
OTHER CLUB
Sheffield Wednesday

Season	League		FA Cup		Total	
	App	Goals	App	Goals	App	Goals
1892/93	14	0	0	0	14	0
Total	**14**	**0**	**0**	**0**	**14**	**0**

Jamieson, R

One-game mystery man who went on to play for Bootle

Season	League		FA Cup		Total	
	App	Goals	App	Goals	App	Goals
1889/90	1	0	0	0	1	0
Total	**1**	**0**	**0**	**0**	**1**	**0**

Jardine, David

Everton's first League Championship winning goalkeeper

Season	League		FA Cup		Total	
	App	Goals	App	Goals	App	Goals
1890/91	10	0	0	0	10	0
1891/92	17	0	0	0	17	0
1892/93	8	0	0	0	8	0
1893/94	2	0	0	0	2	0
Total	**37**	**0**	**0**	**0**	**37**	**0**

Jefferis, Frank

Inside forward who propelled Everton to League Championship success

Everton's signing of inside right Frank Jefferis in March 1911 came at a time when they were still remodelling the great forward line that had served them so well through the previous decade. Jack Sharp had called time on his Everton career the previous summer and the days of Sandy Young and Bertie Freeman were drawing to a close. With their tight and well-organised defence, Everton had at one stage in the 1910/11 season threatened a title challenge, briefly topping the table in early February. But goals were a perennial problem and the board sought to redress this with fresh blood.

That month the club brought Tom Fleetwood from Rochdale, inside left Tom Gracie from Morton, Louis Weller from Chesterfield and Jefferis – for a fee of £1500

– from Southampton. 'Everton have been making very energetic raids on certain club reserves with the intention of building up their team in its weakest department –namely forward,' reported the Liverpool Echo. 'Everton have a number of forwards who touch a certain standard, and do not get beyond that standard. The club's officials, I have reason to believe, have adopted this attitude. We give every man a splendid chance to show his worth, and for those failing to come up to the proper mark we must find better exponents of the game.'

'Jefferis,' recorded the Echo, 'has been the idol of Southampton for some years and he would never have been released but for his club's financial difficulties. Jefferis is a very steady fellow, well behaved and abstemious, and

maybe he is stronger at twenty-six than some footballers are at twenty-three.' His debut came three weeks later, in a 1-0 win at Blackburn. Of this 'early impression' the Echo wrote: 'Jefferis has had much experience, and can make some very neat transfer to [George] Beare. He is dainty in his movements and is an old Everton platform. Much like Wilford Toman in appearance on the field. Jefferis played a quiet game, and effectively yesterday against that able half-backs, Bradshaw.' Jefferis played five times in the 1910/11 season run-in, scoring once. But he couldn't propel the club to an unlikely league title and they finished fourth, seven points behind Manchester United.

Jefferis would start the first 28 matches of the 1911/12 season,

and although goals were still hard to come by, by January the club had risen to second place and a title challenge was on the cards. A 4-0 win at home to champions United in January showed Everton's title credentials. 'This was acknowledged to be Everton's most convincing performance for a long time,' wrote the Merseyside football historian, Percy Young. '[Frank] Bradshaw scored two goals and he and Jefferis were scintillatingly brilliant at inside forward, while [Willie] Davidson was a fine outside left and [Harry] Makepeace the best wing-half on the field.' Everton faltered in early March, but were still in the league running when they travelled to Roker Park to face title favourites Sunderland in what was effectively the Championship decider on 6 April. Jefferis lined up at inside right, but in a story that will be familiar to generations of Evertonians the team capitulated, losing 4-0. Three weeks later the season concluded with Everton runners-up to Sunderland, just three points off the pace.

What a succession of talented Everton teams through the first years of the 20th century sorely lacked was a prolific centre forward. In the exuberant Bertie Freeman they briefly had one, but the board let him go in a period of transition. But in December 1913 a fitting replacement finally arrived from Glasgow Rangers: Bobby Parker. He scored 17 times in just 24 matches in the remainder of the 1913/14 season and, reported one correspondent, 'Parker and Jefferis displayed a perfect understanding.' The next season Parker would score 36 goals from 35 appearances and finally edge Everton to League Championship glory.

JEFFERIS HAD sat out the second half of that season due to a knee injury but would figure in the regional leagues throughout the war years. By the time peace came he was in his mid-thirties and chances were harder to come by. In January 1920, a £1500 bid from Preston North End was accepted. Jefferis would carry on playing until nearly aged 43, combining

A 4-0 WIN AT HOME TO CHAMPIONS UNITED IN JANUARY SHOWED EVERTON'S TITLE CREDENTIALS

player-coach roles at Preston with two spells at Southport. He later worked as a coach at Millwall and died of a heart attack at their training ground in 1938.

[FACTFILE]

BORN
Fordingbridge, Hampshire, 3 July 1884

DIED
New Cross Ground, 21 May 1938

OTHER CLUBS
Southampton (1905–11); Preston North End (1920–23); Southport (player-coach, 1923–25 and 1927)

HONOURS
1914/15 League Championship, 2 England caps (1912)

Season	League		FA Cup		Total	
	App	Goals	App	Goals	App	Goals
1910/11	5	2	0	0	5	2
1911/12	36	7	5	1	41	8
1912/13	27	5	5	2	32	7
1913/14	27	3	1	0	28	3
1914/15	18	4	0	0	18	4
1919/20	12	1	1	0	13	1
Total	**125**	**22**	**12**	**3**	**137**	**25**

Jeffers, Francis

Gifted striker who never overcame injuries or a troublesome temperament

Francis Jeffers first came to Evertonians' attention as a fresh-faced 15-year-old in the mid-1990s, writing a monthly column for the Evertonian newspaper about life at the FA Centre of Excellence while studying for his GCSE exams. Much was expected of the highly rated striker, who made his debut as a 16-year-old substitute in December 1997 and would represent England from schoolboy to senior level.

A member of the 1998 FA Youth Cup winning team, Jeffers made his full debut against Derby County in February 1999 and impressed immediately. The possessor of an excellent first touch and outstanding off-the-ball movement, Jeffers was also fast and a clinical fisher. In many ways his play resembled that of another boyhood Evertonian – although Ian Rush slipped through the net to haunt Goodison. After also losing out to Liverpool on other boyhood Blues such as Robbie Fowler and Michael Owen, it appeared Everton finally had

a home-grown hero of their own. Subsequently linking up with Kevin Campbell, Jeffers' goals would play a part in saving Everton from relegation in the 1998/99 season. So impressive was their fledgling partnership that it represented a cause for genuine optimism going into the following season.

JEFFERS' GOALS WOULD PLAY A PART IN SAVING EVERTON FROM RELEGATION IN THE 1998/99 SEASON

On the eve of 1999/2000 season, however, Jeffers shocked Everton by demanding a transfer after contract negotiations broke down. The spat was played out messily in the press, before subsiding, but it wasn't the last time the striker was to fall foul of the Goodison hierarchy. He returned to impress in flashes, but an ankle ligament injury, sustained in an England under-21 game in February 2000, brought an end to his season.

JEFFERS returned to score five goals in the first five matches of the 2000/01 season before the injury curse struck again. Although sidelined for much of the campaign, by spring a record contract offer remained unsigned amid rumours that Jeffers and Walter Smith did not get along and counter-rumours that the player had an inflated sense of his own self-worth. Despite his abundant potential, injuries had restricted Jeffers to less than 50 appearances in four seasons.

In June 2001 he joined Arsenal in a deal reputed to be worth £10million, dependent on add-ons. Amid supporter anger and disenchantment, Toffeeweb. com gave the most erudite assessment of Jeffers' sale:

His departure to Arsenal came as a terrible indictment on a club regime that continues to denigrate the once-great name of Everton – despite the lip-service paid to boyhood dreams, statutes to past heroes, and belated testimonials.

Jeffers may be injury-prone and lightweight. But under Arsenal's more intelligent coaching scheme than that offered by Archie Knox's baseball bat and fisticuffs, he could reasonably expect to improve his chances of playing for England and winning medals.

With the current Everton set-up, he had no chance. His sale sadly confirms Everton's continuing decline as a Club quite content with selling its best players.

Yet his time at Highbury was an unmitigated disaster. Placed alongside players such as Thierry Henry, Dennis Bergkamp and Sylvain Wiltord, chances were invariably difficult to come by, but Jeffers could surely have expected more than four league starts in two seasons.

In August 2003 Jeffers returned to Goodison on a year-long loan. But hopes that the prodigal son would make a lasting impression were quickly confounded. Beset by more injuries, he barely figured in the Everton line-up, and when he did make the team he looked a shadow of his former self. A huge bust-up with David Moyes as the season petered out to its disappointing conclusion saw Jeffers vow to never play for him again. Although he recanted and apologised, it was little surprise when Moyes let him leave at the end of the season. Jeffers joined Charlton Athletic in August 2004

for a cut-price £2.6million, but played fewer than 15 games before his release. Spells with Blackburn, Ipswich and Sheffield Wednesday proved fruitless and he eventually tried his luck in Scotland and Australia.

[FACTFILE]

BORN
Liverpool, 25 January 1981
POSITION
Striker
OTHER CLUBS
Arsenal (2001–04);
Charlton Athletic (2004–06);
Rangers (loan, 2005);
Blackburn Rovers (2006–07);
Ipswich Town (loan, 2007);
Sheffield Wednesday
(2007–10);
Newcastle Jets
(Australia, 2010–11 & 2011–);
Motherwell (2011)
HONOURS
1 England cap (1 goal)
(2003)

Season	League		FA Cup		League Cup		Total	
	App	Goals	App	Goals	App	Goals	App	Goals
1997/98	0 (1)	0	0	0	0	0	0 (1)	0
1998/99	11 (4)	6	2	1	0	0	13 (4)	7
1999/2000	16 (5)	6	4 (1)	0	0 (2)	0	20 (8)	6
2000/01	10 (2)	6	0	0	2	1	12 (2)	7
2003/04	5 (13)	0	0 (3)	2	1	0	6 (16)	2
Total	**42 (25)**	**18**	**6 (4)**	**3**	**3 (2)**	**1**	**51 (31)**	**22**

Jenkins, Iain

Home-grown full back who earned international honours while playing in the lower leagues

[FACTFILE]

BORN
Whiston, 24 November 1972
POSITION
Full back
OTHER CLUBS
Bradford City (loan, 1992);
Chester City (1993–98);
Dundee United (1998–2000);
Chester City (2001–02)
HONOURS
6 Northern Ireland caps
(1997–98)

Season	League		FA Cup		League Cup		Total	
	App	Goals	App	Goals	App	Goals	App	Goals
1990/91	1	0	0	0	0	0	1	0
1991/92	1 (2)	0	0	0	0	0	1 (2)	0
1992/93	1	0	0	0	0 (1)	0	1 (1)	0
Total	**3 (2)**	**0**	**0**	**0**	**0 (1)**	**0**	**3 (3)**	**0**

Jelavić,
Nikica

Hugely talented centre forward whose arrival has given Evertonians hope for the future

Croatian international centre forward Nikica Jelavić completely revitalised Everton's disappointing 2011/12 season, breaking scoring records along the way and giving every Evertonian hope in their hearts.

A £5million acquisition from financially stricken Rangers in January 2012, Jelavić had made his name with Hadjuk Split in his native Croatia. There followed spells with S.V. Zulte Waregem in Belgium and then a turn with Austrian champions Rapid Vienna between 2008 and 2010. Rangers made him a £4million signing in August 2010 and he immediately impressed, scoring 19 goals in 27 league matches.

NOT SINCE TOMMY BROWELL EXACTLY A CENTURY EARLIER HAD A NEW SIGNING SCORED TEN LEAGUE GOALS FOR EVERTON SO QUICKLY

His move to Goodison came as the Scottish giants neared financial administration and his arrival completely altered the complexion of Everton's season. A lithe, intelligent centre forward, he combines supremely intelligent movement off the ball with composure and imagination on it. While not a target man in the traditional sense, he possesses the physicality to hold his own amid the rough and tumble of the Premier League.

And then there were the goals – lots of them. Not since Tommy Browell exactly a century earlier had a new signing scored ten

league goals for Everton so quickly. He scored them with his head, he scored them with his feet, he scored them against teams battling relegation and sides challenging for the title. He scored in an FA Cup quarter-final replay and on a different day his first-half strike in the semi-final against Liverpool may have brought a victory. Very rarely did he need more than one touch when striking with the ruthlessness of an assassin.

Few goals scored anywhere in England were better than that which he plundered against Newcastle United on the last day

of the season. Superbly collecting a long ball from Johnny Heitinga, Jelavić brought the ball down and shot low and hard, forcing a fine save from Tim Krul. The ball rebounded back into his path and Jelavić recovered and elected to volley home the rebound with his right foot. It was by no means a spectacular goal but one executed with technical brilliance.

'His all-round play has given us a lift,' said David Moyes. 'We had badly needed a centre forward for a couple of seasons and he felt as if he had something to prove. This has been a bit of a step up for Nicky but he is a bit of a silent assassin. Some of the players we have brought in over the years have needed time to settle but he has got on with it.

'We have needed him and are very happy with what he has done for us. He was well recommended by people like Davie Weir and Walter Smith. We had £5million to spend and we spent it wisely.'

[FACTFILE]

BORN
Capljina, Yugoslavia,
27 August 1985

POSITION
Centre forward

OTHER CLUBS
Hadjuk Split (2002–07);
Zulte Waregem (2007–08);
Rapid Vienna (2008–10);
Glasgow Rangers (2010–12)

HONOURS
21 Croatia caps
(3 goals) (2009–)

Season	League		FA Cup		League Cup		Total	
	App	Goals	App	Goals	App	Goals	App	Goals
2011/12	10 (3)	9	3	2	0	0	13(3)	11
Total	10(3)	9	3	2	0	0	13(3)	11

Jevons, Phil

FA Youth Cup winning centre forward who forged a solid lower league career

Season	League		FA Cup		League Cup		Total	
	App	Goals	App	Goals	App	Goals	App	Goals
1998/99	0 (1)	0	0	0	0	0	0 (1)	0
1999/2000	2 (1)	0	0	0	1	0	3 (1)	0
2000/01	0 (4)	0	0	0	0	0	0 (4)	0
Total	2 (6)	0	0	0	1	0	3 (6)	0

[FACTFILE]

BORN
Liverpool, 1 August 1979
POSITION
Centre forward
OTHER CLUBS
Grimsby Town (2001–04);
Hull City (loan, 2002–03);
Yeovil Town (2004–06);
Bristol City (2006–08);
Huddersfield Town
(loan, 2007–08, permanent
2008–10);
Bury (loan, 2009);
Morecambe (loan, 2009–10,
permanent 2010–12)

Jô (João Alves de Assis Silva)

Brazilian international forward of unrealised potential

A prolific goalscorer in the Russian Premier League, 21-year-old Brazilian international Jô was an £18million record signing for Manchester City in July 2008. A tall centre forward of grace and skill, he found it difficult to establish himself at a time when Sheikh Mansour's billions were dramatically shifting the fortunes of the Mancunian underachievers.

AN OUTSTANDING DEBUT PERFORMANCE IN A 3-0 HOME ROUT OF BOLTON WANDERERS

THE following January he joined Everton on loan and put in an outstanding debut performance in a 3-0 home rout of Bolton Wanderers. Clearly a confidence player, he impressed in flashes through the remainder of the season, his fine link play and several further goals helping Everton's rise to fifth. A brief FA Cup appearance as a substitute for City in January meant that he missed out on Everton's run to the FA Cup Final, but he had nevertheless done enough to convince David Moyes to extend his loan spell by a further year with provisions for a permanent deal if it proved successful.

Alas, this was to end in acrimony. Jô, like the rest of the team,

struggled for form in the first half of the 2009/10 season, and the player found himself in and out of the Everton line-up without making much impact. During Christmas he took unauthorised leave to return to Brazil and Moyes terminated the deal.

HE FOUND his way back to Manchester via a loan spell at Galatasaray and in the summer of 2011 returned to South America in an attempt to revive his career with Internacional.

[FACTFILE]

BORN
Sao Paolo, 20 March 1987
POSITION
Centre forward
OTHER CLUBS
Corinthians (2003–05);
CSKA Moscow (2005–08);
Manchester City (2008–11);
Galatasaray (loan, 2010);
Internacional (2011–)
HONOURS
3 Brazil caps (2007–8);
Olympic bronze medal
(2008)

Season	League		FA Cup		Europe		Other		Total	
	App	Goals	App	Goals	App	Goals	App	Goals	App	Goals
2008/09	6 (5)	2	1 (5)	1	0	0	0	0	7 (10)	3
2009/10	3 (8)	2	0	0	2	1	6 (1)	0	11 (9)	3
Total	9 (13)	4	1 (5)	1	2	1	6 (1)	0	18 (19)	6

Johnson, Albert

Outside right who was Everton's oldest living player at the time of his 2011 death

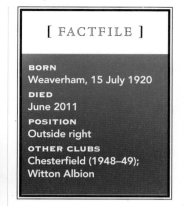

[FACTFILE]

BORN
Weaverham, 15 July 1920
DIED
June 2011
POSITION
Outside right
OTHER CLUBS
Chesterfield (1948–49);
Witton Albion

Season	League		FA Cup		Total	
	App	**Goals**	**App**	**Goals**	**App**	**Goals**
1946/47	3	0	0	0	3	0
1947/48	6	0	0	0	6	0
Total	**9**	**0**	**0**	**0**	**9**	**0**

Johnson, Andrew

Fleet-footed striker who struck derby gold

Signed from Crystal Palace for a club record £8.6million in May 2006, Andrew Johnson arrived at Goodison with a burgeoning reputation as one of the best natural finishers in England.

Something of a late developer, Johnson had started out at Birmingham City, his boyhood club, at the start of the decade, but having failed to make a

significant breakthrough was sold to Crystal Palace in 2002 as a makeweight in the deal that brought Clinton Morrison to St Andrews. Under the management of Iain Dowie his all-round play improved significantly at Selhurst Park and Johnson finished the 2003/04 season – the year Palace won promotion – top scorer with 32 goals. Johnson's streak of form continued the following year, when he scored 21 Premier League goals (half of Palace's total) – a tally bettered only by Arsenal's Thierry Henry. Despite Palace's relegation, Johnson stayed at Selhurst Park for a further year but his club failed to return to the top flight.

Small and lean, with a lightning turn of pace, quicksilver feet and a low centre of gravity, Johnson seemed to be the goal-poacher Everton had so desperately lacked since the days of Tony Cottee and Gary Lineker. First impressions bore this out: a debut goal against Watford was taken clinically, likewise a cool finish that brought a rare victory away at Tottenham.

JOHNSON'S finest hour unquestionably came in only his fourth Everton appearance, against Liverpool at Goodison. Already 1-0 up, on 35 minutes he coolly took advantage of Jamie Carragher's mistake to make it 2-0. Then in the final minute, Pepe Reina fumbled Lee Carsley's shot and Johnson headed home from close range to seal a famous win. 'Andrew Johnson is an unbelievable striker and is going to get goals,' said David Moyes afterwards. 'He fought hard and showed character and now he knows what it means to be a Blue.'

Yet Johnson's partnership with James Beattie never gelled, and as Moyes eased the latter out of contention, increasingly reverting to his favoured 4-5-1 formation, Johnson was left to take on additional responsibilities, often straying out into wide positions. Although his work rate was excellent and he never shirked these new tasks, it seemed to decrease his effectiveness in front of goal. The ease with which he took his early goals left him, and Johnson sometimes seemed to be afflicted with hesitancy when it seemed easy to score. The goals did not entirely dry up, however, as witness his excellent last-minute

shot through a crowded penalty area that sealed a memorable victory over Arsenal in March 2007. The arrival of Yakubu the following August saw Everton's reliance on Johnson diminish, and Moyes increasingly used him as a substitute to stretch games late on. Although a valuable member of the squad and one of the few pacy outlets Everton possessed, his contribution was overshadowed by the scintillating Nigerian, and at the season's end he found himself outscored not just by Yakubu, but Tim Cahill and even Joleon Lescott. With a paucity of transfer funds in summer 2008, Moyes deemed Johnson sacrificable and accepted an offer of £10.5million from Fulham for the striker.

Born in Bedford, but of Polish stock, Johnson chose England over his grandparents' country, making eight appearances, the last against Israel in September 2007.

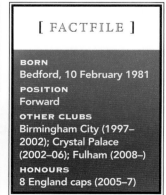

[FACTFILE]

BORN
Bedford, 10 February 1981
POSITION
Forward
OTHER CLUBS
Birmingham City (1997–2002); Crystal Palace (2002–06); Fulham (2008–)
HONOURS
8 England caps (2005–7)

Season	League		FA Cup		Europe		Other		Total	
	App	**Goals**	**App**	**Goals**	**App**	**Goals**	**App**	**Goals**	**App**	**Goals**
2006/07	32	11	1	1	2	0	-	-	35	12
2007/08	20 (9)	6	1	0	2	0	6 (1)	4	29(10)	10
Total	**52(9)**	**17**	**2**	**1**	**4**	**0**	**6 (1)**	**4**	**64(10)**	**22**

Johnson,
David

Forward prospect whose premature departure was a disastrous mistake

The November 1972 sale of David Johnson to Ipswich Town surely ranks among the most catastrophic lapses of judgement an Everton manager has made. In exchange for £50,000 plus Johnson – a highly promising young striker who had already scored on his First Division, FA, European and League Cup debuts as well as a rare derby winner – Everton received Rod Belfitt, an honest trier frankly not up to the standards demanded by the School of Science. Johnson went on to collect England caps, and in 1976 joined Liverpool, where a succession of domestic and European honours followed.

One of the stream of local lads to make good and progress through the Everton youth ranks during Harry Catterick's last years as Everton manager, Johnson made his debut in January 1971 against Burnley. He quickly affirmed himself as a favourite amongst Evertonians, scoring a dramatic scrambled equaliser in the European Cup quarter-final with Panathinaikos two months later. A raw striker with pace and a poacher's instinct in front of goal, many of his early appearances came in the wide forward role previously occupied by Jimmy Husband, or on the left wing.

His talent was palpable, however, and in November 1971 he struck the only goal of the Goodison derby. Scarcely could Evertonians have imagined then that they would not beat Liverpool for a further seven years, or that just four more league wins would follow all season. Johnson ended the 1971/72 season top scorer with 11 league and cup goals.

CATTERICK was desperate to strike the winning formula at Goodison. But many of his managerial decisions – from the sale of Alan Ball to the blatant misuse of talented players, like Henry Newton – defied logic during these last years. Alas, the sale of Johnson was one such bad choice. In May 1975, Johnson made his England debut against Wales at Wembley.

His £200,000 move to Liverpool came in August the following year. Johnson won the First Division and European Cup three times while at Anfield. In April 1978, he became the first player to score the derby winner for both Everton and Liverpool, when he struck the only goal of the Goodison meeting between the two clubs.

Although he made a £100,000 Goodison return in August 1982, he was by then past his best, his presence in the Everton team mostly serving as a reminder of one of their most potent lost talents.

[FACTFILE]

BORN
Liverpool, 23 October 1951
POSITION
Striker
OTHER CLUBS
Ipswich Town (1972–76);
Liverpool (1976–82);
Barnsley (loan, 1984);
Manchester City (1984);
Tulsa Roughnecks (1984);
Preston North End (1984–85)
HONOURS
8 England caps (6 goals) (1975–80)

Season	League App	League Goals	FA Cup App	FA Cup Goals	League Cup App	League Cup Goals	Europe App	Europe Goals	Total App	Total Goals
1970/71	10 (1)	1	2	1	0	0	0 (2)	1	12 (3)	3
1971/72	27	9	4	1	1	1	-	-	32	11
1972/73	10 (2)	1	0	0	1	0	-	-	11 (2)	1
1982/83	25 (6)	3	0	0	4	1	-	-	29 (6)	4
1983/84	7 (2)	1	0	0	1	0	-	-	8 (2)	1
Total	**79(11)**	**15**	**6**	**2**	**7**	**2**	**0 (2)**	**1**	**92(13)**	**20**

Johnson,
Peter

Controversial chairman and owner who oversaw calamity and success

The son of a Birkenhead butcher, Peter Johnson (b.1940) was one of Merseyside's wealthiest businessmen, in the 1990s holding an estimated fortune of £150million. In the late 1960s he had expanded the family business into Christmas hampers, for which people would save through the year. It reaped vast profits and at its peak his business Park Foods packed one million hampers per year. Johnson later diversified into such interests as freight haulage and consumer credit.

His entry into football came with Tranmere Rovers in 1987. He saved them from the financial abyss and relegation from the Football League. Later his investment on such players as Gary Stevens, Pat Nevin and Kevin Sheedy brought Tranmere to the verge of top-flight promotion. But Johnson recognised Tranmere's limitations and when Everton came on the market following John Moores' death in

September 1993, he made his move, buying the club for £10million several months later.

As a former Liverpool season-ticket holder and shareholder, Johnson was always going to find it hard to win over Evertonians, but after years of underinvestment and off the field mismanagement he started well. After Everton avoided relegation in 1994, Johnson injected

around £10million into the club via a rights issue. Mike Walker was given a pot of money to spend, but despite Everton being linked to some of the biggest names in European football, including the Germany striker Jurgen Klinnsman, they opened the 1994/95 season with only Vinny Samways added to the threadbare squad.

Johnson soon proved to be a hands-on chairman. In October 1994, while on a visit to Glasgow to see how Rangers had redeveloped Ibrox Stadium, Johnson agreed the loan signings of Iain Durrant and Duncan Ferguson – who was to arguably prove the club's most significant player over the next decade. Quite what say Walker had in this deal is not known.

Johnson also showed the sort of decisive flourish that would have brought a wry smile from his predecessor Moores, sacking Walker, who was just ten months into the job, and replacing him with Joe Royle in November 1994. Little over six months later, Royle had saved Everton from the threat of relegation and won the FA Cup.

JOHNSON set about reinvigorating Everton's commercial strategy, which even by the standards of the time was second rate. The megastore was constructed and various new initiatives, such as the relaunch of the Evertonian newspaper and the creation of Radio Everton. He also showed some understanding of the club's history and paid for much-needed conservation work on St Rupert's Tower, which appears on the Everton crest. Later he won a mandate to move Everton to a new 65,000-seater stadium, although practical matters – such as location and funding –were skirted over.

Yet many of Johnson's efforts, notably the stadium move, were ultimately botched or deemed insensitive to the club's traditions. One of the first acts of the new regime was to ditch the iconic Z-Cars theme tune, a nonsensical decision which was soon reversed after causing outrage. Distribution of FA Cup Final tickets descended into farce when thousands of Evertonians sat through the night to get their hands on one, but were left disappointed and angry after poor stewarding saw scenes of chaos. Ultimately the problem lay with the way in which the ticket eligibility had been laid out by senior officials. Johnson also set about hiring a chief executive, but the position went unfilled for years before Michael Dunford, the club secretary, was appointed to the position and was an inauspicious custodian of the role.

Johnson's boost to the club's income streams did, however, see the Everton transfer record broken three times in his first year, with the addition of Nick Barmby in November 1996 seeing it broken for a fourth time. Other targets came and went. Claims that Everton were in the market for Alan Shearer and Roberto Baggio as they were about to sign for other clubs were met with derision. Sometimes his leadership was farcical. In July 1996, Johnson's fellow director, Clifford Finch, was left to conclude the transfer of Nigel Martyn from Crystal Palace, but allowed him to leave without signing so that he could talk to Leeds. Martyn, of course, moved to Elland Road.

EVERTON by-and-large continued to underperform, despite finishing sixth in 1995/96. How much of this was down to the chairman and how much was down to Royle is a matter of debate. What is certain is that in March 1997, after a disastrous three months on the pitch, Johnson vetoed Royle's transfer deadline day attempts to sign Tore Andre Flo, Claus Eftevaag and Barry Horne. When Royle met with Johnson at Park Foods headquarters – where, to great bemusement, much of Everton's business seemed to be conducted during this time – the Everton manager parted company with the club. (Later Royle claimed that he never resigned and Johnson never sacked him; that it was all some strange misunderstanding.)

There followed a highly public and humiliating three-month search for a manager, which was finally concluded when Howard Kendall returned for a third spell as Everton boss. What followed during the 1997/98 season, where Everton escaped relegation by nothing other than luck, was one of the most disgraceful episodes in the club's history. Everton were a shambles on the pitch, but off it chaos seemed to reign, with Kendall not given funds to sign players of any great calibre, and high-profile sales of such as Andy Hinchcliffe and Gary Speed seemingly rushed through to balance the books.

AT THE club's annual general meeting in January 1998, Johnson pointed to net spending of £26million since he took over the club less than four years previous. But this ignored his disastrous management. As a shareholders' representative pointed out: 'If your businesses had been run like this club, they would have been bankrupt years ago.' Several protests were staged against Johnson, notably on the last day of the season when relegation was miraculously averted against Coventry, and thousands of fans streamed onto the pitch calling for his head and pelting the directors' box with sods of turf.

Johnson later berated Kendall, saying Evertonians would have been 'appalled' by his signings if he had been allowed to make them. Worse still was his treatment of the manager. At the end of the season the board agreed to sack Kendall and the story leaked to the press. But Johnson flew out on holiday leaving Everton's greatest-ever manager to answer questions on his future as the sword hovered over his head for several weeks before finally swinging.

With the appointment of Walter Smith as manager, Johnson made one last attempt to make things work. Over the summer of 1998 he sanctioned one final, massive spending spree. But it was funded by short-term lending and when, that November, Everton's overdraft needed to be plugged, Johnson sold Duncan Ferguson to Newcastle behind an incandescent Smith's back.

There followed 48 hours of intense backroom activity, but instead – as predicted – of the furious Smith walking away from Everton, it was Johnson who resigned. It took a further 13 months for him to sell his shares to a consortium led by Bill Kenwright and end all ties with Everton.

There was one final footnote to this sorry story in 1999, when Everton and Tranmere were threatened with suspension from the FA Cup when it emerged that Johnson still held a controlling interest in his former club – as well as Everton. Shares that he was meant to have passed on to former Tranmere chief executive Frank Corfe had somehow been retained. It was a messy saga and added to the sulphurous stench.

Johnson has been castigated for his time as Everton chairman, but many of his ideas were forward-thinking and necessary to revitalise the club's torpid commercial set-up. He also took decisive action to remedy the disastrous

managerial reign of Mike Walker, and the appointment of Joe Royle in his place proved – in the short term, at least – a master stroke.

THE PROBLEM he continually came up against was that he lacked the personnel or personal wherewithal to implement these strategies. Not until the following decade, when Keith Wyness and subsequently Robert Elstone became Everton CEOs, did Everton's commercial set-up begin to meet the expectations of the club's fans.

After finally selling Everton to Bill Kenwright's consortium, shortly before Christmas 1999, Johnson formally returned to Tranmere where he became club president. Subsequent attempts to sell the club from 2002 onwards failed. In 2009 he returned as Tranmere chairman, but his habit of attracting controversy followed too. A group of American businessmen instructed to sell the club listed it on ebay.com, while his appointment of John Barnes as manager was disastrous. 'His investment and management of the club saved Tranmere Rovers from slipping

out of the Football League in the 1980s, and he financed the heady years when the club was near the top of what is now the Championship,' Lorraine Rogers, Tranmere's outgoing chairman, said in 2009. 'Few people have been involved in football for as long as him or are as experienced. I can't think of anyone else who has been chairman of a football club in all four divisions.'

Johnson, Tommy (b.1901)

Veteran inside forward who served Everton with distinction through trophy-studded years

On 15 September 1928, Manchester City inside left Tommy Johnson gave one of the most extraordinary performances Goodison Park has ever witnessed.

'Perhaps the most thrilling game of recent years was that at Goodison Park in September 1928,' recalled the Liverpool Evening Express five years later. 'Manchester City were late in arriving – they were fined for it. Everton had them guessing. [Tom] Weldon scored in the first two minutes. But gradually the City improved and eventually left the field winners by 6-2. Tommy Johnson was Everton's bugbear on that occasion. He was playing the unusual position of centre-forward. He rattled in four fine goals, paused to let [Eric] Brook score a fifth and then completed his "nap hand" with a lovely shot.'

JOHNSON WAS THEN a 27-year-old England international and had already established a reputation as one of the finest goalscorers in Manchester City's history. He had scored more than 20 goals in each of the previous

three seasons, and would end the 1928/29 season with 38 goals – a City record that still stands.

His tormenting of Everton that September afternoon summed up a troubled season for the League Champions, who fell from top spot to 18th place by the season's end. The Everton board recognised that too much of the goalscoring burden lay with an increasingly injury-prone Dixie Dean and sought to redress it by bolstering the forward line. Johnson was identified as a key target during the autumn of 1929 but approaches to the City board were rejected. Over the following winter Everton's form collapsed and relegation became a genuine threat. Everton's board spent heavily – some £20,000 – on players including Jock Thomson and Billy Coggins. Surprisingly, when they went back to City in March and asked after Johnson, a £6500 bid was accepted, despite supporter protests. Johnson became an Everton player and overnight 7000 was knocked off the Maine Road gate.

'His nature, judgment, skill and experience should prove of immense worth in the critical

days ahead,' reported the Liverpool Post and Mercury of the new signing. 'A fine positional player, he has a good shot, and his shrewd judgment and placing are excellent. He stands 5ft 9 and half inches and weighs 11st 11lb. Manchester City are well endowed with inside forwards, and no doubt Johnson realises that a change will be of benefit to him.' Johnson joined a team in turmoil. Everton were in the midst of a record run of six straight defeats and although they would win four of their last five games they finished the 1929/30 season rock bottom. Johnson, who had encountered relegation with City, had suffered it again.

But Everton had already laid the basis of their next great side and the next three years were to be among the most thrilling in the club's history. Johnson was at the heart of this revival, with Dean, Jimmy Dunn, Jimmy Stein and Tommy White forming one of the greatest forward lines Goodison has ever seen. They won the Second Division Championship at the first time of asking, scoring an incredible 121 goals – Johnson claiming 14. Their return to the First Division was just as impressive. Champions again, 116 goals scored, 22 by Johnson, who missed only one game. A year later they reached the final of the FA Cup at Wembley, where Johnson had been on the losing side with City seven years earlier. This time he faced his former club and Everton ran out easy 3-0 winners.

Season	League		FA Cup		Other		Total	
	App	Goals	App	Goals	App	Goals	App	Goals
1929/30	10	4	0	0	-	-	10	4
1930/31	36	14	5	4	-	-	41	18
1931/32	41	22	1	0	-	-	42	22
1932/33	40	13	6	4	1	1	47	18
1933/34	19	3	1	0	-	-	20	3
Total	**146**	**56**	**13**	**8**	**1**	**1**	**160**	**65**

Johnson was one of the most popular members of this outstanding Everton team, as an Evening Express profile recorded on the eve of the Cup Final: 'Known familiarly as "Tosh", he is the club comedian. Dean's bridge partner, so beware! His [stage comedian and actor] Sydney Howard expression is nothing to go by. Once scored five goals for Manchester City against Everton and rarely forgets to mention it to his colleagues. Says he only makes up the eleven, but that's his way. Wonderful shot, with his left foot.'

And yet, despite the high regard in which he was clearly held, to be a 1930s footballer was to be a commodity, to be bought and sold at the whim of your directors. The team that had thrilled over the previous three years started the 1933/34 season poorly. Dean was injured again, which cannot have helped. But finding themselves in mid-table mediocrity, in March 1934 the board circulated the names of eight players available for transfer to other clubs. The list, which included Johnson, Dunn and Ted Critchley, was leaked to the press. A furious Will Cuff said, 'Unless there is confidence in football matters, the sport cannot go on. The effects of any club divulging the names of players will eventually stop clubs sending out lists altogether.'

None of this stopped the fire-sale and within days Liverpool came in with a £650 offer, which was duly accepted. Johnson had rendered Everton four years excellent service and at Anfield he enjoyed an Indian summer. In 1936 he dropped out of league football, serving Darwen of the Lancashire Combination until the outbreak of war.

Johnson, Tommy (b.1971)

Former England under-21 striker who failed to impress during brief loan spell

[FACTFILE]

BORN
Gateshead, 15 January 1971
POSITION
Striker
OTHER CLUBS
Notts County (1989–92);
Derby County (1992–95);
Aston Villa (1997–2001);
Sheffield Wednesday (2001);
Kilmarnock (2001–02);
Gillingham (2002–05);
Sheffield United (2005–06);
Scunthorpe United (2005);
Tamworth (2006)

Season	League		FA Cup		League Cup		Total	
	App	Goals	App	Goals	App	Goals	App	Goals
1999/2000	0 (3)	0	0	0	0	0	0 (3)	0
Total	0 (3)	0	0	0	0	0	0 (3)	0

Johnston, Leslie

Local inside left who was tried out during the 1913/14 season without apparent success

[FACTFILE]

BORN
Liverpool, 1890
POSITION
Inside left

Season	League		FA Cup		Total	
	App	Goals	App	Goals	App	Goals
1913/14	8	1	0	0	8	1
Total	8	1	0	0	8	1

[FACTFILE]

BORN
Dalton-in-Furness, 19 August 1901
DIED
29 January 1973
POSITION
Inside forward / centre forward
OTHER CLUBS
Manchester City (1918–30);
Liverpool (1934–36);
Darwen (1936–37)
HONOURS
1930/31
Second Division Championship,
1931/32
League Championship,
1933 FA Cup;
5 England caps (5 goals) (1926–33)

Johnston, Maurice

Controversial striker who failed to live up to hefty price tag

One of the most notorious footballers of his generation, in 1989 Scottish international striker Maurice Johnston swapped the green hoops of Celtic – via a spell in France – for the blue of Rangers to become the first high-profile Catholic to play for the Glasgow club. Vilified on either side of Glasgow's sectarian divide, Johnston handled the uproar with outstanding maturity, forming a fearsome partnership with Ally McCoist before losing his place to Mark Hateley.

A prolific goalscorer wherever he had played, Johnston came to Goodison in November 1991 for a hefty £1.5million charged with reviving Howard Kendall's second term in charge. Quick, adroit and

clinical, Johnston nevertheless represented a strange piece of business, for with such diminutive players as Peter Beardsley, Tony Cottee and Stuart Barlow to call upon, what Everton needed – what they were crying out for – was a forward with physical presence. Johnston flickered in a declining Everton team, scoring three goals in five games, including the strike that earned a draw in a Goodison derby three days after Christmas 1991. Then injuries struck – including an implausible incident with a rocking horse – and from thereon he was in and out of the Everton team.

There was, however, one last hurrah from Johnston. Included to face Liverpool in the December 1992 derby, his turn and shot from the edge

of the Liverpool penalty area brought Everton an equaliser just a minute after conceding; Peter Beardsley scored Everton's second six minutes from full time to record a 2-1 win.

That was Johnston's last goal for Everton and from thereon he looked on largely from the sidelines, before being granted a free transfer in summer 1993. Spells with Hearts and Falkirk failed to witness a return to previous form and in 1996 he joined up with former Scotland team-mate Richard Gough at Kansas City Wizards in the MLS, subsequently building a coaching career in America.

Season	League		FA Cup		Europe		Other		Total	
	App	Goals	App	Goals	App	Goals	App	Goals	App	Goals
1991/92	21	7	1	0	1	0	1	0	24	7
1992/93	7 (6)	3	0	0	1 (1)	0	-	-	8 (7)	3
Total	28 (6)	10	1	0	2 (1)	0	1	0	32 (7)	10

Joliffe, Charles

Reserve goalkeeper during Everton's first league years

Season	League		FA Cup		Total	
	App	Goals	App	Goals	App	Goals
1887/88	-	-	2	0	2	0
1888/89	4	0	-	-	4	0
1889/90	1	0	0	0	1	0
Total	5	0	2	0	7	0

Jones, Dave

Versatile defender who made a name for himself as a manager

A home-grown defender of endless enthusiasm, Dave Jones was one of a sizeable Scouse contingent to represent Everton through the mid-1970s. A clever, versatile defender with strength and guile, his ability to adapt worked against him, because he was constantly shuffled around the Everton back four, never really making any one position his own. Much of 1976 was spent at left back, and the two following calendar years he was right back. 'If he had settled in one position, it might have propelled him from the England under-21s to the senior side,' wrote the Everton-supporting journalist Brian Viner.

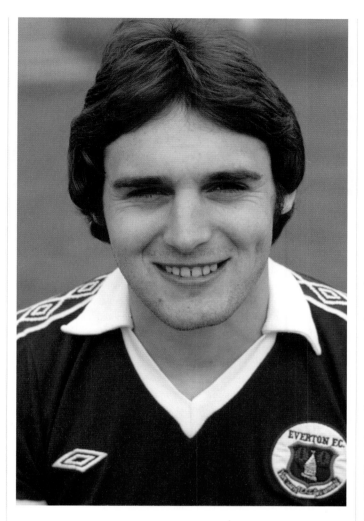

But full back was never his position of choice. Jones always saw himself as a centre half, but after playing no more than a handful of games here for Everton sought a move to a club where such chances would be more forthcoming. At the end of the 1978/79 season – a campaign that had been wrecked by injury – Jones made a £275,000 switch to Coventry City.

'I was a good defender, solid, I could pass,' he wrote in his autobiography. 'I think the

Everton supporters would always take to someone who would give 100% – and that's what I always tried to give.'

JONES'S TIME at Highfield Road was dogged by injury. He spent 18 months in Hong Kong and played out his career with Preston North End.

His subsequent switch to management from the mid-1990s was perhaps more notable than his playing days. He led Stockport County to their highest league

position in half a century, a spell that in 1997 earned him the Southampton job. Later Jones led Wolves back to the top flight following a two-decade absence, and Cardiff City to the 2008 FA Cup Final.

Further reading:

JONES, DAVE AND ANDREW WARSHAW, *No Smoke, No Fire: The Autobiography of Dave Jones*, Know the Score Books, 2009

> 'I THINK THE EVERTON SUPPORTERS WOULD ALWAYS TAKE TO SOMEONE WHO WOULD GIVE 100% – AND THAT'S WHAT I ALWAYS TRIED TO GIVE'

[FACTFILE]

BORN
Liverpool, 17 August 1956
POSITION
Full back
OTHER CLUBS
Coventry City (1979–81);
Seiko (Hong Kong, 1981–83);
Preston North End (1983–85)
AS MANAGER
Stockport County (1995–97);
Southampton (1997–2000);
Wolverhampton Wanderers (2001–04);
Cardiff City (2005–11);
Sheffield Wednesday (2012–)

Season	League		FA Cup		League Cup		Europe		Total	
	App	Goals	App	Goals	App	Goals	App	Goals	App	Goals
1975/76	11 (2)	0	0	0	0	0	0	0	11 (2)	0
1976/77	28	1	4	1	7	0	-	-	39	2
1977/78	29 (5)	0	1	0	4 (1)	0	-	-	34 (6)	0
1978/79	11	0	0	0	0	0	0	0	11	0
Total	**79 (7)**	**1**	**5**	**1**	**11 (1)**	**0**	**0**	**0**	**95 (8)**	**2**

Jones, Gary

Exciting winger who failed to live up to his considerable potential

At his very best Gary Jones was a sublime winger, occasionally untouchable in the way in which he wriggled past opposing defenders with an aura of effortless skill. He had all the technical attributes to make a name for himself as one of the era's great showmen: acceleration, change of pace, and an abundance of flair that could ignite the Goodison crowd into raptures. Others, however, said he was tactically naive, a showboater who put individual glory before team effort.

Jones emerged from the Everton youth team in the 1970/71 season, a time when it was proving to be especially fruitful, having seen Mick Lyons and David Johnson progress from the same group. Jones's solitary appearance came in a 2-1 3-0 home defeat against Wolves of Coventry, the sort of result that epitomised a rare ray of light in a disastrous campaign in which Everton had failed to capitalise upon the previous year's title victory.

ALTHOUGH JONES made a further five appearances the next season, not until Billy Bingham's appointment as manager in April 1973 did he make a proper breakthrough, with the new boss favouring the youngster ahead of Jimmy Husband. Although naturally a right-footer, Jones was more effective on the left wing where he could cut inside and wreak havoc. Despite Bingham's initial faith Jones remained on the periphery of the first team until the 1974/75 season.

Brought back into the side in October 1974, he made an immediate impact, scoring in three consecutive games; after the regular left winger John Connolly broke his leg, he was able to fit into his favoured left-sided position as Everton challenged for the league title.

Yet when Everton's form faltered over the 1975/76 season, so too did that of the winger, who became increasing mercurial. After being substituted at home to Leeds in March 1976 he publicly criticised Bingham and never again appeared in an Everton shirt.

After a brief spell at Birmingham City, he played in the NASL for Fort Lauderdale Strikers before returning to his native Merseyside to run a pub. Alas nobody ever really made the most of Jones's talents and the man who was once wistfully likened to George Best slipped quietly into obscurity.

[FACTFILE]

BORN
Liverpool, 5 January 1951
POSITION
Winger
OTHER CLUBS
Birmingham City (1976–78);
Fort Lauderdale Strikers
(1978–79)

Season	League		FA Cup		League Cup		Europe		Total	
	App	Goals	App	Goals	App	Goals	App	Goals	App	Goals
1970/71	1	0	0	0	0	0	0	0	1	0
1971/72	5	0	1	0	0	0	-	-	6	0
1972/73	11 (1)	0	0 (1)	0	0	0	-	-	11 (2)	0
1973/74	10 (3)	0	2 (1)	0	0	0	-	-	12 (4)	0
1974/75	25 (1)	6	3	0	0	0	-	-	28 (1)	6
1975/76	24 (1)	6	1	1	5	1	2	0	32 (1)	8
Total	**76 (6)**	**12**	**7 (2)**	**1**	**5**	**1**	**2**	**0**	**90 (8)**	**14**

Jones, George

Reserve outside right called upon in the post-World War One years

Season	League		FA Cup		Total	
	App	Goals	App	Goals	App	Goals
1919/20	18	1	0	0	18	1
1920/21	7	0	0	0	7	0
1921/22	8	0	0	0	8	0
Total	**33**	**1**	**0**	**0**	**33**	**1**

[FACTFILE]

BORN
Crook, 28 June 1895
POSITION
Outside right
OTHER CLUBS
Wigan Borough (1922–24);
Middlesbrough (1925);
Southport (1925–28);
Yeovil & Petters United;
Great Harwood

Jones, Jack

Stylish left back for whom honours were cruelly elusive

A centre forward who became a defender and gave up scoring goals to devote his career to stopping them, Jack Jones was an accomplished left back for Everton through the 1930s. It was his misfortune that his time in the Everton first team came between two periods studded with success and that he was unable to add medals to a war-interrupted career.

Spotted playing non-league football for Ellesmere Port Town – where one of his team-mates was Joe Mercer – Jones signed professional terms for Everton in March 1932. His debut came in April 1934 in a 2-0 win over Leeds United in which he deputised for the injured Billy Cook, and he impressed immediately. The debutant, wrote Ernest 'Bee' Edwards, 'provided fine length kicking and a nice judicious style almost suggesting the confidence of a Cresswell'. Edwards noted him playing 'a delightful cool and calm game showing anticipation for the next pass, and making a telling length with his easily delivered clearance'. It was, reflected the journalist, 'quite an excellent start for this Bromborough boy in senior circles'. 'Pilot' in the Evening Express was equally complimentary: 'I like Jones. In the first place he is a two-footed player, and that means a lot. He can punt and volley with either foot, no matter how the ball comes to him, and he has a keen sense of position.'

Cook, however, was a senior figure in the Everton team and would be difficult to dislodge. Jones's chance came in the 1935/36 season when injuries to Cook, the regular right back Ben Williams and the decline of Warney Cresswell saw him given a chance. Such was his progress that Cook moved to right back to accommodate him. A similar arrangement was repeated over the following seasons when the regular right back, George Jackson, was injured

and Cook switched to replace him with Jones coming in on the left. Yet the arrival of Norman Greenhalgh in February 1938 saw Jones's chances stymied overnight. Everton now had three top-class left backs, Greenhalgh – captain from the start of 1938/39 – first choice, Cook playing on the right, and Jones nowhere to be seen. He did not play a single game the year Everton won their fifth league title.

Jones played intermittently for Everton through the war years and when peace came he joined Sunderland, where he played out his career.

Season	League		FA Cup		Total	
	App	Goals	App	Goals	App	Goals
1933/34	5	0	0	0	5	0
1934/35	10	0	3	0	13	0
1935/36	34	0	1	0	35	0
1936/37	16	0	4	0	20	0
1937/38	33	0	2	0	35	0
1938/39	0	0	0	0	0	0
Total	**98**	**0**	**10**	**0**	**108**	**0**

[FACTFILE]

BORN
Bromborough, 3 July 1913
DIED
1995
POSITION
Left back
OTHER CLUB
Sunderland (1945–47)

Jones, Robert

Rarely used defender who gained a Welsh cap after taking the Mancunian way

Season	League		FA Cup		Total	
	App	Goals	App	Goals	App	Goals
1888/89	1	0	-	-	1	0
1889/90	1	0	0	0	1	0
1890/91	0	0	0	0	0	0
1891/92	3	0	0	0	3	0
1892/93	2	1	0	0	2	1
Total	**7**	**1**	**0**	**0**	**7**	**1**

[FACTFILE]

BORN
Wrexham, 1868
POSITION
Right back / centre half
OTHER CLUBS
Wrexham Grosvenor; Ardwick (1894); South Shore
HONOURS
1 Wales cap (1894)

Jones, Robert 'Bob'

Reserve goalkeeper born in the shadow of Goodison who became a Bolton stalwart

[FACTFILE]

BORN
Everton, 9 January 1902
DIED
1989
POSITION
Goalkeeper
OTHER CLUBS
Southport (1926–29);
Bolton Wanderers
(1929–36);
Cardiff City (1937–38);
Southport (1939)

Season	League App	League Goals	FA Cup App	FA Cup Goals	Total App	Total Goals
1924/25	3	0	0	0	3	0
Total	3	0	0	0	3	0

Jones, Tommy (T.E.)

Centre half and captain through Everton's hard times

When the great T.G. Jones left Everton in 1950, it seemed oddly fitting that his successor shared not only his position, but his name too. Tommy Edwin Jones would perform admirably throughout the 1950s – a decade that can count among the most troubled in the club's history – as captain and centre half in a succession of teams for which defending with their backs to the wall seemed a perennial habit.

TOMMY JONES · EVERTON F.C. (1955)

Despite the similarities in name and position, the difference between the two men in their style of play was vast. Whereas T.G. Jones played as a continental-style sweeper, a forerunner of the likes of Franz Beckenbauer, T.E. was a centre back in the traditional mould. Rugged, physical, a doughty tackler and competent man marker, he lacked some of the finesse that marked his predecessor out as one of the game's greats. But then comparisons were never really fair, for while T.G. Jones came into a team that possessed the likes of Tommy Lawton and Joe Mercer, his successor had to play in some of the worst teams in Everton history.

JONES SIGNED professional terms in 1948, aged 18, but had to wait a further two years before making his debut, against Arsenal in September 1950. By Christmas that year he had established himself as first-choice centre half, ahead of David Falder and Maurice Lindley, but the 1950/51 season was catastrophic for Everton and ended in relegation. Jones said later that the team's struggle strengthened him as an individual.

Through these grim years in the Second Division, Jones improved his play and it seemed fitting that on the day Everton were promoted in April 1954, with a 4-0 win at Oldham, he scored his first goal for the club.

Considered one of the game's gentlemen and a fine ambassador for the club, it was appropriate that he succeeded Peter Farrell as captain in 1957. But sometimes his sense of fair play was considered a weakness and exploited by his opponents. Jones was centre back on some of the grimmest days ever experienced by Everton's defences: they conceded six against Portsmouth and Sheffield Wednesday in 1950; eight against Huddersfield in 1953 and Newcastle in 1959; and ten against Tottenham in 1958 – the club's record defeat.

Season	League App	League Goals	FA Cup App	FA Cup Goals	League Cup App	League Cup Goals	Total App	Total Goals
1950/51	30	0	1	0	-	-	31	0
1951/52	37	0	0	0	-	-	37	0
1952/53	42	0	5	0	-	-	47	0
1953/54	37	1	3	0	-	-	40	1
1954/55	41	4	2	0	-	-	43	4
1955/56	39	2	4	0	-	-	43	2
1956/57	39	3	1	0	-	-	40	3
1957/58	31	0	3	0	-	-	34	0
1958/59	38	4	4	0	-	-	42	4
1959/60	35	0	1	0	-	-	36	0
1960/61	13	0	1	0	3	0	17	0
1961/62	1	0	0	0	0	0	1	0
Total	383	14	25	0	3	0	411	14

International honours eluded Jones, although he did play for an England XI against the British Army at Maine Road and also captained the FA side which toured Ghana and Nigeria in 1958.

Towards the end of the 1950s Jones's chances became more limited with the emergence of Brian Labone. Unruffled by the youngster's emergence, Jones moved to left back, a position he held until the arrival of George Thomson from Hearts in late 1960. In a Central League game against Barnsley Jones shattered his kneecap. He tried, valiantly, to regain his fitness, but at the end of the 1961/62 season he called time on his playing career.

'As a gentleman who oozed decency I have met few to compare him with,' Alex Young recalled of him. 'I had the pleasure of playing a couple of games alongside him. Of course, he was approaching the conclusion of his career but nevertheless remained a formidable and honest defender. I suspect he must have yearned for a taste of the footballing success which we enjoyed the following season – the 1962/63 Championship winning campaign.'

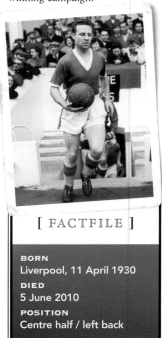

[FACTFILE]

BORN
Liverpool, 11 April 1930
DIED
5 June 2010
POSITION
Centre half / left back

Jones,
Tommy George (T.G.)

The Prince of Centre Halves

In 1948 Roma launched an extraordinary £15,500 bid to make T.G. Jones among the first foreigners to play in Italy. At the eleventh hour, the deal collapsed over currency details. Jones, the prince of centre halves, an unruffled, elegant defender, remained at Goodison Park.

THOMAS G. JONES,
Everton F.C.
TOPICAL TIMES.

Jones bestrode the First Division and the Welsh national team in the 1930s and 1940s, winning the First Division title in 1939. But for the Second World War he would have become a household name, and might have been considered among the finest players of all time. On Merseyside and in North Wales he was considered a true giant, but despite his title medal and caps, his greatest accolades were bestowed upon him by his fellow players and fans.

Born in Connah's Quay, Jones played for Flint Schoolboys and Wales Schools before joining Wrexham in 1934, aged 17. Scouted by bigger clubs, after just six first-team games he was signed by Everton in 1936 for £3000. At Goodison Park, he linked up with youngsters like Joe Mercer and, later, Tommy Lawton, but initially he struggled to arrest Everton's decline.

He made just one appearance in the 1936/37 season, but the

[FACTFILE]

BORN
Connah's Quay,
12 October 1917
DIED
Bangor, 3 January 2004
POSITION
Central defender
OTHER CLUB
Wrexham (1933–36)
HONOURS
1938/39
League Championship;
17 Wales caps (1938–50)

following year established himself in place of the sometime England centre half Charlie Gee, a traditional, uncomplicated centre back. Jones was a defender with the skill and composure of an inside forward. Cool and relaxed when in possession, few defenders of his ilk had been seen before. A forerunner of Franz Beckenbauer, Jones's forte was dribbling out of trouble, and spraying the field with passes.

'He had the great capacity to stroke the ball around,' recalled Tommy Lawton. 'He also had the best right foot in the business and so complete was his positioning and balance that he always seemed to receive the ball on his right foot.' And yet little ever got past him. 'His calmness in a crisis was supreme,' said Lawton, 'Built as he was, he was very good in the air but also delicate and sophisticated on the ground.'

'I think he was the only player I ever knew who could dribble a ball on his own six-yard line and come out with it still between his feet,' said the Liverpool player Cyril Done. 'He was a brilliant

Season	League		FA Cup		Total	
	App	Goals	App	Goals	App	Goals
1936/37	1	0	0	0	1	0
1937/38	28	0	2	0	30	0
1938/39	39	0	5	0	44	0
1946/47	22	3	1	1	23	4
1947/48	24	1	0	0	24	1
1948/49	37	0	2	0	39	0
1949/50	14	0	0	0	14	0
Total	**165**	**4**	**10**	**1**	**175**	**5**

footballer. I jumped up to head a ball with him once, and he came down, fell awkwardly and hurt his ankle very badly. I'm not sure if he broke it. A lot of people seemed to think that I had injured him. I was very upset at the very idea that I could be considered as injuring the great T. G. Jones.'

ALONG WITH Lawton and Mercer, he was instrumental in Everton's renaissance, lifting the 1938/39 League Championship. One of the most attractive and youthful sides of their era, Everton looked set to dominate English football into the 1940s.

War, however, changed everything, and Jones worked in a factory, while still turning out for Everton during the seven years that the Football League was suspended. He also added 11 wartime appearances for Wales to the 17 full caps he earned.

When normal play resumed in 1946, Everton had lost Lawton to Chelsea and Mercer was on his way to Arsenal. The departure of his friends (Jones was best man to both) was a blow to him and Everton, who plummeted into mediocrity.

JONES, nevertheless, continued to illuminate Goodison Park during these years of decline. In 1947 the Liverpool Echo's Ernest 'Bee' Edwards wrote: 'Jones is the finest centre playing football today. He is a class by himself.

Everything he does has the hallmark of a consummate artist. He is the essence of style, neatness and precision and a gentleman on and off the field. I have never seen him guilty of shady action. He is a credit as well as an ornament to the game.'

BUT NOT EVERYBODY agreed and Jones fell foul of Theo Kelly, the club's prickly manager. Amazingly he made little over a dozen appearances in 1947, the bulk coming at its end. Five times through 1947 he asked to leave and each time met the same negative response. The spat with the management then broke out into an unprecedented public argument. 'Could it be,' asked Jones in the local press, 'that having lost Tommy and Joe, when both might have been kept if different methods had been adopted, they are frightened of public opinion if they let me go?'

In fact Jones had a long-standing dispute with the Everton hierarchy, dating to a wartime game in which he was accused by a director of feigning a serious injury in a Lancashire Cup game with Liverpool. His bitterness was compounded by the fact that the injury kept him out of action for six months.

1948 saw Jones back in the first team and the arrival of Cliff Britton as manager seemed to coincide with better times. Then the Italian giants AS Roma came in with a lucrative offer, including an undisclosed lump sum in advance,

a contract from two to four years (depending on his wishes), a wage of £25 per week (double his Everton salary) plus bonuses and a house in the best part of Rome. He was even offered a coaching job upon his retirement. Jones verbally agreed but the deal collapsed.

In August 1949, Jones was reinstalled as captain in place of Peter Farrell but, a handful of games in, lost his place to Jack Humphreys, then David Falder. The situation got so bad that at times he was unable to make the reserve side and would secretly turn out for Hawarden Grammar Old Boys. Finally, on 26 January 1950 he asked for his release, which was agreed.

ON LEAVING Everton, Jones became Pwllheli part-time manager and ran a hotel. In 1962, as manager of Bangor City, the Welsh Cup winners, he ventured into the European Cup Winners' Cup and, incredibly, won the home leg 2-0 against Italian giants Napoli, losing 1-3 in Italy. Alas, there was no away goals rule, and at the replay at Highbury Bangor fought gallantly but lost 3-1.

Later, Jones ran a newsagents' shop in North Wales, and filed a weekly column for the Liverpool Daily Post. He was, said Stanley Matthews, 'a beautiful player'. But the ultimate epithet came from Dixie Dean: 'He had everything. No coach could ever coach him or teach him anything. Tommy was the best all-round player I've ever seen.'

Jordan,
Rev. William Charles 'Willie'

Amateur forward turned preacher who brought Godly presence to the Everton forward line

Season	League		FA Cup		Total	
	App	Goals	App	Goals	App	Goals
1911/12	2	0	0	0	2	0
Total	2	0	0	0	2	0

[FACTFILE]

BORN
Langley, 9 December 1885
DIED
1949
POSITION
Centre forward / inside forward
OTHER CLUBS
Langley St Michaels; Liverpool (1903);
West Bromwich Albion (1906–08);
Oxford University;
Wolverhampton Wanderers (1912)

Juliussen, Albert

**Ill-fated record signing
whose name brought shudders
to Evertonian hearts**

Season	League		FA Cup		Total	
	App	Goals	App	Goals	App	Goals
1948/49	10	1	0	0	10	1
Total	10	1	0	0	10	1

[FACTFILE]

BORN
Blyth, 20 February 1920
POSITION
Centre forward
OTHER CLUBS
Huddersfield Town
(1938–48);
Portsmouth (1948)

Jutkiewicz, Lucas

**Lower-league signing
who enjoyed just five minutes
of first-team action**

[FACTFILE]

BORN
Southampton,
28 March 1989
POSITION
Centre forward
OTHER CLUBS
Swindon Town (2005–07);
Plymouth Argyle
(loan, 2008);
Huddersfield Town
(loan, 2009);
Motherwell (loan, 2009–10);
Coventry City (2010–12);
Middlesbrough (2012–)

Season	League		FA Cup		League Cup		Europe		Total	
	App	Goals	App	Goals	App	Goals	App	Goals	App	Goals
2008/09	0 (1)	0	0	0	0	0	0	0	0 (1)	0
Total	0 (1)	0	0	0	0	0	0	0	0 (1)	0

EVERTON
·ENCYCLOPEDIA·

Andrei **Kanchelskis,** Peter **Kavanagh,** Tony **Kay,** Joseph **Kearslake,** Jason **Kearton,** Glenn **Keeley,** Thomas **Keates,** Jackie **Keeley,** Sam **Keeley,** Jerry **Kelly,** Theo **Kelly,** Bob **Kelso,** Howard **Kendall,** Jack **Kendall,** Andy **Kennedy,** Fred **Kennedy,** Billy **Kenny** (Jnr), Billy **Kenny,** Jack **Kent,** Bill **Kenwright,** Roger **Kenyon,** Martin **Keown,** Jasper **Kerr,** J **Keys,** Brian **Kidd,** Kevin **Kilbane,** Andy **King,** Frank **King,** John **King,** George **Kirby,** Dan **Kirkwood,** Billy **Kirsopp,** Jack **Kirwan,** George **Kitchen,** Per **Kroldrup**

Kanchelskis, Andrei

World-class Ukrainian winger who set Goodison alight with his blistering pace

Handed a reputed £10million transfer kitty following Everton's 1995 FA Cup win, that summer Joe Royle spent a good chunk of it on Manchester United's Russian international winger, Andrei Kanchelskis. United's leading goalscorer during the 1994/95 season and a key member of the double-winning side a year earlier, he was a player of impeccable pedigree, but had become available after a public spat with Alex Ferguson.

BORN IN January 1969 in Kirovograd, a Ukrainian mining city 600 miles south-west of Moscow, Kanchelskis began his career with Dynamo Kiev in the Soviet League, where he became known for his blistering pace and deadly finishing that would become his hallmarks in England. Ironically he was once told as a teenager that he wasn't quick enough to become a footballer – news he reacted to by undergoing a daily ritual of bizarre jumping exercises, which reputedly aided his pace. He joined Shakhtar Donetsk in 1990, and a year later, shortly before the collapse of the Soviet Union, Manchester United paid £650,000 to export him from the Ukrainian mining belt, where Kanchelskis earned 1000 roubles per month – approximately £10. At Old Trafford he won back-to-back Premier League titles and the 1994 FA Cup, but fell out with Ferguson after becoming frustrated with his squad rotation policy.

Kanchelskis's first days at Goodison were beset by frustration. His £5.5million record transfer was protracted by haggling, causing Kanchelskis to miss the start of the 1995/96 season and registration

for Everton's European campaign. Following his belated debut, in only his third game – against his former club – he was carried off with a shoulder injury. A further month on the sidelines followed and although it took the Ukrainian a few more weeks to bed into the Everton team, when he was settled he announced his arrival in grand style: both goals – a header and a trademark low shot – in a 2-1 derby victory at Anfield. It was Everton's first win there in a decade.

Confidence restored, a Kanchelskis-inspired Everton overcame a sluggish start to soar up the table. The Ukrainian was at his best when playing alongside Anders Limpar or Andy Hinchcliffe, who would play him into space with searching diagonal balls from the left. Equally confident

shooting with his left or right foot, the strength and accuracy of his shots, which were usually hit low and at high velocity, were frightening. His acceleration and close control were remarkable; few defenders could keep up with him. Often the only way he could be stopped was to double-mark him, a tactic which only gave the other forward players more space. When Duncan Ferguson overcame disciplinary and injury problems to partner him in attack, the effect was devastating: one or other player made the score sheet in all but one of the 14 matches they played together.

Kanchelskis finished the 1995/96 season top scorer with 16 goals in 32 league appearances, including a hat-trick against Sheffield Wednesday and another derby goal. Many expected Kanchelskis's end of season form (which earned him the April Premier League Player of the Month award) to carry over into the European Championships, but Kanchelskis and Russia were disappointing. Rumours linking him with moves to Italy forced the player to issue a public rebuttal on the eve of the 1996/97 season. 'I am a loyal person,' he said, 'and Everton have been loyal to me. I have another three years of my contract to run and I am very happy here.'

Yet the transfer talk was clearly unsettling and Kanchelskis's form dipped. Initially this was attributed to post Euro-96 fatigue, but as the season progressed and Kanchelskis began to miss chances or take shots from impossible angles when a simple pass would have set up a team-mate, it became increasingly evident that he was not the same player to have previously set

> KANCHELSKIS FINISHED THE 1995/96 SEASON TOP SCORER WITH 16 GOALS IN 32 LEAGUE APPEARANCES

Season	League		FA Cup		League Cup		Europe		Total	
	App	Goals	App	Goals	App	Goals	App	Goals	App	Goals
1995/96	32	16	4	0	0	0	0	0	36	16
1996/97	20	4	2	1	2	1	-	-	24	6
Total	**52**	**20**	**6**	**1**	**2**	**1**	**0**	**0**	**60**	**22**

Goodison alight. Antagonism with his team-mates also became noticeable: after scoring against Sheffield Wednesday in September no one congratulated him.

The sense among many fans was that Kanchelskis was playing for a move. As an injury-decimated Everton team embarked upon their worst run of results in 25 years over December and January, Kanchelskis cut an anonymous figure on the Everton wing. The nadir came in an FA Cup fourth round tie with Bradford City when he was pressured into making a stray pass near the halfway line and Chris Waddle let fly with a 40-yard lob shot that dipped into the net.

Just days later, Kanchelskis joined Fiorentina in an £8million deal. His spell in Italy was short-lived and he returned to Britain 18 months later in a £5.5million switch to Glasgow Rangers. Injuries overshadowed his later career, and brief spells in England – with Manchester City, where he was reunited with Royle, and Southampton – were fruitless. After a lucrative sojourn in Saudi Arabia, he returned to the Russian Premier League, retiring in February 2007.

Kanchelskis said on the day he signed for Everton, 'My aim is to give the people who pay to watch our matches pleasure. I hope I achieve that.' Few will disagree that in his first season at Goodison he did just that.

[FACTFILE]

BORN
Kirovograd, USSR, 23 January 1969
POSITION
Winger
OTHER CLUBS
Dynamo Kiev (1988–90);
Shakhtar Donetsk (1990–91);
Manchester United (1991–95);
Fiorentina (1997–98);
Rangers (1998–2002);
Manchester City (loan, 2001);
Southampton (2002–03);
Al Hilal (2003);
Saturn Moscow Oblast (2004–05);
Krylia Sovetov (2006–07)
AS MANAGER
FC Torpedo Zil-Moscow (2010);
FC UFA (2011–)
HONOURS
17 USSR caps (3 goals) (1989–91);
6 CIS caps (1992);
36 Russia caps (4 goals) (1992–98)

Kavanagh, Peter

Rookie winger who was unable to revitalise Johnny Carey's last days as manager

[FACTFILE]

BORN
Romford, 3 November 1938
POSITION
Left wing
OTHER CLUB
Fulham

Season	League		FA Cup		League Cup		Total	
	App	Goals	App	Goals	App	Goals	App	Goals
1960/61	6	0	0	0	0	0	6	0
Total	6	0	0	0	0	0	6	0

Kay, Tony

Outstanding wing half whose career was brought to a premature end by betting scandal

Few of those to ever witness Tony Kay in an Everton shirt would dispute that had his past not caught up with him, his place among the Everton greats would be beyond dispute. A hard, energetic wing half, he played with verve and energy and swaggered with a sense of self-belief that enthused his team-mates.

Kay possessed the talent to be Everton's Billy Bremner or Danny Blanchflower, and longevity would surely have bestowed such a reputation upon him. But he squandered his formidable gifts with an ill-judged part in a bribery scandal that brought him a prison sentence, life ban and disgrace, simultaneously depriving Everton of their captain and leading light.

Harry Catterick signed Kay from his former club, Sheffield Wednesday, in December 1962 for £55,000 – a record fee for a wing half. At Hillsborough, Kay had been Catterick's captain and many had expected the Everton manager to move for him earlier. His arrival was, nevertheless, timely and refocused the team on their title ambition. A tenacious yet skilful player, Kay possessed a bite in the tackle and outstanding distribution. Although Brian Harris was desperately unlucky to lose his place to the new boy, the powerful redhead was a crucial factor in Everton's successful title challenge.

AN ENGLAND CAP came at the end of the 1962/63 season, and the belief was that Alf Ramsey had earmarked Kay as his 'hard man' for the 1966 World Cup Finals. Within a year of joining Everton, Kay succeeded Roy Vernon as captain, and as winter became spring Everton looked a good bet to retain their league title. But as the 1963/64 season was set for its dramatic conclusion, Kay was sidelined when dramatic news broke.

On Sunday 12 April 1964, the Sunday People printed allegations that several players had received bribes to 'throw' games. To astonishment, Kay was named as one of them. The allegations, relating to his time at Sheffield Wednesday, were made by Jimmy Gauld, a former Everton inside forward. Gauld alleged that three Wednesday players – Kay, Peter Swan and David Layne – had thrown Wednesday's match with Ipswich Town in December 1962 and bet against their own team. Kay reportedly told the People that he was convinced that Ipswich would win anyway. 'It was money for old rope,' he allegedly said. Ipswich won 2-0, but Kay was awarded man of the match and even the People noted that Kay 'put up a fine performance'.

> 'I RECEIVED AN INCREDIBLE OVATION FROM THE FANS. THE WARMTH OF THEIR RECEPTION MEANT EVERYTHING TO ME'

Everton suspended Kay immediately and he denied the comments attributed to him. But nine months later, on 26 January 1965, he was sent to prison for four months for his part in the scandal and subsequently banned for life by the Football Association. The ban was lifted in 1974, by which time his best days were long past him, and he never again played beyond amateur level. Harry Catterick was as bemused as anybody by the case. Not only had he lost one of his best players and captain for a crime committed at another club, but he had also lost the then huge £55,000 transfer fee. Although a disciplinarian himself, Catterick said that the punishments meted out by the courts and the FA were 'far too severe for the offence'. He added, 'I read three newspaper reports for the match in which the offence was alleged to have been committed and Kay had rave notices.'

Speaking to the Observer in 2004 Kay was asked if he regretted placing the bet. 'I think I was harshly punished,' he said. 'I won only £150 from the bet, but my whole career was destroyed. They took away the game I loved and I have never really recovered from that.' However, Everton remained close to his heart: 'One of my happiest experiences was when I returned [in 2003] to Everton, to Goodison Park, for the club's centenary celebrations [sic]… When I returned that day, walking out on to the pitch, I received an incredible ovation from the fans. The warmth of their reception meant everything to me, not least because I hadn't been back to Everton for years and yet they still remembered me.'

[FACTFILE]

BORN
Sheffield, 13 May 1937
POSITION
Wing half
OTHER CLUB
Sheffield Wednesday (1954–62)
HONOURS
1962/63 League Championship,
1 England cap (1963)

Season	League		FA Cup		Europe		Total	
	App	Goals	App	Goals	App	Goals	App	Goals
1962/63	19	1	2	0	0	0	21	1
1963/64	31	3	3	0	2	0	36	3
Total	**50**	**4**	**5**	**0**	**2**	**0**	**57**	**4**

Kearslake, Joseph

Centre forward whose solitary royal blue appearance yielded a goal

[FACTFILE]

BORN
Southampton, 1895
POSITION
Centre forward
OTHER CLUBS
Wigan Borough;
Stockport County (1921–22)

Season	League		FA Cup		Total	
	App	Goals	App	Goals	App	Goals
1919/20	1	1	0	0	1	1
Total	**1**	**1**	**0**	**0**	**1**	**1**

Kearton,
Jason

Long-standing understudy to Neville Southall

[FACTFILE]

BORN
Ipswich, Australia,
9 July 1969
POSITION
Goalkeeper
OTHER CLUBS
Brisbane Lions (1987–88);
Stoke City (loan, 1991);
Blackpool (loan, 1992);
Notts County (loan, 1995);
Preston North End
(loan (1996);
Crewe Alexandra
(1996–2001);
Brisbane Strikers
(2001–04)

Season	League App	Goals	FA Cup App	Goals	League Cup App	Goals	Total App	Goals
1992/93	2 (3)	0	1	0	0	0	3 (3)	0
1993/94	0	0	0	0	1	0	1	0
1994/95	1	0	0	0	0	0	1	0
Total	**3 (3)**	**0**	**1**	**0**	**1**	**0**	**5 (3)**	**0**

Keeley,
Glenn

Experienced defender whose derby day loan appearance saw him embroiled in Goodison infamy

[FACTFILE]

BORN
Barking, 1 September 1954
POSITION
Central defender
OTHER CLUBS
Ipswich Town (1972–74);
Newcastle United (1974–76);
Blackburn Rovers (1976–87);
Oldham Athletic (1987–88);
Colchester United
(loan, 1987–88);
Bolton Wanderers (1988–89);
Chorley (1989–90);
Colne Dynamoes (1990)

Season	League App	Goals	FA Cup App	Goals	League Cup App	Goals	Total App	Goals
1982/83	1	0	0	0	0	0	1	0
Total	**1**	**0**	**0**	**0**	**0**	**0**	**1**	**0**

Keates, Thomas

Former director who became the first chronicler of Everton's history

Thomas Keates (1849–1928) was an Everton director and the club's first historian. His jubilee history of the club, published posthumously in 1929, is a crucial document full of insights and anecdotes into the way the club was run in its early years. Although its narrative is somewhat old-fashioned and prone to flowery digressions, Keates's work is an unparalleled first-hand account of Everton's rise from church team to football giant.

ACCORDING TO the 1901 census, Keates was a Liverpool coal merchant who originally hailed from Cheadleton, near Leek in Staffordshire. A resident of Anfield, Keates was a director of Everton between 1897 and 1900. The board paid him 100 guineas for his history, but he never lived to see it published. A foreword, inserted into the book, records the 'deep regret' of the Everton directors and 'thousands of followers of football in the city' at his passing. The directors 'feel that this book, so full of information and reminiscence, will tend to keep his memory green among the army of supporters of the 50 years old Everton club.'

Further reading:

KEATES, THWOMAS, *History of the Everton Football Club 1878–1928: A Jubilee History*

Keeley, Jackie

Home-grown inside forward who scored an FA Cup brace during a rare outing

[FACTFILE]

BORN
Liverpool, 18 October 1936
POSITION
Inside forward
OTHER CLUB
Accrington Stanley (1959)

Season	League App	Goals	FA Cup App	Goals	Total App	Goals
1957/58	4	1	3	2	7	3
Total	**4**	**1**	**3**	**2**	**7**	**3**

Keeley, Sam

Centre forward who made a solitary outing in royal blue

Season	League		FA Cup		Total	
	App	Goals	App	Goals	App	Goals
1897/98	1	0	0	0	1	0
Total	1	0	0	0	1	0

Kelly, Jeremiah 'Jerry'

League Championship winning half back

EVERTON DIVISION 1 CHAMPIONS 1928

EVERTON 1928 CHAMPIONS
Back - **T.H.McKintosh, Kelly, Hart (Captain), Davies, O'Donnell, Virr, H.E.Cooke**
Front - **Critchley, Martin, Dean, Cresswell, Weldon, Troup**

In the spring of 1927, as Everton were faced with the unimaginable spectre of relegation, the board sought to secure the club's future by bringing in fresh blood to tighten a leaky defence and strengthen the resolve of a team in freefall.

From Sunderland they bought right back Warney Cresswell, once the world's most expensive player, and from Huddersfield Town the England international goalkeeper, Ted Taylor. The inside forwards Dick Forshaw and Tom Weldon would soon be added to this number and from Ayr United came the half back Jerry Kelly. Not only would these men avert the calamity of relegation during the 1926/27 season, but within barely a year of their arrivals they would help propel Everton to their third League Championship success.

The 25-year-old Kelly took the place of William Brown and immediately brought some composure and resolve to a back line that would concede nearly 100 League and FA Cup goals by the season's end. 'In Kelly Everton would seem to have acquired a half-back of the right type,' reported the Liverpool Post and Mercury of his debut against Liverpool at Anfield. 'Splendidly built (tall and slim) he played a capital game once he found his feet and plied the forwards with excellent passes.'

'I like this man Kelly; he is quick to size up a situation, and with

Cresswell behind him we have a right flank of defenders who can become a secure attacking number,' added the distinguished hand of Ernest 'Bee' Edwards. 'Cresswell's nonchalance is not out of place; he believes in working a ball, just as does Kelly, and with Hart finding his captaincy and team care less arduous, he is producing first-class defence and attack.'

The turnaround in Everton's fortunes after Kelly's arrival was astounding. But although a league champion within 14 months of joining Everton, injuries to Dixie Dean meant Everton struggled in

the 1928/29 season and Kelly found his place under threat from Tom Griffiths. He was restored to the team for the start of the 1929/30 season but Everton's form was poor and so too was Kelly's.

'Kelly was a weakness,' reported the Post and Mercury of a 2-3 home defeat to Manchester City. 'He was out of touch with the line, got little of the ball, and most of the City's damaging raids came from Kelly's wing.' He played just once more in an Everton shirt and was subsequently transfer-listed. After Everton were relegated at the end of the season Kelly joined Carlisle United for £500. He is later recorded as playing for Rennes University Club.

Season	League		FA Cup		Total	
	App	Goals	App	Goals	App	Goals
1926/27	14	0	0	0	14	0
1927/28	40	1	2	0	42	1
1928/29	21	0	0	0	21	0
1929/30	6	0	0	0	6	0
Total	81	1	2	0	83	1

Kelly,
Theo

Controversial administrator and manager of Everton during the late 1930s and 1940s

THEO KELLY was a controversial and divisive administarator of Everton during the 1930s, rising to the role of secretary in 1936, and, in 1939 becoming secretary-manager, a position he held for a decade. During this period Everton were one of the best run clubs in England off the pitch. His enemies, however, said he was a self-serving autocrat, who cared nothing for either his players or the Everton fans. His presence as Everton boss was ultimately destructive in the extreme. When he left in 1948, Everton were not only bottom of the First Division, but Kelly's influence had directly led to the departures of Dixie Dean, Tommy Lawton and Joe Mercer, and also paved the way for the end of T.G. Jones's Goodison days.

Kelly arrived at Goodison in August 1929 as A-team trainer-coach on wages of £4.10.0 per week. His duties included scouting opponents and transfer targets, general administration and his A-team duties. In April 1934 he was appointed assistant secretary on wages of £6 per week.

AT THIS TIME, Everton's long-standing secretary-manager was Tom McIntosh. The role that he occupied was a good deal different to the manager's role which we know today. The position was part administrator, part selector and middle-man between the coach, captain and team, and members of the board, who retained a say in selection. The role of captain – in Everton's case Dean – was more like that of a modern-day cricket captain, with some say in team affairs and a responsibility for the daily running of the team, in partnership with the coach, Harry Cooke. McIntosh was most famous for spotting and signing Dean, but beyond that was well respected and liked by both board and players alike. A kind, patient, articulate man, his 'system of management,' wrote the Everton historian Thomas Keates in 1928, 'seems to approach the ideal.' Yet in October 1935, Everton mourned his death from cancer, aged just 56.

At a special board meeting, convened a fortnight after McIntosh's death, there was division as to whether Everton should have a team manager, as clubs such as Arsenal had started to adopt, or continue with the system of secretary-manager. It was decided to wait until the full-time appointment of a new secretary. Kelly was appointed acting secretary and, in February 1936, to the position full time on a salary of £500. The appointment of such a fiercely ambitious individual was to alter the course of Everton history.

Kelly was never well liked by Dean, and he later described him as both an autocrat and despot. But over the course of the 1936/37 season, the relationship between the two men deteriorated as Dean saw Kelly's ambitions begin to surface. 'This chap Kelly had no time for the older lads,' he would recall. 'I just couldn't get on with him. He was secretary but I didn't care what he was. I knew what was happening. He wanted to get rid of me and also one or two other people who looked like being in with a chance of becoming manager one day.'

Three games into the 1937/38 season Dean was dropped. He played just twice more for Everton: a 1-2 defeat at Grimsby, and finally on 4 December 1937, against Charlton Athletic at the Valley. Everton lost 3-1 in Dean's 399th appearance for the club. He continued to play for the reserves, eventually winning a Central League Championship medal, but Kelly had cut off any prospect of his returning back to the first team. Dean recalled: 'Kelly started telling lies about me and things got worse. He wanted to have that manager's job and definitely wanted to get rid of me. I could see that. So I had it out with him and decided to move on.' On 11 March 1938, the unthinkable happened. Dean was sold to Notts County for £3000. The ever-astute Kelly made certain that Everton recouped the money paid out to Tranmere thirteen years earlier. Disgracefully, Everton's greatest ever player was allowed to leave without a farewell or thanks, and understandably he did not return to Goodison for many years after.

Kelly was enjoying success off the field, however. Everton's bank balance doubled to around £30,000 and he was enjoying greater control over first-team matters. For the 1939/40 season he was given charge of first-team affairs, although the intervention of war meant this was short-lived.

HOWEVER, his prickliness and ability to make enemies got him and Everton in trouble. Following the outbreak of war Kelly embroiled the club in an unseemly dispute with the FA over the issue of call-ups of Everton players for matches whose purposes were to raise funds for the Red Cross. The amount of Everton players selected was 'absurdly out of proportion', he moaned, ignoring the fact that they were reigning champions. When Sagar, Jones and Mercer were called up for an FA XI in April 1940 Kelly wrote to Stanley Rous, secretary of the FA, complaining. Rous offered to substitute Sagar and Jones but said that they would need Mercer. Kelly refused to allow the half back to join up, prompting an FA investigation. The sanctions were harsh: the chairman, Ernest Green, was banned from football for 15 months, the director W.C. Gibbons banned for two months, and they recommended Kelly be 'censured' for failing to keep the Everton board properly informed of the FA's decisions. The whole mess seemed emblematic of his form of management.

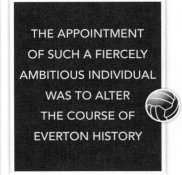

THE APPOINTMENT OF SUCH A FIERCELY AMBITIOUS INDIVIDUAL WAS TO ALTER THE COURSE OF EVERTON HISTORY

WAR ALSO posed challenges to the playing staff and when peace came the squad was significantly changed in terms of readiness for football. Players were older, slower, scarred by war or just wanting away. Dean's replacement and Everton's golden boy, Tommy Lawton, sought a move away from Goodison owing to marital problems. A soothing word in his ear may have sorted the problem, but Kelly was no pacifier. Summoning the striker to his office, Kelly looked down his glasses and said: 'You want a transfer do you, Lawton? Well, let me tell you, we've been trying to give you away for four months and nobody wants you.

There's the door, go out and get your training done and stop wasting my time.' It was vintage Kelly. But he could not sustain the façade of the Dickensian factory owner. A second transfer request was subsequently accepted and Lawton was sold to Chelsea for £11,500.

Soon following him out of the Goodison door was Joe Mercer. In an England v. Scotland international in April 1946, Willie Waddell of Rangers inadvertently landed on Mercer's leg during a challenge. Mercer struggled on gamely, though his injury stunted his efforts. Accusations that he was somehow feigning injury stung the player, but more hurtful was the fact that the Everton management also seemed to believe the allegations. At the heart of the dispute, once more, was Kelly. When the 1946/47 season reopened Mercer was still struggling for fitness and the intimation that he wasn't trying resurfaced. Everton's manager offered no support and the relationship between the two men first broke down then became martial. His injury had cost him his fitness and, sapped of his stamina, he had lost the attacking part of his game. Kelly's unremitting hostility persisted, so Mercer met with the director Cecil Baxter and asked for a transfer, saying that he would quit football altogether if he was not allowed to leave.

Days later Joe Mercer, who six months earlier had captained his country, was serving customers in the grocery wholesalers he co-owned with his father-in-law. The impasse lasted three weeks when Kelly finally summoned him to the Adelphi Hotel, where Arsenal's manager George Allison met him. A transfer was agreed and within minutes he had joined the Gunners for £8000. 'It was a terrible blow for me to go,' Mercer said later, 'because I was so crazy about Everton.' In a final snub,

Kelly brought his boots to the Adelphi preventing Mercer – as he had Dean – from returning to Goodison to say his farewells.

These defections caused apoplexy in the dressing room. T.G. Jones, the finest player left at the club, was deeply unimpressed. But Kelly refused to play him and over the course of 1947 he made just a dozen appearances. On five occasions that year he asked for a transfer, only to be denied each time by Everton. The spat then broke out into a public argument – something which was then absolutely unprecedented – between Jones and the club.

A reluctance to invest in replacing these lost legends did little to help Everton on the field. They finished 1946/47 in 10th place and plunged to 14th a year later. But worse was to come. The start of the 1948/49 season was disastrous. After a 3-3 opening day draw with Newcastle, Everton's results read as follows: 0-4, 0-1, 0-5, 0-5, 2-1, 0-6, 0-1. With Everton bottom of the First Division a board meeting was called in mid-September to discuss the situation. Kelly, perhaps sensing what was to happen, couldn't make it owing to a 'car mishap'. At the meeting it was resolved that he revert to his old position of secretary and the position of a manager concerned with football affairs be advertised. A month later Cliff Britton formally became Everton manager.

FOR THE next two years the pair worked alongside each other in what must have been an awkward relationship. In December 1950 Kelly was given a three-month leave of absence by the Everton board for reasons that are unclear. It was subsequently agreed to give him a payment of £500 and '50 cigarettes per week'. Kelly did not return to work and in March 1951 was replaced by Bill Dickinson.

Kelso, Bob

Victorian half back who previously starred for the 'World Champions'

Bob Kelso was one of the most distinguished Scottish players during the country's international football golden age of the 1880s, an era that included a nine-year-long unbeaten run. Born in Renton, he was part of his home-town team when they won the Scottish FA Cup in 1885, the same year he became an international. In 1888 he was part of the Renton team that beat the English FA Cup holders, West Bromwich Albion, and thus became known as 'World Champions'.

Like many Scottish footballers in this era, he journeyed south in search of a living from the game he played so well – professionalism being prohibited in Scotland until the 1890s. After a spell with Newcastle West End he signed for Everton, but made just one appearance, against Preston North End in January 1889. Evidently he did enough to impress Everton's opponents, for he left to join them at the season's end and would claim League Championship honours with them in 1890.

Everton re-signed Kelso over the summer of 1891 and he replaced Dan Kirkwood, who had served as half back in the League

Championship winning team, occasionally deputising at right back too. Indeed, on one occasion, against Aston Villa in September 1892, he even deputised for the injured David Jardine in goal. He soon earned plaudits of watching reporters. 'The work done by Kelso since his inclusion in the team is of the highest order, and if there was as reliable a man on the opposite wing, the half backs would be complete,' reported the Daily Post. 'He was widely respected as a no-nonsense defender with a granite tackle – which occasionally bordered on bone crunching,' added David France and David Prentice in their history of the era, Virgin Blues.

Season	League		FA Cup		Total	
	App	Goals	App	Goals	App	Goals
1888/89	1	0	-	-	1	0
1891/92	23	2	1	0	24	2
1892/93	14	1	7	0	21	1
1893/94	26	1	1	0	27	1
1894/95	19	1	4	0	23	1
1895/96	6	0	1	0	7	0
Total	**89**	**5**	**14**	**0**	**103**	**5**

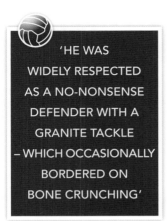

'HE WAS WIDELY RESPECTED AS A NO-NONSENSE DEFENDER WITH A GRANITE TACKLE – WHICH OCCASIONALLY BORDERED ON BONE CRUNCHING'

Kendall, Howard

An illustrious member of Harry Catterick's 1970 Championship side, he went on to become the club's most successful manager, serving in three spells through the 1980s and 1990s.

Kelso's finest hour came in an FA Cup semi-final second replay against Preston North End at Trent Bridge. Playing at right back, the Scot was immense as Everton overcame their opponents 2-1 to reach their first FA Cup Final. '[Bob] Howarth and Kelso, in particular had to exert themselves to the utmost and but for their Herculean work Everton must have met with a reverse,' reported the Liverpool Mercury. Another reporter noted: 'Kelso sustained his later-day form, and his clean kicking did much in the cause of victory.'

Kelso lost his place to James Adams during the 1895/96 season and at the end of the campaign was sold to Dundee for £35. Back in his homeland he regained his place in the national team.

Few men can claim the length or distinction of association with Everton Football Club as Howard Kendall, who, over a period spanning more than three decades and totalling some 18 years, claimed three league titles, an FA Cup and European Cup Winners' Cup.

As a midfielder in the 1960s and 1970s he was part, with Colin Harvey and Alan Ball, of the famed 'Holy Trinity', which drove Everton to title success in 1970 and thrilled football purists of all hues. As manager, he served Everton over three spells through the 1980s and 1990s, masterminding the unprecedented successes of the mid-1980s. Such glories were to elude him later in his career, perhaps clouding some judgements. But after electing to leave following the club's ninth title win in 1987, Kendall realised that he could never escape Everton. He might share love affairs with other clubs, but Goodison was in his blood – it was his 'marriage', he famously quipped, and when Everton called he returned and did his best.

A son of the Northeast, Kendall started his career at Preston North End, first attracting national prominence in May 1964 when, aged 17 years, 345 days, he became the youngest player to turn out in an FA Cup Final.

Twice Preston held the lead, only to lose 3-2 to a last-minute goal. Playing in the Second Division, the young wing half continued to attract positive notices.

A creative wing half, he was a strong and precise tackler who, it was soon quite obvious, was head and shoulders above the rest of his team-mates. Frustrated at Preston's inability to break out of the Second Division, Kendall became restless. For a long time, Liverpool looked the most likely destination for the young player, with Bill Shankly making frequent visits to his former club to scout Kendall. A bid in October 1966 was rejected, and the rumours persisted for so long that the Preston crowd took to chanting, 'Stay away, Shankly.'

In March 1967, Kendall's long-rumoured move to Merseyside finally came. When the Liverpool Echo carried the headline 'Kendall Signs' scores of expectant Liverpudlians bought the newspaper – only to discover that their target had joined Everton for £80,000. To Shankly's fury, the Anfield board failed to back their manager with the funds (causing Shankly to offer a letter of resignation, which remained unretracted in a cabinet in the

[FACTFILE]

BORN
Renton, Dumbartonshire, 1 October 1865

DIED
10 August 1942

POSITION
Right half / full back

OTHER CLUBS
Renton;
Newcastle West End;
Preston North End
(1888–89);
Dundee (1896–)

HONOURS
7 Scotland caps (1 goal)
(1885–98)

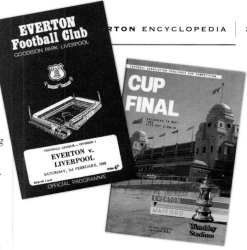

club secretary's office for years), leaving Kendall with a choice between Everton and Stoke. When he and his father discussed a move with Stoke manager Tony Waddington and Alan Ball senior, a member of Stoke's coaching staff, Kendall senior asked Ball, 'If Stoke is the right move for my lad, why didn't your boy come here?' From that moment Kendall knew that he would become an Everton player.

The start of Kendall's 30-year-long association with Everton was nevertheless undermined by injury, limiting him to just four appearances in the final months of the 1966/67 season. But in the 1967/68 season he established himself in place of Jimmy Gabriel in a side that brimmed with potential. Since winning the 1966 FA Cup, Catterick had reconfigured his team into one that oozed youth and panache. Kendall, along with his other new additions – Alan Ball, John Hurst and Joe Royle – were all in their early twenties or younger. So too were Colin Harvey and Tommy Wright, veterans of the cup win.

The renaissance was born in the Everton midfield. Starting in five-aside matches in Bellefield's gym, a unique understanding developed between Kendall, Harvey and Ball. 'Sometimes I wished we could have got the games televised,' Catterick later said of the training sessions. 'It was absolute magic.' It did not take long for this to be transferred onto the Goodison pitch. Each man complemented the others perfectly: Ball the firebrand was offset by the cool panache of Harvey; what Harvey lacked in bite or aggression Kendall made up; if Kendall was occasionally lacking in goals, it was compensated by Ball's incredible strike rate – 51 league goals in his first three seasons at Goodison, including 20 from 34 games in the 1967/68 campaign. 'As three players we hardly ever needed any coaching,' recalled Ball. 'We could find each other in the dark.'

> HE SECURED HIS PLACE IN BLUE HEARTS BY SCORING THE ONLY GOAL IN THE GOODISON DERBY IN FEBRUARY 1968

If Kendall did not immediately win over Evertonians, some still mourning the departure of Jimmy Gabriel, in February 1968 he secured his place in blue hearts by scoring the only goal in the Goodison derby. 'I see the best two teams in Liverpool won today,' said Catterick afterwards, recycling the old Shankly jibe and

goading his rival who he knew to be still smarting from the previous spring's transfer. 'Without a doubt: Everton's Kendall was man of the match,' recorded the Daily Post. 'Whether he was creating opportunities, forcing his attentions on the Liverpool defence or breaking up attacks he hardly put a foot wrong. It was almost as if he was setting out to show what a player Liverpool missed when he decided to go to Everton.'

In May 1968, Kendall returned to Wembley for the FA Cup Final, against West Bromwich Albion – but again left empty-handed. It was his last visit there as a player, for although he would be called up to several England squads, he would never play a full international, causing many observers to dub him the finest English player never to play for his country.

For the next two seasons, Gwladys Street's Holy Trinity reigned supreme, thrilling Goodison with some of the finest football the old stadium has ever seen. There is a school of thought that the brand of football played in the 1968/69 season was purer, more uninhibited than that which ultimately won the league title the following year. Certainly, it was no coincidence that Everton's 1968/69 title challenge waned when an injury suffered in a 1-0 win over Queens Park Rangers on 1 February kept Kendall out for most of the remainder of the season. The following year the three were finally reunited for the run-in after injuries and a suspension served by Ball. Everton embarked on an eight-game unbeaten streak and the title came to Goodison for the seventh time.

According to Colin Harvey, their midfield partnership 'was all very instinctive – not something we worked on in training. Our games complemented each other. Alan liked to push forward in support of Joe Royle while myself and Howard were more defensively minded.'

AND YET AFTER shining so brightly, Everton began to fail. The trio played more games together in 1970/71 than they had a year earlier – but finished only 14th. In December 1971 Ball was sold to Arsenal in a move that shocked Evertonians.

Over the following few seasons of flux, Kendall was one of the few positives in Catterick's waning team. Injured early in September 1973, he missed many of the opening stages of Billy Bingham's managerial reign and when, in February 1974, the Everton manager sought to make Bob Latchford a British record

signing, he deemed Kendall expendable, selling him to Birmingham as a makeweight in the £300,000 deal.

At St Andrews he performed admirably for 115 games before moving to Stoke City during summer 1977. Now aged 31, he also took on coaching responsibilities and played a pivotal role in the club's return to the First Division in 1979. But rather than make a playing return at the top level, in June that year he joined Blackburn Rovers who had just sacked their manager John Pickering, having been relegated to the Third Division.

In his debut season as manager – 1979/80 – Kendall immediately won promotion back to the Second Division. The following year Rovers finished fourth, missing out on promotion only on goal difference to Swansea City.

Kendall's rise at Blackburn did not go unnoticed at his former club. When Gordon Lee was sacked at the end of the 1980/81 season, Kendall, who had already rejected the Crystal Palace manager's job, was appointed Everton boss.

Seven years had passed since his unceremonious departure to Birmingham and much had changed at Goodison: average attendances were down by a third; the Moores millions had dried up; and Everton, once considered perennial title contenders, were merely treading water at the wrong end of the First Division.

'Nothing has happened here since 1970,' Kendall announced on his return. 'And it will take a bit of time to put it right. But we are geared to win trophies and that is what we aim to do.' But despite the limited resources available to him, expectations remained incredibly high. As one newspaper put it, 'They're not asking much from Howard Kendall – only a three minute mile, a century before lunch and a successful assault on Everest.'

From Blackburn he brought Mick Heaton as his assistant manager and over the summer of 1981 engaged in a frenzy of buying and selling. Bob Latchford and John Gidman were high-profile departures, and Kendall memorably brought in seven close-season signings: Alan Ainscow, Jim Arnold, Alan Biley, Mick Ferguson, Neville Southall, Mickey Thomas and Mike Walsh.

> KENDALL OPENED EVERY WINDOW OF THE DRESSING ROOM. 'JUST LISTEN TO THAT,' HE SAID. 'ARE YOU GOING TO LET THEM DOWN?'
>
> EVERTON WON 2-0

Over the course of the 1981/82 season the majority of these new players would make little or no impact as Kendall tried to rebuild. Asa Hartford joined the exodus, and after the new manager failed in a British record bid to sign West Bromwich Albion's Bryan Robson in the autumn, he broke the Everton transfer record to sign Stoke City's Adrian Heath in January 1992. On four occasions, Kendall called upon himself as a midfield stand-in – the final outings in a 600-appearance playing career.

In a season of transition, Everton finished 1981/82 eighth. From the perspective of time this can be considered progress. Several outstanding young players – Kevin Ratcliffe, Kevin Richardson, Gary Stevens and Graeme Sharp – were given extended first-team runs, and although his transfers were more miss than hit, Kendall nevertheless made two inspired signings in Heath and Southall. Each of these young players would play crucial parts in the success that was to follow.

IN SUMMER 1982, Kendall adopted less of a scattergun approach in the transfer market. Old-boys Andy King and David Johnson made returns, and Kendall brought in a couple of young unknowns: the Liverpool reserve midfielder Kevin Sheedy and Tranmere's lanky centre back Derek Mountfield. The former was thrust straight into the first team as Everton showed promise in the first stages of the season, opening their Goodison campaign with a 5-0 win over newly crowned European Champions Aston Villa.

But on 6 November 1982, any progress made under Kendall seemed to grind to an abrupt halt. Facing Liverpool in the Goodison derby, Kendall drafted in his former Blackburn captain centre back Glenn Keeley, who he had signed on loan, for his debut. It would be an unmitigated disaster. Keeley was sent off on the half-hour mark for tussling with Kenny Dalglish. Already a goal behind, it left Everton with a hopeless task, but scarcely could anybody have imagined the ease with which Liverpool cut through them. Ian Rush scored four times, Mark Lawrenson grabbed the middle goal. Everton were humiliated. 'People have gone overboard about the game,' said Kendall, attempting to rationalise in the days after the debacle. 'We were beaten by a very good side and we only had ten men for most of the time. Any side is going to have to do it all against Liverpool.' But Kendall's honeymoon was at an end.

The defeat marked a watershed of sorts. Gary Stevens reclaimed his right back shirt from Brian Borrows. Neville Southall was dropped and loaned to Port Vale – but returned by the season's end, a tougher and more complete player. Billy Wright would soon be phased out from the first team, and Kevin Ratcliffe, hitherto misused as a left back, made a triumphant return in central defence. And the defeat added to the sense that Everton's midfield needed hardening: six weeks later, Everton's overdraft was stretched to breaking point to acquire Bolton midfielder Peter Reid. Although his initial impact would be limited by injuries, Kendall later described him as 'Everton's most important signing since the war'.

Things picked up: six wins in the final eight games of the season saw Everton finish seventh, and they could be considered unfortunate to have been knocked out in an FA Cup quarter-final. Yet Merseyside was gripped with mass unemployment and economic recession. Average attendances stood at barely 20,000 – the lowest since the First World War – impacting on Everton's effectiveness in the transfer market.

During summer 1983 Kendall was able to add just Trevor Steven and Alan Harper – a discarded Liverpool reserve – to his promising squad, while Steve McMahon, one of the best players at the club, was sold to Aston Villa, having failed to agree a new contract.

As 1983/84 began, Goodison was a grim place, and Kendall was on the edge. Attendances dropped below 20,000. Goals were hard to come by – just 11 in the league before New Year. An action group set up by the fans distributed leaflets before home games calling for Kendall's sacking. A spokesman for the group announced: 'We believe something drastic needs to be done because we fear for this great club's Division One future. We have tremendous respect for Howard Kendall as a past player, but we do not rate him highly as manager of Everton. He has been quoted as saying that he thinks the team is on the right lines. If that's the case I'd hate to see what the wrong lines are.' Philip Carter delivered a vote of confidence in the manager, but the fan protests continued. One day, Kendall returned home from training to find his garage daubed with graffiti calling on him to resign.

Kendall persisted. He changed his backroom team, promoting Colin Harvey – previously youth team manager – to his assistant. In an attempt to end the goal drought, he signed Wolves' Andy Gray in November. Peter Reid returned from long-term injury, Derek Mountfield was promoted to the first team and Kevin Ratcliffe was made captain.

THE GREEN shoots of recovery did not show until January 1984, however, when there were a couple of turning points that have subsequently entered Goodison lore. The first came on 6 January, when Everton faced Stoke City in an FA Cup third round tie. Evertonians colonised the Victoria Ground and Kendall's team talk became legendary. With the pre-match noise from visiting fans deafening, Kendall opened every window of the dressing room. 'Just listen to that,' he said. 'Are you going to let them down?' Everton won 2-0. Twelve days later, they faced Oxford United in a Milk Cup semi-final. Trailing 1-0 until the closing stages of the match, Kevin Brock's famous back-pass let in Adrian Heath, who equalised to set up a replay. Everton won that match 4-1, and Kendall never looked back.

The turnaround in a team that at Christmas had looked set for a relegation battle was remarkable. Eleven league goals in the first half of the season became 44 by the season's end as Everton once more finished seventh. They reached the Milk Cup Final, losing to Liverpool after a replay. Seven weeks later Everton returned to Wembley to face Watford in the FA Cup Final. Everton won 2-0 and Kendall, who six months earlier had been vilified by sections of the Everton support, was a hero once more.

That summer he added Sunderland's promising young midfielder Paul Bracewell to his squad, but remained loyal to the

youthful side that had brought him such great success in the first half of 1984. By November Everton were top after a run of results that included a 5-0 demolition of Manchester United and an Anfield derby win, sealed by Graeme Sharp's awesome volley. It was only Everton's third win over Liverpool since Kendall's playing days. Everton, reported The Times, had 'completed the transformation from an ordinary team to a formidable one'.

Although Everton briefly ceded top spot over Christmas, it would soon be reclaimed. From Boxing Day until the beginning of May, when the league title was won, Everton went on a 17-match unbeaten streak, winning 15 and drawing just twice. Never before had a title been won in such a fashion: Everton amassed a record 90 points (surpassed in 1994 by Manchester United), which would surely have been closer to 100 had Kendall not been forced, due to the fatigue of his senior professionals, to play youngsters in the last four games of the season. The tally of 88 goals had not been reached by any top-flight club for 17 years. He led Everton to a second consecutive FA Cup Final, which was lost to Manchester United. In his first European campaign, Kendall led Everton to success in the European Cup Winners' Cup Final. For these achievements, Kendall was named Bell's Manager of the Year.

EVERTON
'WORLD TEAM
OF THE YEAR'

In 18 months Howard Kendall had dragged a team from the depths to being the best in the world – a fact acknowledged by World Soccer magazine, who named Everton 'World Team of the Year'. With the exception of Adrian Heath, he made no big-money signings and made optimum use of his youth players, astute bargains and veterans. They played in a manner and spirit befitting the finest traditions of the School of Science and after sitting for so long in the shadow cast by Liverpool had come marching out of it.

> FROM BOXING DAY
> UNTIL MID-MAY
> EVERTON WENT ON
> A 17 MATCH UNBEATEN
> STREAK, WINNING 15
> AND DRAWING JUST
> TWICE. NEVER BEFORE
> HAD A TITLE
> BEEN WON IN SUCH
> A FASHION

In Harry Catterick, Kendall had once come under the charge of one of the most ruthless managers in the game. While the model of affability himself, he was sometimes also prone to making decisions that flew in the face of supporter opinion. Early in the 1984/85 season, he had replaced the popular John Bailey with Birmingham City's grizzled hard man, Pat Van Den Hauwe. And as he plotted his retention of the league title, so he made another hard choice, selling Andy Gray, who had become a crowd idol. In his place he bought Gary Lineker for a club record £800,000.

LINEKER WAS A huge success, scoring 40 goals in all competitions. For much of the 1985/86 season, spearheaded by Lineker's goals, Everton looked

set to retain the title, also reaching the FA Cup Final for the third year running. But at the last they ran out of steam: the title was conceded to Liverpool after a devastating defeat to Oxford United with just three games remaining; Liverpool then completed the double, overcoming a 1-0 half-time FA Cup Final deficit.

PERHAPS more cruelly, Liverpool had also deprived Everton of the opportunity of competing in the European Cup after their supporters' murderous behaviour prior to the previous season's final led to the deaths of 39 Juventus fans at Belgium's Heysel Stadium. English clubs were given an indefinite European ban, and while Kendall nobly took the line that he did not want to discuss the merits of its fairness because so many had died, he later admitted: 'The ban came as a massive body blow to Everton Football Club. We had won the league and with it the right to contest what is arguably the most sought after piece of silverware in world football. I had been so looking forward to seeing the cream of Europe play at Goodison Park in front of one of British football's most knowledgeable crowds.'

There remained a sense that the Heysel ban left Kendall with unfinished business to conduct – that he needed to prove himself in Europe. Obviously this ambition could no longer be realised at Everton and so speculation started to link him with jobs in Europe and, in particular, Spain.

The Heysel ban would see English clubs lose their best players to European and even Scottish rivals as they sought European competition. Among the first to leave was Lineker, who Kendall sold to Barcelona in July 1986 for £2.2million. Lineker later claimed that he never wanted away from Everton: could it have been that Kendall thought he might be reunited with his supreme goalscorer at the Nou Camp?

Certainly, as the 1986/87 season kicked off there was some truth behind the rumours linking Kendall with the Barcelona job. The Catalan giants approached Kendall at the start of the season, when it emerged that its incumbent manager Terry Venables may be leaving. Kendall met club president Jose Lluís Núñez and chief executive Joan Gaspart at London's Connaught Hotel, even signing a provisional contract. In the event Venables signed for a further year (against his better judgement, as he later admitted) and Kendall's deal fell through. Despite Kendall's obvious disappointment the idea of managing abroad had been firmly implanted in his head. It was 'a longing which burned deep inside of me and one which I knew I had to get out of my system'.

Everton's 1986/87 title win arguably represented the apex of Kendall's managerial skills, for the odds were insurmountably stacked against him. Not only had he lost Lineker to Barcelona, but Paul Bracewell and Derek Mountfield had succumbed to long-term injuries. Neville Southall and Peter Reid both missed the start of the season to injury too.

At the start of the campaign, Kendall added the Norwich City captain Dave Watson, a £900,000 record signing, and Manchester City's 33-year-old captain, Paul Power, for £65,000. If his arrival prompted incredulity, he soon assuaged doubters, filling in a number of roles throughout the team with distinction. Kendall improvised and patched up his squad, adding further inspired signings in Ian Snodin and Wayne Clarke at crucial points in the season as Everton lifted their ninth league title.

Kendall had now eclipsed Harry Catterick to become Everton's most successful manager. But rather than build an empire, as successive

Liverpool managers had done, he sought fresh challenges. In April 1987, as Everton stood on the brink of the championship, Kendall met with a representative from a second Spanish club. Athletico Bilbao, the representatives of Spain's Basque capital, were the unlikely team that had managed to capture his imagination. Like Yorkshire Cricket Club, they had a strictly adhered to policy of only using indigenous players. Normally considered La Liga underachievers, under the management of Javier Clemente, their all-Basque teams had won La Liga twice in the early 1980s, and their representative, Fernando Ochoa, managed to sell the club to Kendall. Despite the efforts of the Everton board – Kendall was offered and turned down a contract that would have made him the highest paid manager in England – he would not stay at Goodison.

On 19 June 1987, after feverish speculation, he revealed his departure to a press conference held at Goodison Park. 'After six years something inside you says go out and start again,' he said. 'There are many aspects to management in England and I felt that I just could not devote enough of my time to the aspects of my job I find important. I am at the stage where I do not want to spend my life sitting behind a desk.' Philip Carter, also making reference to Lineker's transfer a year earlier, rued his departure. 'Spain has had its fair share as far as Everton are concerned.' He added, 'It is a problem for English football.'

Kendall was a moderate success in Spain, taking Bilbao to fourth and seventh in La Liga in his two full seasons at San Marmes, but was sacked in November 1989 after a poor run of results. A month later he returned to England as Manchester City manager, where he surrounded himself with former Everton players. When Everton met Manchester City in April 1990, of the 25 players to take part, 19 appeared for Everton at some time in their career.

Kendall's spell at Maine Road lasted just eleven months. The sacking of Colin Harvey in November 1990 created a vacancy that he could just not resist. While Manchester City had been a 'love affair', said Kendall as he was unveiled for his second spell in charge, Everton was like a 'marriage'.

He inherited a team in a state of turmoil. Several mid-80s stalwarts – Gary Stevens, Trevor Steven, Peter Reid – had already departed, and others, such as Graeme Sharp,

CONSIDERED AMONG THE BRIGHTEST MANAGERIAL TALENTS IN THE ENGLISH GAME AT THE TIME OF HIS RETURN TO GOODISON

Kevin Sheedy and Kevin Ratcliffe, were past their best. Big-money signings, such as Tony Cottee, had failed to deliver. Everton were rooted at the foot of the First Division and the squad was beset by bitter divisions between Kendall's old players and Harvey's signings. A night out in a Chinese restaurant to boost team morale ended in a well-publicised punch-up between Kevin Sheedy and Martin Keown.

KENDALL steadied the ship, leading Everton to ninth and respectability. In these first 12 months back at Goodison there was a frenzy of transfer activity. Sharp was the most notable departure, but Sheedy and Ratcliffe were also marginalised to the point of exclusion. Promising Harvey signings, such as Mike Newell and Stuart McCall, were sold on at a profit, while the dead wood – such as Mike Milligan and Neil McDonald – were also moved on. Kendall brought in Peter Beardsley, Maurice Johnston and Mark Ward each for in excess of £1million, but despite some good football, his team lacked edge or imagination and finished the 1991/92 season 12th.

As had happened a decade earlier, in the midst of an economic recession Everton were struck hard. Average attendances threatened to drop below the 20,000 mark and there was no investment in the team. Less than two years after Kendall's return, Everton were stagnating. Limited transfer funds in summer 1992 saw only the arrivals of Barry Horne and Paul Rideout – both of whom would make crucial contributions to Everton's history, but who at the time left fans underwhelmed.

After another disappointing season in 1992/93, Everton finished thirteenth. Kendall seemed to be running out of ideas. Mid-season, his best player, Martin Keown, was sold to Arsenal, ostensibly to fund the signing of a target man. More money was raised with the sale of Peter Beardsley to Newcastle that summer. But, Graham Stuart aside, much-needed reinforcements never came. A promising start to the 1993/94 season was soon undermined

by the perilously thin squad. Three consecutive wins in the opening week of the campaign were followed by three straight defeats; a 2-0 derby win in September was followed a week later by a 5-1 home thrashing by Norwich City.

On 4 December 1993, Everton faced Southampton at Goodison in front of just 13,667 – the lowest league attendance in a decade. Everton won thanks to a solitary Tony Cottee goal, but if there was any sense that another corner had maybe been turned Kendall soon confounded it, announcing his resignation after the game. It emerged later that a move for Manchester United's Dion Dublin had been vetoed by the board and he felt his position undermined.

Considered among the brightest managerial talents in the English game at the time of his return to Goodison, Kendall's career, like Everton, had by 1993 gone into decline. With no managerial opportunities in England, in 1994 Kendall ventured to Greece for a brief, unsuccessful spell in charge of Xanthi.

In January 1995 he returned to England as manager of Notts County, then of Division One and facing a relegation battle. Kendall made a big impact, leading them to victory in the Anglo-Italian Cup Final and seemingly bringing them clear of relegation. But in April he spectacularly fell out with his chairman and was sacked. County's form nose-dived and they were relegated a month later.

In December 1995, Kendall was appointed manager of Sheffield United, also in Division One and facing a relegation battle. This time he avoided relegation, and in 1996/97 led them to the play-off final, which they lost to Crystal Palace. It represented a renaissance of sorts and brought him to the attention of new Everton chairman Peter Johnson, in the midst of an excruciating three-month-long search to bring a 'world class' manager to Goodison following Joe Royle's departure. When that descended into high farce, after Andy Gray's belated withdrawal from the running, Johnson offered the job to the only man who would still take it – Kendall.

EVERTON'S 1997/98 season represented the worst Goodison campaign in living memory. Everton, by rights, should have been relegated, and owed their salvation not to themselves, but the failure of Bolton Wanderers to overtake them at the last. Who was to blame for this mess? In truth it lies somewhere between

Johnson, who failed to provide adequate transfer funds, leaving Kendall to horse-trade in the bargain basement; the players, who were often inadequate, lacking spirit or pride in their shirts; and Kendall himself.

In fairness, there were a couple of bright spots amid this tale of football carnage. There was a wonderful derby win in October, inspired by the impetuous dreadlocked teenager, Danny Cadamarteri. The signings of Don Hutchison and Thomas Myhre rekindled memories of Kendall's eye for a bargain or young unknown. But what of the rest of his acquisitions? John Spencer, a £1.5million striker who never scored a goal? Danny Williamson, a bog-standard midfielder, traded for David Unsworth plus £1million. Graham Stuart, an underrated hero, swapped for Carl Tiler and Mitch Ward, who – like Tony Thomas, bought from Tranmere – may have been good enough in a lower league, but were patently inadequate for the Premiership.

Amid Everton's slide to the foot of the table, there were rumours of unrest, indiscipline and rancour. Twice player unhappiness with the manager boiled over into outright mutiny. After a 4-1 League Cup hammering at Coventry, the players refused Kendall's orders to warm down, which then descended into a messy on-the-field argument between manager and team. Then in January, Gary Speed, who had succeeded Dave Watson as captain, apparently refused to travel to an away fixture at West Ham. Promptly fined and transferred to Newcastle, with secrecy clauses inserted into his contract, the truth about what actually caused Speed to leave has never fully come to light.

IT WOULD be difficult to credit anything but luck to Everton's dramatic escape from relegation in May 1998. Yet irrespective of Kendall's blame in this unholy mess, history decreed that he deserved better treatment by the club at the season's end. Yet for several weeks, his head lay in the hangman's noose, as Peter Johnson publicly procrastinated over his sacking before finally putting him out of his misery. He then used his position as chairman to publicly berate Kendall. Some of the criticism was justified, but its manner was crass and undignified and Kendall's earlier contribution to the club demanded more respect.

THERE FOLLOWED, during the 1998/99 season, a brief spell in charge of the Greek side Ethnikos Pireaus, but this proved unsuccessful. Kendall returned to England, at the age of 52 his professional career essentially over. In later years he wrote a column for the Liverpool Echo and remained a regular visitor to Goodison Park.

But where, exactly, do Howard Kendall's achievements as player and manager place him among the pantheon of Everton greats?

[FACTFILE]

BORN
Ryton-on-Tyne, 22 May 1946
POSITION
Wing half / midfield
OTHER CLUBS
Preston North End
(1963–67);
Birmingham City (1974–77):
Stoke City (1977–79);
Blackburn Rovers
(player-manager, 1979–81)
HONOURS AS PLAYER
1969/70 League
Championship
AS MANAGER
Athletico Bilbao (1987–89);
Manchester City (1989–90);
Xanthi (1994);
Notts County (1995);
Sheffield United (1995–97);
Ethnikos Pireaus (1998–99)
HONOURS AS MANAGER
1984/85 League
Championship;
1986-87 League
Championship; FA Cup 1984;
European Cup Winners' Cup
1985; Manager of the Year
1985, 1987

As a Player

Season	League App	League Goals	FA Cup App	FA Cup Goals	League Cup App	League Cup Goals	Other App	Other Goals	Total App	Total Goals
1966/67	4	0	0	0	-	-	0	0	4	0
1967/68	38	6	6	1	2	2	-	-	46	9
1968/69	28 (1)	1	3	0	4	0	-	-	35 (1)	1
1969/70	36	4	1	0	4	1	-	-	41	5
1970/71	40	2	6	2	-	-	7	3	53	7
1971/72	34 (2)	4	4	0	0	0	-	-	38 (2)	4
1972/73	40	4	2	0	1	0	-	-	43	4
1981/82	4	0	1	0	1	0	-	-	6	0
Total	**231 (3)**	**21**	**24**	**3**	**12**	**3**	**7**	**3**	**274 (3)**	**30**

As a Manager
Kendall also led Everton to the 1991 ZDS Final, which was lost 1-4 to Crystal Palace

Season	P	W	L	D	F	A	Pts	Position	FA Cup	League Cup	Europe
1981/82	42	17	13	12	56	50	64	8th	3rd Round	4th Round	N/A
1982/83	42	18	10	14	66	48	64	7th	6th Round	3rd Round	N/A
1983/84	42	16	14	12	44	42	62	7th	Winners	Runners-up	N/A
1984/85	42	28	6	8	88	43	90	1st	Runners-up	4th Round	Winners
1985/86	42	26	8	8	87	41	86	2nd	Runners Up	4th Round	N/A
1986/87	42	26	8	8	76	31	86	1st	5th Round	5th Round	N/A
1990/91	38	13	12	13	50	46	51	9th	6th Round	3rd Round	N/A
1991/92	42	13	14	15	52	51	53	13th	4th Round	4thRound	N/A
1992/93	42	15	19	8	51	53	53	13th	3rd Round	4th Round	N/A
1993/94*	42	12	22	8	42	63	44	17th	3rd Round	4th Round	N/A
1997/98	38	9	16	13	41	56	40	17th	3rd Round	3rd Round	N/A

*Kendall resigned December 1993

Kendall, Jack

Reserve goalkeeper during the early 1920s

[FACTFILE]

BORN
Broughton, Lincolnshire,
9 October 1905
DIED
1961
POSITION
Goalkeeper
OTHER CLUBS
Lincoln City (1922–23);
Preston North End (1927);
Lincoln City (1928–29);
Sheffield United (1929–33);
Peterborough United

As a player he distinguished himself, playing in good teams and bad, with grace, élan and passion. He was a key component of the 1969/70 Championship team, and one of the few positive forces in the teams that subsequently laboured in Harry Catterick's last days. Taken as a whole with the rest of Gwladys Street's Holy Trinity, the fame and plaudits earned by the triumvirate have no post-war comparison.

As manager there is no disputing Kendall's achievements in the 1980s, when he assembled a team on a shoestring that for three years ruled England and wowed the world. Who is to say what might have happened had it not been for the grotesque injustices imposed by the post-Heysel ban? But at the same time these staggering achievements must be tempered by the reality that Kendall could have built a Goodison dynasty, but passed on the opportunity to do so in favour of personal ambition. Moreover, his difficult second spell as manager tarnishes his record, while his controversial third period as Everton boss is a blemish.

But taking all this aside, Kendall remains a giant in the history of Everton Football Club. When everything he did over his seven years as player and 11 years as manager is totted up and combined, his achievements and importance to the club's history lies, perhaps, second only to Dixie Dean. Given that Dean lies among football's immortals, can there be higher praise than that?

> HIS ACHIEVEMENTS AND IMPORTANCE TO THE CLUB'S HISTORY LIES, PERHAPS, SECOND ONLY TO DIXIE DEAN

	League		FA Cup		Total	
Season	App	Goals	App	Goals	App	Goals
1923/24	1	0	0	0	1	0
1924/25	12	0	2	0	14	0
1925/26	8	0	0	0	8	0
Total	**21**	**0**	**2**	**0**	**23**	**0**

Kennedy, Andy

Stalwart of Herbert Chapman's great Arsenal teams who was surprisingly limited to a solitary Everton appearance

[FACTFILE]

BORN
Belfast, 1 September 1895
POSITION
Left back / centre half
OTHER CLUBS
Belfast Celtic; Glentoran;
Crystal Palace (1920–21);
Arsenal (1922–27); Tranmere
Rovers (1930)
HONOURS
2 Ireland caps (1923)

	League		FA Cup		Total	
Season	App	Goals	App	Goals	App	Goals
1928/29	1	0	0	0	1	0
Total	**1**	**0**	**0**	**0**	**1**	**0**

Kennedy, Fred

Inside forward and one of Les Rosbifs who in the 1930s joined the nascent French league

Season	League		FA Cup		Total	
	App	Goals	App	Goals	App	Goals
1924/25	10	3	0	0	10	3
1925/26	19	8	0	0	19	8
1926/27	6	0	0	0	6	0
Total	35	11	0	0	35	11

[FACTFILE]

BORN
Black Lane, 23 October 1902
DIED
14 November 1963
POSITION
Inside forward
OTHER CLUBS
Manchester United (1923–25);
Middlesbrough (1927–29);
Reading (1929–30);
Oldham Athletic (1930–31);
Northwich Victoria (1931–32);
Racing Club Paris (1932–33);
Blackburn Rovers (1933–34);
Racing Club Paris (1934–37);
Stockport County

Kenny (Jnr); Billy

Gifted and troubled midfielder who let his talents fade away

When Billy Kenny was made man of the match in the Premiership's first Merseyside derby in December 1992, Peter Beardsley christened the 19-year-old the 'Goodison Gazza'. If only he knew just how apposite the comparison would be.

Kenny, whose father and namesake had been a fringe player for the club in the 1970s, was a midfielder blessed with sublime skill, especially in his passing. He had a range and scope of imaginative distribution that was on a par with some of Goodison's finest. An immaculate double-footed player, he was no show pony either and could mix it with the best. Playing Wimbledon, he was scythed down by Vinnie Jones; Kenny took his punishment uncomplainingly, before giving Jones a taste of his own medicine a few minutes later. He possessed the sort of energy and aggression which could later be likened to Steven Gerrard.

After making just a handful of Everton appearances he was called up to the England under-21 squad.

Kenny, however, was a troubled soul. 'Playing came easily,' he would recall. 'It was what happened off the pitch that was difficult to deal with.' After succumbing to shin splints, Kenny was operated on, but lacking the daily camaraderie of training became bored and sought solace in booze and drugs. 'Some mornings I got home at four or five, had a couple of lines of cocaine, slept for an hour and then went to training,' he said. 'Sometimes I could hardly see the ball. I was a joke.'

In 1994 he was finally sacked by Everton. At the instigation of the PFA he was given a second chance at Oldham – but was sacked again and drifted out of the professional game. In 2003, he wrote: 'I played for other clubs but my heart was not in it. The only team I wanted to play for was Everton … I play football with my friends and work with a cousin in property development. I am bitter at what happened. I have two children and I should have saved a fortune for them from a successful career, but I've got nothing. I still sometimes cry at night about it. It was an utter waste.'

[FACTFILE]

BORN
Liverpool, 19 September 1973
POSITION
Midfielder
OTHER CLUB
Oldham Athletic (1994–95)

Season	League		FA Cup		League Cup		Total	
	App	Goals	App	Goals	App	Goals	App	Goals
1992/93	16 (1)	1	2	0	4	0	22 (1)	1
Total	16 (1)	1	2	0	4	0	22 (1)	1

Kenny (Snr); Billy

Home-grown midfielder whose son would follow him into the heart of the Everton midfield

[FACTFILE]

BORN
Liverpool, 23 October 1951
POSITION
Midfielder
OTHER CLUB
Tranmere Rovers (1974–77)

Season	League		FA Cup		League Cup		Other		Total	
	App	Goals	App	Goals	App	Goals	App	Goals	App	Goals
1970/71	1	0	0	0	0	0	0	0	1	0
1971/72	6 (1)	0	0	0	0	0	-	-	6 (1)	0
1972/73	0 (1)	0	0	0	0	0	-	-	0 (1)	0
1973/74	1 (1)	0	0	0	0	0	0	0	1 (1)	0
1974/75	2	0	0	0	0	0	-	-	2	0
Total	**10 (3)**	**0**	**0**	**0**	**0**	**0**	**0**	**0**	**10 (3)**	**0**

Kent, Jack

Left back who played a solitary game during Everton's final Anfield season

[FACTFILE]

BORN
1869
POSITION
Left back
OTHER CLUB
Loughborough Town

Season	League		FA Cup		Total	
	App	Goals	App	Goals	App	Goals
1891/92	1	0	0	0	1	0
Total	**1**	**0**	**0**	**0**	**1**	**0**

Kerr, Jasper

Reserve full back during Everton's transitional mid-1920s

[FACTFILE]

BORN
Burnbank, 1 January 1903
POSITION
Full back
OTHER CLUBS
Larkhill Thistle; Bathgate;
Preston North End
(1926–31);
New Brighton (1933);
Lancaster Town

Season	League		FA Cup		Total	
	App	Goals	App	Goals	App	Goals
1924/25	2	0	0	0	2	0
1925/26	1	0	0	0	1	0
1926/27	15	1	3	0	18	1
Total	**18**	**1**	**3**	**0**	**21**	**1**

Kenwright, Bill

Bleed-blue Evertonian whose tenure as chairman has divided some of his fellow Blues

In completing a deal to purchase Everton FC in December 1999, the former Coronation Street actor turned theatre impresario Bill Kenwright (b. 4 September 1945) achieved a lifelong ambition. A boyhood Evertonian who had been taken to the Goodison Boys Pen atop the handlebars of his Uncle Cyril's bicycle, there were few more enthusiastic or better-known supporters of the club.

Kenwright had started his career as an actor in the 1960s, notably playing Betty Turpin's son, Gordon Clegg, in Coronation Street in the late 1960s (and subsequently reappearing in cameos since then). He turned to theatre production and found great success with such works as Blood Brothers and Joseph and the Amazing Technicolor Dreamcoat.

He joined the Everton board in 1989 and following the death of John Moores in 1993 and the subsequent availability of the club led a consortium that attempted to buy it. He lost out to Peter Johnson but retained his place on the board. Following Johnson's decision to sell the club in 1998, Kenwright emerged – for many Evertonians – as their proverbial knight in shining armour. The deal to buy Johnson's 68 per cent stake in the club for £20million was announced at Christmas 1999 and a holding company called True Blue (Holdings) Ltd was formed in January 2000. The board included Paul Gregg, the millionaire owner of Apollo Leisure Group, Britain's largest theatre owner. Kenwright was vice chairman and Sir Philip Carter chairman.

'I cried when I was told we had succeeded,' said Kenwright at the time. 'It has been a very difficult year because there was no guarantee that I would manage it. My mum thinks I'm mad but I am a very happy man. We have no magic wand, but there is hope for us now.'

There were, nevertheless, hurdles along the way to making Everton a successful force again. One of his first priorities was to find a media company that would invest in the club, a tactic that at the time was becoming prevalent. A subsidiary of NTL was understood to be close to confirming a deal in the summer of 2000 but it fell through at the last moment. However, several high-profile signings had been made in the expectation of the deal's completion, forcing Everton to sell Francis Jeffers, Michael Ball and Richard Dunne to appease the banks.

A second priority was the future of the club's home, either entailing the redevelopment of Goodison or a move away. One of Kenwright's first acts in charge of the club was to commission a feasibility study, which concluded that the limitations of an inner-city site were such that the club should seek pastures new. The suggested location for Everton's new home was the Kings Dock area, just south of Liverpool city centre, and the proposals for the waterside stadium outlined one of the most advanced and magnificent stadiums of its kind in the world. It was to be built in conjunction with public finance and private partners, which would provide Everton with a 49 per cent share of the project. However, the proposals fell down when Everton were unable to come up with their share of the cash in 2003.

The disarray over Kings Dock led to a spectacular falling-out with Paul Gregg in summer 2004, which culminated in Gregg telling TV crews outside Goodison Park that Kenwright should step down in order to attract new investment. In the midst of this crisis, CEO Trevor Birch resigned just six weeks into the job.

Kenwright would hold on to the club, replacing Sir Philip Carter with himself as chairman of a revised board and the London-born American-based millionaire Robert Earl buying Gregg's stake in Everton. But a tortuous summer, culminating in the sale of Wayne Rooney to Manchester United, made many fans permanently suspicious of the chairman, despite his obvious infatuation with the club.

There was, nevertheless, something of a revival under way on the pitch after years of torpor and instability. In March 2002, Kenwright had sacked Walter Smith as manager and replaced him with David Moyes. The pair forged a uniquely close relationship and under Moyes Everton qualified for the Champions League in 2005, the UEFA Cup in 2007 and 2008 and the Europa League the following year. The club's transfer record was broken repeatedly for the signings of James Beattie, Andy Johnson, Yakubu and Marouane Fellaini. There was also an FA Cup Final in 2009.

Yet the influx of oligarch sugar daddies had altered the complexion of the Premier League and Everton were now expected to compete with clubs who were run at a huge loss but had their overdraft covered by a billionaire owner. The club – and chairman – were now playing a sport in which no natural justice applied.

The pressure was on Bill Kenwright to provide money for Moyes to bring Everton up to the 'next level', but facing him was a huge dilemma. Sell the soul of a club to an outsider – as had happened in the 1990s – and chance success. Or keep the blue blood running through Goodison's heart and hope for the best. Everton has been nominally up for sale since 2007, but no new investor has been found. Other schemes to raise the non-matchday income of Everton, such as an attempt to relocate the club to Kirkby, have failed. This has caused frustrations among the supporters to bubble over, and protests were carried out by a vociferous minority of fans during the 2011/12 season. It seemed a harsh outcome for a passionate and decent man. One wonders if given his time again he would have taken the plunge in 1999.

'Sometimes I think the problem is that I am a fan,' Kenwright told the Daily Mail in 2011. 'Philip Green [the retail magnate] calls me the Romantic Evertonian, and that's me. I am what I am. I jump up when we score, I jump up when we don't score, I jump up for corners sometimes. I'm the most nervous chairman in history. I can't even eat lunch before a game and I haven't enjoyed watching us in 10 years.

'I wish I could be like some of the other guys and take it in my stride, but my days are governed by Everton. It is there all the time. I call it The Pain, and it is permanent. But so is the pride.'

Kenyon, Roger

Long-serving defender whose hunt for medals proved cruelly elusive

When injury ruled Brian Labone out of the Everton side during the final weeks of the 1969/70 season, it was left to Roger Kenyon, a virtually untried 21-year-old, to fill the sizeable hole left by his skipper's broad shoulders. Kenyon rose to the challenge with a maturity that wholly belied his inexperience. In the remaining eight games of the season Everton remained undefeated, winning seven and drawing one to lift the First Division title for the seventh time. 'Kenyon will be difficult to move from this side,' marvelled the Liverpool Echo at the season's end. 'He improves with every match and is already a model of composure with a bite in every tackle.'

Born in Blackpool in January 1949, Roger Kenyon was another product of Everton's highly productive youth system. He made his debut as a substitute for Howard Kendall against Newcastle United in October 1967 and went on to make a further 17 league and cup appearances that season. He was also named substitute for the FA Cup Final against West Bromwich Albion, but was never called on to the hallowed Wembley turf. After impressing in Everton's title run-in, he established himself in the first team during the 1970/71 season after Brian Labone was beset by the injury problems that would prematurely end his career.

A hard and ruthless tackler, Kenyon combined these attributes with precise aerial timing and exceptional pace. And yet he was always more than a mere defensive destroyer. He possessed intelligent and accurate distribution that was capable of turning defence into attack. Amid the perpetual transition of the 1970s, Kenyon was a rare constant, one of the few players to be at the core of both Harry Catterick's and Billy Bingham's Everton teams. By the decade's end he was the last remnant of the title winning season.

Kenyon's career was briefly threatened by a serious traffic accident in 1974, but he recovered sufficiently to be called up to the England squad and was, in 1975, named by Don Revie as substitute for three different internationals, without ever being called upon to win his first cap. Again it seemed that Kenyon, who was never awarded a Championship winners' medal in 1970 (as he had played one game too few) was Everton's nearly man. Having missed out on the 1968 FA Cup Final, Kenyon was omitted from the team that faced Aston Villa at Wembley in the 1977 League Cup Final. Included in the replay at Hillsborough, he scored an own goal and was left out of the second replay, which Everton lost.

A SUCCESSION of niggling injuries saw Kenyon's Everton career go into decline. In 1979 he joined Vancouver Whitecaps and at the age of 30 won his first medal, lifting the NASL Soccer Bowl in his one full season there. A brief stint at Bristol Rovers followed before he announced his retirement.

Still a well-recognised figure at Goodison, Kenyon retains close links to the club and is well known for his work as a director of Blue Nose Promotions, which organises events with former players.

> EVERTON REMAINED UNDEFEATED, WINNING SEVEN AND DRAWING ONE TO LIFT THE FIRST DIVISION TITLE FOR THE SEVENTH TIME

[FACTFILE]

BORN
Blackpool, 4 January 1949
POSITION
Centre back
OTHER CLUBS
Vancouver Whitecaps (1979–80);
Bristol City (1980)

Season	League App	League Goals	FA Cup App	FA Cup Goals	League Cup App	League Cup Goals	Other App	Other Goals	Total App	Total Goals
1967/68	12 (4)	0	2	0	0	0	-	-	14 (4)	0
1968/69	4 (3)	0	0 (1)	0	0 (2)	0	-	-	4 (6)	0
1969/70	8 (1)	0	0	0	0 (1)	0	-	-	8 (2)	0
1970/71	28 (2)	0	2	0	0	0	4	0	34 (2)	0
1971/72	34 (2)	0	3	1	1	0	-	-	38 (2)	1
1972/73	40	2	2	0	1	0	-	-	43	2
1973/74	36	2	1	0	2	0	2	-	41	2
1974/75	40	0	2	1	2	0	-	-	44	1
1975/76	28 (2)	1	1	0	4	1	2	0	35 (2)	2
1976/77	14	1	1	0	3	0	-	-	18	1
1977/78	7	0	1	0	0	0	-	-	8	0
1978/79	3	0	0	0	0	0	1	0	4	0
Total	**254(14)**	**6**	**15 (1)**	**2**	**13 (3)**	**1**	**9**	**0**	**291 (18)**	**9**

Keown, Martin

Outstanding centre back whose best days lay beyond Goodison

Martin Keown was arguably the best of Colin Harvey's signings, overcoming a slow start to his Goodison career to establish himself as one of the finest centre backs in the nascent Premier League.

A FEISTY, snarling player, his outstanding performances in the heart of the Everton defence elevated him to the England team before financial necessity dictated that his destiny lay elsewhere.

The tall, curly-haired Oxonian started his career at Arsenal, but after a promising start fell out with the club hierarchy over the award of a new contract and in 1986 joined Aston Villa. He spent three seasons at Villa Park, but with the expiry of his contract sought fresh challenges and the move to Goodison came on his 23rd birthday, the £750,000 fee decided by a tribunal.

A cool, quick, hard player, with outstanding aerial presence and the capacity to smother even the most formidable opponents with his man-marking, Keown would emerge as the ideal foil for Dave Watson. And yet, in his first days at Goodison, Keown must have seriously considered whether he had made the right move. Through 1989/90 he featured in barely half of Everton's matches, while Villa pushed Liverpool strongly for the First Division title. The 1990/91 season was scarcely more productive and he often found himself deputising, out of position, for Andy Hinchcliffe, while Harvey and then Howard Kendall preferred the more experienced centre half pairing of Kevin Ratcliffe and Dave Watson.

RATCLIFFE, however, was nearing the end of his career and injuries had diminished the pace that was once his hallmark. During the 1991/92 season, Keown got his

chance and an extended run alongside Watson was one of the few bright factors in a mediocre campaign, leading to an England call-up. When England played Czechoslovakia in Prague in March 1992 Keown got on the score sheet – something he would never manage for Everton – with a spectacular 25-yard effort and would play in all of his country's matches at that summer's European Championship Finals in Sweden.

After missing the first two months of the 1992/93 season through injury, Keown's fine form resumed when he returned to the Everton team. But with his team struggling to score goals and desperately needing transfer funds to sign a striker, Howard Kendall deemed a £2million offer from Arsenal in February 1993 good business.

ON HIS RETURN to Highbury, Keown initially struggled to hold down a first-team place and was often derided for his awkward demeanour. However, the arrival of Arsène Wenger in 1996 saw his career undergo a late and lengthy renaissance that continued until he was in his late thirties.

[FACTFILE]

BORN
Oxford, 24 July 1966
POSITION
Centre back
OTHER CLUBS
Arsenal (1984–86);
Brighton (loan, 1985–86);
Aston Villa (1986–89);
Arsenal (1993–2004);
Leicester City (2004–05);
Reading (2005)
HONOURS
43 England caps (2 goals)
(1992–2002)

ARGUABLY THE BEST OF COLIN HARVEY'S SIGNINGS

Season	League		FA Cup		League Cup		Other		Total	
	App	Goals	App	Goals	App	Goals	App	Goals	App	Goals
1989/90	19 (1)	0	4	0	2	0	-	-	25 (1)	0
1990/91	21 (3)	0	4 (1)	0	1	0	5	0	31 (4)	0
1991/92	39	0	2	0	4	0	1	0	46	0
1992/93	13	0	2	0	4	0	-	-	19	0
Total	**92 (4)**	**0**	**12 (1)**	**0**	**11**	**0**	**6**	**0**	**121 (5)**	**0**

Keys, J

One-game man of mystery during Everton's first league outings

Season	League		Total	
	App	Goals	App	Goals
1888/89	1	0	1	0
Total	**1**	**0**	**1**	**0**

[FACTFILE]

BORN
1865
POSITION
Centre forward

Kidd, Brian

Striker of enviable pedigree who failed to lift Everton from mediocrity

A £150,000 acquisition from Manchester City in March 1979, Brian Kidd was among the First Division's best known and most prolific scorers through the 1970s. On his 19th birthday he memorably scored Manchester United's third goal in their 1968 European Cup Final win over Benfica. Subsequent spells with Arsenal and Manchester City added to his reputation.

Tall, skilful and with a powerful shot, his signing was intended to ease Bob Latchford's goalscoring burden. While Kidd held his own and finished the 1979/80 campaign Everton's leading goalscorer, his contribution was not enough to lift a team in decline. Through that season, Everton won just nine league matches. There were, however, glimpses of his supreme talent – as witness his headed strike against Liverpool in the October 1979 derby.

But most Evertonians will remember the magic and madness when Everton faced West Ham in the FA Cup semi-final in April 1980. Called upon to take an early penalty, Kidd showed great composure to give Everton the lead, but was later sent off after clashing with Ray Stewart. West Ham grabbed a late equaliser and stole the replay, for which Kidd was suspended.

That was virtually Brian Kidd's last action in an Everton shirt and, aged 31, he was sold to Bolton Wanderers in May 1980 for £150,000. He later embarked upon a hugely successful coaching career, notably at Manchester United, where he was Alex Ferguson's long-term assistant, and for England, where he performed the same duties under Sven Göran Eriksson.

> MOST EVERTONIANS
> WILL REMEMBER
> THE MAGIC
> AND MADNESS

[FACTFILE]

BORN
Manchester, 29 May 1949
POSITION
Striker
OTHER CLUBS
Manchester United (1967–74);
Arsenal (1974–76);
Manchester City (1976–79);
Bolton Wanderers (1980–82);
Atlanta Chiefs (1981);
Fort Lauderdale Strikers (1982–83);
Minnesota Strikers (1984)
AS MANAGER
Preston North End (1986);
Blackburn Rovers (1998–99)
HONOURS
2 England caps
(1 goal) (1970)

Season	League App	League Goals	FA Cup App	FA Cup Goals	League Cup App	League Cup Goals	Europe App	Europe Goals	Total App	Total Goals
1978/79	9	2	0	0	0	0	0	0	9	2
1979/80	31	10	4	4	5	4	2	0	42	18
Total	**40**	**12**	**4**	**4**	**5**	**4**	**2**	**0**	**51**	**20**

Kilbane, Kevin

Irish international winger who provided Goodison with unstinting service

> DUBBED
> 'ZINEDINE' BY
> EVERTON'S
> SUPPORTERS

A former team-mate of David Moyes at Preston North End, Kevin Kilbane had long been linked with a reunion with his former captain when the Everton manager made a £1.1million deadline day move for him in August 2003.

A left winger, Kilbane had been harangued by Sunderland fans during the latter stages of his time at the Stadium of Light, prompting some scepticism among Evertonians when Moyes made his move. But the adopted Irishman soon confounded any doubters, providing solid service down the Everton left.

Strong, tall and with no little pace, Kilbane was at his best knocking the ball past opponents and running on to it. He was a good header of the ball, but lacked a

Season	League App	League Goals	FA Cup App	FA Cup Goals	League Cup App	League Cup Goals	Europe App	Europe Goals	Total App	Total Goals
2003/04	26 (4)	3	3	1	0	0	-	-	29 (4)	4
2004/05	37 (1)	1	3	0	2	0	-	-	42 (1)	1
2005/06	21 (13)	0	4	0	1	0	3 (1)	0	29(14)	0
2006/07	2	0	0	0	0	0	-	-	2	0
Total	**86(18)**	**4**	**10**	**1**	**3**	**0**	**3 (1)**	**0**	**102(19)**	**5**

killer instinct in front of goal and his strike rate was disappointing for a player whose attacking duties were his primary responsibility. At the same time he was an adept makeshift left back and was called to fulfil the role on several occasions. For Ireland, for whom he qualified through Irish parentage, he was a fixture in the national team, often taking up a more central role.

Moyes, a man who always expects a strong work ethic, got just that from Kilbane. Dubbed 'Zinedine' by Everton's supporters, there was nothing mocking or ironic in this nickname, for there was a healthy respect for a player who never gave anything less than his all. In 2004/05, Kilbane was ever-present as Everton confounded expectations to qualify for the Champions League.

Thereafter, as Moyes sought a more expansive style, increasingly preferring Mikel Arteta on the Everton left, Kilbane's chances became more limited. Included in two of Everton's first three games of the 2006/07 season, his was a

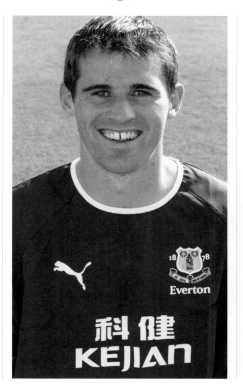

surprise departure to Wigan on August transfer deadline day – exactly three years after his arrival. Nevertheless the £2million fee represented a healthy profit on a good servant who was nearing his 30th birthday.

> ### [FACTFILE]
>
> **BORN**
> Preston, 1 February 1977
> **POSITION**
> Left midfield
> **OTHER CLUBS**
> Preston North End (1995–97);
> West Bromwich Albion (1997–99);
> Sunderland (1999–2003);
> Wigan Athletic (2006–09);
> Hull City (2009–);
> Huddersfield Town
> (loan, 2011);
> Derby County (loan, 2011)
> **HONOURS**
> 110 Republic of Ireland caps (8 goals)
> (1997–)

King, Andy

Charismatic midfielder whose famous drive restored some pride to Goodison

An effervescent, charismatic midfielder with a voracious appetite for the game, Andy King was one of a handful of players to capture Evertonian hearts during the 1970s. In a difficult decade, his goals – notably his decisive strike in the October 1978 derby – helped ease the burden of lying in Liverpool's shadow, while his impudence and smart skills brought real élan to Everton's play. Yet King was always more than an outstanding player – he was a character at a time when Everton lacked such figures.

SIGNED FROM Luton Town in April 1976, King's £35,000 fee would represent one of the real bargains in Everton's history. Billy Bingham put him straight into a team charged with gaining four points from the last three games of the 1975/76 season, with a trip to Spain the reward. King made an immediate impression, scoring a memorable double against reigning champions Derby County and securing a 3-1 victory and the holiday.

> GOODISON WAS A 53,000 ALL-TICKET SELL-OUT WITH A BANNER IN GWLADYS STREET PROCLAIMING 'ANDY IS OUR KING'

Slight, adroit and technically gifted, King retained his place at the start of the 1976/77 campaign – severely limiting Bryan Hamilton's opportunities. Possessing a deft first touch and fine distribution, he could be counted upon to provide the unexpected in a team often lacking a creative cutting edge. And then there were the goals: double figures in all but one of his six full Everton seasons. In an era of extrovert footballers, King was Everton's livewire, always playing with a smile on his face and infecting his team-mates and the crowd with his enthusiasm. To the Goodison faithful he was an immediate favourite, endearing himself to them with his proclamation that he was an adopted Scouser – 'a northerner with a funny accent'.

His most famous moment came in October 1978 when facing Liverpool in a Goodison derby. Everton had failed to beat Liverpool in 362 weeks – at a time when their neighbours were

sweeping all comers in domestic and European competition – and faced the indignity of watching the run pass seven years if they failed to beat them this encounter. There was, however, a sense that the tide was turning in Everton's favour, and they went into the game still unbeaten.

Goodison was a 53,000 all-ticket sell-out with a banner in Gwladys Street proclaiming 'Andy is our King'. And so it was to be, with his fierce shot into the top corner of the Park End net the only goal of the afternoon. 'Micky Pejic played a long, high ball that Martin Dobson nodded down,' King would recall of the moment that saw him enter Goodison lore. 'As it fell to me, I saw Graeme Souness showing his foot, so I hit the shot first time with the outside of my boot. It was one of those that commentators call "great goals".'

By February 1979 Everton were top, after King's hat-trick brought a 4-1 home victory over Bristol City. But they were unable to sustain the form, winning just four of their last 18 games. King finished top league scorer with 12, but fourth place was to be the closest he ever came again to a First Division title. In the 1979/80 season Everton dropped to 19th place and at the season's end Gordon Lee, seeking to reshape his team, raised some much-needed cash by selling King to

Queens Park Rangers for £425,000.

He spent barely a year at Loftus Road, joining West Bromwich Albion in September 1981, where he was groomed – perhaps unfairly – as Bryan Robson's replacement. When he struggled to fulfil these lofty expectations he sought a return to Goodison. In summer 1982 Howard Kendall decided to exchange Peter Eastoe for King, who was still aged only 25. Although he started in impressive fashion, with a 25-yard curler against Aston Villa, a persistent knee injury limited his chances. With the blossoming of an outstanding new generation of Everton footballers through the latter half of the 1983/84 season, King found himself an outsider, his opportunities severely restricted. He was a substitute in the Milk Cup Final replay against Liverpool, but played no part in the FA Cup Final win over Watford.

In June 1984 he joined Dutch side SC Cambuur, returning to England within a year with

Wolverhampton Wanderers. There followed a brief return to the First Division with Luton Town during the 1985/86 season before King played out his career with Aldershot.

Following his retirement he had short spells in charge of Runcorn and Waterford in the Irish League, before a return to Luton as commercial manager. In 1993 he became manager of Mansfield Town, a position he held for three years. There followed two spells in charge of Swindon Town at the start of the new century and six weeks as manager of Grays Athletic in the Conference in late 2006. King subsequently took up scouting positions with Plymouth Argyle and Colchester United before his appointment in November 2011 as Northampton Town assistant manager.

Reflecting on his famous derby-winning goal, he once said, 'If I die tomorrow, I've done something that millions would give their right arm to have done.' Trophies might ultimately have

proved elusive for King – perhaps cruelly so, given that his career touched a period in which a succession of honours came Everton's way after many barren years – but he at least brought some smiles at Goodison during hard times.

Season	League		FA Cup		League Cup		Europe		Total	
	App	Goals	App	Goals	App	Goals	App	Goals	App	Goals
1975/76	3	2	0	0	0	0	0	0	3	2
1976/77	36 (1)	7	4 (1)	0	9	5	-	-	49 (2)	12
1977/78	42	8	2	1	5	2	-	-	49	11
1978/79	40	12	1	0	3	0	3	4	47	16
1979/80	29	9	4	1	4	0	2	0	39	10
1982/83	24	9	4	2	4	2	-	-	32	13
1983/84	19 (1)	2	1	0	4 (1)	1	-	-	24 (2)	3
Total	**193(2)**	**49**	**16 (1)**	**4**	**29 (1)**	**10**	**5**	**4**	**243 (4)**	**67**

King, Frank

Ted Sagar's understudy during the mid-1930s

Season	League		FA Cup		Total	
	App	Goals	App	Goals	App	Goals
1934/35	5	0	0	0	5	0
1935/36	5	0	1	0	6	0
1936/37	3	0	0	0	3	0
Total	**13**	**0**	**1**	**0**	**14**	**0**

King, John

1950s wing half who made his name across the River Mersey

There was a brief, uncomfortable period in the mid-1990s when it looked as though Everton might swap places with their second-tier neighbours, Tranmere Rovers.

Although the systematic mismanagement of Everton had done much to aid their decline, Tranmere's unlikely ascent owed much to their charismatic manager, John King. In the space of five years he led Tranmere, the club where he had spent the bulk of his managerial and playing career, from the verge of extinction to the precipice of the top flight. Meanwhile, Everton, where he had started out as a player, were in the doldrums.

FORTUNATELY for Evertonians, Tranmere never overtook their Mersey rivals and in 1996, unable to slake the expectations he created, King was 'moved upstairs' by the Tranmere board. Not since then have Tranmere come so close to entering English football's elite.

Without question, King is remembered most for his time at Prenton Park. An astute and gregarious man, he had started out at Everton in the mid-1950s, making his league debut away at Preston in October 1957. A quick and hard wing half, King perhaps lacked the flourishes that would have seen him prosper at the highest level. After making a smattering of starts in the remainder of the 1957/58 season, he was a regular for stretches of the subsequent two campaigns, but ultimately overshadowed by Brian Harris and Jimmy Gabriel. In July 1960 he joined Bournemouth, but returned north the following February, embarking on his lengthy affair with Tranmere.

	League		FA Cup		Total	
Season	App	Goals	App	Goals	App	Goals
1957/58	5	0	0	0	5	0
1958/59	17	1	0	0	17	1
1959/60	26	0	1	0	27	0
Total	**48**	**1**	**1**	**0**	**49**	**1**

[FACTFILE]

BORN
Marylebone, 15 April 1938
POSITION
Wing half
OTHER CLUBS
Bournemouth (1960–61);
Tranmere Rovers (1961–68);
Port Vale (1968–71)
AS MANAGER
Tranmere Rovers
(1975–80 & 1987–96)

Kirby, George

1950s rookie striker who forged a solid career beyond Goodison

GEORGE KIRBY - EVERTON

[FACTFILE]

BORN
Liverpool, 20 December 1933
DIED
24 March 2000
POSITION
Striker
OTHER CLUBS
Sheffield Wednesday;
Plymouth Argyle;
Southampton; Coventry City;
Swansea Town; Walsall;
New York Generals;
Brentford; Worcester City
AS MANAGER
Halifax Town
(1970–71 & 1978–81);
Watford (1971–73)

	League		FA Cup		Total	
Season	App	Goals	App	Goals	App	Goals
1955/56	2	0	0	0	2	0
1956/57	22	8	1	0	23	8
1957/58	2	1	0	0	2	1
Total	**26**	**9**	**1**	**0**	**27**	**9**

Kirkwood, Dan

League Championship winning defender-cum-forward turned club administrator

[FACTFILE]

BORN
Linlithgow, 28 May 1867
DIED
1 December 1928
POSITION
Wing half / inside forward
HONOURS
1890/91 League
Championship

	League		FA Cup		Total	
Season	App	Goals	App	Goals	App	Goals
1889/90	11	0	2	1	13	1
1890/91	19	1	1	0	20	1
1891/92	5	0	0	0	5	0
Total	**35**	**1**	**3**	**1**	**38**	**2**

Kirsopp, Billy

Inside forward who won the League Championship but found plaudits harder to come by

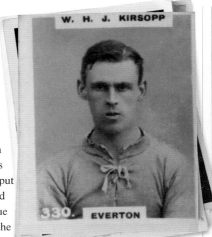

W. H. J. KIRSOPP

330 EVERTON

[FACTFILE]

BORN
Wallasey, 21 April 1892
DIED
1978
POSITION
Inside forward
OTHER CLUBS
Bury (1921–22);
Grimsby Town (1922–23);
New Brighton (1923–24)
HONOURS
1914/15 League
Championship

The ascent of Billy Kirsopp in the mid-1910s carried elements of Roy of the Rovers fantasy. Spotted playing for Wallasey Borough against Ormskirk in the obscurity of the Liverpool Combination in March 1914 by Harry Makepeace, he was trailed over the following month by Everton who, when they got scent of interest by Blackburn Rovers, signed him up. Within a year he was a League Champion.

On 1 January 1915 injury to Frank Jefferis saw Kirsopp called up to the first-team fold for the visit of Tottenham Hotspur. He scored Everton's only goal in a 1-1 draw that was described as 'exceedingly fortunate'. But it put Everton up to second place and in many ways launched a league title challenge. For the rest of the season Kirsopp, a small, slight inside right, who barely weighed 10 stone, occupied Jefferis's shirt and contributed nine goals in just 16 appearances, which were to prove crucial in Everton's eventual title victory by a single point over Oldham.

AND YET FOR all his goals, Kirsopp won only grudging praise. When he scored journalists seemed obliged to highlight his shortcomings. Even the Everton programme damned him with faint praise. 'Possessing a good knowledge of the requirements of an inside forward, he needs to be more alert in dealing with a pass and transferring the ball to a favourably-placed comrade,' it sniped. 'There is a tendency on

THE ASCENT OF BILLY KIRSOPP IN THE MID-1910S CARRIED ELEMENTS OF ROY OF THE ROVERS FANTASY

Season	League		FA Cup		Total	
	App	Goals	App	Goals	App	Goals
1914/15	16	9	5	1	21	10
1919/20	29	14	0	0	29	14
1920/21	13	5	0	0	13	5
Total	**58**	**28**	**5**	**1**	**63**	**29**

his part to keep the ball too long, thereby enabling the opposing half back to baffle him. Quickness of action and rapidity in making an opening are essential qualities for an inside forward to show if he means to be a success.'

Kirsopp played regularly in the regional leagues during the First World War until the end of 1916, when he was presumably called into action. He resurfaced for the 1919/20 season, where he scored almost a goal every other game, but never seemed to win the adulation of the crowd. He lost his place to Stan Fazackerley the following campaign and was sold to Bury for £450 in May 1921. His departure came on the same day another 1915 hero, Bobby Parker, joined Nottingham Forest.

Kirwan, Jack

Irish international winger turned Dutch coaching pioneer

[FACTFILE]

BORN
Wicklow, 25 April 1872
DIED
9 January 1959
POSITION
Outside left / inside forward
OTHER CLUBS
Southport; Tottenham
Hotspur (1899–1905);
Chelsea (1905–08);
Clyde (1908–09); Leyton
Orient (1909–10)
AS MANAGER
Ajax Amsterdam (1910–15);
A.S. Livorno (1923–24)
HONOURS
17 Ireland caps (2 goals)
(1900–09)

Season	League		FA Cup		Total	
	App	Goals	App	Goals	App	Goals
1898/99	24	5	2	0	26	5
Total	**24**	**5**	**2**	**0**	**26**	**5**

Kitchen, George

Early twentieth-century goalkeeper who lost out to Billy Scott

[FACTFILE]

BORN
Fairfield, Derbyshire, April 1876
POSITION
Goalkeeper
OTHER CLUBS
Stockport County (1897–98);
West Ham United (1905–12);
Southampton (1912–14)

Season	League		FA Cup		Total	
	App	Goals	App	Goals	App	Goals
1898/99	1	0	0	0	1	0
1899/1900	2	0	0	0	2	0
1900/01	0	0	0	0	0	0
1901/02	27	0	2	0	29	0
1902/03	26	0	0	0	26	0
1903/04	31	0	1	0	32	0
Total	**87**	**0**	**3**	**0**	**90**	**0**

Kroldrup, Per

Expensively acquired Danish international defender deemed unsuitable to the rigours of English football

[FACTFILE]

BORN
Farso, Denmark, 31 July 1979
POSITION
Centre back
OTHER CLUBS
B.93 (1998–2001);
Udinese (2001–05);
Fiorentina (2006–)
HONOURS
33 Denmark caps (2001–)

Season	League		FA Cup		League Cup		Europe		Total	
	App	Goals	App	Goals	App	Goals	App	Goals	App	Goals
2005/06	1	0	0 (1)	0	0	0	0	0	1 (1)	0
Total	**1**	**0**	**0 (1)**	**0**	**0**	**0**	**0**	**0**	**1 (1)**	**0**

EVERTON
·ENCYCLOPEDIA·

Brian **Labone**, Bill **Lacey**, Kevin **Langley**, Bob **Latchford**, Alex **Latta**, Bobby **Laverick**, David **Lawson**, Tommy **Lawton**, Gordon **Lee**, Jack **Lee**, Fred **Leeder**, Cyril **Lello**, Joleon **Lescott**, Gwyn **Lewis**, Tommy **Lewis**, William **Lewis**, Charlie **Leyfield**, Harry **Leyland**, Li **Tie**, Walter **Lievesley**, Micky **Lill**, Anders **Limpar**, Tobias **Linderoth**, Maurice **Lindley**, Billy **Lindsay**, Jack **Lindsay**, Gary **Lineker**, Archie **Livingstone**, Duggie **Livingston**, Bert **Llewellyn**, Alex **Lochhead**, Paul **Lodge**, Harry **Lowe**, Mick **Lyons**, Everton and **Liverpool**

Labone, Brian

Captain and doyen of Everton's golden era

In the pantheon of Everton greats, few stand as tall as Brian Labone. Long-serving captain, stalwart of Everton's defence, double league title winner, and FA Cup hero, few can match his achievements or length of service. But Labone was always more than just a great player. On the field he cut a noble, distinguished figure, his style of play reflecting not just his personality, but values that every Evertonian held dear – honesty, fair play, composure. In many ways, he was a throwback to a gentler, less cynical era in the game's history. He represented Everton more times than any other outfield player and long after he hung up his boots remained a fine ambassador wwfor a club he dearly loved. Most famously he said that one Evertonian was worth twenty Liverpudlians. This may have been true, but few would dispute that the untimely death in April 2006 of such a great Evertonian surely diluted his calculation.

Born in Liverpool in 1940 and raised an Evertonian, Labone was always a man to defy convention. As a grammar schoolboy in the 1950s, for a period he considered following his studies through to university ahead of a footballing career. The lure of playing for Everton was too much to resist, however, and on leaving Liverpool Collegiate he signed as a professional in July 1957, simultaneously turning down the opportunity to join Liverpool. Skipping the legion of junior sides, he was put straight into Everton's reserves and attracted immediate attention when called upon to mark Dave Hickson in the annual reserves versus seniors pre-season game. Later Labone would liken his ascent from schoolboy football to professionalism to 'climbing the Matterhorn' and admitted to turning white with concern every time T.E. Jones, Everton's first-choice centre half, stumbled – lest he be called upon to deputise.

LABONE MADE HIS EVERTON DEBUT in March 1958 in a 2-1 defeat at Birmingham City and made a further three appearances that season, and four during the 1958/59 season. Although he had experienced just glimpses of the first team at this stage, by the start of the 1959/60 season

Johnny Carey deemed the 19-year-old ready for an extended first-team run, even moving Jones to left back in order to accommodate the teenager. By then, John Moores' millions had started to see several big-name arrivals at Goodison, but Labone kept his place and held his own. During the 1960/61 season Labone was ever-present as Everton finished fifth; still aged only 21 at the season's end, he had become the cornerstone around which the Everton defence was built.

> 'ONE EVERTONIAN WAS WORTH TWENTY LIVERPUDLIANS'

Labone by then was an England under-23 international and in making his England debut against Northern Ireland the following year he became Everton's first England international since the war and would feature throughout Alf Ramsey's tenure as England manager. Later, he credited Harry Catterick's arrival in May 1961 and subsequent faith in him as being key to his progress. He told Ken Rogers in 1989: 'When he first came, he was very straight and fair with me. Many of the papers were saying "Labone is promising, but it's a tender age to hold the Everton defence together." He stuck with me and we began to build an excellent side.'

Tall and composed, even at such a young age Labone seemed to exude a natural authority and command of the Everton defence. His rise was at a time when centre halves were still expected to be cold-hearted, bone-crunching hatchet men who would do weekly battle with equally ruthless and full-blooded centre forwards. But Labone never resorted to such physical excess and could hold his own without letting his polished and unflappable style of play descend into ugliness. Such cruel tricks were the preserve of lesser men, and in 530 Everton appearances Labone was booked just twice.

There is, however, a school of thought that decrees his good nature was a weakness and that he lacked the killer instinct that might have brought him wider recognition. In his 2008 biography Alex Young said that he still believed Labone to be 'too honest on the ground' and admitted criticising him 'for not kicking enough legs'. In an era when the likes of Young were marked men, he felt that Labone should have used his own physical prowess to protect less imposing players. But Labone never compromised his own standards and remained a gentle giant. He would, recalled Young, 'knock opponents down, then pick them up'.

LABONE missed just two games in Everton's title winning season in 1962/63, and following Tony Kay's disgrace the following April succeeded him as captain. In 1966 he led Everton to FA Cup glory but, always something of an idiosyncratic figure, turned down the chance of appearing for England in that summer's World Cup. His wedding to Pat Lynam, a former Miss Liverpool, clashed with the tournament and Labone asked to be overlooked. 'I had fixed the date, made all the arrangements, issued all the invitations. What could I do?' he said in later life, as if it were the entirely logical decision.

A year later, Labone dropped an even bigger bombshell. On 21 September 1967, he announced his retirement from football. The 27-year-old revealed that he wasn't enjoying playing and would be quitting the game at the end of his contract – or sooner if Everton could find a suitable replacement. He said that it was too much of a responsibility to continue playing such a key part in the Everton defence when he wasn't enjoying the game and that he would sooner go into his father's business. Labone was one of the few middle-class footballers of his generation, and his father, who ran a successful central heating business, was a well-known figure in the city,

recognisable from his Bentley and the fleet of company vans that bore his name. It is possible that Labone junior may have even found the family business a more prosperous alternative to professional football.

HARRY CATTERICK, not normally one to single an individual for praise, took the opportunity to give the defender a rare glowing reference. 'It's typical of Brian's top-class character that he has told me 18 months before the end of his contract that he is going to leave the game,' said Catterick. 'Many a player would not have told his club until the last possible minute. Brian is one of the greatest club men I have ever known … and we shall be sorry to see him go.' Yet the announcement marked an upturn in form and soon after he returned to the England team in place of Jack Charlton. It took 14 months for Labone to change his mind, but both Everton and England were delighted when, in January 1969, he put pen to paper and signed a new two-year contract.

> IN 1969/70
> HIS WAS A MAJESTIC PRESENCE
> AS HE LIFTED THE LEAGUE TITLE
> AS CAPTAIN

By now, he was the most experienced player in the Everton dressing room and England's first-choice centre back. This know-how, derived from more than 400 appearances, was integral to an otherwise predominantly youthful Everton team. In 1969/70 his was a majestic

presence as he lifted the league title as captain. That summer, he travelled to Mexico for England's defence of the World Cup, the last appearance of a 26-cap international career coming in England's devastating 3-2 defeat to West Germany in Leon.

Football, over Labone's lengthy career, had changed considerably, but the Everton captain had adapted his play to fit in with the shifting realities. He said: 'As time went on, strikers became much more subtle. The old 2-3-5 formation was replaced by 4-2-4. The long ball down the middle was not quite so prevalent. Teams had to operate with twin centre backs, which is when John Hurst joined me at the heart of the Blues' defence. The game became much harder and made you think a lot more, simply because centre forwards were becoming much more mobile. It was no longer a case of the five marking the nine, the traditional battle. Forwards would try to pull you out of the position and so you stopped marking numbers and had to concentrate that little bit harder.'

Catterick had, by this stage, christened Labone 'the last of the great Corinthians' and it was to be little coincidence that as Labone's career went into sharp decline, so too did Catterick's fortunes as Everton manager. In total, he made just 26 further appearances post-Mexico after being plagued by persistent back and Achilles injuries. His early withdrawal from an FA Cup semi-final with Liverpool in March 1971 – with Everton leading and on top – is credited as a turning point in Everton's history. Liverpool came back to win 2-1, and neither Catterick nor Labone came close to winning further honours again. Labone's final Everton

Season	League		FA Cup		League Cup		Other		Total	
	App	Goals	App	Goals	App	Goals	App	Goals	App	Goals
1957/58	4	0	0	0	-	-	-	-	4	0
1958/59	4	0	0	0	-	-	-	-	4	0
1959/60	31	0	1	0	-	-	-	-	32	0
1960/61	42	0	1	0	4	0	-	-	47	0
1961/62	41	0	3	0	-	-	-	-	44	0
1962/63	40	0	3	0	-	-	2	0	45	0
1963/64	34	0	4	0	-	-	3	0	41	0
1964/65	42	0	4	0	-	-	6	0	52	0
1965/66	37	2	8	0	-	-	3	0	48	2
1966/67	40	0	6	0	-	-	5	0	51	0
1967/68	40	0	6	0	2	0	-	-	48	0
1968/69	42	0	5	0	4	0	-	-	51	0
1969/70	34	0	1	0	4	0	-	-	39	0
1970/71	16	0	3	0	-	-	3	0	22	0
1971/72	4	0	0	0	1	0	-	-	5	0
Total	**451**	**2**	**46**	**0**	**15**	**0**	**22**	**0**	**534**	**2**

appearance came in a League Cup tie against Southampton in September 1971. In retirement, Labone finally went to work for his father. When the family business was sold in the 1980s he worked in insurance and latterly in corporate hospitality at his beloved Goodison.

Labone was a gregarious character and could often be found holding court in one of several Liverpool public houses, usually with a former colleague from either side of the Merseyside football divide. He was a relic of an era in which the players still mingled with the fans and he always had time for supporters, even those who followed great rivals Liverpool.

WHEN RIBBED BY them about Everton's perennial underachievement, he would always delight in countering that no matter what Liverpool's success, 'one Evertonian was worth twenty Reds'. When news came through of his unexpected death in April 2006, shortly after a supporter function, that was the phrase for which the blue half of Merseyside instantly remembered him.

'Brian was quite rightly known as the last of the Corinthians – a fitting title which was given to him by Harry Catterick,' said the Everton chairman, Bill Kenwright, in one of the most moving tributes after Labone's death. He continued:

In a world where we very seldom use the word 'never' I am pretty certain that it will be a very long time before we again see a one-club player with more than 500 senior appearances to his name.

Brian Labone was not only a truly great footballer and a marvellous leader of men, he was – both on the football pitch and away from it – a true gentleman – something which is under-scored by the fact that he was only ever booked twice in a lengthy career. I will always remember his nobility. When I arrived at Goodison Park for a game, he was always the first to greet me – when I left afterwards he was always there to say 'goodnight – safe home'.

He did that not because I am the chairman of the club he always loved but because he was my friend; he was also my idol. Everything that is good and wonderful about Everton Football Club can be summed up in two words – Brian Labone.

On the foot of the Dixie Dean statue outside Goodison Park are the words 'Footballer – Gentlemen – Evertonian'... those words summed up Dixie – and they apply, equally, to the great Brian Labone.

Further reading:

ROGERS, KEN, *Everton Greats*, Sportsprint Publishing, Edinburgh, 1989

[FACTFILE]

BORN
Liverpool, 23 January, 1940
DIED
Liverpool, 24 April 2006
POSITION
Central defender
HONOURS
1962/63, 1969/70
League Championship;
1966 FA Cup;
26 England caps (1962–70)

Lacey, Bill

Goalscoring half back who crossed Stanley Park and became a Liverpool legend

[FACTFILE]

BORN
Enniscorthy, Wexford,
24 September 1889
DIED
30 May 1969
POSITION
Half back
OTHER CLUBS
Shelbourne (1906–09);
Liverpool (1912–24);
New Brighton (1924–25);
Shelbourne (1925–27);
Cork Bohemians (1927–31)
AS MANAGER
Irish Free State; Bohemians

	League		FA Cup		Total	
Season	**App**	**Goals**	**App**	**Goals**	**App**	**Goals**
1908/09	1	0	0	0	1	0
1909/10	6	1	0	0	6	1
1910/11	24	8	2	0	26	8
1911/12	6	2	1	0	7	2
Total	**37**	**11**	**3**	**0**	**40**	**11**

Langley, Kevin

Lower league midfielder who rose to the Goodison challenge and claimed a title medal

Signed from Wigan Athletic for £120,000 in the summer of 1986, all of Kevin Langley's Everton appearances came within a three-month-long window. But in that short period he did enough to be remembered by many Evertonians and earn himself a League Championship medal.

Never seeming overawed by the leap in divisions, Langley came straight into the Everton team at the start of the 1986/87 season. A constructive, composed midfielder who used the ball thoughtfully and effectively, he was well able to find the net too: as witness his equalising goal at Sheffield Wednesday in only his second league appearance.

When Everton faced Manchester United at Goodison in September 1986, Langley put in a masterful display, overshadowing his more

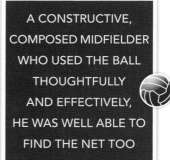

A CONSTRUCTIVE, COMPOSED MIDFIELDER WHO USED THE BALL THOUGHTFULLY AND EFFECTIVELY, HE WAS WELL ABLE TO FIND THE NET TOO

illustrious midfield opponents – Bryan Robson and Norman Whiteside – as he helped inspire Everton to a 3-1 victory. And yet Langley was never the quickest player nor the strongest of tacklers and when his early good form started to desert him he was dropped. Nevertheless, given his promising start, it was still something of a surprise when Howard Kendall sold him to Manchester City before the season was out.

HE STRUGGLED to make an impression at Maine Road and the following season joined Birmingham City. In 1990 he returned to Wigan for a second spell before turning to non-league.

[FACTFILE]

BORN
St Helens,
24 May 1964
POSITION
Midfield
OTHER CLUBS
Wigan Athletic (1981–86);
Manchester City (1987–88);
Chester City (loan, 1987);
Birmingham City (1987–90);
Wigan Athletic (1990–94); Halifax Town (1994–95);
Bangor City (1995–96)
HONOURS
1986/87 League Championship

Season	League App	League Goals	FA Cup App	FA Cup Goals	League Cup App	League Cup Goals	Other App	Other Goals	Total App	Total Goals
1986/87	16	2	0	0	4	1	2 (1)	0	22 (1)	3
Total	16	2	0	0	4	1	2 (1)	0	22 (1)	3

Latchford, Bob

Prolific centre forward whose goals eased Everton through dark years

A player who followed in Everton's famous tradition of number nines, only Dixie Dean and Graeme Sharp have ever bettered Bob Latchford's phenomenal goalscoring for Everton. Latchford may have lacked the charisma of a Dave Hickson, the grace of an Alex Young or the scintillating pace of Roy Vernon, but in an Everton career that spanned more than seven years he was a Goodison icon, a player who, the fans used to chant, 'walks on water'. A modest, articulate man, he helped restore pride to Evertonians during a time when living in Liverpool's shadow had become a way of life.

Born in Birmingham in 1951 into a footballing family, Latchford's elder brother, David, was a goalkeeper at Birmingham City, while a younger brother, Peter, another goalkeeper, played for West Brom and Celtic. Their destinies as goal-stoppers and goalscorers, according to Bob, were forged in kickarounds in the family back garden. Bob joined David at Birmingham, making his debut at the age of 18 in 1969. He would later play in attack alongside another teenage prodigy, Trevor Francis.

Latchford averaged nearly a goal every other game in more than 190 appearances for Birmingham, leading them into the First Division in 1972. But Birmingham were not a wealthy club and when, in February 1974, Everton came in with a bid for Latchford, manager Freddie Goodwin held out for a players-plus-cash offer, eventually accepting Howard Kendall, Archie Styles and £80,000 in a deal worth £350,000 – a British record fee that stood for more than three years.

Everton's post-1970 decline was partly the result of a hideous lack of goals – they had finished the First Division's third lowest scorers with only 41 goals during the 1972/73 season and second lowest scorers the season before with 37 (a total considerably boosted by an 8-0 hammering of Southampton) – and Latchford was signed to redress this problem. Yet he failed to score in his first two games, which made him even more anxious about the move, but in his third – a 2-1 defeat at Leicester – he did and 'everything lifted off my shoulders. That weight that was there, that expectation, fell away.' For the next five years, he barely stopped scoring and even during his brief spell in an Everton shirt during

the 1973/74 season finished second top scorer with seven goals from 13 games.

Following the transfer of Joe Royle to Manchester City at the start of the 1974/75 season, Latchford was given the responsibility of being the Blues' principal goalscorer. He responded brilliantly to the task. In his first full season he scored 17 league goals as Everton finished fourth, just three points behind champions Derby, having led the First Division into April. 'We should have won the title,' he told this author in 2006. 'We had two really bad results against Carlisle, who finished bottom. We were 2-0 up at Goodison and lost 3-2 and they turned us over 3-0 away. If we'd beaten them twice we'd have won the League by a point. That's how close we came. Those two games could have turned my career and kick-started an era of Everton winning things.'

Injury limited Latchford's effectiveness during the 1975/76 season as the club, under Bingham's management, started to wane. At one point, he requested a transfer after Everton refused to accede to his request for a pay rise amid rising inflation, before backing down.

Season	League App	League Goals	FA Cup App	FA Cup Goals	League Cup App	League Cup Goals	Europe App	Europe Goals	Total App	Total Goals
1973/74	13	7	0	0	0	0	-	-	13	7
1974/75	36	17	3	1	2	1	-	-	41	19
1975/76	31	12	1	0	4	1	2	0	38	13
1976/77	36	17	5	3	9	5	-	-	50	25
1977/78	39	30	2	1	5	1	-	-	46	32
1978/79	36	11	1	0	3	6	4	3	44	20
1979/80	26	6	5 (1)	5	2	2	0 (1)	0	33 (2)	13
1980/81	18 (1)	6	-	-	3	3	-	-	21 (1)	9
Total	235 (1)	106	17 (1)	10	28	19	6 (1)	3	286 (3)	138

Rejuvenated for the 1976/77 season, he scored 25 league and cup goals as Everton reached the League Cup Final and FA Cup semi-final – but he was unable to save Bingham's job.

Under his successor, Gordon Lee, Latchford played the best football of his career under a man whose life, Latchford claimed, 'revolved around football'. His first full season – 1977/78 – under the new Everton manager was also his most famous. With the signing of Dave Thomas – a direct winger whose speciality was early accurate crosses – the big striker prospered and the net bulged. After taking five games to get onto the scoresheet he opened his account in the 5-1 mauling of Leicester and after a goal against Man City hit four past QPR – the most he had ever scored in a senior match. Commenting on Latchford's second goal, a diving header from a Thomas cross, Lee said, 'That was the kind of goal I was dreaming about when I bought Thomas. Latchford is deadly when he gets the ball in the area at the right time and with the right pace behind it. Thomas can do this for him.'

'I MIGHT HAVE STARTED AT BIRMINGHAM BUT MY SOUL IS AT GOODISON'

That season the Daily Express had offered a £10,000 prize to a player who could claim 30 league goals. Although the contest may seem parochial by today's standards it generated enormous interest and enthusiasm from Everton's success-starved fans. By New Year Latchford was two-thirds of the way to reaching the magical total. After a lean patch, in which he scored just twice in the first nine games of 1978, five goals in four games over the Easter period saw him well on course for the prize.

WITH 28 GOALS to his name and three games remaining, Latchford then struck two blanks. It left him with the Herculean task – reminiscent of Dixie Dean half a century previous – of having to score a brace in Everton's final league game of the season, against Chelsea.

Nearly 40,000 packed Goodison to see the game and when Everton swept into a commanding 3-0 lead – without Latchford getting onto the score sheet – it was assumed to be one of those freak days when anybody would score but the main man. However, he scored the fourth and with ten minutes remaining Everton were awarded a penalty. Latchford finished off a 6-0 drubbing from the penalty spot to collect the money. And yet his success would plague him for years: half of the £10,000 prize was donated to the PFA benevolence fund and he kindly shared the rest of it out among the other players and ground staff, taking home just £192 himself. Years later Latchford was still trying to convince the taxman that he didn't owe anything!

By now Latchford was an England international, the first of 12 caps coming against Italy in a November 1977 World Cup qualifier. In August 1978, Latchford made headlines again after scoring five times in a League Cup tie against Wimbledon – overshadowing Martin Dobson's hat-trick in the same game. But that represented a high point of sorts, for thereafter he found goals harder to come by. He scored 11 league goals through 1978/79 as Everton made a faltering title challenge, but this tally fell to six in an injury-hampered 1979/80 season, three of which came in a 5-1 drubbing of Leeds United. There was a glimpse of the Latchford of old in September 1980, when he scored five goals in two games, but injury struck again in November and he missed most of the last six months of Gordon Lee's tenure, making only a solitary substitute appearance in the last game of the season against Wolves.

THIS WAS to be his final action in an Everton shirt. When Howard Kendall replaced Lee, one of his first acts as manager was to approve the £125,000 sale of Latchford to Swansea City. The irony of Kendall's arrival bringing an end to Latchford's Everton career, as his had once done to Kendall's, was lost on no one.

'We qualified for Europe, we got to FA Cup semi-finals, we were competing for championships,' Latchford told this author. 'But it was dark days because we ended up coming short. And Liverpool were so dominant. If you took

that Everton team and put it in the era we have now, the fans would be jumping for joy.' At John Toshack's Swansea, Latchford scored a nine-minute hat-trick on his debut against Leeds as the Welsh club rose, improbably, to the top of the First Division table. He later played in Holland for NAC Breda, and then for Coventry, Lincoln and Newport County. Finally, he joined non-League Merthyr Tydfil in 1986, winning the Welsh FA Cup in 1987.

Although he was for a period in the 1990s a youth coach at Birmingham City, where a young Andrew Johnson came under his charge, Latchford slipped out of the game, preferring to concentrate on his business interests. Following the death of his wife in 2000, he immigrated to Germany to be with his new partner and young son. He retains ties to Everton through the Former Players Foundation, for whom he is a generous and committed fundraiser. 'Evertonians are so enthusiastic about their players,' he said. 'It staggers me every time I come over.' I asked him, with his Midlands roots and home in Germany, where his heart lies. 'I might have started at Birmingham,' he said, 'but my soul is at Goodison.'

[FACTFILE]

BORN
Birmingham,
18 January 1951

POSITION
Centre forward

OTHER CLUBS
Birmingham City (1968–74);
Swansea City (1981–84);
NAC Breda (1984);
Coventry City (1984–85);
Lincoln City (1985–86);
Newport County
(loan, 1986);
Merthyr Tydfil (1986–87)

HONOURS
12 England caps (5 goals)
(1977–79)

Latta, Alex

Goalscoring winger who was one of Everton's early greats

Alex Latta was one of the succession of brilliant players Everton reaped from the bountiful Scottish burgh of Dumbarton. John Bell, Richard Boyle, Abraham Hartley and, a century later, Graeme Sharp, all hailed from the same town. Signed after Everton's first league season, Latta was to be one of the outstanding figures in the club's final years at Anfield and first seasons at Goodison, winning the League Championship in 1891 and appearing in the losing side at the FA Cup Final two years later.

The summer of 1889 was one of intense rebuilding after Everton's moderate start to league football. On the eve of the new season the Liverpool Mercury was excited enough by the transfer activity to report: 'The efforts of the executive, have almost solely been directed to the delicate task of scoring really reliable players, the result of continuous negotiations being the engagement for certain of four "stars" Latta (Dumbarton Athletic and Scotch International); and [Alec] Brady, (Renton and Burnley); will join [Fred] Geary, [Edgar] Chadwick and [Charlie] Parry in forward work, and the attack thus promises to be a very keen one, and altogether different to the incohesive formation, so often seen last year.' Certainly the optimism was not misplaced and Latta started his Everton career in fine form, scoring nine times from 19 appearances as his new club finished runners-up to Preston.

Accounts of Latta's pace and incision down the right wing recall memories of Andrei Kanchelskis, the club's great Russian winger who followed him in an Everton shirt a century later. 'The outside right combined lightning acceleration with intricate dribbling skills and also packed a powerful shot in both feet,' wrote David France and Dave Prentice in Virgin Blues, the history of Everton's first years. 'His pairing with Alec Brady was often overlooked by the fans of Chadwick-Milward but was equally as productive throughout the title-winning season.' That came in 1890/91, although Latta would be missing for over half of Everton's games through injury. He scored four times in ten appearances in what was a great team effort.

'In the cherished opinion of many veteran enthusiasts this was one of the best teams that ever played for the Club,' wrote Thomas Keates. 'Every member of it has some rhapsodic eulogists; Geary for his electric runs, tricking out opponents; Chadwick and Milward (left wing) and Latta and Brady (right) as superb exponents; Hannah and Doyle as giant barriers, tacklers and sensational kickers; and the half-backs as reliable resisters and feeders.'

When the trophy was handed over by the club president, John Houlding, he was joined by members of the team. 'As each mounted the stage,' reported the Liverpool Mercury, 'The cheering was terrific.' Houlding said he received the trophy with 'great pleasure' and gave a speech to the assembled crowd. 'Since the Everton Club had been started they had scored many brilliant victories, the crowning point was reached when they brought home the League Championship. It was only by continued perseverance and pluck that this cup could be won. The committee had surprised him by the knowledge they displayed not only as regards the game but also as regards players. If a good player were to be had they would capture him, and when they had them it was their duty to keep them.' Houlding then gave out gold medals to each of the players and Latta 'met with a tremendous reception' from the assembled masses.

If the League Championship winning season represented the collective highpoint of his Everton career, 1891/92 was one of personal triumph for Latta. He finished Everton's top goalscorer with 17 goals, including hat-tricks against West Bromwich Albion and Notts County. It provided conclusive proof that he was an ace finisher as well as a creator of goals.

The hat-trick against Notts County came when he was partnered by Geary on the wing. The pair, wrote a local correspondent, were 'especially prominent as they made rings around the Notts defence'. Latta's first goal came after he 'had the best of a hot tussle with Henry' and combined with Milward to score 'a clinking goal'. The winger then 'got round Henry, and sprinting down with the ball at his toe, finished up by beating Toone for a second time'. The third – and his final goal – came after he was set up by Kelso. It was a brilliant display of pace, power and precision.

Latta's contribution from the wing in the first seasons at Goodison Park were equally telling. He scored 18 league goals in 1892/93 and nine a season later. He started the 1894/95 season – like his team-mates – in irrepressible form as the club shot to the top of First Division. But when injury ruled him out after Christmas it seemed to impact the whole team. The top spot

Everton had held for most of the first half of the season was never regained and they finished runners-up to Sunderland by five points. Hamstrung by injuries and erratic form, pressure was mounting on certain players. Of a friendly at Glasgow Rangers the Mercury reported 'the wretched and terribly aggravating shooting form of the visitors'. Perhaps the selectors held Latta responsible; certainly they increasingly favoured Latta's fellow Dumbartonian, John Bell, on the Everton right. After making just five appearances in the 1895/96 season he was sold to Liverpool for £35 in September 1896. But his return to Anfield was unhappy and he never made a senior appearance in English football again.

[FACTFILE]

BORN
Dumbarton, 1 September 1867
DIED
Bebington, 25 August 1928
POSITION
Winger
OTHER CLUBS
Dumbarton Athletic (1881–89);
Liverpool (1896)
HONOURS
1890/91 League Championship; 2
Scotland caps (2 goals) (1888–89)

Season	League		FA Cup		Total	
	App	Goals	App	Goals	App	Goals
1889/90	19	9	2	0	21	9
1890/91	10	4	1	0	11	4
1891/92	25	17	1	0	26	17
1892/93	28	18	7	1	35	19
1893/94	29	9	1	0	30	9
1894/95	20	11	0	0	20	11
1895/96	5	1	0	0	5	1
Total	**136**	**69**	**12**	**1**	**148**	**70**

Laverick, Bobby

Young winger who failed to make an impression

High hopes were held after the acquisition of former England youth international Bobby Laverick – a contemporary of Jimmy Greaves – when he signed for Everton for a fee of £5000 in February 1959. He joined a club still finding its way after the arrival of Johnny Carey as manager but was never able to make the left wing berth his own.

According to the football historian Ivan Ponting, 'Bobby was quick, could control the ball at speed and could shoot with crispness and accuracy.' Yet he 'never evinced the burning desire to succeed that is crucial to any professional footballer'. A chipped bone sustained barely a month after joining would not have helped his progress.

'He was quite a decent player: he was quick and a good crosser of the ball,' recalled his team-mate Derek Temple who, speaking in 2011, expressed some mystification as to why Laverick never realised his potential. 'You get these fellas who have a great deal of ability and they don't seem to make it. I don't know why it is. I suppose it's consistency and luck, particularly at the start where you need to be in the right place at the right time. I've seen it many many times where someone gets injured, their understudy might be injured and you get a youngster put in and suddenly they're away.' In January 1960 Johnny Carey brought in Scottish international Tommy Ring and in June that year Laverick was allowed to leave for Brighton and Hove Albion for a fee of £3500.

[FACTFILE]

BORN
Castle Eden, County Durham, 11 June 1938
POSITION
Outside left
OTHER CLUBS
Chelsea (1953–59); Brighton and Hove Albion (1960–62); Coventry City (1962–63)

Season	League		FA Cup		Total	
	App	Goals	App	Goals	App	Goals
1958/59	11	5	0	0	11	5
1959/60	11	1	1	0	11	1
Total	22	6	1	0	22	6

Lawson, David

Costly goalkeeper who struggled to justify his lofty price tag

It is an unenviable task to pick up the mantle of a distinguished predecessor, but taking up the gloves after the departure of an illustrious goalkeeper seems to have been a recurrent problem through Everton history.

HARRY CATTERICK SPENT £80,000 TO MAKE DAVID LAWSON THE MOST EXPENSIVE GOALKEEPER IN BRITISH TRANSFER HISTORY

Harry Leyland, Jimmy O'Neill, Albert Dunlop and Albert Harris all tried – with varying levels of success – to fill the void left by Ted Sagar before Gordon West proved a fitting replacement. Several custodians were tried over eight years before Tim Howard was deemed a capable long-term successor to Neville Southall. And so, as Gordon West's Everton career went into decline in the early 1970s, did Everton struggle to replace him too.

Dai Davies had already been given a brief opportunity when, in summer 1972, Harry Catterick spent £80,000 to make David Lawson the most expensive goalkeeper in British transfer history. In many ways, a strange career path led Lawson to Goodison. He had started out as an apprentice at Newcastle, but was released without making an appearance. He joined Bradford Park Avenue, but was not even first choice at a team that would eventually slip out of the Football League, and wound up at Huddersfield Town. Here he got his chance after Huddersfield's first-choice keeper broke his leg, and his rise was thereafter meteoric.

Initial signs were good, and for the first two seasons Lawson was Everton's first-choice goalkeeper. Courageous and dexterous, he provided a solid last line of defence in a transitional side, while his quick distribution – usually with a long, accurate throw – served as a springboard for Everton attacks.

But after this initial good showing, inconsistency became apparent. In particular, Lawson – who as a soft-spoken Geordie was a rare thing – lacked the verbosity to command his defence, breeding uncertainty among his defenders.

He struggled to dominate his penalty area and there was an unwillingness to come off his line.

He lost his place to Davies early in the 1974/75 season and thereafter the two men vied for the green jersey. It was a battle neither would win: George Wood's arrival in summer 1977 precipitated both of their departures – Lawson's to Luton Town in a £15,000 deal in October 1978.

[FACTFILE]

BORN
Wallsend, 22 December 1947
POSITION
Goalkeeper
OTHER CLUBS
Newcastle United (1964–67);
Bradford Park Avenue
(1967–69);
Huddersfield Town
(1969–72);
Luton Town (1978–79);
Stockport County (1978–81)

Season	League		FA Cup		League Cup		Europe		Total	
	App	Goals	App	Goals	App	Goals	App	Goals	App	Goals
1972/73	38	0	2	0	1	0	-	-	41	0
1973/74	42	0	3	0	2	0	-	-	47	0
1974/75	7	0	0	0	2	0	-	-	9	0
1975/76	22	0	0	0	3	0	1	0	26	0
1976/77	15	0	7	0	5	0	-	-	27	0
1977/78	0	0	0	0	0	0	-	-	0	0
Total	**124**	**0**	**12**	**0**	**13**	**0**	**1**	**0**	**150**	**0**

Lawton, Tommy

Supremely talented heir to Dixie Dean, his story represents the ultimate 'if only'

Seventy years after he last pulled on an Everton shirt, the questions about the career of Tommy Lawton, a player many fans considered the finest all-round centre forward they ever saw – superior, inconceivable though it might seem, even to Dixie Dean – remain as pertinent as they ever did. What if war had never intervened? What if a troublesome marriage had never influenced his career? What if he had never sought a move from the First Division while still in his prime? What if he had been given a run of more than 32 months in an Everton shirt?

WILLS'S CIGARETTES

T. LAWTON (EVERTON)

LAWTON REGRETTED LEAVING EVERTON FOR THE REST OF HIS LIFE

Born in Farnworth, near Bolton, in October 1919, like Dean Lawton's father was a railwayman, while his mother worked in one of the town's cotton mills. As a youngster Lawton idolised Dean, and would score 560 goals in three years of schoolboy football. He joined Burnley as a 16-year-old and, included in the first team as a teenager, flourished. A hat-trick against Tottenham in October 1936 brought him national prominence. Two months later, he was an Everton player – the £6500 fee a record for a teenager. Lawton later suspected that the deal had long been set up. Eight weeks earlier, the left wing partnership of Jimmy Stein and Willie 'Dusty' Miller had arrived

at Turf Moor on free transfers. Were they a down-payment for the teenager?

Signed as Dean's long-term replacement, the now veteran centre forward took him under his wing. 'He impressed me right away,' Dixie said. 'He was quiet and listened.' Lawton was aware of his natural abilities and improved under Dean's guidance to the extent that he came to be considered the superior all-round player.

LAWTON made his Everton debut in February 1937 in a 7-2 defeat against Wolves. He made the score sheet via the penalty spot but the critic of the Sporting Star dismissed the new boy: 'Lawton did not have a bad match, for he was rarely given the support necessary to successful leadership.' In these first days he played inside forward, deputising in the centre whenever Dean was injured. But it was increasingly obvious that the older man's days were numbered.

'He [Dean] was always so high in praise of Tommy and all the young lads,' Joe Mercer recalled. 'I remember Tommy coming into the side for a Cup replay at Tottenham. He scored a goal in the first half, turning on the ball beautifully, and Dean said, "Well

that's it. That's the swansong, that's the end of it."' 'He [Dean] helped me a lot when I first joined the club,' Lawton later said. 'He had his faults, he was a boisterous character, but everyone liked him.'

During a summer tour of Denmark in 1937 Lawton led the Everton attack and four games into the 1937/38 campaign Dean was dropped. The stage was set for Lawton. He responded by finishing the First Division's leading goalscorer with 28 goals. 'If Lawton is not the best centre forward playing today,' wrote the Sporting Star, 'I have yet to see one better … he is not merely a proposition, but a ready made player, and I have never seen anyone, including [Ted] Drake, hit the ball so swiftly and accurately on the turn.'

Lawton was nicknamed 'the floater' for his famous heading ability ('I used to take him out to play head tennis and with us it was just like Wimbledon,' Dean recalled) and was soon being championed for an England

call-up. 'Lawton is undoubtedly England's centre forward,' Charlie Buchan wrote in the News Chronicle. 'His great headwork, moulded on the pattern of Dixie Dean, and his clever footwork, stamps him as England's leader for many years to come.' The first of 23 caps came against Wales in 1938.

During the 1938/39 season Lawton maintained his scintillating form, with 34 goals in 38 appearances as Everton lifted the league title. 'They were a bloody good side,' Lawton recalled, 'and the next year we should have won the League again, the FA Cup and the bloody boat race if they'd put us in it.'

War, however, put paid to such aspirations. Lawton's unstoppable form nevertheless continued in the regional leagues in which he scored 85 times in 108 games for Everton. He also guested for Aldershot (eight games, 13 goals) and made 23 England wartime international appearances.

When peace came, Lawton was still young enough to star for the Everton team for years to come, and was still aged only 26 when the 1946/47 season kicked off. But he was no longer an Everton player – amazingly he had been allowed to join Chelsea for £11,500 in 1945. For years the deal was a mystery, but later in life Lawton admitted it was to escape his marriage to a local girl. 'The marriage just wasn't working out, in fact it was purgatory,' he said. 'Home was hell, something had to be done.'

From hereon Lawton's career suffered as the result of several staggering career choices. In 1947 he joined Notts County, who played in the Third Division South, for a British record fee of £20,000 – the equivalent, perhaps, of Wayne Rooney deserting Manchester United for Macclesfield for £50million. There was a spell at Brentford, and in the veteran part of his career he joined Arsenal, where he was reunited with Joe Mercer. Never again did he hit the same heights as he had done for Everton.

Lawton regretted leaving Everton for the rest of his life. He never won another trophy and although he continued to represent

England until 1948, his domestic career was a pallid imitation of what had preceded it. 'On reflection,' he later admitted, 'I should have stayed and transferred the wife.'

On leaving Highbury in 1955, Lawton struggled to find a life outside football. His intermittent spells in charge of Notts County and Kettering were interspersed with unemployment, debts, depression, drink problems and petty crime. On more than one occasion he contemplated suicide, the same fate that had befallen his contemporary Hughie Gallagher in 1957. Mercer eased some of his friend's financial worries by arranging his testimonial in 1972, only the second such match (after Dean's) Everton had granted one of their former players. Eventually he found a niche of sorts, writing a twice-weekly column for the Nottingham Evening Post right up until his death in November 1996.

Further reading:
LAWTON (JR), TOM, AND BARRIE WILLIAMS, *Get in There! Tommy Lawton – My Friend, My Father,* Vision Sports Publishing, 2010**MCVAY, DAVID AND ANDY SMITH,** *The Complete Centre Forward,* SportsBooks, 2000

[FACTFILE]

BORN
Farnworth, 6 October 1919
DIED
Nottingham, 6 November, 1996
POSITION
Centre forward
OTHER CLUBS
Burnley (1935–36);
Chelsea (1945–47);
Notts County (1947–51);
Brentford (1951–53);
Arsenal (1953–55)
AS MANAGER
Brentford (1953);
Kettering (1956);
Notts County (1957–58);
Kettering (1963–64)
HONOURS
1938/39 League Championship,
23 England caps (22 goals) (1938–48)

Season	League		FA Cup		Total	
	App	**Goals**	**App**	**Goals**	**App**	**Goals**
1936/37	10	3	1	1	11	4
1937/38	39	28	2	0	41	28
1938/39	38	34	5	4	43	38
Total	**87**	**65**	**8**	**5**	**95**	**70**

Lee, Gordon

Late-1970s manager dealt a harsh hand by Everton lore

Gordon Lee was a decent, astute and unfairly maligned manager, who brought Everton to the brink of success in the late 1970s, but was ultimately plagued by comparisons to his illustrious predecessor, Harry Catterick, and neighbour, Bob Paisley. With his gaunt face and preference for solid over spectacular players, history has dealt him a bad hand, but it ought to be remembered just how close he came to breaking Everton's barren run and some of the outstanding players that flourished under his watch.

As a player Lee's towering figure had for eleven years been a mainstay of the Aston Villa defence before he set out on a managerial path that took him from Port Vale to Newcastle United via Blackburn Rovers (whom he led to promotion in the 1974/75 season). He was passionate and committed but had garnered a reputation – perhaps after selling Malcolm MacDonald to Arsenal when Newcastle manager – for dour, workmanlike teams rather than (in his own, frequently twisted, words) 'coffee-house ball jugglers' or 'Flash Harrys'.

His arrival at Goodison in January 1977, three weeks after Billy Bingham's dismissal, came after the Ipswich Town manager Bobby Robson had changed his mind on a 10-year contract he had agreed with the Everton board. Lee, however, was undeterred at being second choice. 'When I entered Goodison Park for the first time as manager of Everton FC, I was well

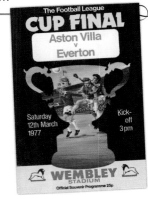

prepared for the fact that I was taking charge of a famous club which stands for everything that is special about English football,' he wrote in his first programme notes. 'But I was still taken by surprise. I suddenly discovered that Everton meant more to me than I thought it would.' He then went on to describe walking out before 40,000 for a cup tie against Swindon. 'I said to myself, "Flipping heck! What is it?" Then it sank in. This is Everton … THE club.'

> WALKING OUT BEFORE 40,000 FOR A CUP TIE AGAINST SWINDON. 'I SAID TO MYSELF, "FLIPPING HECK! WHAT IS IT?" THEN IT SANK IN. THIS IS EVERTON… THE CLUB'

Lee steadied Everton's slide down the table. Mike Pejic, a £150,000 purchase from Stoke City and one-time England international, added some steel to the left side of the defence and a couple of the long unbeaten runs for which his team became well known followed. After a slow start Lee steered his team up to the relative respectability of ninth place by the end of the 1976/77 season. By then, however, greater dramas had taken place in both domestic cup competitions. Already with one foot in the League Cup final, one of his first tasks as Everton

manager was to steer Everton through a semi-final second leg against Bolton, which Everton won 1-0 (2-1 on aggregate). In the epic, twice-replayed final against Aston Villa, Everton eventually fell 3-2 after extra time in the second replay. The disappointment of losing that game was eased by the knowledge that they had an FA Cup semi-final ten days later. Everton looked set to win that when, with the scores tied at 2-2, Bryan Hamilton bundled a late winner home. Or so he thought. The referee, Clive Thomas, inexplicably disallowed the goal and Everton lost 3-0 in the replay.

Lee spent the summer of 1977 making his mark on his new club. George Wood was signed from Blackpool for £150,000 in an effort to address a goalkeeping problem that could be traced back to the start of the decade, and the outstanding winger Dave Thomas was signed from Queens Park Rangers to supply Bob Latchford. Everton lost their first two games, but then went on an unbeaten run that lasted until Boxing Day. 'Attractive football is developed from players with the correct outlook,' said Lee. 'If you want a constructive footballing side you must start by giving 100 per cent physically and mentally.'

Although such a philosophy was bringing Everton results it left him open to criticism, too. His treatment of crowd favourite Duncan McKenzie, whom he left out for long stretches, annoyed and perplexed fans – and the forward. There was a sense that McKenzie was too extrovert, too much of a maverick to ever be allowed to thrive under the new boss and his system. 'I think he was more comfortable dealing with ordinary players than superstars,' said Bryan Hamilton in Three Sides of the Mersey. 'He seemed to be able to understand people better when they worked hard.'

'It has always been my style to demand 100 per cent effort,' said Lee. 'This was something inborn in me and, if I give everything I have got for Everton, then I am entitled to expect that the players do the same. If people think that makes me a hard task master then I wouldn't argue with them. But is it asking so much to expect a total contribution?'

Everton finished the 1977/78 season third, but nine points off League Champions Nottingham Forest. The 30 league goals scored by Bob Latchford was some consolation for another trophyless

season. At the end of it McKenzie was sold and replaced by Mick Walsh. The midfielder Geoff Nulty, signed from Newcastle, was another less than auspicious choice, and while former footballer of the year Colin Todd arrived, he was largely played out of position at right back.

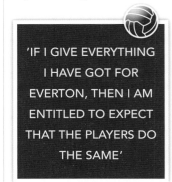

> 'IF I GIVE EVERYTHING I HAVE GOT FOR EVERTON, THEN I AM ENTITLED TO EXPECT THAT THE PLAYERS DO THE SAME'

Yet after the 1978/79 season kicked off, Everton went unbeaten in the league until Christmas and ended a seven-year-long hoodoo against Liverpool, beating them in the October derby thanks to an Andy King strike. They topped the table for a week after beating Bristol City in February, but from then onwards their title challenge slipped away. As under Billy Bingham four years earlier, too many draws were the problem. Everton won just five games after Christmas, losing six and drawing the remainder, and Latchford's

As Manager											
Season	P	W	L	D	F	A	Pts	Position	FA Cup	League Cup	UEFA Cup
1976/77	20	8	4	8	31	24	24	9th	SF	R/up	-
1977/78	42	22	9	11	76	45	55	3rd	4th Round	QF	-
1978/79	42	17	8	17	52	40	51	4th	3rd Round	4th Round	2nd Round
1979/80	42	9	16	17	43	51	35	19th	SF	4th Round	1st Round
1980/81	42	13	19	10	55	58	36	15th	QF	3rd Round	-

goals dried up – he managed just three of his total of 19 (only 11 of which came in the league) – after Boxing Day. Not even the late-season additions of Brian Kidd and Peter Eastoe could bolster Everton's championship challenge and they finished fourth on 51 points, well behind champions Liverpool.

The wheels somewhat fell off Lee's managerial reign after that. Martin Dobson and Dave Thomas left, as did Todd, and expensive new signings like Trevor Ross and John Gidman did not ease the decline. At the same time the faith placed in such young players as Gary Megson, Kevin Ratcliffe and Graeme Sharp was too early. Supporters lacked optimism as the 1979/80 season opened. Only John Bailey had been added to Everton's ranks and season ticket sales were down 24 per cent. 'Goodison will never warm to the sight of players passing the ball

around their own area,' wrote Wilf Heslop of Crosby in the Football Echo's letters pages. 'They should go forward.' Other fans were less generous. 'Gordon Lee is too small for Everton,' said C. Smith of L15. 'I blame everything on him.' Chairman Philip Carter nevertheless spelled out his intentions for the season: he stated in his annual report his ambition was to win the league. Lee admitted, 'I am under pressure. I realise this. But I will do things my way and sink or swim on that basis.' Everton finished the season one place off relegation but a run to the semi-finals of the FA Cup probably saved the manager. Everton, typically for this era, were defeated after a replay.

Time was fast running out for Lee. He spent a frustrating summer of 1980 fruitlessly trying to bring inspirational new faces to Goodison, most notably Peter Reid, but had more fallings out with his players. One of them, Andy King – Lee's most consistent performer during his three-and-a-half years in charge – was sold to Queens Park Rangers for £425,000; while another, the previous season's player of the year, John Bailey, also looked set to leave for a period. Undaunted by his critics Lee announced his faith in youth. He opened the 1980/81 season with the relatively untried novices Megson, McMahon, Ratcliffe and Sharp in his line-up to face Sunderland. It was a bold experiment and in the early stages of the season Everton flourished. But after October they only won six more times in the league all season. Some pride was restored with a win over Liverpool in the FA Cup fourth round, the first and only time Mick Lyons played for the victorious side in 20 derby appearances, but it wasn't enough. Just 15,352 watched the last home match, a 1-0 defeat to Stoke City. Everton finished the season 15th and it was announced that Lee's contract would not be renewed.

LEE SOON returned to management with Preston North End. There was a spell in Iceland with KR Reykjavik and a period as caretaker manager of Leicester City, whom he also served as coach and assistant manager. As time has passed history has tended to be kinder in judging his achievements at Goodison.

[**FACTFILE**]

BORN
Cannock, 13 July 1934
PLAYING CAREER
Aston Villa (1955–66);
Shrewsbury Town (1966–67)
MANAGERIAL CAREER
(excluding Everton):
Port Vale (1968–74);
Blackburn Rovers (1974–75);
Newcastle United (1975–77);
Preston North End
(1981–83);
KR Reykjavic (1985–87);
Leicester City
(caretaker) (1991)

Lee, Jack

Reserve defender who experienced the briefest of Goodison careers

[FACTFILE]

BORN
1880
POSITION
Left back

Season	League		FA Cup		Total	
	App	Goals	App	Goals	App	Goals
1902/03	2	0	0	0	2	0
Total	2	0	0	0	2	0

Leeder, Fred

Full back who dropped into lower leagues and then the semi-professional game

[FACTFILE]

BORN
Seaton Delaval, 15
September 1936
POSITION
Left back
OTHER CLUBS
Darlington (1958–60);
Southport (1960–62);
Runcorn

Season	League		FA Cup		Total	
	App	Goals	App	Goals	App	Goals
1957/58	1	0	0	0	1	0
Total	1	0	0	0	1	0

Lello, Cyril

Model of consistency through Everton's darkest years

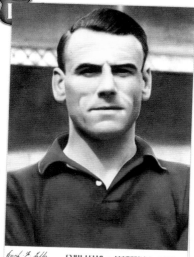

CYRIL LELLO - EVERTON F.C. (1956)

Cyril Lello was a model of consistency and commitment through one of Everton's most difficult periods. A late developer who did not make his top-flight debut until the age of 28, Lello was considered one of the finest uncapped wing halves of his generation. As a steady head in a dismal side, his important contribution to the Everton cause was underlined when, with him absent through injury for the entirety of the 1950/51 season, his club suffered the indignity of relegation.

Lello was born in Ludlow, Shropshire, an area which produced two of Wolves' great post-war players, Billy Wright and Johnny Hancocks. While serving in the RAF during the war, he made appearances for Millwall, Norwich and Lincoln. At the latter club, in December 1943, Lello scored seven goals in a League North fixture against Notts County. His reputation in the wartime leagues prompted Shrewsbury Town to make a move for him when he left the armed forces at the war's end.

At Gay Meadow, Lello continued to build a reputation as a consistent inside forward. He attracted the notice of the Everton director W.R. Williams, who watched him on a number of occasions. With Wolves also interested, in September 1947 Everton made their move, paying £2500 for the forward. He was given his debut in a Central League fixture against Wolves a few days later, and the Everton board – who had expected to pay substantially more for the player – were delighted to hear 'completely favourable' reports of his play.

His arrival was nevertheless low key, and Theo Kelly tried to suppress his age – Lello was 27 when he first signed and 28 when he made his debut – from the local press, who pointedly referred to him as a 'youngster' for several years. His full debut came against Wolves at a snow-covered

Molineux in February 1948. He was, concluded a local journalist, 'the Everton type, good ball control, a nice passer of the ball and one with a fighting quality'. A week later Lello capped his home debut against Middlesbrough with both goals in a 2-1 victory.

Chances were nevertheless initially difficult for the inside forward to come by. Wally Fielding was first choice in the number ten shirt, and a veteran Alex Stevenson was usually preferred ahead of him as well. Lello's career changed when Cliff Britton succeeded Theo Kelly as manager from the start of the 1948/49 season. The new manager converted Lello into a wing half and by the end of the season he had built up a good partnership with Peter Farrell.

In a largely dire team that hung on to its First Division life by a thread, Lello and Farrell provided some solidity and experience in a side sorely lacking it. Yet on 4

February 1950 disaster struck: Lello limped off 27 minutes into a league game at Aston Villa with a serious knee injury. This eventually necessitated a cartilage operation and Lello was largely absent for the next 18 months.

By the time of his next appearance in an Everton shirt, on the opening day of the 1951/52 season, Everton were a Second Division side. Progress after his lay-off was slow and Lello had to vie with Don Donavon and Jackie Grant for his old berth. But midway through the 1952/53 season he finally reclaimed the number six shirt as his own and would retain it for the next three years. In so doing he became the first Everton player to make 150 consecutive league and cup appearances.

During this time Lello, now in the veteran stage of his career, was an important part of the team that secured promotion in 1954 and subsequently re-established itself

as a top-flight force. 'I am as sure now as I was then that I could not have picked a better team,' he said in 1970. 'The atmosphere among the players was terrific. There were no small cliques like you might find in other clubs and Peter Farrell was a great skipper and a tremendous organiser. I could sum it up as "One for all – all for one".'

Cliff Britton's departure in February 1956, however, marked uncertain times for Lello. First the managerial subcommittee instructed to succeed Britton until the end of the 1955/56 season, and subsequently Ian Buchan, preferred to give Ken Birch and Ken Rea a chance to partner Farrell at wing half in his place.

But his value, even at the age of 36, was still recognised, and in November 1956 his former team-mate Harry Catterick, now manager of Rochdale, paid £750 to bring the veteran to the Lancashire moors.

Lello spent less than a year at Spotland before becoming player-manager of Runcorn. After leaving football he worked for Bootle Corporation, but continued to follow Everton, a stone's throw from his old club house on Goodison Road, where he lived until his death in 1997.

Further reading:

RIDGWAY, BARBARA, *From Dinham Mill to Goodison: The Story of Cyril Lello – A Craftsman Footballer,* Scenesetters, 2001

Season	League		FA Cup		Total	
	App	Goals	App	Goals	App	Goals
1947/48	9	2	-	-	9	2
1948/49	20	0	1	0	21	0
1949/50	35	0	2	0	37	0
1950/51	0	0	0	0	0	0
1951/52	21	1	0	0	21	1
1952/53	26	0	5	0	31	0
1953/54	42	2	3	0	45	2
1954/55	42	2	2	0	44	2
1955/56	37	2	4	0	41	2
1956/57	5	0	0	0	5	0
Total	**237**	**9**	**17**	**0**	**254**	**9**

[FACTFILE]

BORN
Ludlow, 24 February 1920
DIED
1997
POSITION
Wing half
OTHER CLUBS
Shrewsbury Town (1946–47);
Rochdale (1956–57)

Lescott, Joleon

England international defender whose Goodison reputation was marred by his messy exit

A fine and versatile defender, Joleon Lescott was a consistent and formidable performer who proved one of David Moyes's most astute buys. Three of Everton's best six defensive seasons of all time coincided with Lescott's three-year spell with the club, but memories of him are ultimately sullied by the manner of his departure.

A boyhood Aston Villa fan, whose older brother Aaron played for Bristol Rovers, Lescott made his league debut as a 17-year-old for Wolves at the start of the 2000/01 season. He quickly established a reputation as Wolves' most outstanding player and was a crucial part of the team that won promotion to the Premier League in 2003. He missed the duration of Wolves top-flight campaign after sustaining a serious knee injury, but made a return the following year.

Lescott continued to impress for the Midlands club, and Wolves attracted covetous glances from the top flight. It was Everton who took the plunge, paying £5million for him in the summer of 2006. David Moyes later revealed that he had had Lescott scouted on more than 20 occasions and never had anything but positive reports back.

Immediately identifiable because of the prominent scar on his forehead – the result of a childhood

traffic accident – Lescott was a prominent member of the Everton back line. Tall, quick and rangy, he first entered the team in the left back berth, where his grounding as a schoolboy winger showed. He was a potent attacker in a team lacking natural width, overlapping or cutting inside, and added real cut and thrust to the Everton left.

But it was at centre back where his long-term ambitions lay and he emerged as an excellent defensive partner to Joseph Yobo, his presence marginalising Alan Stubbs and David Weir and bringing an end to their long Everton careers. Theirs was one of the quickest central defensive partnerships in the league and despite occasional lapses in concentration it was soon one of the most formidable. Later Phil Jagielka would usurp Yobo, and the all-English partnership looked even better.

Lescott was unlucky to miss out to Mikel Arteta for the Everton Player of the Year award in 2007

as the team qualified for the UEFA Cup. A year later he would wrest the award from the Spaniard in a campaign in which he grabbed as many headlines for the goals he scored as the ones he kept out. With Tim Cahill and Andrew Johnson he was second top scorer with 10, and his strike rate was reminiscent of Derek Mountfield's contribution to the great 1980s teams.

BY NOW HE was an England international, making his debut against Estonia in October 2007. It was the natural progression for a player who had represented his country at every level – under-18, under-20, under-21 and B international.

Although one of Everton's most consistent performers there were, however, glimmers of frailty. He scored a last-minute own goal in the 2008 League Cup semi-final that brought a 2-1 defeat in a game Everton should have won. Asked to play left back at the start of the 2008/09 season, he was palpably

unhappy in the role and less than convincing in a position in which he had previously excelled.

LESCOTT was nevertheless an important part of the Everton team that reached the 2009 FA Cup Final. His goal in the fourth round tie with Liverpool gave a depleted Everton team the initiative in a game they were predicted to lose.

Yet rumours linking him with a transfer to Manchester City would never quite go away. In September 2008 Manchester's perennial underachievers had been transformed from national laughing stock to the richest team in the world following a takeover by an Abu Dhabi investment group. Like a gauche lottery jackpot winner they flouted their new-found wealth, paying scant heed to the common courtesies and protocols of British football.

Speculation intensified following Everton's 2009 FA Cup Final defeat to Chelsea, but a firm bid did not come until the eve of the 2009/10 season. The intention of City was seemingly to unsettle one of its main rivals ahead of the new season – a rival, it should be mentioned, that had risen to the top of English football through merit, not the petro-billions of a foreign tycoon.

Bids of £15million and £18million were rejected by Everton and Moyes was adamant that Lescott was going nowhere. On the first day of the 2009/10 season he included him in the team to face Arsenal at Goodison, despite Lescott allegedly telling him he didn't want to play.

> WITH TIM CAHILL AND ANDREW JOHNSON HE WAS SECOND TOP SCORER WITH 10 IN THE 2007/08 SEASON

THE DEFENDER received a mixed reception from the Goodison crowd, although cheers were louder than the boos that greeted his name. Yet Lescott did not acknowledge the supporters and his body language suggested he would sooner be elsewhere.

Although by no means wholly culpable for what happened, his restlessness seemed to undermine the team as Everton were hammered 6-1 – their heaviest home defeat in 50 years.

In the wake of this humiliation, Moyes omitted Lescott from Everton's midweek Europa League tie, publicly berating his poor attitude. Days later he finally joined City for £24million – the third highest fee ever paid for a defender – on a reported basic weekly salary of £94,000.

[FACTFILE]

BORN
Birmingham, 16 August 1982
POSITION
Defender
OTHER CLUBS
Wolverhampton Wanderers (2000–2006);
Manchester City (2009–)
HONOURS
14 England caps (2007–)

Season	League		FA Cup		League Cup		Europe		Total	
	App	Goals	App	Goals	App	Goals	App	Goals	App	Goals
2006/07	36 (2)	2	1	0	3	0			40 (2)	2
2007/08	37 (1)	8	0 (1)	0	5	0	10	2	52 (2)	10
2008/09	35 (1)	4	7	1	1	0	2	0	45 (1)	5
2009/10	1	0	0	0	0	0	0	0	1	0
Total	**109(4)**	**14**	**8 (1)**	**1**	**9**	**0**	**12**	**2**	**138(5)**	**17**

Lewis, Gwyn

Welsh centre forward who later brought a flurry of goals to Saltergate

Season	League		FA Cup		Total	
	App	Goals	App	Goals	App	Goals
1951/52	1	0	0	0	1	0
1952/53	2	3	0	0	2	3
1953/54	3	2	0	0	3	2
1954/55	3	1	0	0	3	1
1955/56	1	0	0	0	1	0
Total	**10**	**6**	**0**	**0**	**10**	**6**

[FACTFILE]

BORN
Bangor, 22 April 1931
POSITION
Centre forward
OTHER CLUBS
Rochdale (1956);
Chesterfield (1956–61)

Lewis, Tommy

Goalscoring outside left and inside forward who later set the lower leagues alight

Season	League		FA Cup		Total	
	App	Goals	App	Goals	App	Goals
1928/29	1	0	0	0	1	0
Total	**1**	**0**	**0**	**0**	**1**	**0**

[FACTFILE]

BORN
Ellesmere Port, 11 October 1909
POSITION
Outside left / inside left
OTHER CLUBS
Wrexham (1930–32);
Bradford Park Avenue (1933–38);
Blackpool (1938)

Lewis, William

One of Everton's Virgin Blues, he went on to have a long career in the red of Wales

[FACTFILE]

BORN
Bangor, 1864

DIED
1935

POSITION
Centre forward

OTHER CLUBS
Bangor Rovers; Bangor City (2 spells); Crewe Alexandra; Chester City (2 spells)

Season	League		FA Cup		Total	
	App	Goals	App	Goals	App	Goals
1888/89	3	1	-	-	3	1
Total	3	1	-	-	3	1

Leyfield, Charlie

Versatile winger who dropped out of favour before Everton's late 1930s heyday

[FACTFILE]

BORN
Chester, 30 October 1911

DIED
1982

POSITION
Outside left / right

OTHER CLUBS
Sheffield United (1937–38); Doncaster Rovers (1938–39)

Season	League		FA Cup		Total	
	App	Goals	App	Goals	App	Goals
1934/35	11	7	0	0	11	7
1935/36	17	5	0	0	17	5
1936/37	10	1	0	0	10	1
Total	38	13	0	0	38	13

Leyland, Harry

Capable young goalkeeper given the difficult task of succeeding Ted Sagar

Signed as a 16-year-old amateur following the Second World War, Harry Leyland was one of several contenders for the ageing Ted Sagar's green jersey in the early 1950s.

He made his Everton debut in September 1951, shortly after the club's relegation to the Second Division, and was able to supplant the veteran. However, Jimmy O'Neill was also a capable candidate to be Everton's number one and for the next five years the two men vied for the chance to keep goal for Everton. It was a battle in which the Irishman always seemed to have the edge over Leyland, and having made just five appearances in the 1955/56 season, he left to join Blackburn Rovers that summer.

At Ewood Park chances were easier to come by and Leyland blossomed. In 1957/58 he won promotion with Blackburn and two years later was part of the team that reached the FA Cup Final. In 1961 he joined Tranmere Rovers and ended his competitive career with a stint as player-manager of Wigan Athletic, then a non-league team.

In common with Gordon West and England's Gordon Banks,

HIS OUTSTANDING BRAVERY MADE HIM A NATURAL TO THE POSITION

Leyland was a late convert to the goalkeeping position, but his outstanding bravery made him a natural to the position.

[FACTFILE]

BORN
Liverpool, 12 May 1930

DIED
6 December 2006

POSITION
Goalkeeper

OTHER CLUBS
Blackburn Rovers (1956–1961); Tranmere Rovers (1961–1967)

AS PLAYER-MANAGER
Wigan Athletic (1967–68)

Season	League		FA Cup		Total	
	App	Goals	App	Goals	App	Goals
1951/52	12	0	2	0	14	0
1952/53	6	0	0	0	6	0
1953/54	14	0	0	0	14	0
1954/55	1	0	0	0	1	0
1955/56	3	0	2	0	5	0
Total	36	0	4	0	40	0

Li Tie

The so-called Chinese Beckham, who flickered then failed amid scepticism

Chinese international midfielder Li Tie arrived at Goodison with his compatriot Li Weifeng in July 2002 as part of the club's sponsorship deal with the electronics manufacturer Keijan. The loan deal initially seemed like a publicity stunt, with David Moyes appearing bemused at the duo's arrival. Indeed Li Weifeng made just a solitary appearance before returning to China.

BUT LI TIE would feature prominently through Everton's 2002/03 campaign and at the season's end Moyes elected to make the deal permanent. Dubbed the 'Chinese Beckham', Li Tie had featured for his country during their first ever World Cup Finals campaign the previous summer. A defensive midfielder, he had spent years at training camps in Brazil prior to embarking on his professional career. He possessed good technique, was an adept passer of the ball over short distances and showed reasonable pace, with a willingness

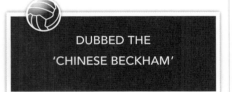

DUBBED THE
'CHINESE BECKHAM'

to support attacks. Confounding expectations that he would be a lightweight, at six foot Li Tie could hold his own amid the physicality of English football, but perhaps lacked some of the grit necessary to emerge as a top-class holding midfielder.

After impressing in the early stages of 2002/03, Li Tie's form waned towards the end of his debut campaign and he was dropped. Introduced as a substitute against Arsenal on the opening day of the 2003/04 season, he was sent off within 12 minutes for two bookings for clumsy challenges. Shortly after, he broke his shin while with the Chinese national team, and did not return to full training until October 2004. Thereafter he was beset by continual niggling injuries that effectively ended his competitive career, although he continued to play for China. On the expiry of his contract in 2006, he joined Sheffield United, who were also trying to break into the Chinese market, but he played just once before being farmed out to Chengdu Blades, United's Chinese feeder club.

[FACTFILE]

BORN
Liaoning, China, 18 September 1977
POSITION
Midfield
OTHER CLUBS
Liaoning Fushen (1997–2003);
Sheffield United (2006–08);
Chengdu Blades (2008);
Liaoning Whowin (2009–11)
HONOURS
89 China caps (5 goals) (1995-2007)

Season	League		FA Cup		League Cup		Europe		Total	
	App	Goals	App	Goals	App	Goals	App	Goals	App	Goals
2002/03	28 (1)	0	0 (1)	0	3	0	-	-	31 (2)	0
2003/04	4 (1)	0	0	0	1 (1)	0	-	-	5 (2)	0
2004/05	0	0	0	0	0	0	-	-	0	0
2005/06	0	0	0	0	0	0	0	0	0	0
Total	**32 (2)**	**0**	**0 (1)**	**0**	**4 (1)**	**0**	**0**	**0**	**36 (4)**	**0**

Lievesley,
Walter

Non-league centre half given a chance at the end of the 1919/20 season

[FACTFILE]

BORN
Haydock, 1888
POSITION
Centre half
OTHER CLUBS
Haydock Colliery; Reading

Season	League		FA Cup		Total	
	App	Goals	App	Goals	App	Goals
1919/20	5	0	0	0	5	0
Total	**5**	**0**	**0**	**0**	**5**	**0**

Lill, Micky

Thrilling winger undermined by injuries who tried his luck in South Africa

Rejected by his local club West Ham, Micky Lill made his name as a goalscoring winger with Wolverhampton Wanderers in the late 1950s. Attracted by his prowess, Johnny Carey made him a £25,000 signing in February 1960. With Tommy Ring acquired just weeks earlier it meant that Everton had one of the most attractive wing pairings in the First Division.

Lill fitted into his new surroundings immediately and was a popular member of the Everton dressing room. He was, recalled Brian Labone, ' a very nice man indeed'. The Everton captain recalled: 'He fitted the bill of a stereotypical cockney: always friendly, chirpy and had a very sharp dress sense. He was a handsome fellow as well – I think a few of the lads in the squad were quite envious of him. In fact, we used to joke that he turned up to training the way most of us would dress for a wedding! On the pitch, he was lively, very quick – and scored a fair few goals.'

Indeed he did: seven from the first eight games of the 1960/61 season. Alas, he was quickly undermined by injuries and a mysterious leg infection kept him out of action, with the club even sending him to a Harrogate sanatorium in an attempt to clear it up.

EVERTON 1959
*Back - **Sharples, Parker, Labone, Dunlop, Gabriel, Meagan, Bramwell***
*Front - **Lill, Collins, Harris, Vernon, Ring***

He was given another chance by Harry Catterick in the 1961/62 season, but the new manager seemed to prefer alternatives. Lill asked for a transfer and joined Plymouth Argyle for £12,500, later immigrating to South Africa, where he ended his career.

'He was quite a slight fellow – and he wasn't helped by the injuries he had,' recalled Labone. 'But he did have talent.'

[FACTFILE]

BORN
Romford, 3 August 1936
DIED
Johannesburg, October 2004
POSITION
Winger
OTHER CLUBS
Wolverhampton Wanderers (1957–60);
Plymouth Argyle (1962–63);
Portsmouth (1963–65);
Guildford City (1965–66);
Germiston Callies (1966–68)

Season	League		FA Cup		League Cup		Total	
	App	Goals	App	Goals	App	Goals	App	Goals
1959/60	12	3	0	0	-	-	12	3
1960/61	8	7	0	0	1	0	9	7
1961/62	11	1	2	1	-	-	13	2
Total	31	11	2	1	1	0	34	12

Limpar, Anders

Fabulously talented winger whose footballing gifts were a throwback to a different era

Although Mike Walker's troubled managerial reign yielded just five wins, one unquestionable triumph was the £1.6million capture of Swedish wing wizard Anders Limpar. On his day, Limpar was a hark back to the golden era of the 1960s; a slight but sublimely gifted player whose impish, impudent skills were occasionally redolent of such predecessors as Alex Young and Tommy Ring.

Brought up watching Everton on Swedish television in the early 1980s, Limpar, the son of a Hungarian immigrant, evidently saw something of himself in their half-Hungarian striker Imre Varadi and so adopted the Blues as his team. The journey that took him to Goodison from Stockholm's suburbs was nevertheless long and exotic. Beginning his career in the mid-1980s with Gothenburg's second club, Orgyte, he split his time between

football and university where he studied for an economics degree. Making his international debut in 1987, he attracted the notice of Swiss club Young Boys of Berne, signing as a professional in 1988.

In 1989 he joined Cremonese, and despite his team's relegation from Serie A was considered an individual success, named third best foreigner in a league that boasted the likes of Maradona, Marco Van Basten and Ruud Gullit. After the 1990 World Cup Finals he joined Arsenal, an early forerunner of the magnificently talented foreigners who would dominate the club's ranks from the mid-1990s, and inspired them to the 1991 First Division title. Differences with manager George

Graham subsequently left him a marginalised figure, leading to his departure on transfer deadline day 1994.

Immediately pitched into an Everton side dangerously close to the relegation zone, his class in a side lacking finesse was immediately apparent. Just two games into his Everton career he was dubbed the 'Blue Brazilian' after an audacious lob over the Aston Villa goalkeeper, Mark Bosnich, missed by inches.

Yet when Everton faced Wimbledon on the last day of the 1994/95 season, needing a win to avoid relegation, Limpar was both hero and villain. Just four minutes in he inexplicably handled the ball in his own area leading to a penalty, which Dean Holdsworth converted. But when Everton slipped 2-0 behind, Limpar led the comeback, winning a dubious penalty that Graham Stuart converted.

An unhappy substitute through the summer's World Cup in the United States as Sweden finished third (but Limpar played just 17 minutes), on his return he

HE WAS DUBBED THE 'BLUE BRAZILIAN' AFTER AN AUDACIOUS LOB OVER THE ASTON VILLA GOALKEEPER

An entirely different player to the Swede, he added the power and pace of an express train and thrived on Limpar's searching passes. Never was this better evidenced than when Limpar danced past three defenders to feed the Ukrainian for his second, and decisive, goal in the Anfield derby in November.

TROUBLED BY inconsistency towards the end of the 1995/96 season, at the campaign's conclusion Royle brought in Gary Speed after trying to offload Limpar to Marseilles. There was always a nagging sense that the Everton manager preferred the solid over the spectacular, or the physically imperious Kanchelskis to the somewhat slight Limpar. From hereon his chances were limited, and with the addition of Nick Barmby in November 1996 his days at Everton were all but over. He made his last appearance as a substitute in a lacklustre game against Wimbledon in December 1996, briefly adding flair to a team devoid of invention. Royle had decided that he no longer required the services of the man who, in his own words, was 'occasionally reminiscent of Cruyff' and offloaded him to Birmingham City the following month for £100,000. It was an unsatisfactory end for a dazzling talent.

subsequently fell out with the calamitous Mike Walker. By the time Joe Royle became manager in November, speculation linked the Swede to moves to the continent and Japan, but the new boss persuaded him to stay. 'When I first came here I was amazed by what I saw,' said Royle. 'He is incredible. In terms of pure skill I have never worked with anyone like him.' This was high praise indeed from a man who once played alongside Alex Young and Colin Harvey.

Arguably Limpar's two best games in an Everton shirt came in the 1995 FA Cup run. In the semi-final against Tottenham, he made a mockery of Stuart Nethercott's attempts to mark him, inspiring a crushing 4-1 victory. In the final against Manchester United, it was Limpar who robbed Paul Ince of the ball before running 50 yards and releasing Matt Jackson, who set up Paul Rideout's winner. It was, he later said, 'probably my best performance for Everton' – despite hobbling off after an hour due to injury.

During the 1995/96 season Limpar was unquestionably at his best when playing with new signing Andrei Kanchelskis on the opposite wing.

[FACTFILE]

BORN
Solna, Sweden, 24 September 1965

POSITION
Winger

OTHER CLUBS
Orgyte (Sweden, 1986–88); Young Boys (Switzerland, 1988–89); Cremonese (Italy, 1989–90); Arsenal (1990–94); Birmingham City (1997); AIK Fotboll (Sweden, 1998–99); Colorado Rapids (US, 1999–2000); Djurgardens IF (Sweden, 2000–01)

HONOURS
1995 FA Cup; 58 Sweden caps (1987-96) (6 goals)

Season	League		FA Cup		League Cup		Other		Total	
	App	Goals	App	Goals	App	Goals	App	Goals	App	Goals
1993/94	9	0	0	0	0	0	-	-	9	0
1994/95	19 (8)	2	5 (1)	1	0	0	-	-	24 (9)	3
1995/96	22 (6)	3	2 (2)	0	1	0	4	0	29(8)	3
1996/97	1 (1)	0	0	0	1	0	-	-	2 (1)	0
Total	**51 (15)**	**5**	**7 (3)**	**1**	**2**	**0**	**4**	**0**	**64 (18)**	**6**

Linderoth, Tobias

Anonymous Swedish international midfielder beset by injury woes

Signed in the dying days of Walter Smith's managerial reign, Everton reputedly beat off a whole host of Premier League and Serie A clubs to capture the £2.5million signing of Swedish international defensive midfielder, Tobias Linderoth. He came from good footballing stock: his father, Anders Linderoth, was in the 1970s a distinguished international and later a well-regarded coach in Sweden.

Hopes that Linderoth may emerge as the midfield anchor Everton had been crying out for since the days of Joe Parkinson or Peter

Reid were soon confounded. The only attributes he shared with his forbears was a hideous susceptibility to injury, which sidelined him for most of his first 18 months at the club. Given his chance in the disastrous 2003/04 campaign, he showed glimpses of composure and good positioning, but no adventure or sense that he might ever take the game by the scruff of the neck. Indeed for the most part he was hugely ineffective.

With just a year remaining on his contract, in the summer of 2004 David Moyes decided that a £1million offer from FC Copenhagen was too good to resist, and Linderoth returned to

Scandinavia. This fee was reinvested in the acquisition of Tim Cahill – proof, perhaps, that every cloud has a silver lining.

[FACTFILE]

BORN
Marseilles, 21 April 1979
POSITION
Midfield
OTHER CLUBS
Elfsborg (1996–98); Stabaek (1998–2002);
FC Copenhagen (2004–07);
Galatasatay (2007–10)
HONOURS
76 Sweden caps
(2 goals) (1999–2008)

Season	League		FA Cup		League Cup		Total	
	App	Goals	App	Goals	App	Goals	App	Goals
2001/02	4 (4)	0	2 (1)	0	0	0	6 (5)	0
2002/03	2 (3)	0	0	0	1	0	3 (3)	0
2003/04	23 (4)	0	0	0	1 (1)	1	24 (5)	1
Total	**29(11)**	**0**	**2 (1)**	**0**	**2 (1)**	**1**	**33(13)**	**1**

Lindley, Maurice

Long-standing servant whose first-team opportunities were fleeting

Maurice Lindley was part of a generation whose prospects for a top-class playing career were wrecked by the outbreak of the Second World War.

The Yorkshireman was signed as a raw 19-year-old in 1935, but scarcely could he have imagined then that over a decade would

pass before he turned out before the Goodison faithful.

INCREDIBLY, although he played in wartime games, Lindley's full Everton debut did not come until September 1947, when he was nearing his 32nd birthday and had been on Everton's books for some 12 years. He served as a deputy to wing half Jackie Grant and also to the up and coming T.E. Jones at centre back. A first-team shirt was never assured, however, and his career was little more than that of a journeyman's in a dire Everton team.

In 1953, after barely a half-century of senior games in an Everton career that had spanned almost two decades, Lindley

joined the coaching staff of Swindon Town. He was appointed manager a year later, but the spell was short-lived. He spent six months as secretary-manager of Barry Town, then in 1955 he followed the path set by his former Everton team-mate Harry Catterick and became Crewe manager, a position he held for three years.

Lindley then joined the Leeds United coaching staff at a time when the club was revolutionised by the management of Don Revie. Lindley was responsible for player recruitment and brought such players as Peter Lorimer,

Billy Bremner, Terry Cooper and latterly David Seaman through the Elland Road ranks. Later he served as Bradford City's chief scout, continuing to work until his late seventies.

[FACTFILE]

BORN
Keighley, 5 December 1915
DIED
1994
POSITION
Centre back / wing half
OTHER CLUBS AS MANAGER
Swindon Town 1954–55;
Crewe Alexandra 1955–58

Season	League		FA Cup		Total	
	App	Goals	App	Goals	App	Goals
1947/48	17	0	0	0	17	0
1948/49	11	0	1	0	12	0
1949/50	2	0	0	0	2	0
1950/51	8	0	0	0	8	0
1951/52	13	0	2	0	15	0
Total	**51**	**0**	**3**	**0**	**54**	**0**

Lindsay, Billy

Son of the Northeast who deputised in defence during the 1893/94 season

Season	League App	League Goals	FA Cup App	FA Cup Goals	Total App	Total Goals
1893/94	9	0	0	0	9	0
Total	9	0	0	0	9	0

[FACTFILE]

BORN
Stockton,
10 December 1872
DIED
1933
POSITION
Full back
OTHER CLUBS
Stockton St John's;
Stockton Town;
Grimsby Town (1894–97);
Newcastle United
(1897–99);
Luton Town (2 spells);
Watford; Hitchin Town

Lindsay, Jack

Left back who was unlucky with the timing of his Everton career

Jack Lindsay had the misfortune of joining Everton in March 1951, just weeks before they suffered the ignominy of relegation to the Second Division. In April 1954, as the club stood on the cusp of promotion back to the top flight following a campaign in which Lindsay had played an important role, he suffered an horrific leg break in a home draw with Stoke City. He never played for Everton again and thus ended one of the unluckiest careers the club has known.

ONE OF THE UNLUCKIEST CAREERS THE CLUB HAS KNOWN

The left back was a £9500 signing from Glasgow Rangers amid one of the most catastrophic periods in Everton history. Everton were 17th at the time of his arrival but a run of just one win in their last 11 games left them rock bottom. Lindsay took place in the final-day nadir, a 6-0 hammering at Sheffield Wednesday – who were also relegated – that secured them last place.

LINDSAY WAS, like many full backs of the era, a hard, muscular

JACK LINDSAY - EVERTON
... ...NG - EVERTON F.C. (1955)

player; a defender first and foremost, but not averse to hoisting in the odd delivery for the formidable temples of Dave Hickson. In the 1953/54 season he was elected penalty taker and kept his nerve to score a couple of goals.

But then came the injury and everything changed. His break was so horrific as to keep him in hospital for a month and out of the Everton first XI for ever. In May 1956 he was sold to Bury with John Willie Parker in a joint deal worth £3500.

[FACTFILE]

BORN
Auchinair,
East Dunbartonshire,
8 August 1924
DIED
1991
POSITION
Full back
OTHER CLUBS
Glasgow Rangers (1946–51);
Worcester City (1954–56);
Bury (1956–57)

Season	League App	League Goals	FA Cup App	FA Cup Goals	Total App	Total Goals
1950/51	4	0	0	0	4	0
1951/52	40	0	2	0	42	0
1952/53	30	0	5	0	35	0
1953/54	31	2	3	0	34	2
Total	105	2	10	0	115	2

EVERTON FOOTBALL CLUB
GOODISON PARK LIVERPOOL

SEASON 1953-4
OFFICIAL PROGRAMME
3D

Lineker, Gary

Impeccable goalscorer who built his reputation during his Goodison sojourn

Rarely has football enjoyed an ambassador like Gary Lineker. Clean-cut, good-looking and suave, Lineker possessed – and continues to do so – the assuredness and populist touch of a film star or politician. In being considered both footballer and modern icon, he was a forerunner, perhaps, of David Beckham. Second only to Bobby Charlton as England's all-time goalscorer and well remembered for spells at Tottenham and Barcelona, it seemingly eludes popular memory that it was Goodison where Lineker made his reputation during a prolific year-long spell in the mid-1980s.

SELDOM have Everton possessed a goalscorer like Lineker. Although possessing a blistering turn of pace and a good first touch, Lineker had few of the attributes commonly associated with world-class forwards. He was weak in the air and outside the penalty area his contribution was negligible. The rocket shot for which other forwards have found fame was lacking. By his own admission he hated training and felt a series of naps was the best way to prepare for a game. And yet, he had an almost subliminal instinct for being in the right place at the right time. His predatory instincts and timing were impeccable. He anticipated chances like a wildcat waiting upon its prey. If a loose ball fell within yards of him in the penalty area, Lineker was invariably there to meet it, sometimes with only the merest of touches – but usually it was enough.

> **LINEKER'S PHENOMENAL GOALSCORING SAW HIM CROWNED PFA AND FOOTBALL WRITERS' PLAYER OF THE YEAR**

Lineker started out at Leicester City, his boyhood club, in the late 1970s, forgoing the opportunity to represent his county at cricket in favour of football. Even in a mediocre Leicester team, he built a reputation as one of the country's foremost goalscorers, earning a first England cap in 1984. In July 1985, Howard Kendall made him Everton's record signing after paying £800,000 for Lineker and courting opprobrium by selling Andy Gray.

Indeed, Lineker initially did little to relieve the pressure from Kendall, drawing blanks in the Charity Shield game against Man United as well as his first three league outings. His single goal which won the away game against Tottenham signalled the start of a goal deluge, and a hat-trick – the first of three that season – in the 4-1 romp over Birmingham City the following Saturday soon won over Evertonians.

LINEKER, it seemed, could not stop scoring, but by spring the Midas touch had started to elude him. Having been reliant on his goals – 24 in the league alone by 1 March – Lineker scored just one First Division goal in the next seven weeks. Top of the league until late April, Everton needed to win a game in hand at Oxford United on 30 April to remain in touch with their title challenge. Lineker needed to come up with

the goods, but his 'lucky' boots which he had worn all season to great effect, it emerged before the game, were in Liverpool for repairs.

In a tight, scrappy game, on 66 minutes Lineker was played through one-on-one with Alan Judge, the Oxford goalkeeper. Normally clinical in such positions, his shot was blocked. Oxford scored a late winner and the title went to Liverpool. (The boots issue should not be overlooked, for when they were returned to Lineker he scored six goals in Everton's final three games.)

Lineker's phenomenal goalscoring saw him crowned PFA and Football Writers' Player of the Year. He also won the European Golden Boot and second place in

the European Footballer of the Year poll. At that summer's Mexico World Cup he finished top scorer with six goals, including a hat-trick against Poland. By then, speculation was rife about Lineker's future, with Barcelona, who were also closely linked to Howard Kendall, leading the running. In July 1986, Kendall shocked Evertonians by accepting a bid of £2.2million from the Catalan giants.

Lineker spent three years in Spain, returning to England with Tottenham in 1989. He starred in the 1990 World Cup, but Bobby Charlton's England goals record remained elusive. After calling time on his international career in 1992, Lineker made a personally lucrative move to Japan, where he

> EVERTON WERE THE ONLY TEAM I EVER PLAYED FOR WHEN, IF YOU WENT A GOAL UP IN A MATCH, YOU KNEW YOU HAD IT WON

played out an injury-riddled two years with Nagoya Grampus 8 in the nascent J-League. On his return to England in the mid-1990s he set out on a hugely successful broadcasting career, in 1999 becoming host of Match of the Day.

THERE remains a lingering sense among Evertonians that Lineker plays down his time at Goodison. But periodically he attempts to set the record straight. In 2002 he wrote in his Daily Telegraph column that he had never wanted to leave Everton, that they were the best team he had ever played for and possessed a superior side to Barcelona. 'The Cup final apart, Everton were the only team I ever played for when, if you went a goal up in a match, you knew you had it won,' he wrote. 'They were also the only team I played for whose names I can still reel off – Southall, Stevens, Van Den Hauwe, Ratcliffe, Mountfield, Steven, Bracewell, Reid, Sheedy, Sharp and me. And they say I never talk about Everton.'

	League		FA Cup		League Cup		Other		Total	
Season	App	Goals	App	Goals	App	Goals	App	Goals	App	Goals
1985/86	41	30	6	5	5	3	5	2	57	40
Total	41	30	6	5	5	3	5	2	57	40

Livingstone, Archie

Inside forward who cameoed with Everton at the veteran stage of a war-interrupted career

Livingston, Dugald 'Duggie'

Scottish full back turned trailblazing international manager

	League		FA Cup		Total	
Season	App	Goals	App	Goals	App	Goals
1946/47	4	2	9	9	4	2
Total	4	2	0	0	4	2

	League		FA Cup		Total	
Season	App	Goals	App	Goals	App	Goals
1921/22	24	0	1	0	25	0
1922/23	8	0	2	0	10	0
1923/24	38	0	2	0	40	0
1924/25	20	0	0	0	20	0
1925/26	5	0	0	0	5	0
Total	95	0	5	0	100	0

EVERTON F.C. 1956-57

EVERTON 1956
Back row - **Sutherland, Tansey, O'Neill, Jones, Kirby,**
Front - **McNamara, Eglington, Farrell, Llewellyn, Glazzard, Rea**

Llewellyn,
Bert

Pocket-sized reserve forward turned prolific lower league goalpoacher

[FACTFILE]

BORN
Golborne, 5 February 1939
POSITION
Centre forward
OTHER CLUBS
Crewe Alexandra (1958–60);
Port Vale (1960–63);
Northampton Town (1963);
Walsall (1963–65);
Wigan Athletic

Season	League		FA Cup		Total	
	App	Goals	App	Goals	App	Goals
1956/57	10	2	0	0	10	2
1957/58	1	0	0	0	1	0
Total	**11**	**2**	**0**	**0**	**11**	**2**

Lochhead,
Alex

Defensively minded Scottish international who made royal blue Anfield cameos

[FACTFILE]

BORN
12 May 1866
POSITION
Half back
OTHER CLUBS
Third Lanark; Heart of Midlothian
HONOURS
1 Scotland cap (1889)

Season	League		FA Cup		Total	
	App	Goals	App	Goals	App	Goals
1890/91	1	0	0	0	1	0
1891/92	5	0	0	0	5	0
Total	**6**	**0**	**0**	**0**	**6**	**0**

Lodge,
Paul

Young midfielder who failed to make the Goodison grade

[FACTFILE]

BORN
Liverpool, 13 February 1961
POSITION
Midfield
OTHER CLUBS
Wigan Athletic (loan, 1982);
Rotherham United (loan, 1982–83);
Preston North End (1983–84);
Bolton Wanderers (1984–85);
Port Vale (loan, 1984–85);
Stockport County (1985–86)

Along with such other promising youngsters as Kevin Ratcliffe, Graeme Sharp and Steve McMahon, Paul Lodge was a player in whom Gordon Lee vested Everton's 1980s hopes. Handed his debut in a 3-1 defeat to Aston Villa in February 1981, Lodge was given an extended run as the 1980/81 season fizzled to its disappointing conclusion.

Considered a more promising and naturally gifted prospect than McMahon, Lodge was given another run under Howard Kendall's watch midway through the following campaign. While his natural talent was never in question, he seemed to lack the physicality or guile to cut it in the hurly-burly of the First Division. After a couple of loan moves in the first half of the 1982/83 season, Lodge was sold to Preston North End in February 1983. He played in the lower leagues for a couple of years but by his mid-twenties had slipped out of the professional game.

Season	League		FA Cup		League Cup		Total	
	App	Goals	App	Goals	App	Goals	App	Goals
1980/81	8 (3)	0	0	0	0	0	8 (3)	0
1981/82	12 (1)	0	1	0	2	0	15 (1)	0
1982/83	0	0	0	0	0	0	0	0
Total	**20 (4)**	**0**	**1**	**0**	**2**	**0**	**23 (4)**	**0**

Lowe,
Harry

Reserve left back who made cameos in Everton's back-to-back title wins

[FACTFILE]

BORN
Skelmersdale, 19 February 1907
DIED
1975
POSITION
Left back
OTHER CLUBS
Skelmersdale (1927–29);
Preston North End (1932–38);
Swindon Town (1939)

Season	League		FA Cup		Total	
	App	Goals	App	Goals	App	Goals
1930/31	4	0	0	0	4	0
1931/32	1	0	0	0	1	0
Total	**5**	**0**	**0**	**0**	**5**	**0**

Lyons, Mick

Spirited star of the 1970s

Some called him a jinx, citing that he never won a trophy or even a derby match. Others, including Gordon Lee, used to say that if you cut Mick Lyons, he would bleed blue. Of course, this was an oft-used cliché, but – jinx or not – the sentiments underlying it were true: for few men have been as devoted or offered such courageous service to Everton as Lyons.

BORN IN Liverpool and bred an Evertonian, Lyons worked his way through the club's youth system to fulfil a life's dream and make his debut against Nottingham Forest in March 1971, scoring in a 3-2 away defeat. As a boy he had watched Everton from the Gwladys Street, witnessing the 1963 title win and the dramas of the 1966 FA Cup Final. Such was his devotion to his hero, Jimmy Gabriel, that at his confirmation he adopted his name.

Lyons had progressed through the Everton youth teams as a centre forward, but the emergence of David Johnson restricted his progress and Tommy Casey converted him to centre half.

Through the early stages of his first-team career he would alternate between the two positions. Called upon to assist in an injury crisis during the 1971/72 campaign, Lyons seemed to deputise for John Hurst one week and Joe Royle the next. It was a similar story until mid-decade, when Billy Bingham decided that he was most effective deployed as centre back on a permanent basis. Even then he was often thrown up front as an emergency striker if Everton were chasing a late winner or equaliser.

Lyons goal-scoring abilities saw him finish leading scorer during the 1973/74 season, the first campaign in which he could call a first-team shirt his own. Nevertheless his technique was often questioned by exacting sections of the Goodison support. The implication from his critics was that he was a 'crude' player and 'all heart and no brains'. Yet this dismissal was harsh. Not since Dave Hickson had there been a player willing to put his head in places where other players thought twice about putting their feet. And his kamikaze approach was often inspirational at a time when Everton were said to lack spirit.

LYONS PROSPERED under Gordon Lee, who preferred solid players to extroverts such as Duncan McKenzie. He was ever-present during the 1977/78 season as Everton finished third – their highest position during his Everton career – and virtually a permanent fixture the following season, when Everton finished fourth. But thereafter his career went into decline as Everton waned during Gordon Lee's final two seasons at the club. A 40-yard volleyed own goal in a 1979 derby match marked him as an object of derision, and only a television strike meant that his blunder wasn't captured for posterity.

The simultaneous emergence of Mark Higgins, Kevin Ratcliffe and Billy Wright at the turn of the decade brought Lyons' first-team place under threat. Midway through the 1981/82 season, Howard Kendall dropped him in favour of Wright. He returned briefly to the first team, marking his final start in an Everton shirt at Goodison against Manchester United in April 1982 with a goal – just as he had announced his arrival 11 years earlier.

That summer Kendall sold Lyons, now aged 30, to Sheffield Wednesday, where he spent three years. There was a spell as player-manager of Grimsby Town, before he returned to Goodison as reserve team coach under Colin Harvey. Later he filled a similar position at Wigan Athletic. In the 1990s he immigrated to Australia where he is now a highly regarded coach.

IN THREE Sides of the Mersey a (possibly apocryphal) story was recounted by a supporter who claimed to have met Lyons in a pub the day he was sold. The player had been crying his eyes out. 'It was as if his wife had left him,' recalled the fan. 'Of course she hadn't, he'd been sold by the club he loved, but I wonder whether he would have been as upset if she had ditched him!' But such are the realities of football: spirit and devotion are no guarantees for success.

Season	League		FA Cup		League Cup		Other		Total	
	App	Goals	App	Goals	App	Goals	App	Goals	App	Goals
1970/71	1 (1)	1	1	0	0	0	0	0	2 (1)	1
1971/72	20 (4)	3	4	0	0	0	-	-	24 (4)	3
1972/73	19 (6)	2	0 (1)	0	1	0	-	-	20(7)	2
1973/74	37 (4)	9	3	0	1	0	2	0	43 (4)	9
1974/75	36 (2)	8	4	3	2	0	-	-	42(2)	11
1975/76	42	5	1	0	5	1	2	0	50	6
1976/77	39 (1)	4	7	1	9	2	2	0	55 (1)	7
1977/78	42	5	2	1	5	2	-	-	49	8
1978/79	37	6	1	0	2	0	3	0	43	6
1979/80	35 (4)	0	6	0	5	0	2	0	48(4)	0
1980/81	30 (3)	2	5 (1)	1	0	0	-	-	35(4)	3
1981/82	26 (1)	3	1	0	4	0	-	-	31 (1)	3
Total	**364 (26)**	**48**	**35(2)**	**6**	**37**	**5**	**9**	**0**	**445(28)**	**59**

[FACTFILE]

BORN
Liverpool, 8 December 1951
POSITION
Centre half / centre forward
OTHER CLUBS
Sheffield Wednesday (1982–85);
Grimsby Town (player-manager, 1985–87)

Liverpool, and Everton

The enthralling rivalry that defines football – and life – on Merseyside

The relationship between Merseyside's two great clubs is at once more complex, passionate, divisive, irrational and intertwined than anyone gives it credit. The rivalry, in many ways, defines Everton and Evertonians, and although for Liverpool this is less marked, it is a central tenet of the club's identity. In many ways this entry needs an entire book of its own to unravel the shared history and contradictions that cut to the core of Everton and Liverpool and football on Merseyside.

Uniquely, the birth of Liverpool came from a faction within the Everton committee room. The club's father, John Houlding, was Everton's president, Anfield, their home for their entire existance, Everton's former residence. Houlding even tried to name Liverpool 'The Everton Football Club and Atheltic Ground Company Ltd' – an attempt that was rejected by Somerset House. Given such a fissure, the split and its implications might have precipitated civil war in Merseyside football and produced a football rivalry akin to that of Rangers and Celtic.

But from the outset there were constant interactions between the two clubs. Many of Everton's first big stars - Fred Geary, Alex Latta, Andrew Hannah – went on to play for the new club. An Everton committeeman, John McKenna,

became Liverpool chairman and shared a long and close friendship with his Everton counterpart, Will Cuff. The death of Houlding in March 1902 undoubtedly eased tensions, and after it flags were flown at half-mast at Goodison and three Everton players joined three Liverpool players as pall-bearers. In the 1920s a former Everton player, Tom Compton, would succeed McKenna as Liverpool chairman. Thomas Keates recalled: 'The breach caused great bitterness of feeling, which, after a time, gradually subsided. For many years the directors and members of Liverpool and Everton have been on friendly terms.' Between 1904 and 1935 the two clubs even printed joint match programmes, a collaboration which fostered some sense of unity and shared identity.

What emerged in the first sixty years of the twentieth century was a traditional city rivalry, with the added complexity of Liverpool's birth. Football, ultimately, was the winner for the intensity of emotions it provoked. Merseyside boasted English football's premium derby encounter. There were no real sectarian or geographic splits in the fanbases, and supporters of each club would often attend each other's matches. There was a perception that Everton were the aristocrats and Liverpool the plucky outsiders. Certainly, a glance around their stadiums – Anfield basic and rudimentary, Goodison a veritable football palace – would heighten that impression.

The dynamics started to change in the late-1950s. Although Everton's patrician owner, John Moores, held stakes in both clubs, divisions started to emerge. First there was Dave Hickson's hugely controversial transfer across Stanley Park to Liverpool in 1959. Then there was Bill Shankly's arrival as Liverpool manager a year later, which changed the course of Liverpool's history and

the world's perceptions of the club. From being rooted in the Second Division, within less than a generation Liverpool were transformed into the greatest club in Europe. This shift in the status quo came at a time when football was starting to be transformed by the television revolution, and millions of long distance fans became entranced by Liverpool's ascent. From having a local fanbase, Liverpool became one of the first clubs in the world to not only have genuinely national support, but a global fanbase too.

The shifting sands of Merseyside football also coincided with Liverpool's rise as the ultimate bogey team. Four times they met Everton in FA Cup semi-finals; twice in the FA Cup final and once in the League Cup final and each time the outcome was depressingly familiar: Liverpool victorious. In 1986 they pipped Everton to both the League and FA Cup at the very death, rubbing salt into the wound caused by the Heysel Stadium riot twelve months beforehand, when the actions of Liverpool's supporters led to the deaths of 39 fans, a ban on English clubs' entry into European competition, and with it the break up and demise of arguably Everton's greatest ever team. Other incidents have also grated: Clive Thomas in 1977; Alan Hansen's handball in the 1984 Milk Cup Final; the departure of Nick Barmby in 2000. Even in otherwise inconsequential league derby matches, favour has invariably favoured the red side of Merseyside, as witness Graham Poll's outrageous decision to blow his final whistle when a goalbound winner was sailing into the Liverpool net in the 2000 Goodison derby. Or Jack Rodwell's dismissal for a completely legitimate tackle on Luis Suarez in 2011.

Heysel was a defining moment for football on Merseyside. It took several years for its full implications

to sink in, and even a year after the riot Everton and Liverpool fans stood alongside each other at Wembley in the first all-Merseyside FA Cup Final, chanting 'Merseyside, Merseyside'. But as Everton went into a late-1980s decline and Liverpool were welcomed back into European competition a year ahead of their ban ending, the injustice of what had passed began to take hold on Merseyside football.

From the mid-1990s the friendly derby deteriorated markedly. It became virtually impossible to openly sit with opposing fans on derby day and though violence remains limited to small incidents, bad feeling dominates. 'It's only really crept in the last ten years,' Graeme Sharp told this author in 2006. 'I don't really know why it is. People come up with their own reasons – Heysel, Man United's dominance – but I just think you have a younger element now who don't realise the historic importance for both clubs, and have spoiled it. It's not nice coming to derby games now as there could be trouble. That's something that never ever happened before.' A greater readiness to discuss Heysel's implications also exists now than in the past, giving way to resentment.

The dynamic of the derby has changed also: Sky TV has increased the reach and fan base of Liverpool rather than Everton, and supporters from outside the city are more likely to put importance on crunch matches against Man Utd and Chelsea than Everton, where the main significance is on local bragging rights. Evertonians, who are still very localised, are particularly dismissive of the out of towners. The relationship was unquestionably soured by Rafael Benitez's ungracious reference to Everton as a 'small club', while Liverpool fans have never forgiven David Moyes for pronouncing Everton 'The People's Club.'

But despite the divisions, very strong unity does still underpin the rivalry. After the Hillsborough Stadium disaster in 1989 the two clubs united in grief and, fittingly, Liverpool's first game back after the disaster was at Goodison. Despite Colin Harvey's appeals for 'a typical ding dong affair', the occasion was marked not by the standard of football on offer, but for the show of unity between rival sets of supporters. At half time the pitch, previously ringed by the deathly metal fences, was circled by a chain of ninety-five red, blue and white scarves to commemorate the dead. A forty foot banner draped amongst the ranks of Liverpool fans massed at the Stanley Park End gave a message to the watching nation: 'The Kop thanks you. We never walked alone.' Similarly, following the murder of the Everton-supporting schoolboy, Rhys Jones in August 2007, Anfield reverberated to the tune of Z-Cars ahead of a Champions League game against Toulouse a week later; a touching, moving and generous gesture.

Interest and passion for the game and its immersion in the consciousness of every single person on Merseyside is without parallel. One club cities – such as Leeds and Newcastle – are all the poorer for not having their football played against such a backdrop. Other top level rivalries – Birmingham, Sheffield, Manchester and (North) London – have seen the intensity of passions, and with it the standard of their derby matches as spectacles, diluted by the mediocrity of one or both of their teams throughout most of the century long sweep in which they have existed. Indeed, 120 years after Liverpool's birth from a split in the Everton committee room, football on Merseyside remains the city's secular religion, Anfield and Goodison its twin temples.

Key figures
John Houlding

Demonised for being Liverpool's founding father, Houlding was one of the key personalities who brought league football to Goodison and oversaw the club's early rise. A successful brewer and local conservative politician (who later became Lord Mayor of Liverpool), his tenure as Everton President in the 1880s coinicided with the period when the club rose from the embers of a church team, to move into a fine purpose built ground at Anfield, take on professional players and enter the Football League as founder members. Only later did the cost of this influence become apparent, when he tried to profit from his role as Anfield's landlord. This, of course, led to the defection to Goodison and the notorious 'split' which bore his new team at his now empty stadium – Liverpool FC.

Dave Hickson

Players have passed between Anfield and Goodison throughout history, but no transfer has been more controversial or divisive than that which brought Dave Hickson's second spell at Everton to an end in 1959 and brought him to Anfield. Outraged letters filled the pages of the local press from both sets of supporters, with some Evertonians seeing through pledges to go and see their idol at Anfield. Hickson never played in the top flight again and later joined Tranmere Rovers, becoming the first major player to turn out for all three Merseyside clubs.

Key meetings
1971 FA Cup semi final

Has there been a more catastrophic few days in Everton's history than those in March 1971? Everton had had a poor league season defending their seventh league title, but found themselves in the quarter final of the European Cup and the semi final of the FA Cup. On the Wednesday they flew to Greece to face Panathinaikos, where they ran a gamut of intimidation and went out on away goals. 72 hours later Everton's tired players returned to face Liverpool at Old Trafford. Everton made a blistering start and took the lead through Alan Ball in the tenth minute. Five minutes after half time the complexion of the match completely changed when Brian Labone limped off with an injury. Liverpool equalised and scored a second half winner. Labone never fully recovered from his injury and Everton went into steep decline. Liverpool, by contrast, didn't stop winning for the next 20 years.

27 MARCH 1971
Old Trafford; FA Cup Semi Final; 62,144
Everton 1 Liverpool 2 (Ball)
Rankin, Wright, Newton, Kendall, Labone (Brown), Harvey, Whittle, Ball, Royle, Hurst, Morrissey,

1986
FA Cup Final

As late as February, when they beat Liverpool in the Anfield derby, Everton seemed odds on to retain their First Division title. In an ordinary season their tally of 86 points would easily have been enough. But Liverpool's form after that 2-0 defeat was extraordinary while Everton laboured at the last and finished runners up. The first all Merseyside FA Cup Final offered some sort of redemption for Howard Kendall's men, however, and with the city on its knees economically and derided by the rest of the country, a sort of showcase for Merseyside. It seems extraordinary now that fans and players mingled together before and after the match, while shouts of 'Merseypride' went up.

On the pitch, however, the script followed a familiar pattern. Gary Lineker offered hope when his fortieth goal of the season put Everton in front at half time. But Liverpool turned the game around in the second half and ran out 3-1 winners, in the process claiming the double.

10 MAY 1986
Wembley; FA Cup Final; 98,000
Everton 1 (Lineker) Liverpool 3
Mimms, Stevens (Heath), Van Den Hauwe, Ratcliffe, Mountfield, Reid, Steven, Lineker, Sharp, Bracewell, Sheedy

THE

EVERTON
·ENCYCLOPEDIA·

Jock **Maconnachie**, Mickael **Madar**, Teddy **Magner**, Aidan **Maher**, George **Mahon**, Harry **Makepeace**, Willie **Maley**, **Manchester United** and Everton, Joe **Marsden**, Cliff **Marshall**, Ian **Marshall**, George **Martin**, Marco **Materazzi**, Alan **Maxwell**, Derek **Mayers**, Tommy **Mayson**, Conor **McAleny**, Neil **McBain**, Brian **McBride**, Joe **McBride**, Stuart **McCall**, Jimmy **McCambridge**, Gavin **McCann**, Joe **McClure**, Harry **McCormick**, Tommy **McDermott**, Jim **McDonagh**, Alex **McDonald**, Jock **McDonald**, Neil **McDonald**, James **McFadden**, Rab **McFarlane**, Jimmy **McGourty**, Johnny **McIlhatton**, Tom **McInnes**, Jimmy **McIntosh**, Tom **McIntosh**, Duncan **McKenzie**, Archibald **McKinnon**, John **McLaughlin**, William **McLaughlin**, Duncan **McLean**, Kevin **McLeod**, Steve **McMahon**, James **McMillan**, Tony **McNamara**, Ken **McNaught**, Lachlan **McPherson**, Mick **Meagan**, Peter **Meehan**, Gary **Megson**, George **Meiklejohn**, Bob **Menham**, Charles **Menham**, Joe **Mercer**, Sammy **Meston**, James **Meunier**, William **Michaels**, Harry **Miller**, Jimmy **Miller**, Dusty **Miller**, George **Milligan**, Jamie **Milligan**, Mike **Milligan**, Alf **Milward**, Bobby **Mimms**, Frank **Mitchell**, Hugh **Moffatt**, Andy **Moffatt**, George **Molyneux**, Eric **Moore**, Joe-Max **Moore**, Neil **Moore**, Sir John **Moores**, R.**Morris**, Johnny **Morrissey (Jnr)**, Johnny **Morrissey (Snr)**, Harry **Morton**, Derek **Mountfield**, David **Moyes**, Willie **Muir**, C. **Murray**, David B. **Murray**, David J. **Murray**, Joe **Murray**, T. **Murray**, Shkodran **Mustafi**, Thomas **Myhre**

Maconnachie,
John 'Jock'

Talented left back who captained the club and won the 1915 League Championship

For over a decade Scottish defender John Maconnachie was a rock in the heart of the Everton team, a classy dependable lynchpin of the club's backline. The left back captained Everton with distinction for three seasons – almost leading the club to the First Division title in 1911/12 – before winning football's ultimate accolade in 1915 under the leadership of Jimmy Galt.

Signed as a 19-year-old ahead of the 1907/08 season from Hibernian, there were high hopes for the defender, who could play at half back, centre half and full back. 'Maconnachie made a very promising debut, tackling well, and passing nicely, but he would be even more successful with a little dash as he is at times rather inclined to take matters too easily,' recorded the Liverpool Courier of his debut versus Preston North End. He was given an extended run over the Christmas period as half back, and the same newspaper added: 'It seems as if the proper position for Maconnachie has been found. He played a really fine game at right half, a tendency to break the rule as to throws-in being a fault, which can easily be remedied.'

Yet it was at left back that Maconnachie became a genuine first choice at Goodison and ultimately made his name. So good was he that he supplanted William Balmer ahead of the 1908/09 season and was ever-present in the left defensive berth. The player, purred one correspondent, was 'cool and sedate in his clearance' and always a man to play the ball rather than hoof and hope, as many defenders were expected to during this era. The 'fair-haired Scot gave a fine display of cool and polished full back play', wrote Merseyside football historian Percy Young,

which ensured 'classical standards prevailed in defence'.

For the 1911/12 season Maconnachie was elected to captain. Everton started the campaign slowly, winning just two of their first eight games – which would prove costly – before building up form. By April they were neck and neck with leaders Sunderland but the captain suddenly found himself curtailed by injury. He was missing for what was, in effect, the title decider at Roker Park on 6 April. Everton capitulated 4-0 and although Maconnachie returned for the final five games of the season it was too late. Sunderland were champions, three points ahead of runners-up Everton.

ALTHOUGH EVERTON faltered over the subsequent two seasons, Maconnachie's reputation continued to grow. 'Macconnachie

was on the top of his form, and everyone who has followed Everton football knows what that means,' reported one local paper in 1913. 'His anticipation of opponents' movements was accurate throughout, and on two occasions when the situation appeared hopeless he took risks and saved his keeper.'

AFTER EVERTON finished the 1913/14 season in a lowly 15th place, the captaincy passed to Jimmy Galt. Maconnachie was a rock as Everton overcame their serial nearly-men hoodoo and squeaked over the line in 1914/15 as League Champions for the second time in the club's history. Thomas Keates wrote: 'Fairly free from injuries, and the resultant changes they involve, the combination was admirable, the accurate passing methodic, and the attack dashing. The team played so brilliantly and consistently that they also reached the semi-final in the Cup ties, injuries … apparently robbing them of what would have been a splendid double achievement, if the usual team had been able to play in the semi-final.' He added: 'our gratification was chilled by the catastrophe of the Great War. Football players were soon absorbed in the fighting forces, and for four years the ordinary League fixtures were suspended.'

In football terms this was calamitous indeed. Maconnachie barely played in the regional leagues from 1916, suggesting he

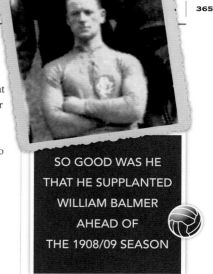

was sent off to fight. When peace came, still aged only 31, he struggled to hold down a first-team place and was sold at the end of the 1919/20 season to Swindon Town. He was also recorded as playing for Djugaarden in Sweden (many years later, Anders Limpar's first club) and in non-league with Barrow and Lowesoft until his forties.

But the financial hardships of a footballer's itinerant life also seem to have taken hold. 'The Chairman reported that the wife of our former player was in very straitened circumstances & it was agreed to grant her assistance of £2 per week until further notice,' reported an Everton board minute in February 1923. 'Secy to make necessary arrangements for payment.' A second grant was made the following July. In October 1930 there was a third request for assistance, but this time it met deaf ears.

Season	League		FA Cup		Total	
	App	Goals	App	Goals	App	Goals
1907/08	21	0	0	0	21	0
1908/09	38	0	2	0	40	0
1909/10	31	0	7	0	38	0
1910/11	22	0	2	0	24	0
1911/12	31	0	5	1	36	1
1912/13	23	4	5	0	28	4
1913/14	35	0	1	0	36	0
1914/15	28	0	3	0	31	0
1919/20	16	2	0	0	16	2
Total	**245**	**6**	**25**	**1**	**270**	**7**

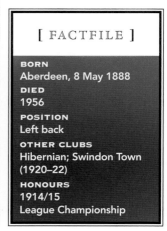

[FACTFILE]

BORN
Aberdeen, 8 May 1888
DIED
1956
POSITION
Left back
OTHER CLUBS
Hibernian; Swindon Town (1920–22)
HONOURS
1914/15 League Championship

Madar, Mickael

Elegant French international centre forward unwanted by Walter Smith

Amid the farcical 1997/98 season, French international centre forward Mickael Madar represented one of the few positives in a dismal campaign. Indeed, in a season in which preservation of the club's top-flight status was only marginal, it could be argued that Madar's six goals saved Everton's skin.

IT COULD BE ARGUED THAT MADAR'S SIX GOALS SAVED EVERTON'S SKIN

SIGNED ON a free transfer from Deportivo La Coruna in December 1997, Madar, who had been part of France's squad at the 1996 European Championships, was still recovering from the effects of a long-term injury. A tall, skilful centre forward, his partnership with Duncan Ferguson made the Everton front line among the most physically imposing in the club's history. But in many ways Madar, with his flicks and shimmies and excellent positional sense, was the antithesis of the physical Ferguson – an elegant contrast to the fiery Scot. He was potent in front of goal and evidently something of a character too. After bravely heading a second-half winner against Blackburn, he memorably ripped off his shirt to reveal an undershirt bearing a photograph of his children to which he pointed manically in celebration.

Yet such theatricals had little place in the new dour order imposed by Walter Smith following his appointment in July 1998. Sent off in a pre-season friendly, Madar was ostracised by the new manager. Asked after a 0-0 draw with Blackburn in September 1998 about his relationship with the manager, Madar responded: 'He's only seen me play twice. The first time I got a hat-trick and the second time, I was sent off too quick for him to make any judgements.' He thought that Everton 'just want to get rid of me and get me off the wage bill'. There followed a brief return to the first team, but in December, just a year after his arrival, Madar was given a free transfer and joined Paris Saint Germain.

[FACTFILE]

BORN
Paris, 8 May 1968
POSITION
Outside left / right
OTHER CLUBS
Sochaux (1987–89);
Stade Laval (1989–90);
Sochaux (1990–92);
Cannes (1992–94);
Monaco (1994–96);
Deportivo La Coruna (1996–97);
Paris Saint Germain (1999–2001);
US Creteil (2001–02)
HONOURS
3 France caps
(1 goal) (1995–96)

Season	League		FA Cup		League Cup		Total	
	App	Goals	App	Goals	App	Goals	App	Goals
1997/98	15 (2)	6	0	0	0	0	15 (2)	6
1998/99	2	0	0	0	0 (1)	0	2 (1)	0
Total	**17 (2)**	**6**	**0**	**0**	**0 (1)**	**0**	**17 (3)**	**6**

Magner, Teddy

Non-league journeyman who made the step up to the big time with Everton

[FACTFILE]

BORN
Newcastle, 1 January 1891
DIED
1948
POSITION
Centre forward
OTHER CLUBS
Stainton Celtic;
West Hartlepool Expansion;
Gainsborough Trinity (1909);
St Mirren

Season	League		FA Cup		Total	
	App	Goals	App	Goals	App	Goals
1910/11	6	2	3	1	9	3
Total	**6**	**2**	**3**	**1**	**9**	**3**

Maher, Aidan

Home-grown wide man limited to a solitary first-team appearance

[FACTFILE]

BORN
Liverpool, 1 December 1946
POSITION
Left winger
OTHER CLUBS
Plymouth Argyle (1968–71);
Tranmere Rovers (1971–72)

Season	League		FA Cup		League Cup		Total	
	App	Goals	App	Goals	App	Goals	App	Goals
1967/68	1	0	0	0	0	0	1	0
Total	1	0	0	0	0	0	1	0

Mahon, George

Committeeman who can be credited as the 'father' of Goodison Park

In the annals of Everton club, few figures have had such a fundamental or lasting effect on the destiny of Everton Football Club as George Mahon. In 1892 he led the rebellion against Everton's president and Anfield landlord, John Houlding, and like a footballing Moses led the club across Stanley Park to the promised lands of Mere Green Field. Here, 120 years later, Goodison Park, one of football's great arenas, still stands.

Born in Liverpool on 7 July 1853, Mahon was brought up and educated in Ireland, returning to Liverpool as a young man to take up an accountancy position with a North John Street firm. Eventually he would become a senior partner with Roose, Mahon and Howard Accountants and well known in the city's courtrooms, where he was often called upon as an expert in bankruptcy cases.

MAHON was a staunch Methodist and organist at St Domingo parish church. There is no evidence that he partook in the church's cricketing or footballing expeditions, but in 1886 he became a member of its offshoot, Everton Football Club. He was first enthused by the club having been to see them play Preston North End around that time by a schoolmaster friend, Sam Crosbie. 'He had a strong prejudice against football, but was so entranced with the wonderful passing of the North End players, that he became a regular attender at the Everton matches,' Crosbie would recall to Thomas Keates, Everton's first chronicler.

He was very much a Victorian reformer, and it is also likely that Mahon was infused with the ideas of 'muscular Christianity' which had born football as an organised sport a quarter of a century earlier. The notion was that sport helped bring order to society by expending the energy of the unruly classes.

Mahon was strongly involved in local politics, allying himself to the Liberal Party, who were trying to end years of Conservative rule in the city. Their reformist platform was centred on an anti-crime programme, and they went to great lengths to emphasise links between alcohol abuse and social problems. This would bring him into conflict with leading Liverpool Conservatives, including brewers such as John Houlding. In 1887 he was elected to the Walton Local Board, defeating Dr John Utting, a protégé of Houlding.

The political differences between Houlding and Mahon were broadly reflected among leading Everton members at this time. On the Conservative side were Houlding, Simon Jude and Edwin Berry; the Liberals, led by George

Mahon, included Dr James Clement Baxter, William Clayton and Will Cuff. In 1889 Mahon and Baxter joined Everton's management board. It was hoped that his position among the city's elite might 'popularise the "great game" among the better classes of the community'.

The split would soon manifest itself in the running of the club. In October 1891 Houlding and Mahon announced that Everton be set up as a limited company. This was a virtually unprecedented move as most football clubs were still run as 'sporting clubs', with members paying an annual subscription. But despite the apparent unity of intent, each man had a radically different interpretation of how Everton should be structured. Houlding proposed that Everton's membership be limited to 500, with each member allocated a single share, but that there be 12,000 shares available – the remainder available to the highest bidder. The proposal was roundly condemned by Mahon and his supporters, one member noting that 'those with longest purses would hold the power'.

MAHON'S PROPOSAL WAS MORE DEMOCRATIC, ANTICIPATING WHAT DAVID MOYES WOULD 111 YEARS LATER DUB 'THE PEOPLE'S CLUB'

Mahon's proposal was more democratic, anticipating what David Moyes would 111 years later dub 'the People's Club'. There would be just 500 shares available, with no member able to own more than 10. According to Mahon, 'We would rather have a large number of individual applications so that there will be more supporters of the club.'

Against this backdrop, Everton was also beset with unrest at Houlding's attempts to bleed as much rent from the club as possible. He sublet the land on which Anfield was built to Everton, but with the onset of league football upped the annual rent from £100 to £240 in 1888, and wanted £370 from 1892. In addition to this he took sole rights for the sale of refreshments from Anfield.

Part of Houlding's vision for Everton was that the club buy Anfield from its landlords, the Orrell Brothers and himself – quite how he entered the property deeds is shrouded in some mystery – for £9237 10s. In September 1891, Mahon raised the amendment which blocked the deal.

A special general meeting met in the college on Shaw Street, on 25 January 1892. The meeting started with Houlding's prospectus again being rejected by the members. George Mahon took to the floor and began to openly talk up the possibility of a new ground. His 'judicial and dignified reasoning' had until then, wrote Thomas Keates, been 'enthusiastically applauded'. But the mention of a new ground caused one heckler to shout out, 'Yer can't find one!' Mahon indolently responded, 'I've got one in my pocket.'

Mahon was referring to Mere Green Field, an area of land on the other side of Stanley Park on which he had gained an option. Today the land is known by its more familiar name: Goodison Park.

Mahon oversaw Everton's bold move from Anfield to Goodison. His skills as an accountant were integral to the club structuring a deal whereby they could afford to build a stadium within six months, buy the land on which it stood within three years, and pay off all the moneys borrowed within a decade.

As chairman, a position he held until June 1895, his vision for the structure of Everton as a limited company was implemented. Paying

tribute to his values, the Everton historian Steve Flanagan wrote: 'Figures show how wildly different the values of Mahon and Houlding apparently were. George Mahon's proposal, which leaned more towards the shared power ethos, spread the power amongst the members as, following the move to Goodison Park in 1892, the 10 original directors owned just 6% of the shares in the club, which rose to 7% in 1902. Contrast this with John Houlding's Liverpool and his apparent power motive, where, in 1892, the original 8 directors owned 52% of the club, which rose to 54% during the same 10-year period.'

Although Mahon remained a director after stepping down as chairman, his later life was blighted by ill health. He died in Parkgate, on the Wirral, on 9 December 1908, aged only 55. In his honour the Liverpool County Football Combination trophy, which Everton donated to the association, was named after him.

According to his old friend Sam Crosbie, Mahon did 'outstanding service in the great crisis, and as chairman of the directors. [He] will be long remembered after the present generation, as there is a George Mahon Cup to be played for – for all time.' But Mahon's name lived on for much more fundamental reasons than that: he is the father of Goodison Park, and, in his own way, Liverpool too. How different might football have been without him.

TODAY THE LAND IS KNOWN BY ITS MORE FAMILIAR NAME: GOODISON PARK

Makepeace,
Joseph William Henry 'Harry'

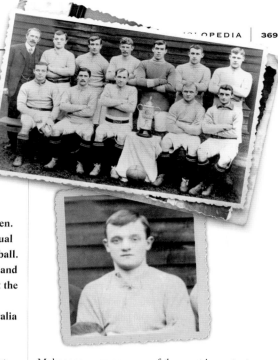

Legendary footballer and cricketer who won every honour each sport offered

Harry Makepeace is arguably the greatest top-class sporting all-rounder England has ever seen. Like Jack Sharp, his team-mate for Everton and Lancashire, he belongs to a select band of dual internationals – numbering just a dozen – who represented England at both cricket and football. His career for Everton lasted more than a decade, and for Lancashire a quarter of a century, and his achievements for both football club and county outstrip even Sharp's. Not only did he lift the 1906 FA Cup with Sharp, but he went on to be the first man to claim both First Division championship and county cricket championship. Throw in a maiden test century against Australia at the age of 40, and the magnitude of Makepeace's sporting achievements become clearer.

BORN in Teesside, Makepeace moved to Liverpool with his family aged 10. He signed for Everton as a forward in 1901, but it was as a wing half that he made his name. After making his debut in an FA Cup tie against Manchester United in February 1903 he established himself in the team during the 1904/05 season while still an amateur. The following season he was persuaded to give up employment and devote himself to Everton full-time through the winter months.

Football's first historians, Alfred Gibson and William Pickford, recorded in their 1906 history of the game, Association Football and the Men Who Made It: '[Makepeace] came into prominence last season, when he swiftly gained a regular place on the side. Cannot now be left out: plays too well. Has already gained honours with the league, and will yet do so for country unless his critics and friends are sadly out in their reckoning.' Indeed by the time of publication he had already fulfilled the authors' prophesy, making the first of four international

appearances for England, against Scotland at Hampden on 7 April 1906. It would be a golden month for Makepeace and just a fortnight later he was at Crystal Palace, facing Newcastle in the FA Cup Final.

Before that match Will Cuff gave a revealing insight into where he believed Everton's true strength lay – namely the back line Makepeace formed with Walter Abbott and Jack Taylor.

'I was fairly confident that we would beat Liverpool in the semi-final, and I feel just as confident that we shall defeat Newcastle United,' said Cuff. 'Mind you, I do not wish in any way to underrate the ability of our opponents, but I rather fancy our half-backs will not allow the United to settle down to their proper game. That is my feeling. Their ten men may be better than our ten men in the field, but as for the eleventh man –the goalkeeper – I am quite confident we have the advantage.' His words were prophetic indeed, and Everton lifted their first FA Cup after a 1-0 win.

Makepeace was now one of the most important members of an Everton squad of which longevity and regularity were its hallmarks. They reached another FA Cup Final in 1907, losing to Sheffield Wednesday, and also fell away in the league that year, finishing third when a better run-in would have brought them another league title. Again in 1908/09 and 1911/12 Everton came tantalisingly close to the championship, on both occasions finishing runners-up. By now the team that had won the FA Cup had been broken up, with the likes of Jack Sharp and Jack Taylor retiring, but Makepeace remained. In the veteran stage of his football career, his crowning moment came in 1914/15 when he was part of the Everton team that defied all odds and won the First Division Championship. It was the final action of a one-club footballing career and a glorious conclusion to it as well.

As a cricketer Makepeace's career was equally distinguished. He made his Lancashire debut in 1906, when he was 24, and played until he was aged nearly 50. In 487 matches he scored 25,207 runs, averaging 36.37.

It was said that his cricketing philosophy was that to show respect to bowlers before lunch was no sign of weakness but merely a necessary prelude to a successful onslaught afterwards. He was 'solid and staid' according to the Lancashire historian, John Kay. But he was also one of the cornerstones of a team that won three consecutive county championships in the late 1920s.

'**MAKEPEACE** gave great service to Lancashire, first as an obdurate opening batsman with strong defence, who relied on pushes, nudges and good placement for most of his runs.

Season	League		FA Cup		Total	
	App	Goals	App	Goals	App	Goals
1902/03	3	0	1	0	4	0
1904/05	19	5	6	2	25	7
1905/06	27	2	6	2	33	4
1906/07	23	0	8	0	31	0
1907/08	31	2	7	0	38	2
1908/09	33	0	2	0	35	0
1909/10	32	4	7	2	39	6
1910/11	33	1	3	0	36	1
1911/12	34	1	5	1	39	2
1912/13	10	0	1	0	11	0
1913/14	16	0	1	0	17	0
1914/15	23	1	5	0	28	1
Total	**284**	**16**	**52**	**7**	**336**	**23**

He was also a good cover fieldsman and occasionally a useful leg spinner,' Robert Brooke and David Goodyear wrote in their history of Lancashire. He was appointed coach in 1931, not retiring until 1951 when he was made an honorary life member.

With England he toured Australia in 1920–21, when England lost the Ashes series 5-0. Despite the grim results, Makepeace was a rare bright light, becoming the oldest player to score a maiden test century in the Fourth Test in Melbourne. The umpire said of it: 'He was typical of the proverbial bull dog pluck, a stern, determined batter, giving no points away and losing none. Watching the ball right up to the handle, Makepeace clipped everything that came along loosely.'

He was, wrote the cricket historian Brian Bradshaw, 'a highly respected, well-loved man. Everybody who came into contact with him spoke fondly about his courtesy, understanding and willingness to help.'

When he died in 1952, the Liverpool Echo's 'Ranger' recorded: 'His death removes one of the finest sportsmen it has been my good fortune to know. The name of Harry Makepeace was always synonymous with the highest standards of skill and clean sportsmanship at both cricket and football.'

[FACTFILE]

BORN
Middlesbrough, 22 August 1881
DIED
Spital, Bebington, 19 December 1952
POSITION
Half back
HONOURS
1906 FA Cup;
1914/15 League Championship;
4 England caps (1906–12)

Maley, Willie

Former Scotland international whose Everton career was notable only for its brevity

Season	League		FA Cup		Total	
	App	Goals	App	Goals	App	Goals
1896/97	2	0	0	0	2	0
Total	2	0	0	0	2	0

[FACTFILE]

BORN
Newry, 25 April 1868
DIED
1958
POSITION
Inside forward / left half
OTHER CLUBS
Cathcart Hazlebank; Third Lanark; Celtic; Ardwick (1895)
HONOURS
2 Scotland caps (1893)

Manchester United, Everton and

Football and inter-city rivals who have contributed to some of Everton's most enduring moments

Manchester United's reputation as England's most famous and, arguably, greatest club is built on the backs of numerous great players – from Duncan Edwards to Ryan Giggs and George Best to David Beckham – outstanding football and an insatiable appetite for success. With 19 league titles, three European Cups and numerous other accolades it is easy to understand why they are England's best supported club, and claim the largest fan base worldwide.

Founded by the workers of the Lancashire and Yorkshire Railway as Newton Heath in 1878, the same year as Everton's inception, they were among the best supported Manchester teams in football's first days. Not invited to join the Football League on its inauguration in 1888, when the league was expanded to 16 teams with a second division in 1892 Newton Heath were inducted into the top flight. Their first meeting with Everton came on 24 September 1892 at Goodison Park and ended in a 6-0 win for the home side. Four weeks later Everton beat them 4-3 at their North Road ground, with Alex Latta scoring all four Everton goals. Newton Heath ended their first league season bottom of the First Division.

THROUGH these early years they were a poor side, beset by financial difficulty and labouring in the shadow of Manchester City. At the start of the 20th century a local businessman, John Henry Davies, saved them from financial ruin and started to turn the club around. He introduced their now iconic red shirts and in 1902 renamed the club Manchester United. He appointed J. Ernest Magnall as secretary-manager, an astute figure who poached many of their rivals' best players. Promotion to the top flight came in 1906 and a first League Championship followed two years later.

In 1908 Everton's outside left, Harold Hardman, became the first significant player to cross between the two clubs. Hardman, an amateur and Manchester-based solicitor, played just four times for United, but went on to serve the club for many years as director and, later, chairman.

In 1909 Manchester United won the FA Cup for the first time. The following February they moved to Old Trafford and in 1910/11 won a second league title. But in 1912 Magnall left for Manchester City and United struggled without him. For the next 30 years they would yo-yo between the First and Second Divisions, seldom threatening a challenge for silverware and on occasion teetering near bankruptcy.

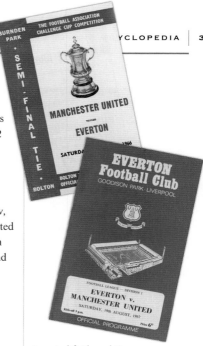

United's predicament during this period seemed to be encapsulated by the transfer of Neil McBain to Everton in January 1923. The elegant wing half was sold to balance the books, but his proposed transfer caused opprobrium among United fans, 1000 of whom attended a public meeting to protest against it. Financial imperatives dictated, however, and McBain became an Everton player because United could not afford to keep him.

UNITED'S fortunes changed markedly following the arrival of Matt Busby as manager in October 1945. Using a mixture of experienced veterans and exciting youngsters, he built a team that narrowly missed out on the league title in three consecutive seasons in the late 1940s, before they finally won it for the first time in 40 years in 1952. At the same time he revolutionised United's youth development and scouting network, which would be the hallmarks of the club's success over 50 years. From the mid-1950s Busby built a second great team with youngsters that he had cultivated, such as Duncan Edwards, Bobby Charlton and Roger Byrne. United won the league title in 1956 and 1957 and became the first English team to enter European competition. Just as Busby's side looked destined for greatness, on their way back from a European tie in Belgrade in February 1958 the team's aircraft was involved in a runway crash at Munich airport. The core of the side was killed and the world's perceptions of United changed overnight.

In the 1960s Everton and United could finally lay claim to great teams in the same era. In the early part of the decade, as United recovered from Munich, Everton had the upper hand, winning the League Championship in 1962/63, although the fates of individual matches could go either way in spectacular fashion:

Everton beat United 5-1 at Goodison in December 1961, but United beat the newly crowned champions by the same score in August 1963. Later that season Everton beat United 4-0 at Goodison. The two teams met in the Inter Cities Fairs Cup in January 1965, and United won 3-2 on aggregate. Fifteen months later Colin Harvey's goal was all that separated the two teams in an FA Cup semi-final. Three years later Everton beat them by the same scoreline at the quarter-final stage.

The 1960s were golden days for both clubs, and the likes of Denis Law, Bobby Charlton and George Best are as imprinted on the fabric of United as many Everton stars of the same era. Both teams went into decline in the early 1970s, although United's was sharper even than Everton's and they were relegated in 1974. After their promotion a year later they would continue to win cup competitions, but their pursuit of league success became something of an odyssey until the early 1990s.

Clashes between Everton and United supporters had been prevalent since the early 1960s and would be particularly malicious during the 1970s. The football rivalry between Liverpool and Manchester was only a symptom of a deeper sense of difference between the two cities. A famous motto – 'The Liverpool gentleman and the Manchester man' – was indicative of Liverpudlians' sense of superiority. Its implication was that Manchester based its prosperity on industry, manufacture and dirt under the fingernails, while Liverpool's was derived from commerce: shipping, insurance, trade, customs and excise. There was an assumption among Scousers that Mancunians were always jealous of the seaport. Liverpool was more cultured, more attractive, wealthier; worthy of greater worldwide renown. As the Liverpool-born writer Linda Grant put it: 'We were famous all over the world because our city, and everything in it, was connected with the sea. Almost everyone had come from the sea. We were multi-ethnic before the phrase was invented. Our backs were turned against the land we were part of.' At the same time there was deep resentment in Liverpool at the Manchester Ship Canal, built in the late 19th century, which bypassed Liverpool's port and signalled the beginning of its decline.

As the city of Liverpool staggered into a post-industrial meltdown during the 1970s, resentment towards Manchester, which suffered less than its neighbour, increased. Often this fierce rivalry was played out on the football terraces between Everton or Liverpool and United and Manchester City fans. Nevertheless, the rivalry would become most pronounced between United and Liverpool; United fans were unable to live with Liverpool's unprecedented success in the 1970s and 1980s, and when the roles were reversed over the subsequent two decades, the antipathy increased.

In October 1984, Everton met Manchester United, in fine form and beaten only once that season on their latest League Championship quest. Everton put five past United without reply in one of the most complete performances in the club's history. It was considered one of many turning points that calendar year as Everton embarked on a record-breaking title-winning campaign. At the end of the 1984/85 season, Everton met United in the FA Cup Final, needing a win to secure a League and FA Cup double, but Norman Whiteside's extra-time goal ended such hopes.

United rested firmly in the shadow of the Merseyside clubs until the early 1990s. However, its manager since 1986, Alex Ferguson, had reverted back to the principles that had once served Matt Busby so well, and

invested faith and time re-establishing the club's youth and scouting apparatus. Allied with some big-money signings this reaped United a Premier League title in 1992/93, their first in a generation and the first of 11 league titles Ferguson would win.

EVERTON by then were in a state of torpor and for the next 15 years victories over United would be rare, but always memorable. In May 1995 Everton met United in the FA Cup Final and, against all odds, beat them 1-0 to avenge the defeat of a decade earlier. It would be their last win over United in a decade, but their next win, in April 2005, on one of Goodison's great nights, effectively secured Champions League qualification. Everton met United in the 2009 FA Cup semi-final, and after a goalless stalemate progressed on penalties.

Everton's team that day contained three former United stars – Tim Howard, Phil Neville and Louis Saha – and in many ways the recent relationship between the two clubs has been defined by transfer activity. In 1995, shortly after the FA Cup Final win, Joe Royle made United's winger Andrei Kanchelskis Everton's record signing. Kanchelskis had fallen out with Alex Ferguson and would provide an outstanding debut season at Goodison, before moving to Fiorentina.

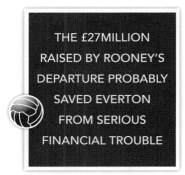

More contentious was the sale of Wayne Rooney to United in August 2004. It came amid accusations of vested interests, tapping up and disloyalty, but the £27million raised by Rooney's departure probably saved Everton from serious financial trouble. Feelings ran high between the two sets of fans for several years and when Everton met United in an FA Cup fifth round tie in February 2005, the aftermath of the game was marred by violence in Everton Valley. More recently there has been renewed solidarity between the two sets of fans in the wake of Liverpool's threatened renaissance and a mutual loathing of the club by Everton and United supporters. Quite how that relationship will fare if rumours that David Moyes is Sir Alex Ferguson's preferred successor are ever realised remain to be seen.

Key Figures

Harold Hardman

An outstanding winger, who appeared in Everton's first FA Cup win in 1906, Hardman combined playing football as an amateur with work as a Manchester solicitor. An England international who won an Olympic soccer gold medal for Great Britain in the 1908 Games, Hardman joined United shortly after. Although his playing career for United was notable only for its brevity, on his retirement he became one of the game's great administrators, serving United as a director for half a century. In 1951 he became Manchester United chairman, a position he held until his death 14 years later. It was a period that coincided with United's renaissance under Matt Busby, and included four league titles and an FA Cup, but was ultimately marked by the Munich air disaster. It remains a crucial period in United's history, from which they emerged a world-famous name.

John Moores

A son of Salford, Moores' interest in football dated back to the 1900s, when, as a boy, he cheered on United's first great teams under the management of J. Ernest Magnall at Bank Street and Old Trafford. After the First World War, Moores recognised the money-making possibilities from football betting, and started a football pools company – Littlewoods Pools. Initially run from an office in Church Street, Liverpool, the very first pools coupons were sold outside Old Trafford in 1923. By the 1930s Moores was a millionaire, his business interests extending to department stores and home shopping. Despite his Mancunian origins, Liverpool remained his business base and he had a great affection for his adopted city and its people. From the late 1950s he retained a financial stake in Everton and Liverpool, becoming Everton chairman in 1960. He would hold the Everton chairmanship over two spells (1960–65 & 1968–73) and remain on the board of directors until 1977.

Wayne Rooney

In making his Everton debut as a 16-year-old in August 2002, Rooney fulfilled a childhood dream. Months earlier, after scoring in an FA Youth Cup tie, he revealed a T-shirt bearing the legend 'Once a Blue, always a Blue' and to Evertonians he seemed to represent the ultimate fantasy footballer: outrageously skilful, fearless, brilliant, one of them. Within two years this special relationship had soured forever, when, on the last day of the August 2004 transfer window, Rooney completed a record £27million move to United. The deal caused outrage among Evertonians with suggestions that United had tapped the player up, that his agent engineered the transfer, that Rooney had sold out and left Everton in the lurch. But the deal represented a new reality in Everton's relationship with Manchester United: that United were so dominant in both financial and footballing senses, that Everton were powerless to keep hold of their best players should the Red Devils come calling. If nothing else, the funds raised from Rooney's sale saved Everton from financial oblivion and helped reinvigorate Everton's renaissance under David Moyes.

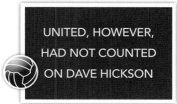

Key matches

14 FEBRUARY 1953   **FA Cup Fifth Round   Everton 2 Manchester United 1**   Attendance: 77,920

In a decade beset by on-the-field mediocrity, Everton's 1953 FA Cup win over the reigning champions stands out like a beacon. Stuck in the Second Division and in the midst of the worst league campaign in their history, Everton were definite underdogs against a formidable United team. Nearly 78,000 packed into Goodison for the famous old ground's second highest attendance. But when Jack Rowley put United in front midway through the first half, it looked as if the game would follow the inevitable script.

United, however, had not counted on Dave Hickson – who had once supported the visitors as a boy. All afternoon he rampaged around the field, upsetting the United defence and handing Everton the initiative. After setting up Tommy Eglington for an equaliser, he suffered a kick to the head that opened up an horrific cut above his right eye. Bravely he carried on into the second half, resisting the referee's appeals that he leave the field. After striking the United post, Hickson hit a fine winner on the hour mark that put Everton in the quarter-finals and Hickson into Goodison lore.

Everton
O'Neill, Clinton, Lindsay, Farrell, Jones, Lello, Buckle, Cummings, Hickson, Parker, Eglington
Scorers: Eglington, Hickson

Manchester United
Wood, Aston, Byrne, Carey, Chilton, Cockburn, Berry, Lewis, Rowley, Pearson, Pegg
Scorer: Rowley

18 MAY 1985 Wembley; FA Cup Final   Everton 0 Manchester United 1   Attendance: 100,000

Everton arrived straight from Rotterdam, where they had won the European Cup Winners' Cup the previous Wednesday, to prepare for the FA Cup Final, knowing that victory over United would make them only the fourth team to win a League and FA Cup double. United had started the 1984/85 season hotly tipped to challenge Liverpool for the League Championship and had led the league early on. But Everton's famous 5-0 win at Goodison in October was a set-back from which they never entirely recovered, eventually finishing fourth. The Monday before the final United concluded their league campaign with a 5-1 defeat at Watford.

EVERTON, riding on a high, were strong favourites. Twice Everton hit the woodwork – when Peter Reid's first-half volley was deflected onto the post by John Gidman; then in extra time, when Bryan Robson headed against his own crossbar – but they could not find a way through, even after United's Kevin Moran became the first player to be sent off in an FA Cup Final. The game seemed to be heading for a replay when, deep into extra time, Norman Whiteside turned Pat Van Den Hauwe and curled a spectacular winner past Neville Southall.

Everton
Southall, Stevens, Van den Hauwe, Ratcliffe, Mountfield, Reid, Steven, Sharp, Gray, Bracewell, Sheedy

Manchester United
Bailey, Gidman, Albiston (Duxbury), Whiteside, McGrath, Moran, Robson, Strachan, Hughes, Stapleton, Olsen
Scorer: Whiteside

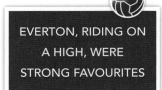

EVERTON, RIDING ON A HIGH, WERE STRONG FAVOURITES

20 MAY 1995 Wembley; FA Cup Final   Everton 1 Manchester United 0   Attendance: 79,592

Everton faced United at the end of a gruelling season in which, for much of its duration, they seemed destined for relegation and United for a third successive Premier League title.

Under Joe Royle's management, Everton were made safe with a game to spare, while United let the championship slip from their grasp on the last day of the season.

Nevertheless, the Mancunians came into the tie hot favourites. In a fiercely contested and closely run match, Everton's dogs of war shaded it. On the half-hour mark a lightning break saw Graham Stuart hit the underside of the United crossbar and Paul Rideout headed the rebound home. Thereafter, Dave Watson marshalled the Everton rearguard magnificently, while Neville Southall was an obstinate and indomitable final barrier. It was enough to bring Everton their fifth FA Cup victory and condemn United to a rare trophyless season.

Everton
Southall, Jackson, Watson, Unsworth, Ablett, Limpar (Amokachi), Horne, Parkinson, Hinchcliffe, Stuart, Rideout (Ferguson)
Scorer: Rideout

Manchester United
Schmeichel, G. Neville, Bruce (Giggs), Pallister, Irwin, Sharpe (Scholes), Keane, Ince, Butt, McClair, Hughes

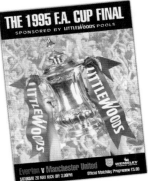

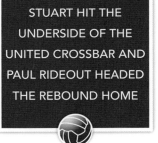

STUART HIT THE UNDERSIDE OF THE UNITED CROSSBAR AND PAUL RIDEOUT HEADED THE REBOUND HOME

Marsden, Joe

Right back who played as many times for his country as he did Everton

Season	League		FA Cup		Total	
	App	Goals	App	Goals	App	Goals
1891/92	1	0	0	0	1	0
Total	1	0	0	0	1	0

[FACTFILE]

BORN
Darwen, 1868
POSITION
Right back
OTHER CLUBS
Padiham; Darwen
HONOURS
1 England cap (1891)

Marshall, Cliff

Ground-breaking winger who was Everton's first black player

Season	League		FA Cup		League Cup		Europe		Total	
	App	Goals	App	Goals	App	Goals	App	Goals	App	Goals
1974/75	2 (1)	0	1	0	0	0	-	-	3 (1)	0
1975/76	4	0	0	0	0	0	0	0	4	0
Total	6 (1)	0	1	0	0	0	0	0	7 (1)	0

[FACTFILE]

BORN
Liverpool, 4 November 1955
POSITION
Winger
OTHER CLUB
Southport (1976–77)

Marshall, Ian

Home-grown defender cum centre forward who enjoyed better times elsewhere

Ian Marshall came at the end of a generation of English footballers reliant on their unrelenting physicality over any discernible technique or natural ability. The tall, physically imposing player got his break as centre back after injury ruled Derek Mountfield out of the Everton line-up in August 1985. After several outings with Kevin Ratcliffe, he returned to Central League football and found his opportunities further limited by the arrival of Dave Watson the following year.

Marshall, however, never saw himself as a centre back but a centre forward, yet was unable to convince Howard Kendall of his aptitude up front. After no more than cameo roles through Everton's glory years, in March 1988 he joined Oldham Athletic for £100,000. At Boundary Park, an injury crisis gave him the stage he sorely craved and in a forward role he thrived. Under the watch of managers – such as Joe Royle and Leicester's Martin O'Neill – reliant on the long ball game, Marshall excelled as a human battering ram, spearheading forward lines with bravery and brute strength. It may not have been sophisticated or pretty, but it was highly effective – particularly in the cut and thrust of the relegation or promotion battles he often found himself in.

A top-flight player until his mid-thirties, in 2000 he won the League Cup with Leicester City and promotion back to the Premier League with Bolton a year later. A short spell with Blackpool followed before Marshall retired to Canada.

[FACTFILE]

BORN
Liverpool, 20 March 1966
POSITION
Defender / centre forward
OTHER CLUB
Oldham Athletic (1988–93);
Ipswich Town (1993–96);
Leicester City (1996–2000);
Bolton Wanderers (2000–01);
Blackpool (2001–02)

Season	League		FA Cup		League Cup		Europe		Total	
	App	Goals	App	Goals	App	Goals	App	Goals	App	Goals
1985/86	8 (1)	0	0	0	1 (1)	1	4	0	13 (2)	1
1986/87	0 (2)	1	0	0	0	0	2	0	2 (2)	1
1987/88	1 (3)	0	0	0	0	0	1	0	2 (3)	0
Total	9 (6)	1	0	0	1 (1)	1	7	0	17 (7)	2

Martin, George

Inside forward whose Goodison career coincided with interesting times

George Martin's Everton career only lasted four years, but it encompassed one of the most dramatic periods in the club's history. He joined in March 1928 as Everton were in the process of winning their third League Championship, played all but two games as they were relegated two years later, encountered a Second Division Championship win and made a cameo as Everton lifted their fourth League title.

THE TALENTED inside forward had first made an impression on the Everton board when starring for Hull City in an FA Cup fourth round win in February 1927. The match had gone to its second replay and was played at neutral

Villa Park; Martin was, according to 'Bee' in the Liverpool Post and Mercury, 'one of their best men in each of the three games'. He got his just reward with the scores tied at 2-2 in extra time: a winner that he struck so hard that it burst the ball.

His arrival at Goodison for a fee of £1750 13 months later was opportune. Everton were in the midst of a 10-game run without a win and league title hopes were drifting away. His addition to the team in place of Bobby Irvine 'certainly improved the line' and 'he played with great dash and determination'. Another correspondent wrote: 'He had a knack of opening out the game, could draw a man and pass the ball. Possibly he will prove deadlier in front of goal.'

He would score three goals before the end of the season, none more crucial than the deciding effort in a 5-3 win at Burnley in the season's penultimate game. A week later he was part of the team that helped Dean score his 58th, 59th, and 60th goals of the season and lift the League Championship.

> HE WAS PART OF THE TEAM THAT HELPED DEAN SCORE HIS 58th, 59th, AND 60th GOALS OF THE SEASON AND LIFT THE LEAGUE CHAMPIONSHIP

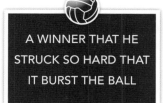

> A WINNER THAT HE STRUCK SO HARD THAT IT BURST THE BALL

That week Jimmy Dunn joined Everton, meaning that just two months after himself joining Everton, Martin's place would always be under challenge. The only campaign he was a cast-iron certainty in the Everton team was the year they were relegated.

In May 1932, having made just two first-team appearances all season, he left to join Middlesbrough in a joint deal with Arthur Rigby for £1800. He played just six times at Ayresome Park before joining Luton and would later serve as coach and manager over two spells at Kenilworth Road. The height of his managerial career came at Newcastle, whom he led to promotion to the First Division in 1948. A subsequent spell in charge of Aston Villa was less happy and he left after falling out with the board.

	League		FA Cup		Total	
Season	App	Goals	App	Goals	App	Goals
1927/28	10	3	0	0	10	3
1928/29	18	6	0	0	18	6
1929/30	40	15	1	1	41	16
1930/31	15	7	0	0	15	7
1931/32	2	0	0	0	2	0
Total	85	31	1	1	86	32

[FACTFILE]

BORN
Bothwell, Lanarkshire, 14 July 1899
POSITION
Inside forward
OTHER CLUBS
Hamilton Academical (1920–22);
Hull City (1922–28);
Middlesbrough (1932–33);
Luton Town (1932–37)
AS MANAGER
Luton Town (1939–47 & 1965–66);
Newcastle United (1947–50);
Aston Villa (1950–53)
HONOURS
1927/28 League Championship, 1930/31 Second Division Championship

Martyn, Nigel

Veteran goalkeeper who impressed after his belated Goodison arrival

It was one of the quiet tragedies of the disruptive 1990s that Nigel Martyn never became an Everton player before he actually did – some seven years too late. In July 1996, Joe Royle had earmarked Martyn, then a 29-year-old sometime England international goalkeeper, as a long-term successor to Neville Southall and had agreed a £2.25million deal to bring him to Everton when the deal collapsed amid high farce.

ROYLE had been called away to attend an urgent hospital appointment with his wife, and Peter Johnson was away on business, leaving an Everton director to conclude the deal. Martyn was summoned to Johnson's Park Foods headquarters, in a Birkenhead industrial park. 'On our way over my agent, who was in the car in front, rang me to say Leeds had just matched the offer so it was in my interests to listen to them,' Martyn told the Daily Telegraph in 2005. 'We told the Everton director about that and, it was weird, he seemed to get a bit flummoxed about the situation. He actually gave us directions on how to get to Leeds. I was all ready to sign for Everton.

'My wife had family in the area but the director, I think, was anxious to seem fair. He even said we'd better get moving because the traffic would be bad! Once we got to Leeds Howard Wilkinson was never going to let us go until I signed.'

FOR THE NEXT seven years, Martyn performed admirable service in Leeds United's rise and subsequent fall. He lost his place to Paul Robinson during the 2002/03 season and with Leeds precipitous financial decline was made available for transfer that summer. In August 2003, after years without a dependable keeper and with uncertainty over Richard Wright's competency and long-term fitness, David Moyes paid a nominal fee to finally bring the 37-year-old to Goodison.

Something of a late developer, Martyn had never played in goal until he was 16, when he was invited to try out for his brother's works team. He subsequently signed for the Cornish amateurs, St Blazey, where he was reputedly spotted in 1987 playing in a pre-season friendly by the Bristol Rovers tea lady who set up the young goalkeeper's successful trial. At the Memorial Stadium he won England under-21 honours before becoming Britain's first million-pound goalkeeper when he joined Crystal Palace in 1989. He spent seven years at Selhurst Park, then seven years at Leeds before the Goodison switch finally came.

MARTYN QUICKLY showed Evertonians what they had missed out on, bringing the sort of calm and composure to the Everton goal largely absent since Southall's departure. A commanding and authoritative figure, he also possessed reflexes that belied his veteran status and was a superb shot stopper. His form through an otherwise troubled 2003/04 season brought him to the verge of an England recall, which he declined so as to focus on his Everton career. Through the 2004/05 campaign, Martyn was a key component in a side that defied all expectations to finish fourth. It was little surprise that when Richard Wright deputised in his place, Everton's form declined dramatically. With Martyn absent for the final two games of the season, Everton shipped 10 goals.

Martyn's reward for his fine form was a year-long extension to his contract. He began the 2005/06 season first-choice goalkeeper, but persistent injuries limited his input. A stress fracture of the ankle kept him out of the final four months of the season, and although another contract was offered to him, medical investigations at the season's close showed that it had not healed. Martyn, in the interests of his future health, announced his retirement, two months short of his 40th birthday.

Season	League		FA Cup		League Cup		Europe		Total	
	App	Goals	App	Goals	App	Goals	App	Goals	App	Goals
2003/04	33 (1)	0	3	0	3	0	-	-	39 (1)	0
2004/05	32	0	1	0	0	0	-	-	33	0
2005/06	20	0	2	0	1	0	4	0	27	0
Total	**85 (1)**	**0**	**6**	**0**	**4**	**0**	**4**	**0**	**99 (1)**	**0**

Materazzi, Marco

Promising Italian centre back whose name entered football infamy

In a single explosive moment in July 2006, Marco Materazzi's name entered football notoriety.

It was deep into extra time of the World Cup Final – a game in which Materazzi had already played a significant role, conceding an early penalty before heading an equaliser – when in an off-the-ball confrontation, Zinedine Zidane, playing the final game of an illustrious career, was provoked into launching a crazy head-butt into the Italian's chest. Zidane was sent off, Materazzi scored in the penalty shoot-out that brought Italy their fourth World Cup victory, and the whole planet pondered the same question: just what did the Italian do to provoke such a violent reaction?

IF WATCHING Evertonians were surprised that Materazzi had scaled such footballing heights, that he was at the heart of controversy was less of a shock. Signed by Walter Smith for £2.8million in the summer of 1998, Materazzi was a tall, hard centre back in the mould of such classic Italian hard men as Claudio Gentile. A good footballing player, he defied the notion that central defenders merely had to hoof the ball at the first opportunity. However, he was let down by an abysmal disciplinary record as Premier League referees baulked at his aggressive style of play. Three times through his solitary season at Goodison he was sent off;

SENT OFF AGAINST COVENTRY CITY, HE SAT BESIDE AN ADVERTISING HOARDING AND WEPT

after his final dismissal, against Coventry City, he sat beside an advertising hoarding and wept. This was the final glimpse Evertonians had of Materazzi, who, as a financial crisis gripped Goodison, was sold back to Perugia that summer. However, controversy did not leave him there, and Everton became involved in a lengthy legal dispute after Perugia reneged on an instalment of the transfer payment. In 2001 he joined Inter Milan for €10million, and at the San Siro his career blossomed with multiple Scudetto wins and the World Cup victory. But just what did he say to Zidane? All through the game, the Italian had shadowed the Frenchman, and Zidane, in a pique of frustration, told him that if he wanted his shirt so badly he would give it to him after the game. To this Materazzi said that he would prefer Zidane's 'whore of a sister'; the Frenchman snapped and Materazzi entered football history.

[FACTFILE]

BORN
Lecce, 19 August 1973
POSITION
Centre back
OTHER CLUBS
Marsala (1993–94);
Trapani (1994–95);
Perugia (1995–98 & 1999–2001);
Carpi (loan, 1996–97);
Inter Milan (2001–11)
HONOURS
41 Italy caps (2 goals) (2001–08);
2006 World Cup

Season	League		FA Cup		League Cup		Total	
	App	Goals	App	Goals	App	Goals	App	Goals
1998/99	26 (1)	1	2	0	4	1	32 (1)	2
Total	26 (1)	1	2	0	4	1	32 (1)	2

Maxwell, Alan

Scottish forward who led the Everton front line during Everton's first season

[FACTFILE]

BORN
Cambuslang, 1870
POSITION
Inside forward / centre forward
OTHER CLUBS
Cambuslang; Darwen (1893–95);
Stoke City (1895–96);
St Bernard's

Season	League		FA Cup		Total	
	App	Goals	App	Goals	App	Goals
1891/92	16	4	0	0	16	4
1892/93	23	7	7	3	30	10
1893/94	4	2	0	0	4	2
Total	43	13	7	3	50	16

Mayers, Derek

Home-grown winger who made a name for himself as Tom Finney's fellow Deepdale flanker

[FACTFILE]

BORN
Liverpool, 24 January 1935
POSITION
Outside right
OTHER CLUBS
Preston North End (1957–61);
Leeds United (1961–62);
Bury (1962–64);
Wrexham (1963–64);
Rhyl

Season	League		FA Cup		Total	
	App	Goals	App	Goals	App	Goals
1952/53	2	2	0	0	2	2
1953/54	1	0	0	0	1	0
1954/55	0	0	0	0	0	0
1955/56	7	2	0	0	7	2
1956/57	8	3	1	0	9	3
Total	18	7	1	0	19	7

Mayson, Tommy

Veteran forward limited to a solitary Everton appearance

	League		FA Cup		Total	
Season	App	Goals	App	Goals	App	Goals
1919/20	1	0	0	0	1	0
Total	1	0	0	0	1	0

[FACTFILE]

BORN
Whitehaven,
8 December 1886
DIED
1972
POSITION
Inside left
OTHER CLUBS
Burnley (1907–11);
Grimsby Town (1911–14);
Pontypridd;
Wolverhampton Wanderers
(1921);
Aberdare Athletic (1922)

McAleny, Conor

Promising young winger whose debut against Arsenal almost brought a goal

	League		FA Cup		League Cup		Total	
Season	App	Goals	App	Goals	App	Goals	App	Goals
2011/12	0 (2)	0	0	0	0	0	0 (2)	0
Total	0 (2)	0	0	0	0	0	0 (2)	0

[FACTFILE]

BORN
Liverpool, 12 August 1992
POSITION
Winger
OTHER CLUB
Scunthorpe United
(loan, 2012)

McBain, Neil

Elegant half back who traversed the Mersey–Manchester divide

IN MODERN TERMS the football journey taken by Scottish international half back Neil McBain would be considered to be wracked by controversy. Not only did he cross the Merseyside divide, leaving Everton to join Liverpool (by way of Perth); but he had earlier played for Manchester United, thus traversing three of England's most hotly contested rivalries. Yet it was his transfer to Everton in January 1923 that attracted most controversy.

The elegant (some said too elegant) wing half had handed in a transfer request at Old Trafford, having fallen out with United's perfidious management. The United board held out for a fee that was described in one newspaper to be 'so sustainable that it quickly frightened possible buyers away, and at the present fee, at any rate, there is no likelihood of the player joining the Everton camp.' Yet the Everton board eventually submitted to pay a huge £4000 fee for the player. The news of his impending departure from Old Trafford precipitated a public meeting to protest at the deal, and more than 1000 angry United fans turned up. It was to no avail and over the following four years McBain was to make more than 100 appearances in the royal blue shirt of Everton.

McBain had started his career with Ayr United and acquired a reputation as a ball-playing half back. This was enhanced after the move to United in 1921, although, as the football historian Percy Young sharply pointed out, 'his meticulous talents were found to be out of place [at Old Trafford]'. At Everton, however, the football philosophy was different. The aim was to build from the back, playing short passes and breaking with subtlety and verve. They would finish 1922/23 fifth and

	League		FA Cup		Total	
Season	App	Goals	App	Goals	App	Goals
1922/23	15	0	0	0	15	0
1923/24	37	0	2	0	39	0
1924/25	35	0	4	0	39	0
1925/26	10	1	0	0	10	1
Total	97	1	6	0	103	1

seventh a year later, although it was believed they played better football then (they also won two more points than the previous year). 'No team in the country has served up more delightful football than Everton,' reported the Athletic News.

In writing about how they played 'the prettiest football in the league', the leading football journalist of the era, Ivan Sharpe, pointed to the influence of defenders like McBain. 'The purpose of Everton is to keep the ball on the ground. Their passes are short and sweet. There is subtlety in attack – mainly because the half-backs (Brown, McBain, and Hart) keep the ball delicately under control in defence and attack, and because in parting they glance it here, glide it there, and, generally, contrive and create, rather than bustle about and bash it to the wings in the manner too prevalent today.'

McBain was a regular until the 1925/26 season after he lost his place to David Bain then suffered injury while playing in the reserves. Local newspapers reported him being 'desirous' to return to Scotland and in the

summer of 1926 he joined St Johnstone for £1000. This move was short-lived and in March 1928 he returned to Merseyside with Liverpool after St Johnstone had had problems meeting their payments of his transfer fee. He then moved to Watford, in 1929 becoming their player-manager, and thus began a 35-year-long managerial career that took him to Luton, Argentina and, finally, back to Ayr, where it had all begun.

In March 1947, aged 51 years and 120 days, McBain, then manager of New Brighton, was called into action in the midst of an injury crisis and selected himself in goal for the Division Three (North) match against Hartlepool. They lost 3-0 but McBain remains the oldest player to turn out in a Football League match.

> **McBAIN REMAINS THE OLDEST PLAYER TO TURN OUT IN A FOOTBALL LEAGUE MATCH**

[FACTFILE]

BORN
Campbelltown, 15 November 1895
DIED
13 May 1974
POSITION
Half back
OTHER CLUBS
Ayr United (1914–21);
Manchester United (1921–23);
St Johnstone (1926–28);
Liverpool (1928);
Watford (1928–31);
New Brighton (1931)
AS MANAGER
Watford (1929–37);
Ayr United (1937–38);
Luton Town (1938–39);
New Brighton (1946–48);
Leyton Orient (1948–49);
Estudiantes de la Plata (1949–51);
Ayr United (1955–56);
Watford (1956–59);
Ayr United (1962–63)
HONOURS
3 Scotland caps (1922–24)

McBride, Brian

Accomplished American international centre forward

A stop-gap loan signing in January 2003, Brian McBride made an immediate impact in an Everton shirt, scoring within 10 minutes of making his debut against Tottenham Hotspur. A week later he scored a brace in Everton's home win over Sunderland, adding much-needed momentum to their push for European qualification.

A tall, strong target man with good positioning and accomplished distribution, McBride had previously come under David Moyes's watch when he played a loan spell with Preston. He impressed during his two months at Goodison, and Moyes tried to extend his loan. However, Major League Soccer, which held his playing registration, would only agree to a permanent

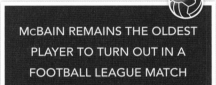

> **McBRIDE MADE AN IMMEDIATE IMPACT IN AN EVERTON SHIRT, SCORING WITHIN 10 MINUTES OF MAKING HIS DEBUT**

move – at a fee variously quoted between £600,000 and £2million. With transfer funds at a premium, the Everton manager deemed the asking price too much for a man who was past his 30th birthday.

McBride returned to the US for the MLS season, but came back to England a year later in an £800,000 deal with Fulham. At Craven Cottage he provided four years distinguished service, assuming the club captaincy and proving that life exists beyond 30.

[FACTFILE]

BORN
Arlington Heights, 19 June 1972
POSITION
Centre forward
OTHER CLUBS
Milwaukee Rampage (1994);
VFL Wolfsburg (1994–95);
Columbus Crew (1996–2004);
Preston North End (loan, 2000–01);
Fulham (2004–08);
Chicago Fire (2008–10)
HONOURS
96 US caps (30 goals) (1993–2006)

Season	League		FA Cup		League Cup		Total	
	App	Goals	App	Goals	App	Goals	App	Goals
2002/03	7 (1)	4	0	0	0	0	7 (1)	4
Total	**7 (1)**	**4**	**0**	**0**	**0**	**0**	**7 (1)**	**4**

·EFC·

McBride, Joe

A winger from illustrious stock, a promising career faltered after Gordon Lee's departure

Joe McBride came from a strong footballing heritage: his namesake and father was a former Scotland international and Celtic striker who ranks among Scotland's most prolific post-war goalscorers. Perhaps given this upbringing, steeped within the Scottish football establishment, it was a surprise that McBride junior chose Everton on leaving school.

After two seasons of Central League football, Gordon Lee pitched the 19-year-old winger in the Everton first team on Boxing

Day 1979. A slight player, who jinked and dribbled his way along the Everton left, there were high hopes that McBride might be part of the youthful renaissance Lee was trying to instil at Goodison. When Everton kicked off the 1980/81 season, McBride was one of five Everton players aged 21 or younger, and a sixth – Billy Wright – was only 22.

ALAS, this inexperience often showed and it was not enough to sustain Everton through the new season. After finishing 15th, Lee left the club and under Howard

Kendall's charge McBride struggled to get a game. In August 1982 he joined Rotherham United and, after a couple of years in England's lower leagues, followed the illustrious path set by his father and joined Hibernian. A fine career in his homeland followed.

Season	League		FA Cup		League Cup		Europe		Total	
	App	Goals	App	Goals	App	Goals	App	Goals	App	Goals
1979/80	17 (1)	1	4	1	0	0	1	0	22 (1)	2
1980/81	27 (4)	7	2	0	3	1	-	-	32 (4)	8
1981/82	7 (1)	1	0	0	3	0	-	-	10 (1)	1
Total	51(6)	9	6	1	6	1	1	0	64 (6)	11

McCall, Stuart

Zestful midfielder whose abundant energy was not always matched with composure

An £875,000 signing from Bradford City in the summer of 1988, Stuart McCall was earmarked as one of the cornerstones of Colin Harvey's Goodison rebuilding programme. Unfortunately, like many of the Everton manager's acquisitions, his talent did not match that of his illustrious predecessor – in McCall's case, Peter Reid – and his Goodison career must be considered one of comparative failure.

The Yorkshire-born son of Scottish winger Andy McCall – who played on the opposite flank to Stanley Matthews at Blackpool in the 1940s – Stuart McCall made his name as an energetic midfielder at Bradford City and was a key part of the club's mid-1980s revival. Signed by Harvey, he quickly earned comparisons to Tony Kay and Alan Ball – as much for his diminutive stature, flame-red hair and lung-busting energy levels as anything else – but struggled to make the desired impact in a transitional Everton team. There was little faulting his effort and he never stopped running, but he frustrated fans by appearing rushed and reckless in his passing. And yet there remained a perpetual sense that if he properly channelled his energy and gained some composure he could emerge as a leading light in an Everton revival.

His finest moments came in the 1989 FA Cup Final, when called upon as a substitute for Paul Bracewell. With Everton trailing 1-0, in the final

minute McCall stabbed home from close range to bring extra time. When Everton fell behind again, McCall was on hand to make it 2-2 with a fabulous dipping volley from the edge of the penalty area that brought raptures from Evertonians, before Ian Rush ultimately ensured the day ended in disappointment.

HIS FINEST MOMENTS CAME IN THE 1989 FA CUP FINAL, WHEN HE SCORED TWO DRAMATIC EQUALISERS

HE WAS a regular through the following two seasons and yet there remained a sense that he was never quite indispensable. Nevertheless it was still something of a surprise when, in August 1991, Howard Kendall accepted a £1.2 million bid from Glasgow Rangers.

Better suited to the Scottish game, he was a key figure in Rangers' domination of Scottish football through the decade. Given a free transfer in 1998, he rejoined Bradford City, captaining them to the Premier League in his first season back. In 2002 he joined Sheffield United and continued playing until just short of his 41st birthday.

McCall won youth caps for England and under-21 caps for Scotland, before earning the first of 40 caps for his father's country in 1990.

An articulate man and strong personality, McCall had long combined his playing duties with coaching and was a popular choice to succeed Colin Todd as Bradford manager in 2007.

OFFICIAL
MATCH DAY PROGRAMME £3.00

F.A. CUP
FINAL
1989
EVERTON
v
LIVERPOOL
SATURDAY 20 MAY
KICK-OFF 3 P.M.
WEMBLEY

[FACTFILE]

BORN
Leeds, 10 June 1964
POSITION
Midfielder
OTHER CLUBS
Bradford City (1982–88);
Glasgow Rangers (1991–98);
Bradford City (1998–2002);
Sheffield United (2002–04)
AS MANAGER
Bradford City (2007–10);
Motherwell (2010–)
HONOURS
40 Scotland caps
(1 goal) (1990–98)

Season	League		FA Cup		League Cup		Other		Total	
	App	Goals	App	Goals	App	Goals	App	Goals	App	Goals
1988/89	29 (4)	0	4 (1)	3	4	1	3 (1)	0	40 (6)	4
1989/90	37	3	7	0	4	0	-	-	48	3
1990/91	33	3	5 (1)	0	3	0	6	0	47 (1)	3
Total	**99 (4)**	**6**	**16 (2)**	**3**	**11**	**1**	**9 (1)**	**0**	**135 (7)**	**10**

McCambridge,
Jimmy

Irish forward never able to supplant Dixie Dean during his three-month Goodison spell

[FACTFILE]

BORN
Larne, 1 September 1905
DIED
1980
POSITION
Centre forward
OTHER CLUBS
Larne; Ballymena United;
Cardiff City (1930–32);
Bristol Rovers (1933–35);
Exeter City (1935);
Sheffield Wednesday (1936);
Hartlepools United (1936);
Cheltenham Town
HONOURS
4 Ireland caps (1930–31)

Season	League		FA Cup		Total	
	App	Goals	App	Goals	App	Goals
1930/31	1	0	0	0	1	0
Total	**1**	**0**	**0**	**0**	**1**	**0**

McCann, Gavin

Home-grown midfielder who enjoyed a successful Premier League career beyond Goodison

Season	League App	League Goals	FA Cup App	FA Cup Goals	League Cup App	League Cup Goals	Total App	Total Goals
1997/98	5 (6)	0	0	0	0	0	5 (6)	0
Total	5 (6)	0	0	0	0	0	5 (6)	0

[FACTFILE]

BORN
Blackpool, 10 January 1978
POSITION
Midfielder
OTHER CLUBS
Sunderland (1998–2003);
Aston Villa (2003–07);
Bolton Wanderers (2007–11)
HONOURS
1 England cap (2001)

McClure, Joe

Defender whose Goodison career coincided with some dramatic times

Season	League App	League Goals	FA Cup App	FA Cup Goals	Total App	Total Goals
1929/30	2	0	0	0	2	0
1930/31	15	1	5	0	20	1
1931/32	7	0	0	0	7	0
1932/33	5	0	0	0	5	0
Total	29	1	5	0	34	1

[FACTFILE]

BORN
Cockermouth,
3 November 1907
DIED
1973
POSITION
Right half / centre half
OTHER CLUBS
Workington;
Preston North End (1926);
Workington; Wallsend;
Brentford (1933);
Exeter City (1934);
Nuneaton Town
HONOURS
1930/31 Second Division
Championship

McCormick, Harry

Irish winger who gained league representative honours in his native Ulster

Season	League App	League Goals	FA Cup App	FA Cup Goals	Total App	Total Goals
1948/49	4	0	0	0	4	0
Total	4	0	0	0	4	0

[FACTFILE]

BORN
Coleraine, 10 January 1924
POSITION
Outside left
OTHER CLUBS
Derby County (1946–48);
Coleraine (1949–56)

McDermott, Tommy

Itinerant inside forward whose Goodison career almost touched glory

[FACTFILE]

BORN
Bridgeton, 12 January 1878
DIED
1961
POSITION
Inside forward
OTHER CLUBS
Cambuslang Hibs; Dundee; Celtic; Chelsea (1905–06); Dundee; Bradford City (1907–08); Gainsborough Trinity (1908); Kilmarnock; Bradford City; Dundee Hibernian; Anfield Royal; St Helens Recreation; Wirral Railway; Vale of Leven; Broxburn Shamrock; Clyde

Season	League		FA Cup		Total	
	App	Goals	App	Goals	App	Goals
1903/04	29	7	1	0	30	7
1904/05	29	7	6	4	35	11
1905/06	6	1	0	0	6	1
Total	64	15	7	4	71	19

McDonagh, Seamus 'Jim'

Ireland international goalkeeper whose Goodison career was cut short by Neville Southall's arrival

Former Bolton Wanderers goalkeeper Seamus 'Jim' McDonagh was the last in a succession of goalkeepers who filled a largely unhappy void between two of Everton's great custodians, Gordon West and Neville Southall.

A £250,000 recruit from Bolton Wanderers in July 1980, McDonagh came in for George Wood, considered the finest of West's many successors. Those who tried to fill the green jersey without success included David Lawson, Dai Davies, Drew Brand and Martin Hodge. McDonagh, in his season-long spell, was considered more on a par with Wood than the hapless 'Dai the Drop' or Lawson – competent, commanding, reliable and yet not destined to greatness or to fundamentally alter the fortunes of a declining team.

Yet his time at Goodison started well and he supplanted Gerry Peyton (himself later on Everton's books) in the Republic of Ireland team. Everton also overcame some poor early performances to rise to third by October. 'Everton's scintillating form this season has been a revelation to the whole of football and they have finally rid themselves of the tag of being the second best team on Merseyside,' recorded the Manchester United programme when Everton visited Old Trafford on 25 October. 'Football at top level is very much an attitude of mind. Everton have had skilful players in abundance for years. Now Gordon Lee seems to have got them thinking positively.'

If only that was the case. Everton lost 2-0 that day and their form nosedived thereafter. A run to the quarter-finals of the FA Cup was ended by Manchester City and they took just a single point from the following eight games. Everton's final three home games of the season witnessed the club's three lowest post-war league attendances. At the end of the season Lee was replaced by Howard Kendall, who initiated a clean sweep.

'He was inclined to trust in experience but I don't think the older players who were already at the club, the likes of Trevor Ross, Peter Eastoe and the goalkeeper Jim McDonagh, were his type of player,' Kevin Ratcliffe later told the Liverpool Echo. 'When you inherit players who are under contract you are stuck with them.

He was trying to balance things. It does take time for a manager to make the changes he wants and it was no different for Howard.'

Kendall brought in Jim Arnold and – crucially – Southall, and McDonagh was on his way back to Bolton in a part-exchange deal that brought Mick Walsh to Goodison.

[FACTFILE]

BORN
Rotherham, 6 October 1952
POSITION
Goalkeeper
OTHER CLUBS
Rotherham United (1970–76); Manchester United (loan); Bolton Wanderers (1976–80 & 1981–83); Notts County (1983–85); Birmingham City (loan, 1984); Gillingham (loan, 1985); Sunderland (loan, 1985); Wichita Wings (US indoor); Scarborough (1987); Huddersfield Town (loan, 1987–88); Charlton Athletic (1988–89); Galway United (player-manager, 1988–89)
HONOURS
25 Republic of Ireland caps (1981–85)

Season	League		FA Cup		League Cup		Total	
	App	Goals	App	Goals	App	Goals	App	Goals
1980/81	40	0	5	0	3	0	48	0
Total	40	0	5	0	3	0	48	0

McDonald, Alex

Well-travelled inside forward who served Everton at the turn of the 19th century

Season	League		FA Cup		Total	
	App	Goals	App	Goals	App	Goals
1899/1900	5	2	0	0	5	2
1900/01	18	4	0	0	18	4
Total	23	6	0	0	23	6

[FACTFILE]

BORN
Greenock, 12 April 1878
POSITION
Inside forward
OTHER CLUBS
Jarrow;
Southampton;
West Ham United;
Portsmouth;
Wellingborough;
Luton Town;
Croydon Common

McDonald, John 'Jock'

Record-breaking full back who provided seven years of fine – but barren – service

For nearly 90 years Jock McDonald held an undistinguished Everton record: the longest run of any outfield Everton player without scoring a goal. Not until March 2011 did Tony Hibbert – another Everton full back whose uncertainty in front of goal led to declarations that Goodison would 'riot' if he ever found the net – surpass his record of 224 goalless appearances.

EVERTON F. C.

The left back had earned Victory International honours while at Motherwell, but it was his form for Airdrieonians that attracted the attention of the Everton directors. They pursued his signature through the 1919/20 season but received repeated denials from the Airdrie board. Finally, ahead of the 1920/21 season, they submitted and McDonald became an Everton player for £2200.

McDonald was what would be described as a 'traditional' or uncompromising full back in an era when the position was defined by a lack of flourishes. His first instinct was to stop attackers; his second to dispatch the ball as quickly as possible. This was, however, in contrast to the pattern of the Everton defence at this time, which was considered to be the team's first line of attack; something that made the team

pleasing to the eye, but was considered by others to be its soft underbelly.

For the 1921/22 season McDonald was made captain, which began in stunning fashion. Everton recorded a 5-0 victory over Manchester United at Goodison on the opening day of the season, and the Liverpool Post and Mercury reported that McDonald was 'particularly brisk in his clearances, which were of

the requisite length and kept well in play'. Its correspondent added: 'The new skipper was fairly in his element, and was entitled to all the applause which came his way.' However, the season quickly went downhill and McDonald was missing for large parts through illness then injury. Everton narrowly escaped relegation and the captaincy reverted to Hunter Hart.

This coincided with an upturn in Everton form and they finished the subsequent two seasons fifth and seventh, playing brilliant

football. But they were inconsistent too, and by the middle of the decade were again flirting with relegation. After another near miss in 1926/27 – when Everton conceded a staggering 90 league goals – the board initiated sweeping changes. McDonald was sold to New Brighton for £100 where his goalless run quickly came to an end. He later gave fine service in the Cheshire League until long past his 40th birthday.

Season	League		FA Cup		Total	
	App	Goals	App	Goals	App	Goals
1920/21	39	0	5	0	44	0
1921/22	26	0	1	0	27	0
1922/23	29	0	0	0	29	0
1923/24	24	0	2	0	26	0
1924/25	29	0	4	0	33	0
1925/26	37	0	2	0	39	0
1926/27	24	0	2	0	26	0
Total	208	0	16	0	224	0

[FACTFILE]

BORN
Dykeland, 4 January 1896
POSITION
Full back
OTHER CLUBS
Motherwell (1913–19);
Airdieonians (1919–20);
New Brighton (1927–31);
Connah's Quay (1931–39)

McDonald, Neil

Versatile Geordie who always faced an uphill struggle to win over the fans

LIKE SO many of Colin Harvey's signings, Neil McDonald faced the difficult – if not impossible – task of succeeding a member of Everton's most illustrious team, in his case Gary Stevens. Ultimately it was a challenge he was unable to meet, but in 100 Everton starts, McDonald could not be faulted for his efforts – the fruition of which saw him successfully reinvented as a central midfielder.

A son of Tyneside, like two men – Peter Beardsley and Steve Watson – who were to follow him into a blue shirt, McDonald was

spotted as a youngster at the famous Wallsend Boys Club and signed by Newcastle. Still a teenager, he established himself in the Magpies' team and was called upon to represent the England under-21 team on five occasions. In August 1988 the £525,000 switch to Everton came and he was immediately installed in place of the recently departed Stevens.

TALL AND SLIGHTLY ungainly, McDonald was a different proposition to the athletic Stevens. If early hesitancy was excused on account of his relative youth, Evertonians soon became impatient after several ponderous displays. McDonald was replaced as first-choice right back by Ian Snodin, whose performances elevated him to the England squad, and he subsequently found himself pushed behind Dutchman Ray Atteveld. Undaunted, McDonald fitted in when called upon, sometimes also as left back.

In autumn 1990, as the Harvey regime went through its death throes, McDonald was called upon as an auxiliary central midfielder and performed with distinction. Showing a previously unseen range of passing and a powerful shot, he looked an entirely different player. Yet this renaissance was brief, and in September 1991 McDonald found himself a victim of a transitory period and was sold to Oldham Athletic. After playing spells with Bolton and Preston, a coaching career of great variation ensued.

[FACTFILE]

BORN
Wallsend, 2 November 1965
POSITION
Full back / midfielder
OTHER CLUBS
Newcastle United (1983–88);
Oldham Athletic (1991–94);
Bolton Wanderers (1994–95);
Preston North End (1995–98)
AS MANAGER
Carlisle United (2006–07);
Ostersunds FK (2007)

Season	League App	League Goals	FA Cup App	FA Cup Goals	League Cup App	League Cup Goals	Other App	Other Goals	Total App	Total Goals
1988/89	22 (3)	1	4	0	1	1	5	0	32 (3)	2
1989/90	26 (5)	1	7	0	3	0	-	-	36 (5)	1
1990/91	27 (2)	2	6	0	3	2	5 (1)	0	41 (3)	4
1991/92	1 (4)	0	0	0	0	0	0	0	1 (4)	0
Total	**76(14)**	**4**	**17**	**0**	**7**	**3**	**10 (1)**	**0**	**110(15)**	**7**

McFadden, James

Gifted Scottish forward who lacked the composure to make his talents count

Amid Scottish football's seemingly terminal decline in the early 21st century, James McFadden was a rare thing. Technically gifted, flamboyant, a natural showman – the young Glaswegian was a throwback to an era when Scotland was renowned for producing some of the game's most entertaining players. In coming to Goodison from Motherwell for a knockdown fee of £1.25million in August 2003, he followed a noble tradition set by the likes of Torry Gillick, Tommy Ring, Alex Young and Pat Nevin.

Indeed, McFadden's full debut, against Leeds United in September 2003, was one of the most memorable Goodison has witnessed in recent years. As Everton romped to a 4-0 win, McFadden was at the heart of everything positive, wowing with his dribbling, close control and trickery – and thoroughly upstaging Wayne Rooney, who was returning from injury. There would be other occasions too when McFadden thrilled Evertonians. His April 2007 flick over the head of a Charlton defender and volley into the back of the net for a late winner was one of the finest and most dramatic goals

Goodison has seen in many a season. And few of McFadden's strikes in an Everton shirt were more important than the one that brought the scores level in the away leg of a UEFA Cup tie against Metalist Kharkiv the following October.

BUT ALL too often, McFadden seemed more like Jim Pearson than the Golden Vision. He was not ruthless enough in front of goal and it took him 16 months to get his first Everton goal. Although he possessed formidable talents, pace was not one of them. Always a slight figure, he was prone to be subsumed by more physical opponents. On other occasions he was let down by overelaboration – the cause of immense

frustration among the Goodison crowd. Or a trick wouldn't come off, McFadden's head would drop and he would drift out of a game.

Part of the problem was that he lacked a regular first-team berth and made more Premier League appearances from the bench than he started. There was also a tendency to play him on the wing, rather than in his preferred central role. And yet when opportunities did come McFadden's way, he never fully seized the moment.

One of his final games – the 2008 League Cup semi-final against Chelsea – seemed to represent everything infuriating and mesmeric about McFadden. Asked to play on the Everton left, he was repeatedly caught out of position and failed to track back as Chelsea romped forward. Given a glimmer of an opening, however, he brilliantly wriggled past Ricardo Carvalho's despairing lunge and broke into the left of the Chelsea

box, but one-on-one with the goalkeeper elected to shoot from a tight angle instead of squaring to the unmarked Tim Cahill. The ball hit the post, Chelsea won the match and within days McFadden was no longer an Everton player – the £4.75million bid from Birmingham representing a good price for a player nearing the end of his contract.

McFADDEN spent four injury-troubled years at St Andrews. Following the expiry of his contract in 2011 he was released from the club and linked with a return to Scotland. It was therefore some surprise that in September that year the out-of-contract player returned to Everton. His opportunities were nevertheless limited in his second spell at Goodison and he was released at the end of the 2011/12 season.

Season	League App	League Goals	FA Cup App	FA Cup Goals	League Cup App	League Cup Goals	Europe App	Europe Goals	Total App	Total Goals
2003/04	11(12)	0	1	0	3	0	-	-	15(12)	0
2004/05	7 (16)	1	3	2	3	0	-	-	13(16)	1
2005/06	24 (8)	6	2 (2)	1	1	0	2 (2)	0	29(12)	7
2006/07	6 (13)	2	0	0	2	1	-	-	8 (13)	3
2007/08	5 (7)	2	1	0	3	2	5	1	14 (7)	5
2011/12	2 (5)	0	1	0	0	0	-	-	3 (5)	0
Total	**55(61)**	**11**	**7 (2)**	**3**	**12**	**3**	**7 (2)**	**1**	**82(65)**	**18**

McFarlane,
Robert 'Rab'

Scotland international goalkeeper not able to make the Everton goalkeeper's jersey his own

Season	League App	League Goals	FA Cup App	FA Cup Goals	Total App	Total Goals
1897/98	9	0	0	0	9	0
Total	**9**	**0**	**0**	**0**	**9**	**0**

[FACTFILE]

BORN
Glasgow, 14 April 1983
POSITION
Forward / left winger
OTHER CLUBS
Motherwell (1999–2003); Birmingham City (2008–11)
HONOURS
41 Scotland caps (13 goals) (2002–)

[FACTFILE]

BORN
Greenock, 14 May 1876
POSITION
Goalkeeper
OTHER CLUBS
Greenock Rosebery; Morton; Third Lanark; East Stirlingshire; Bristol St George; New Brompton; Grimsby Town (1900); Celtic; Middlesbrough (1902); Aberdeen; Motherwell
HONOURS
1 Scotland cap (1896)

McGourty,
John 'Jimmy'

Inside forward who won league representative honours during his time in Ireland

[FACTFILE]

BORN
Fauldhouse, 10 July 1912
POSITION
Inside forward
OTHER CLUBS
Fauldhouse St John's;
Partick Thistle;
Hamilton Academical;
Waterford;
Ipswich Town (1938)

Season	League		FA Cup		Other		Total	
	App	Goals	App	Goals	App	Goals	App	Goals
1932/33	14	2	0	0	1	0	15	2
1933/34	1	0	0	0	0	0	1	0
Total	15	2	0	0	1	0	16	2

McIlhatton, Johnny

Old-school Scottish winger, whose life ended tragically early

Johnny McIlhatton was one of the most highly regarded prospects of wartime football. An old-school Scottish winger who was diminutive, skilful and quick, his performances on Albion Rovers' wing, notably against Rangers' Scotland international full back John 'Tiger' Shaw, brought him growing renown.

He was scouted in spring 1946 by Everton's former captain Jock Thomson, whose enthusiastic report to Goodison saw the director Ernest Green dispatched to Lanarkshire to check him out. Green reported that he was 'small, quick, clever and well built', and recommended Everton buy him.

With hindsight, this was not the smartest move. In pursuing McIlhatton the board agreed to overlook Carlisle's Ivor Broadis and Bristol City's Roy Bentley – both would be England regulars the following decade. The £5000 fee was also a significant sum to pay for a largely untested footballer who had never played beyond amateur level. Later that year Joe Mercer –England's wartime captain no less – would be sold by Everton to Arsenal for just £9000.

McIlhatton was charged with the difficult job of filling the number seven shirt, worn with such distinction by his countryman Torry Gillick in Everton's pre-war title-winning side. Untried and coming into a struggling side, this was always going to be something of a thankless task.

The winger, like his new team, started the 1946/47 season slowly, but pressure quickly gathered on his young shoulders. After a 4-1 defeat to Charlton in October, 'Stork' complained in the Liverpool Daily Post that he had had 'his worst game to date … He did absolutely nothing for the full ninety minutes.'

THERE WERE, nevertheless, by Christmas some brief signs of a return to the form that won him such plaudits as an amateur in Scotland. He was at his best when interchanging with Jock Dodds at centre forward, and their interplay flummoxed opponents.

In an FA Cup third round tie against Southend in January 1947 he had his best game yet, scoring his first goal in a 4-2 win. 'He opened with a fervour and feint and centre quite foreign to his work in recent weeks,' recorded Ernest 'Bee' Edwards. 'His method of tip-and-run beyond a defender succeeded in most instances. As a critic … it is my pleasure to put on record the winger's display and his forging ahead. He was one of an eleven that revelled in a softish turf.'

But the form did not last. Although he continued to feature regularly in a poor Everton team until the autumn he eventually lost his place to Jackie Grant. His irregular appearances dried up altogether following Cliff Britton's appointment as manager in September 1948.

In 1949 McIlhatton joined Dundee and a year later signed for Raith Rovers. At neither club did he succeed in holding down a regular place and he drifted out of football, becoming a marine engineer.

His name re-entered Evertonian minds just a few years later, in February 1954, when supporters learned news of his tragic death, aged 33, from tuberculosis. When news reached Merseyside, the Everton Supporters' Federation immediately sought permission to take a collection at a home game for the benefit of his widow.

BUT WITH THAT incongruous mix of cack-handedness and inherent sense of Evertonian

IN AN FA CUP THIRD ROUND TIE AGAINST SOUTHEND IN JANUARY 1947 HE HAD HIS BEST GAME YET, SCORING HIS FIRST GOAL IN A 4-2 WIN

values with which they frequently governed the club, Everton's board refused the federation's request, while simultaneously investigating the widow's circumstances. When it was reported back that she and her four children were surviving on an income of less than £3 per week, they decided to pay her a grant of £2 per week. Even when she found full-time work as a schoolteacher Everton continued paying her a benefit until autumn 1956.

Season	League		FA Cup		Total	
	App	Goals	App	Goals	App	Goals
1946/47	37	1	2	1	39	2
1947/48	13	0	0	0	13	0
1948/49	5	0	0	0	5	0
Total	55	1	2	1	57	2

McInnes, Tom

Scottish inside forward whose mid-1890s goals almost brought the title to Goodison

Season	League		FA Cup		Total	
	App	Goals	App	Goals	App	Goals
1894/95	23	10	4	0	27	10
1895/96	19	8	1	0	20	8
Total	42	18	5	0	47	18

McIntosh, Jimmy

Forward whose Everton career coincided with the club's nadir

It was the eternal misfortune of inside forward Jimmy McIntosh to have a career defined by being in the wrong place at the wrong time. The young Scot was a prodigy on the wing at Blackpool in the mid-1930s and signed up by Preston while still a teenager.

EVERTON 1951/52
Back row - **Cooke (Trainer), McIntosh, TE Jones**, *Potts, Sagar, Lello,* **Moore, Lindley, Grant**
Front - **Eglington, Lindsay, Catterick, Parker, Buckle, Farrell, Fielding**

BUT THEN war cruelly intervened and cut the bulk of his twenties – a time when he should have been lining up alongside such luminaries as Tom Finney and Bill Shankly at Deepdale. He returned to Blackpool after the war, now playing as a centre forward alongside Stanley Matthews. However, he was dropped for the 1948 FA Cup final and joined Everton for £5500 in March 1949. But again it was a bad time, and Everton were in one of the darkest periods of their history.

Indeed the threat of relegation haunted Goodison at this time. 'Everton are also in the vortex and it may be that we shall not know the members of the relegation fight until the very last day,' recorded the match programme when they visited Sheffield United. 'This has been a very difficult season for Everton.' Yet McIntosh's goals helped elevate Everton above the mire.

There were crucial strikes in 1-1 draws with Sunderland and Stoke, as well as an effort on his debut against his former club Blackpool, a 5-0 hammering. Most crucially he and Eddie Wainwright scored a goal apiece against title contenders Manchester United with two games to go. The victory, according to Liverpool Echo correspondent 'Stork': '… lifted the relegation clouds so that, with the tension eased, Everton can go into their last two matches with easier minds'.

Season	League		FA Cup		Total	
	App	Goals	App	Goals	App	Goals
1948/49	12	5	0	0	12	5
1949/50	17	3	0	0	17	3
1950/51	29	11	1	0	30	11
Total	58	19	1	0	59	19

McIntosh, Thomas

Everton's long-serving secretary-manager who oversaw the signing of Dixie Dean

Tom McIntosh (b. 24 February 1879, d. 29 October 1935) was one of the most respected football administrators in early-20th-century football. He was the natural candidate to succeed W.J. Sawyer as Everton secretary-manager after the latter opted to focus on his other business commitments in late 1919, and McIntosh helped the club move from a state of post-war transition into a golden era. Like so many of the men who succeeded him – Harry Catterick, Gordon Lee and Howard Kendall – he was a Northeasterner and affable, diligent and well liked.

Everton's escape was a temporary reprieve. They would squeak past relegation again the next season before succumbing in 1950/51. Through this succession of on-pitch disasters, McIntosh never quite seemed to settle and was the subject of repeated interest from lower league clubs.

After winning just four of their opening 20 league games in 1949/50 McIntosh was dropped and seemed set to move to Wrexham for £3750, but the deal fell through. He scored 11 goals from 29 games in the relegation season, but it wasn't nearly enough. At the end of that campaign he was sold to Distillery for £1500. He was later their manager, also serving Glentoran and Ballymena United as boss.

McIntosh had been a player with Darlington in the 1890s, reverting to the club's secretary in 1902. Nine years later he became Middlesbrough secretary-manager and was charged with the task of rebuilding the club's sullied reputation after its manager Andy Walker and chairman Thomas Gibson Poole were banned for trying to fix a home game against local rivals Sunderland. He helped transform the club and under his charge they finished third in Division One in 1913/14 – the highest position in the club's history.

His move to Everton in December 1919 came with the consent of his former club. Everton were in a state of flux after the First World War had disrupted their 1915 title-winning side. A total of 35 different players lined up in a blue shirt during the first season after fighting had finished, and McIntosh set about moulding this transitional team into a tighter, more disciplined unit. While never directly responsible for team selection or transfers, he was a key influence on the directors and ran the club on a day-to-day basis.

It took several years, but from the post-war mess he brought a new golden generation to Goodison Park, most famously playing the principal role in the acquisition of Dixie Dean from Tranmere Rovers. A kind, patient, articulate man, his 'system of management', wrote the Everton historian Thomas Keates in 1928, 'seems to approach the ideal'.

'He was someone you looked up to and respected,' recalled Dean. 'When I was made captain we used to have many a chat about this and that and you never had any trouble talking to Tom. He'd always listen and he'd try to do what was best for all concerned.'

Under his watch some of the greatest players in the club's history bestrode Goodison: Dean, Warney Cresswell, Ted Sagar, Alec Troup, Ted Critchley, Tommy White, Jimmy Dunn and Jimmy Stein were all signed. During this period Everton lifted the League Championship in 1927/28 and 1931/32, the FA Cup in 1933, and the Second Division Championship in 1930/31. There was, of course, also the aberration of relegation in 1930.

McIntosh was diagnosed with cancer in 1934 and spent a period away trying to recuperate. However, the illness took his life on 29 October 1935. He was only 56 years old. Dean in particular was devastated. 'He was a great man and when he passed away I was very upset.'

At the following Saturday's match, the Goodison crowd stood in silence to pay respect to one of Everton's great servants. 'There was an impressive two minutes before the match at Goodison Park today,' reported the Football Echo. 'The players lined up and the crowd stood bareheaded as a token of respect to the late Tom McIntosh, the secretary-manager of the Everton club. The Stoke players wore black armbands.'

McIntosh was succeeded by Theo Kelly, but without him the club – as Dean would soon attest – would not be the same place for many more years.

McKenzie, Duncan

Flamboyant forward who illuminated and exasperated during Gordon Lee's tenure

To a generation of Evertonians, Duncan McKenzie personified the club's preference for the solid over the spectacular during its ultimately futile pursuit of glory through the late 1970s. A fabulously gifted forward, McKenzie's skills brought him adulation from Everton fans, deprived of such virtuoso talent since the club's 1960s golden era. But McKenzie was ultimately a free spirit who would not conform to the strictures of Gordon Lee's management. As such, his Goodison career was always doomed to a premature conclusion.

MCKENZIE started out at Nottingham Forest, where he cultivated a reputation as an entertaining forward of skill and bravura with a big-game temperament. Off the pitch, he also became known for his party tricks: leaping over his coach's mini and throwing golf balls phenomenal distances – a technique he had perfected as a youngster throwing stones across the River Trent. He joined Leeds United, during Brian Clough's 44-day stint as manager in 1974, and in 1976 had a spell with Anderlecht. In December 1976, Billy Bingham spent £200,000 to bring him to Everton. It was a move applauded by fans, who willed some flair to Bingham's workmanlike team. But within the game the prevailing wisdom was 'Sign McKenzie and you're

sacked' – a maxim that McKenzie failed to confound. Within a month of signing him, Bingham was fired to be replaced by Gordon Lee.

Lee brought with him a reputation as a dour, dependable man, who had little patience for what he termed 'Flash Harrys' or 'coffee house ball jugglers'. McKenzie, it seemed, belonged to this breed of player, but contrary to the stories of disputes and rancour, Lee and McKenzie had a civil relationship. The player respected the manager

and in turn Lee selected him through his first 18 months as Everton manager.

WIRY AND LITHE, McKenzie possessed pace and a low centre of gravity. He was at his best dropping off the forward line and leading attacks from deep. With his array of flicks, shimmies and dummies he seemed to delight in tormenting his opponents. 'In those days the defenders kicked 10 bells of hell out of us and in many ways they deserved to be on the receiving end occasionally,' he said in 2008. 'It was payback time.'

There was no finer example of this than in Everton's FA Cup fifth round win over Cardiff City in February 1977. McKenzie robbed the Cardiff centre half on the halfway line and set off for goal, with the Cardiff goalkeeper, Ron Healey, advancing to meet his arrival. 'I must have taken it round him six or seven times,' McKenzie told the Guardian's Richard Williams, with a more than a hint of exaggeration. 'And while I was doing that all the Cardiff defenders chased back and got

themselves on the goal line. I pretended to shoot, and they all went one way. I pretended to shoot the other way, and they went that way, too. Then I popped it between the centre half's legs.' And yet Lee was less than impressed by McKenzie's effrontery. 'I got frightful earache off the manager,' McKenzie remembered. 'Gordon Lee said to me, "Why didn't you just hit it?"'

While such antics are invariably remembered with fondness by fans, they cloud other memories of overelaboration and hubris. It was ultimately these which saw McKenzie fall foul of Gordon Lee, who sought a more reliable alternative to the showman.

In September 1978 McKenzie was sold to Chelsea for £165,000, but his time in London was brief and he had returned back north, with Blackburn Rovers, by the end of the 1978/79 season. Still aged only 28, never again did he grace the First Division, instead playing out his career in the NASL.

Since retirement, he has become a popular figure on the after-dinner circuit, an appropriate place, perhaps, for one of the game's natural showmen. 'Entertainment is what it's all about,' he once declared. 'Sure, it's important to win, but there's room for some fun and games along the way.'

> 'I PRETENDED TO SHOOT, AND THEY ALL WENT ONE WAY. I PRETENDED TO SHOOT THE OTHER WAY, AND THEY WENT THAT WAY, TOO. THEN I POPPED IT BETWEEN THE CENTRE HALF'S LEGS'

Season	League		FA Cup		League Cup		Total	
	App	Goals	App	Goals	App	Goals	App	Goals
1976/77	20	5	6	4	4	1	30	10
1977/78	28	9	1 (1)	1	2	1	31 (1)	11
Total	48	14	7 (1)	5	6	2	61 (1)	21

[FACTFILE]

BORN
Grimsby, 10 June 1950
POSITION
Forward
OTHER CLUBS
Nottingham Forest (1969–74);
Mansfield Town (loan, 1970 & 1973);
Leeds United (1974–76);
Anderlecht (1976);
Chelsea (1978–79);
Blackburn Rovers (1979–81);
Tulsa Roughnecks (1981);
Chicago Sting (1982)

McKinnon, Archibald

Prolific outside right who was unable to hold down a place in Everton's debut season, despite his goals

Season	League App	League Goals	FA Cup App	FA Cup Goals	Total App	Total Goals
1888/89	6	4	-	-	6	4
Total	6	4	-	-	6	4

[FACTFILE]

BORN
1865
POSITION
Outside right
OTHER CLUB
Hibernian

McLaughlin, John

Distinctive-looking defender of 1970s vintage

Although he rarely enjoyed a run in the Everton first team, the prematurely balding figure of Scottish defender John 'Tiger' McLaughlin was an image many Evertonians of the early 1970s consider synonymous with the era.

A small, aggressive full back, Tiger – an affectionate nickname he carried south from Scotland – was signed from Falkirk for £50,000 in 1971. A quiet and unassuming member of the Everton dressing room, his arrival effectively marked the end for Keith Newton, less than 15 months after he had starred at the Mexico World Cup. He was a regular through most of the 1971/72 season, but struggled to get a look in the following campaign with midfielder Henry Newton then Archie Styles deployed in his place.

The arrival of Billy Bingham as manager initially prompted a change of fortune. A regular through the first half of the 1973/74 campaign, he lost his place to Steve Seargeant and was thereafter a peripheral member of the Everton squad.

'The balding pate of Everton full-back John McLaughlin makes him look 10 years older than he is,' recorded a Liverpool Echo profile during that season. 'He was thin on top when he joined the Blues two years ago from Falkirk … and then he was only 23. He is deceptive looking in other ways as well. Slightly built,

very quiet off the field, without the strength one would expect from a defender, he gets so involved in a game, particularly with his tackling, that Scottish fans dubbed him "The Tiger" before he moved south to Goodison.'

Unable to supplant either Seargeant or Dave Jones, in summer 1976 Tiger tried his luck in the NASL with Seattle Sounders. He returned to Falkirk the following season, playing out his career at Brockville Park. He settled in the area, later working in the plumbing trade.

[FACTFILE]

BORN
Stirling, 3 January 1948
POSITION
Left back
OTHER CLUBS
Falkirk (1967–71);
Seattle Sounders (1976);
Falkirk (1976–77)

Season	League App	League Goals	FA Cup App	FA Cup Goals	League Cup App	League Cup Goals	Other App	Other Goals	Total App	Total Goals
1971/72	27	0	4	0	0	0	-	-	31	0
1972/73	7	0	0	0	0	0	-	-	7	0
1973/74	21	1	1	0	2	0	2	0	26	1
1974/75	2 (1)	0	2	0	0	0	-	-	4 (1)	0
1975/76	2 (1)	0	0	0	0	0	0	0	2 (1)	0
Total	59 (2)	1	7	0	2	0	2	0	70 (2)	1

McLaughlin, William

Reserve inside forward utilised in the first decade of the 20th century

Season	League		FA Cup		Total	
	App	Goals	App	Goals	App	Goals
1904/05	7	3	0	0	7	3
1905/06	8	2	0	0	8	2
Total	**15**	**5**	**0**	**0**	**15**	**5**

McLean, Duncan

Full back who crossed the new Mersey divide to remain at Anfield after the 'split'

Season	League		FA Cup		Total	
	App	Goals	App	Goals	App	Goals
1890/91	5	0	1	0	6	0
1891/92	20	0	0	0	20	0
Total	**25**	**0**	**1**	**0**	**26**	**0**

McLeod, Kevin

Talented home-grown midfielder who forged a solid league career beyond Goodison

Season	League		FA Cup		League Cup		Total	
	App	Goals	App	Goals	App	Goals	App	Goals
2000/01	0 (5)	0	0	0	0	0	0 (5)	0
2001/02	0	0	0	0	1	0	1	0
2002/03	0	0	0 (1)	0	0	0	0 (1)	0
Total	**0 (5)**	**0**	**0 (1)**	**0**	**1**	**0**	**1 (6)**	**0**

McMahon, Steve

Midfield hard man who became a hated figure at Goodison

Steve McMahon had both the talent and grounding as an Evertonian to become a Goodison great. Were it not for a premature departure – still shy of his 22nd birthday – such hopes may have been realised. But to the unending dismay of Evertonians, McMahon's best years lay at Anfield, and so instead of becoming an Everton hero he became one of the most reviled opponents of his generation.

A boyhood Evertonian, who as a teenager served as a Goodison ballboy and worked his way through the club's youth set-up, McMahon was given his debut as an 18-year-old on the opening day of the 1980/81 season. Immediately showing maturity beyond his young years, he established himself in a transitional Everton team. An energetic player noted for his tough, eager tackling, in many ways he resembled Bolton's Peter Reid, who Gordon Lee had unsuccessfully tried to buy that summer. With his neat and tidy passing, he allowed more expansive players such as Asa Hartford and, later, Andy King and Kevin Sheedy to flourish further up the pitch.

In the 1981/82 season, McMahon – who played more games than any other player – was awarded the Supporters Club Player of the Year award and called up to the England under-21 team. As a youthful Everton team made some

progress under Howard Kendall's management the following season, McMahon was one of its leading lights, outshining Reid, who was now an Everton player.

However, negotiations over a new contract spilled over until the end of the 1982/83 season before reaching an impasse. Kendall insisted he wanted to retain McMahon's services in the teeth of a bid from Liverpool. After a dark night of the soul, McMahon rejected Liverpool's advances,

instead joining Aston Villa on the eve of the 1983/84 season. The £250,000 fee funded the signing of Trevor Steven.

McMAHON spent two years at Villa Park, but remained on Liverpool's radar. In September 1985 he became Kenny Dalglish's first signing as Liverpool manager. At Anfield, McMahon's style became at once more expansive and abrasive. More than just a midfield grafter, he was Liverpool's playmaker as Dalglish led the team to a succession of honours.

And yet at Goodison, the switch smacked of betrayal. The feeling among Evertonians – perhaps unfairly – was that McMahon had

engineered the move to Liverpool. There was also a persistent grudge with his former colleagues in derby matches. Graeme Sharp wrote in his autobiography that McMahon appeared to become a 'Billy Big Time' on signing for Liverpool: 'He had a swagger about him and I felt that he looked down on Everton.' Sharp recounted how McMahon gouged him in the eyes during one encounter, while few Evertonians will forget the bone-crunching challenge he made on John Ebbrell in 1991 – a tackle that ultimately saw McMahon stretchered off.

McMahon played out his career with Manchester City and Swindon Town, where he was player-manager. He enjoyed mixed success at the County Ground and in subsequent spells in charge of Blackpool and Perth Glory, later turning to television punditry.

> IN THE 1981/82 SEASON MCMAHON – WHO PLAYED MORE GAMES THAN ANY OTHER PLAYER – WAS AWARDED THE SUPPORTERS CLUB PLAYER OF THE YEAR AWARD

[FACTFILE]

BORN
Liverpool, 20 August 1961

POSITION
Midfielder

OTHER CLUB
Aston Villa (1983–85);
Liverpool (1985–91);
Manchester City (1991–94);
Swindon Town (player-manager, 1994–98)

AS MANAGER
Blackpool (2000–04);
Perth Glory (2005)

HONOURS
17 England caps (1988–90)

Season	League		FA Cup		League Cup		Total	
	App	Goals	App	Goals	App	Goals	App	Goals
1980/81	34	5	5	0	3	0	42	5
1981/82	31 (1)	2	0	0	4	2	35 (1)	4
1982/83	34	4	4	0	4	1	42	5
Total	**99 (1)**	**11**	**9**	**0**	**11**	**3**	**119(1)**	**14**

McMillan, James

Prolific inside forward unable to claim a regular berth despite his goals

Season	League		FA Cup		Total	
	App	Goals	App	Goals	App	Goals
1892/93	2	1	0	0	2	1
1893/94	4	4	0	0	4	4
1894/95	1	0	0	0	1	0
Total	7	5	0	0	7	5

[FACTFILE]

BORN
1870
POSITION
Inside left
OTHER CLUB
St Bernard's
HONOURS
1 Scotland cap (1897)

McNamara, Tony

Boyhood blue who became the first player to appear in all four divisions in a single season

Tony McNamara was one of a generation of home-grown players charged with the task of restoring Everton from their historic early-1950s low point. His Goodison career, encompassing seven years, witnessed Everton's disastrous 1951/52 campaign, when they finished 16th in Division Two, promotion back to the elite two years later, and the club's re-establishment as a top-flight force in the middle of the decade.

SIGNED as an amateur in the late 1940s, the onset of McNamara's top-class career was delayed by a period of national service with the RAF. He made his debut against Leeds United in September 1951 and in doing so fulfilled a boyhood dream. 'I was always Everton proud and thrilled to watch players like Jimmy McIntosh, Tommy Lawton and T.G. Jones in their wartime team,' he later told Charlie Buchan's Football Monthly.

McNamara was a winger of style and verve and, when given a run in the team, an important contributor of goals. His tally of ten in the 1956/57 campaign made him Everton's top scorer that season. But he was also unlucky with injuries. He had cartilages removed from both legs and made just four appearances in the 1953/54 season when Everton secured promotion.

He returned to play his part in Everton's re-establishment in the top flight and said at the time that the main difference was the scale of the stadia. 'After sampling both divisions now I feel that the First Division is much the better,' he said in 1957. 'There is a lot more positional play, of course, and the players generally think quicker and keep the ball on the move more. But the biggest difference of all is the grounds. Perhaps we are spoilt in having such a wonderful arena at Goodison. But having played there before lofty stands and huge crowds it can be disconcerting to turn out on a small cramped pitch with the spectators virtually able to shake hands with you.'

LITTLE could McNamara have known when he said those words that he was heading back to such insalubrious arenas. After losing his place to Jimmy Harris during the 1957/58 season, Everton entertained offers for the forward. Sheffield United showed an interest, but it was Liverpool, then languishing in the Second Division, that McNamara went to for a fee of £3500 after Everton had failed in a part-exchange bid for Johnny Morrissey. His time at Anfield was brief, as was a switch to Fourth Division Crewe Alexandra. He eventually settled at Third Division Bury later in 1958, meaning he had played in all four divisions within a year – becoming the first player ever to do so.

But it was Everton with whom his name was synonymous and even into his eighties he was a regular guest at Goodison. Interviewed by the Liverpool Echo in 2009 he singled out Everton's famous 5-2 win over Manchester United's Busby Babes at Old Trafford in October 1956 as his highlight.

'I ran down the middle of the pitch, I only touched the ball once and the keeper started coming towards me and I thought "that's it", so I just chipped it over his head,' he said. 'That was the last goal, it was a great win.'

[FACTFILE]

BORN
Liverpool, 3 October 1929
POSITION
Winger
OTHER CLUBS
Liverpool (1957-58),
Crewe Alexandra (1958),
Bury

Season	League		FA Cup		Total	
	App	Goals	App	Goals	App	Goals
1951/52	33	5	1	0	34	5
1952/53	7	0	0	0	7	0
1953/54	4	1	0	0	4	1
1954/55	27	4	0	0	27	4
1955/56	7	2	0	0	7	2
1956/57	32	10	1	0	33	10
1957/58	1	0	0	0	1	0
Total	111	22	2	0	113	22

McNaught,
Ken

Scottish defender whose best days lay beyond Goodison

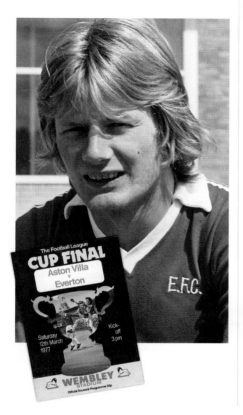

Tall, blond Scottish centre half Ken McNaught came from illustrious footballing stock. His father Willie was, in the 1940s and 1950s, a distinguished left back for Raith Rovers and Scotland; for the former gaining the club's appearance record over a career that spanned 20 years. His influence on his son was immeasurable, and he persuaded the teenage centre forward to swap his position for central defence. He joined Everton as an apprentice on completing his O levels in 1972, making his debut against Leicester City in January 1975.

ALTHOUGH never especially quick, McNaught was tall and imposing in the air and powerful in the tackle. He established himself in the Everton team through the tail-end of the 1975/76 season. Through the next campaign he missed not one of Everton's 58 league and cup matches, and in the League Cup Final epic against Aston Villa was arguably Everton's best player, subduing Andy Gray, who was in the finest form of his career.

Evidently the Scot impressed Villa, for at the season's end Ron Saunders made a £200,000 bid for McNaught, which Gordon Lee, seeking to instil his own vision at Goodison, accepted. Forming a formidable Villa Park partnership

with Allan Evans, McNaught was a key member of Villa's League Championship winning side in 1981. A year later, Villa confounded all expectation to also lift the European Cup. In 1983 McNaught followed Saunders to West Bromwich Albion, and there were later spells with Manchester City and Sheffield United.

> IN THE LEAGUE CUP FINAL EPIC AGAINST ASTON VILLA HE WAS ARGUABLY EVERTON'S BEST PLAYER

[FACTFILE]

BORN
Kirkcaldy, 11 January 1955

POSITION
Central defender

OTHER CLUBS
Aston Villa (1977–83);
West Bromwich Albion (1983–85);
Manchester City (loan, 1984–85);
Sheffield United (1985–86)

Season	League		FA Cup		League Cup		Europe		Total	
	App	Goals	App	Goals	App	Goals	App	Goals	App	Goals
1974/75	4	0	3	0	0	0	-	-	7	0
1975/76	18 (2)	0	0	0	1	0	0	0	19 (2)	0
1976/77	42	3	7	0	9	0	-	-	58	3
Total	**64(2)**	**3**	**10**	**0**	**10**	**0**	**0**	**0**	**84(2)**	**3**

McPherson,
Lachlan

Defensive-minded Scot who played his part in Everton's early 1930s fall and rise

[FACTFILE]

BORN
Cambuslang, 1 July 1900

POSITION
Half back

OTHER CLUBS
Cambuslang Rangers; Notts County (1921–23); Swansea Town (1924–29); New Brighton (1933–34)

HONOURS
1930/31 Second Division Championship

Season	League		FA Cup		Total	
	App	Goals	App	Goals	App	Goals
1929/30	10	0	1	0	11	0
1930/31	17	1	0	0	17	1
1931/32	3	0	0	0	3	0
Total	**30**	**1**	**1**	**0**	**31**	**1**

Meagan, Mick

Irish utility man who went on to manage his country

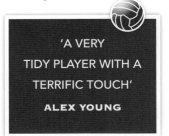

EVERTON 1959

Back - *Sharples, Parker, Labone, Dunlop, Gabriel, Meagan, Bramwell*
Front - *Lill, Collins, Harris, Vernon, Ring*

In 1969, after decades of underachievement and disappointing results, Mick Meagan convinced the FAI administrators that he was the person to become the Republic of Ireland's first full-time manager. In doing so, he set in motion a two-decade-long period of evolution that culminated in the nation's phenomenal footballing successes through the late 1980s and 1990s. In many ways, it was a fitting culmination of a footballing career in which the Dubliner was an impeccable servant for club and country.

Meagan was part of the large-scale 1950s Irish migration to Goodison, signing as an 18-year-old inside forward in 1952. An honest, dedicated professional and the possessor of a fine first touch, he brought a forward's élan to the wing half position when converted there as Peter Farrell's replacement in the 1957/58 season. It said much for Meagan's loyalty that he had stuck around playing junior and Central League football for five years before finally being called upon to make his full debut.

A cool, undemonstrative character, he faced a difficult task not only filling Farrell's illustrious boots but coming into a team for which struggling had become a perennial habit.

Following a disastrous start to the 1958/59 season, in which Everton lost their opening six games, Meagan was dropped and Brian Harris took his place. For the next three seasons this was the pattern of their careers, with managers Johnny Carey then Harry Catterick alternating between the two men.

Towards the end of the 1961/62 season, however, injury sidelined Alex Parker and Meagan was called upon to deputise at right back. He did a fine job, and when Parker returned to full fitness the following October, Catterick switched Meagan to left back in place of the occasionally wayward George Thomsen. His efforts earned him a League Championship medal, and Meagan held his place through much of the 1963/64 season.

But, having passed his 30th birthday at the season's end, Catterick deemed Meagan expendable. Always a wily wheeler-dealer, Catterick used Meagan as a £15,000 down payment in the deal that brought Ray Wilson from Huddersfield Town that summer.

Meagan added to his haul of Ireland caps while at Leeds Road, later playing for Halifax. He returned to Ireland, combining a playing career for Drogheda with management of his country. As Ireland manager until 1971 he did not inspire the results that his inherent decency deserved – indeed they failed to win a single game under his watch – but he had at least established the notion that this was a full-time job and that professionalism was necessary to turn around his country's fortunes.

In 1974, aged 40, he became player-manager of Shamrock Rovers, making history when he played in the same team as his son Mark. Rovers struggled, however, and in 1976 Meagan was sacked as manager, slipping out of the game. 'He was,' recalled Alex Young, 'a very tidy player with a terrific touch. I believe he is someone who would've excelled in the modern game.'

> **'A VERY TIDY PLAYER WITH A TERRIFIC TOUCH'**
> **ALEX YOUNG**

> **HIS EFFORTS IN THE 1962/63 SEASON EARNED HIM A LEAGUE CHAMPIONSHIP MEDAL**

> ### [FACTFILE]
>
> **BORN**
> Dublin 29 May, 1934
> **POSITION**
> Wing half / full back
> **OTHER CLUBS**
> Huddersfield Town (1964–68);
> Halifax Town (1968–69);
> Drogheda (1969–74);
> Shamrock Rovers (1974–76)
> **AS MANAGER**
> Republic of Ireland (1969–71);
> Shamrock Rovers (1974–76)
> **HONOURS**
> 1962/63 League Championship;
> 17 Republic of Ireland caps (1961–69)

Season	League		FA Cup		League Cup		Other		Total	
	App	Goals	App	Goals	App	Goals	App	Goals	App	Goals
1957/58	38	1	3	0	-	-	-	-	41	1
1958/59	21	0	0	0	-	-	-	-	21	0
1959/60	19	0	0	0	-	-	-	-	19	0
1960/61	11	0	0	0	0	0	-	-	11	0
1961/62	18	0	0	0	-	-	-	-	18	0
1962/63	32	0	3	0	-	-	1	0	36	0
1963/64	26	0	4	0	-	-	1	0	31	0
Total	**165**	**1**	**10**	**0**	**0**	**0**	**2**	**0**	**177**	**1**

Meehan, Peter
(aka Peter Meecham)

Distinguished Scotland international full back who was on the losing side in the 1897 FA Cup Final

Season	League		FA Cup		Total	
	App	Goals	App	Goals	App	Goals
1896/97	7	0	4	0	11	0
1897/98	17	0	0	0	17	0
Total	24	0	4	0	28	0

[FACTFILE]

BORN
Broxburn, 28 February 1872
DIED
1915
POSITION
Right back
OTHER CLUBS
Hibernian (1892–93);
Sunderland (1893–95);
Celtic (1895–96);
Southampton (1898–1900);
Manchester City (1900–01);
Barrow (1901–03);
Clyde (1903–04)
HONOURS
1 Scotland cap (1896)

Megson, Gary

Young midfielder who forged a First Division career elsewhere

The son of former Sheffield Wednesday captain Don Megson, Gary Megson was a £250,000 signing from Plymouth Argyle in February 1980.

High hopes were pinned upon the 20-year-old midfielder, as Gordon Lee sought to revive his flagging Everton side. An abrasive tackler, skilful in flashes, and a competent passer, it was nevertheless a challenge too much for one so young, and, lacking the experience to impact upon a declining team, Megson flagged.

Through the 1980/81 season he became no more than a bit-part player and after Howard Kendall's arrival as manager, Megson's was an early departure, sold to his father's former club for £130,000.

There followed the career of a top-flight journeyman, as Megson plied his trade for a succession of middling sides. In the mid-1990s he turned to management and proved his mettle as a sound, authoritarian boss for a succession of teams. In 2002 he was reputedly a boardroom favourite to succeed Walter Smith as Everton manager, but lost out to David Moyes.

HIGH HOPES WERE PINNED UPON THE 20-YEAR-OLD MIDFIELDER

[FACTFILE]

BORN
Manchester, 2 May 1959
POSITION
Midfield
OTHER CLUBS
Plymouth Argyle (1977–80);
Sheffield Wednesday
(1981–84 & 1984–89);
Nottingham Forest (1984);
Newcastle United (1984);
Manchester City (1989–92);
Norwich City (1992–95);
Lincoln City (1995);
Shrewsbury Town (1995–96)
AS MANAGER
Norwich City (1995–96);
Blackpool (1996–97);
Stockport County (1997–99);
Stoke City (1999);
West Bromwich Albion
(2000–04);
Nottingham Forest (2005–06);
Leicester City (2007);
Bolton Wanderers (2007–09);
Sheffield Wednesday (2011–12)

Season	League		FA Cup		League Cup		Europe		Total	
	App	Goals	App	Goals	App	Goals	App	Goals	App	Goals
1979/80	12	1	3	1	0	0	0	0	15	2
1980/81	8 (2)	1	0	0	0	0	-	-	8 (2)	1
Total	20 (2)	2	3	1	0	0	0	0	23 (2)	3

Meiklejohn, George

Centre half with just a single appearance to his name

Season	League		FA Cup		Total	
	App	Goals	App	Goals	App	Goals
1896/97	1	0	0	0	1	0
Total	**1**	**0**	**0**	**0**	**1**	**0**

[FACTFILE]

BORN
1873
POSITION
Centre half

Menham, Bob

Goalkeeper that many felt was culpable for Everton's 1897 FA Cup Final defeat

Season	League		FA Cup		Total	
	App	Goals	App	Goals	App	Goals
1896/97	18	0	5	0	23	0
Total	**18**	**0**	**5**	**0**	**23**	**0**

[FACTFILE]

BORN
North Shields, 1871
DIED
1945
POSITION
Goalkeeper
OTHER CLUBS
Luton Town;
Wigan County;
Swindon Town

Menham, Charles

Reserve goalkeeper in the mid-1920s

[FACTFILE]

BORN
Bromley, 28 August 1896
POSITION
Goalkeeper
OTHER CLUBS
Northern Nomads;
Bradford City (1927)

Season	League		FA Cup		Total	
	App	Goals	App	Goals	App	Goals
1925/26	3	0	0	0	3	0
Total	**3**	**0**	**0**	**0**	**3**	**0**

Mercer, Joe

Home-grown wing half who belongs to the pantheon of English football greats

Joe Mercer typified a generation of footballers who played with a genuine love for the club and an affection for the fans. From the day he first pulled on an Everton shirt in 1933 until the day on which he reluctantly handed it over to his successor Stan Bentham in 1946, his characteristic Cheshire cat grin never once left his face. All the way through his career, through good days and bad, Joe Mercer smiled, because he shared a love affair not just with Everton, but football in general.

Born in Ellesmere Port just after the start of the First World War, Mercer came from footballing stock. His father – Joe senior – had as a youngster played for Ellesmere Port Steelworks with Sam Chedgzoy: scouted by league clubs, Mercer senior joined Nottingham Forest (and later played for Tranmere Rovers), while Chedgzoy went to Goodison. Mercer junior, whose father died when he was 12, grew up idolising the Everton player, however, which marked the start of a lifelong infatuation with the club.

In 1929, aged 15, he was spotted playing as an amateur for Shell and signed for the club he supported as a boy. For the next few years he played in Everton's junior teams and in the Central League, while his tall and skinny frame filled out. But even when he made the step up to the Everton first team, Dixie Dean teased him for his long, bandy legs: 'Blimey, his legs wouldn't last him one day on a postman's round!'

Mercer made his Everton debut a week before the 1933 FA Cup Final and made eight appearances in the 1934/35 season, but had to wait until autumn 1935 before he made a first-team place his own, displacing Jock Thomsen in the Everton half back line. Never noted for his athleticism, he possessed one of the finest footballing brains the English game has witnessed. Mercer, wrote the Everton historian, David France, 'displayed intelligence, vision and guile in all aspects of his game. His precise passing and astute positional play made the game look deceptively easy. Capitalising on his ability to efficiently convert defence into attack, Mercer became the cornerstone of Everton's first School of Science.'

> 'I WAS BROUGHT UP TO BELIEVE THAT EVERTON WAS THE BEST TEAM IN THE WORLD AND NOBODY WAS GOING TO BEAT US'

Mercer later recounted: 'I was brought up to believe that Everton was the best team in the world and nobody was going to beat us.' Yet such hopes took longer to realise than he might have hoped: Everton finished his first full season – 1935/36 – 16th, and the subsequent two campaigns 17th and 14th. If nothing else, Everton were a team in transition, with Dean's golden generation being ushered out and some outstanding new talent – such as T.G. Jones, Torry Gillick, Tommy Lawton and

WILLS'S CIGARETTES

J. MERCER (EVERTON)

Mercer – being introduced. In the 1938/39 season, however, they suddenly clicked and won the First Division title in resounding fashion.

BY THIS TIME Mercer was an England international, having made the first of five international appearances against Northern Ireland in 1938. His finest hour in an England shirt came against Scotland the following April, a match England won after Tommy Lawton struck a late winner. 'Mercer was ever in the thick of the throbbing battle,' the Daily Express wrote of the wing half's man-of-the-match winning performance, 'which, with the wind and pitiless, ceaseless rain, provided the severest of all tests of skill, stamina, and heart. Mercer had them all.'

Aged 24, an England international and league champion – a glittering career beckoned for Mercer. But like all of his generation he was cut off in his prime by the Second World War. Although he had a distinguished career in the wartime leagues and with England – with whom he formed a famous half back line with Cliff Britton and his old schoolmate, Stan Cullis – it was a poor substitute for real football. By the time the Football League recommenced in August 1946, Mercer was past his 32nd birthday.

Everton, by now, were in the grip of Theo Kelly's egocentric management and Mercer was to be a notable casualty of the manager's prickly style. 'He [Kelly] wanted me to play centre half – me, a wing half who used to go diving into action, when the club had T.G. Jones, the best centre half of all in my opinion,' Mercer later said. But a deeper rift was to open between the two men.

In an England versus Scotland victory international in April 1946, Willie Waddell of Rangers had inadvertently landed on Mercer's leg during a

	League		FA Cup		Total	
Season	**App**	**Goals**	**App**	**Goals**	**App**	**Goals**
1932/33	1	0	0	0	1	0
1933/34	0	0	0	0	0	0
1934/35	8	0	0	0	8	0
1935/36	33	1	1	0	34	1
1936/37	39	0	4	0	43	0
1937/38	36	0	2	0	38	0
1938/39	41	0	5	0	46	0
1945/46	-	-	2	1	2	1
1946/47	12	0	0	0	12	0
Total	**170**	**1**	**14**	**1**	**184**	**2**

[FACTFILE]

BORN
Ellesmere Port,
9 August 1914
DIED
9 August 1990
POSITION
Wing half
OTHER CLUB
Arsenal (1946–54)
AS MANAGER
Sheffield United (1955–58);
Aston Villa (1958–64);
Manchester City (1965–72);
Coventry City (1972–74);
England (caretaker, 1974)
HONOURS
1938/39
League Championship,
5 England caps (1938–39)
(plus 26 wartime caps)

challenge. Mercer struggled on gamely, though his injury stunted his efforts. Amazingly, an accusation was levelled after the game that he had not been trying, which was invariably the cause of much hurt for Mercer. The ensuing dispute ended the international career of England's captain – a man with five full and 26 wartime and victory caps – but the sulphuric whiff followed him back to Merseyside, where there was a belief that Mercer was using his injury as an excuse for poor performances .

MERCER was devastated by the allegations and sought to prove everyone wrong, and so consulted an orthopaedic surgeon. When he recommended a cartilage operation, Everton – with whom his association spanned 17 years – refused to pay for it. Unbelievably, Mercer was allowed to pick up the cost himself.

At the heart of the dispute was Kelly and the relationship between the two men first broke down, then became openly hostile. Four games into the 1946/47 season, after Everton played Arsenal at Goodison, Mercer paid a visit to the Arsenal dressing room where

he asked the visitor's physiotherapist, Tom Whittaker, whom he knew from his England days, to inspect his bad leg. Whittaker was shocked by what he saw: the muscles around Mercer's knee were wasted away and the knee itself severely swollen. Turning to the Arsenal players, Whittaker called out: 'Look at this lads – you've been playing against only ten men.'

Mercer persevered, but the injury had cost him his fitness. Kelly's hostility persisted, so Mercer went to meet with the chairman, Cyril Baxter, and asked for a transfer, saying that he would quit football altogether if he was not allowed to leave. Days later Joe Mercer, who six months earlier had captained his country, was serving customers in the grocery wholesalers he co-owned with his father-in-law.

THE IMPASSE lasted three weeks when Kelly finally summoned him to the Adelphi Hotel, where Arsenal's manager George Allison met him. A transfer was agreed and within minutes he had joined the Gunners for £7000. 'It was a terrible blow for me to go,' Mercer said later, 'because I was so crazy about Everton.' In a final snub, Kelly brought his boots to the Adelphi preventing Mercer – as he had Dean – from returning to Goodison to say his farewells. It was an appalling conclusion to Mercer's Everton career, but symptomatic of the way Theo Kelly managed the club.

Written off by Everton in his early thirties, Mercer represented Arsenal until he was 40, captaining them to two League Championships and an FA Cup. In 1955 he became Sheffield United manager, a post he held for three years, moving to Aston Villa in December 1958. He won the inaugural League Cup in 1961, but after suffering a stroke in 1964 was dismissed by the Villa board. Mercer's most auspicious managerial spell came at Manchester City (1965–72) where, in partnership with Malcolm Allison, he won the Second Division Championship, First Division Championship, FA Cup and European Cup Winners' Cup. In 1972 he became general manager of Coventry City, also joining the Highfield Road board. In 1974 he was made temporary England manager between the sacking of Sir Alf Ramsey and the appointment of Don Revie.

Throughout all these achievements at other clubs, he remained an Evertonian at heart, a man who was able to boast, 'I have five shares... which is more than some of the directors have!' After retiring to Merseyside, he remained a regular visitor to Goodison until his death in August 1990.

'We always had fun,' he once said. 'I probably learned more about the game at Arsenal, but I learned how to laugh at Everton.'

Meston, Sammy

Lower-league winger who failed to make the Goodison grade

[FACTFILE]

BORN
Southampton, 30 May 1902
POSITION
Outside right
OTHER CLUBS
Southampton (1921–25);
Gillingham (1926–27);
Tranmere Rovers (1929–31)

Season	League		FA Cup		Total	
	App	Goals	App	Goals	App	Goals
1927/28	1	0	0	0	1	0
Total	1	0	0	0	1	0

Meunier, James

Reserve left back who made just five outings in a royal blue shirt

[FACTFILE]

BORN
Poynton, 1885
POSITION
Left back
OTHER CLUBS
Stockport County (1903);
Manchester City (1904);
Southport Central;
Lincoln City (1912–13);
Coventry City;
Hyde United;
Macclesfield

Season	League		FA Cup		Total	
	App	Goals	App	Goals	App	Goals
1910/11	4	0	0	0	4	0
1911/12	1	0	0	0	1	0
Total	5	0	0	0	5	0

Michaels, William

One-club man whose first-team career was fleeting

Season	League		FA Cup		Total	
	App	Goals	App	Goals	App	Goals
1909/10	3	0	0	0	3	0
Total	**3**	**0**	**0**	**0**	**3**	**0**

Miller, Harry

Lancastrian inside forward whose Goodison career was limited to two outings

Season	League		FA Cup		Total	
	App	Goals	App	Goals	App	Goals
1922/23	2	0	0	0	2	0
Total	**2**	**0**	**0**	**0**	**2**	**0**

Miller, Jimmy

Nomadic winger whose stay at Goodison was no less brief than other postings

Season	League		FA Cup		Total	
	App	Goals	App	Goals	App	Goals
1919/20	8	1	0	0	8	1
Total	**8**	**1**	**0**	**0**	**8**	**1**

Miller, Willie 'Dusty'

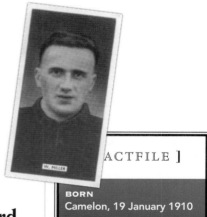

Inside forward whose 1936 transfer to Burnley may have been the makeweight in the Tommy Lawton deal

Season	League		FA Cup		Total	
	App	Goals	App	Goals	App	Goals
1935/36	15	1	1	0	16	1
1936/37	1	1	0	0	1	1
Total	**16**	**2**	**1**	**0**	**17**	**2**

Milligan, George

Defence-minded Lancastrian whose football career ended with the arrival of war

Season	League		FA Cup		Total	
	App	Goals	App	Goals	App	Goals
1938/39	1	0	0	0	1	0
Total	1	0	0	0	1	0

[FACTFILE]

BORN
Fallsworth, 31 August 1917
DIED
1983
POSITION
Left half
OTHER CLUBS
Oldham Athletic (1935–37)

Milligan, Jamie

Home-grown midfielder who returned to league football with Fleetwood Town in 2012 after a decade-long gap

Season	League		FA Cup		League Cup		Total	
	App	Goals	App	Goals	App	Goals	App	Goals
1998/99	0 (3)	0	0	0	0	0	0 (3)	0
1999/2000	0 (1)	0	0	0	0	0	0 (1)	0
Total	0 (4)	0	0	0	0	0	0 (4)	0

[FACTFILE]

BORN
Blackpool, 3 January 1980
POSITION
Midfielder
OTHER CLUBS
Blackpool (2001–03);
Macclesfield Town (2003);
Leigh RMI (2003);
Hyde United (2003–05);
Fleetwood Town (2005–)

Milligan, Mike

Underperforming midfielder who barely flickered in Colin Harvey's last days

A star of Second Division Oldham Athletic's 1990 cup heroics, which saw them reach the League Cup Final and the FA Cup semi-final,

Mike Milligan was one of English football's most desirable transfer targets in the summer of 1990. A hard-tackling, energetic and constructive player, there seemed to be echoes of Peter Reid in his play. Colin Harvey beat off much competition to make the adopted Irishman a £1million signing.

It was unfortunate that Milligan came into a side suffering its death throes under Harvey's management. But as one of the club's most expensive signings he shouldered some of the burden for the malaise and his performances did little to allay the decline. Likened to Bryan Robson,

it was soon obvious that the comparison was hasty and inaccurate. Injured in September 1990, by the time of his recovery Harvey had been sacked.

FOLLOWING Howard Kendall's return as manager in November 1990, Milligan increasingly became a peripheral player at the club. There was a return to the first team in spring 1991, but little sign of the vibrant performances once witnessed in the blue of Oldham. At the season's end, Kendall cut Everton's losses, selling Milligan back to his former club for £600,000.

[FACTFILE]

BORN
Manchester, 20 February 1967
POSITION
Midfield
OTHER CLUBS
Oldham Athletic
(1985–90 & 1991–94);
Norwich City (1994–2000);
Blackpool (2000–02)
HONOURS
1 Republic of Ireland cap (1992)

Season	League		FA Cup		League Cup		Total	
	App	Goals	App	Goals	App	Goals	App	Goals
1990/91	16 (1)	1	1	0	0 (1)	0	17 (2)	1
Total	16 (1)	1	1	0	0 (1)	0	17 (2)	1

Milward, Alf

Brilliant left winger whose partnership with Edgar Chadwick brought the club early success

In Everton history few partnerships have been as enduring or excellent as that of Alf Milward and Edgar Chadwick. The pair dominated the Everton left through the 1890s, a period that encompassed a League Championship win, the notorious split with Liverpool and move to Goodison, two FA Cup Finals and a succession of other near misses.

'There was a personality about the famous "left wing" of the Everton team of the '90s that led people – especially their own followers – to speak and think of them always as a "pair",' recalled Victor Hall in the Liverpool Echo in 1924. 'People always spoke of Chadwick and Milward as the "left wing!" If through injury or illness, or other cause, one or other of the two stood down, then the "left wing" for that day at least, was not playing.' They were, he added, 'the most brilliant left wing pair that Association football had ever seen'.

Born in Marlow, Milward had been spotted as a teenager playing football in London. He started his Everton career as an 18-year-old tyro in the Football League's inaugural season, but his breakthrough campaign came the following year when he was ever-present as Everton finished close runners-up to Preston North End. He was, recalled his captain of that season, Andrew Hannah, 'a capital forward, although one of the youngest members of the team. He formerly played in the London district, where he earned for himself a reputation, which his play here has already enhanced.'

From the outset Milward seems to have built up an almost subliminal understanding with Chadwick. He was short and powerful and aggressive and superbly direct. 'Nothing was more entertaining to the club's spectators than to see Milward at full gallop down the touch line,' reported Victor Hall 30 years later, 'his arms whirling in a mad ecstasy of sheer delight, outpacing every yard the panting defence with the faithful Edgar loping along fifteen or twenty yards in the arrear and slanting in towards goal for the pass he knew would come with mathematical accuracy once Milward had reached the required spot on the goalline.'

Milward, like Chadwick, was ever-present as Everton lifted their first league title in 1891, outscored only by Fred Geary. With 12 goals from 22 games,

he outscored Chadwick by two. But they were friends and team-mates above all. Milward was, wrote Hall, 'an immense admirer of his partner'.

To him, there was no player could hold a candle to Chadwick. In the roar of an exciting game when feelings were wrought and shouting of players and spectators alike were confusing to the ear – the loud shrill voice of Milward might be heard above the din as he raced to get into position for Chadwick's pass: - 'Now! Edgar' his Cockney pronunciation of Edgar's name was unmistakable, and signaled effectually, so that the faithful Edgar need never raise his eye to look for the waiting partner's position; the voice signaled it –and sure enough the pass came true.

Although considered in many minds a homogenous unit, Milward and Chadwick differed greatly in style. While Chadwick was first and foremost a dribbler, Milward was a scrapper, direct and impatient with the flourishes that stood between him and the goal. Chadwick would help in defence, but Milward was an attacker first and last. He was 'not a natural defender', wrote Hall, although he was known to deputise in goal in emergency situations. 'His buoyant spirit called for the wild career down the

wing, for the flying charge, and the flying shot to the goalmouth where Geary or Chadwick could be trusted to meet the rebound, if the first shot found the goalkeeper or the crossbar in the way.'

Milward was among the group of players to resist the overtures of Everton's ousted president, John Houlding, following the split of 1892, and he followed his team-mates to their new home of Goodison. A second title would prove elusive, although after the title win Everton twice finished third and were runners-up in 1895. They were also nearly men in the FA Cup, reaching the final in 1893 and 1897 – the year that Milward scored in the semi-final – but further medals did not come the way of the Marlow man. On four occasions he was capped by England, scoring three times.

Always one of the most popular members of the Everton dressing room, Milward had a reputation as an extrovert character and practical joker. 'Jovial in spirits, fond of song or story, his personality was joyous, and on train journey or in smokeroom, the tedium of travel or training was lightened by his presence,' wrote Hall. 'Of his jokes, practical but harmless, there was no end, [and] of his yarns and experiences one could fill a book.' This self-confidence and swagger he also carried onto the field of play.

Perhaps surprisingly, the second FA Cup Final was to be virtually the last action Milward saw in an Everton shirt. The final had caused a backlog of fixtures, meaning Everton had to play four league games in eight days. In addition to this the directors saw fit to play further friendly matches against Tottenham Hotspur and Reading. It was a gruelling schedule and after Milward refused to play against Spurs he was reprimanded by the board and his wages stopped. Although an apology was accepted, he was left

Season	League		FA Cup		Total	
	App	Goals	App	Goals	App	Goals
1888/89	6	2	-	-	6	2
1889/90	22	10	2	4	24	14
1890/91	22	12	1	0	23	12
1891/92	26	6	1	0	27	6
1892/93	27	11	7	2	34	13
1893/94	24	8	1	0	25	8
1894/95	18	10	3	0	21	10
1895/96	29	17	3	2	32	19
1896/97	27	9	5	3	32	12
Total	**201**	**85**	**23**	**11**	**224**	**96**

out of the final game at home to Bury and sold to New Brighton Tower that summer, still aged only 26.

He returned to prominence with Southampton in the Southern League, where he resumed his partnership with Chadwick. In January 1900 he appeared against Everton in the FA Cup first round and scored a brace as Southampton humbled his former club 3-0. Later that year he made a third, unsuccessful, FA Cup Final appearance.

'Milward called up bright reminiscences that clearly emphasised the loss the Everton club has sustained,' recorded the Liverpool Mercury of his virtuoso cup performance. '[He is] capable of upholding the best traditions of the game [and] probably would be delighted to resume his old associations at Goodison Park, where he has so many well wishers.' Alas, such a return proved elusive.

[FACTFILE]

BORN
Marlow, 12 September 1870
DIED
Winchester, 1 June 1931
POSITION
Left winger
OTHER CLUBS
New Brighton Tower
(1897–99);
Southampton (1899–1901);
New Brompton (1901–03)
HONOURS
1890/91
League Championship;
4 England caps
(3 goals) (1891–97)

Mimms, Bobby

Goalkeeping understudy charged with the thankless task of filling Neville Southall's gloves

There is a common misconception that Everton's league and FA Cup capitulation to Liverpool in 1986 was due primarily to the loss to injury of Neville Southall.

While it is true that the Welsh colossus was a considerable loss, his replacement, the England under-21 goalkeeper Bobby Mimms, was blameless in the subsequent travesty. Indeed Mimms kept clean sheets in six of his first seven games after Southall's injury in late March; and until the FA Cup Final, when Liverpool scored three second-half goals, Mimms had conceded just four times in 10 matches.

BUT HIS WAS always a thankless task, for the chances of making the Everton number one shirt his own were always going to be limited. He made enough appearances at the start of the 1986/87 season to claim a League Championship medal at the season's end, but as soon as Southall returned to fitness Mimms played just a handful more games for Everton.

Born in York, Mimms started his career with Halifax Town, but joined Rotherham in 1981 without playing a game. Howard Kendall signed him for £150,000 in the summer of 1985 and over 37 senior appearances he provided solid and dependable service – certainly a more competent pair of hands than some of the men who succeeded Southall. Following Southall's return in autumn 1986, Mimms was loaned out on three occasions, but having made just a handful of further appearances recognised that his was always an impossible job in Southall's indomitable shadow.

In February 1988 he joined Tottenham Hotspur for £325,000, but never wholly convinced the Spurs faithful. In December 1990 he joined Blackburn Rovers, just as Jack Walker began to plough his millions into the club. He played an important part in their renaissance, but lost his place to Tim Flowers on the eve of Rovers ultimately victorious Premier League campaign in 1994/95. There followed a tour of the lower

league before his retirement at the start of the century.

Mimms now serves as Blackburn's goalkeeping coach, and his son Josh, a former Liverpool trainee, has followed in his footsteps and is a goalkeeper at York City.

[FACTFILE]

BORN
York, 13 October 1963
POSITION
Goalkeeper
OTHER CLUBS
Halifax Town (1979–81);
Rotherham United (1981–85);
Notts County (loan, 1986);
Sunderland (loan, 1986);
Blackburn Rovers (loan, 1987);
Manchester City (loan, 1987);
Tottenham Hotspur (1988–90);
Aberdeen (loan, 1990);
Blackburn Rovers (1990–96);
Crystal Palace (1996);
Preston North End (1996–97);
Rotherham United (1997–98);
York City (1998–2000);
Mansfield Town (2000–01)
HONOURS
1986/87
League Championship

Season	League		FA Cup		League Cup		Other		Total	
	App	Goals	App	Goals	App	Goals	App	Goals	App	Goals
1985/86	10	0	2	0	0	0	0	0	12	0
1986/87	11	0	0	0	2	0	3	0	16	0
1987/88	8	0	0	0	0	0	1	0	9	0
Total	**29**	**0**	**2**	**0**	**2**	**0**	**4**	**0**	**37**	**0**

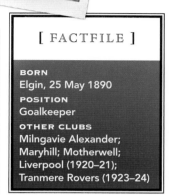

Mitchell,
Frank

Scottish goalkeeper who with Dave Hickson shares the distinction of turning out for all three Merseyside clubs

[FACTFILE]

BORN
Elgin, 25 May 1890
POSITION
Goalkeeper
OTHER CLUBS
Milngavie Alexander; Maryhill; Motherwell; Liverpool (1920–21); Tranmere Rovers (1923–24)

Season	League		FA Cup		Total	
	App	Goals	App	Goals	App	Goals
1913/14	13	0	0	0	13	0
1914/15	2	0	1	0	3	0
1919/20	8	0	0	0	8	0
Total	23	0	1	0	24	0

Moffatt,
Harold 'Hugh'

Widely travelled winger never quite able to call Goodison his home

[FACTFILE]

BORN
Camerton, 1900
POSITION
Outside right
OTHER CLUBS
Arsenal (1923); Guildford United; Luton Town (1925); Oldham Athletic (1927); Walsall (1928); Queens Park Rangers (1929)

Season	League		FA Cup		Total	
	App	Goals	App	Goals	App	Goals
1926/27	2	0	1	0	3	0
Total	2	0	1	0	3	0

Moffatt,
Andy

Early 1920s centre forward discarded after just a solitary start

[FACTFILE]

BORN
Rosewell, 5 September 1900
DIED
1990
POSITION
Centre forward
OTHER CLUBS
Lochgelly United; East Fife; Wrexham (1922); East Fife; Lochgelly United; Dunfermline Athletic; Lochgelly United

Season	League		FA Cup		Total	
	App	Goals	App	Goals	App	Goals
1920/21	1	0	0	0	1	0
Total	1	0	0	0	1	0

Molyneux,
George

Left back who served Everton over two spells and later represented England

[FACTFILE]

BORN
Liverpool, August 1875
DIED
1942
POSITION
Left back
OTHER CLUBS
3rd Grenadiers; South Shore; Kirkdale; Wigan County; Southampton; Portsmouth; Southend United; Colchester Town
HONOURS
4 England caps (1902–03)

Season	League		FA Cup		Total	
	App	Goals	App	Goals	App	Goals
1896/97	1	0	0	0	1	0
1898/99	33	0	2	0	35	0
1899/1900	9	0	0	0	9	0
Total	43	0	2	0	45	0

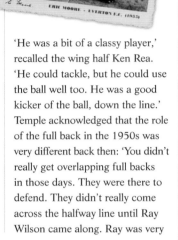

ERIC MOORE - EVERTON E.C. (1955)

Moore, Eric

Respected defender who played through troubled times

Eric Moore was a powerful full back and stalwart of some of Everton's darkest days, a man admired by his team-mates for his footballing integrity at a time when a defender's first and last task was to defend.

Spotted playing local football for Haydock, he was signed with a £20 donation going the way of his former club – a bargain that would be repaid many many times. 'He was from St Helens and classed as a local lad,' recalled Derek Temple, whose Goodison career overlapped with Moore's, in 2011. 'A lot of them were then. It wasn't a matter of signing players for big money and clubs brought in their own local men. He was a big strong full back, a hard player – but then again, they all were! You didn't come across soft defenders. I don't think you

do now, either, but you could tackle from behind then.'

MOORE'S BREAK came in the 1949/50 season when, as a 23-year-old, he took the place of George Saunders. A year later he played in all but five league matches as Everton suffered the ignominy of relegation. Moore lost his place to Tommy Clinton and seldom played in the dark days of the Second Division. But after three seasons away he returned to a regular berth in the 1954/55 season and played in all but one league game over the next two years as Everton re-established themselves in the top flight.

'He was a bit of a classy player,' recalled the wing half Ken Rea. 'He could tackle, but he could use the ball well too. He was a good kicker of the ball, down the line.' Temple acknowledged that the role of the full back in the 1950s was very different back then: 'You didn't really get overlapping full backs in those days. They were there to defend. They didn't really come across the halfway line until Ray Wilson came along. Ray was very

very quick at a time when most full backs were heavy and slow. They weren't built like they are now. They were all heavy-legged and barrel-chested and could kick a ball a long way. They could kick a player a long way as well!'

AFTER Cliff Britton left the club in 1956, Moore never found favour with his replacement, Ian Buchan. He played just once under the new manager – a disastrous 5-1 defeat to Leeds United on the opening day of the 1956/57 season. In November 1956 Buchan presented a list of playing staff to the board with which the club could dispense and Moore was the most senior figure to be included. In January 1957 he joined Chesterfield for £1000 but soon returned to Merseyside with Tranmere Rovers, where he played out his career.

Season	League		FA Cup		Total	
	App	Goals	App	Goals	App	Goals
1949/50	22	0	5	0	27	0
1950/51	37	0	1	0	38	0
1951/52	5	0	0	0	5	0
1952/53	14	0	0	0	14	0
1953/54	9	0	1	0	10	0
1954/55	41	0	2	0	43	0
1955/56	42	0	4	0	46	0
1956/57	1	0	0	0	1	0
Total	**171**	**0**	**13**	**0**	**184**	**0**

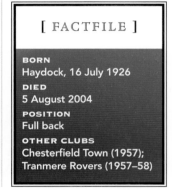

[FACTFILE]

BORN
Haydock, 16 July 1926
DIED
5 August 2004
POSITION
Full back
OTHER CLUBS
Chesterfield Town (1957);
Tranmere Rovers (1957–58)

Moore, Joe-Max

Plucky American striker who failed to build on early promise

Signed from MLS side New England Revolution for a nominal sum in November 1999, Joe-Max Moore arrived on Merseyside a virtual unknown. The son of oil man Carl Moore, who in the 1970s and 1980s had been co-owner of NASL team Tulsa Roughnecks, he had come to Everton on the recommendation of Richard Gough, who played against him in the nascent MLS.

HERE HE was a prolific scorer, and had also been part of two United States World Cup squads. Hard-working and skilful, Moore showed a deft touch in front of goal in his early Everton

appearances – including a run of five goals in five games over winter 2000. Although he appeared for the United States in a variety of roles, including defensive midfield, he appeared predominantly as a striker for Everton.

DESPITE SOME promising shows in these first months as an

Season	League		FA Cup		League Cup		Total	
	App	Goals	App	Goals	App	Goals	App	Goals
1999/2000	11 (4)	6	1 (2)	2	0	0	12 (6)	8
2000/01	8 (13)	0	0 (2)	0	1 (1)	0	9 (16)	0
2001/02	3 (13)	2	2 (2)	0	1	0	6 (15)	2
2002/03	0	0	0	0	0	0	0	0
Total	**22(30)**	**8**	**3 (6)**	**2**	**2 (1)**	**0**	**27(37)**	**10**

Everton player, Moore lacked the power and physicality to make a lasting impression on the Premier League. The goals subsequently dried up, and so did his first-team opportunities.

After appearing in the 2002 World Cup Finals, Moore was released from his Everton contract in December 2002 and returned to New England Revolution. He remains one of the most capped and most prolific American players in US national team history.

[FACTFILE]

BORN
Tulsa, Oklahoma,
23 February 1971
POSITION
Forward
OTHER CLUBS
FC Saarbrucken (1994–95);
1FC Nuremberg (1995–96);
New England Revolution
(1996–99 & 2003–04)
HONOURS
100 US caps (24 goals)
(1992–2002)

Moore,
Neil

Home-grown centre back who had a nomadic lower and non-league career after Everton

[FACTFILE]

BORN
Liverpool, 21 September 1972
POSITION
Centre back
OTHER CLUBS
Blackpool (loan, 1994–95);
Oldham Athletic (loan, 1995);
Carlisle United (loan, 1995–96); Rotherham United (loan, 1996);
Norwich City (loan, 1997);
Burnley (1997–99);
Macclesfield Town (1999–2000);
Telford United (2000–02);
Mansfield Town (2002–03);
Southport (loan, 2002–03);
Nuneaton Borough (2003–09);
Solihull Motors (2009–11)

Season	League		FA Cup		League Cup		Total	
	App	Goals	App	Goals	App	Goals	App	Goals
1992/93	0 (1)	0	0	0	0 (1)	0	0 (2)	0
1993/94	4	0	0	0	0	0	4	0
Total	**4 (1)**	**0**	**0**	**0**	**0 (1)**	**0**	**4 (2)**	**0**

Moores,
Sir John

Patriarchal club owner who oversaw Everton's 1960s transformation

If the extraordinary life and times of John Moores (25 January 1896 – 25 September 1993) were the subject of a Hollywood biopic, it would be difficult to fit the full scale of his achievements into a rags-to-riches epic. His influence upon the people of Merseyside was profound: as a businessman, employer, patriarch and cultural guardian. Of the latter aspect of his rich and varied life, no contribution he made was more far reaching than his ownership of Everton FC.

Born one of eight children into a working-class family in Manchester, Moores left school aged 14, served during the First World War in the Royal Navy and eventually settled in Liverpool in his mid-twenties, working as a telegraph operator. Always imbued by an entrepreneurial spirit and love of sport, in 1923 he combined these two passions by starting a football pool. The idea was that punters would bet on the outcome of football matches, with the payout coming from the accumulated 'pool' of money – less a 10 per cent management fee. What started as a sideline in 1923, with Moores handing out coupons himself outside football stadiums, became, by the late 1920s, a phenomenal success. By the early 1930s Moores was a millionaire at a time when owning a million represented almost unimaginable wealth.

His Littlewoods empire would soon expand into ownership of department stores and, years later, home shopping. Moores' personal interests lay in sport and he played outside right as an amateur footballer until in his mid-forties. As a fan he had been taken to see Manchester United by his father, but switched allegiances to Everton when he moved to Merseyside. One of his first forays into organised sport was his sponsorship of a league for Liverpool baseball teams in the 1930s, which briefly involved Dixie Dean.

IN THE PERIOD after the Second World War, Moores began his financial association with Everton. His friend Dick Searle, a major shareholder at Goodison and later chairman, had encountered some financial difficulties and offered Moores half of his shares. 'It was on the understanding that I always voted with him,' Moores later revealed. 'I agreed to vote with him as long as I didn't think it was against the interests of the club – I reserved that right. So I took half his shares, and he gave me an option to buy the remainder of his shares in the event of his death.'

Over the subsequent several years Moores continued to buy up Everton shares in his name and his family's. In November 1952, following the death of the club chairman W.R. Williams and with Everton mired in the Second Division, there appears to have been an attempt to co-opt Moores onto the Everton board. Always his own man, he 'strongly objected' to this principle and the board respected his wishes. Nevertheless, his presence was increasingly felt at Goodison. His Littlewoods co-founder Colin Askham joined the board in 1955 and in February 1957, with Askham the intermediary, Moores agreed to lend the club £18,000 for new floodlights, to be paid back in three annual instalments from 1960.

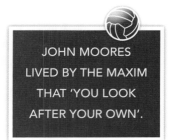

JOHN MOORES LIVED BY THE MAXIM THAT 'YOU LOOK AFTER YOUR OWN'.

A year later Moores was asked to lend money for pitch improvements, and he was subsequently given tickets to the Everton box. Then in February 1960 came a key development. Moores offered the club an interest-free loan of £50,000 repayable over five years. The club accepted. A month later Moores was invited to join the Everton board in place of Askham who had, by coincidence, resigned due to ill health.

A SEARCH through the Everton minute books can see the boardroom culture changing almost overnight. The complacency and inertia that had characterised its affairs for a generation was removed. Moores started to make his presence felt in little ways and large. Blazers, for example, were ordered for the first-team players. Littlewoods agreed to the sponsorship of clocks in the stadium.

In April 1960 a private meeting was held between several of the club's most senior directors 'in order to consider the financial position of the Club'. Moores laid bare the reality facing Everton. 'He was gravely concerned with the Club's financial position which disclosed a total indebtedness at present in excess of £100,000 with hardly any liquid resources to discharge it. He felt that the position could not be allowed to continue and that stringent and overdue economies must be put into operation and recommended that a special committee should be formed charged with the duty of recommending to the Board as soon as possible what economies they recommended for adoption.'

HE WOULD reflect in an interview with World Sports the following March: 'I was very surprised at the lack of business sense of most people in football directorships. I must admit I did not realise until I became involved that running a football club is so much of a business.'

The board accepted Moores' case. In June 1960 the chairman, Fred Micklesfield, stepped aside and Moores was unanimously elected chairman. Everton were about to be transformed and the funds he invested allowed Carey to compete with the best in the transfer market and transform a team of valiant no-hopers. Jimmy Gabriel and Roy Vernon had already been bought and Billy Bingham and Alex Young would, by the end of 1960, join them at Goodison. Everton, invariably, became known as the 'Mersey Millionaires'.

By Christmas 1960, Everton were third and being talked of as genuine title challengers. It was a stark contrast to any season in the 13 that had passed since the war, but Carey's side were entertainers, not winners. They were the sort of side who could thrill with a 3-1 win at Burnley on Boxing Day 1960, then lose miserably (0-3) to the same side in the return fixture at Goodison just 24 hours later. Indeed that very same defeat marked the onset of a run of 10 losses in 13 games. It was not catastrophic and Everton only fell as far as sixth, but it was enough to convince Moores that Carey would never be a winner. He recognised that Carey's team lacked the killer touch that would mark them as winners. Before the end of the season he had dramatically sacked Carey and replaced him with Harry Catterick, a man more in keeping with the Moores mould. He had a reputation as a task master and disciplinarian; for ruthlessness and winning football. 'He had the drive we needed,' Moores later said. 'I told him to aim for a place in the top six by playing good football, and by doing that I was sure that success would come.'

Moores' and Catterick's story is Everton's tale of the 1960s. Their partnership was incredibly successful, bringing two League Championships and an FA Cup to the table. But the chairman did not redefine English football in the way that the petro-dollars of Roman Abramovich and Sheikh Mansour did in the 21st century. He was no arch-benefactor, merely someone who brought sound business logic and soft loans to one of football's aristocrats. Spending heavily at the outset was only a means to an end. 'Our difficulty is that we must have a good team to attract good gates, and good gates to have enough money to get a good team,' Moores said in 1961. 'Buying players and concentrating talent in this way may discourage smaller professional clubs and local talent. But if the big clubs do not survive, the smaller ones certainly will not – and in that case you are left with even less outlet for youthful ambition.' When Everton won the League Championship in 1970, seven of the 13 players they used most regularly were home grown. The Mersey Millionaires had become the School of Science.

MOORES stepped down as chairman in 1965 following the ill health of his wife but retained his place on the board. He returned as chairman for the period 1970–73 and served the following four years as vice-chairman. Now aged 80, he stepped down from the board as one of his Littlewoods executives Philip Carter stepped up to lead the Everton board into a new epoch of the club's history.

In his later years Moores – since 1970, Sir John – would be seen, even in his nineties, at Goodison. He was able to witness the club's 1980s successes, and reflected after the 1985 win: 'I never thought I'd live to see another Championship come to Everton. It's great to feel free of the domination of Liverpool.'

Yet by the early 1990s, with Moores nearing his hundredth birthday, there was a sense that the club were standing still. Too old to impact on its running but not able or willing to break his long ties with Goodison, a paralysis struck the club. On the day of his death in September 1993, Everton were humbled 5-1 at Goodison by Norwich City in front of just 20,531 fans. The result and paltry crowd said much about the state of the club then.

THE following year the Moores family sold Everton to Peter Johnson, another local boy made good. But the relationship wasn't as enduring and Johnson lacked the old man's vision. Although Moores' grandson, John Suenson-Taylor (Lord Grantchester), retained a stake in the club and a place on the board until 2000, it was Liverpool, owned by one of Moores' great-nephews until 2007, that became better known for their association with his family.

John Moores lived by the maxim that 'You look after your own'. In his case his 'own' extended beyond his large family, to include the Littlewoods workforce, the people of Merseyside and Everton Football Club. Everton were lucky indeed to have been part of his life less ordinary.

EVERTON WERE LUCKY INDEED TO HAVE BEEN PART OF HIS LIFE LESS ORDINARY

Morris, R

Centre forward who made a solitary appearance in Everton's debut league season

Season	League		FA Cup		Total	
	App	Goals	App	Goals	App	Goals
1888/89	1	0	0	0	1	0
Total	1	0	0	0	1	0

Morrissey (Jnr), Johnny

Son of the Goodison legend, he wrote himself into Tranmere's record books after just one Everton start

Season	League		FA Cup		League Cup		Europe		Total	
	App	Goals	App	Goals	App	Goals	App	Goals	App	Goals
1984/85	1	0	0	0	0	0	0 (1)	0	1 (1)	0
Total	1	0	0	0	0	0	0 (1)	0	1 (1)	0

Morrissey (Snr), Johnny

Winger who crossed the Mersey divide and became an Everton great

In August 1962, Liverpool's left winger Johnny Morrissey was sold to Everton in a £10,000 deal conducted behind Bill Shankly's back. It was a decision that rankled with the Liverpool manager for the rest of his days, and the first clash in a cold war with his directors that would rumble on for the rest of his career.

The deal represented something of a surprise to all parties, not just Shankly. Morrissey, one of only a handful of players to move from Anfield to Goodison, was also an ardent Liverpool fan, whose early life had centred around his adored club. Everton, now known as the Mersey Millionaires, were supposed to be building a team capable of

challenging for the league title. So why then, was the summer's main transfer business the bargain basement signing of a Liverpool reserve who had never played beyond the Second Division?

Indeed his arrival represented the second attempt by an Everton manager to sign him: Ian Buchan had failed in an attempt to part-exchange Tony McNamara for him in December 1957. And if Morrissey possessed any doubters about his allegiance or ability, he would soon confound them. One month after joining Everton, he came up against his former club in the first league derby to be played in more than a decade. It was 1-1 at half-time and still deadlocked on the hour; a fumble by the

Liverpool goalkeeper, Jim Furnell, saw Morrissey steal in and hit the ball past Liverpool's covering defenders. It was headed away by Ronnie Moran, Liverpool's last defender, but not before crossing the goal line. Liverpool would go on to equalise late on, but Morrissey had allayed much

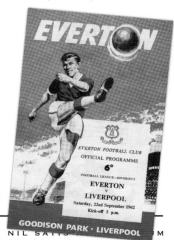

scepticism. 'Morrissey had been abused all his life at the snake pit, until the Blues came in and saved him from those nasty Reds,' wrote George Orr in his chronicle of the era. 'He was re-educated and taught the Gospel according to the Angel Gabriel and the only true God Alex Young.'

Born in April 1940, Morrissey had emerged as one of Merseyside's top young footballers, modelling himself on his hero, left-sided forward Billy Liddell. After scoring almost 60 goals in a season for Liverpool Schoolboys, Liverpool snapped him up and by his 18th birthday he had made his Anfield debut. Yet he found chances difficult to come by: Alan A'Court and a veteran Liddell were difficult to supplant and, despite being highly regarded by Shankly, over five years he made just 36 appearances for Liverpool.

At Goodison, however, Morrissey completed almost as many appearances in his first season, lifting the League Championship in the process. Stocky yet adroit, direct and pacy, Morrissey was a potent part of Everton's attacking armoury. He was at his best taking his ball from deep and running to the by-line, before lofting a lingering cross, but he could also cut in and let fly with a rasping shot. Though not a great stylist, he never lacked finesse and possessed an impeccable first touch and intelligence in his play.

After playing an important part in Everton's 1963 title win, perhaps surprisingly he was a peripheral figure the next season after losing his place to Derek Temple. He returned for much of the 1964/65 season, scoring the final goal in Everton's 4-0 drubbing of Liverpool, but fell out of favour again the next season and missed the 1966 FA Cup Final.

And yet, as Catterick built his second great side around the midfield triumvirate of Colin Harvey, Howard Kendall and Alan Ball, Morrissey was an important part of it. Although he was usually upstaged by the so-called 'Holy Trinity', the Everton manager recognised the winger's importance. 'Johnny Morrissey played a big part in the midfield set-up,' said Catterick. 'We always called Johnny our "safety valve" player because he always made himself available to others when they were in tight situations. When the midfield trio was unable to play the ball forward, Johnny was always there to take a pass, hold the ball until the trio had made room, and feed it back to them.'

Morrissey was more than just a winger, however, he was a genuine hard man in an era when the game was replete with such figures. In particular, Everton's encounters with Leeds United became grudge matches in which Morrissey seemed to up the mutual resentment a notch every time the two teams met. One vivid recollection many Evertonians have of him was during the 1969/70 season, when Everton beat Leeds to the title. Leading Leeds 3-2 in the September encounter at Goodison, Morrissey took the ball to the corner flag to kill time and, so as to goad his opponents, raised his arm as if looking at his watch. Charlton, Billy Bremner, Johnny Giles and the rest of Leeds' so-called hard men never dared go near him.

> JACK CHARLTON, BILLY BREMNER, JOHNNY GILES AND THE REST OF LEEDS' SO-CALLED HARD MEN NEVER DARED GO NEAR HIM

The following year, Morrissey's rivalry with Charlton was laid bare. In an October 1970 TV interview the Leeds player claimed he kept 'a little book with players' names in it. If I get the chance to do them I will. I will make them suffer before I pack it in. If I can kick them four yards over the touchline I will.' Morrissey was one of several players against whom Charlton claimed he sought retribution. Their rivalry stemmed from an incident when Charlton was stretchered off and Morrissey allegedly goaded the Leeds player – 'You won't be getting your win bonus for a while, Jack.' 'John was a dirty bugger,' Brian Labone admitted to Charlton's biographer. 'He was about half the size of Jack and when he was around, you had to look out.'

Perhaps some of the antipathy was football related too. In April 1968, Everton faced Leeds in an FA Cup semi-final and Morrissey was to strike the decisive blow. 'We went into that game as underdogs,' Morrissey would recall. 'John Hurst and Alan Ball were unable

Season	League		FA Cup		League Cup		Europe		Total	
	App	Goals	App	Goals	App	Goals	App	Goals	App	Goals
1962/63	28	7	3	1	-	-	2	0	33	8
1963/64	7	1	0	0	-	-	0	0	7	1
1964/65	25	5	4	0	-	-	4	1	33	6
1965/66	10 (1)	2	1	0	-	-	3	0	14 (1)	2
1966/67	31	6	6	0	-	-	3	1	40	7
1967/68	26	3	5	2	1	0	0	0	32	5
1968/69	40	4	5	0	4	1	0	0	49	5
1969/70	41	9	1	0	3	0	0	0	45	9
1970/71	34	6	4	0	0	0	6	1	44	7
1971/72	15 (1)	0	0	0	0	0	0	0	15 (1)	0
Total	**257 (2)**	**43**	**29**	**3**	**8**	**1**	**18**	**3**	**312 (2)**	**50**

to play and Leeds were the best team in the country.' Shortly before half-time, a plan to frustrate Gary Sprake, the Leeds goalkeeper, paid off. Joe Royle had been instructed to block Sprake's right-footed clearances so eventually he was forced to throw the ball out. When it landed at the feet of Jimmy Husband his lob shot was blocked by the hand of Jack Charlton. Morrissey scored the resultant penalty, but would later admit: 'When I saw it on TV the following day I realised that the Everton fans were behind the goal and if I had missed it I would have had to continue my career with another club.'

After claiming a second league title in 1970, Morrissey played on past his 30th birthday. But during the 1971/72 season he was struck with the injury curse that plagued so many of his colleagues from that team. A persistent Achilles tendon problem limited his outings, and at the end of the season Catterick accepted a bid from Oldham Athletic.

A decade later, Johnny Morrissey was again briefly gracing the Everton team sheet – the son and namesake of the 1960s great worked his way through the youth system to make two appearances for the club where his father made his name. Sold to Tranmere Rovers in October 1985, Morrissey junior went on to make nearly 600 appearances for the Birkenhead club.

Morton, Harry

Experienced goalkeeper who was unable to oust Ted Sagar from the number one jersey

Season	League		FA Cup		Total	
	App	Goals	App	Goals	App	Goals
1936/37	10	0	0	0	10	0
1937/38	16	0	2	0	18	0
1938/39	1	0	0	0	1	0
Total	**27**	**0**	**2**	**0**	**29**	**0**

Mountfield, Derek

Goalscoring central defender who was a popular and important figure in Everton's 1985 title win

For any modern footballer to score 10 top-flight goals in a season is an achievement, but for a central defender to reach that total is a once-in-a-generation occurrence. Yet when Everton won the League Championship in 1985, Derek Mountfield reached that magical number, also weighing in with crucial FA Cup goals. And yet, although he is often most remembered for his attacking prowess, it should in no way diminish his excellent defensive credentials, which saw him on the verge of an England call-up.

A native Merseysider and boyhood Evertonian, Mountfield began his career with Tranmere Rovers. Signed as a 19-year-old by Howard Kendall in June 1982, his £30,000 fee represents one of the great bargains in the club's history. He made his debut against Birmingham City in April 1983, and injury to Mark Higgins by the end of the year allowed him to claim the number five shirt as his own. By then Everton were on the crest of a wave of honours and in May 1984 Mountfield was part of the team that beat Watford in the FA Cup Final.

Thin as a rake and somewhat gangly, Mountfield was a fine and fleet-footed centre half who was always comfortable in possession

and not averse to making long, raking passes up the field. With Kevin Ratcliffe he mastered Everton's zonal marking trap, forming Everton's finest central defensive partnership since the black-and-white days of Labone and Hurst.

And then there were the goals. The 1984/85 season represented Mountfield's annus mirabilis, and not until Joleon Lescott's prime, almost a quarter of a century later, would Everton possess such a dangerous defensive player. His 10 league goals were an important contribution to Everton's League Championship win, and included the strike against Queens Park Rangers that effectively sealed their ultimate victory. But it is the two that Mountfield scored in Everton's run to the FA Cup Final for which he is best remembered.

Losing 2-1 at home to Ipswich, Everton were heading for a quarter-final exit when in the final minute Mountfield slid in with a dramatic equaliser. After easing through the replay, in the semi-final against Luton Mountfield headed home an extra-time winner from Kevin Sheedy's free kick. His ecstatic celebration, open arms stretched to their full width, remains one of the most vivid and enduring images of the era. He would later say of the afternoon: 'If you saw my celebration after scoring you'd understand how I felt. Really we had no right to be in the game at that stage. We didn't play well in the first half and went in 1-0 down, but we came out in the second half with a lot more steel. We equalised very, very late on to get extra time and to score that winner was a great feeling, especially as it got us to Wembley for the second year running.'

At 22, and with a trophy cabinet full enough to make seasoned professionals jealous, a glittering career seemed to beckon for Mountfield. And yet, it was to be cruelly cut short by injury. A torn cartilage wrecked his 1985/86 season and although he returned for its disappointing conclusion, his chances were severely limited the following campaign after Dave Watson became Everton's record signing during the close season.

It seemed an unjust fate for an accomplished defender. Watson initially met a cool reception, with some fans calling for Mountfield's reinstatement. Mountfield would recall: 'Obviously when you sign somebody for £1million, he's going to take preference over somebody else. Even when I got back into the team and played well, Howard would always put Dave back. I was very frustrated but these things happen in football and they'll happen to

better players than me, so you've just got to accept it. At the time Howard thought Dave and Kevin Ratcliffe were the best two together.'

He made enough appearances to win a league title medal in 1987, but after playing just a handful of games during the 1987/88 season he asked for a transfer. In June 1988 he joined Graham Taylor's Aston Villa for £450,000. 'Medals mean nothing and you can't live on memories,' he said at the time. 'The medals will be fine to look at in years to come when I've retired but for now I just want that special feeling of being involved again on a Saturday afternoon. Reserve football is just not the same.'

Villa narrowly missed out on the league title in 1990, and in 1991 Mountfield joined Wolves. There followed spells across the lower leagues and a stint at management before Mountfield slipped out of the game. A devoted Evertonian, Mountfield, who now works as a PE teacher on the Wirral and is shorn of his trademark moustache, remains a well-recognised face at Goodison on match days.

[FACTFILE]

BORN
2 November 1962

POSITION
Central defender

OTHER CLUBS
Tranmere Rovers (1980–82);
Aston Villa (1988–91);
Wolverhampton Wanderers (1991–94);
Carlisle United (1994–95);
Northampton Town (1995);
Walsall (1995–98);
Scarborough United (1999)

AS MANAGER
Cork City (2000–01)

HONOURS
League Championship
1984/85, 1986/87;
FA Cup 1984;
European Cup Winners' Cup 1985

	League		FA Cup		League Cup		Other		Total	
Season	App	Goals	App	Goals	App	Goals	App	Goals	App	Goals
1982/83	1	0	0	0	0	0	-	-	1	0
1983/84	31	3	8	0	8	0	-	-	47	3
1984/85	37	10	7	2	4	2	10	0	58	14
1985/86	15	3	2	0	0	0	2	1	19	4
1986/87	12 (1)	3	0	0	4	1	2 (1)	0	16 (2)	4
1987/88	4 (5)	0	0	0	0	0	-	-	4 (5)	0
Total	100 (6)	19	17	2	16	3	14 (1)	1	147(7)	25

Moyes,
David

Second longest serving Everton manager who has transformed the club, but whose hunt for a trophy goes on

After years of instability and a decade of flirtations with relegation, the arrival of David Moyes as manager in 2002 radically altered the complexion of Everton Football Club. At a time when some clubs have been allowed to buy success through the largesse of foreign benefactors, Moyes has achieved a modern football miracle in making Everton competitive again. His reign in the Goodison manager's office now extends into its second decade and only Harry Catterick has led the club longer in the modern era. Although his lack of rewards in the form of trophies has caused some mutterings among sections of the support, few would question the magnitude of his achievements in bringing pride back to Goodison when serious financial obstacles stand in the club's way.

Born in Glasgow in 1963, Moyes was a graduate of the famous Glasgow junior club, Drumchapel Amateurs, where his father was a coach. Other players to emerge from its ranks included Alex Ferguson, Kenny Dalglish, Andy Gray, Archie Gemmill and Asa Hartford. He joined Celtic and represented Scotland at schoolboy and youth level, breaking into the Celtic team as a teenage centre half. He won the SPL title in 1981/82, but despite the promising start was unable to make a first-team place his own. He sought a move to England and after a transfer to Arsenal fell through, joined Cambridge United in 1983. Besides a spell with Dunfermline in the early 1990s, he never again played in the English or Scottish top flights.

'I don't regret it because it gave me an opportunity to see football in a different way,' he told this author in 2009. 'I was at Cambridge, at Bristol City, I went to Shrewsbury – it's not an illustrious route, but I tell you what, the background I had from Celtic stuck with me all the time. You were required to win, and if you could win with style that was

the way you should do it. But if not, you should win.' He described losing regularly at these clubs, having been at Celtic, as a 'complete shock'.

In 1993 Moyes joined Preston North End, where he spent nearly a decade. He always possessed the natural authority that set him out as managerial material. In January 1998, with the Lilywhites threatened by relegation to Division Three, Moyes became player-manager. By May 1999 he had guided Preston to the Division Two title, and for the next three years Preston were in the hunt for promotion to the Premier League.

Sir Alex Ferguson tried to bring him to Manchester United as his assistant, but Moyes said no. He was linked with several other teams traversing the Premier League / First Division divide, but Everton were the first to fire his imagination. The call to manage Everton came following the sacking of Walter Smith in March 2002.

Bill Kenwright was understood to initially favour Gary Megson, but Moyes was recommended by Smith and after meeting him Kenwright was immediately won over by his force of personality. 'It was midnight when he arrived at my home and we talked for two hours,' Bill Kenwright has recalled. 'He looked at me with those eyes – and when you've not met him before, they're very frightening – and he mentioned the word "win" 10 times in the first minute.'

His unveiling as Everton manager has become the stuff of Goodison

> HIS UNVEILING AS EVERTON MANAGER HAS BECOME THE STUFF OF GOODISON LORE

lore. Moyes immediately endeared himself to every Evertonian by claiming at the press conference that he was joining the 'People's Club'.

'It had been a hectic day and my brother was driving me into the city and we were driving in through this tight old part of the city,' Moyes told this author. 'The kids were playing out on the street – it was nearly back to the old days in Glasgow – and all the ones I saw were in Everton kits. Maybe it was just my eye getting dragged to it, but everyone was wearing an Everton strip. It made me think that people on the streets support Everton.'

Moyes's first task as Everton manager was to save the club from a looming relegation battle. There followed four victories from nine games, which edged the club to 15th place and safety. But facing him were many challenges: an ageing squad with underperforming players on bloated contracts; financial constraints; a club that had been in a state of torpor for the best part of a decade. It was a place, Moyes later recalled, where finishing 13th was considered 'a good season'.

Moyes acknowledged that it was 'a fight' just to establish himself at first. 'I had to change it from a club that was just surviving,' he said. He wanted 'a younger football club, a fresher football club', but he set about imposing himself on the challenges that lay ahead immediately. David Ginola, Paul Gascoigne and Jesper Blomqvist – the sort of past-their-best players who had come to typify the Smith-era – were swiftly discarded.

In their place Moyes used what little funds he had at his disposal both well and imaginatively. He made good use of the loan system to try out players before deciding whether to make their stays permanent. Joseph Yobo was an early success; Juliano Rodrigo less so. He made use of Chinese international Li Tie, who was brought over as part of a sponsorship deal, and was even flexible enough to bring the exiled Alex

Nyarko back from the cold. He was also helped by the emergence of a 16-year-old superstar called Wayne Rooney.

For the first year, Moyes seemed to revitalise Everton through sheer force of personality. Helped by Rooney, Everton finished 2002/03 seventh, having occupied a Champions League spot for most of the season. Only at the very last did they slip out of contention for European qualification. Evertonians were smitten after the club's best showing in years; a campaign of many memorable moments. At its conclusion Moyes was named the League Manager's Association Player of the Year. 'I believe he's destined to be a great Everton manager,' said Bill Kenwright. 'And I'm convinced he will become one of the greatest managers in the world.'

With their youthful manager and brilliant young tyro Rooney, hopes were high for the 2003/04 season. Everton were frustrated in the transfer market, losing out on goalkeeper Petr Cech and midfielder Michael Essien, who both moved to French clubs. Moyes's eye for players rich in potential when they were virtual unknowns was telling.

Instead he brought in Nigel Martyn, Kevin Kilbane, James McFadden and Francis Jeffers on loan. They were steady rather than spectacular players, but (with the exception of the volatile Jeffers) completely reliable and improved the squad. An unhappy season nevertheless ensued, with Everton struggling to click. There was a deteriorating relationship between Moyes and Rooney; the manager's attempts to shield the young star from the glare of the football world were not always met gratefully. Everton dropped out of the early rounds of the League and FA Cup. A poor league campaign ended with defeat in all of their last four games and the season concluded with Everton

having scored fewer goals than in any season of their history. The nadir was a dire 5-1 defeat at Manchester City on the final day. Everton finished just one place off the relegation spots.

Moyes later described this to me as the hardest time of his Everton career. 'I think in those periods, it was a fight for me in the early days to establish myself, there's no doubt about that. But what young manager going in to a club such as Everton was going to have it easy?'

His problems were compounded by boardroom splits and a worsening financial crisis sweeping the club. That summer he had to sell Rooney to Manchester United, while the boardroom went into a state of meltdown. Transfer funds were minimal and expectation low. Journeyman Marcus Bent, a quick, hard-working forward, who made up for a lack of finishing with an extraordinary work ethic, was signed from Ipswich Town. There was Tim Cahill, a promising midfielder at Millwall, but who had never played at the top level. Cahill would be one of the most inspired signings in modern Everton history.

After an opening-day mauling by Arsenal, a relegation battle seemed certain in 2004/05. But in the teeth of this adversity something, improbably, seemed to click. Everton began winning games, and once they started they just couldn't stop. Lee Carsley's winning goal in the Goodison derby in early December saw them rise to second.

Moyes was threatening to achieve the equivalent of a modern footballing miracle. Amid the delirium of Everton's miracle season he signed a new five-year contract. Although a title challenge was never a serious possibility, the belief that Everton would simply drop out of the running for a Champions League

place never happened. They finished the season fourth, a place ahead of Liverpool, and Moyes won the manager of the year award for a second time.

Everton's fourth-place finish was the ultimate expression of teamwork; a blend of youth and experience, astute signings and rookies. Moyes afforded prominent berths to Tony Hibbert and Leon Osman, who were part of Everton's victorious FA Youth Cup run in 1998. He revitalised journeymen, like Bent and Lee Carsley, and made them effective components in a winning system. Although there were mistakes in the transfer market – James Beattie and (later that year) Per Kroldrup and Simon Davies, would be conspicuous failures – he wheeled and dealed brilliantly. Thomas Gravesen was sold to Real Madrid for £2.5million four months before he could have left for nothing on a Bosman free. In his place Moyes signed Real Sociedad's elegant 22-year-old midfielder Mikel Arteta on loan with a view to a permanent move – which was completed at the season's end at a cost of just £2million. Arteta, like Cahill, would become an Everton great.

During summer 2005 he also signed Phil Neville, the experienced and versatile Manchester United player, who became the manager's eyes and ears – and voice – on the pitch. Appointed captain 18 months

later, he has proved one of the best and most influential captains Everton have ever had. Another difficult season followed, however. In all competitions, Everton lost 11 of their first 14 matches, dropping out of the Champions League, UEFA Cup and League Cup at the first hurdles. They recovered to finish the season 11th. Astonishingly, it was still Everton's fourth best showing in 15 years – three of which had now been accomplished on Moyes's watch.

At the end of the 2005/06 season, David Moyes quickly set about adding to his improving squad. As patchy as his summer business had been a year earlier, it was decisive and good in the summer of 2006. Again he brought in younger, fresher players who were completely reliable. There was pacey forward Andy Johnson; Wolves' fast and powerful centre back Joleon Lescott, who would be the mainstay of an excellent defence, also adding some crucial goals; the US international goalkeeper Tim Howard on a year's loan, with an option – which he took up – of a £3million transfer. Everton finished the 2006/07 campaign in sixth place, qualifying for the UEFA Cup and playing some excellent football on the way. Not only were they increasingly competitive, but a more potent footballing force too. Their defence was outstanding and conceded a measly 36 goals – one of the best showings in Everton history.

Moyes spent well again in the summer of 2007. Wigan Athletic's left back Leighton Baines signed for £6million and, although it took him time to settle, he would go on to be one of the Premier League's best attacking full backs, earning England honours. International recognition would also come the way of Sheffield United centre half Phil Jagielka, a bargain at £4million, and a rock-solid pillar on which to build the Everton defence. From Borussia Dortmund on a loan with an option to buy (again taken up for £1.8million) came South African midfielder Steven Pienaar. He became the energetic heartbeat of the team, keeping Everton's finest midfield in a generation ticking with endless running, passes and shimmies. There was also the record signing of the Middlesbrough forward Aiyegbeni Yakubu.

Everton played some sumptuous football during the 2007/08 season. It was another year of great memories and the club finished fifth. But despite the huge promise, Everton weren't quite good or experienced enough to make the breakthrough into the top four again, or to win a major trophy. They reached the semi-finals of the League Cup, where they faced Chelsea, but lost over two legs. Despite beating the competition's eventual winners Zenit St Petersburg in the group stage, they were beaten by Fiorentina in the UEFA Cup

As a Manager										
Season	P	W	L	D	F	A	Pts	Position	FA Cup	League Cup
2001/02*	38	11	10	17	45	59	43	15th	Quarter-Final	2nd Round
2002/03	38	17	8	13	48	49	59	7th	3rd Round	4th Round
2003/04	38	9	12	17	35	57	39	17th	4th Round	4th Round
2004/05	38	18	7	13	45	46	61	4th	5th Round	4th Round
2005/06	38	14	8	16	34	49	50	11th	4th Round	3rd Round
2006/07	38	15	13	10	52	36	58	6th	3rd Round	4th Round
2007/08	38	19	8	11	55	33	65	5th	3rd Round	Semi-Final
2008/09	38	17	12	9	55	37	63	5th	Runners-up	3rd Round
2009/10	38	16	13	9	60	49	61	8th	4th Round	4th Round
2010/11	38	13	15	10	51	45	54	7th	5th Round	3rd Round
2011/12	38	15	11	12	50	40	56	7th	Semi-Final	4th Round

* Moyes appointed 14 March 2002 with Everton 15th and out of both cup competitions

Round of 16 when they should have won. They were knocked out in the third round of the FA Cup by Oldham. Moyes faced criticism from sections of the support, who claimed that his team lacked the fortitude to go on and win things. But the reality was that the club were punching above their weight. The economics of the Premier League were so badly skewed that Liverpool during this period spent £6 on players for every £1 that Everton did.

In the summer of 2008 Moyes broke the Everton transfer record for the fourth time, with the deadline-day signing of Belgian international midfielder Marouane Fellaini for £15million. The deal was funded by the sale of Andy Johnson to Fulham for £10million and James McFadden to Birmingham City for £5million the previous January. Everton started the 2008/09 season frustratingly slowly, losing their first two home games to Blackburn Rovers and Portsmouth. Fellaini took time to settle and Everton were knocked out of the UEFA Cup by his former club Standard Liege in the opening round. Form slowly returned and Everton started 2009 in sixth place, a position they were to retain at the end of the season.

Moyes had possessed a poor FA Cup record since joining the club. A third round humiliation to Shrewsbury Town in 2003 ranked among the club's worst ever results. Defeat to Oldham in 2008 was not much better. But in 2009 Everton overcame a relentlessly difficult run – with ties against Liverpool, Aston Villa and Manchester United – to reach the final against Chelsea.

Unfortunately there was no happy ending for the Everton manager. Everton had already lost Mikel Arteta and Yakubu to long-term injury. Phil Jagielka snapped his cruciate ligament six days after dispatching the winning penalty against Manchester United in the semi-final. It was a patched-up Everton team that faced Chelsea in their 13th FA Cup Final, and although they took the lead after just 25 seconds, Chelsea – funded by the largesse of a Russian billionaire – had too much and won 2-1.

'This team is still growing,' said a defiant and proud Moyes afterwards. 'The team is young and hungry enough to keep going but it will be hard because there's a lot of clubs wanting the best. We have to keep our progress going. We have to believe if there wasn't any money maybe we could win a cup or squeeze into fourth again. We have to keep doing that. The gap is there, but we should all be hoping that somebody does break into that top four because that might alter the whole dynamic of football. If it's going to keep being money, money, money we all know something is going to go wrong in the future. But football goes in cycles. Teams are at the top at different times. I think Everton's cycle is a lot closer to coming around again. Everton had great teams in the 1980s and I think we're getting much closer to that.'

Unfortunately for Everton the hangover of defeat and the absence of big stars unsettled them in the opening stages of the 2009/10 season. So too did the covetous attention of other clubs. Manchester City, a club

that had been as badly run as Everton were managed with expert precision since Moyes's ascent to power in 2002, had been taken over in August 2008 by oil-rich Arab sheikhs, who tried to buy what good management had achieved elsewhere.

Joleon Lescott was tapped up by City and unsettled in such a way that it entirely disrupted Everton's pre-season plans. An opening-day mauling by Arsenal at Goodison – at 6-1 it was a record home defeat – set in motion another slow start to the season. But in the last 24 league matches of the campaign they displayed near title-winning form, losing just twice. Bolstered by the loan signing of US international forward Landon Donovan, they laid to rest the hoodoo of seldom beating the big four with back-to-back defeats of Chelsea and Manchester United. An eighth-place finish owed much to the shaky start, but also the highly competitive nature of the Premier League.

The reality was that Moyes was competing in a league where the competitive factor was being destroyed. Chelsea and Manchester City showed that it did not matter how good a manager you were or how good your team was; if you were a threat they would just poach your best players or spend their wealthy owners' money on better players. Nothing was more ludicrous or insidious than Manchester City spending 108 per cent of their 2010 income on wages. This is without taking into account the £117million they blew on transfer fees in the same period.

On a practical level City's financial doping inflated transfer fees and player wages, leaving Moyes with little scope to wheel and deal. In the 29 months to January 2012 the Everton manager did not pay a fee for a senior player, a drought that ended with the acquisition of Darron Gibson.

It has at times felt that Moyes has spent the period since 2009 treading water; awaiting investment or something more fundamental to change in the governance of football. His contract is due to expire in 2013 and at the time of writing (in July 2012) no new deal is imminent. His decade in charge at Goodison has – given the context in which he has operated – been an astonishing success. But there are many who also say that this success is qualified by the lack of silverware.

Certainly Moyes is not one to talk publicly about the iniquities of the Premier League. And despite the dour personality, the obsessiveness in making Everton even better, he remains at heart an optimist.

'We're all not wanting there to be a glass ceiling that people are talking about,' said Moyes in 2009. 'We all want progress every year … I've got to build on it, somehow I've got to find something that can make Everton move on.'

Europe as Manager			
Season	Champions League	UEFA Cup	Europa League
2005/06	3rd Qualifying Round	1st Round	-
2007/08	-	Round of 16	-
2008/09	-	1st Round	-
2009/10	-	-	Round of 32

Muir, Willie

Scottish goalkeeper who kept guard at the end of the 19th century

In the last years of the 19th century Everton were posed with a telling on-the-field problem. A team that included such talented players as Jack Taylor, John Bell, Johnny Holt and Edgar Chadwick were let down by a succession of erratic goalkeepers. 'In the season 1896/97 the club had got together an array of talented players for every position except in goal, and the weak link in the chain cost the side dearly,' wrote the Everton director and historian Thomas Keates. He added that Everton had lost the FA Cup Final to Aston Villa 'through feeble goalkeeping. The League position, too, was also weakened.' Bob Menham, Everton's hapless cup final custodian, was sold to Wigan that summer.

In his place Everton brought in two replacements: Third Lanark's Rab McFarlane and Kilmarnock's Willie Muir. 'Macfarlane [sic] a Scottish international player [he had one cap] will be entrusted with the position of custodian, and Muir, who also comes with a capital credentials, will doubtless have an opportunity of displaying his ability between the upright,' reported the Liverpool Mercury. McFarlane lasted nine games but was dropped after a 1-4 home defeat to Sheffield United. Muir, a £45 buy, was a more suitable choice for Keates, who described him as 'not a showy, but a most effective custodian'.

Despite conceding twice on his debut, away at West Bromwich Albion, Muir impressed the watching Mercury reporter, who wrote: 'Muir made a very successful debut in league football, and is certainly worthy of further trials.' With the new custodian the club's erratic early season form stabilised and they finished the 1897/98 season fourth, also reaching the FA Cup semi-final.

MUIR WAS A TALL, slender goalkeeper, described as 'steady, cool, and fast'. The addition of the highly rated George Kitchen from Stockport County a year after his Goodison arrival did little to allay his progress in a fine Everton team. The Blues finished the 1898/99 season fourth, with Muir missing just a solitary game, and may have lifted the League Championship had it not been for a disastrous run-in that witnessed just one win in their final eight games.

But inconsistency was never far away. Everton finished the 1899/1900 season 11th and the next campaign seventh; Muir missed just two games during these disappointing seasons. A new-look Everton started the 1901/02 season in excellent form and topped the table for the early part of the campaign. But a crushing 4-0 defeat at Nottingham Forest saw Muir

A NEW-LOOK EVERTON STARTED THE 1901/02 SEASON IN EXCELLENT FORM

made the fall guy. Kitchen took his place the next week and the local press recorded 'no custodian could have given a better display than the man who usually guards the reserve citadel'. Muir never turned out for Everton's first team again, and returned to Scotland the following summer where he found success once more with one of Dundee's greatest teams.

Season	League		FA Cup		Total	
	App	Goals	App	Goals	App	Goals
1897/98	21	0	5	0	26	0
1898/99	33	0	2	0	35	0
1899/1900	32	0	1	0	33	0
1900/01	34	0	2	0	36	0
1901/02	7	0	0	0	7	0
Total	**127**	**0**	**10**	**0**	**137**	**0**

[FACTFILE]

BORN
Ayr, 20 September 1877
POSITION
Goalkeeper
OTHER CLUBS
Kilmarnock;
Dundee (1902–07);
Heart of Midlothian (1907);
Dundee; Hibernian;
Dumbarton
HONOURS
1 Scotland cap (1907)

Murray, C.

Mysterious goalkeeper who made just two FA Cup appearances before disappearing from the records

Season	League		FA Cup		Total	
	App	Goals	App	Goals	App	Goals
1892/93	0	0	2	0	2	0
Total	**0**	**0**	**2**	**0**	**2**	**0**

[FACTFILE]

BORN
Unknown
POSITION
Goalkeeper

Murray, David B.

Full back who crossed the great Mersey divide

Season	League		FA Cup		Total	
	App	Goals	App	Goals	App	Goals
1903/04	2	0	0	0	2	0
Total	2	0	0	0	2	0

Murray, David J.,

Everton's trailblazing first foreign footballer

Season	League		FA Cup		Total	
	App	Goals	App	Goals	App	Goals
1925/26	2	1	0	0	2	1
1926/27	1	0	0	0	1	0
Total	3	1	0	0	3	1

Murray, Joe

Rarely used inside forward whose career traversed the 'Split'

Season	League		FA Cup		Total	
	App	Goals	App	Goals	App	Goals
1891/92	4	0	0	0	4	0
1892/93	1	0	0	0	1	0
Total	5	0	0	0	5	0

Murray, T.

Defender who played twice in Everton's first recognised FA Cup run

Season	League		FA Cup		Total	
	App	Goals	App	Goals	App	Goals
1887/88	-	-	2	0	2	0
Total	-	-	2	0	2	0

Mustafi,
Shkodran

Highly rated German youngster given just a solitary outing

[FACTFILE]

BORN
Bad Hersfeld, Germany, 17 April 1992

POSITION
Centre back

OTHER CLUBS
Sampdoria (2012–)

Season	League		FA Cup		League Cup		Europe		Total	
	App	Goals	App	Goals	App	Goals	App	Goals	App	Goals
2009/10	0	0	0	0	0	0	1	0	1	0
Total	0	0	0	0	0	0	1	0	1	0

Myhre,
Thomas

Charismatic Norwegian international goalkeeper who failed to build on early promise

As Neville Southall's Goodison career wound down in the mid-1990s, speculation as to who would succeed him seemed to persist for an eternity. Given the high-profile names linked to Everton, it was perhaps some surprise when in November 1997 Howard Kendall brought in Thomas Myhre, an unknown from the obscurity of the Norwegian First Division, to fill the mantle soon to be left vacant by the great Welshman.

'SOUTHALL IS A HERO TO ME'

The Norwegian had been tracked by Everton scouts for 18 months, already impressing for the reserve team while on trial at Goodison, when Kendall made him an £800,000 signing. The Everton manager had sufficient confidence to put Myhre straight into the team in place of Southall for an away game at Leeds. He impressed immediately against the resurgent Yorkshiremen, providing a stirring performance that helped Everton earn a 0-0 draw.

Standing 6 ft 3 in tall, the Viking colossus was similar in stature to his illustrious predecessor.

He commanded the penalty area with great self-assurance and, like Southall, his agility and reflexes belied his imposing frame. He possessed charisma too, and struck up a great rapport with Everton's travelling support, who never ceased to be amused by his off-the-ball antics – from celebrating goals to berating misses. Ironically it was the man he replaced who provided the Norwegian with inspiration long before he came to Goodison. 'I used to watch English matches on the television back home and Neville was always everybody's favourite goalkeeper when I was younger,' Myhre said. 'Southall is a hero to me.' Months after Myhre's arrival Everton's most decorated player was allowed to leave Goodison after nearly 17 years.

MYHRE consolidated his position as Everton's number one through the 1998/99 season, when he possessed one of the Premier League's best clean-sheet records. Although there were occasional lapses – as witness the late goal he conceded in Everton's so-called Great Escape against Coventry, when the ball slipped from his grasp and into the net – his overall form saw him linked with a move to Manchester United as Peter Schmeichel's long-term replacement. He also established himself as first-choice Norway goalkeeper. However, at the end of the season Myhre broke his ankle while on international duty, an injury that saw him lose his place to Paul Gerrard. After a couple of loan spells he finally returned to the Everton team in early 2000. This time his form was less spectacular and an abject display in an FA Cup quarter-final against Aston Villa saw him dropped.

This effectively marked the end of Myhre's Everton career. Walter Smith was obdurate in his refusal to play him again, purportedly to avert triggering an appearance clause in his transfer that would have led to Everton paying Viking Stavanger a further instalment of his fee. The impasse seemed to impair the goalkeeper's confidence in a series of unsuccessful loan moves. Eventually he joined Besiktas in November 2001 for a knockdown £325,000.

MYHRE subsequently blamed Smith for the unsatisfactory end to his Everton career. 'I felt that I wasn't treated right by Smith,' he said. 'You could say that our relationship was full of conflict and very turbulent. This wasn't about money. This was about personal things. There was bad chemistry between us.'

[FACTFILE]

BORN
Sarpsborg, 16 October 1973
POSITION
Goalkeeper
OTHER CLUBS
Viking Stavanger (1993–97);
Glasgow Rangers (loan, 1999);
Birmingham City (loan, 2000);
Tranmere Rovers (loan, 2000);
FC Copenhagen (loan, 2001);
Besiktas (2001–02);
Sunderland (2002–05);
Crystal Palace (loan, 2003–04);
Fredrikstad (2005);
Charlton Athletic (2005–07);
Viking Stavanger (2007–10);
Kongsvinger (2010–)
HONOURS
56 Norway caps (1998–2007)

Season	League		FA Cup		League Cup		Total	
	App	Goals	App	Goals	App	Goals	App	Goals
1997/98	22	0	1	0	0	0	23	0
1998/99	38	0	4	0	3	0	45	0
1999/2000	4	0	2	0	0	0	6	0
2000/01	6	0	2	0	0	0	8	0
2001/02	0	0	0	0	0	0	0	0
Total	**70**	**0**	**9**	**0**	**3**	**0**	**82**	**0**

THE

EVERTON

·ENCYCLOPEDIA·

Carlo **Nash,** Gary **Naysmith,** Lucas **Neill,** Phil **Neville,**
Pat **Nevin,** Mike **Newell,** Henry **Newton,** Keith **Newton,**
Geoff **Nulty,** Tommy **Nuttall,** Alex **Nyarko**

Nash, Carlo

Reserve goalkeeper who made just a solitary first-team appearance

Season	League		FA Cup		League Cup		Europe		Total	
	App	Goals	App	Goals	App	Goals	App	Goals	App	Goals
2009/10	0	0	0	0	0	0	1	0	1	0
Total	0	0	0	0	0	0	1	0	1	0

[FACTFILE]

BORN
Bolton, 13 September 1973
POSITION
Goalkeeper
OTHER CLUBS
Crystal Palace (1996–98);
Stockport County
(1998–2001);
Wolverhampton Wanderers
(loan, 2000–01);
Manchester City (2001–03);
Middlesbrough (2003–05);
Preston North End
(2005–07);
Wigan Athletic (loan,
2007–08);
Stoke City
(2008 loan & 2010–)

Naysmith, Gary

Scottish Young Player of the Year who ultimately fell short of the Goodison grade

Signed for £1.7million by Walter Smith in October 2000, Naysmith, a 21-year-old left back and former Scottish PFA Young Footballer of the Year, was already a Scotland international and veteran of nearly 100 league appearances by the time of his arrival. Hailed as one of his country's most promising footballers, in a way Naysmith came to symbolise for Evertonians Scotland's decline as a footballing power. In the past, such Goodison greats as Alex Young and Jimmy Gabriel were frequently omitted from the Scotland team; Naysmith, by contrast, was an international regular even at a time when he couldn't make the Goodison bench.

Initially a quick overlapping full back, Naysmith's pace seemed to diminish over time – perhaps as a consequence of the injuries that often plagued his time on Merseyside. Utilised as both a full back and auxiliary left midfielder, he showed occasional dead-ball prowess. Never was this more in evidence than when he struck a sweet curling free kick that aided a 3-1 victory against Tottenham on Good Friday 2004. Despite signing a new three-year contract in 2005, Naysmith found himself an even more peripheral player in his last two years at Goodison. With just a year left on his contract, a £1million bid from Sheffield United in summer 2007 seemed too good to turn down and the full back was allowed to leave for Bramall Lane.

[FACTFILE]

BORN
Edinburgh,
16 November 1978
POSITION
Full back
OTHER CLUBS
Heart of Midlothian
(1996–2000); Sheffield
United (2007–10);
Huddersfield Town (2010–)
HONOURS
46 Scotland caps
(1 goal) (2000–)

Season	League		FA Cup		League Cup		Europe		Total	
	App	Goals	App	Goals	App	Goals	App	Goals	App	Goals
2000/01	17 (3)	2	1	0	0	0	-	-	18 (3)	2
2001/02	23 (1)	0	4	0	0	0	-	-	27 (1)	0
2002/03	24 (4)	1	1	0	2 (1)	1	-	-	27 (5)	2
2003/04	27 (2)	2	2 (1)	0	2	0	-	-	31 (3)	2
2004/05	5 (6)	0	3	0	1	0	-	-	9 (6)	0
2005/06	7	0	0 (1)	0	0	0	0	0	7 (1)	0
2006/07	10 (5)	1	0 (1)	0	1	0	-	-	11 (6)	1
Total	113 (21)	6	11 (3)	0	6 (1)	1	0	0	130 (25)	7

Neill,
Lucas

Australia captain who briefly plugged Everton's back line

Lucas Neill captained his country, played at two World Cup finals and made more than 400 appearances in English football.

BUT HIS CAREER will, in many minds, always be defined by his decision to eschew a 2007 transfer to Liverpool and instead join West Ham on a reported weekly salary of £72,000. The decision seemed to epitomise an era when footballers' financial considerations came before footballing interests.

Neill had made his way in English football with Millwall where he was a young team-mate of his compatriot and great friend, Tim Cahill. His Premier League reputation was forged as a no-nonsense defender with Blackburn in a six-year spell at Ewood Park before the move to London came.

Thirty-two months later Neill found himself on Merseyside after all. Released from his onerous West Ham contract he was drafted in by Everton as a free agent following early-season injury to Phil Neville. He deputised ably at right back and centre half in a busy autumn of 2009. But with the Everton captain's return and cash in short supply, when Galatasaray made a £700,000 bid for Neill in the following January's transfer window, Everton accepted and his Goodison career came to an end after just a dozen starts.

[FACTFILE]

BORN
Sydney, 9 March 1978

POSITION
Full back / centre back

OTHER CLUBS
Millwall (1995–2001); Blackburn Rovers (2001–07); West Ham United (2007–09); Galatasaray (2010–11); Al Jazira (United Arab Emirates, 2011–)

HONOURS
80 Australia caps (1996–)

Season	League		FA Cup		League Cup		Europe		Total	
	App	Goals	App	Goals	App	Goals	App	Goals	App	Goals
2009/10	10 (2)	0	1	0	1 (1)	0	0	0	12 (3)	0
Total	10 (2)	0	1	0	1 (1)	0	0	0	12 (3)	0

Neville, Phil

Veteran captain and Moyes's on-field lieutenant

One of the golden generation of early-1990s Manchester United players, Phil Neville was one of the most decorated footballers of his era when David Moyes paid £3.5million to sign him in the summer of 2005. An England international of a decade's standing, Neville had graduated through the youth ranks with David Beckham, Paul Scholes and his older brother Gary, and could lay claim to winner's medals for six Premier Leagues, three FA Cups and a Champions League as well as more than 50 caps.

An outstanding schoolboy cricketer, who had focused on football when a top-class cricket career was also a viable option, Neville was a versatile and underrated member of United's great 1990s squad, usually filling in at full back. Later he became frustrated at the lack of first-team opportunities and sought a transfer at the end of the 2004/05 season.

At Goodison Neville started out as a central midfielder, but was usually more effective at full back and his experience and tenacity have been important components of the club's progress since his arrival. Yet for Everton Neville has always been more than just a versatile and talented player; he was the possessor of great experience and a terrific winner's mentality too, which enthused the Goodison dressing room. It was no surprise when Neville succeeded David Weir as captain in January 2007, but by his own admission it had not been an easy journey.

'I thought, "Wow, I could be upsetting a whole dressing room here," and I think at the time I did,' he told the Guardian in 2009 of his first days at the club. 'No one said anything to me but I could feel the vibe. Maybe it

wasn't me as a person but the way I came in from Manchester United. "Who does he think he is?" I had to be strong and I was. At the start I had to grit my teeth but I think once people worked out that all I wanted was the best for Everton they accepted me.'

As Moyes's lieutenant he was crucial to Everton: the manager's eyes and ears – and voice – on the pitch. 'Phil is someone who may be part of a dying breed, he's a great leader,' Moyes would say some five years after signing him. 'We have a good squad and there was consideration about Phil's position but the team just seems to function better when Phil plays. It might get to the stage where he might not be the best player but the team still needs his leadership qualities.

'You should see and hear him in the dressing room before a game. He's a top man. He prepares himself right and that's why he has had nearly 60 England caps and why he's got longevity in his career. He is terrific at motivating and cajoling and is always the first one to put his hands up if he's not on his game.'

proved crucial to the team. His leadership qualities are exemplary. One of the fittest members of the Everton dressing room, it came as no surprise when Neville signed a new two-year contract in 2011, having previously extended his first deal with the club. 'I feel really proud and this club has never let me down,' said Neville. 'It's shown faith in me again and for the next two years I'm going to give my all for this football club.'

[**FACTFILE**]

BORN
Bury, 21 January 1977
POSITION
Full back / defensive midfielder
OTHER CLUB
Manchester United (1994–2005)
HONOURS
59 England caps (1996–2007)

Neville accepted he was part of the manager's attempt to alter the mentality at Goodison. 'The gaffer had a vision of where he was going and I was an important part of that,' he said. 'I am not a shouter or bawler. I lead through my professionalism, through my training, and that is what he wanted. He wanted to change the mentality at Everton.'

A fine athletic defender, with a good tactical brain and the ability to seamlessly slot into a defensive midfield position, Neville has continually

'I'M GOING TO GIVE MY ALL FOR THIS FOOTBALL CLUB'

Season	League		FA Cup		League Cup		Europe		Total	
	App	Goals	App	Goals	App	Goals	App	Goals	App	Goals
2005/06	34	0	4	0	1	0	4	0	43	0
2006/07	35	1	1	0	2	0	-	-	38	1
2007/08	37	2	0	0	4 (1)	0	8	0	49 (1)	2
2008/09	36 (1)	0	7	0	1	0	2	0	46 (1)	0
2009/10	22 (1)	0	2	0	0	0	4	0	28 (1)	0
2010/11	31	1	3	0	1	0	-	-	35	1
2011/12	24 (3)	0	6	0	2 (1)	1	-	-	32 (4)	1
Total	**219(5)**	**4**	**23**	**0**	**11 (2)**	**1**	**18**	**0**	**271 (7)**	**5**

Nevin, Pat

Bohemian winger who defied the modern footballer stereotype

A man who refused to conform to the notion that all footballers are inherently bland, boorish and self-obsessed, Pat Nevin was a rare breath of fresh air during Everton's late-1980s decline. Signed in summer 1988 for £925,000, along with Stuart McCall, Tony Cottee and Neil McDonald, his arrival marked the start of Colin Harvey's rebuilding plans.

Rejected as a teenager by his boyhood club Celtic for being too slight, Nevin had started out as an amateur with Clyde in the early 1980s, combining football with study for a commerce degree at Glasgow Tech. He resisted the switch to professional football for a couple of years, winning the Scottish Second Division title in 1981/82, before joining Chelsea a year later for £95,000. He spent five years at Stamford Bridge, garnering a reputation as one of the country's most stylish wide men.

Indeed, Nevin in many ways represented a throwback to the illustrious Scottish wingers of old. Diminutive and highly skilful, he seemed to dance along the Everton wing, dodging and weaving and sending defenders sprawling with his slights and checks. He was a fine and accurate crosser of the ball and possessed a good finish. Off the pitch, his interest in classical literature, alternative music and modern art set him apart from other players, attracting cult status among the 'thinking' sections of the Everton support.

Nevin's Everton career nevertheless got off to a slow start. Ligament damage sustained in only his third game sidelined him until Christmas, and thereafter it took him some weeks to capture his best form. By April 1989, however, he was firmly established in the side, scoring a fine winner against Charlton: dancing past two defenders, Nevin played a wall pass to Graeme Sharp, then scooped the ball over goalkeeper Bob Bolder. 'It was,' commented the watching Scotland manager, Andy Roxburgh, 'just about the best goal I've seen all season. It was quite brilliant.' A week later Nevin struck the FA Cup semi-final winner against Norwich City, a feat that was inevitably overshadowed by the Hillsborough disaster.

Through the 1989/90 season there were other memorable moments: a beautifully judged lob that he dinked over Jim Leighton's head and into a Manchester United net in September; a superb brace against champions Arsenal the following month. That win put Everton within reach of the top of the First Division, but Everton ultimately finished well short. Amid the dismal last days under Harvey's management, Nevin was a rare bright light and through the remainder of the 1990/91 season enjoyed some of the best form of his career, sometimes in a striking role. Yet Nevin soon fell foul of Howard Kendall, who preferred Robert Warzycha and latterly Mark Ward to the Scot. 'He didn't rate me and I didn't rate him,' Nevin later admitted to Toffeeweb.com.

With only a cameo role in the 1991/92 season, in March 1992 Nevin, still aged only 28, was loaned to Tranmere Rovers, a switch that became permanent the following August for a fee of £300,000. It was one of those dark ironies of Everton history, that just as the club so desperately needed some impudence and guile the manager deemed one of its most likely sources surplus.

NEVIN ENJOYED something of an Indian summer at Prenton Park, later returning to Scotland and playing out his career with Kilmarnock and Motherwell. One of the game's most thoughtful and articulate voices, he has since embarked on a successful career as a broadcast pundit.

> PAT NEVIN WAS A RARE BREATH OF FRESH AIR DURING EVERTON'S LATE-1980S DECLINE

[FACTFILE]

BORN
Glasgow, 6 September 1963

POSITION
Winger

OTHER CLUBS
Clyde (1981–83);
Chelsea (1983–88);
Tranmere Rovers (1992–97);
Kilmarnock (1997–98);
Motherwell (1998–2000)

HONOURS
28 Scotland caps (5 goals) (1986–96)

Season	League App	League Goals	FA Cup App	FA Cup Goals	League Cup App	League Cup Goals	Other App	Other Goals	Total App	Total Goals
1988/89	20 (5)	2	5 (1)	2	1	0	5	1	31 (6)	5
1989/90	23 (7)	4	1 (3)	0	4	1	-	-	28 (10)	5
1990/91	31 (6)	8	5 (1)	0	2 (1)	1	3 (3)	0	41 (11)	9
1991/92	7 (10)	2	1 (1)	0	3	0	1	0	12 (11)	2
Total	**81 (28)**	**16**	**12 (6)**	**2**	**10 (1)**	**2**	**9 (3)**	**1**	**112 (38)**	**21**

Newell, Mike

Local-born centre forward who struggled to win the hearts of the Goodison crowd

Mike Newell was never really ever given a chance to settle at Goodison in a largely disappointing two-year spell. He did not seem to entirely convince either Colin Harvey or Howard Kendall, while Everton's supporters never really warmed to him either – perhaps unwilling to forgive his Liverpool-supporting past.

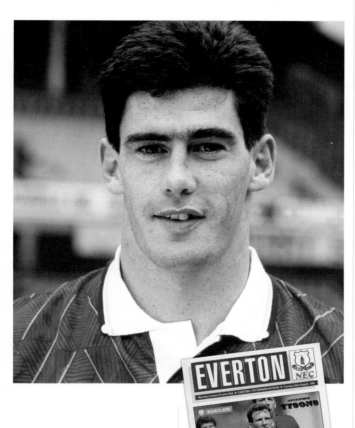

NEWELL HAD first come to prominence in October 1986 as a 21-year-old Luton Town forward who scored a hat-trick in his club's surprise 4-1 demolition of Liverpool. There was a spell with Leicester City before Colin Harvey brought him to Goodison in a £1.1million deal in the summer of 1989.

Immediately displacing Tony Cottee, who was still the British transfer record holder, Newell opened his Everton career in electrifying fashion, with nine goals in his first 13 appearances. Tall and robust with good distribution and quick feet, Newell was an intelligent centre forward who perhaps lacked some of the aggression Graeme Sharp brought to the role. Nevertheless, he proved an eloquent foil for the Scot and his early-season form earned him an England call-up.

But then injuries struck and Newell found himself in and out of a struggling side. After Harvey's sacking, Howard Kendall initially showed a preference for Newell in the second half of the 1990/91 season, but his strike rate had started to decline. Following the arrival of Peter Beardsley during the 1991/92 close season, Kendall plumped for Cottee as his new signing's first-choice partner. In November 1991 he sold Newell to Blackburn for £1.1million, using the proceeds to sign Mo Johnston from Rangers.

It was a costly mistake, as Johnston laboured and Everton struggled without a discernible target man for some three years. At Ewood Park, Newell was an

important part of Blackburn's renaissance and an excellent strike partner to Alan Shearer before losing his place to Chris Sutton. There followed, in his early thirties, a tour of the lower leagues. Newell subsequently emerged as a talented young manager, whose propensity for speaking his mind tended to undermine him.

> **NEWELL OPENED HIS EVERTON CAREER IN ELECTRIFYING FASHION, WITH NINE GOALS IN HIS FIRST 13 APPEARANCES**

[FACTFILE]

BORN
Liverpool,
27 January 1965

POSITION
Centre forward

OTHER CLUBS
Crewe Alexandra (1983);
Wigan Athletic (1983–86);
Luton Town (1986–87);
Leicester City (1987–89);
Blackburn Rovers (1991–96);
Birmingham City (1996–97);
West Ham (loan, 1996–97);
Bradford City (loan, 1997);
Aberdeen (1997–99);
Crewe Alexandra (1999);
Doncaster Rovers
(1999–2000);
Blackpool (2000–01)

AS A MANAGER
Hartlepool United (2002–03);
Luton Town (2003–07);
Grimsby Town (2008–9)

Season	League		FA Cup		League Cup		Other		Total	
	App	Goals	App	Goals	App	Goals	App	Goals	App	Goals
1989/90	20 (6)	7	4 (2)	0	4	3	-	-	28 (8)	10
1990/91	20 (9)	7	2 (2)	0	1 (2)	0	5	1	28 (13)	8
1991/92	8 (5)	1	0	0	2 (1)	1	1	1	11 (6)	3
Total	**48 (20)**	**15**	**6 (4)**	**0**	**7 (3)**	**4**	**6**	**2**	**67 (27)**	**21**

Newton, Henry

Expensive midfielder who failed to slake lofty expectations

In October 1970 Henry Newton became the third most expensive footballer in English football, after Harry Catterick paid Nottingham Forest £150,000 plus Northern Irish midfielder Tommy Jackson for their captain. In joining Everton, the former England under-23 midfielder had rejected the advances of Brian Clough's Derby County.

SOMETHING OF A midfield general, who matched brave and effective tackling with sharp and constructive distribution, Newton was considered among the most talented midfielders in the country. But his addition to a team already boasting the illustrious Harvey-Kendall-Ball triumvirate seemed strange, if not wholly incongruous. Indeed he was never able to break into this part of the Everton team — even after the departure of Alan Ball the following year. Instead, he was inserted as a straight replacement for his namesake, Keith, at left back.

Newton was perfectly adept in this position, and in a declining side his efforts could never be faulted. A competitive player who did the simple things well, there was nevertheless a perpetual sense that he was a square peg in a round hole at full back. Indeed his best performances came during the 1971/72

> IN JOINING EVERTON, THE FORMER ENGLAND UNDER-23 MIDFIELDER HAD REJECTED THE ADVANCES OF BRIAN CLOUGH'S DERBY COUNTY

season when called upon to deputise for Colin Harvey and Howard Kendall in the Everton engine room.

Offered the chance of a return to his native Midlands in September 1973, he accepted a £110,000 move to Derby. Clough had finally got his man and Newton was restored to midfield. The following season, his midfield partnership with Bruce Rioch and Archie Gemmill was instrumental in bringing the First Division title to the Baseball Ground. In the process Derby had pipped Everton to the post: Newton had had the last laugh.

> NEWTON WAS CONSIDERED AMONG THE MOST TALENTED MIDFIELDERS IN THE COUNTRY

[FACTFILE]

BORN
Nottingham, 18 February 1944

POSITION
Midfielder/ full back

OTHER CLUBS
Nottingham Forest (1963–70);
Derby County (1973–77);
Walsall (1977–78)

Season	League		FA Cup		League Cup		Other		Total	
	App	Goals	App	Goals	App	Goals	App	Goals	App	Goals
1970/71	23	3	5	1	-	-	0	0	28	4
1971/72	24	1	2	0	0	0	-	-	26	1
1972/73	23	1	0	0	1	0	-	-	24	1
1973/74	6	0	0	0	0	0	1	0	7	0
Total	76	5	7	1	1	0	1	0	85	6

Newton, Keith

Talented left back who replaced Ray Wilson for club and country

In December 1969 Harry Catterick paid Blackburn Rovers £80,000 for their left back, Keith Newton, and charged him with the same unenviable task he had carried off with distinction for England: filling on a long term basis the number three shirt vacated by Ray Wilson.

COMING into one of the finest Everton teams in the club's history, Newton rarely looked out of place and by the end of the 1969/70 season had won a League Championship medal – his first major honour in a career that already spanned more than 300 senior appearances.

Born in Manchester in June 1941, Newton had been scouted as a schoolboy inside forward, but after joining Blackburn as an apprentice was converted to centre back. Unable to supplant Mike England as Rovers' centre half, he converted to left back. With his forward's touch, turn of pace and imaginative distribution he established a reputation as one of the First Division's finest attacking full backs. Indeed, sometimes he seemed almost an auxiliary winger. And yet he had the aerial ability and combative streak necessary in any outstanding defender. In swapping the Blackburn forward line for the left back berth, he completed an exact reverse of the transition his colleague Fred Pickering – soon to join Everton – had managed around the same time.

Named as part of Alf Ramsey's provisional squad for the 1966 World Cup Finals, Newton made his England debut against West Germany in February 1966. He was one of five unlucky players left out of the 27-man squad on the eve of the finals, but after the World Cup he started to make a sustained challenge for Wilson's England shirt.

At club level there were other parallels with Wilson. Blackburn were relegated at the end of the 1965/66 season, and just as the Everton left back had once had to stake his claim for an international place in the Second Division with Huddersfield, so Newton now had to do so with Blackburn. Newton realised that Ramsey was unlikely to choose somebody who wasn't regularly playing First Division football. 'Without wanting to sound disrespectful to Second Division players,' he proclaimed, 'I am worried that the standard of wingers I am likely to come up against will not be high enough to play for England.'

Such outbursts earned him the opprobrium of the Blackburn board, who transfer-listed him for £100,000. But no top-flight manager was prepared to make him the first English defender to command a six-figure sum. Catterick's £80,000 offer came after years of speculation linking him with a move away from Ewood Park.

NEWTON came into the Everton team in place of Sandy Brown and made enough appearances to claim a title medal before he succumbed to injury during the 1969/70 season run-in. He returned for England's World Cup campaign in Mexico, playing alongside Alan Ball, Brian Labone and Tommy Wright. Post-World Cup, however, he never seemed to capture the confidence of Harry Catterick, who criticised him for overelaborating when in possession, even converting his namesake, Henry Newton, from midfield to left back in his place.

Newton was by no means responsible for Everton's slide in Catterick's last years, but at the end of the 1971/72 season he was allowed to join Burnley. At Turf Moor he provided more than 200 games of service until the late 1970s. The Everton left back berth, meanwhile, remained problematic for a generation.

> COMING INTO ONE OF THE FINEST EVERTON TEAMS IN THE CLUB'S HISTORY, NEWTON RARELY LOOKED OUT OF PLACE AND BY THE END OF THE 1969/70 SEASON HAD WON A LEAGUE CHAMPIONSHIP MEDAL

[FACTFILE]

BORN
Manchester, 26 June 1941
DIED
Blackburn, 16 June 1998
POSITION
Left back
OTHER CLUBS
Blackburn Rovers (1959–69);
Burnley (1972–78)
HONOURS
1969/70
League Championship;
27 England caps (1966–70)

Season	League		FA Cup		League Cup		Other		Total	
	App	Goals	App	Goals	App	Goals	App	Goals	App	Goals
1969/70	12	0	1	0	-	-	-	-	13	0
1970/71	21 (1)	1	1	0	-	-	7	0	28 (1)	1
1971/72	15	0	0	0	1	0	-	-	16	0
Total	**48 (1)**	**1**	**2**	**0**	**1**	**0**	**7**	**0**	**58 (1)**	**1**

Nulty, Geoff

Doughty utility man whose career was ended by derby day savagery

In March 1980, Geoff Nulty was on the receiving end of one of the most notorious incidents in Merseyside derby history. Just minutes into the Goodison encounter, Liverpool's purported midfield hard man, Jimmy Case, the latest in a tradition of Anfield hatchet men, launched a knee-high assault on Nulty that destroyed his knee and ended a lengthy career.

IT WAS AN outrageous challenge still recalled with horror by watching Evertonians. Nearly 30 years later, Alan Kirwin wrote on Toffeeweb. com: 'I can still hear the crack of Geoff Nulty's leg as Jimmy Shithouse Case's boot made contact with his upper tibia about 7 mins after the ball had gone. And the complete lack of remorse, or even interest in the plight of a fellow professional, whose career he had just ended.'

Nulty had joined Everton 20 months previously from Newcastle for £40,000. At St James's Park he had been Gordon Lee's captain, dependable, experienced and adept in midfield or central defence. It was his versatility and professionalism that attracted Lee back to his former charge, and although his performances never really won over the Goodison faithful, his commitment was never in doubt.

Following the horror challenge Nulty was appointed to Lee's Goodison coaching staff and later followed him to Preston North End.

	League		FA Cup		League Cup		Europe		Total	
Season	App	Goals	App	Goals	App	Goals	App	Goals	App	Goals
1978/79	13 (4)	1	0	0	2	0	2 (1)	0	17 (5)	1
1979/80	9 (1)	1	0	0	4	0	2	0	15 (1)	1
Total	22 (5)	2	0	0	6	0	4 (1)	0	32 (6)	2

[FACTFILE]

BORN
Prescot, 13 February 1949
POSITION
Defender / midfield
OTHER CLUBS
Burnley (1969–74);
Newcastle United (1974–78)

Nuttall, Tommy

Versatile forward who played a cameo role in Everton's second title winning season

[FACTFILE]

BORN
Bolton, January 1889
DIED
October 1963
POSITION
Inside forward
OTHER CLUBS
Manchester United (1911–12);
St Mirren; Rochdale;
Northwich Victoria;
Southend United (1920–21);
St Mirren;
Nelson (1923)

	League		FA Cup		Total	
Season	App	Goals	App	Goals	App	Goals
1913/14	14	7	0	0	14	7
1914/15	5	0	0	0	5	0
Total	19	7	0	0	19	7

Nyarko, Alex

Ghanaian misfit who proved a catastrophic transfer error by Walter Smith

Expectations of Alex Nyarko were sky-high when Walter Smith made him a £4.5million signing from RC Lens in August 2000. Likened by the Everton manager to the Arsenal midfield powerhouses Emmanuel Petit and Patrick Viera, the 26-year-old had impressed when he came up against the duo in the previous season's Champions League. Tall, composed and tough, he promised to be the sort of all-action midfielder Everton were crying out for.

> AN EVERTON FAN NAMED STEPHEN PRICE ENTERED THE PITCH AND OFFERED TO EXCHANGE SHIRTS WITH NYARKO

Although there were glimpses of Nyarko's unquestioned ability on the few occasions he pulled on an Everton shirt, his languid style seemed to beg questions of his motivation and will to win. Amid high expectation after a busy summer of transfer activity, Smith's Everton faltered through the 2000/01 season.

NYARKO was by no means the only underperfomer, but he was the most expensive of the manager's white elephants and seemed to symbolise a group of players who cared little about the declining club they played for.

Things came to a head during Everton's customary hiding at Highbury in April 2001. Losing 3-1 and being toyed with by an impressive Arsenal team, an Everton fan named Stephen Price entered the pitch and offered to exchange shirts with Nyarko – the implication being that he was unfit to wear the blue of Everton. Nyarko was understandably flustered by the intervention and asked to be substituted.

AFTERWARDS an unimpressed Smith did nothing to play down the situation or suppress his bemusement. He said: 'It is not a good example to set and it raises a lot of questions, not only about his commitment to the club, but also the mentality of the player to handle it. He showed a lack of strength mentally. Not many footballers will go through their careers without receiving a bit of criticism and he's obviously not accepted it too well.'

Nyarko was hawked around Europe and there were loan moves to Paris Saint-Germain and Monaco, but nobody would make a permanent move for him – even at a knockdown price.

In 2003/04 he returned to Goodison and there was an attempt at rehabilitation under David Moyes. But at the end of the season, and still with a year remaining on his five-year contract, it emerged that only a four-year work permit had been acquired when he signed – a ludicrous situation that meant Everton held his playing registration and were obliged to pay his wages but could not play him.

Now aged 30, Nyarko attempted to revive his career in the Norwegian and Swiss leagues, but the damage to his reputation and confidence was seemingly irreparable.

[FACTFILE]

BORN
Accra, Ghana, 15 October 1973

POSITION
Midfield

OTHER CLUBS
Asante Kotoko Kumsai (1992–93);
Dawu Youngstars (1993–94);
Sportul Studentesc Bucuresti (1994–95);
FC Basel (1995–97);
SC Karlsruher (1997–98);
RC Lens (1998–2000);
AS Monaco (loan, 2001–02);
Paris Saint-Germain (2002–03);
IK Start Kristiansand (2005);
Yverdon-Sports (2006–08)

HONOURS
4 Ghana caps (2000)

Season	League		FA Cup		League Cup		Total	
	App	Goals	App	Goals	App	Goals	App	Goals
2000/01	19 (3)	1	0	0	2	0	21 (3)	1
2001/02	0	0	0	0	0	0	0	0
2002/03	0	0	0	0	0	0	0	0
2003/04	7 (4)	0	2	0	1	0	10 (4)	0
Total	**26 (7)**	**1**	**2**	**0**	**3**	**0**	**31 (7)**	**1**

THE
EVERTON
·ENCYCLOPEDIA·

Jonathan **O'Connor**, Jack **O'Donnell**, Eddie **O'Hara**, John **O'Kane**, Eamon **O'Keefe**, Wilfred **Oldham**, Darren **Oldroyd**, Frank **Oliver**, **Olympians**, Jimmy **O'Neill**, W. **Orr**, Leon **Osman**, John **Oster**, Billy **Owen**, Terry **Owen**

O'Connor, Jonathan

Hugely promising England youth international who drifted out of football

[FACTFILE]

BORN
Darlington, 29 October 1975
POSITION
Centre back / right back
OTHER CLUBS
Sheffield United
(1998–2000);
Blackpool (2000–02)

Season	League		FA Cup		League Cup		Europe		Total	
	App	Goals	App	Goals	App	Goals	App	Goals	App	Goals
1995/96	3 (1)	0	0	0	0	0	0	0	3 (1)	0
1996/97	0	0	0	0	0	0	-	-	0	0
1997/98	0 (1)	0	0	0	0	0	-	-	0 (1)	0
Total	**3 (2)**	**0**	**0**	**0**	**0**	**0**	**0**	**0**	**3 (2)**	**0**

O'Donnell, Jack

League Championship winning left back who left Everton under a cloud

The arrival of left back Jack O'Donnell from Darlington at the end of January 1925 saw Everton plunged into one of the most bitter transfer disputes of the era. The Everton board had sanctioned a £4000 double purchase of the defender and the Darlington forward Tom Scott. The joint bid was accepted and O'Donnell became an Everton player, but Scott delayed and a week later emerged as a new signing for Liverpool.

> JANUARY 1925 SAW EVERTON PLUNGED INTO ONE OF THE MOST BITTER TRANSFER DISPUTES OF THE ERA

A furious Will Cuff announced immediately that Everton would take action through the FA, the Football League and, if necessary, a civil court. 'We have legitimate grounds of complaint against Darlington Club,' he said. 'We consider their action should be subject for inquiry.' Darlington insisted that they had done nothing wrong and merely gave the player a free hand to decide who he should join. The matter was eventually resolved the following August, when Darlington compensated Everton to the tune of £250.

THE PLAYER Everton got from Feethams for an eventual fee of £2700 was considered by the Daily Courier 'one of the most promising defenders in the country'. In acquiring him Everton saw off the interest of Liverpool, Cardiff City, Blackburn Rovers, Leeds United and reigning champions Huddersfield Town. Standing 5ft 8in tall, O'Donnell was a muscular player who had been converted from centre forward to defence. For a stretch of the 1925/26 season he would partner Dixie Dean as inside left, a local newspaperman reporting, 'What his play may have lacked in polish; it undoubtedly atoned for in dash and vim.' But it was at left back that he made his reputation.

'O'Donnell's work roused the admiration of the home spectators,' reported the Daily Courier's 'McN' of an early outing at Bury. 'The Darlington lad had a fast wing to face, but he stood up to them in great style, his interventions being splendidly timed and his kicking strong and of good length.'

Season	League		FA Cup		Other		Total	
	App	Goals	App	Goals	App	Goals	App	Goals
1924/25	13	1	0	0	-	-	13	1
1925/26	27	5	2	0	-	-	29	5
1926/27	24	3	2	0	-	-	26	3
1927/28	42	1	2	0	-	-	44	1
1928/29	41	0	1	0	1	0	43	0
1929/30	41	0	2	0	-	-	43	0
Total	**188**	**10**	**9**	**0**	**1**	**0**	**198**	**10**

O'DONNELL was ever-present as Everton lifted the League Championship in 1928 and missed just a single game in each of the following two campaigns, the latter of which ended in the ignominy of relegation. O'Donnell was, nevertheless, something of what could euphemistically be described as a 'colourful' character. In August 1930 a board minute recorded that he was 'suffering from a disease owing to his own misconduct'. The defender was suspended for 14 days and never played for Everton again. Reading between the lines it seems as if he picked up some sort of sexually transmitted disease – the 'ungentlemanly' conduct of the day.

In December 1930 he was sold to Blackpool for £2500, but disciplinary problems followed him and his contract was eventually terminated. He played out his career in the lower leagues and in Dublin.

[FACTFILE]

BORN
Gateshead, 25 March 1897
POSITION
Left back
OTHER CLUBS
Darlington (1922–25);
Blackpool (1930–32);
Hartlepool United (1932–33);
Wigan (1933–34);
Dolphin FC (1934–35)
HONOURS
1927/28 League Championship

EVERTON F.C. 1959-60
Left to right: (Back row) T. Jones, K. Rea, A. Parker, A. Dunlop, J. Bramwell, M. Meagan, J. Tansey, G. Watson (Trainer); (Front row) A. Sanders, J. Harris, E. Thomas, D. Hickson, R. Collins, E. O'Hara B. Harris,

O'Hara, Eddie

Scottish winger who struggled to make the Goodison grade

On 24 April 1957 a Hampden Park crowd of 80,000 witnessed the greatest moment in Falkirk's long and mostly inauspicious history: a 2-1 Scottish Cup Final replay victory over Kilmarnock. 'Falkirk won because they lasted the pace much better in extra time,' recorded the Falkirk Herald.

'It was the type of game that made the knees knock, an all-action hard-fought match.'

Within a year of their triumph two of their number had wound up at Goodison Park. Right back Alex Parker would go on to be one of Everton's most distinguished servants and lift the 1963 League Championship. Eddie O'Hara, by contrast, would spend two years at Goodison as a largely peripheral player before enjoying a stint in the lower leagues.

The £7500 outside left was a hark back to the classic, jinking winger of Scottish football lore. He had been something of a goalscorer north of the border, but in a transitional team at Goodison he struggled. Everton lost his first five matches in a royal blue shirt and only a handful of games into his Merseyside career he was part of the team that suffered a 10-4 pasting by Tottenham Hotspur.

By then Ian Buchan, who had signed him, had been replaced and his replacement, Johnny Carey, seemed more disposed to alternatives. His cause wasn't helped by a long-term injury, either. In March 1959 a board minute recorded: 'It was reported that O'Hara was suffering from a 3-year-old ankle injury which may mean that he would not be 100% fit to play football again.' A second opinion 'confirmed' this was the case and recommended 'that the operation to shorten the ligaments be done and this was approved'.

By then he was a fringe player and after losing his place again at the start of the 1959/60 season he was sold to Rotherham United for £3500.

[FACTFILE]

BORN
Glasgow, 28 October 1935
POSITION
Winger
OTHER CLUBS
Falkirk (1955–58);
Rotherham United (1960–61);
Morton (1961–62);
Barnsley (1962–65)

Season	League		FA Cup		Total	
	App	Goals	App	Goals	App	Goals
1958/59	21	2	2	0	23	2
1959/60	8	0	0	0	8	0
Total	**29**	**2**	**2**	**0**	**31**	**2**

O'Kane, John

Graduate of Manchester United's famous youth team whose career failed to take off at Goodison

With David Beckham, Ryan Giggs, Nicky Butt and Gary Neville, John O'Kane was part of the illustrious Manchester United team that lifted the 1992 FA Youth Cup. Yet while his team-mates went on to gain international recognition, the right back found first-team opportunities nearly impossible to come by at Old Trafford. In January 1998, Howard Kendall took him on a week's trial, but after just two days was sufficiently convinced that he could cut it as an Everton player.

> NATURALLY ATHLETIC, COMFORTABLE ON THE BALL AND POSSESSING INTELLIGENT DISTRIBUTION

THE £400,000 signing went straight into one of the worst Everton teams in history. While clearly lacking experience, there was obvious potential within O'Kane. Naturally athletic, comfortable on the ball and possessing intelligent distribution, O'Kane bore all the hallmarks of a player tutored by Alex Ferguson. Despite the turmoil of the closing months of the 1997/98 season, O'Kane never seemed overawed by the mess he had found Everton in.

This gradual progress was brought to an abrupt halt by Walter Smith, who became manager in July 1998. As part of his bizarre defensive permutations, Smith preferred playing centre backs or midfielders in the full back berth. After slipping behind Alec Cleland and Mitch Ward in the pecking order, the arrival of David Weir in February 1999 effectively spelled the death knell of O'Kane's Everton career. One month later, he made his final appearance in the right of midfield against Manchester United: it was, ironically, after seven years as a United player, his first Premier League game at Old Trafford.

In December 1999, O'Kane joined Bolton Wanderers on a free transfer. There was a spell at Blackpool before he slipped out of league football.

[FACTFILE]

BORN
Nottingham,
15 November 1974
POSITION
Right back
OTHER CLUBS
Manchester United (1991–98);
Bury (loan, 1996 & 1997);
Bradford City (loan, 1997);
Burnley (loan, 1998);
Bolton Wanderers (1999–2001);
Blackpool (2001–03);
Hyde United (2003–06)

Season	League App	League Goals	FA Cup App	FA Cup Goals	League Cup App	League Cup Goals	Total App	Total Goals
1997/98	12	0	0	0	0	0	12	0
1998/99	2	0	1 (2)	0	0	0	3 (2)	0
1999/2000	0	0	0	0	0	0	0	0
Total	**14**	**0**	**1 (2)**	**0**	**0**	**0**	**15 (2)**	**0**

O'Keefe, Eamon

Non-league star who rose to play in the First Division

There were echoes of a Roy of the Rovers comic strip fantasy in Eamon O'Keefe's ascent from the Northern Premier League to the international stage in the space of two years. O'Keefe was a 25-year-old amateur midfielder who combined playing for Mossley – then managed by future Leeds manager Howard Wilkinson – and driving a van for the Guardian by day when, in the summer of 1979, Gordon Lee paid £25,000 to bring him to Goodison. A boyhood Manchester United fan who had once cheered Brian Kidd from the Old Trafford terraces, O'Keefe suddenly found himself playing alongside him for Everton.

O'KEEFE had, as a youngster, been on Plymouth Argyle's books but left without making an appearance. He developed a formidable reputation in non-league circles, appearing for England's semi-professional team, and even spent a period playing in Saudi Arabia. But league football was something he resisted until Everton came along. Even when they did, such was the nature of 1970s football that he was at first better financially rewarded driving his van and playing non-league.

Standing just 5ft 7in tall, he was quick and aggressive, a tenacious addition to Lee's quota of forwards. Chances were difficult to come by

> LEAGUE FOOTBALL WAS SOMETHING HE RESISTED UNTIL EVERTON CAME ALONG

during the 1979/80 season, but Kidd's departure and injuries to Bob Latchford meant he got more chances the following term. His transformation from non-league into a top-class professional was complete when he made his Republic of Ireland debut against Wales in Dublin in February 1981.

Later, he credited Colin Harvey with aiding his ascent into the big time. 'He was always pulling me up to one side, advising me and being firm when it was necessary,' he told the match-day programme in 1981. 'The first year went as well as I could have hoped. I had three first-team appearances and I felt confident that I could be a First Division player if I could bring myself out a little more.'

When Howard Kendall became manager the following summer, O'Keefe initially found favour with the new manager. But as Kendall sought to instil his own vision upon the club, the Irishman found himself surplus to requirements. In January 1982 Everton accepted a £65,000 bid from Wigan Athletic and a well-travelled and successful lower-league career followed.

[FACTFILE]

BORN
Manchester, 13 March 1953
POSITION
Midfielder / forward
OTHER CLUBS
Wigan Athletic (1982–83);
Port Vale (1983–85);
Blackpool (1985–86);
Cork City
(as player-manager, 1987–88);
St Patrick's Athletic (1989);
Chester City (1989–90);
Bangor City (1990–91)
HONOURS
5 Republic of Ireland caps
(1 goal) (1981–85)

Season	League		FA Cup		League Cup		Europe		Total	
	App	Goals	App	Goals	App	Goals	App	Goals	App	Goals
1979/80	3 (1)	0	0	0	0 (1)	0	0	0	3 (2)	0
1980/81	15(10)	3	4	1	0 (1)	0	-	-	19 (11)	4
1981/82	8 (3)	3	0 (1)	0	4	1	-	-	12 (4)	4
Total	**26 (14)**	**6**	**4 (1)**	**1**	**4 (2)**	**1**	**0**	**0**	**34 (17)**	**8**

Oldham, Wilfred
Reserve centre forward who briefly shone at the turn of the 19th century

Season	League		FA Cup		Total	
	App	Goals	App	Goals	App	Goals
1898/99	19	11	0	0	19	11
1899/1900	3	0	0	0	3	0
Total	**22**	**11**	**0**	**0**	**22**	**11**

[FACTFILE]

BORN
1875
POSITION
Centre forward
OTHER CLUB
Blackburn Rovers (1900)

Oldroyd, Darren
Reserve right back who made a single appearance during Everton's dark days

Season	League		FA Cup		League Cup		Total	
	App	Goals	App	Goals	App	Goals	App	Goals
1983/84	1	0	0	0	0	0	1	0
Total	**1**	**0**	**0**	**0**	**0**	**0**	**1**	**0**

[FACTFILE]

BORN
Ormskirk,
1 November 1966
POSITION
Right back
OTHER CLUBS
Wolverhampton Wanderers
(1986–87);
Southport;
Barrow

Oliver, Frank

Reserve centre forward who scored a debut hat-trick before fading from view

[FACTFILE]

BORN
Southampton, 1882
POSITION
Inside forward
OTHER CLUBS
Brentford;
Clapton Orient (1906–12);
Southport Central;
Clapton Orient (1912)

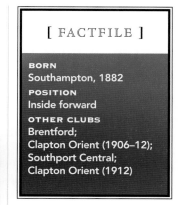

Season	League		FA Cup		Total	
	App	Goals	App	Goals	App	Goals
1905/06	4	4	1	0	5	4
Total	4	4	1	0	5	4

Olympians

Evertonians who have competed and won at the greatest show on earth

Three Everton players claimed gold at the 1908 Olympics as part of the Great Britain squad that ultimately prevailed over Denmark in the final at White City.

IT WAS a tradition that continued nearly 90 years later with Everton's Nigerian international Daniel Amokachi, who won gold after Nigeria's amazing victory over Brazil at the Atlanta games.

In 2008, Victor Anichebe, a son of Lagos who was brought up in Crosby, became Everton's fifth Olympic football medal winner, after taking silver in the Beijing Games football tournament.

Jo, who joined Everton in a loan move from Manchester City the following January, claimed a bronze medal after Brazil beat Marouane Fellaini's Belgium in the third-place play-off.

Player	Country	Medal	Year
Harold Hardman	*Great Britain*	Gold	1908 (London)
George Barlow	*Great Britain*	Gold	1908 (London)
Arthur Berry*	*Great Britain*	Gold	1908 (London)
Daniel Amokachi	*Nigeria*	Gold	1996 (Atlanta)
Victor Anichebe	*Nigeria*	Silver	2008 (Beijing)

*Berry won a second gold in 1912 as a Liverpool player

GOALKEEPER

Ben Howard-Baker competed in high jump and standing jump contests at the 1912 and 1920 games, but without claiming a medal.

O'Neill, Jimmy

Irish goalkeeper charged with the difficult task of succeeding Ted Sagar

As Ted Sagar's career drew to its 1950s conclusion, one of the most urgent tasks facing Cliff Britton was that of finding an adequate replacement for Everton's long-standing goalkeeper. There was no shortage of talented candidates – Harry Leyland, George Burnett and Albert Dunlop all challenged for the Everton goalkeeping gloves – but it was Jimmy O'Neill who provided the most convincing case to succeed the illustrious Sagar.

Born in Dublin in 1931, the son of Moses O'Neill, a professional golfer, the young goalkeeper started as a youth international with Brentford, but was scouted by Everton and signed professional forms in May 1949. His debut came against Middlesbrough in August 1950 and he made 10 appearances during the 1950/51 campaign as Britton alternated the green jersey between O'Neill, Burnett and Sagar. The latter eventually reclaimed the goalkeeping berth as his own, but the season ended in disaster as Everton were relegated for the second time.

As his illustrious forbear was edged out of contention over subsequent years, O'Neill was afforded his chance to stake a claim. A slim and slightly gangly man who stood just 5 ft 10 in tall, he was scarcely a giant. But with his long spindly arms O'Neill had the capacity to draw crosses from the air and reach for shots from distance. Like the very best of goalkeepers

JIMMY O'NEILL · EVERTON F.C. (1951)

WALLY FIELDING · EVERTON F.C. (1955)

he was a natural showman too, utilising his outstanding reflexes like a gymnast to add some theatre to his shot-stopping. By the time of Everton's return to the First Division in 1954 he was established as the club's first-choice goalkeeper.

By then he had earned the first of 17 Ireland caps, although his first international outing was a disaster. Called up to face Spain in Madrid in June 1952, Ireland were thrashed 6-0 and were 2-0 down before O'Neill had touched the ball other than to lift it from the net.

AT GOODISON he fared better and his consistency between the posts helped Everton consolidate their top-flight status in the mid-1950s. However, the arrival of Ian Buchan as manager in 1956 saw O'Neill an early casualty of his regime. Dropped after a quarter of the 1956/57 campaign, Buchan favoured Albert Dunlop, a player O'Neill considered his inferior. For most of the rest of his Everton career, O'Neill played second fiddle to Dunlop and yet, when called upon, provided satisfactory service. Two games into the 1958/59 season this perseverance seemed to

LIKE THE VERY BEST OF GOALKEEPERS HE WAS A NATURAL SHOWMAN TOO

pay off when Dunlop was dropped. But the return was brief: O'Neill conceded ten goals in Everton's record defeat to Tottenham that October and was consigned to the reserves once more. O'Neill only made five further appearances for the club.

In July 1960, Tony Waddington, the new manager of Stoke City, offered £5000 for O'Neill and the bid was accepted. At the Victoria Ground Waddington assembled a good, experienced team, many of whom – including O'Neill, Dennis Viollet and Stanley Matthews – had been prematurely written off by more prominent clubs. In 1962/63 Stoke returned to the top flight with O'Neill ever-present. Still aged only 32, the Irishman might have expected a top-flight Indian summer, but Waddington had different ideas and replaced him. In March 1964, O'Neill joined Darlington, later returning to the Potteries to play out his career at Port Vale.

On retirement, O'Neill settled with his family in Ormskirk, where he ran a taxi firm. He remained a regular visitor to Goodison until his death in December 2007.

Season	League		FA Cup		Total	
	App	Goals	App	Goals	App	Goals
1950/51	10	0	0	0	10	0
1951/52	20	0	0	0	20	0
1952/53	35	0	5	0	40	0
1953/54	28	0	3	0	31	0
1954/55	41	0	2	0	43	0
1955/56	34	0	2	0	36	0
1956/57	13	0	0	0	13	0
1957/58	6	0	0	0	6	0
1958/59	9	0	0	0	9	0
1959/60	5	0	0	0	5	0
Total	**201**	**0**	**12**	**0**	**213**	**0**

[FACTFILE]

BORN
Dublin, 13 October 1931
DIED
Ormskirk, 15 December 2007
POSITION
Goalkeeper
OTHER CLUBS
Stoke City (1960–64);
Darlington (1964–65);
Port Vale (1965–66)
HONOURS
17 Republic of Ireland caps (1952–59)

Orr, W.

Mysterious centre forward who scored on his only Anfield appearance for Everton

[FACTFILE]

BORN
1868
POSITION
Centre forward

Season	League App	League Goals	FA Cup App	FA Cup Goals	Total App	Total Goals
1889/90	1	0	0	0	1	0
Total	**1**	**0**	**0**	**0**	**1**	**0**

Osman, Leon

Hero of the 1998 FA Youth Cup victory and mainstay of the Goodison engine room

Unsung, underrated and yet a crucial component of Everton's rise under David Moyes, Leon Osman was the last of the 1998 FA Youth Cup winning team to break into the Everton first team. Richard Dunne, Tony Hibbert, Francis Jeffers and Danny Cadamarteri had all stepped up by the time Osman's chance belatedly came in 2004 (with Jamie Milligan and Phil Jevons earning cameos too), but the wait was certainly worth it. Indeed his contribution to the Everton cause has outshone those whose chance came earlier.

Born in Billinge to an English mother and Turkish-Cypriot father, Osman rose through the Everton academy and represented England Schoolboys. He shone in the first leg of the FA Youth Cup Final victory, scoring a spectacular third goal, but then suffered a

serious injury which brought question marks over his entire career. 'It was a long way back but I never thought I was finished,' he told the Daily Mail in April 2012. 'It just felt that it was another hurdle I had to get over. It dragged on for three years in total but it never came to the point where I thought to myself: "I'm struggling to make it here."'

During this wilderness period most of his Youth Cup winning team-mates moved on, some earning international recognition too. Osman was loaned out to Carlisle United in the 2002/03 season and then to Derby County a year later. His first-team breakthrough with Everton came at the end of the disappointing 2003/04 season, as his 23rd birthday neared. He has never looked back.

Diminutive, composed, versatile and technically excellent, Osman

Season	League App	League Goals	FA Cup App	FA Cup Goals	League Cup App	League Cup Goals	Europe App	Europe Goals	Total App	Total Goals
2002/03	0 (2)	0	0	0	0	0	-	-	0 (2)	0
2003/04	3 (1)	1	0	0	0 (1)	0	-	-	3 (2)	1
2004/05	24 (5)	6	3	1	2 (1)	0	-	-	29 (6)	7
2005/06	28 (7)	3	3 (1)	1	0 (1)	0	1 (1)	0	32 (10)	4
2006/07	31 (3)	3	1	0	2	0	-	-	34 (3)	3
2007/08	26 (2)	4	0	0	4	1	7	2	37 (2)	7
2008/09	32 (2)	6	6	1	1	0	2	0	41 (2)	7
2009/10	25 (1)	2	0 (1)	1	1	1	6 (1)	0	32 (3)	4
2010/11	20 (6)	4	3	0	2	1	-	-	25 (6)	5
2011/12	28 (2)	4	3	0	1	0	-	-	32 (2)	4
Total	**217(31)**	**33**	**19 (2)**	**4**	**13 (3)**	**3**	**16 (2)**	**2**	**265(38)**	**42**

blossomed in his first full first-team season – 2004/05 – which concluded with Everton qualifying for the Champions League. Perhaps lacking some of the pace that might have elevated him to the international stage, he was an important part of Everton's developing short-passing game. His willingness to fill positions on the right, in central midfield and occasionally operating behind a forward were integral to Everton's progress. Purportedly more glamorous players – like Simon Davies, Manuel Fernandes and Royston Drenthe – came and went, but Osman was always someone who David Moyes could rely upon.

His best form came in late 2007 when he was given a run in his favoured central midfield role. It was no coincidence that with Osman as the fulcrum Everton

embarked on a lengthy unbeaten run, playing some sumptuous football. Osman also scored some glorious goals during this period, few better than a 22-yard effort against AS Larissa in the UEFA Cup: a brilliant counterattack started by Tim Cahill, an overlapping run from Leighton Baines, a flick from Steven Pienaar and a swerving finish from Leon Osman. A 30-yard dribble past three opponents and dinked finish against Sunderland a month later ran this effort a close second.

There have occasionally been question marks posed over a lack of pace and ability to dominate games. Sometimes he has seemed a victim of his own versatility; pushed out of one position to accommodate another player. But those who have watched him week in week out are appreciative of his

true value to the Everton team. 'He is a player who has often divided opinion at L4, with some questioning his lightweight frame,' records the Everton tactics blog, Executioner's Bong. 'For me, Ossie is a top player; he has two quick feet, possesses vision, great touch, can score goals and always puts in a shift. In a national game like ours obsessed with physicality and pace, Osman is something of an oddity.'

OSMAN appeared in the 2009 FA Cup Final and his return to fitness in the second half of the 2011/12 season coincided with Everton's return to Wembley for the FA Cup semi-final with Liverpool. A fortnight after that disappointment he made his 300th Everton appearance.

'Ossie's been a terrific player for the club over the years and he's

continued to grow over the years. He's a massively important player for us now,' said Leighton Baines after that landmark was passed in a 4-0 home romp against Fulham. 'Since I've been here, I think he's got better every year really and become more and more important to us. I thought last season he was great and this year he's been fantastic again. He's a vital part of the squad and the team.'

[FACTFILE]

BORN
Billinge, 17 May 1981
POSITION
Midfielder
OTHER CLUBS
Carlisle United
(loan, 2002–03);
Derby County (loan, 2004)

Oster, John

Gifted wide man who struggled amid Everton's late-1990s upheaval

In July 1997, Grimsby Town's 18-year-old wide man, John Oster, rejected the advances of Manchester United to become a £1.6million addition to Howard Kendall's Everton squad. A highly skilful flanker, boasting a low centre of gravity, tremendous balance and an electrifying turn of pace, it seemed inevitable that the Welshman earned comparisons with Ryan Giggs.

> JOHN OSTER, REJECTED THE ADVANCES OF MANCHESTER UNITED TO BECOME A £1.6 MILLION ADDITION TO HOWARD KENDALL'S EVERTON SQUAD

PRODIGIOUS and mercurial, the baby-faced winger came straight into a woeful Everton team. But the burden of carrying his less gifted team-mates was simply too much: while Andrei Kanchelskis had done so just a year previous on the Everton right, he was a seasoned international. Oster, by contrast, was a 19-year-old with barely a

season of third-tier football to his name. Too often he was caught in possession or went missing. Sometimes when a trick failed to come off there was a noticeable drop of his head. Goodison's unforgiving crowd took out its frustrations on the teenager, and his confidence waned.

Walter Smith, who showed little trust in Everton's talented bunch of youngsters, virtually excluded him after his arrival as manager in July 1998. After transfer-listing him at the end of the 1998/99 season, Oster joined Sunderland for £1million in August that year. He was, lamented Toffeeweb.com: 'An enigmatic, problematic,

Season	League		FA Cup		League Cup		Total	
	App	Goals	App	Goals	App	Goals	App	Goals
1997/98	16 (15)	1	0 (1)	0	3	1	19(16)	2
1998/99	6 (3)	0	2 (2)	1	1 (1)	0	9 (6)	1
Total	22 (18)	1	2 (3)	1	4 (1)	1	28(22)	3

Owen,
Billy

Defender with an eye for goal

Season	League		FA Cup		Total	
	App	Goals	App	Goals	App	Goals
1898/99	13	3	0	0	13	3
Total	**13**	**3**	**0**	**0**	**13**	**3**

Owen,
Terry

Home-grown forward who had a journeyman's career, he is the father of England international Michael Owen

Season	League		FA Cup		League Cup		Total	
	App	Goals	App	Goals	App	Goals	App	Goals
1967/68	2	0	0	0	0	0	2	0
Total	**2**	**0**	**0**	**0**	**0**	**0**	**2**	**0**

idiosyncratic artisan in the Duncan McKenzie mould; perhaps there is no longer any room for such characters in the Premiership.'

ALAS, Oster never really lived up to his potential in the Northeast. There followed a series of loan moves and free transfers that saw him play on the fringes of the top flight for some years, but the youthful promise was never realised.

Speaking later of his experience at Goodison, Oster highlighted the arrival of Smith as marking the beginning of the end. 'We never spoke. Looking back, I went to the Premiership too early: I was only 20, and Everton was a different world to Grimsby. There, we'd play in front of 3000, while there were 40,000 at Goodison. It was a different lifestyle as well; the lonely nights

in a hotel in Liverpool have left their mark. I used to sit alone and worry about Everton, knowing I'd have to impress the fans, especially in the early games.'

EVERTON
ENCYCLOPEDIA

Jack **Page,** Tom **Page,** Bill **Palmer,** John **Palmer,** Alex **Parker,** Bobby **Parker,** John-Willie **Parker,** Thomas **Parker,** Henry **Parkinson,** Joe **Parkinson,** Ray **Parnell,** Charlie **Parry,** Frank **Parry,** Peter **Paterson,** John **Patrick,** Jimmy **Payne,** Joe **Peacock,** Jim **Pearson,** Mike **Pejic,** Mark **Pembridge,** Terry **Phelan,** Fred **Pickering,** Steven **Pienaar,** Cliff **Pinchbeck,** Ernie **Pinkney,** Archibald **Pinnell,** Alessandro **Pistone,** Neil **Pointon,** H. **Pollock,** Harry **Potts,** Aubrey **Powell,** Paul **Power,** Charles **Pratt,** FA **Premier League,** John **Proudfoot**

J. PAGE

Page, Jack

Reserve
right back who
endured
a war-interrupted
career

[FACTFILE]

BORN
Liverpool, 24 March 1886
DIED
1951
POSITION
Right back
OTHER CLUBS
South Liverpool;
Rochdale;
Cardiff City (1920–25);
Merthyr Town (1926–28)

Season	League		FA Cup		Total	
	App	Goals	App	Goals	App	Goals
1913/14	1	0	0	0	1	0
1914/15	0	0	0	0	0	0
1919/20	8	0	1	0	9	0
Total	**9**	**0**	**1**	**0**	**10**	**0**

T. PAGE

PORT VALE

Page, Tom

Reserve
inside forward
who made a
name for himself
as a veteran in
the Potteries

[FACTFILE]

BORN
Kirkdale, 15 November 1888
DIED
1973
POSITION
Inside forward
OTHER CLUBS
Liverpool; Rochdale;
St Mirren; Port Vale
(1920–28);
New Brighton (1929)

Season	League		FA Cup		Total	
	App	Goals	App	Goals	App	Goals
1913/14	7	2	0	0	7	2
Total	**7**	**2**	**0**	**0**	**7**	**2**

Palmer, Bill

League
Championship
winning winger

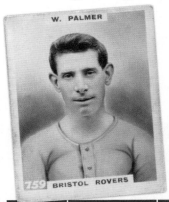

W. PALMER

BRISTOL ROVERS

[FACTFILE]

BORN
Barnsley, 1888
POSITION
Outside left
OTHER CLUBS
Barnsley (1907);
Nottingham Forest (1909);
Rotherham County;
Bristol Rovers (1920–21);
Gillingham (1922);
Doncaster Rovers (1923)
HONOURS
1914/15
League Championship

Season	League		FA Cup		Total	
	App	Goals	App	Goals	App	Goals
1913/14	5	1	0	0	5	1
1914/15	17	1	1	0	18	1
Total	**22**	**2**	**1**	**0**	**23**	**2**

Palmer, John

Reserve
goalkeeper
limited to just
a single
appearance
in an Everton
shirt

[FACTFILE]

BORN
1876
POSITION
Goalkeeper
OTHER CLUB
Luton Town (1898)

Season	League		FA Cup		Total	
	App	Goals	App	Goals	App	Goals
1896/97	1	0	0	0	1	0
Total	**1**	**0**	**0**	**0**	**1**	**0**

Parker,
Alex

Elegant right back who lifted the League Championship in 1963

Alex Parker was one of a litany of gifted Scots to journey south of his country's border to play for Everton in the late 1950s and early 1960s. A graduate of the famous Scottish junior team, Kello Rovers, he made his name with Falkirk, lifting the Scottish Cup with The Bairns in 1957, and winning the first of 15 Scotland caps in 1955.

The right back signed with winger Eddie O'Hara in summer 1958 in a joint deal worth £25,500, with Parker valued at £18,000. His Everton debut was delayed by his national service commitments with the Royal Scots Fusiliers in Cyprus, but his belated introduction in November 1958 helped lift a team shorn of confidence. Everton were facing a relegation battle having lost their opening six games of the season and had suffered their record defeat a month earlier. Parker, with Bobby Collins – signed shortly before his debut – and new manager Johnny Carey, helped steady a listing ship and lift Everton to relative respectability by the end of the 1958/59 season.

Thereafter, he rarely looked back and was an important part of Everton's renaissance. Although stockily built and slightly lacking in pace, Parker compensated with an impeccable sense of timing when entering a tackle. It was said that Parker had 'elevated the sliding tackle into an art form'. He was also renowned for his last-ditch clearances from the goal line. Bert

Slater, who kept goal for Falkirk and Liverpool, used to joke that he was the best full back he ever played in front of. And yet, Alex Parker was always something more than just a defender. He possessed the skill and poise of a winger and his fine distribution was of particular benefit to his wingers. Billy Bingham later described Parker as the best full back he ever played alongside.

Parker was a fine exponent of the overlapping full back role, passing the outside right and playing an early ball to one of the centre forwards. He scored just five goals in his Everton career but few were better than a 30-yard effort in the 6-1 drubbing of Nottingham Forest in January 1960. On one of his forays up the field, and not seeing an Everton player in a forward position to pass to, he curled the ball past the Forest goalkeeper, John Armstrong, to send the crowd wild. 'It wasn't Parker's first goal,' the Daily Post reported, 'but he will never score one so meritoriously.'

Parker also possessed the unusual distinction of being both an Everton player and close friend of Liverpool manager Bill Shankly. Both were Ayrshire sons, and long-standing family friends. At Falkirk, Parker played under his brother Bob Shankly, then a year after his arrival on Merseyside Bill Shankly took the Liverpool job. 'Bill would always give me stick for playing for Everton and he was a terrible swearer,' Parker would recall. 'Bill would say, "How are you getting on with those blue so and so's?" He told me it was the only mistake I ever made in my life!'

Arguably the right back played in the final era of great wingers. For Everton and Scotland he came up against such figures as Tom Finney, Stanley Matthews, Cliff Jones and even a young George Best. But seldom did he look ruffled, he always seemed cool and composed. 'He was,' recalled Alex Young, 'the best right back in Great Britain during the late 50s and early 60s … His technique was laser-like. His timing was unparalleled, his execution was fluent. And his appearance was sophisticated. Possibly the only British players to have possessed his defensive skills were Jimmy

Armfield at Blackpool and Ray Wilson at Huddersfield.' In 1964, a year after Parker had won the First Division title, Wilson became an Everton player. It should have been a world-class full back partnership, but the reality was that persistent hamstring injuries had started to erode the right back's career. Parker and Wilson played just two games together at the start of the 1964/65 season and then injuries struck again. In his place a young Tommy Wright proved an excellent replacement, lessening the burden of his absence.

In September 1965 Parker, now aged 30, joined Southport for £2000. In 1968 he was appointed manager of Ballymena United in Northern Ireland. In 1970 he returned to Haig Avenue as Southport manager, but lasted just a year. He subsequently slipped out of the game, becoming a publican in the Scottish borders.

Season	League		FA Cup		League Cup		Other		Total	
	App	Goals	App	Goals	App	Goals	App	Goals	App	Goals
1958/59	26	1	4	0	-	-	-	-	30	1
1959/60	38	2	1	0	-	-	-	-	39	2
1960/61	41	0	1	0	5	0	-	-	47	0
1961/62	31	0	3	0	-	-	-	-	34	0
1962/63	33	2	3	0	-	-	2	0	38	2
1963/64	17	0	0	0	-	-	2	0	19	0
1964/65	12	0	0	0	-	-	0	0	12	0
Total	**198**	**5**	**12**	**0**	**5**	**0**	**4**	**0**	**219**	**5**

Parker, Bobby

Goalscorer extraordinaire whose career was ravaged by the First World War

But for the angry knocking of the First World War, the forward Bobby Parker may have become regarded as one of the greatest forwards English football has ever witnessed. War cruelly destroyed his career in two ways: first, by extracting a four-year chunk of it while in his mid-twenties pomp; second, by giving him an injury from which he never fully recovered. Instead we can only reflect on a glorious 18-month period in which he changed the course of Everton history following years of underachievement, giving later generations of Evertonians plenty to ponder as to what might have been.

HE WAS born in Glasgow, just days after Everton secured their first League Championship in March 1891, and made his way as a professional footballer at Ibrox. He was a highly rated if seldom called upon prodigy and understudy to Rangers legend Willie Reid when Everton – the perennial nearly men of the era – came calling for his services in November 1913. Rangers were reluctant to sell, even when a fee of £1500 was offered. Lengthy negotiations went on between the clubs and, perhaps surprisingly, a fee of £800 was agreed with John Fulton, an unheralded left back signed the previous May from Greenock Morton and who was still to play for the first team, also heading north. It was among the finest bargains in Everton history.

Goals had been hard to come by all season: just 20 in 14 matches, shared between 12 different players. It was hoped Parker could rectify this problem. 'At last Everton have succeeded in their quest for Parker, the clever centre forward of Glasgow Rangers,' recorded the Liverpool Courier with some relief. 'Though Parker was only a reserve player for Glasgow Rangers he had few superiors in Scotland, and the

brilliance of Reid alone kept him out of the first team. He has a splendid shot, and his record certainly appears to confirm this, seeing that already this season he has three "hat-tricks" to his credit. Last season Parker played in 14 League matches for the Rangers, and found the net in almost every one of them. He is 22 years of age, 5ft 8in height, and weighs 11 and half-stone.'

And yet when he made his debut against Sheffield Wednesday, scoring Everton's goal in a 1-1 draw, the same paper was quick to criticise. 'Like other Scottish players who have come to Everton, he was not quick enough at times,' they sniped. 'It would be unfair to judge him by his first turnout, and he certainly had a tremendous obstacle in McSkimming, the Sheffield centre half. He did secure a goal, and that was more than any of the others could do.' A fortnight later the same paper whined: 'Everton also were weak at centre-forward, for Parker not only showed little or no resource himself, but he was anything but a good general, showing poor judgment in distributing his attack.'

How foolish they were to jump to such hasty conclusions. On Christmas Day Everton travelled to Old Trafford to face Manchester United. Parker scored the only goal of the game. A day later at Goodison, in the return fixture, he scored a hat-trick as Everton romped to a 5-0 win. 'There was no better player on the field than Parker, the Courier eulogised. 'He played magnificent football. His long passes to the wings were always well judged and accurately placed, and he was always alert for openings.'

PARKER'S stunning Christmas performances set the example he would follow over the next 18 months. He finished the 1913/14 season

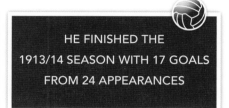

HE FINISHED THE 1913/14 SEASON WITH 17 GOALS FROM 24 APPEARANCES

with 17 goals from 24 appearances and hopes laid firmly on his shoulders at the start of the 1914/15 season. 'Parker did well in the short time he was at Goodison Park last season – a resumption of that form is hoped for; should it materialise, and his colleagues get into proper understanding with one another, then the supporters can confidently look forward to a successful time,' reported the Football Echo. 'If all goes well, then perhaps when April arrives a share of the honours so long over due will find their way to Walton.'

These would be prophetic words indeed. Six times since the Football League's formation just 26 years previously Everton had finished league runners-up. In 1905 they finished with 47 points from 34 games, but still ended up a point behind champions Newcastle. In 1909 and 1912 they ended up with 46 points in an expanded division. But in 1914/15 the same tally was enough to secure the long-elusive crown. Without question Parker's incredible total of 36 goals from 35 games was the key to Everton's success. It included one four-goal haul, four hat-tricks and five braces.

And yet Everton's success was overshadowed by the war in Europe. Even the Football Echo shoved Everton's title triumph to the back pages, with the front of the paper dominated by drawings of the battle front at Ypres.

UNLIKE many of his fellow champions, Parker left almost immediately to join the fighting. But he was seriously wounded in the final year of the war and dispatched home to convalesce with a bullet lodged in his back. Everton gave him time to recover and he returned for the 1919/20 season. He made his long-awaited comeback in December 1919 in an Anfield derby. Parker, predictably, scored – in a 1-3 defeat – but the Daily Post meanly reported: 'Parker was hardly a success.'

Season	League		FA Cup		Total	
	App	Goals	App	Goals	App	Goals
1913/14	24	17	1	0	25	17
1914/15	35	36	5	2	40	38
1919/20	8	4	0	0	8	4
1920/21	17	11	2	1	19	12
Total	**84**	**68**	**8**	**3**	**92**	**71**

He remained at Goodison until May 1921, his outings restricted but always peppered with goals. He joined Nottingham Forest for £500 and later resettled in Ireland. In 1927/28, while his successor at Goodison, Dixie Dean, was making history, so was Parker as manager of Bohemians, managing them to the 'Clean Sweep': the League of Ireland, FAI Cup, Shield and Leinster Senior Cup.

The war injury increasingly took its toll, however, but Everton never forgot a man who had brought them greatness. The Football Echo reported soon after the end of the Second World War: 'Bobby Parker today lies at his Dublin home, a cripple through a hole in his back – the last-but-one war caused this. Everton FC, to their everlasting glory, have never said a word about it, but I will tell you they have pensioned Bobby Parker all these years – a good deed done, without stealth or advertisement.'

[FACTFILE]

BORN
Maryhill, Glasgow, 27 March 1891
DIED
28 December 1950
POSITION
Centre forward
OTHER CLUBS
Glasgow Rangers (1909–13);
Nottingham Forest (1921–23)
HONOURS
1914/15 League Championship

Parker,
John-Willie

Outstanding goal-poacher whose strikes were essential to Everton's 1954 promotion

John-Willie Parker was very much the man for his time; the ultimate late developer, he did not make his league debut until in his mid-twenties, having cost just £10 from the anonymity of St Lawrence CYMS in 1948. It was a victory for the prudence that governed the club during these austerity years and one in the eye for those critics of Cliff Britton who said that Everton needed to spend big in order to halt their decline. Through Everton's darkest days the £10 man's goals would be crucial to the club.

An inside left by trade, Parker could also spearhead the attack as centre forward and in either position was a clinical finisher and prolific goalscorer. As 'Ranger' observed in the Liverpool Echo: 'His deceptively lazy and nonchalant style lulls defenders into a false sense of security. By the time they wake up to it it is usually too late.' Like T.E. Jones he made his bow in the relegation campaign though it was not until the onset of life in Division Two that he fully staked his claim in the first team, eventually concluding the 1951/52 season as Everton's top scorer with 15 goals.

PARKER was a clinical, instinctive six-yard box player who formed a lethal partnership with Dave Hickson. Their goals would not only save Everton from the abyss of Second Division mediocrity, but see them rise triumphantly above the mire and to promotion. They were contrasting players: Hickson big, bold and brash; Parker, small and deceptively casual.

Half a century later Hickson told the author Becky Tallentire: 'I always believed there are players for players and they hunt in pairs. You've got to have that blend and I think John-Willie was ideal; we used to read each other.'

DURING the 1953/54 season the pair formed the deadliest post-war forward partnership that Goodison has seen, between them scoring 56 goals – Parker 31, Hickson 25 – without which Everton would not have been promoted. Their partnership made a promising start to life back in the top flight and with 10 games left in the 1954/55 season, Everton moved up to fourth, four points behind league leaders Chelsea, and with three games in hand. Could this most ordinary of Everton teams put together an unlikely title challenges? The team's overall lack of quality shone through: Everton lost seven, drew two and won just once, finishing the season 11th; the forwards between them scored 31 league goals, Parker contributing 19. He fell out of favour the following season and was sold to Bury. At Gigg Lane the goals flowed again, and he set a record, scoring in seven consecutive games.

[FACTFILE]

BORN
Birkenhead, 5 July 1925
DIED
August 1988
POSITION
Inside forward
OTHER CLUB
Bury (1956–59)

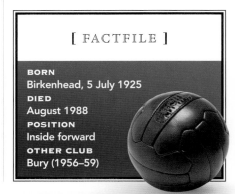

Season	League		FA Cup		Total	
	App	Goals	App	Goals	App	Goals
1950/51	7	0	0	0	7	0
1951/52	36	15	2	1	38	16
1952/53	32	13	4	4	36	17
1953/54	38	31	3	2	41	33
1954/55	34	19	0	0	34	19
1955/56	20	4	0	0	20	4
Total	**167**	**72**	**9**	**7**	**176**	**79**

Parker, Thomas

Winger who briefly supplied the ammunition for Dixie Dean

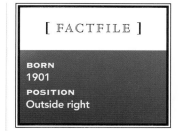

[FACTFILE]

BORN
1901
POSITION
Outside right

Season	League App	League Goals	FA Cup App	FA Cup Goals	Total App	Total Goals
1926/27	6	0	1	0	7	0
Total	6	0	1	0	7	0

Parkinson, Henry

Left half who made a solitary appearance in Everton's debut season

[FACTFILE]

BORN
1866
POSITION
Left half

Season	League App	League Goals	FA Cup App	FA Cup Goals	Total App	Total Goals
1888/89	1	0	-	-	1	0
Total	1	0	-	-	1	0

Parkinson, Joe

Defensive midfielder whose career was cut short by injury

A transfer deadline day signing in March 1994, Joe Parkinson arrived at Goodison a 22-year-old unknown – despite boasting a wealth of lower-league experience. On signing the £250,000 midfielder, Mike Walker admitted that it might take the Mancunian a year to break into the first team, but Parkinson had other ideas, making his senior debut as a substitute on the opening day of the 1994/95 season.

By the end of this debut season, Parkinson was an FA Cup winner, having been one of Joe Royle's 'Dogs of War' – the foundation stones on which the new manager built Everton's recovery. A hard, willing player who sat just in front of the back four, Parkinson was the archetypal midfield harrier, tackling, passing and moving, before stepping back to shield his defence again. Safety and simplicity were Parkinson's principal objectives, and seldom could he be seen rampaging into his opponent's half. Yet there were goals, few more finely crafted than his side-footed winner from the edge of the Aston Villa penalty area on the last day of the 1995/96 season. Tactically his was one of the most difficult positions, and traditionally only more experienced players excel in it. And yet Parkinson never looked out of place and brought a veteran's composure to the heart of the Everton team.

By the end of the 1995/96 season Parkinson was considered among the most important members of the Everton squad. More expansive players thrived in his presence and the team appeared a more cohesive unit when he played. He was attracting the notice of the England and Wales international managers – both of which he was eligible to play for.

> PARKINSON WAS CONSIDERED AMONG THE MOST IMPORTANT MEMBERS OF THE EVERTON SQUAD

Season	League App	League Goals	FA Cup App	FA Cup Goals	League Cup App	League Cup Goals	Other App	Other Goals	Total App	Total Goals
1994/95	32 (2)	0	6	1	2	0	-	-	40 (2)	1
1995/96	28	3	2	0	1	0	3	0	34	3
1996/97	28	0	1	0	2	0	-	-	31	0
Total	88 (2)	3	9	1	5	0	3	0	105 (2)	4

But just as he approached his prime, so he was cut down by injury. A knee cartilage injury suffered over Christmas 1996 waylaid the midfielder for a month, during which time Everton's form collapsed dramatically, signalling the beginning of the end of Royle's managerial reign. So vital was Parkinson to his faltering team that he was recalled prematurely, apparently propped up by pain-killing injections. But this was a disastrous step, aggravating the existing injury. Parkinson hobbled out of Everton's encounter with Leicester City in April 1997 with their Premier League status nearly assured, but the midfielder's part in saving Everton had cost him his career.

There followed a fruitless 30-month battle to save Parkinson's career, but despite having his knee reconstructed the damage caused by playing on through the pain was just too great. In November 1999, still aged only 28, Parkinson announced his retirement from professional football. 'I could be bitter about it, but that's not the way I am,' he said at the time. 'Yes, my career was cut short, but I've looked after myself, I've got a nice house, good family, a decent life and I've won a few medals. I look back on football as a chapter of my life that's closed now. I've got the videos and the cuttings, kept all my shirts and my medals. But what's the point in being bitter? It only rubs off on the people around you and they end up disliking you.'

Parnell, Ray

Young full back never quite able to make the first-team breakthrough

[FACTFILE]

BORN
Birkenhead, 8 October 1943
POSITION
Right back
OTHER CLUBS
Tranmere Rovers (1964–67); Bury

Season	League		FA Cup		League Cup		Europe		Total	
	App	Goals	App	Goals	App	Goals	App	Goals	App	Goals
1960/61	1	0	0	0	0	0	-	-	1	0
1961/62	1	0	0	0	-	-	-	-	1	0
1962/63	0	0	0	0	-	-	0	0	0	0
1963/64	1	0	0	0	-	-	0	0	1	0
Total	**3**	**0**	**0**	**0**	**0**	**0**	**0**	**0**	**3**	**0**

Parry, Charlie

Welsh half back who was a stalwart through Everton's final Anfield days, and their first at Goodison

[FACTFILE]

BORN
Llansillin, 1870
POSITION
Half back / full back
OTHER CLUBS
Ardwick; Newtown; Aberystwyth; Oswestry United
HONOURS
1890/91
League Championship

[FACTFILE]

BORN
Eccles, 11 June 1971
POSITION
Midfield
OTHER CLUBS
Wigan Athletic (1989–93); Bournemouth (1993–94)
HONOURS
1995 FA Cup

Season	League		FA Cup		Total	
	App	Goals	App	Goals	App	Goals
1889/90	22	4	2	0	24	4
1890/91	13	0	1	0	14	0
1891/92	1	0	0	0	1	0
1892/93	10	0	0	0	10	0
1893/94	11	0	1	0	12	0
1894/95	27	1	4	0	31	1
1895/96	2	0	0	0	2	0
Total	**86**	**5**	**8**	**0**	**94**	**5**

Parry,
Frank

Reserve outside right who deputised through the early 1920s

[FACTFILE]

BORN
Aigburth, 14 June 1898
DIED
1973
POSITION
Outside right
OTHER CLUBS
Grimsby Town (1926);
Accrington Stanley
(1927–28);
Nelson (1929)

Season	League		FA Cup		Total	
	App	Goals	App	Goals	App	Goals
1922/23	3	0	0	0	3	0
1923/24	4	0	0	0	4	0
1924/25	4	0	1	0	5	0
1925/26	1	0	0	0	1	0
Total	**12**	**0**	**1**	**0**	**13**	**0**

Paterson,
Peter

Scottish forward whose Goodison career was short-lived

[FACTFILE]

BORN
Glasgow, 1880
POSITION
Inside forward
OTHER CLUB
Grimsby Town (1902)

Season	League		FA Cup		Total	
	App	Goals	App	Goals	App	Goals
1901/02	5	1	0	0	5	1
Total	**5**	**1**	**0**	**0**	**5**	**1**

Patrick,
John

Scottish international goalkeeper who was limited to a solitary Everton appearance

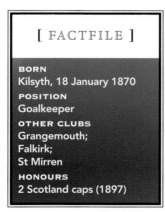

[FACTFILE]

BORN
Kilsyth, 18 January 1870
POSITION
Goalkeeper
OTHER CLUBS
Grangemouth;
Falkirk;
St Mirren
HONOURS
2 Scotland caps (1897)

Season	League		FA Cup		Total	
	App	Goals	App	Goals	App	Goals
1896/97	1	0	0	0	1	0
Total	**1**	**0**	**0**	**0**	**1**	**0**

Payne,
Jimmy

Former Liverpool winger whose switch to his boyhood club was cut short by injury

[FACTFILE]

BORN .
Bootle, 10 March 1926
POSITION
Winger
OTHER CLUB
Liverpool (1948–56)

Season	League		FA Cup		Total	
	App	Goals	App	Goals	App	Goals
1955/56	1	0	0	0	1	0
1956/57	4	2	1	0	5	2
Total	**5**	**2**	**1**	**0**	**6**	**2**

Peacock,
John 'Joe'

**Versatile
forward-cum-
wing half who
earned England
honours late on**

EVERTON F.C.

EVERTON 1924
Back row - **Hart, Brewster,
Peacock, Fern,
McDonald, Chedgzoy**
Front - **Harrison, Downs,
Irvine, Forbes, Williams**

Joe Peacock's career dovetailed
two of the most incredible
goalscoring achievements in
football history. In May 1927
he left Everton to join
Middlesbrough, who had just
lifted the Second Division
Championship. Their success
had come on the back of centre
forward George Camsell's
59 league goals. Yet the record
some believed would last forever
existed only for one season.
At Goodison Peacock's former
team-mate Dixie Dean plundered
60 goals in 1927/28. Peacock
ended the campaign relegated
with his new club.

Peacock joined Everton as an amateur from Atherton Town of the
Lancashire Combination following the end of the First World War.
Nominally a wing back, he would fulfil a number of roles for the Everton
first team, including full back and centre forward. Indeed some of his
first appearances for Everton during the 1919/20 season came leading
the Everton forward line. 'The play of Peacock as centre forward was
frequently promising though he occasionally appeared lost at the critical
moment,' reported the Liverpool Courier of Everton's 'experiment'
during a 1-1 draw with Sheffield United.

IN AUTUMN 1920 he was given a further run at centre forward and
rewarded the Everton selectors with a hat-trick in the visit to Derby.
'Everton came out of their scoring shell and Peacock's three goals
showed the value of giving a junior a trial as compared with scouring
the country with bags of gold,' reported the Football Echo. 'I believe
it is true to state that Everton were prepared to pay quite a number of
thousands of pounds for the right man and while they were angling for
men whose clubs would not part company force of circumstances made
them turn to Peacock, with happy results.'

By mid-October Everton were top but Peacock had added no further
goals. He shifted to half back, then wing half and would remain there for
the bulk of his Everton days. The player 'acquitted himself very creditably
in the right half position' according to one report, 'and it was evident that
his abilities lie more in this direction than as leader of attack'.

EVERTON in this period were talented underachievers. They narrowly
avoided relegation in 1921/22 but the board spent heavily and they
played great football to finish fifth and seventh over the following two
campaigns. Defence, however, was regarded as the soft underbelly of the

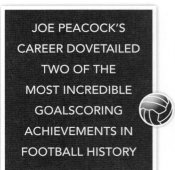

> JOE PEACOCK'S
> CAREER DOVETAILED
> TWO OF THE
> MOST INCREDIBLE
> GOALSCORING
> ACHIEVEMENTS IN
> FOOTBALL HISTORY

Everton team and Peacock would
fall victim to the directors'
chopping and changing to find
the right formula.

He moved to Middlesbrough for
£500 in 1927 and while success
was elusive at Ayresome Park
his own performances were
rewarded with England
recognition in 1929. Following
spells with Sheffield Wednesday
and Clapton Orient he moved to
Sweden in a player-coaching
role in 1933. Later in his career
he served as Wrexham trainer.

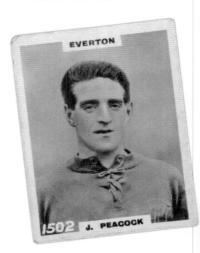

EVERTON

1502 J. PEACOCK

Season	League		FA Cup		Total	
	App	Goals	App	Goals	App	Goals
1919/20	9	2	0	0	9	2
1920/21	28	3	2	0	30	3
1921/22	29	1	1	0	30	1
1922/23	39	4	2	0	41	4
1923/24	8	1	1	0	9	1
1924/25	17	0	1	0	18	0
1925/26	18	1	2	0	20	1
1926/27	3	0	1	0	4	0
Total	**151**	**12**	**10**	**0**	**161**	**12**

[FACTFILE]

BORN
Wigan, 15 March 1897
DIED
1979
POSITION
Wing half
OTHER CLUBS
Middlesbrough (1927–30);
Sheffield Wednesday
(1930–31);
Clapton Orient (1931–33)

Pearson,
Jim

Promising Scottish forward whose career was ravaged by injury

Little known outside his native Scotland when Everton paid St Johnstone £100,000 for him in July 1974, Jim Pearson was one of a succession of forwards designated to share Everton's goalscoring burden with Bob Latchford.

A SCOTTISH youth, schoolboy and under-23 international, Pearson had also been selected to represent the Scottish League prior to joining Everton. A tall, rangy, somewhat gangly striker, invariably there were comparisons with another blond Scottish forward to have passed south to Goodison a generation earlier. But living up to the reputation of Alex Young was always going to be a tough call. Indeed, one writer said that Pearson was less the new 'Golden Vision' than the 'Golden Toothpick', 'so spare and bony was his frame that his kit seemed to hang on him'.

Shortly after his arrival Joe Royle joined Manchester City and Pearson was given an extended run up front with Latchford.

A gregarious character, popular with his team-mates, in August 1978, still unable to guarantee a first-team place after four years at the club, Pearson sought a fresh start at Newcastle, whom he joined for £70,000. However, the injuries that had troubled him at Goodison became a plague at St James's Park. Still in his mid-twenties, a persistent knee ligament injury brought an end to his professional career.

PEARSON then turned to non-league football, taking on a variety of playing and managerial roles with Barrow, Gateshead, North Shields and Blyth Spartans. He also worked in a business development role with Nike and for a period, when Walter Smith was manager, served as Everton's north-east scout. 'When you're an Evertonian, you stay an Evertonian as everyone knows, so it was great to be invited back and still be involved with such a great club,' he said.

Alas, he never provided the sort of goal return necessary to justify his inclusion as an out-and-out striker. Often used from the bench or in unfamiliar wide roles, he was always a willing runner but never found the form to guarantee him a first-team place.

'I wasn't the type ever to be overawed and I settled in well,' he told the Evertonian in 2001. 'My problem was always the injuries I got throughout my career. They meant I didn't really get a long run in the side, but for all that I do look back with pleasure on my time at Everton.'

[FACTFILE]

BORN
Falkirk, 24 March 1953
POSITION
Striker
OTHER CLUBS
St Johnstone (1970–74);
Newcastle United (1978–80)

Season	League		FA Cup		League Cup		Europe		Total	
	App	Goals	App	Goals	App	Goals	App	Goals	App	Goals
1974/75	17 (13)	3	4	1	0 (1)	0	-	-	21 (14)	4
1975/76	26 (3)	5	1	0	5	0	2	0	34 (3)	5
1976/77	12 (4)	4	3	1	1 (1)	0	-	-	16 (5)	5
1977/78	21 (2)	3	1	0	4	2	-	-	26 (2)	5
Total	**76 (22)**	**15**	**9**	**2**	**10 (2)**	**2**	**2**	**0**	**97(24)**	**19**

Pejic, Mike

Former England left back cut off in his prime by injury

Enigmatic, taciturn, unsmiling; outwardly Mike Pejic resembled less a professional footballer than the hero of a spaghetti western. On the field he possessed many of the attributes synonymous with a rugged outsider: hardness, resolve, and an unflinching desire not to let his opponents win. His arrival at Goodison in February 1977 strengthened a shaky back four whose waywardness had brought Everton to the brink of a relegation battle and he was crucial to Everton's subsequent renaissance under Gordon Lee.

Born in Staffordshire, the son of a Serbian father and English mother and elder brother of Mel – a lower-league full back of the 1980s – Pejic started out at Stoke City. Under Tony Waddington's management the left back was an important part of one of the Potters' greatest teams, in 1972 winning the League Cup – Stoke's only major honour. In 1974 his Stoke form earned him an England call-up, but he was allegedly dropped by Joe Mercer because he did not smile enough. Perhaps this is an apocryphal story, but it has lingered.

His £150,000 Goodison switch came in the midst of crippling financial problems at the Victoria Ground. Pejic settled in straight away to a position that had proved problematic through the 1970s. A supremely fit and mobile player, Pejic added much needed steel to the Goodison back line, his ferocious tackles still recalled with relish by fans of the era. With the arrival of Dave Thomas at the start of the 1977/78 season he formed a formidable left-sided partnership, and was always quick and willing on the overlap and a reliable crosser of the ball.

By the 1978/79 season there was talk of an England recall as Pejic and Everton flourished,

but a pelvic injury had started to trouble him. In a home fixture against Leeds United in December 1978 the ailment caused his breakdown and he never played for Everton again. Perhaps it was no coincidence that Everton's title challenge faded after his withdrawal.

PEJIC recovered to play in Everton's 1979/80 pre-season tour of Egypt, but Gordon Lee, perhaps sensing what the injury had taken out of him, accepted a £250,000 bid from Aston Villa. Pejic played just 10 games for Villa before the pelvic injury forced his retirement in 1981. Subsequently he turned to youth coaching, although there was a spell as Chester City manager in the mid-1990s.

> BY THE 1978/79 SEASON THERE WAS TALK OF AN ENGLAND RECALL AS PEJIC AND EVERTON FLOURISHED

[FACTFILE]

BORN
Chesterton, 25 January 1950
POSITION
Left back
OTHER CLUBS
Stoke City (1968–77); Aston Villa (1979–81)
AS MANAGER
Chester City (1994–95)
HONOURS
4 England caps (1974)

Season	League		FA Cup		League Cup		Europe		Total	
	App	Goals	App	Goals	App	Goals	App	Goals	App	Goals
1976/77	17	1	4	0	0	0	-	-	21	1
1977/78	40	1	2	0	4	0	-	-	46	1
1978/79	19	0	0	0	3	0	4	0	26	0
Total	**76**	**2**	**6**	**0**	**7**	**0**	**4**	**0**	**93**	**2**

Pembridge, Mark

Experienced and hard-working Welsh international midfielder

Mark Pembridge represented one of Walter Smith's more astute purchases, providing four years of solid if unspectacular service on the left side of Everton's midfield.

[FACTFILE]

BORN
Merthyr Tydfil,
29 November 1970
POSITION
Midfield
OTHER CLUBS
Luton Town (1989–92);
Derby County (1992–95);
Sheffield Wednesday
(1995–98);
Benfica (1998–99);
Fulham (2004–07)
HONOURS
54 Wales caps
(6 goals) (1991–2004)

An £800,000 signing from Portuguese giants Benfica on the eve of the 1999/2000 season, Pembridge had made his name with Sheffield Wednesday and Luton Town earlier in the decade. A diligent player who made up for what he lacked in flair and impudence with hard work and application, he was a useful addition to Smith's squad, yet was never able to elevate it from the mediocrity in which it was mired.

Possessing the versatility to play across the midfield, Pembridge was palpably more comfortable on the left. He was a fine crosser of the ball, particularly from corners, but his overall distribution was somewhat pedestrian and unimaginative. He was, nevertheless, a hard worker – always willing and prepared to track back and help his defence. Walter Smith found such virtues particularly endearing and, injury permitting, Pembridge was a regular through Smith's final 30 months at Goodison.

Equally, David Moyes found such qualities virtuous and, despite his limitations, Pembridge was a stalwart through the 2002/03 season. He started the next campaign for Everton too, but was a surprise £750,000 departure to Fulham in August 2003. Days later, Kevin Kilbane arrived in his place.

PEMBRIDGE made his Wales debut as a 21-year-old in 1991 and continued representing his country until 2004, making 54 international appearances.

> AN £800,000 SIGNING FROM PORTUGUESE GIANTS BENFICA ON THE EVE OF THE 1999/2000 SEASON

Season	League		FA Cup		League Cup		Total	
	App	Goals	App	Goals	App	Goals	App	Goals
1999/2000	29 (2)	2	5	0	0	0	34 (2)	2
2000/01	20 (1)	0	2	0	0	0	22 (1)	0
2001/02	10 (4)	1	1 (1)	0	0	0	11 (5)	1
2002/03	19 (2)	1	0	0	1	0	20 (2)	1
2003/04	4	0	0	0	0	0	4	0
Total	**82 (9)**	**4**	**8 (1)**	**0**	**1**	**0**	**91 (10)**	**4**

Phelan, Terry

Irish international left back who confounded Goodison doubters

Once the most expensive full back in English football, Terry Phelan's career had started to stagnate at the time of his arrival at Goodison in December 1996. Signed for £850,000 after

serious injury had ruled Andy Hinchcliffe out for the remainder of the season, he was seen as another of Joe Royle's panic purchases, another second-rate player not befitting of Everton's famous motto.

Despite being plunged straight into a team suffering its worst run of form in a quarter of a century, Phelan soon proved his doubters wrong. An enthusiastic, committed player who possessed

Season	League		FA Cup		League Cup		Total	
	App	Goals	App	Goals	App	Goals	App	Goals
1996/97	15	0	1	0	0	0	16	0
1997/98	8 (1)	0	0	0	0 (1)	0	8 (2)	0
1998/99	0	0	0	0	0	0	0	0
1999/2000	0 (1)	0	0	0	1	0	1 (1)	0
Total	**23 (2)**	**0**	**1**	**0**	**1 (1)**	**0**	**25 (3)**	**0**

outstanding athleticism and pace as well as a biting tackle, the Ireland international looked as if he had been part of the Everton defence for years.

But just as injury had opened up a place in the Everton team for him, so it cut short his Goodison career. After starting the 1997/98 season in the first team, a serious cartilage injury kept him out for the bulk of the season and most of the 1998/99 campaign. Phelan regained his fitness for the 1999/2000 season, but was loaned out by Walter Smith, who made clear his preference for David Unsworth and Michael Ball ahead of the adopted-Irishman.

In December 1999 he was given a free transfer and three months later joined Fulham.

> THE IRELAND INTERNATIONAL LOOKED AS IF HE HAD BEEN PART OF THE EVERTON DEFENCE FOR YEARS

Pickering, Fred

The Blackburn 'Boomer' whose name will forever be remembered for his FA Cup Final disappointment

Fred Pickering was a centre forward for whom scoring came as naturally as breathing. A player who marked his Everton and England debuts with hat-tricks, the powerful Lancastrian was one of the most prolific number nines in Everton history. And yet his Goodison career is defined not by goals, but controversies. His 1964 arrival was supposed to beckon the end of Alex Young, causing protests and utter consternation on the terraces – despite Pickering's outstanding efforts on the pitch.

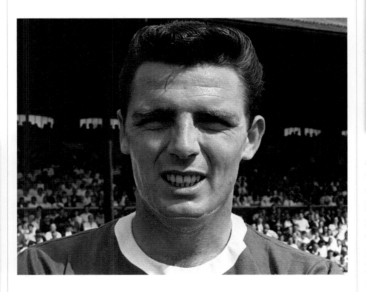

Later he was infamously left out of the 1966 FA Cup Final side, with Mike Trebilcock, hitherto a Cornish unknown, taking his place. For Everton it was a gamble that paid off, but for Pickering it marked the end of what should have been a glittering Goodison career.

A son of Blackburn, Pickering joined his home-town club in the 1950s. A somewhat pedestrian left back, Rovers manager Jack Marshall experimented with him in the centre forward's role. The results were dramatic and from being an ordinary defender Pickering emerged as one of the First Division's outstanding centre forwards. His goals – 59 from 123 appearances – transformed Blackburn from the division's also-rans to title dark horses. As such, it was with understandable frustration and anger from Blackburn fans – who had already seen Roy Vernon depart for Everton four years previously – that the local boy departed to Goodison in March 1964, for a British domestic record fee of £85,000.

The record move, however, was also greeted with bemusement by Evertonians. It was known on the terraces that Harry Catterick's relationship with Alex Young was cool, and it was always assumed that the manager considered his artistry a mere decoration to his team rather than an integral part of it. He had been linked with a move for Sheffield Wednesday's David Layne, a powerful centre forward whose style was not unlike Pickering's, and the assumption was that Young would be dispensed with as soon as a new signing came.

> HIS IMPACT ON A TEAM FIGHTING TO RETAIN THEIR LEAGUE TITLE WAS IMMEDIATE: A HAT-TRICK ON HIS DEBUT

And so it came to pass. Young, who had just returned from injury, was dropped and Pickering took his place. His impact on a team fighting to retain their league title was immediate: a hat-trick on his debut, a 6-1 win over Nottingham Forest. A week later, Everton's 2-1 victory over Pickering's former club Blackburn sent them top for the first time in the 1963/64 season.

Pickering would go on to score nine goals in nine games during the title run-in, but there remained a sense of unease that his inclusion compromised the balance of the team. For all his goals, Everton managed just three points from their final five games and finished third – five points behind champions Liverpool. 'While it wasn't Fred's fault,' Young recalled, 'the fan's reaction to him was tempered. They celebrated his goals then complained bitterly about the sacrificed points.' Indeed Tony Kay's match-fixing disgrace – uncovered in the final weeks of the season – was more disruptive than Pickering's arrival.

PICKERING'S form earned him an England call-up for the end of season tour to the Americas. He scored a hat-trick on his debut – a 10-0 romp over the US – and goals in each of his other international appearances, against Northern Ireland and Belgium. And yet despite this formidable record, beyond 1964 further international recognition would prove elusive.

At Goodison, despite supporter suspicions, Young survived Pickering's arrival and it was Roy Vernon who would eventually be sacrificed. All three players started the 1964/65 season, in which Pickering was the star man – scoring 27 league goals in 41 appearances. Nicknamed 'Boomer' for his explosive shot, Pickering was a burly, uncompromising centre forward, completely unlike the lithe and slight Young and Vernon. And yet he possessed considerable skill for one so big – a reminder, perhaps, of his full back days. Some of his best goals were scored after cutting in from the flank and letting fly with a shot.

'He was free of any serious illusion about his own athletic prowess yet evolved into a top-class striker with shoulders broad enough to carry his bags of skill and courage,' Young recalled. 'Fred was more than a bruiser and had developed a wonderful touch as well as impressive close-control for such a big man.'

Pickering's fine form carried into the 1965/66 season when he scored 18 league goals, plus a further four in Everton's FA Cup run. However, a knee cartilage problem had proved increasingly painful as the season reached its conclusion. He missed the first of Everton's quarter-final triple-header against Manchester City, and three of Everton's last seven league games. Perhaps more crucially he also missed the semi-final victory against Manchester United. Yet he returned to play in Everton's final three league games.

In the run to the FA Cup Final, Catterick darkly hinted that Pickering would not make the team, saying that he was not 'playing with the confidence he was showing in his play' before he was injured. The choice facing him seemed straightforward, however: on the one hand he could play Pickering, an England international who had averaged more than a goal every other game for Everton; on the other he could pick Mike Trebilcock, a novice with just eight Everton appearances and two goals to his name. But Catterick was never predictable and in the end he plumped for Trebilcock. Pickering was said to be 'angry and upset' at the decision, as well he might. Decades later, the snub still seems to define memories of the player.

He returned for the start of the 1966/67 season, but injuries were to limit the impression he made. Yet even when fit, Catterick used him sparingly.

At the season's end he accepted a £50,000 offer from Birmingham City. At St Andrews, Pickering kept on scoring, and his experience helped ease the progression of Bob Latchford – a future Everton number nine. There was a spell at Blackpool and in 1971 a brief return to Blackburn, where he retired.

[FACTFILE]

BORN
Blackburn, 19 January 1941
POSITION
Centre forward
OTHER CLUBS
Blackburn Rovers (1959–64);
Birmingham City (1967–69);
Blackpool (1969–71);
Blackburn Rovers (1971)
HONOURS
3 England caps
(5 goals) (1964)

Season	League		FA Cup		Europe		Total	
	App	Goals	App	Goals	App	Goals	App	Goals
1963/64	9	9	0	0	0	0	9	9
1964/65	41	27	4	4	6	6	51	37
1965/66	39	18	5	4	3	0	47	22
1966/67	8	2	0	0	0	0	8	2
Total	97	56	9	8	9	6	115	70

Pienaar, Steven

Diminutive midfielder who throbs and bustles with energy

Steven Pienaar represented another of David Moyes's great bargains, one of the proverbial rabbits the Everton manager regularly pulled from a hat to infuse his Everton side with fresh impetus and vim at a time when they struggled to compete financially with rivals that they outperformed on the pitch.

The South African first achieved prominence at Ajax Amsterdam, having originally been picked up playing for the Dutch giant's South African satellite club, Ajax Cape Town. Indeed Pienaar's rise to the elite of European football was impressive indeed. He grew up under the shadow of apartheid and gang violence in the Johannesburg township of Westbury, where drug-dealing and shootings were commonplace.

'One thing that sticks in my mind is watching television sitting on the floor. We had a couch, but I wasn't allowed on it, because you never knew when a bullet was going to come flying in through the window,' he recalled in a 2010 interview with the Daily Mail.

'It has calmed down a bit now, but in those days, when I was eight or nine, you witnessed violence and drug-dealing at close quarters on a daily basis. You grew up with it.

It was part of your life, and no one ever dared try to do anything about it.'

As a 20-year-old Pienaar was a member of South Africa's World Cup squad that competed in the 2002 finals in Japan and South Korea. In 2006 he joined Borussia Dortmund as a replacement for Arsenal-bound Tomas Rosicky. Scarcely then could he have imagined that he would soon be following the Czech star to the Premier League.

THE SOUTH African's stay in the Ruhr was brief and unhappy. In the summer of 2007 Moyes signed him on a season-long loan with an option to sign him permanently. He was, in effect, a direct replacement for the disappointing Simon Davies, who had joined Fulham in the previous transfer window.

FEW ON Merseyside knew much about Pienaar at the time. A slight figure, who stood just 5ft 7in tall, with his hair matted into dreadlocks he looked an unlikely Premier League star. Indeed when he made his debut as a substitute on the opening day of the 2007/08 season, one wag sitting near this author in Goodison's Main Stand opined to guffaws of laughter that he looked 'more like a single mother from Toxteth than a footballer'.

How wrong he would be. Pienaar was a beautifully balanced player, speedy of thought and foot, always moving, probing, seeking to find gaps in the opposition's rearguard. In a vibrant, skilful midfield that included Mikel Arteta, Tim Cahill, Leon Osman and, later, Marouane Fellaini, he was often the heartbeat, omnipresent and energetic, keeping the possession football that Everton were increasingly playing ticking. An evangelical Christian, on scoring he would often lift his royal blue shirt in celebration to reveal a T-shirt bearing the slogan 'God Is Great'. At the end of the 2007/08 season Moyes took up the option to sign Pienaar permanently, the £2.05 million fee representing another staggering bargain for the Scot.

With left back Leighton Baines Pienaar would develop a formidable left-sided partnership, the midfielder feeding through balls to the defender's overlapping runs to beautiful effect. Between them the pair would have a telling impact on Everton's rise to fifth in the 2008/09 season and their FA Cup Final appearance against Chelsea. The following season they were Everton's most

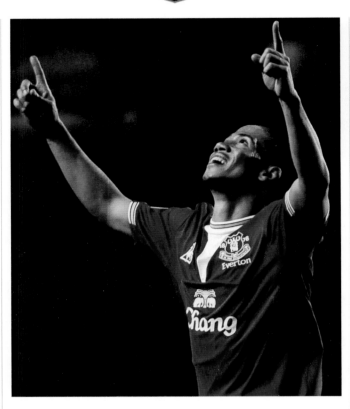

influential players as the club overcame a difficult start to finish eighth. Pienaar was awarded Everton's Player of the Year award in May 2010.

'I believe that he has grown this year,' said the Arsenal manager, Arsène Wenger, soon afterwards. 'He was usually a very busy player where the final ball was missing a little bit, but this year he has gained in personality, and he has kept his work-rate, so he has been much more efficient. I believe what also played a big role in his growth was that [Mikel] Arteta was not there for a while, and that he had to take the responsibility of being the playmaker of the team. In fairness, he was one of the best players in England this year.'

AT THAT summer's World Cup, Pienaar was the face of his home nation. He was outstanding in South Africa's group match victory over France, but it was not enough to see the hosts through to the second round. In England speculation abounded over Pienaar's Everton future. With 12 months left on his existing deal a new contract remained unsigned. He remained an Everton player as the 2010/11 season kicked off and never let transfer talk undermine his perennially excellent performances. But with Everton mired in financial difficulty, a £2.5 million offer from Tottenham Hotspur in January 2011 was always too good to turn down when the player was able to leave for free the following summer.

'I really have to admit that Everton and especially David Moyes made me the player in the Premier League that I am today,' said Pienaar on his departure. 'I will be always thankful for that.'

However, the move to White Hart Lane proved unhappy and there was a successful return on loan to Everton minutes from the January 2012 transfer deadline. With Mikel Arteta now an Arsenal player, Pienaar was the uncontested Everton playmaker and the team thrived under his influence, overcoming a slow start to the season to finish seventh – finishing above Liverpool for only the fourth time in 40 years. At the season's end a £4.5million fee secured his permanent return to Everton.

[FACTFILE]

BORN
Johannesburg,
17 March 1982
POSITION
Midfield
OTHER CLUBS
Ajax Cape Town (1999–2001);
Ajax Amsterdam (2001–06);
Borussia Dortmund (2006–08);
Tottenham Hotspur (2011–12)
HONOURS
57 South Africa caps
(2 goals)

Season	League		FA Cup		League Cup		Europe		Total	
	App	Goals	App	Goals	App	Goals	App	Goals	App	Goals
2007/08	25 (3)	2	1	0	3	0	8	0	37 (3)	2
2008/09	27 (1)	2	6	0	0	0	0 (1)	0	33 (2)	2
2009/10	30	4	2	0	0	0	6	3	38	7
2010/11	18	1	0	0	1 (1)	0	-	-	19 (1)	1
2011/12	14	4	0	0	0	0	-	-	14	4
Total	**114 (4)**	**13**	**9**	**0**	**4 (1)**	**0**	**14 (1)**	**3**	**141(6)**	**16**

Pinchbeck, Cliff

Reserve forward who forged a solid career lower down the league pyramid

Season	League		FA Cup		Total	
	App	Goals	App	Goals	App	Goals
1947/48	3	0	0	0	3	0
Total	3	0	0	0	3	0

[FACTFILE]

BORN
Cleethorpes,
20 January 1925
POSITION
Forward
OTHER CLUBS
Brighton & Hove Albion
(1948–49);
Port Vale (1949–51);
Northampton (1951–52);
Bath City (1953–55);
Salisbury City

Pinkney, Ernie

Scottish winger whose wartime career meant he represented all three sides of the Mersey

Season	League		FA Cup		Total	
	App	Goals	App	Goals	App	Goals
1909/10	4	0	0	0	4	0
1910/11	4	1	0	0	4	1
Total	8	1	0	0	8	1

[FACTFILE]

BORN
Glasgow,
23 November 1887
POSITION
Outside right
OTHER CLUBS
Barrow;
Gillingham;
Liverpool;
Tranmere Rovers;
Halifax Town (1921);
Accrington Stanley (1922)

Pinnell, Archibald

Reserve goalkeeper during Goodison's first season

Season	League		FA Cup		Total	
	App	Goals	App	Goals	App	Goals
1892/93	3	0	0	0	3	0
Total	3	0	0	0	3	0

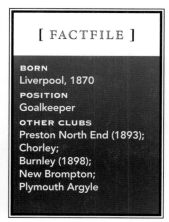

[FACTFILE]

BORN
Liverpool, 1870
POSITION
Goalkeeper
OTHER CLUBS
Preston North End (1893);
Chorley;
Burnley (1898);
New Brompton;
Plymouth Argyle

Pistone, Alessandro

Injury-prone left back who showed flourishes of genuine ability

TALL AND COMPOSED,
HE WAS AN ELEGANT PLAYER,
ALWAYS COMFORTABLE
IN POSSESSION AND CRISP
IN THE TACKLE

An incident at a Newcastle United players' Christmas party in 1998 for many years seemed to define and haunt Alessandro Pistone. As novelty gifts were handed out, Pistone was presented with a sheep's heart, because, it was said, he lacked one of his own. Witnessing the left back in action, one could sometimes recognise how such an aspersion was cast, for Pistone could seem languid to the point of lethargy. And yet such an impression was ultimately misplaced, for on his day, when the injuries that plagued him were overcome, he was one of the finest full backs in the league. Alas, such glimpses were all too rare.

PISTONE arrived in English football in July 1997, his £4.5million move from Inter Milan to Newcastle United representing something of a coup for the Magpies. Captain of the Italian

under-21 team who had also represented his country at the 1996 Olympics, the left back seemed assured of a glittering future. Tall, pacy, strong and two-footed, he settled into English football quickly, with Newcastle manager Kenny Dalglish arguing for him to be included in Italy's 1998 World Cup squad. However, his progress came to an abrupt halt when Ruud Gullit succeeded Dalglish in August 1998 and refused to play him. Pistone spent 14 months out of the team, and thereafter made stuttering progress – a broken leg in February 2000 further setting him back.

The Italian had barely recovered from this injury when, in July 2000, Walter Smith made him a £3million signing. Evertonians barely had a chance to assess Pistone's worth when a knee injury, sustained in September, sidelined him for seven months. His return against Manchester City the following April was marred by a late sending off – and subsequent suspension – for a touchline dust-up with Paul Dickov. As the dark final days of Walter Smith were played out, Pistone made little discernible impression upon his new club.

THERE WERE, however, glimpses of the full back's potential after David Moyes's arrival in March 2002. In particular, he looked strong on the overlap and his crossing was swift and accurate. But injury continued to impair his input and, as a result, his consistency. Not until the 2004/05 season would Pistone put together a season's worth of matches and yet when he did, he fulfilled some of his unrealised promise. Tall and composed, he was an elegant player, always comfortable in possession and crisp in the tackle. He never seemed hurried and preferred to jockey an opponent out of

possession than dive in with a tackle. His crossing was a potent attacking weapon when called upon, and few were better than the diagonal ball he played onto Duncan Ferguson's head for a goal when Everton beat Bolton Wanderers in December 2004.

Nearing his 30th birthday at the end of 2004/05, Moyes offered Pistone a new one-year contract. The Italian held out for two years and seemed set to move. But after a switch to Lecce collapsed, Moyes relented and Pistone signed on. Two games into the 2005/06 season, however, disaster struck. A clumsy challenge on Bolton's Henrik Pederson saw him tear his cruciate ligament. Pistone was stretchered off and never sufficiently regained his fitness to play for Everton again.

[FACTFILE]

BORN
Milan, 27 July 1975
POSITION
Left back
OTHER CLUBS
Solibiatese (1993–94);
Crevalcore (1994–95);
Vicenza (1995–96);
Inter Milan (1996–97);
Newcastle (1997–2000);
Venezia (loan, 1999);
RAEC Mons (2007–08)

Season	League App	League Goals	FA Cup App	FA Cup Goals	League Cup App	League Cup Goals	Europe App	Europe Goals	Total App	Total Goals
2000/01	5 (2)	0	0	0	1	0	-	-	6 (2)	0
2001/02	25	1	1	0	0	0	-	-	26	1
2002/03	10 (5)	0	0	0	2	0	-	-	12 (5)	0
2003/04	20 (1)	0	2	0	1	0	-	-	23 (1)	0
2004/05	32 (1)	0	2 (1)	0	2 (1)	0	-	-	36 (3)	0
2005/06	2	0	0	0	0	0	1	0	3	0
2006/07	0	0	0	0	0	0	0	0	0	0
Total	**94 (9)**	**1**	**5 (1)**	**0**	**6 (1)**	**0**	**1**	**0**	**106 (11)**	**1**

Pointon, Neil

Reliable lower-league bargain who lifted the league title in 1987

Signed for £75,000 from Scunthorpe United in November 1985 as cover for Pat Van Den Hauwe, Neil Pointon was initially seen as a player for the future, but went on to immediately play a more prominent role than had been first expected. An injury crisis at Goodison had forced Van Den Hauwe to switch to the centre of the Everton defence, freeing up the left back position for Pointon.

HE WENT ON to make 22 appearances during the 1985/86 season, eventually ceding his place to Derek Mountfield as Everton finished runners-up to Liverpool.

EVERTONIANS GOT AN EARLY GLIMPSE OF HIS ATTACKING PROWESS ON HIS DEBUT – A 6-1 DRUBBING OF ARSENAL IN WHICH HE RATTLES THE POST

Still to turn 21 when he joined Everton, Pointon arrived at Goodison with a wealth – almost 160 senior appearances – of lower-league experience. Among the fittest players at the club and renowned for his love of press-up marathons, he was a quick and staunch tackler, keen to assist in attack. Evertonians got an early glimpse of his attacking prowess on his debut – a 6-1 drubbing of Arsenal – when Pointon broke into the Arsenal box and hit a post.

Although chances were limited during the 1986/87 season following the arrival of Paul Power, Pointon made enough appearances to claim a League title medal. Over subsequent seasons he proved a capable deputy to Van Den Hauwe, slotting in when the left back was struck down with the most unexpected ailments. While the acerbic nickname 'Dissa' was unnecessarily harsh, never did Pointon really make a convincing case to claim the number three shirt as his own.

In summer 1990, he joined Manchester City as a £600,000 makeweight in the £900,000 deal that brought Andy Hinchcliffe to Everton from Manchester City. He continued performing in the top flight until the mid-1990s, later turning out for Joe Royle's Oldham Athletic. A three-year spell at Hearts was followed by time in the English lower leagues. Pointon now works as a coach at Bolton Wanderers youth academy.

[FACTFILE]

BORN
Church Warsop, 28 November 1964
POSITION
Left back
OTHER CLUBS
Scunthorpe United (1981–85);
Manchester City (1990–92);
Oldham Athletic (1992–95);
Hearts (1995–98);
Walsall (1998–2000);
Chesterfield (2000)
HONOURS
1986/87 League Championship

Season	League		FA Cup		League Cup		Other		Total	
	App	Goals	App	Goals	App	Goals	App	Goals	App	Goals
1985/86	14 (1)	0	5	0	0	0	2	1	21 (1)	1
1986/87	10 (2)	1	1 (1)	0	1 (1)	0	2 (1)	0	14 (5)	1
1987/88	32 (1)	3	7	0	3	0	1 (1)	0	43 (2)	3
1988/89	20 (3)	0	3 (1)	0	0 (1)	0	4	0	27 (5)	0
1989/90	19	1	0	0	2	0	-	-	21	1
Total	**95 (7)**	**5**	**16 (2)**	**0**	**6 (2)**	**0**	**9 (2)**	**1**	**126(13)**	**6**

Pollock, H.

Right half who played a cameo during Everton's first season

[FACTFILE]

BORN
1866
POSITION
Right half

Season	League		FA Cup		Total	
	App	Goals	App	Goals	App	Goals
1888/89	1	0	-	-	1	0
Total	**1**	**0**	**-**	**-**	**1**	**0**

Potts, Harry

Club record signing who created football lore as a 1960s manager

EVERTON F.C. 1953-54

LEFT TO RIGHT - BACK ROW :- LINDSAY, PARKER, CLINTON, O'NEILL, DONOVAN, POTTS, LELLO, C.LEYFIELD (Trainer). FRONT ROW :- FIELDING, MOORE, HICKSON, FARRELL, JONES, BUCKLE, EGLINGTON.

Harry Potts never shared the fame of his managerial contemporaries, but in sustaining Burnley as a major First Division force throughout the 1960s he arguably outshone the achievements of other more revered managers. His time at Everton as a player in the first half of the 1950s, however, can mostly be categorised as a failure, as he struggled to play a meaningful part in the lowest ebb in the club's history.

> HIS £20,000 ARRIVAL AT GOODISON IN OCTOBER 1950 WAS A STAGGERING PIECE OF BUSINESS

EVERTON 1953

Back row - **Lindsay, Parker, Clinton, O'Neill, Donovan, Potts, Lello, Leyfield (Trainer)**

Front - **Fielding, Moore, Hickson, Farrell, Jones, Buckle, Eglington**

BORN IN Hetton-le-Hole, County Durham, Potts was a contemporary of Bob Paisley, and their careers would share many parallels – particularly in their latter stages. He joined Burnley in 1937 as a 17-year-old, showing vast promise as an inside left. He combined pace and trickery with a prolific record in front of goal. Nor was Potts above gamesmanship. As one Burnley fan recorded years later in When Saturday Comes, 'As a player he was the diver of his day, tumbling forward unlikely yardages to claim to have been felled in the penalty box.'

WAR, HOWEVER, intervened and cut off his prime. In 1946/47, the first season back, he was top scorer as Burnley won promotion to the First Division, also reaching the FA Cup Final, in which he struck the crossbar before Charlton Athletic emerged victorious in extra time.

His £20,000 arrival at Goodison in October 1950 was a staggering piece of business and represented a club record transfer fee. Potts was a good First Division player, but fell short of international standard and there was a definite sense that his best days lay behind him – after all, his Everton debut came just a day before his 30th birthday. But Goodison was a peculiar place in those days: T.G. Jones had been allowed to leave for nothing earlier in the year, while vast sums were frittered on players like Albert Juliussen, who were below standard and had seemingly been bought with the minimum of scouting.

POTTS WAS better than that and was one of the few bright lights in a dire 1950/51 season, which Everton spent mostly lurching around the relegation places. In their penultimate game, away at Derby County, he

scored the only goal, lifting them out of trouble. It meant Everton travelled to Sheffield Wednesday, who were rooted to the bottom, needing a single point for survival. Yet Wednesday annihilated Everton 6-0, still tumbling down to the Second Division with their vanquished opponents.

Although he would remain an Everton player for another five years, Potts' part in this dismal season witnessed the bulk of his Everton appearances. At the start of the 1951/52 campaign he lost his place to John-Willie Parker and was thereafter seen only intermittently prior to his retirement in 1956.

Season	League		FA Cup		Total	
	App	Goals	App	Goals	App	Goals
1950/51	28	5	1	0	29	5
1951/52	4	1	0	0	4	1
1952/53	19	8	1	0	20	8
1953/54	1	0	0	0	1	0
1954/55	4	1	2	1	6	2
1955/56	3	0	0	0	3	0
Total	**59**	**15**	**4**	**1**	**63**	**16**

Powell, Aubrey

Record signing who failed to fulfil lofty expectations

EVERTONIANS' EXPECTATIONS WERE BRIEFLY SATED ON HIS DEBUT – A 3-3 THRILLER AGAINST NEWCASTLE – WHICH HE MARKED WITH A GOAL

The club record signing of Welsh international inside forward Aubrey Powell was supposed to revitalise Everton's torpid start to football's post-war era. Signed from Leeds United for £11,000 in August 1948, Powell's arrival captured the imagination of Evertonians, who were disappointed after two dismal seasons.

Despite his playing career fizzling out disappointingly, Potts had garnered a reputation as one of the game's thinkers. On leaving Goodison, he joined Wolves – then one of the strongest teams in England – as coach, before becoming Shrewsbury Town manager in 1957. A year later he returned to Turf Moor as manager, and oversaw one of the great miracles of modern football – Burnley's First Division championship win in 1959/60. They remained a top-four side for the next three years, also finishing third in 1965/66.

In 1970 Potts was shifted 'upstairs' as general manager, but perhaps only then the club and fans realised the true value of his achievements, for they were relegated in 1971. He later managed Blackpool, returning to Turf Moor for a second stint later in the 1970s.

In arriving at Goodison as a 30-year-old, Powell had already overcome significant adversity in getting so far. He was overlooked as a teenager by his local club, Swansea Town, and instead played as an amateur for Lower Cwmtrych. In 1935 he was spotted by Leeds and quickly made a breakthrough to their first team. But after suffering an horrific leg break in 1937 he was told by doctors that he would never play again.

Powell was an exception among his contemporaries in that the outbreak of war in 1939 worked to his advantage. He worked as a PT instructor and built up strength in his injured leg, eventually making a complete recovery. In 1946 he belatedly made his Wales debut.

Evertonians' expectations were fulfilled on Powell's debut, a 3-3 thriller against Newcastle, which he marked with a goal. But in Everton's second game of the 1948/49 season – a dismal 4-0 defeat at Portsmouth – he was injured and thereafter struggled for form.

A month after he joined, Cliff Britton succeeded Theo Kelly as manager and Powell never seemed to gain his full confidence. Billy Higgins and Peter Corr often kept him out of the side, even though he was a regular for Wales. It was a situation which shared parallels with T.G. Jones, who frequently struggled to get a game for Everton despite captaining his country.

In the summer of 1950 Powell refused the new terms offered him by Everton. A swap move for Sheffield United's Jimmy Hagan was rejected by the Yorkshire club, but hearing he was available Birmingham City revived their long-standing interest in Powell and signed him for £7300. The move was nevertheless ill-fated, and a year later he was forced to quit the game because of severe arthritis.

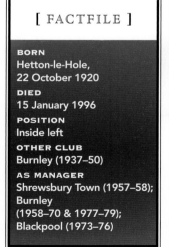

[FACTFILE]

BORN
Hetton-le-Hole,
22 October 1920
DIED
15 January 1996
POSITION
Inside left
OTHER CLUB
Burnley (1937–50)
AS MANAGER
Shrewsbury Town (1957–58);
Burnley
(1958–70 & 1977–79);
Blackpool (1973–76)

[FACTFILE]

BORN
Cwmtwrch, 19 April 1919
DIED
Leeds, 27 January 2009
POSITION
Inside forward
OTHER CLUBS
Leeds United (1935–48);
Birmingham City (1950–51)
HONOURS
8 Wales caps
(1 goal) (1946–50)

Season	League		FA Cup		Total	
	App	Goals	App	Goals	App	Goals
1948/49	19	3	0	0	19	3
1949/50	16	2	0	0	16	2
Total	**35**	**5**	**0**	**0**	**35**	**5**

Power, Paul

Versatile and experienced Mancunian who was a surprise hero in Everton's last title triumph

Evertonians greeted the £65,000 signing of Paul Power in the summer of 1986 with a chorus of barely suppressed bemusement. Power had served Manchester City for more than a decade, including many years as captain, but had never won anything beyond the odd England B cap, and at the age of 32 was considered by many to be past his best.

Scarcely could he have imagined how quickly this was to change, nor Evertonians how crucial he would be to the club's future success.

Nearing his mid-thirties, Power was a supremely fit player and his experience gave him a reading of the game that meant his diminishing pace was rarely exposed. He possessed accurate distribution and was capable in the air. For a player whose responsibilities were primarily defensive he also weighed in with a fair share of goals, including one in a 3-1 win against his former club in November 1986 that he refused to celebrate – a respectful touch that earned admiration from both Everton and City fans.

ARRIVING AT a club in the midst of an injury crisis, he first slotted in as left back in place of Pat Van Den Hauwe, then as Kevin Sheedy's replacement in left midfield. There were even a couple of appearances in central midfield.

Everywhere he was asked to play, however, Power did so with commitment and dedication. His importance to Everton's title victory at the end of the 1986/87 season was recognised by the Everton Supporters' Club, which made him its joint Player of the Year with Kevin Ratcliffe.

As Everton's injury crisis abated through the 1987/88 season, Power's appearances became more sporadic. At the end of the season he announced his retirement and took up a position on Colin Harvey's coaching staff. An articulate man, who had completed a law degree before entering professional football, he later took on several administrative roles in the game, before returning to Manchester City as part of its youth coaching set-up.

> FOR A PLAYER WHOSE RESPONSIBILITIES WERE PRIMARILY DEFENSIVE HE ALSO WEIGHED IN WITH A FAIR SHARE OF GOALS

[FACTFILE]

BORN
Openshaw, 30 October 1953

POSITION
Left back / midfield

OTHER CLUB
Manchester City (1975–86)

HONOURS
1986/87 League Championship

Season	League App	League Goals	FA Cup App	FA Cup Goals	League Cup App	League Cup Goals	Other App	Other Goals	Total App	Total Goals
1986/87	40	4	3	0	5	0	4	0	52	4
1987/88	12 (2)	2	2	0	1	0	2	1	17 (2)	3
Total	52 (2)	6	5	0	6	0	6	1	69 (2)	7

Pratt, Charles

Centre half who made fleeting appearances in the 1909/10 campaign

Season	League App	League Goals	FA Cup App	FA Cup Goals	Total App	Total Goals
1909/10	2	0	0	0	2	0
Total	2	0	0	0	2	0

[FACTFILE]

BORN
1888

POSITION
Centre half

OTHER CLUBS
Barrow,
Exeter City

Premier League, FA

The league that transformed English football forever

The beginning of the 1992/93 season marked the onset of a new era for English football with the inception of the FA Premier League. After years of deliberation England's elite clubs had finally broken away from the rest of the Football League, having submitted their resignation en masse twelve months earlier. This 'Super League' had in fact been agreed in principle in the Everton boardroom in March 1991, in a meeting presided by Philip Carter, and confirmed the following summer. Everton – with Aston Villa and Blackburn Rovers – were the only three clubs to be founder members of both the Premier League and, 104 years previously, the Football League as well.

Originally envisaging an 18-team division replete with minimum standards for pitches, floodlights, stadium facilities and so on, it actually emerged as little different from the old First Division, albeit with 20 teams instead of 22 from the start of the 1994/95 season. In fact, as David Dein, the Arsenal vice-chairman, admitted shortly after its formation: 'I'm getting increasingly embarrassed when people say, what is the difference between the Premier League and the old First Division? I have to face them and say, "Nothing, except there's more money swishing about."'

ALTHOUGH English football had already started to undergo something of a revival following its mid-1980s nadir, the Premier League, its rebranding of the sport and, above all, the influx of vast domestic and overseas television revenues hastened the transformation of the game at an unimaginable rate. The crumbling stadia, poor facilities, hooliganism and underachievement of English clubs in Europe were, by the late 1990s, rapidly diminishing memories.

Criticisms of the Premier League have centred on the huge gulf that

exists between its 20 members and the remaining 72 members of the Football League. Its wealth has meant that talented foreign players have been imported at the expense of native players and, ultimately, the national teams of the home nations. Extensive overseas broadcasts and proposals such as the controversial '39th game' to be played outside England also threaten the future of rival leagues. A longstanding gulf between a so-called 'big four' and the rest of the Premier League make it predictable: in its first 17 years, just four teams lifted the Premier League, with Manchester United claiming 12 of those titles.

And yet the wealth of the Premier League has seen some of the most exhilarating players in world football ply their trade in England. Although some of the old atmosphere has been lost, the new generation of stadia are a world apart from what preceded them. Contrary to common belief, the

allocation of TV money between its members is far more equitable than in most rival leagues. English clubs are better resourced, better run and better equipped than at any previous time in the game's history.

For the first part of its existence it was branded the Premiership under sponsorship deals with Carling (1993–2001), Barclaycard (2001–04) and Barclays (2004–07). From 2007 it has been known as the Barclays Premier League.

Although Everton – as one of the old 'big five' (with Manchester United, Liverpool, Arsenal and Tottenham) – were one of the driving forces behind the Premier League's creation, they have traditionally fared badly. In the first 10 years of its existence they only finished in the top 10 on one occasion. Although faring better under David Moyes, fourth place in 2004/05 represents Everton's best ever showing.

'I'M GETTING INCREASINGLY EMBARRASSED WHEN PEOPLE SAY, WHAT IS THE DIFFERENCE BETWEEN THE PREMIER LEAGUE AND THE OLD FIRST DIVISION? I HAVE TO FACE THEM AND SAY, "NOTHING, EXCEPT THERE'S MORE MONEY SWISHING ABOUT"'
DAVID DEIN

Proudfoot,
John

**Scottish forward
who supplied
Everton's goals at
the start of
the 20th century**

[FACTFILE]

BORN
Airdrie, 27 February 1874

DIED
1934

POSITION
Centre forward / inside right

OTHER CLUBS
Partick Thistle;
Blackburn Rovers (1896–97);
Watford;
Partick Thistle;
Hamilton Academical

Season	League		FA Cup		Total	
	App	Goals	App	Goals	App	Goals
1898/99	28	12	2	1	30	13
1899/1900	20	8	1	0	21	8
1900/01	29	10	2	0	31	10
1901/02	7	0	0	0	7	0
Total	**84**	**30**	**5**	**1**	**89**	**31**

THE

EVERTON
·ENCYCLOPEDIA·

Predrag **Radosavljevic** (Preki), Tomasz **Radzinski,** Daniel **Rafferty,** David **Raitt,** Andy **Rankin,** Bruce **Rankin,** George **Rankin,** Kevin **Ratcliffe,** Syd **Rawlings,** Ken **Rea,** Harry **Reay,** Barrie **Rees,** Stefan **Rehn,** David **Reid,** Peter **Reid,** Alex **Rennie,** Kevin **Richardson,** Paul **Rideout,** Arthur **Rigby,** Bert **Rigsby,** Neil **Rimmer,** Stuart **Rimmer,** Tommy **Ring,** Bruce **Rioch, Roberts,** James **Roberts,** Hope **Robertson,** Jack **Robertson,** Tom **Robertson,** Alfred **Robinson,** Billy **Robinson,** Neil **Robinson,** Tom **Robson,** William **Roche,** Juliano **Rodrigo,** Jack **Rodwell,** Wayne **Rooney,** Leigh Richmond **Roose,** Nick **Ross,** Trevor **Ross,** Fred **Rouse,** Gary **Rowett,** Joe **Royle,** John **Ruddy,** John **Russell**

Radosavljevic, Predrag (Preki)

Serbian playmaker who struggled with the physicality of the English game

Plucked from the obscurity of the North American Indoor Soccer League on the eve of the 1992/93 season, Preki, as he was universally known, represented one of the more unusual pieces of transfer business in Goodison history. An entirely unknown quantity on his £100,000 arrival, he had helped Red Star Belgrade to a mid-1980s league title, before trying his luck in the United States.

> HIS RANGE OF PASSING AND FABULOUS FREE KICKS WERE ON A DIFFERENT PLANE TO MANY OF HIS TEAM-MATES

Although a fringe player in a struggling Everton team, there were tantalising glimpses of the Yugoslav's sublime footballing gifts. Boasting fabulous technical ability and imaginative passing, at his best he was reminiscent of Kevin Sheedy. His range of passing and fabulous free kicks were on a different plane to many of his team-mates at a moribund Goodison. But all too often he laboured in poor teams, and lacked the pace or strength to thrive in the Premier League.

In July 1994, aged 31, he was sold to Portsmouth and spent a season on the south coast. He returned to the US for the onset of Major League Soccer in 1996. Now in the veteran part of his career, Preki experienced an incredible Indian summer that extended almost a decade. Twice he was named the MLS Most Valuable Player and twice he was the MLS Scoring Champion (based on a formula of assists and goals). In 2005, at the time of the MLS 10-year anniversary, he was named as part of its greatest XI.

IN 1996, Preki took US citizenship and was called up to the national team. He appeared for the US at the 1998 World Cup Finals, turning out, ironically, to face Yugoslavia.

In 2005, aged 42, Preki announced his retirement, scoring in the last minute of his last game for Kansas City Wizards. He subsequently turned to management and after succeeding Mike Bradley as Chivas manager in 2007 was awarded Manager of the Year in his debut season.

[FACTFILE]

BORN
Belgrade, Yugoslavia,
24 June 1963
POSITION
Left winger
OTHER CLUBS
Red Star Belgrade (1983–85);
Tacoma Stars (1985–89);
St Louis Storm (1989–92);
Portsmouth (1994–95);
San Jose Grizzlies (1995);
Kansas City Wizards
(1996–2000);
Miami Fusion (2001);
Kansas City Wizards
(2002–05)
HONOURS
28 United States caps
(4 goals) (1996–98)

Season	League		FA Cup		League Cup		Total	
	App	Goals	App	Goals	App	Goals	App	Goals
1992/93	13(10)	3	1	0	1	0	15(10)	3
1993/94	9 (14)	1	0	0	1 (4)	0	10(18)	1
Total	22 (24)	4	1	0	2 (4)	0	25(28)	4

Radzinski, Tomasz

Pacy striker who was never quite as indispensable as he thought

Signed from Anderlecht for £4.5million in the summer of 2001, Tomasz Radzinski was supposed to allay some of the disappointment attached to Francis Jeffers' departure from the club. In many ways, the 27-year-old striker was a similar player to the lamented prodigy: quick, a fine dribbler, and a reasonable finisher.

At the time of his arrival, Radzinski was virtually unknown to English football fans – save for a brace in an October 2000 Champions League fixture that brought Anderlecht an unexpected win over Manchester United. Born in Poland, Radzinski's parents fled Communism in the 1980s, eventually settling in Canada. He started out in the Canadian leagues, moving to Europe with Germinal Ekeren of Antwerp, then Anderlecht.

THE MOVE to Everton came after a month-long stand-off between Radzinski and the Belgian champions, with player power and his desire for a lucrative move to England eventually winning through.

The onset of Radzinski's Everton career was delayed through injury – a persistent impediment through his three-year-long Goodison spell – and his belated involvement was not enough to prevent the unravelling of Walter Smith's managerial reign. He fared better under David Moyes and was an important factor in the club's initial renaissance under the new manager – his pace a rarity among an ageing squad. Yet while quick, Radzinski's movement and reading of the game were not always on the same level, and too often he was static when a midfielder tried to play him through. Nor was his finishing particularly remarkable: when put through one-on-one with a goalkeeper, one always fancied his opponent. There were, however, some glorious moments – none better than his last-minute winner against Southampton in February 2003, a piledriver that almost ripped the Gwladys Street net from its stanchions.

In a small squad his contribution was nevertheless valued by David Moyes, who at the end of the 2003/04 season offered the 30-year-old a new three-year contract – in contravention of his own policy that ordinarily saw players of that age offered just a

single year. His response? Public criticism of Moyes's management while also urging Wayne Rooney to move elsewhere to 'better himself'. Moyes promptly sold the striker to Fulham for £1.75million, where his form over three years was less than impressive, while Everton went from strength to strength without him.

Following his release from Craven Cottage at the end of the 2006/07 season, Radzinski moved to Skoda Xanthi in Greece, before returning to Belgium, where he found his level again in the country's second tier.

[FACTFILE]

BORN
Ponznan, Poland,
14 December 1973
POSITION
Striker
OTHER CLUBS
North York Rockets
(Canada, 1990–93);
St Catherine's Roma
(Canada, 1993-94);
Germinal Ekeren
(Belgium, 1994–98);
Anderlecht (1998–2001);
Fulham (2004–07);
Skoda Xanthi
(Greece, 2007–08);
Lierse (Belgium, 2008–11);
Waasland-Beveren (2012–)
HONOURS
28 United States caps
(4 goals) (1996–98)

HIS LAST-MINUTE WINNER AGAINST SOUTHAMPTON IN FEBRUARY 2003 WAS A PILEDRIVER THAT ALMOST RIPPED THE GWLADYS STREET NET FROM ITS STANCHIONS

Season	League		FA Cup		League Cup		Total	
	App	Goals	App	Goals	App	Goals	App	Goals
2001/02	23 (4)	6	2	1	0	0	25 (4)	7
2002/03	27 (3)	11	1	0	2 (1)	0	30 (4)	11
2003/04	28 (6)	8	2	0	0 (2)	0	30 (8)	8
Total	78 (13)	25	5	1	2 (3)	0	85(16)	26

Rafferty, Daniel

Provided defensive cover during the first decade of the 20th century

Season	League		FA Cup		Total	
	App	Goals	App	Goals	App	Goals
1907/08	3	0	0	0	3	0
1908/09	1	0	0	0	1	0
1909/10	3	0	0	0	3	0
Total	7	0	0	0	7	0

Raitt, David

Skilful full back who was unable to plug Everton's 1920s defensive problems

D. RAITT

EVERTON FOOTBALL CLUB 1927

David Raitt was a skilful, hard, yet not especially quick full back who played for Everton's attractive but underachieving team of the early 1920s.

RAITT, who had played for the Scottish League's representative team, signed from Dundee in the summer of 1922 for £2200. Everton had tried to conclude a double deal with his former club that would have seen Alec Troup join Everton too, but they had to wait another six months before signing the winger. Raitt made his debut in a 2-0 defeat at Tottenham but the new boy did not impress the watching press pack.

'It was Raitt's debut in English League football, and he was naturally taken aback early on by the clever work of masters like [Jimmy] Dimmock and [Bert] Bliss,' wrote the Liverpool Daily Post and Mercury reporter. 'Raitt's real fault was kept till near the end,

when he dared to dribble and showed such a lack of pace that he was beaten at his own game. That was bad football, and it was characteristic of other of the Scottish members – [George] Brewster and [Hunter] Hart –and at times by the Wigan boy, [Joe] Peacock.'

THE NEW BOY eventually won over Everton's exacting observers, although one correspondent noted, 'he is somewhat given to reckless kickings'. Perhaps he didn't kick hard enough. Everton's Achilles heel through this era was their defence, and although they at times played sumptuous football their lack of mean streak cost them honours. Ivan Sharpe, the leading football journalist of the day, wrote after the 1923/24 season's seventh-place finish: 'Everton, by reason of their exemplary contribution to the season's play, are in the honours list, if not among the rewards.' The reason, he added, that

'they are out of presentation of prizes [was] because of uncertainty in defence'. This would become an increasing problem over subsequent seasons. In finishing 1925/26 11th they conceded 70 goals, including seven against Sunderland and five against Liverpool. The next season was worse: 20th place, 90 goals conceded.

The board had by then made significant attempts to redress this problem and made six significant signings in the second half of the season. These included Warney Cresswell, formerly the world's most expensive player and England's sometime right back. He took Raitt's place and although the Scot made six appearances during the next season, which saw the League Championship come to Goodison, he was sold to Blackburn at that campaign's conclusion for £325.

Season	League		FA Cup		Total	
	App	Goals	App	Goals	App	Goals
1922/23	36	0	2	0	38	0
1923/24	19	0	0	0	19	0
1924/25	20	0	4	0	24	0
1925/26	30	0	2	0	32	0
1926/27	11	0	1	0	12	0
1927/28	6	0	0	0	6	0
Total	122	0	9	0	131	0

Rankin,
Andy

1960s goalkeeper who was a long-term understudy to Gordon West

Andy Rankin was faced with the thankless task of having to supplant Gordon West during the 1960s peak of the goalkeeper's career. A home-grown talent who progressed through the Everton ranks with Colin Harvey, Rankin was widely considered the best reserve goalkeeper in England – although there must have been times when he wondered what else he had to do to make the green jersey his own.

WATCHED BY ALF RAMSEY IN SEPTEMBER 1964, HE PUT IN THE PERFORMANCE OF HIS LIFE AS EVERTON BEAT LIVERPOOL 4-0 AT ANFIELD

A Bootle boy who earned England under-23 international honours, there was a sense that Rankin might have gone to the very summit of his profession. In 1963/64, with Everton chasing a consecutive league title, 19-year-old Rankin was thrust into the first team after West suffered a loss of form. He did not disappoint and although the championship was elusive, the rookie kept his place for the first half of the following campaign. Watched by Alf Ramsey in September 1964, he put in the performance of his life as Everton beat Liverpool 4-0 at Anfield – a scoreline that barely hints at the succession of outstanding saves he made.

But always West came back, often better than before. After taking West's place for an FA Cup quarter-final against Nottingham Forest in 1967, Rankin endured a nightmare, and was at fault for all three of Everton's goals as they slipped to a 3-2 defeat – it was the last sight Evertonians glimpsed of him for three-and-a-half years.

HE RETURNED to the team in September 1970, after West was dropped for remonstrating with supporters during a European Cup game. Later that year Rankin made his mark in the same competition, saving a crucial penalty in the shootout victory over Borussia Moenchengladbach. His heroics saw him keep his place until the end of the season. But at the start of the 1971/72 season, West was back and Rankin was kicking his heels in the Central League again.

IN NOVEMBER 1971, Catterick accepted a £20,000 bid from Watford, and Rankin moved south, ousting Mike Walker – later to become Everton manager – as first-choice goalkeeper at Vicarage Road. Later he joined Huddersfield Town, his career extending until in his late thirties.

[FACTFILE]

BORN
Liverpool, 11 May 1944
POSITION
Goalkeeper
OTHER CLUBS
Watford (1971–80);
Huddersfield Town (1980–82)

Season	League		FA Cup		League Cup		Other		Total	
	App	Goals	App	Goals	App	Goals	App	Goals	App	Goals
1963/64	20	0	2	0	-	-	0	0	22	0
1964/65	22	0	0	0	-	-	4	0	26	0
1965/66	9	0	0	0	-	-	2 (1)	0	11 (1)	0
1966/67	6	0	1	0	-	-	0	0	7	0
1967/68	0	0	0	0	0	0	-	-	0	0
1968/69	0	0	0	0	0	0	-	-	0	0
1969/70	0	0	0	0	0	0	-	-	0	0
1970/71	28	0	5	0	-	-	5	0	38	0
1971/72	0	0	0	0	0	0	-	-	0	0
Total	**85**	**0**	**8**	**0**	**0**	**0**	**11 (1)**	**0**	**104(1)**	**0**

Rankin, Bruce

Scottish winger who supplied the Goodison frontline during the early 20th century

Season	League		FA Cup		Total	
	App	Goals	App	Goals	App	Goals
1901/02	1	0	0	0	1	0
1902/03	13	2	1	0	14	2
1903/04	3	2	0	0	3	2
1904/05	16	1	0	0	16	1
1905/06	4	2	0	0	4	2
Total	37	7	1	0	38	7

[FACTFILE]

BORN
Glasgow, 21 July 1880
POSITION
Outside right
OTHER CLUBS
West Bromwich Albion (1905–06);
Manchester City (1906);
Luton Town, Wrexham

Rankin, George

Liverpool Schoolboys defender who failed to win a regular first-team berth

EVERTON FOOTBALL CLUB 1952-53

Strapping full back George Rankin was one of the same group of Liverpool Schoolboys footballers as Jimmy Tansey and T.E. Jones. But while his contemporaries would between them make more than 550 Everton appearances, Rankin was largely a peripheral player at Goodison and struggled to make a first-team shirt his own in an Everton career that lasted more than a decade.

AFFILIATED with the club since the war years, he was signed as a part-time professional in November 1947 on wages of £3 per week. His break came in the catastrophic 1950/51 season, when manager Cliff Britton constantly reshuffled his full backs in an attempt to plug a leaky defence that would ultimately see the club relegated. Rankin's progress was then stunted by a call-up to national service, and although he was belatedly made a full-time professional in 1953, he struggled to dislodge Jack Lindsay and, subsequently, Don Donovan from the left back berth. Rankin represented the British Army in 1951 in a match against Ireland and was the subject of interest from Torquay United, who had a £2000 bid accepted for him in November 1953. Rankin declined to move south and made occasional appearances for the Blues over the subsequent three seasons. Finally, after the dismissal of Cliff Britton in 1956, he was placed on the transfer list. In July that year Southport had a £500 bid accepted, and in Lancashire Rankin flourished.

Season	League		FA Cup		Total	
	App	Goals	App	Goals	App	Goals
1950/51	18	0	1	0	19	0
1951/52	2	0	0	0	2	0
1952/53	10	0	0	0	10	0
1953/54	1	0	0	0	1	0
1954/55	3	0	2	0	5	0
1955/56	2	0	0	0	2	0
Total	36	0	3	0	39	0

[FACTFILE]

BORN
Liverpool, 29 January 1930
DIED
1989
POSITION
Full back
OTHER CLUB
Southport (1956–60)

Ratcliffe,
Kevin

Imperious Welsh international defender and Everton's most decorated captain

Looking back, it seems inconceivable that Kevin Ratcliffe's Everton career nearly ended before it had even really begun. In 1981, still short of his 21st birthday, Ratcliffe was the subject of a bid from Bobby Robson's Ipswich Town. Everton resisted, but a year later, unhappy at flitting in and out of the team and having to play in an unfamiliar left back role, Ratcliffe was on the verge of requesting a transfer. Before this happened, however, he returned to the team in December 1982 as first-choice centre back and within a year he was captain, set to embark on an adventure that would make him Everton's most successful ever skipper.

AN ADVENTURE THAT WOULD MAKE HIM EVERTON'S MOST SUCCESSFUL EVER SKIPPER

A BOYHOOD EVERTONIAN, Ratcliffe's long association with the club began when he signed as an apprentice on leaving school in June 1977. Already a Wales schoolboy international, he went on to represent his country's under-18 team before making his Everton debut against Manchester United at Old Trafford in March 1980. The Liverpool Echo concluded that he had had an 'impressive debut' giving Joe Jordan 'little scope'. A month later he was a surprise inclusion in the team that lost to West Ham in the FA Cup semi-final replay. Ratcliffe later recalled how the day stayed with him. He told Bluekipper.com: 'Looking around the dressing room and on the coach, people like Peter Eastoe Bob Latchford were crying, saying, "You've got plenty of time to get to another final, we'll not get another chance." They were quite right.'

Still a novice, there followed an early international call-up and he was included in the Wales team to face Czechoslovakia in a World Cup qualifier in September 1981. 'It was as if he'd been playing international football all his life, dealing comfortably with opponents like [Marian] Masny and [Zdenek] Nehoda,' Rolant Ellis later wrote in Gwladys Sings The Blues.

But at Goodison, all was not well. Gordon Lee was sacked at the end of the 1980/81 season and replaced by Howard Kendall. Kendall initially preferred Mick Walsh or Mark Higgins as Mick Lyons' central defensive partner, eventually settling on a Billy Wright–Higgins partnership, with Ratcliffe left back. Kendall resisted pairing Ratcliffe and his fellow left-footer Higgins together for as long as possible, but Ratcliffe's unhappiness at full back was palpable, leading to talk of a Goodison exit. Ipswich, Stoke and Blackburn were all linked with the young defender, but Kendall would not sell. 'Howard told me at the PFA awards that Stoke were after me,' he recalled. 'I said, "Are they?" and Howard said, "Yes, I've told them to fuck off!" which was nice to hear.'

Ratcliffe's perseverance finally paid off in December 1982. Everton were still reeling from a 5-0 mauling to Liverpool the previous month, when Kendall decided to reshape his team, dropping Billy Wright and pairing Ratcliffe with Higgins. There followed a marked improvement in form, as Everton rose from 15th to finish the campaign seventh, also reaching the FA Cup quarter-final.

ONE OF THE MOST OUTSTANDING CENTRE BACKS IN THE CLUB'S HISTORY

At last Evertonians were offered a proper glimpse of the qualities that would set Ratcliffe apart as one of the most outstanding centre backs in the club's history. He was an astute reader of the game, a player who would anticipate rather than dive in. Somewhat one-footed, his distribution was nevertheless accurate and consistent. Although never a physical giant he was powerful in the air and not averse to mixing it with his opponents. Indeed, Ratcliffe was in many ways the antithesis of a gentle giant like Brian Labone: hard, uncompromising, not averse to using dirty tricks if the occasion demanded it. After retirement, he was open about kicking Bayern Munich's Ludwig Kogl out of Everton's famous 1985 encounter with the Germans. Later his grudge encounters with Wimbledon's Vinnie Jones would be notorious.

Ratcliffe's hallmark was his pace, however, and few forwards – Ian Rush being a notable exception – ever seemed to trouble him.

Evertonians would joke that he left scorch marks on the pitch, and through his mid-80s heyday he could justifiably boast of being the First Division's fastest defender.

Ratcliffe struck up a solid partnership with Higgins, but by December 1983 injury had effectively wrecked his team-mate's career. Derek Mountfield came in alongside Ratcliffe, and Higgins' captaincy went to the Welshman. Within three months, Ratcliffe had also assumed captaincy of his country and within six had become the youngest captain since Bobby Moore to lift the FA Cup, after Everton's 2-0 victory over Watford.

Although his contribution is often overlooked in favour of some of his more glamorous colleagues, between 1984 and early 1988 Ratcliffe was virtually ever-present, picking up an FA Cup, two League Championships and a European Cup Winners' Cup in the process – an unprecedented haul for a Blues' captain. His footballing talents were obvious to anyone who saw him play, but as captain he was at the centre of team building, a man adept at fomenting the unique 'one for all, all for one' mentality that was so crucial to Everton's successes.

SPEAKING TO Bluekipper.com, he said of these great teams and their philosophy:

> Everyone had a different talent in them. Eighty per cent of the goals came from Kevin Sheedy. Trevor was very skilful. Nev was probably the best keeper in the world at the time, and with Reidy, Sharpy, Andy & Inchy it was just such a good mixture. But the biggest thing about it was that we were nasty!! We were a nasty bunch who wanted to win every game. We had a big togetherness, a team spirit like I've never come across before or since.
> Now you just see a few on the bench, we had about 10, it was our trademark, when you scored everyone on the bench was up dancing. Them lads weren't playing but they were made to feel one of the lads. We never treated anyone any differently, the lads on the bench were just as important. Your Kevin Richardsons and Alan Harpers, whoever it was, they were made to feel part of the team.'

Despite playing more than 450 times for Everton, Ratcliffe's attacking contribution was minimal. Kendall rarely let him venture past the halfway line, and in more than a decade he managed just two goals, although

[FACTFILE]

BORN
Mancot,
12 November 1960

POSITION
Central defender

OTHER CLUBS
Dundee (1992);
Cardiff City (1992–94);
Derby County (1994);
Chester City (1994–95)

AS MANAGER
Chester City (1995–99);
Shrewsbury Town
(1999–2000)

HONOURS
FA Cup 1984;
League Championship
1984/85, 1986/87;
European Cup Winners' Cup
1985;
59 Wales caps (1981–93)

both were memorable efforts. The first came against Norwich City in January 1983 when he ran half the length of the pitch before slipping the ball past Chris Woods in the Norwich goal. The second came in February 1986 when a mishit half-volley trickled past Bruce Grobelaar to record a famous victory over Liverpool. The shot, Ratcliffe later joked, had 'a bit of swerve on it' and not even Southall would have stopped it.

Still aged only 26 at the time of lifting his second league title, greatness beckoned for Ratcliffe. And yet he was cut off in his prime. Struck down with groin and hernia problems during Everton's futile defence of their 1987 title, he returned after a lengthy absence in October 1988 shorn of some of the pace that had once been his hallmark. He led Everton to the 1989 FA Cup Final, but Evertonians grumbled that he was no longer the same player. Niggling injuries curtailed his impact through the 1989/90 season and lessened hopes that there would be a renaissance. Sometimes he was played at left back in order to accommodate Martin Keown.

Season	League		FA Cup		League Cup		Other		Total	
	App	Goals	App	Goals	App	Goals	App	Goals	App	Goals
1979/80	2	0	1	0	0	0	0	0	3	0
1980/81	20 (1)	0	5	0	2	0	-	-	27 (1)	0
1981/82	25	0	1	0	1	0	-	-	27	0
1982/83	29	1	5	0	3	0	-	-	37	1
1983/84	38	0	8	0	11	0	-	-	57	0
1984/85	40	0	7	0	4	0	10	0	61	0
1985/86	39	1	5	0	5	0	5	0	54	1
1986/87	42	0	3	0	5	0	4	0	54	0
1987/88	24	0	1	0	4	0	2	0	31	0
1988/89	30	0	8	0	4	0	4	0	46	0
1989/90	24	0	7	0	2	0	-	-	33	0
1990/91	35 (1)	0	6	0	3	0	5 (1)	0	49 (2)	0
1991/92	8 (1)	0	0	0	2	0	0	0	10 (1)	0
Total	**356 (3)**	**2**	**57**	**0**	**46**	**0**	**30 (1)**	**0**	**489 (4)**	**2**

FOLLOWING Howard Kendall's return as manager in November 1990, Ratcliffe was restored as one of the manager's first choices each week. But all too often he was called upon to carry Kendall's sometimes baffling defensive experiments, not just at centre back, but full back and even sweeper too. His ailing form saw him the target of some terrace abuse – an undeserved outcome for one of the club's greatest servants. Yet Ratcliffe was characteristically selfless in his response, saying he would sooner take criticism than have a young player experience it.

After a torrid first half in a League Cup tie against Leeds United in December 1991, described by When Skies Are Grey as 'the nadir of Kendall's defensive madness', Ratcliffe was substituted and never again played for the first team. It was, wrote WSAG, 'a sad end'.

A month later, following the signing of Gary Ablett, the captain's armband was handed to Dave Watson and Ratcliffe was placed on the transfer list. It was assumed that the centre half, who had only just turned 31 and who had stood out just months earlier when Wales rose to their finest ever victory against World Champions Germany, would immediately be snapped up. Sadly that was not the case and he spent an undeserved year languishing in the reserves before he was signed by Cardiff City.

With the South Wales club his career enjoyed a brief resurgence and he returned to the international fold, playing his last game in Wales' 1993 win over Belgium. With Cardiff he added another medal to his collection, lifting the 1992/93 Third Division Championship. At the end of the 1992/93 season, the fanzine O Bluebird of Happiness recorded: 'Everyone connected with City will recognise the galvanising effect the arrival of Kevin Ratcliffe had on the team … we won 17, drew 2 and lost 2 of 21 league games [he played in].'

THERE followed a brief spell at Derby County. In 1994 Ratcliffe joined Chester City as assistant manager and continued to play for a year. The following summer he was appointed manager, leading Chester to the 1997 Third Division playoffs and retaining mid-table respectability the following term in the midst of crippling financial problems. He left in August 1999 after falling out with the Chester chairman, becoming Shrewsbury Town manager in November that year. In January 2003, Ratcliffe masterminded the most humiliating result in Everton's history, when his Shrewsbury team defeated his former club 2-1 in the FA Cup third round. However, a disastrous run of results followed and in May that year, Shrewsbury were relegated from the Football League. Ratcliffe resigned within days and has since built a career as a football pundit.

'Casting my mind back over the past ten years,' said Ratcliffe in 1989, when he became only the fifth Everton player to be granted a testimonial, 'it is amazing how many of my best memories are of the fans rather than the matches or goals. Even during the lean years there was a massive

hardcore at every away game who lifted us more than they could imagine. And by the time we had lifted ourselves to Wembley and Rotterdam, they brought tears to our eyes. To play before supporters like that, to share their joy has been an honour.'

SUCH modest words can be seen as defining Kevin Ratcliffe: a fine player and great servant, perhaps most importantly he was also a true-born and blue Evertonian.

> 'IT IS AMAZING HOW MANY OF MY BEST MEMORIES ARE OF THE FANS RATHER THAN THE MATCHES OR GOALS'
>
> **KEVIN RATCLIFFE**

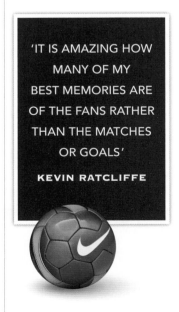

Rawlings, James Sidney Dean 'Syd'

Lower-league winger who made a post-war FA Cup cameo with Everton

Season	League		FA Cup		Total	
	App	Goals	App	Goals	App	Goals
1945/46	-	-	2	0	2	0
Total	-	-	2	0	2	0

[FACTFILE]

BORN
5 May 1913
DIED
1956
POSITION
Winger
OTHER CLUBS
Preston North End (1932–34);
Huddersfield Town (1934–35);
West Bromwich Albion (1935–36);
Northampton Town (1936–37);
Millwall (1937–39);
Plymouth Argyle (1946–48)

Rea, Ken

Home-grown wing half versed in 'ordinary' working life

Wing half Ken Rea was one of a generation of footballers versed in the realities of civvy street, combining his passion for football – and Everton – with working life as an apprentice mechanical engineer.

Signed as a 15-year-old amateur in 1950, Rea worked through the week in factories – training on Tuesday and Thursday evenings – and played on Saturday for the A team. A former Liverpool Schoolboy, he had rejected the overtures of Liverpool because, he told this author in 2011, 'Everton was where I wanted to be.' Only after completing national service with the army did he sign professional forms and not until he had been associated with the club for six years did he make his debut.

His break came in the summer of 1956 when he travelled with the first team on Everton's six-week tour of the United States and played in most of the games. On his return new manager Ian Buchan gave him a run in the side. 'When things were going bad Buchan gave me a go in the first team,' he said. 'It was great playing for the first team, it was the thing

EVERTON 1956
Back row - ***Sutherland, Tansey, O'Neill, Jones, Kirby,***
Front - ***McNamara, Eglington, Farrell, Llewellyn, Glazzard, Rea***

I'd always wanted to do and I had my chance. Cyril Lello was getting a bit older. I played until I got dropped.'

'Though a gifted passer who offered subtle service to his forwards, he rarely asserted himself in the tackle and was a ponderous runner, doubtless being handicapped by the injuries that dogged him throughout his professional career,' opined the football historian, Ivan Ponting. Indeed the recurrent injuries hindered his progress and after Buchan's departure in 1958 chances were

harder to come by. Rea dropped down to non-league football with Runcorn and returned to work on civvy street. 'I missed all the lads,' Rea said, when asked if he had any regrets. 'It was such a great club, Everton, the lads that were there. I still see them now: Tony McNamara, we've just lost Tommy Jones – who was one of us – and Don Donovan.'

[FACTFILE]

BORN
Buckhaven, Fife, 1897
POSITION
Right back
OTHER CLUBS
Dundee (1919–22);
Blackburn Rovers (1928–29);
Forfar Athletic (1929)

Season	League		FA Cup		Total	
	App	Goals	App	Goals	App	Goals
1956/57	15	0	3	0	18	0
1957/58	27	0	2	0	29	0
1958/59	4	0	0	0	4	0
Total	46	0	5	0	51	0

Reay, Harry

Outside right who made a couple of cameo appearances during Goodison's first years

Season	League		FA Cup		Total	
	App	Goals	App	Goals	App	Goals
1893/94	1	1	0	0	1	1
1894/95	0	0	1	0	1	0
Total	**1**	**1**	**1**	**0**	**2**	**1**

[FACTFILE]

BORN
Tyneside, 1870
POSITION
Outside right
OTHER CLUBS
Gateshead;
Shankhouse Black Watch;
Newcastle East End;
Newcastle United

Rees, Barrie

Young wing half tragically killed in a car crash soon after departing Goodison

Season	League		FA Cup		Other		Total	
	App	Goals	App	Goals	App	Goals	App	Goals
1963/64	3	2	0	0	0	0	3	2
1964/65	1	0	0	0	0	0	1	0
Total	**4**	**2**	**0**	**0**	**0**	**0**	**4**	**2**

[FACTFILE]

BORN
Rhyl, 4 February 1944
DIED
1965
POSITION
Wing half
OTHER CLUB
Brighton & Hove Albion
(1964–65)

Rehn, Stefan

Everton's first foreign signing whose career blossomed beyond Goodison

Signed as a 22-year-old from Djurgardens for £400,000 in the summer of 1989, Stefan Rehn was touted as a long-term successor to Paul Bracewell as Colin Harvey sought to rebuild Everton according to his own vision.

THE SWEDEN international midfielder, who became Everton's first foreign signing, was considered among the finest Scandinavian players of his generation – but his Everton career was notable only for its brevity: two starts, four substitute appearances.

INDEED it never really recovered after an incident in a bruising First Division clash with Millwall in October 1989. Called upon as a first-half substitute, Rehn was immediately marked by the Lions' combative midfielder Terry Hurlock. So completely was he physically overshadowed by his opponent that on the hour mark he himself was substituted, his credibility shattered.

Sold to IFK Gothenburg the following summer, he was a key component of the team that won four Swedish titles in five years. Rehn also featured in the Sweden squad that finished third in the 1994 World Cup. A five-year spell in Switzerland was followed by a return to Djurgardens in 2000.

In 2002, his last season as a player, he was an instrumental part of the Stockholm club's first league title win in 36 years. Subsequently he turned to management, taking charge of IFK Gothenburg in 2007.

[FACTFILE]

BORN
Stockholm,
22 September 1966
POSITION
Midfield
OTHER CLUBS
Djurgardens (1984–89);
IFK Gothenburg (1990–95);
Lausanne Sports (1995–2000);
Djurgardens (2000–02)
AS MANAGER
IFK Gothenburg (2007–10);
Jitex BK (2011–)
HONOURS
45 Sweden caps (6 goals)
(1988–95)

Season	League		FA Cup		League Cup		Total	
	App	Goals	App	Goals	App	Goals	App	Goals
1989/90	1 (3)	0	0	0	1 (1)	0	2 (4)	0
Total	**1 (3)**	**0**	**0**	**0**	**1 (1)**	**0**	**2 (4)**	**0**

Reid, David

1920s utility man who made the unlikely transition from winger to centre half

HIS STIRRING DISPLAYS IN THE CLOSING STAGES OF THE 1925/26 SEASON SAW HIM ELEVATED TO VICE-CAPTAIN THE FOLLOWING CAMPAIGN

Everton's history is replete with the endeavours of fine but largely unsung utility men. Alan Harper and Sandy Brown are the most conspicuous examples of this crucial breed of player, but others have also donned the mantle. Few, however, have been as versatile as David Reid. Signed as a left winger, Reid played out his Everton career as an inside forward and half back before eventually settling as a makeshift centre half, where he played the finest football of his career.

Signed from Distillery in Northern Ireland in the summer of 1920, he was intended to form a left-sided partnership with Charlie Crossley, who had joined Everton from Sunderland. 'These two players are likely to make their mark when the real competition starts,' reported the Liverpool Courier of the annual Blues v. Whites trial match. 'Reid's runs and centres, and Crossley's dribbling, were pleasing factors.'

YET REID scarcely got a chance on the flank once the 1920/21 season got under way and when he did play there he flattered to deceive. The Liverpool Post and Mercury were regularly critical of his displays, saying he lacked incision and was prone to overelaboration. '[Reid's] only fault was a super abundance of passes to his partner on the right instead of a variety of methods, especially down the centre,' they sniped of one performance. 'Reid seemed to lack the necessary dash to forge his way through the home defence,' recorded another correspondent of a rare outing on the wing. Indeed the bulk of his 21 league appearances in 1920/21 came as inside forward. By the time of the 1921 Blues v. Whites match it was noted: 'Reid does not progress.'

As Everton struggled to make an impression in the early 1920s, Reid was a peripheral player. The turning point came when Neil McBain was injured at the end of 1923 and Reid was surprisingly called to deputise at centre half. 'Considering the position he was playing in,

[Reid] gave a highly creditable display,' recorded the Post and Mercury of his new role. His performance in an FA Cup tie against Preston North End prompted another correspondent to opine that he 'was the best man on the field. Everton are indeed fortunate in having such an understudy to Neil McBain.'

McBain recovered his place but thereafter Reid was considered an adept reserve to call upon for the Everton defence. His stirring displays in the closing stages of the 1925/26 season saw him elevated to vice-captain the following campaign, which he started as first choice alongside Hunter Hart and William Brown. But, alas, injury struck and he struggled thereafter to reclaim his place from Albert Virr.

REID LATER returned to Ireland with Ballymena and although international honours eluded him he represented the Irish League on four occasions.

[FACTFILE]

BORN
Glasgow, 1897

POSITION
Utility player

OTHER CLUBS
Distillery,
Ballymena

Season	League		FA Cup		Total	
	App	Goals	App	Goals	App	Goals
1920/21	21	5	0	0	21	5
1921/22	16	4	0	0	16	4
1922/23	13	0	1	0	14	0
1923/24	6	0	0	0	6	0
1924/25	23	2	3	0	26	2
1925/26	11	0	0	0	11	0
1926/27	7	0	0	0	7	0
Total	**97**	**11**	**4**	**0**	**101**	**11**

Reid, Peter

Talismanic midfielder who was one of the driving forces behind Everton's mid-1980s successes

The signing of Peter Reid would be hailed by Howard Kendall as 'Everton's most important since the war'. In a seven-year-long Goodison career, his contribution as the midfield enforcer more than justified his manager's claim. But Reid was always more than just a great player. He was a snarling inspirer of his colleagues, a formidable opponent; the brave, vociferous heartbeat of the team whose tirelessness made Everton tick. He was, so the cliché goes, the sort of man you would want alongside you in the trenches. He was integral to Everton's mid-1980s heyday.

Hailing from Huyton, Reid was overlooked by the two Mersey giants as a teenager and signed as a trainee with Bolton Wanderers in the early 1970s. After breaking through to the first team mid-decade he was part of the Bolton side that won the Second Division Championship in 1977/78. After Reid experienced relegation with Bolton in 1979/80, Gordon Lee tried to sign him for Everton in a £600,000 deal that would have

represented a club record transfer. But the transfer fell through and Reid remained at Burnden Park for 30 injury-plagued months.

When Howard Kendall moved for the midfielder in December 1982, Reid had been so ravaged by injury that he was by then valued at just one tenth of the fee Lee had tried to pay. Kendall was nevertheless desperate to get his man, and when Midland Bank refused to extend Everton's overdraft to facilitate the purchase, the club changed banks to TSB who would.

And yet the move quickly threatened to be a disaster. Because of yet more injury Reid played just 10 times in remaining six months of the 1982/83 season. Kendall considered the move a mistake and Colin Harvey, who had scouted Reid, reputedly apologised for his part in the deal.

However, Reid returned to the Everton team in autumn 1983 and for the first time in years put in a run of appearances without succumbing to injury. Gradually he began to impart his influence upon the team, and by January 1984 Goodison had witnessed the genesis of the side that would dominate English football over the next 40 months.

REID WAS never the most technically accomplished nor polished of players. By the time he was an Everton player, injuries had diminished his pace. He was potent neither in the air nor in front of goal. In many ways he resembled a pub footballer – inelegant, stocky, prematurely balding. Evertonians sang, 'He's fat, he's round, he's worth a million pounds' – but, as When Skies Are Grey would later point out, Reid was worth 'much, much more than that to Everton'.

His technique was successful because of its simplicity. He rarely needed more than two touches: he would get it, give it, move into space and demand it back. His distribution was precise and effective; but he could also spray balls over long distances – as witness the 50-yard chipped pass that set up Gary Lineker's goal

in the 1986 FA Cup Final. He was a formidable and effective tackler whose perceptive reading of the game gave him an edge over more athletic opponents. The litany of injuries he had recovered from hinted at the intense willpower that seemed to drive him. This rubbed off on his team-mates, who seemed invigorated by his very presence.

WITHOUT QUESTION, Reid played his finest football in the 1984/85 season when Everton swept aside virtually all comers. Reid added League Championship and European Cup Winners' Cup medals to the FA Cup he had won a year earlier. He also became the first Everton player to win the PFA Player of the Year award. Recording the fact, Rothmans Football Annual paid the following tribute: 'A few years ago injury and disputes seemed to have ruined the first-class career of this midfield player. During one spell of almost five years at Bolton Wanderers he failed to make a score of appearances in any one season. Transfer to Everton proved the breakthrough he needed and last year he was the mainspring in the Goodison Park midfield machinery which churned out Championship and European success in impressive fashion. Then winning his first full international cap for England at

last put his career in pole position.' Reid said of his award: 'When you talk about awards, you can't be given a greater honour than one voted for by your own profession. Winning that is something I'll never forget.' In June 1985, on the eve of his 29th birthday, Reid was awarded the first of 13 England caps, against Mexico.

HAVING BARELY missed a game in nearly two years, in September 1985 injury struck Reid again – this time it was his Achilles tendon and he underwent successive operations on his left and right sides. His return in February 1986 helped shore up Everton's occasionally leaky rearguard, as they narrowly missed out to Liverpool in the race for the League Championship and FA Cup. But in total Reid made just 15 league appearances – who knows how Everton might have fared had he managed more.

With Gary Lineker, Trevor Steven and Gary Stevens, Reid was part of a strong Everton contingent at the 1986 World Cup Finals in Mexico. But on his return the injury curse struck again and Reid was missing at the start of the 1986/87 season and absent until February. His return to form that spring coincided with a seven-match winning streak that propelled Everton to a second league title in three seasons.

When Howard Kendall left Everton for Spain at the end of that season, Reid, now aged 31, was appointed player-coach by his successor, Colin Harvey. Reid insisted, 'I'm still more a player than a coach,' and during the 1987/88 season he played more league games than in the two preceding campaigns combined, many as captain in the injured Kevin Ratcliffe's absence. But as Everton went into their late-1980s decline, an ageing Reid was made a scapegoat by some supporters. He lost his place during the 1988/89 season and in February 1989 was granted a free transfer.

Yet Reid's playing days were far from over. He joined Queens Park Rangers but later on that year, when Howard Kendall became Manchester City manager, he returned north to be reunited with his former manager. In November 1990 Kendall returned to Everton and Reid succeeded him as Manchester City player-manager. He was arguably City's most successful manager since Joe Mercer, twice leading them to fifth, but was, to the surprise of the club's fans, sacked early in the 1993/94 season by a chairman impatient for success. Reid subsequently put in brief playing stints with Southampton, Notts County and Bury.

In 1995 he was appointed Sunderland manager. This would be Reid's most successful managerial spell, spanning seven years. In 1999 he won the First Division title with a record number of points and the following year was briefly called upon to manage the England under-21 team. He was dismissed as Sunderland manager in October 2002, but returned to management with Leeds United in March 2003.

After staving off relegation in his first months in charge, Reid was awarded the job on a permanent basis. But amid the serious financial crisis engulfing Elland Road, Reid struggled to maintain results in the first months of 2003/04 and was sacked. There followed an eight-month spell in charge of Coventry City, which proved fruitless. In September

2008, Reid was the surprise choice to take charge of the Thai national team.

THROUGH this lengthy playing and managerial career it has always been Reid's insatiable hunger for success that has driven him forward – often in the face of adversity. While an Everton player this was, perhaps, best expressed on two occasions during the summer of 1986. The first incident followed Everton's FA Cup Final defeat to Liverpool when Reid was so gripped with disappointment that he refused to take his place on the open-topped bus shared by the two teams. The second came after England had lost to Argentina in the World Cup quarter-final; in his diary of the season, Everton Winter, Mexican Summer, Reid simply recorded: 'We showed them too much respect.' It wasn't that he was a bad loser, he simply wanted to win. 'After all,' he once said, 'it's only the winning that counts.'

Season	League		FA Cup		League Cup		Other		Total	
	App	Goals	App	Goals	App	Goals	App	Goals	App	Goals
1982/83	7	0	3	0	0	0	-	-	10	0
1983/84	34 (1)	2	8	1	9 (1)	1	-	-	51 (2)	4
1984/85	36	2	7	1	4	0	10	1	57	4
1985/86	15	1	5	0	0	0	2	0	22	1
1986/87	15 (1)	1	2	0	0	0	0	0	17 (1)	1
1987/88	32	1	8	1	6	0	2	0	48	2
1988/89	16 (2)	1	2	0	4 (1)	0	2	0	24 (3)	1
Total	**155 (4)**	**8**	**35**	**3**	**23 (2)**	**1**	**16**	**1**	**229 (6)**	**13**

Rennie, Alex

One of Everton's reserve custodians during Goodison's debut campaign

[FACTFILE]

BORN
1868
POSITION
Goalkeeper

Season	League		FA Cup		Total	
	App	Goals	App	Goals	App	Goals
1892/93	4	0	0	0	4	0
Total	**4**	**0**	**0**	**0**	**4**	**0**

Richardson, Kevin

Versatile midfielder who was an important component of the mid-1980s squad

Capable, versatile, committed, Kevin Richardson was a fine midfielder who progressed through Everton's ranks in the early 1980s and was an important member of the squad that reaped so much success in the middle of the decade. The blond Geordie was a popular member of the Everton dressing room – he was Graeme Sharp's best man when he got married – and is remembered fondly by Evertonians who witnessed the club's most successful period.

Greatly valued by his fellow professionals, there was nevertheless sometimes a sense that in supporter's affections he paled in the shadow of his more illustrious colleagues. Diminutive and mobile, hard-working yet lacking the élan that Kevin Sheedy brought to his favoured left-sided

> HE SCORED WHAT WOULD PROVE A DECISIVE GOAL IN EVERTON'S 1984 FIRST-LEG LEAGUE CUP SEMI-FINAL AGAINST ASTON VILLA

position, Richardson was an effective squad player but never quite looked like claiming an Everton shirt as his own. A dedicated, energetic player, a brisk tackler and accurate yet unspectacular passer of the ball, he filled in a number of roles across the Everton midfield with conviction and commitment.

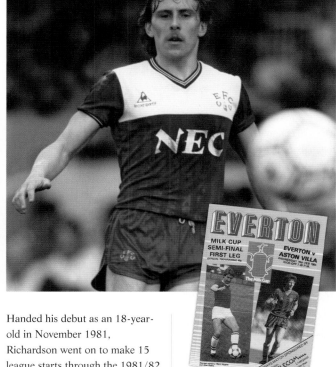

Handed his debut as an 18-year-old in November 1981, Richardson went on to make 15 league starts through the 1981/82 season, 24 the next campaign, and 25 in the 1983/84 season. Perhaps his most telling contributions came in cup competitions. He scored what would prove a decisive goal in Everton's 1984 first-leg League Cup semi-final against Aston Villa, and in the FA Cup Final later that year it was his cross that set up Graeme Sharp's Wembley opener.

With the arrival of Paul Bracewell in the summer of 1984 and the return of Kevin Sheedy from long-term injury soon after, Richardson's chances were restricted through the 1984/85 season. He was recalled to play in the European Cup Winners' Cup semi-final first leg at Bayern Munich, and gave a performance of high discipline and composure as Everton claimed a vital goalless draw. Yet come the second leg at Goodison, Sheedy had reclaimed his place.

Season	League		FA Cup		League Cup		Other		Total	
	App	Goals	App	Goals	App	Goals	App	Goals	App	Goals
1981/82	15 (3)	2	1	0	0	0	-	-	16 (3)	2
1982/83	24 (5)	3	2	0	1 (2)	0	-	-	27 (7)	3
1983/84	25 (3)	4	5	1	6 (1)	2	-	-	36 (4)	7
1984/85	14 (1)	4	0	0	1	0	3 (1)	0	18 (2)	4
1985/86	16 (3)	3	5	0	2	1	3 (1)	0	26 (4)	4
1986/87	1	0	0	0	0	0	1	0	2	0
Total	**95(15)**	**16**	**13**	**1**	**10 (3)**	**3**	**7 (2)**	**0**	**125(20)**	**20**

By the start of the 1986/87 season, Richardson had been part of the Everton squad for five years, but seemed no closer to holding down a permanent place of his own. In September 1986 he joined Watford for £225,000 and a year later signed for Arsenal. At Highbury he finally flourished and was part of the team that secured the 1988/89 League Championship in dramatic circumstances at Anfield. In 1990 he joined Real Sociedad, but returned to England a year later with Ron Atkinson's Aston Villa. Atkinson converted him into a defensive midfielder, and his performances in front of the Villa back four brought them close to the league title in 1993 and a year later, when Richardson was 31, he won a solitary England cap. Richardson subsequently followed Atkinson to Coventry City and continued to play in the top flight until his mid-thirties. He now works as a youth coach at Newcastle United.

[FACTFILE]

BORN
Newcastle, 4 December 1962
POSITION
Midfield
OTHER CLUBS
Watford (1986–87); Arsenal (1987–90); Real Sociedad (1990–91); Aston Villa (1991–95); Coventry City (1995–97); Southampton (1997–98); Barnsley (1998–2000); Blackpool (2000)
HONOURS
FA Cup 1984; League Championship 1984/85; 1 England cap (1994)

Rideout, Paul

Experienced centre forward who overcame a shaky start to become an FA Cup hero

Initially considered a journeyman on his £500,000 arrival on the eve of the 1992/93 season, few Evertonians could have envisaged then the importance Paul Rideout would have on the club's destiny over the following few years. In August 1992 the 28-year-old, who had had relatively short spells with Swindon Town, Aston Villa, Southampton, Notts County, Glasgow Rangers and Italian team Bari, was not the sort of player most fans hoped they would get.

Indeed the start of Rideout's Goodison career was punctuated by niggling injuries and inconsistency. He struggled to form a partnership with either Tony Cottee or Peter Beardsley and bore heavy criticism from a crowd frustrated at Everton's decline.

With the sale of Beardsley in summer 1993, he and Cottee were left to sink or swim as a partnership. Although they impressed only in flourishes as Everton escaped relegation by the skin of their teeth, Rideout's contribution should not be understated as Cottee enjoyed his most prolific league campaign at Goodison. Hard-working and with good ball control, he compensated for a conspicuous lack of pace with good reading of the game. Never a particularly clinical finisher, he possessed the knack – shared by all good centre

forwards – of being in the right place at the right time. He was capable in the air too, without ever being imperious. Cottee, who had played alongside such illustrious names as Graeme Sharp and Peter Beardsley, later cited Rideout as his favourite forward partner.

Mike Walker, however, broke up this burgeoning partnership, selling Cottee in August 1994. After four goals in the opening six games of the 1994/95 season, Rideout was also dropped by Walker and, unhappy at his treatment, demanded a transfer. Transfer rumours came to nothing before Walker's sacking six weeks later.

Restored to the squad for Joe Royle's first game in charge against Liverpool, Rideout was introduced as a half-time substitute with the scores goalless. He seemed to add new balance and fresh impetus to the Everton

attack. Just minutes after coming on he struck the inside of the Liverpool post – a mere warning shot. After Duncan Ferguson gave Everton the lead, Rideout added a second to seal a famous win. Thereafter galvanised, he was restored to the Everton attack, partnering either Ferguson or Graham Stuart to great effect. Although his contribution was often overlooked because of the controversial and charismatic Ferguson, it was Rideout who finished Everton's top league scorer; his 14 league goals included the one that secured Premier League survival against Ipswich Town in May.

The crowning moment of Rideout's career came eleven days later – 20 May 1995 – in the FA Cup Final. Leading the Everton forward line, after injury precluded Duncan Ferguson's involvement, in the 30th minute

he provided the game's decisive moment. A break initiated by Anders Limpar on the Everton right saw Matt Jackson cut into the Manchester United penalty area and square the ball to Stuart. When his shot crashed down off the United crossbar, Rideout held off Denis Irwin's challenge to head into the empty goal – the ball seeming to take an eternity to lift the net. Rideout later told this author that it was a difficult header to place, because the pace of the ball had diminished in the rebound. At first, he said, he wasn't even sure he had scored and had to check before embarking on his celebration.

The goal hero withdrew because of injury on 51 minutes and watched the rest of the game from the Everton bench. When victory was secured, he said: 'This has

been the biggest moment of my career. I can't tell you the feelings we had on the final whistle! It was nerve-racking because we were hanging on to 1-0 and it seemed like an age before the final whistle blew.'

His efforts were rewarded that summer with a new three-year contract. Persistent speculation linked Everton with new striking talent throughout the summer, but it was Rideout, his 31st birthday coming on the eve of the 1995/96 season, who partnered Ferguson on the opening day. He held his own until a sickening head injury against Sheffield Wednesday saw him lose his place. Thereafter, he was called upon mostly as a squad player, but his diminishing pace limited his impression.

Towards the end of the 1996/97 season, Rideout agreed a personally lucrative move to Huang Dao Vanguards in the Chinese league. But his time at Everton was not yet over. After Joe Royle's departure in March 1997, caretaker manager Dave Watson recalled Rideout from the Far East to boost his injury-depleted squad. Thrust into an unfamiliar defensive midfield role, he performed magnificently. His final appearance in an Everton shirt, in a 1-0 win over Tottenham that allayed most relegation concerns, was also possibly his best. Rideout controlled the midfield as a spirited Everton held on to a crucial lead.

RIDEOUT returned to China and there followed a spell in the MLS with Kansas City Wizards before a second term in China with Shenzhen Jianlibao. In 2000 Rideout, now aged 36, joined Tranmere Rovers for a fruitful spell. With his new team he returned to Goodison for an FA Cup fourth round tie in January 2001, playing an important part in Tranmere's 3-0 humiliation of Everton.

After retiring in May 2002, Rideout returned to Kansas, where he runs Wizards' extensive youth academy.

Season	League		FA Cup		League Cup		Other		Total	
	App	Goals	App	Goals	App	Goals	App	Goals	App	Goals
1992/93	17 (7)	3	1	0	4	2	-	-	22 (7)	5
1993/94	21 (3)	6	1	1	3	4	-		25(3)	11
1994/95	25 (4)	14	5	2	1 (1)	0	-		31 (5)	16
1995/96	19 (6)	6	1(1)	0	2	0	5	1	27 (7)	7
1996/97	4 (6)	0	0	0	1 (1)	1	-	-	5 (6)	1
Total	**86 (26)**	**29**	**9 (1)**	**3**	**11 (2)**	**7**	**5**	**1**	**111(29)**	**40**

Rigby, Arthur

Winger and inside forward whose career traversed one of Goodison's most dramatic eras

Season	League		FA Cup		Total	
	App	Goals	App	Goals	App	Goals
1929/30	25	7	2	0	27	7
1930/31	14	4	0	0	14	4
1931/32	3	0	0	0	3	0
Total	**42**	**11**	**2**	**0**	**44**	**11**

Rigsby, Bert

Inside left whose career was shortened by the First World War

Season	League App	League Goals	FA Cup App	FA Cup Goals	Total App	Total Goals
1919/20	14	5	0	0	14	5
Total	14	5	0	0	14	5

Rimmer, Neil

Home-grown midfielder who enjoyed a lengthy career with Wigan

Season	League App	League Goals	FA Cup App	FA Cup Goals	League Cup App	League Cup Goals	Other App	Other Goals	Total App	Total Goals
1984/85	1	0	0	0	0	0	0	0	1	0
Total	1	0	0	0	0	0	0	0	1	0

Rimmer, Stuart

Home-grown forward who became Chester City's record goalscorer

Season	League App	League Goals	FA Cup App	FA Cup Goals	League Cup App	League Cup Goals	Total App	Total Goals
1981/82	2	0	0	0	0	0	2	0
1982/83	0	0	0	0	0	0	0	0
1983/84	1	0	0	0	0	0	1	0
Total	3	0	0	0	0	0	3	0

Ring, Tommy

Sublime winger whose career was cut short by injury

Tommy Ring's Everton career stretched for only the briefest of periods, but his mesmerising talents left a deep impression upon Evertonians.

The Scottish international left winger was approaching his 30th birthday when Johnny Carey made him an £8000 signing in January 1960. Although Ring had spent all of his career with Scottish minnows Clyde, it was one distinguished by remarkable success. Twice he lifted the Scottish Second Division title, but even more remarkably Clyde also twice won the Scottish FA Cup during this period, in 1955 – when Ring struck the replay winner against Celtic – and again in 1958. His signing was designed to add fresh impetus to a team hovering perilously close to the relegation zone. The impact was immediate and remarkable. Everton beat Nottingham Forest 6-1 on his debut and the Daily Post's Horace Yates wrote: 'If one signing, that of Tommy Ring from Clyde, can convert a team of non scorers in four successive matches into a side which can take six goals, with at least as many opportunities wasted in one game, what sort of transformation can be expected when Johnny Carey completes the first instalment in his reconstruction programme with the two or three captures which are necessary.'

RING – along with fellow new signing Roy Vernon – helped exact a remarkable transformation in fortunes: Everton climbed from 20th to 16th and safety. Invariably the winger was an instant crowd favourite, his dazzling runs and change of pace being his most potent weapon. 'Ring is the most complete outside left I have seen at Goodison in a royal blue jersey since Eglington's brightest days,' wrote Yates. 'He beats an opponent effortlessly, inside or outside, and having done that centres the ball with an accuracy which is an open scoring invitation to forwards with any competence for their job.' And yet as Everton stood on the verge of a golden era Ring's career was brought to an untimely end. In October 1960, a collision with the Chelsea goalkeeper Reg Matthews resulted in a broken leg. The break healed, but Ring never returned to top-flight football, playing out his career in a brief spell with Barnsley.

Season	League		FA Cup		Total	
	App	Goals	App	Goals	App	Goals
1959/60	16	2	0	0	16	2
1960/61	11	4	0	0	11	4
Total	**27**	**6**	**0**	**0**	**27**	**6**

[FACTFILE]

BORN
Glasgow, 8 August 1930
DIED
5 October 1997
POSITION
Left winger
OTHER CLUBS
Clyde (1950–60)
Barnsley (1961–63)
HONOURS
12 Scotland caps
(2 goals) (1953–57)

Rioch, Bruce

Widely travelled Scotland international signed in Billy Bingham's last days

Season	League		FA Cup		League Cup		Total	
	App	Goals	App	Goals	App	Goals	App	Goals
1976/77	22	2	7	1	0	0	29	3
1977/78	8	1	0	0	2	0	10	1
Total	**30**	**3**	**7**	**1**	**2**	**0**	**39**	**4**

[FACTFILE]

BORN
Aldershot, 6 September 1947
POSITION
Midfielder
OTHER CLUBS AS PLAYER
Luton Town (1964-69), Aston Villa (1969-74), Derby County (1974-76 & 1977-79), Birmingham City (loan) (1978), Sheffield United (loan) (1979), Seattle Sounders (1980-81), Torquay United (player manager from 1982) (1981-84)
AS MANAGER
F.C. Seattle (1985), Middlesbrough (1986-90), Millwall (1990-92), Bolton Wanderers (1992-95), Arsenal (1995-96), Norwich City (1998-2000), Wigan Athletic (2000-01), Odense Boldklub (2005-07), Aalborg (2008)
HONOURS
24 Scotland caps (1975-78) (6 goals)

Roberts

Unknown centre half who made a solitary appearance in Everton's debut league season

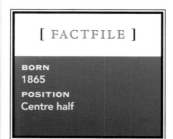

[FACTFILE]

BORN
1865
POSITION
Centre half

Season	League		FA Cup		Total	
	App	Goals	App	Goals	App	Goals
1888/89	1	0	-	-	1	0
Total	1	0	-	-	1	0

Roberts, James

Welsh international winger whose Everton career was limited to a solitary appearance

[FACTFILE]

BORN
Mold, 7 January 1891
POSITION
Outside left
OTHER CLUBS
Mold Villa;
Mold Town; Wrexham;
Crewe Alexandra (1921);
Tranmere Rovers (1921);
Wrexham (1922);
Mold Town
HONOURS
2 Wales caps (1 goal) (1913)

Season	League		FA Cup		Total	
	App	Goals	App	Goals	App	Goals
1914/15	1	0	0	0	1	0
Total	1	0	0	0	1	0

Robertson, Hope

Half back whose career spanned the Anfield and Goodison eras

[FACTFILE]

BORN
Whiteinch, 17 January 1868
POSITION
Half back
OTHER CLUBS
Minerva; Partick Thistle;
Woolwich Arsenal; Bootle
(1892);
Walsall Town Swifts (1894)

Season	League		FA Cup		Total	
	App	Goals	App	Goals	App	Goals
1890/91	3	1	1	0	4	1
1891/92	20	0	1	0	21	0
1892/93	7	0	0	0	7	0
Total	30	1	2	0	32	1

Robertson, John Tait 'Jack'

Scottish international left half who was another of Dumbarton's great sons

[FACTFILE]

BORN
Dumbarton,
25 February 1877
DIED
1935
POSITION
Left half
OTHER CLUBS
Morton; Southampton;
Glasgow Rangers; Chelsea
(1905–06);
Glossop (1906–08)
HONOURS
16 Scotland caps
(3 goals) (1898–1905)

Season	League		FA Cup		Total	
	App	Goals	App	Goals	App	Goals
1897/98	26	1	5	0	31	1
Total	26	1	5	0	31	1

Robertson, Tom

Little-known-about centre half of the mid-1890s

Season	League		FA Cup		Total	
	App	Goals	App	Goals	App	Goals
1895/96	1	0	0	0	1	0
1896/97	3	0	0	0	4	0
Total	**4**	**0**	**1**	**0**	**5**	**0**

[FACTFILE]

BORN
Unknown
POSITION
Centre half

Robinson, Alfred

Inside forward limited to a single Everton outing

Season	League		FA Cup		Total	
	App	Goals	App	Goals	App	Goals
1919/20	1	0	0	0	1	0
Total	**1**	**0**	**0**	**0**	**1**	**0**

[FACTFILE]

BORN
Birkenhead,
30 January 1898
POSITION
Inside forward
OTHER CLUBS
Tranmere Rovers (1921–22);
Wallasey United

Robinson, Billy

Half back who slipped out of league football on leaving Goodison

Season	League		FA Cup		Total	
	App	Goals	App	Goals	App	Goals
1897/98	7	0	0	0	7	0
Total	**7**	**0**	**0**	**0**	**7**	**0**

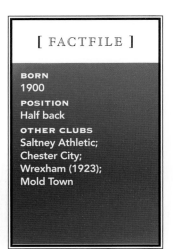

[FACTFILE]

BORN
1900
POSITION
Half back
OTHER CLUBS
Saltney Athletic;
Chester City;
Wrexham (1923);
Mold Town

Robinson, Neil

Local defender who followed his own unique path

Free-thinking full back Neil Robinson sat on the fringes of the Everton team through the mid-1970s and provided solid cover for Mick Bernard and Terry Darracott during this period. Called upon to deputise in the ill-fated League Cup semi-final in one of his very first outings for the club, the 19-year-old let nobody down.

Alas, competition for places meant he was never able to make a first-team place his own and in October 1979 a £70,000 fee took him to John Toshack's Swansea City. His untapped potential was realised at the Vetch Field and he played an important role in the Welsh club's early-1980s ascent.

ROBINSON was part of a family of free-thinkers, and his older brother is the famous

educationalist Sir Ken Robinson. Always one to follow his own path, Neil turned vegetarian as a young teenager and became a vegan after joining Swansea City in 1980. Although the Blackburn forward Jason Roberts later followed this trend, Robinson is credited with being the first modern professional to follow such a rigorous diet.

'I can safely say that my diet was never a limiting factor during my training or playing. In fact I was almost always one of the fittest players at every club I played at,' he told the summer 2006 issue of The Vegan magazine.

'I became a vegetarian at 13 years of age because I was disgusted by the cruelty to animals just for human consumption and became vegan after finally coming to my senses and realising how cruel the dairy industry was to animals. I fully believe that veganism is the most compassionate and only way for vegans to live.'

Season	League		FA Cup		League Cup		Europe		Total	
	App	Goals	App	Goals	App	Goals	App	Goals	App	Goals
1975/76	1	0	0	0	0	0	0	0	1	0
1976/77	4	0	1	0	2	0	-	-	7	0
1977/78	4	1	0	0	0 (1)	0	-	-	4 (1)	1
1978/79	4 (3)	0	0	0	1	0	-	-	5 (3)	0
Total	**13 (3)**	**1**	**1**	**0**	**3 (1)**	**0**	**0**	**0**	**17 (4)**	**1**

[FACTFILE]

BORN
Liverpool, 20 April 1957
POSITION
Full back
OTHER CLUBS
Swansea City (1979–84);
Grimsby Town (1984–88);
Darlington (1988–89)

Robson, Tom

Young half back whose only action came during Everton's disastrous relegation season

Season	League		FA Cup		Total	
	App	Goals	App	Goals	App	Goals
1919/20	1	0	0	0	1	0
Total	**1**	**0**	**0**	**0**	**1**	**0**

[FACTFILE]

BORN
Morpeth, 1909
POSITION
Half back
OTHER CLUBS
Blyth Spartans;
Sheffield Wednesday
(1930–31);
Yeovil and Peters United;
Northampton Town
(1934–37);
Kettering Town

Roche, William

Winger who made just a single league outing

Season	League		FA Cup		Total	
	App	Goals	App	Goals	App	Goals
1901/02	1	0	0	0	1	0
Total	1	0	0	0	1	0

[FACTFILE]

BORN
1879
POSITION
Outside right

Rodrigo, Juliano

Brazilian midfielder whose Goodison hopes were cut short by serious injury

Season	League		FA Cup		League Cup		Total	
	App	Goals	App	Goals	App	Goals	App	Goals
2002/03	0 (4)	0	0	0	0	0	0 (4)	0
Total	0 (4)	0	0	0	0	0	0 (4)	0

[FACTFILE]

BORN
Santos, Brazil,
7 August 1976
POSITION
Midfield
OTHER CLUBS
Guarani (1997);
Gama (1998);
Botafogo (1999–2003);
Atletico Mineiro
(loan, 2002);
Corinthians (2004);
Juventude (2005);
Atletico Paranaense (2005);
Vasco da Gama (2005);
Boavista (2006–07);
Parana (2007);
Boavista (2008);
Fortaleza (2008)

Rodwell, Jack

Elegant home-grown England international midfielder for whom there are high hopes

Five days before Christmas 2007, Everton's stylish home-grown centre half turned midfielder Jack Rodwell became – aged 16 years and 284 days – the youngest Everton player to appear in a European match. The progress was scarcely surprising for those who followed the progress of the club's youth teams. The tall, athletic defensive-minded player had been talked about in excited whispers for years. Indeed the first signs from the boyhood Blue appeared excellent: a powerful, stylish player possessing something of the swagger of Steven Gerrard.

Eased into the Everton team over the following six months, he was a surprise starter on the opening day of the 2008/09 season, making 25 appearances – half of them starts – over the subsequent campaign. He brought elegance and natural composure to the Everton team, offering glimpses of his potential when he chose to break free of his shackles and burst forward.

Speaking to this author in September 2009, David Moyes described him as 'an elegant midfield player'. The Everton manager said: 'He can run, he's quick, he's good on the ball.

What he needs is time and maturity and that will make him a very good player ... He's got things he needs to work on but I think a lot of them will come with maturity and with games. He's a really level-headed boy, he wants to learn, and because of that we've got high hopes that he'll continue to develop.'

RODWELL burst into national consciousness when he scored a fine goal to round off a famous 3-1 win over Manchester United at Goodison in February 2010. Introduced as a late substitute he applied a brilliant coup de grâce in the last minute. Taking a short pass from Arteta near the centre circle, the teenager marched through a retreating defence, finding space for himself until he was one on one with Van der Sar. His low finish was emphatic, the Everton fans ecstatic.

Steady progress followed over the next two years, although there were some grumbles that Rodwell was still to fully impose himself on the Everton team. By the time of his 21st birthday he had made more than 100 Everton appearances and was an England international, having also played at every youth level for his country.

Moyes had spoken to me in 2009 of his hopes that Rodwell would break into the international set-up following the 2010 World Cup. His international debut came as a second-half substitute against Spain at Wembley in November 2011. Rodwell immediately caught the eye as England overcame their opponents 1-0.

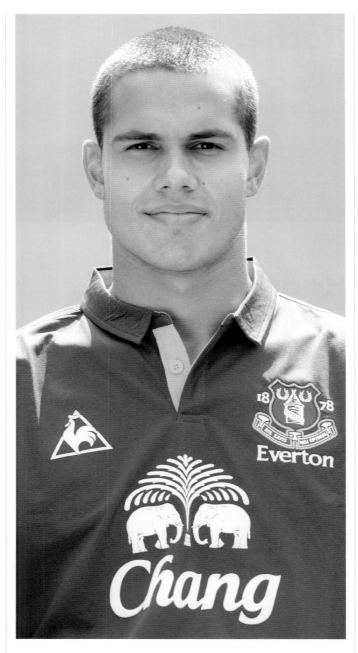

Alas, the midfielder's 2011/12 season was cut short by a recurrent hamstring injury. It cost the midfielder a place in the England squad for the 2012 European Championships or at the very least the Great Britain Olympic team, for whom he had modelled the kit. Hopes, nevertheless, remained high that a rest will see him realise his potential. 'David Moyes will doubtless hate any hysteria over one of his players,' wrote the admiring Winter, 'but all at Goodison should take pride from the prominence of a home-grown product ... Yet he never seized a game until this season. Moyes has clearly challenged him to produce more. Now he is looking good in an Everton shirt, in an England shirt, even an Olympic shirt.'

But a week before the start of the 2012/13 season, Rodwell was a surprise departure from Goodison after a £12 million bid – potentially rising by another £6m depending on the move's success – from Manchester City was accepted. Gloomy resignation greeted the transfer as it was almost accepted by the club's support that City's insidious petro-billions could buy anybody, while Everton had to sell in order to survive.

'The suspicion for some of an Evertonian persuasion was that Rodwell was "too much Birkdale and not enough Kirkdale",' wrote the elegant hand of the Daily Telegraph's Henry Winter. 'Not now. There's a bit of bite in his game. Rodwell's on the rise. One impressive cameo hardly makes a career, and this was only a debut in a friendly, but there were undeniable signs during his enterprising 33-minute shift for England against Spain that Rodwell may mature into a midfielder of genuine substance.'

> [FACTFILE]
>
> **BORN**
> Southport, 11 March 1991
> **POSITION**
> Midfielder
> **HONOURS**
> 2 England caps (2011–)

HIS LOW FINISH WAS EMPHATIC, THE EVERTON FANS ECSTATIC

Season	League		FA Cup		League Cup		Europe		Total	
	App	Goals	App	Goals	App	Goals	App	Goals	App	Goals
2007/08	0 (2)	0	0	0	0	0	0 (1)	0	0 (3)	0
2008/09	9 (10)	0	2 (3)	1	1	0	0	0	12 (13)	1
2009/10	17 (9)	2	0	0	2	0	6 (2)	2	25 (11)	4
2010/11	14 (10)	0	2 (1)	0	1	1	-	-	17 (11)	1
2011/12	11 (3)	2	0	0	3	0	-	-	14 (3)	2
Total	**51 (34)**	**4**	**4 (4)**	**1**	**7**	**1**	**6 (3)**	**2**	**68 (41)**	**8**

Rooney, Wayne

World-class prodigy who slipped away amid financial disarray

At the start of the 21st century excited whispers emanated from Everton's academy of an outstanding prospect, touched by genius, who boasted strength, élan, speed and fabulous technical ability. Periodically such talk emerges but comes to nothing: the prodigy's team-mates catch up physically; his skill set levels out; or he discovers other distractions. But when Evertonians saw Wayne Rooney, a forward who was barely 16 and still at school, carry his team-mates to the 2002 FA Youth Cup Final they could see straight away that he was the real deal. Better still, he was a born-and-blue Evertonian who, after scoring in one youth team game, revealed a T-shirt that said, 'Once a blue, always a blue'.

An unused substitute for a game at Southampton at the tail-end of the 2001/02 season, Rooney made his full debut on the opening day of the 2002/03 season against Tottenham at Goodison. By later standards he had a quiet game, but he set up Mark Pembridge for Everton's opener. His first goals came six weeks later, late in a League Cup tie at Wrexham.

> 'ROONEY WAS THE MOST EXCITING ENGLISH TALENT SINCE PAUL GASCOIGNE IN THE 1980S'

On 19 October 2002, reigning Premiership Champions Arsenal came to Goodison. Top of the table and unbeaten in their 29 previous league matches, their manager Arsène Wenger had, leading up to the game, spoken of the possibility of Arsenal going through the season unbeaten – a feat unparalleled in the modern English game. It was a measure of just how good his side were that nobody mocked his temerity. Rooney – still a week shy of his 17th birthday – entered as an 80th-minute substitute, the game tightly balanced at 1-1. In the final minute of normal time a high awkward pass from Gravesen was played to Rooney 35 yards from goal. His first touch was immaculate; he turned instantaneously and hit a fearsome swerving shot that dipped over Seaman and rebounded off the Park End crossbar to nestle in the back of the net. Goodison exploded. It was one of those 'I was there' moments – like Dean's 60th or Graeme Sharp's derby volley – that pass but once every generation.

Stocky, adroit, the possessor of an explosive turn of pace and – as the whole world saw against Arsenal – one of the most fearsome shots in football, Rooney was the most exciting English talent since Paul Gascoigne in the 1980s. He played entirely without fear and was as instinctive as he was brilliant. 'He's quick, skilful, strong and nasty, something I hope he doesn't lose,' said David Unsworth. 'It's hard not to

get excited about how far he might go.' In an era in which professional footballers had become divorced from their public, Rooney was also – initially, at least – of the people, living out his dream of playing for the club he adored. When newspaper reporters turned up on his doorstep in the wake of his Arsenal goal, they photographed an Everton pennant hanging from the window of his parents' modest Croxteth home.

THERE WERE more sublime moments to come: a fiercely struck winner at Leeds that brought Everton their first Elland Road victory in 51 years; another winner at Blackburn; a mesmerising performance against Bolton that astonishingly yielded no goals. In February 2003, he became England's youngest debutant when, aged 17 years 3 months, he appeared against Australia. His form for Everton brought his club within touching distance of European qualification for the first time in eight years.

Everybody wanted a piece of Rooney and commercial endorsements rolled in. This, however, brought with it its own

problems. His messy defection from Liverpool-based agent Peter McIntosh to Paul Stretford's Proactive Sport Management was tarred by allegations of underworld involvement. Rooney retained his image rights as part of his first professional contract, which he sold to Stretford for a nominal sum. Stretford formed a separate company, allowing him to negotiate with other sponsors such as Ford, Coca-Cola and Pringles. Barely out of school, Rooney had a portfolio of endorsements worth as much as £10million.

Moyes seemed unimpressed by the teenager's burgeoning stardom, and as the 2003/04 season kicked off cracks in their relationship started to show. Rooney started the season injured, scored in Everton's third game against Charlton, then not again until mid-December. Often he started from the bench and was alternately petulant or too eager to please when introduced. There were some great performances, however, notably when he came on as a half-time substitute when

Everton faced Manchester United at Goodison in February 2004. Trailing 3-0, Rooney put in a dazzling performance and transformed the game, inspiring Everton to pull level – although in a twist that typified their season, they fell to a last-minute United winner.

EVERTON finished the season just a place clear of relegation, their tally of points only 39 – the lowest since 1889. In most other seasons such a measly haul would have merited relegation. The season's nadir came on its final day, when Everton fell to a 5-1 defeat against Manchester City – who started the day beneath them.

At the 2004 European Championships in Portugal, Rooney was England's talisman and most outstanding player before he succumbed to injury in the quarter-final. Without him, England limped out on penalties.

Back home a new five-year contract offer promised to make Rooney the most highly paid player in Everton's history. David Moyes spoke of making Rooney Everton's captain and building a team around him. But off the field the club were in disarray. There was talk of Moyes losing the dressing room. There was no money for new signings. The club's new chief executive walked out after six weeks. A boardroom split between Bill Kenwright and Paul Gregg, Everton's other major shareholder, was played out messily before the press. Kenwright spoke of Rooney as a £50million player, but unless he signed the contract he could leave for a fee decided by tribunal – likely to be substantially lower – two years later.

All year rumours persisted that Rooney would be sold to save Everton's future. As the contract remained unsigned speculation intensified. It was suggested his head had been turned by his agent and his new England colleagues. Alex Ferguson was spotted playing golf with Stretford. Then an extraordinary story broke in which it was revealed Rooney had used local prostitutes. Suddenly a footballing dilemma had become a personal crisis. Rooney met Moyes and told him he wished to leave Everton. A £20million bid from Newcastle was rejected, but by the end of August 2004 he was a £27million Manchester United player.

THE ANGER of Evertonians, many of whom thought he had engineered the move, was palpable. The day he joined United something of football's magic seemed to fade. One fan summed up the mood, daubing the walls of Gwladys Street: 'HE COULD HAVE BEEN A GOD, BUT CHOSE TO BE A DEVIL'.

Invariably Rooney ran the gamut of hatred whenever he returned to Everton, notably for an FA Cup fifth round tie in February 2005, which afterwards spilled over into violence between Everton and United fans. Rooney has since inflamed the situation by kissing his United badge on his return. He claimed in his autobiography that his feelings towards Everton had 'changed' in view of his treatment by Evertonians, and yet he has also hinted in the press that his affection for the club has not entirely died.

At Old Trafford Rooney lived up to his potential and has become

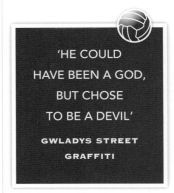

'HE COULD HAVE BEEN A GOD, BUT CHOSE TO BE A DEVIL'

GWLADYS STREET GRAFFITI

one of the most revered and feared footballers in the world. In 2005 and 2006 he was named PFA Young Player of the Year. In 2007 he won the first of a hat-trick of Premier League titles, and in 2008 was part of the United teams that won the Champions League and World Club Cup. For England he goes from strength to strength. For United his trophy cabinet continues to swell.

[FACTFILE]

BORN
Liverpool, 24 March 1985
POSITION
Forward
OTHER CLUB
Manchester United (2004–)
HONOURS
PFA Young Player of the Year (2005, 2006);
76 England caps (29 goals) (2003–)

Season	League		FA Cup		League Cup		Total	
	App	Goals	App	Goals	App	Goals	App	Goals
2002/03	14 (19)	6	1	0	2 (1)	2	17 (20)	8
2003/04	26 (8)	9	3	0	2 (1)	0	31 (9)	9
Total	**40 (27)**	**15**	**4**	**0**	**4 (2)**	**2**	**48 (29)**	**17**

Roose, Leigh Richmond 'Dick'

Illustrious goalkeeper whose form almost inspired Everton to the league title

Leigh Roose's Everton career lasted just months, but as one of the finest and most idiosyncratic players of his era – his goalkeeping in this short period very nearly brought Everton their second league title – his story is worth closer scrutiny.

A physically imposing figure, he was born in Holt, North Wales, to a middle-class family in 1877. His father was a Presbyterian minister and friend of the writer H.G. Wells. Roose studied at Aberystwyth University and played for a succession of amateur clubs, where he earned a reputation as one of the game's finest custodians. In 1900 he won the first of 24 Wales caps, and a year later made his league bow – now in his mid-twenties – with Stoke City.

His form in the Potteries earned him many plaudits. The Bristol Times described being impressed by 'his vivacity, his boldness, his knowledge of men and things'. He was, they wrote, 'a clever man undoubtedly, but entirely unrestrained in word or action'.

Of his playing style, the newspaper recorded: 'He rarely stands listlessly by the goalpost even when the ball is at the other end of the enclosure, but is ever following the play keenly and closely. Directly his charge is threatened, he is on the move. He thinks nothing of dashing 10 or 15 yards, even when his backs have as good a chance of clearing as he makes for himself. He will

rush along the touchline, field the ball and get in a kick too, to keep the game going briskly. Equally daring and unorthodox are his methods of dealing with strong shots. He is not a model custodian by all means. He would not be L.R. Roose if he was.'

But, like all great goalkeepers, Roose was also an unashamed eccentric. Despite playing in the Midlands he continued to live in London, living the life of a playboy and using his 'expenses' as an amateur footballer help fund his lifestyle. Stories about his quirks abound. There was the time he missed the train to a match and so commandeered a private charter train – as was available at the start of the 20th century – at enormous cost and sent the bill to the club. He feigned injury before matches to give opponents a false sense of security. He always wore dirty kit, but no one knew why.

Always one to forgo convention, in 1904, when seemingly at the peak of his career, Roose announced he was quitting football to train as a doctor. He left Stoke to study at Kings College, London, but soon missed the great game.

In November 1904 Everton were beset by a goalkeeping crisis. Billy Scott was absent with a shoulder injury, while his deputy George Kitchen was out with flu. On 17 November, Everton made an approach and Roose agreed to help out. 'He is one of the finest, if not the finest, goalkeepers in the land,' Scott told journalists. 'At least I know my colleagues are in the best of hands. Leigh Richmond Roose won't let them down.'

But Roose did just that, dropping a cross that led to the only goal of the game on his debut at home to table-topping Sunderland. The result left Everton ambling in mid-table. Lesser figures may have withered, but not Roose.

A week later he played in a 4-1 win over former club Stoke, saving a penalty from Frank Whitehead. It proved a turning point in Everton's season. Everton won 12 and drew three of their next 16 games and by late January were top of the table. Their form saw them reach the semi-finals of the FA Cup too, in which they were unfortunate to lose to Aston Villa in a replay. Roose's form was so outstanding that he kept both Scott and Kitchen out of the team.

But the Cup runs and earlier postponements ultimately proved a distraction. It left Everton needing to play their final four league games in nine days, including an infamously rearranged match against Woolwich Arsenal. Everton lost that, having travelled to London straight from the North-west where they had played Manchester City the previous day.

Afterwards Roose had a bust up with Will Cuff, questioning the wisdom of playing so many important games so close together. He certainly had a point, but Cuff didn't like his authority challenged and so restored Billy Scott to the line-up for the final game of the season. Roose, who had never been dropped before, refused to travel with his team-mates to the match and that was to prove the end of his Everton career. Although he later wrote a letter of apology to Cuff, he received no reply.

Everton's loss was the gain of numerous other clubs, including Aston Villa, Woolwich Arsenal and Sunderland. He continued to play for his country and live the high life in London – in 1905 the Daily Mail listed him as the city's second most eligible bachelor, after the cricketer Jack Hobbs – all the while fulfilling the maxim that goalkeepers are somehow different.

Season	League		FA Cup		Total	
	App	Goals	App	Goals	App	Goals
1904/05	18	0	6	0	24	0
Total	18	0	6	0	24	0

HE ALWAYS WORE DIRTY KIT, BUT NO ONE KNEW WHY

Ross, Nick

Victorian superstar who captained Everton through their first league campaign

Considered one of the greatest players of football's Victorian era, Nick Ross captained Everton through the inaugural Football League season. His time at Goodison was brief and seemingly unhappy, but he is worthy of recognition as one of football's first genuine legends.

Born in Edinburgh, Ross was part of the first generation of Scots to play football and started out aged 12 with Edinburgh Rovers, one of the country's first teams. Later he played for Hibernian and Heart of Midlothian, whom he captained aged 20.

Ross came to England in 1883 as part of Preston manager William Suddell's Scottish recruitment drive, which saw many of the best players drawn to England by the promise of financial incentives. These were, of course, illegal until the Football Association gave in to professionalism in 1885. But Preston's willingness to make under-the-table payments gave them a head start, allowing them to assemble the best team in the land.

Ross's greatness was immediately apparent. 'If one were asked to name three of the greatest

full-backs that ever graced the Association game, one would be compelled to include the late Nicholas J. Ross as one of the illustrious three,' wrote William Gibson and Alfred Pickford in 1906. 'Nick Ross could kick artistically – and otherwise; he could "place" the ball beautifully to his comrades; he could take care of himself in a charge; he rarely came second best out of a scrimmage, but it was not all nor any of these qualities that made him a man in a million. Ross was probably the best full-back that ever lived, [not] because he knew everything that a back ought to know, but because he had the faculty of winning matches. He possessed the indefinable something, that magic quality which, for lack of a better word, we call genius.'

OPPOSING wingers seemed to fall apart when faced by Ross. If they tried to go around him they would lose the ball or be forced into touch. If they tried to pass to another player, Ross would anticipate the movement and intercept. He was neither tall nor particularly thin, but seemed a dapper, elegant figure on the field. He was aware of his abilities, but never egotistical. 'He was supposed to play back – and he did – but as a matter of fact he played practically everywhere,' wrote Gibson and Pickford. 'He was quick to discern not only the weakness of his own side, but also the weaknesses of his opponents … In actual play … he seemed

like a man possessed, yet in spite of all his fire, all his dash, all his activity, he always remained cool in an emergency, collected in a scrimmage, calm in the wild whirl that often sends twenty-two strenuous men wild with excitement.'

Ross joined Everton on the eve of the inaugural Football League season in 1888. He represented a fine bargain, with the club's management committee paying just £17 10/- to secure his services – which equated to his summer wages at Preston. He was paid £10 per month – a substantial amount at a time when Everton's annual turnover was only £2251 – but such incentives were necessary to lure one of the finest players of the era.

Everton, however, were no Preston and in some respects had represented a surprise addition to the Football League. Throughout this debut league season they struggled to find their rhythm and Ross, who also filled in as an auxiliary centre forward on occasion, at times seemed like a luxury.

THERE was also a sense that Ross, as captain, was treated badly by Everton's management committee. A letter to the Liverpool Courier in February 1889 recalled an incident prior to the game against West Bromwich Albion at Anfield.

The opposing captain complained about the condition of the ball and asked Ross to request a new one, but when he did he was publicly rebuked by a member of the committee. 'Such treatment of a first-class player is sufficient

'In other positions on the field, success is dependent on combined effort and the dovetailing of one player's work with another,' he once wrote. 'With the goalkeeper, it is a different matter entirely. He has to fill a position in which the principle is forced upon him that it is good for a man to be alone.'

On the outbreak of war in 1914, Roose signed up to fight for the British Army. He was promoted to lance corporal and won the Military Medal for bravery, but never returned to Britain, having perished in the bloodbath on the Somme. It was a short but eventful life and Everton have encountered the services of few others like him.

Further reading:
VIGNES, SPENCER,
Lost In France: The Remarkable Life And Death Of Leigh Richmond Roose, Football's First Playboy, Stadia (2007)

[FACTFILE]

BORN
Holt, North Wales, 27 November 1877
DIED
7 October 1916
POSITION
Goalkeeper
OTHER CLUBS
Stoke City (1901–04 & 1905–07); Sunderland (1908–10); Celtic (1910); Port Vale (1910); Huddersfield Town (1910–11); Aston Villa (1911); Woolwich Arsenal (1911–12)
HONOURS
24 Wales caps (1900–11)

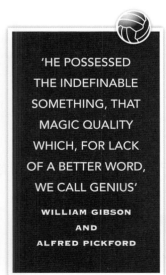

'HE POSSESSED THE INDEFINABLE SOMETHING, THAT MAGIC QUALITY WHICH, FOR LACK OF A BETTER WORD, WE CALL GENIUS'

WILLIAM GIBSON
AND
ALFRED PICKFORD

'threats and foul abuse' according to the Everton executive. As the season drew to a disappointing conclusion they were forced to issue a public statement of confidence in their star player and declared anyone guilty of 'hooting or mobbing' players and referees to be 'enemies' of the club.

ROSS, however, had evidently had enough of Everton's fickle fans and at the end of the season rejoined Preston. He had missed their 'Invincibles' season when they won the League and FA Cup double without losing a game, but trophies were not far away. Indeed if it was revenge he sought after his unhappy year at Anfield, he soon got it as the Lilywhites pipped his former club to the 1889/90 title by just two points. Twice in the subsequent two seasons he finished a league runner-up. In March 1893 Everton were to end Preston's FA Cup ambitions, beating them in the semi-final after two replays.

This was to be Nick Ross's last stab at glory. The following year he took ill with tuberculosis – an often lethal condition in the Victorian era – and

died, aged just 31. 'He had the dual temperament of fire and water,' recalled Gibson and Pickford. 'His flame never danced and flickered; it glowed steadily and lit up all the scene.'

[FACTFILE]

BORN
Edinburgh, 6 December 1892
DIED
1894
POSITION
Full back
OTHER CLUBS
Hibernian;
Heart of Midlothian;
Preston North End
(1883–88 & 1889–1894)

to cause him to be most careful in giving him content to play for the Everton club,' noted the correspondent.

Worse still for Ross, he attracted the opprobrium of some 'so-called supporters' and was subjected to

Season	League		FA Cup		Total	
	App	Goals	App	Goals	App	Goals
1888/89	19	5	-	-	19	5
Total	19	5	-	-	19	5

Ross, Trevor

Young midfielder who struggled to live up to his high price tag

For a player who made nearly 150 appearances over a six-year spell at Goodison, Trevor Ross made a remarkably small dent in Evertonians' consciousness. A former England schoolboy international who qualified to appear for Scotland under-21s, Trevor Ross was signed from Arsenal in November 1977 for a hefty £170,000. The midfielder was intended to add some defensive solidity to a midfield shorn of Bruce Rioch, who had recently left to rejoin Derby County.

Certainly the early signs were good; Everton finished his first season in third place, and came fourth the next year, having topped the table as late as February. However, for all the industry and aggression he

Season	League		FA Cup		League Cup		Europe		Total	
	App	Goals	App	Goals	App	Goals	App	Goals	App	Goals
1977/78	18 (2)	4	2	1	0	0	-	-	20 (2)	5
1978/79	26 (1)	6	1	0	2 (1)	0	4	1	33 (2)	7
1979/80	31 (1)	3	3	1	4	0	1	0	39 (1)	4
1980/81	17	2	6	1	0	0	-	-	23	3
1981/82	27 (1)	1	1	0	2	0	-	-	30 (1)	1
1982/83	1 (1)	0	0	0	0	0	-	-	1 (1)	0
Total	120(6)	16	13	3	8 (1)	0	5	1	146 (7)	20

brought to the right of Everton's midfield, there was a lack of élan and guile that might have significantly improved the team. He was troubled by inconsistency too, particularly after Everton began to wane under Gordon Lee's charge.

After an unhappy 1979/80 season Ross requested a transfer, but no one came in for him and he instead spent the first half of the 1980/81 season on the sidelines. Eventually he repaired his differences with Lee and returned to the team, with promises of a fresh start.

'I didn't see any future for myself here,' he told the match-day programme in January 1981. 'I was down and depressed but I was fortunate to have the encouragement of [reserve team coach] Colin Harvey. He nagged at me and told me to keep my head up.' His enthusiasm, he said, had returned and 'slowly everything slipped back into place. I hope that's how it stays from now onwards.'

Despite Lee's demise at the end of the season and the frenetic transfer activity of his successor Howard Kendall that summer,

Ross remained an Everton player and was a regular on the left of midfield through the 1981/82 season. But as Kendall started to shape his own team during 1982 Ross slipped from contention.

Loan moves to Portsmouth and Sheffield United came to nothing and he eventually joined AEK Athens, which he later described as 'the worst mistake of my life'. He returned six months later to Sheffield United and later played out his career with Bury, where he was reunited with Martin Dobson – the Shakers' player-manager.

Rouse, Fred

Inside forward who went on to earn league representative honours

Season	League		FA Cup		Total	
	App	Goals	App	Goals	App	Goals
1906/07	6	1	1	0	7	1
1907/08	3	1	0	0	3	1
Total	**9**	**2**	**1**	**0**	**10**	**2**

Rowett, Gary

Defender plucked from obscurity who forged a solid career beyond Goodison

Season	League		FA Cup		League Cup		Total	
	App	Goals	App	Goals	App	Goals	App	Goals
1993/94	0 (2)	0	0	0	0	0	0 (2)	0
1994/95	2	0	0	0	0	0	2	0
Total	**2 (2)**	**0**	**0**	**0**	**0**	**0**	**2 (2)**	**0**

Royle, Joe

Distinguished centre forward who went on to manage Everton to FA Cup success

An outstanding centre forward in Harry Catterick's great teams of the late 1960s and early 1970s, with Howard Kendall Joe Royle is part of an exclusive club to enjoy success as both an Everton player and manager. One of the finest goalscorers in the club's history, Royle first emerged as a gangly teenager in the mid-1960s and ably succeeded Alex Young as the club's number nine. His most effective footballing business was conducted at a young age – because of injuries Royle was never quite the same player beyond his 22nd birthday – and he departed Goodison still aged only 25. Twenty years later, he made a long-awaited return as manager, saving the club from relegation and leading them to FA Cup glory in 1995. Although further success remained elusive, he remains one of Goodison's most favourite sons.

Born in Liverpool and an alumnus of Quarry Bank School, Royle was an outstanding schoolboy athlete who attracted the attention of several clubs, including Manchester United, before signing on at Goodison.

AS A PLAYER, Royle's Everton career began in contentious fashion. Aged 16 years, 9 months, in January 1966 he became the club's youngest ever player when he was selected in place of Alex Young for a First Division game at Blackpool. His debut was quiet as Everton lost 2-0, but the fury at Young's omission – considered sacrilege by some of his most ardent fans – caused some supporters to attack Harry Catterick outside the ground. A week later Royle was back in the reserves, Young was reinstated and continued to rule the royal blue Mersey for a further few years.

However, there was a beckoning realisation that Royle represented

a special talent. At the end of the 1966/67 season Catterick recalled Royle, who had been scoring prolifically for the reserves. By now the gangly former Lancashire Schoolboys skipper was more the complete article, and he duly repaid Catterick's faith by scoring three times in four games. At the start of the 1967/68 season, Catterick handed the 18-year-old the illustrious number nine shirt. His reward over the next four years was 95 goals in 190 games, spanning an FA Cup Final in 1968 and two semi-finals in 1969 and 1971, a League Championship triumph in 1970 and the first of six England caps in 1971.

Unlike Young, who he came to replace, the 6ft 1in, 13-stone Scouser was very much the archetypal target man. An imperious aerial presence, he thrived on the wide play of Johnny Morrissey and Jimmy Husband. With his large flat forehead adding to his prowess, Royle was also able to use it intelligently, regularly bringing into play his team-mates from midfield. Although lacking Young's delicate skills, he possessed good feet and was a fine finisher. Never in the club's history has a home-grown centre forward made so vast a goalscoring impact at so young an age: 16 league goals from 33 starts in 1967/68; 22 from 42 starts the following season; 23 goals when Everton lifted the league title in 1970 and Royle was ever-present; and 17 goals from 40 starts in 1970/71. Before long Evertonians idolised Royle – the local lad made good. 'They're peculiar about their number nines here, the way Liverpool are about their number sevens,' Royle later said, modestly omitting his own

> WITH HOWARD KENDALL JOE ROYLE IS PART OF AN EXCLUSIVE CLUB TO ENJOY SUCCESS AS BOTH AN EVERTON PLAYER AND MANAGER

name from the pantheon. 'Whether it was Bob Latchford or Alex Young or Dixie Dean or Tommy Lawton, they've always loved them.'

Royle was always a man for the big occasion and never was he better than in Everton's famous top of the table clash with Leeds in August 1969. Although just seven games into the new season, the outcome of the match was psychologically crucial so early in the title race. Jimmy Husband put Everton ahead after just four minutes, but it was Royle who stole the show with a virtuoso display. On 20 minutes he crashed a header against the Leeds bar but recovered quickly to head into the empty net. Four minutes prior to the interval he span and shot into the top-right corner to make the score 3-0. Leeds pulled the score back to 3-2, but thanks to Royle – who the Football Echo claimed had had 'the game of his life' – Everton took full points and retained their place at the top of the league, where they remained almost uninterrupted until the end of the season. In total, 19 of Everton's record haul of 65 points could be directly attributed to the centre forward's goals – even without taking into account his wider role within the team.

STILL A WEEK short of his 21st birthday when Everton lifted the league title, this was to be the apex of Royle's playing career. Like many of his colleagues, persistent injuries started to impair his effectiveness. Royle was struck with a back problem which put severe limitations on his involvement in the Everton team. Having been virtually ever-present in the four years leading to the end of the 1970/71 season, Royle made just 58 league starts over the next three years.

During this period, Harry Catterick was replaced as manager by Billy Bingham and Bob Latchford was signed from Birmingham City. Although Latchford and Royle partnered each other on a handful of occasions, their styles were, perhaps, too alike for one to be the ideal foil for the other. When Manchester City made a £200,000 bid for Royle in December 1974, Bingham deemed it too good to resist. Yet who knows what might have happened had Royle stayed a few months longer? Everton led the First Division going into April 1975, but just two wins in their final ten games saw any title hopes fade. Could Royle have made an impact at this critical juncture?

Royle spent three years at Maine Road, where his form earned him a brief England recall. In November 1977 he joined Bristol City, moving to Norwich City for £60,000 following the

Robins' relegation in 1980. Despite a second successive relegation in the 1980/81 season, he was a popular figure among the Norwich support, winning the club's Player of the Year award. Knee injuries limited his contribution the following season, at the end of which he called time on his 16-year-long playing career.

In July 1982, Royle was appointed manager of Second Division Oldham Athletic where, on severely limited resources, he proved to be among the most outstanding young managers in the league. In 1990 he led Oldham to the FA Cup semi-final and League Cup Final – the year he was short-listed for the England manager's job. The following season he led Oldham out of the Second Division as Champions, and kept them in the top flight for three seasons. In 1994 he again led Oldham to the FA Cup semi-final where, as in 1990, they were thwarted by Manchester United.

By this point, Royle was among the most sought after managers in England and had already rejected a plethora of bigger clubs. Most famously he turned down Manchester City in 1989 after Oldham fans paid for a scoreboard message which read, 'Please Joe, don't go'.

He always hoped that Everton would make a move, but after Mike Walker's appointment as manager in January 1994, admitted that he felt the chance had passed him by. In November 1994, with Everton rooted to the bottom of the Premier League, Walker was sacked and Royle made his long-awaited Goodison return. It was a month short of 20 years since he had been sold to Manchester City.

EVERTON had suffered their worst ever start to a season in 1994/95 and had won just one of their opening dozen games and been knocked out of the League Cup. Player morale was shattered, while individuals were failing to live up to their potential. Royle fostered a new team spirit in a hitherto morbid dressing room. He was helped by a 16-day break between fixtures, allowing him to reorganise and reinvigorate his team.

When Everton emerged for the first time under Royle's charge – against Liverpool on 21 November 1994 – they were a very different proposition from the side last seen under Walker. The midfield was packed tight with harriers and scrappers – Royle dubbed them his 'dogs of war' – who chased every last ball and played for their shirts as if their very lives depended upon it. The club's senior players

– Neville Southall, Dave Watson, Barry Horne and Paul Rideout – all seemed to be enthused with an additional sense of responsibility. Duncan Ferguson, a hitherto misfiring loan signing, seemed a different player. Although 21 points and 18 positions separated the two sides, on the night Everton were the only team in it, running out 2-0 winners.

Everton embarked on a seven-match unbeaten run, without conceding a goal. But as his new team rose up the table, Royle had his critics. Purists claimed that he was 'borstalising' the School of Science with his no-nonsense tactics. The Liverpool manager Roy Evans claimed that his team were 'hacked' out of the January derby and Kevin Keegan accused Everton of 'indiscipline' when two players were sent off and a further five booked when Everton met Newcastle at St James's Park the following month. It was true that the 'dogs of war' bore little resemblance to the elegant teams in which Royle had once played, but such an approach was necessary given the dire situation he inherited.

THE MIDFIELD WAS PACKED TIGHT WITH HARRIERS AND SCRAPPERS – ROYLE DUBBED THEM HIS 'DOGS OF WAR'

Everton escaped relegation with a game to spare, but the highlight of the season was, without question, the club's fifth FA Cup win. After narrow early-round victories over Derby County and Bristol City, Everton faced Premier League opponents from the fifth round onwards. A 5-0 fifth round thrashing of Norwich City was followed by a close 1-0 victory over high-flying Newcastle. That set up a semi-final against Tottenham Hotspur at Elland Road. Media talk in the run-up to the fixture had been of a Spurs v. Manchester United 'dream final', but Everton defied all such expectations with a resounding 4-1 win. 'I shouldn't be here, should I?' a defiant Royle asked reporters after the game.

'Sorry about the dream final, lads. It could have been more in the end. I was disappointed when they got a penalty which TV will tell whether it was or wasn't. We played a lot of good football, which is perhaps surprising to one or two of you having read the previews. So bollocks to you. And that's double L!' The 1-0 victory over Manchester United in the final seemed, in many ways, inevitable, and appropriate given how the same team had thwarted Royle at Oldham. It also served as vindication for the Everton manager's approach.

Royle's short-term objective had been to save Everton from the nightmare of relegation. Long-term, it was to revitalise the club, and substantial transfer funds were made available to this end. Despite the FA Cup win, Everton needed significant fresh blood. Already he had made Duncan Ferguson's loan signing permanent and acquired Earl Barrett; but just two new names – Craig Short and Andrei Kanchelskis – were added during the summer of 1995 when more were needed to bring not just success but the brand of football Evertonians demanded.

Everton overcame cup disappointments and a slow start to the 1995/96 season to finish sixth, but European qualification was denied them by UEFA, who removed an English berth after farcical representations in the previous summer's Inter-Toto Cup by Wimbledon and Tottenham Hotspur.

Again, Royle was cautious in the transfer market during 1996/97 pre-season, adding only Paul Gerrard and Gary Speed to his squad, while cup winners Barry Horne, Gary Ablett and Daniel Amokachi were allowed to move on. A reputed world record bid for

Alan Shearer failed, while other high-profile links came to nothing. Everton began the new season in brilliant fashion, beating title hopefuls Newcastle in the opening game and running Manchester United close in the next match. But the old frailties soon became apparent. A lack of quality, in part because of Royle's inability to bring enough of the right players in, cost Everton dearly, while the rugged brand of football had evolved too slowly for the liking of Everton's demanding support. The signing of Nick Barmby in November 1996 for £5.75million – the third time in two years Royle had broken the club record

– briefly lifted his team, amid some suggestions that Everton might emerge as title dark horses. But such talk proved vastly premature and Royle's tenure unravelled spectacularly.

Things started to go badly wrong for Royle shortly before Christmas 1996 when Andy Hinchcliffe suffered a cruciate ligament injury. Not only did Royle lose one of his best defenders, but a player who was capable of turning defence into attack with one sweeping pass and whose set pieces were one of the most potent parts of Everton's attacking armoury. The following month Andrei Kanchelskis joined Fiorentina and Anders Limpar – who had been frozen out of the team – joined Birmingham City, severely blunting Everton's attack. Claus Thomsen, a comical midfield harrier, was signed from Ipswich Town, but it was not enough to replenish Everton's diminished and flair-starved squad. Long-ball tactics became even more prevalent. Not only did this make Everton predictable, but they were boring too. The responsibility ultimately rested with Royle, for he had continually resisted the opportunity to bring in creative options since he became manager, always preferring the solid over the spectacular.

January and February 1997 became Royle's winter of discontent. Dumped out of the FA

As a Player

Season	League		FA Cup		League Cup		Other		Total	
	App	Goals	App	Goals	App	Goals	App	Goals	App	Goals
1965/66	2	0	0	0	-	-	0	0	2	0
1966/67	4	3	0	0	0	0	0	0	4	3
1967/68	33 (1)	16	6	3	1	1	-	-	40 (1)	20
1968/69	42	22	5	4	4	3	-	-	51	29
1969/70	42	23	1	0	4	0	-	-	47	23
1970/71	40	17	5	2	-	-	7	4	52	23
1971/72	26 (2)	9	3	0	1	0	-	-	30 (2)	9
1972/73	14	7	0	0	1	0	-	-	15	7
1973/74	18	2	3	0	1	0	0	0	22	2
1974/75	8	3	0	0	2	0	-	-	10	3
Total	**229(3)**	**102**	**23**	**9**	**14**	**4**	**7**	**4**	**273(3)**	**119**

As a Manager

Season	P	W	L	D	F	A	Pts	Position	FA Cup	League Cup
1994/95	42	11	14	17	44	51	50	15th	Winners	2nd Round*
1995/96	38	16	11	11	65	45	61	6th	4th Round	2nd Round**
1996/97	38	10	16	12	44	57	42	17th	4th Round	2nd Round***

* Royle appointed November 1995   ** Everton reached the 3rd round of the European Cup Winners' Cup   *** Royle left by 'mutual consent' March 1997 with Everton in 13th position

Cup by Second Division Bradford and in the midst of six straight league defeats, Royle reacted to press criticism by blanking journalists and banning the press from Bellefield. It was, concluded the Daily Post, 'Madness of course. Childish of course [and] it makes Everton look stupid.' Another critic wrote: 'We do not sign the players, pick the team or tell them how to play. You do and you have spent £26million in the last 27 months. By blaming the press for some of your problems you reveal a fundamental weakness in your ability as a manager of a top club.' The criticism was harsh, but possessed more than a germ of truth.

By March 1997, Everton seemed to have turned the corner.

The football was still dire, but the team had stopped haemorrhaging points. Then on transfer deadline day, Royle unexpectedly left the club. A triple transfer – the re-signing of Barry Horne from Birmingham and the Brann Bergen duo, Tore Andre Flo and Claus Eftevaag – had been earmarked. Flo was considered one of Europe's outstanding young centre forwards, but Eftevaag was a mere makeweight and the wisdom of signing back Horne at a loss was open to question too. Peter Johnson blocked the deal, and Royle felt he had no choice but to depart – just 29 months into a job he had coveted for years.

In February 1998, Royle returned to management with Manchester

City, now in the First Division. They were unexpectedly relegated the following May, but Royle led them through back-to-back promotions to the Premier League. When Everton met City at Maine Road in December 2000, Royle had the last laugh – leading his team to a 5-0 victory. And yet it was not enough to preserve City's Premier League status. After relegation in May 2001 he was sacked, despite previous promises that he had 'a job for life' at Maine Road. In November 2002, Royle returned to football as Ipswich Town manager. In the teeth of a perilous financial situation, he twice led them to the Championship playoffs but was unable to bring a return to the Premier League and left the club in May 2006.

[FACTFILE]

BORN
8 April 1949
POSITION
Centre forward
OTHER CLUBS
Manchester City (1974–77);
Bristol City (1977–80);
Norwich City (1980–82)
HONOURS AS PLAYER
1969/70
League Championship;
6 England caps
(2 goals) (1971–77)
AS MANAGER
Oldham Athletic
(1982–94 & 2009);
Manchester City
(1998–2001);
Ipswich Town (2002–06)
HONOURS AS MANAGER
FA Cup 1995

Ruddy,
John

Talented goalkeeper limited to a solitary appearance in five years at Goodison, he subsequently rose to the England squad

Season	League		FA Cup		League Cup		Total	
	App	Goals	App	Goals	App	Goals	App	Goals
2005/06	0 (1)	0	0	0	0	0	0 (1)	0
Total	0 (1)	0	0	0	0	0	0 (1)	0

[FACTFILE]

BORN
St Ives, 24 October 1986
POSITION
Goalkeeper
OTHER CLUBS
Cambridge United (2004–05);
Walsall (loan, 2005);
Rushden & Diamonds
(loan, 2005);
Chester City (loan, 2005–06);
Stockport County (loan, 2006);
Wrexham (loan, 2007);
Bristol City (loan, 2007);
Stockport County
(loan, 2008); Crewe
Alexandra (loan, 2009);
Motherwell (loan, 2009–10);
Norwich City (2010–)

Russell, John

Reserve centre half at the start of the 20th century

Season	League		FA Cup		Total	
	App	Goals	App	Goals	App	Goals
1902/03	3	0	0	0	3	0
Total	3	0	0	0	3	0

[FACTFILE]

BORN
1880
POSITION
Centre half
OTHER CLUB
West Ham

THE EVERTON ENCYCLOPEDIA

Ted **Sagar,** Louis **Saha,** Ernie **Salt,** Vinny **Samways,** Alan **Sanders,** Kenny **Sansom,** George **Saunders,** Ron **Saunders,** Alf **Schofield, Scotland** and Everton, Alex Scott, Billy Scott, Peter **Scott, Screen Sport Super Cup,** Steve **Seargeant,** Phillippe **Senderos,** Jimmy **Settle,** Alan **Shackleton,** Bert **Sharp,** Greame **Sharp,** Jack **Sharp,** George **Sharples,** Stuart **Shaw,** Kevin **Sheedy, Shirt Sponsorship,** Craig **Short,** Sammy **Simms,** Steve **Simonsen,** Bobby **Simpson,** Tom **Simpson,** Harry **Singleton,** Donald **Sloan,** Robert **Smalley,** David **Smallman,** Derek **Smith,** Joe **Smith,** John **Smith,** Walter **Smith,** Ian **Snodin,** Neville **Southall,** Jack **Southworth,** Gary **Speed,** Henry **Spencer,** John **Spencer,** Garry **Stanley,** Jimmy **Stein,** George **Stephenson,** Trevor **Steven,** Dennis **Stevens,** Gary **Stevens,** Leo **Stevens,** Thomas **Stevens,** Alex **Stevenson,** Billy **Stevenson,** Alex **Stewart,** Billy **Stewart,** David **Storrier,** Mike **Stowell,** Denis **Stracqualursi,** Samuel **Strettle,** Graham **Stuart,** Alan **Stubbs,** Archie **Styles,** Frank **Sugg,** John **Sutherland,** William **Sutton**

Sagar, Ted

Illustrious goalkeeper whose Everton career spanned four decades

Longevity is often the mark of greatness, and in Ted Sagar's case the facts speak for themselves. In a Goodison career that extended from Dixie Dean's heyday to the pomp of Dave Hickson nearly a quarter of a century later, Sagar was a consistently excellent custodian of the Everton goal, becoming one of the most decorated and renowned players in its history.

> SAGAR WAS A CONSISTENTLY EXCELLENT CUSTODIAN OF THE EVERTON GOAL, BECOMING ONE OF THE MOST DECORATED AND RENOWNED PLAYERS IN ITS HISTORY

NO PLAYER has served has served an English club for longer than Sagar, and few goalkeepers of his generation combined such bravery, technical excellence and charisma. Oddly, his 450 Everton appearances seem a comparatively small tally given the length of his service, but this was an age before European or League Cup football and war also cut seven years from his prime.

Like Gordon West – Everton's next great goalkeeper – Sagar hailed from the South Yorkshire coalfields. His childhood was marked by poverty and privations. When he was aged six, two of his sisters died within a week of each other. Within days a third catastrophic blow was dealt when news of his father's death fighting on the Somme reached home. As soon as he was old enough, Sagar's family relied upon him as a breadwinner, and the teenage Sagar went down the coal mine working 'permanent nights' to stave off the spectre of the workhouse.

Football was a release for the youngster and he was spotted playing for Thorne Colliery in the Doncaster Senior League by Hull City. The East Yorkshire side were nevertheless slow in offering him a contract, and in March 1929 Everton took advantage of their hesitancy.

SAGAR made his Everton debut on 18 January 1930 in place of Arthur Davies, keeping a clean sheet in a 4-0 victory. This was a rare bright spot in a travesty of a season in which Everton were relegated for the first time. Sagar made a further eight appearances, but his spirit in a demoralised Goodison must have been sapped further when Everton signed Billy Coggins from Bristol City towards the end of the season.

Coggins was ever-present through the 1930/31 season as Everton swept to the Second Division title, but in the long run Sagar's quality showed

through. He reclaimed his place on the opening day of the 1931/32 season and missed just a single game as Everton lifted the First Division title. A year later – with Sagar keeping goal as football's first 'number one' – Everton won the FA Cup for the second time. In 1938/39 Sagar won his second league title as Everton goalkeeper.

Although relatively slight in build for a goalkeeper, particularly in the days when it was not uncommon for a centre forward to bounce both keeper and ball into the net, Sagar belied his relative frailty with superb athleticism and bravery. 'Every goalkeeper is a specialist,' he said in 1969. 'And each man has his own strongest point. Some are brave to come out and challenge at a man's feet. Others are fast and agile on the goal line. In my case, my biggest asset was a fair eye and a good pair of hands.'

In an age of dazzling wingers and powerful centre forwards, a crucial part of his game was stopping supply lines from out wide. 'I tried to make collecting crosses my life's work,' he once said. 'I would practise for hours on end, week in, week out, with a couple of lads pushing high balls into the box while another came in to challenge me. I very seldom got it knocked out of my hands.'

EVERTON F.C. 1939 - DIVISION I CHAMPIONS

He was also a penalty kick specialist and saved many spot kicks; his strategy being to 'kid' the taker into shooting into a desired part of the goal. 'My idea was to give the penalty taker plenty of net to shoot at,' he recalled. 'So I would stand nearer my left-hand post than the right. Presented with all this room to shoot at, the kicker would almost automatically shoot in the direction I wanted and not realise he was being kidded. Of course, it was always an additional advantage if you could get away with moving before the ball was kicked. I saved many a spot kick because I was moving before the ball was and knew which way the shot was going.'

He was, wrote 'Red Rick', in a 1938 profile of Sagar in the Everton programme, 'the most daring 'keeper that ever played for Everton' whose attitude 'made one think of those glorious words: "thou shalt not pass".

'Many people say he runs out too much, I think he does too,' recorded the correspondent. 'But he gets the ball nine times out of ten. He should be locked up for stealing – look at the times without number he has snatched the ball from bobbing heads in the goalmouth.' 'Red Rick' went on to rate Sagar second behind Billy Scott as the club's greatest goalkeeper, but said he was ahead of Leigh Roose.

SAGAR made his international debut in October 1935, when England defeated Northern Ireland 3-1 in Belfast. It was the first of a four-cap career that was ultimately cut short by war. During the war, when stationed in

E. SAGAR
EVERTON

Portadown with the Signal Corps, in the midst of an injury crisis Sagar was called upon to keep goal for Northern Ireland against the Irish Free State.

Like Neville Southall, whose diatribes at his own team-mates used to reverberate around Goodison in the 1980s and 1990s, Sagar was renowned for his vocal contribution to the Everton team. His first nickname was 'The Cat' but as he became increasingly known for his outbursts, it was not long before he was rechristened 'The Boss'.

He believed the ball had no business in the penalty area unless it was in his hands, and screamed at his team-mates to clear it. When, at the end of the 1930s, T.G. Jones – a great footballing centre half – broke into the Everton team, Sagar's short patience was tested on many occasions as the Welshman coolly dribbled the ball away, instead of launching a hoofed clearance.

'Ted didn't say a lot in the dressing room, but on the field he was a different kettle of fish entirely,' recalled Jimmy O'Neill. 'If the full backs weren't doing their job, he let them know in no uncertain terms. He had quite a temper but after a game was over it was completely forgotten.'

'He was so comical and then serious, and you never knew how to take him,' recalled Tommy Lawton. 'Like all goalkeepers, it was always somebody else's fault when he was bending his back to pull it out the net.'

Although war sucked the prime from many players, some reckon Sagar's peak came after peace returned and he was in his late thirties. Certainly he had more work to do as he was faced with shot after shot in a struggling Everton team. In 1950/51, as Sagar – now in his fifth decade – was being edged from contention, Everton succumbed to relegation for the second time in his career. He played just eleven more games for Everton, finally calling an end to his career in 1953.

AFTER FOOTBALL, like many footballers of his era he entered the pub trade, running the Chepstow Castle on County Road, before taking over the Blue Anchor pub in Aintree. He died suddenly in 1986, his ashes being laid at Goodison Park,

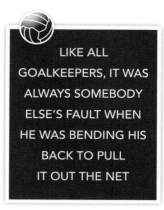

LIKE ALL GOALKEEPERS, IT WAS ALWAYS SOMEBODY ELSE'S FAULT WHEN HE WAS BENDING HIS BACK TO PULL IT OUT THE NET

which had become his spiritual home. 'It made his heart sing when he was surrounded by Evertonians,' his widow Dolly told the author Becky Tallentire in 2004. 'The fans loved Ted – they would always tell me to look after him because he played such an important part in Everton's success.'

Season	League		FA Cup		Other		Total	
	App	Goals	App	Goals	App	Goals	App	Goals
1929/30	8	0	1	0	-	-	9	0
1930/31	0	0	0	0	-	-	0	0
1931/32	41	0	1	0	-	-	42	0
1932/33	42	0	6	0	1	0	49	0
1933/34	40	0	1	0	1	0	42	0
1934/35	35	0	4	0	-	-	39	0
1935/36	37	0	0	0	-	-	37	0
1936/37	29	0	4	0	-	-	33	0
1937/38	26	0	0	0	-	-	26	0
1938/39	41	0	5	0	-	-	46	0
1946/47	29	0	2	0	-	-	31	0
1947/48	42	0	5	0	-	-	47	0
1948/49	40	0	2	0	-	-	42	0
1949/50	18	0	0	0	-	-	18	0
1950/51	24	0	1	0	-	-	25	0
1951/52	10	0	0	0	-	-	10	0
1952/53	1	0	0	0	-	-	1	0
Total	**463**	**0**	**32**	**0**	**2**	**0**	**497**	**0**

Saha,
Louis

France international forward whose injury record undermined his great natural talent

At the top of his game, Louis Saha was a supremely talented centre forward, boasting an intoxicating combination of technical ability, strength, power and deadly accuracy in front of goal. Alas, it took peak fitness for these facets to be fully unveiled and, as through much of his career, his time at Goodison was dogged by a succession of niggling injuries.

A graduate of the famous Clairefontaine football academy, Saha began his career with Metz and joined Fulham as a 21-year-old for £2.1million in 2000, a year after a failed loan move at Newcastle United. His goals helped propel the London club to the Premier League and after proving his worth in the top flight he was a £12.8million acquisition by Manchester United in 2004.

His time at Old Trafford was a qualified success, with 42 goals in a period that won him two Premier League titles, the League Cup and also saw a Champions League win – although he was absent from the United squad for the final. But there was also a sense that he could have achieved much more and he made just 76 starts spread over 4½ injury-troubled years.

HE JOINED Everton for an undisclosed fee in the summer of 2008, initially as an understudy to Yakubu. When Yakubu suffered a serious injury against Tottenham at the end of November 2008, Saha was called in to deputise, but lasted just 60 minutes before himself succumbing to injury, which kept him out for three months. He recovered to score the winning goal in Everton's FA Cup quarter-final against Middlesbrough and played 70 minutes of the successful semi-final victory over Manchester United. In the final against Chelsea he put Everton in front after just 25 seconds – the fastest goal in an FA Cup Final – but it was too little too early and Everton fell to a 2-1 defeat.

Saha's best form came the following winter when he seemed to have overcome his previous injury problems to have a sustained run in the team. A fine brace against Chelsea in a night match at Goodison brought Everton a deserved victory and he agreed a new contract soon afterwards.

'My game is instinctive,' he told the March 2010 edition of the Evertonian. 'I'm not a big thinker. I feel like I'm doing things instinctively at the moment and it's the way I like to play because I feel that's when I'm at my best.

I don't really think about the game before I go out to play in it.

'It's the way I've always been and maybe the reason I made it as a professional. I never got under pressure when I was younger for some reason. I think that's a quality which has made me the player I am.'

Alas, the injury problems continued to dog him and he could never be relied upon as a regular goalscorer. When Tottenham Hotspur made a surprise move for his services in January 2012, David Moyes let him leave on a free transfer.

A thoughtful, intelligent man, in 2012 a thought-provoking book he had written about life as a footballer was published to critical acclaim.

Further reading:

SAHA, LOUIS,
Thinking Outside The Box,
Vision Sports Publishing, 2012

> IN THE FINAL AGAINST CHELSEA HE PUT EVERTON IN FRONT AFTER JUST 25 SECONDS – THE FASTEST GOAL IN AN FA CUP FINAL

[FACTFILE]

BORN
Paris, 8 August 1978
POSITION
Centre forward
OTHER CLUBS
Metz (1997–2000);
Newcastle United
(loan, 1999);
Fulham (2000–04);
Manchester United
(2004–08);
Tottenham Hotspur (2012)
HONOURS
20 France caps
(4 goals) (2004–)

Season	League		FA Cup		League Cup		Europe		Total	
	App	Goals	App	Goals	App	Goals	App	Goals	App	Goals
2008/09	10 (14)	6	2 (1)	2	1	0	1	0	14 (15)	8
2009/10	26 (7)	13	1	0	1	0	3 (2)	2	31 (9)	15
2010/11	14 (8)	7	3	2	0 (1)	1	-	-	17 (9)	10
2011/12	15 (3)	1	0	0	1 (1)	1	-	-	16 (4)	2
Total	**65 (32)**	**27**	**6 (1)**	**4**	**3 (2)**	**2**	**4 (2)**	**2**	**78 (37)**	**35**

Salt, Ernie

Reserve goalkeeper limited to a handful of early 1920s outings

Gallaher's Cigarettes.

[FACTFILE]

BORN
Walsall, 10 February 1897
POSITION
Goalkeeper
OTHER CLUBS
Accrington Stanley;
Wigan Borough

Season	League		FA Cup		Total	
	App	Goals	App	Goals	App	Goals
1921/22	4	0	0	0	4	0
Total	**4**	**0**	**0**	**0**	**4**	**0**

Samways, Vinny

Subtle midfielder who found himself unwanted by Joe Royle

If ever there was a player whose plight epitomised Joe Royle's preference for the workmanlike over the mercurial it was Vinny Samways. Signed by Royle's predecessor, Mike Walker, in August 1994 for a hefty £2.1million, on his arrival Samways was seen as a playmaker who befitted the finest traditions of the School of Science.

SAMWAYS STARTED THE 1995/96 SEASON IN MEMORABLE FASHION, SCORING THE LOBBED GOAL THAT WON EVERTON THE CHARITY SHIELD

Slight, intelligent and with a sharp eye for a cutting pass, Samways had lifted the FA Cup with Tottenham in 1991. But his career had plateaued and he had fallen out of favour at White Hart Lane by the time of his move north. In an Everton shirt he showed glimpses of a talent that had once earned him comparisons with Glenn Hoddle, his illustrious predecessor in the Tottenham midfield. But he lacked the guile to turn around Everton's worst ever start to a season. With better players, the feeling was that he might have excelled.

Joe Royle, however, didn't see it that way, and after becoming Everton manager in November 1994 barely used Samways – no matter how thin his other midfield resources appeared. Even as he tamed his 'dogs of war' and introduced a more expansive brand of football there was no way in for the playmaker.

SAMWAYS started the 1995/96 season in memorable fashion, scoring the lobbed goal that won Everton the Charity Shield. But this was a mere cameo in a blue shirt, and after loan moves to Wolves and Birmingham City failed to earn him a permanent move, he joined Las Palmas. In Spain, the footballing climate was more conducive to Samways' undoubted talents and the midfielder finally thrived.

[FACTFILE]

BORN
Bethnal Green, 27 October 1968
POSITION
Midfield
OTHER CLUBS
Tottenham Hotspur (1986–94);
Wolverhampton Wanderers
(loan, 1995–96);
Birmingham City (loan, 1996);
Las Palmas (1996–2002);
Seville (2002–03);
Walsall (2003–04);
Algeciras (2004–05)

Season	League		FA Cup		League Cup		Other		Total	
	App	Goals	App	Goals	App	Goals	App	Goals	App	Goals
1994/95	14 (5)	1	0	0	2	1	-	-	16 (5)	2
1995/96	3 (1)	1	0	0	1	0	2	1	6 (1)	2
Total	**17 (6)**	**2**	**0**	**0**	**3**	**1**	**2**	**1**	**22 (6)**	**4**

EVERTON F.C. 1959-60

Left to right: (Back row) T. Jones, K. Rea, A. Parker, A. Dunlop, J. Bramwell, M. Meagan, J. Tansey, G. Watson (Trainer); (Front row) A. Sanders, J. Harris, E. Thomas, D. Hickson, R. Collins, E. O'Hara B. Harris

Sanders, Alan

Mischievous Mancunian who filled Everton's right back berth in the 1950s

Fun-loving full back Alan Sanders was one of a generation of young home-grown players vested with the unenviable task of restoring Everton in the 1950s back to their pre-war splendour.

His chance came in the 1957/58 season when Everton's long-standing right back, Don Donovan, was called upon to replace the injured T.E. Jones in the centre of defence. Sanders impressed enough to supplant the Irishman and his first-team career would extend into the tenure of Johnny Carey before he made way for the classy Scot, Alex Parker.

HE WAS, wrote the football historian Ivan Ponting, 'a flamboyant right back with the stature of a body builder who radiated confidence; unfortunately, although he was blessed with a fair degree of ball skill for such a strapping man, he was a rather cumbersome mover who found it difficult to recover his ground if given the slip by a fleet footed opponent.'

DEREK TEMPLE remembered: 'Alan Sanders was a lad from Manchester: big, strong, not to be unkind, I didn't think he was the greatest player we ever had. He was a character – a bit mad. We had a billiard room at Everton. You went up a little spiral staircase from the dressing room and there were chairs in there and benches and two or three snooker tables. It's where we would relax after training and have something to eat.'

I always remember Alan Sanders getting Eddie Thomas and tying him to a chair and putting a load of newspaper under him and lighting it and then doing an Indian war dance around him! Old Frank Blundell who ran the place was going mad. He was crackers, Alan. There was mischief, but we were all young fellas with lots of energy.'

Parker's arrival saw chances limited for Sanders. It was a fate shared with many of his generation of home-grown players as the Moores millions started to make an impression on the club. In November 1959 he was allowed to join Swansea Town and in the lower leagues his career flourished.

Season	League		FA Cup		Total	
	App	Goals	App	Goals	App	Goals
1957/58	26	0	3	0	29	0
1958/59	25	0	4	0	29	0
1959/60	5	0	0	0	5	0
Total	**56**	**0**	**7**	**0**	**63**	**0**

Sansom, Kenny

Former England full back who joined Everton at the end of an illustrious career

Season	League		FA Cup		League Cup		Total	
	App	Goals	App	Goals	App	Goals	App	Goals
1992/93	6 (1)	1	0	0	0	0	6 (1)	1
Total	**6 (1)**	**1**	**0**	**0**	**0**	**0**	**6 (1)**	**1**

Saunders, George

Post-war era full back who came to Goodison on the back of a lofty commendation

EVERTON FOOTBALL CLUB 1948-49

LEFT TO RIGHT :- BACK ROW :- STEVENSON, LINDLEY, SAUNDERS, SAGAR, HEDLEY, FARRELL, T.COOK (Trainer).
FRONT ROW :- CORR, BENTHAM, CATTERICK, FIELDING, EGLINGTON, JONES.

A Birkenhead-born right half, George Saunders was first brought to the attention of the Everton management in the 1930s by his town's greatest son, Dixie Dean. Saunders had been playing for his former school's Old Boys team, when a friend of Dean's recommended the youngster. So strong was the commendation that Dean urged the Everton management to check him out without himself seeing him play, and so began a 15-year association with Everton.

Saunders – whose younger cousin Ron Saunders made a handful of first-team appearances for Everton in the 1950s and later managed Aston Villa to the First Division title – was, noted a pre-war profile, 'of very quiet disposition, and is very popular with his colleagues'. At golf, it recorded, he was 'no mean performer'. While honing his trade in the Everton A team and in the Central League, he converted from right half to right back – and would later in his career fill in as an auxiliary left back.

Like so many players of his era, Saunders saw the bulk and prime of his career ravaged by war. He was aged 19 when he signed professional terms with Everton in January 1938, but had to wait until he was 28 before making his league debut, in September 1946.

DESPITE possessing a good first touch, Saunders was an uncomplicated full back, who believed foremost in a safety-first mentality. Clearing his lines quickly was his principal responsibility; not for him the fancy touches

and embellishments of other defenders. He was strong in the air and possessed the ability to outjump other more physically imposing rivals. Although he was a committed and reliable member of the Everton team, he played in some of the poorest teams in the club's history. Everton were relegated in 1950/51, although by then Saunders had started to fall out of favour with Cliff Britton.

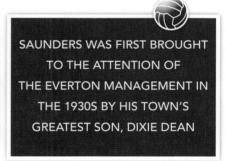

SAUNDERS WAS FIRST BROUGHT TO THE ATTENTION OF THE EVERTON MANAGEMENT IN THE 1930S BY HIS TOWN'S GREATEST SON, DIXIE DEAN

In March 1952, Tranmere Rovers came in for Saunders, now aged 34 and out of the team for most of the 1951/52 season. Everton asked for £3500 for the player, but Rovers pleaded poverty and said they could afford no more than £1000. The Everton board dismissed the bid and Saunders remained an Everton player, even though he never again played for the first team.

The entire predicament spoke much about the limits of player power in this era and the hold that clubs had over footballers. In fairness to Everton, they paid up Saunders' accrued benefit of £675 in July the following year. But their refusal to let him go and the way that the club effectively ended his career must surely have rankled with the right back in years to come.

Season	League		FA Cup		Total	
	App	Goals	App	Goals	App	Goals
1946/47	23	0	1	0	24	0
1947/48	37	0	5	0	42	0
1948/49	36	0	1	0	37	0
1949/50	24	0	0	0	24	0
1950/51	10	0	0	0	10	0
1951/52	3	0	0	0	3	0
1952/53	0	0	0	0	0	0
Total	**133**	**0**	**7**	**0**	**140**	**0**

[FACTFILE]

BORN
Birkenhead, 1 March 1918
DIED
1982
POSITION
Right back

Saunders, Ron

Home-grown forward who made a triumphant return as player and League Championship-winning manager after dropping out of league football

Season	League		FA Cup		Total	
	App	Goals	App	Goals	App	Goals
1948/49	4	0	0	0	4	0
Total	**4**	**0**	**0**	**0**	**4**	**0**

Schofield, Alf

Local winger who made a name for himself with Manchester United after failing to make the Goodison breakthrough

Season	League		FA Cup		Total	
	App	Goals	App	Goals	App	Goals
1895/96	2	1	0	0	2	1
1896/97	1	0	0	0	1	0
1897/98	0	0	0	0	0	0
1898/99	7	1	0	0	7	1
1899/1900	3	0	0	0	3	0
Total	**13**	**2**	**0**	**0**	**13**	**2**

Scotland, Everton and

The breeding ground of a succession of legends who fill every chapter of club history

Scottish football's dire state in the first years of the 21st century betrays its historic status as a powerhouse of British football. It also disguises the reality that it has until recent years always been one of the most potent talent sources for English clubs, not least Everton.

Indeed few clubs have benefited more from this southern emigration of players than Everton, and a tradition of Scots turning out in the blue of the club extends back to the very first years of its existence. The names of Alex Latta, Richard Boyle, Sandy Young, Jimmy Galt, Alec Troup, Jimmy Stein, Torry Gillick, Bobby Collins, Alex Young, Alex Parker, Alex Scott, Graeme Sharp, Andy Gray, Duncan Ferguson and Richard Gough – among others – bear testament to the strength of this shared tradition.

The Scottish Football Association (SFA) was founded at a meeting held at Glasgow's Dewar's Hotel on 13 March 1873. Its formation came a few months after the first international match was staged in the city between Scotland and England and its origination owed much to the missionary zeal of the FA, elements of which sought to spread the word of football to every corner of the planet. The SFA is the second oldest federation in the world, and its historic importance to football is reflected in the fact that it carries a permanent seat on football's law-making council, the International Football Board.

The FA's role in planting football's seed in Scotland was phenomenally influential. The Scottish game's great clubs largely originate from

the 1880s but the growth of the game north of the border immediately gave rise to a succession of highly talented players. The Scots also mastered far more quickly one of football's fundamentals – passing – and the superiority of their early players was reflected in the results of some early international matches. They won 3-1 at Kennington Oval in 1877; 7-2 at Hampden Park a year later; and, best of all, 6-1 at Kennington in 1881. After the 1878 match, Bell's Life had published a letter signed by 'A Disgusted Englishman' who struck at the heart of the problem: 'The England players we had down this time were a splendid lot of players individually, but to my idea they played very selfishly, each one of them appearing to play for himself and not for the success of the side.'

In 1885, the FA, recognising the growth of some of its member-clubs, the fact that they were attracting increasingly significant numbers of paying supporters and were in turn financially rewarding their players, allowed professionalism. It was a move that the conservative SFA took a further eight years to follow. This led to a drain of Scotland's best talent south of the border, which was hastened with the inauguration of the Football League in 1888 (the Scottish Football League followed two years later, but was initially shackled by its amateurism).

EVERTON benefited from this exodus immediately, and Alec Dick, 'a daring and reckless full back' signed from Kilmarnock in 1885, was in its first batch of professional players. Former Heart of Midlothian captain Nick Ross, who was one of the game's first superstars, was signed to captain Everton into the Football League era three years later, and this steady trickle became a flow. Alex Latta, Abraham Hartley, John Bell and Richard Boyle all made the journey to Liverpool from the

town of Dumbarton in the late 1880s and early 1890s; all would play important roles for Everton through the 1890s, with Latta winning a League Championship medal in 1891. Latta was joined in that success by Alec Brady, a Scottish international inside forward, Dan Doyle, a half back, and their captain Andrew Hannah, who had played for Renton when they were declared 'World Champions' in 1888 having beaten the FA Cup holders, West Bromwich Albion.

The cross-border trade in players continued through these early years, although it subsided slightly through the rise of Glasgow Rangers and Celtic as genuine powers. Their ascent meant that Scotland had clubs that were greater forces than even their strongest English rivals. In 1902 Everton faced Rangers in the British League Cup, an end-of-season competition to raise funds for the victims of the Ibrox Stadium disaster that was considered an unofficial British Championship. Everton, however, fell at the first hurdle.

The impact of Scottish players on the Everton team continued to be great, however. In 1906 Alex 'Sandy' Young scored the goal that saw Everton lift the FA Cup for the first time. Nine years later ex-Rangers star Bobby Parker's 36 goals in 35 appearances resulted in Everton's second League Championship, a trophy that was lifted by another former Ibrox man, Jimmy Galt.

In March 1928 Scotland recorded their greatest international result,

a 5-1 win over England at Wembley. A month later Everton signed one of these 'Wembley Wizards', an inside forward named Jimmy Stein. He joined fellow Scot Alec Troup in an Everton team that was dominated by Dixie Dean, but included several notable Scots. These included the left half Jock Thomson and, later, the dazzling winger Torry Gillick. In December 1932 Everton caused a sensation by prising the Northern Ireland international Billy Cook from Celtic. It was the first time a major player had left Parkhead mid-season.

Post-war Everton's great poaching ground reverted to Ireland. But a second great influx of players arrived from north of the border in the late 1950s and early 1960s and included Bobby Collins, Alex Parker, Alex Young, Jimmy Gabriel and Alex Scott. They formed the basis of the team that won the 1963 League Championship and also the British Championship against Rangers later that year. The 1980s and 1990s were defined by Everton's great Scottish centre forwards: Graeme Sharp, Andy Gray and Duncan Ferguson.

PLAYING for Everton enhanced these players' reputations and saw their name enter the pantheon of Goodison lore. What it didn't do was enhance their chances of playing for their country. Throughout history, the 'Anglos' – namely those who appeared in the English league – were overlooked in favour of home-based players. It is one of the tragedies of football that Ferguson, Gabriel, Gray, Sharp and Young collectively earned less than ten Scotland caps while playing for Everton.

In 1998 Walter Smith, the most successful Rangers manager in history, was appointed Everton boss. It was in the midst of a 13-year spell that would see frenetic trading between Everton and Rangers: Gary Stevens, Trevor Steven and Michael Ball

heading north; Duncan Ferguson, Iain Durrant, Richard Gough and Alec Cleland moving south. There was a theory at this time that this signified some deeper link between the two clubs, that Everton and Rangers were somehow linked in the way that Liverpool and Celtic were (they had in common their greatest player, Kenny Dalglish). But such links were simplistic and tended to overlook the complicated religious constituency of Everton supporters. Anyone who held illusions about Everton and Rangers' 'special relationship' should have been present at Dave Watson's testimonial between the two clubs in July 1997 to see the reality. Crowd violence from marauding hordes of drunken Rangers fans and omnipresent shouts of 'Fenian bastards' were indicative of the falsity of this myth. Indeed one only need listen to the lyrics of Evertonian favourite 'We Hate Bill Shankly...' ('To hell with Liverpool and Rangers too, We'll throw them all in the Mersey ...') to recognise that the relationship is only special in terms of animosity.

Four years after Smith took over he was succeeded by a former Celtic player, David Moyes. He twice restored Scots (David Weir and Duncan Ferguson) to the Everton captaincy but has otherwise carried out little business in his home country, besides twice signing James McFadden. Moyes's lack of interest in Scottish footballers speaks of the new reality facing Scottish football this century: that it is a fallen power that produces players below the standard demanded by the Premier League. British football is poorer for this state of affairs.

·EFC·

Scott, Alex

Lightning winger who won trophies and adulation on both sides of the Scottish border

The £39,000 signing of Alex Scott in February 1963 brought to a conclusion one of the most closely fought transfer sagas in Everton's history. Amid the great freeze of that winter, Harry Catterick caught wind that Tottenham, Everton's principal League Championship rivals, were closing in on Scott's signature. Catterick intervened at the eleventh hour and, as he so often did, got his man. In turning down the reigning champions he joined their heirs apparent, and by May 1963 had become one of the few players to claim league title honours in both England and Scotland.

Scott arrived on Merseyside with a formidable reputation. Rangers had acquired him as a teenager from Scottish junior football and he marked his debut as an 18 year-old against Alex Parker's Falkirk, his home-town club, with a hat-trick. In his eight years at Ibrox, Scott scored 108 goals in 331 matches and won four league championships. However, he would thrive most on the European stage, then in its infancy, and his goals propelled Rangers to the semi-finals of the 1960 European Cup.

AN EXPLOSIVE player with a devastating turn of pace, Scott was the sort of player who could conjure something from nothing. To opposing full backs he was the stuff of nightmares: if they marked tightly, he would knock the ball past them and run onto it; if they stood back, then he would cut inside and run through the available space. Scott would exploit such indecision mercilessly, and had a degree of consistency almost unparalleled among wide men.

Perhaps Scott would have played his entire career at Ibrox, but in 1962 his place came under threat from Willie Henderson, an outstanding young tyro, and he sought opportunities elsewhere. At Everton he immediately came into the team in place of Billy Bingham, who moved on to Port Vale in the wake of Scott's arrival, and with fellow new signing Tony Kay added fresh impetus to Everton's ultimately successful title challenge. Alas, Scott fell short of the appearances necessary to also win himself a Scottish Championship medal for his efforts with Rangers that season – which would have constituted a remarkable achievement.

Six months after winning the title Scott was back at Ibrox playing against his former team in a British Championship match. He scored once in a 3-1 victory, but in the return leg at Goodison the visiting supporters gave him a torrid time. George Orr remembered in his diary of the era: 'The whole length and width of the running track, from the Street End to the halfway line, was full of bottles and glasses taken from Rangers fans. There were fights everywhere.' The game ended 1-1, Scott's compatriot Alex Young scoring the Everton goal.

Among his team-mates Scott was known as 'The Head Waiter' in reference to his habit of running with one arm held stiffly, as if holding a tray – the result of a childhood broken arm. Evertonians dubbed him 'Chico', after

ONE OF EVERTON'S MOST OUTSTANDING PLAYERS IN THEIR FA CUP FINAL VICTORY IN 1966

a television promotion that starred a cut-out figure of a Mexican Indian. Many of the cardboard cut-outs featuring Chico the Indian eventually found their way to Goodison on match days.

SCOTT was a determined figure, and his desire to win sometimes brought him into conflict with his team-mates. Brian Glanville recalled one incident: 'With Everton Scott was quite capable of intruding if he felt that a team-mate was playing selfishly. In a game against Tottenham Hotspur in January 1965, when, exasperated by the individualism of Everton's big centre forward, Fred Pickering, he simply tackled his own man. The stratagem seemed to work, since from that point the two combined sweetly and Scott gave Cyril Knowles, Spurs' English international left back, a torrid afternoon.'

Scott continued to shine through the mid-1960s, and was one of Everton's most outstanding players in their FA Cup Final victory in 1966. But as Harry

Season	League		FA Cup		Europe		Other		Total	
	App	Goals	App	Goals	App	Goals	App	Goals	App	Goals
1962/63	17	4	0	0	0	0	-	-	17	4
1963/64	40	7	5	2	2	0	1	0	48	9
1964/65	36	6	4	0	4	1	-	-	44	7
1965/66	35	5	8	0	2	0	-	-	45	5
1966/67	21	1	0	0	2	0	1	0	24	1
Total	**149**	**23**	**17**	**2**	**10**	**1**	**2**	**0**	**178**	**26**

Catterick reshuffled his pack and out-and-out wingers fell out of vogue, Scott was required to play deeper and track back and defend. Alex Young later likened the situation to using a Ferrari to deliver pizzas.

AGED 30 at the end of the 1966/67 season, Scott had already seen his position come under threat and Catterick deemed him expendable, selling him to Hibernian for £15,000. Ironically he replaced his younger brother Jim, also a winger, who had left Easter Road to join Newcastle.

Over the course of a decade, Scott won just 16 caps. He would have earned more, but for the fierce competition then between wingers in Scotland. In 1966 alone, the year of his last international appearance, Scotland also used Celtic's Jimmy Johnstone, Charlie Cooke of Chelsea and Willie Henderson, his successor at Ibrox – all of whom are regarded as incomparable by their respective clubs' supporters.

He retired after a spell with Falkirk, later running a pub in the town with Jim.

[FACTFILE]

BORN
Falkirk, 22 November 1936
DIED
Falkirk, 13 September 2001
POSITION
Winger
OTHER CLUBS
Glasgow Rangers (1954–63);
Hibernian (1967–69);
Falkirk (1969–72)
HONOURS
League Championship
1962/63; FA Cup 1966;
16 Scotland caps
(5 goals) (1956–66)

Scott, Billy

Goalkeeping legend and perennial nearly man

Billy Scott was one of Everton's great custodians; a brave, agile player who kept the Everton net safe through the Edwardian era. He was also one of the most unlucky players to be associated with Everton; three times a League Championship runner-up, once an FA Cup final loser, and also on the losing side at the competition's semi-final stage, he left Goodison in 1912 with almost 300 appearances to his name but just one medal – that of the 1906 FA Cup win.

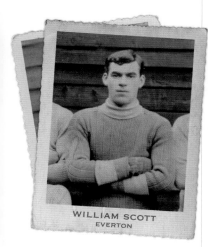

WILLIAM SCOTT
EVERTON

He arrived at Everton in the summer of 1904 as a 22-year-old already with inter-league and international honours to his name. Twice with Linfield, in 1902 and 1904, he had won the Irish League and Cup double. He cost Everton £600, with the full back, McCartney, also coming as part of the deal. Expectations were high because, in George Kitchen, Everton already had an excellent goalkeeper. 'The only new recruit in the Everton ranks was Scott, the Irish international from Linfield,' reported the Liverpool Mercury of his debut against Notts County. 'Although not subjected to any severe trial, he showed that he is a custodian of real ability. A word of caution, however, would not be out of the place. Coolness is an excellent qualification in a goalkeeper, but there is such a thing as carrying it

to excess. On more than one occasion when he might have punted strongly down the field, he threw the ball to the backs, and if the Notts forwards had been more alert the Everton citadel might have been captured.'

Yet Scott quickly allayed any doubts about his ability. The 'famous Irish international', recorded Thomas Keates, was a 'safe custodian'. 'The goalkeeper was equal to the challenges of his most intimidating adversaries and dominated the penalty area,' wrote David France. 'He made up for his lack of size with an abundance of courage, composure and cat-like agility.'

INDEED the Irishman quickly made a formidable impression at Goodison. Not only did he see off the challenge of Kitchen in the

Everton goal but also a second great goalkeeper, Leigh Richmond 'Dick' Roose, a Welsh international. Injured in November 1904, Roose – who had walked away from football to train as a doctor earlier that year – was drafted in as cover. Everton went on a run of 12 wins and three draws over a sequence of 16 matches and narrowly missed out on the league title. But a squabble between the Welshman and Will Cuff – allied to Scott's excellence – meant that the Irishman was preferred in the long term.

Scott's debut season – 1904/05 – nearly brought a League Championship medal. He had to wait just a further year to win the FA Cup, but thereafter his story was one of near misses. He was on the losing team in the 1907 FA Cup Final, a league runner-up again in 1909 and 1912. In 1910 he was in the Everton team for an FA Cup semi-final replay against Barnsley that ended in 3-0 defeat and a football catastrophe. Everton's captain, Jack Taylor, suffered a freak career-ending injury to his throat, while Scott also suffered serious injury.

'With Barnsley's first goal came the disablement of Scott,' reported the Liverpool Mercury. 'Scott was on the ground when the ball was put through, and [by] some means

or other the first two fingers of his right hand were injured. The bleeding was profuse, and when the injury had been attended to Scott was little good in goal. A couple of goals were put past him in the closing stages, and the wounds were reopened to such an extent that he had to leave the field just before the whistle blew.'

Through these years of heartbreaking near misses, Scott was a consistently excellent custodian. In the Athletic News a lengthy controversy arose between the merits of Scott, Roose and Liverpool's England international Sam Hardy; Scott was eventually decreed the finest of the three. 'The nonchalant Irishman seemed to be always chewing, had wonderful anticipation, rarely left his goal and did everything in a quiet cool manner that evoked admiration,' wrote 'Red Rick' in a 1930s

profile in the Everton programme. The author cited Scott as the greatest Everton goalkeeper in their 60-year history.

Perhaps surprisingly, Everton replaced Scott with James Caldwell at the end of the 1911/12 season and the Irishman joined Leeds City, where he spent just two seasons. His departure from Goodison surely impacted on his former team, who dropped from runners-up in his final year at the club to 11th in the first year without him.

Scott's younger brother Elisha emerged in the 1920s as Liverpool's greatest goalkeeper. Twelve years Billy's junior, Everton tried on several occasions to buy Elisha. 'Elisha Scott, the Liverpool keeper, was the greatest I have ever seen,' Dixie Dean would recall, and the pair shared a formidable rivalry. But the two

Scott brothers, despite their shared background and position, were very different people. 'I don't suppose there were two such contrasting characters as William and Elisha, but in spite of that they were parallel cases when they took the sport and kept goal,' recalled Ernest 'Bee' Edwards in the Liverpool Echo in 1936. 'In fact, one would call William Scott the stolid goalkeeper and in dealing with the best shot of old times. William Scott was unequalled in his ability using a knuckle to knock down the hottest shot from a Hampton, a Shepherd, or any other driving force.' After years of working in the pub trade, Scott died of pneumonia in August 1936, aged just 54.

	League		FA Cup		Total	
Season	App	Goals	App	Goals	App	Goals
1904/05	16	0	0	0	16	0
1905/06	35	0	6	0	41	0
1906/07	35	0	8	0	43	0
1907/08	34	0	7	0	41	0
1908/09	36	0	2	0	38	0
1909/10	27	0	7	0	34	0
1910/11	31	0	3	0	34	0
1911/12	37	0	5	0	42	0
Total	**251**	**0**	**38**	**0**	**289**	**0**

[FACTFILE]

BORN
Belfast, 17 May 1882
DIED
Liverpool, 16 August 1936
POSITION
Goalkeeper
OTHER CLUBS
Cliftonville (1901–03);
Linfield (1903–04);
Leeds City (1912–14)
HONOURS
FA Cup 1906,
25 Ireland caps (1903–13)

Scott, Peter

Versatile defender who forged a successful lower-league career

A promising and adaptable full back, Peter Scott progressed through Everton's youth ranks, turning professional in July 1970 and making his debut in place of Colin Harvey on the opening day of the 1971/72 season, aged 18. Serious injury suffered by Tommy Wright in that same game gave Scott an opportunity at

right back, and the bulk of his appearances in a blue shirt came in that position.

A local lad, who had represented England at youth level and was eligible for Northern Ireland through his parentage, Scott was enthusiastic and hard-working, though perhaps lacking in the technique that would have seen a sustained challenge to the ailing Wright's place. After his debut season first Harry Catterick, then Billy Bingham, tried a string of full backs with Scott only ever flitting in as an understudy. He made his international debut for Northern Ireland against Wales in May 1975, but joined York City in December that year without making a further appearance for Everton.

At Bootham Crescent he suffered consecutive relegations, giving him the ignominy of appearing in all four league divisions in successive seasons. He remains York's most capped player and the only Aldershot player to win international honours.

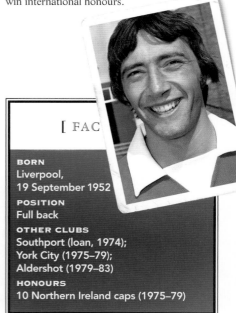

	League		FA Cup		League Cup		Other		Total	
Season	App	Goals	App	Goals	App	Goals	App	Goals	App	Goals
1971/72	28 (1)	1	3	1	1	0	-	-	32 (1)	2
1972/73	8 (1)	0	0	0	0	0	-	-	8 (1)	0
1973/74	0	0	0	0	0	0	-	-	0	0
1974/75	6	0	2	0	0	0	-	-	8	0
1975/76	0	0	0	0	0	0	0	0	0	0
Total	**42 (2)**	**1**	**5**	**1**	**1**	**0**	**0**	**0**	**48 (2)**	**2**

[FAC

BORN
Liverpool,
19 September 1952
POSITION
Full back
OTHER CLUBS
Southport (loan, 1974);
York City (1975–79);
Aldershot (1979–83)
HONOURS
10 Northern Ireland caps (1975–79)

Screen Sport Super Cup

Short-lived competition that represented a poor alternative to European football

The Super Cup was an invention of the Football League in an attempt to provide financial and sporting compensation following UEFA's European ban on English clubs after the 1985 Heysel Stadium disaster.

It was an invitational competition consisting of the six European qualifiers – Everton, Manchester United, Liverpool, Tottenham Hotspur, Norwich City and Southampton – from the 1984/85 season. They were split into two groups of three teams, who played each other home and away. The top two teams from each group qualified for two-legged semi-finals, with the winners facing each other in a final, also played over two legs.

The competition received a lukewarm reception from supporters and Howard Kendall soon lost interest in it, filling his team with fringe players and never-seen-before (or after) reserves, such as Darren Coyle and Peter Billing. Despite this half-heartedness, Everton did well, reaching the final.

But it was indicative of how poorly the competition was received that the Football League was unable to attract sponsorship until the final in September 1986, when Screen Sport, a long-forgotten cable TV channel, stepped in.

IN A DARK IRONY, Liverpool, whose supporters' actions had caused the competition's inception in the first place, won the competition, beating Everton 7-2 on aggregate in a two-legged final. The two games were the most poorly attended derby matches in generations. Afterwards the competition was scrapped, unlamented by clubs and fans alike.

Everton's record

Group stage

18 SEPTEMBER 1985
v. Manchester United [A]
4-2 *Sheedy 2, Lineker, Sharp;* **33,859**
Southall, Stevens, Van den Hauwe, Ratcliffe, Marshall, Harper, Steven, Lineker (Heath), Sharp, Bracewell, Sheedy

2 OCTOBER 1985
v. Norwich City [H] 1-0
Lineker; **10,329**
Southall, Stevens, Van den Hauwe, Ratcliffe, Marshall, Harper, Steven, Lineker, Sharp, Bracewell, Sheedy

23 OCTOBER 1985
v. Norwich City [A] 0-1; **12,196**
Southall, Stevens, Van den Hauwe, Ratcliffe, Harper, Heath, Steven, Lineker (Richardson), Sharp (Wilkinson), Bracewell, Sheedy

4 DECEMBER 1985
v. Manchester United [H] 1-0
Stapleton own goal; **20,542**
Southall, Harper (Pointon), Van den Hauwe, Ratcliffe, Stevens, Heath, Steven, Lineker, Wilkinson, Bracewell, Richardson

Team	P	W	D	L	GF	GA	GD	Pts
Everton	4	3	0	1	6	3	+3	9
Norwich City	4	1	2	1	3	3	0	5
Manchester Utd	4	0	2	2	4	7	-3	2

Semi-Final

5 FEBRUARY 1986
Semi-final 1st leg v. Tottenham Hotspur [A] 0-0; 7548
Southall, Stevens, Pointon, Marshall, Van den Hauwe, Reid, Steven, Coyle, Wilkinson, Billing, Richardson

19 MARCH 1986
Semi-final 2nd leg v. Tottenham Hotspur [H] 3-1 [AET] (aggregate 3-1) *Heath, Mountfield, Sharp;* **12,008**
Southall, Billing (Van den Hauwe), Pointon, Marshall, Mountfield, Richardson, Harper, Heath, Wilkinson (Sharp), Coyle, Sheedy

Final

16 SEPTEMBER 1986
Final 1st leg v. Liverpool [A] 1-3 *Sheedy;* **20,660**
Mimms, Billing, Power, Ratcliffe, Marshall, Langley, Adams, Wilkinson, Sharp, Steven, Sheedy (Aspinall)

30 SEPTEMBER 1986
Final 2nd leg v. Liverpool [H] 1-4 (aggregate 2-7) *Sharp (pen);* **26,068**
Mimms, Billing, Power, Ratcliffe, Mountfield, Steven, Adams, Heath (Aspinall), Sharp, Wilkinson, Sheedy (Pointon)

Seargeant, Steve

Left back who later enjoyed time in the sun with Brazilian legend

A former England schoolboy international who had progressed through Everton's youth ranks, Steve Seargeant first came into the Everton teamas John Hurst's understudy in the early 1970s. The blond defender was a fine and aggressive tackler, but there was a sense that he lacked the physical stature to make a sustained challenge for a central defensive berth.

Billy Bingham converted Seargeant to left back following his arrival as manager in 1973, and Seargeant initially flourished. He made 35 appearances during the 1974/75 season as Everton narrowly missed out on the League Championship and started the following campaign as first-choice left back. But loss of form saw him cede his place, first to Dave Clements, then Dave Jones. After Bingham was sacked, Seargeant found himself frozen out under Gordon Lee, and left in February 1978 to join Detroit Express. He played out his career on the other side of the Atlantic, linking up with Carlos Alberto Torres in California in 1981.

> AGAINST COVENTRY CITY, HE SAT BESIDE AN ADVERTISING HOARDING AND WEPT

Sergeant later embarked on a successful youth coaching career in the United States. His son Christian was on Everton's books under David Moyes but left without making an appearance, later forging a career with Bangor City, where he played alongside Graeme Sharp's son, Chris.

Season	League App	League Goals	FA Cup App	FA Cup Goals	League Cup App	League Cup Goals	Europe App	Europe Goals	Total App	Total Goals
1971/72	1	0	0	0	0	0	-	-	1	0
1972/73	8	0	0	0	0	0	-	-	8	0
1973/74	12 (1)	0	0	0	0	0	-	-	12 (1)	0
1974/75	35	1	2	0	2	0	-	-	39	1
1975/76	17 (1)	0	0	0	3	0	2	0	22 (1)	0
1976/77	4	0	0	0	0 (1)	0	-	-	4 (1)	0
1977/78	0 (1)	0	0	0	0	0	-	-	0 (1)	0
Total	**77 (3)**	**1**	**2**	**0**	**5 (1)**	**0**	**2**	**0**	**86 (4)**	**1**

[FACTFILE]

BORN
Liverpool, 2 January 1951
POSITION
Left back
OTHER CLUBS
Detroit Express (1978–80);
California Surf (1981)

Senderos, Phillippe

Loan star whose Goodison switch did not work out

[FACTFILE]

BORN
Geneva, 14 February 1985
POSITION
Centre back
OTHER CLUBS
Servette (2001–03);
Arsenal (2003–10);
AC Milan (loan, 2008–09);
Fulham (2010–)
HONOURS
44 Switzerland caps
(5 goals) (2005–)

Season	League App	League Goals	FA Cup App	FA Cup Goals	League Cup App	League Cup Goals	Europe App	Europe Goals	Total App	Total Goals
2009/10	1 (1)	0	0	0	0	0	1	0	2 (1)	0
Total	**1 (1)**	**0**	**0**	**0**	**0**	**0**	**1**	**0**	**2 (1)**	**0**

Settle, Jimmy

Inside forward of pace and élan

England international Jimmy Settle arrived at Goodison in April 1899 amid one of the most dramatic overhauls of personnel in the club's short history.

EVERTON had been strongly challenging league leaders Aston Villa all through the 1898/99 season, but in the final weeks of the campaign their form collapsed dramatically, winning just one of their final eight league games and finishing three positions and seven points off the top of the table.

Frustrated by the team's decline the Everton board were spurred into action, spending big to ensure that they would not be nearly men again. From Burnley came the centre forward Wilf Toman, from Aston Villa the brothers Jack and Bert Sharp, a winger and a full back respectively. And from Bury, Everton sought the centre half Joe Leeming and England forward Jimmy Settle. The defender remained at Gigg Lane, but the forward was Everton's for the sum of £400.

Toman's career would be ended by a devastating compound fracture of his leg 17 months later, while Bert Sharp never made the Goodison grade. But Jack Sharp and Settle would be mainstays of an Everton attack through the rest of the decade. League Championship honours would prove elusive, but the pair shared international recognition and the 1906 FA Cup success.

Settle had started out with Blackburn Rovers, but found success as an inside forward after joining Bury, then playing in the top flight. His form was prodigious,

notching 28 goals in just 63 league appearances and earning an England call-up in the spring of 1899. Weeks later he was an Everton player, part of the 'strenuous endeavours' by the Everton board 'to improve the team'.

'The forward's line promises to be a stronger and better balanced lot than has represented the club for some seasons,' reported the Liverpool Mercury. 'J. Sharp will, with Settle, form the right wing, with Toman in the centre. The left will probably cause some difficulty in deciding upon, as there appears to be a wealth of talent to select from.'

Settle was a tough, stocky, but skilful player, who possessed a devastating turn of pace and was an instinctive finisher. In teams that were not prolific he was an important contributor of goals, and his tally of 18 in the 1901/02 season saw him ranked as the First Division's top scorer.

A hat-trick display against Wolves in September 1901 exemplified his skill and illustrated his omnipresent threat to opponents. 'Suddenly Settle got the ball and passed out to Bell, and dashed away, and sent in a shot, which struck the goalkeeper,' reported the Liverpool Courier of his first goal. 'In the melee Settle rushed up and banged the ball into the net, scoring the first goal for Everton.' His second came soon after: 'Sharp had the misfortune

to place the ball into the wrong side of the upright, but coming again, Taylor got in a timely pass to Settle, who after leaving the ball followed it up and planted it in the net, amid terrific cheering. The second goal was distinctly pleasing to the crowd.' By half-time his treble was complete: 'He dodged several opponents very trickily, and finished up by crediting himself with the third of the match. It was a brilliant effort, which deserved the applause, with which it was received. From now to the interval the ball was rapidly transferred from end to end, but nothing further was secured.'

'Full of dash and trickery, he was a constant source of danger to the Wolves defence, and nothing could have been more deftly executed than the movements, which enabled him to score goals number two and three,' added the Liverpool Mercury. 'The second was the result of pretty manoeuvre, but the third was the outcome of pure doggedness, and irresistibility of purpose, for he beat fully half a dozen opponents before shooting.'

His form saw him recalled to the England team. But although he was to score a goal per game, his international career was marked by tragedy. On Saturday 5 April 1902, England met Scotland in the Home International Championship decider at Ibrox and Settle was in the forward line. 'One minute the game was proceeding calmly and being

keenly followed by the vast concourse,' recalled Steve Bloomer, who was lining up alongside him in the forward line. 'The next minute there was a terrible crash like the many peals of thunder in a great storm joining together in unison. The players stood as though rooted to the spot and there before our eyes we saw part of a huge stand, packed with people, crashing to the ground. The memory of that awful picture is still with me, with people crashing through iron railings as if they were matchwood. The groans, cries of fear and the uproar which followed beggars description.' A wooden stand had collapsed, plunging spectators 40 feet through broken boards, killing 26 and injuring 500.

More happy times lay at Goodison. The perennial nearly-men of the era twice finished league runners-up, but in 1906 Settle finally got his hand on silverware when Everton beat Newcastle to win the FA Cup. He was in the side that lost the final to Sheffield Wednesday a year later, but a poor 1907/08 season, in which Everton finished 14th, suggested a team in decline. At the end of the season the Everton directors, who had recently brought in Val Harris, Bert Freeman and John Coleman, sought a clean sweep. Settle, along with fellow stalwarts Tom Booth, Jack Crelley and Walter Abbott, were transfer-listed and for £200 Stockport County were the beneficiaries of the forward's experience.

Season	League		FA Cup		Total	
	App	Goals	App	Goals	App	Goals
1898/99	1	0	0	0	1	0
1899/1900	26	10	1	0	27	10
1900/01	30	10	2	1	32	11
1901/02	29	18	0	0	29	18
1902/03	20	5	2	0	22	5
1903/04	29	8	1	0	30	8
1904/05	32	9	6	4	38	13
1905/06	28	11	5	1	33	12
1906/07	21	6	8	4	29	10
1907/08	21	7	7	3	28	10
Total	**237**	**84**	**32**	**13**	**269**	**97**

[FACTFILE]

BORN
Millorn, 1876
POSITION
Inside forward
OTHER CLUBS
Bolton Wanderers (1894–96);
Bury (1896–98); Stockport
County (1908–09)
HONOURS
6 England caps
(6 goals) (1899–03)

Shackleton, Alan

Unheralded forward of the Carey years who dropped out of league football after Everton

Within weeks of his September 1959 arrival at Goodison Park, the hitherto unsung forward Alan Shackleton found himself cast at the centre of Evertonian hopes. Dave Hickson had been controversially sold to Liverpool and Shackleton, who had previously played on the left wing and twice deputised for the talisman, was given the lofty task of filling the number nine shirt.

> SHACKLETON FOUND HIMSELF CAST AT THE CENTRE OF EVERTONIAN HOPES

Signed from Leeds United for £8450, the Lancastrian had a reputation as a prolific yet underrated striker. At Burnley he had averaged a goal every other game without making the centre forward's shirt his own. In a year at Leeds his record was even better: 16 league goals from just 28 appearances. And yet he was allowed to leave after just a year at Elland Road.

At Goodison there were some promising early signs: a brace from the wing at home to Sheffield Wednesday brought Everton two points, and this was followed seven weeks later by a hat-trick against Birmingham. But at the same time there was also a sense that he and Everton were not destined to be. Within a month of his arrival the Everton board tried to part-exchange him for Huddersfield Town's Denis Law.

Johnny Carey persisted with Shackleton until February 1960, but the arrival of Roy Vernon spelled the end. Jimmy Harris was initially the Welshman's favoured forward partner and Shackleton dropped out of contention. When Carey and the board settled on Everton's retained list at the end of the season, Shackleton's name was initially on it but was then – quite literally – crossed out with biro. He was given notice to quit his club house and joined Nelson in the Lancashire Combination. It seemed an astonishing fall from grace.

A year later Everton received a £500 payment from Oldham Athletic for his playing registration, but Shackleton remained at Boundary Park for just a year. At 28 he dropped out of league football for good, settling in Kent where he played for Tonbridge.

	League		FA Cup		Total	
Season	App	Goals	App	Goals	App	Goals
1959/60	26	10	1	0	27	10
Total	26	10	1	0	27	10

[FACTFILE]

BORN
Padham, 3 February 1934
DIED
26 April 2009
POSITION
Striker
OTHER CLUBS
Burnley (1954–58);
Leeds United (1958–59);
Nelson (1960–61);
Oldham Athletic (1961–62);
Tonbridge

Sharp, Bertram 'Bert'

Younger brother of the illustrious Jack who provided defensive cover over two Goodison spells

	League		FA Cup		Total	
Season	App	Goals	App	Goals	App	Goals
1899/1900	3	0	0	0	3	0
1901/02	6	0	1	0	7	0
Total	9	0	1	0	10	0

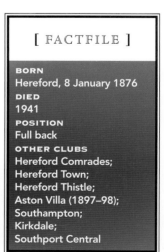

[FACTFILE]

BORN
Hereford, 8 January 1876
DIED
1941
POSITION
Full back
OTHER CLUBS
Hereford Comrades;
Hereford Town;
Hereford Thistle;
Aston Villa (1897–98);
Southampton;
Kirkdale;
Southport Central

Sharp, Graeme

Illustrious centre forward who ranks second only to Dixie Dean in Everton's all-time goalscorers

Graeme Sharp was a constant through the 1980s, his career coinciding with the rise, remarkable success and decline of Everton during this decade. A gifted, no-nonsense centre forward, and – for the majority of his career – a prolific goalscorer too, Sharp and his goals were crucial to Everton throughout the era. Although his reputation as an Everton number nine is often overshadowed by Alex Young, Bob Latchford and even Duncan Ferguson, Sharp was as underrated as he was prolific; his 150 first-class career goals put him behind only Dixie Dean in Everton's list of all-time goalscorers.

Brought up just outside Glasgow, Sharp was a boyhood Rangers fan. He started out in the city's junior leagues and was spotted by Dumbarton, for whom he signed as a part-time professional in

> HE KICKED OFF THE 1982/83 SEASON WITH A BRACE IN THE 5-0 THRASHING OF NEW EUROPEAN CHAMPIONS, ASTON VILLA

1978, aged 17. He quickly developed a reputation as one of the most promising young players in the Scottish First Division and was linked with moves to Celtic, Rangers, Aberdeen, Aston Villa and Arsenal. But it was Gordon Lee who followed up this initial interest with a firm offer, and his £120,000 bid in April 1980 proved successful.

'He is enthusiastic and clearly has potential,' said Lee when he unveiled his new signing. 'I've been looking for a young striker like Graeme because I think we need one.' But it would take Sharp a further, often frustrating, 18 months to make any impact at Goodison, while Aston Villa and Aberdeen, who had both tried to sign him from Dumbarton, rode high in Europe. In May 1981 Lee was replaced as manager by Howard Kendall, who immediately invested heavily in two forwards, Alan Biley and Mick Ferguson. Sharp was linked with a return to Scotland.

Finally, in October 1981, with Everton beset by injuries and suspension, Sharp's chance came. Given a rare start against Notts County he seized his opportunity, scoring in a 2-2 draw. He retained his place in the team, and by the season's end Biley and Ferguson were distant memories as Sharp finished top league scorer with 15 goals from just 27 appearances.

Scarcely did he look back over the next decade. He kicked off the 1982/83 season with a brace in the 5-0 thrashing of new European champions, Aston Villa, and his partnership with Adrian Heath, who also scored twice in the same game, seemed to hold vast potential. 'When Inchy [Heath] signed for a club record £700,000 he was struggling as a midfield player,'

he would recall. 'And I don't know what made Howard push him up front but the two of us hit [it] off straight away. It was something we didn't even have to work on. It just came automatically.' A late-season flourish meant that Sharp matched his previous season's total of 15 league goals.

Although he was quickly gathering a reputation as a prolific goalscorer, Sharp's all-round play was increasingly worthy of note. He was a brave and hard old-school centre forward, not averse to taking knocks – or handing them out. He was more than just an aerial playmaker, however, and possessed a deft first touch; his distribution was unselfish and accurate. The sometime England centre back Terry Fenwick said: 'Graeme Sharp has really come into his own as a target man in the last couple of years. His strength and power in the air make him one hell of a handful.'

BUT AS Everton's form and confidence dipped in the early stages of the 1983/84 season, Sharp struggled too. After scoring on the opening day of the campaign he failed to record another league goal until the end of February. His return to form can ultimately be credited to the arrival of Andy Gray, who was Sharp's boyhood hero. Signed in November 1983, his unshakable sense of self-confidence and desire to win rubbed off on his beleaguered team-mates. 'He was just the sort of character we needed,' Sharp recalled in his autobiography. 'He was terrific: a breath of fresh air … He had an unbelievable will and a desire to win football matches and although our fortunes didn't turn around immediately, he made sure we were never down for too long after a poor result, which is important to a group of young players.' In footballing terms they were a formidable and heavyweight partnership, with the ability to batter their opponents into submission. In the FA Cup

Final they scored a goal apiece as Sharp lifted his first major honour.

For the next two years Sharp's form was magnificent. During this period he started 100 games for Everton, scoring 51 times. None were better nor more deeply enshrined in Everton lore than the stunning volley he hit against Liverpool in the Anfield derby in 1984. Latching on to Gary Stevens' long ball, he flicked the ball past Mark Lawrenson and hit a sublime volley from 30 yards that nestled into the top corner of the Liverpool net. The goal ended 14 years without an Anfield victory, also proving a worthy winner of Match of the Day's Goal of the Season competition. Even Joe Fagan, so often defiant in defeat, was moved to say, 'It was a bloody good goal, worth winning any game. It would almost have been a shame for us to score after a goal like that.'

In September 1985 Sharp won his first Scotland cap in a World Cup qualifier in Iceland. At the end of the 1985/86 season he was part of the squad that travelled to the 1986 World Cup finals in Mexico. Later he attracted criticism for not scoring in his first 11 games for his country, his only international goal coming in his last appearance in a Scotland shirt, against Malta in 1988.

Gray left in summer 1985, and with his successor, Gary Lineker, Sharp formed Everton's most prolific forward line since the 1930s. Between them they scored 64 goals in all competitions; Sharp's share including an extra-time winner in the FA Cup semi-final win over Sheffield Wednesday. But Everton ultimately fell short, narrowly losing out to Liverpool in the league and FA Cup. At the season's end Lineker was sold to Barcelona and the Sharp–Heath partnership was restored. Sharp was far less prolific during the 1986/87 season, but the goals were shared out and he won a second league title medal. Despite scoring just five league goals, none were more important than the strike that saw off Queens Park Rangers on their much criticised plastic pitch in January – earning a 1-0 win that added crucial momentum to Everton's title challenge.

The 1987/88 season saw some vintage performances from the centre forward, even though Everton struggled collectively. His first ever hat-trick came when he scored all four goals in the away victory over Southampton. In the FA Cup, with the third round tie against Sheffield Wednesday deadlocked after three attempts, he hit a stunning first-half hat-trick in the third replay as Everton recorded a 5-0 victory.

This was to be as good as it got for Sharp, and his decline after the end of the 1987/88 season seemed to mirror that of the team. His partnership with Tony Cottee, a British record signing in summer 1988, was unsuccessful, amid rumours that the two failed to see eye to eye. His tally of league goals for his final three years at Everton fell from seven in 1988/89 to six in 1989/90 and just three the following season. His last goals for Everton came in one of Goodison's most memorable matches, the 4-4 FA Cup draw with Liverpool in February 1991.

AT THE end of the season Howard Kendall, now in his second spell as manager and seeking to revitalise his team, deemed Sharp expendable. The two had sometimes shared a testy relationship, Sharp feeling he was under-appreciated by Kendall, and the manager critical of his goalscoring record. (Even in Sharp's own autobiography, when paying tribute to him in an appendix Kendall recorded: 'I still say to this day that he could have been better. Had he got simpler tap-ins we would have had the perfect centre forward because he had everything else.') In July 1991 he joined Joe Royle's Oldham, newly promoted to the top flight, for £500,000. Here, he was a key figure in securing their survival over the next two seasons. In November 1994, when Royle left to manage Everton, Sharp was appointed player-manager at Boundary Park, with Colin Harvey joining as his assistant. However, after failing to make a promotion challenge

and amid crippling financial difficulties, in March 1997 Sharp resigned his position. He then spent a season in charge of Bangor City in the League of Wales. In 1998 he won the Welsh FA Cup, but left the club soon after.

SHARP has since embarked on a successful media career, which he combines with an ambassadorial role for Everton. A dignified and erudite spokesman who always makes time for the fans, he has an enhanced reputation among a generation of Evertonians too young to have seen his pomp.

And yet, it was for his forthright and brave contribution during Everton's glory years that Sharp will always be remembered. 'Even though he was still right at the top of the tree, I think, strangely enough, that he was still under-rated,' Alan Hansen would recall. 'A lot of players didn't realise how good Sharpy was. But the players did.' When Ian Rush was asked in 1987 by his new club Juventus who, out of all the players in the world, he would most like as a strike partner, the Welshman named Graeme Sharp. High praise indeed from the greatest Liverpool forward of his generation to the finest Everton forward, and a true reflection of the high esteem in which Sharp was held.

[FACTFILE]

BORN
Glasgow, 16 October 1960

POSITION
Centre forward

OTHER CLUBS
Dumbarton (1978–80);
Oldham Athletic (1991–97
(Nov. 1994 – March 1997
as player-manager)

HONOURS
FA Cup 1984;
League Championship
1984/85, 1986/87;
European Cup Winners' Cup
1985;
12 Scotland caps
(1 goal) (1985–88)

Season	League App	League Goals	FA Cup App	FA Cup Goals	League Cup App	League Cup Goals	Other App	Other Goals	Total App	Total Goals
1979/80	1 (1)	0	0	0	0	0	-	-	1 (1)	0
1980/81	2 (2)	0	0	0	0	0	-	-	2 (2)	0
1981/82	27 (2)	15	1	0	1	0	-	-	29 (2)	15
1982/83	39 (2)	15	5	2	4	0	-	-	48 (2)	17
1983/84	27 (1)	7	5 (2)	1	11	3	-	-	43 (3)	11
1984/85	36	21	6	2	4	3	9	4	55	30
1985/86	35 (2)	19	7	1	5	1	4 (1)	2	51 (3)	23
1986/87	27	5	1	2	5	2	4	4	37	13
1987/88	32	13	8	6	6 (1)	1	2	2	48 (1)	22
1988/89	26	7	6	3	4	2	2	1	38	13
1989/90	30 (3)	6	7	1	3 (1)	0	-	-	40 (4)	7
1990/91	24 (3)	3	6	2	3	3	1	0	34 (3)	8
Total	**306 (16)**	**111**	**52 (2)**	**20**	**46 (2)**	**15**	**22 (1)**	**13**	**426 (21)**	**159**

Sharp, Jack

Illustrious all-rounder who wrote his name into Everton and Lancashire lore

In Jack Sharp and Harry Makepeace Everton possess two exceptional figures in the history of British sport. Just 10 other men have represented England at both cricket and football, many, such as C.B. Fry, relying on social connections to be able to represent their country. But Sharp and Makepeace were bona fide sportsmen, professionals who helped shape the face of sport in the first part of the 20th century. Both made outstanding contributions to Everton at football and Lancashire at cricket, and Sharp was one of the most well-known sporting figures of the era, his face appearing on 14 different cigarette cards.

EVERTON FA CUP WINNERS 1906

ELLIOTT (TRAINER) MAKEPEACE BALMER W. TAYLOR (C) SCOTT CRELLEY ABBOTT
SHARP BOLTON YOUNG SETTLE HARDMAN

SHARP WAS born in Hereford in 1878, the year of Everton's foundation. He started out as an amateur with Hereford Thistle, briefly filling his days working as a clerk, but he abhorred office life and quit after three weeks. 'I preferred to breathe rather than be asphyxiated, even if I was going to make nothing of games,' he would say.

JACK SHARP
EVERTON

'THE BEST OUTSIDE RIGHT HE'D EVER SEEN, BETTER EVEN THAN BILLY MEREDITH OR STANLEY MATTHEWS'

J.T. HOWCROFT

Instead, he came to Merseyside aged 17, but not as a footballer, instead taking up a position as apprentice groundsman at Liverpool Cricket Club in Aigburth. He held a similar position at Leyland CC, combining the summer sport with football. In 1897 he joined Aston Villa and in 1899 joined Everton, the year he lifted the First Division title with Villa.

Joining him on Merseyside was his elder brother Bert, whose football and cricketing career ran parallel to his brother's but would always be overshadowed by it. Bert represented Herefordshire at cricket and also played at Aston Villa. He had two spells at Everton wrapped around a spell at Southampton but without ever making a first-team shirt his own. In total he made a total of just 10 appearances, but eventually settled on Merseyside.

Despite his illustrious reputation, Jack Sharp's Everton career got off to a slow start. The Everton historian Thomas Keates was not wholly convinced by the new arrivals. 'The ability of ... [Sharp and Walter Abbott] was not perceptible to the Executive in the first season,' he noted. He had good reason to be sceptical – Everton finished the 1899/1900 season 11th, their worst ever

league showing. Nevertheless, the two men began to impress in their second season at Goodison and the directors 'eyes were opened ... and kept open for many years by the sheer and fascinating merits of both'.

Indeed Everton were an improving team, and such outstanding young players as Sharp, Abbott, Jimmy Settle and Sandy Young were still honing their craft in the first years of the 20th century. Everton finished the 1900/01 season seventh, but a year later narrowly missed out on the First Division title, finishing runners-up to Sunderland. It set an unfortunate pattern, for Sharp would be a perennial nearly man in his time at Goodison – three times finishing a league runner-up, twice in third place, but never a league champion.

He was, nevertheless, developing a reputation as one of the most thrilling wingers of his day. Although short and rather stocky he was described as a 'pocket Hercules' and possessed all the attributes found in many a great wide man: pace and acceleration, supreme accuracy on his crosses, as well as the ability to cut inside his defender and let loose with a rocket shot. J.T. Howcroft, who spent 30 years refereeing, described him as the best outside right he'd ever seen, better even than Billy Meredith or Stanley Matthews.

Season	League		FA Cup		Total	
	App	Goals	App	Goals	App	Goals
1899/1900	29	5	1	0	30	5
1900/01	25	7	2	0	27	7
1901/02	32	6	2	1	34	7
1902/03	27	6	2	1	29	7
1903/04	31	6	1	0	32	6
1904/05	21	8	6	2	27	10
1905/06	29	9	6	2	35	11
1906/07	27	7	6	3	33	10
1907/08	23	4	7	0	30	4
1908/09	31	6	2	1	33	7
1909/10	25	4	7	2	32	6
Total	**300**	**68**	**42**	**12**	**342**	**80**

Such views were widely shared by football's opinion makers throughout the Edwardian era. According to Alfred Pickford and William Gibson, authors of the 1906 book Association Football and the Men Who Made It, Sharp possessed 'beautiful control of the ball, and a wonderful eye for a vulnerable part of the defence. Cool, resourceful, determined, he makes the most of smallest openings, and if opportunities do not present themselves he has a wonderful faculty for creating them.'

INDEED THE authors seemed thoroughly enamoured with the Everton winger. 'He is an artist because he does all his work with the ease and certitude of a man who can touch the whole gamut of a forward's possibilities. He knows the game through and through. He is not, however, one of those artistic beings who require someone to fetch and carry for them, who only exert themselves when there are possibilities of individual glory ahead. Sharp does not play for Sharp; he plays for Everton.'

Yet Sharp was more than just a cog in the Everton machine. He was the supreme showman, they wrote: 'Dodging, dribbling, feinting, passing, shooting, he is surely one of the neatest-footed men playing the game.'

Perhaps surprisingly he earned just two England caps, the first against Northern Ireland in 1903, the other against Scotland two years later.

THE CROWNING moment of his Goodison career came in 1906 when he lifted the FA Cup – his only major trophy with Everton, despite several brushes with success. In an insipid final against Newcastle it was his moment of inspiration, when he cut past the Newcastle full back McWilliam and put in a fine cross that led to Sandy Young's winning goal 15 minutes from the end. 'Needless to say, the pent-up feelings of the Everton multitude broke forth in such a volume of sound that it was a wonder the threatening rain clouds overhead did not discharge their deluge,' recorded one excitable journalist.

Twelve months later Everton returned to Crystal Palace, strongly fancied to retain the FA Cup when they faced Sheffield Wednesday in the final. Everton threatened on the break – Young shot over the bar, Hardman missed an open goal – but it was Wednesday who took the lead on 20 minutes. Everton rallied, and two minutes before half-time, Sharp equalised. Yet his goal failed to serve as a rallying point for his team-mates, and Everton never seriously looked like getting the breakthrough. Six minutes from full time Wednesday scored the winner and Sharp, once again, was a runner-up. It had been a bad game for Everton and a poor advertisement for football. 'I doubt,' the Football League's founding father, William McGregor, commented, 'if we have ever had a final in which there has been more loose play … [It was] one of the poorest finals.'

Although Everton went close to winning the First Division title in 1908/09, they were a team in transition and Sharp was now the wrong side of 30. In 1909/10 Everton finished 10th – a calamitous position for a team that prided itself on its 'Nil Satis Nisi Optimum' motto. With Jack Taylor forced into retirement after a freak accident, Sharp also decided it was time to call an end to his lengthy football career to concentrate on his business and cricketing interests.

SHARP had started out for Lancashire as a 21-year-old, in 1899. In a 26-year career he played 518 matches, scoring 22,015 runs. He was, wrote the Lancashire historian John Kay, 'reliable and self-effacing – a cricketer of such all round prowess and always doing something useful'.

In 1909 he was selected to represent England at cricket for the first of three Tests, and many felt that he would have played more cricket internationals were it not for his footballing commitments, which prevented him from partaking in winter tours in remote outposts. Australia, in those days before air travel, was still a six-week voyage away.

In 1923, aged 45, Sharp took over the captaincy of Lancashire. 'For years this dapper Merseysider had done sound all-round work with bat and ball,' wrote Kay. 'Like Makepeace, he was an all-round sportsman. Each gained international honours at soccer and cricket and it is Lancashire's proud boast that few if any other county had ever fielded two "double" internationals in the same side.'

NAMED AN
EVERTON MILLENNIUM GIANT –
A FITTING TRIBUTE
TO ONE OF THE CLUB'S MOST
ILLUSTRIOUS NAMES

In 1924 he became the first Test selector who had previously been a professional player. A year later, when most men are nursing beer bellies and grey hair, his fitness as a top-class sportsman finally left him. 'Unfortunately Sharp contributed little,' wrote Kay. 'Far from fit, he tended to bulkiness and was suspect in the field. His crowning error was to drop a simple catch off Parkin at the start of the temperamental bowler's benefit match … Sharp's blunder not only precipitated a big opening partnership but roused the big crowd to sarcastic comment and unmerciful barracking. Sharp was upset and at the end of the season he resigned the captaincy and retired from a game he had served nobly and well.'

SHARP turned to the eponymous sports shop he ran in Whitechapel. The shop would bear his name until the 1980s. He also continued his association at Everton, serving as a director, a position that his son – Jack junior – would also assume. He died in 1938, aged just 60, his name burned into Lancastrian and Goodison lore. More than 60 years after his death he was unanimously named an Everton Millennium Giant – a fitting tribute to one of the club's most illustrious names.

[FACTFILE]

BORN
Hereford, 15 February 1878
DIED
Wavertree, 28 January 1938
POSITION
Winger
OTHER CLUB
Aston Villa (1897–99)
HONOURS
FA Cup 1906;
2 England caps
(1 goal) (1903–05)

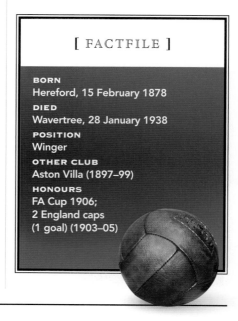

Sharples, George

Home-grown centre back unable to dislodge the imperious Brian Labone from the starting XI

Season	League		FA Cup		League Cup		Europe		Total	
	App	Goals	App	Goals	App	Goals	App	Goals	App	Goals
1960/61	5	0	0	0	1	0	-	-	6	0
1961/62	0	0	0	0	-	-	-	-	0	0
1962/63	2	0	0	0	-	-	0	0	2	0
1963/64	3	0	0	0	-	-	0	0	3	0
Total	**10**	**0**	**0**	**0**	**1**	**0**	**0**	**0**	**11**	**0**

[FACTFILE]

BORN
Ellesmere Port, 20
September 1943
POSITION
Central defender
OTHER CLUBS
Blackburn Rovers (1964–69);
Southport (1971–72)

Shaw, Stuart

Promising winger for whom a regular first-team spot proved elusive

Season	League		FA Cup		Europe		Total	
	App	Goals	App	Goals	App	Goals	App	Goals
1964/65	1	0	0	0	0	0	1	0
1965/66	2	0	0	0	0	0	2	0
Total	**3**	**0**	**0**	**0**	**0**	**0**	**3**	**0**

[FACTFILE]

BORN
Liverpool, 9 October 1944
POSITION
Winger
OTHER CLUBS
Crystal Palace (1966);
Southport (1966–69);
Port Vale (1969–70);
South Liverpool

Sheedy, Kevin

Left-footed maestro who was the creative heart of Everton's glory years

On 9 March 1985, in an FA Cup quarter-final tie with Ipswich Town, Kevin Sheedy was involved in one of the most remarkable pieces of skill Goodison has ever witnessed.

Called upon to take an early free kick, Sheedy took his time and curled a shot around the wall and into the right-hand corner of Paul Cooper's goal. As the crowd roared his opening goal, the referee, deciding Sheedy had taken too long with his effort, called play back and ordered him to retake it. Sheedy kept his cool, and indolently curled the ball to Cooper's left and into the Ipswich net. This time the goal stood. 'I still fancied it,' said Sheedy, later. 'I think after putting the first one in that [corner] Paul

Cooper had over-compensated to stop me doing the same again. It was a good feeling.'

Such effortless composure and technical excellence epitomised Sheedy, who wowed Goodison throughout the 1980s. Never a physical or hard-working player, who sometimes seemed out of place in an era when modern midfielders raced around as if their very lives depended upon doing so, Sheedy possessed something which set him apart from his contemporaries: the finest left foot in football.

Born the son of a publican in Builth Wells in the Welsh borders, Sheedy began his career with Hereford United in the mid-

1970s. Always a delicate player, his precise, imaginative passing soon attracted a score of top-flight scouts to this footballing backwater. In 1978, Sheedy travelled north to complete a move to Merseyside – but not to Goodison. Bob Paisley, always a man with an astute eye for lower league talent, had seen the promise Sheedy so emphatically possessed and paid Hereford £80,000 for the teenager.

If the cloud created by Liverpool's domestic and European domination had a silver lining, it was that Sheedy could not break into the Liverpool machine. Faced with competition from the likes of Graeme Souness, Terry McDermott and Ray Kennedy, chances were always going to be difficult to come by. In four years at Anfield Sheedy started just three games for Liverpool. Frustrated at the lack of opportunities, in the summer of 1982 he asked for a transfer. Paisley was determined to keep him, but the promise of first-team football was too alluring and he joined Everton in August that year after a tribunal fixed a fee of £100,000. In making the switch to Everton he was the first player to cross Stanley Park since Johnny Morrissey 20 years previously.

SHEEDY was an instant success at Goodison, belying the initial scepticism of some Evertonians. During the 1982/83 season he scored 11 league goals and also

played more games than any other Everton player. A delicate player of grace and élan, he defied the notion that football was becoming a mere athlete's game. His precise passing over long distances gave an additional dimension to Everton's play, allowing them to break quickly and penetrate opponent's rearguards. His crossing from set pieces and the wing allowed Graeme Sharp to

prosper, while he started to weigh in with his own contribution of goals from free kicks. In many ways he was a hark back to the old-fashioned footballers that preceded the game's tactical and physical changes in the 1960s, a modern-day Johnny Haynes or Danny Blanchflower.

In October 1983, Sheedy was called up to the Republic Of

Ireland squad, for which he qualified through his parents, and made his international debut in a 3-2 defeat to Holland. He was ever-present through Everton's Milk Cup run, but limped out of the final against Liverpool with the recurrence of an old injury, missing the replay and the rest of the 1983/84 season, including the FA Cup Final.

Sheedy made up for such disappointment by becoming a vital figure during Everton's all-conquering 1984/85 season. When the midfielder wasn't taking teams apart with his pinpoint passing from open play, he did so with the dead ball. Derek Mountfield scored 14 goals – an unprecedented total for a central defender – that season, many of which came from corners or free kicks taken by Sheedy. When he wasn't providing goals Sheedy scored them, his tally of 17 goals in all competitions a remarkable figure for a midfielder. Howard Kendall said of Sheedy: 'In terms of a provider of goals and scorer of goals Kevin will always be up there with the best. He is one of the best left-footed players I have ever seen. Kevin was never a tackler or a player you'd look to chase back defensively, but when he was on the ball he really was something special.' Indeed Sheedy truly prospered after the arrival of Pat Van Den Hauwe in September 1984, who took on many of his defensive responsibilities.

DURING the 1985/86 season, Sheedy's penetrating through balls were keenly exploited by Gary Lineker and his formidable runs from deep. Although beset by niggling injuries, he was again Everton's creative ace as they narrowly missed out on a League and FA Cup double to Liverpool. The following season he suffered again because of injury, but put in a season's best tally of league goals: 13 from 28 starts – a tally of which many a striker would

Season	League		FA Cup		League Cup		Other		Total	
	App	Goals	App	Goals	App	Goals	App	Goals	App	Goals
1982/83	40	11	5	2	3	0	-	-	48	13
1983/84	28	4	6	2	10	4	-	-	44	10
1984/85	29	11	6	4	2	0	5	2	42	17
1985/86	31	5	3	0	4	2	5	2	43	9
1986/87	28	13	1	0	4	1	4	2	37	16
1987/88	14 (3)	1	0	0	1	0	3	0	18 (3)	1
1988/89	24 (2)	8	8	4	1 (1)	0	5	0	38 (3)	12
1989/90	33 (4)	9	6	2	4	2	-	-	43 (4)	13
1990/91	20 (2)	4	3	1	0	0	2	0	25 (2)	5
1991/92	16	1	0	0	2	0	1	0	19	1
Total	**263(11)**	**67**	**38**	**15**	**31 (1)**	**9**	**25**	**6**	**357(12)**	**97**

have been proud. Few were more memorably celebrated than his strike against Liverpool in the Anfield derby, which he marked by waving a V-sign at the Kop.

DURING the 1987/88 season Sheedy completed just 10 of the 17 games he played, as injuries again took hold. Colin Harvey bought Ian Wilson from Leicester City to deputise in his absence, but he was a pale imitation of the Everton great. After starting the 1988/89 season on the substitutes bench, as the season progressed Evertonians saw more of the Sheedy of old. Often dropping into a more central position to accommodate Pat Nevin and Trevor Steven on the flanks, he impressed in flourishes with the vision and penetration of old. He scored in each of Everton's first four FA Cup ties as they made a fourth FA Cup Final in five years. But Sheedy was substituted late in the final as Everton slumped to a 3-2 defeat to Liverpool: it was his third defeat in an FA Cup Final.

Now entering the veteran stage of his career, Sheedy was promoted to chief penalty-taker after Trevor Steven's departure to Rangers. Finally, it seemed, during the 1989/90 season he had overcome the injuries that had so undermined his career. However, his pace – never one of his greatest facets – had diminished further with age. Allied to this, during English clubs' exile from Europe many teams had sacrificed a slower build-up for a faster, more powerful style of football less suited to the likes of Sheedy. Benfica once expressed an interest in him and maybe he should have taken his talents to the continent, as players like Liam Brady, Glenn Hoddle and Ray Wilkins had done with success. But by the age of 30 such a move was increasingly unlikely.

Sheedy was included in the Republic of Ireland squad for the 1990 World Cup Finals in Italy,

and attained footballing immortality in the Emerald Isle after scoring the equalising goal in Ireland's group match with England. On his return to Goodison he found his chances restricted by Colin Harvey, but was given another run in the team with the return of Howard Kendall that November. Eventually he lost his place to Peter Beagrie, and in February 1992, Kendall brought a close to an Everton career that had spanned almost a decade, allowing Sheedy to join Newcastle on a free transfer.

At St James's Park he was an important part of the first stages of the Kevin Keegan-led renaissance, helping stave off relegation to the old Third Division during the 1991/92 season and win promotion to the Premier League the next year. In summer 1993 he joined Blackpool and played one final season before his retirement. John Aldridge brought Sheedy back to Merseyside in June 1996 as his assistant at Tranmere Rovers, and he held a similar position at Hartlepool early the following decade, where he was reunited with Mike Newell. In August 2006 Sheedy returned to Everton as an academy coach – a move he described as 'like coming home'.

[FACTFILE]

BORN
Builth Wells,
21 October 1959
POSITION
Midfield
OTHER CLUBS
Hereford United (1975–78);
Liverpool (1978–82);
Newcastle United (1992–93);
Blackpool (1993–94)
HONOURS
League Championship
1984/85, 1986/87;
European Cup Winners' Cup
1985;
45 Republic of Ireland caps
(9 goals)

Shirt Sponsorship,
and Everton

From Danish processed meat to Thai beer, an eclectic range have decorated the Everton shirt over the years

As with so many developments in English football, Merseyside led the way when shirt sponsorship was first introduced.

Shirt sponsorship had been a growing trend in Europe through the 1970s and in 1979 Liverpool became the first senior English club to seize the possibilities that it presented. They signed up with the Japanese industrial conglomerate Hitachi for the 1979/80 season, but the move was not universally welcomed. Sponsors' logos were limited in size by the Football League in order to placate fans and the 'non-advertising' BBC. Restrictions on certain products, mainly cigarettes, were also imposed. Sponsorship of players' shorts and the backs of their shirts was also prohibited. Not until the 1983/84 season were sponsored shirts allowed to be worn in the FA Cup and there were restrictions until around this time when clubs were appearing in televised games.

Everton soon followed their neighbours, signing up with the Danish processed meat

manufacturer Hafnia. As with the majority of Everton's shirt deals, it was a long-running arrangement. Indeed, over the subsequent 30 years Everton have been less likely to change their shirt sponsor than their manager.

The club's current sponsorship with the Thai brewery Chang was extended in 2011 for a further three years. Worth more than £4million per year at the time of its expiry, it will mean Everton have worn the Chang logo longer than any other sponsor. The partnership is also the longest-running shirt deal in the Premier League.

Speaking to the official Everton website on concluding the deal in Bangkok, chief executive Robert Elstone said that he sees Chang as part of the club's extended family: 'Chang have always been very supportive of Everton since we first signed with them and have been extremely proactive in driving the partnership forward, helping Everton grow internationally, whilst we have assisted in supporting Chang in key markets around the world.'

Everton Shirt Sponsors

Hafnia	Processed meat manufacturers:	1979/80–1984/85
NEC	Electronics manufacturer:	1985/86–1994/95
Danka	Photocopier manufacturer:	1995/96–1996/97
One2One	Mobile phone network:	1997/98–2001/02
Keijan	Electronics manufacturer:	2002/03–2003/04
Chang	Thai Brewery:	2004/05–

Short, Craig

Expensive central defender who fell short of the standard demanded for Dave Watson's successor

Touted as a long-term replacement for an ageing Dave Watson, Craig Short was signed from Derby County for £2.75million and the services of Gary Rowett following Everton's 1995 FA Cup win. The tall centre half had once been the most expensive defender in English football, and had played at every level in league football, having joined Scarborough from non-league Pickering in 1987, shortly after their promotion to the Fourth Division.

ALTHOUGH Short had played just a solitary top-flight season, with Notts County in 1991/92, he subsequently captained Derby County, and Joe Royle's long pursuit of the defender suggested he was a player with sufficient stature to inherit Watson's central defensive berth and maybe even his captaincy. Royle introduced Short gradually over the opening months of the 1995/96 season and by the middle of the campaign he had ousted Gary Ablett.

Tall, yet mobile for such a big player, Short was a fine header of the ball and an expert at the last-ditch tackle. He was composed in possession and Royle encouraged his forward runs with the ball. One such excursion in the October 1997 derby set up Danny Cadamarteri's memorable goal.

And yet Short never really convinced in an Everton shirt. He was horribly prone to getting

caught out of position and his concentration sometimes lapsed at crucial moments. At 27 he was a late arrival to regular top-flight football and sometimes his lack of experience at the highest level was exposed. At other times he looked a fine player, but not near the calibre of Dave Watson on a weekly basis.

SHORT was never guaranteed first-team selection and after the arrival of Walter Smith in 1998, he fell behind such players as Richard Dunne and Marco Materazzi in the Goodison pecking order. With his contract running down he looked a likely departure, lest he leave for nothing on a Bosman transfer. But after rejecting a move to Nottingham Forest, he returned for the run-in to the 1998/99 season and at the campaign's end signed a new three-year deal.

IT WAS SOME surprise then, that before the opening of the 1999/2000 season Short was offloaded to Blackburn Rovers for £2million. The new contract had inflated his price and smacked of sharp practice from the Everton management; certainly, it was no way to repay the defender's loyalty.

Short retired at the end of the 2004/05 season to run a sailing school in the Lake District, but was tempted out of retirement to join Sheffield United, who had just been promoted to the Premier League. He retired again two years later, but in a strange twist in 2008 was persuaded to join Ferencváros in the Hungarian league as a player-coach. He later had short spells in charge of the same club, and also Notts County, before returning to Derby County as head of player recruitment.

[FACTFILE]

BORN
Bridlington, 25 June 1968
POSITION
Central defender
OTHER CLUBS
Scarborough (1987–89);
Notts County (1989–92);
Derby County (1992–95);
Blackburn Rovers (1999–2005);
Sheffield United (2005–07);
Ferencváros (2008)
AS MANAGER
Ferencváros (2009–10);
Notts County (2010)

Season	League App	League Goals	FA Cup App	FA Cup Goals	League Cup App	League Cup Goals	Europe App	Europe Goals	Total App	Total Goals
1995/96	22 (1)	2	3	0	2	0	3	0	30(1)	2
1996/97	19 (4)	2	1	0	1	0	-	-	21 (4)	2
1997/98	27 (4)	0	0	0	2	0	-	-	29 (4)	0
1998/99	22	0	0	0	2	0	-	-	24	0
Total	**90 (9)**	**4**	**4**	**0**	**7**	**0**	**3**	**0**	**104 (9)**	**4**

Simms, Sammy

Reserve centre forward limited to just a couple of outings

[FACTFILE]

BORN
Atherton, 1888
POSITION
Centre forward
OTHER CLUBS
Tyldesley Colliery;
Ton Pentre; Atherton;
Swindon Town;
Leicester Fosse (1914);
Swindon Town (1920);
Gillingham (1921)

Season	League App	League Goals	FA Cup App	FA Cup Goals	Total App	Total Goals
1912/13	2	1	0	0	2	1
Total	**2**	**1**	**0**	**0**	**2**	**1**

Simonsen, Steve

Record-breaking goalkeeper who failed to make the number one shirt his own

In 1998 Steve Simonsen became the most expensive goalkeeper in British football history when he crossed the Mersey, swapping Tranmere Rovers for Everton in a £3.1 million deal. The transfer was mired in controversy, however, as the Everton chairman Peter Johnson was later found to retain interests at Prenton Park and was alleged to have used this influence to secure the deal.

Simonsen had made his Tranmere debut during the 1997/98 season aged just 18, and immediately broke the club's clean-sheet record with seven consecutive shut-outs. Such form earned him both England under-18 and under-21 recognition as well as the Goodison switch.

His new manager Walter Smith was, however, noted for his reluctance to stake his faith in youth, and for Simonsen's first three years as an Everton player, Evertonians barely caught a glimpse of the young Geordie as he was alternatively second or third choice.

Following Thomas Myhre's sale and Smith's final loss of patience with the erratic Paul Gerrard, in November 2001 Simonsen was given his belated Premier League debut away at Bolton. His previous cameos, mostly in the League Cup, had been beset by nerves and plagued by error, but

his return to the Everton team was initially marked by a show of command and composure.

AFTER David Moyes's arrival four months later, he alternated between Simonsen and Gerrard as he worked out his best options. While there was a general upturn in form, neither man shone as Everton conceded 22 goals in nine matches. At the season's end, Moyes bought Richard Wright from Arsenal, and while Gerrard was eventually released, the purchase of Nigel Martyn in August 2003 was a signal that there was little confidence in Simonsen. Although he was offered a one-year contract extension, in July 2004 he joined Stoke City on a free transfer, making a belated Premier League return some four years later.

Season	League		FA Cup		League Cup		Total	
	App	Goals	App	Goals	App	Goals	App	Goals
1998/99	0	0	0	0	0	0	0	0
1999/2000	0 (1)	0	0	0	2	0	2 (1)	0
2000/01	0 (1)	0	0	0	0	0	0 (1)	0
2001/02	25	0	5	0	0	0	30	0
2002/03	2	0	0	0	0	0	2	0
2003/04	1	0	0	0	0	0	1	0
Total	**28(2)**	**0**	**5**	**0**	**2**	**0**	**35(2)**	**0**

[FACTFILE]

BORN
South Shields, 3 April 1979
POSITION
Goalkeeper
OTHER CLUBS
Tranmere Rovers (1996–98);
Stoke City (2004–10);
Sheffield United (2010–)
Chester City

Simpson, Bobby

Versatile full back who provided cover through Everton's victorious 1914/15 season

Season	League		FA Cup		Total	
	App	Goals	App	Goals	App	Goals
1912/13	10	0	0	0	10	0
1913/14	2	0	0	0	2	0
1914/15	9	0	2	0	11	0
Total	**21**	**0**	**2**	**0**	**23**	**0**

[FACTFILE]

BORN
Redcar, 1889
POSITION
Full back
OTHER CLUBS
Redcar Juniors; Old Corinthians; Teeside Amateurs; South Bank; Grangetown Athletic; Wrexham (1921); Chester City

Simpson, Tom

Reserve winger limited to just a solitary outing in an Everton shirt

[FACTFILE]

BORN
Keyworth, 13 August 1879
POSITION
Outside right / left
OTHER CLUBS
Notts County (1899–1901);
Leicester Fosse (1902);
Nelson

Season	League		FA Cup		Total	
	App	Goals	App	Goals	App	Goals
1903/04	1	0	0	0	1	0
Total	**1**	**0**	**0**	**0**	**1**	**0**

Singleton, Harry

Local winger who was unable to make a first-team breakthrough

[FACTFILE]

BORN
Prescot, January 1877
DIED
1948
POSITION
Outside left
OTHER CLUBS
Stockport County (1900);
Bury (1900);
Grimsby Town (1902);
New Brompton;
Queens Park Rangers;
Leeds City (1905–06)

Season	League		FA Cup		Total	
	App	Goals	App	Goals	App	Goals
1901/02	3	0	0	0	3	0
Total	**3**	**0**	**0**	**0**	**3**	**0**

Sloan, Donald

Goalkeeper who gained Irish league representative honours and crossed the Mersey divide

[FACTFILE]

BORN
Rankinston, 31 July 1883
POSITION
Goalkeeper
OTHER CLUBS
Belfast Distillery; Linfield;
Liverpool (1908); Belfast Distillery

Season	League		FA Cup		Total	
	App	Goals	App	Goals	App	Goals
1906/07	2	0	0	0	2	0
1907/08	4	0	0	0	4	0
Total	**6**	**0**	**0**	**0**	**6**	**0**

Smalley, Robert

Everton's goalkeeper as league football arrived at Anfield

Season	League		FA Cup		Total	
	App	Goals	App	Goals	App	Goals
1887/88	-	-	2	0	2	0
1888/89	18	0	-	-	18	0
1889/90	17	0	2	0	19	0
1890/91	1	0	0	0	1	0
Total	**36**	**0**	**4**	**0**	**40**	**0**

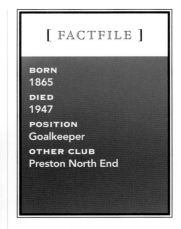

[FACTFILE]

BORN
1865

DIED
1947

POSITION
Goalkeeper

OTHER CLUB
Preston North End

Smallman, David

Great white hope whose career was ravaged by injury

David Smallman was one of football's great might-have-beens. Signed from Wrexham for £75,000 in March 1975, the young striker was considered one of the most outstanding young prospects outside the top flight. Comparisons were invariably made with Roy Vernon, and Smallman shared many of the physical and footballing characteristics of his countryman. Dark and rakishly slim, he possessed whippet-like pace and a poacher's instinct in front of goal; he even liked a cigarette, earning the sobriquet 'Smokey'.

Billy Bingham considered him the ideal foil for Bob Latchford and the early signs were excellent: the new partnership yielded eight goals from the opening eight games of the 1975/76 season. But then an appalling litany of injuries struck with the persistence of a jinx: a dislocated shoulder, torn hamstring, phlebitis of the calf, knee ligament damage, a broken leg in a reserve match and finally a broken leg sustained in a training accident at Bellefield. Evertonians caught but a glimpse of him in 1976/77 and then not at all in the subsequent three seasons. He returned to Wrexham in July 1980, but never played another senior match.

HOW GOOD might Smallman have become? He started just 23 games, but in that time his natural talents made a distinct impression on those who saw him. No less astute an observer as David Prentice, then a young fan and later the Liverpool Echo's chief sports writer, once considered him among the 10 best players he had ever seen in an Everton shirt: high praise indeed for one of football's ultimate maybes.

[FACTFILE]

BORN
Connah's Quay,
22 March 1953

POSITION
Forward

OTHER CLUB
Wrexham (1972–75)

HONOURS
7 Wales caps
(1 goal) (1974–76)

Season	League		FA Cup		League Cup		Europe		Total	
	App	Goals	App	Goals	App	Goals	App	Goals	App	Goals
1974/75	4	1	0	0	0	0	0	0	4	1
1975/76	14 (1)	5	0	0	2 (1)	1	2	0	18 (2)	6
1976/77	1 (1)	0	0	0	1	0	-	-	2 (1)	0
Total	**19 (2)**	**6**	**0**	**0**	**3 (1)**	**1**	**2**	**0**	**24 (3)**	**7**

Smith, Derek

**Home-grown forward
who prospered
on the other side
of the Mersey**

[FACTFILE]

BORN
Liverpool, 5 July 1946
POSITION
Forward
OTHER CLUBS
Tranmere Rovers (1967–70);
Ellesmere Port

Season	League App	League Goals	FA Cup App	FA Cup Goals	Europe App	Europe Goals	Total App	Total Goals
1965/66	2	0	0	0	0	0	2	0
1966/67	1 (1)	0	0	0	0	0	1 (1)	0
Total	**3 (1)**	**0**	**0**	**0**	**0**	**0**	**3 (1)**	**0**

Smith, Joe

**Outside right who
went on to earn Irish
League representative
honours with
Belfast Distillery**

[FACTFILE]

BORN
West Stanley, 1886
POSITION
Outside right
OTHER CLUBS
West Stanley; Hull City (1905–11);
Belfast Distillery;
Bury (1913–14);
West Stanley

Season	League App	League Goals	FA Cup App	FA Cup Goals	Total App	Total Goals
1911/12	8	0	0	0	8	0
1912/13	2	0	0	0	2	0
Total	**10**	**0**	**0**	**0**	**10**	**0**

Smith, John

**Local winger who
failed to claim a
regular first-team
place**

[FACTFILE]

BORN
Liverpool, 14 March 1953
POSITION
Right winger
OTHER CLUBS
Carlisle United (1976–77);
Marine

Season	League App	League Goals	FA Cup App	FA Cup Goals	League Cup App	League Cup Goals	Other App	Other Goals	Total App	Total Goals
1973/74	2	0	0	0	0	0	0	0	2	0
Total	**2**	**0**	**0**	**0**	**0**	**0**	**0**	**0**	**2**	**0**

Smith, Walter

Dour and authoritarian manager who saved Everton from the abyss

One of the most decorated managers in Scottish football history, Walter Smith arrived at Goodison in July 1998 seeking to enhance his reputation south of the border. A decade earlier, in swapping Aberdeen for Manchester United his friend and sometime colleague Alex Ferguson had done just that. But rather than Ferguson, Smith would follow a tradition set by Jock Wallace, Jock Stein and Graeme Souness: managers for whom success was habitual in Scotland, but elusive in England.

Smith's appointment represented Peter Johnson's final throw of the dice as chairman. Although Smith was initially backed with the sort of financial resources needed to rebuild Everton's thin squad, this proved short-lived. Indeed Smith's time as Everton manager would be undermined by boardroom battles and perennial financial crises. On the field the standard of football was largely turgid and often poor – but efficient enough to stave off relegation. By the time of his departure in March 2002 Smith's reputation had been dented, but he had just about done enough to save Everton from catastrophe.

Like many other great Scottish managers, Smith's playing career was mostly inauspicious. On leaving school he worked as an apprentice electrician, playing as a defender for the north Glasgow junior team, Ashfield. In 1965 he was spotted by Dundee United and signed as an amateur, for several years combining his trade with football before turning fully professional. As with the playing career of Alex Ferguson (and later David Moyes) it was largely undistinguished and in 1975 he joined Dumbarton, later returning to Dundee United, where he retired in 1980, due to a pelvic injury.

In October 2001 he told the Evertonian of his playing career: 'To be honest I was average. I was at Dundee United for 20 years and during that period of time I probably spent the majority of my time as a player-coach. I didn't manage to play an awful lot of games for them but I was always a good professional and I always tried my best.'

By the time of his retirement, Smith had already embarked on a coaching career and was highly rated within Scottish football. In 1978 he was appointed manager of Scotland under-18s and in 1982, with a team including Pat Nevin, won the European Youth Championships. Smith combined this work with his role as assistant manager of Dundee United during the most successful period in their history. In 1983 they won the Scottish Premier Division title and the following year reached the semi-final of the European Cup, only losing to AS Roma in contentious circumstances. In 1986 Smith served as Alex Ferguson's assistant when, following Jock Stein's death, he managed Scotland in the World Cup Finals in Mexico.

That same year, Smith left Tannadice to become Graeme Souness's assistant manager at Glasgow Rangers. It was a vastly successful partnership and, by combining Scotland's best players with the cream of English talent – desperate for the chance denied them in their own country to play European football – a glut of trophies followed.

After winning League Championships in 1987, 1989 and 1990, in April 1991 Souness left Rangers to manage Liverpool and Smith was the natural choice to succeed him as manager. Such continuity assured success, and the following month Smith won the first of seven consecutive Scottish league titles. On three occasions he also won the double, but, despite narrowly missing out on a Champions League final place in 1993, the European success demanded by Rangers fans was never forthcoming. In spring 1998 it was announced that Smith was to be succeeded at the end of the season by Dutch coach Dick Advocaat.

Smith quickly attracted the notice of several English clubs eager to utilise his experience and pedigree. In June 1998, he was set to succeed Ron Atkinson as Sheffield Wednesday manager, when Everton came calling.

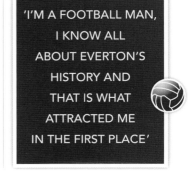

'I'M A FOOTBALL MAN, I KNOW ALL ABOUT EVERTON'S HISTORY AND THAT IS WHAT ATTRACTED ME IN THE FIRST PLACE'

Following a disastrous 1997/98 season and the sacking of Howard Kendall, Peter Johnson embarked on a search for another manager. Mindful of the previous summer's toe-curling odyssey, this time he moved comparatively quickly and poached Smith and his assistant Archie Knox from under the nose of Wednesday chairman Dave Richards.

'I'm a football man, I know all about Everton's history and that is what attracted me in the first place when I was approached,' Smith told reporters when he was unveiled as Everton manager on 1 July 1998. 'Everton's traditions were some of the reasons that I accepted the job. They are a club that can get themselves into a winning position in terms of going for trophies and I intend to help them along in that respect … It's a big challenge, it's one of the reasons we are both here.'

Smith had always spent heavily at Rangers, buying such big names as Paul Gascoigne, Michael Laudrup, Trevor Steven and Britain's first £4million player, Duncan Ferguson. At Goodison he wasted no time in splashing the cash, buying Olivier Dacourt, Marco Materazzi, David Unsworth, John Collins, Steve Simonsen and Ibrahima Bakayoko for a combined total of nearly £20million within his first months in charge. Even a decade later this represented the most lavish spending spree in the club's history.

However, despite the assurances of Peter Johnson, the money was not there to pay for these players. In November 1998 Duncan Ferguson was sold behind Smith's back to Newcastle for £8million in order to plug the gaping hole in Everton's overdraft. Smith was incandescent and only the intervention of Bill Kenwright prevented his resignation. Instead, Johnson resigned as chairman and Kenwright embarked on his purchase of the club. For the rest of his time as Everton manager, lack of money would be a defining characteristic of Smith's reign.

Ferguson's sale made little impact on the 1998/99 season, which began in abysmal fashion. Everton failed to score a home goal until Halloween and only won their first home match on 23 November, the evening before Ferguson's sale to Newcastle. Everton lined up

that day with five centre halves in their starting line-up – which was indicative of the pattern of play under Smith. Throughout his reign he preferred the solid over the spectacular, invariably filling his teams with physical giants, and the play was attritional.

Not only did they lack style, but discipline and composure were sorely absent in Everton's play. Materazzi and Dacourt – the two initial signings to impress most – possessed woeful disciplinary records, as indeed did the entire team under Smith's charge. There was also an infuriating habit of cracking under pressure and falling apart at the seams. Everton reached the quarter-final of the FA Cup in Smith's first season and played Newcastle. But despite drawing 1-1 on the hour mark, they meekly capitulated and were thrashed 4-1.

Despite hints of progress, four straight league defeats in March and April 1999 left Everton facing yet another relegation battle. Smith called upon 18-year-old Francis Jeffers and loan signing Kevin Campbell and their thrilling partnership rescued Everton's season, with Campbell scoring 10 goals in nine games, as Everton finished the campaign 14th.

The 1999/2000 pre-season represented one of consolidation, with Smith forced to balance the books after the earlier spending binge and continued uncertainty over Everton's ownership. Craig Short, Bakayoko, Materazzi and Dacourt were all sold, with Campbell, whose transfer was made permanent, the only major acquisition. Over the course of the summer and through 1999/2000, Smith also added a succession of cut-price and free transfers to his squad. Some of these were inspired, such as Richard Gough and David Weir (an earlier bargain, signed from Hearts); others, like Stephen Hughes and Mark Hughes, less so.

There was an upturn in form through 1999/2000 with Smith's team playing flourishes of slick football in between excruciating lapses, such as a 5-1 hammering at Old Trafford and an insipid FA Cup quarter-final defeat to Aston Villa. For a period they were an outside bet for a European place, but after winning just twice in their last 12 games they dropped to 13th on the final day of the season.

More frenetic transfer activity followed over the summer of 2000, with new owner Bill Kenwright betting on a lucrative media deal

'IT WAS EVIDENT TO FANS THAT SMITH VIEWED CERTAIN PLAYERS AS TROUBLEMAKERS'

with the cable media company NTL. Steve Watson, Alex Nyarko, Niclas Alexandersson, Duncan Ferguson, Alessandro Pistone and, perhaps most eye-catchingly of all, Paul Gascoigne were signed for a combined total of £18.5million, with £11million recouped from player sales.

Gascoigne came to personify the infuriating contradictions of Smith's management style. At Rangers, when he came under Smith's charge, Gascoigne had put in one of the finest and most consistent stints of his career; Smith, for his part, was generous and patient with the troubled star, which seemed to bring out the best in him. There were hopes that this could be replicated at Goodison. But Gascoigne was no longer physically nor mentally able for the rigours of the Premiership, despite Smith's efforts to nurture him. In his painfully honest autobiography, Gazza – My Story, Gascoigne details the benders and breakdowns that defined his 20 months at Goodison. Most of this remained hidden from public view; Smith was understanding, while Gascoigne continued to draw his £20,000 per week wages.

The flip side of this was that Smith was notoriously intolerant towards the perceived excesses and lapses of younger players. Sometimes he was justified, such as when he fined several players for overindulging during the millennium celebrations. Other times he seemed thin-skinned and petty, such as when he dropped Michael Ball and Richard Dunne for the heinous crime of laughing on the coach home after a League Cup defeat to Bristol Rovers in September 2000.

It was evident to fans that Smith viewed certain players as troublemakers. Don Hutchison, a consistent performer throughout his time at Goodison, had already been moved on. Dunne was next, three weeks after the laughing incident. Ball, who would be Everton's player of the 2000/01 season, was sold to Rangers at the campaign's end. Francis Jeffers, who had publicly fallen out with Smith in the past, was also moved on, to Arsenal.

for every Evertonian. Absolutely horrible ... Everton cannot celebrate avoiding relegation. However, we can be thankful for it and grateful for it.'

None of Smith's signings had been successful; indeed many of them spent most of the season injured. The lamentable Nyarko so infuriated one fan in an away game at Arsenal that he marched across the pitch and demanded his shirt – the implication being that he was unworthy of it. Nyarko begged to be substituted and afterwards, showing a staggering lack of empathy with a player he had invested heavily in, Smith seemed to side with the disgruntled fan, implying that he would never play Nyarko again (which he didn't). But what of Everton's £4.5million investment in the Ghanaian? Of course, it would eventually be written off.

Despite the sums raised by player sales during summer 2001, Smith had little money to play with. Alan Stubbs joined on a Bosman free transfer from Celtic and Tomasz Radzinski signed from Anderlecht as Jeffers' replacement. Given the paucity of resources available it was scarcely surprising that there was little upturn in fortunes. But the football was dour and passionless and most players seemed to be going through the motions. Five straight defeats over Christmas forced Kenwright to issue a vote of confidence in Smith. An FA Cup third round tie at Stoke seemed to hold the key to his future – as indeed it had over Howard Kendall in 1984. A 1-0 win earned a stay of execution. But there was no dramatic turnaround. Everton progressed to the quarter-finals of the FA Cup, but won just one more league game under Smith. After the quarter-final, an abject, tactically clueless 3-0 hammering by Middlesbrough, Smith was relieved of his duties on 12 March 2002.

When news of his sacking came it seemed like a release for every Evertonian. The standard of football had become abysmal, with results to match.

On the other hand, there was some sense that Smith had done well in trying circumstances. He showed great patience in the teeth of Peter Johnson's meddlesome running of the club, and was instrumental in ousting him. As the public face of the club he always conducted himself with dignity and was a worthy ambassador. Best of all, he steered Kenwright towards the appointment of David Moyes as his successor, when the chairman was apparently considering different targets.

Given the context of all the off-the-pitch acrimony at the club – takeover battles, crippling debts, lack of transfer funds – he had, on the surface, done well just to ensure survival. Indeed, one only had to look at the club he had turned down to take charge at Goodison, Sheffield Wednesday, who teetered on the brink of relegation to the Second Division and bankruptcy at the time of his sacking, and ponder just what might have been. Perhaps then, Walter Smith was a man for the time. As Kenwright said when he announced his departure: 'Walter Smith brought a stability and dignity to Everton when it desperately needed it most.'

Smith subsequently spent two years out of football. In March 2004 he was a surprise choice as Sir Alex Ferguson's temporary assistant as

Some of this was also dictated by financial necessity. The eleventh-hour collapse of the NTL deal left a gaping hole in Everton's finances and by 2001 plunged the club into another financial crisis. The Dunne, Ball and Jeffers sales raised around £18million and Smith can be credited for getting top dollar at the negotiating table. But at the same it was wholly demoralising to witness Everton sell its best young players in order to balance the books. And whatever the perceived excesses of Everton's young players, Smith failed to nurture their undoubted potential, seemingly treating them like children while simultaneously tolerating the ailing Gascoigne. More than anything else, it was this glaring contradiction that grated with fans.

Everton finished the 2000/01 season 16th, eight points clear of relegation and 20 off European qualification. They were humiliated in the FA Cup fourth round by Tranmere Rovers. It was a wretched season and even the normally ebullient Kenwright admitted: 'This season has been miserable. It has been miserable

> WALTER SMITH BROUGHT A STABILITY AND DIGNITY TO EVERTON WHEN IT DESPERATELY NEEDED IT MOST

> BEST OF ALL, HE STEERED KENWRIGHT TOWARDS THE APPOINTMENT OF DAVID MOYES AS HIS SUCCESSOR

Manchester United manager. In December that year he succeeded Bertie Vogts as Scotland manager. Scotland were in the international doldrums, but Smith oversaw a remarkable renaissance with the national team rising 70 places in the international rankings. It marked a rehabilitation of his reputation and in January 2007 he returned to Rangers, who were languishing in Celtic's shadow. Again Smith turned things around. In 2008 he led Rangers to the UEFA Cup Final, and a year later to their first Scottish title since 2005.

[FACTFILE]

BORN
Lanark, 24 February 1948
POSITION
Defender
CLUBS AS PLAYER
Dundee United
(1965–75 & 1977–80);
Dumbarton (1975–77)
AS MANAGER
Glasgow Rangers
(1991–98 & 2007–11);
Scotland (2004–07)

As Everton Manager											
Season	P	W	L	D	F	A	GD	Pts	Position	FA Cup	League Cup
1998/99	38	11	10	17	42	47	-5	43	14	Quarter-final	Fourth round
1999/2000	38	12	14	12	59	49	10	50	13	Quarter-final	Second round
2000/01	38	11	9	18	45	59	-14	42	16	Fourth round	Second round
2001/02	29	7	9	13	27	35	-8	30	15*	Quarter-final	Second round

* Everton finished 15th under David Moyes

Snodin, Ian

Versatile midfielder whose glittering potential was wrecked by injury

Signed at a crucial juncture of the 1986/87 season, in electing to join Everton from Leeds for £840,000 Ian Snodin snubbed Liverpool and immediately endeared himself to a generation of Evertonians. A fine, competitive midfielder, who combined a vigorous, energetic style with rare grace, Snodin was a hugely effective – even inspirational – component during Everton's title run-in.

A fiercely proud Yorkshireman, who later took the step of having his son born within the county boundaries so that he was eligible to play for its cricket team, Snodin had started off at Doncaster Rovers, amassing nearly 200 appearances by the age of 21, before making the switch to Leeds United in the summer of 1985. He succeeded Peter Lorimer as Leeds captain and his performances in the Second Division earned him the Goodison move 18 months later.

Gritty, composed, an accomplished passer of the ball and a formidable tackler, Snodin had attracted comparisons to Bryan Robson during his Leeds days and in his early appearances the hype seemed to be justified. Certainly at the age of just 23, the potential was there for Snodin to blossom into an outstanding player. He plugged the gap left by Paul Bracewell, a long-term injury absentee, and as the season approached its critical phase Snodin's form, like that of his new team, was magnificent.

His best form for Everton came when he was tried as an auxiliary right back during the 1988/89 season. Snodin slotted in as if he had played his entire career there. His form earned him an England call-up for a friendly against

Greece in February 1989 and there were hopes that he could oust Gary Stevens, now a Rangers player, from the national team. Alas, Snodin, who earned England B and under-21 recognition, was forced to withdraw prior to the game with a hamstring problem, which over the following year proved recurrent – limiting his chances at Goodison.

There followed a two-year-long injury nightmare, in which Snodin failed to make a single appearance. Defying fears that injury would force his premature retirement, Snodin returned to the Everton team in autumn 1992. Howard Kendall likened Snodin's return to the signing of a 'million-pound player'. Such was his commitment that he was often found wearily hobbling away after the match

following a bruising battle. Injury and age, however, had taken their toll on Snodin, while Everton were a poor side. During the 1993/94 season, after another injury-hampered start, Snodin returned at right back, then centre back, before returning to right back again; offering heart and experience in Everton's ultimately successful fight for Premiership survival.

Snodin was edged from contention during the 1994/95 season and allowed to join Oldham Athletic on a free transfer in January 1995. He later played for Scarborough, before returning to Doncaster for 18 months as player-manager in 1998. Snodin, whose older brother Glynn played for a number of Yorkshire clubs and alongside Ian at Doncaster, has since forged a successful media career. He remains a regular visitor to Goodison Park and is a popular figure among fans.

[FACTFILE]

BORN
Rotherham, 8 March 1963
POSITION
Right back / midfield
OTHER CLUBS
Doncaster Rovers (1980–85);
Leeds United (1985–87);
Sunderland (loan, 1994);
Oldham Athletic (1995–97);
Scarborough (1997–98);
Doncaster Rovers (1998–2000)
HONOURS
League Championship
1986/87

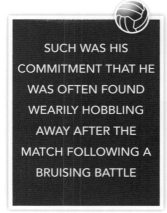

SUCH WAS HIS COMMITMENT THAT HE WAS OFTEN FOUND WEARILY HOBBLING AWAY AFTER THE MATCH FOLLOWING A BRUISING BATTLE

Season	League		FA Cup		League Cup		Other		Total	
	App	Goals	App	Goals	App	Goals	App	Goals	App	Goals
1986/87	15 (1)	0	2	1	0 (1)	0	1	0	18 (2)	1
1987/88	29 (2)	2	8	1	7	1	1	0	45 (2)	4
1988/89	23	0	5	0	5	0	2	0	35	0
1989/90	25	0	7	0	3	0	-	-	35	0
1990/91	1	0	0	0	0	0	0	0	1	0
1991/92	0	0	0	0	0	0	0	0	0	0
1992/93	19 (1)	1	2	0	2	0	-	-	23 (1)	1
1993/94	28 (1)	0	2	0	1 (2)	1	-	-	31 (3)	1
1994/95	2 (1)	0	0	0	1 (1)	0	-	-	3 (2)	0
Total	**142 (6)**	**3**	**26**	**2**	**19 (4)**	**2**	**4**	**0**	**191(10)**	**7**

Southall, Neville

Charismatic goalkeeper blessed with genius, he pulled on an Everton shirt more times than any other player

Neville Southall was a fixture in the Everton goal for an entire generation, wowing crowds with his goalkeeping, which seemed at times to defy the laws of gravity and age. A man of intense contradictions, Southall was at once grumpy, unsociable and eccentric, but carried a charisma that made him adored by all who saw him in an Everton shirt. He is the club's greatest servant and most decorated player, as unconventional as he was brilliant, and one of the few genuinely world-class players to have served the club.

Born in Llandudno, Southall was a boyhood Manchester United fan who initially escaped the notice of league clubs. As a schoolboy he played for the Caernarfon district team, both as a goalkeeper and centre half. His manager was a fortunate man indeed because he had two youngsters in his side who would go on to keep goal for Wales. Southall's rival at that time was Eddie Niedzwiecki, later to play for Wrexham and Chelsea before injury prematurely ended his career. Southall also played for Llandudno Swifts and on leaving school played for a succession of semi-professional teams in order to supplement his income. His full-time jobs were as unglamorous as the teams he played for (Bangor City, Conway United and Winsford United) and he took up roles as a labourer, a hod carrier, bin man and waiter in a Llandudno café, called The Ritz, where he worked seven days a week for £18.

In 1980 his break into league football finally came when he joined Bury for £6000. Under the tutelage of the club's assistant manager, former Manchester United boss Wilf McGuinness, Southall overcame a shaky start to his league career to attract notice further up the league. In July 1981 Howard Kendall paid £150,000 to make Southall one of his first signings as Everton manager; the goalkeeper learned of the move from his local newspaper.

Initially an understudy to Jim Arnold, Southall's chance came in October 1981 in a 2-1 win over Ipswich Town. Mick Lyons said of the debutant: 'At no time did the defence feel nervous because we had a new keeper. Neville had impressed us all with his ability in training and when it came to the crunch that ability was there along with the right temperament. He came through a test with flying colours.' Arnold reclaimed his place after recovering from injury, but shortly before Christmas Southall claimed the number one jersey.

ARNOLD HAD been 'on edge' according to Kendall. 'I felt it was time for Jim to take a break,' added the manager. 'How long that break will be depends on Neville Southall.' The 23-year-old kept his place for over a year. Arnold later recalled: 'I started the first season. But Neville's ability later came through and I ended up being more of a spectator than a goalkeeper ... It was never a case of hoping he would slip and I'd get a chance. I am sure that goes for Neville too.'

His performances for Everton led to a Wales call-up, and Southall made his international debut against Northern Ireland at Wrexham in May 1982. But this swift progress came to an abrupt halt in November 1982, after Everton's cataclysmic derby defeat to Liverpool. Southall conceded five times, including four goals to his international team-mate Ian Rush, and was dropped and subsequently loaned to Port Vale. He returned to reclaim his place in April 1983, and would hold on to it for the next 15 years.

HIS MANTRA WAS 'THOU SHALT NOT PASS'

A great colossus of a man, few players of Southall's physical stature had been seen in an Everton shirt before. He imposed himself on the penalty area like a great bear, plucking even the most fiercely whipped crosses from the sky as if the ball had been tossed to him in an underarm throw. His mantra was 'Thou shalt not pass', and he pursued this ethic with the relentlessness of a fundamentalist, flinging himself in front of opponents, trailing ankles and arms in an effort to stop the ball from entering the net. He was hideously brave, throwing himself through barrages of opponents and colleagues to claim the ball. Always dishevelled – hair plastered to his forehead, socks rolled around his ankles, overheating in

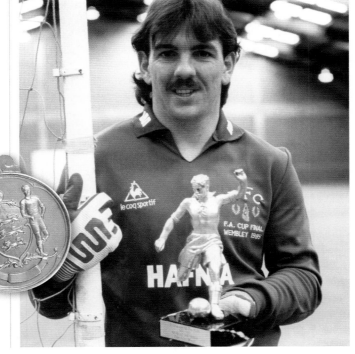

layer upon layer – he never looked much of an athlete, but could always pull off the most spectacular reflex save with the grace and seeming ease of a gymnast.

SOUTHALL controlled his defence with verbal barrage after verbal barrage. Sometimes, on a bad day at Goodison when crowds were stuck below the 20,000 mark, Southall's expletive-laden outbursts at his own defence were louder than the crowd itself. A teetotaller in an age when most footballers drank heavily, Southall was always one to spurn convention. Pat Nevin later described him as 'The classic eccentric with a complex character.' At times he seemed a mass of contradictions. A man who trained religiously, whose idiosyncrasies and indifference to the press have cultivated the image of a former bin man: sullen and withdrawn, happier in domestic bliss with his wife and daughter than living it up with his team-mates.

Yet there was another side to Southall that few saw. He was a committed helper of charities, particularly Alder Hey hospital. He always shared a great rapport with young fans. He possessed a droll sense of humour and delighted in mocking his colleagues. A favourite training ground jape was standing against a post to give a team-mate a full goal to shoot into. Invariably Southall would make it across for a save. Graeme Sharp described such antics as 'soul-destroying'.

Barely a year after his return from the Potteries, Southall was appearing at Wembley in the 1984 Milk Cup Final. His form was integral to Everton's renaissance and he returned in May to lift the FA Cup, the first trophy of an illustrious career. The 1984/85 season saw Southall at the height of his powers as he lifted the League Championship and European Cup Winners' Cup. His part in Everton's successes was recognised by the Football Writer's Association, which made him only the third goalkeeper to be awarded its Player of the Year.

ONE SAVE that lingers long in the memory came on 3 April 1985, with a dozen games remaining. Everton were top of the league and travelled to Tottenham, their principal title challengers. If Everton won, it would underline their title credentials; but if Spurs got a result it would open up the title race again. Everton were leading 2-1 after goals by Andy Gray and Trevor Steven, but with two minutes remaining Mark Falco bulleted a header towards the roof of the Everton net. It looked goal-bound, but Southall acrobatically twisted his body through

the air and somehow tipped the ball over the crossbar. After the game, Spurs manager Peter Shreeves said: 'The talk in our dressing room was all about the save near the end that stopped us getting the draw. It was world class.' Southall's description was typically modest. 'Everyone went on about it,' he shrugged, 'but it was straight at me.' The importance of the save was less in the points that it secured, but the psychological blow it dealt Everton's rivals. Spurs dropped out of the title race, while Everton kept on winning. 'The '85 side was the best I've ever played in by miles,' Southall later told this author. 'The only thing I'd maybe change is have Dave Watson in it.'

Southall's fine form continued into the 1985/86 season, by which time he was considered the best goalkeeper in the world. As he looked set to win a second consecutive League Championship medal, disaster struck. In March 1986, with Everton top of the league, he was playing for Wales against the Republic of Ireland at Lansdowne Road. On a ragged, divot-ridden pitch, Southall slipped in a pothole and suffered a severe dislocation of his ankle and ligament. At first doubts emerged about his future, but he managed to pull through, and was back in the Everton team within seven months. Despite the worthy efforts of stand-in keeper Bobby Mimms, many supporters believe that his absence in the season's concluding months ultimately cost Everton the League and FA Cup double that season. On his eventual return to first-team action, 15 games

> SOUTHALL'S FINE FORM CONTINUED INTO THE 1985/86 SEASON, BY WHICH TIME HE WAS CONSIDERED THE BEST GOALKEEPER IN THE WORLD

into the 1986/87 season, he helped inspire Everton to their ninth League title and remained there, virtually ever-present, in the decade which followed.

Subsequently he was a constant in a fluctuating side and as consistently outstanding as the majority of his team-mates were mediocre. In a succession of teams lacking character he remained as irrepressible as ever. He refused to collect his losers' medal after the 1989 Zenith Data Systems Final ('Who wants a ZDS runners-up medal?' he asked) and, after being denied a transfer request, walked out of Colin Harvey's half-time talk on the opening day of the 1990/91 season. Southall has always insisted that it was no a protest; he merely sought to clear his head. Neither Harvey nor Everton's fans were impressed, however, and he was hit with a fine of two weeks' wages. At the next home game the banner of one disgruntled supporter bore the legend, 'Once a bin man, always a bin man'. Typically Southall let his play do the talking and he remained an Everton player. During the 1993/94 season he surpassed Ted Sagar's Everton league appearance record, which he would eventually trump by more than 100 appearances. The same season he also overtook Peter Nicholas's Welsh international caps record, and would go on to claim 92 appearances for his country.

A succession of understudies – Bobby Mimms, Alec Chamberlain, Mike Stowell and Jason Kearton – were all seen off, but had the talent to forge good careers elsewhere. In his mid-thirties when Joe Royle became manager in November 1994, Southall was one of the core of veterans around whom Everton's survival hopes were placed. His response was magnificent: a record-breaking run of seven league clean sheets in Royle's first weeks in charge. Most memorably he was outstanding

as Everton lifted the FA Cup, with a superlative double save from Paul Scholes crucial to securing victory. After the match Southall told reporters that he intended on playing for another ten years – and then drove home to spend the evening with his family.

Despite Southall's assertion that he intended to stay around, it was inevitable that thoughts turned to a successor. In 1996, Royle signed former England under-21 goalkeeper Paul Gerrard, and earmarked him as a long-term successor to the Welshman. Southall held talks about a transfer to Wolves, but decided that his heart still lay at Goodison and signed a new two-year contract. All Evertonians were united in their appreciation when, on the opening day of the 1996/97 season, he made his 700th Everton appearance and showed that he'd lost none of his brilliance by making a succession of excellent saves, denying new world-record signing Alan Shearer a goal on his Newcastle debut.

Now aged 38, Southall held his own against Gerrard's challenge. But after Everton were dumped out of the FA Cup against Bradford the following January, Royle unwisely made Southall a scapegoat and dropped him. Gerrard, however, did little to impress and when form failed to pick up, Royle was out of a job. After he took over as caretaker manager, Dave Watson restored Southall to the team and he helped Everton move clear from another relegation dogfight.

Southall, however, was nearing the end. He kept his place at the start of 1997/98 season during Howard Kendall's disastrous third spell in charge. But after a 2-0 home defeat to Tottenham left Everton bottom of the Premiership, Southall was again dropped – but this time for good. It was an inauspicious end to a great career.

Later that season he joined Southend United on loan, but was never on the winning side in nine appearances. He then joined Stoke City as player-coach, but Stoke were relegated – the same fate endured by Southend. He was presented to the Goodison crowd for an emotional send-off on the last day of the 1997/98 season, when Everton played Coventry City needing to stay up, and told the ground that they never wanted to play outside the Premiership for it was a 'horrible place'. His words carried great resonance and seemed to stir the crowd: Everton just about held on to their top-flight status, in the process saving Southall the ignominy of playing for three relegated clubs in a single season. Did Southall's parting shot have a subliminal effect on his old club?

Barely a week later, he was released by Stoke and joined Doncaster Rovers, now managed by Ian Snodin. In November 1998 he embarked on a 15-month spell at Torquay United. Southall then returned to the Premier League with Bradford City, aged 41. There was then a tour of lower league and non-league clubs as he searched for a role within the game.

As early as 1995, Southall had applied for the Wales manager's job, but was overlooked. He was Bobby Gould's assistant (1995–99) within the Wales set-up and subsequently worked with Mark Hughes. He had spells in charge of Dover Athletic (2001–02) and Hastings United (2004–05); but it seemed that he was too outspoken to get a role in professional football that his experience and talents surely merited. And yet his services to the game deservedly earned him an MBE in 1996.

When he joined Everton from Bury Southall was asked why he'd played for so many non-league sides. 'I dunno,' he replied, 'maybe I get fed up easily.' At Goodison he clearly found a second home, seemingly becoming a permanent fixture. As such, it was a strange day indeed when the tragi-comic hero that is Neville Southall moved to Stoke City and Evertonians knew once and for all that he was never again to occupy the Everton goal.

Further reading:

SOUTHALL, NEVILLE, *The Binman Chronicles*, deCoubertin Books, 2012

[FACTFILE]

BORN
Llandudno,
16 September 1958
POSITION
Goalkeeper
OTHER CLUBS
Bury (1980–81);
Port Vale (loan, 1983);
Southend United
(loan, 1997–98);
Stoke City (1998);
Doncaster Rovers (1998);
Torquay United (1998–2000);
Huddersfield Town
(loan, 1999);
Bradford City (2000);
York City (2001);
Rhyl (2001);
Dover Athletic (2001);
Shrewsbury Town (2001–02);
Dagenham and Redbridge
(2002)
HONOURS
FA Cup 1984, 1995;
League Championship
1984/85, 1986/87;
European Cup Winners' Cup
1985;
Football Writer's Player of
the Year 1985;
Member of the British Empire
(MBE) 1996;
92 Wales caps (1982–98)

Season	League		FA Cup		League Cup		Other		Total	
	App	Goals	App	Goals	App	Goals	App	Goals	App	Goals
1981/82	26	0	1	0	0	0	-	-	27	0
1982/83	17	0	0	0	2	0	-	-	19	0
1983/84	35	0	8	0	11	0	-	-	54	0
1984/85	42	0	7	0	4	0	10	0	63	0
1985/86	32	0	5	0	5	0	7	0	49	0
1986/87	31	0	3	0	3	0	2	0	39	0
1987/88	32	0	8	0	7	0	2	0	49	0
1988/89	38	0	8	0	5	0	4	0	55	0
1989/90	38	0	7	0	4	0	-	-	49	0
1990/91	38	0	6	0	3	0	6	0	53	0
1991/92	42	0	2	0	4	0	2	0	50	0
1992/93	40	0	1	0	6	0	-	-	47	0
1993/94	42	0	2	0	4	0	-	-	48	0
1994/95	41	0	6	0	2	0	-	-	49	0
1995/96	38	0	4	0	2	0	5	0	49	0
1996/97	34	0	2	0	2	0	-	-	38	0
1997/98	12	0	0	0	1	0	-	-	13	0
Total	**578**	**0**	**70**	**0**	**65**	**0**	**38**	**0**	**751**	**0**

Southworth, Jack

Double hat-trick hero who went on to make a musical career

On 30 December 1893 Jack Southworth made Goodison history by becoming the first and only Everton player to score a double hat-trick. It came in a 7-1 victory over West Bromwich Albion, a match described by the Liverpool Daily Courier, with Victorian understatement, as 'exceptionally interesting'.

A CROWD of 25,000 braved foggy weather to see the game. Within a minute of kickoff they witnessed John Bell put Everton ahead and by half-time Everton were leading 4-0 after Southworth had struck his first hat-trick of the day. Alex Latta and Bell had combined to give him his first goal, and the second came when Reader, the Albion goalkeeper, failed to hold a shot from Bell. Southworth's third was an outstanding solo effort. In the second half the goals kept coming. Southworth added his fourth shortly after the break and although Albion battled back, the Everton forward was insatiable. His fifth goal came after Bell had beaten three men to set him up, and he finished the rout after Latta played him through. Southworth's tally could have been even higher, had Latta not rushed in to finish the forward's late goal-bound header (for which he was ruled offside).

'Southworth gave one of his wonderfully good displays,' reported the Football Echo. 'There is not the slightest doubt but that the whole of the Everton successes now are traceable to the skilful manipulation of the ball by Southworth. The rest of the team apparently recognises Southworth's grand form and unselfishly afford him every opportunity for displaying it.'

> THE FIRST AND ONLY EVERTON PLAYER TO SCORE A DOUBLE HAT-TRICK

Southworth's Christmas heroics unquestionably represented the highlight of his Everton career. Born in Blackburn in 1866, he had started his competitive career with Chester City, where he combined playing with work at the local Royalty Theatre. Southworth was a talented musician and formed a double act with his brother James, who was also a footballer. After a spell with Blackburn Olympic, Jack and James Southworth signed for Blackburn Rovers for the inaugural Football League season. Jack, a centre forward, outshone his brother, a left back, but both played in the 1890 FA Cup Final against Sheffield Wednesday, which Rovers won 6-1.

This was James's final game for Rovers, but his brother, by now an England international, went from strength to strength. In 1891 he won a second FA Cup and over three years Rovers never lost a match with him in the team. His nickname, 'The luck of the Blue and Whites', was fitting and Southworth was considered among the finest players in the league's early days. A contemporary wrote: 'His dodging, his neat passing, his speed and general accuracy in shooting won the hearts of the spectators … He is built for speed, he plays an unselfish game; he's good at tackling and has excellent judgment.' He finished the 1890/91 season top league scorer with 26 goals from 22 appearances, and added a further six in the FA Cup.

Southworth would surely have remained a Blackburn player, but the club were beset by financial problems after the cost of redeveloping Ewood Park had not been covered by a consummate rise in attendances. To avert financial crisis they were forced to sell their star player and in September 1893 Southworth

joined Everton for £400. After scoring on his debut against Derby County, the goals kept coming. His six-goal haul came just a week after he had scored four times in the 8-1 demolition of Sheffield Wednesday. His tally of 27 goals in 22 matches during the 1893/94 season saw him finish the First Division's top scorer for a second time.

SOUTHWORTH began the 1894/95 season in the same scintillating fashion that he had left off the previous year. Nine goals in his first nine matches saw Everton rise to the top of the league. However, a serious leg injury sidelined him in October and without him Everton stumbled, eventually finishing runners-up to Sunderland. Scarcely could Southworth have imagined when he turned 28 on 16 October 1894 that he would play his last professional game less than a fortnight later.

Post-football, Southworth returned to his pre-Football League career as an entertainer, becoming a professional violinist with Manchester's Halle Orchestra.

[FACTFILE]

BORN
Blackburn, 11 December 1866

DIED
16 October 1956

POSITION
Centre forward

OTHER CLUB
Blackburn Rovers (1888–93)

HONOURS
3 England caps (3 goals) (1889–92)

Season	League		FA Cup		Total	
	App	Goals	App	Goals	App	Goals
1893/94	22	27	1	0	23	27
1894/95	9	9	0	0	9	9
Total	31	36	1	0	32	36

Speed,
Gary

**Lifelong
Evertonian who
captained his
boyhood club in
a tumultuous
18-month spell
and whose life
ended in tragedy**

A boyhood Evertonian, Gary
Speed made his name as an
outstanding young left-sided
midfielder in the Leeds United
team that lifted the
last of the old First Division
League Championships in 1992.
Tall and composed, a powerful
striding forward who possessed
crisp and intelligent passing as
well as an eye for goal, Speed
was very much the archetype of
the modern midfielder.

> A FINE HAT-TRICK
> – TWO HEADERS AND
> A 20-YARD DRIVE –
> IN THE 7-1 DEMOLITION
> OF SOUTHAMPTON
> IN NOVEMBER
> WAS A PARTICULAR
> HIGHLIGHT

By the mid-1990s his Elland Road
career had started to plateau.
Speed had long been linked to a
Goodison switch and it finally
came in the summer of 1996
when Joe Royle paid £3.5million
for the 26-year-old. His Everton
career started with great promise,
as he coolly scored on his debut in
a 2-0 win over Premiership title
favourites Newcastle. But despite
this good start, there was a sense
in the first few months as an
Everton player that he flattered to
deceive on the left of midfield.

Royle subsequently moved him to a
more central role and he flourished.
A fine hat-trick – two headers and a
20-yard drive – in the 7-1 demolition
of Southampton in November was
a particular highlight. Speaking
about his positional change, he
told the Evertonian: 'It doesn't
exactly give me a free role because
I have responsibilities, but it
allows me to bomb on and that's
helped. It's my favourite position
and suits mygame. I like to be
able to do a lot of running
and from that position I can.'

By Christmas 1996, Everton were
sixth and spoken by some as
Premiership title dark horses.
However, the season dramatically
fell apart: Andrei Kanchelskis left
for Fiorentina; crucial players,

such as Andy Hinchcliffe and Joe
Parkinson, were struck by
long-term injury, while others
were also hit with injuries and
suspensions; confidence and form
plummeted, and by March Royle
was out of a job. Amid the
turmoil, Speed maintained his
consistency and, along with some
valuable goals, his ceaseless efforts
were one of the few bonds that
held a directionless team together.

He was rewarded with the Everton
captaincy – like that fellow son of
Mancot, Kevin Ratcliffe, he was
also Wales captain – at the start of
the 1997/98 season. But Everton
were a mess on and off the field.
Speed was one of the few to be
counted upon in a dismal side, but
he was displeased with the
disarray that pervaded at every
level of the club. Through January
1998 rumours abounded that he
wanted a transfer to Newcastle.
The situation came to a head at
the end of the month when Speed
refused to travel with the team to
West Ham after supposedly
learning from a journalist that he
would be dropped and stripped
of the captaincy. The midfielder
was left to hang out and dry
by Everton before completing a
£5.5million transfer to the
Northeast later that week. Speed
never broke his silence on the
true reasons behind his departure.

SPEED subsequently conducted
himself with nothing but dignity
whenever he returned to
Merseyside, despite facing catcalls
and a barrage of abuse from
the same fans who once revered
him. He remained at Newcastle
until 2004, later joining Bolton
Wanderers, and he continued to
play in the Premier League
until his late thirties. In January
2008 he joined Sheffield United,
becoming the club's manager in
2010. Later that year he took
over as Welsh national manager.

Always an articulate observer of
the game, Speed was a natural at
management, overseeing a

Season	League		FA Cup		League Cup		Total	
	App	Goals	App	Goals	App	Goals	App	Goals
1996/97	37	9	2	1	2	1	41	11
1997/98	21	6	0	0	3	0	24	6
Total	58	15	2	1	5	1	65	17

dramatic turnaround in the fortunes of the Welsh national team. Under his stewardship Wales rose from an all-time low of 117 in FIFA's rankings to 48th and were the best movers of 2011; a glittering future seemed assured.

BUT ON the morning on Sunday 27 November 2011, the news broke to a bewildered public that Speed had taken his own life. There was no note and no explanation to the shattering news; only a day earlier he had appeared on BBC's Football Focus, and seemed the same as always: erudite, charming, smart.

'I found out by text message on the Sunday morning and thought someone was playing a joke on me,' said Neville Southall. 'If I thought this would happen to anyone I knew, he would have been the last person on the list. He was a lovely lad, a really great manager. Everyone's bewildered.

'He had a way with people, everyone liked him. Even with fans from other teams, he never got booed, he always got clapped. He's the only one I know that's ever happened to. He was fit, he always looked after himself, he was looking at his diet years before anyone else did in the sport. And he was old school. He was the footballer's footballer.

'It's absolutely tragic and absolutely baffling. He was a humble fella, but he was also a battler. This is not the lad I knew. What a tragic waste of life.'

[FACTFILE]

BORN
Mancot, 8 September 1969
DIED
Huntingdon, Cheshire,
27 November 2011
POSITION
Midfield
OTHER CLUBS
Leeds United (1988–96);
Newcastle United
(1998–2004);
Bolton Wanderers (2004–08);
Sheffield United (2008–10)
AS MANAGER
Sheffield United (2010);
Wales (2010–11)
HONOURS
85 Wales caps
(7 goals) (1990–2004);
Member of the British Empire (MBE)
(2010)

Spencer, Henry

Inside forward who struggled to find his niche in Everton's transitional early 1920s team

[FACTFILE]

BORN
Southampton, 17 July 1895
POSITION
Inside forward
OTHER CLUBS
Wigan Borough (1922–24);
Walsall (1924)

Season	League		FA Cup		Total	
	App	Goals	App	Goals	App	Goals
1921/22	9	2	0	0	9	2
Total	9	2	0	0	9	2

Spencer, John

Diminutive journeyman striker whose Goodison spell was destined for failure

[FACTFILE]

BORN
Glasgow, 11 September 1970
POSITION
Forward
OTHER CLUBS
Glasgow Rangers (1988–92);
Morton (loan, 1988–89);
Lai Sun (Hong Kong, 1989–90);
Chelsea (1992–97);
Queens Park Rangers
(loan, 1996–97, then 1997–98);
Motherwell
(loan 1998–99 loan, 1999–2000);
Colorado Rapids (2001–04)
AS MANAGER
Portland Timbers (2011–)
HONOURS
14 Scotland caps (1994–97)

Season	League		FA Cup		League Cup		Total	
	App	Goals	App	Goals	App	Goals	App	Goals
1997/98	3 (3)	0	0	0	0	0	3 (3)	0
1998/99	2 (1)	0	0	0	0	0	2 (1)	0
Total	5 (4)	0	0	0	0	0	5 (2)	0

Stadiums

Everton have resided in four homes, and appear committed to moving to a fifth. But Goodison Park looms large in its history

Stanley Park

Everton's early homes are as modest as their origins as the team of St Domingo's Church. In 1870 the Liverpool corporation acquired around one hundred acres north of the city centre for £115,566 and – following the path taken with Sefton Park in the 1860s and Birkenhead Park (the world's first public park) in 1844 – turned it into a public park, Stanley Park. The motives of Victorian era reformers were to give the urban classes respite from the horrors of the polluted and chaotic cities and a place for exercise and recreation.

It was here that St Domingo's started playing cricket and, when its Parishioners turned their attention to soccer in the winter of 1878, football on its south eastern corner. There was no dressing room, no stands, no gate receipts and few spectators. All expenses were paid by the members. The brand of football, according to Thomas Keates, was of 'a very crude character' defined by an 'every-man-for-himself scramble for possession.' But Everton were successful and popular and by 1882 were attracting crowds of between 800 and 1500. Suddenly the need to move into a private ground, where admission fees could be charged and the crowds better accommodated became more pressing.

Priory Road

Everton's switch to Priory Road in 1883 was short-lived and unhappy. The club leased a field adjoining the house of a Mr Cruitt and seemed set to profit from football's growing popularity as a spectator sport. But, recalled Thomas Keates, it was a 'long, long walk to Priory Road and no buses come near it.' The club's hopes of making money from their own ground were soon confounded and the first match at Priory Road earned just 14 shillings in gate receipts. Indeed Everton were reliant on a benefit concert by to help boost its sagging coffers after the move. Nor did Mr Cruitt have much time for his new neighbours. Having had his 'pastoral serenity' disturbed, he gave Everton notice to cancel their lease after just a single year.

Anfield

A new home was quickly found just outside the city boundary, on Walton-Le-Hill. Here two fields belonging to Orrell Brothers' Brewers stood, with one of them belonging to Joseph Orrell undeveloped. He agreed to loan it to the club on the terms 'That we the Everton Football Club, keep the existing walls in good repair, pay the taxes, do not cause ourselves to be a nuisance to Mr Orrell and other tenants adjoining and also pay a small sum as rent, or subscribe a donation each year to the Stanley Hospital in the name of Mr Orrell.' Everton's president John Houlding arranged to be the club's representative tenant and collect the annual monies.

The new ground was closer to the club's headquarters at the Sandon Hotel and the switch attracted great enthusiasm from Everton's members and players. According to Keates 'they turned themselves into a gang of labourers, with spades and barrows, boards and hammers and nails. A hoarding of boards was fixed on the walls and rails around the playing pitch. Spectators stood on the intervening sods, a very humble stand crouching on the east side for officials, members, pressmen and affluents.'

Everton flourished in their new home and within a year of moving to Anfield were doing well enough out of it to be able to pay their first professional players. The advent of league football in 1888 saw Anfield host its first matches. But its success as a home had started to cause problems within Everton, with John Houlding using his status as representative tenant to his advantage. While it is true that he had 'found' Anfield, advanced money for the construction of its stands, and possibly talked Everton into being Football League founder members, there was a profit motive too. From being representative tenant he became Everton's landlord. The club's rent rose from £100 to £240 in 1888 and £250 a year later. He also granted himself sole rights for sale of refreshments at Anfield.

Within the Everton committee room there was uproar and a resolution to find a new home that Everton could call its own. Houlding assumed – by holding the keys to what had become one of football's finest arenas – that he had the club trapped in this marriage of convenience. But a committee room coup by George Mahon and James Baxter saw Everton move once again in 1892. Houlding was left with an empty stadium while Everton stepped into the unknown.

Goodison Park

Mahon had secured a piece of land on the far side of Stanley Park called Mere Green Field.

Today it is known by its more familiar name: Goodison Park.

Much work needed to be done at Everton's new home: the field still had to be cleared and levelled, turf lain and a basic drainage system put in place. A Mr Barton was contracted to do this on 29,471 square yards at 4 1/2d per square yard – 'a formidable initial expenditure.' A Mr J Prescott was engaged as architect and surveyor and Kelly Bros., builders signed on 7 June 1892, to erect two uncovered stands to accommodate 4,000 each, and a covered stand to hold 3,000. The cost was £1,640, with a penalty clause in the event of none-completion by 31 July. Two weeks later another contract was agreed with them to erect outside hoardings at a cost of £150. Twelve turnstiles were ordered at a cost of £7.15s apiece. In August a third contract was signed with Kelly Bros. for gates and sheds which were completed by 20 August at a cost of £132 10s.

Goodison Park officially opened on 24 August 1892. After an inaugural dinner at the Adelphi Hotel, where the guest of honour was President of the Football Association, Lord Kinniard, a late afternoon procession of open carriages made its way to Goodison during which they received an enthusiastic welcome from flag waving crowds. On Kinniard's entry to the ground he declared it open. The ensuing ceremony was witnessed by 12,000 spectators and concluded with a firework display.

A week later, on Friday 2 September 1892, Goodison witnessed its first match. A friendly, kicked off by George Mahon, with Bolton Wanderers ended in a 4-2 win for Everton. The following day Everton met Nottingham Forest in the opening league fixture of the season. Fred Geary and Alf Milward goals secured a 2-2 draw in front of 14,000 people. Three weeks later,

Goodison saw its first win, a 6-0 trouncing of Newton Heath.

Kelly Bros. had faced a formidable challenge in building Goodison in so short a period, but they stuck to their deadlines and built a wonderful arena. Less than two years later Goodison hosted the 1894 FA Cup Final between Notts County and Bolton Wanderers.

The decision to buy Mere Green Field was made three years later at an outlay of £8,090, the mortgage for which was cleared a decade later. Everton's nomadic period was finally over, Goodison Park, its home for at least the next 110 years was secured.

Everton's committee were never complacent and continued improving the stadium. In 1895 a new Bullens Road stand was built at an outlay of £3,407 and another £403 building a roof on the Goodison Road stand. The profit from winning the 1906 FA Cup was invested in a new £13,000 double decker stand at the Stanley Park End. A huge new Main Stand, designed by the legendary stadium architect, Archibald Leitch, was built on the Goodison Road side of the stadium. At a cost of £28,000 it was a fine investment and stood until 1971. The terracing was concreted and the cinder running track replaced. It was the finest club stadium in England, hosting the 1910 FA Cup Final replay and in July 1913 becoming the first league ground visited by a reigning monarch, King George V.

Leitch returned to Goodison in 1926 to build a new two tier steel and wooden Bullens Road Stand, which feature his hallmark steel trusses at the front of the stand. Besides modifications to the roof, and the seating of the Lower Bullens (in 1963) and Paddock (following the Taylor Report), this stand appears virtually the same as it did when it was built. In 1938 Leitch was commissioned to

rebuild the Gwladys Street stand at the cost of £50,000. In completing it Goodison became the first completely two-tiered stadium in the country.

Goodison suffered bomb damage during the Second World War after the Gwladys Street took a direct hit. It was rectified by a £5,000 grant from the War Damage Commission and the late 1940s and 1950s were a golden age for attendances. 78,299 witnessed the Division One match against Liverpool in September 1948 and 1962/63 saw the highest average attendance (51,603) in the club's history. Further developments came during this period: undersoil heating and floodlighting in 1958, modifications to the Park End and an electronic scoreboard – the first in the country – the following decade.

In 1966 Everton was one of the main stadiums as England hosted the World Cup. It served as the base for Pele's Brazil and witnessed the South Americans' surprise exit, as well as splendid displays by Eusebio and Florian Albert. It hosted the dramatic quarter final between North Korea and Portugal, in which the Portuguese clawed back a 3-0 deficit to win 5-3, as well as the semi final between West Germany and the USSR.

During the 1969/70 season the Archibald Leitch Main Stand was demolished and the current three storey structure was opened in its place at a cost of £1million in 1971. Modifications demanded by the Taylor Report saw the Gwladys Street made all seater in 1991, and the terracing in the Paddock and Main Stand was also replaced by seats. The Park Stand was demolished three years later and replaced by the current cantilever stand for the start of the 1994/95 season. Since then, as the club has sought an alternative home, only small modifications have been made to the stadium,

such as the construction of big screens and the removal of the scoreboard.

Now in its 120th year, Goodison carries a charm and sense of history lacking in its modern rivals. On a cold January evening, with the crowd roaring and the floodlights illuminating their heroes there is no better place on earth. But the sense of history often masks the reality that the current stadium lacks the facilities, the sightlines and comforts demanded by twenty-first century fans. With football clubs so often dependent on ancillary revenue, Goodison lacks the facilities to provide significant non matchday revenues. Its shortcomings pose a significant challenge to the club's owners present and future.

The future

Speculation about Everton leaving Goodison first reared its head during the 1980s glory years when the possibility of Liverpool and Everton sharing a stadium on Aintree Race Course was widely mooted in the local press. The notion of three iconic and world famous sporting arenas being bulldozed to make way for a mega stadium maybe had some relevance in the perverse world of 1980s planners, but was thankfully never realised.

The possibility of a move was again raised by Peter Johnson in the mid-1990s. Johnson noted that Goodison was 'very much landlocked' and foresaw the emergence of a European Super League. To be among the 'big clubs with the big grounds and the big followings' it was an issue, he said, that Everton needed to 'address'. In 1997 he held a ballot among Evertonians to secure a mandate to move way from Goodison. Of 37,000 brochures distributed, 21,974 fans took part in a ballot with nearly 84% giving Johnson a mandate to move. Sketches of a two-tier bowl-like

60,000 capacity stadium were unveiled, with a museum, hall of fame and hall of remembrance. Alas, there was no immediately obvious site for this stadium, with an array of venues as diverse as the South Docks, Liverpool Airport, Kirkby Golf Course and even Cronton Colliery near distant Widnes mentioned. Johnson talked of moving into the new Goodison by the start of the 2001/02 season, but he was long gone as chairman by then.

His successor as Everton owner, Bill Kenwright, also foresaw the need to move and commissioned a feasibility study as one of his first acts as owner. Again it identified the need to move from Goodison and Kings Dock, just outside the city centre emerged as the likely location. The world class plans unveiled fitted Everton's Nil Satis Nisi Optimum mantra, but the move fell through in 2003 after Everton failed to find the £30million needed to buy a 51% stake in the project.

As outstanding as the move to Kings Dock promised to be, so the subsequent plan to move to Kirkby was less than enticing. The deal, in partnership with Tesco supermarket, would have seen a new 50,000 stadium built as part of a £400 million retail development. Although Kenwright was given a mandate by a poll of season ticket holders to go ahead with the move, neither the stadium design – which was based on FC Koln's somewhat utilitarian design – nor the fact that it would result in Everton moving out of town, captured the imagination. A protest group, Keep Everton in Our City, led protests with a well organised campaign that saw aeroplanes dragging its banner across the Liverpool sky on matchday. Eventually, in November 2009, a public enquiry rejected the plans and confirmed that Everton will reside in L4 for the foreseeable future.

Stanley, Garry

Extravagantly coiffured midfielder who fell short of the Goodison standard

Garry Stanley never seemed to quite overcome the slow start to his Goodison career. Signed from Chelsea for £300,000 in the summer of 1979, a contractual tie with the NASL's Fort Lauderdale Strikers meant he missed the opening weeks of the 1979/80 season. Underwhelming performances on his arrival saw Evertonians dub the midfielder 'Jetlag' Stanley. Later he ascribed a pelvic strain – a persistent injury that many players find difficult to remedy – as the underlying cause of his patchy form, but he never seemed to improve.

With his flowing locks, the strapping Midlander had the look of the archetypal 1970s footballer. At Chelsea he had garnered a reputation as a dynamic midfielder, capable of lung-busting runs and with a keen eye for goal. In a team that finished the 1978/79 season rock bottom of the First Division, he was deemed one of Stamford Bridge's most attractive and saleable assets.

SUCH POTENTIAL went largely unrealised at Goodison in a stay that was memorable mostly for his sending off with Liverpool's Terry McDermott in

the October 1979 derby, following an uncharacteristic scrap. In doing so they became the first players to be dismissed in a Merseyside derby.

Despite his underwhelming displays Stanley remained optimistic about his chances at Goodison, and there were signs of a return to form in autumn 1980 as Everton rose up the table.

'Certainly I have not been disappointed at Everton,' he professed to the match day programme in November 1980. 'The set-up is first class, and while 1979/80 was a disappointing year, that's forgotten now. What happens in 1980/81 is all that counts.' Stanley felt sufficiently enamoured with the club to describe 'signing on the dotted line for Everton' as his 'career highlight'.

Yet Howard Kendall did not share an appreciation of Stanley when

he became manager in the summer of 1981. Stanley found himself excluded from the first team and in October 1981 Everton accepted a £150,000 bid from Swansea City, where he played an important role in their initial successes in the First Division. Following their relegation in 1983 Stanley never returned to the top flight.

> [FACTFILE]
>
> **BORN**
> Burton-on-Trent,
> 4 March 1954
> **POSITION**
> Midfield
> **OTHER CLUBS**
> Chelsea (1974–79);
> Fort Lauderdale Strikers (1979);
> Swansea City (1981–83);
> Portsmouth (1983–86);
> Wichita Wings (Indoor, 1986–88);
> Bristol City (1988–89)

Season	League		FA Cup		League Cup		Europe		Total	
	App	Goals	App	Goals	App	Goals	App	Goals	App	Goals
1979/80	24	1	2	0	4 (1)	0	0	0	30 (1)	1
1980/81	28	0	0 (1)	0	3	0	-	-	31 (1)	0
1981/82	0	0	0	0	0	0	-	-	0	0
Total	**52**	**1**	**2 (1)**	**0**	**7 (1)**	**0**	**0**	**0**	**61 (2)**	**1**

Stein, Jimmy

Scottish wing wizard who inspired Everton's 1933 FA Cup win

In the last week of April 1928, while Dixie Dean was setting a Football League scoring record that will never be broken, Everton's board were in the process of forming the club's next great forward line. From Hibernian they acquired inside forward Jimmy Dunn for a fee of £5000, and from Dunfermline Athletic the winger Jimmy Stein for £1400. Over subsequent years this pair of canny Scots would help propel Dixie and Everton to even greater glories.

Prior to his arrival, Stein had already spent an unsuccessful period in England as a youngster with Blackburn Rovers, but returned to Scotland with Dunfermline. He helped the Fife club to promotion from the Scottish Second Division in the 1925/26 season and was soon attracting the attention of several English clubs. But it was Everton who made the move, and Stein's fee would represent a fine bargain.

Yet Stein's early days at Goodison were spent unhappily. He mustered just five appearances in 1928/29 season, and when he did establish himself in the side, at the expense of fellow countryman

Alec Troup, he was part of the team which slumped to relegation for the first time in the club's history. Stein's qualities, nevertheless, were abundantly obvious to all who saw him. 'When in the mood this dashing Scot is a most persistent raider, who shoots hard from acute angles,' recorded one newspaper profile. 'A corner kick specialist … [Stein] also knows how to curl his centres to Dean, who has obtained many of his goals as a result of Stein's ability to place the ball at the required altitude and distance.' A speciality of his came in a corner kick routine in conjunction with the inside forward Tommy Johnson: Johnson would block the path of the goalkeeper and Stein would curl a kick straight into the net. The tactic earned him three goals in the 1932/33 season alone, when he finished Everton's second leading scorer.

SUCCESS followed the crushing failure of his first days at Goodison. He won the Second Division Championship in the 1930/31 season and the League Championship a year later. Full international honours were nevertheless elusive,

a fact surely attributable to the prevailing bias of the country's selectors against the so-called 'Anglos' who plied their trade in England.

Stein's crowning glory came in the 1933 FA Cup Final against Manchester City. He had been in scintillating form all season and he had already scored five goals in Everton's five-game march to the final. Evertonians even composed a doggerel in tribute to the wing wizard:

> After the ball had been centred,
> After the whistle blew,
> We passed it to Tommy Johnson, and he
> showed them what to do.
> He slipped it along to Stein – and down,
> the wing he flew,
> He lobbed it into the goalmouth, and
> Dixie banged it through.

Stein did not disappoint. 'We had a good, solid, fit, tidy team and we just seemed to take City for a ride,' recalled Dixie Dean. 'Our lads played well and one of the sharpest in our forward line was Jimmy Stein, the outside left. There was no getting away from it, he was a good player, that lad.' Stein's moment of glory came in the 40th minute when Len Langford, the City goalkeeper, dropped a cross from Cliff Britton and Stein stabbed home from close range to open the score. 'When I saw the ball strike the back of the net I knew it was a match-winning goal,' reported 'Pilot' in the Liverpool Evening Express. 'Without exaggeration you could see the Manchester players reel under this blow. It took the heart out of them, and they never recovered.' Dean remembered: 'I told the lads in the dressing room at half-time: "Whatever else you do, get the ball into that goal area. Don't be trying to beat another man. Just get that ball over."' Another Britton cross yielded another fumble from the hapless City keeper and Dean doubled the score. The victory was completed with 10 minutes to go when Dunn headed home a Geldard cross.

'Stein, always a match winner, was kept idle for long stretches, but in the first half showed unmistakably how he had rattled the City defences,' reported the Liverpool Post and Mercury. 'Stein had not one of his spectacular "running" days any more than Geldard had his share; the truth was the ball did not go that way to any degree. This match was won through team spirit and consistent endeavour through the combined measures.' He was, added 'Pilot', 'the chief foil. His sweeping touch-line runs and cunning swirling centres often caught Langford in two minds, and with any luck they would have brought goals. His corner-kicking, too, was perfect. Congratulations to Stein on getting the most important goal of the game! He proved himself a fine match winner.'

STEIN was ever-present in the 1933/34 season, but found the lively Jackie Coulter vying for his place thereafter. He moved to Burnley in October 1936 in a £2000 joint deal that also took Dusty Miller to Turf Moor. It was later suggested that this transfer laid the ground for Tommy Lawton's move in the opposite direction several months later. Stein briefly played alongside the young prodigy before he joined Everton. The Scot later returned to Merseyside to play for New Brighton. Upon his retirement from playing, he returned to Burnley where he took up a scouting job.

[FACTFILE]

BORN
Coatbridge, 7 November 1907
POSITION
Winger
OTHER CLUBS
Blackburn Rovers (1924);
Dunfermline Athletic (1924–28);
Burnley (1936–37);
New Brighton (1938–39)
HONOURS
Second Division Championship 1930/31;
League Championship 1931/32;
FA Cup 1933

Season	League		FA Cup		Total	
	App	Goals	App	Goals	App	Goals
1928/29	4	0	1	0	5	0
1929/30	29	10	2	0	31	10
1930/31	28	10	5	3	33	13
1931/32	37	9	1	0	38	9
1932/33	40	16	6	5	46	21
1933/34	42	8	1	0	43	8
1934/35	19	4	0	0	19	4
Total	**199**	**57**	**16**	**8**	**215**	**65**

Stephenson, George

Right half in Everton's league debut season, his single appearance came in a 5-0 defeat to Wolves

[FACTFILE]

BORN
1865
POSITION
Right half

Season	League		FA Cup		Total	
	App	Goals	App	Goals	App	Goals
1888/89	1	0	-	-	1	0
Total	1	0	-	-	1	0

Steven, Trevor

Brilliant wide man who was a driving force behind Everton's mid-80s successes

Over the years Evertonians have enjoyed an embarrassment of riches on the right wing. Players like Jimmy Husband, Andrei Kanchelskis and Mikel Arteta have all held down the berth with distinction. But nobody has sustained the same levels of excellence as Trevor Steven did during his six years with the club in Everton's mid-1980s glory years.

A **DEBATE** on the merits of past and present Everton players always generates a healthy and fulsome response. But when, in 2009, a Toffeeweb.com contributor was perceived as underplaying the genius of Steven, he provoked a furious – but entirely valid and accurate – response. 'Where you there in the 80s?' asked one respondent. 'Did you see Trevor Steven play? Do you remember his nickname from the terraces? GOD! The lad had everything, he could tackle, he could score, defend, attack with brilliance, show people his arse as they slipped in his wake. Today he would be one of the most sought after midfielders in Europe.'

Signed for £300,000 from Burnley in the summer of 1983, many Evertonians first thought it a hefty fee for a virtually unknown 19-year-old – not least given that the hugely promising Steve McMahon was sold to fund the deal. Steven had been scouted by many First Division teams, including Liverpool, but only Everton possessed the confidence to pay so much for a relative unknown.

The start to Steven's Everton career was nevertheless slow. Patchy form in the opening stages of the 1983/84 season saw him lose his place to Alan Irvine. But after a successful spell in the Central League his confidence was restored, and he returned to the first team as the season reached its climax, appearing in the FA Cup semi-final win over Southampton, then in the final itself. It was Steven's deep cross that set up Andy Gray's goal.

Years later, he told the author Becky Tallentire: 'For me, the turning point was the FA Cup win with Everton. To win there and take Everton on to a new level was brilliant, and that medal is the one I cherish the most.' Indeed Steven seemed galvanised by the FA Cup win and was one of the most outstanding performers through the triumphant 1984/85 season. Not only was he a prolific contributor of assists, many destined for the head of Graeme Sharp or Andy Gray, but after Sharp he was second top scorer with twelve league goals. None of these efforts were more memorable than the

> STEVEN WAS SOON RECOGNISED AS ONE OF THE FINEST WIDE MEN IN THE CLUB'S HISTORY

brace he contributed to Everton's European Cup Winners' Cup run. Deep into the semi-final second leg against Bayern Munich, Steven was played in by Andy Gray, and, one on one with the Bayern keeper, coolly chipped from the edge of the penalty area to seal a 3-1 victory. In the final against Rapid Vienna, his close-range volley from a corner was the decisive goal in a 3-1 win.

A player of pace and composure who combined intricate dribbling with surging runs down the Everton right, Steven was soon recognised as one of the finest wide men in the club's history. He possessed all the facets of a great winger: speed, flair, dazzling footwork and a cool head in front of goal. But Steven was always much more than an orthodox flanker. His work rate was exceptional. He could tackle. He was versatile and able to play through the middle, up front and even – as he sometimes did for England – at right back. He was one of the best penalty-takers Everton have seen. With Gary Stevens he formed an outstanding right-sided partnership for club and country: a formidable defensive barrier and electrifying overlapping pairing that hit opponents hard on the break.

ALREADY an England under-21 international, in February 1985 Steven received a full international call-up, making the first of 32 England appearances against Northern Ireland. Steven picked up where he left off during the 1985/86 season, scoring nine goals and providing countless through balls and crosses for the productive Lineker–Sharp partnership. Although the campaign ended trophyless, 'Tricky' – as he was now known – was part of the England World Cup squad in Mexico. With Gary Stevens, Peter Reid and Gary Lineker he formed a strong Everton contingent, playing in

the quarter-final against Argentina. Four years later he would appear in the World Cup semi-final against West Germany.

Although still aged only 22 at the start of the 1986/87 season, Steven always seemed an old head on young shoulders. As Everton were obliterated by injuries that year, he seemed to grow in stature. Steven ended the season top league scorer, his contribution decisive as Everton were again crowned League Champions.

Dark clouds, however, lay ahead. Among the Everton squad, the UEFA ban on English clubs competing in Europe was most keenly felt by its young players, such as Steven, who had many years still ahead of them. With age on his side, by rights Steven should have been

a key component of Everton's domestic and European challenges until the mid-1990s. But he was robbed of this opportunity and after Howard Kendall's departure in 1987, discontent seeped through the club.

After a disappointing 1987/88 season, Steven refused the offer of a new contract. With his existing deal due to expire in summer 1989, speculation abounded about his future. With the signing of Pat Nevin in summer 1988 he found himself playing in a much deeper role, and there were barely suppressed hints at his unhappiness. 'I've hardly played in my traditional wide position,' he said in an interview at Christmas 1988. 'While I've been happy to help Colin Harvey out when we've had injuries, I still prefer to play out on the right.' Linked with moves to Liverpool and

Manchester United, discontent began to permeate from the terraces. During the 1989 FA Cup Final, an Everton fan invaded the pitch to remonstrate with Steven, whose transfer to Liverpool was rumoured to be imminent.

This was his last action in an Everton shirt, a disappointing conclusion to a dazzling career. However, it was not Liverpool he joined that summer, but Glasgow Rangers (Liverpool manager Kenny Dalglish remained an avowed admirer and later recommended Steven to Marseille). The move came after a bitter wrangle over a transfer fee: because Steven was out of contract and the two clubs could not agree a price, it was set by a tribunal at just £1.5million – £1million less than Everton's valuation. It was to prove a hideous under-valuation: just two years later Steven joined Marseilles for three times that amount.

A glut of club honours followed, and for the next seven years he was also able to display his talents in the European Cup and Champions League – opportunities denied him at Everton. In October 1994 he was linked with a return to Goodison as part of the deal that brought Duncan Ferguson from Rangers, but Steven was recovering from long-term injury and the move came to nothing. He retired at the end of the 1996/97 season, later combining a career in punditry with work as a football agent.

LATER, speaking of his decision to leave Everton, he cited the European ban as a major factor. 'We were all set to challenge for the European Cup the following season and that was a crashing blow. It threw a hell of a cloud over the English League. It's one of the reasons I came away from English football. At the time it didn't look as though we'd get back into Europe.'

Season	League		FA Cup		League Cup		Other		Total	
	App	Goals	App	Goals	App	Goals	App	Goals	App	Goals
1983/84	23 (4)	1	2	0	3	1	-	-	28 (4)	2
1984/85	40	12	7	2	4	0	10	2	61	16
1985/86	41	9	6	0	5	0	6	1	58	10
1986/87	41	14	3	0	5	1	5	1	54	16
1987/88	36	6	8	2	6	0	1	0	51	8
1988/89	29	6	7	0	4	2	3	0	43	8
Total	**210 (4)**	**48**	**33**	**4**	**27**	**4**	**25**	**4**	**295 (4)**	**60**

[FACTFILE]

BORN
Berwick-upon-Tweed,
21 September 1963
POSITION
Right winger
OTHER CLUBS
Burnley (1980–83);
Glasgow Rangers (1989–91 & 1992–97);
Marseilles (1991–92)
HONOURS
League Championship 1984/85, 1986/87;
FA Cup 1984;
European Cup Winners' Cup 1985;
36 England caps (4 goals) (1985–92)

Stevens, Dennis

Unsung hero of Everton's 1963 title triumph

If Evertonians had been surprised by the sale of Bobby Collins to Leeds United in March 1962, more than a few eyebrows were raised at the man who replaced him. Dennis Stevens possessed a reputation as a solid, workaholic inside forward, but was neither considered a spectacular player nor of the same calibre as the lamented Collins. His early days at Everton were marred by a vociferous faction of the Everton supporters blaming him for the departure of their hero. Stevens soon won them over.

Born in Dudley, Stevens began his career with Bolton Wanderers, forming part of a potent Bolton attack with Nat Lofthouse. In May 1958 he was at the centre of one of the most poignant games in English football history, when Bolton met Manchester United in the FA Cup Final. Three months earlier eight United players had perished in the Munich air disaster, including Stevens' cousin – the great and much-lamented Duncan Edwards. Against all odds, a makeshift United made it to the final, but sentiment was dispensed with: Bolton won 2-0 in the game 'nobody wanted to win'.

Stevens £35,000 arrival added grit and guile to the heart of the Everton team. Like Collins he was no giant, standing just 5ft 7in tall, but was a similarly strong man who added much needed bite to the Everton midfield. Neither possessing the artistry or skill of Alex Young or Roy Vernon, Stevens' task was less in supplying the magic than assisting the magicians. He was a tireless runner and always willing to assist in both attacking and defensive duties. Given such attributes it was unsurprising that at Burnden Park he had been greatly admired by a young trainee, named Alan Ball.

EVERTONIANS soon warmed to his energy and work rate and he quickly won over the boo-boys. For 30 months, Stevens was ever-present in the Everton team and would emerge as the unsung hero of the 1962/63 league title triumph. Older fans likened him to Stan Bentham, whose graft and work rate had been so indispensable to Everton's flair players in the 1930s. At Bolton he had succeeded Lofthouse as their most potent goalscorer, but many of his attacking responsibilities were shed for the benefit of the team. Often he served as a minder for less physical players, such as Alex Young and Roy Vernon. One fan of the era later recalled in a letter to the Guardian: '[He] used to run a yard or two ahead of a player dribbling the ball (usually Alex Young). As he was technically within playing distance he used to get away with it game after game, and Everton won the championship. I suppose the Americans would call it "running interference". I think it was probably illegal even then, and was certainly against the spirit of the game.'

Following the arrival of Fred Pickering, Catterick reshuffled his pack and Stevens dropped back to wing half. But he was now in the veteran stage of his career and the Everton manager started to look to the future. Brian Harris regained his place as wing half, and a young Colin Harvey was deployed in Stevens' previous role. He remained an Everton player until December 1965, but made just a handful of appearances in his final year at the club. Oldham paid £20,000 for him, and after 15 months at Boundary Park he returned to Merseyside, playing out his career with Tranmere Rovers.

'Dennis had strength, courage, experience and shared the DNA of Duncan Edwards,' recalled Alex Young. 'Like many players of his type he was under-rated and unsung. In a later era I'm sure he would have been better appreciated.'

> STEVENS WAS EVER-PRESENT IN THE EVERTON TEAM AND WOULD EMERGE AS THE UNSUNG HERO OF THE 1962/63 LEAGUE TITLE TRIUMPH

Season	League		FA Cup		Other		Total	
	App	Goals	App	Goals	App	Goals	App	Goals
1961/62	12	4	0	0	0	0	12	4
1962/63	42	7	3	1	2	1	47	9
1963/64	42	9	5	0	3	1	50	10
1964/65	18	0	2	0	6	0	26	0
1965/66	6	0	0	0	2	0	8	0
Total	**120**	**20**	**10**	**1**	**13**	**2**	**143**	**23**

[FACTFILE]

BORN
Dudley, 30 November 1933
POSITION
Inside forward / wing half
OTHER CLUBS
Bolton Wanderers (1953–62);
Oldham Athletic (1965–67);
Tranmere Rovers (1967–68)
HONOURS
League Championship 1962/63

Stevens, Gary

Athletic right back who graduated through Everton's youth ranks to embark on a magnificent career

Supreme fitness and athletic magnificence would underpin Gary Stevens' long and illustrious career, but he was more than just a fine athlete and defender. As well as providing an often impenetrable barrier on the right side of Everton's defence, as an overlapping full back he was an important part of the Everton attack, forming a magnificent right-sided partnership with Trevor Steven. This would span a decade, at Everton, for England, and latterly Glasgow Rangers.

BORN in Barrow, Stevens first made the breakthrough to the Everton team in October 1981 during Howard Kendall's first months as manager. Although he would be a central figure in Everton's glory years, over the next 13 months Kendall alternated between Stevens and Brian Borrows, a fellow youth team graduate. Stevens won through after Borrows was among the scapegoats in the wake of Liverpool's 5-0 Goodison massacre in November 1982. His rival never played in a blue shirt again and was sold to Bolton the following spring. 'There was not much to choose between us,' Stevens recalled. 'For virtually two seasons, it was Brian or me at right back. I played first, he took my place, then I got it back. I don't now what grounds the decision to sell Brian were made on, but it could just as easily have been me who moved on.'

Stevens' career truly took off following the arrival of Trevor Steven in summer 1983. The two shared a similar work ethic and seemed to form an innate understanding down the Everton right. 'I think Trevor has helped him a lot and they worked well together and complemented each other perfectly,' said Tommy Wright. 'He has great attacking qualities with a good eye for goal and did play more as a right winger. But gradually he changed and I think he was told to restrict himself by the coaches. He adjusted and stopped belting helter-skelter down the wing and realised he was meant to be a defender and that was when his skills in that department improved.'

Stevens' form during the 1984/85 season brought him an England debut against Italy at the season's end. He became a fixture for the national team and was in the England squad for the 1986 and 1990 World Cup Finals, and the 1988 and 1992 European Championship Finals. Many of his 46 international appearances were made alongside Trevor Steven.

Fast, powerful and hard-working, Stevens worked the Everton right tirelessly until 1988. He seemed to be blessed with the innate capacity of running constantly, and possessed such a fine turn of pace that few opponents got past him with speed alone. There were, however, some shortcomings. Sometimes he was derided for his lack of technique. Over the years this improved, although he was still prone to hoofing the ball up the field. (Sometimes this was to great effect: it was a Stevens' long ball with which Graeme Sharp connected to score his stunning volley against Liverpool in October 1984.) There were occasional lapses of concentration too – none more costly than the stray pass that let in Ian Rush to score the equaliser in the 1986 FA Cup Final.

IN ATTACK his long throw-ins became a potent weapon, particularly with target men of the calibre of Andy Gray and Graeme Sharp to aim for. For a full back with few set-piece responsibilities, his goals tally was comparatively healthy; none were considered more important by Evertonians than the deflected shot which knocked Liverpool out of the League Cup in the third round in October 1987.

By this stage, however, Stevens was becoming disenchanted with life at Goodison. Having won virtually every honour available to him, he sought European football and the higher wages on offer in Scotland. In summer 1988 he joined Glasgow Rangers for £1.25million. Here he won numerous further honours and Trevor Steven linked up successfully with him a year later. In 1994 he returned to Merseyside with Tranmere Rovers, where he played out his career. Later he turned his hand to physiotherapy.

[FACTFILE]

BORN
Barrow-in-Furness,
27 March 1963
POSITION
Right back
OTHER CLUBS
Glasgow Rangers (1988–94);
Tranmere Rovers (1994–98)
HONOURS
League Championship
1984/85, 1986/87;
FA Cup 1984;
European Cup Winners' Cup
1985;
46 England caps (1985–92)

Season	League		FA Cup		League Cup		Other		Total	
	App	Goals	App	Goals	App	Goals	App	Goals	App	Goals
1981/82	19	1	1	0	4	0	-	-	24	1
1982/83	28	0	5	0	2	1	-	-	35	1
1983/84	26	1	8	0	8	0	-	-	42	1
1984/85	37	3	7	1	4	0	10	0	58	4
1985/86	41	1	6	1	5	0	6	0	58	2
1986/87	25	3	3	0	1	0	0	0	29	3
1987/88	31	0	8	0	6	1	1	0	46	1
Total	**207**	**9**	**38**	**2**	**30**	**2**	**17**	**0**	**292 (1)**	**13**

Stevens, George Leopold 'Leo'

A prolific lower league scorer, he failed to displace his fellow Wirraler, Dixie Dean

Season	League		FA Cup		Total	
	App	Goals	App	Goals	App	Goals
1932/33	2	0	0	0	2	0
Total	**2**	**0**	**0**	**0**	**2**	**0**

Stevens, Thomas

Outside left who struggled to make a first-team berth his own

Season	League		FA Cup		Total	
	App	Goals	App	Goals	App	Goals
1912/13	5	0	0	0	5	0
Total	**5**	**0**	**0**	**0**	**5**	**0**

Stevenson, Alex

Diminutive inside forward whose career spanned both sides of the war

Alex Stevenson was Everton's 'Celtic Sorcerer' of the 1930s and 1940s, with Jackie Coulter forming one of the most magical wing partnerships to ever grace Goodison Park.

FOOTBALL · A STEVENSON. EVERTON

STEVENSON first made his name at Dublin's Dolphin club, where he was part of the team that reached the 1932 Irish FA Cup Final. Spotted by Arthur Dixon, a legendary Glasgow Rangers player turned coach, he joined the Scottish club in August 1932. Gifted and mercurial, the inside left made just a dozen appearances for Rangers but played in the team that would lift the Scottish League Championship in breathtaking fashion during the 1933/34 season. Before Stevenson could witness that success, however, in January 1934 he was persuaded to join Everton. Astonishingly, no Irish Catholic has played for Rangers since Stevenson's departure.

Standing just 5ft 3in tall and weighing barely 10 stone, he cut a diminutive figure but took strength in the old saying – 'the player who is good enough is big enough'. Like many smaller players who thrived amid the physical challenges posed by the First Division, he was a deceptively strong footballer, but never needed to descend to the skulduggery that defined other players. For Stevenson was among the finest ball players of his generation and, blessed with perfect control, was able to dodge and weave his way through opposing sides with ease.

He soon formed a formidable left-sided partnership with the winger Jackie Coulter, and in his first days at Goodison, before they were given first-team opportunities, word of the pair attracted up to 15,000 curious onlookers to Central League games. A few years later, the sight of Stevenson and Coulter lining up in the first team alongside mavericks such as Torry Gillick and Tommy Lawton must have been as exhilarating for Evertonians as it was terrifying for their opponents. According to Tommy Lawton, Stevenson possessed the capacity to roll 'the ball across to me like we were playing on a billiard table'.

STEVENSON SCORED HIS 13TH GOAL OF THE SEASON AND EVERTON WERE VIRTUALLY ASSURED THE LEAGUE CHAMPIONSHIP

Coulter's Everton career was cut short by a broken leg sustained while playing for Northern Ireland and he was transferred to Grimsby Town in 1937. Stevenson, however, continued to provide the link between Everton's defence and attack and Coulter's replacements, Wally Boyes and, after the war, Tommy Eglington, proved to be equally proficient.

STEVENSON was a crucial part of Everton's League Championship success in the 1938/39 season, when he was among their most consistent performers. His most memorable contribution came during Everton's Easter triple-header. With the title race tightly balanced, Everton beat Sunderland 2-1 in the Good Friday fixture at Roker Park. There then followed a lengthy train journey to London, where Everton faced Chelsea. Tired and below par, Everton laboured and with 15 minutes remaining the match was still goalless. Then Stevenson intervened with what Lawton dubbed the 'miracle' of Stamford Bridge. 'Alex Stevenson headed a goal!' he recalled to his biographers. 'When you think that Stan Matthews headed the ball more often than Stevie you can see why I call it a miracle.' On account of his size Stevenson was dubbed 'Mickey' – after Mickey Mouse – but as Gordon Watson remembered: 'For that header he was up above [Chelsea centre half] Bobby Salmond. It was a great moment because Stevie had played so well all season, he was probably our most consistent player – and that's saying something because we were a great side.' On Easter Monday Everton beat Sunderland again, 6-2 at Goodison. Stevenson scored his 13th goal of the season and Everton were virtually assured the League Championship.

Stevenson won the first of seven Republic of Ireland (then Irish Free State) caps while playing for Dolphin in 1932. Like several players of his generation, he also won Northern Ireland honours, the first of 17 caps coming as a Rangers player in 1933.

A. E. STEVENSON *(EVERTON)*

[FACTFILE]

BORN
Dublin, 9 August 1912
DIED
1985
POSITION
Inside left
OTHER CLUBS
Dolphin (1930–32);
Glasgow Rangers (1932–34);
Bootle (1949–51)
HONOURS
League Championship 1938/39;
17 Northern Ireland caps
(5 goals) (1933–47);
7 Republic of Ireland caps (1932–48)

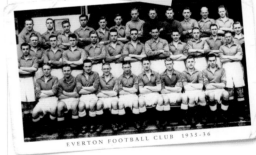

EVERTON FOOTBALL CLUB 1935-36

Like so many of his colleagues, the intervention of the Second World War cut Stevenson off in his prime. He continued to be a regular for Everton in the wartime leagues, also guesting for Tranmere Rovers and Blackpool. When football resumed in 1946, he was in his mid-thirties and playing for a declining team. His footballing brain remained as acute as ever, but his diminishing pace saw him overshadowed by Wally Fielding. Although he continued to represent Everton until the end of the 1948/49 season, he increasingly became a peripheral figure.

In May 1949 he was released by Everton and joined Bootle as player-manager. Later he returned to Ireland, managing the Republic of Ireland between 1953 and 1955.

Season	League		FA Cup		Total	
	App	Goals	App	Goals	App	Goals
1933/34	12	1	0	0	12	1
1934/35	36	15	5	3	41	18
1935/36	29	10	0	0	29	10
1936/37	41	19	3	2	44	21
1937/38	35	13	2	1	37	14
1938/39	36	11	5	2	41	13
1946/47	30	8	0	0	30	8
1947/48	17	3	0	0	17	3
1948/49	19	2	1	0	20	2
Total	**255**	**82**	**16**	**8**	**271**	**90**

Stevenson, Billy

Right back stalwart and Central League captain

Billy Stevenson was a solid, not especially quick right back, who spent much of his Everton career on the fringes of the first team, deputising for the first choice in the berth, Robert Balmer.

> 'CLEVER IN ANTICIPATING OPPONENTS MOVEMENTS AND SPEEDY IN RECOVERY'

He joined Everton for £30 from Accrington Stanley in April 1906 but had to wait until December the following year to make his first-team debut, against Newcastle at St James's Park. Reports suggest it was inauspicious, with the watching Balmer given 'considerable cause for anxiety' and the defender was 'repeatedly disturbed' by the opposing winger, although he 'played better as the game wore on'.

STEVENSON usurped Balmer midway through the 1910/11 season and held the right back berth for the subsequent two campaigns. He was, noted one contemporary report, 'clever in anticipating opponents movements and speedy in recovery'. On this particular occasion, the Lancastrian 'had no superior in defensive work'. During this period Everton finished fourth and then runners-up, missing out on the league title by just three points.

Everton dropped to 11th in 1912/13 and as the directors sought to find the winning formula, Stevenson was a victim. Leicester Fosse's Bob Thompson was drafted in to replace him in April 1913 and proved an excellent choice, helping Everton lift the League Championship in 1914/15.

Stevenson was by now Everton's Central League captain, quite a responsibility at a time when reserve games were played in front of several thousand fans. Following the outbreak of war he remained on Everton's retained list for the 1915/16 season, but is not listed as making a senior appearance in the wartime leagues.

[FACTFILE]

BORN
Accrington, 1886
POSITION
Right back
OTHER CLUB
Accrington Stanley (1903–06)

Season	League		FA Cup		Total	
	App	Goals	App	Goals	App	Goals
1907/08	8	0	1	0	9	0
1908/09	2	0	0	0	2	0
1909/10	3	0	0	0	3	0
1910/11	22	0	3	0	25	0
1911/12	32	0	5	0	37	0
1912/13	36	0	5	0	41	0
1913/14	8	0	0	0	8	0
Total	**111**	**0**	**14**	**0**	**125**	**0**

Stewart, Alex

Defensive-minded Scot who played through Everton's ultimately unsuccessful run to the 1893 FA Cup Final

Season	League		FA Cup		Total	
	App	Goals	App	Goals	App	Goals
1892/93	12	1	7	0	19	1
Total	**12**	**1**	**7**	**0**	**19**	**1**

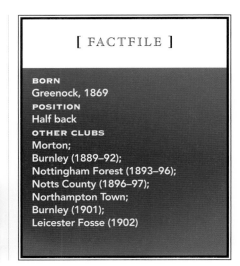

[FACTFILE]

BORN
Greenock, 1869
POSITION
Half back
OTHER CLUBS
Morton;
Burnley (1889–92);
Nottingham Forest (1893–96);
Notts County (1896–97);
Northampton Town;
Burnley (1901);
Leicester Fosse (1902)

Stewart, Billy

Scottish defender who brought military levels of fitness to the Everton defence

The Scottish left half Billy Stewart first rose to prominence playing for the regimental team of the famous Black Watch regiment.

After attaining his discharge so that he could play professionally, he joined Preston North End via a spell with Belfast Distillery. A move to Everton came in 1893 and he brought a new level of professionalism and fitness to the Everton team. 'As a stylist Bill Stewart had few points of character play to distinguish him from the average first-class half-back of today,' recorded a 1925 profile. 'It was in his results for the team that he can best be judged.'

Stewart joined a defence that was overseen by the mighty 'wee devil' Johnny Holt and brought 'untiring skill and ceaseless vigilance … not only in tactical defence, but inventing and developing constant attack, which is, of course, the most perfect form of defence.' A vivid portrait of the former army man was painted by Victor Hall in the Football Echo in 1925.

Stewart had developed his football under Army conditions, and speed, strength, and stamina were the prime essentials. He had learned in the hard school of experience to stand up to grueling players, to take hard knocks, and to give them in return. There is or was, no school so serve for testing perfect physical fitness as the Army gyms, and playing fields, and Stewart had come through the ordeals with honours. Therefore, professional football had nothing to teach him in strength, stamina, or physique, and the skill and intuition of the finer points of the game were born in him.

According to Hall, Stewart was renowned for the power of his throw-ins, which were often said to be equal to the velocity of a free kick 'and contemporary players of those days claimed that he could drop the ball into the goalmouth from a touchline throw-in'.

He was a regular over four seasons through the mid-1890s, but after captaining Everton to the 1897 FA Cup Final fell out of favour with the Everton selectors. After losing his place to Jack Robertson he joined Bristol City in the Southern League, where he played out his career.

Season	League		FA Cup		Total	
	App	Goals	App	Goals	App	Goals
1893/94	29	1	1	0	30	1
1894/95	27	2	3	0	30	2
1895/96	28	0	3	0	31	0
1896/97	29	3	4	0	33	3
1897/98	9	0	4	0	13	0
Total	**122**	**6**	**15**	**0**	**137**	**6**

[FACTFILE]

BORN
Arbroath, 1867
POSITION
Left half
OTHER CLUBS
Strathmore;
Arbroath;
Black Watch;
Belfast Distillery;
Preston North End
(1890–92);
Bristol City

Storrier, David

Powerful full back who went on to captain Celtic

Season	League		FA Cup		Total	
	App	Goals	App	Goals	App	Goals
1893/94	1	0	0	0	1	0
1894/95	1	0	1	0	2	0
1895/96	3	0	1	0	4	0
1896/97	25	0	3	0	28	0
1897/98	25	0	5	0	30	0
Total	**55**	**0**	**10**	**0**	**65**	**0**

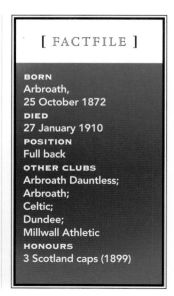

[FACTFILE]

BORN
Arbroath,
25 October 1872
DIED
27 January 1910
POSITION
Full back
OTHER CLUBS
Arbroath Dauntless;
Arbroath;
Celtic;
Dundee;
Millwall Athletic
HONOURS
3 Scotland caps (1899)

Stowell, Mike

Reserve goalkeeper who thrived away from
Neville Southall's considerable shadow

Season	League		FA Cup		League Cup		Other		Total	
	App	Goals	App	Goals	App	Goals	App	Goals	App	Goals
1988/89	0	0	0	0	0	0	1	0	0	0
Total	**0**	**0**	**0**	**0**	**0**	**0**	**1**	**0**	**0**	**0**

Stracqualursi, Denis

Big-hearted Argentine
centre forward whose
endeavours captured
Evertonian hearts

Season	League		FA Cup		Europe		Total	
	App	Goals	App	Goals	App	Goals	App	Goals
2011/12	7 (14)	1	2 (3)	2	1 (1)	0	10 (18)	3
Total	**7 (14)**	**1**	**2 (3)**	**2**	**1 (1)**	**0**	**10 (18)**	**3**

Strettle, Samuel

Cheshire-born
defender unable to
carve out a regular
first-team berth

Season	League		FA Cup		Total	
	App	Goals	App	Goals	App	Goals
1906/07	2	0	0	0	2	0
1907/08	1	0	0	0	1	0
1908/09	1	0	0	0	1	0
Total	**4**	**0**	**0**	**0**	**4**	**0**

Stuart, Graham

Everton's underrated diamond whose goals staved away relegation

Scarcely in Everton's history has there been a player more befitting of his nickname than Graham 'Diamond' Stuart. Stuart's debut season was drawing to its miserable conclusion in May 1994, with Everton staring down their noses at relegation. Losing 2-0 to Wimbledon, in the season's make-or-break fixture on the final day of the campaign, Everton were handed a lifeline from the penalty spot shortly before half-time.

Goodison was a cauldron simmering with anxiety, and there were senior players who clearly baulked at the task in hand. But Stuart, an unassuming 23-year-old who'd had a mixed debut season on Merseyside and had never taken a spot kick for the club before, took possession of the ball and smartly despatched it into the back of the Wimbledon net. Everton's revival was set in motion, and nine minutes from the end Stuart completed the turnaround with a scuffed shot from the edge of the penalty area that bobbled past Hans Segers and brought a 3-2 win and safety.

Stuart, a former England under-21 international and graduate of the FA School of Excellence, had signed from Chelsea the previous summer for £850,000. Nominally a right winger he would, over his four-year-long Goodison career, fit into a variety of roles across the Everton midfield, also as a forward and wing back. A good dribbler and fine and accurate passer of the ball, always eager and willing, Stuart had nevertheless been slow to adapt to life at Goodison. Prior to the Wimbledon game he

'ONE OF THE BEST AND WORST DAYS OF MY LIFE'

had often flattered to deceive and had scored just once as Everton neared the abyss.

That crazy afternoon changed everything, however, as Stuart

entered Goodison lore. Stuart later recalled it as 'one of the best and worst days of my life'. 'I have seen people celebrate Cup wins less passionately,' he told the Liverpool Echo in 2009. 'It rattles me a little bit. The whole thing does. I hate the fact that we were even in that position to start with because it tells me that we must have been pretty woeful for the whole of the season.'

Things, nevertheless, improved with the arrival of Joe Royle later that year. Stuart was greatly valued by the new manager, who often used him in his favoured role as a deep-lying forward. It was here that he started the 1995 FA Cup Final, and it was his shot against the crossbar that set up Paul Rideout's decisive goal. Royle persevered with him as a forward throughout much of the 1995/96 season, talking him up as a possible England contender. Stuart proved a more reliable

alternative to the enigmatic Duncan Ferguson and finished second top scorer. But he lacked the pace and ruthlessness in front of goal that would have marked him out as a top marksman. His versatility worked against him too, and he lacked the sort of lengthy run in a single position that might have seen him excel.

Still, he was a valued and respected member of the Everton squad, and his departure to Sheffield United as a makeweight in the deal that saw Carl Tiler and Mitch Ward arrive in November 1997 was widely mourned. He subsequently returned to the Premier League with Charlton Athletic, whom he captained at the start of the century, later playing out his career with Norwich City.

On retirement he returned to Merseyside, which the effusive Londoner came to regard as his home. 'The days I spent at Goodison were the happiest of my career,' he said in 2009. 'Don't get me wrong; I had a great time at Chelsea and had a magnificent upbringing there. But Everton is just a special club; it's a still place [that] gets to you. Once you've played here, you don't forget it.'

Season	League		FA Cup		League Cup		Other		Total	
	App	Goals	App	Goals	App	Goals	App	Goals	App	Goals
1993/94	26 (4)	3	1 (1)	0	2	0	-	-	29 (5)	3
1994/95	20 (8)	3	3 (2)	2	2	1	-	-	25 (10)	6
1995/96	27 (2)	9	4	3	1	1	2 (1)	1	34 (3)	14
1996/97	29 (6)	5	2	0	1	0	-	-	32 (6)	5
1997/98	14	2	0	0	3	1	-	-	17	3
Total	**116(20)**	**22**	**10 (3)**	**5**	**9**	**3**	**2 (1)**	**1**	**137(24)**	**31**

[FACTFILE]

BORN
Tooting, 24 October 1970
POSITION
Midfield / forward
OTHER CLUBS
Chelsea (1989–93);
Sheffield United (1997–99);
Charlton Athletic
(1999–2005);
Norwich City (2005)
HONOURS
FA Cup 1995

Stubbs, Alan

Centre back who recovered from cancer to captain his boyhood team

A Kirkby-born boyhood Evertonian who watched Everton's mid-80s glory days from the Gwladys Street terrace, Alan Stubbs first made his name as part of Bolton Wanderers' mid-1990s revival. The tall centre half was a fine reader of the game, a good header and, even if his ball-playing skills were sometimes overhyped in these early years, a doughty and brave player. He won England B honours in 1994, and joined Celtic in a £4million deal in 1996.

PERHAPS full international recognition may also have come Stubbs's way, but in 1999 his life changed forever. After giving a blood sample following the Scottish Cup Final, he was diagnosed with testicular cancer. An operation and chemotherapy saw a recovery, but in November 2000 it emerged that he had suffered a relapse and he was admitted to hospital for further treatment. He underwent surgery in January 2001 and was again given the all-clear.

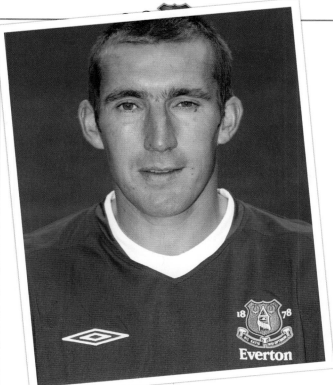

Six months later, Stubbs was an Everton player, having signed on a Bosman free transfer. It was, he acknowledged, his 'dream move' and pulling on an Everton jersey for the first time was 'the best feeling I've ever had in football'. He had by now entered the veteran stage of his career and was nearing his 30th birthday. One of the most noticeable things in these early appearances was a discernible lack of pace – something that was easily exploited by opponents. Stubbs was dropped barely a month after his debut, and although he returned soon after was unable to remedy the terminal decline of Walter Smith's regime.

And yet after the arrival of David Moyes in March 2002, Stubbs looked a different player.

Particularly when picked to play alongside Joseph Yobo, whose fleet-footedness complemented Stubbs's impeccable reading of the game, he shone, often captaining the team too. Alongside David Weir, he shared a solid and occasionally imperious central defensive partnership. While against better opponents their lack of pace showed, sometimes their experience counted for more as the Everton defence absorbed onslaught after onslaught.

STUBBS possessed many of the attributes – a boyhood love of the club, passion, commitment – to make him a firm crowd favourite, a legend even. And yet the bonds between supporter and player were sometimes undermined. Stubbs shared the same agent as Wayne Rooney, which fanned conspiracy theories when the youngster

joined Manchester United. Later he publicly backed Everton's unpopular proposed move to Kirkby. In July 2005 he skulked out of the club, turning down the chance of a new contract and Champions League football in favour of a better deal at Sunderland. He then accused Everton of demanding a contractual clause relating to the cancer – claims that were untrue and for which Stubbs later apologised.

The switch to the Stadium of Light was an unmitigated disaster. Sunderland were relegated from the Premier League with a record low points tally, but Stubbs had by then left the Northeast. Chastened after his earlier outbursts, Stubbs was a surprise return to Goodison in January 2006 and soon confounded any lingering doubts with some fine performances through the remainder of the season, and in Everton's successful push for European qualification in 2006/07.

Following the arrival of Phil Jagielka in July 2007, Stubbs fell down the Everton pecking order. In January 2008 he was given a free transfer and joined Derby County. But the move was less than successful, with Derby even beating Sunderland's dismal low points record. Following relegation he made just one more appearance, before announcing his retirement due to a persistent knee injury. In September 2008, he returned to Everton as part of Moyes's coaching staff.

Season	League		FA Cup		League Cup		Europe		Total	
	App	Goals	App	Goals	App	Goals	App	Goals	App	Goals
2001/02	29 (2)	2	5	1	1	0	-	-	35 (2)	3
2002/03	34 (1)	0	1	0	1 (1)	0	-	-	36 (2)	0
2003/04	25 (2)	0	2	0	1 (1)	0	-	-	28 (3)	0
2004/05	29 (2)	1	3	0	2	0	-	-	34 (2)	1
2005/06	13 (1)	0	0	0	0	0	0	0	13 (1)	0
2006/07	23	2	0	0	1	0	-	-	24	2
2007/08	7 (1)	1	1	0	2	0	1 (1)	0	11 (2)	1
Total	**160(9)**	**6**	**12**	**1**	**8 (2)**	**0**	**1 (1)**	**0**	**181(12)**	**7**

[FACTFILE]

BORN
Liverpool, 6 October 1971
POSITION
Central defender
OTHER CLUBS
Bolton Wanderers (1990–96);
Celtic (1996–2001);
Sunderland (2005–06);
Derby County (2008)

Styles,
Arthur 'Archie'

Local left back who was a makeweight in Bob Latchford's record transfer

A former England schoolboy international, there must have been times when Archie Styles wondered if his chance for Everton would ever come. After working his way through the club's youth ranks through the later half of the 1960s, he was aged 23 when he made his belated debut in December 1972.

But the long wait seemed worth it, for Styles immediately proved the cause of great optimism to an increasingly beleaguered Goodison crowd.

Replacing Henry Newton in the left back berth, the local youngster would retain his place for much of the remainder of the 1972/73 season. A player tutored in the traditions of Harry Catterick's School of Science, he was a fine ball player, possessing a sure first touch and decent range of passing.

HOWEVER, at the end of the season Catterick was replaced by Billy Bingham, who did not share

Wolverhampton W. Saturday 9th December 1972 kick-off 8 p.m. · Football League Div. 1
official magazine 8p

his predecessor's faith in the full back. After giving him a handful of chances, in February 1974 he was sold to Birmingham City – a £90,000 makeweight in the British transfer record deal that brought Bob Latchford to Goodison. The comparatively high price paid for him was indicative of how highly Birmingham coveted him.

Styles never seemed to live up to his promise after leaving Goodison, however, and a journeyman career followed.

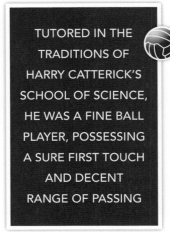

[FACTFILE]

BORN
Liverpool,
3 September 1949
POSITION
Left back
OTHER CLUBS
Birmingham City (1974–78);
Peterborough United
(1978–79);
Portsmouth (1979–80)

Season	League		FA Cup		League Cup		Total	
	App	Goals	App	Goals	App	Goals	App	Goals
1972/73	16 (1)	0	2	0	0	0	18 (1)	0
1973/74	6	0	1	0	1	0	8	0
Total	22 (1)	0	3	0	1	0	26 (1)	0

Sugg, Frank

Versatile defender-cum-striker who played his part in Everton's first league season

Season	League		FA Cup		Total	
	App	Goals	App	Goals	App	Goals
1888/89	9	0	-	-	9	0
1889/90	1	0	0	0	1	0
Total	10	0	0	0	10	0

[FACTFILE]

BORN
Ilkeston, 11 January 1862
POSITION
Centre half / centre forward
OTHER CLUBS
Bolton Wanderers;
The Wednesday;
Derby County;
Burnley

Sutherland, John

Defender who was the last of the post-war Irish invasion of Goodison

Season	League		FA Cup		Total	
	App	Goals	App	Goals	App	Goals
1956/57	6	0	2	0	8	0
Total	**6**	**0**	**2**	**0**	**8**	**0**

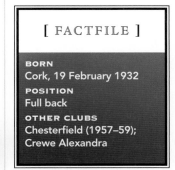

[FACTFILE]

BORN
Cork, 19 February 1932
POSITION
Full back
OTHER CLUBS
Chesterfield (1957–59);
Crewe Alexandra

Sutton, William

Goalkeeper who was among Everton's early one-game wonders

Season	League		FA Cup		Total	
	App	Goals	App	Goals	App	Goals
1894/95	1	0	0	0	1	0
Total	**1**	**0**	**0**	**0**	**1**	**0**

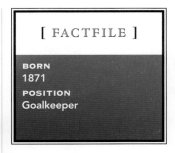

[FACTFILE]

BORN
1871
POSITION
Goalkeeper

THE

EVERTON
· ENCYCLOPEDIA ·

Idan **Tal,** Jimmy **Tansey,** Jack **Taylor,** Ted **Taylor,** George **Telfer,** Derek **Temple, Texaco Cup,** Dave **Thomas,** Eddie **Thomas,** Mickey **Thomas,** Tony **Thomas,** William **Thomas,** Bob **Thompson,** Robert **Thompson,** Claus **Thomsen,** George **Thomsen,** Jock **Thomson,** Sammy **Thomson,** Carl **Tiler,** Colin **Todd,** Wilf **Toman,** John **Tomlinson,** Mike **Trebilcock,** Douglas **Trentham,** Alec **Troup,** Bob **Turner,** Dave **Turner,** Edward **Turner,** George **Turner,** Iain **Turner,** Joe **Turner**

Tal, Idan

Well-travelled Israeli international who never settled at Goodison

Idan Tal joined Everton for an undisclosed fee variously estimated to be between £700,000 and £925,000 after impressing during a trial at the club's Italian training camp during the summer of 2000.

His transfer was delayed until he had played two further internationals and could thus satisfy the Department of Employment's work-permit restrictions. His early forays as a substitute were impressive, with some wistful Evertonians likening him to Pat Nevin. Walter Smith gave him a run in the team over the winter of 2000 but ultimately preferred a string of other players on the Everton left as disparate as Mark Pembridge, Gary Naysmith, Jesper Blomqvist and David Ginola.

TAL MADE just one league start during the 2001/02 season and disappeared from view after David Moyes succeeded Smith as manager. After his release in early 2003 he moved to Spain then back to Israel, briefly returning to the Premier League with Bolton in the 2006/07 season.

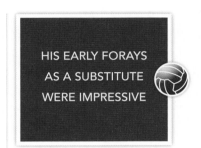

HIS EARLY FORAYS AS A SUBSTITUTE WERE IMPRESSIVE

[FACTFILE]

BORN
Jerusalem,
13 September 1975
POSITION
Winger
OTHER CLUBS
Hapoel Jerusalem (1994–96);
Maccabi Petah Tikva
(1997–98);
Hapoel Tel Aviv
(1998–2000);
CP Merida (loan,
1999–2000);
Maccabi Petah Tikva (2000);
Rayo Vallecano (2003);
Maccabi Haifa (2003–06);
Bolton Wanderers (2006–07);
Beitar Jerusalem (2007–11),
Hapoel Jerusalem (2011–)
HONOURS
69 Israel caps (5 goals)
(1998–2007)

Season	League		FA Cup		League Cup		Total	
	App	Goals	App	Goals	App	Goals	App	Goals
2000/01	12 (10)	2	0 (2)	0	0	0	12 (12)	2
2001/02	1 (6)	0	0 (1)	0	1	0	2 (7)	0
2002/03	0	0	0	0	0	0	0	0
Total	**13 (16)**	**2**	**0 (3)**	**0**	**1**	**0**	**14 (19)**	**2**

Tansey, Jimmy

Wise head among Everton's 1950s young Turks

EVERTON 1956
Back row - Sutherland, Tansey, O'Neill, Jones, Kirby,
Front - McNamara, Eglington, Farrell, Llewellyn, Glazzard, Rea

'HE WAS
A GOOD PLAYER, JIMMY,
A GOOD MAN TO
HAVE ON YOUR SIDE'

KEN REA

Local left back Jimmy Tansey was a stalwart of Everton's mid-1950s strugglers, a man senior in age to many of the young hopefuls on whom Everton's future was staked, though not in terms of first-class appearances. Indeed, in a career interrupted by national service, Tansey had to wait until his mid-twenties for a regular run in the Everton first XI.

Yet when given the chance he showed himself to be a leader among Everton's young Turks. 'He was a good player, Jimmy, a good man to have on your side,' the wing half Ken Rea told this author in 2011. 'He used to talk to you all on the field. He advised people and was a smashing fella within himself. He never shouted at you or bawled at you, he just told you what to do. He was a bit of a leader.'

His chance came at the start of the 1955/56 season when he took the place of Irish left back Don Donovan. Yet although popular with his team-mates, the Goodison faithful could be unforgiving. 'With his bandy-legged gait and rather deliberate style, left back Jimmy Tansey presented an at times irresistible target for frustrated Goodison Park fans as Everton struggled throughout the 50s,' wrote the football historian Ivan Ponting. 'Yet behind the

occasional baiting was genuine respect for a whole-hearted and thoughtful competitor.'

DEREK TEMPLE, himself then a young hopeful, said that Tansey was underrated. 'Jimmy was a cracking fella, a real character,' he said in 2011. 'Not the quickest – none of them were quick and Jimmy didn't like a quick player chasing at him. But he used to figure them out. It was a question of tactics then: getting someone to help him a bit. He made quite a number of appearances so he didn't do too badly.'

Temple, who came up against many a fearsome full back, said that the position was far less elaborate in the 1950s than its modern

equivalent. 'Full backs in those days were good footballers, but they didn't play football in the way they do now,' he said. 'The game has changed in that respect. They were strong, they could hit a long ball for fellas to make a break from deep. If they had quick players they could very often get goals from it.' Not until he found himself lining up alongside the lithe, whippet-like Ray Wilson the following decade did he play alongside someone that could be construed as a modern defender-cum-attacker in the full back berth.

Tansey held his own in the Everton team until the 1958/59 season, when John Bramwell was preferred to him. The following year T.E. Jones was moved to left back to facilitate the emergent Brian Labone at centre half and chances became even harder to come by. Now past his 30th birthday, he was enticed by a £500 move to Crewe Alexandra in June 1960 and he played out his career at Gresty Road.

[FACTFILE]

BORN
Liverpool, 29 January 1929
DIED
Liverpool, 7 July 2012
POSITION
Left back
OTHER CLUBS
Crewe Alexandra (1960–61)

Season	League		FA Cup		Total	
	App	**Goals**	**App**	**Goals**	**App**	**Goals**
1952/53	3	0	0	0	3	0
1953/54	0	0	0	0	0	0
1954/55	5	0	0	0	5	0
1955/56	39	0	4	0	43	0
1956/57	42	0	3	0	45	0
1957/58	39	0	2	0	41	0
1958/59	3	0	0	0	3	0
1959/60	2	0	0	0	2	0
Total	**133**	**0**	**9**	**0**	**142**	**0**

Taylor, Jack

Captain and utility man extraordinaire, Taylor was the first man to bring the FA Cup to Merseyside

In the pantheon of Everton greats, the elegant, moustachioed figure of Jack Taylor stands tall if not slightly underappreciated.

Just six men – Neville Southall, Brian Labone, Dave Watson, Ted Sagar, Kevin Ratcliffe and Mick Lyons – have worn the blue of Everton more times than him, and were it not for the club's perennial underachievement at the start of the 20th century, his medal cabinet would almost certainly be fuller than most of his successors. Three times – in 1902, 1905 and 1909 – he was a league runner-up, and twice – in 1897 and 1907 – an FA Cup runner-up too.

> HE WAS IN 1906, AS EVERTON CAPTAIN, THE FIRST MAN TO BRING THE FA CUP BACK TO LIVERPOOL

IN RETIREMENT he could, nevertheless, reflect on the fact that he was in 1906, as Everton captain, the first man to bring the FA Cup back to Liverpool.

Taylor was one of Goodison's early heroes, revered by Evertonians for epitomising all the qualities found in a traditional sporting gentleman. Willing to adapt to any position in order to benefit the good of the team, Taylor played in a variety of roles during an Everton career that lasted for 14 years.

Another son of that prolific Scottish town of Dumbarton – the burgh that bore Dickie Boyle, John Bell, Alex Latta and Graeme Sharp – Taylor joined Everton in 1896 from St Mirren. He had started out at Dumbarton and already had five Scotland caps to his name, a tally that was, astonishingly, never added to. His first days at Goodison were played at inside forward and on the right wing, and it was here that he partook in the 1897 FA Cup Final, which Everton were unlucky to lose to League Champions Aston Villa.

With his fellow Dumbartonian John Bell, Taylor formed one of the finest wing partnerships the club has witnessed. He was as revered off the field as he was on it, and Everton's first historian, Thomas Keates, who was a director at this time, wrote: 'He played anywhere readily and played well everywhere, and had a fine record during 13 years service … No Everton player has left Evertonians with a more fragrant memory …' The influence of the 'three Jacks' (Taylor, Bell and Sharp) on the dressing room was immense, believed Keates, and 'their high standard code of life, mentality and lingual purity had a most beneficial influence on the habits and tone of their players and the influence did not cease with their exit.'

For the 1898/99 season Taylor was made captain and reverted to half back, where his cool and accomplished play and eye for attacking move were instrumental to Everton's progress. It was telling that when he shifted to the wing late in the season he was sorely missed. A run of seven games without a win cost Everton the title and they finished fourth.

Taylor continued to split his time between the Everton back line and positions in its attack. He gave up the captaincy for the first five years of the new century to first Jimmy Settle then Tom Booth, but took it triumphantly back for the 1905/06 campaign. The league season was mediocre, but in the FA Cup Everton seemed destined to win the trophy. He captained Everton all the way to Crystal Palace, and had a decisive impact in the final against Newcastle United. With 13 minutes remaining Taylor – sole survivor of Everton's previous final – found Sharp with a searching pass. He evaded the Newcastle left back Carr, who had not previously given the Everton wide man an inch, before sending a beautifully centred cross which Young slotted home for Everton's winner.

Although Everton had previously won the League Championship in 1891, the 1906 FA Cup win was without doubt the biggest occasion in the first 30 years of the club's history. The scenes that greeted them in Liverpool were incredible. It was 'the most remarkable popular demonstration that has ever taken place within the city boundaries', wrote Keates, and it was Taylor who led the celebrations.

EVERTON 1909/10
Back - **Cuff (Secretary), Harris, R.Balmer, Scott, Maconnachie, Taylor, Makepeace, Elliott (Trainer)**
Front - **Sharp (Captain), Coleman, White, Freeman, Young, Turner**

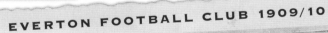

EVERTON FOOTBALL CLUB 1909/10

Back - **Cuff (Secretary), Harris, R.Balmer, Scott, Maconnachie, Taylor, Makepeace, Elliott (Trainer)**
Front - **Sharp (Captain), Coleman, White, Freeman, Young, Turner**

JACK TAYLOR
EVERTON

Arriving at Central Station, a thunderstorm of cheering greeted Jack Taylor, Cup in hand, and his victorious comrades as they stepped from a saloon carriage. After a preliminary reception, on the platform, by the Lord Mayor, surrounded by football directors of Liverpool as well as Everton, a host of officials of other clubs and local notables, the Lord Mayor ascended a gorgeously carpeted truck, and delivered a neat congratulatory oration that would have swelled the heads of ordinary mortals. But Jack and his comrades were not ordinaries. Conscious, however, that they were having the time of their lives, they were compelled to keep smiling, couldn't help it, if they could. From the station on a four-in-hand (the players outside); Jack Taylor, on the driver's seat, proudly waved the Cup to the cheering thousands that lined the route to Goodison Park, via Church Street, Whitechapel, Byrom Street and Scotland Road. The enclosure was crammed with enthusiasts. The team (escorted by mounted police) had a great reception. More ceremony, more speeches. Refreshments, a lull; fatigue, dispersal; followed by a welcome rest after a prolonged hour of glorious life.

'NEVER HAD A CLUB HAD A MORE LOYAL AND HARD-WORKING SERVANT OR ONE WHO WAS EVER DOING THE UTMOST FOR HIS TEAM AND CLUB'

The players were deified for their achievement. At the club's AGM a month later, the chairman, George Mahon, paid tribute to the Everton captain. 'With regard to the players who brought that honour, to them; the duties of the captaincy fell upon the old and well tried comrade Jack D. Taylor,' he said to a round of applause. 'Never had a club had a more loyal and hard-working servant or one who was ever doing the utmost for his team and club.' Taylor returned to Crystal Palace with Everton 12 months later, but the final against Sheffield Wednesday was a damp squib, and they fell to a 2-1 defeat.

By now in the veteran stage of his career, he reverted to centre half and with Jack Sharp the captain, he pushed for his first League title. By Christmas in the 1908/09 campaign, and boosted by Bert Freeman's goals, Everton were way ahead. But they faltered in the second half of the campaign and the perennial nearly men ended a place and seven points behind champions Newcastle.

STILL TAYLOR played on, and although injuries had started to take their toll, another stab at glory seemed to be on the cards. Everton reached the 1910 FA Cup semi-final against Second Division Barnsley. After a hard-fought goalless draw at Elland Road, the teams met at Old Trafford for the replay five days later. But the match was a disaster for Everton and Taylor.

After just 10 minutes Taylor was struck in the throat and collapsed to the ground. 'Few of those on the grand stand really saw what happened,' reported the Liverpool Courier. 'The fact is that Taylor received a kick in the throat. At first the impression was that he had swallowed something, for the doctor and the trainer seemed to be directing their attention to his throat. He was obviously suffering, and after Dr Baxter and Dr Whitford had examined him in the dressing room it was seen that he would be unable to take any further part of the match. His larynx had been injured, and it was with difficulty that he could speak.' With 10 men Everton missed two first-half penalties, then their goalkeeper Billy Scott was also badly injured. Barnsley won 3-0.

This was not only the end of Taylor's hopes for another trophy, but so severe was the injury that it was the end of his top-class career. He returned a couple of years later, playing for South Liverpool as a fortysomething, but his best years had lain in the north of the city. Taylor remained on Merseyside after the end of his career and was regularly seen at the club he had helped make great throughout this time. He died in a car accident on the Wirral in 1949.

[FACTFILE]

BORN
Dumbarton, 27 January 1872
DIED
West Kirby, 21 February 1949
POSITION
Winger / inside forward / half back / centre forward
OTHER CLUBS
Dumbarton Athletic (1891–94);
St Mirren (1894–96)
HONOURS
1906 FA Cup;
5 Scotland caps (1 goal) (1892–95)

Season	League		FA Cup		Total	
	App	Goals	App	Goals	App	Goals
1896/97	30	13	5	2	35	15
1897/98	30	3	5	3	35	6
1898/99	34	3	2	1	36	4
1899/1900	32	7	1	0	33	7
1900/01	25	11	2	1	27	12
1901/02	26	8	2	0	28	8
1902/03	33	3	3	1	36	4
1903/04	22	6	1	1	23	7
1904/05	34	4	6	0	40	4
1905/06	36	4	6	2	42	6
1906/07	34	1	8	2	42	3
1907/08	23	2	7	0	30	2
1908/09	27	1	1	0	28	1
1909/10	14	0	7	1	21	1
Total	**400**	**66**	**56**	**14**	**456**	**80**

Taylor, Ted

Veteran goalkeeper of great pedigree who returned to his home city to lift the 1928 League title

Gallaher's Cigarettes.

[FACTFILE]

BORN
Liverpool, 7 March 1887
DIED
1956
POSITION
Goalkeeper
OTHER CLUBS
Marlborough Old Boys;
Liverpool Balmoral;
Oldham Athletic (1912–21);
Huddersfield Town (1921–26);
Ashton National;
Wrexham (1928)
HONOURS
League Championship 1927/28;
8 England caps (1922–26)

	League		FA Cup		Total	
Season	**App**	**Goals**	**App**	**Goals**	**App**	**Goals**
1926/27	14	0	0	0	14	0
1927/28	26	0	2	0	28	0
Total	**40**	**0**	**2**	**0**	**42**	**0**

Telfer, George

Local-born forward who slipped from view

George Telfer was one of a succession of gifted players to progress through Everton's youth set-up in the early 1970s, but who perhaps lacked that little extra something necessary to thrive at the very highest level.

A stocky, powerful forward, always full of running, Telfer first came onto the scene in the 1973/74 season. Hard-working and fast when at full pelt – though perhaps lacking some of the acceleration that would have marked him out for the top – the teenager's effervescent performances on the Everton wing saw some observers state that the club possessed a future England international. He was a fine finisher and possessed a powerful shot, yet sometimes lacked subtlety in his approach play.

His finest season came in 1975/76 when he was frequently utilised as Bob Latchford's foil. Towards the end of the season Telfer was asked to play as centre forward and although the 20-year-old gave his all, for demanding sections of the support it was not good enough. He became a whipping boy as Everton lost five straight league games.

FOR A CLUB with League Championship ambitions, what they needed was a top-class partner for Latchford. What they got, later on that year, was Duncan McKenzie, whose cavalier approach divided fans. Telfer outlasted him, but his confidence and chances seemed to be stunted thereafter. By his mid-twenties his career was drifting, and he left Goodison shortly after Howard Kendall's arrival in May 1981. In retirement he became involved with youth football in his native Liverpool.

[FACTFILE]

BORN
Liverpool, 6 July 1955
POSITION
Forward
OTHER CLUBS
San Diego Sockers (1981);
Scunthorpe United (1981–83);
Preston North End (1983);
Runcorn

> HIS FINEST SEASON CAME IN 1975/76 WHEN HE WAS FREQUENTLY UTILISED AS BOB LATCHFORD'S FOIL

	League		FA Cup		League Cup		Other		Total	
Season	**App**	**Goals**	**App**	**Goals**	**App**	**Goals**	**App**	**Goals**	**App**	**Goals**
1973/74	15	3	1 (1)	0	0	0	-	-	16 (1)	3
1974/75	11 (4)	2	2 (2)	0	0	0	-	-	13 (6)	2
1975/76	20 (4)	8	0	0	2 (1)	0	1	0	23 (5)	8
1976/77	17 (2)	4	0 (1)	0	3	0	-	-	20 (3)	4
1977/78	7 (5)	1	1	1	0 (1)	1	-	-	8 (6)	3
1978/79	10 (2)	2	0	0	0	0	0	0	10 (2)	2
1979/80	0	0	0	0	0	0	0	0	0	0
1980/81	1 (1)	0	0	0	0	0	-	-	1 (1)	0
Total	**81(18)**	**20**	**4 (4)**	**1**	**5 (2)**	**1**	**1 (1)**	**0**	**91 (25)**	**22**

Temple, Derek

Long-serving winger and inside forward whose goal brought FA Cup glory

Two names are intrinsically linked to Everton's 1966 FA Cup triumph. The first is the unheralded Cornishman, Mike Trebilcock, who, with Everton losing 2-0, seemed to come from nowhere to hit a rapid-fire brace that levelled the tie. The second is Derek Temple, who struck a spectacular winner 17 minutes from the final whistle. But unlike Trebilcock, Temple was far from a one-match wonder and by 1966 his career at the club had already spanned nearly a decade.

A son of Dovecot who progressed through Everton's youth ranks in the mid-1950s, Temple first broke into the Everton team at the end of the 1956/57 season and played in each of the final seven games, scoring three times. He impressed immediately and the following season he established himself in the first team as a speedy inside right partnering the irrepressible Dave Hickson. After a productive first half to the season, his progress was halted by a national service call-up. He joined the King's Liverpool Regiment because their headquarters were in Formby and was

HIS ACCOMPLISHMENT – COMING LATE IN THE MATCH AND WITH TIRED LEGS, AGAINST AN ENGLAND INTERNATIONAL GOALKEEPER – WAS TRULY MAGNIFICENT

assured that his Everton career would not be unduly hampered, but he ended up in Kenya.

BY THE time of his return to Merseyside in 1960, a crucial part of his early career had been lost. Everton, moreover, had changed too, with the Moores millions starting to eradicate the 1950s gloom. Temple initially struggled with the transition as chances were difficult to come by. His perseverance seemed to have paid off when Harry Catterick rewarded him with a run in the team during the closing stages of the 1961/62 season. This proved to be particularly productive and he scored five goals in Everton's last ten games of the season from the left wing, bringing his tally for the season to ten, which included an early season hat-trick against eventual champions Ipswich.

But just as Temple re-established himself in the Everton team, once more his progress was stunted, this time by a cartilage injury. In the 1962/63 season he made just five appearances, but his return in April 1963 was timely and he struck a crucial goal against West Ham that kept Everton's title bid on track. Alas, he never made enough appearances to claim a League Championship medal. The following season Catterick dropped Johnny Morrissey and brought in Temple on the left wing, where he remained until his transfer to Preston North End in 1967.

Equally skilful with both feet, Temple played on both wings and as an emergency centre forward. A reliable goalscorer, he averaged a goal every three games – a tally of which many an out-and-out striker would be proud. But it wasn't just the number of goals Temple scored that made him a favourite, more their nature – often a rasping shot at the end of a spectacular dash upfield.

Season	League		FA Cup		League Cup		Other		Total	
	App	Goals	App	Goals	App	Goals	App	Goals	App	Goals
1956/57	7	3	0	0	-	-	-	-	7	3
1957/58	28	8	1	0	-	-	-	-	29	8
1958/59	4	2	0	0	-	-	-	-	4	2
1959/60	0	0	0	0	-	-	-	-	0	0
1960/61	20	4	0	0	3	0	-	-	23	4
1961/62	17	10	0	0	-	-	-	-	17	10
1962/63	5	1	0	0	-	-	0	0	5	1
1963/64	41	12	5	0	-	-	3	1	49	13
1964/65	39	11	4	1	-	-	6	2	49	14
1965/66	38	9	8	6	-	-	4	0	50	15
1966/67	27 (1)	12	3	1	-	-	5	0	35 (1)	13
1967/68	5	0	0	0	1	0	-	-	6	0
Total	**231 (1)**	**72**	**21**	**8**	**4**	**0**	**18**	**3**	**274(1)**	**83**

NONE WERE better or more important than his effort against Sheffield Wednesday in Everton's FA Cup Final victory. It came on 73 minutes, after the ball had slipped away from the control of Wednesday centre half Gerry Young on the halfway line. 'As Gerry was the centre half, I knew there was nobody behind him except the goalkeeper, Ron Springett,' recalled Temple. 'I also knew that I would be expected to score. I was helped by the fact that Springett did not come far off his line. As I got to the edge of the penalty area, I aimed for the far post, and although the keeper got his fingers to the ball, he could not keep it out of the net.' Perhaps Temple's telling makes his goal sound easy, but his accomplishment – coming late in the match and with tired legs, against an England international goalkeeper – was truly magnificent.

> FOR TEMPLE IT WAS THE FITTING CONCLUSION OF A DECADE'S SERVICE, GUARANTEEING HIS PLACE IN EVERTON LORE

For many Everton supporters it was the first time they had seen their team win the FA Cup, and it sparked epic celebrations. Yet Temple's first thought was relief. 'Not thrilled or excited, although that came later,' he would recall. 'Just relieved that the ball had

gone in, because if it hadn't I would have been branded a villain.' For Temple it was the fitting conclusion of a decade's service, guaranteeing his place in Everton lore.

As Harry Catterick reconstructed his team around the Kendall-Harvey-Ball axis, Temple was a casualty, with Everton's manager preferring Johnny Morrissey on the Everton left through the latter half of the 1966/67 season. Despite featuring five times in the opening stages of the 1967/68 campaign, when Preston North End made a £35,000 offer in September 1967, the Everton manager accepted it.

In 1970 Temple dropped out of league football to combine playing semi-professionally with Wigan Athletic with the running of a newsagents he owned in Maghull. He subsequently worked in insurance sales, then for a double glazing company, before working for a chemical company. Still a regular and popular visitor to Goodison Park, his lengthy Everton career is invariably defined by memories of his FA Cup-winning goal. It was, said Albert Geldard, who had played on the Everton left when they previously won the FA Cup in 1933, 'One of the greatest goals I have ever seen. Those sort of openings can be missed so easily.'

> [FACTFILE]
>
> **BORN**
> Liverpool,
> 13 November 1938
> **POSITION**
> Inside left / left winger
> **OTHER CLUB**
> Preston North End (1967–70)
> **HONOURS**
> 1966 FA Cup;
> 1 England cap (1965)

Texaco Cup

Pan-British cup competition that failed to rouse enthusiasm

The Texaco Cup was a competition involving clubs from across Britain and the Republic of Ireland that had not qualified for European competitions. It ran between the 1970/71 season and 1974/75. Irish clubs withdrew from the competition in 1973/74.

Sponsored by American petroleum giant Texaco, in its first two seasons attendances for many games were comparable to those for European matches and Scottish clubs fared well against their English counterparts. However, from 1973 onwards, English sides dominated, causing all-English fixtures and spectators to stay away. Texaco withdrew sponsorship in 1975 and the competition was renamed the Anglo-Scottish Cup, but at that stage few top-flight teams entered the competition.

EVERTON entered the competition just once, in the 1973/74 season, but their record was inauspicious and they were knocked out in the first round by Heart of Midlothian.

Everton's record

18 SEPTEMBER 1973
First round, first leg v. Heart of Midlothian [H] 0-1; 12,536
Lawson, Darracott, McLaughlin, Buckley, Kenyon, Hurst, Newton, Lyons, Belfitt (Bernard), Harper, Connolly

3 OCTOBER 1973
First round, second leg v. Heart of Midlothian [A] 0-0; 24,903
Lawson, Darracott, McLaughlin, Clements, Kenyon, Hurst, Buckley, Husband, Lyons, Harper, Connolly

Thomas, Dave

Winger who supplied the crosses for Bob Latchford's goals

It was the brilliant and often unerring accuracy of Dave Thomas's crosses which led to Gordon Lee paying Queens Park Rangers £200,000 for his services on the eve of the 1977/78 season. Thomas replaced the more mercurial Ronnie Goodlass on the Everton wing as Lee formed the side that he hoped would push strongly for League Championship honours at the end of the season. The title never came, but Thomas's contribution of crosses and assists to the Everton goal tally during his two years at Goodison is almost immeasurable.

Starting out as a 16-year-old, the dashing flanker originally made his name with Burnley, later winning England under-23 honours. Inevitably he was sought by bigger clubs, with Everton, Leeds and Manchester United all seeking to acquire him in the early 1970s. Perhaps surprisingly, he joined Queens Park Rangers in October 1972 for £165,000. At Loftus Road he won promotion in 1972/73 and came agonisingly close to winning the League Championship in 1975/76. Don Revie, who had once tried to sign him for Leeds, awarded him the first of his eight England caps against Czechoslovakia in October 1974.

It was with Bob Latchford in mind that Gordon Lee made Thomas an Everton player. With his socks rolled around his ankles and without shin pads – a brave habit in an era of defensive hatchet men – Thomas cut a slight figure, but was nevertheless a formidable addition to the Everton team. Quick and skilful, he dodged a path down the Everton flank, lulling his opponents into challenges and, with a flick of his boot, skipping around them with the ball to deliver cross after cross. He was a teasing presence, lithe and brilliant. But it was his end

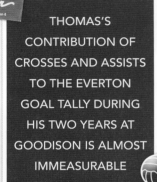

product that brought him such great renown, for his crosses were supremely accurate. With him in the side, Latchford thrived, scoring 30 goals in Thomas's debut season – many of which originated from the winger's left boot.

DESPITE Latchford's goals during the 1977/78 season, Everton fell short of the League Championship, finishing third. In 1978/79 they finished fourth, but were knocked out in the early stages of both domestic cup competitions and the UEFA Cup. Still firmly in Liverpool's shadow, the pressure was on Lee to bring success, and, as he sought to raise funds

and refashion his team, Thomas, was a surprising departure – sold to Wolves in October 1979 for £420,000. That season, without such a regular supply from the Everton flanks, the strike force of Latchford and Brian Kidd could muster only 16 goals between them. Indeed Latchford never hit such lofty heights again.

AFTER ONLY a short spell at Molineux, Thomas played out his career with Middlesbrough and Portsmouth via a spell in the NASL with Vancouver Whitecaps. Subsequently he left football and worked as a PE teacher in Sussex.

[FACTFILE]

BORN
Kirkby-in-Ashfield, 5 October 1950

POSITION
Winger

OTHER CLUBS
Burnley (1966–72);
Queens Park Rangers (1972–77);
Wolverhampton Wanderers (1979–80);
Vancouver Whitecaps (1981);
Middlesbrough (1981–82);
Portsmouth (1982–85)

HONOURS
8 England caps (1974–75)

Season	League		FA Cup		League Cup		Europe		Total	
	App	Goals	App	Goals	App	Goals	App	Goals	App	Goals
1977/78	38	2	1	0	5	1	0	0	44	3
1978/79	33	2	1	0	2	0	4	1	40	3
1979/80	0	0	0	0	0	0	0	0	0	0
Total	71	4	2	0	7	1	4	1	84	6

Thomas, Eddie

Prolific inside forward used to lure Roy Vernon to Goodison

EVERTON F.C. 1959-60

Left to right: (Back row) T. JONES, K. REA, A. PARKER, A. DUNLOP, J. BRAMWELL, M. MEAGAN, J. TANSEY, G. WATSON (Trainer); (Front row) A. SANDERS, J. HARRIS, E. THOMAS, D. HICKSON, R. COLLINS, E. O'HARA B. HARRIS

EVERTON 1959/60
Back - ***Jones, Rea, Parker, Dunlop, Bramwell, Meagan, Tansey, Watson (Trainer)***
Front - ***Sanders, J. Harris, Thomas, Hickson, Collins, O'Hara, B. Harris***

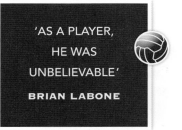

'AS A PLAYER, HE WAS UNBELIEVABLE'
BRIAN LABONE

Eddie Thomas seemed the very antithesis of a professional athlete. Fragile and gaunt, when up against some of the hatchet men of his era one would always have bet against him. But, recalled Brian Labone, 'As a player, he was unbelievable. He looked so slight, but he didn't half possess a powerful shot and he was so nippy. He was a nightmare to mark.'

THOMAS worked his way through the Everton youth ranks, national service delaying his debut until March 1957, when he was well past his 23rd birthday. His impact was almost immediate, however, and he scored a brace in only his second game, a 3-1 victory at Birmingham City. Throughout his Everton career his scoring record would remain enviable, despite always playing in poor teams.

As John Moores' influence began to draw a better standard of player to the club, Thomas initially held his own. He was Everton's top scorer through the first half of the 1959/60 season, outshining even Bobby Collins. But in February 1960 a bid was accepted for Blackburn's Roy Vernon and Johnny Carey deemed Thomas expendable, a makeweight in the deal that brought the Welshman to Goodison.

He spent two years at Ewood Park, before moving to Swansea Town. There followed spells with Derby County and Leyton Orient, before his retirement in 1968 – well into the veteran stage of his career.

AFTER his retirement he settled in Derby, home of the club that had arguably witnessed his best years. But he remained an Evertonian at heart and was a regular visitor to Goodison up till his death in 2003.

OFFICIAL PROGRAMME
EVERTON FOOTBALL CLUB
GOODISON PARK LIVERPOOL

Everton v. Preston North End
3d.   3d.

Season	League		FA Cup		Total	
	App	Goals	App	Goals	App	Goals
1956/57	7	2	0	0	7	2
1957/58	26	15	3	0	29	15
1958/59	32	10	4	2	36	12
1959/60	21	12	0	0	21	12
Total	**86**	**39**	**7**	**2**	**93**	**41**

[FACTFILE]

BORN
Newton-le-Willows, 23 October 1933
DIED
Derby, 12 November 2003
POSITION
Inside forward
OTHER CLUBS
Blackburn Rovers (1960–62); Swansea Town (1962–64); Derby County (1964–67); Leyton Orient (1967–68)

Thomas, Mickey

Colourful Welsh international winger whose Goodison exit was hastened by a managerial falling out

Season	League App	League Goals	FA Cup App	FA Cup Goals	League Cup App	League Cup Goals	Total App	Total Goals
1981/82	10	0	0	0	1	0	11	0
Total	10	0	0	0	1	0	11	0

Thomas, Tony

Long-serving Tranmere defender who failed to make the step up to the Premier League

Season	League App	League Goals	FA Cup App	FA Cup Goals	League Cup App	League Cup Goals	Total App	Total Goals
1997/98	6 (1)	0	1	0	1	0	8 (1)	0
1998/99	0 (1)	0	0	0	0	0	0 (1)	0
Total	6 (2)	0	1	0	1	0	8 (2)	0

Thomas, William

Goalkeeper who found his career limited to a solitary first-class appearance

Season	League App	League Goals	FA Cup App	FA Cup Goals	Total App	Total Goals
1892/93	1	0	0	0	1	0
Total	1	0	0	0	1	0

Thompson, Bob

League Championship winning right back

Right back Bob Thompson signed for Everton as part of a £750 joint deal that also saw winger George Harrison join Everton from financially stricken Leicester Fosse. It would prove to be a fine piece of business, with both footballers playing important roles in Everton's second League Championship win in 1915.

Thompson was a tough, uncomplicated defender as was the way with full backs of this era. Seldom did they venture past the halfway line and the attacking flourishes expected of today's generation of defenders were beyond the comprehension of most fans.

With a growing reputation in the reserves, Thompson was given a chance six games into the 1913/14 season and his presence marked the end of William Stevenson's tenure in the right back berth. He and John Maconnachie were, according to one local reporter, 'a pair of very reliable backs' and 'misgivings' about their ability were 'rare'.

Thompson played in all but five of Everton's matches as they lifted the League Championship. The intervention of war came when he was still in his mid-twenties and on his return he was unable to hold off the challenge of Dickie Downs. He joined Millwall Athletic in the Southern League, before returning north to Tranmere where he made a further 35 appearances.

	League		FA Cup		Total	
Season	App	Goals	App	Goals	App	Goals
1913/14	30	0	1	0	31	0
1914/15	33	0	5	0	38	0
1919/20	17	0	0	0	17	0
1920/21	3	0	0	0	3	0
Total	**83**	**0**	**6**	**0**	**89**	**0**

[FACTFILE]

BORN
Newcastle,
27 February 1890
POSITION
Right back
OTHER CLUBS
Blaydon;
Swawell;
Scotswood;
Leicester Fosse (1911–12);
Millwall Athletic (1921);
Tranmere Rovers (1922)
HONOURS
1914/15 League
Championship

Thompson, Robert

Defender who made just a single appearance, during Goodison's first season

	League		FA Cup		Total	
Season	App	Goals	App	Goals	App	Goals
1892/93	1	0	0	0	1	0
Total	**1**	**0**	**0**	**0**	**1**	**0**

[FACTFILE]

BORN
1870
POSITION
Left back

Thomsen, Claus

Lumbering midfielder, not up to the Goodison grade

Signed in January 1997, during the dying days of Joe Royle's managerial reign, Claus Thomsen represented the nadir of his manager's transfer policy. Acquired for a hefty £900,000, for a defensive midfielder Thomsen couldn't defend particularly well, nor did he add the flourishes expected of a midfield player. At Ipswich Town he had attracted impressive notices, but it was difficult to see why. Tall, gangly, lacking mobility and largely ineffective, he simply seemed too badly co-ordinated to cut it at the top level of the English game.

Perhaps unfairly, as Everton's form nosedived under Royle, Thomsen became a supporters' scapegoat, seeming to typify his manager's preference for the solid over the spectacular. When Howard Kendall succeeded Royle, Thomsen was virtually ostracised – not even

able to make it into one of the worst Everton teams in history – and eventually sold for £500,000 to AB Copenhagen in March 1998.

[FACTFILE]

BORN
Aarhus, Denmark, 31 May 1970
POSITION
Defensive midfield
OTHER CLUBS
Aarhus (1989–94);
Ipswich Town (1994–97); AB
Copenhagen (1998);
VFL Wolfsburg (1998–2002)
HONOURS
20 Denmark caps (1995–99)

Season	League		FA Cup		League Cup		Total	
	App	Goals	App	Goals	App	Goals	App	Goals
1996/97	15 (1)	0	0	0	0	0	15 (1)	0
1997/98	2 (6)	1	1	0	0	0	3 (6)	1
Total	17 (7)	1	1	0	0	0	18 (7)	1

Thomson, George

Scottish full back whose life ended tragically

For many years George Thomson's career mirrored that of his compatriot, Alex Young. The stylish left back had emerged through Heart of Midlothian's part-time ranks in the mid-1950s, when he was an apprentice plasterer and Young an engineer. The two had subsequently turned professional and won Scottish League Championship medals in 1958 and 1960. In November 1960, Thomson joined Everton as part of the deal that made Young an Everton player; Thomson was valued at £15,000.

A POLISHED AND COMPOSED PLAYER

EVERTON FOOTBALL CLUB 1960

LEFT TO RIGHT - BACK ROW - GORDON WATSON (Trainer), JIMMY GABRIEL, ALEX PARKER, ALBERT DUNLOP, BRIAN LABONE, GEORGE THOMSON, BRIAN HARRIS
FRONT ROW - BILLY BINGHAM, FRANK WIGNALL, BOBBY COLLINS, ROY VERNON, DEREK TEMPLE

EVERTON 1960
*Back row - **Watson (Trainer), Gabriel, Parker, Dunlop, Labone, Thomson, Harris** Front - **Bingham, Wignall, Collins, Vernon, Temple***

THE FULL BACK slotted in immediately to Johnny Carey's rapidly evolving team, taking the place of T.E. Jones, who had reverted to left back following the emergence of Brian Labone. A polished and composed player, Thomson's arrival effectively spelt the death knell of the former captain's first-team career.

And yet for all the composure he brought to the Everton defence, Thomson struggled with the rapid pace of First Division football. Brian Harris provided sound cover from the wing half position, but when he pushed forward Thomson was left terribly exposed. Though Thomson was first-choice left back for two

years, Harry Catterick eventually preferred Mick Meagan and dropped Thomson midway through 1962/63. He played enough games to claim a League Championship medal that season, but was sold to Brentford the following November.

WITH HIS dark good looks, it seemed inevitable that Thomson should be compared to his fellow Scot, Sean Connery, who was making a name for himself as James Bond in Ian Fleming's Dr No. To the unending amusement of his team-mates, he would announce his arrival: 'The name is Thomson, George Thomson.' He was, recalled Alex Young, something of a 'suave rascal', but a sad character too, who often appeared lonely. Young would recall in his memoirs that in retirement Thomson struggled with life after football, becoming something of a drifter who would turn up unexpectedly, looking for hand-outs. Alas, he fell foul of the law, and died while serving a custodial sentence in Preston Prison for murder.

Season	League		FA Cup		League Cup		Other		Total	
	App	Goals	App	Goals	App	Goals	App	Goals	App	Goals
1960/61	22	0	0	0	2	0	-	-	24	0
1961/62	32	1	1	0	-	-	-	-	33	1
1962/63	19	0	0	0	-	-	1	0	20	0
Total	**73**	**1**	**1**	**0**	**2**	**0**	**1**	**0**	**77**	**1**

Thomson, Jock

Highly decorated half back who captained Everton to League Championship success in the Indian summer of his career

Jock Thomson was one of a succession of fine Goodison servants whose first months at the club were defined by football fiasco.

Like Ben Williams, Ted Sagar, Billy Coggins and Tommy Johnson, Thomson was no sooner an Everton player than he was, with his new Everton team-mates, tasting the unfamiliar waters of the Second Division. Less than two months and just nine games after signing in March 1930, Thomson was part of Everton's first relegation side. This was, nevertheless, a black mark in an association with the club that was otherwise defined by glory.

THE FORMER Dundee left half had arrived at Goodison after Everton were given an option to sign him as part of the deal that had brought Alec Troup to Dens Park in January 1930. Everton had actually been following the

EVERTON F.C. 1939 - DIVISION I CHAMPIONS

EVERTON 1939
*Back - **Lawton, T.G. Jones, Sagar, Cook (Trainer), Mercer, Greenhalgh,***
*Front - **W. Cook, Gillick, Bentham, Thomson, Stevenson, Boyes***

player for some months, but his performances split the Everton directors. It was only after being watched by the former Everton player John Bell, who recommended him, that Everton made their move, paying £3650 for his services.

The half back position had been problematic for Everton all through the 1929/30 season and the 23-year-old Thomson was expected to rectify this. Standing 5ft 11in tall he was, reported the Liverpool Post and Mercury,

'a really class half-back whose mode of play is the right one. He keeps the ball on the floor, when at all possible and Everton should be strengthened by his inclusion to the team.' The correspondent added ominously: 'He will be tested to the full in Everton's remaining games and he may expect a strenuous time during the next few weeks.'

Indeed he was, although Thomson made a sound start himself – despite the shortcomings of his colleagues. 'Thomson made a successful initial appearance and added strength to the middle line,' the Post and Mercury reported of his debut against West Ham at Goodison. 'He was particularly effective in dribbling and delivering his pass at the most opportune moment. In attack he did excellent work, his good shooting being another point in his favour.' Yet that match ended in a 1-2 defeat and such poor form over the coming weeks would cost Everton their top-flight place.

However, Thomson would be crucial to Everton and their revival over subsequent years. 'A strong and forceful left half, Thomson toiled in the Goodison midfield trenches and strove to do the simple things well,' wrote David France. 'He relished the heat of battle and was respected for his resolute tackling which helped shore up a far from watertight rearguard.' Over the coming years Everton would win the Second Division Championship, the League Championship and FA Cup with Thomson at the heart of the team. 'One of the three Scots in the team, whose dainty footwork greatly help Johnson and Stein on the left wing,' read one profile ahead of the 1933 FA Cup Final, '[Thomson is] a good tackler and a fine feeder, he is always in the thick of the fray, and he is very enthusiastic.'

Yet Everton's board were ruthless and showed time and again that no one was indispensible in their pursuit of success. After three fallow years following the Cup win Thomson was dropped in favour of the promising youngster Joe Mercer ahead of the 1936/37 season. For nearly two years Thomson was sidelined and although he captained Everton to

EVERTON F.C. - F.A. CUP WINNERS 1933

LEFT TO RIGHT - BACK ROW :- H.F. COOKE (Trainer). BRITTON, CRESSWELL, SAGAR, COOK, WHITE, THOMSON.
FRONT ROW :- GELDARD, DUNN, DEAN, JOHNSON, STEIN, CRITCHLEY.

EVERTON 1933
Back row - Cooke (Trainer),
Britton, Cresswell, Sagar, Cook,
White, Thomson
Front - Geldard, Dunn, Dean,
Johnson, Stein, Critchley

the Central League title in 1938 it looked as if his career was, to all intents and purposes, over.

BUT LATE in the 1937/38 season, with Everton battling relegation, Mercer was injured and Thomson returned. Now a veteran, his experience and guile helped elevate Everton above the mire, and they were steered to the sanctuary of 14th place. Everton's directors recognised his impact and the following season Mercer was switched to right half to accommodate him. Thomson was made captain as Everton raced to the League Championship in breathtaking fashion.

War, of course, changed everything. Post-conflict the Scot became Manchester City manager and enjoyed mixed success in the Maine Road hot seat. He subsequently left football and worked as a licensee.

Season	League		FA Cup		Other		Total	
	App	Goals	App	Goals	App	Goals	App	Goals
1929/30	9	0	0	0	-	-	9	0
1930/31	41	0	5	0	-	-	46	0
1931/32	39	0	1	0	-	-	40	0
1932/33	41	3	6	0	1	0	48	3
1933/34	38	0	1	0	1	0	40	0
1934/35	42	1	5	0	-	-	47	1
1935/36	25	0	0	0	-	-	25	0
1936/37	2	0	0	0	-	-	2	0
1937/38	9	1	0	0	-	-	9	1
1938/39	26	0	4	0	-	-	30	0
Total	**272**	**5**	**22**	**0**	**2**	**0**	**296**	**5**

[FACTFILE]

BORN
Thornton, Renfrewshire,
6 July 1906
DIED
Carnoustie, 1979
POSITION
Left half
OTHER CLUBS
Dundee (1925–30)
AS MANAGER
Manchester City (1947–50)
HONOURS
Second Division
Championship 1930/31,
League Championship
1931/32 & 1938/39, FA Cup
1933; 1 Scotland cap (1933)

Thomson, Sammy

One of Preston North End's Invincibles, he failed to settle on Merseyside

Season	League		FA Cup		Total	
	App	Goals	App	Goals	App	Goals
1891/92	3	1	0	0	3	1
Total	**3**	**1**	**0**	**0**	**3**	**1**

[FACTFILE]

BORN
Lugar, 14 February 1862
DIED
1943
POSITION
Centre forward /
outside forward
OTHER CLUBS
Glasgow Rangers;
Preston North End
(1888–89);
Wolverhampton Wanderers
(1890); Accrington (1891)

Tiler, Carl

Centre back who fell short of the Goodison standard

In the early part of his career, Carl Tiler, an imposing Yorkshireman, was talked of as a future England centre half. One of Brian Clough's last big-money signings at Nottingham Forest, whom he joined for £1.4million in 1991, his potential seemed to wane as Clough's career unfolded. A move to Aston Villa in 1995 failed to resurrect his potential.

In March 1997, Howard Kendall signed him for Sheffield United and eight months later, as Everton manager, brought him to Goodison with Blades' team-mate Mitch Ward, in exchange for Graham Stuart and £500,000.

These moves were initially met with consternation by Evertonians, hungry for big-money signings. After his debut – a home defeat to Tottenham – Everton found themselves propping up the Premier League table. But once he had settled, Tiler comfortably outperformed Slaven Bilić, who had arrived amid much hullabaloo the previous summer. Tall, angular and solid, he helped shore up a leaky defence. And yet the suspicion remained that he was merely a Division One defender outperforming in the top flight – and the second tier seemed precisely where he was headed as Everton's form took a disastrous turn.

Following Walter Smith's arrival as manager in July 1998, Tiler found himself an early casualty of the new regime. In September 1998 he joined Charlton for £700,000 and he subsequently played out his career outside the Premiership – a more suitable level, perhaps, for an honest player not quite up to the standard Evertonians expect.

[FACTFILE]

BORN
Sheffield, 11 February 1970
POSITION
Central defender
OTHER CLUBS
Barnsley (1988–91);
Nottingham Forest (1991–95);
Swindon Town (loan, 1994);
Aston Villa (1995–97);
Sheffield United (1997);
Charlton Athletic (1998–2001);
Birmingham City (2001);
Portsmouth (2001–03)

Season	League App	League Goals	FA Cup App	FA Cup Goals	League Cup App	League Cup Goals	Total App	Total Goals
1997/98	19	1	1	0	0	0	20	1
1998/99	2	0	0	0	1	0	3	0
Total	21	1	1	0	1	0	23	1

Todd, Colin

Outstanding central defender asked to play out of position in a blue shirt

Considered among the finest English footballers of his generation, when Gordon Lee paid Derby County £300,000 for Colin Todd's services in September 1978 he equalled the Everton transfer record fees spent on Martin Dobson and Bob Latchford.

Once considered the 'new Bobby Moore', Todd had outdone his illustrious forbear domestically, winning two League Championships with Derby County in 1972 and 1975 – the same year he was crowned PFA Player of the Year.

TODD was an impeccable, unflustered defender; a perceptive reader of the game and strong tackler who had brought poise and assurance to the Derby and England defences. In short, he was a footballing thoroughbred who had proved one of the finest central defenders of the era. And yet, to the incredulity of Evertonians, and no doubt Todd himself, Gordon Lee insisted on playing Todd out of position at right back, preferring the novice Billy Wright as Mick Lyons' central defensive partner.

Season	League App	League Goals	FA Cup App	FA Cup Goals	League Cup App	League Cup Goals	Europe App	Europe Goals	Total App	Total Goals
1978/79	29	1	1	0	2	0	0	0	32	1
1979/80	3	0	0	0	0	0	0	0	3	0
Total	32	1	1	0	2	0	0	0	35	1

THE EXPERIMENT never worked and the blond Northeasterner failed to recapture the form of his Baseball Ground heyday. He played just three more games after the end of the 1978/79 season before joining Birmingham City for £275,000 exactly a year after his arrival.

A FOOTBALLING THOROUGHBRED WHO HAD PROVED ONE OF THE FINEST CENTRAL DEFENDERS OF THE ERA

[FACTFILE]

BORN
Chester-le-Street,
12 December 1948
POSITION
Defender
OTHER CLUBS
Sunderland (1966–71);
Derby County (1971–78);
Birmingham City (1979–82);
Nottingham Forest (1982–84);
Vancouver Whitecaps (1984);
Luton Town (1984)
AS MANAGER
Middlesbrough (1990–91);
Bolton Wanderers (1995–99);
Swindon Town (2000);
Derby County (2001–02);
Bradford City (2004–07);
Randers FC
(Denmark, 2007–09);
Darlington (2009–)
HONOURS
27 England caps (1972–77);
PFA Player of the Year (1975)

Toman, Wilf

Centre forward who turned out in two Goodison spells; he died fighting for his country on the Western Front

[FACTFILE]

BORN
Bishop Auckland, 1873
DIED
France, May 1917
POSITION
Centre forward
OTHER CLUBS
Victoria United;
Aberdeen Strollers;
Dundee;
Burnley (1896–99);
Southampton (1900–01);
Stockport County (1904–05);
Oldham Athletic (1905–06);
Newcastle United (1906–07)

Season	League		FA Cup		Total	
	App	Goals	App	Goals	App	Goals
1898/99	2	1	0	0	2	1
1899/1900	25	8	0	0	25	8
1901/02	2	1	0	0	2	1
Total	29	10	0	0	29	10

Tomlinson, John

Local winger who was on the periphery of Ian Buchan's young team

[FACTFILE]

BORN
Bebington, 26 June 1934
POSITION
Outside right
OTHER CLUB
Chesterfield (1957–59)

Season	League		FA Cup		Total	
	App	Goals	App	Goals	App	Goals
1956/57	2	0	0	0	2	0
Total	2	0	0	0	2	0

Trebilcock, Mike

Journeyman striker whose 15 minutes of fame earned him Wembley immortality

Mike Trebilcock played just 14 times during his two-year-long Goodison sojourn, yet made an indelible imprint on the club's history.

THE 21-year-old Cornishman joined Everton from Plymouth Argyle for £20,000 on the last day of 1965. Harry Catterick initially used him sparingly, as an occasional forward partner to Fred Pickering, but by April Pickering was beset by injury problems and the rookie was called up in his place, notably for the FA Cup semi-final against Manchester United.

Although Trebilcock held his own in the England forward's absence, Pickering, who played in the final three games of the 1965/66 season, was expected to reclaim his place for the final, against Sheffield Wednesday. But Catterick had other plans, and felt Pickering had not sufficiently recovered. Having played just eight previous games for Everton, Trebilcock was in. It was the biggest gamble of Catterick's managerial career, and for the first hour it looked doomed to failure. Wednesday scored in the fourth and 57th minutes.

Nobody, however, had counted on Trebilcock. Two minutes after

going 2-0 down, Derek Temple's header was blocked and fell into the path of Trebilcock, who fired home from 12 yards. Five minutes later, Alex Scott's free kick was only half cleared and Trebilcock fired home a volley from the edge of the area. On 73 minutes Temple completed the turnaround to give Everton their FA Cup win.

'I was looking forward to it because I had never been to Wembley and I would be sitting at Wembley with a new suit,' said Trebilcock afterwards. 'Then, after lunch on the Friday before the game, the manager called me. I expected to have to help out with the gear. Instead he told me I would be playing in place of the England centre forward Fred

Pickering, who had been injured. If ever I have fallen off the back of my seat, that was it.

'Every schoolboy dreams of playing at Wembley and scoring the winner in a cup final,' said Trebilcock. 'But I didn't score the winner!'

TREBILCOCK kept his place for the Charity Shield game with Liverpool the following August, but made just two league appearances during the 1966/67 season and two more the next season. He joined Portsmouth for £35,000 in January 1968 and after playing out his professional career with Torquay United and Weymouth immigrated to Australia.

Season	League		FA Cup		Europe		Total	
	App	Goals	App	Goals	App	Goals	App	Goals
1965/66	7	2	2	2	0	0	9	4
1966/67	2	0	0	0	1	0	3	0
1967/68	2	1	0	0	-	-	2	1
Total	11	3	2	2	1	0	14	5

[FACTFILE]

BORN
Gunnislake, Cornwall,
29 November 1944
POSITION
Striker
OTHER CLUBS
Plymouth Argyle (1962–65);
Portsmouth (1968–72);
Torquay United (1972–73)
HONOURS
1966 FA Cup

Trentham, Douglas

Outside right who made a goalscoring cameo during the all-conquering 1938/39 campaign

Season	League		FA Cup		Total	
	App	Goals	App	Goals	App	Goals
1937/38	15	6	1	0	16	6
1938/39	1	1	0	0	1	1
Total	16	7	1	0	17	7

[FACTFILE]

BORN
Chirbury, 2 November 1917
POSITION
Outside left
OTHER CLUBS
Mickle Trafford;
Ellesmere Port Town

Troup, Alec

Outstanding Scottish winger who provided much of the ammunition for Dixie Dean

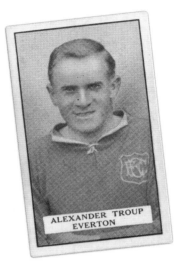

ALEXANDER TROUP
EVERTON

A four-day spell in January 1923 marked one of the most prolific periods of transfer activity in Everton history. In an effort to save a season that was spiralling out of control – Everton were in the unheard of depths of 14th place and out at the first stage of the FA Cup – the Everton board spent heavily to bring three internationals to Goodison.

FROM Manchester United came Scotland defender Neil McBain, and from Chelsea the England centre forward Jack Cock. But the signing that would have the most significant impact on the club was Scotland international winger Alec Troup, signed for a fee of £1950.

Troup was a classic wide man, a feinter and crosser of deadly, unerring accuracy. 'There could

be no doubt of the class of Troup when he was on the move,' recorded the Liverpool Echo in a prescient assessment of him on his debut, a 4-1 horror show at Stoke. 'He did not run along the wing and lift the ball into the centre heedless of his colleague's positions, but he placed the ball well and also made use of a delicious inward pass, as deceptive as it was neatly done.'

Troup, in tandem with the new arrivals, revived a flagging team. Newspaper eulogies said things like: 'Troup's dandy runs and dribbles have captivated the Mersey crowd.' 'Troup has put the "ton" back in Everton'. He was a 'magic' and 'charismatic little Scot' who brought out 'the best in players like Cock and [Wilf] Chadwick'. By the season's end, something had been redeemed from the disappointing campaign and the club finished fifth.

TROUP'S creativity and verve had a transformative effect on the team. When he played forwards prospered and with Sam Chedgzoy on the opposite flank Everton had arguably the finest pair of wide men in the league. They combined with great success in the 1923/24 season, providing the crosses and attacking impetus that made Wilf Chadwick the First Division's leading goalscorer with 28 goals.

But it was his understanding with Dixie Dean, who arrived in March 1925, for which Troup became renowned. Dean, a classic target man and incredible finisher, thrived from the teasing crosses put in by the Scot. 'He stood only 5ft 5in, but was full of bravery and skill,' recalled Dean. 'Because of a weak collarbone, which kept slipping out of joint, he had to play with a strapping on his shoulder every game … I think we had a perfect understanding and I think I have to thank him more than anyone else for the part he played in scoring the goals I did. I'd rate him as one of the best wingers there's ever been.'

Countless goals came from the pair combining. Still only a teenager, Dean managed 32 goals in the 1925/26 campaign – his first full season – and 21 next, a year that was largely wrecked by his near-fatal motorcycle accident. But it was 1927/28 for which Dean became a legend. 'It's much better for a centre forward to be able to head a fast-moving centre,' Dean would recall in later life. 'I could either head it directly or flick it on to someone else, and Troup's centres were made to order.' Chedgzoy was another winger who he praised, but Troup 'was even more accurate than Sammy, and used to hit them harder'.

According to Troup's biographer, David Potter, Evertonians adopted a Victorian music hall song, 'Nellie Dean', that paid tribute to both Dixie and his wide man.

> **That's another goal you've scored, Dixie Dean,**
>
> **Another goal for our team, Dixie Dean,**
>
> **For when Troup sends it o'er**
>
> **Above them all you'll soar,**
>
> **It's a goal, we love you, Dixie Dean!**

INEVITABLY it was a Troup corner from which Dean got his legendary 60th Everton goal of the 1927/28 season. 'Troup's determination equalled that of Dean himself,' wrote Potter. 'His ever-alert football mind went back to his days with Forfar North End at the Market Muir before the First World War. There he was always told about corners, "If ye're geaeing tae float it in, mun, hit it higher than ye think ye need. The wind'll get a haud o' it, and yer man'll be better able tae judge it. He'll hae time tae get in alo' it'." This is exactly what he did.'

From the corner Dean rose in front of the Arsenal goalkeeper, Bill Patterson, and above the defence and headed powerfully home. Goodison erupted as history was made. 'You talk about explosions and loud applause,' Thomas Keates recalled. 'We have heard many explosions and much applause in our loud pilgrimage but believe us, we have never

INEVITABLY IT WAS A TROUP CORNER FROM WHICH DEAN GOT HIS LEGENDARY 60TH EVERTON GOAL OF THE 1927/28 SEASON

EVERTON FOOTBALL CLUB 1923

Back - Brown, Mr Barks (Director), Fern, Elliott (Trainer), Livingstone, Forbes, Macdonald, Mr Coffey (Director), Chadwick
Front - Chedgzoy, Irvine, Cock, Hart (Captain), McBain, Troup

EVERTON 1923
Back row - **Brown, Mr Barks (Director), Fern, Elliott (Trainer), Livingstone, Forbes, Macdonald, Mr Coffey (Director), Chadwick**
Front - **Chedgzoy, Irvine, Cock, Hart, McBain, Troup**

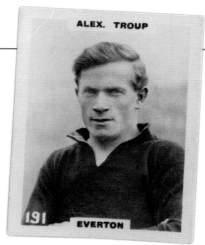

heard before such a prolonged
roar of thundering congratulatory applause as
that which ascended to heaven when Dixie
broke his record.'

Dean's place in history was secured, but the
supporting role of his team-mates was often
overlooked. Yet Dean was always sure to pay
tribute to his supply lines. 'Out of those sixty
goals I scored this season I must have scored
forty from centres by Troup, most of them
with my head,' he later said.

> 'OUT OF THOSE SIXTY GOALS
> I SCORED THIS SEASON
> I MUST HAVE SCORED FORTY
> FROM CENTRES BY TROUP'
>
> **DIXIE DEAN**

Troup remained a regular through the 1928/29
campaign but thereafter the continual injuries
he suffered began to take their toll and his
fellow Scot, Jimmy Stein, supplanted him. 'Old
Harry Cooke used to take him down to the
dressing room when the shoulder came out of
place, jerk it back and the shoulder would come
right again,' recalled Dean.

In February 1930 a delegation from Dundee
visited Merseyside in an effort to entice the
veteran reserve back to Scotland. Everton
sought £500 for Troup, but the Dundee
directors had a better offer: first option on their
outstanding left half, Jock Thomson. If Everton
did not take up that transfer, they could accept
a £200 fee. Troup returned to Scotland and a
month later Everton took up the option to buy
Thomson. Thus as one of the most successful
associations in the club's history ended, so
another began.

Further reading:
POTTER, DAVID, *Wee Troupie*,
Tempus Publishing, 2002

[FACTFILE]

BORN
Forfar, 12 May 1895
DIED
2 January 1952
POSITION
Winger
OTHER CLUBS
Forfar Athletic (1910–15);
Dundee (1915–23);
Dundee (1930–33)
HONOURS
League Championship 1927/28,
5 Scotland caps (1920–26)

Season	League		FA Cup		Other		Total	
	App	Goals	App	Goals	App	Goals	App	Goals
1922/23	17	2	0	0	-	-	17	2
1923/24	41	1	2	0	-	-	43	1
1924/25	32	2	0	0	-	-	32	2
1925/26	38	6	2	0	-	-	40	6
1926/27	37	5	4	2	-	-	41	7
1927/28	42	10	2	1	-	-	44	11
1928/29	38	5	0	0	1	0	39	5
1929/30	4	1	0	0	-	-	4	1
Total	**249**	**32**	**10**	**3**	**1**	**0**	**260**	**35**

Turner, Bob

Winger of East Midlands stock who flitted in and out of the Everton left wing role

[FACTFILE]

BORN
Leicester, 15 July 1885
DIED
1959
POSITION
Outside left
OTHER CLUBS
Grasmere Swifts;
St Andrews (Leicester);
St Marks;
Leicester Imperial;
Leicester Fosse (1906–08);
Preston North End (1911);
Darlington;
Coventry City;
Durham City

Season	League		FA Cup		Total	
	App	Goals	App	Goals	App	Goals
1908/09	5	1	0	0	5	1
1909/10	19	0	0	0	19	0
1910/11	10	0	0	0	10	0
Total	**34**	**1**	**0**	**0**	**34**	**1**

Turner, Dave

Young right back limited to a single appearance by the continued excellence of Tommy Wright

[FACTFILE]

BORN
Derby, 26 December 1948
POSITION
Right back
OTHER CLUBS
Southport (1970–73);
Bootle

	League		FA Cup		League Cup		Total	
Season	App	Goals	App	Goals	App	Goals	App	Goals
1967/68	1	0	0	0	0	0	1	0
Total	1	0	0	0	0	0	1	0

Turner, Edward

Right back who went on to enjoy a varied career in the Southern League

[FACTFILE]

BORN
Skerton, 1877
POSITION
Right back
OTHER CLUBS
Skerton;
Kendal; Royal Artillery (Portsmouth);
Portsmouth; Northampton Town;
Portsmouth Fulham; Luton Town;
Carlisle Co-operative

	League		FA Cup		Total	
Season	App	Goals	App	Goals	App	Goals
1898/99	2	0	0	0	2	0
Total	2	0	0	0	2	0

Turner, George

Widely travelled winger who briefly supplied the crosses for Dixie Dean

[FACTFILE]

BORN
Mansfield, 5 May 1910
DIED
1996
POSITION
Outside left
OTHER CLUBS
Sneiton; Notts County (1930);
Luton Town (1931); Bradford City (1934);
Luton Town (1935);
Northampton Town (1935–36)

	League		FA Cup		Total	
Season	App	Goals	App	Goals	App	Goals
1932/33	2	0	0	0	2	0
Total	2	0	0	0	2	0

Turner, Iain

Scotland B international who failed to make a first-team breakthrough during eight years at Goodison

Season	League		FA Cup		League Cup		Europe		Total	
	App	Goals	App	Goals	App	Goals	App	Goals	App	Goals
2005/06	2 (1)	0	1	0	0	0	0	0	3 (1)	0
2006/07	1	0	0	0	1	0	-	-	2	0
Total	3 (1)	0	1	0	1	0	0	0	5 (1)	0

[FACTFILE]

BORN
Stirling, 26 January 1984
POSITION
Goalkeeper
OTHER CLUBS
Stirling Albion (2002–03);
Chester City (loan);
Doncaster Rovers (loan, 2005);
Wycombe Wanderers (2005);
Crystal Palace (loan, 2006);
Sheffield Wednesday
(loan, 2007);
Nottingham Forest
(loan, 2009);
Coventry City (loan, 2010);
Preston North End (2011–12);
Dunfermline Athletic
(loan, 2012)

Turner, Joe

Outside left who provided Goodison with a year of fine service

Season	League		FA Cup		Total	
	App	Goals	App	Goals	App	Goals
1899/1900	1	2	0	0	1	2
1900/01	31	6	2	1	33	7
Total	32	8	2	1	34	9

[FACTFILE]

BORN
Burslem, 1 March 1872
POSITION
Outside left
OTHER CLUBS
Newcastle Swifts;
Dresden United;
Southampton;
Stoke City (1898–99);
Southampton;
New Brompton;
Northampton;
Eastleigh Athletic;
South Farnborough Athletic

Turnstile Fraud, The Great Everton

Scandal that was exposed in Goodison's early years

As one of the first giants of the Football League, Everton's popularity brought some of football's first mass attendances. The crowd of 44,000 that bore witness to Everton's 3-0 demolition of Liverpool in the first ever Merseyside derby in October 1894 was a world record for a league match and Everton were the best supported team in the Football League. However, something perplexed Everton supporters and directors alike for some time. A discrepancy seemed to exist between the attendances estimated by journalists visiting Goodison Park and the official attendance tallied from the turnstiles at the end of each match.

> A WORLD RECORD FOR A LEAGUE MATCH AND EVERTON WERE THE BEST SUPPORTED TEAM IN THE FOOTBALL LEAGUE

'A vague suspicion developed into a disagreeable conviction of misappropriation by somebody,' noted Thomas Keates, an Everton director and later club historian. Yet the starting numbers on the machines were noted by one or more of the directors before the gates were opened each week, and again at half-time when they were closed. The takings of each turnstile was correct, so any discrepancy between the official attendance and the estimated crowd was surely a trick of the eye.

WHEN EVERTON met Sunderland on 16 November 1895, one of the directors – as usual – accompanied the groundsman for the weekly inspection to note the turnstile numbers half an hour before the gates opened. Then, ten minutes before they were due to open, two other directors went to re-inspect the turnstiles. This time, however, they found several of the gates had been clocked back by 200 units.

A Goodison employee was arrested and plain-clothed officers watched the working of every stile. Realising they had been uncovered, seven turnstile men each brought in £5 more than their stiles registered. None could account for the irregularity, pleaded ignorance and were released. However, the Goodison employee confessed all he knew under police questioning and the conspiracy was unmasked. The result was that a dozen turnstilemen, the mechanic and groundsman appeared in Dale Street Court the following Monday. All, save for the instigators, were treated leniently by the stipendiary magistrate and new turnstiles were subsequently installed. With their introduction the 'Everton turnstile fraud' – which had caused a great sensation – was brought to an end and the club have never had subsequent cause for such trouble.

Tyrer, Alan

Young midfielder who found his niche in the lower leagues

Season	League		FA Cup		League Cup		Total	
	App	Goals	App	Goals	App	Goals	App	Goals
1959/60	4	1	0	0	-	-	4	1
1960/61	3	1	1	0	0	0	4	1
1961/62	2	0	0	0	-	-	2	0
Total	**9**	**2**	**1**	**0**	**0**	**0**	**10**	**2**

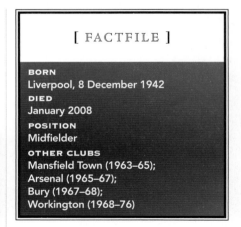

[FACTFILE]

BORN
Liverpool, 8 December 1942
DIED
January 2008
POSITION
Midfielder
OTHER CLUBS
Mansfield Town (1963–65);
Arsenal (1965–67);
Bury (1967–68);
Workington (1968–76)

THE

EVERTON
·ENCYCLOPEDIA·

UEFA Cup, David **Unsworth,** Harold **Uren**

UEFA Cup

European club football's second-tier competition

The successor to the Inter Cities Fairs Cup, the UEFA Cup was first played in the 1971/72 season. Its renaming reflected the changing face of European football: the competition was now governed by UEFA and had dropped the links with trade fairs that had marked its inception in the 1950s. In reality it was little changed from its predecessor and still consisted of 64 teams that had finished in or near the runners-up spot in their domestic leagues. It was a straight knockout competition consisting of home and away ties up until and including the final. A European Super Cup was played between the UEFA Cup winners and European Cup winners at the end of the calendar year.

IN FACT it was Everton that enacted the first fundamental change in the competition's structure. In 1974/75 Everton finished fourth in the First Division – high enough to qualify for the UEFA Cup. But Liverpool had finished the season runners-up and UEFA still implemented a 'one club per city' rule – a hangover of its Inter Cities Fairs Cup days, when the competition was meant to stimulate foreign commerce by being accompanied by a trade fair. Everton appealed, arguing that this was an anachronism, and won.

Until the 1990s the competition remained virtually unchanged. The collapse of the Soviet Eastern bloc and UEFA's expansion into Central Asia saw numerous new national federations established and as a consequence the UEFA Cup's preliminary round was significantly expanded.

In the 1997/98 competition the two-legged final was dropped in favour of a single match played at a neutral venue. In 1999 the European Cup Winners' Cup was disbanded and domestic cup winners joined the UEFA Cup from the 1999/2000 season.

From the 2004/05 season a group stage was incorporated after the first round. Somewhat confusingly, groups consisted of five teams who played each other once, either at home or away. Three teams could qualify from a group and they were joined in the next knockout round by the best losers from the Champions League. In short, a lot of football was played in order to eliminate only a handful of teams. Moreover, there was a clear sense that the competition was becoming devalued by the cash-rich Champions League, which invariably attracted all of Europe's biggest teams. Even when Champions League qualifiers were not up to the challenge in its group stage they had a second chance by way of the UEFA Cup. In 2009 the last UEFA Cup Final was played between Shakhtar Donetsk and Werder Bremen in Istanbul. From 2009/10 the competition was rebranded the Europa League (see separate entry).

Everton's record in the UEFA Cup is largely inauspicious. Over the course of 38 UEFA Cup competitions, Everton partook just six times, on just one occasion progressing beyond Christmas. They were denied qualification for the 1988/89 season and, possibly, the 1990/91 season due to the Heysel ban. In 1996 Everton were again denied entry, despite finishing sixth, after UEFA cut the number of English clubs. This was punishment for Tottenham and Wimbledon's farcical representation in the previous year's Inter Toto Cup.

EVERTON'S BEST year in the UEFA Cup came in 2007/08. Following a shaky start against the Ukrainian team Metalist Kharkiv, Everton progressed to the group stage. Faced with one of the toughest sets of teams, Everton topped the group playing some of the most sumptuous football Evertonians had seen in a generation. Highlights included: Leon Osman's sublime deciding goal against AE Larissa; 8000 Evertonians invading Nuremburg and seeing their team win 2-0; a Goodison victory over eventual competition winners Zenit St Petersburg; and a 3-2 victory over Dutch team AZ Alkmaar – their first ever home defeat in European competition.

Going into the competition for the first ever time after Christmas, Everton played the Norwegian team SK Brann and steam-rollered them 8-1 on aggregate. In the last 16 they faced a tough challenge against Italian giants Fiorentina. In Florence, a rare off night and defensive naivety undid Everton and they lost 2-0. At Goodison a week later, Everton threatened to produce one of the old stadium's great nights – overturning the deficit and battering the Italians over 120 minutes. But the third goal proved cruelly elusive and when it came to penalties, Yakubu hit a post and Phil Jagielka saw his shot saved while Fiorentina scored their four spot kicks.

Everton's UEFA Cup Record

1975/76

17 SEPTEMBER 1975
Rd 1 1st leg v. AC Milan [H]
0-0; 31,917
Lawson, Bernard, Seargeant, Pearson, Kenyon, Lyons, Buckley (Clements), Dobson, Latchford, Smallman (Hurst), G. Jones

1 OCTOBER 1975
Rd 1 2nd leg v. AC Milan [A]
0-1 (aggregate 0-1); 66,000
Davies, Bernard, Seargeant, Pearson, Kenyon, Lyons, Buckley, Dobson, Latchford, Smallman, G.Jones

1978/79

12 SEPTEMBER 1978
Rd 1 1st leg v. Finn Harps [A]
5-0 *King 2, Latchford, Thomas, Walsh;* **5000**
Wood, Darracott, Pejic, Lyons (Higgins), Wright, Nulty, King, Ross, Latchford, Walsh, Thomas

26 SEPTEMBER 1978
Rd 1 2nd leg v. Finn Harps [H]
5-0 (aggregate 10-0) *Dobson, King, Latchford, Ross, Walsh;* **21,611**
Wood, Darracott, Pejic, Lyons (Higgins), Wright, Ross, King, Dobson, Latchford, Walsh, Thomas (Nulty)

18 OCTOBER 1978
Rd 2 1st leg v. Dukla Prague [H] 2-1 *King, Latchford;* **32,857**
Wood, Darracott (Robinson), Pejic, Lyons, Wright, Ross, King, Dobson, Latchford, Walsh, Thomas (Nulty)

1 NOVEMBER 1978
Rd 2 2nd leg v. Dukla Prague [A]
0-1 (aggregate 2-2; Dukla Prague won on away goals); 35,000
Wood, Darracott, Pejic, Kenyon, Wright, Nulty, Ross, Dobson, Latchford, Walsh, Thomas

1979/80

19 SEPTEMBER 1979
Rd1 1st leg v. Feyenoord [A]
0-1; 37,000
Wood, Barton, Bailey, Lyons, Higgins, Ross, Nulty, Wright, King, Kidd, Eastoe

3 OCTOBER 1979
Rd 1 2nd leg v. Feyenoord [H]
0-1 (aggregate 0-2); 28,203
Wood, Barton, Bailey, Lyons, Higgins, Nulty, McBride (Varadi), Wright, King, Kidd, Eastoe

2005/06

15 SEPTEMBER 2005
Rd 1 1st leg v. Dinamo Bucharest [A] 1-5 *Yobo;* **15,000**
Martyn, Hibbert, Yobo, Weir, Valente, Osman, Cahill, Neville, Davies (Kilbane), McFadden (Ferguson), Bent

29 SEPTEMBER 2005
Rd 2nd leg v. Dinamo Bucharest [H] 1-0 (aggregate 2-5) *Cahill;* **21,843**
Martyn, Hibbert (Weir), Yobo, Ferrari, Valente (Bent), Arteta, Cahill, Neville, Kilbane (Beattie), McFadden, Ferguson

2007/08

20 SEPTEMBER 2007
Rd1 1st leg v. Metalist Kharkiv [H] 1-1 *Lescott;* **37,120**
Wessels, Hibbert, Yobo, Lescott, Baines, McFadden, Neville, Carsley (Jagielka), Osman, Yakubu (Anichebe), Johnson

4 OCTOBER 2007
Rd 1 2nd leg v. Metalist Kharkiv [A] 3-2 (aggregate 4-3) *Lescott, McFadden, Anichebe;* **27,500**
Howard, Neville, Stubbs, Yobo, Lescott, Arteta, Jagielka (Anichebe), Osman, Pienaar, Yakubu (Baines), McFadden (Hibbert)

UEFA Cup Group A

v. AE Larissa [H] 3-1 *Cahill, Osman, Anichebe;* **33,777**
Howard, Hibbert, Yobo, Lescott, Baines, Arteta, Osman, Carsley, Cahill (Gravesen), Pienaar (Stubbs), McFadden (Anichebe)

v. Zenit St Petersburg [H] 1-0 *Cahill;* **38,407**
Howard, Neville, Jagielka, Lescott, Baines, Arteta, Cahill, Carsley, Pienaar, Johnson (Vaughan), McFadden (Anichebe)

v. 1FC Nurnberg [A] 2-0 *Arteta, Anichebe;* **43,000**
Howard, Neville, Yobo, Lescott, Valente, Pienaar (Hibbert), Cahill (Jagielka), Carsley, Osman, Arteta, Yakubu (Anichebe)

v. AZ Alkmaar [A] 3-2 *Johnson, Jagielka, Vaughan;* **16,578**
Wessels, Hibbert, Jagielka, Lescott, Valente, Carsley, Gravesen (Rodwell), Pienaar (Vidarsson), McFadden, Johnson (Vaughan), Anichebe

Team	P	W	D	L	GF	GA	GD	Pts
Everton	4	4	0	0	9	3	+6	12
1FC Nurnberg	4	2	1	1	7	6	+1	7
Zenit St Petersburg	4	1	2	1	6	6	0	5
AZ Alkmaar	4	1	1	2	5	6	-1	4
AE Larissa	4	0	0	4	4	10	-6	0

13 FEBRUARY 2008
Round of 32, 1st leg v. SK Brann [A] 2-0 *Osman, Anichebe;* **16,207**
Howard, Neville, Jagielka, Yobo, Lescott, Osman, Cahill, Carsley, Fernandes (Hibbert), Johnson (Anichebe), Yakubu (Baines)

6 MARCH 2008
Round of 16, 1st leg v. Fiorentina [A] 0-2; 32,934
Howard, Hibbert (Johnson), Jagielka, Yobo, Lescott, Neville, Osman (Arteta), Carsley, Cahill, Pienaar, Yakubu

21 FEBRUARY 2008
Round of 32, 2nd leg v. SK Brann [H] 6-1 (aggregate 9-1) *Yakubu 3, Johnson 2, Arteta;* **32,834**
Howard, Neville, Jagielka, Lescott, Valente, Arteta, Cahill (Hibbert), Carsley (Fernandes), Pienaar, Johnson, Yakubu (Anichebe)

12 MARCH 2008
Round of 16, 2nd leg v. Fiorentina [H] 2-0 (aet) (aggregate 2-2 Fiorentina won 4-2 on penalties) *Johnson, Arteta;* **38,026**
Howard, Neville, Jagielka, Yobo, Lescott, Arteta, Carsley, Pienaar (Anichebe), Johnson (Gravesen), Yakubu

2008/09

18 SEPTEMBER 2008
Rd 1 1st leg v. Standard Liege [H] 2-2 *Yakubu, Castillo;* **28,312**
Howard, Neville, Yobo, Jagielka, Lescott, Anichebe (Vaughan), Cahill, Castillo, Osman, Arteta, Yakubu

2 OCTOBER 2008
Rd1 2nd leg v. Standard Liege [A] 1-2 (aggregate 3-4) *Jagielka;* **27,406**
Howard, Hibbert (Anichebe), Jagielka, Lescott, Baines, Osman, Cahill, Neville (Yobo), Arteta, Saha (Pienaar), Yakubu

Unsworth, David

Nominated Everton's penalty taker, over the years he would prove one of the most superb takers in the club's history

Just as Mick Lyons seemed to typify Everton's 1970s malaise, so David Unsworth has become synonymous with the wretched 1990s and early 21st century, when Everton lurched from crisis to crisis. A fiercely proud Evertonian who always wore his heart on his sleeve, Unsworth was a brave, physical, hard player, sometimes lacking sophistication in his approach, but usually effective, committed and always giving his best. Alas, this wasn't quite enough to allay the worst period in Everton's recent history, but if nothing else, Unsworth brought heart to a team sorely lacking in it.

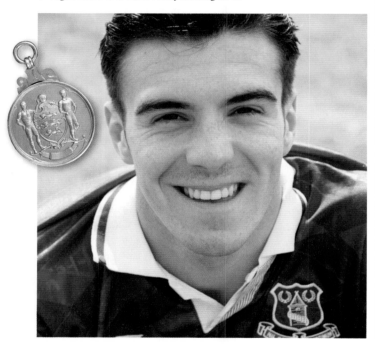

Born in Preston, Unsworth came through the Everton youth ranks in the early 1990s. Only John Ebbrell had made the step up in the previous decade, but Unsworth immediately made his mark, scoring on his debut against Tottenham Hotspur in May 1992. Chances were subsequently rare until Mike Walker's appointment as manager in January 1994.

WALKER invested huge faith in the 20-year-old, but he took his chance. Everton's defence was a one-paced disaster zone and it was left to Unsworth to sweep up, to charge back down the lines and clear up the unfolding mess. His tackles were crisp, precise and hard – hard enough to rev up a crowd deprived of other meaningful action in a moribund three-sided Goodison.

Come the start of the 1994/95 season, Unsworth was a first choice in the Everton defence and a crowd favourite. He had played his early football in midfield, but by then was usually partnering Dave Watson in central defence, although he also played left back too. Tall, strong and fast, he seemed the embodiment of the modern defender. Powerful in the air – yet never quite as indomitable as Dave Watson – and an outstanding tackler, he soon attracted plaudits, despite playing in a team that was propping up the Premier League. He was also

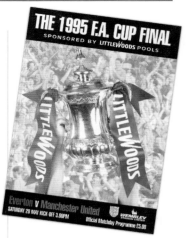

nominated Everton's penalty-taker, and over the years would prove among the most superb takers in the club's history.

UNSWORTH was outstanding in Everton's 1995 FA Cup run, subduing Jurgen Klinsmann in the semi-final and proving equal to the challenges posed by Manchester United's formidable forwards in the final. His form saw him rewarded with an England call-up at the end of the season, and he made his international debut against Japan at Wembley.

And yet when the 1995/96 season kicked off, it seemed as if Unsworth had spent all summer in the gym. Bulked up like a heavyweight boxer, it seemed to diminish some of his pace and agility. Mistakes crept in and his head dropped. He was left out of the England squad, then the Everton team, with Royle preferring the doughty but limited Craig Short in his place.

Season	League		FA Cup		League Cup		Other		Total	
	App	Goals	App	Goals	App	Goals	App	Goals	App	Goals
1991/92	1 (1)	1	0	0	0	0	0	0	1 (1)	1
1992/93	3	0	0	0	1 (1)	0	-	-	4 (1)	0
1993/94	7 (1)	0	0	0	0	0	-	-	7 (1)	0
1994/95	37 (1)	3	5	0	2	0	-	-	44 (1)	3
1995/96	28 (3)	2	2	0	0 (1)	0	4	1	34 (4)	3
1996/97	32 (2)	5	0	0	2	0	-	-	34 (2)	5
1998/99	33 (1)	1	3	1	3	0	-	-	39 (1)	2
1999/2000	32 (1)	6	5	3	1	0	-	-	38 (1)	9
2000/01	17 (12)	5	1	0	2	0	-	-	20(12)	5
2001/02	28 (5)	3	3 (1)	0	0	0	-	-	31 (6)	3
2002/03	32 (1)	5	1	0	3	1	-	-	36 (1)	6
2003/04	22 (4)	3	3	0	1 (1)	0	-	-	26 (5)	3
Total	**272(32)**	**34**	**23 (1)**	**4**	**15 (3)**	**1**	**4**	**1**	**314 (36)**	**40**

> NOMINATED EVERTON'S PENALTY-TAKER, AND OVER THE YEARS WOULD PROVE AMONG THE MOST SUPERB TAKERS IN THE CLUB'S HISTORY

As some of David Unsworth's limitations came to be exposed, so too did those of Joe Royle's game plan. When things became really dire, less than two years after the FA Cup win, it seemed as though the solitary tactic began with Unsworth's left foot and ended with Duncan Ferguson's head. Some fans began to take their frustration out on Unsworth, his confidence dropped further; Joe Royle left, and with little more than 100 appearances under his belt, the defender was left to contemplate life under a fourth different manager.

In June 1997, Howard Kendall returned as Everton manager for a third time. He had always been reluctant to use Unsworth in his second spell, and this time deemed him expendable, exchanging him for West Ham's Danny Williamson and £1million. It was a bum deal, with Williamson playing just a handful of appearances before his retirement from injury.

UNSWORTH spent a successful season in London, but sought a return north after just a year. In the summer of 1998 there

followed a bizarre interlude at Aston Villa, whom he joined for £3million, but immediately sought to leave when he caught word that Everton, now managed by Walter Smith, were interested in signing him back. Without playing a single game for Villa, he returned to Everton for £3million.

Smith, who admired physical presence in his charges, utilised Unsworth mainly as a left back, although he slotted in as an auxiliary centre half on occasion too and on the left of midfield. He became something of an enigma: at times an excellent defender, his form was undermined by lapses of concentration and poor distribution. There were several low points – with Marco Materazzi he conspired to hand Sheffield Wednesday's Benito Carbone two goals in a fixture at the end of the 1998/99 season that left Everton in serious relegation trouble; and he was abysmal in Everton's 2001 FA Cup humiliation to Tranmere – but Unsworth always had the strength of character to bounce back. He may have sometimes resembled a pub footballer, but at a time when the loyalty and motivations of some of his team-mates could be called into question, Unsworth always gave his all. In 2002 he was awarded a testimonial.

In 2004 he fell foul of David Moyes's policy of awarding older players just one-year contracts and, offered a three-year deal at Portsmouth, moved to the south coast. When that move did not work out, in January 2005 he joined Ipswich Town on loan, where he was reunited with Joe Royle. Released from his Portsmouth contract in summer 2005, he joined Sheffield United on a free transfer, returning to the Premier League a year later. In the January 2007 transfer window, Unsworth joined Wigan Athletic, and his penalty goal on the last day of the 2006/07 season condemned Sheffield United to relegation. Unsworth spent the 2007/08 season at Burnley and subsequently joined Huddersfield Town. However, persistent injuries restricted him and he announced his retirement in spring 2009.

Although he never really lived up to his potential, Unsworth was a fine and dedicated servant, who always spoke with the same affection and pride for the club that he showed each time he pulled on an Everton shirt. Shortly after his 2004 departure, he attended a Merseyside derby in the

EVERTONIANS ALWAYS KNEW THAT, AT HEART, UNSWORTH WAS ONE OF THEM

Gwladys Street. His arrival on the old terrace was marked with less incredulity than may have been expected – for Evertonians always knew that, at heart, Unsworth was one of them.

[FACTFILE]

BORN
Preston, 16 October 1973
POSITION
Left back / centre half
OTHER CLUBS
West Ham United (1997–98);
Aston Villa (1998);
Portsmouth (2004–05);
Ipswich Town (loan, 2005);
Sheffield United (2005–07);
Wigan Athletic (2007);
Burnley (2007–08);
Huddersfield Town (2008–09)
HONOURS
1995 FA Cup;
1 England cap (1995)

Uren, Harold

Winger who crossed the Mersey divide and fathered England rugby international sons, Harold and Richard

	League		FA Cup		Total	
Season	App	Goals	App	Goals	App	Goals
1911/12	8	1	0	0	8	1
1912/13	16	2	0	0	16	2
Total	**24**	**3**	**0**	**0**	**24**	**3**

[FACTFILE]

BORN
Barton Regis,
23 August 1885
DIED
1955
POSITION
Outside left
OTHER CLUBS
Northern Nomads;
Wrexham (3 spells);
Liverpool (1907 & 1908);
Lochgelly United

THE
EVERTON
ENCYCLOPEDIA

Nuno **Valente**, Pat **Van Den Hauwe**, Andy **Van der Meyde**, Imre **Varadi**, Alfred **Vaughan**, James **Vaughan**, Ray **Veall**, Apostolos **Velios**, Roy **Vernon**, Bjarni **Vidarsson**, Albert **Virr**

Valente, Nuno

Champions League winner who wound down his career at Goodison

A fine and experienced Portuguese international left back, Nuno Valente arrived at Goodison in August 2005 after Alessandro Pistone was struck by a career-ending injury. Valente had previously been a member of Jose Mourinho's FC Porto team that won back-to-back UEFA Cup and Champions League accolades in 2003 and 2004 and came on the recommendation of his former manager, who was by then in charge of Chelsea. Indeed Mourinho clearly rated Valente highly: in 2002, when he left União de Leiria to manage Porto, Valente followed his manager, becoming his first signing at Estádio do Dragão.

Nearing his 31st birthday when the £1.5million transfer was completed, Valente's signing ran counter to David Moyes's stated policy of signing only younger players. The onset of his Everton career was replete with mistakes and hesitancy. In one of his early appearances – a UEFA Cup horror show against Dinamo Bucharest – Valente suffered a nightmare and was constantly caught out of position and second best to the Romanians' winger, even seeming to dive out of the way of a goal-bound shot.

that reached the World Cup semi-finals, and was outstanding in his country's quarter-final victory over England.

Alas, injuries diminished his contribution to the Everton cause beyond this first season. In his absence Joleon Lescott proved an outstanding auxiliary left back, and after Leighton Baines's arrival in 2007, Valente slipped further down the pecking order. Moyes nevertheless recognised his value as a squad member, twice extending his contract so that he remained an Everton player until June 2009, when he announced his retirement.

But over the course of the 2005/06 season, after settling in, Valente proved his value, bringing experience, composure and a touch of gamesmanship to the Everton squad. A tough, cloying full back, Valente liked to get in close to his opponents and jockey them out of possession. His passing was accurate and intelligent and, although never particularly quick, his forward runs were a useful outlet for the attack. Never the most naturally athletic of players, he was sometimes caught for pace, but overall his astute reading and veteran's calm set him apart as a fine left back. At the end of his debut campaign he was part of the Portugal squad

[FACTFILE]

BORN
Lisbon, Portugal,
12 September 1974
POSITION
Left back
OTHER CLUBS
Sporting Lisbon (1992–99);
Portimonense
(loan, 1993–94);
Maritimo (loan, 1996–97);
União de Leiria (1999–2002);
FC Porto (2002–05)
HONOURS
33 Portugal caps
(1 goal) (2002–06)

Season	League		FA Cup		League Cup		Europe		Total	
	App	Goals	App	Goals	App	Goals	App	Goals	App	Goals
2005/06	20	0	4	0	0	0	2	0	26	0
2006/07	10 (4)	0	1	0	2	0	-	-	13 (4)	0
2007/08	8 (1)	0	0	0	3	0	3	0	14 (1)	0
2008/09	1 (1)	0	0	0	0	0	0	0	1 (1)	0
Total	**39 (6)**	**0**	**5**	**0**	**5**	**0**	**5**	**0**	**54(6)**	**0**

Van Den Hauwe, Pat

Defensive hard man whose antics were revered by the Goodison faithful

In September 1984 Howard Kendall caused some surprise when he paid Birmingham City £100,000 for the services of 'Psycho' Pat Van Den Hauwe. As befitted his nickname, Van Den Hauwe had cultivated a hard man reputation during his St Andrews days and some purists believed the left back might borstalise Goodison's School of Science. Moreover, he was to replace the popular John Bailey.

His arrival immediately shored up a defence that occasionally leaked goals. Twice already that season Everton had conceded four goals, and would do so on another three occasions – once when Van den Hauwe was substituted, again when he was injured and on a third occasion when all the season's main business had been concluded. Fortunately his team-mates scored with abandon, and Everton won the League Championship in record-breaking fashion.

Born in Belgium, Van Den Hauwe had come to Britain as a young child and progressed through the ranks at Birmingham City. In opting out of national service in the country of his birth he turned his back on the opportunity to play for Belgium (and perhaps play in the 1986 and 1990 World Cup Finals), instead choosing to play for Wales, making his international debut against Spain in February 1985.

In an era of footballing hard men, Van Den Hauwe belonged to the heavyweight class. Scowling, rugged and with an explosive temper, he was a man who not only struck fear in his opponents,

but apprehension in his colleagues too. Evertonians gained an early glimpse of his love of a fight in December 1984, when he ran the length of the Loftus Road pitch to embroil himself in a dust-up between Everton and Queens Park Rangers players. Van Den Hauwe

punched the first QPR player he set eyes upon and the fisticuffs became a twenty-man brawl, which concluded with Van Den Hauwe's dismissal and an appearance on the nine o'clock news.

The reputation that such incidents earned him clouded over the reality that Van Den Hauwe was an outstanding player. He was commanding in the air, quick and, of course, supreme in the tackle. With the defensively shy Kevin Sheedy usually playing in front of him, he shouldered the entire defensive burden of the Everton left. His distribution was proficient and his crosses yielded Graeme Sharp and Andy Gray a number of goals. His versatility was of great use to Kendall, and much of the 1985/86 season was spent deputising for

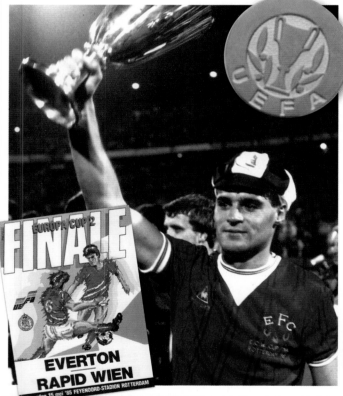

the injured Derek Mountfield at centre back, where he excelled. Alas, Van Den Hauwe was struck down with his own ailments the following campaign, but returned for the season's run-in. A rare goal against Norwich City in May 1987 sealed Everton's ninth League Championship success.

An extrovert character who was popular among his team-mates, Van Den Hauwe was prone to go missing from training for days and turn up without a word. He played in the 1989 FA Cup Final against Liverpool, but was on the losing side – his third straight defeat at that stage of the competition. This was to be Van den Hauwe's last appearance in an Everton shirt and that summer Colin Harvey sold him to Tottenham Hotspur for £575,000.

In 1991, his perennial FA Cup disappointments were overcome when he was part of the Tottenham team that defeated Nottingham Forest - a match best remembered for the horrific knee injury sustained by Paul Gascoigne after his reckless challenge on Gary Charles. By now his relationship with Mandy Smith, the ex-wife of Rolling Stone Bill Wyman, whom he married in 1993, had made him tabloid fodder. Van Den Hauwe later played for Millwall and after retiring immigrating to South Africa.

[FACTFILE]

BORN
Dendermonde, Belgium, 16 December 1960
POSITION
Left back / centre half
OTHER CLUBS
Birmingham City (1978–84); Tottenham Hotspur (1989–93); Millwall (1993–95)
HONOURS
League Championship 1984/85, 1986/87; European Cup Winners' Cup 1985; 13 Wales caps (1985–89)

Season	League		FA Cup		League Cup		Europe		Total	
	App	Goals	App	Goals	App	Goals	App	Goals	App	Goals
1984/85	31	0	7	0	3	0	5	0	46	0
1985/86	40	1	7	1	5	0	6 (1)	0	58 (1)	2
1986/87	11	1	2	0	0	0	1	0	14	1
1987/88	28	0	8	0	7	0	2	0	45	0
1988/89	24 (1)	0	6	0	5	0	1	0	36 (1)	0
Total	**134 (1)**	**2**	**30**	**1**	**20**	**0**	**15 (1)**	**0**	**199 (2)**	**2**

Van der Meyde, Andy

Gifted Dutch winger whose Goodison career was ravaged by poor discipline

Andy van der Meyde was an old-school winger, a veritable box of tricks who combined mesmerising skills with unerringly accurate crosses. A product of Ajax's famed youth academy, he first showcased his skills to a wider audience during its 2002/03 Champions League campaign, scoring the goal which knocked out Arsenal and sent the Dutch side through to the quarter-finals.

At the end of the 2002/03 season he joined Inter Milan for £4million, but failed to settle. David Moyes tried to sign him for Everton in summer 2004, but had to wait a year to complete a £2million move for the winger.

Almost from day one, Van der Meyde seemed doomed to failure at Goodison. He arrived with a groin problem that he struggled to shake off and was injured soon after his belated debut in October 2005. Just as he seemed to be nearing full fitness, he was victim of a ludicrous sending off in the March 2006 derby match and suspended. All the while rumours seeped from the Everton dressing room of a poor attitude and a liking for the good life.

In fact, at the end of the 2005/06 season, Van der Meyde was forced to issue a public denial that he

suffered from alcoholism. Then on the eve of the next campaign he was admitted to hospital with breathing problems, claiming a drink had been spiked. On his return he missed a training session and was disciplined again. Although there were no further public lapses, the rumours about 'Shandy' Andy would never quite go away.

Not until December did he make his first start of the 2006/07 season. There were some tantalising glimpses of his talent, but he never seemed to win Moyes over and made just a handful of further appearances over the next 30 months.

THERE WAS, however, one brief and glorious interlude at the very end of his Everton career, that perhaps made all the excess and ill discipline forgivable. Introduced as an extra-time substitute in the 2009 FA Cup fourth round replay against Liverpool, with just seconds remaining he broke down the

right wing and scooped a delicious far-post cross to Dan Gosling, who turned his marker and curled home a glorious late winner.

That was the high point and also virtually the end of Van der Meyde's Everton career. Although he continued to be named among the seven substitutes, he was rarely called upon and as the end of the 2008/09 season neared did not even make the bench.

It was entirely unsurprising when he was released at the end of that season and his departure was marked with a blistering attack on David Moyes. 'Moyes is a worthless man who tried to destroy me, but he didn't succeed,' he said. 'You cannot write me off.'

> THERE WAS, HOWEVER, ONE BRIEF AND GLORIOUS INTERLUDE AT THE VERY END OF HIS EVERTON CAREER, THAT PERHAPS MADE ALL THE ILL DISCIPLINE FORGIVABLE

[FACTFILE]

BORN
Arnhem, Netherlands,
30 September 1979
POSITION
Winger
OTHER CLUBS
Ajax (1997–2003);
FC Twente (loan, 1999–2000);
Inter Milan (2003–05);
Blackburn Rovers (2009)
HONOURS
18 Netherlands caps
(1 goal) (2002–04)

Season	League		FA Cup		League Cup		Europe		Total	
	App	Goals	App	Goals	App	Goals	App	Goals	App	Goals
2005/06	7 (3)	0	0	0	0 (1)	0	0	0	7 (4)	0
2006/07	5 (3)	0	1	0	1	0	-	-	7 (3)	0
2007/08	0	0	0	0	0	0	0	0	0	0
2008/09	0 (2)	0	0 (1)	0	0	0	0	0	0 (3)	0
Total	**12 (8)**	**0**	**1 (1)**	**0**	**1 (1)**	**0**	**0**	**0**	**14 (10)**	**0**

Varadi, Imre

Itinerant striker who secured derby glory

Without question the defining moment of Imre Varadi's short Everton career was the deciding goal he scored in Everton's FA Cup fourth round win over Liverpool in January 1981. Liverpool had been wholly dominant through the 1970s, while Gordon Lee's managerial reign was in its death throes. The game nevertheless attracted all the inevitable fanaticism of a Mersey derby. 54,000 fans paid record receipts to see the Goodison tie and were treated to a rare display of Everton superiority.

Peter Eastoe opened the scoring with a low shot, but it was Varadi with whom the game has become synonymous. His back-post half-volley into the Liverpool net prompted elation among Evertonians. As he celebrated in front of the Park End, a Liverpool fan, with characteristic graciousness, hurled a meat pie that hit Varadi square on the side of the face. Jimmy Case pulled a goal back for Liverpool, but Varadi's strike was enough to put Everton into the fifth round.

A LITHE, quick-footed striker who liked to bamboozle defenders with his cavalier feats of dribbling, Varadi, a young Londoner of Hungarian immigrant stock, had been plucked from amateur football by Sheffield United in the late 1970s. After just 10 appearances at Bramall Lane, Lee paid £80,000 for him in March 1979. Chances were initially scarce, but after Bob Latchford was struck down by serious injury in November 1980, Varadi got an extended run.

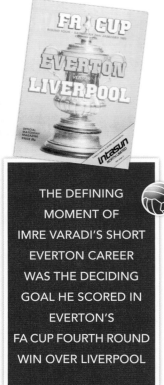

THE DEFINING MOMENT OF IMRE VARADI'S SHORT EVERTON CAREER WAS THE DECIDING GOAL HE SCORED IN EVERTON'S FA CUP FOURTH ROUND WIN OVER LIVERPOOL

Alas, his chance probably came at the wrong time. Everton were labouring under Lee and struggling without their talisman, Latchford. It was always asking much for a young player to take on such a striking burden and Varadi often struggled, running down blind allies or retaining possession when a simple pass would have sufficed. Everton won just four league games after Latchford's injury, and at the end of the season Varadi was an early departure under Lee's successor, Howard Kendall. His £125,000 move to Newcastle was another stop in a lengthy tour that, by the end of his career in the mid-1990s, would see him turn out for a dozen clubs. Varadi is now a well-known football agent based in Sheffield.

Despite the brevity of his Everton career, Varadi left a lasting impression on at least one young Evertonian. Treated to a diet of televised English football at his Swedish home, because of Varadi the teenage son of a Hungarian immigrant became an Evertonian, for they were the only club with a discernible link to his father's homeland. His name? Anders Limpar.

[FACTFILE]

BORN
Paddington, 8 July 1959
POSITION
Striker
OTHER CLUBS
Sheffield United (1978–79);
Newcastle (1981–83);
Sheffield Wednesday (1983–85);
West Bromwich Albion (1985–86);
Manchester City (1986–88);
Sheffield Wednesday (1988–90);
Leeds United (1990–93);
Luton Town (loan, 1992);
Oxford United (loan, 1993);
Rotherham United (1993–95);
Mansfield Town (1995);
Boston United (1995);
Scunthorpe United (1995)

Season	League		FA Cup		League Cup		Europe		Total	
	App	Goals	App	Goals	App	Goals	App	Goals	App	Goals
1978/79	0	0	0	0	0	0	0	0	0	0
1979/80	2 (2)	0	0 (1)	0	0	0	0 (2)	0	2 (5)	0
1980/81	20 (2)	6	6	1	0	0	-	-	26 (2)	7
Total	**22 (4)**	**6**	**6 (1)**	**1**	**0**	**0**	**0 (2)**	**0**	**28 (7)**	**7**

Vaughan, Alfred

Centre half and man of mystery who played just a solitary game before disappearing from view

Season	League		FA Cup		Total	
	App	Goals	App	Goals	App	Goals
1898/99	1	0	0	0	1	0
Total	1	0	0	0	1	0

Vaughan, James

Youngest goalscorer in Everton and Premier League history

On 10 April 2005, centre forward James Vaughan became, at the age of 16 years and 270 days, the youngest goalscorer in not only Everton's history, but that of the Premier League too.

JAMES VAUGHAN BECAME, AT THE AGE OF 16 YEARS AND 270 DAYS, THE YOUNGEST GOALSCORER IN NOT ONLY EVERTON'S HISTORY, BUT THAT OF THE PREMIER LEAGUE TOO

His goal, the fourth in a 4-0 rout of Crystal Palace, added fresh impetus to Everton's ultimately successful pursuit of a Champions League place and there were high hopes for the teenager.

THE YOUNG Midlander had been a champion schoolboy sprinter and followed the likes of Wayne Rooney, Francis Jeffers and Michael Ball off the prolific Goodison youth production line. Many tipped the forward to follow them into the national team.

Season	League		FA Cup		League Cup		Europe		Total	
	App	Goals	App	Goals	App	Goals	App	Goals	App	Goals
2004/05	0 (2)	1	0	0	0	0	-	-	0 (2)	1
2005/06	0 (1)	0	0	0	0	0	0	0	0 (1)	0
2006/07	7 (7)	4	0 (1)	0	0	0	-	-	7 (8)	4
2007/08	0 (8)	1	1	0	0 (2)	0	0 (2)	1	1 (12)	2
2008/09	1 (12)	0	0 (2)	0	1	0	0 (1)	0	2 (15)	0
2009/10	0 (8)	1	1 (1)	1	0	0	0 (1)	0	1 (10)	2
2010/11	0 (1)	0	0	0	0	0	-	-	0 (1)	0
Total	8 (39)	7	2 (4)	1	1 (2)	0	0 (4)	1	11 (49)	9

In cameos over the subsequent couple of seasons, Vaughan showed not only an electrifying turn of pace, but surprising upper-body strength and aerial ability too. His finishing showed an initial calmness but as injuries began to blight Vaughan's career he often seemed beset by nerves and became increasingly erratic. Capped at England under-17 and under-19 level, he was called up to the England under-21 team aged just 18, in 2007. He was awarded Everton's young player of the year for the 2006/07 season.

THAT WAS as good as it got for Vaughan as progress at Goodison was stunted by continual injury. Long stretches on the sidelines were interspersed with loan spells at Derby County, Leicester City and Crystal Palace. He did make one more telling impact in a royal blue shirt: brought on as a substitute in the FA Cup semi-final v. Manchester United, Vaughan boldly elected to take a penalty in the shootout and promptly buried it. He appeared as a second-half substitute in the final defeat to Chelsea.

After a second loan spell at Crystal Palace in 2011 speculation persisted about his future. In the summer of that year Everton accepted a bid believed to be worth £2.5million from Premier League newcomers Norwich City and he took up the fresh start his stalling career needed.

[FACTFILE]

BORN
Birmingham, 14 July 1988
POSITION
Forward
OTHER CLUBS
Derby County (loan, 2009);
Leicester City (loan, 2010);
Crystal Palace
(loan, 2010 & 2011);
Norwich City (2011–)

Veall, Ray

Young winger who contributed to Everton's 1963 League Championship win

Season	League		FA Cup		Europe		Total	
	App	Goals	App	Goals	App	Goals	App	Goals
1962/63	11	1	0	0	0	0	11	1
Total	11	1	0	0	0	0	11	1

[FACTFILE]

BORN
Skegness, 16 March 1943
POSITION
Left wing
OTHER CLUBS
Skegness Town (1960–61);
Doncaster Rovers (1961);
Preston North End (1965);
Huddersfield Town
(1965–68);
Los Angeles Wolves (1968);
Maritzburg (1971);
Gisbourne City (1972–74)
HONOURS
League Championship
1962/63

Vellios, Apostolos

Promising Greece under-21 international centre forward

Season	League		FA Cup		League Cup		Total	
	App	Goals	App	Goals	App	Goals	App	Goals
2010/11	0 (3)	0	0	0	0	0	0 (3)	0
2011/12	2 (11)	3	0 (1)	0	0 (1)	0	2 (14)	3
Total	2 (14)	3	0 (1)	0	0 (1)	0	2 (17)	3

[FACTFILE]

BORN
Thessaloniki, 8 January 1992
POSITION
Centre forward
OTHER CLUB
Iraklis

Vernon,
Roy

Rapier-like forward whose goals propelled Everton to League Championship glory

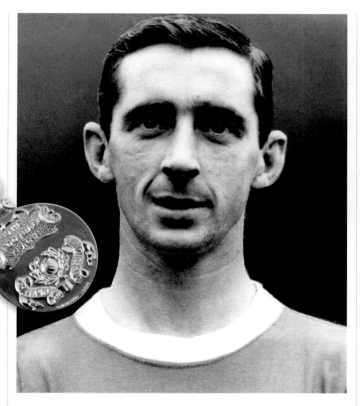

After a succession of physically imposing, hurly-burly centre forwards in the traditional mould through a generation starved of Goodison glory, the slight, unathletic figure of Royston Vernon was the unlikely figure to propel Everton back to success in the early 1960s.

'He was about 10 stone wet through and looked about as athletic as Pinocchio,' Brian Labone once said, conjuring a less than complimentary image of his former team-mate and captain. 'He had no left peg and couldn't head the ball,' added Alex Young. And perhaps such jibes bore some truth. After all, Vernon was a player who was once accused by a fan of smoking on the pitch (he was inhaling an ammonia capsule), was a poor trainer and was once sent home from a tour of America for breaking a curfew. However, such off-the-pitch antics in no way detracted from his superb goalscoring prowess. He was, acknowledged Labone, a 'brilliant player'. In five years at Goodison he scored 110 goals in 200 games and captained Everton to their first post-war League Championship. Asked in the mid-60s to name the county's most talented goalscorers, Vernon answered, 'There's Denis Law, there's Jimmy Greaves and there's me!' Such self-confidence had more than some basis in fact.

Born in 1937, as a schoolboy Vernon had originally turned down the chance of joining Everton, preferring instead to sign professional terms with Blackburn Rovers where he was first acquainted with Johnny Carey. Under his tutelage he emerged as one of the most deadly young goalscorers in English football and was recognised by Wales, with whom he travelled to the 1958 World Cup in Sweden. Carey became Everton manager in October 1958 and as the Moores millions started to make an impression upon his new club the search for a top-class forward was a priority. Attempts to buy Denis Law and Joe Baker were thwarted, but when the Everton manager heard that his former charge was available, in February 1960 he made his move. A part-exchange, which saw Eddie Thomas and £27,000 go to Ewood Park, saw Vernon sign for Everton.

Vernon's impact at Goodison was immediate and he helped revive the fortunes of Carey's struggling side by scoring six times in his first five games. His performance in the 6-1 defeat of Chelsea in March 1960 led the Daily Post to marvel, 'Vernon was man of the match and is destined to play a leading role in the good things which promise to come Everton's way.' He was indeed set to have a key role in the Blues' revival and was to finish top scorer for four successive seasons.

EVERTON 1959
Back - Sharples, Parker, Labone, Dunlop, Gabriel, Meagan, Bramwell
Front - Lill, Collins, Harris, Vernon, Ring

Season	League		FA Cup		League Cup		Europe		Total	
	App	Goals	App	Goals	App	Goals	App	Goals	App	Goals
1959/60	12	9	0	0	-	-	-	-	12	9
1960/61	39	21	1	0	4	1	-	-	44	22
1961/62	37	26	3	2	-	-	-	-	40	28
1962/63	41	24	3	3	-	-	2	0	46	27
1963/64	31	18	5	2	-	-	2	0	38	20
1964/65	16	3	0	0	-	-	3	1	19	4
Total	**176**	**101**	**12**	**7**	**4**	**1**	**7**	**1**	**199**	**110**

HIS BEST football in an Everton shirt came after the arrival of Alex Young from Hearts later on in 1960. Vernon was primarily a penalty area player feeding off the supply of balls from the brilliant Scot. 'He developed into a tremendous runner off the ball, which suited me down to the ground,' recalled Young. 'Roy loved to make surging runs down the middle, just like Eusebio, and could slip through defences like sand through fingers. He claimed that it takes two to make a pass, one to strike the ball and another to receive it. We honed our inter-passing and reaped the rewards with nets full of goals.' Vernon's shot was one of immense power and from an early age he developed the technique of rifling the ball low and hard into the corner, with little backlift. He was also an outstanding penalty-taker, missing just one of the 20 he took in a royal blue shirt. 'It could be said that Vernon made Alex Young, rather than the other way around,' this author's grandfather, Charles Mills, told me. 'I rather think he made Vernon: he provided the flicks and the through balls and Vernon was of course dynamite anywhere in the penalty area.'

Vernon scored 26 league goals in the 1961/62 season and to add to his growing goalscoring burden came the club captaincy following Bobby Collins' shock departure to Leeds United in March 1962. And yet his off-the-pitch behaviour seemed in stark contrast to the responsibilities one would expect the Everton captain to assume. He was a heavy smoker and it was reckoned that he could hold a cigarette at such an angle as to be able to smoke in the shower.

He was outspoken and his sharp tongue had a propensity to upset the club management.

And yet his formidable talent saw such waywardness tolerated, even by an arch-disciplinarian like Catterick. This is unsurprising for through the 1962/63 season Vernon, in concert with Young, was exceptional. Missing just one league match between the two of them, they scored 46 league goals, 24 of which came from Vernon's boots. These included a hat-trick on the last day of the season against Fulham, which effectively sealed the title win. 'I was delighted – for everyone's sake,' Vernon reflected to Charles Buchan's Football Monthly. 'The pressure had been on since Easter when we knew we had a good chance of the title and we all felt it was in our grasp when we scored two goals in the first eleven minutes of this game.' He claimed that the single biggest factor in the win was 'team spirit, of which we have plenty at Goodison', adding, 'Not that we always agree – we don't. But our differences are thrashed out at meetings. They REALLY are discussions, with everyone chipping in.'

Vernon and Young's partnership was exceptional and from the start of the 1961/62 season to the midway point of the 1963/64 campaign it yielded more than 100 league goals. But Catterick was never satisfied and in March 1964 he went back to Blackburn to buy their centre forward Fred Pickering for a British domestic record fee. Vernon retained the captaincy and Young seemed to be the one the Everton manager sought to replace. But over the next year it was Vernon that was edged out and he was allowed to join Stoke City in the summer of 1965, Young later saying that 'his tongue must have upset Harry too many times'.

WITHOUT him, Everton went on to win the FA Cup a year later – the trophy that Vernon coveted the most. He enjoyed good times in the Potteries, later playing out his career with Halifax Town. Post-football he went into the antiques business, but the years of heavy smoking left their legacy and he died when only in his mid-fifties. Goodison mourned the death of a man who had left so deep an impression in only a relatively short period at the club. 'When a great player leaves the club,' wrote Young, 'there is a period of mourning. After emptying Roy's ashtray, we all grieved so much that someone forgot to replace him.'

[FACTFILE]

BORN
Ffyynnongroew, 14 April 1937
DIED
4 December 1993
POSITION
Forward
OTHER CLUBS
Blackburn Rovers (1955–60);
Stoke City (1965–70);
Halifax Town (loan, 1970)
HONOURS
League Championship 1962/63;
32 Wales caps (8 goals) (1957–68)

Vidarsson, Bjarni

Young Icelandic midfielder who rose through the Everton youth system to represent his country

[FACTFILE]

BORN
Reykjavik, Iceland, 5 March 1988
POSITION
Midfielder
OTHER CLUBS
Bournemouth (loan, 2008);
FC Twente (2008–09);
Roeselare (2009–10);
Mechelen (2010)
HONOURS
1 Iceland cap (2008)

Season	League		FA Cup		League Cup		Europe		Total	
	App	Goals	App	Goals	App	Goals	App	Goals	App	Goals
2007/08	0	0	0	0	0	0	0 (1)	0	0 (1)	0
Total	0	0	0	0	0	0	0 (1)	0	0 (1)	0

Virr,
Albert 'Ted'

Half back whose goal revived Everton's 1927/28 title challenge

EVERTON DIVISION 1 CHAMPIONS 1928

EVERTON 1928

*Back - **T.H.McKintosh, Kelly, Hart (Captain), Davies, O'Donnell, Virr, H.E.Cooke***
*Front - **Critchley, Martin, Dean, Cresswell, Weldon, Troup***

It was a goal by unsung half back Ted Virr on the last day of March 1928 that reawakened Everton in pursuit of what would be one of their greatest triumphs. Everton had started the 1927/28 season on fire and by January were far ahead at the top of the table, while Dixie Dean had scored nearly 40 goals. But with 1928 came an unusual torpor.

FROM 7 January until 31 March, when Everton met Sunderland at Roker Park, the club went without a league victory. Dean was away on international duty when Everton visited the Northeast and without him they struggled for inspiration. Early in the second half Virr found what they were looking for.

'From a corner kick, well placed by Troup, Virr, who was standing almost on the goal-line, headed the ball through the goal,' reported the Daily Courier. 'From then onwards Everton monopolised the attack, most of the raids being made by Critchley.' A second goal by Bill Easton secured victory and from then on there was no stopping Everton. In the final seven games of the season, with Dean restored to the side, they won five and Dean scored 15 more goals. It took his tally up to 60 and earned Virr a League Championship winners medal.

Without question this was the highlight in Virr's 127-match Everton career. He was spotted playing local football as a teenager and signed as a professional with Everton in April 1922. He had to wait another three years for his debut, but impressed the watching Daily Courier correspondent, 'F. McN', who wrote of his debut: 'Virr, the local boy, showed great promise, his defensive tactics, under trying conditions, being extremely good.'

Everton's half back line in the early 1920s had been problematic, with winger David Reid even lining up in it. In the 1926/27 season, however, the tall, slender figure of Virr made a first-team shirt his own on the left side of the defence. Everton were wildly inconsistent, narrowly avoiding relegation that season before winning the title a year later. 'Virr has come on splendidly during the season,' it was recorded at the end of that victorious campaign.

VIRR'S place would come under threat from Tom Griffiths from the 1928/29 season but he was still deployed frequently. On Christmas Day 1929 he picked up a knee injury in a match against Sheffield Wednesday. Extensive treatment at a sanatorium over subsequent months brought no improvement and in February 1930 the Everton board were informed that his playing career was at an end.

> EVERTON HAD STARTED
> THE 1927/28 SEASON ON FIRE
> AND BY JANUARY
> WERE FAR AHEAD AT
> THE TOP OF THE TABLE

[FACTFILE]

BORN
Liverpool 1902
DIED
1959
POSITION
Half back
HONOURS
League Championship 1927/28

Season	League		FA Cup		Other		Total	
	App	Goals	App	Goals	App	Goals	App	Goals
1924/25	1	0	1	0	-	-	2	0
1925/26	16	0	2	0	-	-	18	0
1926/27	32	1	4	1	-	-	36	2
1927/28	39	1	1	0	-	-	40	1
1928/29	24	0	1	0	1	0	26	0
1929/30	5	0	0	0	-	-	5	0
Total	**117**	**2**	**9**	**1**	**1**	**0**	**127**	**3**

THE
EVERTON
· ENCYCLOPEDIA ·

Eddie **Wainwright**, **Wales** and Everton, Robbie **Wakenshaw**, Jack **Walker**, Mike **Walker**, Alec **Wall**, James **Wallace**, Mickey **Walsh**, Mike **Walsh**, Mark **Ward**, Mitch **Ward**, Billy **Wareing**, Harry **Warmby**, Robert **Warzycha**, Dave **Watson**, John **Watson**, John Gordon **Watson**, Robert **Watson**, Steve **Watson**, Gordon **Watson**, David **Waugh**, Walter **Weaver**, Keith **Webber**, **Websites**, Li **Weifeng**, David **Weir**, James **Weir**, Tony **Weldon**, Lewis **Weller**, Stefan **Wessels**, Gordon **West**, Sander **Westerveld**, Tommy **White**, Wattie **White**, John **Whitehead**, Norman **Whiteside**, Jack **Whitley**, Alan **Whittle**, Frank **Wignall**, William **Wildman**, Monty **Wilkinson**, Paul **Wilkinson**, Ben **Williams**, Bill **Williams**, Billy **Williams**, Graham **Williams**, Owen **Williams**, Richard **Williams**, Danny **Williamson**, Alan **Wilson**, David **Wilson**, George **Wilson**, Ian **Wilson**, Ray **Wilson**, Walter **Wilson**, Arthur **Winterhalder**, Sam **Wolstenholme**, George **Wood**, Ronald **Woodhouse**, Matt **Woods**, Bernie **Wright**, Bill **Wright**, Billy **Wright**, Mark **Wright**, Richard **Wright**, Robert **Wright**, Tommy **Wright**, Tom **Wylie**

Wainwright, Eddie

Popular post-war forward whose prime was wrecked by a broken leg

A talented and dedicated forward, Eddie Wainwright was one of a committed band of young footballers in whom Everton's post-war hopes were vested.

Plucked from one of Southport's amateur leagues as a teenager in 1939, Wainwright was subsequently farmed out to Fleetwood to hone his trade. In September 1943 he made his Everton debut in the wartime league, immediately impressing the club's management, who recommended he turned professional. He did so in April 1944.

A deep-lying forward who could also fit in on the Everton wing, he was, recalled Dave Hickson, 'a really good, direct winger who could really cross the ball'. Hickson also remembered him as a popular figure in the dressing room. 'He was already at Everton when I arrived and he was a lovely man. He seemed to get on with everyone around him. He had a kind word for everyone because that's the type of man he was.'

Wainwright made an immediate impression in post-war football. Before the Football League had even commenced he was selected to play for an FA XI at White Hart Lane in May 1946. In 1946/47, Wainwright's debut season, he averaged a goal every other game and over the next few years was one of the few bright spots in an ailing Everton team.

BY 1950 there was talk of an England call-up – this in the age of such luminaries as Wilf Mannion, Len Shackleton and Tom Finney. In April that year Wainwright represented the Football League against Ireland and was then picked to tour the

United States and Canada with an FA team that infamously included Stanley Matthews – thus delaying the legendary winger's arrival at the World Cup in Brazil.

Despite playing in a poor Everton team, Wainwright was at the peak of his career when, in December 1950, disaster struck. A tackle by Derby County's Chick Mussock broke his leg in two places and effectively ruled him out for three years.

Wainwright's absence – coupled with that of Cyril Lello who was also seriously injured – through much of the 1950/51 season was to have a huge effect on Everton as they finished rock bottom of the First Division and were relegated for only the second time. Wainwright missed all of the 1951/52 season and played just a handful of games the following season.

These wilderness years must have been incredibly hard for Wainwright to take. Beyond the physical torment of three years on the sidelines, in an age when players were not particularly well remunerated, appearance fees and win bonuses would have constituted a big part of his income. These were, of course, lost.

A request by Wainwright for a club house – possibly to ease the financial burden he was facing – was made to the Everton directors in 1952 and eventually accepted. But in a note on the club ledgers accompanying his request, the directors sniffily recorded that all players suffering long-term injury should in future refer to the Football League insurance scheme for compensation. It seems that they took umbrage at a player seeking to have his hard times eased – even though he was injured in action for the club.

DESPITE his injury problems, Wainwright was the subject of transfer interest from Leeds and Swindon – who saw a £3500 bid rejected in October 1953 – but remained an Everton player.

When he finally returned to a regular first-team berth in the second half of the 1953/54 season

WAINWRIGHT MADE AN IMMEDIATE IMPRESSION IN POST-WAR FOOTBALL

it coincided with Everton's successful promotion push. Now in the veteran part of his career, Wainwright continued to be a regular for the two seasons that followed the club's return to the First Division. Always a reliable source of goals, the kind of form that once brought him to the verge of an England call-up was nevertheless elusive.

In June 1956 Wainwright, with Gwyn Lewis and Jackie Grant, joined Rochdale – now managed by Harry Catterick – for a combined fee of £2500. He played 100 games for the Spotland club, retiring in 1959. He later settled on the Wirral and ran the Acorn Hotel in Bebington.

Season	League		FA Cup		Total	
	App	Goals	App	Goals	App	Goals
1946/47	27	13	2	2	29	15
1947/48	30	9	4	2	34	11
1948/49	17	10	1	0	18	10
1949/50	37	11	5	2	42	13
1950/51	11	1	0	0	11	1
1951/52	0	0	0	0	0	0
1952/53	7	4	0	0	7	4
1953/54	23	8	3	0	26	8
1954/55	24	4	2	0	26	4
1955/56	31	8	4	2	35	10
Total	**207**	**68**	**21**	**8**	**228**	**76**

[FACTFILE]

BORN
Southport, 22 June 1924
DIED
Ellesmere Port,
30 September 2005
POSITION
Inside forward / winger
OTHER CLUB
Rochdale (1956–59)

Wales, and Everton

Situated less than 30 miles from the Welsh Border, Everton's relationship with the principality has always been strong

Everton's bonds with Wales – through its players, supporters, and the Welsh national team – have always been tight, and the club has made important contributions to the landscape of Welsh football. Merseyside's geographical proximity to Wales and the traditional flow of immigrants from North Wales to Liverpool has ensured such a close relationship, which extends back almost back to the birth of Everton.

THOMAS G. JONES, Everton F.C.   TOPICAL TIMES

Football in Wales originates in the country's north east and this area has been a fertile poaching ground for Everton players and supporters throughout the game's history there. The Welsh FA was founded in 1876, making it amongst the oldest federations in the world, and while football struggled to forge an identity in the face of rugby's dominance elsewhere in Wales, the north east remained one of its heartlands.

'Throughout its history, football in Wales has struggled against the popularity of rugby union, financial constraints, divisions between north and south and perceptions that there was something un-Welsh about the sport,' writes Martin Johnes in the Encyclopaedia of British Football. 'There is little that is actually distinct about Welsh football, and it is intimately linked to the game in England, but throughout its history its players, fans and administrators have all shared a pride in Wales.'

The district of Everton, from which the football club's first supporters were drawn, had a strong Welsh immigrant presence, with a Welsh Baptist Church in Everton Village, a Welsh Church in Kirkdale, and Welsh Presbyterian Churches on Anfield Road and in Walton Park. Many of these congregations would take on a new royal blue faith and impart it to their families back across the Welsh border.

INVARIABLY this influence soon found its way onto the pitch and Smart Arridge and Robert Jones became, in 1894, the club's first Welsh internationals. This started a proud tradition that took in such great players as Leigh Richmond Roose, T. G. Jones and Roy Vernon. The highpoint of Everton's Welsh influence was the 1980s, when Pat Van Den Hauwe, Neville Southall and Kevin Ratcliffe were pillars in what was arguably the most talented Welsh team of all time. With teammates such as Mark Hughes and Ian Rush it seems difficult to believe that they failed to qualify for a major tournament. Alas, the sad reality is that no Wales team has done so since the 1958 World Cup Finals.

Since the end of the Second World War, Everton have always maintained a leading presence in the Wales team. Jones, Vernon, Ratcliffe and Southall all captained the team, as did Ben Williams in the 1930s and Barry Horne and Gary Speed in the mid-1990s.

B. WILLIAMS

Mark Hughes combined playing for Everton with managing Wales, while Speed went on to manage the national team. Southall has the record number of caps (92) for the country.

Such strong footballing influence along with the close geographic ties have played their part in making Everton one of the most popular clubs in Wales. No one example is more instructive of the hold the club has on the country than that of the club's most successful captain, Kevin Ratcliffe. 'I was always going to play for Everton. Everton had the pull, because I used to go and watch them play regularly as a boy,' he wrote in the foreword of Dean Hayes's Everton's Welsh Legends. 'Everyone in our house was brought up as an Evertonian… We had a lot of support at Everton from north Wales. Lots of coaches would go from the north Wales area to Goodison. I knew that every Saturday there'd be coaches going and stopping off on the way for a drink, because I used to pass them myself on the way to matches from my home in Flintshire. Sometimes I even travelled with them.'

Wakenshaw, Robbie

Prolific reserve team striker who never quite made the first-team grade

Season	League		FA Cup		League Cup		Europe		Total	
	App	Goals	App	Goals	App	Goals	App	Goals	App	Goals
1983/84	1	1	0	0	0	0	-	-	1	1
1984/85	1 (1)	0	0	0	0	0	0 (2)	0	1 (3)	0
Total	**2 (1)**	**1**	**0**	**0**	**0**	**0**	**0 (2)**	**0**	**2 (3)**	**1**

Walker, Jack

Reserve defender who deputised occasionally during Goodison's second season

Season	League		FA Cup		Total	
	App	Goals	App	Goals	App	Goals
1893/94	3	1	0	0	3	1
Total	**3**	**1**	**0**	**0**	**3**	**1**

Walker, Mike

Maligned mid-1990s manager, but is his reputation entirely warranted?

There's a belief, bound up in fact, that goalkeepers do not make good managers. So when Everton moved to appoint Mike Walker in January 1994, following Howard Kendall's resignation a month earlier, Everton's board should, perhaps, have been more cautious.

WALKER had been a lower-league goalkeeper in the 1960s and 1970s, laying out a lengthy career at a variety of inauspicious postings – Reading, Shrewsbury, York, Watford and Colchester. Although he won Wales under-23 honours, his playing career is perhaps best remembered for a penalty save when Watford knocked Liverpool out of the FA Cup quarter-finals in 1970.

In 1986 Walker was appointed manager of Colchester United, for whom he had played more than 450 times, but his reign lasted just a year and he was sacked with his team top of the Fourth Division. He took charge of Norwich City's youth team in 1987, and in May 1992 succeeded Dave Stringer as manager. His debut season, the Premier League's inaugural campaign, was an

outstanding success. Norwich led the league for much of the season, before slipping back to third position – the highest in their history. They did so with extremely limited resources and Walker based his success around a mixture of unheralded veterans and exciting young players, such as Chris Sutton and Ruel Fox.

THE FOLLOWING season, Norwich knocked Bayern Munich out of the UEFA Cup, before succumbing to Inter Milan. Walker made his mark on Evertonians in September 1993, when his Norwich team humbled Everton 5-1 at Goodison – Everton's biggest home defeat in more than a decade.

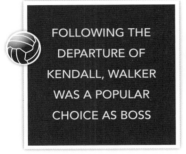

FOLLOWING THE DEPARTURE OF KENDALL, WALKER WAS A POPULAR CHOICE AS BOSS

Following the departure of Kendall, Walker was a popular choice as boss: a bright manager who would bring the clean sweep the club so desperately needed. Such optimism was heightened by resounding victories over Swindon Town and Chelsea early on in his career. But hope soon turned to despondency as defeat after defeat followed. Only the famous Wimbledon game on the final day of the 1993/94 season kept Everton from relegation.

That summer Walker was given a sizable transfer war chest. But although he was linked to a succession of illustrious internationals, such as Muller, Jurgen Klinsmann and Martin Dahlin, he seemed incapable of getting anybody to sign. Everton opened the 1994/95 season with Vinny Samways the only new face in the team. Although a string of signings came soon after – Daniel Amokachi, David Burrows and Duncan Ferguson – it was too late to stop Everton's worst ever start to a season. The first win of the campaign came only at the start of November, and although there were some signs that Walker had started to turn things around, a week later he was sacked– just ten months and six wins into his Goodison reign.

WALKER'S regime was an absolute disaster in terms of results. He was disliked by many of the squad and brought in players like Brett Angell and Burrows – swapped for the prolific Tony Cottee – who are considered among the worst to wear the blue shirt. Yet he was also responsible for the signings of favourites such as Joe Parkinson (an unknown bargain from Bournemouth), Anders Limpar, Amokachi and Ferguson.

Moreover, he inherited a team in a dire state. Although Everton finished the 1992/93 season 13th they were just four points off relegation and sold their best player, Peter Beardsley, that summer having already lost

Martin Keown mid-season. They had lost five straight league games when Walker took over and lay in 17th place.

'Standards are not as high as they should be,' he told the Independent in April 1994. 'They've been allowed to slip. People talk about resurrecting Everton and winning things again, but we've got to raise our levels of performance everywhere before we can do it. I don't think the players train hard enough. They think a little running session is hard work, but we're only talking about what was normal at Norwich. The Everton lads hadn't been used to doing any running. Their training routine was a few five-a-sides and a bit of head tennis. That was it. It shows. That's why they can't do certain things I want. They're not fit enough.'

In 1996 he returned to manage Norwich City, but was sacked at the end of the 1997/98 season having failed to restore them to the Premier League. Later he managed in Cyprus before dropping out of the game.

[FACTFILE]

BORN
Colwyn Bay,
28 November 1945

CLUBS AS A PLAYER
Reading (1963–64);
Shrewsbury Town (1964–66);
York City (1966–68);
Watford (1968–73);
Charlton Athletic (loan, 1973);
Colchester United (1973–83)

AS MANAGER
Colchester United (1986–87);
Norwich City
(1992–94 & 1996–98);
APOEL (Cyprus, 2000–01)

As Everton Manager										
Season	P	W	L	D	F	A	Pts	Position	FA Cup	League Cup
1993/94	17	5	8	4	20	28	19	17	3rd Round	N/A*
1994/95	14	1	8	5	12	20	8	22	N/A	2nd Round**

* Walker appointed 7 January 1994 ** Walker sacked 8 November 1994

Wall, Alec

Early-1920s inside forward for whom a regular starting berth proved elusive

Season	League		FA Cup		Total	
	App	Goals	App	Goals	App	Goals
1919/20	3	0	0	0	3	0
1920/21	2	0	0	0	2	0
1921/22	8	3	1	0	9	3
1922/23	1	0	0	0	1	0
1923/24	0	0	0	0	0	0
1924/25	2	0	0	0	2	0
Total	16	3	1	0	17	3

[FACTFILE]

BORN
Liverpool,
31 October 1899
DIED
1978
POSITION
Inside forward
OTHER CLUB
Swindon Town (1925–26)

Wallace, James

England youth international for whom high hopes are held

[FACTFILE]

BORN
Fazackerley,
19 December 1991
POSITION
Midfielder
OTHER CLUBS
Bury (loan, 2010);
Stockport County
(loan, 2011);
Shrewsbury Town
(loan, 2011–12);
Stevenage (loan, 2012);
Tranmere Rovers
(loan, 2012-) (after initial loan)

Season	League		FA Cup		League Cup		Europe		Total	
	App	Goals	App	Goals	App	Goals	App	Goals	App	Goals
2009/10	0	0	0	0	0	0	0 (1)	0	0 (1)	0
Total	0	0	0	0	0	0	0 (1)	0	0 (1)	0

Walsh, Derek

Teenage midfielder whose solitary appearance came in a Goodison derby victory

[FACTFILE]

BORN
Hamilton, 24 October 1967
POSITION
Midfielder
OTHER CLUBS
Hamilton Academical
(1987–88);
Carlisle United (1988–93);
Hamilton Academical
(1993–94);
Gretna

Season	League		FA Cup		League Cup		Europe		Total	
	App	Goals	App	Goals	App	Goals	App	Goals	App	Goals
1984/85	1	0	0	0	0	0	0	0	1	0
Total	1	0	0	0	0	0	0	0	1	0

Walsh,
Mickey

Striker who was unable to replicate his goal-of-the-season form at Goodison

> EVERTONIANS EXPECTED THE SORT OF FORM THEY HAD GLIMPSED ON MATCH OF THE DAY

In many ways Mick Walsh's career was defined by a glorious moment at its very dawn. Aged 20, he lined up for Blackpool against Sunderland in front of Match of the Day's cameras at Bloomfield Road in February 1975.

With the scores balanced at 2-2, five minutes from the end Walsh made the game's decisive intervention: taking a high ball down on his chest on the edge of the centre circle, he broke into the

Sunderland half, and, meandering with the menace of a wildcat, turned his defender on the edge of the penalty area and curled an instantaneous piledriver into the far corner of the Sunderland net. Later that year it would be awarded Goal of the Season.

When Walsh arrived at Goodison three years later for a hefty £325,000, the burden of expectation hung heavily over the forward, the latest partner for Bob Latchford. He had averaged nearly a goal every other game for Blackpool and Evertonians expected the sort of form they had glimpsed on Match of the Day.

Alas, this proved elusive, as Walsh was struck by erratic form and pure bad luck. The sort of brilliant strike that may have changed his fortunes was never forthcoming and the following March Gordon Lee swapped him for Queens Park Rangers' Peter Eastoe.

WALSH fared little better at Loftus Road, and in 1981 he moved to Porto. In Portugal his career underwent an extraordinary resurgence and he won the Portuguese Cup in 1983 and the league title two years later, also appearing in the 1984 European Cup Winners' Cup Final, which Porto lost to Juventus.

[FACTFILE]

BORN
Chorley, 13 August 1954
POSITION
Striker
OTHER CLUBS
Blackpool (1971–78);
Queens Park Rangers
(1979–81);
FC Porto (1981–86);
Salgueiros (1986–87);
Espinho (1987–88)
HONOURS
22 Republic of Ireland caps
(3 goals) (1976–85)

Season	League		FA Cup		League Cup		Europe		Total	
	App	Goals	App	Goals	App	Goals	App	Goals	App	Goals
1978/79	18 (2)	1	1	0	3	0	4	2	26 (2)	3
Total	**18 (2)**	**1**	**1**	**0**	**3**	**0**	**4**	**2**	**26 (2)**	**3**

Walsh, Mike

Defensive stalwart whose Goodison opportunities were fleeting

One of Howard Kendall's 'magnificent seven' signings in the summer of 1981, Mike Walsh was a strapping centre half, who had earned a reputation for dependability during a lengthy spell with Bolton Wanderers.

WITH HIS striking blond hair, the defender – not to be confused with the Everton forward of the same name – was one of the acquisitions said to herald a new era at Goodison. Exchanged for £90,000, plus goalkeeper Jim McDonough, his Everton career started promisingly, but like so many of Kendall's initial signings – Mickey Thomas, Alan Ainscow, Alan Biley – it quickly petered out. By autumn he had lost his place to fellow left-footer Mark Higgins, and although he returned briefly at left back there was no way back in his favoured position.

In 1983 Walsh joined Fort Lauderdale Strikers in the NASL, but within months of his signing they filed for bankruptcy. He returned to England with Manchester City, but joined Blackpool after only four appearances. In September 1990 Walsh was appointed Bury manager, leading them to the playoffs on three different occasions, including, in 1995, their first Wembley appearance in the playoff final. He was later assistant manager of Swindon Town and Southport manager at the start of the century. He has since left professional football and settled in Spain, where he runs a restaurant.

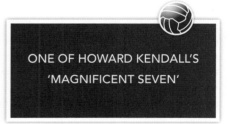

ONE OF HOWARD KENDALL'S 'MAGNIFICENT SEVEN'

[FACTFILE]							

BORN
Manchester, 20 June 1956
POSITION
Centre half
OTHER CLUBS
Bolton Wanderers (1974–81);
Norwich City (loan, 1982);
Burnley (loan, 1982);
Fort Lauderdale Strikers (1983);
Manchester City (1983–84);
Blackpool (1984–89)
HONOURS
5 Republic of Ireland caps (1982–83)

	League		FA Cup		League Cup		Total	
Season	App	Goals	App	Goals	App	Goals	App	Goals
1981/82	18	0	0	0	1	0	19	0
1982/83	2	0	0	0	0	0	2	0
Total	20	0	0	0	1	0	21	0

Ward,
Mark

Feisty midfielder who struggled with life after football

In joining Everton in the summer of 1991, Mark Ward resurrected a dream that had seemingly died a decade earlier. The Huyton-born midfielder, a fan who had once served as a Goodison ball boy, had worked his way through Everton's youth ranks, but was released by the club for being too small without making an appearance.

He resurrected his career in non-league football, before getting his chance at Joe Royle's Oldham. He broke into the First Division with West Ham in 1985, before Howard Kendall twice paid more than a million pounds for him at the end of the decade: while Manchester City manager in December 1989 and again for Everton 18 months later.

A feisty right-sided midfielder, who belied his diminutive frame with snarling aggression and a relentless will to win, Ward added tenacity and bite to the Everton midfield. Not for nothing was he dubbed 'Mark the nark' and Stuart Pearce described him as his 'toughest opponent'. He was comfortable in possession and running with the ball, though was

never particularly pacy, nor a possessor of the dazzling dribbling skills that came naturally to a player like Pat Nevin.

He had a fierce shot and scored some spectacular long-range goals. On his home debut against league champions Arsenal, Ward scored twice in an effervescent display as Everton won 3-1. It was, he recalled, 'the best game of my career'.

But after such a fine start, what followed was tinged with disappointment. Everton underachieved and Ward, who was in his late-twenties, looked as if he had already peaked elsewhere. There were a few memorable moments, notably a fierce drive that opened the scoring in the September 1993 derby match, but these were few and far between. With the arrival of Mike Walker as manager in January 1994, chances became sparse and Ward joined Birmingham City for £500,000 two months later.

After two years at St Andrews, Ward struggled to find a meaningful role within the game. He managed non-league Altrincham for a period but was sacked. After spells of unemployment and illness, he fell into crime

and in October 2004 was convicted of possession of cocaine with intent to supply and sentenced to eight years imprisonment. It was a shocking outcome for a man who had played at the top for so long.

'I've never been in trouble before and have never dealt in drugs,' he told the Observer, shortly after his conviction. 'Adapting to life after football was too much for me at times. When today's Premiership stars retire they'll be set up for life. But the biggest contract I ever had was £2,000 a week and, when my playing career ended, I soon wound up with nothing. When the money, fame and glamour disappear it's hard to adjust.'

Further reading:
WARD, MARK, *Hammered,* John Blake, 2010

STUART PEARCE DESCRIBED HIM AS HIS 'TOUGHEST OPPONENT'

[FACTFILE]

BORN
Prescot, 10 October 1962
POSITION
Midfield
OTHER CLUBS
Northwich Victoria (1982–83);
Oldham Athletic (1983–85);
West Ham (1985–89);
Manchester City (1989–91);
Birmingham City (1994–96);
Huddersfield Town (1996);
Wigan Athletic (1996);
Northwich Victoria (1997–98)
AS MANAGER
Altrincham (2000–01)

Season	League		FA Cup		League Cup		Other		Total	
	App	Goals	App	Goals	App	Goals	App	Goals	App	Goals
1991/92	37	4	2	0	2	0	1	0	42	4
1992/93	19	1	0	0	0	0	-	-	19	1
1993/94	26 (1)	1	2	0	4	1	-	-	32 (1)	2
Total	**82 (1)**	**6**	**4**	**0**	**6**	**1**	**1**	**0**	**93 (1)**	**7**

Ward, Mitch

Lower league midfielder who failed to hit the mark

Experienced, versatile and hard-working, Mitch Ward had been one of Howard Kendall's most reliable performers during the manager's spell in charge of Sheffield United. A right-sided midfielder, who could also play at full back, wing back and even in central midfield, he was renowned for whipping in crosses from the flank, and also for his fiercely struck penalties.

In October 1997, Kendall brought him to Goodison along with Carl Tiler in a part-exchange deal that saw the popular Graham Stuart leave for Bramall Lane, plus £500,000. He arrived at Goodison at a dire time, and his debut at Chelsea was inauspicious – giving away the first of two late penalties, which sealed a 2-0 defeat and Everton's place at the foot of the Premiership table.

Ward played just a handful of games before being struck down by a succession of ankle injuries that ruled him out of much of the remainder of the 1997/98 season. By the time he returned to fitness, Kendall was gone and his replacement Walter Smith seldom used him, although he did once name him captain in a League Cup tie against Oxford United in September 1999. At the end of the 1999/2000 season, Ward joined Barnsley for £200,000, a more fitting level, perhaps, for an honest trier.

RENOWNED FOR WHIPPING IN CROSSES FROM THE FLANK, AND ALSO FOR HIS FIERCELY STRUCK PENALTIES

[FACTFILE]

BORN
Sheffield, 19 June 1971
POSITION
Midfield
OTHER CLUBS
Sheffield United (1989–97);
Crewe Alexandra
(loan, 1990);
Barnsley (2000–03);
York City (2003–04)

Season	League		FA Cup		League Cup		Total	
	App	Goals	App	Goals	App	Goals	App	Goals
1997/98	8	0	0	0	0	0	8	0
1998/99	4 (2)	0	2	0	1	0	7 (2)	0
1999/2000	6 (4)	0	0	0	1 (1)	0	7 (5)	0
Total	**18 (6)**	**0**	**2**	**0**	**2 (1)**	**0**	**22 (7)**	**0**

Wareing, Billy

Lancastrian defender on the fringes of Everton's 1915 title winning side

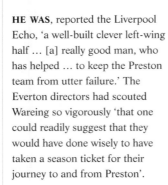

W. WAREING
EVERTON F.C.

A £900 signing from Preston North End in October 1912, Billy Wareing was purchased with the intention of shoring up an Everton back line that was proving prone to damaging lapses. Six months earlier the club had run Blackburn Rovers a close second in the hunt for the First Division title, but they were now plummeting towards mid-table.

'A WELL-BUILT CLEVER LEFT-WING HALF'

HE WAS, reported the Liverpool Echo, 'a well-built clever left-wing half … [a] really good man, who has helped … to keep the Preston team from utter failure.' The Everton directors had scouted Wareing so vigorously 'that one could readily suggest that they would have done wisely to have taken a season ticket for their journey to and from Preston'.

Alas, his debut was a catastrophe: a record 6-0 home defeat to Newcastle United. 'One can hardly remember Everton being made to look such exceedingly small fry as they did on Saturday,' reported the Liverpool Courier of the 'Everton debacle'. 'Six clear goals does seem a big margin, but it in no way over-emphasises the superiority of the Newcastle team in a game which was played under the most trying circumstances. Everton never had a look in … and in the later stages the side as a whole became completely demoralised.'

WAREING kept his place in the Everton team, nevertheless, switching to centre back later on in the season. Everton finished the campaign in 11th place, one of their worst ever showings. When form did not improve the following season, Wareing lost his place to Tom Fleetwood and was just a fringe player throughout the remainder of his war-interrupted career.

Season	League		FA Cup		Total	
	App	Goals	App	Goals	App	Goals
1912/13	24	2	4	1	28	3
1913/14	17	2	0	0	17	2
1914/15	8	0	1	1	9	1
1919/20	15	0	0	0	15	0
Total	64	4	5	2	69	6

[FACTFILE]

BORN
Southport, 1888
POSITION
Left half / centre half
OTHER CLUBS
Chorley; Preston North End (1910–12); Swindon Town (1920–24)

Warmby, Harry

Centre half who played in Everton's third ever league game before drifting into obscurity

[FACTFILE]

BORN
1865
POSITION
Centre half

Season	League		FA Cup		Total	
	App	Goals	App	Goals	App	Goals
1888/89	1	0	-	-	1	0
Total	1	0	-	-	1	0

Warzycha, Robert

Enigmatic Pole who made it big in America

Signed from Gornik Zabrze for £500,000 in March 1991, Robert Warzycha was a surprise and exotic signing who added some colour to the Everton line-up as another pallid season faded to grey. A tantalising and lightning quick winger, Warzycha – affectionately dubbed 'Bob the Pole' – was a seasoned Polish international and among the first of a succession of talented footballers to cross over from the former Soviet bloc.

With his blend of pacy and powerful running and his unerring habit of running through his opponents' challenges, Warzycha was a popular addition to the Everton squad. He had a powerful shot too, and it would not be unkind to describe him as a 'poor man's' Andrei Kanchelskis – a player who would replace him on the Everton flank a few years later.

AMONG THE FIRST OF A SUCCESSION OF TALENTED FOOTBALLERS TO CROSS OVER FROM THE FORMER SOVIET BLOC

Some of his early performances were outstanding – he scored a goal in the ill-fated Zenith Data Systems Cup Final against Crystal Palace shortly after his arrival, and at the start of the following season tore apart Manchester United at Old Trafford in one of the very first Premier League encounters. Alas injuries curtailed his impact as time went on, and whenever he recovered he seemed to struggle with the tactical intricacies of English football.

HIS ABSENCE from the Everton team cost him his place with the Polish national side, which in turn saw his work permit revoked. At the end of the 1993/94 season he joined Pesci Munkas of Hungary, later crossing the Atlantic to play in the nascent MLS. Like so many of Everton's enigmatic 1990s stars, he found his level here, becoming something of a legend with Columbus Crew, whom he later managed.

[FACTFILE]

BORN
Siemkowice, Poland,
20 August 1963
POSITION
Winger
OTHER CLUBS
Gornik Walbrzych (1985–87);
Gornik Zabrze (1987–91);
Pesci Munkas SC
(Hungary, 1994–95);
Kispest Honved
(Hungary, 1995–96);
Columbus Crew (1996–2002)
AS MANAGER
Columbus Crew (2009–)
HONOURS
47 Poland caps
(7 goals) (1987–93)

Season	League		FA Cup		League Cup		Other		Total	
	App	Goals	App	Goals	App	Goals	App	Goals	App	Goals
1990/91	7 (1)	2	0	0	0	0	3	2	10 (1)	4
1991/92	26(11)	3	1 (1)	0	1 (1)	0	1	0	29 (13)	3
1992/93	15 (5)	1	0 (1)	0	3 (1)	0	-	-	18 (7)	1
1993/94	3 (4)	0	0 (1)	0	0	0	-	-	3 (5)	0
Total	51(21)	6	1 (3)	0	4 (2)	0	4	2	60 (26)	8

Watson,
Dave

Imperious centre half who captained Everton to FA Cup glory

After narrowly missing out on a League and FA Cup double in 1986, Howard Kendall set to strengthening Everton's defence, where injuries and suspensions had ultimately proved devastating during the previous campaign. For a club record fee of £900,000 he signed Norwich City's centre back and captain, Dave Watson, bringing the sometime England international back to his native city. Norwich's manager Ken Brown likened losing Watson to having his right arm cut off. Considered managerial hyperbole at the time, after Watson gave 15 years service to Everton, spanning more than 500 appearances, Evertonians came to understand just what Brown meant.

Watson started his career with Liverpool, but in November 1980 left to join Norwich City for £50,000 without making an appearance. Later in the decade Watson's younger brother, Alex, also a centre half, played a handful of games for Liverpool before forging a successful lower-league career.

At Carrow Road, Watson's career finally picked up and he emerged as one of the most outstanding young players outside the top flight. He was part of the team that won promotion back to the First Division in 1982, where they remained until 1985. In June 1984, when Watson was 22, he made his England debut against

Brazil in the Maracana, on the same day that John Barnes scored his famous solo goal. Watson was made Norwich captain, in 1985 lifting the Milk Cup. A year later he captained them to the Second Division Championship – his final act as Norwich skipper.

Still aged only 24 when he became an Everton player, Watson possessed a wealth of experience. And yet in his early days at Goodison, there was a sense of naivety as he struggled to adapt from man-marking to the zonal marking system that had been the hallmark of the club's defensive solidity through the mid-1980s. Some of his early appearances in a blue shirt were wracked with hesitancy and errors that later seemed wholly uncharacteristic of the player. The start of his Goodison career was made more difficult by a section of the support baying for the return of their hero Derek Mountfield, the man Watson had replaced.

HOWARD KENDALL kept faith in his record signing, and slowly Watson began to justify his hefty fee. 'The fans gave me some stick because I wasn't playing well,' Watson would recall of the most turbulent time of his Goodison career, 'But I don't just think it was me. If anyone is playing badly, they are likely to get on his back, but I must say that Evertonians are as quick to praise you.' As the season progressed Watson got to grips with his new role and the campaign ended with Everton crowned League Champions for the ninth time.

From thereon, Watson never looked back. The 1987/88 season was one of collective disappointment as Everton finished the season fourth.

But having conceded just 27 goals all season, it marked the meanest defensive campaign in the club's history. Watson's role in this was acknowledged when he was voted Supporters Player of the Year and selected as part of England's 1988 European Championship squad.

Like his contemporaries Tony Adams and Terry Butcher, Watson was very much the archetypal English centre half. Commanding in the air, hard and crisp in the tackle, there was nothing glossy or complicated about his style. But he was always consistent, always committed and always did his best when he pulled on an Everton shirt. Never the quickest of players, Watson made up for this deficiency – which, with the onset of his thirties, became more pronounced – with supreme reading of the game. He relished physical battle, but his disciplinary record was exemplary, and he was sent off just once in more than 500 Everton appearances.

In 1991 he succeeded Kevin Ratcliffe as captain and, as Everton went into their early-1990s decline, Watson, along with Neville Southall, was one of the few constants in a succession of failing sides. Everton went downhill further after Watson's successful central defensive partnership with Martin Keown was broken up in February 1993. He continued to marshal a mixture of young players – such as David Unsworth and Mathew Jackson – and those not quite up to the task – Paul Holmes and Kenny Sansom – as best he could. But 15 months later, Everton only avoided relegation by the skin of their teeth.

The start of the 1994/95 season was disastrous, with Everton only recording their first league win at the start of November. Mike Walker was sacked as manager soon after and Joe Royle, whom Watson was first acquainted with as a Norwich City youngster, succeeded him. Much was made

of Royle's midfield 'dogs of war' and how they steered the club clear of another relegation scare, but the new boss also handed responsibility for rectifying Everton's abysmal position to the senior squad members – Barry Horne, Paul Rideout, Southall and Watson. It was a challenge to which the captain responded magnificently – not least in Everton's FA Cup success.

WATSON was never as prolific a goalscorer as Derek Mountfield, but throughout his Everton career he was a regular on the score sheet and weighed in with a number of crucial goals, such as that which finally saw off Liverpool after their epic FA Cup tussle in 1991. But no goal he scored was more invaluable than that which defeated Newcastle in the 1995 FA Cup quarter-final. With Everton still in a relegation battle, high-flying Newcastle were strong favourites for the tie and only a string of outstanding first-half saves from Southall denied them the lead. In the 66th minute, a long free kick from David Unsworth found the head of Duncan Ferguson; his header was only half cleared into the air, and Watson rose majestically to power the ball into the Newcastle net from close range for the game's only goal. Two months later Watson lifted the FA Cup, his outstanding marshalling of the

defence and man-marking of Mark Hughes sealing a man-of-the-match winning performance. With typical modesty, Watson would always play down his role in the final. 'There was no "special ingredient" or "secret" from our team in that game,' he said in 2008. 'It was just 11 players performing to their maximum level on the day. We had it then and were able to beat Manchester United.'

With Watson now in the veteran stage of his career, Royle sought a long-term successor to him, earmarking Craig Short and, later, Slaven Bilic for the role. But both men would ultimately fall short of what it took to fill his boots, and while the likes of David Weir and Alan Stubbs would prove fine centre backs, not until the signing of Phil Jagielka in 2007 would there be a worthy successor to his shirt.

In the meantime he continued to provide staunch service as captain and centre back, his diminishing pace compensated by astute reading of the game. Injuries started to trouble him, but Watson never let it show. In many ways, he was a throwback to an era in which football was a man's – not an athlete's – game. 'Dave Watson was brilliant and what he put out, game after game, was beyond the call of duty,' Jimmy Gabriel told the author Becky Tallentire. 'He would go out and play with injuries and he never let anyone know about it. We knew because we were on the staff, but he just got on with it because he was a fine man. So if you want to talk about somebody as hard as nails then Dave Watson was that man and what a great servant to Everton.'

In March 1997, Watson's duty suddenly extended beyond the pitch when he was made caretaker manager after Joe Royle's unexpected departure. Everton again found themselves in the relegation mire, but with his customary level-headedness he calmed the storm engulfing Goodison. Three draws and a win in seven games were enough to bring Everton clear of the trailing pack and at the end of the season he returned to playing duties.

SENSING that Watson was nearing the end of his playing days, Howard Kendall, now in his third spell as manager, made Gary Speed captain for the 1997/98 season, giving Watson a place on his coaching team. Still he played on and after Speed's departure in January 1998 became club captain to Duncan Ferguson's team captain. It was a position he retained for the rest of his playing days.

He made 22 appearances through the 1998/99 season under Walter Smith's management – the sixth managerial reign he had experienced as an Everton player. The following campaign he famously formed a brief central defensive partnership with Richard Gough – combined age 75 – but injuries and age had started to impair his involvement. His last game came in January 2000 against Tottenham Hotspur, and although he remained an Everton player for another year, he was not seen in a royal blue shirt again.

In summer 2001 Watson was appointed Tranmere Rovers manager, but the move was ill-fated and he was sacked after a year having failed to win promotion to Division One. There followed spells in schoolboy coaching, and in 2008 he was reunited with his former Norwich defensive partner, Steve Bruce, who appointed him Wigan Athletic youth team manager, a position he subsequently took up with Newcastle United. It was a return to the level his talents and experience merited.

[FACTFILE]

BORN
Liverpool, 20 November 1961

POSITION
Central defender

OTHER CLUBS
Liverpool (1977–80);
Norwich City (1980–86)

AS MANAGER
Tranmere Rovers (2001–02)

HONOURS
League Championship 1986/87;
FA Cup 1995;
12 England caps (1984–88)

Season	League		FA Cup		League Cup		Other		Total	
	App	Goals	App	Goals	App	Goals	App	Goals	App	Goals
1986/87	35	3	3	0	2	0	2	0	42	3
1987/88	37	4	8	1	7	1	2	0	54	6
1988/89	32	3	7	0	4	1	4	0	47	4
1989/90	28 (1)	1	4	0	3	0	-	-	35 (1)	1
1990/91	32	2	6	2	3	0	5	2	46	6
1991/92	35	3	2	0	4	0	2	1	43	4
1992/93	40	1	2	0	6	0	-	-	48	1
1993/94	27 (1)	1	0	0	3	3	-	-	30 (1)	4
1994/95	38	2	6	1	2	1	-	-	46	4
1995/96	34	0	4	0	1	0	2 (1)	0	41 (1)	0
1996/97	29	1	2	0	0	0	-	-	31	1
1997/98	25 (1)	0	0	0	3	0	-	-	28 (1)	0
1998/99	22	0	3	0	1	1	-	-	26	1
1999/2000	5 (1)	0	0 (1)	0	0	0	-	-	5 (2)	0
2000/01	0	0	0	0	0	0	-	-	0	0
Total	**419(4)**	**22**	**47(1)**	**5**	**39**	**7**	**17 (1)**	**3**	**522(6)**	**37**

Watson, John

Left back during the first years of the twentieth century

Season	League		FA Cup		Total	
	App	Goals	App	Goals	App	Goals
1899/1900	3	0	0	0	3	0
1900/01	24	0	0	0	24	0
1901/02	17	0	0	0	17	0
Total	**44**	**0**	**0**	**0**	**44**	**0**

[FACTFILE]

BORN
Dundee, 1876
POSITION
Left back
OTHER CLUBS
Dundee Wanderers;
New Brompton;
Dundee;
Tottenham Hotspur

Watson, John Gordon

Young attacker whose Goodison career was limited to a couple of outings

Season	League		FA Cup		Total	
	App	Goals	App	Goals	App	Goals
1932/33	1	0	0	0	1	0
1933/34	1	0	0	0	1	0
Total	**1**	**0**	**0**	**0**	**1**	**0**

[FACTFILE]

BORN
Wolsingham, 1912
POSITION
Outside right
OTHER CLUBS
Blyth Spartans;
Coventry City (1934–35);
Crystal Palace (1936);
Ashington

Watson, Robert

Inside forward who was a regular through Everton's first league campaign

Season	League		FA Cup		Total	
	App	Goals	App	Goals	App	Goals
1887/88	-	-	4	2	4	2
1888/89	18	4	-	-	18	4
Total	**18**	**4**	**4**	**2**	**22**	**6**

[FACTFILE]

BORN
1866
POSITION
Inside right
OTHER CLUB
Gorton Villa

Watson, Steve

Popular right back who filled a variety of roles with commitment and enthusiasm

In English football history there are not many full backs who, among their footballing souvenirs, can boast ownership of a match ball – the prize typically awarded for scoring a hat-trick. Steve Watson, however, is one of the very few. His day of glory came in September 2003, when Everton met Leeds United at Goodison and Watson, playing as an auxiliary midfielder, dispatched a treble with the aplomb of a centre forward – including a superlative 30-yard lob.

SUCH A goalscoring flurry was not too surprising to watching Evertonians. Anyone who had seen Watson's brilliant overhead kicked goal from the edge of the Bolton penalty area the previous January knew that he possessed rare composure in the penalty area. But Watson was more than merely a goalscoring full back. He was a supremely versatile footballer who always played with commitment, verve and a smile on his face, no matter what role he was asked to fill.

NOT MANY FULL BACKS CAN BOAST OWNERSHIP OF A MATCH BALL IN THEIR SOUVENIRS FOR SCORING A HAT-TRICK

Signed from Aston Villa for £2.5million in the summer of 2000, Watson had previously turned down a £4million move to Goodison from Newcastle in 1998. Tall, powerful and calm in possession, he was a fine attacking right back whose slight lack of pace occasionally saw him exposed defensively. For a defender he possessed a fine footballing brain and was called upon to fill a variety of roles across the Everton defence and midfield and, once, also as centre forward.

His best form came following the arrival of David Moyes in March 2002, when he was pushed forward to right midfield and permed alongside the more athletic Tony Hibbert. His experience and Hibbert's pace made them a formidable barrier down the Everton right.

During the 2004/05 season Watson was edged out of contention by Leon Osman, but was regularly called upon to deputise in a variety of positions. Never was he better than as an auxiliary left back when Everton played Manchester United towards the season's end, almost entirely subduing Cristiano Ronaldo as Everton secured a famous win and effectively sealed Champions League qualification. Late on Ronaldo theatrically threw himself to the ground in the Everton penalty area, but it was as much a show of frustration at being overshadowed by the veteran as an attempt to cheat a way back into the game.

AT THE season's end, Watson, now aged 31, was offered a year-long contract extension, but instead chose to join West Bromwich Albion on a three-year deal. In 2007 he joined Sheffield Wednesday and was later appointed club captain.

[FACTFILE]

BORN
North Shields,
1 April 1974

POSITION
Full back / midfield

OTHER CLUBS
Newcastle United
(1991–98);
Aston Villa (1998–2000);
West Bromwich Albion
(2005–07);
Sheffield Wednesday
(2007–09)

Season	League		FA Cup		League Cup		Total	
	App	Goals	App	Goals	App	Goals	App	Goals
2000/01	34	0	2	1	2	0	38	1
2001/02	24 (1)	4	0	0	1	0	25 (1)	4
2002/03	14 (4)	5	0	0	0 (1)	1	14 (5)	6
2003/04	22 (2)	5	0 (1)	0	1	0	23 (3)	5
2004/05	12 (13)	0	0	0	3	0	15(13)	0
Total	**106 (20)**	**14**	**2 (1)**	**1**	**7 (1)**	**1**	**115 (22)**	**16**

Watson, Thomas 'Gordon'

Much-loved figure who devoted his life to Everton

Although his Everton career spanned just 66 games spread over some 15 years, Gordon Watson is considered one of the club's great servants – over more than half a century – serving as player, trainer, administrator and even barman in one of the club's lounges.

Spotted in 1933, playing for Blyth Spartans, one of his native Northeast's most illustrious amateur clubs, Watson was blooded in the Central League and had to wait more than three years for his full Everton debut. He nevertheless made a stir for the reserves, and after Preston North End failed to sign him in November 1933, he looked set to join Coventry City a year later only for the move to fall down at the last moment.

Their loss was undeniably Everton's gain, and as the great side of the late 1930s gained momentum, Watson earned a deserved reputation as the club's twelfth man: unfussy, reliable, entirely committed whatever the role he was asked to fill. All of Everton's great teams have been underpinned by great utility men – whether it be Sandy Brown in the 1960s or Alan Harper in the 1980s – and Watson was of such ilk.

EVERTON 1960
Back row - **Watson (Trainer), Gabriel, Parker, Dunlop, Labone, Thomson, Harris**
Front - **Bingham, Wignall, Collins, Vernon, Temple**

His contribution to the great title-winning side of 1938/39 – when he played 16 games – should not be dismissed. He was twelfth man on so many occasions that his team-mates reputedly clubbed together to buy him a cushion so that he could be more comfortable on the trainer's bench when he missed out. But his role as Jock Thomson's deputy in the title run-in was crucial.

Watson would have walked into many First Division teams as a regular and being called upon as a reserve should not minimise his many footballing talents. He was once called up for the England B team, but Everton would not let him play as the fixture clashed with an end of season tour.

Aged 25 when the Second World War broke out, the conflict invariably took its toll on his Everton career and he would have made many more senior appearances had it not cast its shadow. Watson made more than 200 wartime appearances in an Everton shirt and was still with the club when peace came. In 1947/48 he made 22 league and cup appearances, the most in his career, and he appeared before Goodison's record crowd, against Liverpool in September 1948.

AS EARLY as 1945, Watson had sought a coaching position at Goodison and approached the Everton board with a request that he be considered should such a role arise. As his playing career petered out, he took up the role as trainer, a position he held until the 1960s. Subsequently he worked in the club offices, fulfilling a variety of roles.

He was a well-known and highly regarded figure, much loved by the fans. Never was this more keenly felt than when in 2001, shortly before his death, he paraded the FA Cup into one of the Gwladys Street Hall of Fame's legendary dinners. The roar that greeted him nearly carried the roof off the Adelphi and lives long in the minds of all who were there.

> HIS CONTRIBUTION TO THE GREAT TITLE-WINNING SIDE OF 1938/39 – WHEN HE PLAYED 16 GAMES – SHOULD NOT BE DISMISSED

Season	League		FA Cup		Total	
	App	Goals	App	Goals	App	Goals
1936/37	2	0	0	0	2	0
1937/38	9	1	0	0	9	1
1938/39	16	0	1	0	17	0
1946/47	12	0	0	0	12	0
1947/48	18	0	4	0	22	0
1948/49	4	0	0	0	4	0
Total	**61**	**1**	**5**	**0**	**66**	**1**

[FACTFILE]

BORN
Wolsingham, 1 March 1914
DIED
2001
POSITION
Wing half / utility man
HONOURS
League Championship 1938/39

Waugh, David

Inside forward who played in Everton's first ever league match

Season	League		FA Cup		Total	
	App	Goals	App	Goals	App	Goals
1888/89	7	2	-	-	7	2
Total	7	2	-	-	7	2

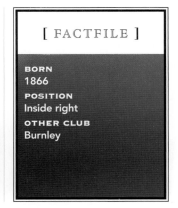

[FACTFILE]

BORN
1866
POSITION
Inside right
OTHER CLUB
Burnley

Weaver, Walter

Local winger who failed to break the stranglehold of Alec Troup on the Everton left

Season	League		FA Cup		Total	
	App	Goals	App	Goals	App	Goals
1924/25	9	2	0	0	9	2
1925/26	4	1	0	0	4	1
1926/27	5	0	0	0	5	0
Total	18	3	0	0	18	3

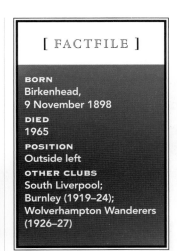

[FACTFILE]

BORN
Birkenhead,
9 November 1898
DIED
1965
POSITION
Outside left
OTHER CLUBS
South Liverpool;
Burnley (1919–24);
Wolverhampton Wanderers
(1926–27)

Webber, Keith

Early 1960s starlet who made a name for himself in the lower leagues

Season	League		FA Cup		League Cup		Total	
	App	Goals	App	Goals	App	Goals	App	Goals
1960/61	1	0	0	0	2	1	3	1
1961/62	3	0	0	0	-	-	3	0
Total	4	0	0	0	2	1	6	1

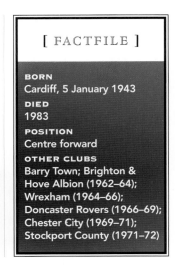

[FACTFILE]

BORN
Cardiff, 5 January 1943
DIED
1983
POSITION
Centre forward
OTHER CLUBS
Barry Town; Brighton &
Hove Albion (1962–64);
Wrexham (1964–66);
Doncaster Rovers (1966–69);
Chester City (1969–71);
Stockport County (1971–72)

Websites

Tracing two decades of Everton's online history

The origins of Toffeeweb.com, the earliest and most comprehensive Everton website, was Toffeeweb.org. Initially conceived in 1994 by a Finnish fan, Marko Poutianen, it combined up-to-the-minute Everton news and information with low-resolution graphics, affording it quick loading times – a bonus in the Internet's pre-broadband era. Michael Kenrick, an expatriate Evertonian based in Seattle, eventually took over site management.

Evertonia.com was conceived in the 1990s by a South African blue, Lyndon Lloyd, which combined comprehensive Everton news with slick layout and the adoption of new computer technologies, such as WAP. The two sites merged as Toffeeweb.com in March 2001 and continue to go from strength to strength, jointly edited by Kenrick and Lloyd, claiming 40,000 to 70,000 visitors to the site every day.

A plethora of other fine fan websites have also cropped up over the years. One of the most popular and irreverent is Bluekipper.com, which combines its own passionate and sometimes bizarre take on all things Everton with an unrelenting hatred of everything red and white. NSNO. co.uk was founded by Simon Paul in 2004 and is often the first source for breaking Everton news and gossip. The long-running fanzine, When Skies Are Grey entered the web as part of the rivals.com platform at the start of the century. Its messageboard, in particular, was bitingly funny, irreverent (or maybe that should be irrelevant – long-running debates included 'greatest crisp flavours' and whether the restaurant chain, Little Chef, ought to be boycotted by its members) and a source of unending fascination on all things Everton. In 2008 rivals.com pulled the plug on WSAG at short notice. A messageboard was set up by the fanzine's owners but later discontinued. Followtonians, established by Pete McPartland and Kansan Eric Howell in 2010, is one of the most popular club-specific podcasts and claims several thousand weekly listeners.

EVERTON itself were, by contrast, comparatively slow to develop a web presence, not launching Evertonfc.com until 1996. Combining news, interviews and a subscription-based internet TV channel, it is one of the leading club sites.

Perhaps surprisingly, given its strong fanzine heritage, Evertonians have been slow to adopt blogging. Several have disappeared soon after their creation. Arguably the best are Dixie's 60, edited by the expatriate Evertonian Edward Bottomley, and Executioner's Bong – a fascinating tactical deconstruction of the team.

Weifeng, Li

One of China's greatest players, his Everton career was limited to just two outings

Season	League		FA Cup		League Cup		Total	
	App	Goals	App	Goals	App	Goals	App	Goals
2002/03	1	0	0	0	1	0	2	0
Total	1	0	0	0	1	0	2	0

[FACTFILE]

BORN
Changchun, Jilin, China, 1 December 1978
POSITION
Centre back
OTHER CLUBS
Shenzen (1998–2002 & 2003–05);
Shanghai Shenhua (2006–08);
Wuhan Guanggu (2008);
Suwon Bluewings (2009–10);
Tianjin Teda (2011–)
HONOURS
114 China caps
(14 goals) (1998–)

Weir, David

Fine centre half who was a stalwart in Everton's early 21st -century renaissance

David Weir represented the finest bargain of Walter Smith's Everton reign – a time of frenetic transfer activity at Goodison.

A late starter who had studied in the US on a football scholarship, in 1992, aged 22, Weir finally embarked on a professional career with Falkirk. Weir came onto Walter Smith's radar while playing in Scotland and twice he tried to sign him for Rangers. But the deals fell through and in 1996 Weir joined Heart of Midlothian. He excelled at Tannadice, earning his first Scotland cap in 1997, and as his contract ran down towards the end of the decade began attracting the notice of English clubs keen to sign him on a Bosman free transfer.

IN FEBRUARY 1999, Smith stole a march on his rivals, which included Liverpool, paying Hearts – who risked losing Weir for nothing in the summer – £200,000 for the defender. Tall, slim, a fine header of the ball and a good reader of the game, Weir initially struggled to adapt to English football. Bafflingly, Smith initially played him at right back, wing back and even in midfield, positions to which he was patently unsuited. Never the fastest of players, nor possessing the technical attributes necessary in such positions, it was unsurprising that his form at the start of his Goodison career was faltering.

During the 1999/2000 season Weir was given more opportunities at centre half, his natural position, and began to prove his worth. A calm,

unflustered player, with Richard Gough alongside him he brought composure and experience to the Everton back line. When Gough was ruled out for most of the 2000/01 season through injury, Weir assumed the Everton captaincy and was one of the few bright points in another disappointing campaign.

With the arrival of David Moyes in March 2002, Weir became one of the foundation stones upon which Everton's renaissance was built. Now one of Goodison's senior professionals, over the next two years the captaincy rotated between himself, Kevin Campbell, Alan Stubbs and Duncan Ferguson. He was at his best when partnered by Joseph Yobo, his experience aiding the rookie's development, and the Nigerian's blistering pace compensating for Weir's lack of speed.

Weir started the 2004/05 season open that it would likely be his last for Everton and that he was playing to attract the notice of another club. But after injury to Joseph Yobo, he was recalled to the heart of the defence and was among the most consistent performers as Everton defied all expectations and finished fourth. His

outstanding form earned him at the age of 34 a recall for Scotland, now managed by Walter Smith. At the end of the season Weir signed a contract extension, and following Alan Stubbs' departure to Sunderland was named club captain.

Perhaps this was one season too many for the Scot. Although he continued to appear regularly through 2005/06, he was now in his mid-thirties and his waning pace became exploited by opponents. Although by no means wholly culpable for these reversals, Weir played in the 7-0 humiliation to Arsenal at the end of the 2004/05 season, the 5-1 hammering at Dinamo Bucharest and the 4-0 defeats to Bolton Wanderers and West Bromwich Albion in the first half of the following season. At other times his experience under pressure was excellent, and off the field he remained an outstanding and articulate ambassador for the club.

WEIR retained the Everton captaincy for the 2006/07 season, but with the arrival of Joleon Lescott chances were harder to come by. In January 2007, Walter Smith, who had returned to manage Rangers, signed him on a free transfer. There followed an Indian summer: for Rangers, he was instrumental in their reaching the final of the 2008 UEFA Cup; for Scotland he was a key component in their team that unexpectedly beat France in a 2007 European Championship qualifier.

Weir, who had once professed his ambition to play at 40, did just that, also continuing to turn out in the blue of Rangers until midway through his 42nd year. The Scot left amid the club's crippling financial problems in January 2012 and after spending a few weeks on a pay-as-you-play deal with Sheffield United returned to Everton as an academy coach. He displayed his supreme fitness on the day of his return, turning out for the reserve derby with Liverpool and playing his part in a 1-1 draw.

Season	League		FA Cup		League Cup		Europe		Total	
	App	Goals	App	Goals	App	Goals	App	Goals	App	Goals
1998/99	11 (3)	0	1	0	0	0	-	-	12 (3)	0
1999/2000	35	2	5	0	2	0	-	-	42	2
2000/01	37	1	1	0	1	0	-	-	39	1
2001/02	36	4	5	0	1	0	-	-	42	4
2002/03	27 (4)	1	1	0	2	0	-	-	30 (4)	1
2003/04	9 (1)	0	0	0	2	0	-	-	11 (1)	0
2004/05	34	1	0 (2)	0	1	0	-	-	35 (2)	1
2005/06	32 (1)	1	4	0	1	0	3 (1)	0	40 (2)	1
2006/07	2 (3)	0	0	0	1	0	-	-	3 (3)	0
Total	**223(12)**	**10**	**17 (2)**	**0**	**11**	**0**	**3 (1)**	**0**	**254(15)**	**10**

[FACTFILE]

BORN
Falkirk, 10 May 1970
POSITION
Centre half
OTHER CLUBS
Falkirk (1992–96);
Heart of Midlothian (1996–99);
Glasgow Rangers (2007–12);
Sheffield United (2012)
HONOURS
63 Scotland caps (1 goal) (1997–2010)

JAMES WEIR
EVERTON F.C.

Weir, James

Defender through Everton's first years of competitive football

Season	League		FA Cup		Total	
	App	Goals	App	Goals	App	Goals
1887/88	-	-	2	0	2	0
1888/89	16	0	-	-	16	0
Total	16	0	2	0	18	0

[FACTFILE]

BORN
1864
POSITION
Half back
OTHER CLUBS
Hibernian;
Third Lanark;
Sunderland Albion

Weldon, Tony

Inside left who partnered Dixie on his 60-goal romp

WELDON
MADE AN IMMEDIATE
IMPRESSION,
SCORING IN HIS FIRST
THREE MATCHES,

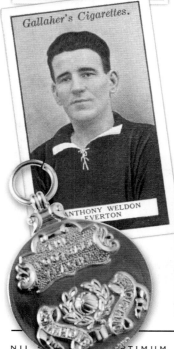

Gallaher's Cigarettes.

ANTHONY WELDON
EVERTON

Inside left Tony Weldon was one of an astonishing succession of highly talented forwards to emerge from the relative obscurity of Airdrieonians during the 1920s. During this era Broomfield Park witnessed the emergence of Scottish internationals Willy Russell and Hughie Gallagher, and saw the Scottish Cup come its way in 1924. Weldon, who was signed as Gallagher's replacement in December that year, immediately carried on the club's attacking tradition, soon attracting scouts from England.

Everton had an interest in the player from April 1926, but it took several failed bids and nearly a year before, in March 1927, he finally moved to Goodison for a fee of £3750. Everton were in the midst of a spending spree and his arrival followed those of players such as Warney Cresswell, Dick Forshaw, Jerry Kelly, Ted Critchley and Tommy White. These men would form the basis of Everton's success-laden immediate future.

WELDON made an immediate impression, scoring in his first three matches, including winners against Leeds United and Arsenal. But judgement remained reserved on the player. 'Weldon scored in all his matches so far, though his general play has not reached expectations,' bemoaned the Liverpool Post and Mercury.

'He did not do much in this game, but he got his usual goal and that covered a multitude of sins. Still there were many faults all round though the heavy state of the turf made accuracy a difficult proposition even to the skilled artist ... To attempt to dribble was courting disaster.'

EVERTON   DIVISION 1 CHAMPIONS 1928

Standing just 5ft 7in tall, Weldon, declared one newspaper profile, was a 'decidedly dangerous forward and shall do well with Everton'. His 'forte is his shot, his surprise shot with either foot is his best work' and he possessed the trickery to 'entrance the crowd'.

After narrowly avoiding relegation in 1927 the next season belonged to Everton and Dixie, who scored his unforgettable 60 goals as Everton lifted their third League title. Weldon played in all but four of Everton's games, scoring seven goals. Yet Everton were erratic and after plunging back into mediocrity he lost his place in autumn 1928 to George Martin and never regained it. After playing just three times in the 1929/30 relegation season he was sold to Hull City for £1000.

EVERTON 1928
Back - T.H.McKintosh, Kelly, Hart (Captain), Davies, O'Donnell, Virr, H.E.Cooke Front - Critchley, Martin, Dean, Cresswell, Weldon, Troup

[FACTFILE]

BORN
Croy, Scotland,
12 November 1900
POSITION
Inside left
OTHER CLUBS
Airdrieonians (1924–27);
Hull City (1930–31);
Lovells Athletic (1932–33);
Rochdale (1933–34);
Dundalk (1934);
Bangor (Northern Ireland,
1934–36)
HONOURS
League Championship
1927/28

Season	League		FA Cup		Other		Total	
	App	Goals	App	Goals	App	Goals	App	Goals
1926/27	9	3	0	0	-	-	9	3
1927/28	38	7	2	0	-	-	40	7
1928/29	20	3	1	0	1	0	22	3
1929/30	3	0	0	0	-	-	3	0
Total	70	13	3	0	1	0	74	13

Weller, Lewis

Journeyman defender who received unexpected international recognition

The high point of Lewis Weller's life in football came at Goodison Park, though not in the blue of Everton, with whom he spent his entire professional career. At the height of the First World War, in May 1916, the left half appeared for England in a wartime international. Twenty-two thousand supporters watched a thrilling encounter, with the home nation prevailing 4-3.

SIGNED FROM Leek United* in 1909 for £10 'with a promise of a further £10 if Weller did well for us', Weller was, in essence, a squad player throughout the entirety of his 15-year-long Everton career. He made his debut against Blackburn Rovers as a reserve for the injured Harry Makepeace in April 1910 and marked it with a rare goal. 'He had indulged in a passing bout with [James] Gourlay, and after Ashcroft had saved the latter's

effort, Weller pounced upon the ball, and netted with a fast rising shot, which struck the under part of the bar, leaving the custodian helpless,' reported the Liverpool Courier. The debutant, it added, was 'the pick' of the Everton backs and was subsequently described as a 'clever and resourceful defender'.

Yet there was no rapid ascent for Weller and although he was part of the team that lifted the 1914/15

League Championship, his contribution was not enough to earn a medal. His best season came in 1919/20, when he appeared in 28 league matches, mostly at left back. Although he remained on Everton's books until May 1924, when he was given a free transfer, he did not make a first-team appearance in either of his final two years at the club. In the 1930s he returned to Everton in a scouting capacity.

> HE MADE HIS DEBUT AGAINST BLACKBURN ROVERS AS A RESERVE FOR THE INJURED HARRY MAKEPEACE IN APRIL 1910 AND MARKED IT WITH A RARE GOAL

Season	League		FA Cup		Total	
	App	Goals	App	Goals	App	Goals
1909/10	1	1	0	0	1	1
1910/11	5	0	0	0	5	0
1911/12	1	0	0	0	1	0
1912/13	0	0	0	0	0	0
1913/14	10	1	0	0	10	1
1914/15	6	0	0	0	6	0
1919/20	28	0	1	0	29	0
1920/21	9	0	4	0	13	0
1921/22	5	0	0	0	5	0
Total	**65**	**2**	**5**	**0**	**70**	**2**

[FACTFILE]

BORN
Stoke-on-Trent, 7 May 1887
DIED
1952
POSITION
Left half
OTHER CLUB
Leek United

* Some accounts erroneously claim Weller joined from Chesterfield, but Everton's minute books confirm that this is not the case.

Wessels, Stefan

Former Germany under-21 international who was reserve goalkeeper during the 2007/08 season

[FACTFILE]

BORN
Rahden, Germany, 28 February 1979
POSITION
Goalkeeper
OTHER CLUBS
Bayern Munich (1999–2003);
1FC Köln (2003–07);
VFL Osnabrück (2008–09);
FC Basel (2009–10);
Odense Boldklub (2011–)

Season	League		FA Cup		League Cup		Europe		Total	
	App	Goals	App	Goals	App	Goals	App	Goals	App	Goals
2007/08	2	0	1	0	2	0	2	0	7	0
Total	**2**	**0**	**1**	**0**	**2**	**0**	**2**	**0**	**7**	**0**

West, Gordon

Talented and charismatic goalkeeper who was Everton's last line during the sixties

Images of Gordon West in his 1960s heyday invariably show a great cat of a goalkeeper clawing the air in an attempt to keep the ball from crossing the line. Stopping shots was what he did, and West elevated goalkeeping into an art form. He never set out to be a spectacular goalkeeper and was scornful of those who liked to show off between the posts. But his combination of magnificent agility, relentless desire to guard the Everton goal and natural charisma meant he was one of the most eye-catching custodians of his era. He matched these attributes with great consistency. One of the most successful players in the club's history, with Neville Southall and Ted Sagar he ranks among the genuine greats to have worn the Everton goalkeeper's jersey.

Born in Darfield, South Yorkshire, West's was a meteoric rise. As a teenager he had been a Sunday league centre back, but when a friend was invited to Blackpool for a trial and asked to bring a friend along West said to say that he was a goalkeeper. Little did he know that this was the beginning of a career as goalkeeper which would eventually see him challenge Gordon Banks, the greatest of them all, for his England jersey.

Blackpool signed him straight away and by 1960 he started to challenge their first-choice goalkeeper, Tony Waiters, for the green jersey. Waiters, like West, would represent Alf Ramsey's England. West played 33 times for Blackpool, but when Harry Catterick offered £27,500 – a record fee for a goalkeeper – to bring him to Goodison in March 1962, the bid was accepted.

Still aged only 18, West immediately replaced Albert Dunlop as Everton's first-choice goalkeeper. Brave, agile and strong, it was immediately apparent that West bore all the hallmarks of a great goalkeeper – something the club had not possessed since Ted Sagar's 1930s heyday. He was a supreme shot-stopper and commanded his penalty area with authority. West was also noted for his long throws, which he modelled on Manchester City's great German goalkeeper, Bert Trautmann. This provided the basis for numerous

Everton breakaway attacks. He was virtually ever-present through Everton's League Championship season in 1962/63.

The great football writer Brian Glanville once wrote a book called Goalkeepers are Different and there is much truth in his adage. In a sport in which its professionals are renowned for their blandness West – like Neville Southall after him – bucked this trend and was one of the game's great characters.

Despite his reputation as one of the best goalkeepers in the country, he was a player plagued by self-doubt and before games was wracked with nerves. He reputedly vomited before games because of the tension, but has since said that such suggestions were overplayed – he was in fact too nervous to even eat anything. 'I have gone home and cried after defeat,' he said. 'It was all immaturity I suppose.'

With the Kop, who dubbed him 'Mae West', he shared a lively relationship, defined by their presentation of a handbag to him before a game. 'I remember my first derby game and I didn't know about the rivalry between the two clubs,' he told the Evertonian in 2001. 'So I went down and stood in front of the Kop and they were all sticking two fingers up at me, poking and swearing – all aimed at me. I just couldn't believe anybody could be like that.

'The year after I thought I would sort the Liverpool fans out, so I started blowing them kisses and

> HE WAS VIRTUALLY EVER-PRESENT THROUGH EVERTON'S LEAGUE CHAMPIONSHIP SEASON IN 1962/63

showing them a bit of my bottom. I thought it was really funny. The following year, that's when I got the handbag. It ruined my life. You ask anybody in Liverpool about Gordon West and they will mention Sandy Brown's goal and the handbag – and I've played for England. It is unbelievable. All my life I have gone out and had a pint and I have had people asking, "Where's your handbag?"'

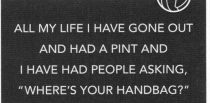

> ALL MY LIFE I HAVE GONE OUT
> AND HAD A PINT AND
> I HAVE HAD PEOPLE ASKING,
> "WHERE'S YOUR HANDBAG?"

His weight, particularly by the 1970s, was often a source for criticism. In Three Sides of the Mersey, Catterick's trainer, Stewart Imlach, recalled Fridays at the club when each player would be weighed, and if they were caught overweight would be sent back for an afternoon training session. 'Westy was always overweight,' he said, 'and he'd come into the room and take all the plasters off his leg. He had a little razor and he'd go into the medical room and shave his legs. There was a little table just by where they weighed, and Westy used to stand by this and he'd be pushing his hand on the table to take half a stone off!'

But West was no clown. He was a giant in a team of great players and was integral to the club's successes through its 'golden era'. 'Westy was an intelligent and acrobatic giant who commanded his defenders like Field Marshal Montgomery during the heat of the battle,' recalled Alex Young. 'He had soup bowls at the end of his wrists which he combined with near-flawless judgement to pluck the ball out of the air. The legendary Lev Yashin and Pat Jennings had similar anatomical extremities.'

There were, however, occasions when it was not just West who asked questions of his ability. Harry Catterick was ruthless, and dropped West on several occasions, sometimes at the merest hint of lost form. Twice during the 1963/64 season he was dropped in favour of Andy Rankin, who maintained his place in the Everton goal for the first half of the 1964/65 season. Injuries troubled West during the 1965/66 campaign, but he returned to win an FA Cup winners medal. For the remainder of the decade he was Everton's first-choice goalkeeper.

IN 1968 West made his England debut, which he described as the pinnacle of his career. Only the excellence of Gordon Banks restricted him to three caps, although more may have been forthcoming had he taken up the chance to travel to the 1970 World Cup Finals in Mexico. Perhaps the course of football history would have been radically different had he done so. Banks was struck down with food poisoning on the eve of England's quarter-final with West Germany and was replaced with Chelsea's Peter Bonetti – included in the squad because of West's withdrawal. But the move was a disaster – Bonetti was at fault as England let slip a two-goal lead and lost 3-2.

West lost his place to Rankin early in the ill-fated 1970/71 season, but returned to be ever-present through the 1971/72 season, putting in one of his most consistent seasons. It was surprising then when Catterick broke the transfer record for a goalkeeper a second time in the summer of 1972, when he bought Huddersfield's David Lawson for £80,000. West was stunned by his arrival, later claiming he'd never even heard of Lawson before Everton signed him. Still only aged 29, he persevered, but when Billy Bingham became manager a year later there was no way back.

He dropped out of the game, working as a sales representative for a bakery, before returning in the mid-1970s with Tranmere Rovers, where he combined goalkeeping back-up with coaching duties. In the early 1980s West dropped out of football, working as a security guard at Woodvale air base. Still based in Merseyside during his retirement, he remained a regular visitor to Goodison and a much-loved figure among fans until his death in June 2012.

> **[FACTFILE]**
>
> **BORN**
> Darfield, 24 April 1943
> **DIED**
> Liverpool, June 10 2012
> **POSITION**
> Goalkeeper
> **OTHER CLUBS**
> Blackpool (1958–62);
> Tranmere Rovers (1976–81)
> **HONOURS**
> League Championship
> 1962/63, 1969/70;
> FA Cup 1966;
> 3 England caps (1968–69)

Season	League App	League Goals	FA Cup App	FA Cup Goals	League Cup App	League Cup Goals	Other App	Other Goals	Total App	Total Goals
1961/62	12	0	0	0	-	-	-	-	12	0
1962/63	38	0	3	0	-	-	2	0	43	0
1963/64	22	0	3	0	-	-	3	0	28	0
1964/65	20	0	4	0	-	-	2	0	26	0
1965/66	24	0	8	0	-	-	2	0	34	0
1966/67	36	0	5	0	-	-	5	0	46	0
1967/68	41	0	6	0	2	0	-	-	49	0
1968/69	42	0	5	0	4	0	-	-	51	0
1969/70	42	0	1	0	4	0	-	-	47	0
1970/71	12	0	1	0	0	0	2	0	15	0
1971/72	42	0	4	0	1	0	-	-	47	0
1972/73	4	0	0	0	0	0	-	-	4	0
Total	**335**	**0**	**40**	**0**	**11**	**0**	**16**	**0**	**402**	**0**

Westerveld, Sander

Former Liverpool goalkeeper who joined on a short-term loan deal

	League		FA Cup		League Cup		Other		Total	
Season	App	Goals	App	Goals	App	Goals	App	Goals	App	Goals
2005/06	2	0	0	0	0	0	0	0	0	0
Total	2	0	0	0	0	0	0	0	0	0

White, Tommy

Utility man whose versatility was crucial to Everton's 1930s successes

When Tommy White arrived at Goodison as a teenager from Southport in February 1927 the Everton board were in the midst of a flurry of transfer activity that would not only save the club from the ignominy of relegation that year, but would lay the basis of a team that would win an unparalleled haul of trophies over the subsequent six years. Twice during this time the League Championship would reside at Goodison, as would the Second Division title and the FA Cup. White would be in the thick of most of this action.

EVERTON F.C.

EVERTON 1932
*Back row - **Cooke (Trainer), White, Britton, Sagar, Thomson, Cresswell, Cook***
*Front - **Critchley, Geldard, Dunn, Dean, Johnson, Stein***

SIGNED AS a centre forward, White would fill a number of roles – centre half, inside forward, right half – for Everton over the subsequent decade with distinction. With Sandy Brown and Alan Harper he can be considered among the club's great utility men, an underappreciated breed of player that has always been fundamental to Everton's success.

His debut came as centre forward in the 1927/28 campaign, a season defined by Dixie Dean's astonishing haul of 60 goals. Yet Everton were no one-trick ponies and with Dean absent and White in his place Everton recorded their biggest win of the season, a 7-0 hammering of West Ham in which White scored twice. 'The game was developed on the flanks, so that not so much depended upon White the ex-Southport player, as distributor and leader,' reported the Daily Courier. 'The young centre is coming along nicely in this class of football, and his goal each half should be a message of confidence for the future.'

WHITE made no further appearances that season but plenty more opportunities were to

TOMMY WHITE
EVERTON F.C.

come his way over the following two years as the club was rocked by injuries to many of its key players. Through 1928/29 he was called up in place of Jerry Kelly at right half, Albert Virr at left half and Dean at centre forward. He also partnered Dean in place of George Martin and Jimmy Dunn, Everton's regular inside forwards. Everton finished 18th.

At the start of the 1929/30 season White re-emerged as Everton's centre half. Never the tallest of players, he was nevertheless hard and uncompromising. 'He had no pretentions to cleverness, but he adopted the line of least resistance every time, and did not stand on

ceremony,' reported one newspaper. Yet Everton's form was disastrous: just two wins from their first 11 matches. Tom Griffiths replaced him in the heart of defence and White pushed up to more advanced roles, but on occasion also reverted to the half back role. A record run of six straight defeats in March 1930 saw Everton fall to the bottom of the division. Worse still, Dean was injured. White returned to his favoured centre forward berth and scored seven goals in the final five games of the season, including a hat-trick in the last match against Sunderland. But there were no celebrations afterwards: Everton were relegated.

Amends were made in the 1930/31 season, which ended with Everton Second Division Champions and a record haul of 121 league goals. But for injury White would have taken a more active role in this goal gluttony: he had managed nine in the first seven games as inside forward before injury struck. A year later he won his second medal – the League Championship – after scoring 18 goals from 23 games

as inside forward. But his third success – the 1933 FA Cup – came at centre half, as did his solitary England cap, a month later against Italy in Rome.

White continued to serve Everton in a number of roles, mostly defensive, until the 1936/37 season, when he played just a single game. At the end of that season he was transfer-listed for just £50 and joined Northampton

Town, a year later returning to Merseyside with New Brighton. He later worked at Liverpool Docks and was killed in a dockside accident in 1967.

[FACTFILE]

BORN
Pendleton, 29 July 1908
DIED
Liverpool, 13 August 1967
POSITION
Centre back / centre forward / inside forward
OTHER CLUBS
Southport (1925–27); Northampton Town (1937–38); New Brighton (1938–39)
HONOURS
Second Division Championship 1930/31, League Championship 1931/32, FA Cup 1933; 1 England cap (1933)

Season	League		FA Cup		Other		Total	
	App	Goals	App	Goals	App	Goals	App	Goals
1927/28	1	2	0	0	-	-	1	2
1928/29	21	6	0	0	-	-	21	6
1929/30	35	11	0	0	-	-	35	11
1930/31	10	10	0	0	-	-	10	10
1931/32	23	18	1	0	-	-	24	18
1932/33	34	2	6	0	1	0	41	2
1933/34	28	14	1	0	1	0	30	14
1934/35	5	0	0	0	-	-	5	0
1935/36	35	3	1	0	-	-	36	3
1936/37	1	0	0	0	-	-	1	0
Total	**193**	**66**	**9**	**0**	**2**	**0**	**204**	**66**

White, Walter 'Wattie'

Versatile Scottish international who filled a variety of positions

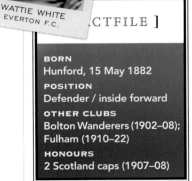

WATTIE WHITE
EVERTON F.C.

[FACTFILE]

BORN
Hunford, 15 May 1882
POSITION
Defender / inside forward
OTHER CLUBS
Bolton Wanderers (1902–08); Fulham (1910–22)
HONOURS
2 Scotland caps (1907–08)

Season	League		FA Cup		Total	
	App	Goals	App	Goals	App	Goals
1908/09	18	3	2	1	20	4
1909/10	23	6	7	2	30	8
1910/11	2	1	0	0	2	1
Total	**43**	**10**	**9**	**3**	**52**	**13**

Whitehead, John

Goalkeeper who turned out for a trio of Merseyside clubs

[FACTFILE]

BORN
1871
POSITION
Goalkeeper
OTHER CLUBS
Bootle (1892); Liverpool (1894–95)

Season	League		FA Cup		Total	
	App	Goals	App	Goals	App	Goals
1893/94	2	0	0	0	2	0
Total	**2**	**0**	**0**	**0**	**2**	**0**

Whiteside, Norman

Irish firebrand whose career was prematurely wrecked by injury

Until the ascent of Manchester United's 1990s golden generation, Norman Whiteside was the player who came closest to living up to the lofty tag of being the 'new' George Best. Whiteside was every bit the teenage prodigy, in 1982 becoming the youngest player to appear in a World Cup Finals. A year later he became the youngest player to score in an FA Cup Final, scoring the second in United's 4-0 replay victory over Brighton. It was a feat he infamously repeated against Everton two years later to deny an historic treble. 'I scored a very good goal but the thing that made it more important for me was that I scored against the best keeper in the world at that time – which was Neville,' he would recall.

TALL, hard and powerful, Whiteside was among the most outstanding and prolific attacking midfielders of his generation. At Old Trafford, however, Whiteside fell foul of Alex Ferguson, who sought to end the booze culture he felt was undermining United's pursuit of success. Along with Paul McGrath and Bryan Robson, Whiteside was deemed one of the instigators of United's infamous 'drinking club' and in the summer of 1989 Ferguson broke this up, selling McGrath to Aston Villa and Whiteside to Everton for £600,000.

Barely past his 24th birthday on his arrival at Goodison, Whiteside already seemed something of a veteran. But his contribution during the 1989/90 season, playing behind the Everton forward pairing, was replete with the effervescence and energy once shown as a teenager. A regular on the score sheet, his guile and aggression were integral to a side that was showing some signs of renaissance under Colin Harvey's management.

ALAS, knee injuries had always plagued Whiteside and he was forced to undergo surgery at the end of the 1989/90 season. His recovery was stuttering and he made just one further start for Everton, in a dismal 2-1 defeat by Wimbledon watched by just 6000 spectators. It was a sad end to what should have been a glittering career.

Speaking to Evertonfc.com in 2008, Whiteside said that it was the memory of the Goodison crowd that remained most vivid. 'I remember the Gwladys Street took to me unbelievably. What I can say about both sets of fans – Everton and United – is that they're working-class people, and they took to a working-class guy like me. When I was down at Everton it was just like being at home in Belfast. The kettle was always on the boil, with people asking, "Do you want a cup of tea?" It was so friendly.'

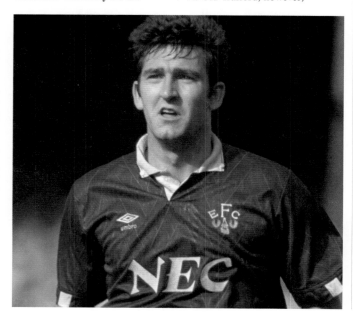

[FACTFILE]

BORN
Belfast, 7 June 1965
POSITION
Midfield
OTHER CLUB
Manchester United (1981–89)
HONOURS
38 Northern Ireland caps (9 goals) (1982–89)

Season	League		FA Cup		Other		Total	
	App	Goals	App	Goals	App	Goals	App	Goals
1989/90	26 (1)	9	6	3	2	1	34 (1)	13
1990/91	1 (1)	0	0	0	0	0	1 (1)	0
Total	27 (2)	9	6	3	2	1	35 (2)	13

Whitley, Jack

Reserve goalkeeper who went on to serve as Chelsea's custodian

Season	League		FA Cup		Total	
	App	Goals	App	Goals	App	Goals
1902/03	8	0	3	0	11	0
1903/04	3	0	0	0	3	0
Total	11	0	3	0	14	0

[FACTFILE]

BORN
Seacombe, 1 April 1880
POSITION
Goalkeeper
OTHER CLUBS
Liscard YMCA;
Darwen (1898);
Aston Villa (1900–01);
Stoke City (1904–05);
Leeds City (1905–06);
Lincoln City (1906);
Chelsea (1907–13)

Whittle, Alan

Prodigy whose goals fired Everton to their 1970 League Championship success

Often the key to league title success is as much the timely addition of fresh blood as it is the pedigree of the team that started the season. In 1962/63 the mid-season signings of Tony Kay and Alex Scott added fresh impetus to Everton's successful title challenge. Twenty-four years later Howard Kendall added Wayne Clarke to the Everton squad as they neared their ninth league title, and his goals ultimately did much to push Everton over the finishing line.

But the most dramatic intervention to an Everton season came with the call-up of Alan Whittle from the reserves in December 1969. Hitherto a highly rated but virtually untested teenage striker, the 'blond bomber' deputised for the injured Jimmy Husband and breathed new life into Everton's ultimately successful assault on the league title. By the season's end he had claimed 11 goals from just 15 starts as Everton lifted their seventh championship with a record points haul.

Born and bred in Merseyside, in signing as an Everton youth player Whittle rejected the advances of a succession of their Northwest rivals. On first witnessing Whittle's accession to Everton's first team Manchester United's chief scout, Joe Armstrong, admitted: 'I wish we'd got him. [He is] a great prospect. I'd have felt like putting my head in a gas oven if he'd been Manchester-born and gone to Everton.'

His Everton debut came in March 1968, a week past his 18th birthday. He made a handful of appearances during the closing weeks of the 1967/68 season and again over

the course of the following campaign. But with more senior colleagues playing so well, Evertonians wondered whether the promising youngster would make the breakthrough or simply fall by the wayside like so many gifted Everton youngsters of this era.

Whittle's big chance came in December 1969 when injury struck Jimmy Husband and he was recalled for the Goodison derby. Everton were beaten 3-0 but Whittle did enough to keep his place for the following week's fixture at West Ham. Having to play on a quagmire of a pitch, the game was heading for a stalemate until a poor back pass by Bobby Moore was intercepted by Whittle. He sped 50 yards down the pitch, evading challenges by the West Ham full back Alan Stephenson and Moore, before hitting the ball into the back of the Hammers' net. It was the game's only goal and the Liverpool Echo reported: 'All credit to Whittle for the chance was brilliantly taken.'

THAT WINNING goal, wrote historian George Orr in his chronicle of the era, 'was to start a fire in him that not many defenders were able to put out in the following months'. Likened to

Denis Law, Whittle was an effervescent, quick-footed forward, who thrived when running at his opponents with the ball at his feet. Zestful, enthusiastic and possessing deceptive strength, he was a fine and, in these early stages of his career, prolific finisher. His 11 goals were to directly lead to 11 of Everton's final tally of 66 points that season. But his strikes were to have a more fundamental impact, instilling confidence at crucial stages in the season. Six goals from six games in March and April 1970 effectively sealed the title for Everton.

WHITTLE retained his place for the first half of the 1970/71 season, but his form suffered as Everton were beset by baffling inconsistency. The following campaign he started 18 league games – often asked to play in midfield – but failed to score once. After barely featuring in the opening stages of the 1972/73 season, he was sold to Crystal Palace in December 1972 for £100,000 on the same day that Harry Catterick paid Aberdeen £180,000 for his replacement, Joe Harper.

Whittle became a firm favourite at Selhurst Park without hitting the same heights he had once scaled at Goodison. Palace were relegated from the First Division at the end of the 1972/73 season and from the Second Division a year later. In 1976 he joined Orient and a year later made a lucrative move to Iran, where he became the first Briton to play. Forced to flee the country after the Iranian Revolution, Whittle played out his career with Bournemouth – a disappointing conclusion to a career that once seemed replete with promise.

Season	League		FA Cup		League Cup		Europe		Total	
	App	Goals	App	Goals	App	Goals	App	Goals	App	Goals
1967/68	6	0	0	0	0	0	-	-	6	0
1968/69	4	0	0	0	1	2	-	-	5	2
1969/70	15	11	1	0	2	0	-	-	18	11
1970/71	24	7	2	1	-	-	5 (1)	2	31 (1)	10
1971/72	18 (1)	0	4	2	1	0	-	-	23 (1)	2
1972/73	5 (1)	3	0	0	0	0	-	-	5 (1)	3
Total	**72 (2)**	**21**	**7**	**3**	**4**	**2**	**5 (1)**	**2**	**88 (3)**	**28**

[FACTFILE]

BORN
Liverpool, 10 March 1950
POSITION
Forward
OTHER CLUBS
Crystal Palace (1972–76);
Orient (1976–77);
Persepolis (Iran, 1977–78);
Bournemouth (1980–81)
HONOURS
League Championship 1969/70

Wignall, Frank

Underrated centre forward who hit his stride beyond Goodison

THE GOALS SEEMED TO COME EASILY: 15 FROM 19 LEAGUE AND CUP GAMES

There must have been times in Frank Wignall's career when he wondered what else he need do to earn the recognition his goals surely merited. After scoring on his Everton debut in September 1959, the centre forward bettered a goal every two games over the next four years – but the chances handed to him were sporadic at best. In November 1964, now no longer an Everton player, he made his England debut against Wales at Wembley and scored both goals in a 2-1 win. A glittering international career surely beckoned, but Wignall played just once more for his country, against the Netherlands a month later, and was never picked again.

IT SEEMED a harsh outcome for a talented footballer who enjoyed a productive First Division career elsewhere. A brave, strong player, Wignall, a Lancastrian who grew up modelling himself on Nat Lofthouse, was very much the archetypal English target man. Never the most naturally graceful player, he was nevertheless powerful, energetic and a handful for any defender. He possessed a fearsome shot and the goals seemed to come easily: 15 goals from 19 league and cup games in 1960/61 and five from 11 league games the following year.

But with the arrival of Harry Catterick, Wignall's chances became more limited as he struggled to break the stranglehold of Alex Young and Roy Vernon on the Everton forward line. After making just a solitary appearance during the 1962/63 League Championship winning season, Wignall sought fresh challenges and joined Nottingham Forest for £20,000, where he was reunited with Johnny Carey. An England call-up came a year later, and in 1966/67 his goals brought Forest within touching distance of the League Championship. There was talk of a Goodison return, but it never came and there followed a year at Wolves. Wignall later joined Brian Clough's Derby County, before playing out his career with Mansfield and as player-manager of King's Lynn.

[FACTFILE]

BORN
Chorley, 21 August 1939
POSITION
Centre forward
OTHER CLUBS
Nottingham Forest (1963–68);
Wolverhampton Wanderers (1968–69);
Derby County (1969–71);
Mansfield Town (1971–73)
HONOURS
2 England caps (2 goals) (1964)

Season	League		FA Cup		League Cup		Other		Total	
	App	Goals	App	Goals	App	Goals	App	Goals	App	Goals
1959/60	6	1	1	0	-	-	-	-	7	1
1960/61	15	8	1	0	3	7	-	-	19	15
1961/62	11	5	0	0	-	-	-	-	11	5
1962/63	1	1	0	0	-	-	0	0	1	1
Total	**33**	**15**	**2**	**0**	**3**	**7**	**0**	**0**	**38**	**22**

Wildman, William

Reserve full back who was limited to just two Everton appearances

Season	League		FA Cup		Total	
	App	Goals	App	Goals	App	Goals
1904/05	1	0	0	0	1	0
1905/06	1	0	0	0	1	0
Total	**2**	**0**	**0**	**0**	**2**	**0**

[FACTFILE]

BORN
Liverpool, 1883
POSITION
Full back
OTHER CLUB
West Ham United

Wilkinson, Jonathan Montague 'Monty'

Reserve outside right who made cameos in Everton's early 1930s relegation and promotion seasons

J. M. WILKINSON
EVERTON F.C.

[FACTFILE]

BORN
Esh Winning, Co. Durham,
20 July 1908
DIED
1979
POSITION
Outside right
OTHER CLUBS
Durham City (1925);
Crook Town;
Newcastle United (1927–28);
Blackpool (1931–32);
Charlton Athletic (1932–39)

Season	League		FA Cup		Total	
	App	Goals	App	Goals	App	Goals
1929/30	6	0	0	0	6	0
1930/31	5	2	1	0	6	2
Total	**11**	**2**	**1**	**0**	**12**	**2**

Wilkinson, Paul

Young centre forward whose Goodison grounding provided a solid career

It was a last-gasp goal from Grimsby Town's Paul Wilkinson in November 1984 that unexpectedly sent Everton crashing out of the League Cup. In doing so he not only dealt a rare blemish on Everton's otherwise impeccable record for the 1984/85 season, but alerted Howard Kendall to his burgeoning talent. Four months later the Everton manager paid £250,000 for the strapping 20-year-old centre forward.

Acquired as an understudy to Graeme Sharp and Andy Gray, Wilkinson soon made his mark in a royal blue shirt. Included for the final four games of the 1984/85 season, with the league already won and most minds focused on forthcoming cup finals, Wilkinson struck his first goals for the club, including the only goal of the Goodison derby.

Chances were hard to come by through the 1985/86 campaign, but Wilkinson played enough games the following season to win a league title medal. He scored freely in the League Cup, but it was never enough to threaten Graeme Sharp's place in the team. Before the campaign was over, Kendall sold Wilkinson to Nottingham Forest for £200,000, using the fee as down payment for the signing of Wayne Clarke.

Having failed to make a significant breakthrough at the City Ground, in 1988 Wilkinson joined Watford. In 1991 he joined Middlesbrough, where he remained until 1996, and his goals twice helped earn his team promotion. There followed something of an itinerant trail through the lower leagues and after finishing up with Northampton Town he turned to coaching.

[FACTFILE]

BORN
30 October 1964
POSITION
Centre forward
OTHER CLUBS
Grimsby Town (1982–85);
Nottingham Forest (1987–88);
Watford (1988–91);
Middlesbrough (1991–96);
Oldham Athletic (loan, 1995);
Watford (loan, 1995);
Luton Town (loan, 1996);
Barnsley (1996–97);
Millwall (1997–98);
Northampton Town (1998–2000)
HONOURS
League Championship 1986/87

Season	League		FA Cup		League Cup		Other		Total	
	App	Goals	App	Goals	App	Goals	App	Goals	App	Goals
1984/85	4 (1)	2	0	0	0	0	0	0	4 (1)	2
1985/86	3 (1)	1	1	0	0	0	3 (1)	0	7 (2)	1
1986/87	12(10)	3	2	1	3 (1)	7	3 (1)	1	20 (12)	12
Total	**19 (12)**	**6**	**3**	**1**	**3 (1)**	**7**	**6 (2)**	**1**	**31(15)**	**15**

Williams, Ben

Former coalminer and Welsh international who captained Everton to the Second Division Championship

Strapping right back Ben Williams rose from the South Wales coalpits to captain Everton to Second Division Championship success and give Goodison his best years as a footballer. In his thirties during his Goodison pomp, Williams also lifted the 1930/31 League Championship and captained Wales.

Williams was a late developer, not playing league football until his mid-twenties, when he rejected the advances of Cardiff City to sign for Swansea Town and left work down the Glamorganshire coal-belt pits. Tall and slim, he had a reputation for 'tackling stoutly and heading accurately', and his performances in the white of Swansea saw him elevated to the Welsh national team and represent the Welsh League XI on two occasions.

> 'WE HAVE ALWAYS PLAYED A GOOD, CLEAN, AND STYLISH TYPE OF FOOTBALL'

The Vetch Field was, however, no fit stage for a player of such talent. When Everton found themselves in a defensive crisis midway through the 1929/30 season they turned to Williams, paying £4300 for his services after he had been recommended by Jack Sharp. Only three weeks before his arrival Everton had somehow contrived to lose 5-4 at home to Leicester City. It was hoped that Williams could shore up such a leaky rearguard.

In the short term such hopes were elusive. Everton's form through the rest of the campaign was disastrous and they were relegated. 'Everton's plunge into the Second Division will give a fillip to that part of the League, for there is no doubt that the name of the Goodison Park club still enjoys a great reputation for the purely scientific game,' wrote John Peel in the Liverpool Post and Mercury, somehow trying to seek a silver lining from the disaster. 'Whether the style of play will have to be changed to suit the new conditions remains to be seen, but I am sure the team will receive a rousing welcome wherever they go to.'

Although the play was largely unmodified, one thing the directors did do was make Williams captain, believing his knowledge of the Second Division would stand him in good stead. It was a fine move indeed, Everton racing to the title with five games to spare and a record 121 goals scored along the way. They also reached the FA Cup semi-final and were unlucky to fall 0-1 to West Bromwich Albion.

'We have won because we have always played a good, clean, and stylish type of football,' said Williams on being presented the Second Division Championship trophy. 'We are determined to regain First Division status, at the first time of trying. We have been pitted against splendid teams, and the co-operations between the players and the management has proved a deciding factor. The team spirit has been wonderful. Our big disappointment is that we are not going to Wembley on Saturday. I think our success has been largely due to the skilful and never say die tactics of the players.'

John McKenna, the former Everton committee man turned Liverpool chairman and Football League President, said: 'There were many Weary Willies, who predicted that Everton would remain in the Second Division a long time, but their performance has confounded those critics and justified the hopes of their more optimistic supporters.' He added that he saw 'no reason' why Everton should not win the First Division championship a year later. These were prophetic words indeed and, although Williams gave up the captaincy to Dean, he added a League Championship medal to his collection in April 1932.

Williams' form had been so good that he had supplanted Warney Cresswell – formerly the world's most expensive player – from the right back berth, who moved to left back in order to accommodate him. Indeed Williams was enjoying the finest football of his career, and is described in the Liverpool Echo as having the crowd cheer his every move in one encounter. 'Cresswell and Williams as a pair have no superior in First Division football,' reported the Liverpool Post and Mercury. 'Williams has the trace of "devil" necessary, and Cresswell the finesse –a grand combination in two backs.'

However, in December 1932 a knee injury cruelly struck the full back and the Everton board moved immediately, signing Celtic's Billy Cook to replace him. Out injured for more than a year, he returned in January 1934 with Cook switching to the left to accommodate him. But thereafter chances were limited and after making just three appearances in the 1935/36 season he was given a free transfer. He returned to South Wales and, by way of Newport County, to the coalmines where his working life had started.

Season	League		FA Cup		Other		Total	
	App	Goals	App	Goals	App	Goals	App	Goals
1929/30	9	0	2	0	-	-	11	0
1930/31	35	0	5	0	-	-	40	0
1931/32	33	0	1	0	-	-	34	0
1932/33	20	0	0	0	1	0	21	0
1933/34	18	0	0	0	0	0	18	0
1934/35	12	0	0	0	-	-	12	0
1935/36	3	0	0	0	-	-	3	0
Total	**130**	**0**	**8**	**0**	**1**	**0**	**139**	**0**

[FACTFILE]

BORN
Penrhiwceiber, Glamorgan, 29 October 1900
DIED
Bridgend, 5 January 1968
POSITION
Full back
OTHER CLUBS
Cardiff City (1923–25);
Swansea Town (1925–29);
Newport County (1936–38)
HONOURS
Second Division Championship 1930/31;
League Championship 1931/32;
10 Wales caps (1928–35)

Williams, Bill

Winger whose form twice earned him league representative honours

[FACTFILE]

BORN
1874
POSITION
Outside right
OTHER CLUBS
Blackburn Rovers (1898–99);
Bristol Rovers;
Newton Heath (1901)

Season	League		FA Cup		Total	
	App	Goals	App	Goals	App	Goals
1894/95	5	1	0	0	5	1
1895/96	8	1	0	0	8	1
1896/97	1	0	0	0	1	0
1897/98	9	2	1	1	10	3
Total	23	4	1	1	24	5

Williams, Billy

BILLY WILLIAMS
EVERTON F.C.

Talented inside forward whose life ended before he saw his thirtieth birthday

[FACTFILE]

BORN
16 November 1898
DIED
1926
POSITION
Inside left
OTHER CLUBS
Darwen;
Blackpool (1924–25)

Season	League		FA Cup		Total	
	App	Goals	App	Goals	App	Goals
1922/23	28	13	2	0	30	13
1923/24	2	0	0	0	2	0
Total	30	13	2	0	32	13

Williams, Graham

Enigmatic Welsh winger, who earned international recognition beyond Goodison

Wales under-23 international winger Graham Williams was one of a succession of talented young players charged with the task of reviving Everton fortunes in the mid-1950s, but who ultimately found the challenge beyond him.

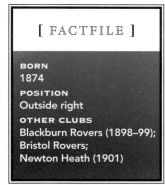

'HIS RETURN LATE IN THE IN 1956/57 SEASON BROUGHT GOALS AND GLIMPSES OF HIS POTENTIAL'

SIGNED from Bradford City in spring 1956, he immediately found himself struck down with serious injury that left him absent from first team action for almost a year. His return late in the in 1956/57 season brought goals and glimpses of his potential. 'Though capable of juggling tricks, he opted more often to knock the ball past his full-back and tear after it before aiming for his centre-forward's head or attempting a long-distance strike himself, finding the net from outside the box on several occasions,' wrote the football historian, Ivan Ponting.

Nevertheless his habit of over elaboration often frustrated the crowd and his fellow teammates too. Some grumbled subsequently that his self-confidence belied his actual ability. Above all though, injuries undermined his progress.

Although given a chance by Johnny Carey following his arrival as manager in 1958, Williams never had the confidence of the new boss and was sold to Swansea Town in 1959. Here he flourished and represented his country in the early-1960s, enjoying successful spells elsewhere in the lower leagues.

[FACTFILE]

BORN
Wrexham,
31 December 1936
POSITION
Winger
OTHER CLUBS
Bradford City (1955-56),
Swansea Town (1959-64),
Wrexham (1964-66),
Tranmere Rovers (1966-68),
Port Vale (1968-69)
HONOURS
5 Wales caps (1961-2)
(1 goal)

Season	League		FA Cup		Total	
	App	Goals	App	Goals	App	Goals
1955/56	2	0	0	0	2	0
1956/57	9	3	0	0	9	3
1957/58	13	2	0	0	13	2
1958/59	7	1	2	0	9	1
Total	31	6	2	0	33	6

Williams, Owen

Welsh defender limited to a couple of Everton appearances

[FACTFILE]

BORN
Holyhead, 2 October 1896
POSITION
Left half
OTHER CLUBS
South Liverpool;
Wigan Borough;
Holyhead

Season	League		FA Cup		Total	
	App	Goals	App	Goals	App	Goals
1919/20	2	0	0	0	2	0
Total	2	0	0	0	2	0

Williams, Richard

Goalkeeper who kept guard of the Everton nets through Goodison's first years

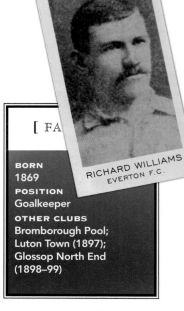

RICHARD WILLIAMS
EVERTON F.C.

[FA

BORN
1869
POSITION
Goalkeeper
OTHER CLUBS
Bromborough Pool;
Luton Town (1897);
Glossop North End
(1898–99)

Season	League		FA Cup		Total	
	App	Goals	App	Goals	App	Goals
1891/92	9	0	1	0	10	0
1892/93	11	0	7	0	18	0
1893/94	26	0	1	0	27	0
1894/95	12	0	3	0	15	0
Total	58	0	12	0	70	0

Williamson, Danny

Injury plagued midfielder whose Goodison career was cut short

After five years' largely unspectacular and injury-plagued service at West Ham, Danny Williamson was a surprise selection to revive an Everton midfield sorely lacking creativity. Williamson was part of a £3million part-exchange deal in August 1997 that valued David Unsworth at £2million. Heralded by Howard Kendall as a player who could sit in front of the back four or play a more creative role, Williamson laboured in a dire team, neither able to add defensive solidity nor attacking impetus.

Struck down by a serious foot injury shortly before Christmas 1997, there followed a lengthy and ultimately futile battle to save his career. In 2000, still aged only 26, he was forced to announce his retirement from the game.

[FACTFILE]

BORN
London, 5 December 1973
POSITION
Midfield
OTHER CLUBS
West Ham United
(1992–97);
Doncaster Rovers
(loan, 1993)

Season	League		FA Cup		League Cup		Total	
	App	Goals	App	Goals	App	Goals	App	Goals
1997/98	15	0	0	0	2	0	17	0
1998/99	0	0	0	0	0	0	0	0
1999/2000	0	0	0	0	0	0	0	0
Total	15	0	0	0	2	0	17	0

Wilson, Alan

Home-grown midfielder who later served Southport over two spells

Season	League		FA Cup		League Cup		Total	
	App	Goals	App	Goals	App	Goals	App	Goals
1971/72	1	0	0	0	0	0	1	0
1972/73	1	0	0	0	0	0	1	0
Total	2	0	0	0	0	0	2	0

[FACTFILE]

BORN
Dingle, 17 November 1952
POSITION
Midfielder
OTHER CLUBS
Southport (1975–78);
Torquay United (1978–79);
Southport

Wilson, David

Scottish defender who provided cover through the 1906/07 season

Season	League		FA Cup		Total	
	App	Goals	App	Goals	App	Goals
1906/07	5	0	0	0	5	0
Total	5	0	0	0	5	0

[FACTFILE]

BORN
Lochgelly, 1883
POSITION
Defender
OTHER CLUBS
Lochgelly Rangers;
Buckhaven United;
Gainsborough Trinity (1901);
Cowdenbeath;
East Fife;
Heart of Midlothian;
Portsmouth

Wilson, George

Maverick forward, controversially omitted from the 1907 FA Cup Final

Season	League		FA Cup		Total	
	App	Goals	App	Goals	App	Goals
1906/07	28	3	6	1	34	4
Total	28	3	6	1	34	4

[FACTFILE]

BORN
Lochgelly 1884
POSITION
Outside left / inside left
OTHER CLUBS
Thomson Rovers; Lochgelly
Rangers; Buckhaven United;
Cowdenbeath; Heart of
Midlothian; Distillery;
Newcastle United (1907–14);
Raith Rovers; East Fife;
Albion Rovers; St Andrew's
(Vancouver, Canada)
HONOURS
6 Scotland caps (1904–09)

Wilson, Ian

Underwhelming understudy to Kevin Sheedy

In September 1987, Colin Harvey paid Leicester City £300,000 to make Ian Wilson his first senior signing since his appointment as Everton manager. The left-sided midfielder was a current Scotland international and was intended as cover for Kevin Sheedy, who was the victim of persistent injuries.

A competent yet unspectacular player, he slotted into a great Everton team without ever looking as if he might distinguish himself. 'Although he was neat and tidy, it was felt that he couldn't hold a candle to Sheeds,' recalled Graeme Sharp. 'I thought we could perhaps have set our standards higher and that Everton players should have been more than "neat and tidy".'

IN FAIRNESS to the prematurely balding Aberdonian, Wilson, in common with many Everton signings during this period, faced a thankless task in having to deputise for a member of its most illustrious team. He made 36 appearances over two seasons, without ever looking like making a regular first-team berth his own. In summer 1989, aged 31, he joined Besiktas, later returning to England to play out his career in the lower leagues.

> **[FACTFILE]**
>
> **BORN**
> Aberdeen, 27 March 1958
> **POSITION**
> Midfield
> **OTHER CLUBS**
> Leicester City (1979–87);
> Besiktas (1989–91);
> Derby County (1991);
> Bury (1991–92);
> Wigan Athletic (1992–93)
> **HONOURS**
> 5 Scotland caps (1987)

Wilson, Ramon 'Ray'

World Cup winning left back, he belongs among the Everton greats

Even half a century later, it seems extraordinary that a player widely considered the best in his position in the world should be consigned to spend the majority of his career in the Second Division. But in an era when player power was still a concept footballers and their clubs were coming to terms with, that is precisely the fate suffered by Ray Wilson. Only when he was in his 30th year did he make the leap from Second Division Huddersfield to Everton, the top flight and the level his talents demanded. But despite this delayed ascent, the mark Wilson left on Evertonians' memories and Goodison history remains indelible.

Born in Derbyshire, Huddersfield Town took Wilson on as a schoolboy inside forward in the early 1950s. By his 21st birthday Wilson had still not appeared in the first team and his career appeared to be petering out when Alan Beattie, the Huddersfield manager, converted him to wing half and then full back. Wilson made his debut in April 1956, in a 3-0 defeat by Manchester United's Busby Babes, and played in the subsequent five games, all defeats, as Huddersfield were relegated to Division Two.

Season	League		FA Cup		League Cup		Europe		Total	
	App	Goals	App	Goals	App	Goals	App	Goals	App	Goals
1987/88	13 (3)	0	3	0	4	1	0 (1)	0	20 (4)	1
1988/89	11 (7)	1	0 (2)	0	5	0	1 (1)	0	17(10)	1
Total	**24(10)**	**1**	**3 (2)**	**0**	**9**	**1**	**1 (2)**	**0**	**37(14)**	**2**

He remained at this level until Everton signed him eight years later, nurtured by Beattie then Bill Shankly, who managed the Terriers between 1956 and 1959, until he became the most outstanding full back in the Football League. In 1960 he won the first of 63 England caps when he was selected to play Scotland, and Wilson would collect a third of all his international appearances while playing outside the top flight. He was included in the England squad that travelled to the 1962 World Cup Finals in Chile.

Although footballers had come to enjoy many new freedoms since the start of the 1960s, with the maximum wage and 'retain and transfer' scrapped after a long-running campaign by the PFA, clubs were still in a powerful position when it came to deciding the destiny of their players. Huddersfield, still mired in Second Division mediocrity, resisted repeated attempts from bigger clubs to lure Wilson away. Harry Catterick, who had once tried to sign Wilson for Sheffield Wednesday, was nothing if not persistent, and in July 1964 finally got his man, when he paid £35,000, plus Mick Meagan, for the England star.

And yet, after much anticipation, Wilson's Everton career got off to the worst possible start. On his home debut, against Nottingham Forest, he sustained a hip injury that kept him out for four months, limiting him to just 21 first-team outings in his first season at the club. Despite such injury problems, the class which had attracted Catterick was immediately evident.

WILSON possessed the change of pace more commonly found in attacking players. It enabled him to stick, glue-like, to opposing wingers and with equal proficiency he could either jockey them out of possession or dispossess them with the crispest of tackles. He had a strong tactical awareness and was blessed with precise and imaginative distribution, never playing a team-mate into trouble nor making an ungainly hoof into the back of the stands. 'Superlatives are applied too freely in football, but Ray was unquestionably world class and remains the finest left back that the British game has ever produced,' Alex Young recalled. 'He accelerated like an E-type Jag and no one could outpace him over short distances. He also used his foot speed to great effect in the opponent's half and was always a threat when overlapping. Then there was his sublime ball control. Ray was always available and had the skills to get his team-mates out of trouble.'

WILSON thrived on big occasions. 'He was one of the most resolute defenders I ever played with or against,' recalled Bobby Charlton. 'He was the kind of player you always knew would grow with pressure.' 1966 was to be Wilson's annus mirabilis, with two career-defining games over the course of the summer.

In May, he was part of the Everton side that defeated Sheffield Wednesday in the FA Cup Final. Two months later, he was back at Wembley, Everton's only representative in Alf Ramsey's England team to face West Germany in the World Cup Final. And yet, the day threatened to take a disastrous turn. On 13 minutes Wilson failed to deal with a German cross, making a poor headed clearance that fell to the feet of Helmut Haller, who fired home from close range to put the Germans in front. Nobby Stiles reputedly called across: 'In the fourteen years I have been playing with and against you, the first time you make a fucking mistake is in a World Cup final!' Perfection had for so long been Wilson's trademark, that such

an error seemed wholly uncharacteristic. England, of course, recovered and Wilson became a World Cup winner. A month later he and Liverpool's Roger Hunt paraded the Jules Rimet trophy with the FA Cup and League Championship trophy before the Charity Shield match at Goodison.

Wilson was now aged nearly 32, but still retained the fitness and athleticism of a younger player. He continued to represent club and country with distinction for another two years, but during the summer of 1968 suffered a twisted knee that proved devastating. He made just a handful of appearances for Everton beyond then, and in 1969 was given a free transfer, electing to join Oldham Athletic. In 1970 he joined Bradford City and a year later served as caretaker manager for two months. Shortly after he left football to join his family's undertaking business.

[FAC

BORN
Shirebrook,
17 December 1934

POSITION
Left back

OTHER CLUBS
Huddersfield Town
(1955–64);
Oldham Athletic (1969–70);
Bradford City (1970–72)

HONOURS
FA Cup 1966;
World Cup 1966;
63 England caps (1960–68);
Member of the British
Empire (MBE) 2000

1966 WAS TO BE
WILSON'S
ANNUS MIRABILIS

Season	League		FA Cup		League Cup		Europe		Total	
	App	Goals	App	Goals	App	Goals	App	Goals	App	Goals
1964/65	17	0	4	0	-	-	2	0	23	0
1965/66	35	0	8	0	-	-	4	0	47	0
1966/67	30	0	6	0	-	-	5	0	41	0
1967/68	28	0	6	0	-	-	-	-	34	0
1968/69	4 (2)	0	0	0	0 (1)	0	-	-	4 (3)	0
Total	**114 (2)**	**0**	**26**	**0**	**0 (1)**	**0**	**11**	**0**	**151(3)**	**0**

Wilson, Walter

Full back who played a single game during Everton's debut league season

Season	League		FA Cup		Total	
	App	Goals	App	Goals	App	Goals
1888/89	1	0	0	0	1	0
Total	1	0	0	0	1	0

Winterhalder, Arthur

Young winger who cameoed during the 1907/08 season

Season	League		FA Cup		Total	
	App	Goals	App	Goals	App	Goals
1907/08	4	0	0	0	4	0
Total	4	0	0	0	4	0

Wolstenholme, Sam

England international half back who was part of Everton's early-20th-century revival

With his fellow former-England internationals Steve Bloomer and Fred Spikesley, the Lancastrian half back Sam Wolstenholme would be involved in one of the most remarkable episodes of the First World War.

In their retirement the footballers had moved to Germany as coaches and found themselves there when war unexpectedly broke out. 'I was one of the happy throng of Britishers assembled on the boulevards of Berlin at the start of August 1914,' Bloomer would recall. 'I remember one night we went home, aliens in a strange land, and there was rumour of war in the air. Ah well,

what did it matter? It hadn't been declared and there was plenty of time to do something about it when it was an accomplished fact. So we went home perfectly happy and not a bit worried.'

Four months later, however, there was a mass internment and the footballers were some of the 600 men rounded up and placed in an internment camp at Ruhleben.

The adversity of spending the war in these circumstances was counteracted by the players organising teams –adopting the names of English clubs – to play in leagues in the camp. Wolstenholme also appeared alongside Bloomer for England against a Rest of the World team and the Ruhleben players achieved worldwide fame, with their activities reported globally.

This saga formed a dramatic epilogue to a fine career in English football. Everton acquired the right half as a teenager from the amateurs of Horwich and after a solitary appearance in the 1897/98 season he was given a run in the team in November 1898. The centre half Billy Owen had suffered injury and Everton's regular right half, Dickie Boyle, switched to his position to accommodate Wolstenholme. The youngster, it was reported of his second match in a blue shirt, against Sheffield Wednesday, 'came out of a trying ordeal with great success'.

By the end of the season he had established his place in the Everton team and was, according to one account, 'a brainy and thoughtful right half, as nimble as

Season	League		FA Cup		Total	
	App	Goals	App	Goals	App	Goals
1897/98	1	0	0	0	1	0
1898/99	15	0	2	0	17	0
1899/1900	29	0	1	0	30	0
1900/01	34	2	2	0	36	2
1901/02	27	1	2	0	29	1
1902/03	22	1	2	0	24	1
1903/04	32	4	1	0	33	4
Total	160	8	10	0	170	8

a squirrel'. Yet Everton at this time were in a state of flux, between two great sides. Of the club's 21st year, the 1899/1900 season, Thomas Keates wrote: 'Our coming of age celebrations were a chilling, killing frost. Eleventh on the league table. Shocking!'

Wolstenholme would be one of the young players central to Everton's revival. They narrowly missed out on the League Championship in 1902 and 1904, encountering dismal Aprils as the ultimate crown was theirs for the taking. Wolstenholme's form earned him League representative honours in 1902, and in 1904 he was selected for the England team. Yet at the height of his Everton career it ended abruptly. A refusal to sign terms for the 1904/05 season saw the Everton directors touting him around their rivals, and Wolstenholme became a Blackburn Rovers player for £600. He provided them with four years of fine service, before switching to the Southern League. But greater dramas lay in store.

Wood, George

Popular custodian who defied the Scottish goalkeeper stereotype

Through the 1970s, Everton struggled to replace Gordon West with a worthy successor. Not until Neville Southall's arrival in 1981 did a goalkeeper of such stature fill the Everton goal, but in the interim, George Wood came closest to adequately filling West's gloves.

A £150,000 signing from Blackpool in the summer of 1977, he had started his career with East Stirlingshire, but moved to England before his 20th birthday. The physically imposing Scot endured a nightmare debut, against Nottingham Forest, when he was at fault for all three goals in a 3-1 defeat on the opening day of the 1977/78 season, but soon recovered his composure.

Indeed, the burly stopper quickly embarked on the form of his career as Everton concluded his first two seasons third and fourth. Wood kept 19 league clean sheets through the 1977/78 season, a feat that had only been bettered before by West in Everton's 1970 League Championship winning campaign. Such form earned him a Scotland call-up, and he was part of Ally McLeod's ill-fated squad that travelled to the 1978 World Cup Finals in Argentina.

DESPITE his imposing figure, Wood was athletic and agile, able to stoop to block even the lowest shot. A diligent trainer, he was among the fittest players at the club, and his work in the Bellefield gym unquestionably contributed to the longevity of his playing

career, which extended past his 40th birthday. Quickly he became a popular figure in the Goodison dressing room and on the terraces.

If Wood possessed a weakness it was in the command of his penalty area, and sometimes he flapped at crosses. His confidence seemed undermined by Everton's poor start to the 1979/80 season, and as Gordon Lee sought to find a winning formula Wood was a casualty, finding himself dropped mid-season with Martin Hodge taking his place. Although he returned for the season's conclusion, that summer he was sold to Arsenal – Everton recouping the fee paid to Bolton three years earlier.

WOOD put in a couple of good seasons at Highbury, for a period keeping Pat Jennings out of the Arsenal team. He was later Crystal Palace's long-serving goalkeeper, and finished his playing career at Hereford United in the mid-1990s. On retirement he turned to coaching, serving Cardiff and Hartlepool United as their goalkeeping coach.

Season	League		FA Cup		League Cup		Europe		Total	
	App	Goals	App	Goals	App	Goals	App	Goals	App	Goals
1977/78	42	0	2	0	5	0	-	-	49	0
1978/79	42	0	1	0	3	0	4	0	50	0
1979/80	19	0	1	0	5	0	2	0	27	0
Total	**103**	**0**	**4**	**0**	**13**	**0**	**6**	**0**	**126**	**0**

Woodhouse, Ronald

Experienced forward who never settled into the Goodison groove

[FACTFILE]

BORN
Leyland, 15 January 1897
POSITION
Inside forward
OTHER CLUBS
Preston North End (1919–25);
Wrexham (1927–29);
Halifax Town (1930);
Chorley

Season	League		FA Cup		Total	
	App	Goals	App	Goals	App	Goals
1926/27	2	0	0	0	2	0
Total	2	0	0	0	2	0

Woods, Maurice 'Matt'

Defender who went on to provide many years of fine service to Blackburn Rovers

[FACTFILE]

BORN
Skelmersdale, 1 November 1931
POSITION
Central defender
OTHER CLUBS
Burscough (1949);
Blackburn Rovers (1957–63);
Sydney Hakoah (1963–65);
Luton Town (1965–66);
Stockport County (1966–68);
Drumcondra (1968–69);
Altrincham
AS MANAGER
Stockport County (1970–71)

Season	League		FA Cup		Total	
	App	Goals	App	Goals	App	Goals
1952/53	1	0	0	0	1	0
1953/54	0	0	0	0	0	0
1954/55	1	0	0	0	1	0
1955/56	3	1	0	0	3	1
1956/57	3	0	0	0	3	0
Total	8	1	0	0	8	1

Wright, Bernie

Lower league centre forward who has entered Goodison notoriety

[FACTFILE]

BORN
Birmingham, 17 September 1952
POSITION
Centre forward
OTHER CLUBS
Walsall (1971 & 1972–76);
Bradford City (1976–78);
Port Vale (1978–80);
Kidderminster Harriers;
Trowbridge Town;
Cheltenham Town;
Worcester City;
Gloucester City

Season	League		FA Cup		League Cup		Total	
	App	Goals	App	Goals	App	Goals	App	Goals
1971/72	7 (1)	1	0	0	0	0	7 (1)	1
1972/73	3	1	0	0	0	0	3	1
Total	10 (1)	2	0	0	0	0	10 (1)	2

Wright, Bill

Rookie centre forward who played a cameo role during the Blues' 1915 title triumph

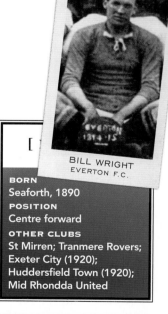

BILL WRIGHT
EVERTON F.C.

[FACTFILE]

BORN
Seaforth, 1890
POSITION
Centre forward
OTHER CLUBS
St Mirren; Tranmere Rovers;
Exeter City (1920);
Huddersfield Town (1920);
Mid Rhondda United

Season	League		FA Cup		Total	
	App	Goals	App	Goals	App	Goals
1914/15	2	0	0	0	2	0
Total	2	0	0	0	2	0

Wright, Billy

Local defender who followed an Evertonian family tradition

In making his Everton debut in a 2-0 win over Leicester City in February 1978, Billy Wright followed a family tradition set by his uncle Tommy a decade earlier.

Like his illustrious uncle, Wright was a local defender who had progressed through the Everton youth ranks to the first team. An accomplished footballer, he belied many of the characteristics typical in English centre halves. Neither especially tall nor quick, he overcame these shortcomings with astute reading of the game and a heading ability that was redolent of a player taller than his 5ft 9in frame. Such assets were replicated across the field and on occasion Wright filled in as a midfielder or in the number two shirt once distinguished by his uncle.

After making just a handful of appearances through the 1977/78 season, Gordon Lee invested considerable faith in the youngster the following campaign, making him first-choice centre back alongside Mick Lyons. Not only did Wright displace the equally promising Mark Higgins and the experienced Roger Kenyon, but he forced new signing Colin Todd, a former England centre back and Footballer of the Year, to play in the unfamiliar right back berth.

> HE FORCED NEW SIGNING COLIN TODD, A FORMER ENGLAND CENTRE BACK AND FOOTBALLER OF THE YEAR, TO PLAY IN THE UNFAMILIAR RIGHT BACK BERTH

With just a handful of first-team appearances, Wright was called up to the England under-21 team. Ron Greenwood, the England manager, who in the 1960s had overseen the emergence of Bobby Moore and was an advocate of 'footballing' defenders, was evidently impressed by what he saw, and at the end of the 1978/79 season called up Wright to the England B team to face Austria. Wright would make a further England B appearance, against Australia in November 1980, but full honours remained elusive.

Wright was virtually ever-present through Gordon Lee's final days as manager, and after Howard Kendall's appointment in 1981 was briefly captain. And yet he soon fell foul of the new manager. Never the most naturally athletic of players, Kendall criticised Wright for being overweight. Matters came to a head in December 1982, when Kendall finally lost patience with the centre back, who was 8lb heavier than his prescribed weight. Prior to an away fixture at Ipswich he reputedly announced to his squad, 'Billy's failed a fatness test,' and dropped him. Although the manager pleaded with the press to be sensitive to the problem, the headlines likening Wright to Billy Bunter were inevitable.

Wright never saw first-team action again and in June 1983 joined Birmingham City on a free transfer. There was a spell with Carlisle United, but by the age of 30, when, under different circumstances, he might have enjoyed his Goodison prime, Wright had slipped out of league football, joining Morecambe, whom he briefly managed.

[FACTFILE]

BORN
Liverpool, 28 May 1958
POSITION
Central defender
OTHER CLUBS
Birmingham City (1983–86);
Chester City (loan, 1986);
Carlisle United (1986–88)
AS MANAGER
Morecambe (1988–89)

Season	League		FA Cup		League Cup		Europe		Total	
	App	Goals	App	Goals	App	Goals	App	Goals	App	Goals
1977/78	3 (1)	1	0	0	0	0	-	-	3 (1)	1
1978/79	39	2	1	0	3	0	4	0	47	2
1979/80	40 (1)	0	6	0	3	0	2	0	51 (1)	0
1980/81	41	2	6	0	3	0	-	-	50	2
1981/82	24	2	0	0	0	0	-	-	24	2
1982/83	17	3	0	0	4	0	-	-	21	3
Total	**164 (2)**	**10**	**13**	**0**	**13**	**0**	**6**	**0**	**196 (2)**	**10**

Wright, Mark

Mancunian defender who enjoyed a brief lower league career before dropping out of the professional game

Season	League		FA Cup		League Cup		Total	
	App	Goals	App	Goals	App	Goals	App	Goals
1989/90	1	0	0	0	0	0	1	0
Total	**1**	**0**	**0**	**0**	**0**	**0**	**1**	**0**

[FACTFILE]

BORN
Manchester,
29 January 1970
POSITION
Central defender
OTHER CLUBS
Blackpool (loan);
Huddersfield Town
(loan, 1991–92,
then 1992–93);
Wigan Athletic (1993–95);
Chorley

Wright, Richard

Accident-prone goalkeeper who proved to be David Moyes's costliest transfer error

Signed for a hefty £4.5million in the summer of 2002 as David Moyes sought to address one of the club's longest-standing problems – the lack of a consistent goalkeeper since Neville Southall's departure five years previous – Richard Wright seemed to fit many of the criteria needed to fill the hefty vacancy left by the great Welshman. A Premier League debutant at 17, he made his England debut five years later and subsequently become one of Arséne Wenger's rare English signings at Arsenal.

In their way these last two factors should have been warning enough. When making his England debut, against Malta prior to the 2000 European Championship Finals, Wright conceded two penalties and scored an own goal. As for Wenger, the Arsenal manager simply doesn't do English signings very well – something to which Francis Jeffers could certainly attest.

Yet after a nervy first few games at the start of the 2002/03 season, Wright seemed to settle down, despite the occasional howler. Indeed all the contradictions within Wright seemed to present themselves in only his second Everton game, away at Sunderland. In the first half he made an outstanding point-blank save from Kevin Phillips; then in the second, he came for a cross shot, missed completely, and the ball sailed into the Everton net – only for the goal to be incorrectly disallowed for offside. Wright then gave away a ludicrous penalty for a foul on Niall Quinn – which he promptly saved!

As Everton finished the season in seventh place – despite occupying a higher league position for most of the campaign – Wright could reflect on an adequate first season. But his Goodison nightmare hadn't yet begun. That summer he fell out of his parent's loft and

injured his shoulder in a freak accident, forcing Moyes to sign Nigel Martyn as cover. Martyn made the goalkeeper's shirt his own over 2003/04 and thereafter Wright's confidence seemed shot.

Unable to displace the older player, when Wright was drafted in – usually for cup games – the occasions resembled comedic interludes. With poor handling and questionable positioning, Evertonians increasingly watched him through cracks between their fingers.

BROUGHT IN for the last game of the 2004/05 season, he vindicated Wenger's decision to sell him by letting in seven. Wright's response? 'I enjoyed the Arsenal game. I know I conceded seven goals but I got a chance to make some saves and get involved.' Warming up for an FA Cup tie at Chelsea the following January, he tripped over

a 'Not In Use' sign warning away players: cue another lengthy spell on the sidelines.

With the arrival of Tim Howard in May 2006, Wright was – mercifully – only unleashed twice more in an Everton shirt before his release at the end of the 2006/07 season.

[FACTFILE]

BORN
Ipswich, 5 November 1977
POSITION
Goalkeeper
OTHER CLUBS
Ipswich Town (1995–2001);
Arsenal (2001–02);
West Ham United (2007–08);
Southampton (loan, 2008);
Ipswich Town (2008–10);
Sheffield United (2010–11);
Ipswich Town (2011–12);
Preston North End (2012–)
HONOURS
2 England caps (2000–01)

Season	League		FA Cup		League Cup		Europe		Total	
	App	Goals	App	Goals	App	Goals	App	Goals	App	Goals
2002/03	33	0	1	0	3	0	-	-	37	0
2003/04	4	0	0	0	0	0	-	-	4	0
2004/05	6 (1)	0	2	0	3	0	-	-	11 (1)	0
2005/06	14 (1)	0	1	0	0	0	0	0	15 (1)	0
2006/07	1	0	0	0	1	0	-	-	2	0
Total	**58 (2)**	**0**	**4**	**0**	**7**	**0**	**0**	**0**	**69 (2)**	**0**

Wright, Robert

Stand-in centre forward who made a single appearance in the 1905/06 season

[FACTFILE]

BORN
1880
POSITION
Centre forward
OTHER CLUB
Burnley

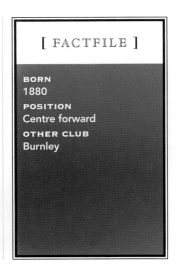

Season	League		FA Cup		Total	
	App	Goals	App	Goals	App	Goals
1905/06	1	0	0	0	1	0
Total	**1**	**0**	**0**	**0**	**1**	**0**

Wright, Tommy

1960s great whom many consider Everton's finest right back

Few full back partnerships in English football history – much less Everton's – have matched the quality of that shared by Ray Wilson and Tommy Wright through the mid-1960s. For four years they were an indomitable presence on the flanks of the Everton defence; dependable, talented, rarely breached, and in their own right as vital a component of Everton's success as the Harvey-Kendall-Ball partnership or Joe Royle's goals. And yet Wright, a brilliant and formidable defender, outstanding athlete and diehard Evertonian, is every bit as unheralded as Wilson has been eulogised. Perhaps it is a reflection of his modest demeanour, but it remains an anomaly of Everton history.

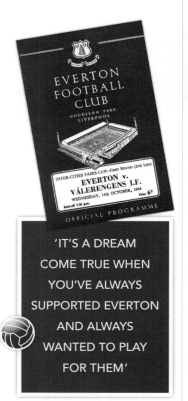

'IT'S A DREAM COME TRUE WHEN YOU'VE ALWAYS SUPPORTED EVERTON AND ALWAYS WANTED TO PLAY FOR THEM'

A boyhood Evertonian who grew up idolising Dave Hickson and Tommy Eglington from the Goodison terraces, Wright was a former Liverpool Schoolboys inside right, where he lined up alongside Liverpool's Tommy Smith. He joined Everton on leaving school and although an A team regular as inside right was eventually converted to right back. After being tried out in the reserves, Wright made his first-team debut in October 1964 in an Inter City Fairs tie against Vålerengen, a week short of his 20th birthday. His debut was 'solid', but thereafter his progress was swift and by Christmas he had ousted Alex Parker as Everton's first-choice right back.

A calm, unflustered player, he always played without fuss, sticking to his opponent relentlessly and dispossessing them with the crispest – and on occasion, fiercest – of tackles. He was never a hard man, but always held his own against even the most formidable of opponents.

Wright was one of the new breed of full backs, along with players like Ray Wilson and Jimmy Armfield. Previously the position had been the preserve of hatchet men, whose first task was to nobble the opposing winger and second was to get rid of the ball as quickly as possible.

But Wright had a fine footballing brain. He never lost the first touch or passing skills learned as an inside forward. And while his first task was always defending, the attacking flourishes of his former position were never forgotten either. One of Everton's most effective attacking movements of the era came when a winger cut inside, allowing Wright to overlap and roam freely; a teasing cross or low first-time ball from the defender would then wreak havoc in the opposition penalty area.

WRIGHT WAS never a flashy or spectacular player, but many Evertonians of the era will confirm that he was the unsung hero of the Everton defence. At the back of the Blues team he was solid, dependable and fiercely brave. Perhaps it was his sheer pride in playing for Everton that inspired such courage. In 1996 this author interviewed Wright at his home in Garston for the fanzine Gwladys Sings The Blues. Wright delighted in telling me how he had first started watching Everton as a seven-year-old in 1951, when the club were rooted in the Second Division. Twenty-five years after leaving the club, he still attended as a season ticket holder and displayed all the passion and enthusiasm of the most ardent fan.

'It's a dream come true when you've always supported Everton and always wanted to play for them,' he said. 'That was always my one ambition in life, to play for Everton.' Of Ray Wilson, he was unstinting in his praise: 'Ray was one of the best left backs I've seen

in any country. He used to help everyone on the pitch … A great asset.' But despite playing a part in some of Everton's most illustrious teams, he remained modest about his own contribution. 'The likes of them [Alan Ball, Alex Young, et al.] took the pressure off if you got the ball. All you did was give it to them and let them do all the work. All my job was to get the ball off the other side and give it to them.'

Following Everton's FA Cup win in 1966, Wright was virtually ever-present over the next five seasons, including Everton's League Championship winning campaign in 1969/70. So omnipresent was he – along with such stalwarts as Brian Labone and Gordon West – that he at times seemed indestructible. But often he played on through the pain barrier, with his knees particularly prone to knocks.

In summer 1968, while Wright was on tour with the England under-23 team, he was called up by Alf Ramsey for the full England squad, which was competing in the European Nations Cup – precursor of the European Championships. Picked to make his debut in the third-place playoff against Russia, he was

judged 'magnifico' by the watching Gigi Peronace, the Italian football agent who had once brought John Charles and Denis Law to Italy. Wright remained part of the England set-up for two more years and was part of a strong Everton contingent in the 1970 World Cup squad. The last of his England appearances came in the group stage match against Brazil, a game made famous for Gordon Banks' gravity-defying save at the feet of Pele.

On his return from Mexico he was a constant in an Everton team that embarked on its mystifying decline from 1970/71. But thereafter injuries started to take hold and he missed large chunks of the 1971/72 and 1972/73 seasons. In an away match against Wolves in April 1973 he limped off injured and was never to play a senior game again; still aged only 29, he announced his retirement soon after. In May 1974 he was awarded a testimonial, against Glasgow Rangers.

Wright left football altogether, working in security and then at Garston docks. Just a few

years after his retirement, his nephew, Billy Wright, became a stalwart of the Everton defence, even playing in the same number two shirt once distinguished by his uncle.

EVERTON struggled to find a sufficient replacement for Wright through the 1970s and he was never properly replaced with anybody of his standard until Gary Stevens' emergence a decade after his retirement. He was, quite simply, 'Magnifico'.

Season	League App	League Goals	FA Cup App	FA Cup Goals	League Cup App	League Cup Goals	Other App	Other Goals	Total App	Total Goals
1964/65	22	0	3	0	-	-	3	0	28	0
1965/66	35 (1)	0	6	0	-	-	4	0	45 (1)	0
1966/67	42	0	6	0	-	-	5	0	53	0
1967/68	38	0	6	0	2	0	-	-	46	0
1968/69	41	1	5	0	4	0	-	-	50	1
1969/70	42	1	1	0	4	0	-	-	47	1
1970/71	40	2	6	0	-	-	7	0	53	2
1971/72	17	0	1	0	-	-	-	-	18	0
1972/73	30	0	2	0	1	0	-	-	33	0
Total	**307(1)**	**4**	**36**	**0**	**11**	**0**	**19**	**0**	**373(1)**	**4**

Wylie, Tom

Dashing winger whose four-goal spree helped Everton to their first League Championship

Season	League App	League Goals	FA Cup App	FA Cup Goals	Total App	Total Goals
1890/91	4	4	0	0	4	4
1891/92	16	1	1	0	17	1
Total	**20**	**5**	**1**	**0**	**21**	**5**

EVERTON

·ENCYCLOPEDIA·

Abel **Xavier,** Aiyegbeni **Yakubu,** Joseph **Yobo,** Eddie **Youds,**
Alex **Young,** Sandy **Young,** Robert **Young, Z-Cars**

Xavier, Abel

Eccentric and controversial Portuguese utility man

With his lurid haircuts and bleached blond beard, Portuguese international Abel Xavier added some colour to Goodison during pallid times. The Mozambique-born utility man was a £1.5million signing from PSV Eindhoven in September 1999. Tall, pacy and sound in the air, he slotted into a variety of positions across the Everton defence and midfield through his 30 months at the club, but was at his best when deployed as centre half.

Xavier arrived at Goodison with an eclectic CV. Having started out in the Portuguese leagues, he had from the mid-1990s become something of a wandering minstrel – playing in Italy, Spain and the Netherlands before his move to England. A sound, technically accomplished player, Xavier was let down by a series of niggling injuries and illnesses as well as a tendency to go missing from games. As such, he was never a cast-iron selection in the Everton team.

HIS FORM through the 1999/2000 season was, nevertheless, enough for him to earn selection for Portugal's European Championship squad at the season's end. Xavier attracted Europe-wide notoriety when a penalty area handball was harshly given against him in extra time against France; Xavier's lengthy and aggressive protests earned him UEFA's opprobrium, who fined him £8000 and banned him from European and international competition for nine months. Xavier announced his disappointment at the ban, because it limited his chances of a move away from Everton!

Inevitably Walter Smith took a dim view of this and in 2000/01 excluded him from the first team, until an injury crisis took hold. Xavier continued to fill in as a squad player, impressing in flashes. But with his contract

running down, in January 2002 Smith decided that an £800,000 offer from Liverpool was too good to refuse.

XAVIER never really settled at Anfield, and thereafter resumed his nomadic career with spells in Turkey, Germany and Italy. In 2005 he returned to the Premier League with Middlesbrough, but was banned for a year after testing positive for an anabolic steroid. Later, there was a spell in the MLS with David Beckham's LA Galaxy. It seemed fitting that one of football's last eccentrics should end up in Hollywood.

Season	League		FA Cup		League Cup		Total	
	App	Goals	App	Goals	App	Goals	App	Goals
1999/2000	18 (2)	0	2	0	1	0	21 (2)	0
2000/01	10 (1)	0	1	0	0	0	11 (1)	0
2001/02	11 (1)	0	1	0	1	0	13 (1)	0
Total	**39 (4)**	**0**	**4**	**0**	**2**	**0**	**45 (4)**	**0**

[FACTFILE]

BORN
Nampula, Mozambique, 30 November 1972

POSITION
Defender

OTHER CLUBS
Estrela Amadora (Portugal, 1990–93);
Benfica (1993–95);
Bari (1995–96);
Real Oviedo (1996–98);
PSV Eindhoven (1998–99);
Liverpool (2002–03);
Galatasaray (2003); Hannover 96 (2003–04);
AS Roma (2005);
Middlesbrough (2005–07);
LA Galaxy (2007–08)

HONOURS
20 Portugal caps (2 goals)
(1993–2002)

Yakubu, Aiyegbeni

Prolific Nigerian international whose Goodison career faded after injury

When he was at the top of his game, Nigerian international centre forward Yakubu was one of the most unstoppable finishers in the Premier League. Stocky, adroit, supremely powerful, he belied a languid manner to score goals with abandon. Alas, after a prolific first season at Goodison, injuries ravaged his career and he never seemed quite the same player when not performing at supreme level of fitness.

Hailing from the southern Nigerian city of Benin City, Yakubu started out with the Bridge Boys (also known as Julius Berger FC after the German company that founded them in the 1970s), a nursery club that had produced internationals such as Taribo West, Sunday Oliseh and Rashidi Yakini. Still a teenager, he joined Maccabi Haifa, where his prolific record earned him two Israeli league titles and the opportunity to play in the Champions League.

A move to England with Derby County collapsed over work permit restrictions, but in 2003 the Nigerian joined Portsmouth, initially on loan. His goals at Fratton Park – one every two games – elevated Portsmouth to the Premier League, and 16 from 35 appearances in 2004/05 maintained Pompey's top-flight status. At the end of that campaign he joined Middlesbrough for £7.5million and he was part of the team that reached the 2006 UEFA Cup Final.

Through the summer of 2007 Yakubu was linked with transfers away from the Northeast, while Everton needed to redress a goalscoring problem and replace the hapless James Beattie, who had joined Sheffield United. Late in the summer transfer window David Moyes made the Nigerian Everton's £11.25million record signing.

Perhaps wary of the vast price tag and his nomadic reputation, Yakubu's arrival wasn't greeted with universal delight by Evertonians. He scored just 10 minutes into his debut versus Bolton Wanderers, but initially looked overweight and off the pace.

EVERTON'S form, nevertheless, picked up through the autumn of 2007, with the team playing sumptuous football. And for Yakubu the goals started to flow. Strikes against Sheffield Wednesday and Birmingham City were followed by a brace in a 7-1 hammering of Sunderland, then a hat-trick against Fulham. He scored a last-minute winner against West Ham in a League Cup quarter-final and followed it with a goal against the same club in the Premier League 72 hours later. By the season's end he had become the first Everton player in a generation to score more than 20 goals in a season. This was despite arriving a month into the campaign and missing a further five weeks to play in the African Cup of Nations.

GOODISON roared to chants of 'Feed the Yak and he will score' but his all-round play was assured too. 'Yakubu played really well up front,' Moyes said after a UEFA Cup tie with SK Brann – pointing to Yakubu's largely unheralded team play. 'He kept hold of the ball, linked the play well and worked really hard for the team. I was pleased with him.'

In finishing the 2007/08 season fifth, Everton had earned their highest points tally (65) in 20 years. Only the uniquely competitive landscape of the Premier League that year prevented a stronger challenge for a Champions League spot. Great things were expected ahead of the 2008/09 season. But Everton's propensity to start slowly cost them badly and Yakubu looked sluggish and was frequently withdrawn before the 90 minutes were up. Then, 14 Premier League games into the new season disaster struck. In an away match at Tottenham, Yakubu went down awkwardly under an innocuous challenge from Ledley King and ruptured his Achilles tendon. The prognosis was dire: 10 months on the sidelines, which saw him miss the 2009 FA Cup Final.

He returned the following August as a substitute in a Europa League tie against Sigma Olomonuc. But, always a man who thrived when at the peak of physical condition, he never again looked the same player. The thrust and hustle and bustle of his play had diminished and the chances that such physicality brought him started to fade.

He appeared at the 2010 World Cup Finals for Nigeria, but at Everton his career was on the wane. Having become a bit-part player at the club, in January 2011 he was loaned to Leicester City. The following August, and now into the final year of his contract, he joined Blackburn Rovers for a fee believed to be around £2million. Following Rovers' relegation in 2012 he made a lucrative switch to China with Guangzhou R&F.

[FACTFILE]

BORN
Benin City, Nigeria,
22 November 1982

POSITION
Centre forward

OTHER CLUBS
Julius Berger FC
(Nigeria, 1995–99);
Gil Vicente (loan, 1998);
Maccabi Haifa
(Israel, 1999–2003);
Hapoel Kfar Saba (Israel,
loan, 1999–2000);
Portsmouth (2003–05);
Middlesbrough (2005–07);
Leicester City (loan, 2011);
Blackburn Rovers (2011–12)
Guangzhou R&F (2012-)

HONOURS
57 Nigeria caps
(21 goals) (2000–)

Season	League		FA Cup		League Cup		Other		Total	
	App	Goals	App	Goals	App	Goals	App	Goals	App	Goals
2007/08	26 (3)	15	0 (1)	0	3	3	7	3	36 (4)	21
2008/09	14	4	0	0	0 (1)	0	2	1	16 (1)	5
2009/10	9 (16)	5	0	0	2	1	4 (5)	0	15 (21)	6
2010/11	7 (7)	1	0	0	1	0	-	-	8 (7)	1
Total	56 (26)	25	0 (1)	0	6 (1)	4	13 (5)	4	75 (33)	33

Yobo, Joseph

Elegant defender who shone at Goodison and captained his country

In the summer of 2002 21-year-old Nigerian international defender Joseph Yobo became the first signing of Everton's new manager David Moyes. His arrival on loan from Marseille saw Everton beat off the attentions of Juventus, Arsenal and Newcastle United and set the standard Moyes sought for his new arrivals. The youthful, elegant figure of Yobo was much in contrast to the overpaid veterans that had largely characterised the reign of Moyes's predecessor Walter Smith.

YOBO had started his career with Mechelen, then Standard Liege, following a route travelled by many promising young African footballers, who see Belgium – with its easier immigration regulations – as the ideal stepping stone to the main European leagues. He appeared 46 times for Liege, making his debut for Nigeria too. In 2001 he joined Marseille and was part of the Nigeria squad that fell at the first stage at the 2002 World Cup in Japan and South Korea.

The nature of Yobo's transfer to Everton later that summer laid a template that Moyes would follow many times over subsequent years. He paid £1million for Yobo's services for a year, with an option to complete the transfer at a fixed additional fee (of £4million) if he impressed. Mikel Arteta and Steven Pienaar would be signed permanently after similar deals proved successful later in the decade, while the likes of Phillipe Senderos, Manuel Fernandes and Jo would be discarded after failing to impress Everton's exacting manager.

Happily, Yobo impressed immediately. In his first days at Goodison he showed himself to be a skilful, ball-playing centre half, with the ability to deputise at right back. Immensely cool in possession, he also had the fastest change of pace witnessed in an Everton central defender since Kevin Ratcliffe's heyday.

Yobo's debut season coincided with this author's grandfather's 75th year of watching the club. Normally difficult to please, Charles Mills was fulsome in his praise of the young African, saying that he overshadowed another young prodigy – Wayne Rooney. 'He had a look of T.G. Jones about him,' he said. 'He is outstanding. In the fifty years since T.G. left I don't think I've ever seen anybody quite like him. Cool as you like, he never once looks flustered. For me, it was him that was the outstanding presence in many of those early games, not Rooney.'

In the summer of 2003 Moyes took up his option to retain Yobo after protracted transfer wranglings with his former club. With his team-mates he suffered a difficult second season but he emerged a stronger player and played his part in Everton's ascent to Champions League football after their fourth place in 2004/05. With the departure of Alan Stubbs at the end of that season Yobo's name was assured as one of the first on the Everton team sheet.

Much of the earlier exuberance of Yobo's first days of the club had, alas, been coached out of him by this stage, and he was as renowned for his clearances into Row Z as he once was for his flourishes and dragbacks in his own half. The transition made him a better, more resolute defender and in 2006/07, with Yobo virtually ever-present, Everton had one of their best defensive seasons of all time, conceding just 36 league goals – a feat they bettered by three goals a year later.

There were, nevertheless, terrible lapses of concentration that

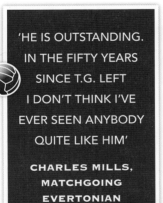

'HE IS OUTSTANDING. IN THE FIFTY YEARS SINCE T.G. LEFT I DON'T THINK I'VE EVER SEEN ANYBODY QUITE LIKE HIM'

CHARLES MILLS, MATCHGOING EVERTONIAN SINCE 1928

perhaps stunted his ascent from top-class Premier League defender to a player of world-class renown. These became less prevalent as he matured, but were the cause for some angst-ridden moments.

Yobo was one of the most popular members of the Everton squad and seemed to possess a sense of level-headedness and inherent decency lacking in many of his Premier League contemporaries. He was a deeply religious man, who took strength from his convictions. 'It's important because I grew up with God,' he said in an interview with the Observer in 2003. 'I say my prayers and go to church in Liverpool every week. It gives me hope and takes me away from bad matches. If I don't play well then I worry.'

> WITH YOBO VIRTUALLY EVER-PRESENT, EVERTON HAD ONE OF THEIR BEST DEFENSIVE SEASONS OF ALL TIME

With Yakubu and Victor Anichebe, Yobo formed a strong Nigerian contingent at Goodison. He participated in the 2004, 2006, 2008 and 2010 editions of the African Cup of Nations, occasions that added to his standing as a footballer, but interrupted his Everton career. In 2010 he captained Nigeria at the World Cup Finals in South Africa. As in his previous finals appearance in 2002, his country were knocked out in the first round.

Yobo found his Everton first-team place threatened by the arrival of Phil Jagielka in 2007 and his emergence as an England international centre back after he had formed a good partnership with Joleon Lescott. But the reality was that in a congested season three top-class central defenders were a necessity. This became apparent when Jagielka snapped his cruciate ligament at a crucial juncture of the 2008/09 campaign; Yobo reclaimed his place and appeared in the FA Cup Final defeat to Chelsea at the season's end.

In the summer of 2009 Lescott joined Manchester City following an acrimonious transfer. Yet rather than cement Yobo's place in the team, Moyes showed a preference for Lescott's replacement, Sylvain Distin, alongside Jagielka. In the second half of the 2009/10 campaign Yobo made just three starts, amid speculation that he had fallen out with Moyes.

At the end of the season he was loaned out to Turkish club Fenerbahce, where his career was revitalised. Yobo scored the goal that clinched the league title for the club in a 4-3 win over Sivasspor, enabling the Istanbul club to pip Trabzonspor to the title on the head-to-head rule after they finished on equal points. It proved to be something of a hollow victory, however, with Fenerbahce implicated in a huge match-fixing scandal and stripped of the right to compete in the following season's Champions League.

That prevented Yobo from making a permanent £6million switch, but he was in no doubt that he did not wish to return to Merseyside. 'I do not want to return to Everton because I have seen the difference in playing in a competitive team on a regular basis and that has helped me to improve,' he said. With this in mind, Everton accepted a second year-long loan deal and Yobo returned to Turkey.

[FACTFILE]

BORN
Kono, Nigeria, 6 September 1980
POSITION
Centre back
OTHER CLUBS
Standard Liege (1998–2001);
Marseille (2001–03);
Fenerbahce (loan, 2010–)
HONOURS
87 Nigeria caps (7 goals) (2001–)

Season	League App	League Goals	FA Cup App	FA Cup Goals	League Cup App	League Cup Goals	Europe App	Europe Goals	Total App	Total Goals
2002/03	22 (2)	0	0	0	2	0	-	-	24 (2)	0
2003/04	27 (1)	2	0 (1)	0	2	0	-	-	29 (2)	2
2004/05	19 (8)	0	3	0	3	0	-	-	25 (8)	0
2005/06	29	1	0	0	1	0	4	1	34	2
2006/07	38	2	1	0	1	0	-	-	40	2
2007/08	29 (1)	1	0	0	2	0	7	0	38 (1)	1
2008/09	26 (1)	1	2 (1)	0	1	0	1 (1)	0	30 (3)	1
2009/10	14 (3)	1	0	0	0	0	6	1	20 (3)	2
Total	**204(16)**	**8**	**6 (2)**	**0**	**12**	**0**	**18 (1)**	**2**	**240(19)**	**10**

Youds, Eddie

Local centre half who worked his way back up to the top flight after his Everton release

Season	League App	League Goals	FA Cup App	FA Cup Goals	League Cup App	League Cup Goals	Other App	Other Goals	Total App	Total Goals
1990/91	5 (3)	0	0	0	0	0	0	0	5 (3)	0
1991/92	0	0	0	0	0 (1)	0	1	0	1 (1)	0
Total	**5 (3)**	**0**	**0**	**0**	**0 (1)**	**0**	**1**	**0**	**6 (4)**	**0**

[FACTFILE]

BORN
Liverpool, 3 May 1970
POSITION
Central defender
OTHER CLUBS
Cardiff City (loan, 1989);
Wrexham (loan, 1990);
Ipswich Town (1991–95);
Bradford City (1995–98);
Charlton Athletic (1998–2002);
Huddersfield Town (2002–03);
Grays Athletic (2003–05)

Young, Alex

Centre forward blessed with genius, he stands among the Everton legends

Everton greats fall into three distinct categories. There are the goalscorers: the illustrious number nines and sublime poachers who form a proud tradition dating back to the days of Fred Geary and Jack Southworth. There are the artistes: the incomparable geniuses who bestowed upon the club the lore of the School of Science. Finally, there are the mavericks: the one-offs, who combined ability and force of personality to find their way into Evertonian hearts.

ALEX YOUNG is a special case because he transcends such ready categorisation. He was a great goalscorer, one of Everton's best. He was also a fabulous, uniquely skilful creator of goals. What sets Young apart, however, was the unique hold he had over Everton fans. It has been said that if he had played for Liverpool or Manchester United he would be as revered as George Best or Kenny Dalglish. But even if the wider public did not come to appreciate Young's sublime talents, no discerning fan of the game – Evertonian or not – could have failed to have been impressed by the man they called the 'Golden Vision'. After all, this was the player who inspired a Ken Loach film about him; who prompted an attack on Harry Catterick, when he was dropped for a game at Blackpool. One of the most enduring images of the era is a fan being led off the Goodison pitch by a bobby, still defiantly holding up a placard with the legend: 'Sack Catterick, Keep Young'.

Young was born in Loanhead, a coalmining village in Midlothian, in 1937. In common with many such communities it was a hotbed of footballing talent – in Young's junior school team alone were Ian King, later of Leicester City, and Malcolm Howieson, who would play for Grimsby Town; John White, who played with Young at Hearts and for Tottenham, went to a neighbouring school. Like many youths from such a background, Young seemed destined for life down the coal pit and he was taken on as a colliery apprentice aged 15.

YOUNG'S escape from such drudgery came via football. He was spotted by Hearts playing junior football for Broughton Star, aged 16. Loaned out to Musselburgh Union and Newtongrange Star, local junior teams, until deemed ready for the rigours of senior football, all the while he combined playing with work at the coalmine. Aged 18, at the start of the 1955/56 season, he made his Hearts debut in a League Cup tie; by the season's end he was an established Tynecastle favourite and had played a part in Hearts' first Scottish FA Cup win in half a century.

This would emerge as the greatest Hearts team in the club's history, and as well as Young it boasted players such as Dave MacKay, Ian Crawford and Willie Bauld. Twice they lifted the Scottish League title, in 1958 and 1960, and would also lift the League Cup in 1959 and 1960. Young quickly cultivated a reputation as a forward of grace and élan. In 1960 he won his first Scotland cap, against Austria; staggeringly, just seven more would follow – the majority of them earned while playing for Hearts that same year.

By now Young had started to attract the attention of a host of English clubs. The financial incentives south of the border made it attractive for ambitious young players and Young was keen on a move. Speculation linked him with switches to Preston North End, West Bromwich Albion and Everton, but it was Preston, managed by Cliff Britton, who in November 1960 followed up their initial interest. Hearts agreed a fee and Young agreed terms with Britton, but when the Preston manager put the move before his board, they would not sanction the signing-on fee. For the sake of £1000, the Lancastrians lost out on a football great.

At this stage Everton moved in, bidding £55,000 for Young and the full back George Thomsen. Young was valued at £42,000, which was a record for a player coming out of Scotland. He arrived at Everton injured and still needing to complete his national

service, which severely restricted his progress through the remainder of the 1960/61 season. He made his debut at Goodison on 17 December 1960 against Tottenham, who would finish the season League and FA Cup winners, but made little impression in a 3-1 defeat. Young stepped down from first-team action for a further six weeks and did not return until a 2-1 defeat at the hands of Bolton – Everton's fifth consecutive defeat, which had seen them drop from third to fifth and knocked out of the FA Cup third round. The poor form continued: Everton lost 4-0 at West Ham and were knocked out of the League Cup by Shrewsbury Town, despite Young's first Everton goal. It was, Young would recall, 'one of the most embarrassing evenings in the club's history'.

But as spring came there were the first stirrings of an understanding building between Young and Roy Vernon. On the last day of March 1961, Young scored a brace and Vernon the other goal in a 3-1 win over Blackburn Rovers. Suddenly the hype that had surrounded his move was beginning to become justified. The Liverpool Echo reported: 'Young is a thoroughbred, a great mover with the ball, fast, active, razor sharp in his reactions. For his size, he is a good header of the ball. He is clever, artistic and can score goals.'

Everton won six of their final seven games, finishing fifth – their highest position since the war. But it was not enough to save Johnny Carey's job as manager, and he was replaced by Harry Catterick. Although Young would remain under his charge for seven years, he never shared a good relationship with the new manager, who seemingly preferred more muscle and brawn in his number nine than the slight Young could ever offer. He was suspicious too of the growing adulation Young received from the Goodison crowd. 'It turned out that the more the fans loved me, the more the manager disliked me,' he recorded in his memoirs. 'I was engaged in a constant battle with Harry and learned not to trust him.'

Part of Young's problem was that he was not a traditional centre forward. He lacked the physicality of the blood-and-thunder striker who characterised the position. He was slim, delicate, even frail, possessing more the physique of a winger or inside forward. He was prone to injury and never a prolific goalscorer. Sometimes he disappeared from play or was outmuscled by the defensive hatchet men who were increasingly fashionable during this time. But none of this lessened his effect on the

Everton forward line. He was a graceful player, who floated around the attack, bringing in colleagues with a flick or a shimmy, or coasting past opponents with a drop of the shoulder. He was a formidable header of the ball, seemingly hanging in the air as if suspended by string. His passing was precise, accurate and, on occasion, visionary. He was a cool finisher in front of goal. Within a year of his arrival, he was a Goodison icon. In October 1961, the Liverpool Echo's Leslie Edwards wrote of Young: 'It is not necessary for a player with his extraordinary gifts to play a blood and guts centre forward game. With a slight feint of the shoulders he gets them going the wrong way. Then he drifts past them almost lazily. Like Matthews and other men of football genius he always seems to have time to think and space in which to move. He won't get a packet of goals, but he'll make hundreds of others.'

YOUNG and Vernon would effectively play just three full seasons together, in which time they claimed some 116 league goals between them. Vernon, clinical and whippet-like – the ultimate penalty area player – was the perfect foil for the Scot and they built up a subliminal understanding. Certainly both men played the finest football of their careers when partnering each other.

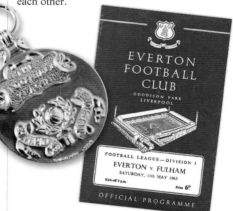

Everton finished the 1961/62 season fourth, Young scoring 14 goals, with poor away form and a bad start costing the club a serious stab at the league title. The following campaign he was ever-present as Everton lifted their sixth league title. Fittingly, as Young was now Everton's talisman, when they met their nearest rivals, Tottenham, in mid-April, it was he who scored the only goal of the game. That victory handed Everton a crucial initiative in the title hunt, and three weeks later, after a 4-1 win over Fulham, they were crowned champions. 'Never shall I forget those final five minutes of the Fulham match,' said Young. 'When the crowd was stamping and shouting so much that my head

was reeling with the noise and it seemed we could feel the playing pitch vibrating under our feet.'

The 1963/64 season was less happy for Young, despite Everton coming close to retaining their title. Injured over Christmas, strong speculation linked Catterick to a replacement centre forward, with Sheffield Wednesday's David Layne his seeming target. Catterick, however, surprised everybody, waiting until March, when Young was recovered, to make Blackburn's Fred Pickering a domestic transfer record signing. Young was consigned to the reserves for much of the remainder of the season, his Everton career seemingly nearing its end. He requested a transfer, which was accepted, but he later retracted the demand.

Yet while speculation linked Young with moves to Rangers, Spurs, Manchester United and even a return to Hearts that summer, only Third Division Brentford bid for his services, and Catterick wanted much more than the £30,000 they offered. At the start of the 1964/65 season, Young was included as inside right in an illustrious forward line that also included Pickering, Vernon, Alex Scott and Derek Temple. Evertonians expected goals galore, but in accommodating so many attackers they had, ironically, become one-dimensional and over-reliant on Pickering, who scored goals with abandon. In March 1965 Vernon was sold to Stoke City. Young scored just three league goals in an injury-hampered campaign as Everton finished fourth.

Young's most persistent injury problem was unnaturally soft feet – which earned him the tag 'tenderfoot' – that were exceedingly prone to blisters. The affliction seems obscure, but it was enough to keep Young out for large tracts of the season and no cure seemed to be able to rid him of the problem. When his ever devoted followers became aware of his affliction he became inundated with suggested remedies. 'My home and the club offices were absolutely deluged with letters giving me advice on just what to do in order to get back into the soccer scene,' he later remembered. They ranged from the bizarre to the ridiculous. One fan suggested he paddle on Crosby beach three times a day, to benefit from the salt water; another that he wrapped his feet in newspaper; others suggested that he rub them down with a lemon, or even a potato.

The 1965/66 season showed Everton to be a team in transition. Rarely did they figure in the top 10, finishing 11th. In September 1965 they

were beaten 5-0 by Liverpool at Anfield. Young continued to partner Pickering in attack, but had had to adapt his game to take on some additional defensive responsibilities, particularly away from home. Evertonians were increasingly unhappy, particularly with Catterick. This bubbled over in January 1966, when the Everton manager left Young out of the line-up to face Blackpool at Bloomfield Road. While Young was playing for the reserves, 16-year-old Joe Royle made his debut in his place, but was unable to stop a 2-0 reverse. After the game, angry supporters surrounded the Everton coach, and in a surge forward Catterick was knocked to the ground and reputedly jostled. The incident, which was exaggerated by the press, was taken as an example of Evertonians' unstinting devotion to their hero.

Perhaps Young's omission was a piece of reverse-psychology on behalf of the Everton manager. The following week, in an FA Cup tie at Sunderland, Young was restored to the line-up and scored as Everton won 3-0. It was the first in a run of games that led Everton to Wembley, and an FA Cup Final against Sheffield Wednesday. Having played virtually the previous two years as inside right, Young was restored as centre forward in the absent Pickering's place, with Mike Trebilcock partnering him.

And yet Young's only Wembley appearance threatened to peter

out in disappointment. Twice he was denied, first when a perfectly valid goal was disallowed for offside, next when he was hauled down by Ron Springett for what seemed a stonewall penalty, but nothing was given. Wednesday took a two-goal lead, which Everton famously overcame to win 3-2. It was, Young recorded, 'a glorious comeback and a tremendous advertisement for the competition'. 'I think Alex Young had a great match,' said an elated Dixie Dean afterwards. 'He did everything right for me.'

The FA Cup victory reinvigorated Young, who, after earning a Scotland recall that summer following a five-year hiatus, started the first 33 league games in the 1966/67 season for Everton. Many of these were in his preferred number nine shirt, and he showed that aged 30 the old magic had not deserted him. On the final day of the season he returned from a month-long injury lay-off to destroy Sunderland. In an outstanding display, in which his mark was clear on each of Everton's four goals, Everton won 4-1 with Johnny Morrissey scoring a hat-trick. 'Young spread

destruction through their ranks with his wonderful ball distribution, artistry and sheer cheek,' wrote Michael Charters in the Liverpool Echo. 'In this he was matched by Ball and their superiority was so pronounced that they almost put on a music hall double act at times.' According to Labone, it was the best individual performance he had ever seen from Young, and Alan Ball wanted him – and not Morrissey – to have the match ball at the end. 'Young beat Sunderland almost on his own that night,' claimed Labone. 'He played on the wing and I never felt so sorry for a man as I did for the Sunderland left back. For him, it was a nightmare. For Young, it was a great personal triumph.' It was the zenith of Alex Young's genius: a virtuoso display of grace and trickery.

CATTERICK had by now rebuilt Everton around the Harvey-Kendall-Ball midfield. Young played the majority of the first half of the 1967/68 season either on the right wing or deputising for Joe Royle at centre forward. But as the campaign progressed he began to be squeezed out in

favour of Jimmy Husband and made only occasional forays from the substitute's bench. He came on as a substitute for Jimmy Husband in the FA Cup semi-final victory over Leeds United, but despite Catterick assuring him of a place on the bench for the final against West Bromwich Albion, Young was left out.

By then Young had played his last game in an Everton shirt. It was at West Ham on 11 May 1968, a month after the screening of The Golden Vision, Neville Smith and Ken Loach's BBC1 play about Young. Although he lined up alongside virtually a reserve side, as Catterick rested players for the following Saturday's FA Cup Final, Young ran the show with an imperious performance that drew loud applause even from the West Ham fans.

IN JULY 1968, Everton accepted a £7500 bid from New York Generals for Young and for a period he seemed set to leave, before changing his mind. Four weeks later, Glentoran paid £10,000 for Young to take over as player-manager. The move was ill-fated, however, and Young was uneasy at Northern Ireland's rising sectarian violence. He returned to England with Stockport County, but the Third Division was no fitting stage for a player like him. After making just a single appearance in the 1969/70 season he called time on his illustrious career.

Young returned to Scotland, where he lived a quiet post-football existence, first running a pub, then working for his family's soft furnishings business. His son, Jason, was a forward for Scotland's youth teams alongside Duncan Ferguson, but after breaking his leg was consigned to a career in the Scottish lower leagues with Livingston and Stranraer.

Everton always retained a place in Alex Young's heart. In 2003, he

Season	League		FA Cup		League Cup		Other		Total	
	App	Goals	App	Goals	App	Goals	App	Goals	App	Goals
1960/61	13	6	0	0	1	1	-	-	14	7
1961/62	40	14	3	0	-	-	-	-	43	14
1962/63	42	22	3	0	-	-	2	0	47	22
1963/64	27	12	3	0	-	-	3	0	33	12
1964/65	20	3	1	0	-	-	3	3	24	6
1965/66	26	7	8	2	-	-	2	0	36	9
1966/67	35	8	5	2	-	-	5	0	45	10
1967/68	24 (1)	5	2 (2)	0	2	2	-	-	28 (3)	7
Total	**227 (1)**	**77**	**25 (2)**	**4**	**3**	**3**	**15**	**3**	**270 (3)**	**87**

Young, Alexander 'Sandy'

FA Cup Final hero who remains one of the club's greatest goalscorers

wrote: 'I left Everton football club in 1968. But I can honestly say that Everton has never left me. Most professional footballers embrace some sort of superstitions. But I am the sort of person who can walk into a room and immediately sense vibes about a place – and when I first walked into Goodison Park in November 1960 I could feel something almost spiritual. People may say that's just so much mumbo-jumbo, but I still get that feeling when I go back. Everton possesses a kind of magic – and it is a magic generated by the quality of players who have graced the stadium over the past 125 years.'

But the relationship was always reciprocal, even among those palpably too young to have witnessed him play. For Alex Young was a rare thing, not just a great footballer but as a man, he was one of the very few: a footballing hero blessed with genius, but possessing the highest virtue of them all – humility.

[FACTFILE]

BORN
Loanhead, 3 February 1937
POSITION
Forward
OTHER CLUBS
Heart of Midlothian (1955–60); Glentoran (player-manager, 1968); Stockport County (1968–69)
HONOURS
League Championship 1962/63; FA Cup 1966; 8 Scotland caps (5 goals) (1960–66)

Centre forward, goalscorer, FA Cup Final hero, murderer, outlaw, felon – the life and times of Sandy Young resembles a Hollywood epic. But in an extraordinary life, the Scottish centre forward traversed the peaks and troughs of human existence and was, within the space of a decade, a nationally renowned figure and a notorious villain, banged up in an Australian jail and awaiting a likely death sentence for the murder of his own brother.

YOUNG, who was no relation to the 1960s 'Golden Vision', joined Everton from Falkirk in 1901. Born in the Stirlingshire village of Slamannan, Young started his career with Slamannan Juniors, attracting attention with his goalscoring feats, which included seven in a single Stirlingshire Cup tie against Bannockburn. In 1899 he joined Scottish First Division team St Mirren, but spent just a year in Paisley before returning to Stirlingshire and Falkirk, who still competed in amateur leagues at this time. Two years later, aged 21, came the move to Goodison and Young's life changed forever.

The Scottish forward made his Everton debut on 28 September 1901 against Aston Villa, but it took him until December to register his first goal in a royal blue shirt. Indeed Young was never prolific in his first few campaigns for Everton, but it is clear that his selfless play allowed others – notably Jimmy Settle and Jack Sharp – to thrive. Everton were perennial nearly men in this time, and they ended Young's debut season runners-up to Sunderland.

The rookie had scored only six league goals in this first year at Everton and would add just a further five during the 1902/03 season, as Everton stumbled to a disappointing finish of 12th – the lowest in their history. But come the 1903/04 campaign, Young was leading Everton's resurgence – finishing the campaign top league scorer with 10 goals as Everton rose back to third.

Young's fine late-season form carried on through the 1904/05 season as goals started to come more freely. Everton led the league table from January and going into April seemed destined to take the League Championship. However, a lengthy FA Cup run, which saw Everton reach the semi-finals, and a series of postponements, including a match from the previous autumn at Woolwich Arsenal that was abandoned with Everton leading 3-1 with 15 minutes remaining. It left a build-up of fixtures through April 1905 that Everton needed to conquer in order to lift the title for the second time.

The run started well, with Young scoring the only goal of the game against Woolwich Arsenal at Goodison on 5 April. Three days later momentum was maintained with a draw at Stoke. On 15 April

Young scored in the win against Small Heath. But then things went badly awry. Everton met Manchester City at Maine Road and the scoring touch proved elusive for Young as Everton fell to a 2-0 defeat to a team with title ambitions of its own. After the match Everton journeyed immediately south for the rearranged fixture at Arsenal. Tired, and with momentum waning, Everton lost 2-1. Young failed to score again.

EVERTON then travelled to play Nottingham Forest, who they beat 2-0, but had to wait helplessly to see if Newcastle would win their last match of the season against Middlesbrough and in doing so pip Everton to the Championship. Newcastle emerged 3-0 winners; Everton, who had led the table for the previous three months, fell down to the runners-up spot at the death. 'Shakespeare wrote of "The uncertain glory of April",' quipped Everton historian Thomas Keates. 'This April is remembered a shocker.'

Might Everton have won it had Young been a more reliable goalscorer? Certainly, at this point of his career, he was like an early version of Tony Cottee – scoring freely against weaker opponents, or in various routs, but going missing when the going got tough. A Liverpool Echo pen portrait of the period was revealing: 'Sandy Young, the centre forward, is a variable sort of man who plays

EVERTON 1906 FA CUP WINNERS
Back - **Wade (Director), Makepeace, Cuff (Secretary), Young, Davies (Director), Bainbridge (Director), Taylor, Mahon (Director), Scott, Kelly (Director), W. Balmer, Wright (Director), Elliott (Trainer)**
Front - **Clayton (Director), Baxter (Director), Sharp, Bolton, Abbott, Settle, Crelley, Hardman, Whitford (Director), Kirkwood (Director)**

one good game in three on average. He takes the bumps a centre forward must inevitably expect smilingly and determination makes up for lack of skill at times.'

But when Everton got their chance to wreak revenge upon Newcastle a year later, Young showed that he was the man for the big occasion. With the exception of a second round strike against lowly Chesterfield, goals had proved elusive to Young throughout Everton's 1906 FA Cup run, which brought them to a final against Newcastle at Crystal Palace on 21 April 1906.

IT WAS, reported the Daily Mirror, 'the tamest final for many years' and its reporter accused Young of marring his 'dashing display' with 'a good many petty tricks, which Mr Kirkham [the referee] generally noticed and always promptly penalised'. But Young was on fine form. On 53 minutes he found the net, but the goal was ruled out for offside ('He was standing almost under the bar,' said the Mirror). Twenty-five minutes later Jack Sharp was sent free down the wing, evading the pursuit of the Newcastle left back Carr, who had not previously given the Everton wide man an inch. Sharp beat Carr and another defender, and sent in a beautifully weighted cross, which Young slotted home for the game's only goal.

'Thrice has the battle been waged, and twice the victory denied, but the third time pays for all,' recorded the Daily Post of Everton's first FA Cup Final win after three attempts. 'Bravo the Blues!' Young's FA Cup Final winner was, in many respects, the defining moment of his career. But his goalscoring through the 1906/07 season threatened to outshine even that achievement.

With the onset of the 1906/07 season it looked as if Everton may wrest the First Division title from Liverpool, quickly rising to the top of the table. Their results at home were hugely impressive and included a 9-1 thrashing of Billy Meredith's Manchester City – a record league win. In all they won 16 times at Goodison, drawing twice and losing just once; but their away form was disastrous. At the season's end they had managed just four away victories, which cost them the title. Everton finished third, Newcastle gained their revenge for the Cup Final and finished six points clear. For Sandy Young it had been a season of personal triumph: he ended the campaign as the First Division's top scorer with 28 League goals.

Yet Young did not match those goalscoring feats in the FA Cup, where for the second season running Everton reached the final. He scored just once in the seven-match path that led Everton to the Crystal Palace, where

they met the previous year's semi-finalists, Sheffield Wednesday. In a poor game Everton fell behind, equalised through Sharp and lost 2-1 after a late goal. Young's scoring touch had again proved elusive. 'I doubt,' the Football League's founding father, William McGregor, said, 'if we have ever had a final in which there has been more loose play ... [It was] one of the poorest finals.'

> 'BRAVO THE BLUES!' YOUNG'S FA CUP FINAL WINNER WAS, IN MANY RESPECTS, THE DEFINING MOMENT OF HIS CAREER

Young's goalscoring exploits during the 1906/07 season earned him a Scotland recall for the fixture against Wales in Wrexham in March 1907. It was his second and last cap – like many so-called 'Anglos' he found himself overlooked in favour of players who remained in their homeland. Even 60 years later, Alex Young, his namesake and successor as Everton number nine, would find himself excluded by Scotland's selectors on similar grounds.

Although Young still managed a goal every other game through the 1907/08 season, Everton dropped

Season	League		FA Cup		Total	
	App	**Goals**	**App**	**Goals**	**App**	**Goals**
1901/02	30	6	2	1	32	7
1902/03	19	5	1	0	20	5
1903/04	22	10	0	0	22	10
1904/05	31	14	6	0	37	14
1905/06	30	12	5	2	35	14
1906/07	33	28	8	1	41	29
1907/08	33	16	6	5	39	21
1908/09	23	9	1	0	24	9
1909/10	24	2	7	3	31	5
1910/11	30	8	3	3	33	11
Total	**275**	**110**	**39**	**15**	**314**	**125**

to 11th. In an effort to revive fortunes, Bertie Freeman was signed late in the campaign from Woolwich Arsenal and took Young's berth. Thereafter the Scot would find himself overshadowed by Freeman's extraordinary exploits and would often be forced to play as an inside forward. He managed just two league goals during the 1909/10 season, and although he showed signs that he may wrest back the number nine shirt the following season, Everton's selectors deemed Young – now aged 30 – to be past his best.

In the summer of 1911 Young was sold to Tottenham Hotspur for £500. His spell in London was brief and inauspicious and he returned north within a year, signing for Manchester City. There followed spells with South Liverpool and Burslem Port Vale. By the outbreak of the First World War Young had dropped out of professional football and immigrated to Australia.

What followed is shrouded by a combination of mystery and urban myth. Some sources have

said Young was hanged for sheep rustling – which is not true – and others have said that he lingered in an asylum for years after killing his brother.

HOWEVER, it seems that a variation of the latter story actually happened. In Australia, Young joined his brother John, who was a dairy farmer in Victoria. But their partnership took a tragic turn. In December 1915 Sandy was charged with John's murder. Following the intercession of English football officials, who testified that Young was prone to bouts of 'temporary insanity', this was, in June 1916, downgraded to manslaughter, and he was given a three-year prison sentence, rather than an execution.

It seems he was then detained in an asylum for some years, before winding up back in Scotland. In October 1945, the Everton board received a letter regarding his 'circumstances', but after considering it, decided to refer the matter to the public assistance officer in Stirlingshire, where Young was seemingly now

based. The next years remain a blank, until news of Young's death in September 1959 in an Edinburgh nursing home.

[FACTFILE]

BORN
Slamannan, 23 June 1880
DIED
Edinburgh, 17 September 1959
POSITION
Centre forward
OTHER CLUBS
St Mirren (1899);
Falkirk (1899–1901);
Tottenham Hotspur (1911);
Manchester City (1912);
South Liverpool (1912);
Burslem Port Vale (1913)
HONOURS
FA Cup 1906;
2 Scotland caps (1905–07)

Young, Robert

Young defender who was part of the team that came close to 1911 League Championship honours

[FACTFILE]

BORN
Swinhill, 1888
POSITION
Right half / centre half
OTHER CLUBS
St Mirren;
West Ham;
Middlesbrough (1908–09);
Wolverhampton Wanderers (1911–13)

Season	League		FA Cup		Total	
	App	Goals	App	Goals	App	Goals
1910/11	31	5	3	1	34	6
1911/12	7	2	0	0	7	2
Total	**38**	**7**	**3**	**1**	**41**	**8**

Z-Cars, Theme from

Iconic music to which Everton run out at Goodison

Z-Cars was a TV police show, popular in the 1960s, set in the fictional northwest town of Newtown. Its theme tune is composed by Fritz Spiegl and performed by Johnny Keating and his orchestra. It is based on the late-19th-century folk song 'Johnny Todd', and reached number 5 in the singles chart in April 1962.

SINCE around this time, Everton have run out to the Z-Cars theme tune. It is believed that one of the actors from the series, Terence Edmonds, was an Evertonian and brought a number of the cast to watch a match against Birmingham City in April 1962. To honour their presence the theme music was played over the Tannoy before the game and has stuck ever since. Watford and, for a period, Sunderland also adopted Z-Cars as their theme tune.

Certainly it is one of the most evocative parts of the Goodison experience, guaranteed to prickle the hair on the neck of every Evertonian. Only once have the club abandoned the music, at the start of the 1994/95 season when Peter Johnson's new management team sought to overhaul what was seen as an outdated tradition. They replaced the Z-Cars theme music with an atrocious version of 'Bad Moon Rising', with lyrics adopted to give it an Everton theme. The result? Everton's worst ever start to a season. 'Bad Moon Rising' was happily abandoned and consigned to the dustbin of Goodison history and Z-Cars restored.

Bibliography

Allen, Robert, *Billy: A Biography of Billy Bingham,* Viking, 1986

Ball, Alan, *It's All About a Ball,* W. H. Allen, 1978

Ball, Alan, *Playing Extra Time,* Macmillan, 2004

Bingham, Billy, *Soccer with the Stars,* Stanley Paul, 1962

Brown, Tony, *The Football League Match by Match series – various volumes,* SoccerData

Buckland Gavin, *Everton Strange But True,* Sport Media, 2007

Corbett, James, *England Expects: A History of the England Football Team,* deCoubertin, 2010

Corbett, James, *Everton: The School of Science,* deCoubertin, 2010

Cottee, Tony, *Claret and Blues - My Autobiography,* Independent UK Sports Books, 1995

Davies, Dai, *Never Say Dai,* Siop y Siswrn, 1987

France, David, *Gwladys Street Hall of Fame,* Skript 1999

France, David, Dr Everton's Magnificent Obsession, Trinity Media 2008

France, David, *Alex Young: The Golden Vision,* Skript 2008

France, David and Prentice, David, *Virgin Blues,* Skript, 2003

France, David and Prentice, David, *Gwladys Street's Blue Book,* Skript, 2002

Geldard, Albert and Rowlands, John, *The Life and Times of a Professional Footballer,* Countryside Press, 1990

Gray, Andy, *Shades of Gray,* MacDonald Queen Anne Press, 1987

Inglis, Simon, *League Football and the Men Who Made It: The Official Centenary History of the Football League, 1888-1988,* Collins Willow 1988

James, Gary, *Football with a Smile, The Biography of Joe Mercer,* Polar Print Co., 1993

Johnson, Steve, *Everton: The Official Complete Record,* deCoubertin, 2010

Joyce, Michael, *Football League Players' Record 1888 to 1939,* SoccerData, 2004

Keates, Thomas, *History of the Everton Football Club 1878-1928,* Desert Islens Books, 1998

Keith, John, *Dixie Dean: The Inside Story of a Football Icon,* Robson Books, 2001

Kendall, Howard, *Playing for Everton,* Arthur Baker, 1971

Kendall, Howard and Ross, Ian, *Only the Best is Good Enough,* Mainstream, 1993

Labone, Brian, *Defence at the Top,* Pelham Books, 1968

Lawton, Tommy, *Football is my Business,* Sporting Handbooks, 1946

Lupson, Peter, *Across the Park,* Trinity Media, 2009

Malam, Colin, *Gary Lineker, Strikingly Different,* Stanley Paul, 1993

Matthews, Tony, *Who's Who of Everton,* Mainstream Publishing, 2004

McKenzie, Duncan, *One Step Ahead,* Souvenir Press, London, 1978

McVay, David and Smith, Andy, *The Complete Centre Forward, The Life of Tommy Lawton,* Sportsbooks, 2000

Mercer, Joe, *The Great Ones,* Oldbourne, 1964

O'Brien, Mark, *The Everton Miscellany,* Vision Sports, 2008

O'Brien, Mark, *The Road to Rotterdam,* Parrs Wood, 2004

Onslow, Tony, *Everton FC: The Men from the Hill Country,* Countryvise, 2002

Orr, George, *Everton in the Eighties, Singing The Blues,* Blueblood, 1998

Orr, George, *Everton in the Seventies, Singing The Blues,* Blueblood, 1996

Orr, George, *Everton in the Sixties, A Golden Era,* Blueblood, 1995

Owen, Mike, *Der Ball Ist Rund,* Countryvise, 2005

Ponting, Ivan, *Everton Player by Player,* Hamlyn, 1998

Reid, Peter, *Everton Winter, Mexican Summer,* MacDonald Queen Anne Press, 1987

Roberts, John, *Everton: The Official Centenary History,* Granada, 1978

Rogers, Ken, *100 years of Goodison Glory,* Breedon Books, 1998

Rogers, Ken, *Everton Greats,* Sportsprint Publishing, 1989

Ross, Ian and Smailes, Gordon, *Everton: A Complete History,* Breedon Books, 1985

Royle, Joe, *The Autobiography,* BBC Books, 2005

Sharp, Graeme, *Sharpy: My Story,* Mainstream, 2008

Shankly, Bill, *Shankly by Shankly,* Mayflower, St Albans, 1976

Smith, Billy, *The Blue Correspondence: Everton Season 3 vols,* Countryvise, 2007-10

Southall, Neville (with Ric George), *Everton Blues, A Premier League Diary,* B&W Publishing, 1998

Southall, Neville (with James Corbett), *The Binman Chronicles,* deCoubertin, 2012

Studd, Stephen, *Herbert Chapman, Football Emperor.* Souvenir Press, 1998

Taylor, Rogan and Ward, Andrew (with John Williams) *Three Sides of the Mersey, An Oral History of Everton, Liverpool, and Tranmere Rovers,* Robson Books, 1993

Taylor, Rogan (ed.), *The Day of the Hillsborough Disaster: A Narrative Account,* Liverpool University Press, 1995

Walsh, Nick, *Dixie Dean: The Life of a Goalscoring Legend,* McDonald and Jane's, 1977

Young, Alex, *Goals at Goodison,* Pelham Books, London, 1968

Young, Percy, *Football on Merseyside,* Stanley Paul, 1963

LIBRARIES AND ARCHIVES
The Everton Collection
The British Library
The British Library of Social and Political Sciences

NEWSPAPERS AND PERIODICALS
Blueblood
Daily Telegraph
The Evertonian
FourFourTwo
The Guardian
Gwladys Sings The Blues
Liverpool Echo
Liverpool Daily Post
Liverpool Mercury
The Times
When Skies Are Grey

WEBSITES
Bluecorrespondent.co.nr
Evertonfc.com
Evertonresults.com
Rsssf.com
Toffeeweb.com

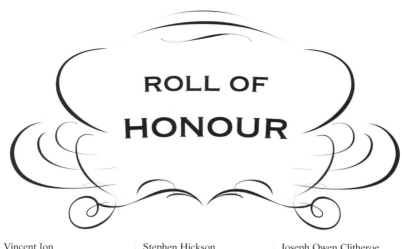

ROLL OF HONOUR

James Corbett
Joshua Corbett
Eleanor Corbett
Catherine Corbett
Charles Mills
John Corbett
Mary Corbett
Leslie Priestley
Daniel Lewis
David Corbett
Andrew Corbett
Anna Corbett
Michael Corbett
Lucy Corbett
Julia Corbett
Charles Mills Jr
Peter Mills
Tom Mills
Ben Mills
Poppy Mills
Lucy and Mark O'Connor
Anne and Joseph Wright
George Orr
Paul Wharton
Neville Southall
Les Read
William Corbett
Catherine Mills
Steve Johnson
Howard Kendall
James and Noreen Miller
Michael Quarry
John Waddington
Bryn Griffith
Barry Sheils
Andy Weir
Robert A. Rice
Nicholas Evans
James Yoxall
Paul Simpson
Alan Khan
David Grundy
Matthew Lewis
Ed Perryman

Vincent Ion
Mark Peter Edwards
Owen Edwards
Tom Mallows
Daniel Salewski
Jason Howarth
Jason Russell
John Francis Mulrooney
Paul Mulrooney
Michael Francis Murphy
Alan Carter
Mark Van Marle
Paul Gornell
Sean O'Brien
Mark Joseph O'Brien
Richard Stolworthy
Alan Robert Newton
Dennis Stevens
Jerome Payne
Mike Saunders
Ralph Saunders
Paul W. Carr
Gary J. Firman
Thomas Goodison Loyden
David Briscoe
Philip Johnson
David France
Neil Entwistle
David Kennedy
Paul Ankers
Thomas Anthony Barker
Thomas O'Reilly
Bonita Mersiades
Michael Mersiades

Stephen Hickson
Liam Rogers
Stephen Rogers
Geoff Harrison
David Roscoe
Peter Roscoe
Ivan Parsons
Andy Clarke
Mark Grogan
Tore Lyse
Paul Mannix
Alan Crowley
Dale Slater
Gabriel Nathaniel Woods-Brown
Alan Bradford
Bryan Maddocks
Mike Byrne
Anthony James Marsh
Peter Walsh
Tony Walsh
Howard Collins
Edgar Francis Collins
Tim Lamb
Mark P. Edwards
Ian Maher
David Roscoe
Philip G. Davies
Adele Muscat
David Jeffery
Michael McGloin
Karen Doherty
Nigel Sartain
M. L. Corley
Graham Anthony Jones

Joseph Owen Clitheroe
Graeme Wilson
Edward Houghton
Joseph Connolly
James Blake
Terry O'Donnell
Alan Bradford
Andrew Joseph Clare
David J. Lane
Christopher Wynne
John Cant
Paul Gabbutt
Keith Daniel Roberts
K. P. Jones
James Rowe
Daniel Tucker
Dr Jamie Hynes
Owen Dodd
Jake Stevens
Francis Everton dadi Dadez
Andrew Walsh
James Harrison
Harry Joseph Campbell
Andy Lindsay
John Lindsay
Diane Lindsay
Eric C. Seeder
Ciaran O'Rourke
Katie Flanagan
David Roy Dickin
Ian Murray
Dave Gillam
Jack Gillam
Gary Koh Chuan Yen

Jasmine Eden Buckle
Steven David Corley
Liam Mulchay
A. J. Jones
Geoff Doe
Robert David McFawn
Stanley McQuillan
Peter Leslie Smith
Mark Rhys Davies
Laurence Cribbin
Richard Buchalter
John Christopher Wing Tat Fong
Barbara Johnson
Joe Peters
John Harrison
Michael Clark
Damian Richard Hayward
Paddy Howlin
David Edward Giles
Gareth Jones
Neil Bennett
Nick Pennick
Bluekipper.com
Alison Priestley
Joan White
Paul Lambert
Gary Lambert
Paul Nelson
Alan Baillie
Greg Baillie
Ryan Baillie
John Sweeney
Brian King
David John Stronach
Joe Grieves
Paul Maguire
Matt Kennedy
Des Bill
Dave Kelly
Michael Murphy
Renzo Spadon
Keith Bruce Entwistle
Matthew John Entwistle
Stephen Muscat

IN MEMORY OF

CHARLES MILLS

1924 - 2012

Husband, brother, father, grandfather,
great-grandfather, Evertonian.

'We all leave our footprints on the sands of time.
But we must advance.
I've had my pleasure of thankfully seeing my offspring
"maintaining the faith".'